# MAN'S CULTURAL HERITAGE

*A World History*

**The Lippincott social studies program**

*Supervised by*

**STANLEY E. DIMOND**
Professor of Education
University of Michigan, Ann Arbor

*Editorial Consultants*

**RALPH H. BOWEN**
Professor of History
Northern Illinois University

**HAROLD E. DAVIS**
Professor of Latin American Studies
School of International Service
The American University

**PAUL M. A. LINEBARGER**
Professor of Asiatic Politics
School of Advanced International Studies
The Johns Hopkins University

**KURT L. LONDON**
Director, Institute for Sino-Soviet Studies
George Washington University

**ROBERT A. LYSTAD**
Professor of African Studies
School of Advanced International Studies
The Johns Hopkins University

**ABDUL A. SAID**
Professor of International Relations
School of International Service
The American University

# CULTURAL HERITAGE

## *A World History*

PAUL THOMAS WELTY

Professor of History
Chicago Teachers College, North

Formerly, Assistant Secretary-General
World Confederation of Organizations of
the Teaching Profession

J. B. LIPPINCOTT COMPANY

Philadelphia · New York

100.656.2

Maps for text by Alan Young

Atlas maps by C. S. Hammond & Company

Cover design by Donald Cooke

Writing has served for thousands of years to transmit man's accumulated knowledge, but printed books have been known for only a few centuries. The art of book design first flourished during the age of the great humanists, and we are the inheritors of their thought and spirit. In keeping with this tradition, the cover for MAN'S CULTURAL HERITAGE is an authentic rendition of an original hand-tooled bookbinding made in Paris about 1560 for Thomas Mahieu, secretary to Catherine de Médicis.

Copyright © 1965 by J. B. LIPPINCOTT COMPANY

Printed in the United States of America

# PREFACE

The history of mankind is of compelling significance and interest. The man of today's world is very much what he is because of the urges, the thoughts, and the deeds of the many men who preceded him. And man today is involved in the process, consciously or unconsciously, of shaping the world of tomorrow's man. There is a close and vital relationship between the past, the present, and the future. Our ancestors conceived ideas and fostered attitudes which continue substantially to direct our lives and color our viewpoint; and they set in motion forces which yet swirl about us, influencing the total fabric of our lives. But we, too, have ideas and attitudes which often modify and expand those inherited from the past, and we shall pass them along in their merged and changed forms to our descendants, shaping and contributing to the future. Just as our ancestors live on in us, we shall live on in our descendants.

If we are to live with understanding and work with satisfying results, it is essential that we know something about the long evolution of the bewilderingly varied life of man. We need to relate ourselves to the past of all mankind and all parts of the earth. We need to know about the birth and growth of ideas and institutions which are yet evolving and affecting our lives. It is also important to understand that man is a social being, to examine the origin and development of social groups, to study past successes and failures in government, and to learn about man's magnificent efforts to create beauty and to satisfy his spiritual needs. Knowing these things and more helps us to understand ourselves.

Our increasing interdependence demands that each of us learn more about ways of life which differ from his own. Actions that stem from the special traditions, desires, and needs of men in one part of the world may influence the lives and shape the destinies of other men in all parts of the world.

Men of good will go forth from one nation to another to help others in peaceful ways with their agricultural and technological techniques, their medical skills, and their skills as teachers in schools. They are frequently frustrated and hampered in their helpfulness until they learn to work within the differing cultural framework of the people they are attempting to assist. Soldiers are sent to alien lands, sometimes to fight an enemy about whom they know very little, for reasons they do not fully understand. And it is all alien to them, the land, the language, the enemy—only the sound and thud of the bullets are truly understood. An understanding of cultures which differ from one's own may not bring a liking and an appreciation for these differing cultures, but it can lead to a more realistic approach to understanding how diverse peoples may live and work together with a minimum of friction. This knowledge is vital in the fast-moving, interdependent world of our time.

In the following pages I have briefly told the tale of man and his works. It is not the complete story of man — such a task would require the labors of thousands of scholars spread over many years of time, and even after their work was done there would still be much left unsaid. Rather, I have summarized man's life. I have broadly sketched him as he grew and matured in the various parts of his world. I have, fundamentally, provided an introduction to the vast and rich diversity of man's past and present. One of the prime purposes of this introduction is to stimulate you, the reader, to go beyond this first meeting and deepen your acquaintance.

The unfolding story of man is a moving and dramatic one, and I have striven to capture the movement and drama of life. Man is shaped by history, but he also has a questing spirit which moves him to uncover the mysteries in himself and the universe. I have, therefore, portrayed man as the dynamic maker, as well as the product, of history.

In MAN'S CULTURAL HERITAGE I have tried to show something of the many facets of men. I have pictured peasants struggling to live on an over-burdened earth as well as kings and nobles ruling in the magnificence and comfort of their palaces. I have spoken of those who built great empires and monuments to their towering pride, and of those who made toys for their little children thousands of years before the birth of Christ. I have shown the women washing clothes at the edge of river and well, and the women who sit in parliaments and sometimes rule. I have written about the artist praised and known by millions, and about the millions whose chief concern was food, not art. I have told about the humanity of the old Greek who sculptured a sitting boy plucking a thorn from his foot, and about the heavenly vision of those who saw only God in their lives. I have used *man* as the central idea of this book. I have written of Asian man, European man, Christian man, the man of the Renaissance, the Frenchman or the Scandinavian, the Russian, and others. Each of these is not a stereotype but is, rather, many different men. Mankind, however, is one in its shared humanity, and I have tried to emphasize this fact. Man is not one; he is many. And an introduction should, at least, hint at this diversity.

The organization of MAN'S CULTURAL HERITAGE has been carefully planned to present in the most interesting way the major cultures of the world in their historic and geographic settings. Each unit of the book treats a major region and the history of its people. Thus, the great cultures of the world are presented in separate units, but they should be viewed as parts of a whole. The chronological graphs called Milestones, which are found in each unit, present a summary of important dates and events. They are intended as aids to review and also as a means of comparing important periods and developments in the history of man in all parts of the world.

I have tried to write this tale of man with clarity and with accuracy. A number of fine, scholarly men have helped me in this task. I am indebted to the editorial consultants who have contributed to the accuracy and clarity of the text in their fields of specialization. I am also indebted to Dr. Nils-Gustav Hildeman, for his critical review of the chapter on Scandinavia; to Dr. Charles Lowry, for his critical review of sections on Christianity; to Dr. Alfred Jospe for critical review of sections on Judaism; and to Rabbi Fredric Kazan for critical review and important contributions to sections on Judaism and Christianity. Miss Cora Prifold, who wrote the chapter-end materials for the book and Mr. Richard E. Marshall, instructor in history at Lower Merion Township High School, who prepared materials for the teacher's edition, also made many valuable suggestions with regard to the content of the book. I acknowledge with deep gratitude the invaluable assistance of all these able and informed persons. A great number of individuals, libraries and museums, embassies, and national agencies were most generous in helping to obtain illustrations for the book; they are mentioned in the credits for photographs. Finally, I shall be always grateful for time and encouragement given generously by family and friends that I might complete the writing of this book.

PAUL THOMAS WELTY

# CONTENTS

## UNIT II The People of the Middle East Molded Man



## UNIT III The European: An Introduction

## UNIT IV The Evolution of the Modern European



## UNIT V The Communist World



## UNIT VI The Two Americas

# MAPS AND TIME LINES



**Milestones of History**
**(Time Lines and Chronological Tables)**

## PROLOGUE

# What Man Has Wrought

THIS IS a story about man. It is our story, for we are men. It is a tale of strivings and yearnings, trials and failures, and of disappointments and achievements during the brief period that man has been writing about his life on earth. Usually history begins with the first written records of man, and, as far as we know now, he began to write three or four thousand years before Christ. The great bulk of our story, therefore, will be confined to the time in which man has been writing.

But this is not the complete story, for we are of ancient stock and our origins but dimly seen. We have written only a minute, but we have lived for hours. With each passing day, knowledge about our past grows through the constant searchings of scholars in every field of learning; but frequently each new addition to our store of knowledge also expands the awareness of our ignorance.

### Man Before He Wrote

We once thought that man began five or six thousand years ago, but as we found older and older bones, our amazement grew with his age. We pushed the age of man back to startling depths of time—20,000 years, 30,000 years, 50,000 years, 100,000 years. Then we found the Java man in Indonesia and the Peking man in China, and it is estimated that they lived as long ago as 500,000 years. More recently, it is claimed, by some who have found remnants of ancient man in Africa, that man has lived on earth for a million years or more. From the remains of some types of ancient men, we know that they had learned the use of fire and that they used stones for tools.

Although these ancients are all called "men," they were not all of the type we call ourselves, *Homo sapiens*, which literally translated from the Latin means "intelligent man." Investigators of the past use this term only to describe those kinds of man having a brain of a certain size and certain other physical characteristics. It is estimated that *Homo sapiens* has been in existence for about 100,000 years or more.

There were several kinds of "intelligent men" who became extinct while our kind survived. Among these was Neanderthal man, who lived as much as 50,000 years ago or more. Neanderthal man refined the stone tools used by earlier men, making sharper and more effective instruments for hunting and daily activities. Examples of his skeleton have been found in Germany and other parts of Europe. He was heavy-set and only about five feet tall. He thought about the state of his dead. Instead of leaving them on lonely surfaces for the beasts to feed upon, as others had done before him, he buried them in graves and placed tools and other man-made objects of value beside them.

And then came men who were much like us. They were rather tall and long-headed, with features more like those of modern men. They lived in the area now known as Europe, and some of these early European men were truly magnificent artists. They were of the kind we call Cro-Magnon man. It is thought that they lived on earth from about 25,000 B.C. until about 10,000 B.C. (B.C. means "before the birth of Christ"; A.D., "anno Domini," means "in the year of the Lord.") Exactly when and how Cro-Magnon man began and ended is one of the mysteries of the past. But we know he was here because he left us an unwritten record of achievements. His tools were not merely of stone, but of horn, bone, and ivory. He invented a bone needle to sew together his clothing of animal skins, fashioned buttons and loops, and further adorned himself with necklaces of shell and teeth. He improved the old-fashioned weapons of stone and became a most efficient hunter of game with his darts, his harpoons, his fishhooks, and his bow and arrow. His mind groped for the unseen, and he was even more careful in disposing of his dead than Neanderthal man had been. The dead of Cro-Magnon man were buried in a certain position and companioned with the products of inventive minds—tools, weapons, and ornaments.

The most impressive account remaining of Cro-Magnon man is in his paintings, which have been found in caves. He mostly painted animals: bison, horses, oxen, deer, mammoths, and other animals that lived around him. He pictured them alone and in groups, in all their variety of motion and stillness—leaping, running, bellowing, chewing, with heads lowered and heads raised, contentedly resting and tensely at bay, and injured and dying from the accurate throws of his lances. He used the natural colors of the earth, red, yellow, and black, and he used the hollow bones of animals to hold his coloring matter. He was natural, spontaneous, and imaginative. The caves within which he imprisoned his art are today the showplaces of his talent.

He seemed not to care whether anyone saw his art or not; he painted, and that was most important. The caverns of his paintings are scattered in many parts of Europe, and among the most striking are those of Lascaux in southern France and Altamira in the north of Spain. Cro-Magnon man is gone, but his art remains, permanently entombed in his and our earth.

### The New Stone Age

Up to this point we have been talking about the hunting man in the Old Stone Age or Paleolithic period (*paleo-*, old; *lith-*, stone). The man of the Old Stone Age had no fixed abode which he could really call home, but moved about, gathering food wherever he could find game, wild roots, berries, and other edibles. He was subject to the uncertainties of the elements and the beasts. Later, other men wandered, perhaps from western Asia, into other parts of the world. These men radically changed their way of life by discovering how to grow food and domesticate animals. This important moment of man's life came in the time known as the Neolithic period (*neo-*, new) or New Stone Age. The entire era is known as the Stone Age because man's tools and weapons were chiefly of stone, although in the New Stone Age he began to experiment with the uses of copper.

The men of the New Stone Age developed agriculture and began to settle down in villages and communities which became centers of their lives. It is estimated that this development began around 5000 B.C. or earlier in Egypt and Southwest Asia, and gradually the knowledge of agriculture spread around the world. (It is believed that in certain parts of Africa and the Americas agriculture was developed independently.) After he had learned to cultivate the land and grow crops, man was no longer forced to roam about, led by the wanderings of animals. He had learned to control nature, to bend her processes of growth to his will where the land was fertile and water was available. The man of the New Stone Age found that he need no more exhaust all his energies in a footloose search for food, which was sometimes fruitless and always dangerous, for he had now but to plant and to plow, and the earth gave of her abundance.

Man's leisure grew because there were times when he had merely to wait until the grains matured, and he now had time to pause and think about himself, his fellows, and new ways of improving his life. His numbers grew because he grew a surplus and could feed more people. Communities grew, and man was forced to find practical methods of accommodating himself to others in a settled existence. He domesticated animals—the cow, the pig, the goat, and the sheep. As these controlled sources of food increased in quantity, the population increased uncontrollably, until the number of people outstripped the resources of land and herds.

The making of glass is among man's most ancient achievements. This vase was made possibly in Mesopotamia or Syria as early as 500 or 1000 B.C. (The Corning Museum of Glass)

Paintings in the caves of Lascaux in southern France show the kinds of animals hunted by Cro-Magnon man. (French Government Tourist Office)

Wheat, top left, was one of the earliest grains cultivated by ancient man. Kernels of wheat have been found in ruins of an ancient village in Iraq more than 6,000 years old. Indigo, top right, is the oldest dye known to man. Cloth dyed with indigo 3,000 years ago in Egypt has been found. Digitalis, a drug still in use, was known to ancient men and was obtained from the foxglove plant. (all photos, USDA)

The aurochs was the native wild ox of Europe, and modern cattle were probably descended from it. The animal above, which closely resembles an aurochs, was bred by Heinz Heck, Director of the Munich Zoo. By mixing modern breeds of cattle and "back-breeding," the ancestral animal was "re-created." (Heinz Heck, Tierpark Hellabrunn)

Man moved on to other lands, where the fields were virgin, planted them with his seeds, and grew new herds from their fertility. And again his numbers swelled so that the grain and the beasts were insufficient to satisfy his hunger. He went on to another good earth, and another, and another, and continued to populate our world. He settled in Asia, in Europe, in Africa; he built boats and rafts and journeyed to Australia, New Zealand, and the islands of the Pacific, including Hawaii; he reached the lands of the Americas; he fished waters rimmed with ice, learned to live in the steaming jungles of Africa, and layered the world with his cultures and his species.

But in his migrations across the vastness of the earth, he did not cease to speculate and invent. His searching mind ever outsped his searching feet. He made fire by rubbing sticks together, and he built houses of mud and wood and thatched them. He sometimes raised his houses on stilts, as in Switzerland, and they became safe refuges from other men and from beasts. He built great walls and roads of stone in Peru. He started to count, learned to weave, knit, and spin, and grew less dependent upon animals as he exchanged clothes of skin for clothes of cloth. He made pottery and decorated it with designs. He developed more fully

The European forest horse pictured below has been extinct since the 1800's. These horses were hunted for food by ancient man. Modern horses bear little resemblance to them. (Heinz Heck, Tierpark Hellabrunn)

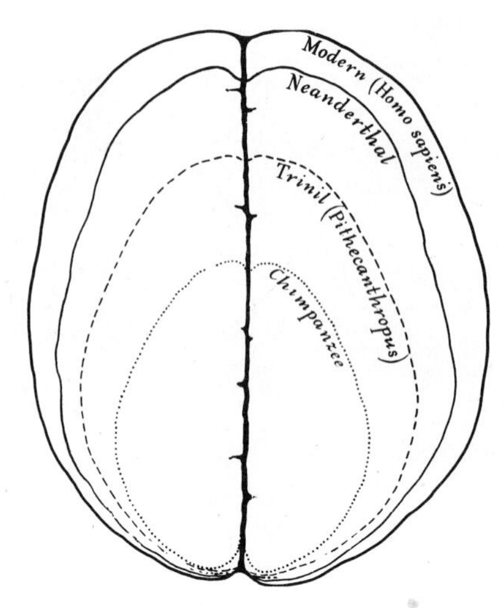


The drawings show how the brain size of modern man compares with that of Neanderthal man, Pithecanthropus, and the chimpanzee. Find out the brain size of Cro-Magnon man. (Courtesy of the American Museum of Natural History)

such basic social institutions as the family and meditated more deeply on that spiritual power which is beyond the self. He thought and acted religiously by erecting great stone monuments in France and England. He also was afraid—of the savagery of the storm, the blinding lightning, the thunders of the sky, and the quaking of the earth. He suspected that there were evil spirits and sought to make peace with them by offerings or attempted to ward them off with magic and charms. He developed customs, means of social control, certain ideas of rights and duties, and a rudimentary sense of government.

### The Wheel, Metal, and Writing

Somewhere near the very end of the New Stone Age, man invented the wheel, which further eased his life and expanded his horizons. Use of the wheel enlarged trade, quickened travel, and bettered work. It is difficult for us to conceive of man without the wheel, but he was without it for more years than he has possessed it.

The New Stone Age ended with two magnificent achievements: man learned to make bronze, beginning the Age of Metal, and he invented writing and started to make records that were the beginning of history.

About 3000 or 4000 B.C. someone found that by melting copper and hardening it with molten tin he could produce an alloy called bronze. From that time on, bronze was man's most valuable metal until the discovery of iron almost two thousand years later. Bronze made much more efficient tools and weapons than stone, tools that were sharper and more accurate. It was also a timesaver and was adaptable to useful and artistic pursuits. Bronze was used for swords and armor, for horses' shoes, and for the wheels of chariots. Man fashioned pitchers of bronze to hold water and wine, basins of bronze to wash from, plates of bronze to eat from, and vases of bronze to decorate his tables and his rooms. He made knives and spoons of bronze and lightened his palaces and his temples with its burnished rays. Bronze became for him what steel is for us today—a necessity for living.

About this time man began to write and record his speculations, activities, and laws, his experiments, his struggles, and his hopes. He began what is properly called history. All of that almost immeasurable span of time before man wrote is called prehistory because no one recorded in writing what he had thought, done, felt, and observed. We have the paintings of Cro-Magnon man, and the fossils and products of other early men. We have learned much through the marvelous detective work of our scholars who piece together a general picture from the few traces of themselves that our prehistoric ancestors left behind. Still, there are very few relics from the past, and our interpretation of them may be only partly true and even partly false. Without the written record, we do not know for sure.

The earliest writings were on stone and clay tablets and on *papyrus*, the pith of a plant pressed into a material somewhat like paper. At first men wrote with pictures, which the Greeks later named *hieroglyphics* or "the writing of priests," for it was the priests who did much of the earliest writing. In the past one hundred and fifty years we have uncovered in Egypt many rolls of papyrus, preserved by the dry air over these many centuries. They show us illuminating pictures of early Egyptian life. The early Egyptian writing consisted of *ideographs*, or conventionalized pictures that represented ideas. In Mesopotamia, the Land between the Rivers, men wrote by making marks that represented syllables or words. These marks were made with an instrument which pressed small wedge-shaped marks into soft clay. It is for this reason that such writing is called *cuneiform*, "wedge-shaped writing." The Chinese wrote with ideographs also. They still do, and we do not know whether they wrote before or after the men of Egypt and Mesopotamia. Their writing was developed independently from the writing of the Western world, but we know that they have been writing from very early times.

The Phoenicians completed the process of developing alphabetical writing by making a single letter represent each sound. It is thought that all the alphabets we have today, including the Hebrew, Sanskrit, and Arabic, are offshoots of this dramatic discovery of the Phoenicians.

1. What is history? When did it begin?
2. Compare man of the Old and New Stone Ages in achievements, physical stature, and mode of living.
3. List the achievements of man during prehistory and give reasons for their importance.
4. Describe some of the earliest forms of writing. Why was the invention of writing important?

## Cities and Civilization

At about the same time men began to write, cities arose, and what we call civilization began. Our English word *civilization* is derived from the Latin word *civis*, meaning "citizen" or "free inhabitant of a town or city." The development of agriculture released numbers of men from the direct hunt for food. In an agricultural society, a smaller number of people could produce enough food to support the entire population. Those men who were released from the production of food turned to other occupations and specializations which often involved the production of goods of one

The invention of the wheel was a great aid to the development of transportation. This gold model of a Persian war chariot shows an early use of wheeled vehicles. (Courtesy of the Trustees of the British Museum)

kind or another. There was a division of labor. Some made baskets, pottery, or weapons. Others drew pictures or carved.

People began to exchange the products of their labor in return for food or other objects they deemed of value. This was the beginning of trade. They bartered at first, and then they began to use money. To make trading easier, and to protect themselves from attacks of enemies, people grouped together in greater numbers and surrounded themselves with walls. Sometimes the mighty walls were wide and towering, and several chariots could ride abreast along their tops. These centers of grouping became man's first cities.

Living crowded together, men soon learned that they needed protection also from some of their companions within the walls. It became necessary to make laws—laws against stealing and killing, laws about property, laws about restitution and punishment for injuries to others, and social laws to regulate relations with those outside and even inside the family. But someone must make the law, enforce it, and interpret it. Chiefs and kings were selected to govern the people so that they might live together more harmoniously. It often happened that ambitious men captured these positions of power without the approval of the people. But, whether good or bad, there was always government within the cities.

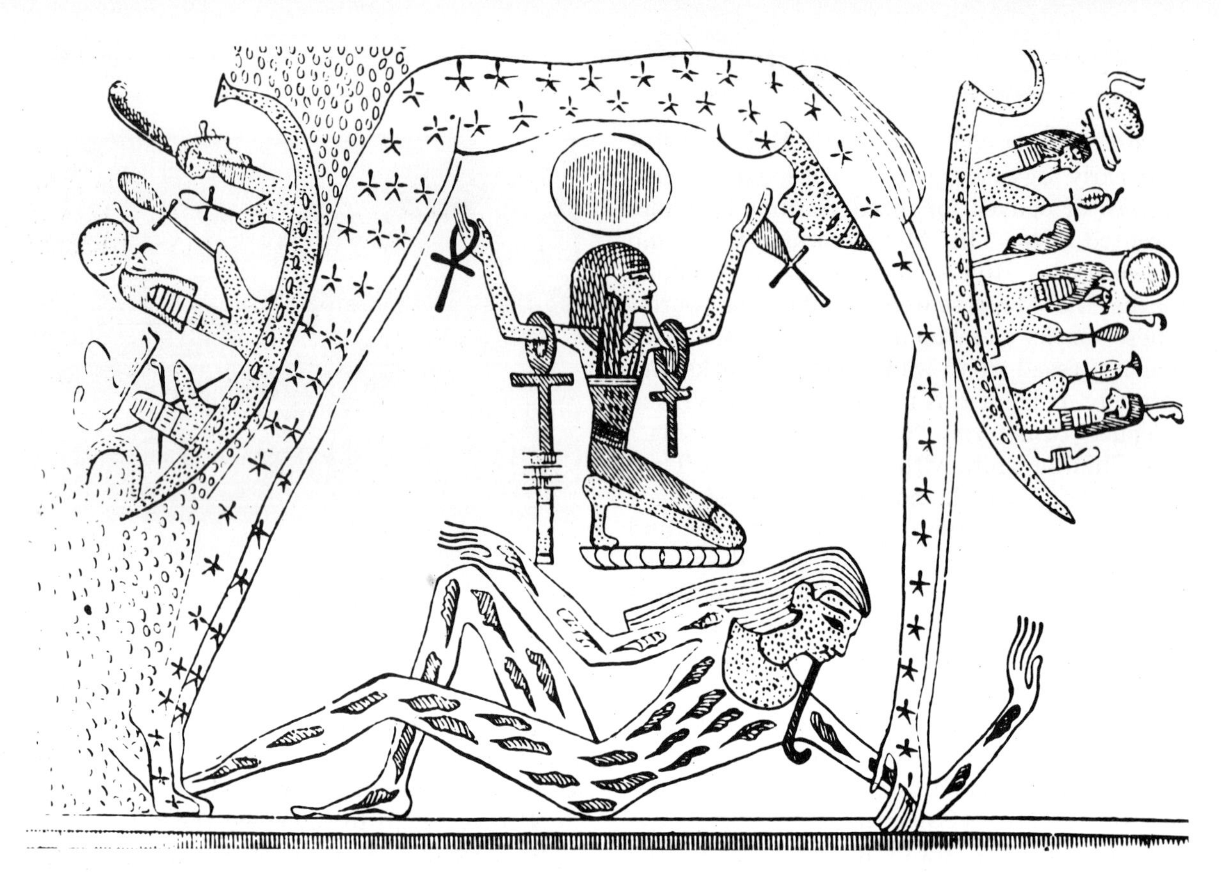

The drawing above shows the Egyptian concept of the universe. The boat of the sun is shown crossing the sky. Since earliest times, men have tried to explain the secrets of the universe and to understand the world in which they live. (Yerkes Observatory, University of Chicago)

As towns developed and civilizations grew, the use of money became common. This "spade" coin of ancient China may have been in use as early as 2000 B.C. (Chase Manhattan Money Museum)

Some men were cleverer, and perhaps luckier, than others, and they amassed greater amounts of goods and objects of value. They became men of property and wealth. They commissioned others to make artistic objects for their personal use and for the decoration of their homes—lockets, bracelets, necklaces, rings, vases intricately carved, paintings, scrolls, and furniture of bronze, wood, and ivory. They commissioned some men also to create music and others to tell stories. And these men of property were the kings, the nobles, and wealthy merchants. The priests, too, demanded the best for their temples, and great buildings of stone were erected to their gods, sometimes hugely simple, and sometimes lavishly ornamented. The arts began to flourish.

Within the cities men had more leisure than those of the rural parts, who frequently worked from early morning until late at night in an unending effort to earn a living from the soil. Some of these city men were inclined to use their leisure to study the stars, to play with numbers, to experiment with healing the sick, to unlock the secrets of nature, and to mix various elements together in order to see what unique and perhaps useful combinations would result. They began to think and brood about the why, whence, and whither of their lives. These thinkers were the first theologians and philosophers. Trade, laws and government, art and literature, science, and religion—all are parts of what we call civilization. In his cities, man produced civilizations.

## Different Civilizations

Man is man wherever he is on earth, but for one reason or another, all men have not sought to find happiness in the same way. Men have founded different civilizations and fashioned approaches to living which distinguish one group from others. These differences among men are still apparent today. There is always change and modification going on among men everywhere. For the past few centuries Western ideas and inventions have penetrated every region of our globe, but the hold of the past is tenacious, and older habits of thought and custom persist. In the cities of Asia there is an exterior somewhat like that of the West, but beneath the surface are the special features of the Asian way.

Man is everywhere, but he is always distinctly *somewhere*—in Asia, in the Middle East, in Europe, gathered within a Communist bloc, in the Americas, and in Africa. In each of these areas he has a point of view, varying cultures, and a regional story of struggle and achievement. But this is not to say that all within the region are alike. They are not. There are some real differences between those who live in Canada and those who live in the United States. Both of these countries differ from Peru, Bolivia, Paraguay, Brazil, Haiti, and other parts of Latin America. The peasant of Latin America often produces his food, views his society, and hopes for the future in a manner significantly different from that of the farmer of the United States. Man bears within himself an almost infinite capacity for variety, and it is obvious within his region as well as outside it.

Man dwells practically everywhere on our planet, but he planted his civilizations earlier in some places than in others. The Egyptians, the people of the Middle East, and the Asians developed the earliest civilizations that we know about. Many people believe that the Egyptian and the Mesopotamian civilizations came before those of India and China. Others think that they developed at the same time. It will take more digging, more uncovering of buried cities and records, and some very good detective work by scholars before this question is finally settled. But one thing is sure—they are all very old civilizations. We shall start our tale of civilized man in Asia, then move to man in the Middle East, in Europe, in the Communist bloc, in the Americas, and in Africa.

1. Discuss the development of cities. What made them possible? What problems did they face? Do they face the same problems today?
2. What were the functions of the first governments? How did they differ from the governments of today?

Transportation has always been important to man. The dhow, left, is a primitive type of sailing ship still used in the Middle East. (Arabian American Oil Company) The camel, above, provides transportation in many parts of the world. (Pakistan Embassy)

### Man Is Many-Sided

There are many sides of man's life, and they are all reflected in his way of life. He toils within a certain physical environment, shaping and being shaped by it. He is endlessly thinking, theorizing, and questioning about his many problems. Sometimes his expressed thoughts are so magnificent in content and structure that they become enduring ideas in which others have faith. And there is a complex web of relationships among men both near and far, for man lives in a society, and he has a social life.

Man is imaginative and, at times, wonderfully talented and deeply sensitive to the drama of his life. He is compelled to picture it in stone, on canvas and on paper, and with brush and pen. The beauty and the heartbreak that are portrayed draw from us tears and ecstasy, contemplation, and sometimes action. Man is politically minded and, too frequently throughout his history, has been overly fond of power. But politics and power are a necessity, and of awful importance in these days when freedom and existence itself seem to be threatened. We must look at all of these many aspects of man's life, even though briefly, if we are to know man at all in history and in the world.

The saga of man is not easy to relate in truth and in depth because the chief character, man, is often strange and formidable, sometimes inspired, and always complex. He takes pleasure in himself, but he must live with others. He is of earth, but he is proud and gladdened that he is not of earth. He creates imperishable beauty, and then a measureless ugliness. His pride is immense, but he is forever humbled. He risks any danger for wealth, and voluntarily wastes his body in poverty. He approaches divinity in his thoughts, and is often corrupt in his acts. He conceives and, with an agony of effort, produces magnificent civilizations, only to wipe them out suddenly in a moment of madness. He enslaves and he frees; he breeds and he slays; he destroys and he restores; but he always moves on from one moment of time to another, with his achievements outweighing his failures, and with hopes high that he will find the perfection he seeks. These are but a few of the many faces of man, whose story now begins in more detail.

Wall paintings from the tombs of Egypt tell us much about life in ancient times. What does this picture tell? (Courtesy of the Oriental Institute, University of Chicago)

When man learned to irrigate his fields, he was no longer dependent upon the unpredictable rainfall. Many modern farmers still use systems of irrigation that are very similar to those used by ancient farmers. (USDA)

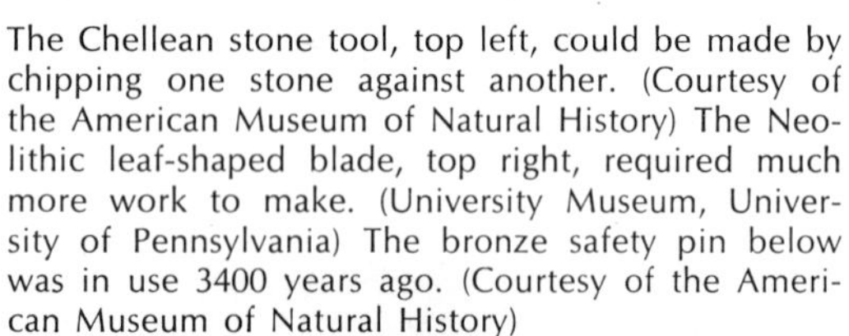

The Chellean stone tool, top left, could be made by chipping one stone against another. (Courtesy of the American Museum of Natural History) The Neolithic leaf-shaped blade, top right, required much more work to make. (University Museum, University of Pennsylvania) The bronze safety pin below was in use 3400 years ago. (Courtesy of the American Museum of Natural History)

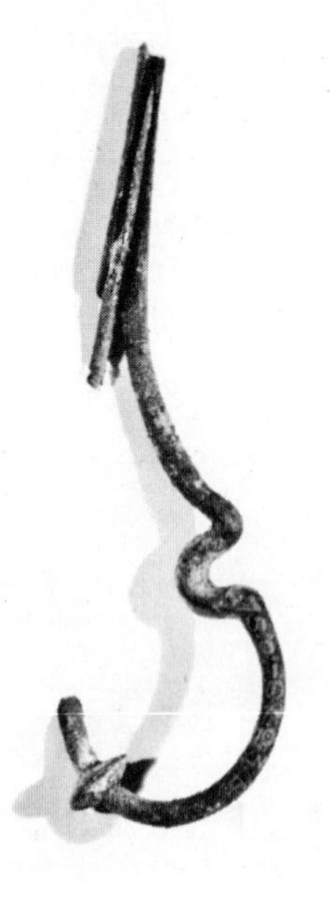

## SUMMING UP THE PROLOGUE

A. Define or explain the following terms, relating them to this chapter.

| | | | |
|---|---|---|---|
| page 1 | A.D. | page 2 | hunting man |
| page 7 | alphabet | page 5 | migration |
| page 1 | B.C. | page 7 | money |
| page 7 | civilization | page 6 | papyrus |
| page 7 | cuneiform | page 6 | prehistoric man |
| page 6 | fossil | page 6 | social institution |
| page 6 | hieroglyphics | page 7 | trade |

B. Identify the following and tell why they are important.

| | |
|---|---|
| Age of Metal | New Stone Age |
| Cro-Magnon man | Old Stone Age |
| Homo Sapiens | Paleolithic |
| Java man | Peking Man |
| Mesopotamia | Phoenicians |
| Neanderthal man | Sanskrit |
| Neolithic | |

C. Chapter review questions.

1. How old is man? Where were the earliest traces of man found?

2. In what geographical regions have we found evidence of ancient men?
3. List the implements used in prehistory. Which tool do you consider to be the most important from the point of view of its impact? Why?
4. When does history properly begin? What do we call the period before history began?
5. Explain the following quotation taken from this chapter: "We have written only a minute, but we have lived for hours."
6. How do we know so much about man's life during prehistory, if man could not write?
7. Contrast life in the Age of Metal with that in the New Stone Age.
8. Approximately when was agriculture developed? In what part of the world was it first developed? Why is this discovery significant?
9. How was Cro-Magnon man more advanced than Neanderthal man?
10. What problems of survival did "hunting man" face? Name two specimens of hunting man and the geographical region in which each lived.
11. What metals were most important to man in each of the periods mentioned in this chapter? What metals are most important today?
12. In what ways was man's life radically changed with the discovery of agriculture?
13. When did man learn to write? Are any of the earliest forms of writing still being used today?
14. What prompted or encouraged the establishment of "the arts"?
15. City life during the Age of Metal was easier than rural life. Explain. Would this be true today?
16. List the most significant dates mentioned in this chapter. Explain their significance.

D. Questions for discussion.
1. How would you explain the differences between various modern civilizations?
2. Early man feared and viewed with awe and wonder many natural phenomena such as the sun, fire, thunder, and lightning. What do his reactions to such phenomena suggest about man's early religion?
3. Cro-Magnon man was an accomplished painter. Why do you suppose he painted?
4. Why do different approaches to life exist within a region as well as between geographical regions?

E. Projects for groups or individuals.
1. Keep a notebook listing the most important names, dates, places, and achievements of man throughout history. You might begin your notebook by listing such items according to the periods listed in this chapter.
2. Select a modern invention or new skill and explain how it has changed our way of life or will change it.
3. Look up in your school library some of the old forms of writing. Trace their influence in any of the forms of writing used today.
4. Do research from books in your school library on what life was like in one of the first walled cities. Do any of these cities exist today?
5. Prepare a chart comparing the men of the Neolithic, Paleolithic, and Metal periods in the following ways:
   a) years on earth
   b) geographical location
   c) method of securing food and clothing
   d) home
   e) tools
   f) skills
   g) religion
   h) government
   i) most important contribution or discovery.

## FURTHER READINGS

ANDREWS, ROY C., *Meet Your Ancestors.* Viking, 1945. A short survey and introduction to the study of ancient and primitive man. Presents what is known to date (1945) based on actual specimens.

BARNETT, ANTHONY, *The Human Species.* Penguin, 1961, paperback. Especially good in treatment of early man.

GOLDMAN, HANNAH AND IRVING, *First Men: The Story of Human Beginnings.* Abelard, 1955; Collier, paperback. Describes the beginnings of man, and discusses primitives who live now.

Editors of LIFE, *The Epic of Man.* Time, Inc., 1961. Based on a series of articles which appeared in *Life* from 1955 to 1957. Vivid illustrations about early man.

LINTON, RALPH AND ADELIN, *Man's Way from Cave to Skyscraper.* Harper, 1947. Easy reading about early and later man.

MEAD, MARGARET, *People and Places.* World, 1959. A well-known authority writes about early man and where he lived.

QUENNELL, MARJORIE AND CHARLES H. B., *Everyday Life in the Old Stone Age.* Putnam, 1956.

———, *Everyday Life in the New Stone, Bronze, and Early Iron Ages.* Putnam, 1955. These two books tell a story of early man with good illustrations.

WHITE, ANNE T., *Lost Worlds: Adventure in Archaeology.* Random, 1941. The archaeologist pries into the past, and the result is better knowledge about our ancestors.

# UNIT I

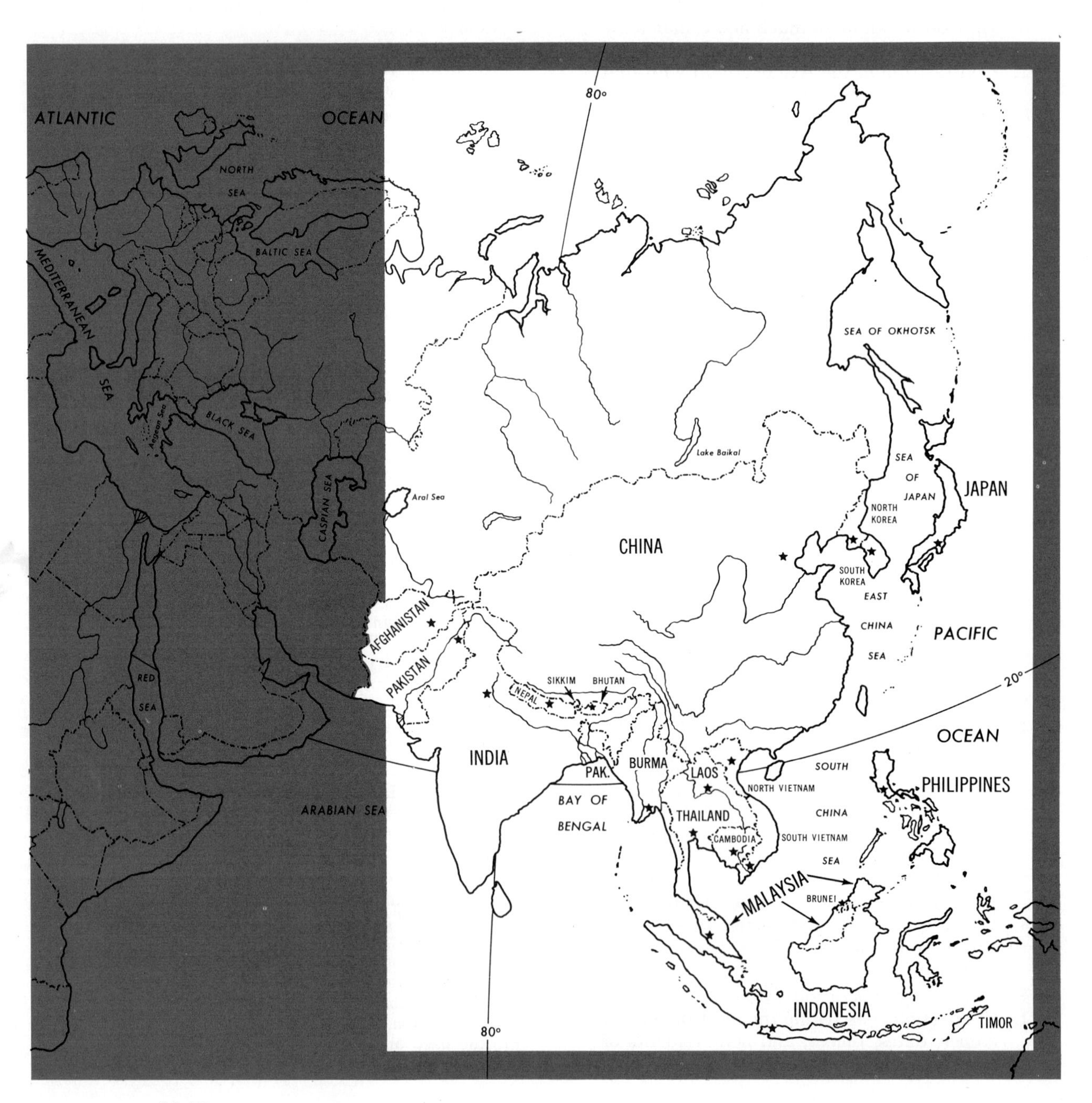

ATLANTIC
OCEAN
NORTH SEA
BALTIC SEA
MEDITERRANEAN SEA
Aegean Sea
BLACK SEA
CASPIAN SEA
Aral Sea
RED SEA
ARABIAN SEA
80°
SEA OF OKHOTSK
Lake Baikal
SEA OF JAPAN
JAPAN
NORTH KOREA
SOUTH KOREA
CHINA
EAST CHINA SEA
PACIFIC
OCEAN
20°
AFGHANISTAN
PAKISTAN
SIKKIM
BHUTAN
NEPAL
INDIA
PAK.
BAY OF BENGAL
BURMA
LAOS
NORTH VIETNAM
THAILAND
CAMBODIA
SOUTH VIETNAM
SOUTH CHINA SEA
PHILIPPINES
MALAYSIA
BRUNEI
INDONESIA
TIMOR
80°

# THE ASIANS BUILT ENDURING WAYS OF LIFE

This political map of Asia is drawn to the same scale as other maps in the unit. As you study the historical maps, compare them with the modern map of Asia. Stars indicate capitals.

# CHAPTER 1

# *Man Came To Asia*

MAN CAME TO ASIA early and continuously, and he has endured there in ever-increasing numbers to the present day. He came walking, dragging supply sleds behind him, and he came riding horses or camels. He came in twos and threes, and in a medley of tribes from all points of the compass—by way of the flat grasslands and the desert, by mountain trail and jungle path, or carried by the river and the sea. He came quietly, looking for food; loudly, with weapons clanging, in search of land, booty, and power; humbly seeking knowledge; and proudly to lead. He came gradually, delayed by many bypaths; and he came swiftly with a purpose. He came to trade, and there was always something that he wanted, something that he gave, and something that he found. And he rarely returned to where he came from. The vast lands were peopled with his variety and his numbers—the Asians.

In the long process of man's coming, he peopled the land with an amazing diversity of his kind. During the long, dim periods of prehistory, different families of man came to Asia from varying directions. Branches of the Caucasian family came from Southwest and Central Asia, and the hazel eyes and curly hair of the Ainu of Japan tell of the extent of their wanderings. They met with the Negritos, a branch of the Negroid family, who drifted into Asia, especially Southeast Asia, from somewhere in eastern Africa. From their meeting came other varieties of man. Then came the Mongols, of the Mongoloid family, from northern and northeastern Asia originally. They mingled with the Caucasians and the Negritos, and with their offspring. From their mingling, other patterns of man were born. From the mixture of these groups, and perhaps others, there emerged the Malays who, in turn, interbred with the others. An example of their interbreeding is the Japanese, who are, in part, of Malayan as well as Mongolian ancestry. Much of this blending of man was done before the Asians fashioned their first civilizations. And the meeting, mingling, and mating of families of man in Asia continued after civilizations began.

## Indian and Chinese Civilizations

The Indians and the Chinese were the first to develop civilizations in Asia. From the evidence we have now, it appears that the civilization of the Indians preceded that of the Chinese. The first civilization in India, called the Dravidian, is estimated to have been flourishing around 3000 or 2500 B.C. The earliest civilization of the Chinese is thought to be about 2500 B.C. or perhaps later.

### Dravidians and Aryans

The Dravidian civilization was already established in India when the Aryans came there about 2000 B.C. The Aryans were tall, fair, blue-eyed nomads who originated in the steppes of Central Asia—lands without forests and with very few hills. Some of the Aryans roamed into Europe and became the ancestors of the Greeks and other Europeans. Others entered Persia and began a civilization there. Still others wended their way through the northwest passages into India and slowly forced the Dravidians south, where they still live today.

The ancient Dravidians were of many physical types—small and slight, tall and robust—and the colors of their skin varied from black to a light brown. Perhaps the lighter ones had come to India as much as a thousand years before the Aryans came, and they may have come by the same northwest mountain passages that the Aryans used.

The ancient Dravidians had one common language. The chief languages of the Dravidians today are Tamil, Kanarese, Malayalam, and Telugu.

We did not know until 1920 what a rather wonderful civilization the Dravidians had created. It was then, by accident, that two of their long-buried cities were uncovered—Harappa and Mohenjo-Daro. Both cities were located on the land watered by the Indus River.

The advances of the Dravidians were startling for that time. Mohenjo-Daro was a well-planned city with wide, regular streets. The one- and two-story houses which lined these streets had the conveniences of courtyards and bathrooms. The Dravidians knew the use of sanitation and made sewers lined with baked brick. They wrote, but we have not yet deciphered the earliest forms of their writing. They worked with gold, copper, silver, bronze, and earth, and the artistry of their hands would be prized in any age. They made toys for their children which were delightful and imaginative. Then, suddenly, a catastrophe befell them—remains of their buildings suggest the ravages of war.

Slowly the Aryans took over much of the land in the west and northwest, and in northern India. The Dravidians retreated southward, but they were not entirely dispossessed. During the slow retreat, their blood had combined with that of the Aryans. The fair Aryan

Excavation of the cemeteries at Harappa have revealed much about the civilization of this ancient site. (Embassy of Pakistan)

The bronze ornaments above show us that the people of the ancient Indus River civilization had attained much skill in metal casting. The child's toy, right, which is worked by a string, was found at Mohenjo-Daro. It is made of terra cotta and is almost perfectly preserved. (Both photos, courtesy of Embassy of India)

skin became a little darker, and the blue eyes changed to brown. These changes happened in spite of the Aryan's struggle to preserve his original fairness, for he was proud of the whiteness of his skin. The fertility of the land held the Aryans. They settled around the Indus and Ganges rivers and never returned to the nomadic life of the steppes again.

The Aryans laid a heavy imprint upon India which, to this day, can be observed. They thought of themselves as nobles and freemen, and they elected their chiefs and their councils. All outside their group were inferior. By insisting upon their separateness and superiority, the Aryans planted the seeds of a caste system which still divides man from man and group from group in India. We shall discuss caste later in some detail. The Aryans loved nature, and their deities personified its beauty and its forces. They honored Ushas, goddess of the dawn, Indra of the storm, Agni of the fire, and Varuna of the sky. The Indians have never lost their regard for nature and its works. The Aryans gave to India their language, of which Sanskrit, Avestan of Iran, and the languages of Europe are offshoots.

The Aryans were lusty, uninhibited men. Cities were too confining for them; they preferred the open spaces, the countryside, the life of the village and the farm. They brawled, raced their chariots, diced, and lamented their gambling losses in song and poem. They were fond of drink, caroused wildly, and relieved the excesses of their energy in song and dance. For a thousand years or more they sprawled their villages and their people over the broad river plains of northern India.

We call the years from around 2000 B.C. to about 500 B.C. the Vedic Period because it was during this time that the Vedas were narrated, collected, and finally written down in Sanskrit. These are the earliest literature of the Indians, composed mainly of religious poems and hymns. The books of the Vedas are the foundation of much of Indian thought about life and afterlife. During the period ranging roughly from 1000 B.C. to 500 B.C., further additions were made to the foundation and structure of the future Indian society, but we know little of the people who came to India during this time. It is often called the Epic Period because two great epic poems were written toward the end of this period: the *Mahabharata* and the *Ramayana*. These two grand works have also contributed much to the thinking, feeling, and orientation of the Indians and others in South and Southeast Asia.

## Legendary and Historical Chinese

The origins of the Chinese people are obscure. Some believe that they have been living in the vicinity of northern China for around 500,000 years, since the time of Peking man. Others

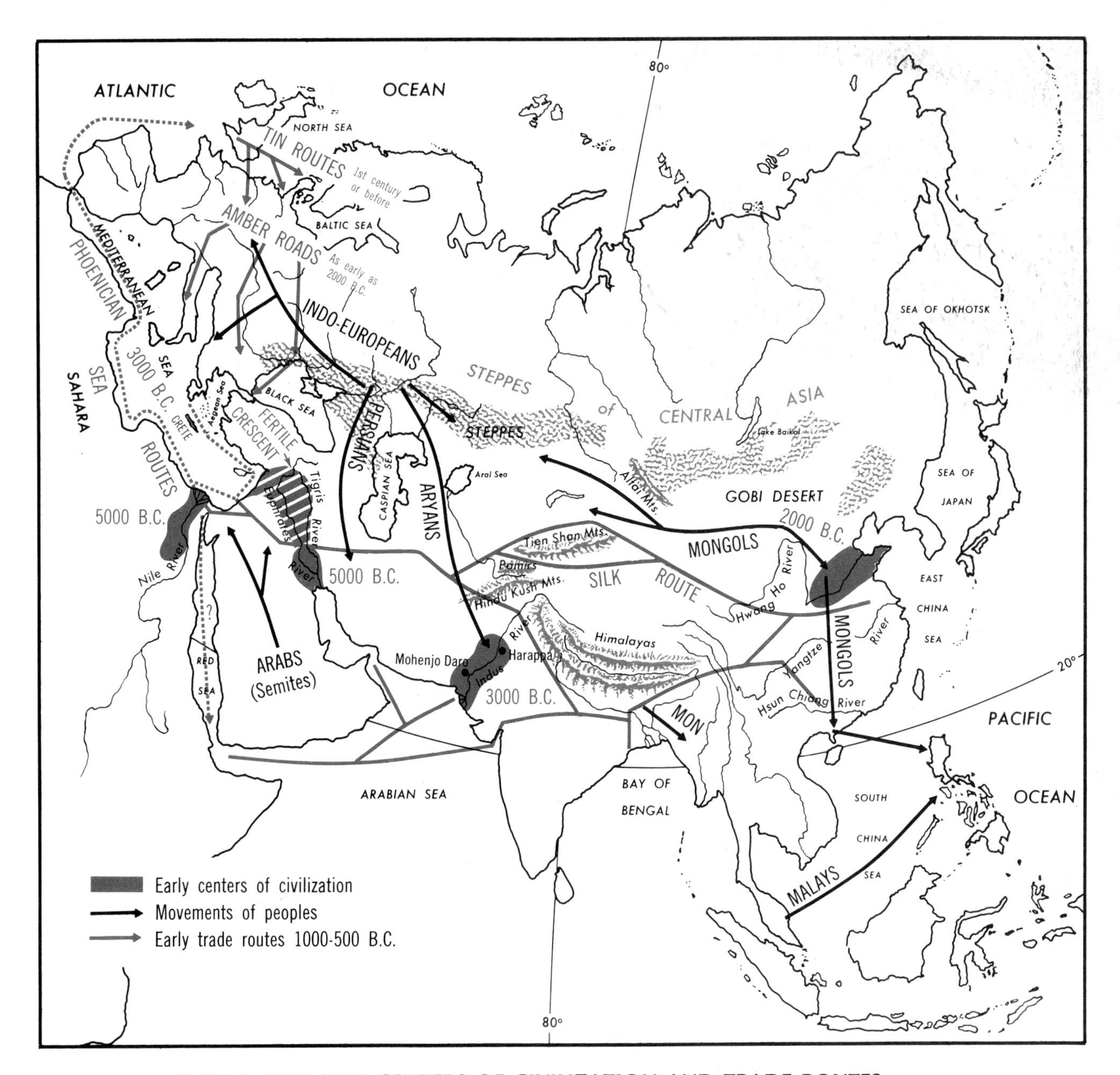


**ANCIENT EURASIAN CENTERS OF CIVILIZATION AND TRADE ROUTES**

Eurasia is the great land mass occupied by countries of Europe and Asia. What similarities can you see between the locations of early centers of civilization? The early trade routes were not lines of continuous commerce. Goods were traded between the peoples who lived along these routes. Thus, goods traveled with no particular destination, and the people who received them often did not know the place of origin. Use reference books to read the history of silk, tin, and amber.

dispute this claim. More believable is the Chinese legend that the more recent origins of their people and their civilization were around 2500 B.C. in northern China.

Around 2000 B.C., the first hereditary dynasty in China began. (By the word *dynasty* we generally mean a succession of rulers who are of the same family line.) It was called the Hsia, and it is thought to have lasted until about 1750 B.C. Up to this time the story of the early Chinese is regarded by many as legendary, but there is often much truth em-

Today the Indus River is spanned by many modern bridges. The photograph shows one of the many canals along the Indus in the Sind. (Embassy of Pakistan)

bedded in legends. One thing on which everyone agrees is that an incredible mixture of men came between prehistoric man and the Chinese of today.

Then came a more historical period, which starts with the Shang dynasty, from 1750 to 1122 B.C. We know from written records that during this period the Chinese lived under a ruler who combined both religious and political duties. Under the Shang emperors the culture and political influence of the Chinese spread north, south, east, and west and gathered great numbers of differing peoples into the body Chinese. The Shang dynasty was overthrown by the House of Chou who justified their deed by declaring that it was right to overthrow an emperor who had lost his virtue. By doing this, the Chinese followed a revolutionary theory that has also been used by many others since. They did not say that the Chou god overthrew the Shang god; they did say that all of heaven was the same and that the revolution reflected the will of a supreme force, making it "the mandate of heaven." They established the Chou dynasty, which lasted from 1122 to 256 B.C., and started the feudal system in China. Under this system the emperor gave a part of his land into the hands of a subordinate, called a vassal, on condition that the vassal lord render him service and obedience in return. But more important, the major Chinese philosophies of Confucianism, Taoism, and Legalism became systematized during the reign of the Chou emperors.

## Chinese Foundations

During the period from their early, uncertain beginnings to the end of the Chou dynasty, the Chinese shaped and laid the foundations of a civilization which has been built upon for several thousand years. The Chinese are of the Mongoloid family of man, but not entirely, for they took in many tribes of men whose ancestry is not always clear. The Chinese gave these tribes such descriptive names as "the spearmen," "the goat men," "the men who use bow and arrows," and others. This ability to take in or assimilate other people is still characteristic of the Chinese.

The early Chinese developed *ideographic* writing—in which pictures or symbols stand for *ideas*—rather than spelling the *sounds* of words as we do with our alphabet. This is the only form of writing known to most Chinese today. They thought deeply and originally about how man should live on earth if he was to be at peace with himself and others.

The early Chinese started an expansion which has yet to cease. The Koreans, the Japanese, the Vietnamese, the Thais, the Burmese, the Malayans and, in truth, most of the people of Asia have felt the striking influence of the Chinese and their culture. They settled the river deltas, farmed, and constructed villages. The river, the farm, and the village are still the dwelling places of most Chinese.

1. What major families of man populated Asia? Where did these families come from originally, and what part of Asia did they settle? During what period did they come to Asia?
2. Who developed the first known civilizations in Asia? Around what period and in what part of Asia did these civilizations develop?
3. Who were the Aryans, and why are they important to the history of Asia? How did they gain access to Asia?
4. What is the period of Indian history from 1000 B.C. to 500 B.C. called? Where did it get its name?
5. Name some of the earliest Chinese dynasties. What is each known for?
6. Describe other kinds of writing that use ideographs. How do these kinds of writing differ from writing that uses an alphabet? What are the difficulties in using ideographic writing for printing and in business?

## Asians Elsewhere

While the Indians and the Chinese were forming Asia's first civilizations, a mosaic of people were stirring, combining, learning, and settling the land elsewhere in Asia. They populated Korea, Japan, and perhaps the islands of Oki-

The Chinese of the Chou period (1122-256 B.C.) are especially remembered for their fine work in bronze. This vase is from the early Chou period. (Courtesy, The Cleveland Museum of Art)

nawa and Formosa in East Asia; they boated to the Philippines and the islands of Indonesia; they came by sea and by land to Vietnam, Laos, Cambodia, Burma, Thailand, Malaysia, and the other territories of Southeast Asia. And they were all swayed and leavened by the emerging, developing ways of life of the Indians and the Chinese. They borrowed and adapted the conceptions and ways of the Indians and the Chinese—sometimes of the one more than the other—to shape their own special mode of life and thought. From this fusion there came forth, in later periods of Asian history, the Korean and Japanese civilizations and civilizations in Cambodia, Burma, Vietnam, Indonesia, Thailand, Ceylon, and elsewhere.

### A Land of Diversity

While the Asians were intermingling, learning, creating, and fusing their ways of life, they settled a land enormous in extent and extreme in its diversity. Karachi, Pakistan, is over four thousand miles from Tokyo, Japan. If we compare some of the Asian countries with countries in other continents, we find that mainland China rivals the United States in size; that India is larger than any European country except Russia; and that Indonesia extends its islands east and west for three thousand miles and is more than three times the size of France. West Pakistan by itself is larger than the state of Texas; East Pakistan is about the size of Wisconsin.

The Asians were obliged to accommodate themselves to a wide range of climate and land features. We see them today, wrapped in layers of padded clothes, laboring as did their forefathers on land hardened and frozen by the cold, or almost naked, working in fields baked by the heat of the sun. They herd their camels, goats, sheep, and horses on the steppes, or live in jungles where the trees are thick, with tops so closely interwoven that they serve as ceilings. Some experience the changing seasons—spring, summer, autumn, winter; others live where it is always warm, and the only change they expect is that it may or may not rain. They cross and recross the dry reaches of the desert with caravans of animals and trucks, and they gather their tea leaves in a land drenched by unbelievable torrents of rain.

Mostly, the early Asians congregated around rivers. The rivers nourished them with fresh waters and carried silt which formed flat, rich land called *deltas* at the river mouths. The Asians eagerly accepted the gifts of the rivers. The Aryans found the Dravidian civilization around the Indus River and its tributaries in the western and northwestern parts of the Indo-Pakistan subcontinent. It is not surprising that they wanted this land and also took to themselves the broad plain in northern India watered by the Ganges River. The Chinese began their early civilization on the earth moistened by the Yellow River (Hwang Ho) and its tributaries. Today the Chinese continue to live in large numbers around their rivers—the Yangtze, the Pearl, the Red, and others. From the earliest times until now, the Asians have thronged the soil beside their rivers—the Indus and its tributaries in India and West Pakistan, the Ganges in India, the Brahmaputra in India and East Pakistan, the Irrawaddy in Burma, the Mekong in Cambodia and Vietnam, to mention a few of the more prominent ones.

The rivers helped them in many ways, and the daily scenes we observe along river banks today are but reflections of long centuries of helpfulness: a woman scooping up water to cook the rice and boil the tea . . . a child protesting a bath . . . a woman kneeling, rinsing and pounding the family wash with a paddle . . . a group of fishermen casting their nets . . . a traveler quenching his thirst. Sometimes the river is the only means of communication between one place and another, and it frequently acts as a sewer, bearing away the waste of village and city.

The river has been a home for many generations of Asians. Its surface teems with people. These are the boat people of Asia. They are born, grow up, marry, beget children, and die on their boats. Sometimes, when the boats are moored together beside a wharf, one can walk for miles on the planks of these floating homes without touching land or wetting his feet. The river is a shopping center, as in Bangkok, the capital of Thailand, where the people trade, buying and selling wares while stroking their boats to and fro.

But the river has often been their sorrow. Too frequently it has broken from its confines and flooded the land with sickness, desolation, and death. For long centuries, the Asians have schemed and fought to contain rushing waters within strong dikes of earth and stone. This is an endless task. The river never ceases to build up its bed and raise its level, and the Asians are compelled to construct higher and higher dikes to restrain it. In some places the surface of the river flows fifteen, twenty, thirty, and more feet above the bordering land. When the dikes weaken and the water gushes out, the river becomes a "River of Sorrow," and the Asians have sadly named their rivers "China's Sorrow," "India's Sorrow," "Vietnam's Sorrow."

On the lands along the river the Asians planted their main crops of rice and wheat, and other grains and vegetables—barley, millet, corn, sorghum, soybeans. They learned to grow a fantastic array of garden vegetables and fruit, and especially sweet potatoes. Sweet potatoes can grow practically everywhere, and they rival rice in relieving the eternal hunger of the Asians. In China, especially, it is a common sight to see a child munching a cooked sweet potato with the same delight we feel in nibbling a candy bar. Hunger is prevalent everywhere, for the Asians have crowded the available tillable land in such numbers that the earth cannot produce enough to feed them adequately. In some places there are over 1,500 persons occupying one square mile of land. They eat mostly grains and vegetables, but little meat and eggs. Some of the poorest are even without the services of the work animals of Asia, the water buffalo, the cow, and the bullock. They must pull their plows over the land by human effort.

For long ages the Asians have been surrounded by towering, sheltering, isolating mountains. Walls of mountains run from a core called the Pamir Knot in Central Asia to Pakistan, India, Southeast Asia, and China. They dissect Korea, are symbolized in Japan by beautiful Mount Fuji, and appear as symmetrical volcanic cones in Indonesia and the Philippines. The mountains are so mightily ever-present and so awesome that the Asians thought of them as the homes of gods and called upon them for protection and aid in hours of affliction.

The mountains were not always helpful. The Himalayas fringing northern India are the highest mountain range in the world. They are an impassable obstacle for the moisture-bearing winds of the Indian Ocean. As a consequence, Central Asia to the north of the mountains is dry and inhospitable to agriculture. The early people who inhabited these steppes led a gypsy-like existence, roaming from place to place in search of food for themselves and their animals. Wherever they pitched their tents of skin was home. They were constantly drawn to the settlements along the rivers and the greener fields which lay beyond the mountains. Year after year and tribe after tribe, these wanderers journeyed through the passes of the mountains to dispute with those before them the ownership of the richer, more productive earth south of the mountains. The history of India is in great part the history of those who came there through mountain passes—the Khyber, the Gumal, the Bolan, and others.

The mountains are greedy. They occupy so much of the land of Asia that there is little left for farming. In Japan the mountains are so prevalent that only about fifteen per cent of the land is tillable. Row after row, the mountains cut through Burma, Thailand, and Vietnam, and only the valleys and narrow coasts are left for the Asians in those countries to cultivate. This is also true of other Asian countries.

But the Asians overcame the mountains. The steep mountains stop the wind and the rain, but only from one side. The Asians learned to live on the side that stops the wind and causes rain to fall. As a result the people have reaped the riches of the mountain obstacle in food and in crops they can barter

The high mountains which occupy much of Asia are broken in a few places by passes. The picture above shows the Khyber Pass. For many centuries the Khyber Pass has allowed movement between Central Asia and the Indian sub-continent. (Embassy of Pakistan)

and sell. They met the challenge of the mountain heights by terracing their slopes and thus produced not only food but a picturesque landscape. They conquered the mountains, but at a great price wrenched from the muscle and sinews of their bodies. The mountains still play a major role in the lives of the Asians.

After they began to engage in agriculture, the Asians discovered that they were dependent for water not only upon the rivers but also upon a seasonal circulation of the winds called *monsoons*. In the summer season, from May to October generally, the intense heat results in the formation of hot, light air, a low-pressure area. The heated air rises and the relatively heavier adjacent air moves in from the ocean, bringing rain to the land. In the winter season, from November to April, this process is reversed. Cool, dry air blows from the continent to the low-pressure ocean areas. Generally, these winds are dry because they blow over land. When they blow over water—as in the case of the wind from China blowing over the Sea of Japan, or from the Asian continent blowing over the Bay of Bengal—the west coast of Japan and the southeast coasts of India and Ceylon receive winter rains. The Philippines and Indonesia are also well watered with winter rains.

When the monsoons come late or bring too little rain, the Asians are in grave trouble, for the rivers cannot supply all the needs of their crops. Also, because of the ever-increasing population, many people have been forced to live farther and farther away from the river banks.

1. To what extent does Asia's physical vastness account for the differing ways of life existing there?
2. Explain how the rivers, mountains, and monsoons can be both an asset and a liability to

the peoples of Asia. How have the Asians overcome these liabilities and developed these assets?
3. What are the major crops and livestock raised in Asia?

## Village Life

From the earliest days, the Asians have lived in villages. They are a farming people, and most of them still live in rural communities. Asia is a continent of villages. It is thought that there are almost two million villages in Asia, and they are the homes of the vast majority of the Asian people. For many Asians, the limits of the village are the limits of their lives, as they were for their ancestors. The Asian male goes to the market town nearest his village, and sometimes beyond. But the Asian female stays near the village into which she was born, or into which she went in marriage, and only rarely does she see the world outside its boundaries. The world of the village has been, for thousands of years, the only world most Asians have known.

These villages are not planned; they just grow. A village is frequently a network of tiny winding lanes and alleys which lead to some courtyard and some door. These alleys and lanes are often filled with refuse and sewage and are seldom covered with anything but mud and filth. Sometimes cobblestones are laid, but they are usually uneven and irregularly spaced. The narrow avenues of a village permit only the passage of man and beast. Around the village lie the fields, which the people of the village cultivate. During the working season, the villagers walk from their homes to the fields, carrying their farming implements and often leading or driving before them a water buffalo, a cow, or a bullock. At dusk—sometimes later if they are busy—they return to their village homes with their implements and animals.

For centuries the Asian has made his farmhouse of mud or mud bricks, stamped, beaten, sun-dried, and hardened. His windows may be covered with paper, but seldom with glass, and they are tiny and barred—he fears the thief, for he is poor, and any loss can be a calamity. His roof is frequently thatched with grass tied down with bamboo strips. Rooms are small and few. It is not uncommon for the Asian to share his house with his animals, especially at night, for they are food and are therefore valuable, and he feels more secure when they are close by, locked in his house with him.

The furniture is simple and essential: an earthen stove, some brass pots, some tin cans, and some dishes made of clay. The bed is of rope, of wooden planks, or simply a mat upon the floor. There are a few benches or chairs and a table. The Asian may also possess a scroll, a vase for his flowers, a picture or two, and little else. This is the home of the average Asian villager.

There are variations of the typical Asian village scene. Sometimes villages are clustered with closely-packed houses. Sometimes the houses stretch out in rows on one or both sides of a river, dike, or highway. In many parts of Southeast Asia, the houses are raised above the ground on stilts. They sit in the middle of a compound, nestling among shade trees of fruit and palm, and have roofed porches which are a comfort to the family during the hot days and nights. The animals live beneath the house. This kind of house is right for a warm climate, for it permits a good circulation of the air.

The number of Asians who live in a typical village varies from several hundred to over a thousand persons. They may all bear the same surname and be the descendants of the common ancestor who founded the village, as in China. This type of village is known by the family name, the Li Village, the Wu Village, the Wang Village. Other villages may be made up of families with several different names, although they are often related through many generations. Or the people of a village may be separated by impenetrable barriers of caste, as in India. The outcastes may live there too—poor, neglected, condemned to a life of wretchedness and degradation—but they belong to the village, and it is the one thing that all the people have in common. It is their village.

Rice is a part of the basic diet in much of Asia. In the Japanese method of cultivation it is transplanted in flooded fields. (Embassy of India)

In parts of Asia, grain is still winnowed in the traditional manner, using the wind as an aid. (Embassy of India)

A village potter makes useful articles with his wheel. (Embassy of India)

The villagers have always been relatively self-supporting. They grow the food they eat. Countless generations of village women have spun, cut, and sewn for long, long hours to make clothes for their children, their husbands, and themselves. They have learned to be practical and have adapted their clothes to the climate in which they live. Clothes are padded with layers of cotton and silk in the cold regions. In warm climates, clothing is loose and scanty. The village, however, is not completely self-sufficient, and some items must be bought—salt, sugar, cooking oil, implements of iron and metal, dyes, and a few others. To obtain these necessities, the villagers raise crops such as peanuts and other vegetables which can be sold for cash. The villagers were more self-supporting in the past than they are today, and the cheaper machine-made products of our modern age are changing the economy and life of the villagers.

Of course, in our own time, there are a few rich villages as well, where electric lights gleam in almost every house, where clean filtered water pours out of modern faucets, where sanitary shops, blaring radios, and occasional TV aerials intrude dramatically on the traditional Asian landscapes. Such villages are found in Japan, in Formosa, in the "model villages" of mainland China, and even, in small numbers, in Malaysia, the Philippines, and India. They are living demonstrations of the threat of promise, of the enormous hard work which must be done by millions of people if all of Asia is to be brought up to their standard.

The life of the villagers in most of Asia, however, is not an easy one. There are too

The earliest known form of printing was probably first done by the Chinese. The Diamond Sutra, below, was printed on paper from a wood block in the ninth century A.D. (Courtesy of the British Museum)

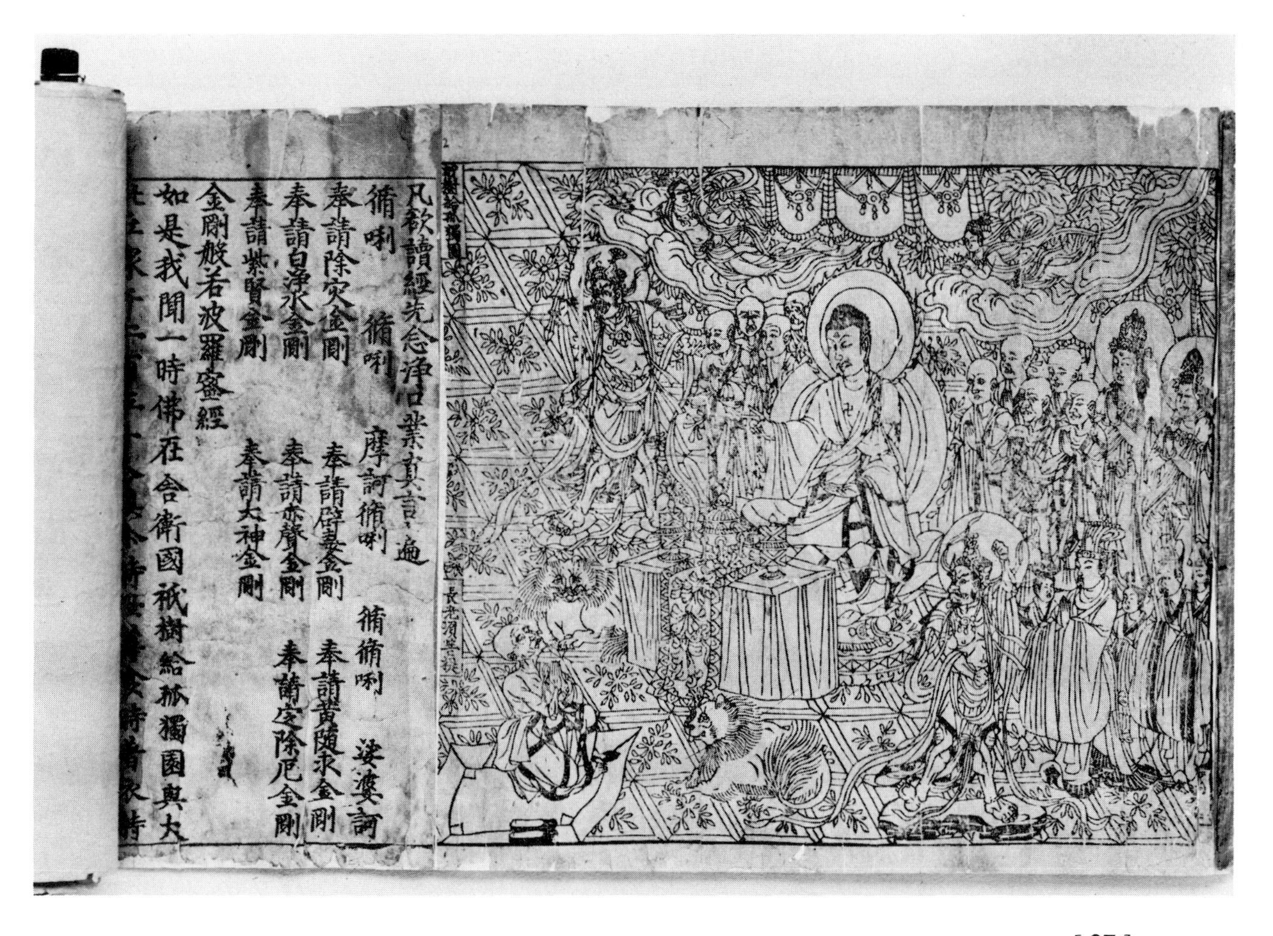

many villagers trying to obtain a living from little plots of earth. The rains may not come, the locusts may come and eat the few grains that are growing, or other insects may blight the crops—but men must eat, and their families must be fed, so they borrow from the money-lender, the village banker. He charges a very high interest, which they too often cannot meet, and soon they find themselves working exclusively for the money-lender. The interest of the original debt has mounted to the point where they can never hope to pay it off.

But the villagers have their moments of happiness. In the past, wandering storytellers visited the village and related to them dramas which often had a moral. A group of players may stage for them tales of revered and heroic men. In every Asian country there are religious and other festivals which give temporary relief from the thought of debt and toil, and the food is sufficient, at least for the day. There are marriages and funerals, which are always occasions for visiting, gossiping, and eating. And there are the times when the villagers merely stand or squat at the village edge to watch the sunset redden their ripening grain, and they are quietly happy.

1. Explain the term *self-sufficiency*. Relate this to village life in Asia.
2. What is a "family village"?
3. How do you explain that modern conveniences have come to a few villages?

### Conclusion

We have watched as various families of man slowly made their way to Asia over many years in the distant past. The Indians and Chinese constructed the first civilizations in this region, and we have observed that their achievements attracted other men. The Asians of today are a mixture of many origins, peoples, and civilizations—all of which are reflected in differing physical characteristics, languages, and ways of life.

As the Asians settled a land which had a variety of features and climates, they chose to make their settlements first along the rivers and the coasts. These were the places where water could be obtained most easily and food could be produced in greater abundance. Over the long centuries the population increased until these fertile lands could not feed any more men. Some moved elsewhere—to the mountains and other less hospitable land—and gradually every bit of Asia's earth came to be cultivated by man.

Today almost half of the world's population is Asian. The land, for the Asians, is a matter of life or death. They spend much of their lives in the search for food. The land's production cannot keep pace with the rapidly increasing numbers of people. Many, if not most, of the people of Asia are hungry, and some starve.

## SUMMING UP THE CHAPTER

A. Define or explain the following terms, relating them to this chapter.

| | |
|---|---|
| caste | money-lender |
| Confucianism | monsoon |
| dynasty | Taoism |
| Legalism | |

B. Identify or locate the following and tell why they are important.

| | |
|---|---|
| Ainu | Hwang Ho |
| Aryan | Khyber Pass |
| Bolan Pass | Mahabharata and Ramayana |
| Caucasian | Mongols |
| Chou dynasty | Negritos |
| Dravidian | Pamir Knot |
| Gumal Pass | Shang dynasty |
| Harappa and Mohenjo-Daro | Vedas |
| Himalayas | Vedic Period |
| Hsia | Yangtze |

C. Identify these dates and indicate their importance.

1. 2000 B.C. (India)
2. 2500 B.C. (China)
3. 1750-1122 B.C. (China)
4. 1122-256 B.C. (China)
5. 1000-500 B.C. (India)
6. 2000-500 B.C. (India)

D. Chapter review questions.

1. What were some of the results of the meeting, mingling, and mating of the first peoples who came to Asia?
2. Where did the Dravidians first settle in India? Why did they move southward from

their original settlements and what happened to them on their move south? Where are they living in India today?

3. Compare the lasting effects of the Dravidian and Aryan cultures. Which effect do you feel was the most important? Why?
4. The Aryan sense of separateness and superiority resulted in the establishment of an important social institution. Name this institution. Does it exist today?
5. Who gave India her classical language, Sanskrit?
6. When was the Epic Period in India? What is known about this period?
7. Why are legends important to historians?
8. When the House of Chou overthrew the Shang dynasty it offered an ideological explanation. What was this justification, and was it used in subsequent attempts to overthrow other dynasties?
9. What do the legends of early China tell us about her accomplishments?
10. Why was the discovery of Harappa and Mohenjo-Daro important?
11. What are the origins of the Chinese people? Why is it difficult to determine their exact ancestry?
12. Why are rivers of central importance to people living in Asia? What crops are grown near their banks? What advantages and disadvantages can you see in living near a river?
13. Describe the formation of summer and winter monsoons. In what ways are the Asians dependent on them?
14. What is the highest mountain range in the world? Where is it located?
15. Explain the following quotation as it relates to this chapter: "Asia is a region of villages." To what extent would this quotation be valid for both historic and modern settings?
16. To what extent were Asians of the past limited to the surroundings of their villages? To what extent would this be true today?
17. Describe several types of Asian villages from the point of view of their dwellings and layout. What accounts for differences in these two things? What can you learn about the topography and climate of Asia by looking at pictures of its villages?
18. Why was survival a problem in historical Asia? Is it a problem today? For the same reasons?
19. On what occasions have Asians traditionally escaped from the hardships of life?

E. Questions for discussion.
   1. Practically all known civilizations developed originally around rivers. What explanation can you give for this? Can you think of any civilizations that did not develop along rivers?
   2. The early history of Asia is in part the history of the intermingling of races from which new races were formed. This process of racial assimilation is not confined to Asia or to the past. How do you account for the fact that new races have not emerged during the modern age?
   3. Can you explain the circumstances and economic processes which often create a class of large landowners and a class of tenants or serfs?

F. Projects for groups or individuals.
   1. List the major river systems of Asia and tell where they are located. Draw a map and label the rivers.
   2. Prepare a scrapbook on the various peoples of Asia mentioned in this chapter. Find pictures which will show the physical features of these different peoples, their villages, major arts and crafts. Label each picture in your collection with a brief description.
   3. Select one of the major mountain passes in Asia. Trace its history and its effect on the development of the region in which it is located.

# CHAPTER 2

# *Lasting Ideologies*

THE PHYSICAL WORLD is but one aspect of the Asian's life—necessary and important, but still only a part of the total. Man is something more than a food-gathering animal. He thinks, dreams, speculates, inspires, and is inspired. He is unsatisfied, and he hopes for something better, either here or hereafter, or in both places. The Asian is no exception to these drives and urges within man. He has talked and written much about man and God, man and nature, and man and his society. It was the Indians and Chinese who spoke earliest and most about these matters. Later, the Japanese and the Southeast Asians contributed their thoughts to these important subjects.

## Early Religion of the Indians

It will be recalled that the Aryans came to India around 2000 B.C. from Central and Southwest Asia. They were an earthy people and boisterous in their manners. Many of their religious beliefs revolved around the exciting exhibitions of nature and its powerful forces—the sky, the sun, the dawn, the fire. They made a god of liquor under the name *Soma*. They sacrificed the flesh of animals as well as milk and grain. They offered fermented wine to their gods in the hope that the gods would aid them here and now. But there was also a faint, undefined feeling that the assistance of the gods might be needed after death.

## The Vedas

We know something about the customs, institutions, and religious practices of the Aryans from four collections of sacred writings called *Vedas*. The Vedas are very ancient. They are made up for the most part of poetic hymns and prayers, and before they were written down they were passed by word of mouth through an unknown number of centuries. Thus, the Indians refer to them as "that which is heard"—the holy men heard the words of God and wrote them down so that others too might know them. Oldest of these is the *Rig-Veda*, written about the middle of the period between 2000 and 500 B.C. The other three Vedas were written toward the end of this period.

Then, over the course of the years, other works were added to the original Vedas. Some dealt with ritual and the interpretation of the original religious hymns of the Vedas; others were legal writings. The best known of these additional works are the Upanishads. *Upanishad* literally means "sitting near." A knowledge of the essential truths of the Vedas was acquired while sitting around wise teachers. The Vedas and the Upanishads might be called the basic scriptures of Hinduism, the religion of the majority of the Indians.

## The *Mahabharata* and the *Ramayana*

There are other writings which are also important to the religious life of the Hindu Indians. Among the more important and best known of these are two epics, the *Mahabharata* and the *Ramayana*. They were written toward the end of the period between 1000 and 500 B.C. These epics are so influential in the thinking and actions of the Hindu Indians that this period of time is called the Epic Period of India.

The *Mahabharata* is the longest poem in the world, around 200,000 lines. It relates the story of a war between two Indian families, the Pandavas and the Kauravas. The Pandavas were the five sons of Pandu, who ruled an area south of Delhi. The Kauravas were the hundred sons of Dhritarashtra, brother of Pandu, whose capital was on the Ganges. The war was fought so savagely that few survived its end. Deep in the heart of the poem is a profound discussion between the god Krishna and Arjuna, a member of the forces of the Pandavas family. This poetic dialogue is known as the *Bhagavad-Gita*, the Lord's Song. Its basic thought—to perform without attachment the work that must be done—became fundamental to the religion of the Indians. One must act, but he should also be detached from his acts or their results. Duty should be done without emotion or desire.

Over the years of Indian history, and today, scenes from the *Mahabharata* have been told by the village storyteller, dramatized on the Indian stage, and repeated in many books. There are few Indians, literate or illiterate, who are not familiar with the content and the teachings of the *Mahabharata*. This epic is also well known to other Asians in Thailand, Cambodia, Ceylon, Laos, Burma, Malaysia, Indonesia, and elsewhere.

The *Ramayana* is a story about Prince Rama and his devoted wife, Sita, who were exiled because of the mad jealousy of a stepmother. It tells of their rovings in the jungle, the kidnaping of Sita by a demon king of Ceylon named Ravana, and of her rescue by Prince Rama with the help of the monkey king, Hanumàn. The story concludes with their happy return to their native land. It is a beloved tale in India and also in Indonesia, Thailand, Burma, and elsewhere in Asia. One of India's gayest festivals, the Diwali (Festival of Lights), celebrates the return of Rama and Sita to their homeland. Every year on this festive occasion trees, streets, and homes are alight in celebration of the safe return of Rama and Sita from the demon king's land of Lanka in Ceylon. This epic is no longer

There are few Indians who are not familiar with the story of the *Ramayana*. The story is often played as a dance-drama, as in the performance pictured below. (Government of India Tourist Office)

Yoga is the Hindu system of philosophic meditation designed to attain spiritual perfection. The postures, or asanas, are intended to develop the power of meditation. (Embassy of India)

regarded as merely a story; it has become a part of the religious life of the people. Prince Rama is the ideal man, and Sita, the ideal woman; they have become examples of what all good Indian men and women should be.

## A Thousand Years of Change

We know from reading the *Rig-Veda* and these two epics, written hundreds of years apart, that during this time the customs, institutions, and religious beliefs and practices of the Indians evolved into something quite different from what they had been. The freedom-loving, unrestrained Aryans became chained, over the course of these many years, by the restrictions of a more rigid society. The people changed somewhat in appearance, as strains of other races, including the Mongoloid, appeared among them. Their loose tribal associations evolved and the land was divided into small kingdoms concerned with the ceremonial and with war. The seeds of division among men, planted by racial attitudes, grew into a system of caste supported by religion. And many other gods replaced the few gods of nature. Three of these many new gods became supreme: Brahma, the Creator; Vishnu, the Preserver; and Siva, the Destroyer. They are still supreme today. The rather simple early religious beliefs evolved into something more complex, more embracing, more meaningful—the religion of Hinduism, a religion that is now followed by the vast majority of the population of India.

1. What are the *Vedas?* Name the most important of them. When were they written?
2. How did the *Upanishads* acquire their name?
3. When were the Epics written? To what Western literature may they be compared?
4. What important ideals are found in the *Mahabharata?* What is the *Bhagavad-Gita?* What is its fundamental teaching?

## Hinduism

In Hinduism, the Indians found a religion which seeks to meet all the needs of man. It is tolerant. It is accommodating. To the mystic, it offers thought at the highest level. For those who prefer the more concrete, it provides impressive temples, a pageant of ritual, and a choice of many gods. The Hindus understand that the intellectual and spiritual cravings of man are almost infinite, ranging from the highest to the lowest levels. Hinduism seeks to satisfy man at every level.

In these sincere efforts to satisfy the many wants of man, the Hindu religion has become almost bewildering in its variety. There are gods beyond number, sects and subsects, and subsects of the subsects. There are commentaries on the scriptures, and commentaries on the commentaries. Religious practices vary from locality to locality, and even from home to home. But the sympathetic, wise Indian sage to whom we take our bewilderment will say that it is all very simple. This almost infinite variety is but the face of Hinduism, and beneath this face there lies a basic unity of thought and action.

### One Ultimate Reality

Reality is one, the wise man would continue, though we speak of it in differing terms. The myriad gods displayed in temples, cities, countryside, and homes are merely symbols of one Ultimate Reality which cannot be limited to a name, a form, or a person. All the gods of stone, wood, gold, silver, clay, or any other element of earth, are but the unceasing, limited efforts of man to portray what can never be truly portrayed, what must forever be really formless and nameless. These many gods of India are concessions to the senses of man. They are attempts to meet the demands of the human heart which require some material expression of a reality that goes beyond the reaches of human understanding and imagination.

Everything in the universe—man, gods, animals, nature—is a manifestation of this Ultimate Reality. We are all related; we are all one through this Ultimate Reality; and nothing, living or nonliving, stands apart from anything else. Within every man there is an essential self, similar perhaps to what the Christians call the soul. The Hindus call it *Atman.* This Atman is one with the Ultimate Reality or *Brahma*, which is the name the Hindus generally use when referring to the Ultimate Reality. And thus man is one with everything in the universe, because he is but one of the countless evidences of Brahma.

### Salvation from the Finite

Hinduism teaches that gods and temples, rituals and creeds, are not of themselves important. They are merely means to assist man in delivering himself from a particular body. The essential self, or Atman, of man is imprisoned in a confining, ignorant, egotistical body. This body is confined by the limitations of the senses; it is ignorant that everything in the world is part of one thing, not separate; and it is egotistical in thinking of itself as unique. The final goal of man is the realization that he is one with the Ultimate Reality. To reach his goal, he must escape from the idea that he is an individual, separate and distinct from others. He must destroy the "I am."

When man finally realizes that he is one with the Ultimate Reality, he is no longer subject to the confinements of the body and the bonds of an individual existence. He is then free of the finite. But our wise Indian teacher would tell us that this is not an easy task, and it generally involves a series of separate existences before salvation from the finite is obtained.

### Rebirth

The Hindus believe that a man may be reborn again and again, perhaps many times. The essential self of man does not die when the body dies, for it is a part of the Ultimate Reality which has no beginning and no end. Nor is it restricted in the form it might assume. In succeeding generations, the self may reign as a god, destroy as a demon, bloom as a flower, crawl as a snake, wander as a tiger, or silently meditate as a Hindu seer.

The form into which a man is reborn is determined by the law of *karma*—which holds that the acts a man performs while he is living determine his future state, and that his present state itself is the result of all his previous acts. Good acts done now will raise him to a higher level in his next rebirth; bad acts will lower his status in his next rebirth. Karma is inexorable, certain, and constant.

The statue above portrays the cosmic dance of the Hindu god Siva. (Government of India Tourist Office)

This statue in the caves of Elephanta in Bombay shows the three faces of Brahma, Siva, and Vishnu. Hindus consider them as personifications of the one Ultimate Reality. (Government of India Tourist Office)

In the idea of rebirth there is a spiritual progress which finally ends when man is liberated from the ever-turning wheel of birth and rebirth. The system of caste is one way in which Hindus measure man's progress toward final liberation.

## Caste

Indians are born into different castes, or separate groups, within their society. In part, the caste system had its origin in the attitude of superiority that the fair Aryans held toward the darker-skinned people they met when they first entered India. Its origin is also partly economic. We shall deal with the social aspects of caste in more detail in a later chapter. We are interested now in how caste conforms to the idea of rebirth and the spiritual progress of man toward liberation.

Basically, there are four castes: the Brahman, the Kshatriya, the Vaisya, and the Sudra. Then there are those with no caste at all, called *outcastes*. This latter group is on the lowest level of Indian society. The caste system indicates the progress man is making towards liberation. The Brahmans, the most spiritual caste, hold the highest position, followed by the Kshatriyas, the Vaisyas, the Sudras, and finally the outcastes, in that order. So the farthest removed from liberation among the Hindus are the outcastes, and the nearest to liberation are the Brahmans.

The Kailasa temple at Ellora is one of the finest examples of ancient Brahmanical architecture in India. There are also Buddhist and Jain temples nearby. Which religion ultimately became dominant? (Government of India Tourist Office)

## Stages of Life

The Hindus have also divided the life of each individual into four progressive stages, which they call *ashramas*. These stages of life move along upward, from the more material to the more spiritual occupations of the individual. In ascending order, these are the student, the householder, the anchorite, and the sannyasi. The stage of the student is one of preparation, study, and discipline. The stage of the householder is the one in which the individual undertakes his responsibilities to his family, his society, his community, and his nation. When he has fulfilled these responsibilities, he should withdraw from the distractions of the world and enter the third stage of his life, that of the anchorite, wherein he immerses himself in study and meditation once again. Finally, he reaches the time of complete denial of all that is material, the stage of the sannyasi: he may become a hermit, living in some remote place, satisfied to be alone with his high thoughts and his God; or he may wander among the people, asking nothing of anyone, nor caring if he receives anything. He has renounced his passions and his desires. He is among the people but not of them. The Indians revere these men above all others. Although the sannyasis do not care, they receive from all the highest honor and respect.

## A Guide for Life

Every Hindu has his duty, his law, his guidebook for life, called *dharma*. Each individual's dharma will vary with his position, his responsibility, his caste, and his stage of life. It is the Hindu's guide for right conduct, and if he carries out his dharma well, he knows that he is on the right path toward final liberation.

The Hindus realize that men have certain material and social needs that must be satisfied. Dharma regulates the satisfaction of these needs in such a fashion as to make every act further the progress toward eventual liberation from the limitations of the body. Ideally, man should act without attachment to the act. He must destroy the desire that accompanies action, but not the action itself.

These, in brief, are some of the basic beliefs that lie beneath the many-hued face of Hinduism. But there is also another religion that was born in India. It has claimed the love and allegiance of millions of Asians both inside and outside India down to the present. That religion is Buddhism.

1. How has the accommodating nature of Hinduism led to great diversities? How is this diversity explained away by the Hindu?
2. Explain the concept of the one Ultimate Reality, or *Brahma*. What is the relationship of *Atman,* the essential self, to *Brahma?*
3. How does the inexorable law of *karma* lead to identification of *Atman* with *Brahma,* and liberation from the wheel of rebirth?
4. What is the religious significance of the caste system? List and describe the divisions within this system.

## Buddhism

Much that has been said about Hinduism can also be said about Buddhism, for each has influenced the teachings of the other. Buddhism began after Hinduism, in the sixth century B.C., when Gautama Siddhartha, later called the Buddha, suddenly understood the cause and solution of man's sufferings. This realization came to him while he was sitting deep in meditation under a tree. The Buddhists refer to this "sudden understanding" as "enlightenment."

A scene on the Meghna River, East Pakistan is shown. Find this river on a map. (Embassy of Pakistan)

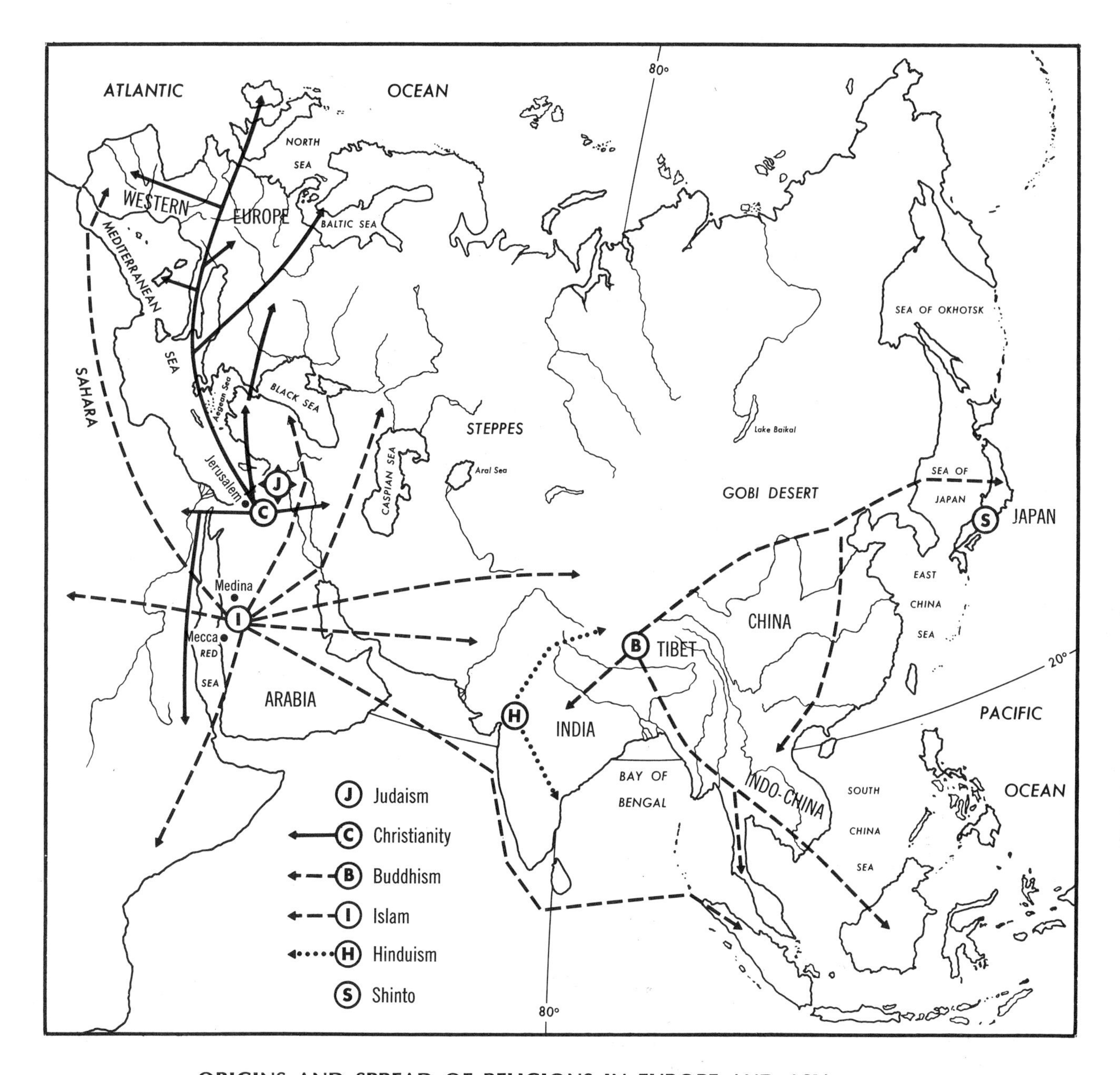


**ORIGINS AND SPREAD OF RELIGIONS IN EUROPE AND ASIA**

Use the text to find the dates of origin of the religions shown. Why do you imagine each religion spread in certain areas but not in others? Which religions became most widely spread?

In a sense Buddhism was an offspring of Hinduism. In another real sense it was a protest against certain teachings and practices of the Hindus, especially those of the Hindu priests, or Brahmans. It was in part a movement against these priests. Another religion called Jainism also arose in India during the sixth century B.C. It, too, was in part a reform movement protesting the rigid, artificial domination of the Brahman priests. Both Jainism and Buddhism had great influence upon the Indians. Today there are still perhaps a mil-

This representation of the Buddha is by Nand Lal Bose, a modern painter of Bengal. (Embassy of India)

lion or more followers of Jainism in India. The influence of Buddhism, however, went far beyond India into practically all of Asia. Buddhism has shaped the beliefs and the lives of untold numbers of Asians since the time of its birth in India almost six hundred years before the Christian era.

Both Hinduism and Buddhism are concerned with the origins and meaning of life. Both were the results of much inspired thinking about the primary problems of life such as the impermanence of existence, the presence of suffering everywhere, the unity that appears amid diversity, and the untouchable spirit that dwells among people and perhaps within —a spirit capable of such feelings.

Some of the answers that the Buddhists found to man's problems eventually were absorbed into the accommodating, tolerant religion of Hinduism; and some were not. For instance, Hinduism taught that man had a soul; Buddhism denied the existence of an individual soul. Hinduism gave many gods to man; Buddhism, in its original form, denied to man any gods or supernatural beings.

## The Founder: Gautama Buddha

Hinduism had no single founder. There is no definite period of time or date when it can be said that Hinduism began; but Buddhism has a founder, and its beginning dates from him. Gautama Siddhartha is generally known as Gautama Buddha, and sometimes he is simply called "the Buddha" or "the Enlightened One." Gautama was born around 563 B.C., and he died about eighty years later in 483 B.C. What we know about his life comes to us through tradition, but there are certain parts of this tradition which are generally accepted as factual.

Gautama was the son of a chief of the Sakya tribe, which lived in the foothills of the Himalaya Mountains, perhaps within the present borders of Nepal. He was born into a family of wealth and power, and he enjoyed its many advantages. He was married and, at the age of 29, became the father of a son. During this same year he was shocked into changing his entire life by successive meetings with an old man, a sick man, a dead man, and a beggar. Suddenly struck by the misery, sorrow, and decay of life, he felt compelled to leave his family and his home to find the reason for these sad facts and the solution for them. For six wearying years he sought the answers to these disturbing questions. He sought in the Vedas, the source of Hindu truths; he sought through the practice of a strict life of self-denial; he sought in the middle ground between ravaging and indulging the body. Then, one day while sitting under a bo tree, he was enlightened, and the answers to his questions about man's life came to him. He had found the way of Buddhism. And Gautama Buddha began to preach to the people of India, telling them what he had discovered.

**Change is everywhere; nothing is permanent.** Everything is in a state of flux, constantly passing from one modification to another. Nothing that we see today is ever the same tomorrow. And while it is changing, it is decaying. The young become old and finally die; and the fresh flower of the dawn droops withered at sunset. Nothing is permanent, not even the essential self or soul of man. The only thing that might be said to endure is the ever-turning wheel of change and decay, the eternal, ever-turning wheel. Basic to the Buddha's teaching are four important truths.

**There are Four Noble Truths:** (1) suffering is universal; (2) the cause of suffering is desire; (3) the elimination of desire will destroy suffering; and (4) the Noble Eightfold Path is a good technique for overcoming desire.

*1. Everyone suffers.* There is no man, no woman, no child who does not suffer in some way almost daily. Even pleasure is a cause of suffering because we know that it will not last, and this knowledge in itself is a sorrow. And these sorrows of man will go on and on, rebirth after rebirth, until he ends his existences through enlightenment. Although Gautama Buddha did not believe in the permanence of a soul, he did believe that, in some way, man was born and reborn again and again until he had crushed his desires and his attachments.

*2. Desire is the cause of suffering.* Until man stops craving for anything, his suffering will continue through the ages, birth after birth. He will go on forever, chained to the wheel of a changing and decaying life. Man must realize that he can never find permanent satisfaction on earth or elsewhere until he suppresses all desires for happiness, pain, individuality, existence—in short, for everything. When he realizes that self is an illusion, that all things are temporary and changing, and that individual existence can only result in suffering, then, and only then, will he become enlightened—a Buddha. His continued existences will cease and he will escape to the bliss of nirvana.

*3. Nirvana is a condition or state in which all desires are extinct.* It is the ultimate goal of all good Buddhists. It is bliss and is a condition of no suffering. It is indescribable because it can be known only by those who are enlightened.

There are certain guidelines that Gautama Buddha offered to those who would escape the tragedies of life and enter nirvana even while living a life in society. These guidelines are incorporated in the Noble Eightfold Path.

*4. The Noble Eightfold Path is as follows:* (1) right knowledge of the cause and ending of suffering; (2) high and worthy intentions; (3) kind, frank, truthful speech; (4) right conduct; (5) right livelihood that does not injure any living thing; (6) right effort to train oneself; (7) a keen and active mind; (8) meditation. If man followed these ethical guidelines carefully and well, he would find his nirvana.

## Buddhism Spreads

Many of the people of India, especially North India, heard and liked the teachings of Gautama Buddha and his disciples. They built monasteries, and many of them donned the robes of monk or nun. Those who entered monasteries sought enlightenment and eventually nirvana. This beginning of monastic life started when the Persians, under the great king Darius, came to India in 518 B.C. Darius made northwest India a Persian province. When Alexander the Great defeated the Persians and appeared briefly in northwest India in 327-326 B.C., Buddhism was still expanding. It reached great heights of influence in India during the Maurya dynasty, 322-185 B.C., which was founded by a clever, cunning man named Chandragupta.

**Chandragupta: founder of the Maurya dynasty.** The Maurya dynasty was the first to unite most of the Indians under one ruler. Chandragupta was an efficient ruler, with a well-organized spy system, a fine road network, and an effective bureaucracy. His well-organized government insured that laws were carried out and that revenues from the land—all of which was state land—came in regularly and in the proper amount. Chandragupta was also a suspicious man. He feared for his life and the security of his dynasty. He maintained an army of around 700,000 soldiers in addition to his army of informers. He traveled protected by a bodyguard of women fighters—sometimes referred to as Amazons—and to break within this bodyguard was to meet with death. Chandragupta feared assassination, and all of his food and drink was tasted by someone else. It is reported that he slept in a different room each night.

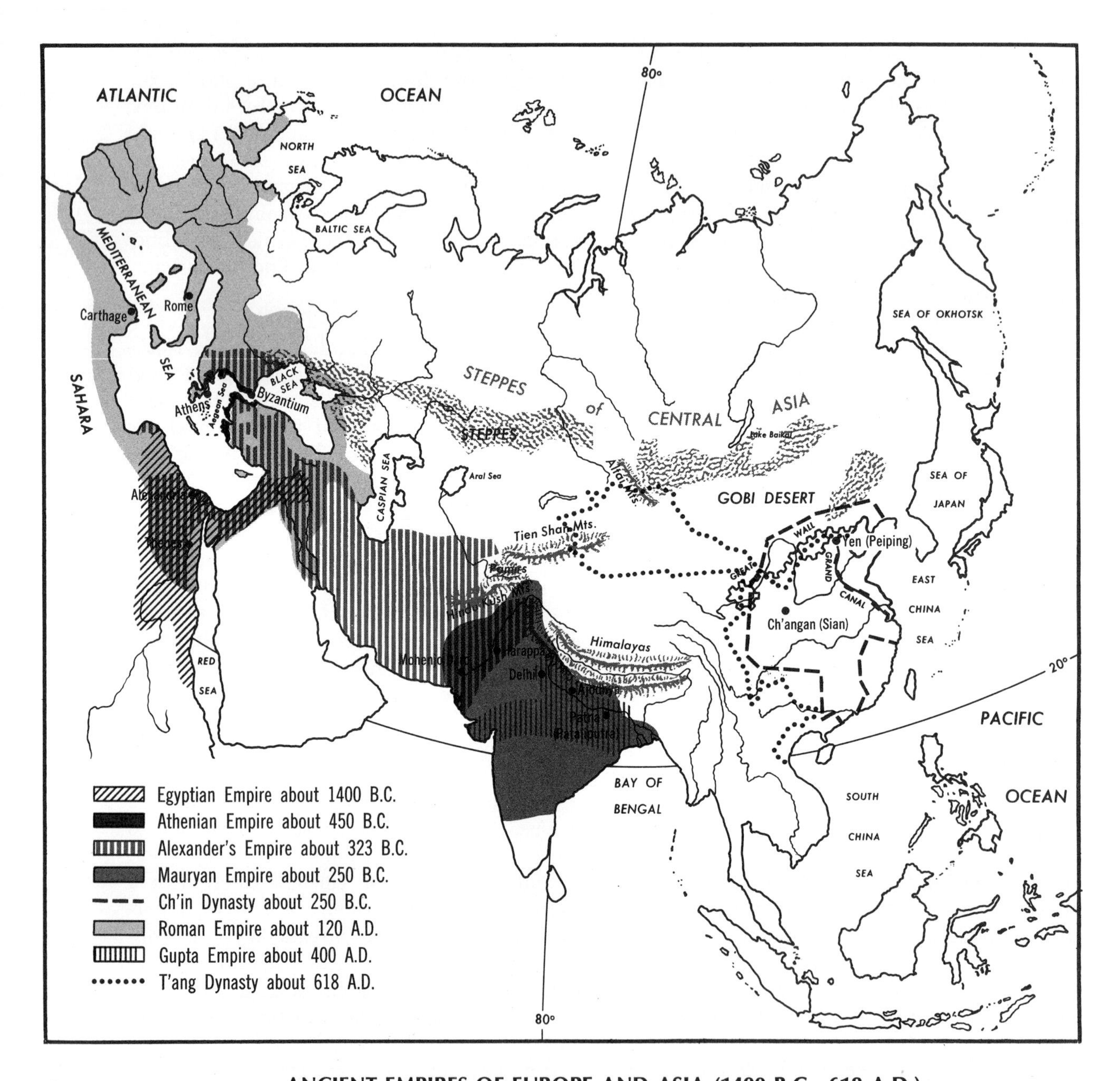


**ANCIENT EMPIRES OF EUROPE AND ASIA (1400 B.C.–618 A.D.)**

Compare the ancient empires shown here with modern political maps of Europe and Asia. Which modern countries correspond most closely in area to the ancient empires shown?

**Asoka: the tolerant king.** It was under Asoka, the grandson of Chandragupta, that the Maurya empire reached its greatest extent and Buddhism flourished in India and expanded abroad. Asoka, who ruled from 273 to 232 B.C., is regarded by the Indians as one of their most remarkable rulers. And indeed he was. At first he embarked upon an expansion of the empire left him by his grandfather and his father, Bindusara. He succeeded so well that most of the India and Pakistan we know today was brought under his control. But the awful, bloody price of his conquest was paid in the dead and mutilated bodies of hundreds of thousands of his people. This turned him from the path of violence and war, and he became one of the most humane, tolerant, and kindly kings of history.

Asoka became a fervent disciple and teacher of Buddhism. He rejected violence. He asked his subjects to be compassionate toward all living things and neither to harm nor to kill them. He himself pursued the way of nonviolence in governing his empire: he forgave his former enemies, pardoned many, and gave up his favorite pastime of hunting. Over all the land of India he carved his edicts on stones and on pillars, some of which still stand, rising forty and fifty feet above the ground. These edicts were most often moral laws and instructions. They urged the people to be kind, gentle, and tolerant of the differing beliefs and practices of others. They taught respect for the aged and advised all subjects to follow the compassionate law of Buddha.

Asoka was concerned with the welfare of his people. He improved their medical services, gave much attention to the irrigation of lands, eased the life of the traveler with rest houses, and beautified the landscape with the planting of trees. The army of informers he had inherited from his grandfather and father was transformed into an army dedicated to the advancement and protection of religion rather than the downfall and imprisonment of the suspicious.

In the reign of Asoka, Buddhism expanded at home and abroad. Asoka's personal example, his rock-carved edicts, the direction of his government—all served to publicize Buddhism throughout his empire. Toward the end of his life, Asoka convened the first council of Buddhists, which is referred to as the "Council of Patna." This council met at Pataliputra, the capital, and settled on the basic texts of Buddhism. Asoka was also filled with a missionary spirit and wanted those beyond his empire to

Asoka was the greatest ruler of the Maurya dynasty. He was converted from Brahmanism to Buddhism, and he made Buddhism the state religion of India. His edicts were carved on pillars which are of great historical value today. The Asoka pillar shown here dates from the third century B.C. and is located in the state of Bihar. (Embassy of India)

hear and accept the truths of Buddhism. His own brother was sent to Ceylon, where he converted the king of that country. Missionaries were sent to Burma and Nepal, and others went to Egypt, Greece, North Africa, and perhaps to Syria. But Buddhism did not take hold in Egypt, Greece, North Africa, or Syria. It spread to Ceylon and Burma, and from there to other parts of Southeast Asia; and today with the exception of Indonesia, Malaya, and the Philippines, the majority of the Southeast Asians are still followers of Buddhism.

The Maurya dynasty did not last long after Asoka's death. It ended with the assassination of the last ruler in 185 B.C.—but Buddhism continued to advance abroad. It entered China around the first century of the Christian era, flowed from there to Korea, and in the seventh century A.D. became entrenched in Japan. In the eighth century A.D. the Tibetans adhered to it.

1. In what way was Buddhism a reaction to Hinduism? Was there any other religious reaction to Hinduism in the sixth century B.C.?
2. What are the "Four Noble Truths"?
3. What are the elements of the "Noble Eightfold Path"?
4. When was India first unified? By whom? How did this expand the influence of Buddhism?

## The Thought of the Chinese

Buddhism made its way to China around the first century of the Christian era, carried by missionaries and travelers over the steppes and the desert of Central Asia. The Chinese already had their own ideas about man and his society and about man and nature. These ideas had been discussed, written, elaborated, and accepted centuries before the arrival of Buddhism. They were quite different from the concepts of Buddhism and, indeed, from those of Hinduism. The Indians were rather pessimistic about man's chances of finding happiness on earth. Their religions of Buddhism and Hinduism advised men to try to escape from the earthly existence, for happiness was to be found elsewhere. The Chinese, on the other hand, were more optimistic about the possibilities of finding some happiness here and now. They concentrated on trying to improve man and his society. They were not too much concerned with what might happen after death, although they did think about it; but they were mightily interested in what happened during life.

The practical quality of the great Chinese philosophies — Confucianism, Taoism, and Legalism—may have been due in large measure to the troubled times in which they originated. This was the period between the fifth and third centuries before Christ. After the Chou warriors overthrew the Shang dynasty about 1122 B.C. (see page 20), their kings set up a system which they thought would best safeguard their regime. Vassal lords were given complete authority over various territories of the Chou empire. In return, they paid tribute to the Chou king and gave full obedience in all questions of concern to the kingdom. This system of lords obeying the king is called *feudalism.* The right to rule was hereditary. It was partly based on the belief that only the ruling aristocrats could call upon supernatural assistance to maintain the security and prosperity of the country. According to this belief, if the rulers discontinued their sacrifices of the land and the grain at the ancestral halls and at the altars, trouble would befall the people and the state. This feudal society was based, therefore, upon the strong bonds between hereditary rulers and the spirits to whom they sacrificed.

As the years went on, this spiritual authority of the Chou kings weakened. The vassal lords became less obedient and began to act more like independent sovereigns rather than rulers whose authority depended ultimately upon the king. The force of the spirits gave way to the force of the sword. By the time of the fifth century B.C., the former lords of the Chou kings had become rulers of independent states. They were generally at war with one another, contending for the mastery of all China. This period of chaos and struggle is called the Warring States Period and runs from about 481 to about 256 B.C. It was during this period of bloodshed and the breakdown of customary ways of life that the great Chinese philosophies were developed.

### Confucianism

Confucius, the first and the greatest of the Chinese philosophers, was born in 551 B.C. and died around 479 B.C. His proposals for a new society were based on a return to the past. This gave Chinese society a backward-looking conservatism which lasted down to our present century. Actually, some of his ideas were new, but they also retained much of the ritual and formality of the past. Confucius especially insisted upon the responsibility of the ruler for the welfare of the people. This was a new concept of the ruler's responsibility.

Some of the ideas and practices that we find in the philosophy of Confucianism were not originated by Confucius alone. Ancestor worship, sacrifices to the dead, and other ceremonies had been practiced among the Chinese long before Confucius. Other schools of thought also contributed ideas to Confucianism as we know it now. But the basic doctrines of this philosophy can be attributed to Confucius and his two most important followers, Mencius and Hsün-tzu. The writings of Confucius and Mencius have been grouped into a collection known as the *Confucian Canon*, which is divided into two parts called the *Four Books* and the *Five Classics*.

**Human-heartedness and sympathy.** The Confucian social philosophy was rather wonderful in its thought. The Confucianists taught that in every man there is something which causes him to want to live among other men. Man, they said, is by nature a social creature.

Ancient rites are performed by Chinese people each year to celebrate the birthday anniversary of Confucius. The picture shows this celebration in Taipei at the Confucius Temple. (Photo by courtesy of the Embassy of the Republic of China)

To live apart from other men is unnatural and harmful; to live with others is natural and will further the growth and development of man. This quality, which they named *jen*, is often translated into English as "human-heartedness," "sympathy," or "benevolence." It means all of these, and more. Jen relates man to man.

This relationship is so close that whatever affects one man also affects all others. Through jen we share the feelings, interests, and common humanity of other men. Jen lies at the very root of society, for without it there could be no society, and it can only exist when there is a society.

Jen permits us to help others more easily because, since all men have it, they merely have to look within themselves to find the solutions for the problems of others. Thus, understanding of himself will give each man an understanding of others. The man who truly understands the importance and nature of jen will want to help others, because in helping others he is really helping himself. If a man faithfully follows the promptings of jen he will know how to behave toward others, for it will always tell him not to do to others what he does not want done to himself. The Confucianists taught that jen must be expressed in action, and they defined some of these actions.

**Right action.** The Confucianists insisted that each person must play definite roles in his lifetime if man was to live in harmony with himself and with others. They taught that there were five fundamental social relationships: those between ruler and subject, father and son, elder brother and younger brother, husband and wife, and between friend and friend. In these relationships there were duties and responsibilities which each person owed to the other. In each case, except in the relationship between friends, one person has authority over the other. The subordinate should give loving obedience to the superior, and the superior should be lovingly responsible for the subordinate. If there is any doubt about the right action, one has merely to ask himself: If I were a ruler how would I wish my minister or subject to serve me? If I were a father how would I want my son to behave toward me? If I were a friend how would I desire my friend to act toward me?

The Confucianists taught that actions should conform to the meaning of the names in social relationships. The ideal conduct that is associated with these names should serve as a model for behavior. A father, a son, an elder or younger brother, a husband, wife, or friend should behave in ways that agreed with the highest ideals expressed by these names. If actions did not conform to the ideal meaning of these names, then they did not conform to the reality, and therefore the relationship did not exist. A father who was not dutifully responsible for his children was not really a father; a son who was not loving and obedient was not a son at all; and a friend who was false could not be truly called a friend.

**Always be humane.** Any just action, they said, must be filled with a humane feeling for others. There is a need for written laws, but above the written law is the quality of sympathy—a wise compassion which must be an essential part of each judgment and each decision. The Confucianists doubted that just decisions could come from a strict obedience to the letter of the law under all circumstances. Custom, circumstances, the human relationships involved in each case—these were much more important to the better functioning of society than a precise interpretation of the law. The law was made for man under varying circumstances, and it should be humanely interpreted. If necessary, it should be modified to meet the changing circumstances of each individual case. Rule by man was much more important to the Confucianists than rule by law.

The Confucianists also believed that it was quite normal and correct at times for people to express outwardly their feelings of sorrow, respect, sympathy, and reverence. They approved of rituals and ceremonies through which men showed respect, for instance, to their ancestors, or their sense of loss over the death of a relative or close friend. But they cautioned that these rituals meant nothing if the individual did not himself experience the sorrow or the respect. Used properly, ceremony and ritual were considered to be instrumental in developing the moral and mental growth of men.

**The family is important.** The Confucianists taught that the family was basic to society. It was within the family that the child and the individual learned to play his basic roles in society at large. If he learned well, he would naturally be a good member of the community and a good official of the government. For the state was but an extension of the family, and an individual owed the same obedience and loyalty to the political authorities that he owed to the seniors in his family. Thus, the emperor was the father of all the Chinese, and he was responsible for the welfare of all his children.

The emperor was responsible to an impersonal force, which was called Heaven, in much the same way that the father of a family was responsible to his ancestors. The Confucianists were very rational in their approach to the problems of man. They had little to say about an afterlife, but they did teach that if the emperor did not maintain a proper relationship with Heaven, he and his people would suffer. In part, this proper relationship demanded that he be a morally good example for his large family and that he be always concerned with the welfare of his people. Otherwise Heaven would disown him. Heaven wanted what the people wanted, and the people wanted a ruler who was morally good and an able administrator, one who would give them peace, order, and prosperity.

**A better society through government.** The Confucianists believed that a well-ordered and happy society could be preserved by good government. The virtue of those who ruled was basic to good government. Both the emperor and his ministers must understand that people could be transformed by their example. It was the function of government officials to reduce corruption by moral teachings and a moral life. This was just as important as the maintenance of the irrigation systems, the defense of the empire, and other affairs of state—perhaps of greater importance.

Because of the supreme importance of men to good government, the Confucianists urged that only the best and the wisest be permitted to govern. Moral as well as secular education was required of those who wanted to serve in the government. Above all, the educated man should be honored. It did not matter into what class a man was born, nor whether he was rich or poor. His sense of moral responsibility, his example, and his education were the things that counted in the selection of a government official. The Confucianists wanted to establish a tradition in government of morally sound, educated men who worked solely in the interests of the people. They felt that if they could establish such a tradition, society would definitely improve, the state would prosper, and the people would be happy.

So they taught that if the emperor did not give them good government, the people could overthrow him; and if they were successful in their revolution, they would know that they had received a mandate from Heaven to change their rulers. Theoretically, there was no absolute king in China, for the king's authority was checked by Confucianist principles and the will of the people, which ultimately was the will of Heaven.

**A powerful force in China.** Starting with the Han dynasty (205 B.C.-220 A.D.) Confucianism became a powerful force in the society and government of China. For two thousand years it dominated the thinking and actions of Chinese scholars and officials. Knowledge of it was required of those who wanted to advance their position in the society and in the state. It became the core and the substance of all Chinese education, and thus learning in China was largely ethical in character. Confucianism gave a certain unity and permanent quality to Chinese civilization; but it also kept the people rather conservative and a bit narrow. Since the leaders were, for the most part, Confucianist in their training and orientation, they were not disposed to accept other ideas of government and society. They were somewhat contemptuous of those outside China, whose social and political thought could not compare with their own.

Marco Polo reported spectacles in use in China about 1275 A.D. (Courtesy of Bausch & Lomb, Rochester, N.Y.)

But during the Period of the Philosophers, extending roughly from the fifth to the second century B.C., Confucianism had not yet been generally accepted as the orthodox philosophy. There were other philosophers who disagreed with the teachings of Confucius and his disciples. They looked at life, society, and politics from other points of view, and much of what they taught also entered into the developing Chinese way of life, influencing literature, customs, and attitudes. Among the most influential of these philosophies were Taoism and Legalism.

1. Describe Chinese life during the Period of the Philosophers. What role did religious observance play in maintaining the power of the Chou dynasty? What is the period of the collapse of the Chou dynasty known as?
2. What quality did the Confucianists see as the basis of society? How does this quality make society both possible and necessary?
3. What are the "Five Relationships"? Which of these does not involve the authority of one person over another?
4. Explain the Confucian principle of the "Mandate of Heaven." What practical effects do you suppose resulted from this?

## Taoism

Taoism received its name from the Chinese word *tao* meaning "The Way." Lao-tzu, "Old Master," is traditionally believed to be the founder of Taoism, and the author of the original source book of this philosophy, the *Tao Te Ching*. Two other men, Chuang-tzu and Tang Chu, also contributed to the teachings of Taoism, and the book of *Chuang-tzu* is another important source of Taoist beliefs. Some believe that Lao-tzu was a little older than Confucius, while others question his very existence; but we know that Taoism originated sometime during the fifth and fourth centuries B.C.

**Let us be natural.** The Taoists taught that the problems of their time were due to man's unnatural life. Man, they said, had been chained by the conventions and restrictions of an unnatural society. The result was suffering, mental and physical pain, bloodshed, and chaos. This was not man's original condition. Formerly he had lived and moved about freely and naturally like the wild deer, unhampered by the artificial restraints that society now placed upon his movements and his actions. In his natural state, man had been happy and in harmony with his nature and the way of the *tao*.

The *tao* is that which is within and beneath all life and movement in nature. It could not be defined, the Taoists said, but it could be suggested. It is beyond measure, endless, unceasing in its flow; its shape is without a shape, and its features are featureless, like the uncarved block. It moves along, like nature, unconsciously, without motive and without effort. The sun beams, the moon shines, the clouds drift, and the rains fall; and the current of time carries us ever along from one minute to the next. There is no purpose to all of these happenings in nature; they just happen. And this is the *tao* or like the *tao*.

Perhaps, they said, we could compare it also to running water. The water prevails over barriers in its way by flowing around them; the *tao* conquers by surrendering. It is like the seas and the rivers which are found in the low places of the earth; the *tao* is supreme because it is humble.

**Tao makes things what they are.** *Tao* gives life and their special natures to all things. It is *tao* that sustains the nature of all things; and all things are different in their natures. A duck differs from a fish, a dog from a cat, a horse from a cow, and so on. It is true, they said, that the *tao* is constantly changing these forms, but always in conformity with the specific nature of each animal or thing.

To act contrary to the particular nature of an animal is to harm it by blocking the preserving flow of the *tao*. Thus, to force fish to live on land and men to live without air would result in death. It is harmful to place halters on horses and whip them, or to make them go long distances without food and water, or to make them walk in regular order, for these things are artificial and contrary to their nature.

**Social conventions are harmful.** The Taoists taught that social conventions such as ceremonies and etiquette are artificial and not of man's nature. Therefore, they are harmful. Man should be free to express himself spontaneously and naturally. He should not be inhibited and constrained by external conventions imposed upon him by society. These harmful practices were forced upon man by the inventors of conventions and rules, and by those, such as the Confucianists, who persisted in urging man to harness himself with rituals and ceremony. The Taoists believed that man should withdraw from conventional society, although not from other men.

The Taoists were very doubtful about the usual notions of right and wrong, or good and evil. They felt that the idea of one thing being good and another evil had been created only by the false standards of society. The Taoists said that we only teach and encourage men to steal and be dishonest by using locks and seals for protection and by using weights and measures to ensure honesty. Both the man of great virtue and the man of great evil are abnormal and unnatural, they said. There should be only the natural man expressing his nature, unhindered by anything external.

**Have no illusions.** Men are led astray, the Taoists said, because they think that things outside of themselves—things perceived by the senses—have an independent existence. Because of this, men either want to own these things, or they fear them, or they seek a knowledge of them. The Taoist sage, on the other hand, because of his union with the *tao*, already possesses all these outward-appearing things. He has no illusion that they are separate from him, and therefore he does not fear, want, or seek a false knowledge of them. He does not fear death, because he is one with the *tao*, which is deathless. Death for him is merely a change of form. He has no intention of seeking anything; therefore, he can have no frustration. He has no ambition for high office or prestige; therefore he knows no envy nor tension. His mind does not stop to feel guilty nor to judge. He wears his thoughts like well-fitting shoes, unthinkingly and naturally.

The Taoists were imaginative and poetic, and they wanted to free man from his routine of thinking. They tried to stimulate and excite thought by statements that seemed to express impossible ideas, such as "Do nothing, and there is nothing you cannot do." They applied this type of thought to the practice of politics. One who was in union with the *tao* would govern without appearing to govern. He would fill the people's stomachs and empty their minds, and everyone would be happy.

**The evolution of Taoism.** As time went on, Taoism took a religious turn, and the Chinese peasant began to associate Taoism with the world of spirits. Gods close to the daily life of the Chinese arose from Taoism; the gods of rain, of fire, of agriculture, and of the kitchen, for example, became superior beings whose aid has been invoked for hundreds and hundreds of years by the Chinese. Taoists are still called upon to select lucky days for weddings and funerals and to select good and fortunate sites for houses and shops. As time progressed, Buddhism and Taoism influenced each other in the development of ritual, ceremony, and a priesthood.

But the basic teachings of Taoism have also intrigued scholars and thoughtful people over the many centuries since its birth. Thus Taoism is mirrored in many Chinese poems, paintings, and books, and in the great appeal that nature has for the Chinese. In their arts, the Chinese are more Taoist than Confucianist.

## Legalism

Legalism is another important philosophy of the Chinese. The main collections of Legalist writings are found in three works written in the period between 350 and 100 B.C. They are *The Book of Lord Shang*, written by Shang Yang; *Han Fei-tzu*, written by Han Fei-tzu; and the *Kuan Tzu*, attributed to Kuan I-wu.

**The ruler was absolute.** The ruler was all-powerful, whoever he might be, the Legalists said. He was subordinate to no one. He determined what the people would do, how they would behave, and what laws should govern them. Heaven and the people had nothing to say about these matters. The people were to be regarded as babies who did not know what was good for them. They had to be instructed in simple, clear, specific language. If they disobeyed instructions, they should know the specific punishment they would receive for each infraction of the rules, or, as the Legalists would say, the laws.

Law was the ruler's main instrument in controlling the people, in securing his power within the state and expanding it abroad, they said. The law was not intended for the protection of the individual and his rights. The Legalists did not conceive of such a use for the law, for the individual existed to serve the ruler and the state; he had no privileges except what the ruler might give him. The laws mostly dealt with punishments; they were penal laws. The Legalists believed that the Confucianists were foolish to think that benevolence or human-heartedness could maintain order within the state. This could only be done through laws supported by harsh penalties.

**Self-interest.** Man is a selfish animal, the Legalists said. He can be moved to act or not to act only by the hope of some reward or the fear of some punishment. He will obey his ruler only if he fears him, or if he will get something from him.

The Legalists thought that the social and political problems of their time were due to the scarcity of goods in relation to the increase of population, and to the increased importance of the position of emperor. In former years, when the population was smaller, there had been more than enough of food and goods to go around. Consequently, there had been no necessity to compete with others for these items. But as the numbers of the people grew, production of goods did not keep pace with the increase of population. People began to struggle among themselves for possession of increasingly scarce materials and foods. They eventually became so concerned with the satisfaction of their own individual desires that they were blinded to the welfare of the people and the state.

Further, said the Legalists, the wars among the various Chinese states were caused by the many rewards that would fall to the one who succeeded in occupying the throne as emperor of China. In the past the office of emperor had not been very rewarding. In those days the ruler lived in poor quarters, ate simple foods, worked like a peasant, and dressed in rough clothes. But now, even the office of the magistrate of a district provided enough to keep a man and his family living well for generations. Naturally men fought among themselves to gain the spoils of the emperor's office.

**The solution.** The solution, they said, was to set up a strong, centralized state under the firm hand of one ruler. Then the ruler should publish a detailed list of laws, stressing the penalties for lawbreakers. There should not be any humaneness nor any circumstances that might excuse the offender from his punishment. Even the most unimportant offenses should be dealt with in a severe manner. For example, they recommended that the hand that threw ashes into the street should be cut off, and that one who hid a lawbreaker should be cut in two. Their reasoning was that if the ruler was harsh in small offenses, the people would not dare break the more important laws.

Following their idea of the nature of man, the Legalists recommended that only two occupations should be encouraged in the state: war and agriculture. Food was essential; and war was the means to the control of all China. The ruler must manipulate his people in such a way that advancement came only from the pursuits of agriculture and war. Life must be made bitter for those who did not farm or soldier. Thus, men would seek the advantages of agriculture and war and shun the bitterness of other occupations.

After he had published his laws and regimented the people into the two occupations of war and agriculture, the ruler should select the right people to carry out the duties listed for each office. And there should be a detailed list of rewards and punishments for them also. He should delegate to them the full responsibility of executing his laws and orders, and he need then do nothing more. Borrowing the words but not the means of the Taoists, the Legalists said that the ruler could rule by doing nothing, and yet there would be nothing that was not done.

**The legacy.** The methods employed by the Legalists were quite successful at first. They were used by the rulers of Ch'in, one of the small states seeking the mastery of China at that time. They proved to be so effective that Ch'in conquered the other contending states and unified the China of that period under one ruler. The ruler of Ch'in began to rule as first emperor around 256 B.C. He continued to use the ideas and methods of the Legalists in governing the country. The first emperor divided China into various administrative districts, standardized such things as weights and measures, and published laws affecting many aspects of the people's lives. Infractions of these laws were severely punished.

But the inevitable happened. The people endured as much as they could of these severe laws and penalties, and finally, about 207 B.C., they revolted. The Ch'in ruler was toppled from his throne. The Han dynasty succeeded the Ch'in and lasted from about 205 B.C. to 220 A.D. With the coming of the Han dynasty, Confucian philosophy began to dominate the social and political scene. There was only one brief period, under the Han emperor Wu, when a disguised Legalism prevailed. Otherwise, Confucianism remained the philosophy of China until the twentieth century, although the codes of each dynasty reflected some of the influence of Legalism. Today the very different doctrine of Communism prevails over the length and breadth of mainland China. Its principles and origins have nothing in common with traditional Chinese philosophies, but it brings again the same arbitrary spirit that marked Legalist China.

1. What was "The Way," or *tao?* What was the Taoist's objection to society?
2. What happened as Taoism became popularized? In what fields did Taoism exert its greatest influence?
3. How did the Legalist view of man's nature determine the form of society and government in China during the third century B.C.?
4. How did the Legalists explain the social, political, and economic problems of the era of the contending states? What form did their solution to these problems take? Was their theory put into practice?

## Conclusion

We have reviewed briefly the religions of Hinduism and Buddhism, which originated in India, and the thought of Confucianism, Taoism, and Legalism, which originated in China. Although these ideas were born in India and China, they were not confined permanently to these countries. Ideas can seldom be imprisoned forever within geographic boundaries, especially if the ideas contain certain grains of truth which others find appealing and useful. As ideas and inspirations grew and matured, they spread abroad and influenced the thinking, action, and institutions of other peoples.

In the next chapter, we shall see how some of these ideas of the Indians and Chinese went forth to mix with, and often to modify, the beliefs and convictions of other Asians.

## SUMMING UP THE CHAPTER

A. Define or explain the following terms, relating them to this chapter.

| | |
|---|---|
| absolutism | Kshatriya |
| anchorite | nirvana |
| Brahman | outcaste |
| caste | Sannyasi |
| dharma | Sudra |
| jen | Vaisya |
| karma | |

B. Identify or locate the following and tell why they are important.

| | |
|---|---|
| Asoka | Maurya dynasty |
| Atman | Mencius |
| *Bhagavad-Gita* | Noble Eightfold Path |
| Brahma | Period of the Philosophers |
| Ch'in dynasty | Prince Rama |
| Confucius | Shang Yang |
| Four Books | Upanishads |
| Four Noble Truths | Vishnu |
| Gautama | Warring States Period |
| Han dynasty | |
| Jainism | |
| Lao-tzu | |
| Mandate of Heaven | |

C. Identify these dates and indicate their importance.

1. 563-483 B.C. (India)
2. 327-326 B.C. (India)
3. 273-232 B.C. (India)
4. 481-256 B.C. (China)
5. 256-207 B.C. (China)

D. Chapter review questions.

1. In what way is the concept of reincarnation on the one hand a concession to human weakness, and on the other hand an ideal transcending human frailty and giving consolation to all whose life on earth is hard?
2. Describe the four periods in the life of each man as taught by Hinduism. Do these correspond to natural divisions of man's life? Is this division unique to Hindu life and thought?
3. What does the wheel symbolize to Buddhists?
4. How can it be said that even pleasure is a source of suffering and sorrow?
5. Why is Buddhism a "tragic" theology? How can it be tragic but not pessimistic?
6. How did Buddhism expand during the mid-third century B.C.? Who was largely responsible for this?
7. What did Buddhism see as the cause of suffering? How is the concept of change important?
8. What is meant when we say that Chinese thought is characterized by great practicality? How does this tend to make Chinese religious and philosophic thought less tragic or pessimistic than Indian?
9. What explanations can you give for the appearance of the great philosophers during the period of the breakdown of Chou authority (fifth to second centuries B.C.)? Has this been true in other countries and times?
10. The Chinese are famous for the examination system of recruiting government officials. Of what do you suppose these examinations consisted? What consequences for the maintenance of a particular governmental (bureaucratic) system can you see in this system?
11. Taoism was not as antisocial as it appears on the surface. Explain how the possessor of *tao* transcends the imperfections of society.
12. What is meant when it is said that Legalism is an absolutist philosophy?
13. In Legalism, as in Taoism and Confucianism, a major political goal is "invisible government." What is meant by this term?

E. Questions for discussion.

1. What weaknesses are there in formalizing sets of roles or relationships? How did the Confucianists believe these rigidities could be overcome?
2. Why was such a great emphasis placed upon ritual and ceremony in the Confucian system? Is there anything inherently good or bad in ritual and ceremony?
3. Are the rights, duties, and responsibilities of government subject to patterning after those of the family, as Confucian political theory and Western theory hold?
4. What are the economic ideas of the Legalists? What was the Legalists' solution to the social, political, and economic problems of the Warring States Period?
5. Contrast Taoism's view of society with the Confucian view. Would you call Taoism a revolutionary political philosophy (aside from its ethical and religious elements)?

F. Projects for groups or individuals.

1. Prepare for classroom presentation a report on one of the following: the early religion of the Indians; Hinduism or Buddhism; Confucianism; Taoism.
2. Study the life of one of the Asian religious leaders. Make a summary of the most significant events in his life for your classmates.
3. Read selections from several of the great religious books of Asia, such as the *Vedas* or the *Confucian Canon*.

# CHAPTER 3

# *The Spread of Ideologies*

IDEAS HAVE a tendency to spread, to live, and to evolve in many forms. This is particularly true of philosophies and religions. Thus, the thoughts of various Asian peoples about the purpose and meaning of life, about God and about man, spread to other Asians, were reshaped by them, and passed along to still others. An example of this process is Buddhism, which changed somewhat from its original form as it traveled eastward from India to China. The Chinese received Buddhism, modified it, and then passed it, together with their own original ideas, along to the Koreans and the Japanese. The Koreans and Japanese received these modified forms of Buddhism and other Chinese ideas and proceeded to add special characteristics of their own. Let us look first at how Buddhism became Chinese.

## Buddhism Becomes Chinese

Buddhism appeared in China about the middle of the Han dynasty (205 B.C. to 220 A.D.). It was not welcomed. At this time the more practical philosophy of Confucianism had already begun its climb to the position of the highest-ranking philosophy of the Chinese. The Buddhist idea that man was reborn again and again seemed like nonsense. The practice of encouraging men to renounce marriage and enter monasteries as monks was considered to be disgraceful. The Chinese felt strongly that every man should have descendants who would look after him in his old age and honor him after death. Finally, there was the question of the family, which was the root and backbone of the state. What would happen to it if these silly and dangerous notions of the Buddhists were accepted by the people? Besides, Buddhism was a foreign religion, and its spread might be subversive and undermine the authority of the officials.

Despite its early lack of acceptance, Buddhism stayed in China and gradually became acceptable to the Chinese. By the time of the sixth century A.D., it was generally acknowledged as an integral part of Chinese life and thought. There are several important reasons why Buddhism became Chinese.

## The Dark Ages and Hope

After the Han dynasty fell in 220 A.D., China was split once again into a number of rival kingdoms. For over four hundred years the land and people of China suffered the blight of civil war. This period is sometimes aptly referred to as the "Dark Ages." Not only were the Chinese fighting among themselves, but invaders poured into China from the north. Among the invaders were the savage Huns, a warlike Mongoloid tribe who were later to invade Europe. The land was ravaged with

This carved jade figure from the period of the Han dynasty represents one of the large winged lions used as tomb guardians. (Embassy of the Republic of China)

The Great Wall of China extends over fifteen hundred miles and is fifty feet high in some places. It was intended to keep out invaders from the north. (Sawders from Cushing)

their greed, brutality, and bloody battling. For hundreds of years the people who worked the land, the common men and women of China, were struck again and again by the banditry, famines, and plagues that followed in the wake of civil wars and barbarous invasions. Life seemed impossible and undesirable, and the Chinese grasped for hope and release from their awful plight. Buddhism was there to offer them hope.

## Theravada and Mahayana Buddhism

Even before Buddhism came to China from India, it had divided into two major forms, both of which still persist in Buddhist practice and thought today. These two divisions are known as *Theravada* (sometimes called *Hinayana* Buddhism) and *Mahayana* Buddhism. Theravada Buddhism follows quite closely the original teachings of Gautama Buddha and is widely accepted in Ceylon and Southeast Asia. But the original teachings of Buddha were too difficult for many individuals who sought chiefly the heart and the compassion of Buddha. The result was the founding of Mahayana Buddhism.

It was the compassion and comfort of Mahayana Buddhism which gave hope to the despairing people of China. This type of Buddhism emphasized the example of Gautama Buddha, who gave completely of himself that others might find the enlightenment, peace, and completion that he had found. The Mahayana Buddhists taught that Buddha had struggled to obtain enlightenment, not for himself so much, but that other men and women might be rescued from the sorrows of life. He had delayed his entrance into nirvana so that he might help others to learn the way there. If he had entered nirvana he would not have been available to other human beings. Those who delayed their entrance into the bliss of nirvana were called *bodhisattvas*. Those who entered nirvana became Buddhas. Gautama Buddha had accumulated great merit as a bodhisattva in many previous existences before he finally entered nirvana.

## The Chinese Wanted Compassion

Mahayana Buddhists urged all to follow the example of Buddha: to feel compassion for those who suffer, to feed the hungry, and to soothe the tormented. They taught that the true follower of Buddha chose the path of unselfishness and sought enlightenment in order to aid others. It was only natural that the great mass of the common people, unenlightened and steeped in misery, eagerly accepted the merits of these saintly ones and the salvation that they offered. The people began to rely more and more upon the mercy and compassionate attitude of these holy ones, to pray to them and adore them. Buddhas and bodhisattvas were represented in bronze, gold, and jade. Prayers and incense were offered to them in temples and pagodas. The Buddhas and bodhisattvas became gods and goddesses in the minds and hearts of the afflicted Chinese people.

Chief among these Buddhas and bodhisattvas was Amitàbha, who had vowed to save all men. He had created a "Western Paradise," a heaven filled with unmatchable beauty, where all could go who called upon his name. Another important one was Kuan-yin, the Goddess of Mercy, who was ever ready to relieve the wretchedness of those who entreated her.

### Desired by Peasant and Scholar

Buddhism began to become a necessity to many of the lowly people of China. By about 380 A.D. most of the Chinese living in the northwest were Buddhists. And Buddhism continued to harmonize itself with Chinese thought and customs. The Buddhists adopted certain ideas and practices of Taoism; they referred to Confucius as a bodhisattva, named temples after him, and stressed the duty of sons and daughters to their parents as a part of their teaching. They set up tablets in special halls to honor their dead monks, and this pleased the Chinese because it showed respect toward ancestors. The many similarities between Buddhist and Confucian morality were emphasized.

Buddhism began to please the scholars and the educated as well as the common people. The Buddhists wrote much, translated many works from the Indian languages into Chinese, and two famous Chinese Buddhists went to India. Fa-Hsien left China in 399 A.D. and lived for fifteen years in India, and Hsüan Tsang left in 629 A.D. and spent sixteen years there. In India they studied and collected many Buddhist books and manuscripts. When they returned to China, they translated these works into Chinese and wrote detailed accounts not only of religion in India, but also of the life of the people there. As a result of the writings of these well-traveled observers we know a great deal about the life of the Indians during these periods.

Thus Buddhism became a part of the life of the Chinese. It complemented and blended with the philosophies of Taoism and Confucianism. This blending of three views of life continued through the Sui dynasty (589-618 A.D.). It was in full flower by the time of the T'ang dynasty (618-907 A.D.). The Chinese people were, as many are even today, Confucianists, Taoists, and Buddhists all at the same time.

1. When did Buddhism come to China? Explain why it was not accepted at that time, but was accepted later.
2. What are the two major sects into which Buddhism is divided? How do they differ?
3. What were the bodhisattvas? How did this idea appeal to the Chinese?

## Chinese and Japanese Meet in Korea

From very early times the Chinese and Japanese have met in Korea, sometimes in peace, sometimes in anger, but always with far-reaching results to themselves and their hosts, the Koreans. Because of the location of Korea, it was only natural that this land should be a meeting place. It borders China on the northwest and is separated from Japan on the east by only a relatively few miles of water.

In part, the racial heritage of the Koreans has been a blending of Chinese, Japanese, and Mongol, as well as Caucasian and other families of man. Their political and cultural history has been tremendously influenced by Japan and China, both of which have played important roles in the evolving life of the Koreans down to the present.

The Chinese are thought to have entered Korea hundreds of years before the birth of Christ, and they have continued their visitations over the long history of both peoples. From early in their history, the Japanese, too, have been interested in the land and people of Korea. As a consequence, most of the history of the Koreans has been, in a real sense, a continuous struggle to preserve political, cultural, and social independence amidst the intrigue and ambitions of these two aspiring neighbors.

Most recently, the Chinese have feared the role played by the U. S. Americans in Korea even more than they used to fear the Japanese. Korea is now divided into two parts. The northern part is controlled by Communist Koreans and closely allied to the Chinese. The southern part is part of the Free World and is tied to the United States by treaty. But the Japanese, by reason of geography and history, will long be concerned with Korean affairs.

The cultural heritage of the Koreans is predominantly of Chinese origin. Under Chinese influence, Koreans learned to use the Chinese written characters, studied Chinese classics, and accepted Confucianism as a directing guide for their society and their government. The administration of the Korean government was modeled after that of China. The Koreans received Chinese drama, art, poetry, and architecture and made them their own. They became Buddhists, Confucianists, and Taoists.

They remained Koreans, however, modifying and enriching whatever was received from other cultures. A Korean alphabet for the Korean language replaced the Chinese written characters. Korean porcelains, lacquer, and ceramics became famous. Koreans learned and used strategic languages, such as Chinese, Japanese, and Mongolian tongues. But they were not disposed to bend their necks for anyone's sword. Because of their independent spirit, the Koreans have been referred to as the "Irish of the Orient."

This fifteenth-century Korean map showed the world in the shape of a man's head. (Courtesy of the British Museum)

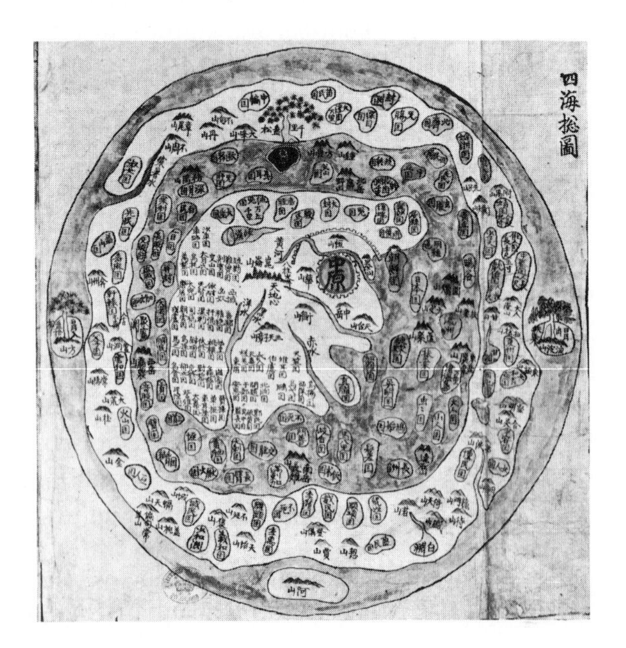

Cultural imports from China, which the Koreans were receiving and adapting to their own special setting and character, began to attract the rulers of Japan. The Japanese were interested in dominating Korea politically and also in receiving from Korea the valuable ideas, artistic products, and patterns of life which could be very useful in their own country. To the Japanese, Korea was a passageway by which they could have direct contact with the Chinese; it was an essential route by which the riches of Chinese culture could come swiftly to them. The Japanese had great respect for the material and cultural achievements of China. Although they continued to war with the Chinese, they have never quite lost that respect which began about 1,500 years ago or more.

It is ironic that the Koreans, who did so much to spread and enrich the culture of eastern Asia, had to pay for the gifts they gave with their blood, their tribute, and their freedoms. A good location may also have great disadvantages.

1. How does the history of Korea illustrate the importance of geography?
2. Of what racial heritage are the Koreans? Does Korea's cultural heritage follow her racial heritage?

## The Early Japanese

Some known and some unknown types of men were the ancestors of the Japanese people. We know of the Ainu, who bear similarities to the Caucasian. They probably came to Japan from the north and by way of Korea. Some of them still live in Hokkaido, the large northern island of Japan. We know, too, of the Malays who came from the southwest. But mostly the

Japanese are of the Mongolian family of man, and the majority of their ancestors probably came to Japan by way of Korea. There probably were other men who came around the same time as the Ainu, Malays, or Mongolians; there may have been others who came earlier. We are not exactly sure of the times any of them came. Perhaps they started coming after 3000 B.C. and continued to make their way to Japan over a period of several thousand years.

Much of what we know about the activities and thinking of the early Japanese is either legendary or guessed from the remains of their life which have been discovered by searchers into the past. Shinto, the religion native to Japan, declares that the land and the people were creations of the gods. Others, more material-minded, are convinced that the Japanese are the offspring of various strains of men.

Several centuries before Christ, the people of Japan grouped themselves into tribes and *clans.* A clan may be described as a group which shares a common ancestor, although sometimes persons are adopted into it. In their earlier days most of the clans lived in southern Japan, not far from Korea. They grew rice, settled in villages, developed their own customs and religious ideas, rode horses, and warred with one another. They were also influenced by ideas from China passed on to them by the Koreans across the Strait of Korea.

### Contact with China and Korea

We are fairly certain that the Japanese were in regular contact with the Koreans at least a hundred years or more before Christ. We are told that a remarkable woman, the Empress Jingo, invaded, conquered, and took booty and slaves from Korea about 200 A.D. It may be that Chinese writing and Buddhism came to Japan for the first time in the third century A.D. We know that by the sixth century A.D. the Japanese had a knowledge of Buddhism and things Chinese. During that century a number of Koreans came and stayed in Japan. They brought to the Japanese a knowledge of the Buddhist religion, medicine, the arts, and other civilized achievements. And during the beginning of the seventh century A.D. the Japanese began a formal diplomatic relationship with China.

The dark ages of the Chinese had just ended around this time, and their country had been reunited once again under the Sui dynasty. The Sui dynasty was followed by the T'ang dynasty, beginning in the seventh century. The T'ang dynasty is considered to be one of China's most magnificent periods of maturity and creativity. The Japanese viewed the wonderful accomplishments during this flowering period of Chinese history, and they were impressed. They were almost overwhelmed by the quality and overflowing abundance of the cultural, scientific, and artistic achievements of the Chinese, and they wanted to possess them all. Over a period of several hundred years they sent group after group of Japanese to learn and bring back all they could of the Chinese creations.

The Japanese studied architecture, painting, and literature. They learned the art of writing Chinese characters, which is called calligraphy, and which the Chinese had made into an art. They studied Chinese philosophies, especially Confucianism; they learned the Chinese system of government administration and the process by which government personnel were chosen; and they looked into city planning and health facilities. The manufacturing of porcelains, ceramics, clothing, utensils of every description, and weapons of war—all were studied by the Japanese. They also learned about Buddhism and imbibed some of the Taoist practices which had become magical and semireligious by this time. They were thorough; they were detailed; and there was little that escaped their notice.

When these visitors returned to Japan, they were welcomed back as the bearers of useful knowledge. The knowledge that they brought with them was put into practice, but not always in a form the Chinese would understand or approve. The Japanese already had some basic ideas about life and society which they were not prepared to give up. In fact,

This Chinese painting, made on silk, is from the period of the T'ang dynasty. (Embassy of the Republic of China)

they intended to use at least a portion of this borrowed learning to strengthen institutions and positions of authority which were already established in Japan.

### Useful Borrowings

By the fourth century A.D. one of the competing Japanese clans, the Yamato, was acknowledged as the strongest, and theoretically it was the ruling group. The Yamato clan was still the ruling group in Japan in the seventh century when Japanese students began going to China to learn and return with their knowledge. But the other clans of Japan were also strong and independent in their thought and action. The Yamato clan ruled through persuasion and intrigue rather than through military strength. The leaders of this clan found their position of dominance always a little uncertain, and they searched for ways to support it. They found such support in their borrowings from China. The other clans gradually came to be dominated by the Yamato clan.

The chief of the Yamato clan became an emperor who was both high priest and secular ruler. Under this emperor a central administration was established. The country was divided into prefectures and subprefectures, and the emperor appointed officials to govern them. This new bureaucracy was financed by imposing a land tax. The new centralized administration was housed in an imposing new capital called Nara, which was modeled after Ch'ang-an, the capital of T'ang China. All of these new impositions upon the people of Japan were learned first by students sent to China and used by the Yamato leaders to strengthen their position of authority in Japan.

Though the system of government was outwardly Chinese in form, it was Japanese in substance and in spirit. The Chinese administration, both central and local, was manned by educated persons who had passed through a series of hard examinations. The Japanese officials were often chosen because of their aristocratic blood and the strength of their family connections. The Chinese emperor was checked by Heaven and by the right of the people to revolt. The Japanese held the emperor to be divine; he could do no wrong, and therefore there could be no revolt. These are but a few of the borrowed Chinese forms which, in Japan, became Japanese.

1. For what purposes did the Japanese borrow Chinese ways? When did contact between the two countries begin? Give examples of ways in which the Japanese adapted Chinese ideas, institutions, and forms to their own unique spirit.
2. How were Chinese political ideas and institutions changed by the Japanese; for example, the administrative system?

### Shinto Is of Japanese Birth

The belief in the divinity of the Japanese emperor goes deep into Japan's past. It has been for many centuries an important teaching of Shinto, "the Way of the gods," which is the legendary and native-born religion of the Japanese. But the emperor is not alone in his divinity, for, says Shinto, all men and every piece of land, the mountains and plains, the trees and the waters, too, were born originally of gods and goddesses.

The god Izanagi and the goddess Izanami dipped a spear into the waters that covered the earth, and from the drops that dripped back to earth the islands of Japan were formed. The god and goddess liked these beautiful islands their drops had made, and they descended from heaven to live in them. They conceived children there, and their children were the rivers, the mountains, and the forests. They gave birth to a daughter who shone so brightly that they sent her to the sky to light all the world; and they named her Amaterasu-o-mi-Kami, the Goddess of the Sun. A son was born, and he, too, was sent to share the sky with his sister, and he was called the Moon God. And the goddess Izanami continued to bear children. There was the cruel Susa-na-wo, who became ruler of the Dark World; and there was the child who burned Izanami so fiercely that she died, and he is the God of Fire.

But creation did not cease with the death of Izanami, for others were born from the tears of her husband. And Susa-na-wo, the God of the Dark World, produced many children who ruled for a time in Japan. The Sun Goddess Amaterasu also begot children, and heaven decided that her grandson should rule Japan forever. His name was Ninigi, and he went first to the island of Kyushu in Japan, carrying with him three treasures given him by his grandmother: a jewel, a sword, and a mirror. These were the symbols of sovereignty. One of his great-grandchildren, Jimmu Tenno—*Tenno* means "Sovereign of Heaven"—moved from Kyushu to central Japan. There he established the state of Yamato. Thus, in the year 660 B.C., began the Empire of Japan. Jimmu is held to be its first emperor.

We know this story of the creation of Japan from two basic Shinto books which were written in the eighth century A.D., not long after the Japanese learned to write with Chinese characters. These books are *Kojiki*, "Record of Ancient Things," and *Nihon-shoki*, "Chronicles of Japan." There are those who say that these books were written primarily to support the position of the ruling Yamato kings and the aristocracy of this period, for there is no greater nor more enduring foundation and authority than that which is divine. But the good follower of Shinto would say that these doubters or skeptics are unduly suspicious. He would tell us that this tale of the beginnings of the Japanese had been handed down for many generations by word of mouth, long before the Japanese learned to use the Chinese characters for writing. Probably both of these statements are partially true.

### Surpassing Nature

Shinto makes nature divine. Divinity dwells within the rock, the tree, the mountain, the sea, and in all of nature's majestic forces. Shinto identifies these divinities with names: the Sun Goddess, the Moon God, the Mountain Goddess, the Fertility God, the Food God, and other gods and goddesses. Most Japanese, whether they admit to being followers of Shinto or not, are reverent before the indescribable beauty of nature and the magnitude of its power. They are grateful and thankful for its creative processes which bring them food and drink.

Shinto taught that all should be thankful for the blessings of nature, for birth, and growth, and life. It taught that death, decay, and sterility—everything that interferes with these blessings—should be regarded as evils to be avoided. Following this teaching, the Japanese have been much concerned with man as a creator of life. Their most joyous festivals are those related to the planting, growing, and harvesting of crops.

Shinto surrounded itself with the beauty of nature. Ancient Shinto had no shrines except those of the soaring tree, the quiet stream, and the lonely mountain top. Sometimes one of nature's small but striking manifestations, a rock of unusual shape, for example, might be enclosed with sticks; but it was only later, under the influence of Buddhism, that symbols of the divine were housed in man-made shrines. Today, the greatest of these shrines are at Ise. These shrines are destroyed and erected again with unpainted wood every twenty years. There is no place there for a congregation. Generally, the people approach the shrine, wash their hands, rinse their mouths, clap their hands, perhaps ring a bell, and make an offering. Then they bow and leave. All of this is done outside the shrine.

The true Shintoist finds his divinity outside the shrine, not within. It is in the magnificent pines surrounding the shrine, in the peaceful air he breathes as he walks among them, and in the green and relaxing landscape he sees as he stands and looks at the beauty that surrounds his shrine.

The Japanese reveal in many ways their love and feeling for nature. The great and the small, the rich and the poor delight in bringing the loveliness of nature into their homes, their restaurants, and frequently, their shops. The arranging of flowers is an accomplishment that every Japanese girl must learn, and a fresh flower, or two, or more, will be found brightening most Japanese homes each day. The Japanese exhaust themselves in patient labor, making artistic gardens of the ground around the house and within its courtyards. The most beautiful gardens, in their eyes, are those which do not reveal the hand of man but the artlessness of nature. Although the smoke, grime, and ugliness of industry are now encroaching upon the natural beauty of their land, the urge to live in harmony with their landscape still moves the Japanese to act. And this, in great part, is the heritage of their Shinto religion.

## Cleanliness

When the Shinto worshiper washes his hands before the shrine, he is really cleansing himself of dirt. The gods would be offended if he approached them carrying anything that might defile him. Those who participate in the rituals of Shinto must be physically pure. There are many things that can defile a worshiper; sickness, injuries, and physical uncleanliness are some of them.

Shinto has not concerned itself with moral guilt or impurities beyond the physical. It is actual physical uncleanliness that must be washed away. Shinto does not speak of sin to be forgiven or confessed. It is concerned only with the defilements of the body that must be avoided. Perhaps it was Shinto that gave to the Japanese their passion for a clean body. There are few Japanese who do not take a hot bath daily. The Japanese delight in many baths each day when they visit their hot-spring resorts.

## Shinto Was Influenced

Shinto was affected by the entrance of Chinese ideas and practices into Japan. Confucianism contributed its emphasis upon forms of behavior and its stress upon ancestor worship and loyalty to the superior, especially the emperor. From popular Taoism certain magical practices were adopted. But the greatest of all influences was Buddhism, which replaced Shinto as the dominant religion in Japan from the ninth to the nineteenth century.

Buddhism first began to make its doctrines felt in Japan perhaps around the early part of the sixth century A.D. It clashed with Shinto, much in the same way that it had clashed with Chinese ideas when it first came to China, but not for doctrinal reasons. Shinto had few doctrines, speculated little, and defined little; it was essentially a means for the Japanese to contact the unseen in nature. But Buddhism and Shinto were used as rallying cries for the clans competing for power during that period of Japanese history. Sides were drawn, and the fight was on. The supporters of Shinto lost. With the victory of its supporters, Buddhism began to establish itself firmly in Japan.

But Shinto remained strong among the common people, and Buddhism undertook to adapt itself to Shinto as it had done with the beliefs and attitudes of the Chinese some centuries before. The gods of Shinto became Buddhist holy ones; and some people proclaimed that the two religions were merely forms of the same religion. Buddhist monks took part in Shinto rituals, and gradually the Japanese became both Buddhists and followers of Shinto at the same time. Buddhist and Shinto shrines stood peacefully side by side representing not contradictions but merely differences of function.

Both religions were used by the ruling groups in Japan to strengthen their power. Both became stabilizing factors in the country, working in the interest of law and order and respect for authority. The Sun Goddess was officially recognized as the ancestress of all the clans, and the emperor was her direct descendant. All owed him the reverence demanded by divinity. Thus Shinto was tied closely to the developing political life and institutions of the Japanese. Its formal ties with the politics of Japan were not cut until the Japanese were defeated in the Second World War.

## Buddhism in Japan

Most of the Japanese Buddhists are followers of Mahayana Buddhism, as are the Chinese, and the most popular sect is known in Japan as Shin-shu. It is ceremonial and colorful in its ritual. The Shin-shu Buddhists also rely upon the merits and mercy of the Buddhas and the saints for their salvation. But there are many Japanese who feel that they should rely upon their own efforts for salvation, rather than the merits of others. They are disciples of a Buddhism known in Japan as Zen Buddhism.

### Zen Buddhism

Zen Buddhism is rather close to the original teachings of Gautama Buddha and the Buddhism called Theravada, which is practiced in Southeast Asia. The Japanese derived their basic ideas about Zen from the Chinese, who started to practice it about 400 A.D., and called it Ch'an Buddhism.

Zen Buddhists believe that the Buddha-nature is everywhere. This idea is graphically caught in the story of a monk who spat one day on a statue of Buddha. When scolded for his nasty behavior, he replied, "Is there a place I can spit where there is no Buddha?" The Zen teacher stood in silence at this.

Zen Buddhism teaches that it is the purpose of man to discover and understand this Buddha-nature. When he does this, he will be enlightened; and he must do it all by himself. There can be no assistance from others, no matter how devout and saintly they may be. The student cannot find much help in books or writings, whether secular or sacred, nor in good works or prayers, but only in meditation. He must meditate and meditate; and this meditation may go on for years before he reaches enlightenment.

If he is to meditate well, he must live a quiet, serene, self-disciplined life. He must conquer himself. He must be austere. He must be simple in his tastes and in his occupations. Zen approves of gardening, the study of nature, and the simplicity of the tea-drinking ceremony of the Japanese. These pursuits are said to help along the way towards enlightenment.

If the Zen teachers think that a student is on the verge of enlightenment, they may suddenly shout at him or strike him in an effort to push him into the blinding, indescribable illumination of enlightenment concerning the nature of all things. This cannot be described in words. It must be sensed, felt, and experienced; and it cannot be shared with others. The student must get it himself, or he can never possess it. And the one who has it remains an ordinary-looking man to all who merely see his outward appearance. But he is not ordinary at all, for he has been radically changed. He may live here, but he is beyond here; he may eat, drink, and clothe himself, but he thinks not of what he eats, drinks, or wears; he is a man, yet not a man. He is enlightened.

Buddhism has lasted in Japan from at least the beginning of the sixth century A.D. to the present day. It has penetrated all levels of Japanese life and has played a major role in molding Japanese customs, thought, literature, and art. It has been for scholar and uneducated alike a comfort, a hope, and a guide for life. Buddhism itself has been enriched by the Japanese, who brought to it their own unique feeling for nature, for society, and for man. They made it their own. It is the Buddhism of the Japanese.

1. How did Shinto and Buddhism take on political significance; that is, how did they serve as props for Japanese governments? What major religious role of the emperor was renounced after World War II?
2. How do you explain the fact that great numbers of Japanese have always been both Buddhists and Shintoists?
3. How did the Japanese emperor trace his divinity back to the god Izanagi and the goddess Izanami? Where is this story of the creation of Japan to be found?
4. To which of the two major divisions of Buddhism do the majority of Japanese Buddhists belong? What is the Japanese name for this sect?

### Conclusion

Buddhism made its way from India to China, was modified there by the Chinese to harmonize with their own special ways of life, and then traveled in its Chinese dress to Korea and Japan. The Koreans and the Japanese also took native Chinese ideas—such as Confucianism and Taoism, methods of government, and other Chinese cultural achievements—and remolded them to fuse with their own special views and practices. Ideas swell and grow and move about, and often change appearance; but the seeds of their basic truths remain and flower in differing, yet still beautiful forms in differing environments.

## SUMMING UP THE CHAPTER

A. Identify or explain the following, relating them to this chapter.

| | |
|---|---|
| Ainu | Kyushu |
| Amaterasu-o-mi-Kami | Nara |
| Ch'an | Nihon-shoki |
| Hinayana | Ninigi |
| Hokkaido | Shin-shu |
| Izanagi | Susa-no-wo |
| Kojiki | Yamato |
| Kuan-yin | Zen |

B. Chapter review questions.

1. Buddhism gained adherents among the Japanese clans which later became successful in the political struggles for power. With the political success of these clans came the rapid expansion of Buddhism in Japan. How did the assimilation of Buddhism to Shinto folk religion aid in this expansion?
2. What groups in China were the first to become Buddhists? How do you account for this?
3. How did Buddhism accommodate itself to Chinese customs and beliefs?
4. To what extent is the following statement true? "The cultural heritage of the Koreans is predominantly Chinese in origin." Give specific examples in your answer.
5. Identify the "Irish of the Orient." For what products were they famous?
6. Describe life in a clan in early Japan. Where did most of the clans live at that time?
7. Trace the history of Japanese-Korean relations from their early beginnings to the present. Describe how the Yamato exercised authority. Were these methods successful? Why?
8. What is the relationship between Shinto and nature?
9. What are the major beliefs and practices of Zen Buddhism?

C. Questions for discussion.

1. How would you explain that the Koreans adopted Chinese and Japanese cultural elements without losing their own unique Korean identity?
2. Can you draw any conclusions from Chinese and Japanese uses of religion to buttress the political system? Is the political use of religion unique to these countries?
3. Why do you suppose Zen Buddhism has such great appeal for artists, whether writers, painters, sculptors, actors, etc., not only in Japan, but in the West as well?
4. In your reading on Confucianism and Buddhism, what insights have you gained into how religions become accepted among both the educated and the uneducated? Are these patterns true of other religions as well?

D. Projects for groups or individuals.

1. Prepare a report on various forms of Japanese art which express the Japanese appreciation of nature.
2. Study early Japanese paintings in reference books, and make a sketch of what you think the Empress Jingo may have looked like.
3. Find pictures of some of the Buddhist gods.
4. Make a chart showing the descendants of Izanagi and Izanami.

CHAPTER 4

# Movement of Men and Ideas in Southeast Asia

WE HAVE SEEN that the Indians and the Chinese were slowly forming the social and cultural foundations of their ways of life during hundreds and hundreds of years. Buddhism made its way to China from India and entrenched itself there. The Koreans slowly absorbed and adopted Chinese ideas and practices. The Japanese also borrowed and modified Chinese ideas, and they were enticed by the land and culture of Korea. During all of this time there was also movement and contact of men and ideas in Southeast Asia.

## Burma: The Burmese

The Mon, a Sino-Tibetan people, came to Burma perhaps more than a thousand years before the Christian era. They settled in lower Burma on lands along the Irrawaddy River. There they mixed with unknown peoples who had preceded them. After the Mon, tribe after tribe, mostly arising from where China and Tibet meet, came southward in successive waves. They pressed each other farther along the narrow valleys leading to the broad lowlands of lower Burma or into the mountains enclosing the valleys and the plains. Even before the beginning of the Christian era there was a merging of men and a contesting for land in Burma.

About 400 B.C., on the coast and land fronting the Bay of Bengal, the people of Burma met with Indian traders and began to learn about the material and spiritual advances of the Indians. They were influenced. Their society and their government became more complex. Civilization was developing in lower Burma. By the time of the fifth century A.D., kingdoms called Prome, Pegu, and Thaton arose there.

But the migrations from the north had not ceased. A people called Burmans moved into central Burma around the beginning of the eighth century and founded there a kingdom called Pagan. As the centuries moved along, the Burmans extended their political control over most of central and lower Burma. At the same time, the religion of Buddhism, brought first by the Indians, extended its control to such a degree that the Burmans began to think of themselves as chosen defenders of Buddhism. Although greatly moved by Indian culture, they did not merely imitate, but evolved their own way of life, which can be called "The Burmese Way." They developed the Burman written language, and they continued to merge their blood with the many people who had come before them to this land.

But they were not left in peace. During all the time the Burmans were fashioning their culture, there was the pressure of more people from the north. These were the Thai people mostly, from southwest China, who were also moving slowly southward under the pressure of the Chinese from the north. The Shan, a branch of the Thai people, also set up a kingdom north of Pagan. It was called the Kingdom of Ava, taking its name from the place where it was located. The Shan people had inherited the culture of their Thai parent stock. However, they were gradually drawn to the ways and thinking of the Burmans to the south of them. The Burmans in turn were influencing and being influenced by the kingdom of Pegu to the south of them. The people of Pegu were still much under the influence of the classical Indian civilization.

During the ninth through the sixteenth centuries A.D. there was a continual milling, merging, and mixing of people and ideas in Burma. The people, for the most part, came from Tibet and China; and the ideas were in large measure of Indian origin. Both the people and the ideas changed somewhat in the process, and there continued emerging a Burmese people and Burmese ideas in the valleys and on the watered plains of Burma.

There was also movement in the mountains surrounding the evolving Burmese. Three peoples, the Chin, the Kachin, and the Naga—all from lands bordering Tibet—occupied parts of the Burmese mountains. The Chin wandered into the west; the Kachin and Naga occupied the northwest; and other peoples moved into the northeast. All of these peoples became a part of the country now called Burma. The Mongol conquerors of China destroyed Pagan in the thirteenth century, and there were other invasions from China and Thailand in the seventeenth and eighteenth centuries. The infusion of new kinds of people and the impact of military might were important influences in the development of the political, cultural, and social patterns, and the outlook of the Burmese.

Then in the early nineteenth century, the British took over the administration and control of Burma. They retained power in the country until 1948, when Burma obtained her independence. But the country is still plagued with the rivalries and the jealousies of the many different groups who have been long resident in the land. The mountain people are still not inclined to bow before the ruling cliques of the lowlands. Even among the lowland rulers there is a struggle for power which reveals itself from time to time in military coups and sudden resignations. The years have brought certain common attitudes toward life to the people of Burma, but the blending of men and cultures is not yet complete.

1. When did the peoples of Burma come into contact with Indian civilization? How did this contact occur? What changes resulted from it?
2. What cultural influences came to Burma from the north? From the south?
3. What influences on Burmese political and social life can be traced to Burma's being a "melting pot" of peoples and cultures in Asia?

## Thailand: The Thais

Thailand takes its name from the Thai people who originally came there from southwest China. One branch of their family, the Shans, went to Burma and established a kingdom there. Another branch, the Lao, gave the country of Laos its name. Still another group fought and infiltrated their way into Thailand (sometimes called Siam). It is thought that they started on their journey into Thailand around the ninth century A.D.

The Thais, before they left China, had been for some centuries exposed to the military power and cultural invasions of the Chinese to the north of them. Perhaps they had also received some knowledge of Indian civilization from those south and west of their Chinese homeland. About the seventh century A.D. they organized the state of Nanchao in Yunnan, China. This state was overrun by Chinese armies around 1000 A.D. Finally, in the thirteenth century A.D., it was conquered by the Mongols and incorporated into the empire of Kublai Khan.

The Thais were gradually moving southward even before the final conquest of their Chinese state by the Mongols. They mixed with the Khmer, a people who were the ancestors of the Cambodians. The Khmer controlled all of that land into which the Thais were moving. At first the Thais gave allegiance to the Khmers and even served as soldiers in their armies. But as the Thais became stronger and more numerous, they began to compete with the Khmers. Then came another great migration of Thais out of southwest China when the Mongols defeated them in war. The newcomers swelled the numbers of the Thais struggling for part of the land ruled by the Khmers. They obtained their first capital at Sukhothai in north-central Thailand, and the period of Thai history from about 1250 A.D. to 1350 A.D. is known as the Sukhothai era.

The Thais continued to move southward, fighting and infiltrating. Around 1350 A.D. they moved their capital to Ayudhya, which is only about forty miles from the present city of Bangkok. Ayudhya remained the capital of Thailand until 1767, when the Burmese destroyed it during one of their invasions. Thereafter Bangkok was made the capital and has remained the capital to the present day.

During the centuries they were journeying to their new state, and afterwards, the Thais picked up other ideas and strains of blood. They were changed in many ways from what they had been when they first left southwest China. They obtained their written language and some political ideas from the Khmers; they intermarried with them and with the Mon people who had also penetrated to this area. They became Buddhists.

From the seventeenth through the nineteenth century, the Thais were able to play the Western powers, particularly France and England, against each other. Thus they escaped the colonial nets of the Europeans which caught so many of their neighbors. But they did not escape the penetration of Chinese immigrants, who came in numbers to trade during this period and on into the twentieth century. Many Chinese intermarried with the Thais; and many of them remained aloof, maintaining the continuity of their blood and

Boats on a canal near Bangkok, Thailand are a part of the great "floating market" of that city. (Pacific Area Travel Association)

These pagodas are among the famous religious shrines of the Ayudhya province of Thailand. (Royal Thai Embassy)

Each motion in the Thai classical dance conveys a meaning. (Royal Thai Embassy)

their customs. Gradually a large part of the resources of Thailand flowed into their pockets. Despite the restrictive and sometimes desperate measures of the Thai government to change this flow, the Chinese remain dominant in the economy of Thailand.

During the twentieth century, the Thais have tried to democratize their government, at least formally. In 1932 the king gave up his absolute powers and established a constitutional and limited monarchy in Thailand. But the road toward a democratic form of government is often a rocky one. Outside forces as well as factions within Thailand have often prevented the formal fulfillment of democratic aims. Marshal Thanarat, who was Premier of Thailand up until his death in 1963, stated in 1952 that, due to the great threat of Communism within the country, the government must resign and the constitution be suspended. It is still suspended. The threat of Communism still remains.

1. Where did the Thais originate? What other peoples merged with them in Thailand?
2. Describe the cultural borrowings of the Thais.
3. How did the Thais escape Western colonial domination?

## Cambodia: The Cambodians

The Cambodians are descendants of the Khmers, a fascinating and creative people. You will recall that the Thais invaded and took a part of the land of the Khmers. But even before the Khmers, there had been people of mixed origins who occupied the present lands of Thailand, Cambodia, and South Vietnam: the Mon from the west, Chinese-Tibetan tribes, a people called Chams, and others. Indian traders had also established trading posts on lands facing the Gulf of Siam, and their influence penetrated the Mekong River area and beyond. Even before the coming of the Khmer, these Indian traders helped to form a state in Cambodia known to the Chinese as Funan. This was around the beginning of the Christian era. It was a loosely organized state, based chiefly upon sea and river communications and held together partly by Buddhist and Hindu concepts brought by the Indians. Funan was not confined to Cambodia, but spread around the coasts of the Gulf of Siam and the South China Sea.

The Khmer people—we do not know where they came from—founded a state to the north of Funan in the sixth century A.D., and became its rival. Between 600 A.D. and 1200 A.D. the Khmers grew in power, intermixed with a great variety of peoples, and combined Hindu, Buddhist, native, and Chinese cultural traits with their own. They built some of man's most magnificent monuments of stone in Asia. The peak of their development was reached in the twelfth and thirteenth centuries A.D. The Khmer empire, with its capital at Angkor, had long since taken over the areas controlled by Funan.

But like all empires, this one, too, faded away and was gradually reduced to approximately the area of the present state of Cambodia. The Khmers were pressed from all sides —by the Thais, the Annamese of Vietnam, and others, who took parts of their land and reduced the supply of labor and the income from the land tax. They were plagued by floods, and it is thought that disease decimated their numbers. Perhaps the spread of the self-denying religion of Theravada Buddhism helped to weaken the power of the Khmers. The Khmer society had been headed by nobles and priests whose position was founded on a combination of Hindu and Mahayana Buddhist doctrines. These are some of the reasons for their decline, and there may be others. In 1432 A.D. the capital was moved from Angkor to the neighborhood of Pnompenh, which is the present capital of Cambodia.

During the period of their glory, the achievements of the Khmers were remarkable. They wrote, and they passed on their alphabet to the Thais. They built reservoirs, stone-surfaced roads, temples that are wonders of art even today, and palaces that amazed even the most sophisticated of visitors. They had towers of gold, bridges of gold, and statues of gold. They made tiles of lead, and everywhere their city was beautified with an abundance of sculpture. When the king rode out from his palace, he was accompanied by carriages of gold and by women carrying objects of gold and silver and hundreds of umbrellas of gold and silver. He was guarded by armed women and by men mounted on elephants and horses. The Khmers had astronomers who were honored, and their science of measurement and location was so exact that Khmer temples were built precisely upon an east-west axis. We are told that the Khmers had over one hundred hospitals for the care of the sick.

Khmer society was headed by nobles and priests. In between were the free middle and lower classes, and at the bottom was a huge mass of slaves. Agriculture was highly developed by the Khmers, and they grew rice, varieties of vegetables, and many kinds of fruit. Their dress was simple, but the use of ornaments such as rings and bracelets was quite common.

Much that we know about the Khmers comes from the writings of visitors. In the sixteenth century the Khmer capital at Lovek was burned by the Thais, and all the records that might have been there are gone. Even the memory of Angkor was almost lost to man for many years. It was the French who rediscovered the mighty stone monuments of the Khmers, nearly forgotten and hidden within the thick jungles of Cambodia.

The French assumed protection over Cambodia in 1863. Cambodia was associated with the French politically until it declared itself independent in 1953. During this period of French control, the Cambodians learned about representative forms of government and now they have a premier, a council of ministers, and a parliament. Their king has given up his royal title and functions simply as Head of the Royal Government. During their period as a protectorate of France, the Cambodians learned the French language, and many of the more educated among them have an appreciation for French ways, French books, and French culture.

But the Cambodians also retained their identity in their religion, in their age-old cus-

Vietnamese civil guards cross a slippery footbridge during a mopping-up operation against Communist-led Viet Cong guerrillas. (Wide World Photo)

toms, and in their political tendencies. They do not want to be regarded as being on either one side or the other in the Cold War. Officially, they are neutrals. They are suspicious of the Annamese of Vietnam, the Thais, and others around them, and border incidents are not uncommon. The Cambodians do not have as much territory and power as their ancestors, the Khmers, but Cambodia is important to the peace and stability of Southeast Asia.

1. Describe some of the achievements of the Khmers.
2. How extensive was the Khmer state at its peak? What countries today are the successors to the Khmer state?
3. Describe the social structure of the Khmers.

### Vietnam: The Vietnamese

The history of Vietnam is the history of a people known as the Annamese. Whereas the cultural orientation of the people of Burma, Thailand, and Cambodia is the result of early heavy Indian penetration, the culture of the Annamese was strongly influenced by the Chinese.

Some centuries before the Christian era, the Annamese migrated from China to the area around the Red River known as Tongking. This area is now the heart of North Vietnam, the Communist part of Vietnam. Over a long period of time, the Annamese fought their way southward along the coast. By the fifteenth century A.D. they had taken over the delta of the Mekong River in the extreme south of

Vietnam. This area is the food-producing center of South Vietnam, the part of Vietnam which has allied itself with the Free World.

From the third century B.C. until the tenth century A.D., the Annamese were ruled by the Chinese. During all this long period of time there was an intermingling between the Chinese and Annamese people. The Vietnamese, however, still distinguish carefully between themselves and the Chinese, who have always composed a minority within their country.

The Annamese political state evolved under the tutelage of Chinese political officials, who brought with them the philosophy of Confucianism, which had molded much of the political and social behavior of the Chinese. It was only natural that the Annamese should adopt many Chinese practices with regard to the government of the state and the roles of individuals within the family. In their religious practices the Annamese accepted the Mahayana Buddhism of China and added some Taoist religious practices to their own native beliefs.

Since the tenth century the Annamese have been relatively free from the domination of the Chinese. But at periodic intervals the Chinese have asserted their sovereignty over the Annamese by demanding tribute, which was evidence of their ultimate control of Vietnam. It is not surprising that today Communist China is vitally interested in the political affairs of Vietnam and would like it to be entirely directed by the same Communist ideas and practices that prevail in Red China. Such a desire has a historical basis.

During the 2,000 years that the Annamese have dwelled in Vietnam, they have made themselves the dominant group in neighboring areas. They have also made themselves the most feared group. Laos, Cambodia, and Thailand have all felt the sometimes fierce blows of the Annamese. They all fear the possible expansion and respect the power of an armed Annamese people.

However, the Annamese have not only fought with their neighbors but have also struggled among themselves. In the seventeenth century they divided into three rival kingdoms which warred among themselves for supremacy for over a hundred years. The king of Annam, with the help of the French, finally became the ruler of all in 1801.

Today the Annamese are divided again, into North Vietnam and South Vietnam; and the Communist North is endeavoring to assert its rule over the free South. Today the history of the Annamese is being repeated in a modern setting to the distress of themselves, their neighbors, and a world more closely related than ever before.

1. What were the origins of the Annamese of Vietnam? What cultural influences have been most important in Vietnam?
2. Describe the historical background of Chinese political interest in Vietnam.

### Laos: The Laotians

The history of Laos is in large measure the history of the Lao people. The Lao people are of the same stock as the Thais of Thailand and the Shans of Burma (see pages 61-62). While the Thais were moving into Thailand, and the Shans into Burma, the Lao were slowly settling the present country of Laos. Much of their history is legend, passed on by word of mouth from one generation to another. Even today in much of Laos, people still listen to tales of their ancestors told by storytellers and singers.

Perhaps the Lao people started their slow occupation of the land of Laos around the ninth century A.D. They gradually pressed out the less advanced peoples who had come before them to this rough and rugged land. These people were collectively called the Kha, which means "slave." The land in which the Lao settled was also under the rule of the Khmers, and, for a time, the Lao lived peacefully under them. More of the Lao people came into the land when the Mongols destroyed the Thai capital of Nanchao in the thirteenth century. As the Khmer power weakened the Lao assumed more and more control of the land.

In the fourteenth century a kingdom called the Lan Xang, "the kingdom of a million elephants," was founded by a man named Fa Ngum. Legend and tradition say that there were over twenty earlier rulers, but the written records start with Fa Ngum, who ruled from 1353 to 1373 A.D.

Fa Ngum was a great warrior and spent much of his time enlarging the boundaries of Laos. He also made Theravada Buddhism the official religion of the state. But the people tired of his military inclinations and demands, and his throne was given to his son, Sam Sene Thai, who was more inclined to peaceful ways and more concerned with the administration of the kingdom. It was a monarchy, with all power concentrated in the hands of the king. The ministers of the king were the royal princes, and there was a hierarchy of command running from the king at the top to the lowest official in the bureaucracy at the bottom. All of the officials served at the will of the king. This administrative structure controlled by the king has lasted to the present day. Even now, though the power may in reality lie elsewhere, the king's consent is formally sought for any major change in policy.

During the fifteenth and sixteenth centuries the succeeding kings of Laos were constantly preoccupied with defending their lands. They fought with the Annamese, and for a rather long period of time with the Burmese, who ruled them for about twenty years during the latter part of the sixteenth century. The Thais eventually defeated the Burmese and drove them from their own land as well as the land of Laos. It was during the sixteenth century that the capital was moved to Vientiane, where it has remained to the present time. The Laotians wanted to be closer to their allies and relations, the Thais.

During the eighteenth and nineteenth centuries the Laotians split among themselves, and independent tribes and kingdoms dotted the country. The history of these two centuries is one of desperate struggles against the Chinese, the Annamese, the Burmese, and the Thais, all of whom sought to take for themselves various portions of the country.

With the extension of French protection in the latter part of the nineteenth century, Laos enjoyed a period of peace until the end of the Second World War. Then the Laotians were again divided amongst themselves by the issues of nationalism, Communism, and neutralism. The interested powers of the world agreed to neutralize Laos in 1962, and an uneasy peace is now being observed.

1. Describe the governmental structure of Laos under the monarchy of Sam Sene Thai. What form of government does Laos have today?
2. Laos for hundreds of years has been the scene of political penetration by neighboring countries. What European nation brought peace to Laos until World War II? What has happened to Laos since then? What is meant when it is said that Laos has been *neutralized?*

## Malaysia: The Malayans

Malays and Chinese make up the bulk of the population of Malaysia. Some of the Malays, who are mostly of the Mongolian family of man, have been in Malaya since prehistoric times. Other Malays from Sumatra and Java in Indonesia migrated to Malaya in varying numbers at varying times. They were joined by migrating Chinese and some Indians.

That familiar figure, the Indian trader, stopped off here also on his trading trips to Burma, Thailand, and Indochina, early in the Christian era. There was little to trade with the Malays at first, but gradually trade began to grow. Some of the Indian traders settled in Malaya and married into Malay families, and there developed an Indian-Malay high society. Priests followed the traders to Malaya and introduced Hinduism and Buddhism into the land. Then around the twelfth century, or perhaps slightly before, other Indians came, and Arabs, too. The Arabs were followers of Islam, a religion which was assuming great importance in India. Gradually the Malays became Moslems, the name given to those who believe in Islam, and they have remained Moslems to the present day.

Small states headed by rulers called *sultans* developed in Malaya. But these states were not always completely independent. Some of them paid tribute to the Chinese emperors and relied upon their protection. Some of them were compelled to acknowledge the overlordship of empires based in Sumatra and Java in Indonesia. With the destruction of one of the strongest of these, the Javanese empire of Majapahit, in the early sixteenth century, the Moslem sultans, with the aid of Moslem Indians and Arabs, began to assume more control over the political and economic life of the areas. Their trade expanded west and east, for their ports lay astride the main sea routes between the Far East and the West. It was a one-way trade, for the people of Malaya had little to export at this time.

Many people from the East and the West were drawn to this thriving trading center. The Chinese came in large numbers and they have continued to come over the centuries. They concentrated on making money and left politics, until recently, in the hands of others. The Portuguese came from the West in the sixteenth century and seized a number of coastal ports, which they held and governed for many years. With them they brought missionaries, for they were interested in converting the Malays as well as making money. The Portuguese traders made money, but few Moslems were converted.

In the seventeenth century the Dutch came and seized the ports from the Portuguese. Then, in the eighteenth century, the British came and established themselves on Penang, an island off the coast of Malaya. In the nineteenth century they relieved the Dutch of control over the ports of Malaya. The British retained control over the political and economic life of the Malayans until 1957 when the Federation of Malaya became an independent country.

The Federation of Malaya did not include the island-city of Singapore on the extreme tip of the Malay Peninsula. Singapore has over 1,500,000 people, 80 per cent of whom are Chinese. In 1958 it became a self-governing state within the British Commonwealth. Neither did the Federation at first include the British Crown Colony of North Borneo, the British Protectorate of Brunei, nor the Crown Colony of Sarawak. Brunei and Sarawak are both located on the north side of Borneo and are composed mainly of Malays. However, in September, 1963 Singapore, Sarawak, and North Borneo joined the Federation of Malaya to form the new country of Malaysia.

1. Malayan history illustrates two cultural contacts—trade and religion—which have been important in many areas of the world. Who were the traders that came to Malaya? What religions were introduced into Malaya? Which of these religions became dominant in Malaya?
2. How did Portuguese political and economic influence extend to Malaya in the sixteenth century? What Western powers succeeded the Portuguese? When did Malaya become an independent nation?

## Indonesia: The Indonesians

Many races of man contributed to the populating of Indonesia. There were the Negritos, a small pygmy branch of the Negro family, and mixtures of the Caucasian and Mongolian families. There were also men called Malays, who were mostly of the Mongolian family of man. They all settled the land over a great period of time, thousands of years before the beginning of the Christian era, and they bred in the many islands of Indonesia a great variety of men, cultures, and languages.

Early in the history of the Indonesians, perhaps around the first century of the Christian era or even sooner, their coasts, too, were probed by the ever-moving, inquisitive Indian traders. The Indians built trade centers along the coasts of Borneo, east Sumatra, and north Java, just as they did along the coasts of Burma and elsewhere in Southeast Asia. The culture they brought with them was superior here also to the culture of the native peoples. The Indians were not only the merchants for the Indonesians but became also their architects and their religious and political teachers.

By the second century of the Christian era, Chinese and Arab traders were also visiting these trading centers established by the Indians, and by the time of the fourth century the main centers of Indonesia were known throughout Asia.

States began to arise in some of the islands, and several of them early became large empires. There was one called Srivijaya, a sea empire, based on the east coast of Sumatra near Palembang. From the seventh through the twelfth century Srivijaya controlled the lanes of the sea throughout this region as far north as Cambodia and dominated the Malay Peninsula. In the thirteenth century another great sea power, the Majapahit, arose in east Java. For a short time the Majapahit ruled the sea almost to the extent of the former empire of Srivijaya. While these two great sea empires were relatively equal in sea power, the Majapahit had, in addition, control over much of the land of Java. During this period of the rise and fall of Indian-Indonesian empires, smaller dynastic states in various parts of the Indonesian islands were being created, destroyed, modified, re-created, and combined again and again. These dynastic kingdoms were generally near the coastal centers of trade, but there were some inland states too.

During much of this period of the development of commerce, politics, and religion in Indonesia, the Indians and their culture prevailed. Indians were everywhere in the highest political and economic positions.

The Indians were dominant especially in the capitals and the trading ports along the coasts. Hindu and Buddhist priests and monks from India taught, built temples and monasteries, and even counseled the ministers of state. Indians intermarried with the Sumatrans and the Javanese. The combining of their blood forged even stronger ties and served to perpetuate and spread the ways and thoughts of the Indians.

The Chinese were also attracted to the profitable and growing trade of the Indonesian ports. A few were also drawn by the religious and political surges of the Indian-Indonesian society. From early in the Christian era, Chinese, singly and in groups, had come to Indonesia to observe and to learn something of the religious and political developments there; and some came to trade. But for the most part the Chinese were just travelers. Beginning with the twelfth and thirteenth centuries more Chinese came to Indonesia to live permanently and to trade. The Chinese were almost exclusively concerned with material gain. They were so successful that the economy and resources of Indonesia eventually lay largely in their hands. They continued to come and reside there until very recently, when President Sukarno braked the flow of their entry.

The Arabs also came very early to this land, for they, too, were great traders, always ready to make long, dangerous voyages for commodities that would bring them profit. After their conversion to Islam, the Arabs continued to come to Indonesia, but now they brought their religion with them as well as their trading goods. They were joined by Indian Moslems who came to preach as well as trade, and Islam began to make great advances in Indonesia. It rapidly supplanted the religions of Hinduism and Buddhism, which had so long been accepted and mingled with native religious practices. The spread of Islam was unbelievably swift. By the early part of the sixteenth century much of Indonesia could be called Moslem. The vast majority of the people have remained Moslem to this very day.

Then, in the sixteenth century, Europeans were attracted by the great profits to be made from spices and other valuable commodities in these ancient market places. The Portuguese came first, and they sought a monopoly of the spice trade. They never quite succeeded, for their methods antagonized the local rulers, and their purposes aroused the jealousy and ambitions of other European peoples. Spanish, Dutch, English, and Danish adventurers and traders followed the Portuguese to Indonesia. The tale of trade and politics in Indonesia during the seventeenth and eighteenth centuries is one of intrigue, struggle, and war between these groups to dominate and reap the harvest of Indonesia's riches. The main rivalry was between the Dutch and the English. It was finally resolved in a peace treaty giving Indonesia to the Dutch and Malaya to the British. The Portuguese retained a part of the island of Timor, and they still possess it today.

Indonesia was governed by the Dutch until 1942, when the Japanese took it during World War II. In 1945, at the end of the war, the Indonesians proclaimed their country a republic, and from that time until 1949 warred with the Dutch to maintain their independence. In 1949, the Dutch formally transferred the land of Indonesia to the new government of the Republic of Indonesia.

1. How did Indian political, economic, and religious influence spread to Indonesia?
2. The political, economic, and religious history of Indonesia and that of Malaysia are very much alike. What are some of the common elements in the history of these countries?
3. How did Indonesia become independent?

## The Philippines: The Filipinos

The story of the Filipinos is also an account of the coming of diverse peoples and the mingling and adaptation of diverse cultures. The Negritos probably came from somewhere in East Africa, and they spread over much of southeastern Asia. They probably arrived in the Philippine Islands first, followed by other men who were somewhat like the Malays. They were hunting peoples. Then, perhaps five or six thousand years before the Christian era, people of the early Mongoloid family of man crossed over from the mainland and settled on the islands. For about 5,000 years, they continued to cross the sea that lies between the Philippines and the Asian mainland. As the Mongolian people evolved, they brought with them their developing culture. Among their earlier contributions to the Philippines were a knowledge of agriculture, the concept of building houses on stilts, and improved tools. Later, the Mongolians introduced methods of working copper, bronze, and gold, and, possibly at the same time, the cultivation of wet rice.

Then, around 500 B.C., the Malays began to stream in, century after century, group after group, and their type of man assumed dominance among the Filipinos. Today most Filipinos will say that they are of Malay origin for the most part. The Malays brought with them their methods of fishing and farming and of building boats and houses. They brought fashions of dress and behavior and their language. They also brought with them some knowledge of Indian advancements—the loom, cotton, the manufacture of iron, and others. Indian traders followed the Malays, or accompanied them, and their influence was felt especially in the language, in architecture, and in the arts. These streams of men and influences continued through the sixth and seventh centuries A.D.

From around the eighth to the fifteenth century, the Chinese, a later Mongolian type of people, crossed the sea in numbers. They

The chief port and former capital of the Philippine Republic is Manila. This city was founded in 1571. The modern buildings along the waterfront reflect little of the Philippines' colonial past. (H. Armstrong Roberts)

Stilt houses serve especially well in the climate of the Philippine Islands. This kind of house was probably first introduced by Mongolians from the mainland. (H. Armstrong Roberts)

settled mostly in Luzon, the large northern island of the Philippines. They intermarried with the other peoples of the islands, and some say that over ten per cent of the Filipinos have Chinese blood. The Chinese came to control a great portion of the trade and wealth of the Philippines.

About the middle of the fifteenth century, Moslems came to Mindanao and Palawan, two of the southern islands of the Philippines. These Moslems were a combination of Malay, Indian, and Arab, but mostly Malay. They brought with them new ideas about social and political life and new religious ideas. Most of the people of Sulu, and a number of people in Mindanao and Palawan, embraced the faith of Islam, and some were converted in other parts of the Philippines. All this happened in a little over a century.

**Spanish influence.** In 1521, the famous Spanish captain, Magellan, found the Philippines, and about forty-five years later the Spanish began their conquest of the islands. They succeeded rather well except in the southern areas occupied by those of the Moslem faith. The Spanish brought more new ideas and practices to the Philippines, and the stamp of their culture is still boldly printed on the land and people of this country.

The Spanish were Roman Catholics, and an important reason for their expansion into other regions of the globe was their desire to convert others to the Catholic faith. On their voyages of exploration and expansion they were generally accompanied by zealous, dedicated priests, who were determined to bring the non-Christian into the fold of the Church. With the aid of the Spanish government authorities, they made the Philippines into a Catholic country during the more than 300 years of Spanish rule. They never succeeded in converting the Moslems, but elsewhere their churches, their monasteries, and their convents dotted the land. They still do.

The Spanish divided the country into local units of government, called *barrios*, and the towns and cities they made into municipalities. They established provinces, which included many barrios and municipalities. Over all of these was the central government of Manila, the capital. These barrios are still basic to the political system of the Philippines, and there are still provinces. The present-day central government is formally located in Quezon City but still actually housed to a great degree in Manila, next-door to the new capital. It is a Filipino government now, democratic, free, and modeled in great part after that of the United States.

The Spanish exploited the Filipinos, taxed their land heavily, forced them to labor without wages, and confiscated much of their property. The Filipino people were drained of their strength and wealth so that their Spanish rulers might live in luxury. In return, the Spanish contributed certain standards of dress and behavior, as well as Spanish architecture, ornamentation, art, and dance.

**Influence of the United States.** Then, at the very end of the nineteenth century, in 1898, the Americans arrived in the Philippines. They were at war with Spain, and a famous American, Admiral George Dewey, carried the war to the Spanish-governed Philippines. Spain was defeated, and the Philippines were handed over to the United States in the peace settlement after the war. The Americans brought with them their passion for good sanitation, their technical knowledge, and a belief that the government has the duty of providing every child with an opportunity for education. They brought the idea of a republican form of government.

The Americans separated the Church from the State, and introduced a public school system which has grown rapidly. As a consequence, the modern Republic of the Philippines is, with Japan, one of the most literate states in Asia. The Filipinos learned about democracy, liked it, and made it their own. A kind of partnership developed between the Americans and the Filipinos. Even the propaganda of the Japanese, who occupied the country from 1941 until 1945, could not destroy this bond. The Americans kept faith with the Filipinos and in 1946 granted the independence that had been promised previously. The Filipinos kept faith with the Americans and have remained loyal friends in the midst of all the uncertainties of political life in Asia today.

1. Describe the numerous racial and cultural inheritances of the Philippines.
2. When and how did Western influence extend to the Philippines?
3. What were the two major incentives to Spanish colonialism in the Philippines?

### Island Homes in the Pacific

The Pacific Ocean is so huge that all of the continents of the world could not cover its surface, and all of their land could not fill its bed. Surrounded by this immense expanse of water are thousands of islands which many men call home. Created by the slow building of coral or the sudden eruption of volcanoes, these islands are often jewels of earth scattered upon the surface of the waters. Beaches, shining whitely in the sun, are cleansed and smoothed by the unceasing surges of blue-green water. Tall palms move and murmur in response to the daily caress of the winds. The green-clad breadfruit, cocoanut, banana, and orange trees produce beauty as well as food for those who live on these island homes. There is a harmony of land and climate which makes these islands irresistible refuges for the restless among men.

Long ago men from the mainland of Asia found these inviting islands and settled them; and there are those who are convinced that some men boated to them from parts of Latin America. A daring few in modern times have experimented with this possibility. The story of their adventures on a drifting raft, carried by the currents of the Pacific from South America to the islands of Polynesia, is told in a book called *Kon-Tiki.* Whatever their earliest history may have been, men have continued to make their way to these Pacific islands and to find them a pleasant place to stay.

The inhabitants of these islands are of various families of man and are called by various names. There are the Micronesians who live in the Marianas and the Carolines. There are the Melanesians who are believed to be Negrito in origin and live in New Guinea, Fiji, the Solomons and other islands. There are the Malays, and they have inhabited many islands, the largest being those which compose the Philippines and Indonesia. There are the Polynesians, a mixture of the Caucasian, the Mongol, and the Negrito, who have lived for centuries on the Hawaiian, Samoan, Society, and other island groups. Tahiti, one of the Society Islands, has become famous for the attractiveness of its land and people.

Captain Bligh and his English crew, made famous by the book *Mutiny on the Bounty,* visited Tahiti in 1788, and the mutineers from the crew settled on Pitcairn Island. The Polynesians have been immortalized in the paintings of Paul Gauguin and the words of great writers. Robert Louis Stevenson described them as the finest of God's works. The European was among the last of the families of man to discover the advantages of these Pacific islands, and during the nineteenth and twentieth centuries he brought most of them under his control.

The Japanese occupied a number of the islands during the Second World War, and the Americans used them as stepping stones in their defeat of Japan. The spirit and knowledge of freedom and independence have also become a part of the atmosphere of these islands. The people who live in the Pacific region, sometimes referred to as Oceania, are reassuming control over their island homes.

The port of Papeete, Tahiti is a busy center of tourist activity set against a background of palm groves and dramatic mountains. (Air France)

## Australia

Man first came to Australia around 50,000 years ago from the islands of Indonesia. Removed from contact with other men who were evolving into different ways of life, the aborigine of Australia remained rather primitive. He used the spear, the boomerang, the club, and the shield in war, and he hunted wild game and gathered wild herbs and nuts for food. He was a nomad, who asked little of the land except the satisfaction of his basic needs. In the warmer areas, he wore no clothing, and his simple culture never developed agriculture, herding, or villages. But in the 1700's English prisoners and adventurers began to share this island-continent with the aborigines. Slowly over the years their share became larger than that of the original inhabitants. Diseases brought by the new settlers ravaged the tribesmen, and their numbers dwindled as the Europeans increased and took more and more of the land. The island-continent became the homeland of the transplanted Englishman who took the name Australian. His culture and his kind dominate Australia today, although the primitive aborigines still roam in a small part of the land.

The European Dutch discovered this island-continent in the 1600's and called it New Holland. They viewed it, however, as a land of little promise, and concentrated their colonizing labors on the islands of the East Indies, which were richer in people and in resources. In 1770, Captain James Cook, an Englishman, claimed Australia for England. The English viewed it as a splendid solution to their problem of overcrowded jails. Offenses were many and punishments were heavy in that period of England's history, and the surplus population of the prisons was sent to this isolated land. The first shipment of convicts and their guards landed near the present location of Sydney in 1788. As prison ships continued to come and discharge cargoes of England's unwanted men, there were those who found that sheep could feed and multiply on the extensive acres of Australia. Soon wool became the "golden fleece," the foundation of Australia's prosperity. The land began to show promise, and a few free settlers also went there. The number of convicts gradually decreased, and by the end of the 1860's the English had ceased to send prisoners there.

In 1851 gold was discovered, and the magic and the promise of quick wealth drew to Australia's shores men from all over the world. They came in numbers and they came voluntarily. The population doubled and tripled, and there was not gold for all. Many turned to farming and to the planting of orchards, but the physical environment of Australia made their task most difficult. Although Australia has a land area more than two-thirds as large as mainland United States, nearly 40 per cent of it is wasteland, and rain is scarce throughout the greater part of the country. There were failures and disasters, and the colonists demanded that the government rescue them. The government responded by building railroads, roads, ports, and public utilities, and by sponsoring an increasing number of economic activities. Minerals were uncovered — coal, lead, copper, and later, bauxite, manganese, and uranium—and the foundations of an Australian mining and manufacturing industry were laid. The government protected these home industries with tariffs and aided them with loans. Today the Australian does not question the major role of government in his economy, and in fact demands it.

Many settlers continued to come to Australia in search of the good life, but they found that there would be little security if they did not band together and seek it in an organized fashion. They founded trade unions, which grew in numbers and in power, and today it is estimated that 40 per cent or more of Australian wage-earners are members of some union. These unions have played a major role in pressing the government to adopt welfare measures such as pensions for the aged, health and unemployment insurance, assistance for widows and children, and other advanced social legislation.

Early in their history the Australians of English and European heritage became jealous and fearful of the Asians within whose region Australia lay. The island-continent loomed large on a map, and its largeness was an invitation to those who lived closely packed together in Asia. These Asians did not know that most Australians lived around the coasts and that the interior of the country was so inhospitable to man that it was sometimes referred to as a "dead heart." Shaken by the thought of being swamped and absorbed by waves of Asian immigrants, the Australian government passed laws forbidding citizenship and permanent residence to those who are not white. These laws are still in force. Most Australians are of English descent, over 90 per cent, but in recent years Europeans from the continent are also finding their way to Australia. The population of Australia now numbers around 10,600,000.

Since 1901 Australia has been an independent self-governing member of the Commonwealth of Nations. In political matters the Australian is a fiercely independent man. Despite his exclusion of others not of his own family of man, he is deeply conscious of his own dignity as a man and of his need to be free. He is democratic. His country, officially known as the Commonwealth of Australia, is a federal union of six states: New South

Wales, Victoria, Queensland, South Australia, Western Australia, and Tasmania. The Australian constitution, like that of the United States, provides that powers not specifically given to the federal government are reserved to the various states. The Australian Parliament consists of two house, the Senate and the House of Representatives, whose members are elected, and the Cabinet is chosen from the majority party in the House of Representatives.

The Australian is Western in appearance and in culture, but Asian in location and in concern. Although tied to England by heritage and long association, the Australian looks to the United States for his ultimate security. Awakened by the Japanese to the potential dangers of his Pacific location, he is seeking greater knowledge of his Asian neighbors and groping for closer ties with those who are friendly. There is yet in him the spirit, the adventure, the vitality, and the bravery of the pioneer. He is a nationalist, but he is also a man who now understands that the wide waters of the oceans no longer isolate him from the affairs of other men. He knows that his destiny is being determined by others as well as himself. His dedication to the freedoms and the peace of the world was dramatized by the courage and the sacrifices of his people in two world wars. There are few of freedom's battlefields where the Aussie is not known with affection and respect. He is a man of toughness of conviction, and he does not yield easily to those who threaten his freedom and independence.

### New Zealand

About 1,250 miles southeast of Australia lie the picturesque and prosperous islands of New Zealand. Consisting of two main islands known as North Island and South Island and some outlying islands, New Zealand is about the size of Italy. A Polynesian people known as the Maoris settled these islands several centuries before the European Dutchman, Abel Tasman, discovered and named them New Zealand in 1642. The English began to know the beauty and potential of the islands in the 1700's. In 1839 a group of English settlers went to New Zealand, and in 1840 the English government annexed the islands. The English royal governor negotiated a treaty with the Maori chiefs which was designed to protect their lands and their rights. Gradually, however, much of the land became the property of the colonists, for this was the period of European migration to more promising and distant lands. The total population today numbers about 2,415,000, of whom more than 90 per cent are of English descent, while the Maoris number about 171,000.

The advance of New Zealand toward constitutional government and independence was rapid. By 1853 a constitution was adopted, and a cabinet system of government evolved which placed political power in a single House of Representatives whose members were elected. By 1879 there was universal male suffrage, and in 1893 women were given the right to vote in national elections. New Zealand was first among the democracies to grant the vote to women. New Zealand became a self-governing member of the British Commonwealth in 1907. Although free to follow an independent foreign policy, the New Zealander tends to support the policy of Great Britain and is intensely loyal to the homeland from whence most of his people originally came.

New Zealand is a land of much natural beauty. The grandeur of the mountains along the west coast of South Island is so magnificent that they are called the Southern Alps. On North Island there is the symmetrical cone of the volcano, the glistening plume of the geyser, and the bubbling warmth of the hot spring. New Zealand has an abundant variety of waterfalls, lakes, forests, and grassy plains, and its climate is largely cool, moist, and suitable for comfortable living and productive work.

The New Zealander has made good use of his fertile earth. Upon it he raises over 47,000,000 sheep, almost 6,000,000 cattle, and around 700,000 hogs. He grows wheat, barley, potatoes, fruits, and a variety of vegetables. Much of this agricultural wealth, dairy products, wool, and meat is exported to other lands, especially to Great Britain and the United States. It is from these riches of the land that New Zealand obtains most of its income. There are manufacturing industries in New Zealand, but they do not compare in scope with agricultural production. Forests provide timber and pulp for a paper industry, and natural steam, rivers, and coal provide power.

The government has built railroads, roads, and public utilities. It also provides for social welfare, old-age insurance, unemployment compensation, insurance against accidents, and health insurance. The New Zealander is a man of neither extreme wealth nor extreme poverty, and he is frequently a small independent farmer. He wants no monopolies and no great holders of wealth in land or in industry, for he is suspicious of those who possess great economic or political power. New Zealand is a member of the Free World and lends support to those who stand for freedom.

Tonga islanders are shown preparing a feast for their ruler. The Tongans are Polynesians. (New Zealand Consulate General)

1. What did the experiment which is related in the book *Kon-Tiki* hope to establish? What term is sometimes used to refer to the islands in the Pacific region?
2. What product formed the foundation of Australia's prosperity?
3. How does the land area of Australia compare with that of the United States?
4. What is the New Zealander's political attitude toward Great Britain?

### Religion and Thought

Many religions have found a home in the hearts of the Southeast Asians. They are a religious people. Everywhere there are shrines, temples, religious buildings—grand or humble, ornate or sometimes unadorned—remembrances of the divinity they seek and cherish.

Originally the Southeast Asians sought the divine in the objects around them. They believed that the mountains, the rivers, the seas, and all of nature's manifestations contained a spirit, sometimes good, sometimes evil, but always of importance to their lives. The Laotians called these spirits *phi*. It was believed that some spirits could cause disease, suffering, and even death; others were good to man. Practically every Thai village has a guardian, portrayed in many ways, and it is the spirit that guards the villagers. The Burmese make their offerings to the *nat*, which is the name they give the spirit whose help they need. Indonesians are careful to placate the powerful spirits of the volcano, the sea, and the river. These spirits are of ancient origin, and their influence still endures, though overlaid with the more complex teachings of Hinduism, Buddhism, Islam, and Christianity.

Hinduism and Buddhism were brought early to the various peoples of Southeast Asia by Indian traders, who traveled practically everywhere in this region. Hinduism did not last, at least not in its pure form; but Buddhism persisted, and, in the form called Theravada, "The Path of the Elders," it is today the religion of the great mass of the people of Burma, Thailand, Cambodia, and Laos.

It will be recalled that there are two forms of Buddhism. One is called Mahayana Buddhism, and it is the more tender or merciful belief, which tries to save man through the merits of others, to uplift him by the examples of holy ones who are kind and merciful. This is the Buddhism of the Chinese, Koreans, Vietnamese, and many Japanese. Then there is Theravada Buddhism, which is more demanding of man and teaches that man must rely upon himself, and not upon others, if he is to reach the peace and bliss of nirvana.

There is a story told about four men who were climbing a mountain. The first man to reach the top looked, gave a great shout, and threw himself out of sight over the other side of the mountain. The second man did the same thing, and so did the third man. When the fourth man reached the top, he, too, looked and gasped in joy and amazement, for there awaiting him was the paradise of all his dreams. He did not go to it, but, instead, turned away, went back down the mountain, and spent the rest of his life showing others the mountain path that led to Paradise. The first three men were followers of Theravada Buddhism; the fourth man was a follower of Mahayana Buddhism.

Because Theravada Buddhism teaches that each man must find his own way to nirvana, a great many adult male Buddhists become monks for short, and sometimes long, periods of their lives. During the time they are monks, they study, meditate, beg their food, teach, and perform other good works. They are respected and welcomed everywhere. They are needed in religious ceremonies and rituals. They are a necessary part of the social, political, and religious fabric of the Asian way of life.

In Malaya, Indonesia, Borneo, and southern parts of the Philippines, the majority of the people are Moslems, followers of the Islamic religion. This religion, too, was brought in part by Indians, and in part by Arabs. It is a religion that preaches that there is only one God, who is the same as the God of the Jews and the Christians. Moslems believe that Mohammed, the historical founder, was God's prophet, as were Jesus, Moses, Abraham, and others. They believe that God revealed Himself and His teachings to Mohammed, as He had to the prophets before Mohammed. Mohammed wrote these revelations down in a book called the *Koran.* The Koran is regarded by the Moslems as the sacred, revealed words of God. They hold it in the same reverence that Christians hold the Bible, and the Jews the Old Testament.

Mohammed preached Islam first in Arabia in the sixth century A.D., and its spread was rapid and wide. It was carried to both the East and the West by the Arabs and their converts. The Arabs, Afghans, Persians, and Turks all helped to propagate Islam in India, and from India and Arabia it spread to Southeast Asia. We shall treat the birth and growth of Islam more fully when our tale of man moves to the Middle East.

The Vietnamese, for the most part, were followers of Mahayana Buddhism because they received their religious and philosophical thought from the Chinese. But officially they were also Confucianists, and, to a small degree, Taoists. They, too, have their spirits who dwell within nature's creations. Many Vietnamese have also embraced Catholicism, which was brought to them by French missionaries. Most of the Filipinos are also Catholics, the result of the efforts of Spanish priests and missionaries; but a number of them still believe in a hidden world of spirits which, though unseen, surrounds them.

1. What are the three major religious faiths in Southeast Asia?
2. Why do you suppose Hinduism failed to take hold and last in Southeast Asia?
3. What is the sacred book of Islam?

## Conclusion

In the past three chapters we have looked at some of the important ideologies of the Asians. There was Hinduism, which was born in India; there were Confucianism, Taoism, and Legalism, which came from China; and there was Shinto, which is exclusively Japanese. There was also the belief in spirits of the land and the waters—a form of religion we call *animism.* In Southeast Asia there was the religion of Islam. And there was Buddhism, which went forth from India and found a home in China, Korea, Japan, and Southeast Asia.

These ideologies have played a significant role in making the Asian what he was in the past and what he is today. There is not one aspect of the Asian's life which has not been touched, and often deeply, by his religious beliefs and the teachings of great philosophers. His beliefs and ideas are evident in social and political life and in the temples, shrines, and mosques which crowd the landscape. The ideology of the Asian frequently determines whether he will act or not act when called upon to make a decision about his own life or the lives of others.

The Asian, like other men, has been exposed to ideas which came from outside his homeland. Ideas often seem to grow wings rapidly and fly forth to many lands and peoples, even over great distances. This is especially true of those ideas which deal with the basic questions that man is always asking himself: Why am I here? How did I get here? How should I live here? Where am I going? For what purpose? All of these are questions which have always plagued and interested man. Some of the answers that have been proposed have frequently found a welcome in the hearts of men. Ideas know no barriers of race, economic position, or distance.

Ideas are durable as well as adaptable. They seldom die. The men who speak, write, and teach ideas may die, but what they have created, or been inspired to say, will linger on for centuries, perhaps forever. An idea may disappear in its original form, as Buddhism did in India, but it will appear in other appealing forms elsewhere. Ideas spoken, written, and taught so many years ago in Asia, and modified and expanded over thousands of years, are still essential to the Asian of today. There can be no understanding of the Asian of yesterday, today, and tomorrow unless there is some understanding of the beliefs and ideas which guide his life and move him to act.

## SUMMING UP THE CHAPTER

A. Identify or explain the following, relating them to this chapter.

| | |
|---|---|
| Angkor | Maoris |
| Annamese | Marshal Thanarat |
| Burman | Mon |
| Khmers | Pagan |
| Kublai Khan | Pegu |
| Lan Xang | Shan |
| Lao | Srivijaya |
| Magellan | Sukhothai |
| Majapahit | Thais |
| Malays | |

B. Chapter review questions.

1. What group became dominant in the economy of Thailand? In what other areas of Asia did this group also gain economic power? What economic, social, and political problems do you think this caused?
2. What does the economic and political history of Malaysia tell you about the nature of Western colonialism? What is the political status of Singapore today?
3. What cultural, economic, and political consequences derive from the vastness of the island empire of Indonesia?
4. How did the British and Dutch carve out political and economic spheres of influence in Southeast Asia in the nineteenth century? What other Western nations were also involved?
5. How did the United States become involved in the Philippines at the turn of the century?
6. In what ways is Islam a very accommodating religion?

C. Questions for discussion.

1. How would you explain that religion seems to have greater influence on daily life in Asia than in the West?
2. Discuss the relation of folk religion to the more intellectually "sophisticated" religions and the political uses of religion in Asia.

D. Projects for groups or individuals.

1. Draw a map of Southeast Asia. Label each country.
2. Read a full account of the history of Australia and New Zealand or any one of the nations of Southeast Asia.
3. Make a list of all the different peoples living in Southeast Asia and the islands of the Pacific. Check in an almanac or encyclopedia to see what percentage of the population is made up by each group. Make a list also of the religions of Southeast Asia.
4. Make a map of the islands of the Pacific and on it indicate the kinds of people found, the earliest explorers, and the present government for each major group.

# CHAPTER 5

# *They Cherished Art and Writings*

THE ASIAN, like other men, has been moved to describe in stone and precious metal, with brush and pen on paper and silk, in music and in dance, the thoughts and the feelings his tongue alone could not adequately express. He has sculptured, carved, painted, and written. He has been moved by religious beliefs, by the magnetism of nature, by feelings for others, and by the many mysterious urges which spur man to try to express what is in his heart. Many of these expressions still remain, preserved in temples of chiseled stone, in sculptured figures, in painting, and in literature. But much, too much, has been lost, eroded away by the changes of time, by the winds and the waters, the dirt, the sand, the insect. And much was looted, burned, and mutilated in wars and through man's carelessness.

From the fall of the Maurya dynasty in India (185 B.C.) until the establishment of the Gupta dynasty (320 A.D.), the Indians were subjected to many invasions from the ever-moving peoples of Central Asia. During this period there was much looting and destruction, and many of the early artistic achievements of the Indians were lost. The Chinese were also subject to invasions of the nomads from the steppes to the north of them. These invasions, as well as civil wars among themselves, resulted in the loss of many of their fine early works. One of the early Chinese emperors, the first Legalist emperor, Ch'in Shih Huan Ti, wanted history to begin with himself, and he burned all the historical and philosophical books he could find in the empire. Much was lost, although a few of the old writings were hidden and saved.

The Koreans, the Japanese, and the Southeast Asians have all experienced the horrors of war throughout their history, and all have suffered the destruction of untold numbers of works of art and writings. The Chinese suffered particularly because their finest architecture was usually done in wood rather than stone. Today Europe has far more temples, castles, and cathedrals than does all of China. The Chinese built constantly, but for most of their ancient or medieval buildings we have nothing to show except the stone outline of the foundations. Fire and chance have taken all the rest.

The Asian today knows of this loss because those who lived before and during these periods of destruction wrote about their achievements. They described palaces with many rooms, well-proportioned and made beautiful with intricately carved wood, inlaid precious and semiprecious stones, and adornments of gold, silver, and bronze. They wrote about monasteries and libraries in which were stored thousands upon thousands of manuscripts and books containing literary works of all kinds. They described marvelous paintings and told of geniuses who created beauty beyond compare; but they rarely told us the names or any details of the lives of these inspired men. The artists of Asia have generally been anonymous. It is through the eyes of these observers that we gain some idea of the value and quantity of the lost artistic expressions of the Asians.

But not all was lost. Much of the work in stone endured the passage of time and the de-

This stupa is located at Taxila, the ruins of an ancient town just east of the Indus River. (Government of India Information Services)

struction of man. Sometimes paintings were made in caves which the vandal and the looter did not find. A few specimens of art and writings were hidden and preserved for posterity.

1. What reasons can you give that might account for the destruction of much of Asia's early art and writing?
2. Why do men express themselves in art? Name some of the forms of art developed in Asia.

## Religion and the Arts in India

Religion has influenced the art and literature of India from very early times. One of the oldest types of religious monument in India is the Buddhist *stupa.* A stupa is a hemispheric mound of brick or stone which houses some sacred relic. An outstanding example, the Sanchi Stupa, dates from the time of Asoka (273-232 B.C.).

The Sanchi Stupa is a huge mound of stone with a flattened top. In the middle of this flat top is the receptacle for holding the holy relics, surrounded by a railing and shaded by an umbrella. The umbrella is the symbol of kingship. This entire mound sits upon a raised terrace and is fenced completely around by a stone railing. This railing is pierced with four large gateways facing north, east, south, and west. These gateways are elaborately carved, with symbolic and imaginative figures in which the closeness between religion and art is evident.

Everywhere one looks on these gates there are carvings of men, women, animals, plants, and symbols. No part of the stone has been left uncarved. Buddha is represented by the wheel, the lotus, the lion, the footprint, and the sacred tree, but never in human shape. Stories called *Jataka tales* are carved here. They tell about the previous existences of Buddha when he was a deer, a king of the monkeys, and an elephant. These picture stories show his goodness and kindness to all even when he was an animal. Buddhist stupas were sacred places, and the followers of Buddha gained merit by merely walking around them.

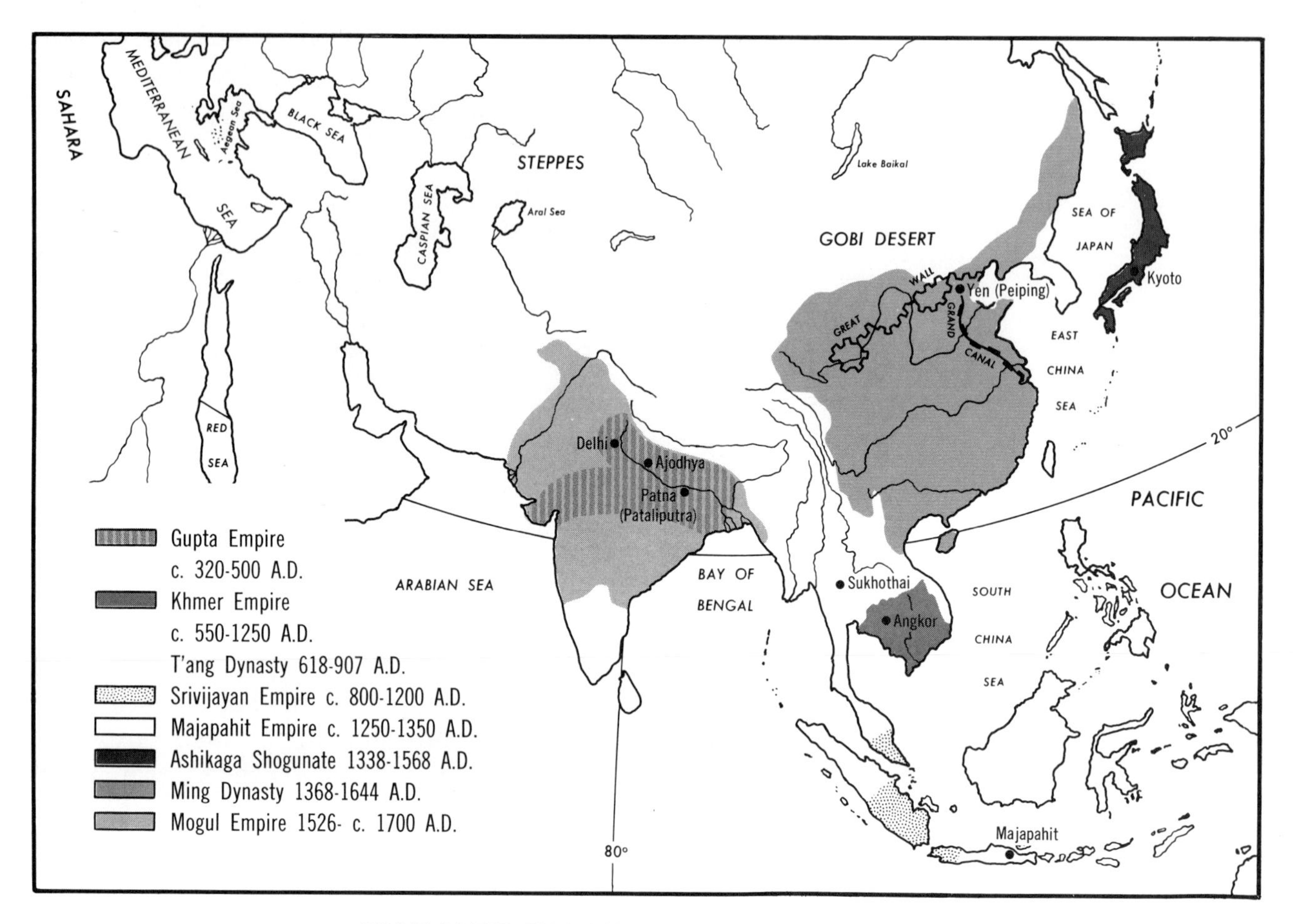


**SOME LATER EMPIRES OF ASIA (320 A.D. to 1700 A.D.)**

Compare the later empires of Asia with empires shown on page 168. Why is it important to study Middle Eastern empires along with those of India, China, and Southeast Asia? Use reference books to read about contacts between the ancient peoples of the Far East and the Middle East.

As time moved along, the Indians undertook the tremendous task of carving temples from the solid rock. They imitated structures of wood and masonry by carving beams from the stone. Pillars of stone carved along the sides of the temple appeared to actually hold up the beams. In the most holy place, the sanctuary, a stupa was placed, and the good Buddhist gained merit here, too, by walking around it.

Gradually, statues of Buddha began to replace the stupa. These statues were not supposed to look like Buddha, but were sculptured to portray his peace of mind, his calmness, and his happiness which was beyond the pleasure of the senses. Many of these representations of Buddha have a swelling or bulge on top of the head, signifying wisdom. Buddha's ear lobes are long and pierced to remind the viewer that Buddha at one time wore jeweled earrings of such weight that they stretched the lobes of his ears. This symbol reminds all that wealth is of little value. A mark was placed on the forehead between the eyes to represent the third eye of virtue and spirituality. The statue of Buddha preaching in the Deer Park of Sarnath is regarded as one of the finest examples of this art.

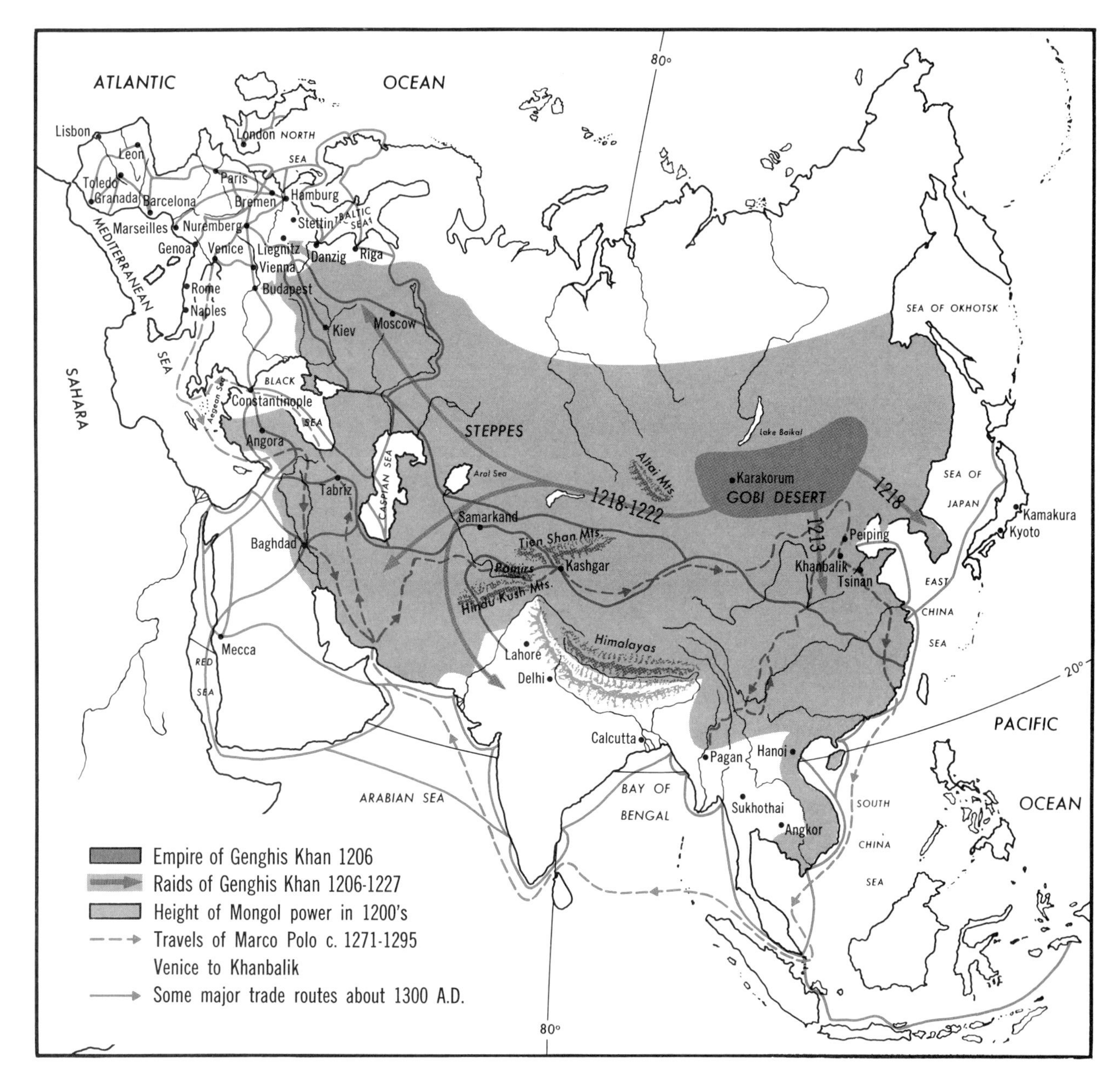


**MONGOL EMPIRES AND MAJOR TRADE ROUTES (1206–1300)**

On page 87 you will read about the Mongols and Turks who invaded India. Study this map and the map on the facing page as you read.

A few of the paintings of these early Indians survived the weathering of the centuries because they were painted inside caves. Among the best of these surviving paintings are those found in the caves of Ajanta in central India. Around 200 B.C. a religious community was started in an isolated jungle above the Wardha River, and for a period of about 700 years a community of monks lived there. While they were living there, they chiseled and dug halls

The picture shows carvings at an entrance to the caves of Ajanta. Find Ajanta on a map. (Embassy of India)

of worship and quarters for the monks from the cliffs of solid rock above the river. The walls of these temple-caves were graced with sculpture and paintings.

These unknown artists of the caves of Ajanta painted a living, moving, colorful picture of India's life. The variety of India is there: the beggar, the rich man, the peasant, and the king. There are also flowers, children, animals of the earth, and forms that are not of earth. On these walls are pictures of palaces and the audiences of the emperor, of great processions, and of people listening intently to the truths of Buddhism. All are clothed in many vivid colors—greens, browns, reds, blues, and white—and seem almost alive.

By the end of the sixth century A.D. Buddhism had withered much in the country of its birth, but it lived on vigorously abroad. In Thailand, Indonesia, Burma, Cambodia, and Ceylon, there are magnificent representations of Buddha. He is pictured reclining in repose, standing tall and strong, and sitting to teach and to meditate. Some of these statues are encrusted with emeralds and enclosed in temples leafed with gold. In these lands the people have erected imposing stupas and carved the stories of Buddha's previous lives on wall, and door, and ceiling. Their art reflects their living faith.

## Gupta Dynasty: Classical Period

Many of the great classical works of the Indians were done during the Gupta dynasty, which lasted from 320 A.D. until the end of the fifth century. A Chinese Buddhist pilgrim who visited India during this dynasty described in glowing language the political and cultural atmosphere he found there. The arts flourished, and there was religious tolerance. The government was mild, and the ruler appeared to have a real interest in the welfare of the people. After the fall of the Gupta dynasty, another great king, Harsha, brought peace, unity, and security to the land from 606 to 647 A.D. He was a tolerant and responsible ruler who worked hard to improve the lot of his people. It was during the time of the Gupta dynasty and the reign of King Harsha that the arts of India also flowered.

Although tolerant of Buddhism, the Gupta kings were Hindus, and during this period Hindu themes and representations of the deity were done with vigor and artistry in stone, bronze, and gold. Over the centuries, Hindu temples were cut from the solid rock and stood proudly displayed, released from the cave and the mountainside. One of the most famous of these Hindu rock temples is the well-known Kailasa Temple. Another is the cave of Elephanta in the Bay of Bombay, which is dedicated to the Lord Siva.

**The three great gods.** Lord Siva is one of of the three great gods of Hinduism. The other two are Brahma and Vishnu. Brahma is sometimes represented with four heads and four arms holding the Vedas. His wife is Sarasvati, the goddess of music and eloquence. Lord Siva is sometimes portrayed in a dancing pose of creation and destruction, and in this pose he is known as Nataraja. He is often shown with his wife, Parvati, who can also destroy and save men. Lord Vishnu is sometimes represented with four arms holding a shell, a staff of authority called a mace, a lotus flower, and a disk indicating the sun. He rides a bird called the garuda, which is part man and part eagle. His wife is named Lakshmi and is the goddess of beauty. There are thousands upon thousands of interpretations of these famous gods of Hinduism carved, molded, and painted with genius and originality.

**Detailed art rules.** Many, if not most, of the great army of artists who have created the masterpieces of India over the passing centuries have worked within detailed and strict rules. There were rules, for example, for the length and width of the nostril. Even the precise placement of the hands was spelled out. The artist used no living model. He had his ideas and his rules. Before he could begin his painting or his sculpturing, he must first meditate and think through every particular of what he was about to describe. Finally, he must identify himself with the idea he was about to portray. It is a mark of the genius of the Indian artists that they were able to produce an art of magnificence and beauty within the limitations of these strict rules. No doubt this was in large measure due to the strength of their religious beliefs.

1. How has religion influenced art in India?
2. What art form took the place of the *stupa* in India? Why do you suppose this change took place?
3. What type of paintings were found in the caves of Ajanta? Who were the artists?
4. Name the three chief Hindu gods. Describe their artistic representations and what they stand for.

## The Indians Wrote Much

The Indians have written almost beyond measure. They have recorded the Vedas, the sacred books of Hinduism. They have written epics, the greatest of which are the *Mahabharata* and the *Ramayana.* To many, the heart of the *Mahabharata* is the *Bhagavad-Gita,* "The Lord's Song." The Indians have written an untold number of religious and philosophical works explaining, extending, and praising their religions. These writings have been read, loved, followed, and believed. They are a part of the heart as well as the literature of the Indians.

Indian writers and scholars have commented on politics, on relations between states, on the practice of diplomacy, and on the strategy of war. They have observed the paths of the stars and written books to guide man's life by them. In ancient times they were fascinated with numbers and gave to us the concept of zero and other mathematical discoveries. The also examined the illnesses of man and suggested possible cures for them.

The technique and art of advising and teaching through fables originated in India. The *Panchatantra,* or "Five Books," is a collection of stories with moral lessons intended for the instruction of the youth. Some of these stories are almost identical with some of the famous tales in *The Arabian Nights* and Aesop's *Fables.* The stories of the *Panchatantra* were written down between 300 and 500 A.D. In them, the lion, the chicken, the mouse, the jackal, and other animals characterize the failings and weaknesses of man.

The Indians wrote much about society and its problems. They believed that the separation of groups by means of a caste system was basic to cooperative living in India. They held that the family was fundamental to all society, and they wrote in detail about the roles required of the family members if the family was to function happily and properly.

Indian poetry and drama rank high in the history of literature. One of the greatest of Indian poets was Tulsi Das (1532-1623), whose work is still read and appreciated. Drama was written in poetic form, and the greatest of the poetic dramatists was Kalidasa, who lived and wrote in the fifth century A.D. His drama entitled *Sakuntala* is considered by many to rival the best of Shakespeare. Sakuntala is the name of the heroine. She is shy, like the animals of the forest in which she lives with her foster-father, a holy sage. She is tender, merciful, generous, and faithful. She has strength of character, beauty of form, and is generous in her love and care for animal, friend, and husband alike. She represents an ideal vision of all women.

It is impossible to list in this brief summary all the great authors of India, for they have lived in every age of Indian history down to the present. Indian writers today are writing in English as well as in Sanskrit, their oldest language. They are writing, too, in their mother tongues. (India does not have one common language. There are several hundred distinct languages and dialects.) These modern writers have been influenced by the changing times and the styles and thoughts of the West. They are attempting to blend the old and the new, the past and the present, and in their latest writings they are evolving new ways of stating old truths.

### Crowds of People Dimly Seen

With the death of the enlightened King Harsha in 647 A.D., a mist envelops the history of India for more than five hundred years. We have only a vague knowledge of this time. This period is a dim divider between the old and the modern India. Hinduism survived it in a modified form. Buddhism was almost completely lost to the Indians sometime during this period. There were empires, but they are like formless shadows passing hurriedly. There were heroes and outstanding men, but we know of them only through folk tales. There were vast and continuous migrations

This stone chariot is one of the ruins at the site of the capital of the Hindu kingdom of Vijayanagar, overthrown by the Moslems in 1565. (Government of India Tourist Office)

into India of people from Central Asia, and they were assimilated and given their places in the layers of the caste society of India. Then, in the eleventh century, there came a people who were not so easily absorbed and who stamped the cultural and the political life of the Indians with an impression that is still very obvious today. They were the Moslems, the followers of the religion of Islam.

### The Moslems

It was the Turks who really brought Islam to India in the eleventh century. They were a restless, warlike people, who burst from Central Asia, that breeding land of wandering warriors, to make themselves rulers in the Middle East. They became Moslems and were greatly influenced by the culture of Persia. But this culture and this religion had not penetrated deeply when the Turks began their raids into India in the early part of the eleventh century. These savage and destructive raids were first directed from the Turkish capital of Ghazni in Afghanistan. The Turkish raiders looted Hindu and Buddhist temples of great quantities of jewels and gold and destroyed the idols, which, they believed, honored false and accursed gods.

Under new leaders, the Turks continued their advance into India, and finally, at the end of the twelfth century, established their capital at Delhi. By the beginning of the thirteenth century most of north and northwest India were under Turkish control. This was the first time that India had been united since the Gupta empire in the fifth century A.D. The Turkish empire in India lasted from 1192 to 1398 and during this period maintained the unity of the country. In the thirteenth century the Mongols under Genghis Khan and his descendants pillaged and ruled the land from the Yellow Sea to the Dnieper River in Russia. The Turks found many brilliant minds and fine soldiers among the refugees who fled the destruction of the Mongols to the north. Although the Mongols attempted to invade India, they could not overcome the strong Turkish empire there.

Then, at the end of the fourteenth century, divisions weakened the empire in India. Timur, sometimes called Tamerlane, was a Turk, and he was one of the greatest conquerors and destroyers of all time. Born in 1336, he took advantage of the dissension among the Mongol successors of Genghis Khan and built for himself a great empire. He ruled a domain from Samarkand (now located in the USSR) that stretched for thousands of miles from Moscow and the Mediterranean to China in the Far East. He invaded India in 1398, and his pillage of the land and the people was so savage that in Delhi it is said not even a bird moved its wings until months after he had left. He did not linger there, but returned to his homeland in Central Asia, leaving behind terror, strife, and divisions. India remained divided until Babur, a direct descendant of Timur, invaded India in 1525 and founded the Mogul Empire. *Mogul* is an Indian pronunciation of *Mongol*, and this name is given to the Indian empire because Timur and Babur, though Turks, claimed legal and family descent from the Mongols.

Babur was a much different man from his ancestor Timur. He was human, warm, and witty. He was sensitive to beauty, a poet and author of prose, and the quality of his writings is still recognized today. He was a rare and appealing figure amidst the trouble, deceit, and pride of his time. In 1530 Babur was succeeded by Humayun, his eldest son. Humayun was a good man, steeped in Persian culture, and lovable but weak. He was addicted to opium. Humayun was driven into exile for several years by an Afghan chief, but later he was able to retake Delhi. He soon died, but left a son, Akbar, who was to become one of the greatest and the best of India's rulers.

**The Emperor Akbar.** Akbar was only thirteen years of age when his father died in 1556. With the help of able and loyal followers while he was young, and later under his own brilliant leadership, the greater part of India was brought under his rule. More than a military leader, he was a fine diplomat and a magnificent organizer; and he had a feeling for the welfare of the people. He gave

Above, the Taj Mahal. Below, a Mogul painting of the eighteenth century. (Both, Embassy of India)

logic, unity, and justice to the land taxes and established a civil service. Akbar was able to reconcile the differences among the often conflicting communities within the land he governed. Under his rule, the Moslem tax on nonbelievers was removed, and the temples of the Hindus were protected.

**The artistry of the Moguls.** Under Akbar and his successors, the culture of Persia merged with that of the Hindu, and from this union there flowered the art of the Moguls.

Persian had been the official language of the court before Akbar's reign but he made it the language of India, much as French used to be the polite language of diplomacy and educated circles in Europe. From this mixture of Persian and Hindi languages came the Urdu language. Urdu is the official language of modern Pakistan and is still spoken today by a great many people in India.

The Moguls were perceptive and enthusiastic patrons and collectors of paintings. Their realistic and detailed landscapes and portraits done in miniature are prized today as among the finest of their kind ever done by man.

**Poetry in stone.** In their architecture the Moguls made poetry of marble and semiprecious jewels. Their palaces, places of worship called mosques, and their tombs are visions of beauty. The style of their architecture is marked by strength and elegance. They introduced the arch and graceful bulb-shaped domes. Their soaring, delicate works of stone were placed in the midst of cultivated parks and mirrored in the still waters of lakes and lagoons. The most beautiful example and glory of Mogul art is the Taj Mahal, a tomb built in the 1600's by the emperor Shah Jahan for his beloved wife.

The Taj Mahal is one of the most harmonious arrangements in stone created by man. It is constructed of white marble, crowned with one large and four small domes, and it is flanked on each corner by four minarets, or towers, which are separated from the main structure. The tomb is of huge dimensions but so well designed that it creates an impression of lightness, as if poised to take flight and soar to heaven. Seen at night, glowing softly in the light of the moon, and shimmering in the quiet waters that lie before it, it casts a spell of serene, lasting, indescribable beauty. By building this tomb the emperor Shah Jahan made the memory of his queen immortal.

**Poetry written and spoken.** The Moguls delighted to write, listen to, and make up poetry. It was regarded as a great honor to come

The two folk dancers of Rajasthan are accompanied by native musicians. Use reference books to learn more about the music of India. (Government of India Tourist Office)

before the emperor and recite poetry, often praising his reign. Sometimes this poetry was of great merit. The Moguls would at times improvise lines of poetry when moved by some event, some passion, or the beauty of the landscape. There was the Mogul princess who, while gazing at a waterfall in Lahore and hearing the sounds of its splashing on the marble below, spoke lines of poetry which are still remembered today. As translated, they are:

> Whose absence, O Waterfall, art thou
> lamenting so loudly,
> Why hast thou cast down thy head in grief?
> How acute was thy pain, that throughout
> the night,
> Restless, like me, thou wast striking thy head
> against the stone and shedding tears profusely![1]

The Moguls prized their books and manuscripts, and they often decorated the borders and bindings of books with gold. They honored those who could write with a beautiful hand. It is said that the great Mogul emperor Aurangzeb was a gifted writer who enjoyed making lovely copies of the Koran with his own hand. It was probably the Moguls who first introduced the Indians to the use and manufacture of paper, a knowledge which had been passed to them by the Chinese.

But, like all empires, theirs, too, was destined to decline. In the seventeenth and eighteenth centuries Mogul control of India was gradually loosened by divisions within and by the growing power of the Europeans who came there. Eventually the British became the rulers of India. But the Moguls left a cultural imprint upon the people of India which has never been erased.

1. What has the Indian written about in the past? In what language does he write today?
2. What were the strengths and weaknesses of the Moslem rule of India? What do you consider to be the greatest single achievement of Islam in India?
3. Who replaced the Mogul rulers during the eighteenth century in India?

[1] From *The Legacy of India,* edited by G. T. Garratt. Quoted by permission of the Clarendon Press, Oxford.

## The Chinese Also Created

The Chinese, like the Indians, have been sculpturing, painting, carving, building, and working in metal from the earliest period of their history. Unfortunately, many of their creations have also disappeared from the sight of man. Fortunately, some have survived the decay and the destruction of the ages. Among the earliest and most famous of these survivals are their works of bronze which were produced during the Shang dynasty, about 1750-1122 B.C.

The Chinese made bronzes for a variety of uses. They made tall, slender cups to drink from and vessels of bronze with three legs and handles to hold their food. To hold their wines, they fashioned containers of bronze which were sometimes in the shape of owls and other animals.

During the Chou dynasty, 1122-256 B.C., the Chinese continued to make bronze bells, mirrors, and vessels. On their bronzes they carved birds and animals, imaginative dragons, and abstract symbols, and thus produced an art which is unique. They made bronze vessels and containers not only for dining and drinking but also for use in rituals honoring their ancestors and in memory of important family and state events. Man has never surpassed the works in bronze of the ancient Chinese.

In their tombs, the ancient Chinese placed small reproductions of houses and other objects of bronze, gold, and shell. On the walls of tombs they carved men, beasts, and scenes from daily life. We have learned much about the early Chinese from their tombs, particularly those of the Han dynasty, 205 B.C.-220 A.D.

Many of their buildings had curving roofs which overhung the walls. The roofs were supported by pillars. The walls filled the spaces between the pillars and kept out the harsh weather but did not support the roofs. Roofs were made of tiles of various colors, mostly blue and green, but the tiles of the royal palace were of yellow, for this was the distinguishing royal color. The Chinese were fond of colors and used them lavishly. The wooden

The ancient Chinese sought to explain natural phenomena, as did other ancient peoples. This drawing pictures a solar eclipse as a dragon devouring the sun. (Yerkes Observatory)

beams and pillars of buildings were carved and brightened with gold, lacquer, and inlays of different kinds. These buildings were, of course, the homes of the wealthy or the palaces of the kings and the nobles, for the average Chinese could not afford these luxuries of art.

Jade is a hard stone which is found in a number of colors, green being the most common. From the earliest times the Chinese have worked in jade. Jade ornaments such as rings, buckles, and hooks, as well as cups, bowls, and vases, were made for personal use. Articles of jade were also made for use in worship, and jade was also used to make seals and badges of authority.

When Buddhism entered China around the first century A.D., it brought other forms of art which grew into a new art combining both Indian and Chinese styles. The evolution of this new art can be viewed as Buddhism slowly made its way eastward from India to China. In North China, caves called grottoes were dug in the sandstone and limestone cliffs. In these caves were placed Buddhas and religious scenes cut from marble. These statues and carvings caught and held for all these centuries the spiritual beauty, the compassion, and the mercy of Mahayana Buddhism. Among the most famous of these are the masterpieces made in the sixth century and found in the caves of Lung-Men.

1. Out of what substance did the early Chinese, especially during the Shang and Chou dynasties, produce most of their works of art? What were these objects of art and why were they created?
2. How have we learned about life during the Han dynasty?

## The T'ang Dynasty: Artistic Peaks

The T'ang dynasty, 618-907 A.D., is one of the greatest periods of all Chinese history. During this period the Chinese reached a cultural and political peak. This was the period when the Chinese dazzled the Japanese with their culture, their learning, and their achievements in many fields. Their influence extended westward into Central Asia and southward into Southeast Asia, and beyond. Merchants, travelers, adventurers, seekers of knowledge, and missionaries of various faiths from all parts of the world were attracted by the brilliance and fame of the T'ang Chinese. They all came in large numbers and were generally welcomed.

The Chinese excelled in many fields, but it is in their art and poetry, their appreciation of the beautiful, that they have rarely been surpassed. At some time before the eighth century A.D., they developed the art of printing with wood blocks. A written page was first pasted on a smooth block of wood; then the wood was carved away, leaving the writing or characters raised. The raised characters were inked and then pressed on the paper of the book. One of the oldest printed books we possess dates from this period. It is a Buddhist text printed in 868 A.D.

The Chinese valued calligraphy, the art of beautiful writing or penmanship. Painting and calligraphy were closely allied since the same brush was used for both painting and writing. The force and skill that gave character and feeling to Chinese picture-writing also gave meaning, strength, and beauty to Chinese paintings.

**Paintings.** Little remains of the paintings of the T'ang Chinese, but we know from copies and observations of those who saw them that they painted much, and they painted well. Then, and in the Sung dynasty which followed, they were inclined to paint scenes from nature. Sometimes they portrayed the horse, the flower, the butterfly, and the bird in fine, minute detail. But they especially loved misty landscapes. Mountain peaks were veiled with fog and cloud, and often the river, the stream, or the lake would be linked with the mountain or the cloud by mist. And always the line and the stroke were important.

Sometimes man was introduced into these landscapes, but he was generally small and insignificant amidst the grandeur and marvelous works of nature. The Chinese were rarely inclined to do portrait painting.

Chinese paintings were not framed. They were painted on scrolls that could be hung and unwound. Many families would not display them on their walls but kept them rolled up in some safe place in the house. They were brought out for a leisurely viewing from time to time.

**Literature.** The Chinese have a vast literature. They have written much and continuously from far back in their history. They have especially been inclined to write history. At the court, there were always scribes taking down in great detail everything that was said and done by the emperor and the great of the kingdom, sometimes including the most trivial matters. There were histories of dynasties, histories of provinces, histories of localities, and detailed histories of various significant and sometimes insignificant events. The past, and its preservation, has always been of the utmost importance to the Chinese.

They compiled dictionaries and genealogies, and they have written at length on Confucianism, Taoism, and Buddhism. They wrote essays. They wrote fiction. They wrote exquisite poetry. And some of their finest poets lived and wrote during the T'ang dynasty.

There was Li T'ai-po (701-762), an original genius, fond of gay parties, who was always ready to drink wine with congenial companions. His unconventional ways eventually led to his exile from the court of the Emperor, and throughout his life he was forced to wander much. Legend tells us that he died as unusually and poetically as he had lived. Restless, and under the influence of too much wine, he went boating on a moonlit lake. The beauty of the moon's image moving gently on the surface of the water attracted him. He leaned from the boat to embrace it, fell into the lake, and was drowned.

It is extremely difficult to translate a poem from one language to another and convey to the reader all the beauty and shades of meaning given in the original language. His weakness for wine did not deter Li T'ai-po from writing poetry that even in translation can stir our thought and feeling. He wrote once about a quiet night.

Here it is night: I stay at the Summit Temple
Here I can touch the stars with my hand.
I dare not speak aloud in the silence
For fear of disturbing the dwellers of Heaven.[1]

Another great poet was Tu Fu who lived at the same time as Li T'ai-po and was a close friend of his. The Chinese regard him as perhaps a greater poet than Li T'ai-po. He was interested in the state of the society in which he lived, and he sorrowed over the sufferings of the poor and the afflicted around him. He wrote of them with warmth and sympathy. Tu Fu was a caustic critic of the government which permitted the miseries of the poor. He, too, had his problems of poverty, which some of us may feel and understand in the following poem. It is called "The Empty Purse."

The bitter pinecone may be eaten,
The mist on high give nourishment.
The whole world takes to go-and-getting;
My way alone is difficult:

My oven is cold as the well at morning,
And the bed wants warmth from coverlets;
My purse ashamed to be found empty
Still keeps on hand a single coin.[2]

The third great poet of the T'ang period was Po Chü-i. His poems were carved on stone tablets by command of the emperor.

Romances and stories of heroism were written during the T'ang period. It was during this period that one of China's most famous tales of love and tragedy began. One of the greatest T'ang emperors was Hsüan Tsung, who reigned from 713 to 756 A.D. Under him the T'ang Chinese reached the summit of their brilliance and power. When he was rather old, Hsüan Tsung fell in love with a lady of great beauty known as Yang Kuei-fei. She became one of his secondary wives—the emperors had many wives—and his favorite. She became a political power in her own right and was a patroness of the arts. She sponsored Tu Fu and other poets. But she encouraged the king to many excesses, and the people grumbled. The military were also angered at her undesirable influence on the emperor. They arose in rebellion against the emperor, and he fled the city. As the price for his return to the throne the life of Yang Kuei-fei was demanded. The emperor prized his throne more than he prized Yang Kuei-fei, and she was sacrificed that he might regain his kingdom. This story

This portrait of Confucius was made by a Manchu prince and is dated 1735 A.D. Members of the Chinese courts especially enjoyed writing commentaries on Confucius. (Photo by Charles Phelps Cushing)

[1] From *The White Pony*, edited by Robert Payne, John Day and Company, New York, 1947. Translations by the editor; quoted by permission.
[2] *Ibid.*

has been written and rewritten, told and retold, throughout the long years since it first began, and there are few Chinese who have not heard or read this drama of the great king Hsüan Tsung and the beautiful Yang Kuei-fei.

1. Why was the T'ang dynasty considered one of the greatest periods of all Chinese history? What do you consider to be the greatest achievement of this period?
2. What subjects were painted during the Sung dynasty? What materials did these artists use?
3. What were the accomplishments of Li T'ai-po and Tu Fu?

## The Sung and Yüan Times

The next great dynasty in China was the Sung (960-1279 A.D.). The Sung emperors never ruled an area as great as that of the T'ang dynasty, and in the twelfth century they were forced to move to southern China, where they located their capital in the city of Hangchow.

It was during this period that Genghis Khan started on his far-reaching conquests. He was a Mongol, the chief of one of the roving tribes of Central Asia. He conquered much of North China, most of Central Asia, and extended his rule as far as modern Russia and the eastern borders of Europe. His grandson, Kublai Khan, overthrew the Sungs about 1279, and until 1368 the Mongols ruled China. Their great realm stretched to the eastern borders of Europe and south to the shores of Southeast Asia.

Kublai Khan established his capital on the present site of Peking and called it Cambaluc. In Chinese history the period of Mongol rule is known as the Yüan dynasty. It was during the reign of the great Kublai Khan that Marco Polo, the Venetian, visited China. Polo won the favor of the emperor and eventually returned to Italy, where he published an account of his travels and his observations. The Europeans of that day were so far behind the culture and the achievements of the Asians that they could not believe what he told them. They branded him a liar for trying to deceive them with tall stories of civilizations beyond the borders of their dreams.

During the Sung dynasty the Chinese continued to write histories and important treatises on medicine, botany, astronomy, and mathematics. They had fine poets too, but none of the stature of those of the T'ang period. The porcelains of the Sung dynasty have rarely been equaled. The white porcelains of the Sung period were of a purity that proclaimed the high skill of their makers. We have complimented the Chinese on the quality of their porcelain by calling all work of this type "china" and "chinaware."

But the Sungs are best remembered through their art. Many say that their landscapes are among the greatest ever painted. It was not the intention of the artists to paint an exact copy of what they saw. They tried, rather, to paint the ebb and flow of life within nature. They painted an impression of the core, the heart, the living essence of what they beheld. These paintings gave to us a magnificent landscape art.

During the rule of the Mongols, the Chinese turned their hands to writing novels and dramas, and the Chinese generally date their development of these forms of literature from this period.

## The Ming Period

The Mongols were overthrown, and the Ming or Glorious dynasty (1368-1644) succeeded them. China became something of a sea power during this period. Chinese ships went as far as Cambodia, Siam, Sumatra, Java, India, and Ceylon.

Peking became one of the world's imposing capitals, with its great walls, its temples, and its palaces. The emperor's palace was so huge that it was like a city within a city, and it was named the "Forbidden City." Within this inner city, there were spacious courtyards, halls, and pavilions, lovely gardens, and waterways. There were walls and terraces of marble which blended harmoniously together to create a massive appearance of grandeur, yet remained pleasing to the eye.

The Altar of Heaven was near here, and the emperor went there at dawn to perform the rituals to Heaven on behalf of his people. The altar was made up of three tiers of terraces, each enclosed by a railing. It was made in the form of a circle, which symbolized the fullness and the completeness of the emperor and of Heaven.

During the Ming dynasty, the Chinese continued to turn out prodigious quantities of writings of all kinds—histories, essays, poems, and prose fiction. They began to paint portraits as well as landscapes and to introduce color into their paintings. The reputation of Chinese porcelains grew, and their cups, saucers, bowls, and vessels of every variety—all of great beauty—became more and more sought after beyond the borders of Ming China.

### The Manchus

The Mings were overthrown by the people of Manchuria, called the Manchus. They ruled China from 1644 to 1912. Their dynasty is known formally as the Ch'ing dynasty. Under two of their early rulers, K'ang Hsi (1662-1722) and Ch'ien Lung (1736-1796), the Manchus reached the zenith of their power and prestige. Chinese influence under these two rulers was equal to that of the greatest dynasties of the past.

During the Ch'ing dynasty, the Chinese wrote much, but not with the originality and power of the writers who preceded them. They were, however, exceptionally good at writing novels. One of the greatest novels of this time, *The Dream of the Red Chamber*, is a love story of a large, rich family. During the Ch'ing dynasty, the Chinese continued to make fine porcelain, to paint, and to carve, but their works in these fields did not rival those of the great artists of the past.

Influences from the outside were beginning to penetrate China during this time. Christian missionaries had begun to come even in the latter part of the Ming dynasty, and traders and adventurers began to come in greater numbers during the Ch'ing dynasty. The ideas and the culture of the Europeans began to change the traditional patterns of the Chinese way of life.

1. For what types of art was the Sung dynasty noted?
2. Did the artists of the Sung dynasty try to paint realistically? If not, what did they attempt to portray?
3. Was the Ch'ing dynasty known for its art? Why?

### The Artistry of the Japanese

We have noted that the Japanese were greatly influenced in their culture and their ways of life by the Chinese. It will also be recalled that they adapted these imported Chinese ideas to their own special patterns of life and temperament. This is true also of the art forms they borrowed from China.

In the seventh century A.D. the Horyuji Monastery was built. It was modeled after the architecture of China. This was during the time of the Empress Suiko, whose reign marks the beginning of real art in Japan. The monastery is largely Chinese in form, but it has a distinctive Japanese artistic touch. Though massive and dignified, the building is colorful, light, and seems a natural part of the beautiful landscape. The monastery is built of cypress and camphor wood, for the Japanese have much wood but little stone. It is thought to be one of the oldest existing wooden structures in the world.

During the eighth century, while the capital was at Nara, the Japanese produced an enormous amount of fine art work, largely influenced by Buddhism. Their statues of Buddhas have the charm, grace, and simplicity that are characteristic of Japanese art. The materials chiefly used were wood, clay, and bronze. Toward the close of the Nara period an anthology of poems was collected which is called the *Manyoshu*, or *Collection of a Myriad Leaves*. These light, delicate poems were probably written by members of the small aristocratic society of that period.

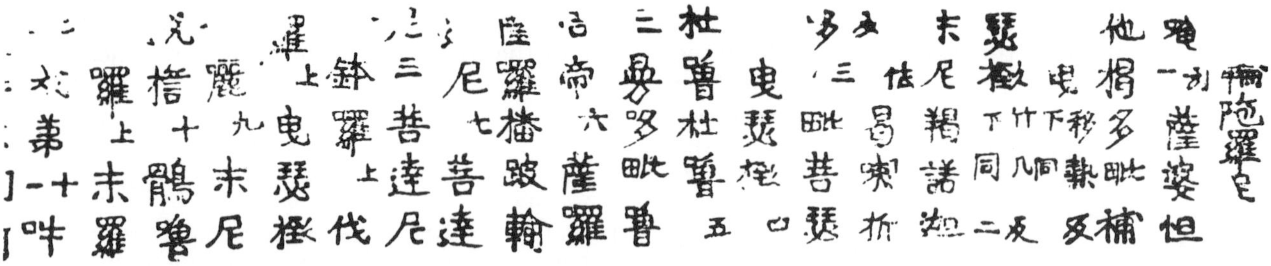

The woodblock print above is a charm against sickness printed for the Empress Shotoku of Japan about 770 A.D. (The Free Library of Philadelphia)

Late in the eighth century the capital was moved to Kyoto, which remained the residence of the emperor until the nineteenth century. Buddhism and Chinese culture continued to have significant influence on the Japanese. It will be recalled that the great T'ang poets, Li T'ai-po, Tu Fu, Po Chü-i, and others created great poetry in China, and the Japanese were influenced by them. The Emperor Go-Saga took poets with him on picnics and outings. Sometimes in the palace courtyard the guests would sit beside an artificial stream and play a game of poetry. A cup of wine was floated on the water, and as it floated by each guest he was required to pick it up, drink, recite a poem, and place the cup back in the water to pass on to the next guest. Though they did not at this time compose poetry of the lasting merit of Tu Fu and Li T'ai-po, the Japanese showed an appreciation of good art that is the sign of a sensitive and gifted people.

The years from 795 to 1185 in Japanese history are known as the Heian period, Heian-kyo being another name for Kyoto, the capital. The court life of this time is well described in a great romantic novel, *The Tale of Genji.* It was written by a lady of the court called Murasaki Shikibu, and its central character is Prince Genji, the son of the Emperor. *The Tale of Genji* is not merely a well-told tale of the life, loves, and thoughts of Prince Genji; it is a vivid picture of Japanese culture and character, especially within the circles of the court. The translation of this tale into English by Arthur Waley ranks of itself as a great work of English prose.

In Japan, as in China, the form of the paintings was extremely important, for basic to Japanese paintings was the Japanese way of writing. The Japanese had borrowed ideographs along with the many other achievements of the Chinese, and they, too, learned to judge and appreciate the force, symbolism, and beauty of the lines they drew to make the ideographs of their picture-writing.

1. During whose reign was the Horyuji Monastery built? Of what significance is this reign in regard to Japanese art?
2. What traces of Chinese culture do you see in Japanese art? Give some examples.
3. Identify the *Tale of Genji* and tell who wrote it. What is it concerned with and why is it important?

## Themes from History

The Japanese, like others, have taken stories from their history and enacted them on the stage or made them the central themes of their novels and poetry. Japanese history from the ninth to the eighteenth century A.D. has provided dramatists, novelists, and poets with many themes for stories.

During the ninth, tenth, and eleventh centuries, control of the imperial government slowly passed from the central administration in Kyoto into the hands of military lords outside the capital. These warlike leaders began to organize private armies of their own, and there emerged a warrior class called *samurai*, or "those who serve." The samurai served their lords, who were called *daimyo*. Some of them began to wield great power. Between the samurai and their lords there grew a tradition and a relationship based upon the virtues of loyalty, courage, obedience, and responsibility. The sword was the symbol of this relationship which forms the basis of much of the art and literature of Japan.

The powerful lords and clans fought among themselves. From this struggle the Taira and the Minamoto clans emerged as the most powerful. In the second half of the twelfth century they waged a ruthless war for dominance in Japan.

From amidst the courage, intrigue, treachery, betrayal, and victory of this war there stood forth two characters who became the central figures of many dramas and stories of Japanese literature. Their names were Yoritomo and Yoshitsune. They were half-brothers, having different mothers but the same father, Yoshitomo, the leader of the Minamoto clan.

The Taira clan was at first successful and defeated the Minamoto clan, killing most of its leaders. But Kiyomori, the Taira leader, spared Yoritomo, the young son of the Minamoto leader, because of his charm and presence. The other young son, Yoshitsune, and his two full brothers were permitted to live in a monastery because the Taira leader desired their beautiful mother for himself. She persuaded him to spare the lives of her sons in return for her surrender to him.

After Kiyomori died, Yoritomo revolted and raised the standards of the Minamoto once again. Yoshitsune, his half-brother, joined him and through his courage, daring, and military genius assisted greatly in bringing about the defeat of the Taira. But Yoritomo was jealous and suspicious; he would not chance any possible rival to his power, so he ordered the execution of his faithful brother Yoshitsune.

Yoshitsune escaped and wandered from place to place in Japan trying to avoid the spies and executioners of his brother. Finally he and his family took refuge in an isolated castle, where they lived safely for a while. At last, he was betrayed, and his brother's forces came to take him. In order to avoid the shame of being murdered by others, he killed his wife and family and then killed himself.

### Kamakura Shogunate

Yoritomo established a military government in Japan which was called a *shogunate*. This name comes from the title *shogun*, or "Barbarian-conquering general," which he assumed. The period which started with his rule is known as the Kamakura shogunate (1192-1333 A.D.). Kamakura is the place where Yoritomo located his capital.

Artistic accomplishments, which had mainly been confined to the court circles of Kyoto, began to spread to other parts of the land during this period. The Kamakura shogunate became interested in Buddhism. Many Buddhist temples were rebuilt and redecorated. Works in sculpture were also patronized. The sculpture of this period was living, vigorous, and simple, reflecting the tastes of the military overlords of Japan. During this period a monk painted *The Naichi Waterfall*, which is one of the world's fine landscape paintings. It reflects both the love of nature and the love of religion in Japan. The life of Japan was represented also on picture scrolls, many of which still exist.

It was during this period that Zen Buddhism began to flourish, for its simplicity and ideal of self-discipline appealed to the austere virtues and stern, harsh life of the military class. The tea ceremony associated with Zen started at this time.

### Ashikaga Shogunate

The Kamakura shogunate was succeeded by the Ashikaga shogunate which lasted from 1338 to 1568. The greater part of this period is known as the Muromachi Period. Muromachi was the name of the part of the city of Kyoto where the Ashikaga shoguns lived.

This was a period of much civil strife and destruction, but it was also a time when the arts took on new vigor and new forms. During the period of the Ashikaga shogunate, the well-known No drama of the Japanese developed from an ancient dance which was accompanied by music. The dance evolved into a play which told a story with posturing, dance, music, and some speech. But the dance remained central to the No drama, and it is primarily through motion and posture that emotions and ideas are conveyed. The No is still performed in Japan today.

It was also at this time that several great Japanese painters, influenced by the Chinese painters of the Sung dynasty in China, produced some of the finest black and white pictures composed by man. The most famous of these painters were Shubun and Sesshu, both of whom lived in the fifteenth century. Sesshu's work is a remarkable example of this school of painting. He captures the inner idea of what he paints with the fewest possible strokes of the brush. He leaves the viewer with a sense of peace and tranquillity and with the impression that the few strokes of his brush are completely satisfying. His was an art of stark simplicity. There is no doubt that he was influenced by the simplicity of Zen Buddhism.

### A Century of War

The sixteenth century was a period of war, and three famous leaders engraved their deeds and their names during this struggle-torn age upon the historical epics of Japan. Their names were Nobunaga, Hideyoshi, and Tokugawa Iyeyasu. Nobunaga was the first of these leaders, and he is described as short, squat, and with the face of an ape. He was called upon by the Emperor to restore order to a disunified Japan. Before this task was completed, Nobunaga was surprised and killed by an enemy. His two lieutenants were Hideyoshi and Iyeyasu. Hideyoshi was the son of a common soldier. He had great ability and determination. Hideyoshi took over the leadership from Nobunaga and completed the unification of Japan.

Hideyoshi was an exceptional man, with great ambitions, and he dreamed of the conquest of all China. For the Japanese, the road to China ran through Korea, but the Koreans refused to permit peaceful passage. Hideyoshi was forced to fight his way through the stubborn resistance of the Koreans to the borders of China. This struggle destroyed his manpower and his supplies, and he died before he could achieve his goal.

### Tokugawa Shogunate

Hideyoshi wanted very much to leave his son in control of Japan. To this end, a council of regents was formed, with Tokugawa Iyeyasu as chairman, to insure the authority of his son. But Iyeyasu had other ideas, and in 1603 he had himself appointed by the Emperor as Shogun of Japan. Thus was founded the Tokugawa shogunate, which lasted until 1867. In part, the end of this shogunate was due to Commodore Matthew C. Perry, the American whose fleet sailed into Tokyo Bay in 1853 and forced Japan to open its ports to the world.

Iyeyasu established his capital at Yedo, which is the present site of Tokyo. To maintain his control over the great lords of the realm, he required them to keep hostages at the capital. The lords themselves also had to visit there periodically. Naturally there had to be services for these many rich lords and their families, and a merchant class arose. The wealth and standard of living of this merchant class eventually rivaled and surpassed that of the aristocratic class they served.

Much of the art, recreation, and entertainment of that period centered in a section of Yedo called the Yoshiwara. This section was a different world within the city. There were theaters, actors and actresses, dancers, wrestlers, tellers of stories, and all that many-hued world of men and women who make a business of providing pleasure. The people of this world became the characters for plays, novels, poems, and the art called *ukiyo-e*, which pictured scenes from this floating world of pleasure. (*Ukiyo-e* is often translated as "floating world.")

The Kabuki, or popular drama, in which the players originally were women but later were exclusively men, began to develop during the Tokugawa shogunate. The lively musical attractions of the Kabuki theater still draw the Japanese and the non-Japanese to admire and to applaud.

Puppet shows—dramatic, realistic, and wonderfully done—took the Japanese into a world of play-acting which was vivid and interesting. Japanese puppet manipulators are still masters of their art, and there are few in their audiences today who are not caught up by their art. The puppets seem to be real persons enacting a drama of life, not fiction. They roll their eyes, lift their eyebrows, wiggle their fingers, and walk, strut, or dance to the beat and rhythm of the music. The plays originally written for puppets were of a quality that was destined to live and to be acted upon the stage with living actors and actresses.

There were painters, such as Hishikawa Moronobu, who were not content merely to suggest in their paintings, but portrayed true-life scenes. They painted the people on the street, passengers on ferry boats, or whatever they saw that reflected life and action. They especially liked to picture rascals, rowdies, rakes, and rogues and to show what they did, how they looked, and what they wore. Their art was colorful and popular, and it sold, and sold, and is still selling today to Japanese and foreigner alike.

Above, the shrine of Byodoin at Uji reflects the Japanese love of nature. Below, the Japanese Kabuki drama remains a favorite entertainment in Japan, and touring companies have made it world-famous. (Both photos, Japan National Tourist Association)

In the period of the Tokugawa shogunate, the Japanese began to write short poems called *haiku*, made up of three lines and seventeen syllables. They were simple. They were definite. They frequently suggested more than was actually said. The poet, Basho, was one of the first to write these poems. It is not easy for the untrained non-Japanese ear and mind to grasp the full meaning and flavor of these poems in miniature. Basho once wrote:

> Old pond—
> and a frog-jump-in
> water-sound.[1]

Another poet, Taniguchi Buson, wrote in the eighteenth century:

> No poem you send
> in answer—O, young lady!
> Spring is at its end![2]

And then the Westerners began to come and to bring with them new ideas which the Japanese also took up, considered, and made their own. But that is another part of their story.

1. Discuss the development of art during the period of the Ashikaga shogunate. Name some of the most important contributions of this period.
2. When did the unification of Japan take place? Name some of the key individuals responsible for bringing about unification and the roles they played.
3. What was Hideyoshi's dream? Did he accomplish it?
4. How did Iyeyasu maintain control as shogun of Japan?

## Conclusion

The buildings the Asians constructed, the figures they carved, the paintings they drew, and the prose and the poetry they wrote were all so many ways of trying to say what was in their minds and hearts. The Asian artists were deeply concerned with telling what they felt within themselves and how they looked at man, at nature, and at God.

Religion was very close and dear to most Asians. Much of what they built, carved, painted, and wrote was an attempt to show in some material way the depths of their religious feelings. They wanted also to teach through their artistic works something of the content, the beauty, and the glory of what they believed. The contentment, the peace, the serenity of their Buddhas could be attained by every man if he followed the right path in life. The thousands upon thousands of differing interpretations of the Hindu's Ultimate Reality were merely to show how all-embracing it really was and is.

The writings and paintings of the Asians also reveal their attitudes toward life and nature. The poetry of the Chinese shows how deeply many of them were concerned about the hardships man must often undergo on this earth. When they wrote of the lonely soldier manning a border post, and the tears of his family far away, they were expressing the discontent of many Chinese who thought this should not be. When they wrote of the poor and the downtrodden, they were voicing the complaints of many against corrupt officials and a government which did not seem to care. When they made man small in their magnificent landscape paintings, they were indicating how insignificant the individual really is when placed beside the wondrous works of nature.

The Asians have often expressed themselves well, and the messages they first conveyed to man many years ago, are still being conveyed to Asian and foreigner alike today. The Asians have wrapped their messages in forms of beauty which are everywhere regarded as beautiful. Theirs have been messages about things that man has always been interested in learning about—his nature, his landscape, his destiny, his God. And man has always learned through the arts and the writings of others. In expressing themselves to the men of each successive time, the Asians have succeeded in expressing themselves to men of all times.

[1] Translated by Harold G. Henderson; from *An Introduction to Haiku,* Doubleday and Co., Inc., New York, 1958. Quoted by permission.
[2] *Ibid.*

## SUMMING UP THE CHAPTER

A. Define or explain the following terms, relating them to this chapter.

| | |
|---|---|
| daimyo | No |
| haiku | samurai |
| Kabuki | shogunate |
| mosque | stupa |

B. Identify the following and tell why they are important.

| | |
|---|---|
| Akbar | Mogul |
| Babur | Muromachi Period |
| Basho | Nara Period |
| Commodore Perry | *Panchatantra* |
| *Dream of the Red Chamber* | Sesshu |
| Empress Suiko | Taira |
| Genghis Khan | Taj Mahal |
| Manchus | Timur the Turk |
| Ming dynasty | Tokugawa Iyeyasu |

C. Identify the following dates and indicate their importance.

1. 185 B.C. (India)
2. 606-647 A.D. (India)
3. 205 B.C.-220 A.D. (China)
4. 618-907 A.D. (China)
5. 1644-1912 A.D. (China)
6. 1338-1568 A.D. (Japan)
7. 1603-1867 A.D. (Japan)

D. Chapter review questions.

1. Describe a typical stupa and explain its symbolism.
2. What were Buddha statues supposed to portray? What were some of the typical symbols used and what did they represent?
3. Trace the political rulers of India from the eleventh to the seventeenth century. During what period or periods did the arts flourish? How do you account for this?
4. What languages were fused together to make Urdu? Where is this language spoken today?
5. How did the Chinese adorn their buildings? What significance did they attach to the color yellow?
6. Identify the most important form of art or individual work of art associated with each of the Chinese dynasties mentioned in this chapter.
7. During what dynasties and in what countries were works of porcelain created?
8. What works of art were created in China during the period of the Sung dynasty? Are they considered truly great today?
9. What major themes of history between the ninth and eighteenth centuries did the Japanese dramatists, novelists, and poets write about?
10. Discuss the relationship between a member of the warrior class and his particular war lord in Japan. What symbol was used to indicate this relationship?
11. Trace the Chinese influence in Japanese art.
12. What influence did Zen Buddhism have on Japanese art? What influence did religion in general have on art in Japan, China, and India? Compare and contrast the effects of this influence in those three countries.
13. What factors led to the establishment of a merchant class in Japan? Contrast the wealth of the merchants with that of the aristocracy.
14. How was the belief in simplicity expressed in Japanese art? Discuss form as well as content.
15. Compare and contrast the arts, in form and content, in Japan, China, and India. Which country first gained stature in the arts? Which country do you consider to be the most advanced today?
16. How has politics influenced the development and preservation of the arts in Japan, China, and India?

E. Questions for discussion.

1. What do the statues of Buddha represent? What explanation can you give for the fact that they are not intended to represent the Buddha himself?
2. How would you account for the lack of art and literature in India from the seventh to the eleventh century?
3. Why is nature of central importance to Asian artists and writers?
4. What evidence do we have that the Chinese were fond of writing? What other peoples are fond of writing? Do you feel Americans are fond of writing? What evidence do you have to support your answer?

F. Projects for groups or individuals.

1. Examine several copies of Asian paintings. Try to determine how the artist feels about the subject he paints, and perhaps something of his philosophy of life.
2. Prepare a report for classroom presentation on the forms of art most appreciated by the Moguls.
3. Prepare a report on religious influences in art. Pay particular attention to the differing types of influences of different religions.
4. Read several of the poems mentioned in this chapter. Which did you like best and why?
5. If your library has a record collection, make arrangements to hear records of traditional or classical Asian music.

# CHAPTER 6

# The Asians and Their Society

MAN DOES NOT LIVE ALONE. As the poet John Donne said, "No man is an island." Man lives in a family, companioned by brothers and sisters, and sometimes other relatives. He has friends, acquaintances, and neighbors. He resides in a community, a village, a town or a city, and a state. He spends most of his life in the company of others of his kind. We refer to this association and companionship with others as *society*.

There are rules and standards which regulate and limit the association between people so that all may live more harmoniously together. These rules and standards of a society stem in part from beliefs, from ideologies and religions such as we have just finished studying. They are also based in part on long years of experience in living with others, in part on the physical environment, and in part on stubborn traditions whose sources are now forgotten.

The Asian is no exception to these common facts of life. He, too, is governed by standards and commandments which have their sources in his religion, environment, experience, and traditions. His social ways are, for the most part, of ancient origin. Until recently, the Asian has been left relatively undisturbed by industrial and political revolutions such as those which have caused so much change in the social life of the Western world. Most Asians continue to follow old, customary practices in their relations with others. This is especially true of the rural Asians. The caste system of India is an example of a social practice which started long ago and is still practiced by the Indians today.

## The Caste System of the Indians

The Indian lives in a segregated society. He rarely, if ever, associates with those in groups other than his own, and he almost never crosses over into another group. He is born into a distinct and destined grouping, and he dies within it. Between his birth and his death, he marries within a group, eats and drinks almost exclusively with its members, is subject to its strict rules and limitations, and often, but not always, works with its members in similar occupations.

This division of groups within the Indian society is known as the *caste system*. Each group is generally referred to in English as a *caste*. The word is borrowed from the Portuguese, who used it to describe the separations of people which they observed when they first came to India in the sixteenth century. This system has old origins and a long history.

### A Long Evolution

When the fair Aryans migrated to India around 2000 B.C., they thought themselves superior to the darker peoples they found there. They introduced into India a separation of peoples based upon skin color. As the history of India moved slowly along, people came to be separated, too, by the kinds of work they did. Those who followed the same occupation developed a closely knit community. In their own minds, and in the minds of others, the members of each group were sharply distinguished from other groups. Sometimes separate groupings grew out of religious differences.

There were instances of people placed within certain castes in wholesale lots. A people called the Rajputs were an example of this process.

The Rajputs, whose ancestors were invaders from Central Asia, were powerful in northern and central India from about 650 to 1150 A.D., and they were politically important until the nineteenth century. They were men of war, brave, proud, clannish, chivalrous, and aristocratic. They proclaimed themselves the royal ones, the sons of kings, which is the meaning of the name Rajput. They were fierce in battle, and they gave and asked no quarter. They fought to the death. Sometimes, when defeat was inevitable, they were known to first kill their women and their children before dying themselves on the swords of their conquerors.

The Brahmans, the powerful priests of Hinduism, found that they could not withstand such valiant warriors, so they linked the Rajputs to themselves by means of the caste system. Even at that time the caste system was a matured social institution in India. The Rajput chiefs became members of the warrior caste. Their followers became members of the agricultural caste. Some of the Rajput priests became Brahmans.

These are some of the ways the caste system evolved in India. There are, no doubt, many other historical reasons for the system we see operating at present, but we know little about them.

## The Substance of Caste

Generally speaking, there are four main caste divisions among the Indians. The Brahman or priestly caste ranks first among them. The Kshatriya or warrior caste ranks second. The Vaisya or mercantile and agricultural caste ranks third. Those of lowest rank are the Sudra, who originally were supposed to serve the other three castes but who now perform many kinds of work.

This ranking has both an occupational and a religious significance. Because of their spiritual and educational work, the Brahmans are held in the highest esteem. They are traditionally the teachers of India. Of next importance is the function of governing and protecting the realm, which is the duty of the Kshatriyas. The production of food and conduct of trade, which are the duties of the Vaisyas, are essential, but these occupations have less prestige than those of the higher castes. Finally, the least important function is that of service to the other three castes, which is the duty of the Sudras.

The caste system is supported by the Hindu religion. It will be recalled that the caste to which one belongs is considered to be an indication of his distance from final salvation. The Brahman is the nearest to salvation, followed in descending order by the Kshatriya, the Vaisya, and the Sudra castes. But the farthest removed from salvation is the *outcaste.*

There are many millions of Indians who have no caste at all, and they are called *outcastes* or *untouchables.* They cannot touch anything without contaminating it for the other castes, and they comprise the lowest layer of Indian society. They perform those occupations which the Indians regard as most degrading: taking care of the dead, sweeping the streets and the floors, removing filth and refuse, and working in leather. The cow is sacred in India, and the Indians consider those who work with its hide to make shoes or other articles as unclean.

## Advantages—Disadvantages—Change

Hindu writers have claimed that the caste system has contributed to the preservation of Indian culture and civilization. Over the thousands of years of Indian history, the people have been afflicted with invasion after invasion, chaos after chaos; but always they have retained their loyalty and devotion to the caste. Thus, they have maintained the stability and continuity of Indian culture. In the face of uncertainty, the caste system has given meaning, direction, and hope to the hard-pressed Indians. It has created cooperation instead of competition, for each man in the community has a special task, a special position, and a special duty in society. There is no reason, no opportunity, to compete for something else.

There are other Indian writers who say that this system has weakened India, especially today. The famous author Rabindranath Tagore has stated that there can be no real political unity in India until all Indians are permitted to mingle freely. Some Indian leaders have declared that there can be no real social progress in India while so many millions remain segregated one from another, bound by a rigid caste system. The great spiritual father of modern India, Mahatma Gandhi, pleaded for more tolerance and justice for the outcastes and named them "Children of God."

And there have been changes. Officially the outcastes are now called the "Scheduled Castes." There are even some members of the Brahman caste who are willing to marry those of another caste. These are mostly of the younger educated generation, and they probably plan to live in cities where their radical step may be less noticed, but it is a sign of change. Industry, transportation systems, hospitals, schools and colleges are all throwing the various castes and outcastes together. From this association, of necessity there will eventually come changed attitudes. But change comes slowly, as we know, when emotions, traditions, and religions support the separation of peoples. Caste separation is still practiced and is still a social force in India. The caste system may evolve, but it will not easily die.

1. What is society? From what sources are its standards and commandments derived?
2. What are the four major castes in India? Explain their occupational and religious significance and trace their historical development up to the present.
3. What changes are taking place in the caste system in India today? What part has education played in bringing about these changes? Do you think these changes are for the good? Why? Why not?

## The Family in India

The family in India is a basic institution. Within the family, the Indian learns his role in society, his duties within the caste, his responsibilities, and his obligations.

The traditional Indian family generally consists of the parents, all unmarried children, and the married sons with their wives and their children. It often includes other persons such as grandparents and even some distant relatives. This kind of a family is referred to as a *joint-family* because the members join together in eating, worshiping, and holding property.

The oldest male is usually the head of the family. He supervises the family property and the finances. The family members pool their resources and their income, and the head of the family spends it according to the needs of each. This is not to say that individuals do not possess personal property. They do. For instance, the jewelry that a bride receives from her parents and her relatives remains her own personal property. There are few women in India, with the exception of widows, who do not adorn their bodies with gold or silver bracelets, earrings, nose-rings, necklaces, and other jewelry. This is generally all they can call their very own except the clothes they wear. Widows are not supposed to wear jewelry, bright clothing, or cosmetics. All brightness, theoretically, has left their lives when the husband is gone; and society frowns upon seeking another husband.

The male head formally possesses all authority within the family, but he is bound by tradition, custom, and public opinion to preserve and not to waste the family holdings. He consults with the elders of the family, and he seeks advice from his mother and his wife if they are living.

Traditionally, the woman occupies a subordinate position to the male in Indian society. The ideal wife is one who is submissive and obedient to the will of the husband. She is modest, retiring, and loyal. She serves her husband and her family quietly, efficiently, and without complaint. When she is the wife

The Brahman cow is sacred in India. Those who worked with leather, under the caste system, were considered unclean. (USDA)

The system of castes in India drew sharp lines of distinction between various occupations. To what caste do you think the village farm workers below and the wood-carver above might belong? (Embassy of India)

of the family head, and the mother of his children, she is an object of respect. Her words and advice on household and other matters are heeded and often followed.

One of the most serious responsibilities borne by Indian parents is the marriage of their children. Marriage in India is not a private romantic affair between two individuals. It is a family matter of grave importance. Two individuals are being brought together to preserve and continue the family, not merely to satisfy their own emotions. Traditionally, the boy and the girl have been given little choice in the selection of a mate. The Indians take the view that love should follow the marriage, not precede it. As a consequence, the boy and the girl may not see each other before their engagement, and sometimes not before their marriage day. They may see only a picture of each other.

It is not always easy for parents to find a proper wife for their son or a suitable husband for their daughter. Many social difficulties surround marriage in India. There is the question of the right caste, the reputation of the family—remember, this is a family matter—and the economic position of the family. The girl must have a trousseau and a dowry. These items are important to the family of the boy, for she will bring these resources to his family. There is the question of matching the horoscopes of the prospective couple. The horoscope of each was cast at birth, and if their stars and signs do not harmonize, it would be extremely foolish to chance marriage. In the face of all these difficulties, and others, parents usually enlist the aid of a third person or go-between to find a suitable mate for their children. He or she undertakes all the arrangements and negotiations and usually receives payment for the services rendered.

A successful marriage results in children. These children are primarily members of the family, not merely the offspring of two individuals. They are the responsibility of the family rather than the parents alone. If the father has more than one wife, the children call them all mother. The same word is used for *brother* and *paternal cousin.* Children absorb a sense of responsibility toward the entire family which rarely deserts them throughout their entire lives. Indian history is filled with stories of sacrifice and suffering undertaken on behalf of the family.

### There Is Some Change Today

There is some change in family life today, especially in the cities and among those educated along Western patterns. The growth of industrialization in India has attracted many people from the villages to the cities. In the cities, crowded conditions and cramped living quarters do not permit the larger joint-families of the countryside. The Indian youth, attracted by imported ideas and seeking greater choice in the selection of a mate, is demanding that he or she be consulted in the marriage negotiations. Sometimes a boy or girl may personally suggest a candidate for the parents' consideration. Formerly, few girls received a formal education. Today more and more of them are attending high school and university and embarking upon professional careers. Supported by their learning, they are more inclined to argue their points and assert their opinions before their husbands and other males.

As in the case of caste, however, traditional attitudes toward the family are still held firmly by the vast majority of the Indians. There will, of course, be certain changes as India passes through its economic and political transitions. No one can say to what extent these changes will penetrate and modify the Indian's attitude toward his family. In the meantime, for most Indians, the family continues to be a beloved center of his life.

1. Name the members of a typical Indian family. What term is applied to a family of this type?
2. Describe and compare the role of the oldest male in an Indian family and that of his mother or wife. How do tradition and custom affect these roles? Do tradition and custom affect your role?
3. Why are marriages in India considered a family matter? What preparations for a marriage

must be made by the family, particularly by the oldest male? What does this tell you about the Indian view of love?

4. What changes have taken place in recent years in Indian family life? What factors have encouraged these changes?

## The Society of the Chinese

The family and clan, the peasant, gentry, and the scholar were important groups in traditional Chinese society. Some of their features have disappeared where the Chinese live under Communism; but they are retained where the Chinese live under a freer and more traditional government. The family has always been basic to Chinese society.

### The Family

Traditionally, the family was so important to Chinese society that even the state was regarded as an extension of it. The Chinese customarily expressed this thought in the phrase "Within the four seas [China] all men are brothers." Confucius stressed the importance of the family in his philosophy. Three of the five basic social relationships he enumerated were concerned directly with the family: the relationship between father and son, between elder brother and younger brother, and between husband and wife. Indeed, traditional China was composed of a large number of families rather than individuals.

Each individual was regarded as a member of some family. The success or failure of the individual was the success or failure of his family. He was responsible to it, and it was responsible for him. If he stole, the family had to pay back what was taken. If he offended another, apology had to come from his family. If he revolted against the government, the family was punished. If he became an honored official, it was a family honor. It was the family that really counted, not the individual.

Traditionally, the ideal family was one which contained a number of generations. But only the wealthy could achieve this ideal of twenty, thirty, forty or more people within a single household. The poorer people had to be content with fewer people under one roof, generally from five to seven people. But whether there were few or many, it was the duty of the parents and the elders of the family to teach the younger ones their proper roles and stations in Chinese society. Those who could afford it started their boys early on the road to scholarship and possibly an appointment in the government. Only the educated and examination-tested individuals could obtain service in the government, thus bringing prestige and wealth to the family.

Girls were taught the care and supervision of the household, for they were destined for marriage and motherhood. Peasant girls also learned to work in the fields. Since ancient times, the peasant women of China have worked beside their husbands and their children in rice and wheat fields and in tending their vegetables.

Boys were taught to perform ancestral rituals and prepared for their future responsibilities as heads of families and elders of the village and community. Here, as in India, the female was subordinate to the male. The woman's life was generally confined before marriage to the household of her parents, and after marriage she moved to the household of her husband's parents. It was the male's job to represent the family in all matters outside the household.

The oldest male was the official and formal head of the family, and all authority was vested in him. In practice, his wife or his mother also wielded great power in domestic matters. From behind the scenes, women also had influence in public matters. For instance, a mother had much to say about the choice of a bride for her son, and this bride came directly under her authority within her household.

Marriage in China followed, with some variations, the same general pattern of arrangement, negotiation, and use of a go-between that we have just described for India. In China it was also a family matter. The most difficult task of both Indian and Chinese brides was the adjustment to a strange household and a demanding mother-in-law. Often a mother-in-law was fierce and exacting in her discipline and treatment of the young, fearful bride. There are tales of Chinese brides who committed suicide or ran away to escape the cruelties of their new homes. Nor could the husband protect his wife, for family obligation required that he support the mother no matter what the provocation.

One of the strictest Chinese social obligations was the respect and care that children owed their parents. Children were required to give their parents loving obedience and support while they lived and to carry out faithfully the ceremonial rites due them after they had died. The Chinese did not fear old age, especially if they had sons, for this was the best period of life. They were respected and supported. It was their one period of tranquillity, outside of childhood. The burdens and the work had shifted to others. They could now rest and prepare to become ancestors.

## The Clan

The clan was an important institution in traditional China. It was an extended family composed of those people who traced their lineage back to a common ancestor. This line of descent was traced from the father's ancestor, not the mother's. Some clans had thousands of members, but others were much smaller. Proof of membership in a clan was demonstrated by means of a family record—a genealogy—which charted the individual's descent from a common ancestor. These were very elaborate records, and they often included biographies of individuals, histories of the locality, and many other details.

There was an ancestral center where there was usually an ancestral hall, and family graves were there. Personal data about the clan members were stored in this hall on ancestor tablets. For each ancestor there was a rectangular piece of wood upon which his name, title, and birth and death dates were written. His spirit was in the tablet, especially when ancestral rites were being performed. It was very important to have male descendants who would perform the necessary ancestral rites. This ceremony is customarily referred to as "ancestor worship," although it is not worship in the usual sense of the term.

The clan also held property, often in the form of fields. The income from the property was used for the welfare of the members, for the support of orphans, widows, and childless members, and to put promising students through school. The clan substituted for state welfare, and the government encouraged these activities because they helped to maintain the stability of the community within an acceptable framework.

## The Gentry and the Scholar

Those who possessed much of the wealth in traditional China made up a special class of the well-born Chinese called *gentry*. The members of the gentry were usually well educated, and it was generally from this group that the governing officials came.

The gentry derived their income, as a rule, from public service and from land which they rented to others. The scholars of the gentry class often eked out a living by teaching and many of the gentry supplemented their income by commercial undertakings such as rice shops and pawn shops. Pawn shops have traditionally served the Chinese community as banks or lending agencies. They were very profitable undertakings, for the Chinese were always subject to crises of one kind or another and often needed cash. The owners of pawn shops were ready to make loans at very high interest rates, which sometimes ran as much as twelve per cent or more a month.

The gentry usually lived in large families, with three, four, or five generations under one roof. The male head of the family ruled as a patriarch, much as a king might rule his kingdom. The gentry stressed etiquette and ritual. They were not expected to do any physical labor. They were the teachers, governors, and patrons of the arts, the writers of poetry and prose, the historians, and the professional men. They were dedicated to preserving the system of thought and practice by which they had benefited. Thus, they were the greatest supporters of Confucianism and the traditional ways of the Chinese.

The gentry in traditional China was an ever-changing class. Families might enter and leave it within the space of three or four generations. There were always forces of division at work within the large families. Jealousies and antagonisms among the brothers and their wives frequently forced a division of the family property. In many cases the separated families could not live in the same manner as before on their smaller share of the property. Sometimes families became so large that they could not be supported adequately by the land they owned, and they were forced to sell the land. This usually led to reduced means, and eventually to loss of gentry status. But there were always those rising from the peasant class to take the places of those who sank from the gentry class.

## The Peasant

The peasants have made up the vast majority of the Chinese throughout history, and they still do. Their income came from the land which they cultivated themselves, and it was supplemented by handicraft work such as basket-making, embroidery, weaving, and other skilled and semiskilled work of the hand.

The Chinese peasants have usually lived on the edge of hunger and sometimes starvation. They have had one main purpose—to get enough to eat. There was little time for literature, the arts, the theatre, and the elaborate ritual. They were often illiterate and always were chained to the task of wresting a living from their tiny plots of earth.

The peasants of China appreciated the finer things of life. They wanted these things for themselves and for their children. They did not question the standards and better way of life of the gentry, and they followed traditional etiquette and rituals to the best of their ability and means. There was always the hope that perhaps one day, through its children, a peasant family might rise to the gentry class.

To this end the peasant family struggled and saved in order to give one or more of their boys an education, which was essential for any official advancement in China. Sometimes the peasants of a village would pool their resources to provide a tutor for one or more promising boys. If a boy succeeded in passing the state examinations and obtained an official position, the entire village would share in his good fortune. The history of China is filled with examples of the peasant boy who made the grade and carried his family along with him. There were few gentry families in China who did not have a peasant origin, and few peasant families who did not have ancestors of the gentry class.

## Changes Have Occurred

Changes were gradually introduced into China from the time Europeans first began to have contacts with the country. The major changes, however, were not formally incorporated into the political, economic, and social life of the people until the period beginning early in the twentieth century under Sun Yat-sen, Chiang Kai-Shek, and others. From this time until 1949, when the Communists took control, substantial changes occurred in China. The National Government, for instance, introduced a system which was entirely different and based on Western ideas. The Communists abolished this system and went even further. They encouraged the youth to disobey and betray their parents. The Communist leaders have commanded the youth of China to look upon the state as the only family to which they owe loyalty, service, and obedience.

The Communists have ridiculed and replaced the traditional Chinese standards and those modern ones which had begun to be introduced earlier. The new standards are those of Communism. The Communists have destroyed the gentry which remained as a class, labeling their way of life subversive and harmful to the new government. They have placed the peasants in communes where all persons work, theoretically, for the common benefit of the community, and no one works for himself. The land and the tools are the common property of all.

The Communists have regimented everyone in the land to better control them. The clan and the family have been subordinated to the state. But it is not easy to obliterate from the minds of the Chinese those social customs and practices which are of such ancient origins. They persist, of course, among the millions of Chinese who live in Formosa, in Southeast Asia, and in other parts of the world.

1. Explain the importance of the family in China. In what way is a Chinese responsible to his family and his family responsible for him?
2. Compare the gentry and peasantry of China in the following categories:
   a) wealth
   b) type of employment
   c) education
   d) concern for survival
   e) interest in the "finer things of life"
   f) major ambition.
3. What is a clan? What is the usual basis of membership in a clan? What important functions did a clan perform in traditional China?
4. What social changes have been brought about in China with the arrival of Communism? What forces have worked against the social changes desired by the Communists?

## The Society of the Japanese

Much of what has been said about the Chinese family also applies to the Japanese. They have been taught to regard themselves as one large family headed by the father of all—the emperor. Traditionally, the individual exists to maintain the continuity of the family. Failures on the part of family members have traditionally reflected upon the entire family. Within the family the Japanese finds the whole social pattern of his society. Within the family he learns etiquette, his role in life, and acceptable behavior towards others.

The oldest male is the head of the Japanese family and represents it in all official matters. He controls the finances and property, but he often allows his wife to handle the household budget. Marriages are also arranged in Japan, and there are the customary negotiations, often undertaken with the assistance of a go-between.

The Japanese love and desire children, especially male children, because the family line is perpetuated by the male. If there are no male offspring, a younger son of the husband's brother, or the son of another relative, may be adopted. Sometimes, if a couple have a daughter but no son, they may adopt a boy who then marries their daughter. He gives up his name and takes the surname of his adopted parents. Some of Japan's great business firms are headed by men who were adopted sons. Of course the adopted son is chosen very carefully, for the continuation of the family is an extremely important matter.

### The Japanese Woman

For more than a thousand years the Japanese woman has been taught that she exists to serve man. The ideal Japanese woman is one who does not question her father's commands nor her husband's wishes. She is gentle, chaste, and submissive, and she seeks always to please in every possible way. She does not raise her voice in anger nor to complain. She accepts the wanderings of her husband in silence and does not feel it her duty or her right to accompany him when he spends some evenings out. These are some of the traditional teachings which have, over the centuries, been imparted to Japanese women.

There are those who say that women in Japanese society did not always occupy a subordinate position. They say that during the early period of Japan's history woman was the equal of man and his companion rather than his subordinate. They tell of ancient Japan and the Empress Jingo, who invaded Korea with a strong army. In those days women fought, governed, and led armies to battle. They were regarded as individuals in those early days, with the same rights and privileges as the male. It was only about the sixth century A.D. that the position of women in society began to change.

The Japanese woman was taught from

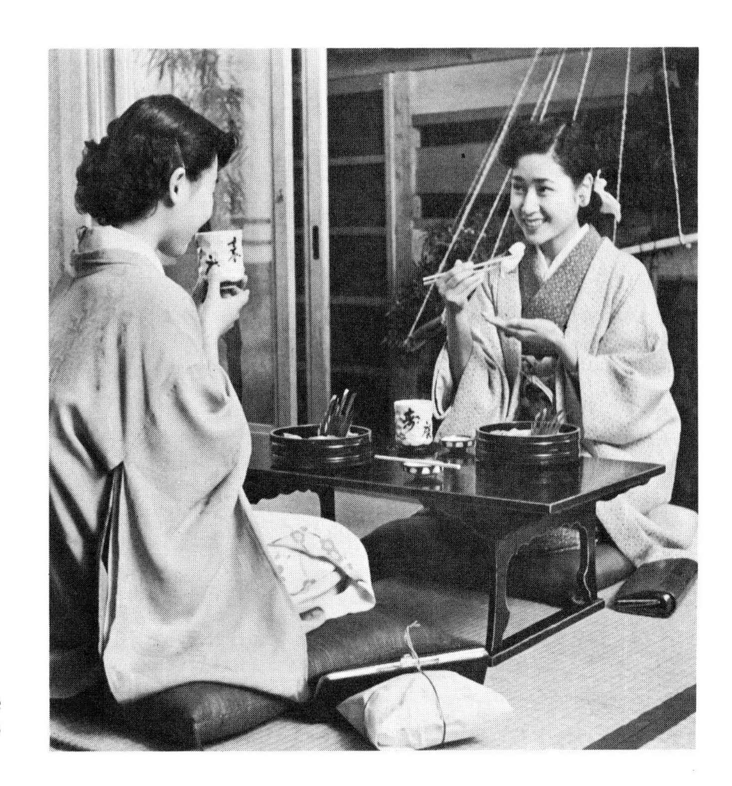

Two Japanese women in traditional costume stop to have tea on a shopping trip. Many Japanese women today dress in Western style. (Japan National Tourist Association)

early childhood that her primary virtues were obedience, devotion to duty, patience, good nature, and self-sacrifice. Public office and a career outside the home were not for her; these were the privileges and the rights of the male. Her goal in life was to be a good wife and a good mother. To this end she was trained in the practical matters of the household. She learned to cook, to sew, and to wash. She was shown the proper way of serving food, of entering rooms, and of greeting guests.

The daughters of farmers learned to do farmwork and helped in the planting and harvesting of crops. Farm women were allowed a greater freedom of association with men because their labor in the fields brought them into a closer and necessary association. But the middle and upper class women maintained their separate, dependent position even with very close male relatives. Many, if not all, learned the rudiments of flower arrangement, and the upper-class women generally learned to play a musical instrument.

With the opening of Japan to outside influences in the nineteenth century, the position of women in society began almost imperceptibly to improve. The new rulers of Japan who assumed control in 1868 with the Meiji Restoration (see page 136) wanted a new political and economic order, but they did not really try to change the traditional role of the Japanese woman. Women were permitted some formal education, but only to assist them in becoming better wives and mothers.

The new economy established by the Meiji Restoration, however, required the services of women, and by 1936 Japanese women were found in many occupations outside the home. Women became telephone operators, bus attendants, "gasoline girls," typists, stenographers, and factory workers. But still the Japanese tried to keep them in a traditional social mold. Those who worked in the factories, for instance, were rarely permitted outside its walls. The management substituted for their parents. The women who worked in factories were encouraged to use their spare time in preparing trousseaus and were offered classes in the traditional womanly subjects. It was impossible, however, to prevent all change.

With the American occupation of Japan in 1945, the legal and actual status of the Japanese woman changed significantly. She was made legally equal to the male. She was given the right to vote, hold political office, and to seek divorce. Today, Japanese girls must be educated for at least nine years, and they often study in the same schools as boys. More and more women are attending colleges and universities, and many of them are embarking upon professional and political careers.

Increasing industrialization and urbanization in Japan are affecting the size and relationships of families. Families are becoming smaller, and in the cities, particularly, husband and wife live in a separate household with their children. In this smaller family unit, the wife is not directly and immediately subject to her mother-in-law and the elders of a larger family.

But still much of the traditional remains. Traditional virtues and customs are still praised and admired. Although the Japanese woman may wear a Western dress, she retains many kimono manners and traits. Some Japanese lovers continue to commit suicide because they fear their parents will not consent to their marriage. The Japanese woman must follow certain traditional patterns of life if she wishes to retain her status as a good woman, wife, and mother. She is becoming modernized, but is yet traditional. She is a blend of her past and her present.

1. Why is a male child especially prized and important to a Japanese family? What might a Japanese family do if a male child was not born to them?
2. What are the traditional values of Japanese womanhood? How have these values been preserved by the modern Japanese woman?
3. Compare the life of a Japanese farm woman with that of a woman in urban society in old Japan. To what extent would these differences and similarities be true today?

## Society of Southeast Asia

The Southeast Asian also practices the joint- or large-family system traditionally practiced elsewhere in Asia. There are some variations, but the system is still recognizable whether it is seen in India, Pakistan, China, Korea, or Japan. The woman of Southeast Asia is familiar with the same traditional education imparted to her other Asian sisters. She, too, has been taught her special role as wife and mother and the traditional virtues of a good woman. The young man of Southeast Asia knows that his marriage has great significance to his family and to his community. He, like the other Asians, must often accept the desires of his parents in this grave matter.

### A Traditional Cooperative Spirit

Until recently, and even now in many parts of Southeast Asia, there has been an air of relaxation among the people. Perhaps it is because many Southeast Asians are not so constantly subject to the fear of hunger and starvation as are other Asians. The sea gives them fish and other marine foods, and some of them have a surplus of rice. Except for a few areas, such as Java, the land is not overcrowded; and the climate is warm and favorable to the production of a variety of vegetables and fruits. The people need not spend all of their time searching for food, and there is time for rest, gossip, and festivals.

There is a spirit of helpfulness among the Southeast Asians. This spirit has stemmed from their environment, their traditions, and their religions. They have traditionally sought to resolve the social conflicts within their community through adjustment and compromise; and they have succeeded more often than not. Perhaps one of the primary reasons for their success is their basic sense of cooperation. They prefer to cooperate rather than to compete with others.

This cooperative trait marks the daily life of the family and the village. The people join together in constructing community buildings, schools, and clinics, and in building roads, dams, irrigation canals, and defense works. They help each other in putting up houses, cultivating the fields, and in finding brides for the men and grooms for the girls. They are generally ready to assist where helpful hands

The houses of this typical Japanese rural village are crowded close together. Most of the houses are thatched with straw, and only a few have tile roofs. What changes might have come to this village in recent years? (Japan National Tourist Association)

are needed—in funerals, in births, and in celebrating the many religious and national festivals.

Sometimes this cooperative attitude extends beyond the community and the village. When the dikes of their rivers burst, and the rushing waters deluge the land, the people come from many communities to repair the damage, to house the homeless, to rescue the stranded, and to feed the hungry. They have been doing this from the early moments of their history. This spirit, this practice of cooperation, is one of the finest distinguishing features of the society of Southeast Asia.

### Life Becomes Complex

As contact between people within each country and between the countries of the world has become closer and closer, the Asian has found life more confusing than before, and he has been faced with decisions that are increasingly harder to make. No longer is it possible to remain isolated from the opinions and actions of others. In the rural villages and even within the family, advice and opinions from outsiders often intrude. Often these new ideas are not welcomed.

The village elder thought that life was difficult enough when he had only village and family affairs to think about. Now he is being asked to think about national and even international matters and to participate in matters which, in his opinion, are no particular concern of his. He listens to the village radio and it tells of disturbing events. He is told that in order to avoid great trouble, he and his countrymen must change their views, or that his rulers must change their policies. He frets because these are events over which he has no control, and yet they may react unfavorably upon his family, his village, and his country.

He goes to a meeting of the village elders, and there he hears a young and eager representative of the central government urge, and sometimes command, them to change their time-honored ways of tilling the soil and producing food. This youngster sometimes even suggests that they plant other crops and change their habits of eating. The village elder may think that the young man is a fool, but he keeps this thought to himself while the government representative is present.

He returns to his home, but there is no peace of mind for him even within the family, which he rules at least in name. His sons and daughters go to school. He still cannot understand why girls must go to school, but the government says they must go at least for a period of time, and he has little choice in the matter. Sometimes the boys and girls go to the same school, and the village elder does not approve of this mixing of the sexes; no good will come of it. Nor does it appear that they are being given a good and sound education. The government and the teachers, who should be upholding the traditional ways, as they have always done in the past, are spreading strange and troublesome ideas. The young people are encouraged to speak these ideas bluntly to their elders. This is a major break with tradition.

The young people speak to him about the unsanitary conditions of the house, the lack of vitamins in the food, the wrongness of his social attitudes, and the inefficiency of his farming methods. They speak about marrying for love. Sometimes the daughters of the family insist upon going on to high school and even the university. Both sons and daughters strongly object when the elder tells them in plain language that it is a girl's destiny to get married, raise a family, and manage a household, and that the only education she needs for this job is education at home. They tell him that he and the other villagers are old-fashioned and that they are obstacles to progress. The young people insist that their country will never be strong and progressive if their elders persist in useless and backward traditions. It is all very perplexing and very troublesome, and the elder knows that he is not alone with such problems, for his friends have spoken to him about these same difficulties.

But the elder is a stubborn man. He does not intend to give up the old ways which have withstood the test of time until it is proven to him that the new ways are better. These were the ways of his father, his grandfather, and other ancestors stretching far back in time, and they are his ways now. They are not to be lightly forsaken. "What was good for them is good for me until proven otherwise" is the principle upon which he works; and this principle holds for all aspects of his traditional way of life.

1. How has life become more complex to the Asian today than it was in the past?
2. What effect has education had on the traditional patterns of life in Asia?
3. What major obstacle in Asia today stands in the way of progress?

## Conclusion

We have seen that the Asian thought the good of the family, the caste, the clan, and the group was of greater importance than his own personal welfare. He was prepared to make great sacrifices in order to preserve and sustain these institutions of his society. He was never alone. Wherever he went, he carried with him responsibilities to his family and to his society.

The social life of the Asian is in the process of a great, monumental change. The change is slow, however, and will not be completed for many years to come, if ever. In the cities, and upon the surface, the change may appear rapid and complete; but man does not give up overnight what he has lived by for centuries. The Asian today still bears the traditional responsibilities to his family and to his group. He cannot shirk them without incurring mental anguish within himself and the condemnation of his group. The Asian may learn Western speech, dress in Western clothing, and entertain in a Western way publicly and among Westerners; but he will also talk, dress, act, and think as an Asian in his home and among fellow Asians.

The hold of the past is difficult to shake, but the lure and the necessity of the new are

inescapable. The Asian is changing, but he is yet unchanged. He is caught up in an agonizing mental and emotional social conflict, for he can deny neither the old nor the new. At present he is desperately trying to reach a satisfactory compromise. He must seek a means of keeping those social ways he cherishes most from the past while he takes of the new that which is essential to his society in this modern age.

In order to build and maintain hydroelectric plants, improve roads and transportation, and develop industry, many Asian countries have had to train mechanics and engineers. These students in Ceylon are learning maintenance and repair of heavy automotive equipment. (United Nations)

## SUMMING UP THE CHAPTER

A. Define or explain the following terms, relating them to this chapter.

| | |
|---|---|
| ancestor | joint-family |
| clan | patriarch |
| communes | pawn shop |
| Communist | sacred cow |
| filial obligation | society |
| gentry | untouchables |
| horoscope | |

B. Identify the following names and tell why they are important.

| | |
|---|---|
| Brahmans | Meiji Restoration |
| "Children of God" | Rabindranath Tagore |
| Empress Jingo | Rajputs |
| Kshatriya | Sudra |
| Mahatma Gandhi | Vaisya |

C. Chapter review questions.

1. Explain the meaning of this quotation by John Donne: "No man is an island." Relate this quotation to ideas expressed in this chapter. Does it have any meaning for you as an individual?
2. What historical events helped to establish a caste system in India? What peoples originated each division?
3. Describe the types of castes in India. What advantages and disadvantages do you see in their existence? What is the relationship between a member of a caste and one who is not a member of a caste?

4. Discuss the family as the basic social institution in Asia. Give examples from each of the countries mentioned in this chapter.
5. Historically could Indian women own property? If so, what kind?
6. In what country was the state considered an extension of the family?
7. Compare and contrast the responsibility of parents in the marriage of their children in India, China, and Japan. How does this differ from the customs of your family?
8. How were social welfare needs met in traditional China?
9. Members of the gentry class in China often became members of the peasantry and vice versa. Explain how this might happen. Are there similar movements up and down the social scale in the United States in the present day?
10. Trace the status of the Japanese woman from the time of Empress Jingo to the present day.
11. Identify this quotation and explain its meaning: "Within the four seas all men are brothers."
12. Traditionally in Asia the oldest male is the absolute head of the family. How is his authority checked and moderated in India, China, and Japan?
13. How radical have the changes in Asian culture been? What part have necessity and industrialization played in bringing about these changes?
14. Compare the role of the family in India, Japan, and China. What similarities and differences do you find in the following categories?
    a) the role of the oldest male
    b) ownership of wealth
    c) continuation of the family
    d) responsibility of the family as a whole for the success or failure of each of its members
    e) education
    f) size
    g) position of women.

D. Questions for discussion.

1. How would you explain the subordinate status of women in Asian society? In what other societies or countries would this also be the case? What is the Western ideal of the status of women? What reasons can you see for the different approaches to a woman's status in the world?
2. Is the joint-family uniquely Asian? Was it also European and even American? If so, what social and economic forces led to its decline in the United States? Are there factors now present in such countries as China, Japan, and India that would bring about the decline of the joint-family? If so, what are the factors?
3. In what sense is government a simple extension of the family? What factors complicate government handling of functions once handled by the family? Do governments follow the ideological and structural patterns of the family? What types of societies are more likely to follow these family patterns? What reasons can you give for not following the family pattern?

E. Projects for groups or individuals.

1. Make a list of the most important social customs of India, China, and Japan. Which of these customs are similar?
2. Write a short story, using facts about family life in Japan, telling what life might be like for a boy or girl of your age.
3. Write a short story illustrating the difficulties a Chinese bride might face in her new household.
4. Keep a scrapbook of pictures and clippings on traditional Asian clothing. Note the differences between countries and regions within a country. Write captions for the pictures, explaining their significance.

# CHAPTER 7

# *Politics in Asia*

The Asian has thought and spoken much about politics. He has discussed the responsibilities and qualities of a good ruler and his advisors, as well as the duties of that ruler's subjects. He has thought and written about the administration of government and the problems of relations with other empires and states. The Asian has viewed the uncertainties and insecurities of life and concluded, like many of us, that good government is the answer to many of his problems.

## The Ruler and the Ruled

Asian thought has generally been in terms of the ruler and the ruled. There was one who ruled and had certain responsibilities; and there was the great mass of the people who were ruled and had certain duties. The ruler was not chosen by the people, nor did he consult them when he made his decisions; it was their duty to obey his commands from on high. It is true that the ruler had advisors, and sometimes he was manipulated by others who really ruled in his name; but officially and formally there was one ruler, whose word was law.

Although the ruler was all-powerful, a number of Asians thought that he had a real responsibility for the welfare of his subjects. Some Indians stated that a king should be judged in terms of whether or not he met the needs of the people. If he failed, he should be replaced. Some even held that he could be assassinated if he showed himself unworthy. The Confucianists taught that the emperor was responsible for the security and happiness of his people. If the emperor failed to carry out this responsibility, he would lose the blessing of Heaven, since Heaven thought as the people thought. Thus, the Chinese were told that they had the right to revolt against an unworthy emperor. But, as is frequently the case, there was often a great difference between theory and practice. In practice, many Asian rulers did not concern themselves with the welfare of their people.

The rulers often appeared to be primarily interested in preserving their own power and in increasing the social, political, and economic rewards of their high position. A few, such as Asoka, Harsha, and Akbar of India, some of the Chinese emperors, and perhaps a few here and there elsewhere in Asia, actually tried to improve the condition of their people; and history has honored their nobility of purpose and soul. Too often, however, rulers regarded themselves as the masters of the people and neglected to uplift the people they governed.

The people, as a rule, were resigned to this state of political affairs. Naturally they disliked the often harsh conditions of their lives, and they dreaded civil wars and invasions. The heavy price of fighting was borne most by them, but they rarely had the opportunity to avoid these conflicts. When the kingdom was badly governed, and the ruler cruel and tyrannical, the subjects often despaired. Many turned to banditry and other forms of lawlessness to survive. They robbed the rich and poor alike.

Sometimes a member of the despairing peasant class or an ambitious member of the ruling class would use the discontented and the lawless to try to seize for himself a part of the kingdom or the throne of the emperor himself. Sometimes these attempts succeeded. But no one tried to change the system; they sought merely to change the rulers. This seemed to be the only solution when political

The royal barge of Thailand is used only on state occasions. (Royal Thai Embassy) The Marble Temple, in Bangkok, Thailand is located in the same compound with the royal palace. (Pacific Area Travel Association)

problems became overwhelmingly bad. And there was generally only one way to be rid of a hated ruler—by force.

The people, for the most part, wanted little to do with the central government. The further it was removed from them, the better they liked it. Their sad experience showed that a ruler gave little but wanted much of them—their grain and money in taxes, their sons for battle, and their free labor for building public works. Under these circumstances they preferred a ruler to ignore them, for to be unnoticed was to be unbothered. They were, however, interested in their village or local government.

## The Village in Politics

A rough democracy was often practiced at the village level. The village was important to the Asians. For practically all of them it was the boundary of their lives. Depending, of course, upon the time and the ruler of the central government, the villagers often had something to say about local government. The villagers knew that their leaders were of their own caste, clan, or family. They knew these leaders well. The lives and fortunes of villagers and those of their leaders were closely intertwined.

In India the village was governed by a council known as the *panchayat*. Usually it was composed of some of the most respected members of the village. Sometimes the village council or committee was chosen by lot or by the householders under a kind of constitutional government. Often all the householders participated in major decisions affecting the village. There was also a headman, who was one of the villagers, and who frequently represented the central government.

In China, and elsewhere in many parts of Asia, the villagers were also governed by their own people. Most of the Chinese were supervised by the elders of the village and by their clans, their families, or their guilds. A guild was an association of people performing the same occupation, such as making bows and arrows, porcelains, or other such products. Guild members banded together for mutual protection and aid. Japanese officials tried to supervise the villagers more closely, but even here the headman was chosen from among those living in the village.

The collection of taxes, settlement of land disputes and quarrels, and construction of irrigation projects and public works requiring a community effort were handled by village councils and village elders. The ruler of the kingdom rarely dealt with anyone below the rank of village representatives, who stood between the ruler and his people.

The institutions of village, caste, clan, and guild gave to the political life of the Asians a certain continuity and stability. These institutions were carried on no matter who ruled the land. The rulers needed the villagers and accepted their institutions as long as they paid taxes, maintained the peace, and provided the

Hawaii possesses the natural beauty that has made the Pacific Islands famous. What historical ties have the people of Hawaii with the people of other Pacific islands? (Hawaii Visitors Bureau)

The Maoris were the native inhabitants of New Zealand. They belong to the Polynesian race of the Pacific. Their wood-carvings are especially skillful. (New Zealand Consulate General)

Australia and New Zealand were colonized chiefly by people from the British Isles. Sheepherding is a major industry in these countries. (Australian News and Information Bureau)

minimum of public work when it was requested of them. The villagers did not care to whom they paid their taxes and gave their labor as long as they were not too oppressed.

## The Coming of the Westerner

When Westerners started to come to Asia in greater numbers at the beginning of the sixteenth century, they found political life to be much as it has been described above. This had been the government of the Asians for centuries. Changes were to come with the opening of Asia to increasing Western influences.

People from the West had visited the Asians before the sixteenth century. In 327-326 B.C. Alexander the Great had opened up trade between India and the West. From that time, Westerners had made their way singly or in small groups to India and other Asian countries. They came for various reasons, but mostly they came to trade. Asian goods were prized by most Westerners, and Asian knowledge was sought by a few. From India the Westerners wanted gems, cotton, spices, and drugs, to mention only a few items. The Romans thought of China as a place from where silk came, and named it "The Land of the Silk." Roman coins have been found in China.

Beyond the few goods they received from the Asians, most Western Europeans knew very little about Asia. It was for them a mysterious land of mysterious people. For many centuries the Westerners exerted no real influence upon the life of the Asians. But beginning in the sixteenth century, a change began.

A number of reasons have been given for the expansion of Europeans into Asia—social, political, religious, and economic reasons—but one of the most immediate and compelling was the need for spices. Western Europeans needed spices, especially pepper, to improve the taste of their frequently rancid meats. The prices of these spices were continually rising. On the long journey from Asia through the Middle East to Europe, spices passed through the hands of many middlemen. These middlemen became increasingly numerous and demanding. The Europeans began to search for a sea route which would bypass the middlemen and allow them to obtain spices from the Asians directly.

The Portuguese and the Spanish started first to look for a sea route to the Indies. Though the Spanish discovered America by sailing west, it was the Portuguese who found a way to India by sailing around the southern tip of Africa and across the Indian Ocean. Vasco da Gama was the Portuguese captain who first sailed to India. His ship brought a cargo of spices back to Portugal in 1499, and it is said that he sold it at a price over sixty times the cost of the venture. In 1520, sailing under the Spanish flag, Magellan discovered a strait around the southern tip of South America. He crossed the Pacific Ocean and found the Philippines, which he claimed for the Spanish. He was killed there, but his ship continued the voyage and reached Spain again in 1522. He had proved that the world was round and uncovered another sea route to Asia.

From this time onward the Westerners went to Asia in increasing numbers and for a variety of reasons. The British, the French, the Dutch, the Danes, and others followed the overland spice trails and the exploring ships of the Portuguese and the Spanish. They fought and intrigued, and eventually they divided the lands, the products, and the peoples of Asia among themselves. The British, French, and Dutch were chiefly interested in the economic rewards they could get from the Asians. The Portuguese and the Spanish were interested in material products and also in converting the Asians to Christianity. In all cases the Europeans found themselves assuming greater and greater political control over the Asians. By the middle of the nineteenth century, most of Asia was directly or indirectly under the rule of Westerners.

The Russians and the Germans also became involved in the economics and politics of the Asians. Unlike the other European nations, Russia spread her influence over the land rather than by the sea, and Russian settlers and armies moved across much of north and northeast Asia. These lands under Russian control still lie today like a thick and heavy roof covering the Asian lands to the south. The Germans arrived late, obtained little, and left after a relatively short stay.

At the end of the nineteenth century, the Americans, too, became rulers of a part of Asia, the Philippines. These islands were formerly Spanish and were ceded to the United States in 1898 by Spain after her defeat in the Spanish-American War.

### The Asians Learned and Acted

In their coming, the Westerners laid the foundations for the present political structure of the Asians. Westerners took control of much of Asia's land and ruled in the place of the former native rulers. They brought with them ideas about nationalism, representative forms of government, the worth and rights of the individual, and new ideas of rulers as the servants rather than the masters of the people. The Asians heard from them about personal liberty and republican forms of government. They learned about some of the advantages of democracy. From enemies of democracy the Asians also learned about Communism, fascism, and imperialism; they were told that the Western democracies would decline and decay.

The Asians thought much about these different ideas. They went to study and observe in Western nations where democracy was practiced. They read about capitalism, socialism, and later, Communism, for all of these ideas originated in the West. In general, they liked the idea of being free, of having self-government and representative government. Many Asians were inclined toward a democratic socialism, but some embraced Communism. Others borrowed the outer forms of the West but retained much of the traditional Asian ruling spirit.

Many Asians began to dislike very much the rulers from the West who were democratic at home and undemocratic in Asia. They resented the implied and frequently expressed attitude that Asians were unfit and unready to govern themselves. They were angered that their resources and products went to foreigners rather than to their own people. Many of the governors from the West showed by their attitude that they thought the Asians were racially inferior. Spurred by their anger, resentment, and yearnings to be free, the Asians acted.

The first really articulate prophet of Asian liberation was the Chinese physician, Sun Yat-sen, who became one of the world's great political theorists and who is still honored as the father of the Chinese republic. Dr. Sun insisted that Asian countries should keep their old moral standards, which he felt to be superior to those of the West. However, he wanted the Asians to adopt Western technology (science, medicine, engineering, and the military arts) so as to achieve a better life for themselves and freedom from European domination. He was an apostle of democracy, who acknowledged that his three great principles of nationalism, democracy, and democratic socialism were inspired by Abraham Lincoln's stirring phrase about government "of the people, by the people, and for the people." Though Dr. Sun died in 1925, many Asian and African governments follow the outlines of his plans—sometimes without even knowing that they do so.

Some Asians spoke violently, and their foreign rulers put them in prison. Some rioted, and blood was shed. Some preached revolt, and they were beaten and also put into prison. Others resisted peacefully, offering their undefended bodies as a sacrifice to freedom. This was the technique of one Asian, Mahatma Gandhi, the spiritual father of modern India. It was called *the way of nonviolence.*

1. How did the village, the clan, and the guild serve as a buffer between the individual and the central government? How did these semi-governmental institutions contribute to stability and order in Asia?
2. What major incentives encouraged European contact with and exploration of Asia? What countries started these explorations?

## Indians and Pakistanis Struggled for Independence

The Portuguese came first to India toward the end of the fifteenth century. Ironically, they were the last of the Western rulers to leave India, when the Indian army in 1961 chased them from the district of Goa, 250 miles south of Bombay. The Portuguese had occupied this small piece of India since the sixteenth century. The British, French, and Dutch followed them to India. There were the inevitable jealousies, clashes, and battles among them, for the spoils of India were very alluring. The British were more clever, and luckier. With the help of discontented and ambitious Indians, through well-placed bribes, and by able military leadership, they took advantage of disunity and gradually secured control over the greater part of India.

By the beginning of the nineteenth century, the East India Company held sovereignty over India. This company was an association of British merchants and manufacturers who had been given a monopoly of the Asian trade by the British king. It was a profit-making organization, but it recruited and led armies in India, and its agents ruled and lived like kings. Greed and mismanagement within the Company sometimes led to civil strife and even mutiny on the part of the Indian soldiers. In 1858 control of India was taken from the Company and given to the British Parliament. And Queen Victoria of Great Britain later became also Empress of India.

By the middle of the nineteenth century, some Indians had already started to clamor for freedom. There was Tilak, a very religious Hindu, who linked independence and Hinduism together. He gave meaning and force to the idea of nationalism and freedom among the Hindu people. Tilak preached violence, and even assassination, if necessary to the cause of freedom. He was put in prison for some years. A more realistic and moderate man was Gokhale, who understood that the British were too strong at this time to be overcome by force. He advocated a slower, less bloody path to freedom.

### Mahatma Gandhi and India

In 1869 there was born in northwest India a man who was destined, more than any other single man, to unify the Indians and gain freedom for his people. His full name was Mohandas Karamchand Gandhi. An adoring Indian people later bestowed upon him the name Mahatma, which means "Great Soul." It is by this name that he is generally known to India and to the world.

Gandhi was a Hindu. He went to London to study law and returned to India, where he practiced law for a time. Then in 1893 he went to South Africa on a law case, and he stayed to fight the degrading discrimination against the Indians that he saw there. He fought for the Indians in the courts of law; but, more important, he conceived and put into practice the idea of mass resistance through nonviolence. He called this *Satyagraha,* which he translated as "soul-force." This soul-force stemmed from certain basic beliefs he held. They were: injure no living being; return love for hate, good for evil, and unselfishness for selfishness. He believed in conquering by the power of goodness.

Mohandas Gandhi practiced what he preached and believed. He was tormented by his enemies, and suffered imprisonment. He was humbled and handled roughly by the police but never struck back. He suffered all in silence and in patience. In the end, the government of South Africa agreed to remedy what Gandhi had fought against in his nonviolent way.

He returned to India in 1914. From that time until he died by the gun of an assassin in 1948, he worked in his nonviolent way for peace, unity, and the freedom of the Indian people. This little man, dressed in a simple piece of white cloth, eating little, owning little, and asking little for himself, went from place to place in India, preaching always his message of brotherhood, love, and nonviolence. If his people rioted, he pleaded for them to stop. If they fought with guns or clubs, or even with their bare hands, he cried for them to cease. When they did not heed his words, he fasted, and he continued to fast until his wishes were met. And his wishes were always met, for he was precious to the Hindu people. There were only a few fanatics who wanted the guilt of his death upon their heads.

Gandhi fought the British with a weapon they had never before encountered—nonviolent protest, or "civil disobedience." He borrowed this term from the writings of the American philosopher Henry David Thoreau. Women and children lay down on the rails of the railroads and upon the streets and the highways, accepting passively and sometimes with smiles the beatings of those who tried to remove them. Gandhi was jailed for "civil disobedience," but to no avail. The resistance stiffened. There was no alternative for the British except to talk and negotiate. They talked for years, and finally in 1947 the British announced that they would leave India in June of 1948.

Despite the magnificent peace efforts of Gandhi, the Indians did not achieve independence without bloodshed. With the sudden announcement that the British intended to leave India within a year, wild emotions and long-restrained enmities erupted. There was conflict between the Moslems, on the one hand, and the Hindus and Sikhs, on the other. The Sikhs are a religious group who have constantly feared Moslem domination. In the struggle that resulted, each of the groups, Moslem, Hindu, and Sikh alike, suffered man's worst cruelty and brutality.

Mahatma Gandhi was sickened to the depths of his being by the savagery of his fellowmen. He pleaded, begged, and finally fasted almost to death in his effort to bring a halt to the needless suffering in India. He succeeded in saving thousands of lives; he could not save them all. He came to be hated by a few Hindu fanatics, and one of them shot and killed him as he walked in the midst of a crowd on January 30, 1948.

Gandhi was succeeded as the leader of the Indian people by his long-time supporter Jawaharlal Nehru. This brilliant, versatile man came of a cultured family of the Brahman caste. He had been well educated at home and

Mohandas K. Gandhi spent much of his life seeking to gain independence for India by peaceful means. After Gandhi's death, Jawaharlal Nehru became the leader of the Indian people. (Embassy of India)

Mohammed Ali Jinnah took the oath of office as Governor-General of Pakistan when independence was granted. (Embassy of Pakistan)

abroad in some of England's best schools. His thinking was not as simple and direct as Gandhi's, but he had worked closely with Gandhi for many years to obtain those freedoms they both desired for their people.

After Gandhi's death, Nehru became the first Prime Minister of India's new parliamentary government, and he remained in that position until his death in May, 1964. India is a democracy now, with a government patterned much after the British system, but not completely. There is a president now, not an emperor. There are judges and a legislature, and the members of the legislature are elected by the people. Unlike that of England, the Indian government is a federal system, with states like those in America. These states have legislatures whose members are chosen by the people. The people are beginning to feel that it is their government, and that it is something like their democratic village government of old.

## The Birth of Pakistan

It will be recalled that Moslems began to come to India as far back as the eighth century A.D. Gradually, under a succession of able military leaders, they conquered most of India and established the Mogul Empire. This is the empire which the British succeeded. The Moslems were different from other invaders before them in that they had a religion and a culture of Middle Eastern and Persian origin. They felt that their culture and religion were equal, if not superior, to the Indian culture. The Moslems refused to be assimilated, as others had before them, into the ever-blending, ever-harmonizing culture and society of the Indians. They remained distinct and separate.

Further, the Moslem culture and religion had a real impact upon the Indians. Persian culture, Persian language and literature, and Persian art and architecture became an integral part of Indian culture and society, particularly among the higher and middle classes. Millions of Indians were attracted to the teachings of Islam, for it denied caste, gave women a better status, preached racial equality, and held to a brotherhood of man in which all are equal before God. Many Indians embraced the hope offered by Islam, and it is estimated that a quarter of the entire population was Moslem when the British decided to leave India.

After the fall of their Mogul Empire in the eighteenth century, the Moslems were dispirited and directionless. No longer guided and protected by their Moslem empire, they were a minority surrounded by a Hindu majority and governed by the foreign British. Direction, purpose, and spirit were given them by the voices of three strong men who led them to dream and eventually to realize a homeland and country of their own. The first voice was that of Sir Sayyid Ahmad Khan (1817-1898), who urged Moslems to learn and borrow from the West so that they might become strong once again. He reinforced their feeling of separateness from the Hindus and urged them to always remember that in an independent India they would be outnumbered three to one.

Next was the great Panjabi poet, Sir Mohammed Iqbal (1873-1938). He inspired Moslems to become the masters of modern science in order that it might assist in furthering their destiny. He was the first to present Moslems with the dream of a separate homeland which he called Pakistan, "The Land of the Pure."

The third voice was that of Mohammed Ali Jinnah (1876-1948), who led the Moslems to their new homeland and is called the "father of Pakistan." He was a lawyer who practiced in Bombay. He was Western in inclination and carefully Western in dress, but he was also a Moslem, a nationalist, and, in the beginning, a supporter of the Hindu-dominated Congress Party. Jinnah was aloof in appearance, cold and logical in his approach to all problems, and rarely aroused to a display of anger and emotion. Once convinced of the truth of his position and the rightness of his purpose, he was a man of unbreakable will and determination.

Mohammed Ali Jinnah had no real intention at first of seeking a division of India when the British left. He thought in terms of a coalition government in which the Moslems would participate. He negotiated for a greater degree of self-rule by Moslems within the future Indian state. It was his aim to guarantee the individual and group rights of Moslems and to prevent a future cultural, economic, and political domination by the Hindu majority. But the Hindu-dominated Congress Party refused to part with any of its power. The leaders of the Congress Party underestimated the determination and organizational ability of Jinnah and his supporters. They did not probe deeply enough the fears of Hindu domination held by the Moslem minority nor the passionate need the Moslems felt for a separate land of their own.

The Moslems asked for partition, and they stood firm on their demands. The British and Congress Party leaders gave in, pushed by the urgency of the situation. On August 14, 1947, Britain gave dominion status to both India and Pakistan.

The partition of India followed roughly the concentrations of Moslem population. Millions of people were uprooted, however, for many Moslems lived in territory assigned to India, and many Hindus in lands assigned to Pakistan. Uncounted numbers of those uprooted had to travel great distances to their new homeland. Thousands did not survive the journey. Passions had been aroused on both sides, and the lurking beast within man came forth to kill and to ravage. Long and unprotected caravans of refugees were ambushed and many people were killed. Property on both sides of the new borders was confiscated and often whole villages were burned to the ground. It was the old, old story of man's great inhumanity to man, and it happened not so many years ago in a land that had produced one of the world's finest modern apostles of peace and love—Mahatma Gandhi.

**Government.** Pakistan is a democracy and its government is much like that of Britain. It has a parliament, a constitution, and a president. The constitution secures the many rights of man and provides for social justice, freedom of religion, and freedom of association. When the republic was founded, its leaders quoted and kept in mind Lincoln's words about a

Pakistan is a Moslem country. Here Moslems are seen offering prayers at a new mosque in Karachi. (Embassy of Pakistan)

government of the people, by the people, and for the people. Pakistan is also a state that bases its principles upon the strong foundation of the teachings of Islam. Shortly after the founding of the republic, Mohammed Ali Jinnah died, and the country is headed now by President Ayub Khan. His views and policies have served as inspiration for other nationalists in Asia. He is considered as a model by the present ruling group in South Korea.

President Khan was a military man originally. He wanted his country to be strong, his people prosperous, and his government to be honest and efficient. He was opposed to the Communists, but he also became disillusioned with the incompetency and corruption of government officials, with too much talk and too little action. Khan became concerned, and in his concern he acted. He took over the government, reorganized the administration, and stamped out many corrupt practices, such as the smuggling of gold, which was a heavy economic drain upon the country. A commission was appointed to draft a new constitution.

Khan's policies were based upon the observation that the people of Pakistan did not yet know what democracy really is. They did not have sufficient experience in its practice. He felt that under these circumstances the people should pause and take a fresh look at themselves and their objectives. Khan wanted to correct the mistakes that were being made in the use and practice of representative government. Democracy should not lead to chaos, to instability, weakness, and corruption. It should be tailored to the special needs and character of the people practicing it. After many years of effort and trial and error, it might emerge with many resemblances to the democracy of the Western countries; but in the meantime the proper foundations for a real democracy must be laid. The people of Pakistan were at the beginning, not the end, of their democratic evolution.

For democracy to flourish in Pakistan, security and stability were needed within the nation. At least a certain minimum of unity and discipline had to be maintained. Educational, social, and agrarian reforms had to be made to strengthen the basic democracy. It was necessary to have a constitution that would reflect these needs in its basic laws. Democracy would remain the cornerstone of the country's political system, but if it was to grow and mature there must be responsive masses and responsible leadership. There would be freedom, but it would be the freedom to construct, not the freedom to destroy.

These observations and conclusions of President Ayub Khan are akin to the thinking and conclusions of many Asian leaders today. Asian society today is in the formative stage. The people are yet naive about democracy, and their countries are beset by subversion from within and possible invasion from the outside. There is a great need for time, for education, for capable leadership, and for stability if the people are to weather their stormy independent beginnings and bring forth a lasting and real democracy.

The road to independence and democracy has been long and thorny for both India and Pakistan. No doubt there is a long and arduous road ahead, but governments based firmly upon the will of the people have hope and endurance beyond all others.

1. What was the East India Company? In what ways did it function as a private government, holding sovereignty over India?
2. Where did Gandhi first practice "nonviolent resistance"? What was the term he applied to it?
3. What are some of the reasons for the success of Islam in India? How did the Indian Moslems maintain their separateness from Indian Hindus?
4. How was the partition of India arrived at? Who were the leading figures in the creation of India and Pakistan?

## Afghanistan

From ancient days the land of Afghanistan has known the tread and the labors of a diversity of men. Their variety is reflected in the present inhabitants of this country—the majority Pushtuns, the Tajiks, the Uzbeks, the Turkomans, and others.

Four thousand or more years ago the Aryan knew the high mountains and deep valleys of Afghanistan before he discovered the wide river-moistened plains of India. The old Persians made this land a part of their empire between 549 and 331 B.C. The Macedonians and the Greeks led by Alexander the Great came, conquered, and left men of their own kind and traces of their culture in Afghanistan around 330 B.C. Conquerors from Central Asia swept through its mountain passes and made its earth their own. Among these were the Kushans in the first century A.D., whose most famous leader was Kanishka. Under his rule Buddhism spread across the steppes of Central Asia and found acceptance in the minds and hearts of the Chinese. The empire of Kanishka fell soon after his death, and a succession of new rulers followed. There were the Persians, who came in the sixth century A.D., and after them Arab Moslems from the west brought new rulers and a new religion to the land. In the seventh century A.D. Islam became entrenched in Afghanistan, and there can be no real understanding of the people today without an understanding of the religion which has shaped their customs, their attitudes, and their law.

But the Arabs did not bring peace to Afghanistan. Its earth continued to tremble under the heavy tread of massed armies and the thundering beat of charging cavalry. Tribes competed for dominance, dynasties came and went, and in the thirteenth century the Mongols of Genghis Khan brought terror and destruction to the land. Tamerlane exerted his control there, and one of his descendants, Babur, founded the Mogul dynasty in India. The Mogul Empire also included Afghanistan. In later years, the Russians expanded eastward over the rolling land of Central Asia, and the English expanded eastward

Many of the tribes of Afghanistan are nomads. (Royal Afghan Embassy)

over the swelling oceans. Both looked at Afghanistan as a possible extension of their growing empires. Neither of them took over the country completely, though they tried. The British assumed a dominant role and controlled Afghanistan's foreign affairs from 1880 until 1919. From this time onward, the people of Afghanistan began to learn something about Western political ideals and technology. They also began the slow and long process of adapting some of these Western features to their own special political, social, economic, and physical environment.

A constitution was adopted, and the king became a constitutional monarch. The forms of representative government began to appear, although it is yet a small elite who govern. In 1946 Afghanistan became a member of the United Nations, and leading Afghan officials began to realize that the future of their country was dependent upon the policy and the actions of powerful nations. Afghan leaders did not wish to offend their Russian neighbor, with whom they shared a common border of over a thousand miles. They therefore embarked upon a policy of neutralism in the Cold War, a policy they have maintained until the present. This policy has worked to their economic interests because both the United States and Russia have given substantial aid to Afghanistan in recent years.

Afghanistan is in need of economic help, for the country is underdeveloped. It is a rugged country—dry, desolate, and inhospitable in many sections. The cloud-reaching peaks of the Hindu Kush march east and west across the land, rising at times to heights of 25,000 feet and more. Roads are few. The camel, the horse, and the bullock are still the chief transportation among a people whose villages are locked within strong mountain walls or isolated by the bleakness of the desert. Nomads still wander in search of good pasture for their wealth of sheep and goats, but most of the people continue to follow a farming life. The chief agricultural products grown are wheat, cereals, fruit, nuts, tobacco, and cotton. Famine is not a serious threat to the population of Afghanistan—around 14,736,000—for the land, slightly smaller than Texas, is capable of supporting many people. But the standard of living is low, manufacturing is negligible, communications are poor, and educational facilities are few. With the aid of other countries, Afghan leaders are trying to meet some of their more pressing economic needs.

The entrance of modern ideas and activities is, however, causing some internal social strains. Young women in the city of Kabul, the capital, and in some of the other cities are taking the radical step of removing the traditional veil which hid their faces from the gaze of man. They are also beginning to dress in the Western style, which reveals rather than hides their figures. This nakedness of face and the display of form are yet offensive to many in Afghanistan, and the new customs are not tolerated beyond the walls of the cities. There is still an intense loyalty to the family, the clan, and the tribe, and it is frequently stronger than the loyalty to a nation-state. Customs, attitudes, and laws shaped by the past are, in many cases, proving unsuitable for the present. There is a need to harmonize the old with the modern practices and appearance which the officials are introducing into the country.

Many tribes of Pushtuns live in northwest Pakistan, and when the partition between India and Pakistan took place in 1947, they elected to go with Pakistan. The leaders of Afghanistan believe that there should be an independent country called Pushtunistan for these tribes. The leaders of Pakistan do not agree, and this issue has caused bad relations between the two countries. Russia has supported Afghanistan on this question, and the Afghans have shown their gratitude by supporting Russia in many votes taken in the UN on other matters. The Shah of Iran has, however, launched efforts that may eventually lead to a conciliation between Pakistan and Afghanistan.

The Afghan has problems, and he has hopes. Neutrality has apparently benefited him in foreign affairs, but the solution of his internal problems will come only with patience, effort, and education.

1. Why is Afghanistan in need of economic help?
2. Why is the entrance of modern ideas and activities causing some internal social strains within Afghanistan?

## Politics in China

During these years of struggle for independence in India, the Chinese were having their own troubles with the Westerners.

The Chinese have been for centuries proud of their own culture and way of life. They could see nothing beyond their borders to compare with their own remarkable political and social system. They thought themselves to be the only truly civilized people in the world, and they thought of all others as barbarians. The Chinese did not object to having barbarians come to China to learn, to inquire, and to pay homage and tribute to the emperor. They did object, however, to any actions or demands on the part of these barbarians which implied that they were equal to the Chinese. The Chinese had much to offer others, but they were convinced that others had little, if anything, of value to them.

In many ways the Chinese were right. They had for centuries been a creative people in many fields. Their philosophers had thought deeply and broadly about man, nature, and the problems of living. They had constructed a social system which was generally accepted by the people. This system gave a certain harmony and definite pattern to their daily relations with each other. Each person had his defined place and role in society, but it was not a static society. There was also movement and flexibility. Chinese works of art were original, distinctive, and often unexcelled. Chinese writers had created sensitive, poignant poems, and literature of power and depth. The scholar stood highest in their esteem; the soldier was among the lowest. But even in military matters there were books which are yet regarded as classics. On the northern borders of their country, the Chinese built a defensive wall which was regarded as one of the wonders of the world. And these are but a few of the achievements in which they took pride.

### A Cold Reception and Retaliation

The Western sailors and traders who came to China in the sixteenth, seventeenth, and eighteenth centuries seemed rough and often uncouth. It is not surprising that the Chinese, with their ancient attitude of mind and impressive background of achievement, received these Westerners with cold indifference and even with contempt. The foreigners were restricted to such ports as Canton and Macao in South China and were denied access to other parts of the country. The Westerners, particularly the British and French, reacted violently to these restrictions upon their trade. They resented the indifference and superior attitude of the Chinese towards them. In the middle of the nineteenth century, they began to use force to obtain a greater freedom to trade and a more equal relationship with the Chinese.

Treaties were forced upon the Chinese which gave the Westerners more ports and the right to make foreign settlements within China itself. Special privileges placed the foreigner beyond Chinese law on Chinese soil and made him subject solely to the representatives of his own government. Gradually the Westerner began to assume greater and greater economic and political control over the Chinese. The Europeans negotiated among themselves to divide China into economic spheres of influence in which each would have an exclusive right to trade. The United States refused to recognize these spheres of influence of the other Western countries. The Americans were opposed to such a division and strove constantly to maintain the "open-door" in China. This meant basically that each country would be free to trade anywhere in China.

The Chinese struggled long to resist influence and pressure from the West, but they failed. Their defenses broke down, and Western methods, ideas, science, and customs began to spread around the land. Christian missionaries made their way to China in numbers. They helped to spread Western ideas about government, health, social life, and technology. Many Chinese began to question their own systems of government, philosophy, and social and economic life. They went to other countries to study, and they studied at home. They concluded that a reform was needed in China and that the Manchu emperor must be overthrown.

1. How did the superior attitude of the Chinese toward the Western diplomat-traders lead to the eventual forced opening of China to the West?
2. How did "spheres of influence" allow the competing Western traders and governments to accomplish their purposes in Asia with a minimum of friction?
3. How did Chinese contact with Western ideas and institutions lead to such increased internal dissatisfaction that the Manchu dynasty was overthrown?

## Sun Yat-sen: Father of the Republic

From among the Chinese there emerged one man, Sun Yat-sen, who was destined to become the father of the new Republic of China. He was born in 1866 near Macao in South China and went to study in Hawaii, where he was converted to Christianity. He returned to China, where he found himself out of place. He then went to British Hong Kong, where he studied medicine and became a physician. But most of his life was spent in political activities directed toward the overthrow of the Manchus and the establishment of a republican government in China. Sun Yat-sen worked at home and abroad to bring about the downfall of the Manchu dynasty.

In 1911 revolution finally broke out in China. Sun Yat-sen became president of the first Chinese republic, which was proclaimed at Nanking in 1912. But he did not remain president for long. The Republic lacked a strong organization and the Chinese people had little understanding of democracy. China remained divided among many factions, each competing for power.

In Peking (now renamed Peiping), the capital of Manchu China, a national assembly was also called. This faction elected Yüan Shih-k'ai, a strong military leader, as Prime Minister under the Manchu emperor. Yüan Shih-k'ai was a cunning, crafty man with little use for democracy and great ambitions to set up a new dynasty of his own in China. He schemed for control of all China.

Yüan Shih-k'ai obtained the resignation of the Manchu emperor. In an attempt to preserve the unity of China, Sun resigned as President of the Republic and recommended that Yüan Shih-k'ai be elected in his place. This was done.

Yüan ruled as a dictator until his death in 1916. After his death, China was again divided among local military chiefs, called *warlords,* who kept personal armies, taxed the people of their territories for support, and fought continually among themselves. There was terror, chaos, and disorder everywhere throughout the land. The embittered and frustrated Chinese people turned hopefully to the West for possible solutions to their many political problems.

Through the continuing efforts of Sun Yat-sen, the Nationalist movement eventually brought most of China under one republican government. In the organization of this movement, Sun was helped immensely by the Russian Communists. He had appealed to other countries of the West for help, but they had delayed giving aid. The Russian Communists, on the other hand, had been quick to see the great possibilities of having a Communist state in China. They sent organizers to China to help Sun Yat-sen in the revolution and to assist in starting a Communist party. Sun's party, the Kuomintang, was reorganized along Communist lines. Students, peasants, laborers, and other groups were organized, and soldiers were taught Communist ideology and methods. Although the Russian organizers became officially a part of the Kuomintang, they were actually strengthening their own party in China.

**The Three Principles.** Dr. Sun worked and traveled tirelessly to preach his doctrine of the "Three Principles of the People" by which he tried to adapt and blend the best of Chinese ideology and the best of Western thought and progress.

The first principle was *Nationalism.* It

called for the Chinese to regard themselves primarily as citizens of a nation and only secondarily as members of a family or clan. This principle added the virtue of patriotism to the traditional Confucian virtues of loyalty, filial devotion, and obedience. Through this combination, Sun hoped to establish and strengthen a new Chinese nationalism.

The second principle was *Democracy*, or popular sovereignty. This principle provided for a democratic and representative type of government and stressed also the duties of each individual toward the state. Sun Yat-sen believed that the individual Chinese possessed enough freedom, for the traditional Chinese central government rarely interfered in his personal life. Personal life was regulated by the family, the clan, or the guild, rather than the central government, and the individual served them rather than the state. Dr. Sun wanted more service to the state and more freedom for the state.

Sun believed that the wise and the creative should rule but that their power should be curbed by the ultimate sovereignty of the people. This popular sovereignty would be exercised through elections and other democratic methods. The government should be run by competent managers, but, as in a corporation, the ultimate power should be retained by the owners, the shareholders.

He thought, however, that the people had to be taught democracy. During the period of teaching, his party, the Kuomintang, would rule the country. When the people had understood sufficiently the how and why of democracy, the Kuomintang would resign from its position as the only governing body, and the people could elect whomsoever they wished.

The third principle was *Livelihood*. Under this principle Sun wanted to raise the standard of living for all the people and, at the same time, increase the wealth of the nation. He advocated two methods to achieve these two ends. One was that the land be divided and equalized among the people. The other was that the government should regulate and control the ownership of capital. Heavy industries and the communication and transportation systems were to be owned by the government. There were to be progressive income and inheritance taxes.

Sun Yet-sen died in Peking in 1925, several years before his dream of a republic headed by his Kuomintang party was realized. His program was carried on by one of his supporters and military leaders, Chiang Kai-shek.

### Chiang Kai-shek

Chiang Kai-shek had begun to support Sun Yat-sen's program as a young military officer. He studied the Communist army organization in Russia and received much of his military training in Japan. He never studied in the Western countries. Chiang was the first commandant of the Whampoa Military Academy, which was established by Sun on the pattern of West Point in the United States to train his army officers. In 1926 Chiang was given command of the Northern Expedition Army of the Nationalist government, and by April 1927, he had established a Nationalist government in Nanking. By December of 1928, he had reunited most of China under the Nationalist government, which was controlled by the Kuomintang party. He broke with the Communists and, after six years of hard fighting, drove their armies to Yenan in northeast central China where he contained much of their armed power until World War II.

Chiang Kai-shek leads the Chinese Nationalists. (Embassy of the Republic of China)

Chiang became the leader of the Kuomintang party, the head of the State, and the commander-in-chief of China's armed forces. His government ruled most of China from 1928 until 1949, when the Communists took over control of mainland China. He continues to rule a part of China today from the island of Formosa (Taiwan), where he established the headquarters of the Nationalist government when it was driven from mainland China by the Communists.

1. Describe the early attempts at setting up a republican form of government in China. What role did the Chinese Communists play in the early Kuomintang?
2. What were Dr. Sun's "Three Principles of the People"? Why did he stress nationalism? Evaluate the usefulness of the three principles.
3. What did Dr. Sun mean by his third principle, *livelihood*? How did he propose to raise the standard of living?
4. What was Chiang Kai-shek's background before he became head of the Kuomintang party and government? When did he break with the Communists? Why?

### Mao Tse-tung

Mao Tse-tung became Chairman of the Communist party in China in 1931. He is still today the leader of the party and the single most powerful man in Communist China. He is of peasant stock, a realist, and a dedicated follower of Communism. He has been toughened by many battles in which he has been both loser and victor. He has endured many hardships and brought many hardships on others in his determined efforts to make China a Communist state.

Mao lived with his army and his followers for many years in Yenan, located among rich unoccupied farmlands. He had been driven there by the armies of Chiang Kai-shek. The Communist forces might have been completely destroyed, but Chiang was forced to concentrate much of his energy and his resources in fighting the Japanese for most of the period in which he headed the government of mainland China.

While the Japanese were ravaging the land of China during the Second World War, Mao's agents were recruiting greater and greater numbers of the Chinese into his forces. In part, his success was due to the moral and economic breakdown which occurred in China as the result of the war with Japan. In part, it was due to widespread corruption among the local, provincial, and even central government officials. And, in part, it was due to the apparent sympathy of the Communist party for the sufferings of the people. The Communists made appealing proposals to solve the land problems of China. Then, too, there was a rather despairing attitude on the part of many Chinese. They felt that things could not be any worse under the Communists than they were already. The Chinese found to their sorrow that things could be worse, but by that time it was too late.

After the war with the Japanese, the Communists were entrenched in strategic positions. There followed a civil war between the Nationalist government of Chiang Kai-shek and the Communists under Mao Tse-tung. The Communists won. By 1949 the Communists were in control of most of mainland China, and the Nationalists established their capital in Taipei on the island of Formosa.

The Communists established their capital in Peiping, the old capital of China, and this ancient city, which has been a capital of Mongol and Chinese rulers for many centuries, remains their capital to the present day.

### China Today

The Nationalists under Chiang Kai-shek are beginning to democratize their government. The people are beginning to have some say in the selection of their local and, in some cases, their provincial officials. There has been great progress also in the economic life of the people living under Nationalist control. But the dominant and prevailing party is still the Kuomintang, and both government and party are supervised by Chiang Kai-shek. Still basic to the party and the government is the ideology of the Three Principles of the People formulated first by Dr. Sun Yat-sen, who is regarded as the founder of Nationalist China. The Nationalists are determined to wrest mainland China back from the Communists, and everything they do and say is fundamentally motivated by this fixed purpose.

The Communists under Mao Tse-tung have, from the beginning of their rule, been engaged in a program of restricting the liberties and activities of the people they govern. In few parts of the world are the people regimented and controlled to the extent that they are in Communist China. There is no real security and no real freedom anywhere. Even within the family circle one must be careful lest mother, father, sister, or brother betray him as a subversive and traitor. The Communists have taught the youth that such betrayal is the highest form of patriotism.

The economic state of the people is, from all reports, rather bad. Food is rationed, and the amount allowed is barely enough to sustain life. For some it is not enough. Relatives abroad send food parcels to them and thus keep many alive; but there are many more to feed.

The Chinese Communists are determined to take Formosa and destroy the Nationalist government. They are also determined to enlarge the boundaries and influence of Communist China in Asia. They are further engaged in a program of making their influence felt abroad, and they have concentrated their efforts in this direction in Africa and in Latin America. It is estimated that the Communist Chinese embassy in Cuba alone has two hundred members.

The Chinese Communists regard the United States as their worst enemy, outside of Chiang Kai-shek. Their hate-America propaganda is continuous, abusive, and widespread both within and outside the borders of Communist China. Their hatred of America is not based on anything that the Americans have done or could do. It is based simply on the fact that the United States is the greatest power of the Free World, and hence the greatest obstacle to Communist victory over all mankind. Chinese Communist theory does not allow for the possibility of peaceful co-existence with the United States and the Free World.

The philosophy of Communism sparks the actions and the words of the Chinese Communists. They are, if that is possible, more Communistic than the Russians, who first practiced Communism on a national scale. They are more inclined to the violent overthrow of capitalism than any of the other Communist states. Their tendency toward violence and the use of force to achieve their ends has even embarrassed and irritated Russia, the formal leader of the Communist bloc of nations. We shall explore in detail the philosophy of Communism later when we deal with the Communist world.

1. How were the Communists under Mao Tse-tung able to expand their power from a small base in Yenan to eventual control of all mainland China?
2. What happened to the social, economic, political, and moral structure of China during and after World War II? How did this contribute to the defeat of the Nationalists by the Communists? Where did the Nationalist government set up headquarters after its defeat in 1949?
3. How has the ideology of Dr. Sun's three principles been maintained in Nationalist China (Formosa)? Compare the two Chinese governments, Nationalist and Communist.

### Politics in Japan

Like the Indians and the Chinese, the Japanese have had their own special political development, and the Westerners brought change to them also. The Japanese system of government, headed by the emperor, has had a long and interesting development.

The emperor of Japan traces his origins back through over 1,500 years of family rulers. The emperor has been central to the political life and thought of the Japanese for most of their history. A primary reason for his importance has been that the emperor was long considered to be of divine origin, his original ancestor being the Sun Goddess. She was first among the gods of Japan, and it seemed right that her descendant should be the ruler.

### The Puppet Masters

The emperor reigned, but he rarely ruled. Power was exercised in the name of the emperor by some person or some group who ruled from behind the throne. This political fact also began deep in Japan's past. The Fujiwara family began this process and this tradition as far back as the seventh century A.D.

The manner in which this was done became standard practice in Japan for many years. To control the emperor, the Fujiwara family married him early to a Fujiwara girl. After he had produced sons, they forced him to give up the throne. The head of the Fujiwara family then took the office of regent and ruled during the youth of the new emperor. This process was repeated when the young emperor became old enough to father sons.

The Fujiwara family assumed the power of appointing the highest officials of the land. As time passed, this power became hereditary in their family. This tendency to the inheritance of offices is another aspect of traditional Japanese political life. An example is found in the *shoguns,* the feudal military dictators, who ruled Japan starting with the Kamakura shogunate (1192-1333), which was succeeded by the Ashikaga shogunate (1338-1568), and ending with the Tokugawa shogunate (1603-1867). The shoguns never abolished the institution of the emperor or the position of the Fujiwara family. The forms of the old imperial government were maintained, but the real rulers were the shoguns. There were even instances of the shoguns themselves becoming puppets in the hands of someone behind them.

Thus, over the years, in seeking the man or men who ruled Japan, it was often necessary to peer over the shoulders of the rulers-in-name to see those who might lurk behind

An artist with Commodore Perry's fleet drew this picture of Tokyo harbor in 1853. (Library of Congress)

them pulling the strings like a puppet manipulator. Sometimes there was a series of puppet masters.

### Military Virtues Were Honored

Beginning in the twelfth century with the establishment of the Kamakura shogunate, military men and military virtues became increasingly important in the political development of the Japanese. From 1192 until 1867 the Japanese were governed by military men called shoguns, "barbarian-conquering generals." They established a feudal type of military government known as the shogunate. The shoguns were supported and assisted in ruling the country by strong military lords who held their lands as grants from the shoguns. These lords, in turn, were supported and upheld by armed followers or warriors called *samurai.* Over the years a certain formal relationship developed between the samurai and their lords. Gradually it became an expected pattern of behavior for all those who fought in war.

During the Tokugawa shogunate (1603-1867) the code of this relationship between warrior and lord was made the basic guide for the lives of all Japanese whether or not they were samurai. The ideals and virtues of the samurai were the ideals and virtues of all. In the Japanese language there is a term which is used to describe the proper behavior of the military man. This term is *Bushido,* which means "the way of the warrior."

**Bushido.** The virtues of courage and obedience were upheld by "the way of the warrior." To lack courage was to lose respect in one's own eyes and in those of one's fellowmen. Superiors must be obeyed promptly and without doubt or question.

Loyalty was valued above all else, and the loyalty of a vassal to his lord was superior to all other kinds. This loyalty might demand that parents substitute their child in the place of the lord's child who was about to be killed by an assassin and watch him be killed with no show of emotion. According to the highest ideals of the Japanese Tokugawa period, such an act was completely understandable and worthy of the highest praise.

Buddhist monks stand before the ruins of Angkor Wat. In what countries is Buddhism a major religion? (Pacific Area Travel Association)

Bushido emphasized the virtues of self-discipline, self-conquest, and self-restraint. It taught that everything should be done in moderation. The ideal man was restrained and touched with simplicity, always shunning excess.

Bushido included a love of nature in all of its manifestations. This love of nature was closely related to a deep and abiding love for the land. To the Japanese, the wonder of nature and the land of Japan are almost inseparable.

All of these teachings of Bushido are an integral part of what the Japanese refer to as their spirit. These teachings supported and strengthened the Tokugawa shogunate. They have in many ways continued to underlie the thinking of the Japanese to this very day. These ideas were born before the Tokugawa shogunate began, and they lived on after it came to an end in 1867.

1. How did the belief in the divine origins of the Japanese emperor assist in the preservation of an imperial family line for a longer time than in any other country?
2. How did the Fujiwara family rule from behind the throne? How does this remind you of a Confucian political ideal?
3. Name the three great military dictatorships of Japan and the dates of their existence. What were the shoguns?
4. How was the samurai code, or *Bushido*, incorporated in the Japanese social system? How is it preserved in present day Japanese "spirit" even though *Bushido* is gone?

## They Moved into the World

It was not until the Tokugawa shogunate was overthrown in 1867 that Japan was transformed into a centralized, outward-looking modern state. Up to that time, the Tokugawas had maintained an attitude of isolationism and a system of feudalism. The beginning of the end of Tokugawa power dates from the time when the American Commodore Perry sailed his black warships into Tokyo Bay in 1853-54. Perry had orders from his government to open diplomatic relations with Japan and to demand fair treatment of American traders and sailors in Japan. For over two hundred years Japan had been cut off from communication with much of the world. In order to understand how Japan was opened to the modern world, it is necessary to keep in mind the background of the Tokugawa shogunate and the changes in Japanese society during that period.

The first Tokugawa shogun was the warrior Iyeyasu. His descendants were determined to preserve the power of their family in Japan for a long time to come. The Tokugawa shoguns encouraged such virtues of the code of Bushido as loyalty and obedience. They feared that any change in the ways of Japanese thinking and acting might undermine their authority. But change might come from outside the country as well as within it, especially from the strange Westerners who were beginning to bring different ideas to Japan. To prevent any alien thinking from entering Japan the Tokugawas sealed the country off from any outside influence. Only one Dutch ship a year and a few Chinese traders were permitted to touch Japan. Even Japanese who were then abroad could not return to the land. If they did, and were discovered, they were killed.

It is impossible, however, to keep a people completely isolated from others and to limit the penetration of all ideas and influences into a country over a long period of time. Nor is it possible to prevent the evolution of a society and economic and political changes within a country. The Tokugawas established their center at a place called Yedo, which is the old name for the present city of Tokyo. As commerce increased in the city, the merchants began to grow rich. A change was taking place in the social structure of Japan. The once-powerful feudal lords often found themselves without jobs and could not keep their armed retainers. Their former soldiers roamed about the country, lordless and penniless. There was a feeling of discontent and frustration and an increasing desire for change among many of the samurai when Commodore Perry forced his way into Japan in 1853-54.

After Perry's display of power had forced the weak Tokugawa government to sign a treaty, the warships of other Western nations began to come to Japan. The Tokugawa rulers still sought, however, to maintain the isolation of Japan. But when incidents occurred, the Westerners bombarded Japanese cities with their guns, and the Japanese found themselves powerless to prevent this retaliation. The restless samurai, being a practical people, decided to learn from those who had humiliated them.

**The reformers.** A group of reforming samurai set things right at home. They removed the Tokugawa shogun and brought the Emperor Meiji from Kyoto, where he had been without power, to Yedo, which was renamed Tokyo (Eastern capital). Tokyo has been the capital of Japan since that time. This movement to Tokyo returned the emperor to the center of the country's power. This event has since been known as the Meiji Restoration.

The reforming samurai re-emphasized the divinity of the emperor and described the shogun as a usurper. The government was further centralized by forcing all the great lords to deed their lands to the central government. The country was then divided into prefectures governed by officials appointed by the government. The samurai were stripped of their special privileges, and all young men were subject to military service. A modern army and navy were set up.

At the same time, these reform leaders started a detailed and systematic study of Western technology, institutions, and science. They adopted a constitution based on that of Germany; their courts and law courts were modeled on those of France. They established a civil service. A banking system was modeled along Western lines, and Japan began to be industrialized. In a relatively few years, Japan, on the surface had many Western features. They were real features, but they covered a core of basic ideas and traditions that remained very Japanese.

### They Remained Japanese

The samurai ruled Japan from behind the emperor. They were joined later by business interests commonly referred to as the *Zaibatsu*, which means "money faction." Another group arose from the bureaucracy of government officials which administered Japan. Thus a combination of three groups of men began to rule Japan—the military, the bureaucrats, and the big business interests. The militarists were probably the dominant faction among the three, but all of them were powerful and sometimes they acted as brakes on each other.

In the reform of Japanese society, universal education for both sexes was made compulsory for six years. The basic purpose was not so much to improve the individual for his own sake as to make him more useful in the service of the state. In the schools, pupils were taught the traditional Japanese virtues of obedience, loyalty, and submission to authority. They were also taught to believe in the divinity of their emperor. They were taught to read and write because a modern industrial state needs workers who can read, and modern soldiers must be literate.

Japan had political parties, but the relationship between leaders of these parties and their followers was like that which had formerly prevailed between lords and their vassals. Personal relations were much more important than law or principle.

### The Second World War

The Japanese began to make their power felt in Asia. In 1895 they defeated the Chinese in war. In 1904-1905 they defeated Russia. By 1910 they had incorporated Korea into their empire, and by the 1930's they had added great areas of Chinese lands to their ever-expanding territory. They dreamed of a mighty empire which would embrace most of East and Southeast Asia.

On December 7, 1941, the Japanese formally launched their great expansion by bombing Pearl Harbor in Hawaii. During the first years of the war they were extremely successful. Japanese troops conquered the Philippines. They occupied Hong Kong and much of China, Burma, Singapore, Malaya, French Indochina, Indonesia, and Borneo. They even penetrated the eastern borders of British India.

But their control of these lands was brief. The Americans, assisted by allies from Asia and the West, began to push the Japanese back to their homeland. Resistance was stubborn, for the Japanese soldiers had been well-indoctrinated with the virtues of Bushido. But the Japanese forces were over-expanded. The strategy of the American military leaders, particularly that of General Douglas MacArthur and Admiral Chester Nimitz, was sound, and the fighting qualities of American soldiers and sailors were great. The Japanese were

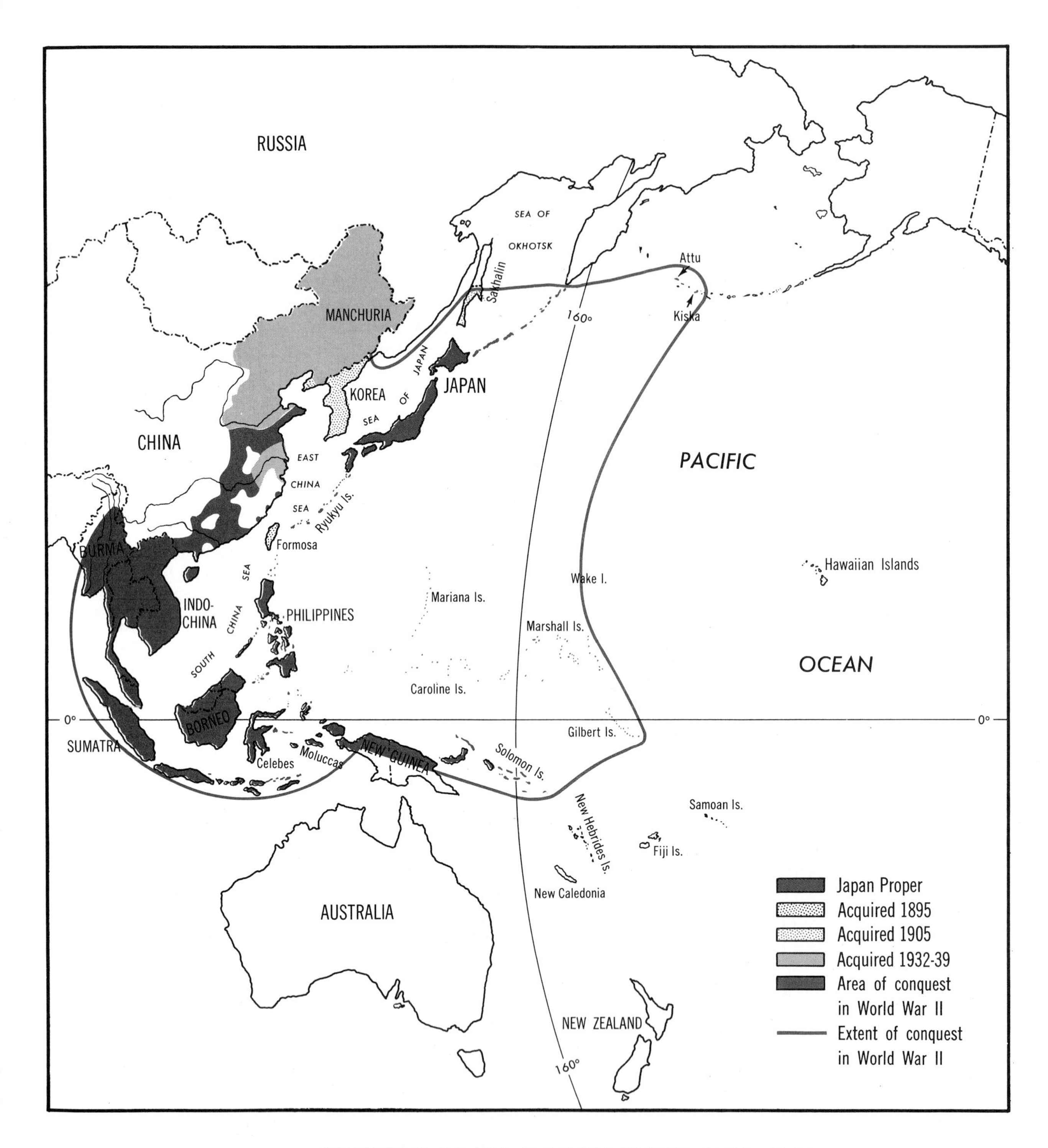


**EXPANSION OF THE JAPANESE EMPIRE (1895–1945)**

In which of the areas shown had Japan been interested before 1895? Many cultural factors influence the territorial expansion of nations. Relate the historical background of Japan to expansion in the twentieth century.

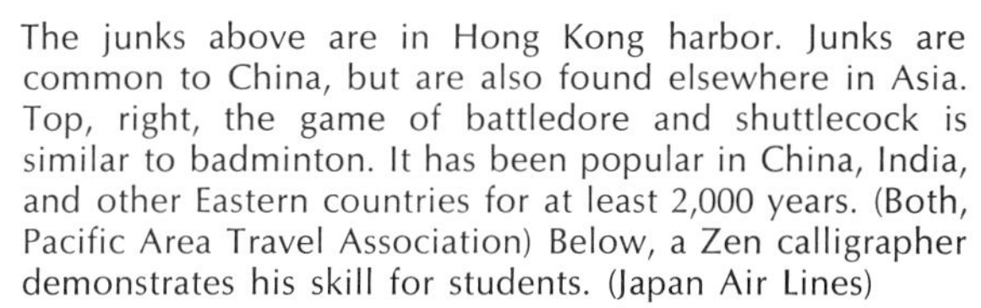

The junks above are in Hong Kong harbor. Junks are common to China, but are also found elsewhere in Asia. Top, right, the game of battledore and shuttlecock is similar to badminton. It has been popular in China, India, and other Eastern countries for at least 2,000 years. (Both, Pacific Area Travel Association) Below, a Zen calligrapher demonstrates his skill for students. (Japan Air Lines)

pushed back island by island until Japan itself was threatened.

The Japanese, no doubt, would have continued to fight on, bringing a great loss of life to themselves and to the military forces of the United States, but for the discovery and use of man's most destructive weapon—the atomic bomb. This bomb was used for the first time in the history of man upon the cities of Hiroshima and Nagasaki. In a brief moment, the A-bomb obliterated most of the life, movement, and structures of great areas of these cities. The will and spirit of the Japanese to continue the war were shattered. They asked for peace and surrendered unconditionally to the United States on August 14, 1945. Thereupon the Americans occupied Japan and, under the command of General Douglas MacArthur, began a reorganization of the political, economic, and social life of the Japanese.

### The Newer Japan

The American occupation authorities began a systematic reform of the Japanese political system. The Emperor was persuaded to speak to the people and tell them that he was a symbol rather than a god. The state religion of Shinto, which was the bulwark of the divine-emperor system, was separated from the state. It became an independent religion, not an official propaganda instrument for government officials. The Japanese were taught that they were important as individuals, not merely because they were members of a family-state. They were informed that they had certain rights and privileges which were a part of their human nature. Equality before the law was due each of them. The laws were made to protect these rights, and they could not be done away with at the whim of a ruler or rulers.

Yokohama harbor, above, was first opened to international trade in 1859. (Japan National Tourist Association)

All of these democratic provisions, dear to the hearts and traditions of the Americans, were incorporated into a written constitution. This constitution has remained as the basic law of the land. A broader parliamentary form of government was established, with a prime minister and a legislative body consisting of an upper and lower house of representatives. The members of these two houses of parliament are elected by the people. Political parties which represented all shades of opinion developed. Two parties gradually emerged to dominate the government: the Liberal-Democratic party, which is basically conservative in attitude; and the Socialist party, which is supported by labor and the more radical groups. The Liberal-Democratic party has controlled the government for many years, and its foreign policy is tied to that of the United States. The Socialists, on the other hand, would like to lead Japan into a neutral position and to forge closer ties between Japan and Communist China and the Communist bloc of nations. The Socialists are also interested in making Japan into a socialist state, with government ownership of industries.

The United States no longer controls the affairs of the Japanese, but the institutions and ideas left behind by the Americans are yet real and vital to Japanese political life. The Japanese are engaged in the practice of democracy, and they are succeeding in making it live because they are practicing it within the Japanese pattern of living. Their democracy is of American origin in large measure, but it does not mirror the image of its American founders. It mirrors the image of a Japanese people who have been influenced by Americans but who still look and act like Japanese in most ways.

Kumamoto castle is a classic example of Japanese architecture of the feudal period. (Japan National Tourist Association)

The elevated expressway and modern buildings show that Tokyo has changed with the times. (Japan National Tourist Association)

1. How did Japan's technological backwardness encourage interest in the West after 1854? How did this lead to the collapse of the Tokugawa shogunate and to the Meiji Restoration?
2. How were Western democratic ideals adopted wholesale into the constitution imposed on Japan during the occupation after World War II? Was this constitution successful?
3. What were some of the reforms of the Meiji Restoration? What groups actually began to rule Japan?

As you study the time line and the chronological list below, compare the historical development of India, China, and Japan. Note differences as well as similarities.

## Conclusion

Our story of the evolving political life of Asia has shown that only the minority were involved in politics at the national level; but most Asians participated, often vehemently and vigorously, in politics at the local level.

As Westerners came to Asia, the people learned something from them about democracy, representative government, socialism, Communism, nationalism, and other foreign social, economic, and political ideas and techniques. Those Westerners who became rulers usually had the greatest influence. Thus, in India, Pakistan, Burma, Malaya, and else-

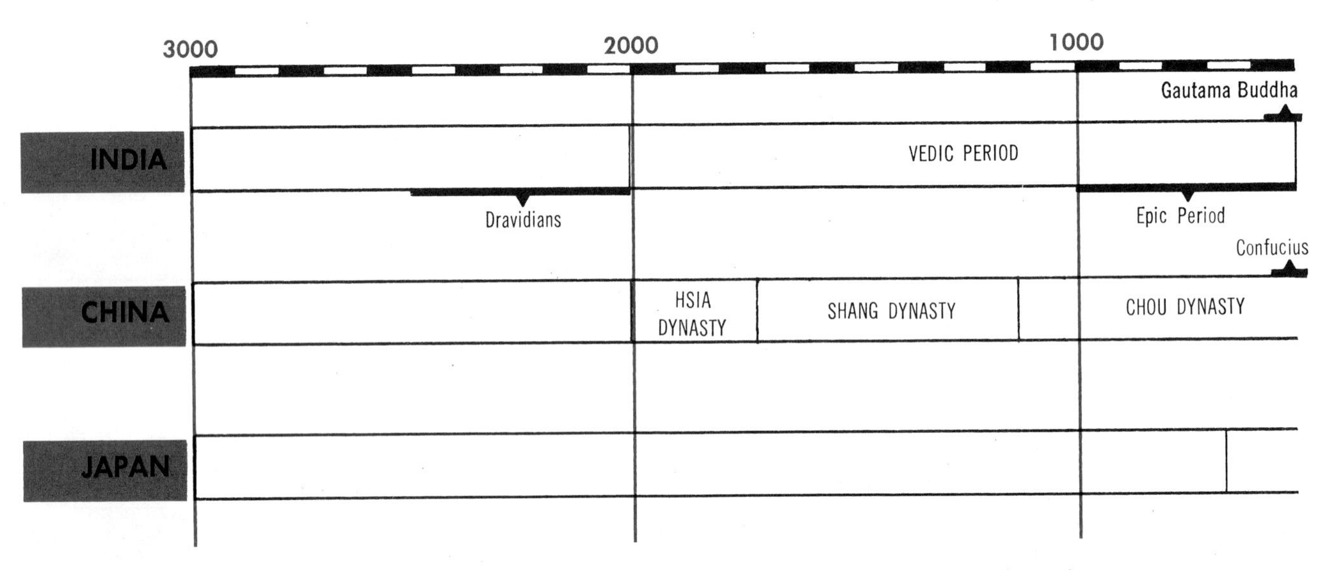


## MILESTONES

### INDIA

B.C.

| | |
|---|---|
| c. 3000-2500 | Dravidians |
| c. 2000 | Aryans migrate into India |
| 2000-500 | Vedic Period |
| 1000-500 | Epic Period; Mahabharata, Ramayana written |
| c. 563-483 | Gautama Buddha |
| 327-326 | Alexander the Great invades India |
| 322-185 | Maurya dynasty (Asoka, 273-232) |

A.D.

| | |
|---|---|
| 320 | Gupta dynasty established |
| 606-647 | Reign of Harsha |
| 1000s | Moslems bring Islam to India |
| 1192-1398 | Turkish empire in India |
| 1498 | Vasco da Gama reaches India |
| 1525 | Babur invades India; founds Mogul Empire |
| 1600 | East India Company chartered |
| 1700s | Fall of Mogul Empire |
| 1858 | English Crown controls India |
| 1869 | Mohandas K. Gandhi born |
| 1876 | Mohammed Ali Jinnah born |
| 1947 | India and Pakistan gain dominion status |
| 1948 | Gandhi assassinated |
| 1961 | Portuguese routed from Goa |

### CHINA

B.C.

| | |
|---|---|
| c. 2000-1750 | Hsia dynasty |
| c. 1750-1122 | Shang dynasty (early works of bronze) |
| 1122-256 | Chou dynasty (beginning of feudal system) |
| c. 551-479 | Confucius |
| 481-256 | Warring States Period |
| 256-207 | Ch'in dynasty (China unified) |
| 205-A.D. 220 | Han dynasty (examination system established) |

where, British political institutions became the pattern for the newly independent nations. In the Philippines, American political institutions are more evident today. There were, however, other influences besides those of Western rulers. Some of the Asians were inclined toward Communism, and they modeled their institutions after those of Russia. In all cases, Asian political life is still being shaped and influenced by the heritage of the past.

Slowly, as the years went by, these ideas and influences brought changes. There was a new sense of obligation to country as well as to family. The Asian began to dream about independence for his nation, to feel concern about its strength and its position of respect and equality among the other nations of the world. Those who shared these dreams struggled, and sacrificed, and finally succeeded in driving out their foreign rulers.

But once a country was independent of foreign control, its troubles had barely begun. The new leaders were a minority in their own country. The vast majority of people lived in villages, and most of them were still more concerned with their families and village matters than with the affairs of the nation. It was good, perhaps, that their own people ruled

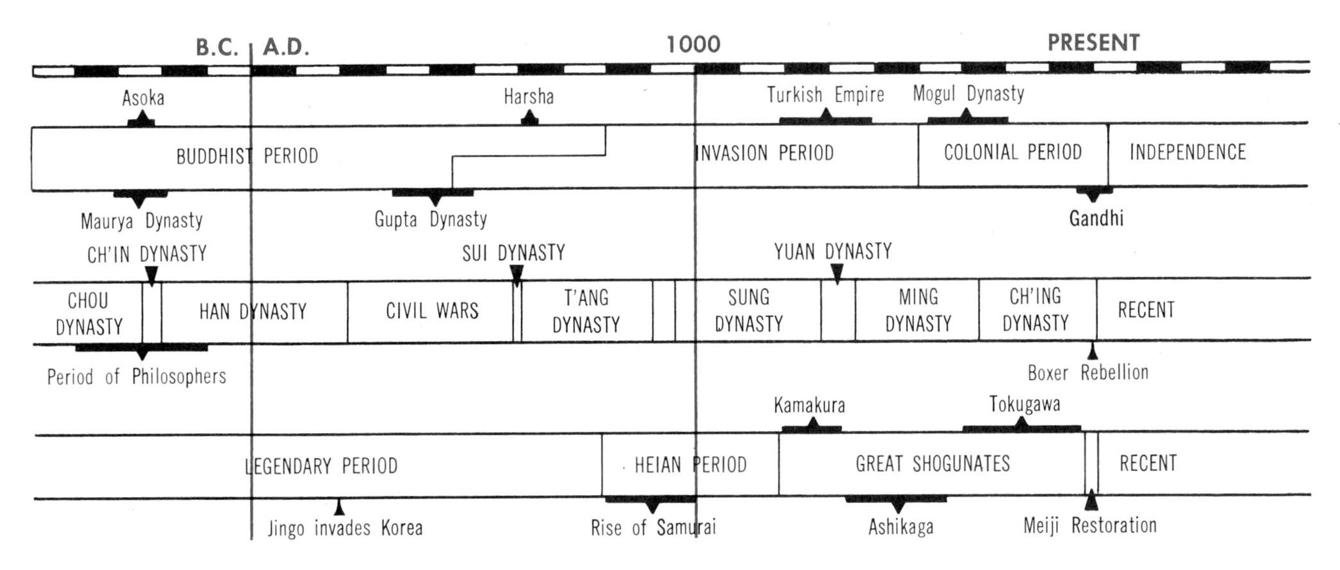


A.D.

| | |
|---|---|
| 589-618 | Sui dynasty |
| 618-907 | T'ang dynasty (China's cultural and political peak) |
| 960-1279 | Sung dynasty |
| 1279-1368 | Yüan dynasty (Kublai Khan overthrows Sungs) |
| 1368-1644 | Ming dynasty (Mongols overthrown) |
| 1644-1912 | Ch'ing dynasty |
| 1866-1925 | Sun Yat-sen |
| 1900 | Boxer Rebellion |
| 1912 | China becomes republic |
| 1927 | Nationalist government established |
| 1949 | Communists take control of Chinese mainland; Nationalist capital at Taipei, Formosa |

JAPAN

A.D.

| | |
|---|---|
| c. 200 | Empress Jingo invades Korea |
| 300s | Yamato clan is ruling group in Japan |
| 500s | Japanese know of China and Buddhism |
| 600s | Japanese begin diplomatic relationship with China; Buddhism entrenched in Japan; Fujiwara family begin rule from behind throne |
| 795-1185 | Heian Period |
| c. 800-1100 | Samurai warrior class emerges |
| 1192-1333 | Kamakura shogunate |
| 1338-1568 | Ashikaga shogunate; Muromachi Period |
| 1500s | Civil wars |
| 1603-1867 | Tokugawa shogunate |
| 1853-1854 | Commodore Matthew Perry arrives in Tokyo Bay; Japan forced to open ports to world |
| 1868 | Meiji Restoration begins |
| 1904-1905 | Japan defeats Russia in war |
| 1910 | Korea incorporated into Japanese empire |
| 1941 | Japanese bomb Pearl Harbor |
| 1945 | Unconditional surrender of Japan; U.S. begins occupation of Japan |

now, but the villagers still wanted to continue undisturbed in their customary ways. The new leaders wanted to make their nations strong. This required modern education for all the youth, development of industry, changes in the economic and social life of the people, and other reforms which sometimes struck at the foundations of the traditional life of the people. The new native rulers found it easier to work with the people of the cities than with the villagers, but they found it difficult among both groups. Life continues to be complex for both the Asian rulers and those they rule. In politics, as in every aspect of his life today, the Asian lives embraced by his traditions as well as the grasping arms of the present.

As the Asian looks outward to see what there is elsewhere to learn and adopt, he sometimes does not understand what he sees. Like all men, he often interprets what he sees according to his own desires. Emotions enter into thought and sometimes become barriers to knowledge. But through intelligent perception, the Asian has often seen and learned much that is good and useful from others.

The Asian is interconnected with all of mankind, and this bond cannot be severed without damaging his own humanity and his own happiness. He would like to be friendly with everybody, but experience has taught him to be wary and suspicious, for the friend of today may be the enemy of tomorrow. Yet it is impossible to live in isolation from others. The Second World War brought soldiers from all the world to Asia. The Korean War, though confined to the physical boundaries of Korea, affected the lives of many people throughout Asia and in the rest of the world. In South Vietnam, on the remote border between India and Communist China, on the small islands between Formosa and mainland China, and within many other Asian countries, blood is being shed by Asian and foreigner alike. All men are caught up in a world web of relations which ties peoples and nations together, and the Asian is a part of that web.

Asia has been a homeland for many peoples, all bound to it by centuries of blood, knowledge, understanding, and love. But all of the peoples of Asia are not bound together by friendship, nor are all who live outside of Asia enemies. In recent years, particularly, the greatest danger has come from within. Once the Asian rallied to the cry "Asia for the Asians," and this cry still touches the wellsprings of his being. But he has sadly learned that this slogan too often means "Asia for one or a few Asians, not all." The Asian still distrusts the intentions of some non-Asians, for he has not forgotten his colonial days; but he is being forced today to look beyond as well as within his own part of the world for friends and allies. The Pakistanis, the Thais, the South Koreans, the South Vietnamese, the Nationalist Chinese, the Japanese, the Filipinos, and the Malayans have allied themselves with Americans and other Westerners to better secure the integrity of their lands. The Communist North Koreans, North Vietnamese, and the Communist Chinese have allied themselves to the Communist bloc of nations headed by Russia. There are other Asians, too, who have not yet aligned themselves with either the Communists or the Free World. But they are finding it increasingly difficult to secure their territories against the advances of the more aggressive Asians, especially the Communists.

The Asian is proud of his heritage and his Asian name. He is proud to be a member of the Asian family of man. But he is becoming more conscious of the importance of his membership in a much larger family—the family of man.

## SUMMING UP THE CHAPTER

A. Identify the following and tell why they are important.

| | |
|---|---|
| Ashikaga shogunate | Jawaharlal Nehru |
| Ayub Khan | Kamakura shogunate |
| Chiang Kai-shek | Kuomintang |
| Commodore Perry | Magellan |
| Congress party | Mahatma Gandhi |
| East India Company | Manchu dynasty |
| Fujiwara | Mao Tse-tung |
| General MacArthur | Meiji Restoration |
| Goa | Mogul Empire |
| Islam | |

| | |
|---|---|
| Mohammed Ali Jinnah | Sun Yat-sen |
| | Tilak |
| Mohammed Iqbal | Vasco da Gama |
| Sayyid Ahmad Khan | Yüan Shih-k'ai |

B. Define or explain the following terms and explain their significance.

| | |
|---|---|
| Bushido | panchayat |
| civil disobedience | Satyagraha |
| nationalism | sovereignty |
| nonviolence | spheres of influence |
| open-door | Zaibatsu |

C. Identify the following dates and indicate their importance.

1. 1858 (India)
2. 1869-1948 (India)
3. 1948 (India)
4. 1949 (China)
5. 1192-1333 (Japan)
6. 1338-1568 (Japan)
7. 1603-1867 (Japan)
8. 1853-1854 (Japan)
9. December 7, 1941 (Japan)
10. August 14, 1945 (Japan)

D. Chapter review questions.

1. What enabled a certain degree of democratic self-government to exist at the local or village level in Asia? How important generally are such extra-legal political institutions? Are they equally important in the West?
2. Trace the history of Moslem influence in India from its beginnings in the eighth century to the partition of Pakistan in 1948. How successful has this partition been? What problems has it created for both Pakistan and India?
3. Why did Dr. Sun feel that the Chinese must go through a transitional period of tutelage before they would be ready for a truly republican form of government? Has Nationalist China completed this transition period yet?
4. What is meant when it is said that the emperor reigned, but he rarely ruled? Why would others who actually ruled want or need to keep the emperor as a figurehead?
5. How did Japanese feudalism operate from the twelfth to the twentieth century?
6. Modern Japanese thought and history have been strongly influenced by almost three hundred years of isolation from the rest of the world imposed by the Tokugawa shogunate. What effect did this isolation have on Japanese political, social, and economic life? What was the Tokugawa objective in sealing off Japan from outside influences?
7. How did the opening of Japan in 1853-54 by Commodore Perry lead to the collapse of the Tokugawa shogunate? What does this tell you about the wisdom of the Tokugawa isolation policy?
8. How did the *samurai* and the *Zaibatsu* join with the professional bureaucracy to rule Meiji Japan? What were their goals in bringing universal education to Japan?

E. Questions for discussion.

1. Why do you suppose Asians have historically tended to view government and politics in terms of ruler and ruled? Does this give a partial explanation of why Asian political revolts generally resulted only in a change in rulers and not a change in the political system?
2. How did the Allied occupation of Japan attempt to divorce the Japanese government from its religious props? How successful was this reform? What elements in Japanese history made this difficult? How did the psychological reaction of the Japanese to their defeat serve to make this easier?

F. Projects for groups or individuals.

1. Trace on a map the travels of several of the great explorers who came to Asia from other parts of the world.
2. Asian engineering projects include some of the greatest in world history, including the Great Wall and the irrigation and flood control projects of China. Read these projects and prepare a report detailing political reasons for their undertaking, means of financing, recruitment and control of labor, and political effects.
3. Prepare a report comparing village government in Asia with village and local government in the West.
4. Read a biography of one of the great ancient or modern Asian political leaders. Compare his life, character, and rule with that of a great Western statesman.
5. Read one or more of the many biographies of Gandhi. Prepare a report analyzing the lasting contributions he made to political and social thought, Western as well as Asian.
6. Discuss in class the Tokugawa policy of isolating the Japanese from the rest of the world. Compare this policy with that of Soviet Russia as symbolized by the Iron Curtain.
7. Prepare a report on the Russo-Japanese War of 1904-1905. Explain how this war whetted the appetite of Japanese leaders for a "Greater Japanese Co-Prosperity Sphere" and encouraged the territorial expansion which led to World War II.

# SUMMING UP THE UNIT

### *Drawing together the main themes*

1. What did prehistoric man contribute to civilization before history began?
2. Give examples of how geography, in the broad sense of the word, can influence the political, economic, social, and cultural development of a nation. In your answer refer to India, China, and Japan. You might also want to do some outside reading on Indonesia and Pakistan, two of the most striking illustrations of this phenomenon in Asia.
3. Man in all ages, past and present, has been concerned with certain basic needs. Identify these needs and describe some of the alternative methods man has devised in meeting these needs. Do these alternative methods suggest anything about the level of development of the society, its resources, or wealth?
4. What advantages and disadvantages can you see in the Asians' general acceptance of authoritarian government? In your answer discuss the type of social arrangement required to support authoritarian governments and the importance of the various levels of government.
5. What factors are most important in regulating the behavior of individuals in Asia? Describe in detail.
6. Perhaps the central feature of Asian politics through the centuries has been the existence of figurehead governments, with those behind the scenes "pulling the strings." Is this phenomenon uniquely Asian? What factors might account for the institution of "shadow governments"? Give at least five examples of such governments in Asia, past and present.
7. What geographical, historical, religious, social, economic, and psychological features illustrate the basic unity of Asia?
8. What factors encouraged and discouraged the flourishing of the arts in Asia? During what period or periods in India, China, and Japan were the most significant contributions to the arts made?
9. Historians have learned a great deal about the character and history of nations by studying their art and writing. In what ways can a nation's art and writing be revealing to a historian?
10. How has religion contributed to the form and the content of the arts?
11. How can tradition be both a weakness and a strength?
12. Explain the meaning of this quotation as it applies to Asia: "The past is not dead." Can you think of any other quotations that illustrate the same point?
13. One of the most important features of the religions of Asia is their accommodating nature. How does this explain the spread of the great religions, Hinduism, Buddhism, and Confucianism? How does this also explain the continuing role of the folk-based religions, such as Shinto?
14. Many nations have passed through or are passing through stages of planned political tutelage, preparing them for the day when they will govern themselves. Describe how this has taken place in Japan, India, China, and Indonesia. How successful has it been?
15. Evaluate Western influence in Asia.

### *Unit projects for groups or individuals*

1. Find out as much as you can about your own ancestry.
2. Prepare for classroom presentation a report on Confucianism, Taoism, or Legalism.
3. Look up the archeological findings made in the Anyang caves of Honan Province of China. On the basis of these findings, how does early Chinese civilization compare with early Indian civilizations?
4. Find photographs and illustrations of ancient Chinese ideographs. Compare these with modern Chinese ideographs. What relationship can you see between them?
5. Locate on a map the countries mentioned in this unit.
6. Read the *Mahabharata* or the *Ramayana* (or parts of either). Prepare reports telling when and how they were composed and read sections aloud to your class.
7. Point out the historical events behind current news stories about Asia.
8. Prepare a report on the Great Wall of China. Include in your report a discussion of its physical size as well as the history of its building. Why is it considered one of the two or three greatest architectural accomplishments of mankind? (Possible source of information: *The Tiger of Ch'in* by Leonard Cottrell.)
9. Get a book on Japanese pen drawing. See if you can imitate the style.
10. Pretend you are a reporter for a weekly news magazine assigned to write a feature story on the man of the year. Pick out a great Asian leader, past or present, and write an account of his life and his contributions to Asia in particular and the world in general.

11. Music and dance are two forms of art which have given great pleasure to many people. Prepare a report on Asian forms of music and dance. If you are so inclined, see if you can perform some Asian music or dances.
12. Prepare a dramatic reading for your class of one of the Japanese folk tales. After the reading, conduct a class discussion to see if the class learned anything about Japan's history or heritage.
13. Read the plots of several *Kabuki* dramas, such as the "Forty-seven Ronin." Analyze them in terms of the ideals that emerge.

## FURTHER READINGS

*ASIA: GENERAL*


ANDERSON, GEORGE L., ed., *Masterpieces of the Orient.* Norton, 1961, paperback. Translations of Asian literature.

Asia Society, *An Introductory Reading Guide to Asia.* 1962. An excellent introductory list of books for the general reader interested in Asia. Annotated.

Association for Asian Studies, *Bibliography of Asian Studies.* Annual. Exhaustive list of books and articles on Asia that appear during the year.

BUSS, CLAUDE A., *Arc of Crisis.* Doubleday, 1961. A perceptive look at the crises exploding and fermenting in Asia.

CEADEL, ERIC B., ed., *Literatures of the East: An Appreciation.* John Murray, 1953. An introduction to the literature of Asia.

GINSBURG, NORTON, ed., *The Pattern of Asia.* Prentice-Hall, 1958. Good maps and good commentaries make a good geography.

MURPHEY, RHODES, *An Introduction to Geography.* Rand McNally, 1961. Good coverage of Asian lands and peoples.

SMITH, HUSTON, *The Religions of Man.* Harper, 1958; Mentor, paperback. Contains clear and concise descriptions of Asian religions.

WELTY, THOMAS, *The Asians: Their Heritage and Their Destiny.* Lippincott, 1963. A basic introduction to the Asians. Covers many aspects of their life. Written especially for beginning students in Asian studies.

YOHANNAN, JOHN D., *A Treasury of Asian Literature.* John Day, 1956; Mentor, paperback. Selections of Asian literature.


*SOUTH ASIA: (AFGHANISTAN, CEYLON, INDIA, PAKISTAN)*


ABBAS, ZAINAB GHULAM, *Folk Tales of Pakistan.* Pakistan Publications, 1957. Everybody will like them. Well illustrated.

BASHAM, ARTHUR, *The Wonder That Was India,* rev. ed. Hawthorn; Grove, 1959, paperback. A magnificent account of traditional India before the arrival of the Moslems.

BOLITHO, HECTOR, *Jinnah: Creator of Pakistan.* Macmillan, 1955. A good biography of the "Father of Pakistan."

BROWN, D. MACKENZIE, *The White Umbrella: Indian Political Thought from Manu to Gandhi.* U. of Calif., 1953, paperback. Excellent presentation of Indian political thought.

CLIFFORD, MARY LOUISE, *The Land and People of Afghanistan.* Lippincott, 1962.

DUBE, SHYAMA C., *Indian Village.* Cornell U., 1955; Humanities. An introduction to the village life of India.

EMERSON, GERTRUDE, *Voiceless India,* rev. ed. John Day, 1944. Well-written and sympathetic portrayal of rural and social life in a part of India.

FISCHER, LOUIS, *The Life of Mahatma Gandhi.* Harper, 1950; Collier, paperback. An understanding and revealing biography of a great man.

GARGI, BALWANT, *Theatre in India.* Theatre Arts Books, 1962. Covers old and modern theatre in India.

GATES, KATHERINE, ed. and trans., *Ramabai Ranade, Himself: The Autobiography of a Hindu Lady.* Longmans, 1938. An insight into the attitudes of an Indian lady.

GOETZ, HERMANN, *India: 5,000 Years of Indian Art.* McGraw, 1959. The story of Indian art with illustrations.

IQBAL, MUHAMMAD, *Poems,* trans. by V. G. Kiernan. Paragon, 1955. Excellent translation of poems the Pakistanis consider among their greatest.

MODAK, MANORAMA, *The Land and People of India,* rev. ed. Lippincott, 1960.

MORGAN, KENNETH W., *The Religion of the Hindus.* Ronald, 1953. A good introduction to the beliefs of the Indians.

NEHRU, JAWAHARLAL, *The Discovery of India,* ed. by Robert Crane. Peter Smith, 1960; Doubleday, paperback. Basic work by India's great modern leader.

PICKTHALL, MOHAMMAD M., ed., *The Meaning of the Glorious Koran.* Mentor, 1954, paperback. Good and inexpensive translation of the Koran with an introduction.

TRESIDDER, ARGUS J., *Ceylon.* Van Nostrand, 1960, paperback. Good for the general reader.

WILBER, DONALD N., ed., *Afghanistan: Its People, Its Society, Its Culture.* Taplinger, 1962. General survey of Afghanistan.

———, *The Land and People of Ceylon.* Lippincott, 1963.


*EAST ASIA: (CHINA, KOREA, JAPAN)*


BARNETT, A. DOAK, *Communist China and Asia: A Challenge to American Policy.* Harper, 1960; Vintage, paperback. A detailed account of Communist China's foreign policy with emphasis upon its activities in neighboring Asian countries.

BORTON, HUGH, ed., *Japan between East and West.* Harper, 1957. Good introduction to the country.

BUCK, PEARL, *The Good Earth.* Day, 1931; Pocket Books, paperback. A classic novel which reveals the traditional life of the Chinese peasant.

CHIA, CH'U AND WINBERG CHAI, *The Changing Society of China.* Mentor, 1962, paperback. A good and inexpensive introduction to China.

CHIANG K'AI-SHEK, *China's Destiny,* trans. by Wang Chung-hui. Macmillan, 1947. The thought of the present leader of Nationalist China who now rules Formosa.

CREEL, HERRLEE G., *Chinese Thought from Confucius to Mao Tse-tung.* U. of Chicago, 1953. A good survey of Chinese thought from ancient days to the present.

CRESSEY, GEORGE B., *Land of the Five Hundred Million: A Geography of China.* McGraw-Hill, 1955. A standard geography of China by a well-known author.

FAIRBANK, JOHN K., *The United States and China,* rev. ed. Harvard U., 1958; Viking, paperback. Another key book by an influential author.

GOODRICH, LUTHER C., *A Short History of the Chinese People,* 3rd rev. ed. Harper, 1959; also paperback. Condensed, clear, and worthwhile introduction to China.

HEARN, LAFCADIO, *The Selected Writings of Lafcadio Hearn,* ed. by Henry Goodman. Citadel, 1949. He loved the Japanese and wrote about them sympathetically.

HUNG, WILLIAM, *Tu Fu: China's Greatest Poet.* Harvard U., 1952. He was a great poet who commented upon the social problems of China.

KANG, YOUNGHILL, *The Grass Roof.* Scribner's, 1931. An autobiography which shows, among other things, the traditional life of a Korean child.

KEENE, DONALD, ed., *Anthology of Japanese Literature: Earliest Era to Mid-Nineteenth Century.* Grove, 1956.

———, *Modern Japanese Literature: An Anthology from 1868 to the Present Day.* Grove, 1956; also paperback. Together these books provide the reader with a rewarding look at the literature of Japan from olden days until the present.

KIM SO-UN, *The Story Bag: A Collection of Korean Folk Tales,* trans. by Setsu Higashi. Tuttle, 1955. The students will like these tales and the illustrations.

KYUNG CHO CHUNG, *Korea Tomorrow.* Macmillan, 1956. A survey of Korea for the general reader.

LINEBARGER, PAUL and others, *Far Eastern Governments and Politics: China and Japan,* 2nd ed. Van Nostrand, 1956. A solid book on the governments of China and Japan.

MEARS, HELEN, *Year of the Wild Boar.* Lippincott, 1942. Gives revealing glimpses of the Japanese woman and family.

SANSOM, GEORGE B., *Japan: A Short Cultural History,* rev. ed. Appleton, 1962. A classic introduction to Japan's history.

SEIDENSTICKER, EDWARD, and the editors of LIFE, *Japan.* Time, Inc., 1961. Well-written and beautifully illustrated.

SPENCER, CORNELIA, *The Land of the Chinese People,* rev. Lippincott, 1960.

SUN YAT-SEN, *The Three Principles of the People,* trans. by Frank Price. Stechert, 1927. The thought of the "Father of the Republic of China."

TSAO HSUEH-CHIN, *Dream of the Red Chamber,* trans. by Chi-chen Wang. Twayne, 1958; Doubleday, paperback. Regarded as the finest novel produced by the Chinese. Gives insight into the traditional social life of old China.

VAUGHN, JOSEPHINE BUDD, *The Land and People of Japan,* rev. Lippincott, 1962.

WALEY, ARTHUR, *Translations from the Chinese.* Knopf, 1955. The author captures the spirit as well as the meaning of Chinese poetry.

WU CHENG-EN, *Monkey,* trans. by Arthur Waley. Grove, 1958. Both teachers and students will enjoy this Chinese gem of literature.

*SOUTHEAST ASIA: (BURMA, CAMBODIA, LAOS, VIETNAM, MALAYSIA, THAILAND, INDONESIA, PHILIPPINES, AUSTRALIA, NEW ZEALAND)*

BAUM, VICKI, *Tale of Bali,* trans. by Basil Creighton. Sun Dial, 1939. Interesting novel that gives the reader a feeling for the life of the Balinese.

BENITEZ, CONRADO, *History of the Philippines,* rev. ed. Ginn, 1954. Good general history.

BLUNDEN, GODFREY, *The Land and People of Australia,* rev. Lippincott, 1963.

BUSCH, NOEL, *Thailand.* Van Nostrand, 1959; also paperback. A simply written introduction.

BUTTINGER, JOSEPH, *The Smaller Dragon.* Praeger, 1958. Detailed history of Vietnam from earliest times to the present.

BUTWELL, RICHARD, *Southeast Asia Today and Tomorrow.* Praeger, 1961; also paperback. National and international problems facing Southeast Asians.

CADY, JOHN F., *A History of Modern Burma.* Cornell U., 1958. One of the best histories of modern Burma.

CHAMPASSAK, SISOUK, *Storm Over Laos; A Contemporary History.* Praeger, 1961. Good account of Laos, especially since World War II. Illustrated.

DOBBY, ERNEST H. G., *Southeast Asia,* 7th ed. U. of London, 1960. Excellent geography of Southeast Asia.

DUBOIS, CORA, *Social Forces in Southeast Asia.* Harvard U., 1959. Teachers will get an understanding of social life and social change in Southeast Asia from this work.

FALL, BERNARD B., *Street Without Joy,* rev. ed. Stackpole, 1963. Fighting in Vietnam since the end of World War II.

FIFIELD, RUSSELL H., *The Diplomacy of Southeast Asia, 1945-1958.* Harper, 1958. Good study of the foreign policies of Southeast Asian countries since the end of World War II.

FISHEL, WESLEY R., ed., *Problems of Freedom: Vietnam.* Free Press, 1961. Studies on present-day problems in Vietnam.

GROSLIER, BERNARD AND JACQUES ARTHAUD, *The Arts*

The Chinese have long been famed for their glazed pottery. The horse, left, is from the period of the T'ang dynasty. The incense burner, above, is from the period of the Sung dynasty. (Courtesy, The Cleveland Museum of Art)

*and Civilization of Angkor,* trans. from French by Eric E. Smith. Praeger, 1957. Wonderful pictures of an old and magnificent civilization.

HALL, DONALD G. E., *A History of South-East Asia.* St. Martin's, 1955. A good general history of the entire region.

KAULA, EDNA MASON, *The Land and People of New Zealand.* Lippincott, 1964.

LE BAR, FRANK M., ed., *Laos.* Taplinger, 1960. Solid work. Good reference book.

PEARSON, HAROLD F., *A History of Singapore.* U. of London, 1956. Quick and useful look at Singapore.

PENDLETON, ROBERT L., and others, *Thailand.* Meredith, 1962. Especially good on Thailand today.

RAVENHOLT, ALBERT, *The Philippines: A Young Republic on the Move.* Van Nostrand, 1962. Covers with fine style the whole life of the Filipinos.

RIZAL, JOSE, *The Lost Eden (Noli Me Tangere),* trans. by Leon M. Guerrero. Indiana U., 1961. A classic novel by one of the great heroes of the Philippines.

SMITH, DATUS C., JR., *The Land and People of Indonesia.* Lippincott, 1961.

VAUGHN, JOSEPHINE BUDD, *The Land and People of the Philippines,* rev. ed. Lippincott, 1962.

VLEKKE, BERNARD H. M., *Nusantara: A History of Indonesia,* rev. ed. Quadrangle, 1960. An excellent history of Indonesia.

WINSTEDT, R. O., *The Malays,* 5th ed. Routledge, 1958. A concise and solid account of the people of Malaya.

WOODMAN, DOROTHY, *The Making of Burma.* Dufour, 1962. Excellent account of the Burmese.

———, *The Republic of Indonesia.* Dufour, 1954. A good work on this country.

# UNIT II

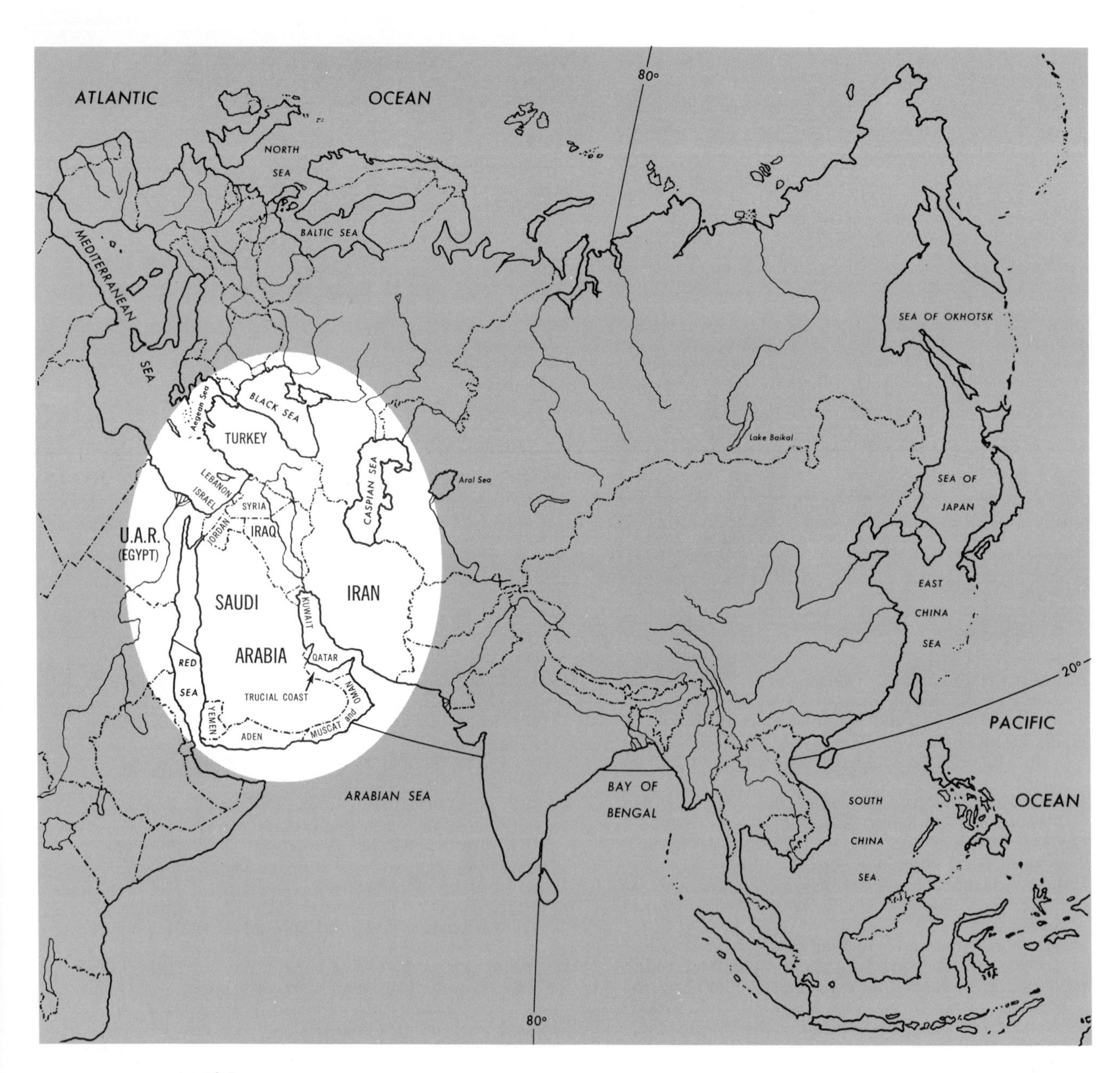

ATLANTIC
OCEAN
NORTH
SEA
BALTIC SEA
MEDITERRANEAN
SEA
Aegean Sea
BLACK SEA
TURKEY
LEBANON
ISRAEL
SYRIA
JORDAN
IRAQ
CASPIAN SEA
Aral Sea
U.A.R.
(EGYPT)
SAUDI
ARABIA
IRAN
KUWAIT
QATAR
RED
SEA
TRUCIAL COAST
OMAN
MUSCAT and
YEMEN
ADEN
ARABIAN SEA
BAY OF
BENGAL
Lake Baikal
SEA OF OKHOTSK
SEA OF
JAPAN
EAST
CHINA
SEA
PACIFIC
OCEAN
SOUTH
CHINA
SEA
80°
20°

# THE PEOPLE OF THE MIDDLE EAST MOLDED MAN

These maps show the modern nations of the Middle East and their location on the Eurasian continent. The Middle East, since ancient times, has formed a bridge between Europe, Asia, and Africa.

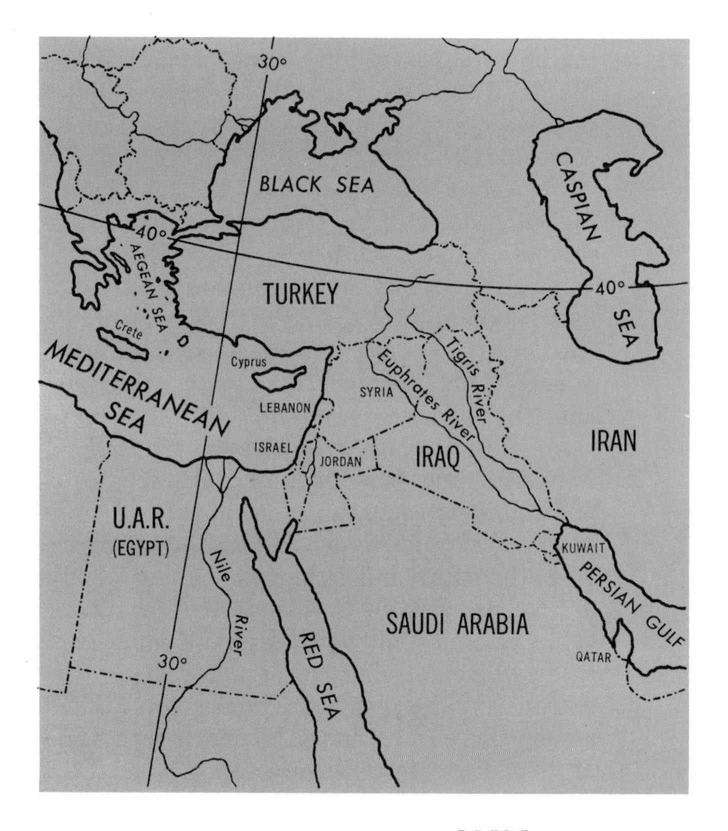

CHAPTER **8**

# *Ancient Civilizations Along the Rivers*

MAN HAS LIVED in the Middle East since very ancient days. He has been tilling its river-watered earth and moving across its dry, hot deserts for years beyond knowledge. Some believe that the first man lived here. We do not know for certain whether or not this land was the birthplace of man. But as we uncover more and more ancient traces of man from the dirt and the sand of the centuries, it does appear that he started to build his civilizations here before he did elsewhere in the world. And the time when man first started to build cities and keep records in writing was farther removed than we are from the birth of Christ by more than a thousand years. The searching and frequently lofty mind of man in the Middle East has, from those ancient times until now, given character and broad vision to all mankind.

It was in the Middle East that the teachings of Judaism, Christianity, and Islam were first proclaimed. And today these three religions give meaning and purpose to the lives of over a billion people. The man of the Middle East invented ways of writing, and we have inherited his alphabet. He charted the stars and the planets, beginning our science of astronomy. He gave us a calendar. He studied, practiced, and experimented with medicine, and countless generations have benefited from his medical lore. He delved into the mysteries of mathematics and fashioned the early foundations of this field which other men later extended and built upon. He built edifices of stone which yet stagger the imagination. His works in gold, silver, and bronze are ranked among the world's finest. He reached to some of man's greatest heights, and from these heights he has been an inspiration, a beacon-light, and a hope for long centuries of man everywhere.

But the people of the Middle East were also subject to the failings of man. There were those who sought power and wealth through war, and the history of these lands is filled with marching armies, the din of battle, the broken walls of cities, and the endless lines of captive peoples trudging into exile and to the slave markets of the conquerors. No one was ever really secure. Whether farmer, desert wanderer, merchant, or king, he had always to be on guard lest others take his life, or goods, or both. Life could be harsh in this land, and constant vigilance was the price of security.

There were four ancient families of man who shaped the times and the environment of the Middle East: the Sumerians, the Semites, the Egyptians, and the Indo-Europeans. The division into these families is based chiefly upon the important languages spoken by these ancient peoples and not upon race. Within the Semite family of man were the Akkadians, Amorites, Chaldeans, Assyrians, Phoenicians, Arameans, Arabs, Hebrews, and others. The Indo-European family included the Hittites, Mitanni, Persians, Greeks, Romans, and others. As the story of man in this region moves along, each of these branches of the Semite and Indo-European families will become better known.

## The Sumerians

The Sumerians came to the land between the Tigris and Euphrates rivers as long ago as 4000 or 5000 B.C., perhaps from somewhere in the lands that make up modern Turkey and Iran, and the land that they settled between the rivers was called Sumer—whence the name Sumerian. The land of Sumer lay near the head of the Persian Gulf between the Tigris and Euphrates rivers. These rivers rise northwest of Sumer in the highlands of Anatolia (in modern Turkey) and Armenia. They flow in a southeasterly direction into the Persian Gulf. The rivers often flooded, and when they receded they left rich dirt on the lands that bordered them. Most of their rich cargo of soil was left on the land near where they entered the Persian Gulf. This earth became the most fertile of all the land between the rivers. The Greeks later named the whole area embraced by the rivers Mesopotamia, which means "the land between the rivers."

On this land the Sumerians began to grow barley, wheat, dates, and other vegetables and grains. They learned to control the rivers by building dikes to contain flood waters. These waters were used to irrigate fields of grain. The Sumerians bred cattle, tended herds of sheep and goats, and started a dairy industry. They used oxen to pull plows and oxen or donkeys to pull carts and chariots. The first known use of the wheel was in this land. These early wheels were made of wood, with leather or copper tires. Agriculture and cattle were the foundations of Sumerian wealth.

The Sumerians began to build cities and to protect them with walls of mud brick. Their

**Ancient Middle Eastern Centers of Civilization**

The earliest known civilizations in the Middle East developed beside rivers and in similar locations where agriculture could support the growth of towns and cities. We have some records but few remains of nomadic herders such as the ancient Hebrews.

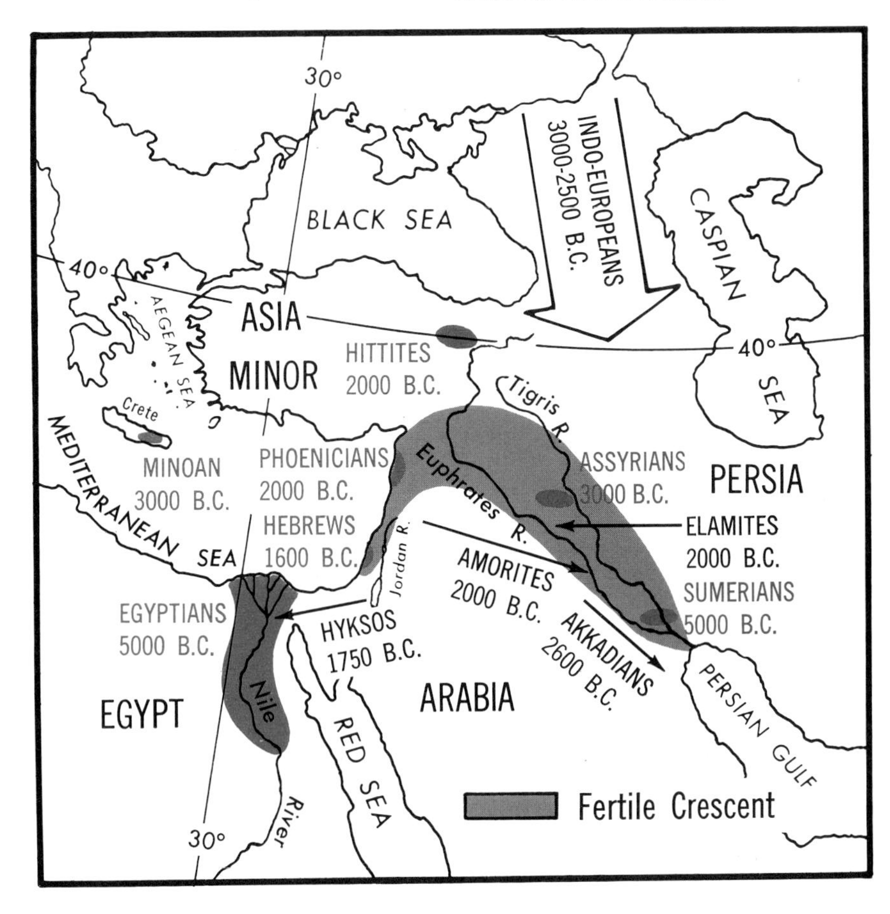

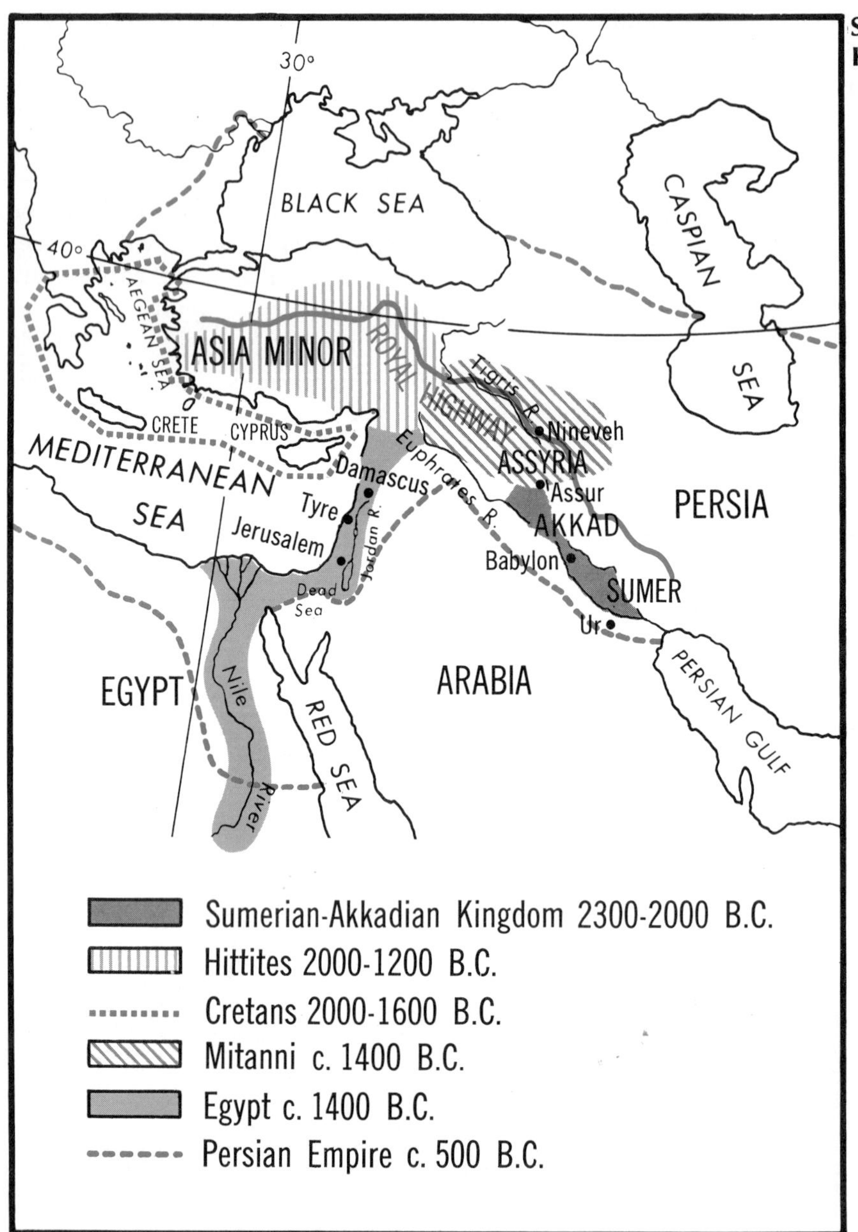


**Some Early Middle Eastern Kingdoms (2300–500 B.C.)**

rulers lived within these cities, and they were both priests and kings at the same time. Much of the farmland around the cities was owned by the priest-king, but there were also free landholders who lived here and used slaves to till their farms. Each city needed the protection of a strong priest-king and his army, for there were other city-kingdoms whose marauding armies often raided farms, took prisoners, and besieged the city itself.

The city was the political, economic, spiritual, and cultural center of Sumerian life, and the heart of the city was the temple compound. From the temple, high-priest and king administered the city and the surrounding land. The temple was a business center, a storehouse for grains, and even served as a bank.

In the cities trade began to develop. Woolen cloth was woven from the wool of flocks; utensils of bronze and copper were fashioned for household use and for the needs of work and trade; and works of art were made of gold and silver. These and other goods were traded with the settled Semites who lived to the north in the land between the rivers and with the nomadic Semites of the Arabian and Syrian deserts to the west. Some of these products found their way to the eastern borders of the Mediterranean Sea and to the Egyptians, who lived far across the deserts to the west around the river Nile. It is likely that there was also trade with the Dravidians, who lived along the Indus River. This, of course, was long before the Aryans came to India around 2000 B.C.

We know many things about the life of the Sumerians because they wrote on clay tablets which outlasted the centuries. The tip of a reed or a sharpened stick was used to make wedge-shaped marks on a soft clay tablet, which was then put into an oven to be baked and hardened. Later, the Sumerians learned to sprinkle powder over the fresh writing and wrap the tablet in a clay envelope. The whole package was then sent to the oven for hardening. The powder prevented the envelope from sticking to the soft clay marks. When the letter reached its destination, the envelope was cracked off, and there was a baked clay letter ready to be read. This type of writing is called *cuneiform*, which means "wedge-shaped."

It is fortunate for our historical knowledge that the Sumerians wrote on such long-lasting materials, for thousands upon thousands of these clay tablets have been found in the rubble of fallen houses, temples, and palaces. From these writings we have learned much about life five thousand or more years ago.

For several thousand years the Sumerians farmed this land, dotted it with cities, traded with their neighbors, practiced their religions, warred with fellow Sumerians, and evolved a civilization. Through conquest and absorption by others, they gradually became an unidentifiable part of the mixture of man in the Middle East, but their civilization lived on. Sumerian culture and achievements were carried on by those who came later. The laws, religion, arts, and wedge-shaped system of writing of the Sumerians were borrowed, adapted, and further evolved in the thinking and practices of their conquerors.

1. What great contributions did the Sumerians make to civilization? Try to imagine what life might be like today without one or more of these accomplishments.
2. Describe the civilization of Sumer, paying particular attention to the location and importance of cities, and ways of earning a living.

### The Semites

The Semites were the second great family of man in the Middle East. They were nomads who roamed the Arabian and Syrian deserts of the Middle East long before the historical records of man. They led a hard life in a harsh land, for in the deserts there was little rain and little water, and there were few pastures where men and animals could settle and live. These nomads were constantly on the move in search of those few desert spots where men and animals could feed and drink. They were a tough and lean people, as fierce as the desert environment with which they struggled daily to survive. They recognized few laws, and there was only one law they truly respected—the law of self-preservation. Every man was on his own, and raiding others, or being raided, was an accepted part of life.

The Semites multiplied, and the deserts could not support their increased numbers. It was inevitable that they should make their way to the green pastures of the Euphrates and Tigris rivers and compete there with those who had come from the mountains and the steppes of the north and east for this rich abundance of water and earth. Some branches of this family—Akkadians, Amorites, Assyrians, and Chaldeans—left their wandering desert life to settle and dominate for centuries these river lands.

There were other groups of Semites who migrated northward and found a promising green strip of land about 350 miles long running along the eastern borders of the Mediterranean Sea. They were called Canaanites,

One of the oldest cities of Mesopotamia is Ur (modern Muqaiyir). This goat caught in a tree was found in the cemetery there. (Courtesy of the Trustees of the British Museum)

Phoenicians, Hebrews or Jews, and Syrians. All this green land which they settled and struggled for, the land bordering the Mediterranean Sea and the land between the Euphrates and Tigris rivers, is often referred to as the *Fertile Crescent*. When pictured on a map, it resembles the curved shape of a new moon.

The ancient Semitic-speaking peoples of the Middle East were mixed with others of their kind and with their conquerors, but the Semitic languages evolved and have survived in their later forms as Arabic, Hebrew, and several other languages. The great religions that developed from those of the ancient Semites have also survived, and the Moslem Arabs and the Jews continue to dominate much of the life of the region. Many of the peoples of the Middle East have migrated to northern and eastern Africa and to other parts of the world, and in their migrations they have contributed beyond measure to the developing civilization of man.

## Akkadians

A branch of the Semite family conquered the Sumerians during the period between 2600 and 2400 B.C., and with this conquest the decline and disappearance of the Sumerians as a people began. One of the chief leaders of the conquering Semites was King Sargon, who lived in Akkad, a city to the north of Sumer. His people were known as Akkadians.

King Sargon of Akkad was the first ruler to unite a great part of Mesopotamia into one kingdom. With his kingdom began a series of Semite-dominated empires and countries in the Middle East, some of which have lasted to the present day. Perhaps even before the conquest of Sumer, the dark-skinned, bearded Semites and the smooth-shaven, round-headed Sumerians had intermixed their blood and ways of life, but certainly King Sargon accelerated the process.

In the long process of intermixing, the culture of the Sumerians survived, but their identity as a people was eventually lost. The Semites spoke a language but they had never written it down. They borrowed the wedge-shaped Sumerian writing and adapted it to their own special language. The Semites had been wanderers before, but now they learned from the Sumerians to live in a settled manner, to build houses, temples, and palaces, and to sculpture and to carve in the Sumerian way. They did not merely copy, but added refinements of their own, and in many ways surpassed the works of their teachers. The Semites learned about trade, began to keep records, and adopted the Sumerian system of weights and measures.

The Akkadian Semites also learned to work in partnership with the Sumerians. About 2300 B.C. they cooperated in throwing off the Gutians, a barbarian tribe who had conquered them some years before. From this time until about 2000 B.C. the Sumerians and Akkadians lived together in peace in one united country. They were ruled at various times by either a Sumerian or a Semite king. The city of Ur was the brightest light of this mixed nation. It was from the city of Ur that Abraham, to whom the Jews trace their descent, went forth to wander toward Palestine on the Mediterranean.

This mixed nation of Sumer and Akkad came to an end around 2000 B.C. when it was overrun by the Amorites, another branch of the Semite family, who came from the northwest.

### Amorites

The Amorite Semites wandered out of the Syrian desert and occupied a small town on the Euphrates River called Babylon. From about 2000 B.C. to 1750 B.C. this city was the political, economic, and cultural center of that entire area. Babylon had such an overwhelming impact upon that region once ruled by the Sumerian and the Akkadian that the land came to be known from that time on as Babylonia.

The greatest and best known of the Amorite kings who ruled during this time was known as Hammurabi. He died around 1900 B.C. Hammurabi extended the boundaries of the Amorite empire, but he is best known as an able administrator and one of man's great lawmakers.

All the cities of this area had their own special laws, but these laws applied only to the people within the city and its immediate neighborhood. There were as many laws as there were cities, and sometimes these laws were contradictory. There was no one law for all the people of the Babylonian empire. Hammurabi found this situation illogical, inconvenient, and harmful to the unity of the kingdom. He remedied it. He had all the laws and usages of past and present collected. From among them, he selected those laws and precedents which he considered useful and just, added some laws of his own, and issued one unified law which, from then on, all must obey. He had these laws cut into shafts of stone and set up in Babylon and the other cities of his realm so that all might know them.

Hammurabi's laws covered many problems of the daily life of man. They dealt with false accusation, slavery, marriage, divorce, alimony, the welfare of children, robbery, looting, the protection of the property of soldiers away on military duties, agriculture, commerce, and the affairs of professional men. Many of these laws were based upon the principle of an eye for an eye, and a tooth for a tooth. For instance, if a nobleman knocked out the tooth of his equal, his tooth also should be knocked out; and if a house fell down and killed the owner, the builder of the house should also be put to death. Women were also safeguarded by these laws, and they were permitted to own property and engage in commerce. The laws of Hammurabi had their influence not only in his own time but long afterwards among the people of the Middle East. Some of his laws are to be found, worded somewhat differently, in the Old Testament of the Bible, indicating that the Hebrews had been influenced by Babylonian laws.

Amorite rule in Babylon did not long survive Hammurabi's death. The Amorites were

Helmets like this one have been found in the ruins of Ur. (University Museum, Philadelphia)

conquered about 1750 B.C. by the Kassites, a non-Semitic people from the mountains to the east, who ruled Babylon until they were conquered by the Elamites during the 1100's. The Elamites were in turn defeated by the Assyrians.

### Assyrians

The Semite was always a warrior, valiant, daring, and sometimes cruel; but for the Assyrian Semite the practice of war was a way of life instilled by circumstance and tradition. Around 3000 B.C. this branch of the Semites settled the highland of Assur, the place from which they took their name. This highland was located on the Tigris River about five hundred miles from its mouth. The Assyrians were always surrounded by those who sought to control them, and they had to fight desperately to survive.

To the northwest in Asia Minor, where Turkey lies today, there was a people called Hittites who spoke an Indo-European language. The Hittites were an extremely dangerous threat because they were the first to use weapons of iron. These weapons were far superior to the softer ones of copper and bronze used by the Assyrians and others in the Middle East. The Hittites were a great power in the northern part of the Middle East from around 2000 to 1200 B.C., and the Assyrians had frequently felt the hurt of their tough iron weapons.

To the west were the Mitanni, also an Indo-European people, who introduced the horse into this region. Their skill in using horses and chariots in war made them a considerable power in this area. To the south were other Semites and the Sumerians, who often came north to make war.

Over many centuries of battle experience with these powerful foes the Assyrian Semites improved their organization and ability to wage war. Around 1200 B.C., they began to expand their power in this region. From the Hittites they had learned to forge weapons and war equipment of iron. From the Mitanni they learned to employ the horse and chariot skillfully in battle. Their own inventive minds produced other techniques and equipment which advanced the science of war and added to its effectiveness and destructiveness. For instance, battering rams, armored towers on wheels, and other siege equipment to batter down the walls of cities were first used by the Assyrians. Most of the city walls of this region were made of sun-dried or baked brick, and such walls were little protection against the science and strength of the Assyrian war machines.

In the thirteenth century B.C. the Assyrians were greatly helped in their expansion by the constant rivalry between the Hittites and the Egyptians, the two greatest powers in the Middle East, who exhausted themselves in wars to control the lands of the Hebrews, the Phoenicians, and the Syrians, which lay between them. These wars drained the strength of the Hittites and the Egyptians and left the Assyrians relatively stronger than they. In the centuries that followed, the Assyrians gradually conquered all but a fraction of that civilized Middle Eastern world, and by the eighth and seventh centuries B.C. they reigned supreme there. The Assyrian was no longer a defender of his tiny land against powerful foes but a conqueror against whom others had to defend themselves. War had become a part of his life, and he could not stop his conquests until all the civilized world he knew was under his domination.

The Assyrians were stern and greedy rulers. They taxed heavily, and the wealth of all that region flowed into their cities in the form of camel-loads of gold and silver, countless flocks of sheep, goats, and cattle, and hundreds of thousands of men, women, and children who were brought as slaves to their cities. Again and again the people they had conquered rebelled, and each time the Assyrians became more and more cruel in crushing these revolts, thinking that they could prevent future rebellions by the severity of their punishment and revenge. Fear, however, was not enough to restrain the conquered people, and they continued to rebel. The Assyrians were forced to keep their armies in the field and in garrison posts. Their strength gradually began to fail and to drain away at home and abroad. Finally, in 612 B.C., the great capital of Nineveh on the Tigris River was breached and destroyed by a coalition of an Indo-European people called Medes, from the mountains to the north, and a branch of the Semite people called Chaldeans, from the deserts to the south.

### Chaldeans

The Chaldean Semites who had helped to conquer the Assyrians made Babylon the capital of their empire and rapidly became the greatest power in the Middle East. They ruled much of the region from 612 to 539 B.C. For a good part of this time, from 605 to 562 B.C., they were governed by the famous king Nebuchadnezzar. Nebuchadnezzar rebuilt Babylon from the rubble into which the Assyrians had smashed it. He transformed it into one of the greatest cities ever built on the ancient earth of the Middle East. It was Nebuchadnezzar who wrenched the Hebrews from their homeland and lodged them captive in Babylon after destroying their city of Jerusalem and their Temple.

The Chaldeans were fine astronomers and specialized in charting the course of the stars and the planets. They maintained accurate records of eclipses and other phenomena of the heavens for over 350 years. They invented the seven-day week, and divided the day into twelve hours of one hundred and twenty minutes each. They knew the length of the year to within less than one half hour, and they devised a lunar calendar. The Chaldeans believed in astrology and studied the heavens because they thought that the heavenly bodies and man's fate were intertwined. Their observations of the stars and planets were amazingly accurate and painstaking, and many men who came after them profited much from these patient recordings and conclusions about the heavenly bodies.

Chaldean power did not last long, for in 539 B.C. Cyrus the Persian, who will be discussed later, took the city of Babylon and its territories.

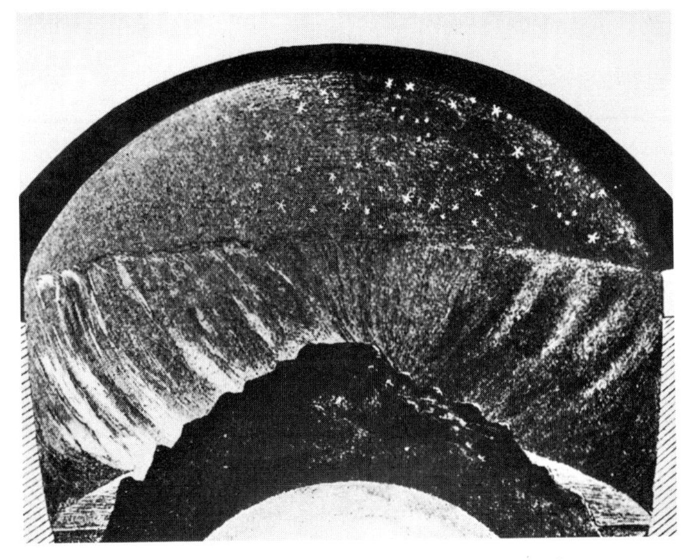

This drawing shows the Chaldean concept of the world. Ancient theories about the universe are an interesting part of the history of science. (Yerkes Observatory)

### Phoenicians

Today we remember the Phoenicians primarily as traders who spread far the fruits and knowledge of civilization, colonized the shores of the western Mediterranean and Africa, and transmitted to modern man the basic alphabet in use in most of the world today.

The Phoenicians lived on a narrow border of land between the Mediterranean Sea and the Lebanon Mountains. The modern country of Lebanon now occupies much of this old land, and the Lebanese sometimes refer to themselves as Phoenicians. Phoenician Semites probably came to this land before 2000 B.C. and reached the height of their greatness between the tenth and eighth centuries B.C. Their slow decline was quickened by the conquering armies of the Chaldean Semites and the Indo-European Persians. Although Phoenicians lived on to trade and to breed, they were but a remnant after Alexander the Great captured their city of Tyre around 332 B.C. But Phoenicia left memories of unusual achievements.

The Phoenician was an adventurous trader of the seas who went to distant and unknown coasts to buy copper, tin, and other raw materials and to sell the products of his skilled hands. The secrets of the sea and its coastal

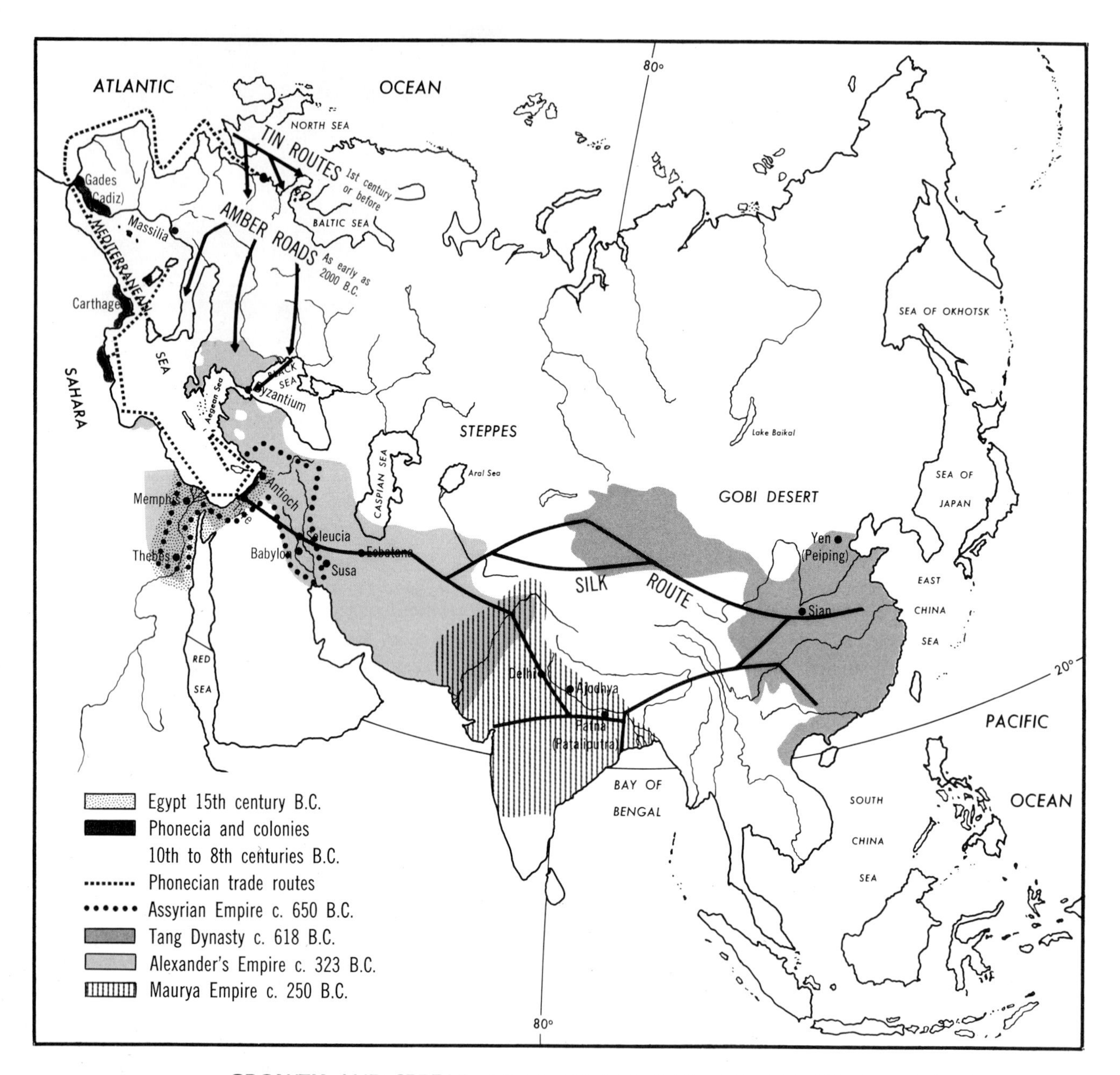


**GROWTH AND SPREAD OF MIDDLE EASTERN EMPIRES (1500—250 B.C.)**

As great empires and civilizations grew up in the Middle East, empires also grew in China and India. Although communications were poor, goods traveled over great distances through trade. Phoenician trade routes reached as far north as the Baltic Sea and may have extended down the eastern coast of Africa. As you read, keep in mind the indirect contacts between peoples through trade in ancient times.

markets became his monopoly. He mapped the northern coasts of Africa and built trading posts where the harbors were good and the trade profitable. Sometimes these trading posts grew into cities. There was the post at Carthage which grew into one of the mightiest cities in the western Mediterranean until it was ravaged and destroyed in wars with the

Romans lasting from 264 to 146 B.C. Pushed along by wind and oar, the Phoenician steered his ships past the Strait of Gibraltar into the Atlantic Ocean and became familiar with the people and the goods of West Africa, Spain, and perhaps the British Isles.

It was the skill of his hands and the imaginativeness of his mind which made trade rewarding to the Phoenician. He was a gifted carpenter who fashioned the beautiful cedars of Lebanon into strong ships and into pillars and furnishings for palace and temple. He helped to build King Solomon's temple in Jerusalem. He learned from the Egyptian the manufacture of glass, and his glass designs were frequently superior to those of his teacher. His woven woolen cloth was considered the

The ship model above shows the probable appearance of a Phoenician merchant ship of the thirteenth century B.C. (Commercial Museum, Philadelphia) Marseilles, a French port, was an important trading colony of the ancient world. Use reference books to learn about its history. (French Government Tourist Office)

best in the Middle East. He used the shellfish called *murex* to manufacture a purple dye with which he colored his woolen cloth. This purple cloth was sold at such fabulous prices that purple clothing became identified with royalty. The Phoenician took raw materials such as tin, copper, ivory, and silver, which his seafaring brothers had collected on far shores, and shaped them into useful and beautiful objects. The products of his art and skill were exported and traded for other needed products in all the trade marts of the known world.

The alphabet of consonants which the Egyptians had invented but rarely used was simplified by the Phoenicians and passed along to the Greeks and to other neighbors. The Greeks used some of these signs to represent vowels, and in this form the alphabet was picked up by the Romans and transmitted to man in Europe. Even the Greek *alpha* and *beta* corresponding to our "A" and "B", from which the word *alphabet* is derived, stem from the Phoenician *aleph* and *beth.*

Though their country was small and their numbers few, the Phoenicians contributed much to the advance and spread of knowledge and civilization among men. Trade can be a powerful force in moving man to improve his standards of work and living and to expand his horizons.

### Arameans

The Aramean Semites lived on a land to the east of Phoenicia, approximately where Syria is located today. In a sense they were the ancient ancestors of the modern Syrians. They had moved northward from the desert before 1500 B.C. and by 1200 B.C. had settled much of the land that is now Syria. They reached the peak of their culture and prosperity during the ninth and eighth centuries B.C. In 732 B.C. Aramean political power was destroyed and the people were scattered to many parts of the Middle East by the Assyrians. But before they died as a distinct people, the Arameans, like the Phoenicians, contributed to the passage of knowledge within and beyond the borders of their region through their trading activities.

The Arameans, too, were well-known and far-roving traders, but they traveled by land rather than by sea. Damascus was the most famous Aramean city, and its inhabitants today proudly declare it to be the oldest of the world's cities with an unbroken history. Ancient Damascus lay astride the main trade routes of the Middle East. The people of Damascus took advantage of this profitable geographic gift by channeling their energies into trade.

The Arameans traded in every variety of goods, and they traded everywhere. Their goods, their faces, and their language became familiar throughout the Middle East. They took the goods of the Phoenicians and carried them inland. They borrowed the alphabet of the Phoenician and adapted it to the special requirements of their own spoken language. In this form it was transmitted to their neighbors.

In the course of time the Aramaic language and alphabet became the common language of the people of the Fertile Crescent. The Assyrians used Aramean in addition to their own language. Under Persian rule it was the official language in which all could communicate with each other. Aramaic became the language of the Hebrews, and it was the language of Jesus and his disciples. The great contribution of the Arameans to man in the Middle East was their language and the alphabet which they had received from the Phoenicians. For centuries the Aramean language permitted an easy and rapid exchange of goods and ideas among the people of the Middle East and thus advanced the cause of knowledge.

The Semite did not cease making contributions to the spiritual and material advancement of man, as we shall see in the following chapters, which will describe the achievements of other branches of his family—the Hebrews, the Arabs, and others. But it is necessary now to interrupt the Semite's story to begin the tale of another famous family of man in the Middle East, the Egyptian.

1. Who was Hammurabi? What do you consider to be his greatest achievement, and why?
2. What skills of war did the Assyrian develop? Which of these skills or techniques were their own invention, and which did they learn from the Hittites and the Mitanni?
3. What did the Phoenicians contribute to the advance of knowledge and civilization?
4. Make a list, giving dates and nations of important rulers of the Fertile Crescent from 4000 B.C. to 538 B.C. mentioned in the section you have read of this chapter.

## The Egyptians

The third great family of men in the Middle East were the Egyptians. The modern Egyptian lives geographically in a part of the vast continent of Africa, but culturally and ethnically he is a part of that long-lived Middle Eastern man who contributed much to the civilizing of man. He is a mixture of the strains of many men—Arab, Turk, and others. His ancestor, the ancient Egyptian belonged predominantly to the Caucasian family of man. The ancient Egyptian language was perhaps related to the Semitic languages and is called a Hamitic language. The ancient Egyptians settled the lower reaches of the Nile River, near where it empties into the Mediterranean Sea, and began to build there one of man's greatest civilizations. Some of their achievements have rarely been equaled and never surpassed. And always Egyptian civilization was centered around the Nile.

It was the Nile River which sustained the Egyptian and made it possible for him to build his civilization. The river gave him life, and he knew it. Beyond the narrow green strips of land along the river there stretched an immense expanse of waterless desert. The Egyptian knew that but for the continuous nourishment of the Nile he would perish quickly or, at best, become a beggarly wanderer of the desert. The river was essential to his way of life and to his life itself.

The Nile is the longest river in the world, starting in central Africa and flowing for about 4,000 miles into the Mediterranean Sea. The last 600 miles of its journey to the sea extend through Egypt, and where it enters the sea it lays down a thick carpet of fertile earth which is shaped like the Greek letter delta (Δ). We generally refer to this placement of earth at the mouth of any river as a delta.

Every year the Nile flooded and poured the rich abundance of its water, which it had picked up and carried from the uplands of Africa, upon the shores of the desert bounding its banks. When its flooding waters returned within their normal banks, a deposit of rich, moist earth, brought down by the river from the uplands of Africa, awaited the hand of the Egyptian. This rich soil was sown with barley, wheat, and vegetables.

It was on the delta of the Nile that the Egyptian started his advance to greatness and to civilization around 5000 B.C. Here he built huts of mud and began community living. He began to build his canals and irrigation ditches here. He observed the movement of the sun and the change of seasons and created our first solar calendar of twelve months, with thirty days in each month, to which he added five extra days at the end of the year. This calendar was made around 4200 B.C., which was probably before the people of Mesopotamia and Asia had evolved their lunar calendars. The ancient Egyptians began to make useful and beautiful pottery and to make implements and ornaments of gold and copper. They started to weave cloth of linen, and few have equaled them in the art of making linen. They began to write with pictures, and they began a government.

These achievements and ways of life traveled from Lower Egypt, where the Egyptians lived, to Upper Egypt, where other people lived around the borders of their common river. With the slow movement of the centuries there gradually evolved among these peoples a common way of living and of looking at life. But politically they were apart; there was a Kingdom of Lower Egypt and a Kingdom of Upper Egypt.

Then around 3200 B.C. an Egyptian named Menes brought the kingdoms together

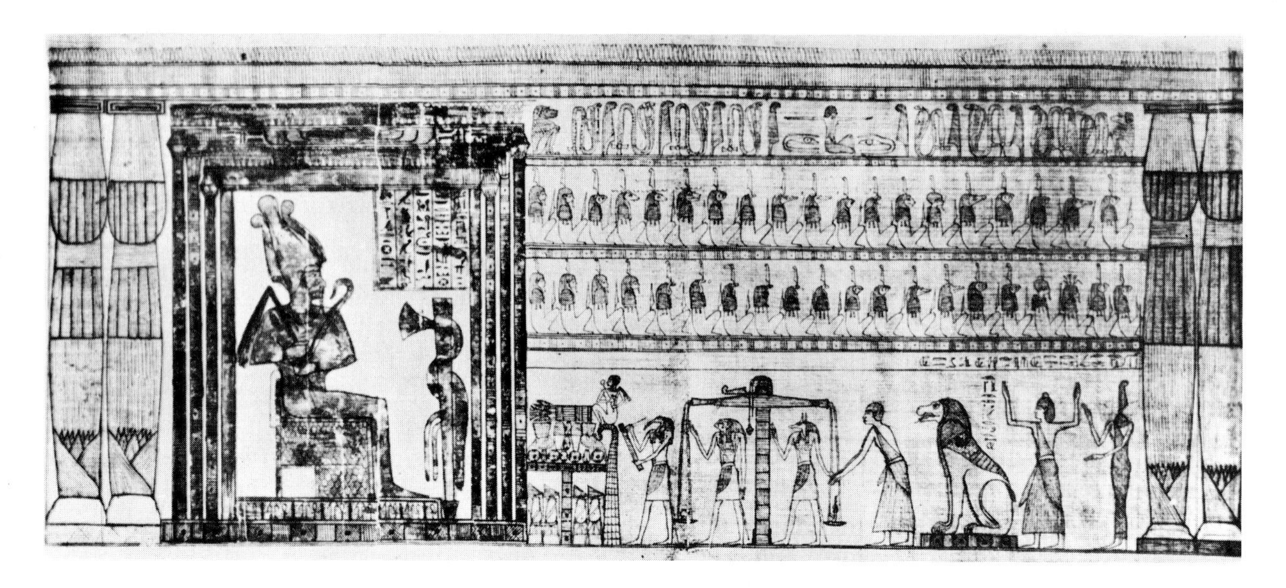

Papyrus scrolls of the Book of the Dead (above) contained spells and prayers. (Oriental Institute, University of Chicago) The Rosetta Stone is inscribed in Greek, demotic, and ancient hieroglyphics. (Courtesy of the Trustees of the British Museum)

under his rule, and for the first time Egypt was politically united. Menes became the first pharaoh or king of a united Egypt. *Pharaoh* means "royal house," and the ruler was always referred to by this title because he was believed to be divine, and a god could not be called familiarly by his name. The ruler was not permitted to marry outside his immediate family, for divinity could not produce another divinity if mated to a mortal. Thus, the pharaoh frequently married his sister, and it was from their union that other divine beings or pharaohs sprung.

## Old Kingdom

The period of a thousand years from about 3200 to 2300 B.C. in Egyptian history is known as the time of the Old Kingdom. This was a time when traditions and customs were being formed and fantastic achievements accomplished. It was the period in which a civilization continued to evolve. The priests and the pharaoh, who was chief priest, became very important in the government and the daily life of the people, for the church and state were one, and the ruler was divine. The position of the pharaoh and other high officials gradually became hereditary. Law courts were established. The pharaoh first located his capital at Heliopolis, but later pharaohs moved it to Memphis. For almost a thousand years, from 3200 to 2300 B.C., the Egyptians lived in peace. The sweeping and forbidding barriers of deserts which surrounded them kept out invaders, and the Egyptians themselves were peacefully inclined toward others. They spent this time in developing their country and advancing their civilization.

The Egyptians of the Old Kingdom built fantastic pyramids which are still wonders of the world today. Egyptian ships were sent to the peninsula of Sinai where Egyptians tunneled the oldest copper mines we know about. Ships also went to Byblos on the Syrian coast where they picked up timber which was used to build houses, furniture, and boats. Papyrus reeds, gathered from the marshes of the Nile, were made into light yellow paper, which was written upon with ink made of water, vegetable gum, and soot. The earliest Egyptian writing was with pictures which represented objects. From this there evolved a kind of writing in which the picture represented a syllable. From these syllables words were formed which might be different from what the pictures originally represented. Thus two pictures would make a word, and groups of two or more picture-words would make a sentence. The Egyptians created an alphabet, too, of twenty-four letters but it was rarely used. Writing for all ordinary business continued to be done with pictures in abbreviated forms, and we call this type of rapid writing *hieratic*. Writing had evolved even before Menes united Egypt into one kingdom.

The sphinx and great pyramids are at Giza, on the west bank of the Nile near Cairo. (Moore-McCormack Lines)

## Middle Kingdom

Around 2300 B.C. troubles began to plague Egypt from inside as well as outside the land. The poor rebelled at their heavy taxes and harsh life, and their complaints were voiced with violence. The nobles thought of themselves as kings and ruled their small domains with little reference to the pharaoh, who was now only nominally their ruler. Africans to the south and Middle Easterners to the east took advantage of this disunity to invade the land and further add to national woes. This time in Egyptian history is often referred to as the Feudal Period because the nobles governed so much of the land. A measure of unity was brought to the land about two centuries later, about 2100 B.C., when a new dynasty of pharaohs assumed the throne. Thus began the Middle Kingdom period in the history of Egypt. This period lasted until about the year 1800 B.C.

During this Feudal Period and the period of the Middle Kingdom, the Egyptians continued to evolve their civilization. The power of the pharaoh was less absolute, and a little more democracy existed in Egypt. A man of merit and ability might rise high despite his birth and the economic condition of his parents. The Egyptians began to evolve a social conscience, and the priestly writings of the time told about the sad conditions of the poor and urged the pharaoh and the nobles to be more humane in their government. They spoke of a wonderful ruler who was to come in the future, a good shepherd who would rescue the poor from the torment of their present life and take them into a period of peace and plenty.

The Egyptians of this time also became concerned with the illnesses of man and started to observe more closely the workings of the

The model shows a Nile River boat of about 3600 B.C. (Commercial Museum, Philadelphia)

organs of the human body. Our oldest known work on surgery was written in this period, and it contained the observations that the brain controlled the limbs and that an injury to the brain could paralyze the limbs. There were also works on mathematics, engineering, geography, and astronomy. Yearly measurements of the rise and fall of the Nile River led to the building of additional reservoirs and irrigation ditches to increase the production of grains. A canal was dug from the delta of one of the branches of the Nile River to the northern end of the Red Sea. This canal opened up the first sea traffic from the Red to the Mediterranean Sea almost four thousand years before the Suez Canal was built.

Then, in 1750 B.C., Egypt was invaded by a mixed group of Semites who came from that part of the Fertile Crescent which bordered Egypt along the Mediterranean. These invaders were called Hyksos, a name sometimes translated into English as "shepherd kings." The Hyksos used horses and war chariots, and the Egyptians did not know how to combat these new instruments of war. This was the Egyptians' first experience with the horse, but it was not to be their last. They were a clever and resourceful people, never too proud to borrow the accomplishments of others. The Egyptians, like the Semites, had borrowed and learned from the Sumerians and other peoples of the Middle East. They now began to explore the usefulness and abilities of the horse in war.

The invasion of the Hyksos also taught another lesson. The Egyptians found that in order to face the invader with a united front it was necessary to bury grievances among themselves. They found, as other men did before and after them, that disunity within a country breeds weakness which others will take advantage of. The Egyptians learned that in unity there is strength, and toward the end of the seventeenth century B.C. they began to fight back.

The Egyptians worshiped cats, and the goddess Bast was represented as having the head of a cat. (University Museum, Philadelphia)

The fight was launched from the capital at Thebes in Upper Egypt, and gradually the conquerors were driven back. By 1580 B.C. all of Egypt was free from the Hyksos. A new pharaoh named Ahmose I took the throne and began another great period in Egyptian history. It is known as the period of the Empire.

### Empire Period

The pharaoh did not disband the grand army that had driven out the invader. He and his people understood that they could no longer live secure behind the wide barriers of the desert, for there were highways into their land which could be used by invaders.

The Hyksos had come along the Mediterranean coast, and some Africans had already come down along the Nile from the south. Like many men before and after them, the Egyptians began to think of their army not merely as a defensive force but as an offensive force which could be used before a potential enemy could strike. They began to reason that Egypt could never be secure unless it actually controlled its immediate neighbors far back on the Nile and the peoples who lived along the Mediterranean to the east. Thus, for several centuries Egypt played a dominant role in the struggle for power in the Middle East. The Empire Period, in which Egyptian power expanded and was finally lost, lasted from about 1580 to about 1000 B.C.

The Egyptians had learned well their lessons in war, and they began a conquest which did not end until it reached the Euphrates River on the east and stretched far back up the Nile to the south. Under Thutmose III Egypt reached the peak of its power and in 1479 B.C. successfully invaded Syria, thus establishing the supremacy of Egyptian power. The Phoenicians, Hebrews, and Syrians were all under Egyptian control, and the borders of Egypt were pushed deep into Africa. The wealth of all these peoples poured into the coffers of Egypt.

The Egyptians became surfeited with wealth and weakened with easy living. Their conquests had made many enemies, and their wealth attracted new enemies. The power of the pharaoh was now absolute, but the foundations of this power among the people had been sapped. Enemies began to harass the land to the north and the south. Libyans, who lived to the west raided Egyptian territories again and again, and Nubians, or Ethiopians, from the south began to push north along the Nile in increasingly menacing numbers. Egyptian strength began to fail, and by the middle of the tenth century B.C. the Libyans had taken over the throne of the pharaoh. They, in turn, were replaced in the eighth century B.C. by the Nubians; and about 670 B.C. the Assyrians conquered Egypt. Then the Egyptians regained their independence for a short while, only to lose it again to the Persians in 525 B.C. But no matter what conquerors came to their land or what strains of people were mingled with them, the Egyptians never lost their identity. They continued as an integral and important part of the Middle East.

1. Where and when did the Egyptian civilization begin? What factors made the location ideal?
2. Describe life during the period of the Old Kingdom. What was the relation between the ruler and the religion at this time? What were the important achievements of Egypt in the time of the Old Kingdom?
3. When did the Egyptian begin to evolve a "social consciousness"? What did this mean for the average individual and what new interests or endeavors did it bring about?
4. What changes in attitude and ways of life did the invasion by the Hyksos bring about in Egypt?

### The Indo-Europeans

The Indo-Europeans, the fourth great family of men in the Middle East, also helped to pattern the ways and thoughts and kinds of man in the Middle East. They are called "Indo-European" primarily because of their language rather than because of body structure or coloring, for the Indo-Europeans evolved into many varieties of man. Their original homeland was somewhere in the steppes of Central Asia, but the Indo-Europeans were wanderers whose feet took them to other lands where they settled and mingled with those who were before them. From this mingling there sprung other men who partook of the characteristics of both the new and the old inhabitants. Indo-Europeans went into India, Persia, Asia Minor, Greece, and the lands of Europe, and in each of these places they became differentiated culturally and in certain physical characteristics from others of their kind. Remaining constant through the centuries of wandering

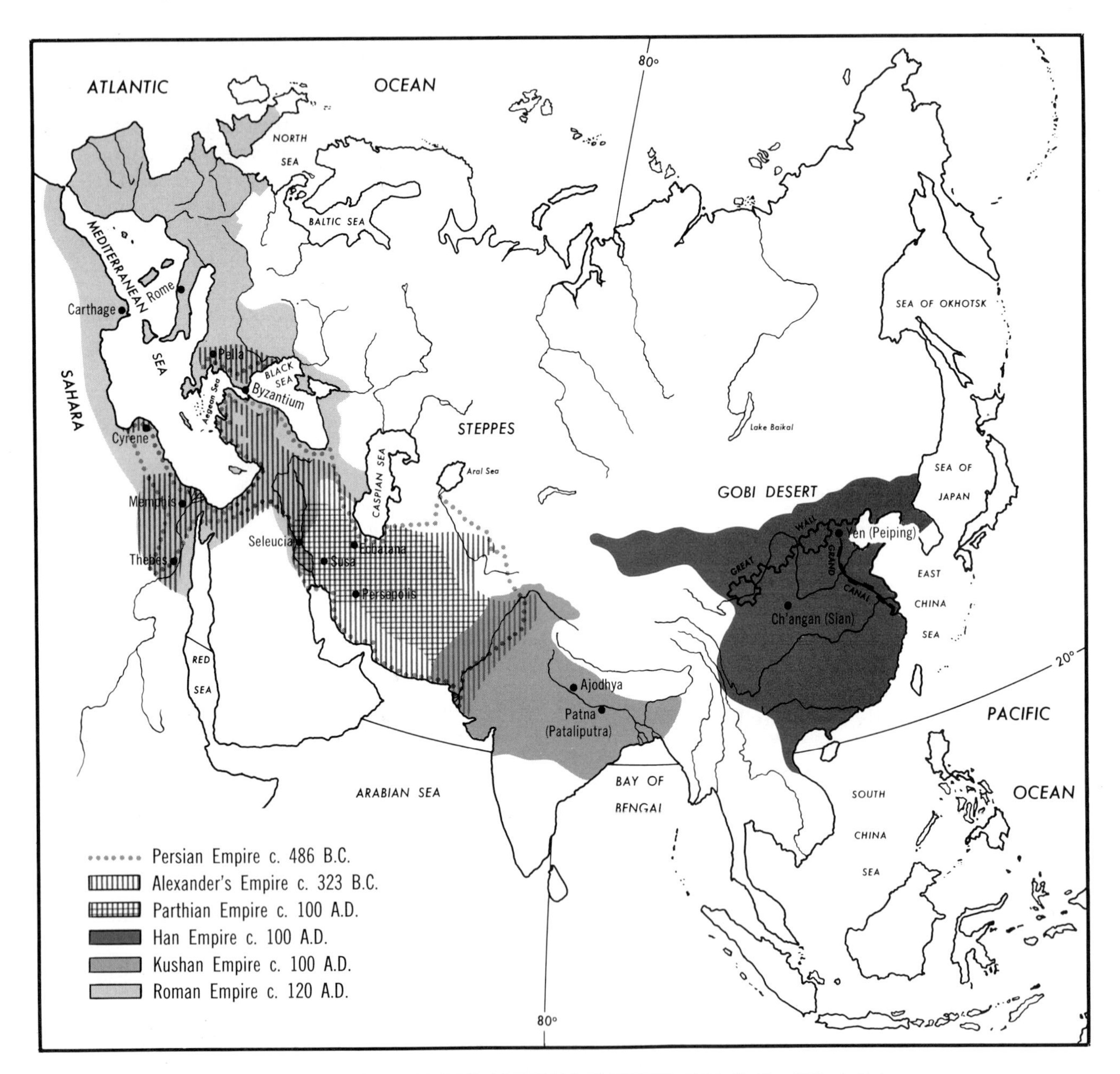


**GREAT MIDDLE EASTERN EMPIRES (486 B.C.–120 A.D.)**

Compare the empires of the Middle East with those of China and India and with the Roman empire in size. How did each successive empire build upon others that had come before it? Note that Alexander's empire extended more to the East than to the West.

and changing were the basic features of the Indo-European language. From the ancient Indo-European have sprung the languages of Sanskrit, old Persian, Greek, Roman, and the modern European languages of today. Thus the Indo-Europeans are given their name, not because of their looks or culture, which varied widely, but because of their language, which gave a certain measure of identity and unity to many later peoples.

The Indo-European Hittites who settled in Asia Minor before 2000 B.C. became a great power in the northern part of the Fertile Crescent for many centuries. They gave to man there the secrets of making iron, among other contributions. There were the Mitanni, who lived west of the Assyrians, and brought to man in the Middle East a knowledge of breeding, training, and using the horse. Both of these Indo-European peoples at times wielded great power and passed along a knowledge of Middle Eastern civilization to other Indo-Europeans of the steppe and to Greece.

The Persians were an Indo-European people. The gold roundel below was made during the period of the Achaemenid dynasty, which ruled from the seventh to the fourth century B.C. (Courtesy of the Oriental Institute, University of Chicago) The mosque was built in Isfahan in the sixteenth century. (Embassy of Iran) The Persian miniature was painted in the sixteenth century. (John Frederick Lewis collection of Oriental Miniatures, Free Library of Philadelphia)

## The Persians

The Persians were a part of the Indo-European family of man who wandered long ago from the flat grasslands of Central Asia and settled the land where Iran is located today. Around 550 B.C. a great military and administrative genius called Cyrus became king of the Persians. He belonged to the Achaemenian dynasty and founded the Persian Empire. Before he died in 529 B.C., he had conquered a great part of the Middle East. His son, Cambyses, conquered Egypt in 525 B.C. Cambyses was murdered on his way home from Egypt, and the throne was taken by a successor known in history as Darius the Great. He ruled from 521 to 486 B.C. Under Darius the Persian Empire became the greatest empire man had seen to that moment. It extended from the river Indus in northwest India to beyond the western borders of the Black Sea, and into the lands of the Greeks.

The Persians were not oppressive and demanding rulers as the Assyrians were, and they generally left conquered peoples free to follow native customs, religions, and ways of living, provided they paid taxes and did not foster rebellions. It was Cyrus the Persian who freed the Hebrews from their captivity in Babylon and permitted them to return to their homeland and rebuild their temple.

It was most difficult, however, to govern and control the huge mass of men and land that made up the Persian Empire. The Empire was divided into twenty-one provinces, and over each of these the king put a governor called a *satrap*. Roads were built connecting the provinces to the various capitals of the Persians—Susa, Persepolis, Babylon, and Ecbatana. The Persians were magnificent road-builders. The king's messengers traveled on roads from one end of the empire to the other in about a week's time on relays of horses. This was incredibly swift for that period of time. Their finest road, called the Royal Road, ran for about sixteen hundred miles from Susa, near the Persian Gulf, to the city of Sardis, near the Mediterranean Sea.

Despite their fine roads and administrative abilities, the Persians began to stagnate and decline. Luxurious living, rebellions, graft, and long-continued incompetency in kings and officials sapped the strength and efficiency of the Empire. Persia succumbed rather quickly when Alexander the Great invaded with his relatively small Macedonian army around 330 B.C.

The Palace of Darius at Persepolis was built in the fifth century B.C. (Erich F. Schmidt, Oriental Institute, University of Chicago)

## The Macedonians and the Greeks

Alexander the Great, king of Macedon, opened the way for a cross-pollination of Greek and Middle Eastern cultures through his conquest of the Persian Empire. The Macedonians and the Greeks were of the Indo-European family of man. The Greeks had made great advances by this time in philosophy, in the arts, and in science, and Alexander had been given a rather thorough Greek education. He was not interested in imposing Greek ideas upon the peoples he had conquered, but he thought the cultures could be merged. Alexander and those who followed him founded cities in the Middle East which became centers of Greek thought and science: Alexandria in Egypt, Antioch in Syria, and Seleucia along the Tigris. Alexander did not live long after his final conquest—he died in Babylon of swamp fever at the age of thirty-three in 323 B.C.—but his generals divided the empire between themselves after his death and founded dynasties which lasted for some centuries.

Greeks flocked into the Middle East to take positions under the Macedonian generals who now ruled in Egypt, in Mesopotamia, in Persia, and elsewhere. Greek became the language of the ruling clique and the educated. Greek philosophy, education, art, and science became a part of the educated man's knowledge in the Middle East. But the Macedonian-Greek rulers also absorbed Middle Eastern ideas and practices. For instance, the new rulers found it useful to encourage the feeling in that region that they were divine and governed by divine authority. In fact, it is believed by many students of this region that the impact of Middle Eastern thought and ways was greater upon the Greeks than the impact of Greek thought and ways upon men in the Middle East. Whether the influence of one or the other was greater may be debatable, but it is true that there was a merging of the ideas, customs, and peoples of Macedonia, Greece, and the lands of the Middle East. Nor was this merging disrupted when, between 146 and 30 B.C., the Romans conquered most of the areas under Macedonian-Greek rule.

### The Indo-European Romans

The Romans were more interested in a peaceful and orderly empire than in changing the accustomed patterns of living of the people they ruled. So long as the people of the Middle East did not rebel or challenge the supremacy of Rome, they were permitted to live as they chose. Moreover, the Romans thought highly of Greek learning, philosophy, art, and science. They hired and bought Greeks to tutor their children and students, and they often adopted Greek ways. The Roman Empire gave long periods of peace and order to many parts of the Middle East. Under Roman rule, the people of the Middle East continued their merging of old ideas and the creation of new ones. The Romans left in the Middle East some of the accomplishments of their engineering genius, and in some places a sense of their law, but few personal traces of themselves.

It was, however, during the period of Roman rule that Christianity was born, and the unified empire did permit it to spread quickly and widely.

1. Who were the Indo-Europeans? Why are these people called Indo-European?
2. Who was Cyrus and what type of ruler was he? What reason did he give for establishing provinces in his kingdom?
3. How was Greek thought introduced in the Middle East? Where were the main centers of Greek influence, and what reasons can you see for the location of these places?
4. What factors contributed to the success of Roman rule in the Middle East?

## Conclusion

The Sumerians, the Semites, and the Egyptians were the earliest builders of civilization in the Middle East. Their earliest civilizations grew up where there was adequate water and good earth to insure a continuous supply of food—in Mesopotamia, "The Land Between the Rivers," and around the Nile. These early settlers were joined later by other Semites who wandered north and settled the narrow coastal lands of the Mediterranean between the rivers and Egypt; and Indo-Europeans came to settle the eastern and western bounds of the region in Persia and in Asia Minor.

These civilizations were not built easily or rapidly. Hundreds of generations of men, working and thinking for thousands of years, constructed the civilizations of the Middle East. Sometimes their creative work was interrupted by wars among themselves and with invaders, and much of what they had previously accomplished perished in the madness of battle. But there were always those among them who continued to move along to greater and greater heights, and whose restless search for knowledge was never stilled.

They built slowly, but they built well and laid the foundations of knowledge upon which later men raised towering achievements. In truth, the people of the Middle East did construct the cradle of civilization. In no area, however, did they affect the total life of man more than in their revelations about God.

## SUMMING UP THE CHAPTER

A. Define or explain the following terms, relating them to the chapter.

| | |
|---|---|
| city-kingdom | law of self-preservation |
| cuneiform | murex |
| delta | nomad |
| hieratic | satrap |

B. Identify or locate the following and tell why they are important.

| | |
|---|---|
| Akkadians | Hyksos |
| Amorites | Mesopotamia |
| Arameans | Nebuchadnezzar |
| Assyrians | Nile |
| Babylon | Persia |
| Chaldeans | Phoenicians |
| Euphrates | Sumerians |
| Fertile Crescent | Tigris |
| Hittites | |

C. Identify the following dates and indicate their importance.

1. 2000 B.C.-1750 B.C. (Babylon)
2. 1200 B.C.-612 B.C. (Assur)
3. 612 B.C.-539 B.C. (Babylon)
4. 3200 B.C.-2300 B.C. (Egypt)
5. 1580 B.C.-1000 B.C. (Egypt)

D. Chapter review questions.

1. Describe the early writings of the Sumerians. Why were these writings important?
2. What functions did the priest-king perform in Mesopotamia? Which do you consider to be the most significant?
3. What did Hammurabi's code deal with? From what source or sources was this law drawn and upon what principles was it based? Why was it important?
4. Compare and contrast the various Semite families with regard to each of the following:
   a) geographic location
   b) most important period of existence
   c) characteristics of most important rulers
   d) manner of life
   e) contributions.
5. Compare and contrast the type of rule and degree of authority exercised by an Egyptian pharaoh during the Old Kingdom, the Middle Kingdom, and the Empire Period.
6. What do you consider to be the five greatest gifts of the Middle East to civilization? Give reasons for your choices.
7. Describe the life of a typical nomad.
8. Identify King Sargon and tell why he is an important historical figure.
9. What was unique about the city of Ur?
10. Name the descendants of the Semite family living in the Middle East today. What happened to the other families?
11. What reasons can you give that might explain why the Assyrian made the "practice of war" his way of life? Describe him as a defender and as a conqueror.
12. Who were the Chaldeans and why were they important?
13. Sketch briefly the history of Babylon, mentioning its most significant rulers.
14. Who were the Arameans? How did they gain their livelihood? What were their greatest accomplishments?
15. Who was Menes and why was he important?
16. When was the Feudal Period in Egypt? Why is it called this? Can you think of a better term?
17. Why was the army not disbanded by the pharaoh upon his defeat of the Hyksos?
18. Compare the Persians, Assyrians, and Greeks as rulers. Under which type of ruler would you prefer to live?
19. What did the Egyptians contribute to civilization?
20. How do you account for the fertile lands of Mesopotamia and Egypt?

E. Questions for discussion.

1. Greed and desire for power are two drives that exist in greater or lesser degree in most men. When these two drives become characteristic of a society or nation, what consequences develop? In answering this question, refer to the experience of the Egyptians, Sumerians, and Semites.
2. Various types of rulers and their methods of administration have been discussed in this chapter. From this discussion can you identify and evaluate the qualities necessary for a successful ruler in the Middle East? To what extent would these qualities contribute to successful leadership in other parts of the world?
3. From this brief introduction to the Middle East, can you pick out the elements common to its nations and peoples that identify the Middle East as a region?

F. Projects for groups or individuals.

1. Make a freehand drawing of the Middle East. Label each country and its capital as well as major rivers and mountains.
2. Prepare a report for class presentation on the life of Hammurabi. Be sure to discuss his contributions to civilization.
3. Find out what happened to the famous cedars of Lebanon.

# CHAPTER 9

# *They Thought Deeply About God*

MAN IN THE MIDDLE EAST has thought deeply and spoken eloquently about his God. What he has been inspired to think and to say has touched the hearts and moved the deeds of unnumbered generations of men everywhere. Very early men searched for the divine in nature and believed that they found it in many forms—in the fertility of the earth, in the light and warmth of the sun, in the stars of the night, in the wind and the rain, and in animals. The search continued, and some found one God who reigned supreme over all nature and the destiny of man. Gradually man in the Middle East came to believe in this one God, who also came to be accepted by a great part of mankind.

## The Many Gods

The Sumerians, the Semites, and the Egyptians thought that there were many gods, although some gods were considered to be superior to others. They pictured these gods in various shapes and built for them monuments of stone and brick, some of which are still standing. Frequently the king was considered as the representative of some great god or gods, and sometimes he also was held to be divine. The Sumerians and the Semites were fearful of their gods and vague or pessimistic about the chances of life after death. The Egyptians feared their gods too, but not so much, and they were convinced that there was a good life after death for those who had lived a good life on earth.

## The Sumerians and the Semites

The Sumerians and the Semites had many gods and goddesses. Among the greatest of these gods were Enlil, the earth god; Shamash, the sun god; and Ishtar, the goddess of love and fertility. Later, the Babylonian god Marduk, and the Assyrian god Assur also became important as Babylon became politically powerful. There were many other gods: the cow goddess, the god of earth, and those of sky and sea. There were also the various gods of the cities, and the people had personal gods from whom they sought favors and protection.

The Sumerians and the Semites needed protection from their gods, who were thought of as subject to all the violent passions of man. It was necessary to sacrifice to these gods and give them gifts. When one of these gods became angry, man might call upon other gods to intercede. And this happened frequently, for these many gods often became angry.

Sumerian legend tells a story of the time when the gods became angry with man and decided to destroy him with a great flood. One of the gods, however, warned a man whom he liked about the decision. This man was told to build a large boat for himself and some others, and thus they could ride out the flood and be saved. The man believed and did as the god had instructed him. When the rains and the storms came, the earth was flooded for seven days and seven nights. Only those who were in the boat survived that great flood of the gods. This story is found in later versions

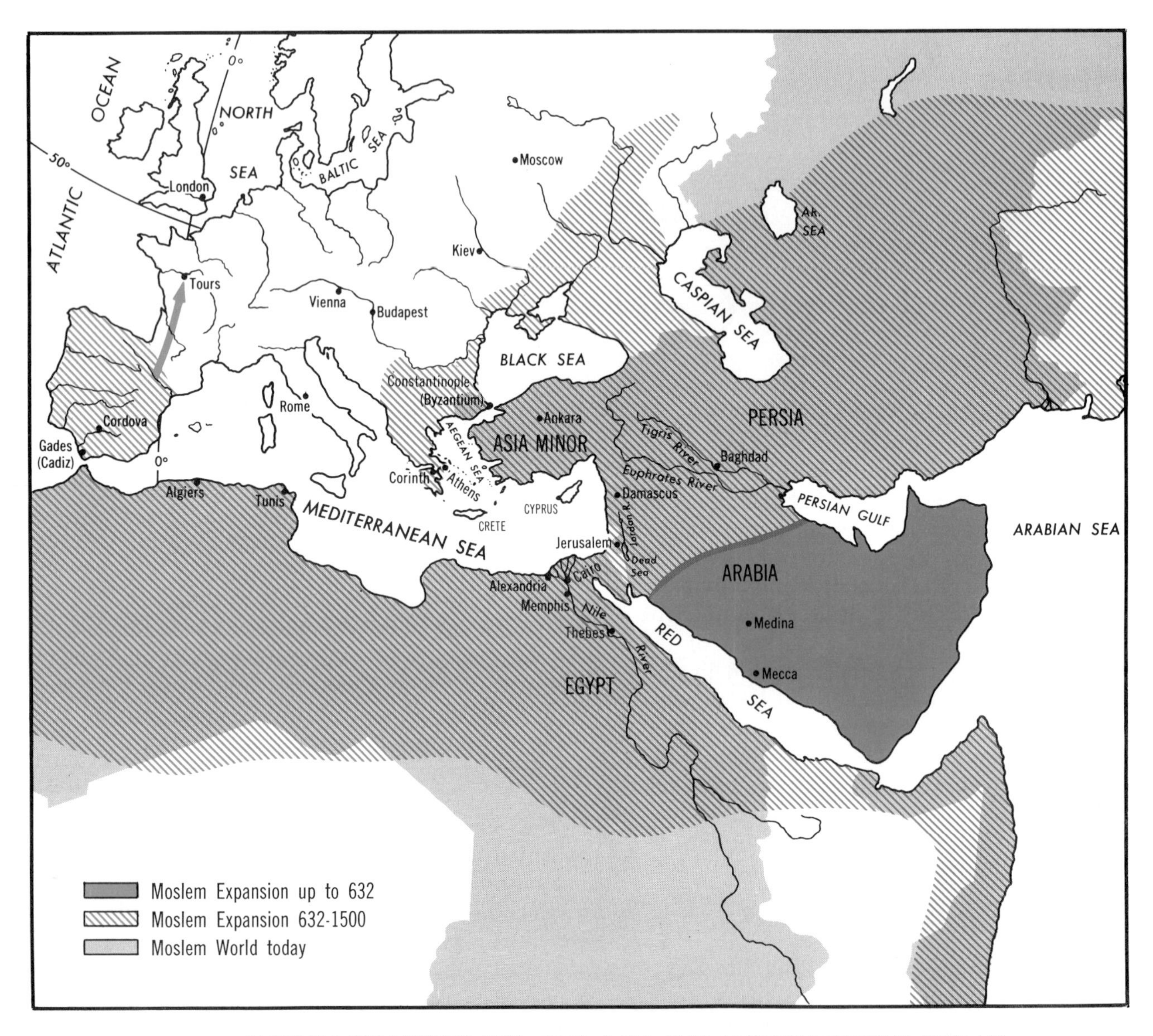


**MOSLEM EXPANSION (632—1500 A.D.) AND MOSLEM WORLD TODAY**

among the Semites, and there is the well-known account in the Old Testament of Noah and the ark.

The Sumerians did not think there was an eternal life after death, for only the gods were immortal. They did, however, show some concern for their dead and often buried them under the floors of their houses. Some of the Sumerian kings, however, did not wish to be alone in death. When a king died, a great pit was dug, and the dead king was escorted to this pit by his male and female court attendants, his bodyguard of soldiers, his servants, and oxen yoked to his carts and chariots. After the king was placed in his tomb within the great pit, the tomb door was closed, and his bodyguard of soldiers, his court attendants, and his servants either killed themselves or were killed. The oxen were killed too, still yoked to their chariots. The great pit was then filled in. The early Sumerians and Semites did not possess a consoling religion.

## The Egyptians

The Egyptians were much closer to their gods. They were more optimistic about the possibilities of help from these gods, and more certain of a life after death than the early Sumerians and Semites. The early Egyptians had many gods, and sometimes they were pictured in the shapes of mixed animals, such as Anubis, who had the head of a jackal and the body of a man.

**Re.** With the beginning of the Old Kingdom in 3200 B.C., the sun god Re began to assume dominance over all the gods of Egypt. He became the state god, and his worship was the official religion. The pharaoh was his living representative on earth. Re, however, was not concerned with the personal affairs and difficulties of the individual but rather with the preservation of the state and the people as a whole. He was the great god who sustained Egypt, but he was indifferent to the individual. The Egyptians felt closer to the subordinate gods of their various cities and localities than to Re. (Re was often called Ammon-Re after the Theban local god Ammon became identified with him in the twelfth century B.C.)

**Osiris and Horus.** There was another god, Osiris, who gradually became even more important in the personal life of the Egyptians than Re. Osiris was the god of the Nile and of life. The river Nile and life were closely associated in Egyptian thinking. Osiris was kind to the Egyptians and taught them agriculture, gave them good laws, and helped them in many, many ways. But he had a wicked brother, named Set, who one day fell upon him and cut him to pieces. Osiris was restored to life, however, by his devoted wife, Isis, who was also his sister. She found the parts of his body and put them back together again. Osiris had a son, Horus, who avenged his father by killing the wicked Set. It was the triumph of good over evil. This was a story of the triumph of life over death, and it appealed to the Egyptian with its promise that the death of the body was not the end of all. The Egyptians believed that man could and would live again in another place after his life on earth.

During the time of the Feudal Period and Middle Kingdom, beginning around 2300 B.C., the Egyptians became extremely concerned about life after death. Horus was now the god concerned with the affairs of man's life on earth, and Osiris had become exclusively the god of the kingdom of the dead. Osiris sat in judgment on all who had died. The Egyptian who appeared before him was asked if he had committed any of forty-two sins, which included murder, theft, anger, and others. He was asked to tell what good deeds he had done on earth, such as feeding the hungry, helping the poor, paying the proper respect to the gods, and other acts of helpfulness to gods and man. His answers were used by Osiris in judging his case. Finally his heart, which represented the conscience, was weighed on a scale which was balanced on the other side by a feather representing the truth. If they balanced out, the man had told the truth, and he was admitted into a happy world of light, peace, and pleasure. If he failed these tests, he entered into a world of darkness, to thirst and hunger forever.

By the end of the Middle Kingdom the sun god Re and Osiris were both important. Re was the god of justice and goodness for the living; and Osiris was the god of the judgment and the dead. But with the beginning of the Empire Period in 1580 B.C., Egyptian religion became debased. Priests sold magical charms which were guaranteed to fool Osiris when he balanced the heart against the feather. The priests became more interested in selling spoken and written formulas which assured entry into heaven than in urging the people to better themselves while still alive.

**Amenhotep IV and the one God.** There was one great pharaoh, Amenhotep IV, who tried to reform and uplift Egyptian religion during this period. Later he changed his name to Ikhnaton. His reign began in 1375 B.C. Ikhnaton was a rare man for his time and his environment. He proclaimed that there was but one God, who was called Aton. Aton was described not merely as the god of the Egyptians but of all men everywhere. He was considered as the good and kind creator of the world, who loved mankind. He had created the moral order in the world, and he rewarded all those who were pure and clean of heart. Ikhnaton curtailed the growing power of the corrupt priests and attempted to abolish the other gods from the minds of the Egyptians, but he did not succeed. After his death the priests regained their power. They restored the old gods and continued the selling of their magic charms. Superstition began to replace once again the high ethical and sublime quality of the earlier Egyptian religion. But the idea of one God was not lost to man in the Middle East and elsewhere. It was preserved by others.

### The Persians and Zoroastrianism

The Persians, or Iranians, as they are called today, gave religious beliefs to man which were lasting and deep. These beliefs were expressed in the religion known as Zoroastrianism, which takes its name from a Persian prophet called Zoroaster who is believed to have lived in the seventh century B.C. or possibly as early as 1000 B.C. It was a revealed religion, for its truths had been told to Zoroaster by the creator of goodness and light, Ahura-Mazda, and then transmitted to man by Zoroaster. The teachings of Zoroastrianism are contained in the Zend-Avesta, which is the sacred book of this religion.

Zoroaster revealed that a powerful battle was being waged between two great forces for the control of the universe and man. One was the creator of goodness and light, called Ahura-Mazda; the other was the maker of evil and darkness, Ahriman. All that was good, hopeful, and constructive in the world was of Ahura-Mazda. All that was evil, despairing, and negative was of Ahriman. The struggle between these two great forces was constant and fierce, but eventually the goodness of Ahura-Mazda would triumph. Ahriman would then be condemned to an abyss from which he would never escape.

With the victory of Ahura-Mazda the dead would arise and would be judged by Ahura-Mazda. He would reward the good with eternal happiness and punish the wicked. The good man, said Zoroaster, told the truth, helped his neighbor, tried to relieve the miseries of others, was kind and loyal, and harmed no one. He was not given to envy, anger, pride, wastefulness, lust, or slander. He was not lazy, but tilled his fields with diligence and care. He was temperate and did not go to excess in indulging or pampering the body. He was a force for good in action.

Darius the Great, who ruled from 521 to 486 B.C., proclaimed his acceptance of the teachings of Zoroaster when he wrote: "I am Darius, King of Kings. I love justice and I hate iniquity. It is not my pleasure that the lower shall suffer because of the higher. By the will of Ahura-Mazda, thus speaks Darius."

The influence of these ideals continued strong even after Persia was defeated by Alexander the Great in 330 B.C. and continued during the rule of the Seleucid dynasty, which was founded by one of Alexander's generals called Seleucus Nicator. The influence of Zoroastrianism continued during the long period from the rise of the Parthians around 250 B.C. to 226 A.D. The Parthians were of the Scythian race and they ruled a great empire from their homeland, which is today a part of northeastern Iran. They were especially well known as horsemen and archers. Zoroastrianism flourished anew at home and abroad when Ardashir I overthrew the Parthians and established a Persian dynasty known as the Sassanian in 226 A.D.

Many of these Zoroastrian beliefs found their way into the hearts and minds of the peoples of the Middle East. Zoroastrianism, like other religions, was changed and some of its basic beliefs were altered with the passage of time. Sects arose. There was Mithraism, which deified Mithra, the chief lieutenant of Ahura-Mazda. Its followers believed that Mithra ascended into heaven but that he would come once again to confer immortality upon the faithful and the good. This cult eventually died out, but it was a strong competitor with early Christianity. There was the sect of Manichaeism, which took its name from Mani, a Persian priest who lived about 250 A.D. He taught that all that was good, bright, and spiritual in the world was of the good God, but all that was material and evil was created by Satan. Man had to repress his sensual desires entirely if he would be perfect. The influence of his teachings was widespread, and it is said that St. Augustine was a follower of Mani before he became a Christian.

Some of the ideas first given to man by Zoroaster concerning the struggle between good and evil have lived on to the present. Some Persians still adhere to Zoroastrianism, but their numbers are few, and today the vast majority of Persians are Moslems. By about 650 A.D. the Arabs had carried the religion of Islam to Persia, and gradually it won the allegiance of the Persian people.

1. How did the development of religious belief and the movement away from polytheism follow political fortunes?
2. Explain how the priests of Egypt derived their power. Why do you suppose the reforms of Ikhnaton failed to survive his reign?
3. What is meant by a "revealed" religion?
4. Discuss the ideals of Zoroastrianism.

## The One God and Judaism

It was the ancient Hebrew who gave to man a lasting knowledge of the one God, whom he called Yahweh. For almost four thousand years the ancient Hebrew and his heir, the Jew of today, have spoken and written of one God with reverence, with love, and with perseverance. Throughout the long ages, the Hebrew, who became the Israelite, and then the Jew (those who were from Judea) were sustained by the conviction that they were entrusted with the duty of preserving the knowledge of the one God and His Torah or Teaching.

The Hebrew Bible or Old Testament forms the Holy Scriptures of Judaism as well as being part of those of Christianity and Islam. The teachings of these thirty-six books, especially of the Hebrew prophets like Amos, Isaiah, Jeremiah, and Ezekiel, emphasize justice and righteousness. All three of the major religions born in the Middle East share this common heritage that grew out of the Hebrews' belief in one God. The belief in one God is called *monotheism.*

The Jewish, Christian, and Moslem faiths teach that the one God created the universe and that He is independent of His creation and above it. His power is subject to no limitations whatsoever (such as other gods, magic, or fate). In the Torah or Five Books of Moses it is explained that God created man in His own image and that all mankind shares in a common "divine" image. The Hebrews, who were the first called to be near and dear to the one God, had a special bond, a covenant between them and their God.

The Hebrews had been a nomadic people who worshiped several gods until some time between the years 2000 and 1600 B.C., when Yahweh took the family of Abraham as his chosen children. At this same time, the family of Abraham was promised a homeland, the land of Canaan—approximately the same land where the state of Israel lies today. Here the Hebrews were to reside, multiply, and love and serve their God.

The grandson of Abraham was Jacob, who was known also as Israel. The twelve sons of Jacob became the heads of the Twelve Tribes of Israel. It is after Jacob (Israel) that the Jews are sometimes called "the children of Israel."

With Jacob's son, Joseph, the Israelites began a sojourn in Egypt, first prospering, then enslaved by a succession of pharaohs, among them Seti I and Rameses II. It was during the 1200's B.C. that a towering man called Moses had a revelation in the wilderness. He returned to the Israelites in Egypt as a messenger prophet and revealed the name Yahweh to them. He told them that God had remembered them and that Egypt's gods were false gods. He also told them that they would be delivered from the bondage of Egypt. The Israelites were electrified by this message, and sometime around 1230 B.C. their Exodus from slavery to freedom occurred. There is an Egyptian monument that mentions "Israel" and a battle in the reign of Merneptah (1225-1215 B.C.).

Every year the Jews of Israel celebrate their independence in synagogues. (Israel Information Services)

While the Israelites journeyed over the barren wastes of the desert toward Canaan, the Covenant between God and the new nation came into being. A national pact began between God and His people, and it was sealed by the act of the Exodus. The Bible tells that Moses went up to the heights of Mount Sinai, where he received the Tablets of the Law to help guide man's actions in accordance with God's will. This teaching is called Torah, and it is for the Jew a fountain of wisdom and a source of infinite strength.

It its broadest sense, Torah embraces all of the revealed instruction and guidance which are the basis of the Jewish way of life. It includes the entire body of law and standards for personal and collective conduct found in the Bible. More specifically, the Torah means the five books of Moses called the Pentateuch.

The Torah deals with the whole life of man, spiritual, social, and physical. Originally Moses received many commandments, including the Ten Commandments, but a number of them were specifically for that time and circumstance and no longer apply to the great mass of the people. Yet many of the commandments are still observed and remain central to the teachings of Judaism. Among these are the commandments to believe in the unity of God and to love and fear Him; to provide for the poor; to love one's neighbor; to honor one's parents; and to pray. Of equal importance are prohibitions that forbid killing, stealing, and the worship of false gods. The Torah is the directing center of Jewish life. It occupies a central place in Jewish thought and worship and can be found today written in Hebrew letters on parchment scrolls in the Ark of every synagogue.

The other books of the Hebrew Bible or Old Testament constitute an anthology of inspired writings that cover the first two thousand years of Jewish history. The earliest Hebrew historical writings were probably first put down sometime between 1000 and 800 B.C. They told of the origins of the Hebrew people, the great flood, the patriarchs, Abraham, Isaac, and Jacob, and the Exodus from Egypt. Modern archaeologists have found evidence of much of the history of the early Hebrews, for instance, the Babylonian version of the story of the flood. Egyptian letters confirming other events of the time have also been found.

Later historical books of the Bible tell us of Joshua and the Judges, who led the tribes of Israel after the death of Moses. The tribes conquered parts of Canaan, but they had great difficulty because of disputes among themselves and with outside enemies such as the Philistines. After the death of the first king, Saul, the tribes of Israel were united and reached the heights of their ancient glory in the reigns of David and Solomon. The tenth century B.C. was Israel's golden age when David and Solomon ruled and Israel dominated a large part of the surrounding area of the Middle East.

About 925 B.C. a division among the Hebrews resulted in the formation of two separate kingdoms: a grouping of two southern tribes into the Kingdom of Judah with their capital at Jerusalem, and a grouping of the ten tribes in the north into the Kingdom of Israel. Around 721 B.C. the Assyrians overran the Kingdom of Israel and carried its people away. These tribes were scattered all over the Middle East and their identity as a people was lost. They are remembered now as the "ten lost tribes of Israel." In 586 B.C. the Chaldean king, Nebuchadnezzar, destroyed Jerusalem and the Temple, and deported most of the population to his capital. This period in Jewish history is known as the "Babylonian Captivity."

After Cyrus the Persian conquered Babylon, he permitted the Jews to return to their homeland and rebuild Jerusalem and the Temple around 539 B.C. Unfortunately their troubles did not end at this time. The Jews, who lived on the land bridge between Asia and Africa, came under the control of the empire founded by Alexander the Great around 332 B.C. Later, in 167 B.C. they revolted against the Seleucid king, Antiochus, and founded their own Hasmonaean dynasty (the family of the Maccabees). The festival of Hanukkah commemorates their war for religious freedom at this time.

The Romans took over Palestine and its people about 63 B.C. There were many revolts during Roman rule, including one which lasted from 66 to 70 A.D. and resulted in the destruction of the Holy Temple in Jerusalem. After the Jews revolted in 135 A.D., they were scattered by the Romans into many parts of the empire. From that time until 1948, when the independent state of Israel was established, the Jews wandered and settled in many nations but remained without a country.

By the end of the Hellenistic Age, Jews were dispersed throughout the Roman Empire. They settled in Europe and the Mediterranean lands, in the *Diaspora*, which means "dispersion" and refers to all lands in which they were scattered. Often, in the medieval and modern period, Jews suffered from discriminatory laws that prohibited them from engaging in certain occupations, limited the places where they could live, and denied them citizenship. This discrimination is usually referred to as *anti-Semitism.* The darkest chapter of Jewish history was written in Hitler's Germany, where six million European Jews were killed outright or tortured to death in concentration camps operated by the Nazis. The Jew has, indeed, sampled beyond measure, man's inhumanity to man.

Yet, the Jews and Judaism have enjoyed a remarkable record of religious creativity. The idea of a Messianic Age with the establishment of the Kingdom of God on earth, prayer, the observation of the Sabbath, and study as a religious obligation—all these sustained them. The institution of the synagogue, the ministry of spiritual leadership of the rabbi, and the Bible with the Oral Law kept the Jews loyal to their tradition.

The Jewish love of learning produced a long continuous chain of scholars and thinkers. There was Philo of Alexandria, who first struggled to bring Greek and Hebrew thought together, and Saadia Gaon, a Babylonian who wrote of reason and revelation. In the eleventh century, Rabbi Solomon ben Isaac of France wrote a commentary on the Talmud and the Bible that is still used today. Moses Maimonides, physician to the Sultan of Cairo in the twelfth century, attempted to reconcile Judaism with Aristotle's philosophy. The Jews were a cultural bridge between the Arabs who continued Greek ideas and medieval Christendom.

The Jews have played an important role in man's struggle for freedom and enlightenment. Out of their long historical experience as a minority, they learned to treasure freedom, and with their great cultural heritage, they made important contributions wherever they went. The contributions to the modern world by Jewish scholars, writers, and scientists like Spinoza, Freud, Einstein, and many others have been immense.

Modern Judaism consists of three major groupings: Orthodox Judaism, which emphasizes tradition and observance; Conservative Judaism, which makes adjustments in traditions; and Reform Judaism, which emphasizes the prophetic heritage. All of these groups are essentially agreed upon the ethical and moral teachings of Judaism, the obligation of prayer and worship, and belief in the one God who chose the Hebrews as His own people with a Covenant to reveal Him to mankind.

### The One God and Christianity

Christianity was born of the worship of the God of the Jews. Its founder was Jesus of Nazareth, a Jew who was born in the land of Israel almost 2,000 years ago. He grew to manhood in a place called Nazareth and, at about thirty years of age, began what might be called His public life. For the next several years He wandered among the people of this land and spoke to them about their God, about the way God wanted men to act toward one another, about mercy and kindness, about life and death, and many other matters of divine and human importance. He touched the hearts of His listeners with the eloquence of His example as well as His tongue. He was gentle, kind, unselfish, sympathetic, and always ready to help those distressed in mind or in body. Peter, one of His followers, described the life of Jesus in these words: "He went about doing good."

The story of Jesus and His teachings is told in four books called Gospels (good tidings) which make up the first part of the New Testament. Jesus, we are told, was born about the year 4 B.C. His childhood was spent in the typical surroundings of the Jews of Galilee.

We know little of the early life of Jesus, but according to the Gospel of Luke, at the age of twelve, He amazed the scholars at the Temple in Jerusalem by His great learning and wisdom. We know from the teachings of Jesus and His emphasis on "loving the Lord" that He knew well the teachings of the great prophets of Israel. But Jesus brought a new message of love and of the coming of God's kingdom.

The Gospels tell of Jesus going to Jerusalem for the festival of Passover, His arrest by Roman soldiers, and His subsequent crucifixion at the command of Pontius Pilate. Roman records tell of the later removal of Pilate as governor because of his excessive cruelty.

After Jesus died upon the cross, the Gospels record that when the disciples went to His tomb, they found it empty. An angel told them that Jesus had risen from the dead. Later in Galilee the disciples reported that Jesus was indeed the Messiah and would return to usher in His Father's kingdom.

Everything Jesus said and did focused around God's great love for man, and the love that people should have for each other. He is, to Christians, living proof that God loved man to the extent of sending Himself in the person of His Son to preach, to suffer, to die, and to rise again, in order that man might be saved. Jesus taught His disciples to love everyone, the good and the bad, the friend and the enemy, the poor and the rich, the weak and the strong, the stupid and the bright, the deformed and the straight. There could be no exception to this love, for God made no exceptions, and Christians were, therefore, obliged to love man as God loved him. They must show this love in action, for a love that is not concretely displayed has little substance and meaning. This love must also be sincere, for Jesus detested hypocrisy. He seemed to prefer the outright bad to the hypocrites.

Not all Christians today agree exactly as to the interpretation of all of the teachings of Jesus. Doctrines vary among the numerous sects of Christianity, but there is substantial agreement on a number of beliefs and principles originating with the life and teachings of Jesus. These have been the basis for traditional Christianity.

Most Christians believe that God is one, but that there are three persons in God: Father, Son, and Holy Ghost. These are distinct persons, but they have one nature, and each is fully God. This teaching is known as the *Trinity.* Jesus is held to be the Messiah promised to man in the Old Testament who came to earth to atone for man's sins and to show how man could be saved by faith and a life modeled after His teachings.

Most Christians accept the word of God as revealed through the Bible, and they place special stress on the New Testament. Christians generally accept the Crucifixion of Jesus as atonement for men's sins, and the Resurrection as final evidence that Jesus was the Son of God.

Christianity teaches that man should love God and his neighbor as Jesus did. The Christian is taught to observe the Ten Commandments, be humble, tolerant, avoid evil, forgive others their offenses against him, and ask God for the forgiveness of his sins. The Christian is promised that some day God will come again to judge all the living and the dead.

Many were drawn by the goodness, warmth, and sincerity of Jesus. He chose twelve of His closest disciples to spread His teachings. The disciples were called Apostles, and the greatest of them was Peter. They established small groups who believed in Jesus as the Messiah (in Greek, the Christ). The earliest Christians, called Nazarenes, were considered a sect of Judaism.

With Saul of Tarsus, called Paul, Christianity began to reach the Gentiles, or those who were not Jews. In his early life Paul fought the Christians, but after a vision around 35 A.D., he traveled throughout the Mediterranean world founding churches. Christian communities were established in Syria, Asia Minor, the Balkan Peninsula, Greece, Egypt, and Rome. Paul was a product of a Greek and Hebrew background and was a Roman citizen. He wrote letters to the different communities interpreting Christian teaching. These letters make up the Epistles of the New Testament. The Gospels, Book of Acts, Epistles and books of the Apocalypse (concerning the end of days) written in Greek, form the books of the New Testament. The books were officially accepted as *canon*, or standard, by Church councils.

The early Christians had many differences regarding the nature of Christ and His relation to God. Despite these differences, Christianity spread. The Roman authorities regarded Christianity as a threat to the empire, and hundreds of Christians were killed at the Circus and the Colosseum in Rome. Peter and Paul were among the early martyrs. But Christianity continued to grow.

In 313 A.D. the Edict of Milan was issued by the Roman Emperor Constantine, granting complete toleration to Christians. Christianity flourished, and a Council was called at Nicaea

Ephesus, above, was an early center of Christianity and the *Epistle to the Ephesians* was directed to the Christian community there. (Turkish Tourism and Information Office)

The Church of All Nations, built with money from many lands, stands beside the olive trees of the Garden of Gethsemane in Jerusalem. In the background is the Russian Church of St. Mary Magdalene. (The Jordan Tourism Authority)

(Nice) in 325 A.D. to settle theological issues. It was decided that Christ was of the *same* substance as God the Father, not, as was claimed by Arius of Alexandria, that Christ was of *like* substance. The Nicene Creed, expressing this, was adopted, though the teachings of Arius continued among many sects. By 400 A.D. Christianity had become the state religion of the Roman Empire, and the pagan gods were made illegal.

During the fourth century A.D., when the Roman Empire began to split up, Constantine, the Emperor of the Romans, built a new capital on the site of the old city of Byzantium, which he named Constantinople. The western part of the old Roman Empire declined and was lost, but this eastern part with its capital at Constantinople continued for another thousand years and gradually became known as the Byzantine Empire. Christianity was the state religion of this empire, which controlled those parts of the old Roman Empire which lay in the Middle East—Syria, Asia Minor, Palestine, and Egypt among others. It shared control of the Middle East with a new Persian Empire which had begun in 226 A.D., and which controlled much of the rest of Mesopotamia.

The control of the Middle East by the Byzantines and the Persians was soon threatened and wrested from them by the followers of a new religion called Islam, which first arose amidst the barrens of Arabia. The followers of this religion were known as Moslems, and the prophet of the religion of Islam was Mohammed.

1. Is the idea of a "chosen people" unique to the Jews? What other religions identify their followers as "chosen people"?
2. What is the Torah?
3. Trace the history of the Jewish "homeland" from Moses to modern Israel.
4. What are the central teachings of Christianity?

## The One God and Islam

The one God of the Jew and the Christian is also the one God of the Moslem. Moslems, the followers of the religion of Islam, believe that there is only one God, called Allah. They believe that Allah is the creator of all things—heaven, earth, and man. They believe that this is the same God who spoke to man through the voices of the prophets Abraham and Moses, as well as through Jesus and their own special prophet, Mohammed.

Islam is in the fullest sense a faith that furnishes its followers with a comprehensive guide for living. It is concerned with the material as well as the spiritual well-being of man. Islam holds that the two are inseparable, for the spirit of man is deeply immersed in a sea of material problems. The Moslem believes that it is good to relieve the misery of the poor and needy, to care for the aged and the afflicted, help the orphan, and free the debtor from the burdens of his debts and the borrower from the devouring of usury. Islam is interested in solving community and world problems as well as in the progress of man towards his creator. It is involved in bettering the status of women, in promoting racial equality, in advancing science, and in fostering international understanding and brotherhood among all men. It is for the Moslem a full way of life.

The faithful Moslem lives in the conviction that the truths of his faith and way are of God. He believes that these truths had been revealed to others before Mohammed, but that Islam was the completion and confirmation of such revelations. Moslems believe that Mohammed was chosen to complete and to seal the long series of revelations to man, and they call him "The Seal of the Prophets."

There was little in the early life of Mohammed which forecast his future greatness. He was born around 570 A.D. in the city of Mecca in Arabia. He was orphaned early in life and raised by an uncle. During his youth he worked as a shepherd. He married a widow named Khadija who was devoted to him, and they lived happily together for twenty-six years. Mohammed seemed like all other men around him until he began to proclaim his revelations, and then he became hugely different and significant to the eyes of man.

Mohammed was moved by that spirit

which impels man to quest for the divine, for that which is above nature, man, and the universe. Although born of a people who worshiped many gods, he was drawn to a knowledge and belief in the one God. He thought and meditated much. In the solitude of a quiet desert cave outside of Mecca, free from the distractions of man, he sometimes spent whole nights wrestling with the mysteries of the divine. Then, as he described it later, one night while he was deep in meditation, God spoke to him through the voice of an angel. "Read!" the angel said. "I cannot read," Mohammed answered. "Read!" the angel said again. Mohammed replied the second time, "I cannot read." "Read!" the angel commanded the third time. Mohammed then asked, "What shall I read?" The reply to his question came quickly:

> Read—in the name of your God
> The Creator!
> Who created man from a clot
> Of congealed blood.
> Read! Your God is most generous
> He who has taught man
> By the pen things he knew not.
> —(Surah XCVI, 1-5) KORAN

After this moment of revelation Mohammed dedicated his life to proclaiming to man the truths which had been revealed to him. These truths are recorded in a holy book called the Koran. The Koran is for the Moslem the written word of God. Due to problems of interpretation and difficulties arising in matters not treated in the Koran, other compilations and commentaries were made. Among these are the *Hadith* and the *Sunna*. The *Hadith* is equally authoritative on matters not treated in the Koran. It contains utterances of Mohammed written down by those who were his companions, and the teachings of these disciples. The *Sunna* contains important customs and Moslem teachings based on the words and deeds of Mohammed. The Koran has many regulations governing the daily life of man, for within Islam the social and material life of man is not divorced from his spiritual life. The Moslem incorporates his religion inseparably into his total life.

**Five basic pillars.** Five basic beliefs support Islam. The first of these is that there is only one God, who is the creator of all things; that Mohammed was the last of a line of prophets which included Abraham, Moses, and Jesus among others, but neither he nor they were God; that God has given each man an eternal soul, and for the good man there is a paradise after his death; that there is also a hell awaiting the evil and the unworthy; that there will be a day of judgment for all men.

The second pillar of Islam is prayer. The Moslem is required to pray five times a day, before sunrise, at noontime, during the midafternoon, at sunset, and after sunset. He calls his church a mosque, and his services at the mosque are held on Friday. But it is not essential that he go to the mosque to pray, for he is taught that the whole world is his mosque. He should pray wherever he might be when the appointed hours of prayer arrive. When he prays, he faces the city of Mecca to remind him of the unity that reigns within

The Sacred Kaaba stands inside the courtyard of the Great Mosque at Mecca. Inside is the Black Stone, said to be of meteoric origin. (Saudi Arabian Information Service)

Islam and as a sign of respect to Abraham, who is said to have built the first Kaaba or shrine in Mecca.

The third pillar of Islam is charity. Islam teaches that man should manifest his love for the one God by loving his neighbor. The Moslem is required to share what he has with others in order that their life on earth be not too harsh. Islam asks that every Moslem pay a tax of two and one-half per cent each year upon his entire holdings, including money, goods, real estate, or other possessions. This is a higher tax than many nations require of their citizens. The money obtained from this tax is used for such charitable and religious purposes as aiding the poor, assisting needy travelers, housing the homeless, and building mosques. Islam teaches its followers to have a social conscience, a sense of obligation for the earthly miseries of other men.

The fourth pillar is the observation of the fast during Ramadan, the ninth month of the Moslem lunar calendar. Ramadan is of special significance to the Moslem because it was during this month that Mohammed received God's revelation through the voice of an angel and migrated from Mecca to the city of Medina. The people of Mecca, to whom he had first preached, rejected his revelation, and Mohammed moved on to Medina where he was received with honor and belief. In memory of these two important events, the faithful Moslem, unless excused by exceptional circumstances, fasts during this month each day from sunrise to sunset. His fast is strict and strenuous, for nothing may pass his lips, neither food, drink, nor smoke, during this period of the day. By this fast, Islam teaches its followers that they are weak and need the constant support of their God; and the suffering of hunger reminds them to be sympathetic and helpful toward others whose hunger is a constant companion.

The fifth pillar is the pilgrimage to the sacred shrine of the Kaaba in the court of the Great Mosque in Mecca. Islam teaches that, if possible, every Moslem should visit this shrine at least once in his lifetime to refortify his faith. This shrine marks the site made holy by Abraham when he erected the first Kaaba there and also marks the place where Mohammed was born. Here on this holy land, as in the mosque, there are no distinctions of wealth and rank. Rich man, poor man, beggar, or king, all wear the same simple garment when approaching the Kaaba, and all kneel side by side in the mosque in prayer and worship. Islam teaches that all are essentially equal before God.

This gathering of Moslems at Mecca also stresses the brotherhood that binds all within Islam and furthers international understanding. Islam teaches that every Moslem should look upon every other Moslem—regardless of race, sex, or social position—as a close member of a common family, a brother to be loved and treated as one should treat a brother or a sister. Moslems come to Mecca from every part of the globe, and they meet and speak with one another there within the embrace of one religion. The unifying factor of Islam allows Moslems of many nationalities to exchange information and opinions with less suspicion and antagonism and to receive and accept knowledge of other lands and people. In this way Islam advances the spiritual growth of man and fosters social growth through international understanding of the brotherhood of man.

**Growth of Islam.** The revelation uttered by Mohammed exploded like a volcano upon the men of the Middle East, and even today its force is felt far beyond the boundaries of this region. Within a century after the death of Mohammed in 632 A.D. most men in the Middle East and many in North Africa had given their allegiance to the one God of Islam. The Moslems carried their faith to Spain and might have greatly changed the life and culture of Western Europe had they not been defeated at the Battle of Tours in 732 A.D. by Charles Martel of France. Islam did not spread farther in Western Europe, but it continued to gain the allegiance of great numbers in Asia and in Africa, and thousands upon thousands of men are embracing its teachings today. There are now five hundred million Moslems in the world, and they are mostly grouped in the Middle East, in Asia, and in Africa.

Although Moslems have been pictured as converting by the sword, there is little evidence which indicates that their spiritual successes were due to the sword. Their law as written down in the Koran forbade them to impose their faith upon the unwilling. Further, throughout their history, the Moslems have regarded both Christians and Jews as people to whom the one God was also revealed. Mohammed himself commanded his followers to be tolerant toward them. Mohammed believed that the Jews had fallen away from the truths revealed to them through Abraham, Moses, and the other prophets, and he objected to the Christian concept of Jesus as God. Jesus, as the Moslems see him, was a great prophet and a holy man, but he was not God. For Islam there was only one God, revealed to Jew, Christian, and Moslem alike.

Shortly after the death of Mohammed in 632 A.D. the beginnings of divisions began to appear among the Moslems which later grew into mature and continuing differences of organized opinions. Most Moslems belong to either the Sunnite or the Shiite sect.

**Sunnites and Shiites.** The large percentage of Moslems are Sunnites, and they take their name from the word *sunna* or "tradition." What Mohammed said or did was also a part of their faith, though it might not be explicitly treated in the Koran. The tradition was also a source of truth and, in a sense, complemented the Koran. The Koran, as the revealed word of God, cannot be modified or amended. The caliph or successor to Mohammed is the head of Islam and, ideally, he should be chosen by the whole community of Moslems. The Sunnites are rather democratic and liberal in their Islamic approach to life.

The Shiites generally rely upon the words of the Koran alone. They believe that only those should be chosen as caliph who are related in some way to the prophet Mohammed by blood or by marriage. Some believe that from time to time God reveals Himself through other men called *imams*, and these imams have the same authority as Mohammed when revealing spiritual truths. Any new teaching of Islam, the Shiites say, should be supported by the authority of these imams.

**The Sufis.** Within Islam there is a group called Sufis, who have been described as a sect. It would, perhaps, be more correct to describe them simply as Moslems who attempt to follow the highest type of religious life within Islam. The Sufis believe that man can reach a spiritual communion with God through fasting, long contemplation, and ascetic practices. Many of them have founded monasteries and lived a life of prayer, meditation, and austerity, or they have wandered about preaching. These missionaries of Islam have been to remote places and carried to unbelieving peoples the knowledge and the salvation of Allah, the one God.

There are many variations of practice and belief among the followers of Islam, just as there are among the followers of Buddhism, Judaism, Christianity, and other religions. All of Islam, however, has a unity of doctrine which is of greater scope and depth than the differences which divide any groups within it, and all of its followers are basically true Moslems.

1. Describe how Islam incorporates the historical figures of other religions. Is this a feature of any other religion?
2. What are the five basic teachings of Islam?
3. What is the significance of Ramadan? What is the life of the Moslem like during Ramadan?
4. What are the three major Moslem sects? How do they differ?

## Conclusion

Belief in the divine, in something less limited than man, was an important part of the civilization that grew in the Middle East. Man's life in much of the world has been greatly influenced by what man in the Middle East has had to say about his God. The earliest men saw divinity in the gigantic displays of nature —in the sky, the sun, the mountain, and in the miracles of life bursting from fertile seeds. Some believed divinity lived within their rulers and in a number of gods. Gradually these beliefs changed, and some men came to accept the belief that divinity was one—that there was only one God who had created the majesty and the miracles of nature. Thoughts and revelations about this one God began in the Middle East and went on to shape and reform the lives of countless men in all parts of the world—in Asia, in Africa, in Europe, and in the Americas. When Moslems pray in the mosque on Friday, Jews in the synagogue on Saturday, and Christians in the church on Sunday, they are praying to the God who was first revealed to man in the Middle East.

It is almost impossible to imagine how much of man's total life has been molded and channeled yesterday and today by the concept of the one God which man in the Middle East passed along to other men. Man in the Middle East was strangely and deeply touched by the divine, and he has been inspired to tell others what he feels and knows. He has gone forth to speak and to write so that others might know his God, and he has been successful in bringing his inspirations and revelations to the hearts and minds of other men in all parts of the world.

## SUMMING UP THE CHAPTER

A. Identify or locate the following and explain their significance.

| | |
|---|---|
| Abraham | Medina |
| Ahura-Mazda | Mithraism |
| Allah | Mohammed |
| Amenhotep | Nazareth |
| Aton | Osiris |
| Cyrus | Pentateuch |
| Darius | Re |
| Koran | Torah |
| Manichaeism | Yahweh |
| Mecca | Zend-Avesta |

B. Chapter review questions.

1. Explain the following sentence and relate it to the Middle East: "The many gods die, the one God remains."
2. Describe the religions of the early Semites and the Sumerians.
3. Who was Ikhnaton? What were his contributions to religion?
4. What religion became dominant in Persia after 642 A.D.? How do you account for this?
5. Explain the belief of the Jew concerning "one God and His Law."
6. Where did the "ten lost tribes of Israel" live originally? Who carried them away from there?
7. Explain the meaning of the term *Messiah.*
8. Trace the "public life" of Jesus Christ. What kind of a man was he?
9. How and by whom was Christianity spread?
10. Identify the Trinity, Resurrection, and the canon. What do they all have in common?
11. Identify the most important teachings of Islam. Are any of these teachings a part of other religious beliefs that you are aware of? What does this suggest to you?
12. Discuss the attitude of Mohammed, as revealed in the Koran, toward Christians and Jews.

C. Questions for discussion.

1. What historical explanations can you find for the progression from polytheism to monotheism?
2. How might you explain the existence of the story of the flood in Sumerian, Semite, and Biblical religion? Can you prove your explanation?
3. How would you explain the animal forms of ancient gods? What existing religions symbolize certain of their gods in animal forms?
4. Why do you suppose the conflict between the forces or gods of good and evil is a persistent theme in all religions? Compare this conflict in the religions discussed in this chapter with the religions of the Far East discussed in the first unit.
5. How would you explain the development of numerous sects or cults from a major religion?

D. Projects for groups or individuals.

1. Read parts of the Koran. Compare it with familiar parts of the Bible.
2. Prepare a report for classroom presentation on the history of Zoroastrianism. Find out in what countries or areas of the world this faith still exists.
3. Make a list of all the religions of the Middle East. Make a chart showing how many people or what percentage of the population in each Middle Eastern country are believers of each religion.

# CHAPTER 10

# *Mighty Creators*

MAN IN THE MIDDLE EAST was a mighty creator in art, in literature, and in science as well as in religion. We know especially of his capacity to create magnificence in brick and stone. Great walls and towers still stand as witnesses and the ruins of cities and temples give mute testimony to his creative genius. These splendid monuments were made to house gods, to insure immortality, to proclaim the greatness of some man or some people, to awe other men, and for many other reasons. Some of these great memorials in stone yet tower over men in this region, but much that was built of sun-dried brick and wood has long since crumbled from exposure over the centuries. The outlines that remain enable us to measure and reconstruct, and from these works we know something of the ambitions and art of man in the Middle East.

The man of the Middle East did not always build hugely. He frequently painted and fashioned objects of beauty on a smaller scale: gems carved and framed in carefully wrought designs of gold and silver; exquisite work in ivory, wood, glass, or pottery. He was a talented artist who displayed his artistry in many materials.

He was also a skilled writer who wrote about the divine, revealed the words of his God, and discussed life here and after death. He told of his perplexities, troubles, and loves, his fantasies, his life with other men, his domestic affairs, and all the various aspects of earthly life. These writings were in both prose and verse, and many of them have endured and are still read today.

Man in the Middle East was also a scientist who delved into the mysteries of astron-

Clay tablets inscribed with cuneiform writing provide much of our information about ancient Mesopotamia. This is a due bill from Babylonia. (Chase Manhattan Bank Money Museum)

omy, mathematics, physics, chemistry, and medicine. Many of his discoveries were lost, but some were handed down to provide the foundations for great edifices of knowledge.

## Lands Between the Rivers

Our knowledge of the earliest artistic creations of the people of the Middle East comes from archaeological finds in the Fertile Crescent region and especially in the land between the rivers, Mesopotamia. Among the most important peoples to make their home in this land and leave behind traces of their creativity were the Sumerians, the Assyrians, and the Chaldeans.

### Sumer

Sumerian art was among the earliest to flourish in Mesopotamia. The *ziggurat*, or terraced tower, which was crowned with a shrine, was first built by the Sumerians. This temple-tower rose above the great city of Ur to a height of seventy feet. It inclined upward like a mountain slope to a flat top where the god of the Sumerians was represented and enclosed. The tower was built to resemble a mountain because the Sumerians had worshiped their gods upon hills and mountaintops in the lands of their origin. Since there were no hills and mountains in the land of Sumer where they now lived, the temple-tower served as a high place for worship. The Semites continued to use this building form for many centuries, and modern architects still use its basic design to construct recessed skyscrapers.

The use of brick for buildings was necessary because there was little stone in Sumer. As a consequence, much of what the Sumerians built was swept away in the course of time by the winds, the rains, and the rivers. But some of their important architectural advances were copied and carried on by those who came after them. The arch, the vault, and the dome are Sumerian inventions that have been used in buildings by generations of men.

Among the Sumerians were gifted and imaginative artists. Their finely carved gems and beautifully fashioned jewelry of gold, silver, and bronze still excite our admiration. They were especially skilled in life-like representations of both humans and animals, and were particularly fond of carving the head and shape of the bull.

### Assyria

The Assyrian was a man of war and the hunt, and this fact is reflected in his art. He delighted in scenes of the calmness of man in facing grave danger, in the savagery of a great beast at bay, and in the death struggles of man and beast. He was excited and gratified by this theme of bravery, struggle, and death, and he surrounded himself with its representations. There is movement and life in his sculptures of the angered lion, the hunter, and men at war.

The Assyrian admired bigness and judged the beauty and usefulness of his architecture by this standard. He had sought to make his capital of Nineveh imposing and impregnable. It was one of the great cities of the Middle East. The massive walls of Nineveh ran for several miles along the Tigris River, and the inner walls of the city were eight miles around. Nineveh was filled with magnificent palaces and tower-temples. In this part of Mesopotamia there was much stone, and it was used to make arches, domes, and other architectural features borrowed from the Sumerians. Man's first great aqueduct to span a valley and bring water to a city and its surrounding land was built by the Assyrians. They felt secure and proud in the bigness of their creations. But their creations and their power were destroyed for all time by conquering enemies.

### Chaldea

Nebuchadnezzar, the greatest king of the Chaldeans, outdid the Assyrians in the magnificence of his city and capital of Babylon. Assyrian invaders had destroyed Babylon and diverted the river waters across the rubbish

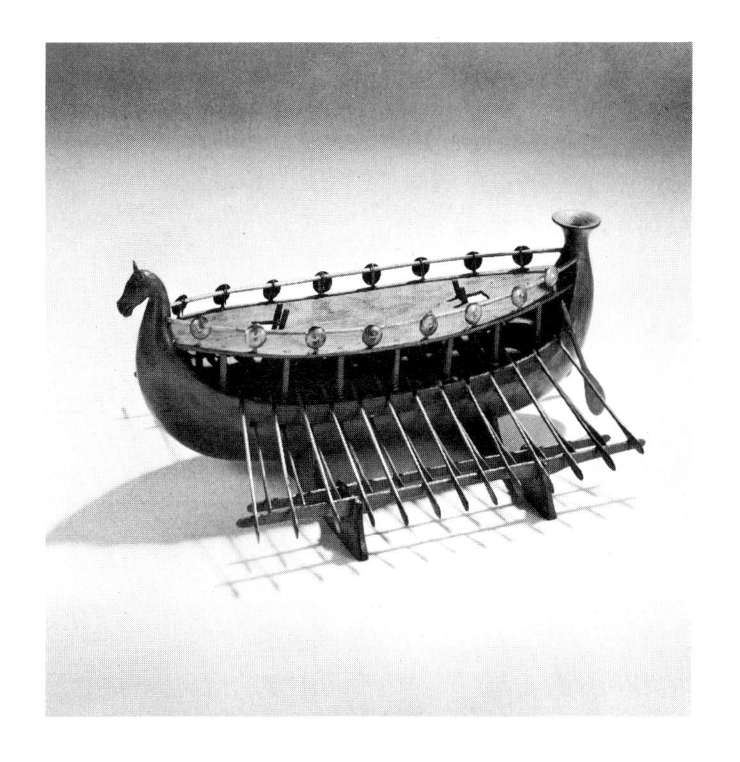

The model shows the Babylonian ship called a "sea horse" of the seventh century B.C. (Commercial Museum, Philadelphia)

of its bricks. But Nebuchadnezzar rebuilt it into a fantastic city.

The city was spread over fifteen square miles of land along both banks of the Euphrates River. Its walls were so wide that chariots could be driven on a road along their tops, and beside the road there were covered sidewalks. One hundred bronze-plated gates gave entry to the city through these massive walls.

Within the city Nebuchadnezzar built his palace. Its surface was covered with brilliantly glazed and patterned tile, and it was surrounded with a profusion of trees and plants. Around this palace terraces were constructed, one above the other, and on these terraces many varieties of trees, plants, and shrubs were planted. They grew in such numbers and to such a length that they hung down like tapestries from the terraces. These were the famous "Hanging Gardens of Babylon," which the Greeks later called one of the seven wonders of the world. It is said that Nebuchadnezzar created these gardens to please his queen, who longed in this brown, dry land for the trees and greens of her homeland.

## Egypt

The Egyptians raised spectacular monuments in stone which have lasted for thousands of years. Many believe that they excelled all other men in this region or any other in their arrangement of grandeur and majesty in stone. Even today, with the assistance of machine and advanced technology, man would find the duplication of these massive achievements a challenge to his knowledge, his economy, his ingenuity, and his imagination.

Four to five thousand years ago, between 3000 and 2300 B.C., the pyramids were built as tombs for Egyptian pharaohs. The pyramids of Egypt were built to insure the immortality of the pharaohs and their people. The people of Egypt would be as indestructible as the tons of granite and limestone blocks which held the body of their representative and ruler, the pharaoh. Some also think that the pyramids were raised to honor the sun god. Whatever the primary reasons for their existence, they are amazing works of man.

The first Egyptian pyramid was built around 3000 B.C., and it is called the Step

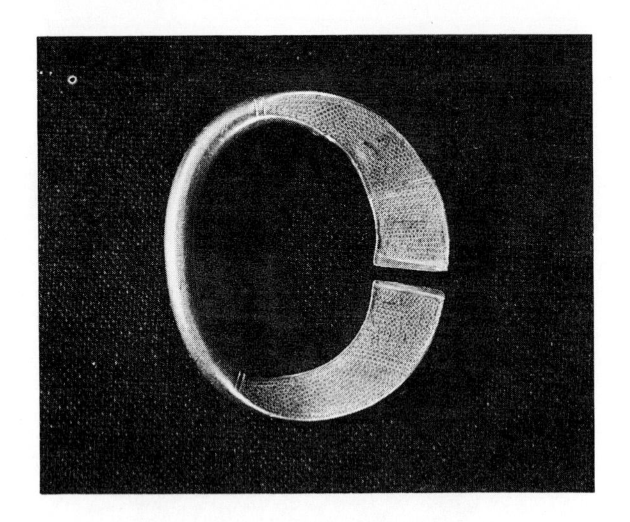

Gold ring money, above, was in use in Egypt about 1000 B.C. (Chase Manhattan Bank Money Museum) The amphora, or wine jar, below, is typical of those used in Egypt about 1400 B.C. (The Corning Museum of Glass)

Pyramid. Larger and larger pyramids followed, and finally the Khufu Pyramid, named after the Pharaoh Khufu, was built. It was the largest ever constructed. The Khufu Pyramid was made of over two million blocks of limestone, each weighing about two and one-half tons, and reached a height of almost 500 feet from a base covering 13 acres of land. Except for a few chambers in the center of the pyramid, where the preserved bodies of the pharaoh and his queen would lie, and a few passageways and airshafts, the pyramid was solid limestone blocks. The blocks were so tightly joined together that in many places the width of the space between them was about one-thousandth of an inch.

It is estimated that one hundred thousand men labored for a period of twenty years to complete the building of this pyramid. The blocks were cut with copper saws, levered along on sledges, and dragged up earthen ramps by hundreds of straining men. As the pyramid grew higher, the height of the earthen ramps was raised and the torture to the muscles of the pulling men increased. The immortality of the pharaoh and his country was built upon the sufferings and the death of many lowly men.

When the pyramid was finished and the dead king placed in his tomb, the entrance to his chamber was sealed and the passageway to his burial place filled in. The entrance to the pyramid was hidden with all the ingenuity at the command of the Egyptian. Nothing must disturb the everlasting body of the pharaoh. But over the centuries, tomb robbers unlocked the secrets of the pyramids, and of the more than sixty pyramids on the west side of the Nile, none have been found unopened. The gold, and silver, and objects of value entombed with the pharaoh for his use in the hereafter were a powerful incentive to those who wanted their use here and now. The millions of tons of granite and limestone still stand, indestructible protectors of empty burial chambers.

The Egyptians stopped building pyramids after the end of the Old Kingdom in 2300 B.C. However, they continued to create huge

The massive statues above are found at Abu Simbul Temple, in Egypt. (Egyptian State Tourist Administration)

works of beauty in stone by building massive, wonderful temples. The temples at Karnak and Luxor are the most famous examples.

The temple of Karnak was the greatest temple ever built by man to honor his god or gods. It was over a thousand feet long, and some of the great columns which supported its roof were about 80 feet high. They were large enough for a hundred men to stand on their tops. Egyptian architecture pioneered in the use of columns and pillars of stone to support roofs. An avenue bordered on each side with a long row of animals carved in stone led up to the entrance of this fantastic temple. Although the temple was vast, it was well proportioned, and its columns were adorned with inscriptions and well-executed carvings.

The Egyptians sculptured their pharaohs massively too. Some of these stone statues reached heights of 70, 80, and 90 feet. The Egyptians also made *obelisks*, tapering pillars of stone, which weighed as much as a thousand tons each. Great stone sphinxes, which had the body of a lion and the head of a man, guarded cities and pyramid-tombs. Few men have thought and constructed on so great a scale with stone as did the Egyptians.

The Egyptian was a versatile artist, however, and not limited to greatness in size. Egyptian paintings caught the movement and flow in nature, the animal running, the bird flying, the stars of the night sky, the opening flower, and the budding tree. Although painting was restrained by strict rules in portraying humans, each subject showed a distinct personality. The Egyptian was human and he wanted to portray the humanness of others even though the conventions of his society required that this portrayal be kept within definite limits.

The Egyptian also worked in many other materials—ivory, ebony, wood, gold, silver, copper, bronze, and glass. It was he who invented the art of glassmaking. He made necklaces, bracelets, pendants, jewelry boxes, containers for cosmetics, and many other objects in which both men and women delighted.

The Egyptian was no ordinary artist. His artistry ranged from the incredibly large to the smallest of man's needs of beauty. From almost the beginning of civilized history to the present, man has stared with appreciation and amazement at thc artistic achievements which emerged from the mind, and heart, and hand of the Egyptian.

1. What does a ziggurat look like? Why are they built in this shape?
2. Describe Assyrian art and tell how it reflected the Assyrian way of life.
3. Identify and describe the "Hanging Gardens of Babylon." What reasons explain their construction?

## An Ancient Literature

In addition to building and carving large and small works of art, the Sumerian, the Egyptian, and the Semite also wrote works still remembered and read. Some of the earliest literature that we know about was written by man in the Middle East. The greatest and most lasting of this literature dealt with religious matters, with the meaning of life, with gods, the creation of the world, and the revelations of God to man. But there were also writings that dealt with more earthly matters—the love of a man for a woman, the faithlessness of wives or husbands, and stories of adventure and battle. There were also tales of magic and tales about heroes who struggled and overcame gods and men. One of the greatest of these tales about heroes is known as the *Gilgamesh Epic*, which takes its name from the hero of the story, Gilgamesh.

The Sumerians probably began this epic of Gilgamesh, and the Babylonians later made it into a stimulating poem, perhaps around 2000 B.C. Gilgamesh was the son of a goddess and a mortal man, and he was endowed with more than ordinary strength. But he was also subject to the limitations of all mortals, for he never escaped the inevitability of death, and he could not uncover many of the mysteries of life. Although he won many victories over those who tormented him, victory was never complete and there were always other obstacles to overcome. Frustration was his fate, for when he almost had the secret of immortality within his reach in the form of a weed, it was stolen from him by a serpent. The lesson of the epic seems to be that man cannot escape death, and death may not bring happiness, so we must try to make the best of what we have here and now on earth.

Some of the best of Egyptian literature was also religious in nature. It included touching hymns to the sun god Re and verse of great merit which spoke to man about eternal life and how to achieve it. Some of these hymns and religious writings were written prior to 3000 B.C. There is also the beautiful hymn to the one god Aton written by Ikhnaton in the fourteenth century B.C. A verse from this hymn reads:

> How manifold are thy works!
> They are hidden before men
> O sole God, beside whom there is no other
> Thou didst create the earth according
> to thy heart.[1]

Ancient Egyptian literature also included love poetry, tales of adventure, and fables which found their way into the *Arabian Nights*. The Egyptians wrote about various aspects of life and made some penetrating observations about man and his various moods and actions. Many of their observations are still pertinent today.

[1] From *Dawn of Conscience* by J. H. Breasted, Charles Scribner's Sons, 1934. Quoted by permission.

To the minds of many, the Bible is the greatest literature produced by ancient man in the Middle East. Many have observed that the literature of the Bible is among the best ever written by man. It is often referred to as the world's greatest book. In its imagery, its flow of events and language, its poetry, its drama, and its depth of content, it is unique among the literature of the world. There are the thundering, stirring, threatening words of the prophets calling upon the people to relinquish their evil ways and return to the ways of God. There is the drama of the puzzled, righteous Job who is afflicted with many sufferings despite his goodness. What suffering man through the ages has not understood his anguished cry "Why? Oh God! Why me?" The lovely psalms of praise and love for God compare with the greatest poetry created by man. During the Babylonian captivity, one of the most deeply moving of these psalms expressed the longing of the Jews for their homeland.

By the rivers of Babylon, there we sat down, yea, we wept, when we remembered Zion.
We hanged our harps upon the willows in the midst thereof.
For there they that carried us away captive required of us a song; and they that wasted us required of us mirth, saying, Sing us one of the songs of Zion.
How shall we sing the Lord's song in a strange land?
If I forget thee, O Jerusalem, let my right hand forget her cunning.
If I do not remember thee, let my tongue cleave to the roof of my mouth; if I prefer not Jerusalem above my chief joy.

—Psalm 137

Then there are the writings of the New Testament, which are familiar to most Christians. There are those today who can recite from memory passage after passage of its books. The New Testament brings to its readers not only a feeling of the beauty of line and word but a sense of comfort, mercy, compassion, and hope. There are the moving gospels of Mark, Matthew, Luke, and John, and the epistles of Paul which are the basis of certain Christian doctrines. There are also epistles of Peter, James, John, and Jude which elaborate on the teachings of Jesus. The Old and New Testaments have had a profound effect upon the standards, values, and beliefs of man.

## Creativity and Science of the Moslem

The Moslems, through their creativity and science, gave much to man. They, too were indebted to other men for some of the bases of their art and science: to the Persian and the Byzantine for the column, the dome, and the arch, and to the Greeks for earlier scientific contributions. But, beginning with the spread of Islam in the seventh century, many older cultures were blended and new ones evolved in the lands of those who accepted the Moslem faith. Moslem conquests covered a spread of nations and lands extending from Spain in the west to India in the east. But whether Spanish, Egyptian, Arabic, Persian, or Indian, the followers of Islam developed a science and art forms that were distinctively Islamic. The creations of the past were adapted to new uses and the Moslems made many new contributions of their own.

**Art and architecture.** The Moslems fashioned unique onion-shaped domes, made curved arches like horseshoes, twisted columns into graceful and intricate forms, and built soaring towers called minarets. From the balconies of minarets each day Moslems were reminded of their appointed hours of prayer. The stone of the walls of Moslem buildings was made to appear as lace, and we call this stone tracery "arabesque." These walls were made appealing to the eye with flowing geometric patterns and Arabic script. Beautiful mosaic patterns were fashioned of inlaid stone and colored glass. Islam frowned upon painting or sculpturing human forms because it was feared that man might turn to the worship of idols again. The Moslem lavished his feeling for architectural beauty upon hospitals, schools, and libraries, as well as mosques.

Moslem art was not limited to buildings. The Moslem artisan had a feeling for color, and his rugs, silks, and tapestries glowed in warm and vivid hues. His inlaid metal was outstanding, and his glass lamps were decorated with colored enamel. He painted pottery, tooled leather, and produced variety and richness in copper, brass, ivory, gold, and silver. He worked in steel, and swords of Damascus

A mosque stands among the modern buildings of Alexandria in Egypt. (Egyptian State Tourist Administration)

and Toledo steel were prized everywhere. He made linen in Damascus of such quality that it is still known as damask. He took endless pains to artfully adorn his manuscripts.

The Moslem Arabs were extremely fond of poetry, and Arab poets composed verses on numerous subjects and for every occasion. The Persians were also famous among the Moslems for their ability to create literature. One of the most famous Persian poets was Omar Khayyám, who is known to many in the world for his collection of poems called the *Rubáiyát.* Omar Khayyám was better known in his time, about 1048 to about 1123, as an astronomer and mathematician.

The Arabic book best known to Western readers is *The Arabian Nights Entertainments*, a collection of several hundred tales taken from many lands and first put together in Arabic translations probably during the ninth and tenth centuries. Countless children and grownups have read about Aladdin and his magic lamp, the story of Ali Baba and the forty thieves, and the adventures of Sinbad the sailor. This collection of stories gives us a picture of life in the political and religious center at Baghdad during some of the peaks of Moslem power.

**Medicine and science.** Moslem creativity was breath-taking in medicine and other sciences. There was the great Persian doctor Avicenna (980-1037) who explained that tuberculosis was contagious and that diseases could be spread by contaminated water and dirt. He was familiar with pleurisy and nervous illnesses of the body. Around the year 1000 he wrote a classic medical book known as the *Canon of Medicine* which was highly respected in Europe and was utilized by the Moslems for centuries. But Avicenna was only one of many who contributed to medical knowledge.

Moslem doctors uncovered the truth about smallpox, diagnosed stomach cancer, treated eye diseases, and knew antidotes for poisoning as well as ways of stopping bleeding and infection. They understood that the plague could be passed along to others through clothes and contact with contaminated eating and drinking vessels as well as by direct contact with the sick person himself. They practiced surgery and started this practice in Europe. They discovered and used many medicines for a variety of ailments. Hospitals were built and administered by a system that was quite modern, with special wards, dispensaries, and libraries. Medical students learned through practical experience and attended lectures. When they had satisfactorily completed their studies, they were given medical diplomas permitting them to practice medicine. Man owes much to the research of Moslem doctors.

Man is also indebted to the Moslem for fundamental contributions in mathematics. The use of the zero and Arabic numerals from 1 through 9 make it possible to deal conveniently with tens, hundreds, thousands, and millions. It is believed that this number system originated in India, but it was passed along to other men by the modern Arabs, who also did basic work in geometry and trigonometry and gave us the word *algebra*.

Moslem astronomers understood that the earth rotates on its axis and revolves around the sun. They had wonderful observatories and spent much time observing the movements of the stars. Omar Khayyám was an astronomer as well as a poet, and he helped to devise a calendar which is superior to the Gregorian calendar in use today. The Moslems were also navigators and knew the use of latitude and longitude. They improved upon the old Greek invention of the astrolabe, which assisted sailors in determining their position when out of sight of land. Columbus used the astrolabe in his voyage across the Atlantic to the Americas.

The Moslems also worked in physics and in chemistry. They studied light—its refraction, speed, and transmission—and were the first to theorize that we see because light rays reflected from objects strike our eyes. They pioneered chemical research and discovered many compounds—sulfuric and nitric acids, carbonate of soda, nitrate of silver, borax, and many other substances. They were among the first to learn the chemical processes of distilling and filtering. Many of these discoveries were the result of alchemy, the medieval science chiefly concerned with the desire to change base metals into gold, but they led to later chemical discoveries of great importance to man.

**Influence on Europe.** Many of these advances were passed to Europe by way of Spain when that country was ruled by Moslems and later by returning crusaders who had first come to take the Holy Land from the "uncivilized" Moslem control in the eleventh century.

Moslem contributions to European civilization were great. The European accompanied his love songs on the *guitar*, *lute*, and *tambourine*, and these instruments as well as their names were originally Arabic. The European used the words *alchemy*, *zenith*, *nadir*, and *alcohol* and gradually forgot their Arabic origin. The works of Aristotle, Plato, and other Greeks were translated into Latin from the Arabic before the original Greek was known. Thus, the European learned much about his cultural ancestors, the Greeks, from their cultural preservers, the Moslems. In science, in the arts, in literature, and in many other areas, man in the West learned much from the followers of Islam.

1. Identify the *Gilgamesh Epic*. Who wrote it and what is it about? Does it have a moral?
2. What advances in the field of medicine do we owe to the genius of the Middle East?
3. How were the knowledge and achievements of the Middle East carried to Europe?

## The Persians

None were more honored among the Moslems than the Persians for the quality of their creative genius. Although the Arab introduced the religion of Islam into Persia about 650 A.D., the cultured Persian in turn had a refining influence upon the Arab. The caliph, the leader of the Moslem world, lived in Baghdad starting around 750 A.D., and many of his ministers were Persian. The culture, literature, and language of Persia spread from this court of the ruling family known as the Abbasids to much of the Middle East.

In the tenth century, Persian literature and genius in other fields continued to develop. There was the poet Firdausi, who wrote the great epic of the Persians entitled *Book of Kings*. There was Avicenna who, in addition to the *Canon of Medicine*, also wrote eighteen volumes dealing with physics, metaphysics, and mathematics, all collected under the title *al-Shifa*. Even when the Seljuk Turks began to control the Persians between 1037 and 1157, their creativity was not dimmed. This was the period when Omar Khayyám made his important contributions in astronomy and mathematics and wrote his imperishable *Rubáiyát*.

Persian cultural vitality survived the savage forays of the Mongol conqueror Genghis Khan in 1220 and the second Mongol invasion of Hulagu Khan in 1256. It flowered to even

This relief carving of a lion attacking a bull is at Persepolis, ancient capital of Persia. (Embassy of Iran)

greater peaks just before and during the period called *Timurid*, 1336-1501. During this period the poets Rumi, Saadi, and Hafiz became known and their works were read and respected throughout the world of Islam. Saadi, who lived from about 1184 to 1291, wrote such works as the *Bustan*, or *Garden of Fruits*, and the *Gulistan*, or *Garden of Roses*. Saadi's feeling for the all-embracing commonality of man is caught for all time in the following verse from the *Gulistan:*

> All of Adam's sons are limbs of one another,
> Each of the selfsame substances as his brother:
> So, while one member suffers ache and grief,
> The other members cannot win relief.
> Thou, who are heedless of thy brother's pain,
> It is not right at all to name thee Man.[1]

Hafiz is regarded as among the best of the Persian poets, and his collection of poems under the title *Divan of Hafiz* is consulted as a spiritual guide.

[1] From *Shiraz: Persian City of Saints and Poets,* by A. J. Arberry. Copyright 1960 by the University of Oklahoma Press.

The creativity of the Persian was not confined to poetry, astronomy, medicine, and mathematics. He was also a magnificent architect, painter of miniatures, worker in metal and ceramics, and maker of fine carpets. The exquisite miniatures painted by Persian artists in the fifteenth century have never been excelled. This art form had great impact upon the Indians, and in the sixteenth century there arose at the Mogul court in India an Indo-Persian school of miniature art.

Between 1502 and 1736, when the Safavid dynasty ruled in Persia, their capital, Isfahan, became a city rich in masterpieces of architecture. The Persians are so enthralled with its beauty that they refer to this city as "Half the World." Its buildings, its mosques, and its pavilions are incredibly beautiful in their covering of colorful glazed tile and sparkling mosaics, and in the skyward-reaching forms of their domes and minarets. Isfahan is a city which only a people steeped in the traditions of creating beauty could erect.

1. What were some of the great achievements of the Timurid Period?
2. Who was Saadi? What were his major accomplishments?

### Conclusion

In art, architecture, literature, and science, man in the Middle East created much that was fine and useful for all men everywhere. The massiveness, richness, and elegance of his buildings have long been admired and frequently imitated. He built and furnished houses and palaces for convenience and comfort. He explored the mysteries of the heavens and learned to regulate time by clocks and calendars and to navigate the seas by positioning himself according to the stars. He probed the machinery of his body and learned to shorten pain and lengthen life. The force, vividness, and content of Middle Eastern literature have influenced the thoughts and writings of countless men down to the present day. Man in the Middle East poured out his passions, questions, problems, and yearnings in verse and prose which touch our understanding and draw our sympathy.

## SUMMING UP THE CHAPTER

A. Define or explain the following terms.

| | |
|---|---|
| aqueduct | obelisk |
| astrolabe | pharaoh |
| caliph | psalm |
| damask | pyramid |
| Gospels | ziggurat |
| minarets | |

B. Identify or locate the following and tell why they are important.

| | |
|---|---|
| Avicenna | Luxor |
| *Gilgamesh Epic* | Omar Khayyàm |
| Hafiz | Sphinx |
| Karnak | Timurid |
| Khufu Pyramid | |

C. Chapter review questions.

1. Why are so few of the buildings of Mesopotamia left today?
2. What important architectural advances were made by the Sumerians? How significant are they today?
3. Identify the Assyrian standards of beauty. What are our standards of beauty? How would you account for these differences in taste?
4. By whom and why were the pyramids built? Name some of the most important pyramids and discuss how they were built.
5. When was the use of the column introduced in architecture? For what types of building was it used?
6. What materials besides stone did the Egyptian use in his art?
7. What did the ancient Middle Easterner write about? What do you consider to be the most important subject?
8. What important contributions to the fields of physics, chemistry, and astronomy did man in the Middle East make?
9. Evaluate the creative genius of man in the Middle East. Compare Middle Eastern accomplishments with those of Asia and America.

D. Questions for discussion.

1. In what countries or areas of the world do walled cities exist? How do you account for this?
2. Why is the concept of zero so important? Do you know any numbering system, other than Roman numerals, that does not use zero?

E. Projects for groups or individuals.

1. Read the *Gilgamesh Epic* and report on it.
2. Write an adventure story similar to those found in the *Arabian Nights*.
3. In your school library, look up pictures of mosques and minarets in various countries of the Middle East. See if they are similar in any way.
4. Prepare an oral report on religious influence on art in the Middle East. Would your findings be true of other areas of the world?

# CHAPTER 11

# Society: the Many and the Few

SINCE ANCIENT TIMES in the Middle East there have been divisions of class which were wide and deep. At times lucky and clever men bridged these divisions and improved their economic and social positions, but they were the exceptions rather than the rule. It was not easy to climb from the lower to the upper social levels, for there were few rungs between the bottom and the top of the social ladder. The middle class was almost nonexistent.

The social system of the Middle East has been described as a pyramid with a broad base of the lowly masses tapering upward to a peak made up of the high and the few. The few people of high positions were supported with difficulty by the masses. For the greater part of man's social existence in the Middle East, this way of life was accepted and endured as inevitable.

But there were instances when men rebelled against a degrading social system and cried out that their fate was overly harsh. The religions of Judaism, Christianity, and especially Islam brought a sharpened sense and consciousness of social equality. They taught that man had a soul which in the sight of God might be better than that of his superior on earth. These religions taught that all men were equals before God. Then in modern times, thoughts from the West began to be felt in the Middle East, and they brought messages about the equality of man based on the idea that the individual possessed certain inalienable rights. In some areas, social life has begun to change rapidly; in others, slowly; but in all instances the changes have brought about more equal terms in social groups. Man in the Middle East, as in Asia, is living now amidst social changes.

## Ancient Social Life

Throughout the lands of the Fertile Crescent and in ancient Egypt the social systems were remarkably similar. There were variations from place to place, but in spirit and in content, society was substantially the same. The king, the priest, the noble, and the government official were the elite of society. They were separated from the humble people below them by a wide chasm of custom, culture, economics, and political power. Far below, on a descending scale, were the scribe, the merchant, and the artisan. Still farther along toward the broadening base were the small farmer, the peasant, and, lowest of all, the slave. The great differences in their manners of living were symbolic of the vast social distances which separated the elite from the artisan and peasant.

A typical Egyptian noble lived comfortably in his spacious, cool, and inviting villa along the river. He walled it for privacy, and within his walls trees shaded and cooled the walks, the gardens, and the house. A typical house had two stories and was built of brick and wood. The floors were of patterned tile, and tapestries hung upon the walls. The furniture had elegance and strength. Chairs and couches were cushioned with soft leather and the wood was inlaid with ivory and ebony. A roof garden was shaded from the sun by linen cloth, and the noble frequently slept there on a soft bed, refreshed by the river breezes.

The master of the villa wore a simple kilt of fine linen, and his wife wore a long dress of linen which left her arms exposed. Her dress was starched and pleated, and often made of cloth so fine as to be almost transparent. She used green eye shadow and a black powder called *kohl* to darken her eyebrows and eyelashes. She used the juice of the henna plant to redden her fingers and her feet. The boxes that held her make-up were artistic in design as well as useful. She adorned herself with lovely necklaces and wore bracelets on her arms and legs. She kept her hair cut short, for she enjoyed wearing wigs of various styles and colors.

The master and his guests dined with tableware and glasses that were artistically shaped. They ate varieties of meats, vegetables, and delicacies served by an abundance of slaves and servants. They were entertained by the music of slave girls playing on wind instruments and stringed instruments. And all this comfort, beauty, and abundance was made possible by the hard labor of the peasant in the fields. The pharaoh had granted this noble the rents of the harvests of many fields to insure the easy living which was his due as a noble of the kingdom.

The peasant struggled desperately during his lifetime to wrest a living from the land which he planted with wheat, barley, and flax for his linen thread. His life was a weary routine of planting, irrigating, and harvesting. He paid high rents to the noble or priestly landowners, which left him barely enough to live on. He lived in a small, stifling, dark house of sun-dried mud brick. His furniture was meager and poor—some pots for cooking, a small bed of wood, and a brick oven outside the house where he cooked his food. He ate little meat, except when he was lucky enough to snare a wild duck in the marshes, but fish was not uncommon. His basic fare was loaves of barley or wheat which he baked himself and washed down with beer.

The peasant toiled long hours in the fields under the hot sun, sometimes helped by an ox which pulled his plough. Sometimes he owned a donkey on whose back he transported his goods and his crops. He scooped up water

The ancient Egyptian relief carvings below show the sowing and harvesting of wheat. (Courtesy of The Cleveland Museum of Art)

from the river Nile for his thirsty fields by means of a bucket attached to one end of a long pole which was weighted on the other end. This irrigation device, called a *shadoof,* is still in use in some parts of Egypt. The peasant had no time to entertain, nor any money to buy his wife jewelry or fine clothes. He felt himself lucky if he was not required to toil for the pharaoh and the noble on the construction of a massive temple, tomb, or public work, which would drain his strength and shorten the few years of his life. His life was known, but it was not shared by king, noble, priest, and government servant, all of whom he nourished and sheltered with the fruits of his labors.

These examples of the different social worlds in which Egyptian lived with Egyptian could be multiplied throughout the Fertile Crescent with some changes in the style and materials of the noble's house and the woman's dress. If anything, there was probably more mobility within the social system of the Egyptian than elsewhere in the Fertile Crescent. The more liberal Greek ideas began to penetrate the Middle East after the defeat of the Persians by Alexander the Great around 330 B.C., but the system remained essentially unchanged.

The Romans did not basically change the system when they came to control the coastal areas of the Fertile Crescent and Egypt several centuries later. Nor was there a fundamental change when the Byzantine rulers succeeded the Romans in the fourth century A.D. and controlled much of the Middle East. And it did not change after the Byzantine capital of Constantinople was conquered by the Ottoman Turks in 1453. In fact, only recently in the twentieth century, have some rulers taken concrete steps to provide the peasant with an opportunity of raising his social status. And there are still a number of areas in the Middle East where the peasant continues to exhaust himself in maintaining the social status of the ruler, the government officials, and the landed aristocrats.

The religions of Judaism, Christianity, and Islam did emphasize beliefs in certain fundamental rights of man. From these beliefs there grew a realization in the Middle East that the more fortunate had a duty to relieve the lowly of some of their economic and social burdens. Islam especially had a great social impact in the Middle East because it became the religion of the majority there.

1. In what way was the social system of the Middle East like a pyramid? What factors inspired man to change this system?
2. Describe the dress, abode, and mode of living of a noble and a peasant. What advantages do you see in each way of life?
3. Did the various foreign rulers of the Middle East attempt to change the existing social system? Do you think they were wise in their decision?

### Social Teachings of Islam

Mohammed, the prophet of Islam, preached a doctrine in the early seventh century A.D. which was socially revolutionary for that age. He taught that all men were equal in the sight of God. In Islam the mighty and the low pray together in the mosque without distinction of rank, and when the Moslem pays homage to his God at the shrine of the Kaaba in Mecca, his social status is unrecognizable, for all must wear a simple sheetlike garment. Mohammed spoke of Islam as a brotherhood of man, and he married an African woman to teach his followers that no social blemish should follow from race. One of the reasons for the tremendous successes of Islam in Asia and in Africa is the practice of racial equality among the Moslems.

Islam imposes upon every Moslem a tax which is used for the social and economic uplift of man. Every Moslem is called upon to treat the unfortunate with the compassion of Allah. The good Moslem should think first of those near him by blood and by proximity, and he should exert himself to help them. Mohammed was an Arab, and his first followers were Arabs. He and they had a keen sense of family, clan, and tribal responsibility. The Arab belonged to a family, to a clan which was composed of closely related families, and to a tribe which was made up of several or more clans. All within the tribe were related because they traced their descent to a common ancestor. The Arab was responsible for the welfare of all of his tribe, and they for him, even to the extent of avenging his death if he was killed by a man of another tribe. This sense of responsibility for the welfare of kinsmen is carried on in Islam.

But the responsibility of the Moslem does not cease when he has helped his relative, for he is responsible for the uplift of every man. This responsibility has found expression among the Moslems in building hospitals, schools, and inns for travelers, giving alms for the poor, and in other charitable works.

## The Spread of Islam

The Moslem Arab and his converts carried the religious and social teachings of Islam far beyond the geographic boundaries of Arabia and the Middle East. After Mohammed's death in 632 A.D., his followers chose caliphs who continued the religious and territorial expansion of Islam which had begun during the lifetime of Mohammed. The name *caliph* means "successor." The caliph was the successor to the religious and political authority of the prophet Mohammed. The Moslem advance in the Middle East was so rapid that by 661 A.D. the capital of the Moslems was moved from Medina in Arabia to Damascus in Syria. There the office of caliph became the exclusive prerogative of the Ommiad clan until around 750 A.D. when the Abbasid family overthrew the Ommiad caliph at Damascus. The Abbasid caliphs established their capital at Baghdad, which is the present capital of Iraq and is located on the Tigris River.

The Abbasid family came to power with the help of the Persians and others who believed that the caliph should be related to the prophet Mohammed by blood or marriage. The Abbasids were descended from a cousin of Mohammed named Abbas. Those who hold that the head of Islam should be only a member of the family of Mohammed are known as Shiites. The Abbasid family continued to formally rule from Baghdad until 1258 when the Mongols under Hulagu, the grandson of Genghis Khan, captured Baghdad and killed the Caliph and many of the people of the city. However, the power of the Abbasids had waned long before this time, and as early as 1055, the Seljuk Turks had actually ruled Baghdad.

The cathedral at Santiago de Campostela, Spain is said to be built on the grave of St. James, the patron of Spain. "Santiago and Spain" was the rallying cry of Spaniards against Moslem Moorish invaders. (Spanish National Tourist Office)

During these early changes of caliphs, the march of Islam went quickly forward. It expanded to Egypt, and along the coast of North Africa which now includes the countries of Libya, Tunisia, Algeria, and Morocco. The people called Berbers, who lived in North Africa, carried the teachings of Islam to Spain. During the eighth century they were stopped

Modern buildings rise in the city of Mecca, birthplace of Mohammed. (Arabian American Oil Company)

from spreading Islam to France by the army of Charles Martel. By 800 A.D. the followers of Islam ruled a great stretch of land which extended from the borders of India and the lands around the Black and Caspian seas to the Pyrenees Mountains separating Spain and France. A vast expanse of lands and peoples was brought under Moslem rule in a phenomenally short period of time.

## War and Social Teachings

This unusually quick and mighty growth of empire did not result, as some have said, from a commandment of Mohammed to his followers to go forth and convert by the sword. On the contrary, Mohammed tried to stem the rush of man to war, for in the Koran he stated: "Defend yourself against your enemies; but attack them not first: for God does not love transgressors." Mohammed sought to limit the horrors of war through the social teachings of Islam, but he was trying to restrain man, and man will not always be restrained. Man's inclinations to seek power and plunder through war and conquest are not always curbed by his conversion to a religion, even though this religion counsels him to love others and to seek his ends by righteous methods. The Moslem, like other men who adhere to a religious faith, gave his allegiance to Islam and has been the better because of its ideals and teachings. But environment, circumstances, strong temptations, and traditions have often prevented his living these ideals continuously and completely.

The Arabs, who sparked the great forward movement of Islam, lived in an environment where raiding and battles were a part of life, and the bravery and skill of a warrior were necessities. When the Arabs of the Arabian desert became unified for the first time under Islam's banner, they felt the possibilities of their unified strength. It was human and natural that they should follow their inclination to test this strength in the regions neighboring them. The Byzantine and Persian empires were in a weakened condition in these areas, and their territories fell readily and easily to Arab raids. It was almost inevitable that the Arabs should carry on until stopped by a stronger power. They and those who joined with them found no stronger power in the Middle East, in North Africa, in Spain, in Persia, or in the steppes of Central Asia, and thus their empire was born.

The social teachings of Mohammed contributed to the acceptance, the spread, the unity, and continuity of Islam within the empire. Although the Arab Moslem was not stopped from conquest by the teachings of Islam, his actions in war and peace were moderated by these teachings. He was tolerant of the Christians, the Jews, and members of other religious faiths he found among the peoples he conquered. He did not always insist with the sword that they become Moslems. He built hospitals, schools, and libraries, and brought vegetables and fruits and goods that made life easier to bear for those he had conquered. Many found him less oppressive than the Byzantine and the Persian, and they welcomed his conquests. Most of those conquered by the Arab admired the teachings and the actions he advocated, and they too became Moslems and helped to spread the teachings of Islam.

**Jihad (Holy War).** Moslems are allowed to resist evil, and Islam teaches the ancient Middle Eastern tradition of an eye for an eye and a tooth for a tooth. The offender may be punished to the full extent of his offense. Moslems also believe in a *jihad* or "holy war," as do many Christians. But such a holy war must be defensive in nature—it must be waged to right an injury or to protect oneself. The Moslem who fights and dies in such a war is a martyr and goes immediately to heaven. But Islam does not permit an offensive war except to right a wrong done.

Even when engaged in a holy war there are certain rules of war which should be observed, for Mohammed wished to soften the barbarities of war even when it was justified. He insisted upon certain rules and a certain code of behavior: the dead and the wounded should not be mutilated, as was the custom in many wars of those days; women and children should be spared; the harvests, the orchards, the sacred objects, and the homes of the poor should be spared. War was just as savage and hellish in those days as it is today, and Mohammed understood well the almost unlimited fiendishness of man which even a "good" war unleashed. The social teachings of Mohammed were directed toward controlling the passions of man at war.

The social teachings of Islam on the conduct of war found their highest expression in the humanity, mercy, and generosity of the great Sultan Saladin—the Turks referred to their rulers as sultans. Although Saladin fought against the Crusaders from Europe and wrested Jerusalem from them in 1187, he was regarded even by them as a man to be respected and honored.

## The Seljuk Turks and the Crusades

Despite the enlightened religious and social teachings of Islam, factional quarrels began to disrupt the empire the Moslems had established. Their empire, which had been unified under one caliph at Baghdad, split into three separate caliphates. An independent caliphate was established at Cordova, Spain, about 929, by some members of the Ommiad family who had formerly ruled in Damascus. The descendants of Ali, a cousin of Mohammed who had married Mohammed's daughter Fatima, founded an independent caliphate in Egypt. The caliphs in Baghdad deteriorated under the great weight of wealth and luxury which were now theirs. Gradually much of their political power moved into the hands of the Persian *viziers* or prime ministers and their Turkish mercenaries. Then, between 1055 and 1057 the Seljuk Turks, who had gradually pushed south from Turkestan, began to conquer much of the Middle East. Among their conquests were Palestine and great portions of the Byzantine Empire in Asia Minor. The Crusades, launched from Europe over a period of several hundred years beginning around 1096, were one of the results of the Turkish invasion.

In 1095 Pope Urban II called for rich and poor, knight and peasant alike, to go forth from Europe and drive out the Turks who now controlled the Holy Land and refused it to the Christian. It was a Christian holy war, and those who lost their lives in this war would die with their sins forgiven. For the Moslems it was also a holy war, for they regarded it as a defensive war. If a Moslem died defending lands regarded as holy, he too would go immediately to heaven. Bolstered by the promise of eternal life, both Christian and Moslem displayed magnificent courage in battle.

Two leaders in the latter part of the twelfth century are respected in history for their expression of high religious ideals despite the pressures of war: Richard the Lion-Hearted of England and Saladin, Sultan of the Turks. They were antagonists, and each was convinced of the rightness of his cause. But they admired and respected each other, and, given the chance, would have welcomed a more permanent and peaceful opportunity of sharing each other's company.

An eyewitness account tells of a humane action by Saladin which also illustrates the ideals of the religion he lived by and the virtues the Crusaders attributed to him. One day while Saladin was besieging a camp of the Crusaders, one of his warriors brought a weeping woman of the Crusaders to him. She told him that the night before some Moslems had stolen into her tent and kidnapped her little girl. The leaders of the Crusaders had advised her to ask the help of Saladin, for he was kind and merciful. Her tears and despair moved Saladin, and he sent one of his staff to the town nearby with orders to buy the little girl from those who had stolen her. Late that day the man returned with the girl riding upon his shoulders. The teller of the tale described the tears of Saladin and those around who were touched by the happy hysteria of the mother whose child had been returned to her. Saladin then ordered the woman and her child escorted to the lines of the Crusaders. His generosity was legendary, and when he died there were few personal effects left which he could call his own because he had given so much to others.

But among the Moslems and Crusaders there were also knaves, opportunists, and men who shadowed the purity of their purposes with greed, treachery, and barbarous acts. The ultimate failure of the Crusaders to maintain themselves in the Holy Land was due as much to their narrow selfishness as to the bravery and skill of the Moslem warrior. Before the end of the twelfth century the Christians were driven from this land, and the Crusades had a greater effect upon the European than upon man in the Middle East.

1. In what ways were the teachings of Mohammed socially revolutionary? What other religious figures also taught revolutionary ideas?
2. How do the teachings of Islam require every Moslem to be responsible for the social and economic uplift of every other Moslem?
3. In what respect did the teachings of Islam oppose aggressive wars?

## Woman in the Middle East

The position and treatment of women in the Middle East has varied with time, place, and circumstance. The Sumerians, the Babylonians, and the Egyptians frequently treated women with respect and as equals. The code of Babylonian laws published by Hammurabi, protected the woman by law. She could own property, do business, and divorce her husband if she was without blame and he had been neglecting her and speaking ill of her.

In Egypt women enjoyed a fine position in society. No man could have more than one legal wife, and descent was traced through the wife's line; she was recognized as a person with intelligence, and consulted on domestic and official matters. If a woman was of the royal family, she often exercised great influence in affairs of state. During the Empire Period, about 1580 to about 1000 B.C., women ruled as pharaohs. There was a queen named Hatshepsut who ruled extremely well and raised her country to new heights of prosperity and peaceful glory.

At other times and in other places the life of women was deplorable. They were viewed as mere pieces of property to be sold, used, or discarded on the mere whim of a male master, who might be father, husband, or owner. One of these times was during the sixth and seventh centuries in Arabia when Mohammed started to proclaim the doctrines of Islam. Girl babies were often unwanted and might be killed soon after birth. Polygamy was practiced, and marriages were frequently temporary. The wife had no recourse if her husband tired of her and cast her off without support. Women were regarded as of small value at this time in Arabia.

Mohammed was sickened by this treatment of women, and through his preaching and commandments he changed their conditions for the better. He forbade the killing of babies, whether female or male. A woman could not be left without any support by either father or husband, and she shared in her father's inheritance with the male. At the time of her marriage the husband or his family must provide a dowry for her which she could claim at any time. If her husband divorced her, he was required to support her for a time or until she remarried. The good Moslem was not permitted to marry more than one wife unless he could love and treat her in the same way he treated his other wives. The Koran permits a Moslem to have four wives at one time, but because of these hard and strict conditions, the vast majority of Moslems have rarely had more than one wife.

Gradually, as the centuries moved along, it became the custom for the Moslem woman to veil her face from the sight of men outside her immediate family. She began to spend much of her life in a special part of the house, often referred to as a *harem.* As the wealth and luxury of the ruling Moslems increased, they bought girls and trained them in the art of entertainment. Many of these slave girls could be found in the palaces of the sultans, the nobles, and the wealthy. By the beginning of the nineteenth century the Moslem woman was living a life apart from males other than those of her family. But she never lost many of the rights given her by Islam. With the onward movement of the nineteenth century and the influx of additional ideas about human rights stemming from Europe, she began to move toward a fuller and more complete equality with the male.

Many women still wear veils in the Moslem world. These women in Morocco are waiting in line to vote. (Wide World photo)

Between 1800 and 1914 social conditions in Europe were in a state of almost continuous and drastic change, and these changes made themselves felt in the Middle East. During the nineteenth and twentieth centuries the British, French, and other Europeans came to rule and to control much of the Middle East. The Europeans brought with them their own evolving ideas about the justice of the social equality of the sexes. Slowly their ideas permeated the minds of some of the men and women of the Middle East.

Some women are still veiled in the Middle East, but their number is dwindling. Despite the opposition of the conservatives of their own and the opposite sex, women in the Middle East are making rapid gains in expanding their social freedoms. The basic social doctrines of Islam and the accepted fundamental rights of man support their endeavors to improve themselves and their status. The life of the woman in the Middle East has been a checkered one, and not always a happy one, but today she is emerging as one of the great human resources upon which man in the Middle East must depend in his political, economic, social, and cultural advancement.

Perhaps no one in the twentieth century made more radical and rapid changes in the social life of his country than Mustafa Kemal Atatürk, the father of modern Turkey, who became its president in 1923. Kemal Atatürk especially improved and advanced the status of women. He was influenced by the need of applying the basic social teachings of Islam to the modern scene in Turkey. The Middle East was already in the process of being altered by the forceful political, economic, and social ideas and practices of the West, especially Europe, when Kemal Atatürk created the strong modern state of Turkey. He was by inheritance the product of the Ottoman Turks who ruled much of the Middle East, Southeast Europe, and North Africa from the fifteenth century until 1918.

### Social Changes Under a Modern Turk

During the thirteenth century, the Mongols from the vast distances of Central Asia bathed the Middle East in blood and left its cities in ruins, destroying Baghdad in 1258. But the Mongols, too, became caught up in the religion of Islam, and by 1300 many of them were Moslems. Around 1400 Tamerlane, a Turk with Tartar blood, came from the area of modern Turkestan—now located within the borders of Russia—and destroyed the bustling cities and lands of the Middle East. He left no lasting influence except in the magnitude of his destruction. But he failed to destroy the Ottoman Turk. The Ottoman Turks, named after the chief Osman or Othman, had started upon a conquest of the Byzantine Empire before the death of Osman in 1326. From this time until 1918, the Ottoman Turks played a prominent role in the affairs of the Middle East, Asia Minor, and Southeastern Europe.

Through conquest, the Ottoman Empire included all the Middle East to the borders of Persia and extended deep into southeastern Europe. It embraced areas around the Black and Caspian seas, other areas now within the borders of Russia, and held sovereignty, at least theoretically, over much of North Africa. In 1453 the ancient Byzantine capital of Constantinople was taken and became the Ottoman capital. The Ottoman Turks conquered areas within the present states of Hungary, Albania, Yugoslavia, Romania, and Greece, and penetrated twice almost to the gates of Vienna, the capital of Austria. In 1683, however, they were defeated in their attempt to take Vienna, and this defeat marked the climax of Turkish conquests. From this time onward began long years of slow decline. During the eighteenth and nineteenth centuries the Turks lost most of their land in Europe, but in 1914, from their capital of Constantinople, they still ruled a considerable territory extending from Persia to the Mediterranean Sea.

Mustafa Kemal Atatürk, father of Turkey's democracy. (Turkish Tourism and Information Office)

The Ottoman Turks allied themselves to Germany in the First World War and became one of the losers. They lost all their lands except those included in the modern state of Turkey. They would have lost much more than this except for the determination and quick action of Mustafa Kemal Atatürk.

Mustafa Kemal was a young army officer from Macedonia who had made a name for himself during the war. He resented the first treaty which the Allies had forced on Turkey and which the Sultan had approved. Kemal led a movement of Turkish nationalists and retook some of the territories that had been lost by the treaty. His forces captured Constantinople, deposed the Sultan, and in 1923 established a new Turkish republic. Also in 1923 Mustafa Kemal became the first president of the Republic. He was almost fanatically determined that the Turks should become modernized overnight. He was a unique man with an unyielding will and purpose.

Mustafa Kemal literally turned the social life of the Turks inside out. Polygamy was discouraged, and the traditional customs of the Turkish female were radically changed. Kemal tore the veil from her face and brought her from the seclusion of the home into the gaze of the public. Education for both boys and girls between the ages of six and sixteen was made compulsory. The traditional fez worn by the Turks was forbidden as being too costly to make, old-fashioned, and unnecessary. Western-style hats were introduced. Both sexes were urged to wear Western clothes. By 1934 Turkish women voted for the first time, and they quickly became familiar figures in public affairs. Since that time women in numbers have entered into public and professional life, and they are found everywhere today working unveiled with men for the common good of their country.

Mustafa Kemal was a whirlwind in Turkey. He believed that the Arabic script which the Turks had adapted to their language was unsuitable for the expression of modern Western ideas. In 1928 the use of the Latin or Western alphabet was made compulsory. To speed up this change, he himself lectured around the country, demonstrating on a blackboard the new way of writing; and he decreed that no one could hold public office in Turkey who did not know the new system of writing. He tried to lift the economic and social life of the peasant by easing taxes. In the tradition of Islam, ownership of small farms was promoted by lending the peasants money to buy them. Agricultural colleges were founded, model farms established, and agencies were set up to distribute seeds and machinery to the peasant farmers. The whole economic position of the country was improved by building railroads, and the state entered into the manufacture of sugar, alcohol, tobacco, salt, and matches. Mustafa Kemal promoted industrialization in every way he could.

There were few aspects of Turkish life that were not changed. It was traditionally the custom among the people of the Middle East to have only first names. Mustafa Kemal insisted that the Turks take surnames, and he himself received the family name of Atatürk ("chief Turk") at this time. The capital of Turkey was moved to Ankara, and the name of the ancient city of Constantinople was changed officially to Istanbul. In addition, Atatürk introduced the Gregorian calendar, took a census, and had new civil and penal codes written. Atatürk was amazing, and through his actions, ideas, and words, he dramatized in an extreme manner the impulse of modern man in the Middle East to adapt the social teachings of Islam to the present needs of man there.

1. What factors contributed to the social and economic betterment of women in the Middle East? Pay particular attention to religious teachings in your answer.
2. List some of the steps Mustafa Kemal took to modernize Turkey.
3. How large was the Ottoman Empire at its height? When and why did it begin to decline?

## Conclusion

Inequality among men in the Middle East has existed since the earliest times. Kings, nobles, priests, and government officials were the elite of society, and the artisans, peasants, and slaves made up the greatest numbers. A vast, almost empty gulf usually separated the few elite from the masses in the social, economic, and political ways of life. A few men climbed from the depths to the peaks in Egypt, and fewer still in other parts of the ancient Middle East. Only because of war or invasion, or by chance, could men scale the social ladder. These conditions began to change with the acceptance of the teachings of Judaism, Christianity, and Islam. Before the God of the Jew, the Christian, and the Moslem there was no rank of social position, wealth, or political power.

It was the religion of Islam which began to give to men in the Middle East a feeling of basic equality. The teachings of Islam had an influence upon attitudes and actions, and though they did not make the social system perfect, they helped greatly to improve it. The social teachings of Islam had their greatest impact in the Middle East because the greatest number of people there became Moslems. Islam gave to woman more freedom, more security, and more male respect for her human dignity. Islam emphasized man's responsibility for the uplift of his fellowman. It urged the building of institutions for the care of the poor, the sick, and the homeless. It made tolerance of others a virtue and sharing with others a command. It sought to soften the cruelties of war and to establish a relationship of brotherhood between men. Most men in the Middle East are still followers of

Islam, and its enduring social principles still give a sense of unity to Moslems there.

Separateness of social classes in the Middle East was further reduced by the entrance and gradual acceptance of modern Western ideas about the inalienable rights of man. These ideas taught that equality should be established by men as well as by God. The process of transforming Western ideas into concrete practices acceptable to Middle Eastern environment, traditions, beliefs, and attitudes is often difficult and frustrating. But these teachings are pushing the peoples of the Middle East toward a greater social flexibility and mobility than they possessed before. They are helping to bring a new evaluation of the basic teachings of Islam.

There is in the Middle East today a resurgence of the social philosophy of Islam, and this philosophy is now being applied with a renewal of energy and a new interpretation.

## SUMMING UP THE CHAPTER

A. Define or explain the following terms, relating them to this chapter.

| | |
|---|---|
| caliph | polygamy |
| harem | shadoof |
| jihad | sultan |
| kohl | viziers |

B. Identify and locate the following and tell why they are important.

| | |
|---|---|
| Berbers | Ommiad |
| Damascus | Osman |
| Fatima | Richard the Lion-Hearted |
| Hatshepsut | Saladin |

C. Chapter review questions.

1. The nobleman in the Middle East often lived a life of leisure. What factors made this possible?
2. How do you account for the success of Islam in Asia and Africa?
3. Who helped the Abbasids to take over the caliphate? Why did they help?
4. In what ways did the following factors tend to obstruct the Moslem from living up to the ideals of his religion:
   a) physical environment
   b) economic circumstances
   c) traditions
5. In what ways did Islam have a moderating influence on social and political life? Support your answer with facts.
6. What teachings of Islam were opposed to waging a war? Was war ever sanctioned? If so, under what circumstances?
7. Describe the basic social relationships of the Middle East existing in the past. Do these same relationships exist today? If not, how and where do they differ and how do you account for the changes?
8. In what way did the laws of Hammurabi contribute to stability and growth in the Middle East?
9. How did the teachings of Islam influence the character of Saladin?
10. Who were the Ottoman Turks? Why were they important?
11. When did the Seljuk Turks invade the Middle East? What were the results of their invasion?
12. When was the Republic of Turkey established? What great leader made this possible?
13. What social and economic changes, especially regarding women, did Atatürk impose on Turkey? Do you think these changes were for the good?

D. Questions for discussion.

1. Why do you suppose Greek, Byzantine, and Roman rulers in the Middle East did not bring about changes in the basic social organization of the area?
2. If Mohammed did not encourage the spread of Islam, what factors do you think caused his followers to spread the religion?
3. Do you think the fact that both Christians and Moslems felt they were fighting a "holy war" during the Crusades contributed a special character to the wars? How do you define "holy war"?
4. How do you account for the changes in the status of women in the Middle East throughout history?

E. Projects for groups or individuals.

1. Draw a pyramid and place cross marks in such a way as to illustrate the various levels of society in the Middle East. Make the lines correspond with the per cent of the population in each social class. How do the proportions in each class compare with the United States? (Perhaps you will want to make a similar drawing for the United States.)
2. Trace the paths of the great crusades, in particular the Children's Crusade and that of Richard the Lion-Hearted.
3. Islam imposes a tax on each believer. Prepare a report for your class on similar practices of other faiths.

# CHAPTER 12

# *They Were Ruled*

MAN IN THE MIDDLE EAST has called his rulers by various names—pharaoh, king, high priest, caliph, and sultan. He has not often questioned the *system* under which they ruled, though he has often questioned the *manner* in which they ruled. He has sometimes hated the one man who ruled him, plotted the downfall of his ruler, and even resorted to assassination. This was done to replace a ruler with someone better, but never with the intent of changing the system. The Middle Easterner did not argue with the political way of life in which one man was supreme, but he did argue about the qualifications of the man who ruled. When Alexander the Great conquered much of the Middle East in the fourth century B.C., he opened a path for later invasions and for the influx of ideas about other ways of governing. But, in practice, these ideas had little effect. More often than not, the invaders themselves were influenced by Middle Eastern ideas about governing.

From very ancient days politics and religion have been almost inseparable in the Middle East. To the Sumerians, the high priest and the king were one and the same person. To the Egyptians, the pharaoh was divine and was the symbol of the immortality of his people and his state. The caliph, the head of the Moslems, represented both the spiritual and the temporal authority of the empire which the followers of Islam had created. Those who came to rule in the Middle East found that it was acceptable, and perhaps expected, that a ruler should have divine as well as secular authority. Many rulers came to really believe that they were divinely appointed. Thus, the political system was buttressed by divine support as well as acceptance by man.

All of this began to change when, during the nineteenth and particularly the twentieth century, thoughts about nationalism, democracy, the political rights of man, and representative government flowed into this region with vigor and without ceasing. After the First World War, with the breakup of the Ottoman Empire and the taking of control by the British and the French in many parts of the Middle East, these thoughts began to assume more importance. European intrusion was resented in the Middle East, and this resentment was expressed through increasingly violent words and violent actions. These Western "trespassers," however, brought economic, social, and political theories and practices which could be learned and put to use. Thus began the slow process of adapting new theories and practices to the special environment, attitude, and tradition of the Middle East.

The lands of the Middle East achieved some measure of independence from their own authoritarian traditions and from European overlords during the period between the two world wars, 1918-1939. The greatest number recovered their independent political authority, however, after the Second World War during the 1940's and 1950's. In this period constitutions were written and made the legal basis of governments. The new independent nations instituted elections, formed political parties, established representative forms of government, and elected men and women to parliaments and to the office of president. The political system began, outwardly at least, to resemble that of the West.

But the traditions and practices of the centuries had also established attitudes and views which were not easily or quickly removed. The ruler was extremely important in the traditions of the Middle East and is still important. Despite the presence of a body of elected representatives sitting in a parliament, the attention and hopes of the people frequently remain fixed upon a single man, whether he be called president, prime minister, premier, shah, or sheikh. The single ruler is important whether he is chosen, appointed, or rules by inheritance. In much of the Middle East it is still the one man who is influential in determining the political practices, methods, and the foreign as well as domestic policies of the nation.

One of the earliest examples of the modern ruler in the Middle East is Mustafa Kemal Atatürk. Atatürk desired his people to become more Western and more oriented to the modern world, and thereby stronger as a nation. He has already been mentioned in terms of his social changes in Turkey. Atatürk was able to make drastic political, social, and economic changes in his country because, although called president and elected, he ruled as the people had always expected their rulers to rule —with firmness, with strength, and with commands.

### Turkey

From 1923, when Mustafa Kemal Atatürk became the first president of the new Republic of Turkey, until 1938, when he died, his will was the will of Turkey. During these few short years he changed the political and social face of Turkey and gave to the people a purpose and direction toward a more democratic and modern way of living which carried on even after his death. He thought of himself as destined to resurrect his people from the ruins in which stagnation, corruption, and war had buried them. He was determined to lead his people by the hand until they could walk alone, and then he conceived his job as finished. Since he was aware that life is short and that the social and political journey on which he must lead the Turks was long and painful, Atatürk wanted his people to move along as rapidly as possible. Thus, with Mustafa Kemal Atatürk pulling them along at a great pace, the Turks went breathlessly from one reform to another until the momentum of their forward progress toward a modern nation-state could not be stopped.

Modern machinery and methods of agriculture have helped to increase Turkey's production of food. (Turkish Tourism and Information Office)

Three important segments of the population helped in this breakneck speed toward modernization: soldiers, teachers, and women. To the soldier, Atatürk was a hero because he was a great leader in battle, and he had won back for Turkey large parts of the country which the Allies had taken at the conclusion of World War I. He was a hero to the teachers because he regarded education as the basis of his policies, made education compulsory for both sexes between the ages of six and sixteen, established a public school system, and gave teachers the respect due their key position in the country. He was a hero to women because he thought of them as valuable individuals, and he made his thoughts concrete by removing restrictions which custom had placed upon their equality and mobility. He gave women an opportunity to show their intelligence, their value, and their energies in the service of the state and its people. Neither Atatürk nor the people regretted the entrance of the Turkish woman into public service.

One of the first political reforms in the creation of modern Turkey was the abolishment of the caliphate, which had been the top political as well as spiritual office in Islam for almost thirteen hundred years. Under the old system the sultan, as caliph, was the spiritual head of the Moslems, and the laws of the state were religious laws. What schools there were, were attached to the mosques. Mustafa Kemal replaced the religious laws and courts with secular laws and courts which he regarded as more scientific and up-to-date. He separated the schools from the mosques and placed them under the government. A directorate of religious affairs was established and it, too, was placed under the government. Thus the government of Turkey became a secular rather than a religious one. All of this was done during the year 1924.

In that same year, Atatürk had the Grand National Assembly adopt a constitution, which substantially remained in force until May of 1960. This constitution vested all executive and legislative power in the Assembly, and it was from the Assembly that the president was to be selected and elected. The president had the right to appoint a prime minister. The prime minister, in turn, had the right to appoint a cabinet. Since Mustafa Kemal, as president, controlled the Assembly, this constitution actually gave him great power.

Six principles guided Mustafa Kemal in leading his people into the modern political world: nationalism, secularism, populism, statism, republicanism, and revolutionism.

*Nationalism* meant a national consciousness, a sense that all within the borders of Turkey—no matter what their origin, their appearance, or their beliefs—were Turks. All should regard themselves as Turks and, theoretically, all would be treated alike in law and in practice. *Secularism* meant separation of the government and organized religion. This principle led to a breaking with religious customs and traditions which were, in the opinion of Mustafa Kemal, holding back the progress of the people. Many of his reforms, in line with this guiding principle, were opposed by the more fanatical and conservative of the Moslems. For instance, the mark of a good Moslem was the fez, a tasseled red brimless hat, which Mustafa Kemal had forbidden Turks to wear. The subject of controversy was a small one, but the implications for this program of secularization were great. Mustafa won.

*Populism* meant the popular will. Reforms were justified by stating that the Grand National Assembly was the agent of the people and expressed the popular will in legislative and executive reforms. *Republicanism* referred to the form of representative elected government. *Statism* was concerned mostly with upgrading the economy of the nation through massive grants of state aid and training of experts in management. The nationalization of railroads, ships, banks, and other industries such as the manufacture of tobacco, matches, salt, alcohol, and sugar was accomplished under this principle. *Revolutionism* was the expression of an attitude of mind to make and accept changes in the political, social, and economic life of the individual and the whole people in order that the country might proceed quickly to the fulfillment of its modern goals.

Mustafa Kemal Atatürk could be ruthless toward his political enemies, yet he was not addicted to the use of terror through secret police; nor did he terrorize minorities except in the case of rebellion; nor did he engage his people in outside wars. He brought his people a long way forward on the path toward becoming a modern nation-state. When he died, succession passed peacefully to Ismet Inönü. In 1946 an opposition political party was formed. Called the Democratic party, it challenged the old Republican People's party in the elections of 1946. It lost, but a measure of real democracy was now coming to Turkey, and in the elections of May, 1950, the Democratic party won the election. Celâl Bayar became president, and Adnan Menderes became prime minister.

The Democratic party started off by continuing the democratic and economic advance of the country. It particularly favored the peasants, the small farmers, and the herders who still make up the majority of the people. Gradually, however, the rule of Menderes became more dictatorial and authoritarian, and the economic condition of the country began to deteriorate. There were riots and criticisms of the regime in the newspapers, and the government retaliated with mass arrests. Unrest and suspicion began to grip the country. Finally, the army leaders took over control of the country in May 1960, declaring that they had done so to prevent a civil war and that their control would be temporary. The government was turned over to a "Committee of National Unity." The policy of the Committee was to return to the road of democracy first constructed by Atatürk.

A new constitution was written and approved by national referendum in 1961. It introduced a system of checks and balances into the government, provided for a legislature divided into two houses (a national assembly and a senate), and established an independent judicial system which could review legislation.

A new election was held in October 1961. Since no one party won a clear majority a coalition government was formed with General Cemal Gursel as president, and Atatürk's old companion, Ismet Inönü, as prime minister. The avowed policy of the new government is to continue the progress toward modernization and democracy begun by Mustafa Kemal Atatürk.

Turkey has a population of 31,118,000, the largest of any country in the Middle East. Its strategic location is of considerable importance in the Cold War between the West and the Communists. Turkey is a member of CENTO (Central Treaty Organization), which is a defensive alliance including Iran, Pakistan, and Great Britain. It also has a defense pact with the United States which was signed in 1959. It is, therefore, aligned with the West in its international policies. Turkey has a correct, but rather aloof, relationship with the Arab nations of the Middle East, and aroused their displeasure by recognizing Israel as a state. The Turkish people, however, are almost 98 per cent Moslem and their ties with the Islamic world through a common religious belief are continuing and strong. Mustafa Kemal Atatürk separated the church and the state in Turkey, but he did not intend to tear Islam from the hearts and minds of the people.

## Iran (Persia)

Iran, the land of the Aryans, is the modern name of old Persia. Within the borders and amidst the exciting scenery of this country live peoples whose ancestors are traced back to before the dawn of the written records of man. It was from here that the Aryans began their journey into India around 2000 B.C. It was from here that a people called Elams penetrated the region of the Sumerians several thousand years before Christ. From here, in the sixth century B.C., Cyrus the Great began the Persian Empire which, under his successors, was to include the whole known civilized world of the Middle East and beyond. The hardy people of this land withstood the armies of the Romans, the Byzantines, and the Ottoman Turks and were never a part of these great empires. They knew defeat and subjugation by the Parthians, the Seljuk Turks, the Mongols, the Tatars, the Arabs, and others,

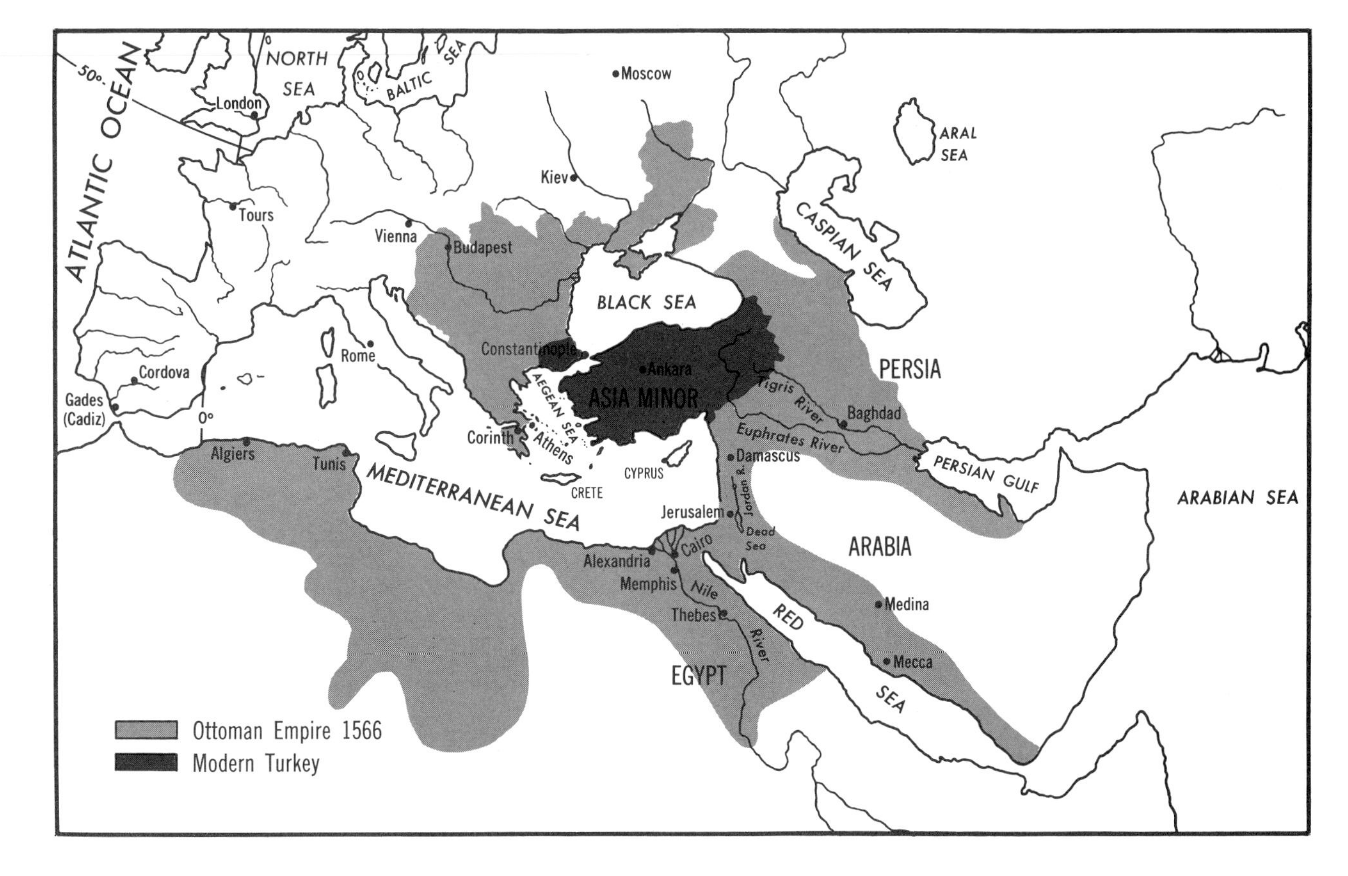


**THE OTTOMAN EMPIRE IN 1566 AND MODERN TURKEY**

The Ottoman Empire extended over lands that had been part of ancient Egypt, the empire of Alexander the Great, the Roman Empire, and the Byzantine Empire. Find other maps that show these ancient empires and compare them.

but Persian culture and blood absorbed these conquerors, and the Persians arose from their defeats to even greater heights of political and cultural glory.

Many peoples have met and mingled in Persia because it is a crossroads land. To the north are the Russians, to the west the Turks and the Iraqis, to the east the Afghans and the Pakistanis, and to the south the Persian Gulf, which from long ages in the past has been a link to the peoples of Africa and the Far East. The cultural and political influence of Persia has made itself felt in all the regions surrounding it, and even today this cultural imprint remains in India and Russia as well as the Middle East.

The last great Persian conqueror was Nadir Shah who established the Afsharid dynasty in 1736. He expelled the Russians from lands they had taken, defeated the Afghans and Turks, and invaded India to the capital of Delhi, where he obtained the Peacock Throne upon which the shahs of Iran are crowned today. A dynasty called the Qajar ruled Iran from the late 1700's until 1925, and during this period of Iran's history there was a gradual decline of political power.

**Russian and British control.** During the nineteenth century, Russia and Great Britain controlled Persia much of the time. Dissatisfaction with the rule of the shah forced him to grant the people a constitution in 1906. A

Above, the Senate Palace in Tehran, capital of Iran. Below is shown one of the modern villages being built in Iran. These villages have electricity and other conveniences, as well as schools, mosques, and playgrounds. (both, Embassy of Iran)

parliament was established consisting of two houses, and a basic law was established for the country. But this did not stop the ambitions of the Russians and the British, who agreed to divide Iran into spheres of influence. The northern sphere was taken by Russia, the southern sphere by Great Britain, and a little in between was left to the shah. From this time until Riza Khan Pahlevi took the throne in 1925, Iran was a scene of political, economic, and social chaos. Russians, British, Germans, and others schemed for control of a disturbed but potentially rich and strategic land.

**Reforms of Riza Khan.** In 1925 an able military man by the name of Riza Khan was proclamed shah of Iran. He founded the Pahlevi dynasty. He ruled until 1941 when he was succeeded by his son Mohammed Riza Pahlevi. Riza Khan was to Iran what Mustafa Kemal Atatürk was to Turkey. With boundless energy and a fixed will, he pushed and pulled the Iranian people into the modern age. He forced the semiautonomous tribes to acknowledge

the authority of the central government and broke the opposition of Moslem religious leaders who opposed reforms. He put to work the begging dervishes who roamed about wearing tall hats and panther skins, holding begging bowl, ax, and antelope horns in their hands. He stopped the fanatics who held bloody passion plays commemorating the martyrdom of Husain, the son of Ali, who had married the daughter of Mohammed. (The Iranians are Shiites, members of the Sh'ia sect of Islam, and they give their spiritual allegiance only to the descendants of Mohammed.) Riza Shah confiscated religious properties, and henceforth the mullahs, who are, in a broad sense, the priests of Islam, were dependent upon the state for their support.

Further reforms included the adoption of Western codes of law, establishment of a single educational system patterned after that of France, and a civil service based upon merit. An American was obtained to revamp the finances of Iran, as Persia was now officially called. Women in particular benefited from reforms. They were no longer required to wear the *chador*, a shapeless garment which disguised the shape and covered the face. Polygamy was discouraged, and a man was not permitted to marry a second wife without the consent of both the first wife and the prospective second wife; nor could girls be married before the age of fifteen.

**World War II and after.** During the Second World War Riza Shah tried to preserve Iranian neutrality and resisted Russian and British demands for a supply corridor through Iran. The Russians invaded from the north and the British from the south. Riza Shah was forced to abdicate, and the British shipped him to South Africa, where he died in 1944. But before he was forced to leave, Riza Shah had given the Iranian people a sense of national consciousness. He observed that the Russians and the British treated his country in the same way that Mussolini treated Greece and Hitler treated Belgium. War is a great leveler of men's actions.

In 1942 the British, the Russians, and the Iranians signed the Tripartite Alliance in which Iran was a full partner. Iran was obliged to declare war on Germany to achieve this partnership. The Iranian people suffered great hardships during the war, and the restlessness of the people manifested itself in national agitation. Communism began to show itself under the Tudeh, or "Masses," party. In 1946 a revolt broke out in the northern provinces, and Russia used this as a pretext to maintain troops in the northern part of Iran. The firmness of the United States during this period, the condemnation of the UN Security Council, but most of all the clever diplomacy of the Iranians caused the Russians to withdraw. Eventually the Iranians controlled their land again without the help of foreign troops.

From that time until now the Iranians have been disturbed by one crisis after another. There was the rise of Dr. Mohammed Mossadegh, who nationalized the oil industry, dissolved the parliament, and denounced the shah. Mossadegh ruled almost as a dictator and tried to overthrow the monarchy. He was removed from office by a coalition of nationalists and the army. Mossadegh's National Front party was dissolved, and the shah returned to power. Efforts have been made to further the democratic development of Iran, but there is still economic and political unrest in the country. Cabinets and premiers have come and gone with some rapidity, and until the country achieves some measure of political and economic stability the future is always uncertain.

The United States has a bilateral treaty with Iran and has supported the country with various forms of material and financial assistance. Iran is a member of CENTO. Its population of 21,227,000 and its strategic location make it an important Middle Eastern country.

1. What did Mustafa Kemal Atatürk think his responsibility to Turkey was?
2. Identify Atatürk's six principles and explain their meaning.
3. What are spheres of influence? Relate this concept to Iran in the twentieth century.
4. What changes did Riza Shah bring about in Iran to bring his country into the modern age?

## United Arab Republic (Egypt)

Egypt, which is today called the United Arab Republic, has been an important country in the Middle East since the beginning of the written history of man. Occupying as it does the corner of northeast Africa, bordering the western portions of the Middle East, and sitting astride the main shipping route between Europe and the huge mass of Asia, Egypt is important to the European, the African, and the Asian as well as to man in the Middle East. The political intentions of Egyptian leaders can have far-reaching effects. From the distant past to the present the Egyptian has set out from this strategic location to carry the political and cultural influence of his country deep into Africa and the Middle East. During the thousands of years of its ancient glory, the influence of Egypt was widespread. There were few in the early days of the civilized world who could successfully resist the vigor of Egyptian power and cultural achievements. Like all men, however, the Egyptian has undergone periods of decline during which he was enslaved and his country humbled by those more powerful though less culturally advanced.

The Assyrian, the Persian, the Libyan, the Macedonian, and the Roman all took turns ruling Egypt before the birth of Christ. To the Roman, the Egyptian was merely a worker in an important granary. The Arab, who overcame the Byzantine-Roman ruler in 640 A.D., brought his Arabic language and the teachings of Islam. He accepted the Egyptian as a brother. Under the spur of a flowering Islamic civilization, Egyptian political power was renewed, and Egypt reached new cultural heights. During the Fatimid dynasty, 968-1171, Cairo became the greatest center of the Moslem world. Its mosques, universities, and libraries were renowned as seats of knowledge and strongholds of culture. The glory of Egypt continued under the kind and strong Saladin and his family, who ruled from 1171 to 1250. Under the Mamelukes, who ruled from 1250 to 1517, it declined once again. The Mamelukes were descendants of the slaves and bodyguards who had been recruited to defend and fight for the sultans of the dynasty of Saladin. They lived only for themselves and permitted the country to deteriorate while they lived in luxury. They were defeated in 1517 by the Ottoman Turks who allowed them to retain much of their power. In 1805 control of Egypt was seized by Mehemet Ali, a Turkish soldier who had been appointed governor. He started a dynasty which ended when the last of his line, King Farouk, was expelled from the country during the revolution led by reforming army officers in 1952.

**The rise of Nasser.** On June 18, 1953 Egypt was proclaimed a republic with General Mohammed Naguib as its first president. In 1954 Colonel Gamal Abdel Nasser became prime minister, and in 1956 he was elected president of Egypt. The history of the United Arab Republic, as Egypt is now called, from the beginning of the republic until today has revolved mainly around the thoughts and purposes of Gamal Abdel Nasser.

President Nasser thinks of himself as the leader of a social and political revolution, not only in Egypt but throughout the Arab world. He has spoken of himself as an Egyptian patriot and an Arab nationalist. He believes strongly that there exists in the hearts of most Arabs a spiritual impulse toward solidarity which rests upon their shared religion, language, culture, and history. He has declared that he does not propose to impose this unity upon Arabs by force. Nasser insists, however, that the Arabs can never reach their full potential in the political, economic, cultural, and social areas until there is a close and voluntary relationship among all Arabs in these fields. Nasser has, therefore, concentrated his energies upon two broad fronts: the political, economic, and social uplift of his own people, and the revival of the political, economic, and social life of all Arabs through cooperation.

In line with these policies Nasser has pushed hard to improve the conditions of the peasants who have tilled the land of Egypt under unbelievably difficult circumstances for years beyond our knowledge. He has loaned them money to buy small plots of land at low interest rates. He is improving and expanding irrigation facilities, and he is fighting to increase agricultural production—for the population of Egypt is increasing at almost the same rate as the food supply. It is for this reason that President Nasser feels the construction of the Aswan dam to be so important, for it will result in the irrigation of some additional three million acres of land. At the same time, the waters of this dam will flood the rocks sculptured by ancient Egyptian artists. This loss of ancient tombs and temples distresses the Egyptians because they take great pride in the achievements of their ancestors. But some of the tombs and temples are being moved to higher ground, where they will be preserved.

Nasser has worked to obtain better health services and to provide a better education for Egyptian youth. He is moving to establish industry in the country, and already Egyptians are making tires, steel, automobile parts, radios, and a large number of other products for use at home and for export. The goal of Nasser's government is to make Egypt as self-supporting as possible in agriculture and in industry.

President Nasser declares himself to be a democratic socialist. He does not accept Communism as a philosophy to guide the people and has outlawed the Communist party in Egypt. Nor does he accept capitalism as it is practiced in the West, for he conceives it to have been one of the reasons why he and others suffered at the hands of the Europeans in the Middle East.

During the nineteenth and twentieth centuries, the French, and later the British, dictated much of the policy of Egypt in their own interests rather than the interests of the Egyptian. After the revolution of 1952, Nasser was determined to rid Egypt and especially the Suez Canal Zone of all British troops. In 1954 he signed an agreement with Great Britain which would result in the removal of all British troops from the Zone by June 1956. In July 1956 he took over and nationalized the Suez Canal under Egyptian control from the international company that owned it.

This dam at Aswan, Egypt, provides irrigation water. (Egyptian State Tourist Administration)

In line with President Nasser's socialist thinking and his determination to remove all foreign vested interests in Egypt, he has nationalized the commercial and industrial holdings of most foreigners there and placed them under Egyptian control. He has also destroyed internal threats to his political control by breaking up the power of the Moslem Brotherhood organization and other opposition elements. At this moment he stands alone as the leader of the Egyptians, who look to him for the fulfillment of their individual and national dreams.

**Arab unity.** President Nasser is dedicated to the advancement of Arab unity. In his National Charter of Socialist Principles which was approved by the National Congress of Popular Forces in 1962, it is stated that "The United Arab Republic, firmly convinced that she is an integral part of the Arab Nation, must propagate her call for unity and the principles it embodies, so that it would be at the disposal of every Arab citizen. . . ." It was this principle which had led to the formation of a new unified Arab state in 1958 consisting of Egypt, called the Southern Region, and Syria, called the Northern Region. Yemen also federated with the new state. This Republic did not last long, however, for Syria and Yemen withdrew in 1961. Revolutions in Yemen in 1962, and in Iraq and Syria in early 1963 brought pro-Nasser rulers to power, and a new federation of these countries with Egypt was proposed in April 1963. The new federation did not materialize, but Nasser continues to press for Arab unity.

In foreign affairs beyond the Arab world, Egyptian policy is described as "positive neutralism." Nasser insists that he will not take sides with either of the great power blocs but will work with other neutrals to reduce the tensions of the cold war, oppose imperialism, increase the voice and power of neutrals in the world, strengthen Afro-Asian solidarity, and pursue other policies in the interest of Egypt. He detests any pact which places an Arab nation in alliance with either the East or the West, for he prefers the Arabs to be uncommitted. Nasser has aroused both antagonism and love in his own region and elsewhere, but he remains an important force in the Middle East.

## Syria

Syria is the modern name for a land upon which many kinds and mixtures of men have warred, traded, settled, and farmed. The Arameans of the early Semite family lived here and evolved a language which was the common tongue of the Middle East when Christ was born. The Hittites, the Egyptians, the Assyrians, the Persians, the Greeks, the Romans, the Arabs, and the Turks all at one time or another sought to control this land. Their blood and their civilizations met and blended in Syria. Damascus, the capital, claims to be the oldest city in the world with an unbroken history, and it was from this city that the Ommiad caliphs ruled a vast Moslem empire for about one hundred years. The last foreign rulers of the Syrians were the French, who governed this land under a mandate from the League of Nations from 1920 until 1941. They did not finally leave Syria until April 1946.

The Syrians have had a hectic political history since gaining their independence. There has been crisis after crisis, and coup after coup, with the military emerging frequently as the strongest single force in the country. However, under the leadership of an Arab Christian named Michel Aflaq—about 13 per cent of the Syrians are Christians—the Baath or Arab Socialist Resurrection Party was formed. This party is now playing a vital role in shaping the political and economic future of the country. Its slogan is "Unity, Freedom, Socialism," which Nasser also adopted in Egypt. Its members are committed to unity of the Arab world. They want the freedoms of speech, assembly, and election which characterize a democracy; and they also want a socialism which will improve the welfare of the people and the economic strength of the country. The ideals and purposes of this party did not remain limited to Syria but went to the neighboring countries of Iraq, Jordan, Kuwait, and Saudi Arabia. The party became strongest in Iraq, and in cooperation with the military pulled off the coup which overturned the dictatorial government of Kassim early in 1963.

The Baathists, as the party members are called, have not had an easy road to success. It was not until 1958 that they were able to enlist the aid of others, more conservatively inclined, against the Communists, who at that time threatened to take over the government of Syria. It was the Baathists who initiated the merger of Syria and Egypt at this time. They feared a Communist takeover, and they believed that the aims of President Nasser and their own were identical. After several years of unity, the policies of President Nasser upset and angered many Syrians. They were especially angered when he dissolved all of the political parties in the country. Syria abruptly became separated from the United Arab Republic. The conservatives came to power again, but the appeal for unity with their Arab brothers was strong among Syrians. In March 1963, the government of Syria was overthrown with the help of pro-Nasser elements of the Syrian army and the Baathist party. The Baathists and the pro-Nasser military again started negotiations with President Nasser to establish a closer unity between Syria and Egypt. It is still too early to predict the path of Syria's political development, but there is every evidence that powerful forces within the country would like unity with all Arabs.

Many difficulties must be overcome before Syria can evolve a working democracy and a working economy. There are authoritarians among the citizens who prefer the old path of political control by the one or the few; they are either dictatorial rightists, dictatorial leftists, or dictators who have borrowed doctrines from both the conservatives and the radicals. The Syrian economy is based chiefly on farming and the herding of animals. The largest export is cotton, followed by a much smaller amount of wool in second place. Half of the land is arable, but only a third is cultivated. Syria has a population of around 5,067,000, but the rich are too few and the poor too numerous. There is unrest in the land, and it embraces all classes—military and civilian, landowner and peasant, intellectual and illiterate. Since Syria gained independence the doors of jails have opened and shut and opened again for individuals of almost every imaginable political persuasion. Although their views are often conflicting, Syrians hope that democracy may reign more peacefully in their country and that their welfare will improve with peace and progress.

The Syrian wants no part of war, and he remains neutral between the two power blocs headed by the United States and the Soviet Union. He is extremely desirous of Arab unity, but he feels it should be on the basis of equality rather than domination by one country. There is a large underground Communist movement within the country, but it is offset by a Moslem and Christian heritage. A strong sense of nationalism and the aim of Arab unity are also opposed to Communism. The new leaders of Syria and those of Iraq met with President Nasser in Cairo and in April 1963 announced their agreement to establish a new federal unity between the three countries. As yet, this federal unity has not been fulfilled.

The Syrian hopes to find policies which will bring peace and prosperity to him and peace to his neighbors and to the world. But he is also prepared to rebel against his own leaders and outsiders if he does not believe their politics are in his best interest.

## Iraq

Iraq is the modern name for old Mesopotamia, the Land between the Rivers where long ago the Sumerian, the Semite, and the Indo-European mingled and passed on to others their civilized accomplishments. It was here in their capital of Baghdad that the Abbasid caliphs of Islam ruled for centuries the mighty civilized world of the Moslems. It was this thronged and prosperous land that the Mongol horsemen visited with destruction during the thirteenth century, and to which Tamerlane the Tatar-Turk brought ruin during the fifteenth century. Less than half the population survived these two destroyers. This was the land which the British removed from the empire of the Ottoman Turks after the First World War and governed under a mandate from the League of Nations until 1932. In 1932 Iraq became a member of the League of Nations and was recognized as a sovereign independent state headed by a constitutional monarch, King Faisal.

The government of the new nation of Iraq was established by an Organic Law which provided for a parliament of two chambers, an independent judiciary, and a rather strong executive branch. The political, social, and economic advancement of Iraq was hampered by great illiteracy, disputes among religious and racial minorities, and a lack of trained leadership dedicated to furthering the progress of the country. Iraq has been torn almost constantly by the intrigues of various factions seeking power, which has resulted in a long series of rising and falling cabinets. There has been little continuity of rule and of policy. Nuri al-Said, the elder statesman of Iraq, was acting as prime minister for the fifteenth time when, in July 1958, General Abdul Karim Kassim led a revolt of army officers. In this revolution the king and his family were killed, as was Nuri al-Said.

Iraq was proclaimed a republic as a result of this revolution. The old constitution was abolished and a new one replaced it. General Kassim became prime minister and governed with the assistance of a Council of Sovereignty. Kassim tried to institute social and agrarian reforms, but his policy of dictatorial government, of reliance upon the Communists, and of opposition to President Nasser disturbed many. Conflicts swirled around him and often broke into open violence. There were counter-revolutions and intrigues against his life. Some members of the military led open rebellions. Warfare broke out with the Kurdish minority within the country. The Iraqis suffered all the harassments of a people who have not yet had time to forge a common unity and tolerance. Kassim was lucky and clever, and he survived in this steaming and scheming political jungle for almost five years. Finally, in February 1963, the Baathists and the pro-Nasser army officers toppled his government and showed his lifeless body on television for all to see. The new rulers have won power, but their remaining problems are monumental.

The social structure of Iraq is still feudal, and tribal chieftains still control many men and many stretching miles of land. Strong minorities with interests yet unsatisfied continue to war with an unbroken spirit. There are the followers of Nasser, the followers of Communism, the Baathists, the nationalists, the doubtful military, the illiterate, the impoverished, and the feudal lords of desert and oasis. The factions intrigue, and their intriguing leads at times to a savagery that streams the land with blood and causes further divisions.

The country is fortunate to have vast reservoirs of oil, which bring millions upon millions of dollars into the Iraqi treasury every year. Iraq also produces 80 per cent of the world's dates and exports wool and barley, among other agricultural products. But these riches have not yet sifted down to the poor of the city, the watered plain, and the desert.

Of Iraq's approximately 7,000,000 people, 75 per cent are Arabs, but 15 per cent are Kurds, who struggle for a country of their own to be called Kurdistan. The Kurds are a mixture of people who trace their ancestry back to ancient inhabitants of this area who lived here as early as 2400 to 2300 B.C. The approximately 300,000 Kurds live in southeast Turkey, northeast Iraq, and Iran. Their dream of an independent Kurdistan involves all of these nations. The Kurds are determined to have an autonomous state, and they have been a continual source of unrest in all three of the countries where they presently live. Uneasy truces have been negotiated between the Kurds and the rulers of these three countries, but the fires of conflict are still smoldering.

Before the advent of General Kassim, Iraq was tied to the West through treaties, but Kassim abolished these treaties and followed a policy of neutralism. Many believed this policy to be more oriented to Russia than to the West. The Iraqis, like the Syrians, Egyptians, and other Arabs, have long been interested in Arab unity; but this unity is easier to proclaim than to make concrete. The government of Iraq has a worrisome and difficult job, but success will bring a glory and a prosperity that the Iraqi has not known since the time long ago of the Abbasid caliphs.

1. Trace the general development of government in the history of Egypt up to June 18, 1953. Which period do you consider the most important and why?
2. Discuss Nasser as a political and social leader in Egypt and as a spokesman for Arab unity.
3. Discuss the evolution of the Iraqi government between 1932 and today. What factors have worked against stability and peaceful change?

## The Arabian Peninsula

The Arab nomad, or Bedouin as he is often called, wandered and warred in the desert wastes of the Arabian peninsula until Mohammed, the prophet of Islam, unified the clans and tribes under the banner of Islam in the sixth and seventh centuries. Strengthened by unity, the Arabs went forth from this peninsula and spread their religion, their language, and their blood in many lands. They settled in new lands and begot vigorous and flourishing civilizations. But the original land of Arabia, with its cities of Mecca and Medina, where Mohammed had lived and preached, remained holy in Moslem memory. This peninsula became important to all who embraced the teachings of Islam, for all Moslems face toward Mecca during their daily prayers. And every Moslem is urged to make a pilgrimage to Mecca, near the Red Sea, at least once during his lifetime. For all of Islam this peninsula has become a spiritual homeland.

The Arabs who remained in the peninsula gradually lost the unity they had gained through their religion, and over the years they separated again into roaming and marauding groups. They remained Moslems but continued in many separate groups. It was the combination of King Ibn Saud and the Wahabi reform movement within Islam which finally brought most of the people and the peninsula within the state of Saudi Arabia in 1926. There are small political entities in the peninsula, such as Yemen, Kuwait, and some British protectorates, but Saudi Arabia is the dominant country.

## Saudi Arabia

In the eighteenth century a reform movement within Islam was founded by Mohammed ibn-Abd-al-Wahab. His followers are known as Wahabis. Abd-al-Wahab was an intelligent man, sensitive and religious, and he became disgusted and indignant with what he conceived to be the corruptions and distortions of the teachings of Islam among the Moslems of his time. He wanted a return to the teachings of Islam as given in the Koran. He denied the spiritual authority of any person, whether sultan or caliph. Ibn-Abd-al-Wahab wanted Moslems to follow the strict teachings of the Koran with regard to prayers, fasting, and the pilgrimage. He believed that the prohibitions with regard to gambling, drinking of wine, smoking, wearing luxurious dress, using tombstones for the dead, and other forbidden acts should be strictly enforced. He was a reformer in the full meaning of the term and almost puritanical in his outlook.

These teachings were rejected by the powerful at first, but eventually Abd-al-Wahab and the Saud family made an alliance. From that time forward the Saud family advanced in power, supported by the teachings of Wahabism and the growing numbers of its followers. By 1814 King Saud II controlled a great state throughout the peninsula. The power of the Saud family was broken temporarily when the Egyptians and Turks gained control of a large part of Arabia. But the Wahabi beliefs and the keen diplomacy of the Saud family could not be destroyed. Gradually, the Sauds began to regain the power they had lost, and by 1926 the Saud family under King Ibn Saud expanded its control to the present boundaries of Saudi Arabia.

The power of the Saud family and the economic condition of the country were greatly improved by the discovery and exploitation of fabulous resources of oil beneath the sands of Saudi Arabia. The first oil concession was granted to a United States company, and in 1936 the Arabian American Oil Company

Most of Arabia's natural wealth consists of oil. Below, oil wells are being drilled. (Saudi Arabian Information Service)

(Aramco), owned by several American companies, was formed. In 1950 Saudi Arabia and Aramco concluded a fifty-fifty profit-sharing agreement and, in general, the relations between the two have been extremely good. The annual income of the ruling family from oil royalties exceeds $300,000,000 a year.

The money that has been received from oil has been used for various purposes. The Saud rulers rely, as did their predecessors, upon the loyalty of the chieftains and sheikhs of the major tribes of the country, who receive grants from oil royalties. Further, the hundreds of members of the Saud family spend money lavishly and ostentatiously. Air-conditioned palaces, expensive cars, private planes, trips to Europe accompanied by great entourages, and gifts to favorites consume millions of dollars. There has been an attempt in recent years to curtail the personal spending of these great oil royalties, for there is much to be done to improve the economic and social conditions of the poor.

The government follows a neutral policy with regard to the Cold War, but the Saud ruler is not on good terms with President Nasser of the United Arab Republic. He has accused Nasser of following policies which are alien to Islam. Nasser has accused the ruler of Saudi Arabia of being a reactionary and of having worked against Nasser in the Arab world. Saudi Arabia is on good terms with Jordan, but it is having problems with Yemen and some of its other neighbors. All the Arabs, however, are agreed on opposing the state of Israel in their midst.

### Yemen

Yemen is a small country located in the southwestern part of the peninsula. The people are Moslems and conservative in their ways. Until recently, Yemen was governed by a ruler whose title was *imam*. The imam held all political power in the country and ruled it as Middle Eastern countries were ruled before the advent of Western democratic ideas. In 1962 a revolt led by army officers overthrew the imam. The new leaders promised a more democratic form of government in the country, but fighting and unrest still continued. The situation was further complicated because Saudi Arabia and Jordan gave armed support to the imam while Nasser, of Egypt, backed the revolutionists. There are a number of Red Chinese and Russian technicians working in the country, but few Westerners. The country is officially neutral, but the direction of its future is at present uncertain. Yemen has a population estimated at 5,000,000.

### Kuwait

Kuwait is a country in the Arabian peninsula located near the northern end of the Persian Gulf. It is ruled by a sheikh of the as-Sabah dynasty, which was founded in 1756. In 1899 Kuwait came under the protection of Great Britain, and its foreign affairs were handled by that country until Kuwait became fully independent on June 19, 1961. It joined the Arab League later in the same year but still retains a defense agreement with Great Britain. This defense agreement proved useful to Kuwait when, on June 25, 1961, General Kassim of Iraq threatened to take over Kuwait, stating that it was an integral part of Iraq. The sheikh called upon the British for armed support, which was promptly given. Later the Arab League guaranteed Kuwait's borders, admitted her as a member, and thus angered Iraq. Kuwait is important because this small bit of land produces more than one-third of the total production of oil in the Middle East. The rulers of Kuwait are using the revenues from oil to raise the economic and social levels in the country, and their educational and health policies are enlightened and progressive. Kuwait has a population of about 322,000.

### Muscat and Oman

The sultanate of Muscat and Oman occupies a portion of southeastern Arabia running along the coast for approximately a distance of 1,000 miles. The present ruler is Sultan Saiyid Said bin Taimur, whose family has ruled since 1741. The principle of inherited rulership has offended the traditions of many of the people, for they believe that the spiritual and temporal authority should be vested in the same person, who should be elected. Tribes in certain portions of the country have elected an imam to whom they give their allegiance. From time to time this imam has attempted to assert his right to rule, but he has always been defeated by the British-trained army of the sultan. The imam has been supported by Arab nationalists who desire to see British influence decline. The population of Muscat and Oman is estimated to be 550,000.

### Bahrain Islands

The Bahrains are a small group of islands lying about twenty miles off the coast of the Arabian peninsula in the Persian Gulf. Control of the islands has long been contested by the Iranians and the Arabs of the peninsula. The authority of the Iranians was generally stronger until the islands were taken under British protection in 1861. Although ruled by a sheikh, there is still strong British influence and control in the islands. Until recently there were almost constant internal problems and riots stemming from the quarrels between the adherents of the two main Moslem sects, the Sunnites and the Shiites. As a growing oil industry brings new economic opportunities, there are signs that the Sunnites and the Shiites are beginning to soften their violence toward each other. The population of the Bahrains is about 156,000.

### Qatar Sheikhdom

Qatar is a small independent sheikhdom which occupies the Qatar peninsula on the eastern coast of Arabia. It is very tiny, having about 45,000 population and an area of 8,000 square miles (about the size of our state of Massachusetts). Oil is important here also, but the revenues have not been used by the rulers with the same progressive wisdom as in Kuwait. Most of the revenues have found their way into the pockets of the ruling family.

### British Protectorates

Running along the southern coast of the Arabian peninsula is an area known as the Aden Protectorate. It consists of the port city of Aden, a small piece of surrounding territory, which is a British Crown Colony, and about twenty-five other British-protected states. The British Crown Colony of Aden is a busy free port and transit air base. It is a headquarters for the British forces in that part of the Middle East. The various British-protected states, ruled by Arab sultans or emirs, range in size from thousands of square miles to a few dusty acres. Their rulers are authoritarian, but they are restrained and limited in some ways by British advisors and policies. In January, 1963 a number of the small states bordering the Red Sea joined in a Federation of South Arabia which includes the former Crown Colony of Aden, now known as the state of Aden. Thus, the British have attempted to form a larger union which will be economically and politically more unified. The success of this plan will depend upon many factors, especially the desire of many states to incorporate their lands with others.

The often conflicting interests and policies of various personalities and countries are felt in these British-protected lands, especially the impulse toward Arab unity, nationalism, and anti-imperialism and opposition to vested interests.

## Jordan

The country of Jordan started its history when the British established the state of Transjordan under the Hashemite King Abdullah in 1922. The British governed Transjordan and Palestine under a mandate from the League of Nations. Transjordan was another parcel of land taken from the former Ottoman Turk rulers and transformed into a country. From the very beginning of Jordan's existence, the British have been deeply involved in almost all aspects of the country's political and economic life. Prior to 1946 the British handled Jordanian foreign policy. The British organized and subsidized Jordan's army, the famous Arab Legion, which has made a good name for itself since its formation early in the country's history. Britain has handled a great part of the finances of the country and, until recently, subsidized it rather heavily. The country became an independent sovereign state in 1946 and formally received the name Hashemite Kingdom of Jordan.

Prior to 1946 Jordan's territory and population were on the east bank of the Jordan River. In the fighting between Arab and Jew in 1948, after the British withdrew from Palestine, the Arab Legion seized territory on the

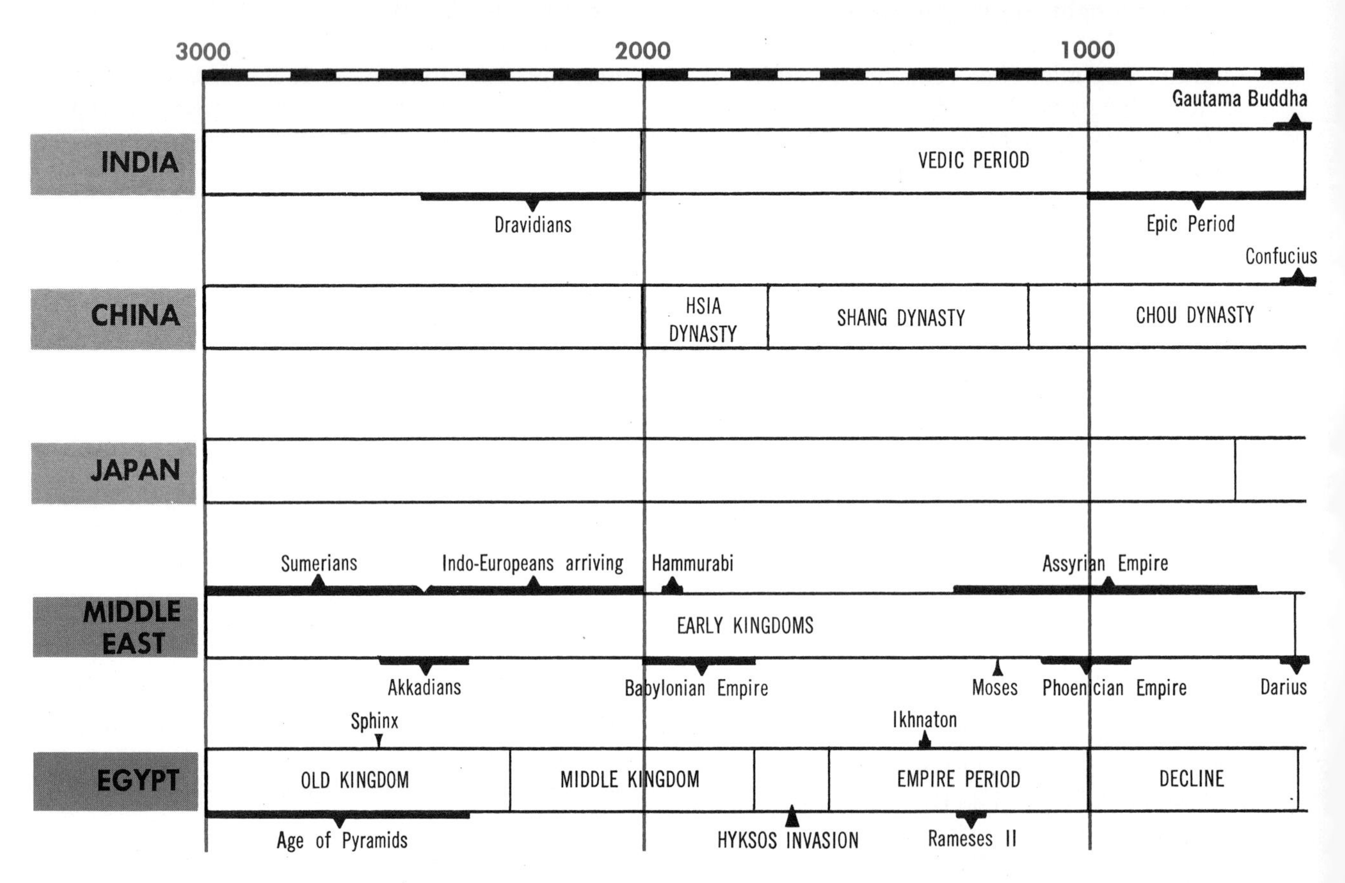


## MILESTONES

MIDDLE EAST

| | |
|---|---|
| B.C. | |
| 5000-4000 | Sumerians settle Tigris-Euphrates valley |
| c. 3000 | Assyrians settle Assur |
| c. 2600-2400 | Akkadian Semites (Sargon I) conquer Sumerians |
| c. 2000-1750 | Amorite dominance in Babylonia (Hammurabi) |
| c. 1225-733 | Peak of ancient Hebrew civilization |
| c. 1100-900 | Height of Phoenician greatness |
| c. 940 | Separate kingdoms of Israel and Judah |
| 612 | Nineveh destroyed |
| 612-539 | Chaldean Empire |
| 586 | Nebuchadnezzar destroys Jerusalem |
| c. 550-529 | Reign of Cyrus the Great |
| 521-486 | Reign of Darius |
| c. 330 | Alexander the Great defeats Persians |
| 264-146 | Punic Wars; Carthage destroyed |
| 146-30 | Rome conquers much of Alexander's empire |
| c. 7-4 | Jesus of Nazareth born |
| A.D. | |
| 70 | Titus destroys Jerusalem |
| 135 | Beginning of the Diaspora |
| 476 | Fall of Roman Empire in West |
| c. 570-632 | Mohammed |
| mid 700s | Most of Middle East converted to Islam |
| 1055-1057 | Seljuk Turks conquer much of Middle East |
| 1096 | Crusades begin |
| late 1100s | Crusaders driven from Palestine |
| 1200s | Mongols overrun Middle East |
| 1220 | Genghis Khan invades Persia |
| 1453 | Constantinople conquered by Ottoman Turks |

west bank of the Jordan. This land on the west bank of the river had been allotted by the United Nations to the Arab Palestinians. Jordan also captured the old city of Jerusalem. By this action Jordan acquired a large population of needy resident refugees which more than doubled its original population. These refugees are restless, discontented, politically powerful, and determined to wrest back from the Israelis the land they once possessed. They are a continual problem for King Hussein I, the present king of Jordan. Sup-

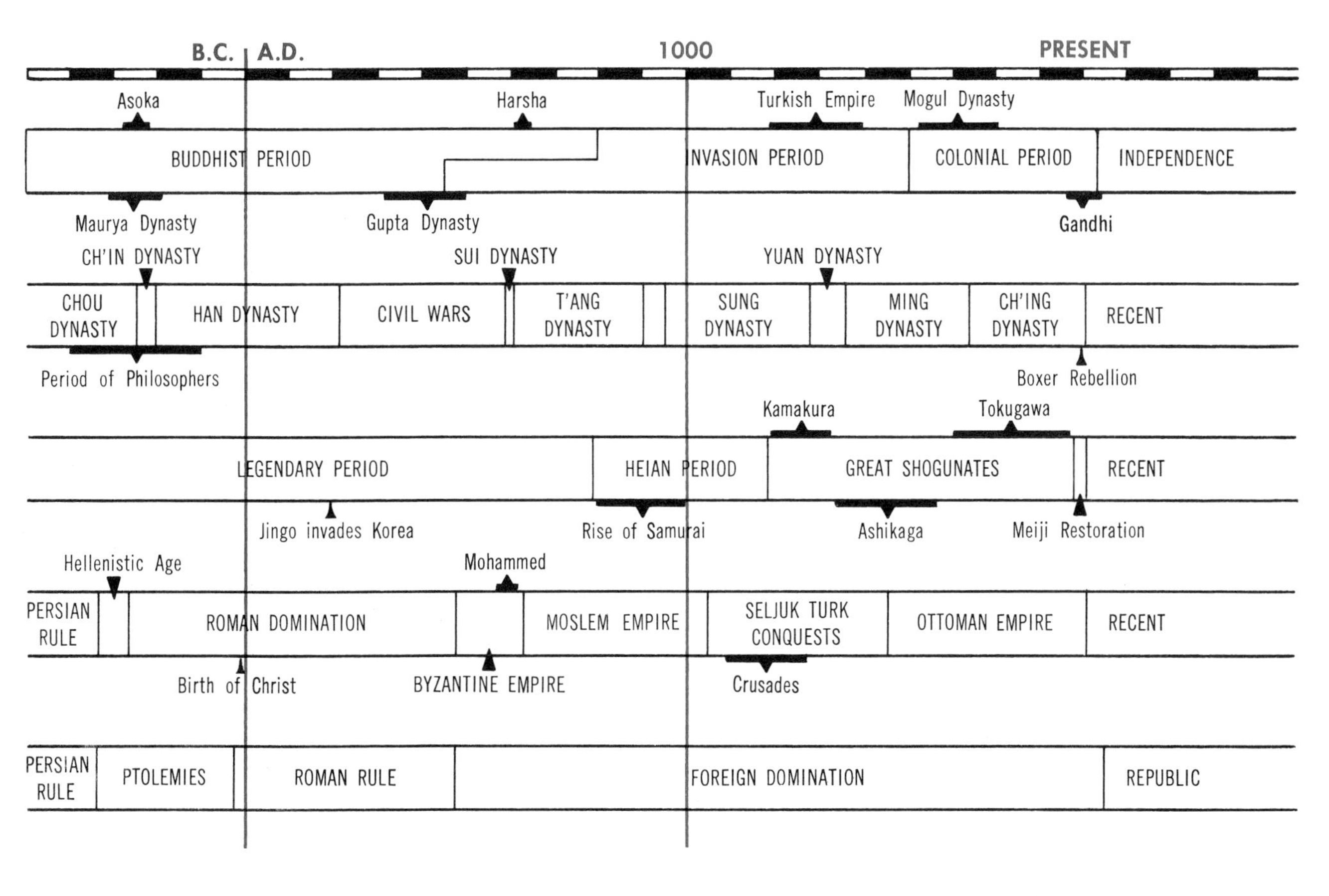


| | |
|---|---|
| 1918 | Ottoman Empire breaks up |
| 1923 | Turkish republic established by Atatürk |
| 1926 | State of Saudi Arabia formed |
| 1945 | Arab League formed |
| 1948 | New state of Israel created |

EGYPT

| B.C. | |
|---|---|
| c. 4200 | Egyptians develop first solar calendar |
| c. 3200 | Menes unites kingdoms of Upper and Lower Egypt |
| c. 3200-2300 | Old Kingdom (pyramids built) |
| c. 2300-1788 | Middle Kingdom |
| c. 1750 | Hyksos invasion |
| c. 1580-1000 | Empire Period |
| c. 1375-1358 | Amenhotep IV (Ikhnaton) reigns; idea of one god |
| c. 670 | Assyrians conquer Egypt |
| 525 | Egypt annexed to Persia |
| 332 | Alexander the Great conquers Egypt |
| 323-30 | Ptolemies rule |
| 30 | Rome conquers Egypt |
| A.D. | |
| 640 | Moslems conquer Egypt |
| 1517 | Turks invade and conquer Egypt |
| 1798 | Napoleon invades Egypt |
| 1805 | Mehemet Ali seizes control of Egypt |
| 1953 | Egypt proclaimed a republic |
| 1956 | Nasser nationalizes Suez Canal |
| 1958 | UAR formed (Egypt and Syria) |
| 1961 | Syria withdraws from UAR |

porters of Nasser, Communists, anti-Western nationalists, Baathists, and others find many followers among these discontented people. It is only the loyalty of the army and of the tribal chieftains of the original population which maintains King Hussein in power.

Jordan has few resources and few sources of income for its population of nearly 1,725,-000. The king must depend upon subsidies and aid from such countries as Britain and the United States to obtain the general expenses for running the country and for the support of his army and government officials. To a certain extent, he also depends upon the United States and Britain to defend his country in case of aggression.

Hussein's relations with President Nasser of Egypt have frequently been characterized by name-calling and threatening gestures. Motivated, at least in part, by antagonism toward Nasser, in August 1962 Jordan and Saudi Arabia declared that they would merge their armed forces and economic policies. Recently, however, Nasser has tried to better his relations with Jordan. But there remains an uncertainty about their relationship.

The silver plate below was made by ancient Phoenicians, ancestors of the Lebanese. (Courtesy of The Cleveland Museum of Art)

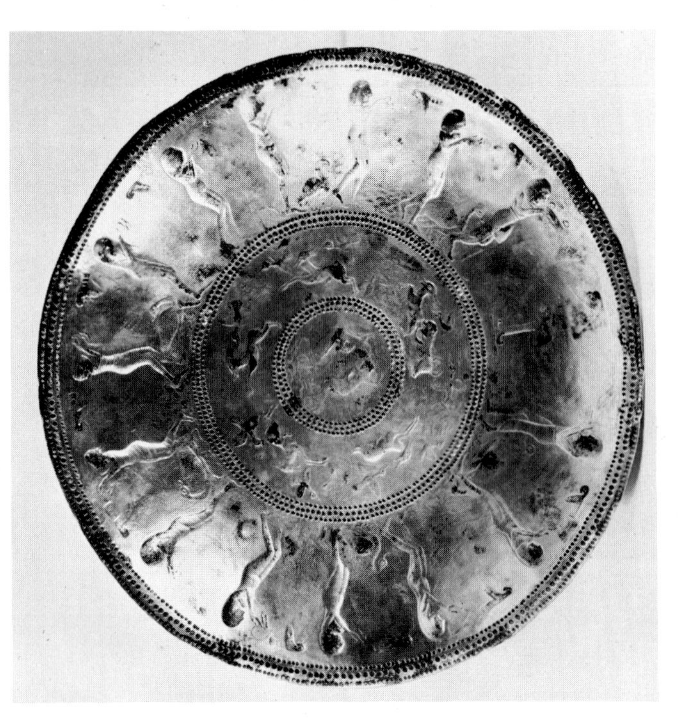

## Lebanon

The Lebanese occupy approximately the same territory which their ancestors, the Phoenicians, occupied many years ago. The Lebanese are traditionally a tolerant people, and their land has been a refuge for those escaping the intolerance of others. There have been differences among the Lebanese, however, and a revolt in 1958 caused President Chamoun to call upon the United States for help, which resulted in the sending of fourteen thousand marines to Lebanon for a short time. Generally, however, the Lebanese have been capable of handling their differences without outside help. They prefer it this way, for trade is in their blood, an essential part of their ancient tradition and way of life. The freer they are to trade and to act, the freer and more prosperous are the people. The Lebanese are divided about equally between the Moslem and Christian faiths—they prefer not to know in exactly what proportion—and by tacit agreement the president is a Christian and the prime minister a Moslem. The population is around 1,822,000.

Lebanon was governed by France under a mandate from the League of Nations from 1920 until 1941, and French troops did not withdraw until 1946. Since then the Lebanese have governed themselves. The legislative body is the Chamber of Deputies of ninety-nine persons, elected every four years. There is democracy in Lebanon, though sometimes it is expressed in a violent manner. The Lebanese have their problems, as do all peoples, but by and large they manage to solve these problems without too much disruption of their own economic and political system or those of their neighbors.

The Lebanese try to live on good terms with everyone, as good traders should, and they seem to be successful in this policy both with their neighbors and those farther removed. Both Christians and Moslems in Lebanon regard themselves as a part of the Arab world, and Lebanon is a member of the Arab League, which was founded in 1945 to safeguard Arab interests and to speak for the

Arabs. The Lebanese are an integral part of the Arab world, and the Arab world is the better for their tolerant presence.

1. Who was Abd-al Wahab? What were his reform teachings?
2. What countries make up the Arabian peninsula? Who are the rulers of each of these countries and why are they important?
3. How is democracy implemented in Lebanon? What personal attribute of the Lebanese helps to make this possible?

### Israel

In the year 70 A.D., Titus, who was later emperor of Rome, destroyed much of the city of Jerusalem and burned the Temple. In 135 A.D. the Roman Emperor Hadrian forbade the Jews to enter Jerusalem. Since that time the Jews have been living dispersed in various parts of the world. This dispersion is called the *Diaspora*. There were a few Jews who remained in Palestine, and over the lengthening centuries of their dispersion some returned to spend their last years and to be buried in its blessed earth. But the great mass of Jews continued to live dispersed around the world. Many of them believed that they could never return to their old homeland until the coming of the Messiah. A few among them did not think they needed to wait for this indefinite day to dawn before returning home. During the nineteenth century many Jews fled from persecution in Russia and settled elsewhere, especially in the United States. Some of the younger persecuted ones slipped quietly into Palestine and thus began the first immigration into this land. Most of these early immigrants died of disease and ill-treatment, but the example they gave was followed by increasing numbers of their people in the twentieth century.

**Zionism.** The movement to make Palestine a real homeland of the Jews came to be identified by the name Zionism. This movement was given greater life and vigor by the publication of a pamphlet called *The Jewish State* and other writings of Theodor Herzl during the latter part of the nineteenth century. Herzl was distressed by the prejudices displayed by Europeans in word and deed against the Jew. He believed that the solution was in a mass and orderly exodus of the Jews from Europe to a place where they could live in freedom.

In 1897 Herzl and others met at the first Zionist Congress in Basel, Switzerland. This Congress decided that Palestine should be a homeland for the Jews and stated the principles upon which Zionism would be based. The movement grew, and further attacks against the Jews in Eastern Europe and in Russia started a second migration to Palestine. Between 1903 and 1913 fifty thousand Jews emigrated from Europe to Palestine. Among those who survived the harshness of man and environment experienced by this group was David Ben-Gurion, a Polish Jew. Ben-Gurion was one of the founders and the first prime minister of Israel.

During the First World War another champion of Zionism, Chaim Weizmann, won British approval for this cause. This approval was expressed in a declaration by Arthur J. Balfour, the British Foreign Secretary, when he formally recognized in writing the historical connection of the Jews and the land of Palestine. This statement was known as the Balfour Declaration, and it was made a part of the League of Nations mandate which gave Great Britain authority to govern Palestine after the end of the war. From this time onward many Jews began to immigrate to Palestine. Their numbers increased to a flood when the Jews in Germany, Austria, and Czechoslovakia began to feel the terrible hate of Hitler during the mid-1930's.

The trials of the Jews did not cease when they reached Palestine, for they frequently escaped imprisonment and death in Europe only to find suffering and death in Palestine. The Arabs particularly feared and resented the coming of Jews in numbers. During many centuries the Jews had been separated from this land, and the Arabs had become the great majority. They held this land by the right of their centuries of toil and ownership and they looked upon the Jews as invaders who must be cast out with violence if necessary. The

Jews regarded this land as rightfully theirs, for their ancestors had been forcibly removed from it. The Jews believed that the Arabs possessed a land not theirs by ancient right. These peoples were determined to maintain their just claims, and there began a history of violence which stained the land with blood and misery. This controversy continues to torture the relations between the Israeli Jews and their Arab neighbors.

After the Second World War the British sought to satisfy the Arabs by limiting the number of Jews who could come to Palestine each year. The conditions of continuous violence increased as the Jewish underground stepped up its terrorist attacks against both the British and the Arabs. The Jews refused to submit to the limitations of the British and would not yield to the attacks of the Arabs. Finally, in 1947, the entire question was submitted to the United Nations.

The Assembly of the United Nations recommended the partition of Palestine into three parts: a Jewish state, an Arab state, and a Jerusalem administered by an international body. The Assembly also called upon the British to leave Palestine in eight months. In May 1948, Ben-Gurion announced the creation of the new state of Israel, and the British began a withdrawal of their troops from the land. War broke out immediately between the Jews and Arabs living within Palestine. The Arabs were supported by troops from Egypt, Iraq, Lebanon, Syria, Jordan, and later Saudi Arabia and Yemen.

The United Nations sent Count Bernadotte of Sweden to mediate between the Arabs and the Jews. Bernadotte was assassinated, and his place was taken by his American assistant, Ralph Bunche. As a result of the patience and tact of these two men, and because the Arab armies were being rather badly mauled by the Jews, an armistice was signed. The armistice agreement between Egypt and Israel was signed in June 1949, followed some months later by agreement with all the Arab states except Saudi Arabia. But violence has not ceased, for there are almost daily border incidents and killings on both sides. As late as 1956 Israel, France, and Britain launched a full-scale attack on Egypt which ended only when the United Nations called for a cease fire.

During these periods of war and terror, hundreds of thousands of Palestine Arabs fled to surrounding countries and territories, where they still live in misery and want. These refugees are a source of antagonism between the Arabs and the Jews. The United Nations attempts to care for the refugees, and would like to relocate them, but they are unwanted. They live on in the hope that one day Palestine will be theirs again.

In the meantime, the Jews are building Israel into a small but powerful state. Ben-Gurion became its first prime minister, and Chaim Weizmann its first president. There is a unicameral parliament known as Knesset. Jews living outside Israel have poured an abundance of money into the country, about a billion and a half dollars over a thirteen-year period. Immigrants from many countries also poured in, many of them with technical skills needed for the advancement of the country. The population is now around 2,338,300. The Jews in Israel are working with devotion, with skill, with imagination, and with purpose to make their country into a land of promise where all Jews can find a haven should they need one. They appear to be succeeding.

1. What is Zionism? Why is it significant as a social and political movement? Name some of its most important leaders.
2. What two major groups claimed a right to Palestine? What evidence exists to support both claims? What was the result of these two conflicting demands?

## Conclusion

Man in the Middle East has lived within the wide borders of empires carved by conquerors and on small spaces of earth governed by members of the same family for generations. There was a long period of time when few had a part in the political struggle for power, and none questioned the political system. Decisions were made by the one or the few, and most people were given no choice or voice in political decisions. The people did not conceive of a change in this system, though they thought often of changing their rulers. Nor was it an easy matter to change a ruler, for many thought their rulers had divine authority. Only the madly daring and unbelieving would have attempted to unsettle the divinely supported. These attitudes began to change and political restlessness grew when the European brought his political behavior and social ideas to the Middle East during the nineteenth and twentieth centuries.

In recent years man in this region has questioned the right of one man to rule without reference to the people. In many cases the divine political authority of the ruler has been denied. The Westerner brought ideas about national independence, about individual freedoms, and about the voice of the people in government. The Middle Easterner was drawn to these ideals. When the Europeans showed no sincere intention of leaving his lands, he began to feel that his political ambitions were being too long frustrated. Suspicion of the Westerners grew and often violence erupted. These suspicions of Western intentions have never been completely dispelled, though most lands of the Middle East now have their own governments. Too often these governments have not brought peace of mind and stability to their people.

There have been only a few years to shape this new political life, to free it from the grasp of the past and to mold it to the needs of the present and the uncertainties of the future. The Middle Easterner is confused by the din of promises and panaceas from those who seek to rule and influence him. He is torn between loyalty to his clan and religion and the loyalty required by his nation. He has trusted some leaders and found them unworthy of trust. He once thought that the pace toward democracy and prosperity would be rapid, but he has quickly learned that it is a plodding and painful journey.

Man in the Middle East is frequently obliged to rely on the armed might and reforming spirit of certain military leaders. This has been especially so during the present uncertain period of transition and adjustment to new realities. Difficulties and disorders have made imperative the disciplined hand of strong and forward-looking leaders. But ultimately, the Middle Easterner wants something to say about how he is governed.

The peasant, struggling to earn from the land enough to eat and to pay the high rent of his landlord, is still a neglected, toiling figure in the Middle Eastern landscape; but the military reformer is conscious of his needs. The illiterate woman must still ask someone to read or write her letters; but many schools are being built for both sexes. Diseases of the eyes, running sores of other diseases, and bad hygienic practices are yet afflicting people in this region with pain; but efforts are being made to improve and expand health facilities. The unemployed still loiter restlessly on city streets, or sit weakly in squalid huts; but jobs are increasing through industrialization, handicrafts, and government work.

Some people complain of the dictatorial methods of the military man and cry out that representative government is being lost in the Middle East. The military man replies that the people do not require the chaos and squabbles of political factions and parties but rather the orderly, disciplined, efficient, and commanding voice of a soldier to lead them during this period of their history. Representative government may come, but it will come only after there have been years of educational and economic progress. In the meantime, the soldier must be the guide through the pitfalls of this transitional time. The military reformer is having his moments of unhappiness, for he is finding that something gained is sometimes something lost.

Man in the Middle East has all the problems of men everywhere in passing through a transitional stage from one type of economic, social, and political system to another. He is often frustrated and angered at the limitations which the past and the present inflict upon him. But he is determined and proud, and he feels that his difficulties will be solved, though perhaps some of the solutions may not be pleasing to others outside his region. He is not disposed towards Communism as a rule because his God has been rejected by the Communists. Neither has the man of the Middle East liked some of the policies of the Western democracies.

Man in the Middle East today does not desire to divorce himself from the rest of the world. However, he does want to evolve his way of living without too much interference from others. He knows himself to be a member of the family of man, and he is part of the brotherhood of Islam, which is not confined by national boundaries. He also realizes that special regional problems must often be solved without outside interference. The question that nags him is: Will he have the freedom and the opportunity to resolve his problems without the intrusion of other men and policies born somewhere else in the world?

## SUMMING UP THE CHAPTER

A. Define or explain the following terms, relating them to this chapter.

| | |
|---|---|
| Bedouin | mullahs |
| chador | pilgrimage |
| imam | Zionism |

B. Identify or locate the following and tell why they are important.

| | |
|---|---|
| Atatürk | Mossadegh |
| Balfour Declaration | Pahlevi |
| Ben-Gurion | Peacock Throne |
| CENTO | Qajar dynasty |
| Farouk | Ralph Bunche |
| Fatimid dynasty | Riza Shah |
| Kurdistan | Tripartite Alliance |
| Mecca | Tudeh party |

C. Identify the following dates, indicating their importance.

1. 968-1171 (Egypt)
2. 1250-1517 (Egypt)
3. 70 A.D. (Palestine)
4. 1925-1941 (Iran)
5. 1923-1938 (Turkey)

D. Chapter review questions.

1. How valid is the following statement? "From very ancient days, politics and religion were almost inseparable in the Middle East."
2. What three groups in Turkish society were the basis of Atatürk's support? Why?
3. Describe Atatürk's reforms.
4. Evaluate the political evolution of Turkey since the death of Atatürk.
5. Discuss Turkey's place in world affairs. What part has her geography played in determining her position?
6. What factors contributed to the downfall of Riza Shah? Which factor do you consider the most significant in this respect?
7. What role did Mossadegh play in Iranian history? Evaluate both his strengths and weaknesses.
8. Has Egypt made any progress in her struggle to become self-sufficient? Do you think her attempts are enough? What alternatives would you suggest?
9. Discuss the importance of the Aswan dam to Nasser and to Egypt.
10. Evaluate the effects of European intervention in Egypt, paying particular attention to the 1956 Suez Canal crisis. Discuss Nasser's reactions, especially his economic policy.
11. What two factors have aided and strengthened the influence of the Saud family? Do you feel that these factors are a wise foundation for a government?
12. How has the Saud family used its oil royalties?
13. What was the reason for the 1963 revolt in Yemen? List the supporters of each group.
14. What strategic position does Aden hold?
15. How do most Lebanese earn a living?
16. What elements, internal and external, support and oppose the present government of Jordan? Which factors do you consider most important?
17. In what ways are the Arab refugees from Palestine a major problem for Jordan?
18. What are some of the reasons for Iraq's internal troubles?
19. What role did the United Nations play in the war over the division of Palestine? Was the UN successful?

E. Questions for discussion.

1. Why do you suppose Atatürk made Turkey a secular state?
2. What is "positive neutralism"? Does Nasser's definition hold up in practice? Can you name any other countries that practice a similar policy?

F. Projects for individuals or groups.

1. Pick a significant political leader in the Middle East and prepare a report on his or her life for classroom presentation.
2. Locate on a map the countries of the Arabian peninsula. Shade the British territories.

# SUMMING UP THE UNIT

### *Drawing together the main themes*

1. What factors brought out in this unit identify the Middle East as a region? Which of these factors do you feel are the most significant?
2. What peoples have inhabited the lands of the Middle East? Tell something that each has contributed to the progress of civilization in the area.
3. Identify and compare and contrast the importance of Ammon-Re and Osiris. What happened to these gods?
4. Who first introduced the concept of one God in the Middle East? Did this concept spread widely when it began, or was it reintroduced at a later period? If so, by whom?
5. Describe the religion of the early Sumerians and Semites.
6. To what degree do the teachings of Islam, Christianity, and Judaism furnish their followers with a comprehensive guide for living?
7. What changes in the social system were brought about by Atatürk and Riza Shah in their respective countries? Compare the way they handled the problems they faced and evaluate their success.
8. In this unit, as in the unit on Asia, we learned that man did not question his system of government; he questioned, rather, the individual ruler and his manner. How do you account for this? Would this be true in the United States?
9. Comment on the following statement: Modernization in the countries of the Middle East has been largely brought about by governmental action. To what degree is this statement true?
10. What role has nationalization played in bringing about change in the Middle East?
11. Discuss the Middle East as a crossroads land.
12. Outside intervention has been an important factor in the Middle East. Discuss the assets and liabilities of such intervention.

### *Unit projects for individuals or groups*

1. Point out the historical events behind current news stories about the Middle East.
2. Read sections of *The Arabian Nights.* Do they remind you of any other piece of literature? If so, what?
3. Try to find pictures of buildings in the United States that are examples of Islamic architecture.

## FURTHER READINGS


BAUMANN, HANS, *The World of the Pharaohs.* Pantheon, 1960. Old Egypt is pictured well by the illustrations in this book.

BREASTED, JAMES H., *Ancient Times,* 2nd ed., Ginn.

———, *A History of Egypt from the Earliest Times to the Persian Conquest.* Scribner's, 1912.

———, *The Conquest of Civilization,* new rev. ed. Harper, 1938. These three books, written by one of the greatest scholars on early man in the Middle East, are a treasury of information.

CERAM, C. W. (Kurt Marek), *Gods, Graves, and Scholars.* Knopf, 1951. Archaeologists uncover ancient mysteries in the Middle East.

CHUBB, MARY ALFORD, *Nefertiti Lived Here.* Crowell-Collier, 1955. The home of the famous Egyptian Queen Nefertiti is explored by the archaeologist.

CONTENAU, GEORGES, *Everyday Life in Babylon and Assyria.* St. Martin's, 1954.

COPELAND, PAUL W., *Land and People of Syria.* Lippincott, 1964.

COTTRELL, LEONARD, *Life Under the Pharaohs.* Holt, Rinehart & Winston, 1960. He writes well about the classical Egyptian.

CRESSEY, GEORGE B., *Crossroads: Land and Life in Southeast Asia.* Lippincott, 1960. Excellent geography of the Middle East.

EDWARDS, I. E. S., *The Pyramids of Egypt,* rev. ed. Penguin, 1961, paperback. All about the pyramids.

FISHER, SYDNEY, *The Middle East: A History.* Knopf, 1959. Good textbook.

HINCKLEY, HELEN, *The Land and People of Iran.* Lippincott, 1964.

HITTI, PHILIP K., *The Near East in History.* Van Nostrand, 1961. Hitti knows the Middle East well and writes informatively about it.

———, *The Arabs: A Short History.* Regnery, 1956, paperback. Survey of the Arab's history.

HOFFMAN, GAIL, *The Land and People of Israel,* rev. Lippincott, 1963.

KRAMER, SAMUEL N., *History Begins at Sumer.* Doubleday, 1959, paperback.

LOVEJOY, BAHIJA, *The Land and People of Iraq.* Lippincott, 1964.

MAHMOUD, ZAKI NAGUIB, *The Land and People of Egypt.* Lippincott, 1959.

PICKTHALL, MOHAMMED M., ed. and trans., *The Meaning of the Glorious Koran.* Mentor, 1954, paperback. Translations and explanations.

SMITH, WILFRED C., *Islam in Modern History.* Princeton, 1957; Mentor, paperback.

SPENCER, WILLIAM, *The Land and People of Turkey,* rev. Lippincott, 1964.


### *ARTICLES*


MENEN, AUBREY, "The Mohammedan World," *Holiday* (March 31, 1962). Excellent photographs.

KHAN, SIR ZAFRULLA, "The Concept of Unity," *Saturday Review* (December 26, 1959). Similarity of Islam to other religions.

# UNIT III

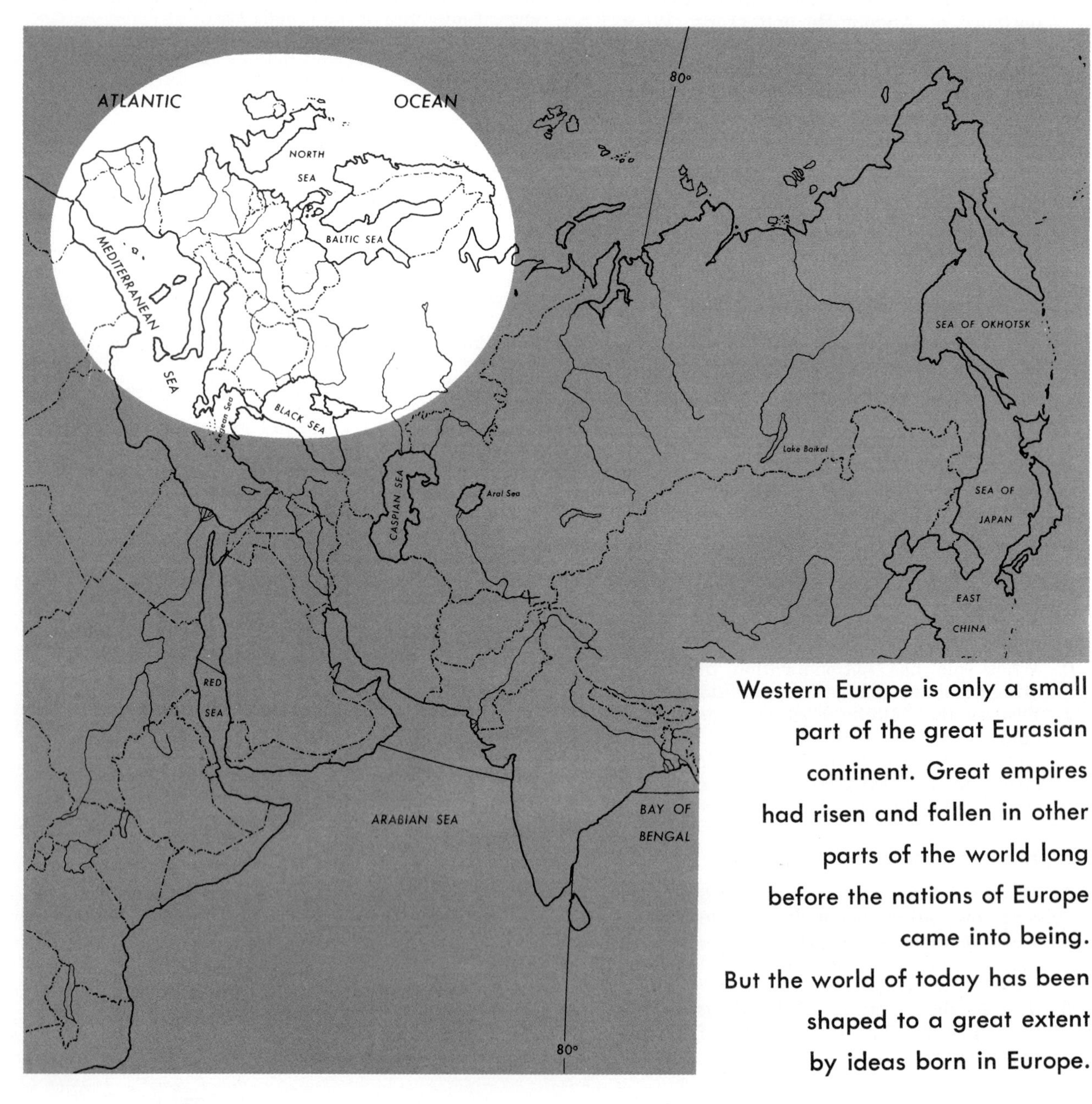


Western Europe is only a small part of the great Eurasian continent. Great empires had risen and fallen in other parts of the world long before the nations of Europe came into being. But the world of today has been shaped to a great extent by ideas born in Europe.

# THE EUROPEAN: AN INTRODUCTION

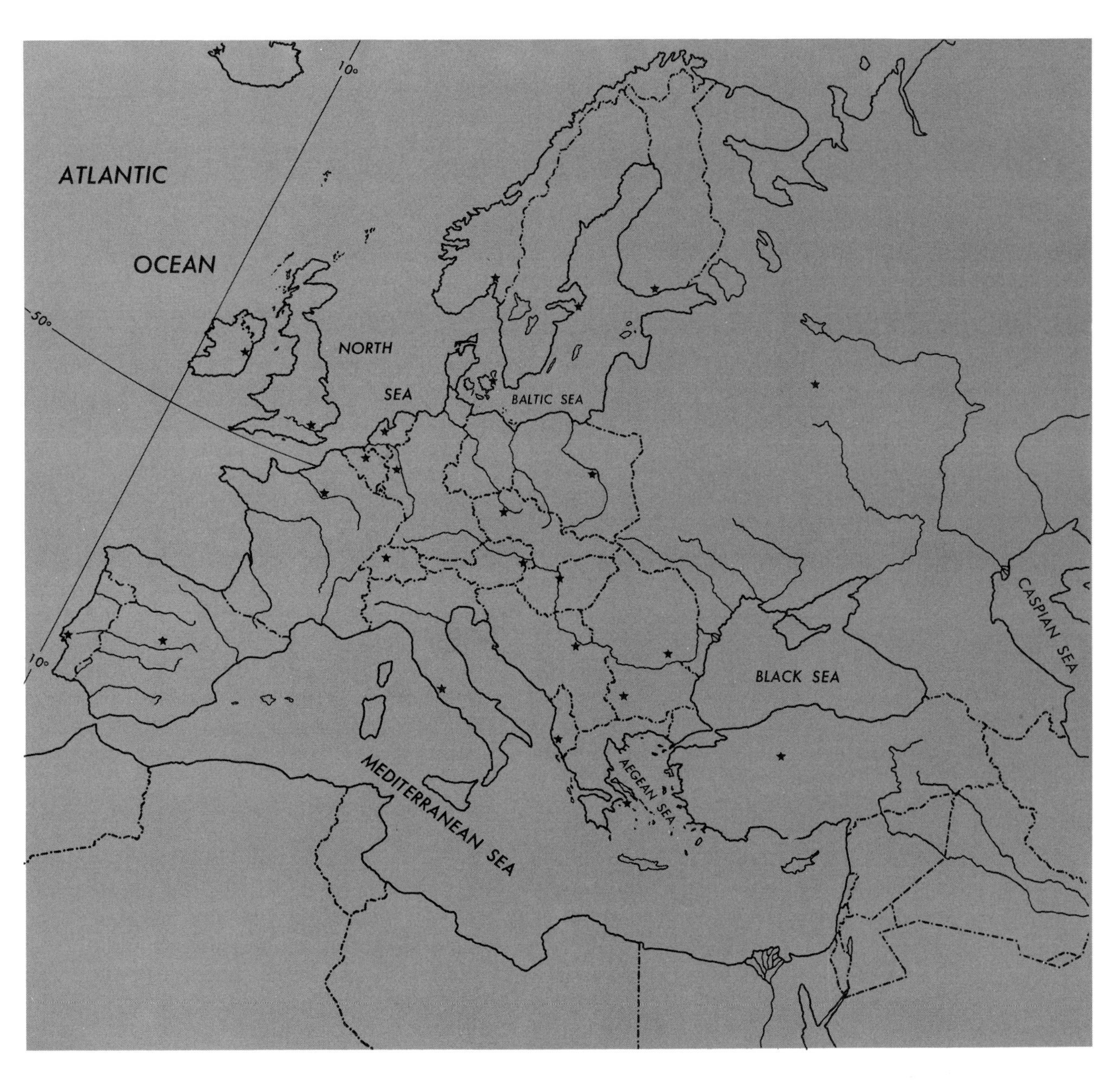

# CHAPTER 13

# *Man Settled Greece*

THE FIRST GREAT CIVILIZATION to which men of the Western world trace their beginnings was that founded by the Indo-Europeans in Greece. Other civilized men had known the shores of Greece before them, but the Indo-European Greeks built a civilization that is still having its impact on much of the world.

## The Cretans Came First

On an island straddling the south entrance into the Aegean Sea, lying between the Middle East and Greece, there lived civilized men called Cretans. Their island is still known as Crete. Perhaps they inhabited this island around 3000 B.C. or earlier. It has been surmised that the Cretans were the end result of the mixing of several strains of man, the Hittites and the Egyptians among others. However, no one is yet definite about their bloodlines and origins. From the surviving portrayals of the Cretans it appears that they were slender and small of stature and that their long heads were crowned with dark, curly hair. Archeological excavations reveal that their principal city was Knossos, and that by 2000 B.C., or possibly earlier, the Cretans had begun a remarkable civilization, which they continued to build to greater heights until they were destroyed around 1200 B.C. Some historians call this civilization *Minoan* after the name of one of the Cretan kings, Minos; others speak of the Cretans as being at the center of the entire area washed by the Aegean Sea and refer to this whole civilized group as *Aegean*.

The Cretans were men of many accomplishments. They were fond of living well. They made their homes more comfortable with hot and cold running water, bathrooms, and good furniture. They protected their things of value with metal locks for which they fashioned keys. The plastered interiors of their homes were colorfully decorated with excellent paintings. (This technique of painting on plaster, called fresco, is still used today.) Cretan art was often bright and cheerful, and the Cretan frescoes seem to reflect great joy in painting. The Cretans were fond of dancing, as well as boxing, racing, and other sports. There was one sport in which perhaps the Cretan was unique, and that was bull-leaping. This seemingly impossible feat has been attested to in Cretan paintings of men and women leaping over the bull's horns, turning a handspring on its back and landing upright on their feet behind the bull.

Today we must depend chiefly upon the art of the Cretans for a knowledge of their culture. Although both men and women could read and write, only in recent years have we been able to read one form of their writing, which archeologists call Linear B. The Cretans also had another kind of writing which has not yet been deciphered. The paintings found on delicate, beautiful vases and on the walls of Cretan dwellings give us a clear picture of how Cretan women dressed. They wore tight jackets and long, bell-like skirts, and they liked to make and wear hats. From what has been uncovered of their achievements, it appears that women held a high position in Cretan society—at least equal to that of the men. The chief deity of the Cretans was a goddess, whose likeness was often carved in gold and ivory in the form of a snake.

Cretan art reveals that the people had a feeling for the interesting and dramatic displays of nature—the bending lily, the startled

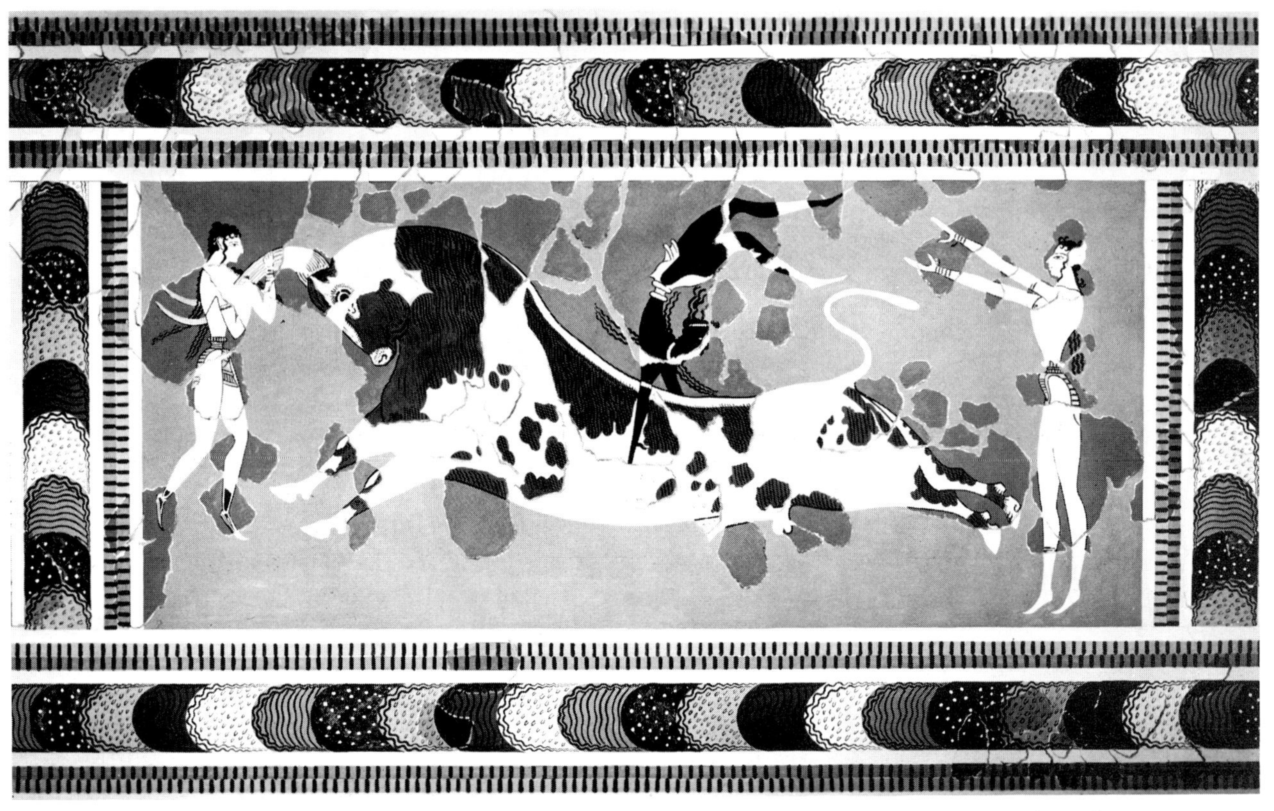

Cretan frescoes show men and women leaping over bulls. Most of our knowledge of the Cretans is from their art. (University of Pennsylvania Museum)

deer, and the stalking cat. They did not portray scenes of war, but rather concentrated their attention on nature and the more peaceful acts of man—landscapes, sports, and festivals. They watched their athletes and entertainers perform while sitting on tiers of stone seats in outdoor theaters.

The Cretans derived their comfortable living from the profits of trade. They were among the earliest of the sea-traders, and their ventures took them to Egypt, Phoenicia, and lands bordering the Aegean Sea. They profitably traded their beautifully designed vases, enameled daggers of bronze, rings, and many other products wrought of gold, silver, and bronze. Trading brought the Cretans to the shores of Greece where they dealt with the early inhabitants who lived along the coasts of this land. These early people of mainland Greece were subdued by and mixed with the invading Indo-European tribes who had been wandering southward through Greece to the shores of the Aegean Sea for centuries.

### The Indo-Europeans Came to Greece

Between 2500 and 2000 B.C., the Indo-Europeans began a slow exodus from their flat lands of grass to the hills, valleys, and coasts of Europe. Moved by forces and reasons which can only be guessed, this migration continued for more than two thousand years. The various groups of Indo-Europeans paused at times to rest, to adjust themselves to a new environment, and to settle; but there were always others who passed them by or pushed them along into other parts of Europe. The westward movement was relentless, and it did not cease until Europe was peopled from the islands of the bordering seas to the grasslands of the steppes of Russia. The Indo-Europeans participated in one of the grandest of man's migrations, and they began one of the grandest of man's civilizations—the civilization of Europe.

It was around 2000 B.C. that the Indo-Europeans started on a series of migrations southward into the peninsula of Greece. The eastern shores and harbors of the Greek peninsula formed the western borders of the Aegean Sea. The Indo-Europeans moved down among the twisting ways of this mountainous land and settled its isolated valleys and hillsides with their families, clans, and tribes. The earliest of the Greek-speaking tribes to invade Greece were known as Achaeans. Near the sea, the earliest of these invaders were introduced to the civilized works of the Cretans, and the result of their meeting was the rise of the Mycenaean civilization, which lasted until about 1200 B.C.

The Mycenaeans built great walled citadels, armed themselves with bronze swords, guarded themselves with great shields, and used chariots to make war. They eventually came to dominate the trade of the Aegean Sea and the products of their trade—bronze daggers, beads, pottery—have been found in the western parts of Europe as well as on the islands of the Aegean and the mainland of the Middle East. But neither their walled cities nor the waters encircling their city at Knossos on Crete could protect them from the tribes that continued to move down the peninsula of Greece. These later tribes were armed with weapons of iron, and the bronze weapons of the Mycenaean were no match for this tougher metal. Some have thought that these new Indo-European conquerors learned about iron weapons and the secret of their manufacture from mercenaries who had served in the armies of the Hittites and others who used and manufactured iron.

Iron was a cheaper metal and easier to make than bronze, and men continue to wonder why the Mycenaeans clung to their less efficient and softer bronze weapons in the face of the iron threat of the invaders. Whatever the reason, these later migrating tribes came to dominate Greece and much of the Aegean area. Some of the civilization which the Cretans and the Mycenaeans had fostered there was destroyed. Not all was lost, however, of this Bronze Age civilization. Upon the remnants that remained, the Greeks began to build another and greater civilization which continues to have its impact upon man.

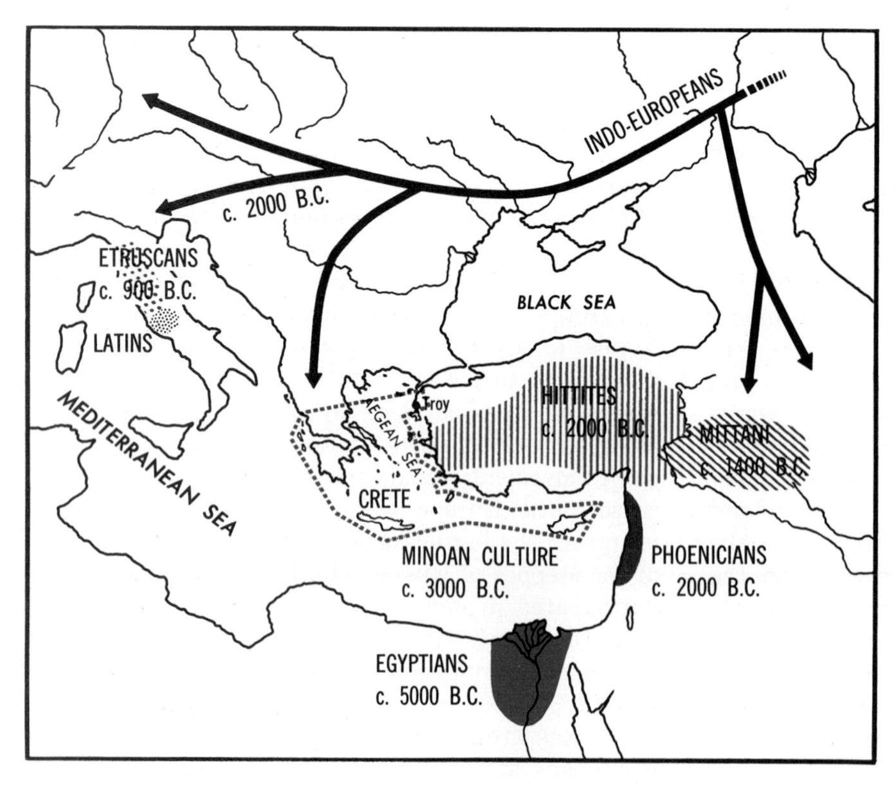


**Ancient Mediterranean Civilizations**

Before the Indo-Europeans came into the lands beside the Mediterranean Sea, great civilizations flourished there. In this unit you will read about some of them.

1. Who were some of the earliest known peoples of Europe?
2. Describe some of the achievements of the Minoan civilization.
3. What permitted the Cretans to live so well?

## The Greeks

On hills and rocky coasts, the Greeks built forts which grew into city-states. The Greek name for a city-state was *polis*, and this name is preserved today in such words as *politics*, *metropolis*, and *policy*. The Greeks acknowledged no authority over the individual or the city except that of the tribal leader. The basic social groups were the family, the clan, and the tribe, and those outside these relations of kinship were considered only as possible enemies to be raided for plunder and fame. The position of the tribal leader became that of the king, and the clan leaders became the nobles. Beyond the few square miles of valley and mountain controlled by each city, there were other city-states which were equally proud and jealous of their independence. Since the Greeks were prone to raid and to war upon their neighbors, who also held submission to be unthinkable, the peninsula became for centuries a scene of shifting battles and alliances. Geography was in great part responsible for the development of small city-states within Greece. The self-reliance and proud apartness of the Greeks were reinforced by the separating mountains and waters and the secluded valleys and coastal cliffs of their land.

There were, however, a few occasions when the city-states temporarily cooperated to raid and to compete in sports.

### The Homeric Age

The Greeks were experienced in living and fighting on land, but where they lived near the sea, they learned to move about and to fight with ships. They became sea-raiders, sea-traders, and colonizers. It is widely believed that their scheming minds and their arms were responsible for the destruction of Knossos, the center of the ancient Aegean civilization on Crete, and the capture of its accumulated riches. Perhaps this happened around 1200 B.C. Two great epic poems narrate the story of the Greek expedition against the city of Troy in Asia Minor, another center of Aegean civilization. One of the poems, *The Iliad*, tells of the Greek siege and plundering of this city, which possibly happened around 1170 B.C. The other poem, *The Odyssey*, relates the fantastic experiences which befell the warrior-hero Odysseus while returning home from Troy. These heroic poems are usually considered to be the work of the blind poet Homer, who lived some time between 1000 and 800 B.C. They are the chief written descriptions we possess of the life and beliefs of the early Greeks. For this reason, the period between 1000 and 800 B.C. is sometimes referred to as the Homeric Age.

### The Olympic Games

The early Greeks gathered together every four years for five strenuous summer days of physical contests in sports. This event was called the Olympic games. The earliest recorded date of these games was 776 B.C. It is from this year that the Greeks calculated their dates in four-year periods called *Olympiads*. The games consisted of contests between athletes in foot racing, chariot racing, hurling of discus and javelin, the broad jump, and other displays of physical fitness. Wreaths of olive branches or laurel were placed upon the heads of the winners, and additional honors and rewards awaited them when they returned to their homes.

The Greeks delighted in watching and in exhibiting the skill and strength of a well-trained body. They came to Olympia from all over Greece to see and participate in these contests. The official purpose of the games was to honor Zeus, the father of the gods and of men, but the Greeks also took great pleasure in these displays of brawn and skill. From the time of the earliest Greek Olympic games to the expanded Olympic games of today, man has enjoyed observing competition between well-muscled athletes.

## The Spartans

The Greeks did not always train their bodies merely for the purpose of receiving peaceful wreaths of olive or laurel. Their intention was also to harden themselves to endure the rigors of war. Probably no Greeks—nor any men since that time—prepared their bodies and minds more systematically for war than the Spartans. Today we still use the word *Spartan* to describe strict self-discipline like that practiced by the ancient citizens of Sparta.

The city-state of Sparta was located in a southern part of Greece called Peloponnesus. The Dorian tribe, ancestors of the Spartans, had migrated there from the north and found themselves in the minority among the original inhabitants. They remained in the minority, but by 600 or 500 B.C. the Spartans ruled the entire area of Peloponnesus. They ruled because their bodies and minds had been toughened and shaped for war since childhood.

**A fighting machine.** While yet a baby, the Spartan was examined by his elders, and if he met their standards of physical fitness, he was permitted to live. Others not so fortunate were taken to a hillside or cave and left to die from harshness of climate or to be eaten by animals. At the age of seven, the Spartan began the severe training that would eventually fashion him into one of the world's finest fighting machines—the soldier of Sparta. From this age until he was sixty, his life was dictated by the unyielding discipline and requirements of Sparta.

Turnips were a common food of both the Greeks and Romans. List the foods that you eat in one day and use reference books to compare them with foods known to the Greeks and Romans. Make a list of foods that were unknown in ancient times. (USDA photo)

The boy in training was given rough and insufficient food so that he would be compelled to steal, for the soldier in the field must learn to live off the land. The boy who was caught stealing was flogged before others, and if he whimpered he was disgraced.

The Spartan learned to endure privations, pain, and indignities in silence. He was given but a single piece of cloth to wear in both summer and winter, and no shoes for his feet. He marched, fought with weapons, wrestled, and hardened his muscles with gymnastics. He was instructed to speak little at all times; his deeds in war would speak for him. At the age of twenty he became a full citizen of Sparta, and at the age of thirty he was married.

The woman he married had also been taught to keep her body healthy and sound for breeding and for work; her first loyalty was to Sparta. The ideal Spartan woman was one who asked first whether Sparta had won or lost a battle, and afterward inquired about the fate of her sons fighting in the battle. If Sparta won, she would be thankful, even though her sons had been killed in battle. The whole purpose of the Spartan was to fight, to breed, and to die for the glory and preservation of Sparta.

Fighting was the primary occupation of the Spartans; everything else, including the making of money, was secondary and even frowned upon. Slaves tilled the fields, which were allotted to each citizen in equal measure; but in a sense the Spartans, too, were slaves. Although their city was governed by men whom they elected, the citizens existed for the state alone. With their training and indoctrination, it is not surprising that the Spartans were incomparable soldiers or that they contributed little to the advancement of the arts and sciences.

1. How did the geography of Greece contribute to the political temperament of the Greek?
2. What were the subjects of the great Greek epics?
3. What was the religious significance of the Olympic games?
4. Describe the training of Spartan youths for service to their city-state.

## The Athenians

There were citizens of other city-states in Greece who were not so Spartan in their inclinations. Some of them, such as the Athenians, surrounded themselves with beauty, enjoyed discussing the arts and politics of man, were fond of making money, and preferred to serve the state by choice rather than compulsion. In their democracy and in their culture, the Athenians were the farthest removed from the Spartans among the citizens of the city-states of Greece. They were named after their city-state of Athens, which was located in the district of Attica in east-central Greece.

Athenian life was not as orderly or as rigidly molded as that of Sparta. As their lives evolved, the Athenians developed into free-thinking men who frequently showed their willingness to die rather than exist without the climate of freedom which they had created. The Athenians did not arrive at the summit of their freedom and civilization, beginning around 500 B.C., without undergoing a lengthy period of painful experience and preparation. They learned that the blessing of freedom is earned only by those willing to sacrifice body and brain, and that it is secured only by those who give it their constant devotion and protection.

The early Athenians had kings who oppressed them and, later, there were nobles who ruled, taxed, and judged them, often unjustly. Most of the people owned little land, and the fields they worked as tenants produced scarcely more than enough to pay the high rents of the noble-landlords. To pay their rent, some of the tenants were forced to borrow, and when they could not pay their debts, they were forced to work for their creditors in virtual slavery. They starved, and their children starved. This oppression continued because the Athenians had no real voice in their government. Merchants, laborers, farmers, and seafaring men were ruled by the noble few who governed for their own benefit. The people saw no solution to their problems except rebellion.

**Tyrants: good and bad.** Around the seventh century B.C. some men began to step forward and offer their single rule as the solution to the Greeks' pressing problem. The Athenians called them *tyrants*. The tyrant's rule was sometimes short and sometimes long; at times it was bad and at times good. From the badness and the goodness of their government, the Athenians learned to construct man's first and perhaps purest democracy in action.

The tyrant Draco, around 621 B.C., gave to the Athenians their first written code of law. Prior to this time there had been no written law; the noble judges decided the cases before them in the interests of the small group of which they were a part. Draco's law was unreasonably severe; even a minor theft was punishable by death, and the law leaned always in favor of the noble. But at least a law was written down. The Athenians, however, were still unsatisfied, and tension grew between the common people and the nobles. The nobles were compelled to hand over their power into the hands of a man called Solon.

Solon was of the noble class, but he was a man of wisdom and moderation. From the moment he assumed power, in 594 B.C., he advanced the Greeks far along the path to democracy and economic reform. He canceled all debts owed the noble-landlords, freed those already enslaved because of debt, and placed a limit on the amount of land a man could own. He urged farmers to take up other trades where the land was already crowded, or to try planting olives and other fruits instead of grains.

Solon gave to the poor and the unpropertied the privilege of belonging to the Assembly, one of the governing bodies of Athens. Membership in this body had formerly been confined to the citizens with property. Solon increased the power of the Assembly by giving it a Council of four hundred members elected by Assembly members. The members of the Council could propose laws and reforms to the highest ruling body of Athens, the Council of Areopagus. The Council of Areopagus was composed exclusively of great nobles. Solon established new courts of justice open to all citizens, and the decisions of judges could be appealed in these courts. Solon was a wise and well-liked man. The story is told that when he was offered a permanent dictatorship over Athens, he politely refused with an inquiry: Where does one step down to from there?

Another good tyrant, called Cleisthenes, brought the Athenians to the beginning of the golden age of their democracy and culture. He assumed power in 508 B.C. Cleisthenes, too, was an aristocrat, but he had a deep sense of obligation and concern for the welfare and freedoms of the citizens of Athens. He acted upon the premise that every citizen was equal and capable of holding office. Every male citizen over the age of twenty became a member of the Assembly. A Council of Five Hundred was established which became the chief administrative and executive body in the government. Its members were chosen by lot from all citizens over thirty. The power of the Assembly was enlarged.

**Ostracism.** There was in Athens a practice known as *ostracism.* To protect his democracy, each citizen once a year was given the right to write on a piece of pottery called an *ostrakon* the name of one who he feared was planning to become a dictator. This piece of pottery was placed in a ballot box. If enough people cast a person's name in the ballot box, he was sent into exile for a period of ten years. Men still ostracize those whom they do not like, but as a rule it is not done today in such a formal fashion.

At about this time in history, the opening flower of democracy was threatened by the blighting hand of the Persians, who ruled the land from the eastern shores of the Aegean across from Greece to the hinterlands of India. This threat from the Persians was due in part to the tendency of the Athenians and other Greeks to wander far beyond the walls of their city-states.

1. Who were the tyrants? How has the meaning of the word *tyrant* changed in popular usage today?
2. What was the Council of Areopagus? What was its function?
3. How was the *ostrakon* used?

## They Went Elsewhere

The citizens of Athens and Corinth and those of other Greek cities started very early to imitate the sea-trading habits of the Phoenicians. They followed the Phoenician custom of building trading posts along the shores of the Mediterranean where the harbors were good and trade was profitable. Between 750 and 500 B.C., they spread their achievements throughout the Mediterranean world and beyond.

They colonized the islands of the Aegean Sea and the coasts of Asia Minor fronting the Aegean. Greek colonies dotted the edges of the Black Sea and included the city of Byzantium, site of the future Constantinople, which is now called Istanbul. The Greeks moved westward and placed great numbers of their people upon the shores of Sicily and mainland Italy. Naples was originally a Greek city. The Greeks had so many cities and people in this area that it came to be known as Great Greece. Later the city-state of Corinth began to dominate the trade of the western Mediterranean. The most famous city its citizens founded was Syracuse, located on the eastern shore of Sicily. The Greeks colonized southern France; their ancient city of Massilia later became the French city of Marseilles. They were the first to locate a town on the site of Nice. They even dared to plant settlers on the shores of North Africa, which had been for centuries the preserve of the Phoenicians.

It was not difficult to recruit Greeks to man the trading posts and colonies. The Greeks did not find it easy to make a living on

The coin shown above is a decadrachm of Syracuse, made in the fifth century B.C. (Chase Manhattan Bank Money Museum)

the barren hillsides and mountain-scattered land of their peninsula. Much of the best soil was owned by the nobles and the wealthy. The Greeks were multiplying and further crowding the already scarce patches of usable earth. In some city-states, democracy may have guaranteed men political equality, but it did not insure them against poverty. In other city-states, there was no equality of any kind—merely the brutal fist of the despot. Many fled to the more promising havens of the colonies. The Greeks left their hearths for one reason or another, but they remained *Hellenes*—living parts of Hellas, which was their name for Greece.

The Greeks carried with them to the colonies their pride of ancestry—their attitudes, customs, philosophy, arts, and literature. They were a part of Greece planted abroad. To them, all non-Greeks were barbarians. They shared the trade of the Mediterranean with the Phoenicians, especially those Phoenicians who traded and governed from the city of Carthage in North Africa, but they shared with no one the ability to transplant and ripen their civilization in distant lands. Greek civilization was often superior to the civilizations of those into whose midst it was carried. "Barbarian" neighbors learned to admire it and flattered the Greeks by imitation. Although the Romans later conquered Greece and went on to rule the world, they never lost their admiration for the accomplishments of the Greeks.

Not all the Greek characteristics pleased those around them in their foreign settlements. In their city-states lodged on the coasts of Asia Minor, they angered the Persians by expressing their independent spirit through rebellion against Persian domination. The Greeks of Asia Minor were often encouraged and aided in their rebellious moods by their Greek brothers across the Aegean Sea. This, too, annoyed the Persian rulers. The Persians resolved to teach the Greeks a lesson. The resulting series of wars tested to the utmost the physical and spiritual endurance of the Greeks.

## They Warred with the Persians

Around 492 B.C. the Persians governed a vast expanse of land from northwest India to the shores of the Aegean Sea. We might think that King Darius, who ruled this great empire, would have felt satisfied with this mass of earth and people. However, conquerors have enormous appetites for power which no amount of men and land appears to satisfy. The Persians were never overly interfering governors. They generally left their subjects in peace to follow their customary ways of life provided the subjects acknowledged Persian overlordship, did not rebel, and paid the required tribute. The Persians offered the same treatment to the Greeks, but it was not in the Greeks to acknowledge that anyone stood above them. They refused the offer. Even be-

Darius of Persia made Persepolis his capital. Remains of the great staircase at the royal palace show that the Persians were magnificent builders. (Embassy of Iran)

fore the Greeks' refusal, Darius had launched a fleet toward the shores of Greece, but it was wrecked along the way.

In 490 B.C. Darius sent another fleet to Greece which landed his soldiers at the Bay of Marathon in the district of Attica, where Athens was located. Ten thousand Athenian soldiers aided by 1,000 Plataeans—soldiers of the city-state of Plataea, which was allied with Athens—engaged the approximately 25,000 Persians in battle on the plain of Marathon and defeated them. The Greeks were fighting for a city and a system they loved. They fought so fiercely that they drove off the Persians, who left thousands of their dead upon the battlefield. The Persians did not attempt to return to Greece until ten years later, in 480 B.C. Then, under a new king, Xerxes, they marched once again against the Greeks.

Xerxes, who was Darius' son, was a cautious man, and he prepared for this war with care. He built a bridge of ships to span the narrow strait of the Hellespont which divided Asia Minor from the continent of Europe and he sent several hundred thousand well-equipped troops across the bridge. He also sent a mighty fleet—some estimate that it totaled around 3,000 ships—to the shores of Greece. Herodotus, the Greek historian, stated that the Persian army was so huge that it drank rivers dry. Estimates vary regarding the size of Xerxes' force, but the total number of both fighting and nonfighting personnel which accompanied this invasion was probably around one-half million.

This awesome threat to the independence and the existence of the Greeks did not bring about a united front against the Persians. There were many Greek city-states which remained neutral or submitted to the invader. But several states did join in an alliance against the common enemy. Sparta and her allied states, Athens, Corinth, and a number of smaller city-states united in a grand effort to repulse the invader. In order to achieve a unity of command at the top, both the land and the sea forces of the Greeks had Spartan commanders-in-chief. Their combined land forces totaled slightly over 100,000, and they had between 400 and 500 ships.

The Persian army approached Greece from the north. They were met in the narrow mountain pass of Thermopylae, leading from Thessaly into central Greece, by about 6,000 Greek soldiers. This army was led by Leonidas, King of Sparta, who had with him a hard-fighting core of about 300 Spartans. The Greek forces held off the frontal attack of the Persians for two days. Then they were betrayed by a Greek from Thessaly who led a part of the Persian army along a secret route around the pass. The Greeks were then surrounded. Leonidas sent most of his army back to meet the Persians attacking from the rear, but the Spartans, the Thespians, and the Thebans stayed on to fight to the end. When, in their last desperate stand, death or defeat seemed inevitable, the Thebans surrendered. But the Spartans and the Thespians fought on until all were dead. This small heroic group demanded a heavy price of Xerxes for his passage into Greece—twenty thousand of his finest infantry soldiers were killed in the final battle.

When Xerxes arrived at Athens with his army he found it almost empty of people. The Athenian leader, Themistocles, had led those who could fight aboard the fleet and evacuated the others to places beyond the reach of Persian anger. Meanwhile the Greek fleet was congregated in the bay of Salamis. Xerxes decided that the quickest way to victory over the Greeks was to destroy their fleet. The Persian fleet at Salamis numbered around 1,200 ships, which was three times the number of Greek ships opposed to the Persians. A number of the Greeks wavered and wanted to withdraw from the coming battle, but the Athenian leader, Themistocles, tricked the Persians into immediate battle. He sent a slave to the Persian admirals to inform them that the Greeks were in disorder and that they intended to flee the next day. The slave was also instructed to tell the Persians that Themistocles was prepared to help them. His stratagem worked, and that night the Persian fleet bottled up the Greek fleet in the bay of Salamis. There was nothing for the Greeks to do but fight.

The next morning King Xerxes sat in a golden chair upon a hill overlooking the battle and saw his vast fleet battered badly by the clever and audacious Greeks. The Greeks enticed the great fleet of the Persians into the narrow channel between Salamis and the coast. There the Persian ships collided with each other, became confused, and exposed their sides to the ramming tactics and boarding parties of the more heavily armed Greek marines. Some Persian ships were wrecked on the coasts, and others could not escape because of the great mass of ships blocking their passage. There was no room for a great fleet to maneuver within these narrows. The Persians disengaged themselves from the battle and fled from the Greeks to more open waters. Although the Persian fleet was still greater than that of the Greeks, Xerxes had had enough of the Greeks, at least for the time being. News of revolts at home, the approach of bad weather, and perhaps other reasons caused him to take the remains of his fleet and part of his army back to his Middle Eastern empire. The following year, the part of his army he had left behind was also defeated by the Greeks. Never again did the Persians try to subdue the Greeks by force alone.

1. Name the major Greek trading settlements.
2. How did the disunity of the Greek city-states almost result in their defeat by the Persians?
3. Who finally brought about the defeat of the Persians?

### The Full Flower of Greek Democracy

With the removal of the menacing shadow of the Persians from their city-state, the Athenians brought their democracy to its fullest glory. The Athenians established man's first real democracy. They had started cultivating this democracy many years before, and now, between the years 461 and 429 B.C., they enjoyed the fullness of its bloom. This time is often called the Age of Pericles because the leadership and words of a statesman named Pericles characterized best the tone and the spirit of this period. Thucydides (471-400

B.C.), the famous Greek historian, quotes Pericles' speech honoring the Athenian soldiers who had died in the war against Sparta in 431 B.C.:

> Our constitution does not copy the laws of neighboring states; we are rather a pattern to others than imitators ourselves. Its administration favors the many instead of the few, this is why it is called a democracy. If we look to the laws, they afford equal justice to all in their private differences; if to social standing, advancement in public life falls to reputation for capacity, class considerations not being allowed to interfere with merit; nor again does poverty bar the way, if a man is able to serve the state, he is not hindered by the obscurity of his condition.[1]

The Athenian citizens ruled and judged themselves, and the Athenian who did not take an active part in his government was a useless and irresponsible citizen. It was the many who governed—the many Athenian citizens. All the citizens belonged to the Assembly which made the laws of their city-state. The Assembly decided on matters of war or peace, sanctioned treaties, and approved the city's budget. When the thousands of citizens met on numerous occasions throughout the year in the open air, any citizen could express his opinions with complete freedom. There were about forty-five thousand citizens of Athens, but decisions could be made only if there were at least six thousand citizens present.

The Assembly was much too large to administer the affairs of the city-state effectively. The daily business of city government was undertaken by a Council of Five Hundred chosen by lot from the various districts or *demes* into which Athens was divided. The Council of Five Hundred was further divided into ten committees of fifty members; these committees took turns in handling the affairs of the city for one-tenth of a year each. In order to give everyone a chance to participate in the government of Athens, no citizen could be a member of the Council for more than two years. Thus the vast majority of Athenians had the opportunity of acting as officials of their government during some period.

Some officials could be re-elected to their posts. The most important of these officials were the generals. Each year the Assembly chose ten generals to oversee the armed forces. If a general was found to be a successful and effective leader, he might be elected to his position over and over again. Pericles was chosen to this position thirty times. Because of the long tenure of his office and the respect the Athenians held for him, Pericles was the single most important leader of Athens during this time.

The Athenians were fearful lest they or their fellowmen might not receive justice; they trusted justice from the many, but not from the few. They remembered the injustices they had experienced in the past from the judgments of the nobles, and they wanted no repetition of these wrongs. Each year the various districts or wards of Athens elected six thousand citizens over thirty years of age to sit on juries and judge cases. When cases were to be heard, the six thousand citizens met in the city and from them large numbers were chosen by lot to hear and judge the various cases. Sometimes the number of citizens needed to try a single case might range from over two hundred to over two thousand. The Athenians reasoned that if the number was large enough there was less chance that the jurors might be swayed by bribery, threat, or prejudice. The jurors determined the guilt or innocence of the parties before them and also fixed the penalty. They were, at the same time, both judge and jury.

From a more modern democrat's point of view, there were some defects in this free system. Women had no political rights, and the Athenians thought it comical to even imagine a woman participating in government. There were many slaves in Athens; they, of course, had no share in Athenian freedoms. Foreigners, whom the Athenians called *metics*, were welcomed to Athens. They were permitted to take up residence in the city-state, but they were not allowed to own land, and only rarely were they permitted to

[1] From *The History of the Peloponnesian War* by Thucydides, translated by Richard Crawley, revised by Feetham. Everyman's Library, E. P. Dutton & Co., Inc., New York. Quoted by permission.

become citizens. The Athenians who lived in the city found it easier to attend the meetings of the Assembly than their fellow citizens who lived in the countryside. It was not easy for the weary farmers, whose lands needed unceasing attention, to leave their fields and orchards and spend a day or more in the city where the Assembly was held. They often disregarded this duty, and the affairs of the Assembly came to be dominated more and more by the city dwellers.

The mountainous, rough countryside of Greece presented many obstacles to communication between the early tribes as well as the later city-states. Greek tribal organization also encouraged a clannish attitude. In addition, the Greek traditions of independence and rivalry contributed to their failure to develop any political organizations larger than the city-state. A number of city-states sometimes did unite to fight against a common enemy, as, for instance, against the invasion of the Persians under Xerxes. But even on this occasion a number of Greeks aided the Persians or remained neutral. Much of the history of Greece consists of rivalry, jealousy, and war among city-states, all of which contributed to a general political decentralization.

Greek political life within the city-states was not without flaws and imperfections. There were rabble-rousers and demagogues who sought to increase their personal influence by inflaming the fears, the envies, and the social discontent of the people. The Greeks, like modern man, also had some leaders who were not devoted to the welfare of the people but to their own personal ends. The Greeks, like many men since, found that freedom of speech and freedom of political life must also permit freedom for those who would act against the common good of the people. The citizens of Greek city-states, under irresponsible leaders, knew periods of anarchy and tyranny as well as of freedom and democracy.

Despite the defects of their system and their human failings, however, we still look to the Greeks as an example of man's earliest and finest democracy.

1. What body actually governed Periclean Athens? How was it organized?
2. How was the Council of Five Hundred chosen? How was it organized?
3. What was Pericles' official position?
4. How were the juries of Athens chosen?

### Conclusion

Almost five thousand years ago the Indo-Europeans began the westward advance which led them throughout Europe and into the peninsula of Greece. Those who settled the rugged land of Greece founded city-states which often struggled among themselves but sometimes joined together against common enemies to preserve their freedom and their civilization. These city-states evolved a form of democracy that is still admired today.

Although the city-states of Greece never formed a single great national government, their citizens enjoyed liberties of mind and spirit that were almost unique in the world of their time. Modern democracies are very different indeed from the Greek ideal of democracy, but the Greeks were among the first to establish governments which assured liberty for the many rather than the few.

## SUMMING UP THE CHAPTER

A. Identify or locate the following and tell why they are important.

| | |
|---|---|
| Assembly | *Odyssey* |
| Carthage | ostrakon |
| Council of Areopagus | Peloponnesus |
| Council of Five Hundred | Pericles |
| Crete | polis |
| Homeric Age | Solon |
| *Iliad* | Troy |
| metics | tyrant |
| Minoan | Zeus |
| Olympiads | |

B. Identify these dates and indicate their importance.
1. 1000-800 B.C.
2. 776 B.C.
3. 594 B.C.
4. 490 B.C.
5. 480 B.C.
6. 461-429 B.C.

C. Chapter review questions.
1. What is the oldest European civilization known to us?
2. How do we know so much about the Minoan civilization?
3. How do we know what the Cretans traded with the Achaeans?
4. Why do you suppose the Cretans did not build walled cities?
5. Describe the early world of the *polis*. How did its natural limits lead to the decline of the Greek city-state?
6. What do we know of the early Greek civilization? What is the source of our knowledge of it?
7. Why did the Greeks place such emphasis upon physical fitness? Has this been a feature of other civilizations? Why was this particularly a goal of the Spartans?
8. Describe the Athenian system of government. Be sure to discuss the organization of each of the institutions of government.
9. How were the Greeks finally able to defeat the Persians?
10. Why was it necessary to have a smaller body than the entire Assembly to govern Athens?
11. Describe the various devices used by the Athenians to spread rule around, such as councils, rotation in office, and election by lot.
12. What was the role of woman in Spartan life?

D. Questions for discussion.
1. Why did Sparta make so few significant contributions to Greek civilization?
2. How is it possible for a people such as the Spartans to base their entire life from birth to death on war? Why do you suppose they never sought the social and cultural amenities and pleasures that almost all other peoples have sought and developed?
3. Why were the restrictions against re-election to Athenian office not applied to the generals? How did this give them political as well as military leadership?
4. Is direct democracy such as that of Athens possible in a large state? Why or why not? What modern attempts at direct democracy have there been?
5. Do you think the Athenians were correct in their belief that the active and direct participation of all citizens in government is essential to the good life?
6. Do you believe that the average man is capable of participating in the decisions of modern government? Explain your answer.

E. Projects for groups or individuals.
1. Find out what languages belong to the Indo-European group. Describe some of the similarities between them.
2. Prepare a report on the prehistoric men of Europe, Asia, and Africa.
3. Read Pericles' "Funeral Oration" (in Thucydides, Bk. II, 35-46) in class. Discuss the civic ideals exhibited in this passage.
4. Read parts or all of the *Odyssey* and the *Iliad*. Compare them with the epics of India.
5. Prepare a report on the Greek Olympic games. Discuss the track and field events included. When and under what circumstances were the Olympic games revived in modern times? What new events are included?
6. Draw an outline map of Greece and pinpoint Sparta, Athens, and other important places in ancient Greece.
7. How much fact is there in the Homeric epics, the *Iliad* and the *Odyssey*?

# CHAPTER 14

# *The Greeks Thought and Achieved Greatly*

THE ORIGINAL and independent thought of the Greeks had great influence upon other men of their own world and served as a basis for men who came long after them. In forming their philosophies, they laid a foundation that men centuries later would build upon in their inquiries into the nature of man and the universe.

The balance and proportion of Greek art, architecture, and sculpture still serve as models, and their dramas are yet played upon the stage. Greek advances in the sciences were carried throughout the empire built by Alexander the Great, and this period is called Hellenistic in honor of the Greeks.

The simple and practical lives of the Greeks were in contrast to the rare heights reached by Greek thinkers and artists. But they built man's first practical and perhaps his purest democracy, and many of their ideas were preserved and passed along to later generations of men when they finally came under the rule of the Romans.

## The Gods of Olympus

The Greeks had a family of gods to whom they looked for protection and aid in their daily lives. Their chief gods were believed to live on Mount Olympus in the north of Greece. These gods were considered to be immortal and had powers far superior to those of man. The Greeks had to be careful at all times lest, through some oversight, one of the gods might be offended, for the anger of a god was extremely fierce and dangerous. Man crouched in fear when Zeus, the father of the gods, roared his anger upon the land in storm and split it savagely with his thunderbolts of lightning. Zeus, however, was only the chief of a great family of gods. There was Hera, the wife of Zeus, who was the guardian goddess of women and marriage. Poseidon, a brother of Zeus, was the god of the sea. Another brother named Pluto was the god of Hades. He ruled the dark underworld where most men went after death. Persephone was the daughter of Zeus and was Pluto's wife. She was concerned with the fertility of earth. She spent the winter months with Pluto in Hades and returned to earth each springtime to insure the budding and harvesting of the seed. Another daughter of Zeus, Aphrodite, was the goddess of beauty and of love. Her son, Eros, was fond of shooting love-arrows into people and making them captives of love. He is generally known today by his Roman name of Cupid.

Each locality and city-state had its special god or gods who were honored as founders and protectors. There was a very close relationship between the people and their gods. Athena was the patroness of Athens. She was the goddess of wisdom because she had sprung full-grown directly from the brain of Zeus, and the Athenians felt themselves to be the wisest of Greeks because of her. When they honored her with ritual and with ceremony they were performing civic as well as religious duties. When they performed well their duties to the state and avoided discord among themselves, they could count upon the aid of Athena. Thus their secular activities also had a religious meaning. This was also true of the relationship between the Greeks in other city-states and their gods.

The Greeks believed that at shrines sacred to certain gods they could receive answers put to the god about their fate or a contemplated course of action. The god often answered through the mouth of a priest or priestess, and the answers were known as oracles. The priest or priestess and the shrine itself were also called oracles. Apollo, another brother of Zeus, represented the perfection of the male. He was the guardian of man's finer callings—music, poetry, and healing. He was also the god of light. Apollo was particularly helpful in advising men at his shrine in Delphi.

The Greeks had other means besides the oracles for discovering the correctness of impending decisions. They observed the behavior of sacred animals, and they frequently studied the entrails of an animal after it had been sacrificed. Their decisions were strongly influenced by observations of the condition of the animal's entrails. These practices were not confined to the Greeks but were practiced by ancient men as widely separated as the Chinese and the Romans.

The religious beliefs of the Greeks had a tremendous influence upon their literature, art, and architecture. The Olympic games grew out of ceremonies honoring Zeus. Some of the greatest sculptured Greek works were portrayals of their gods in stone, wood, marble, and bronze. Among the finest and most magnificent of their public buildings were the temples of their gods. Much of their lyrical poetry was hymns honoring and praising their gods. And the Greek drama had its foundation in religious festivals.

There is in Greek mythology the tragic and inspiring story of Prometheus. He belonged to an ancient group of Greek gods who were giants. Prometheus was favored by Zeus until he opposed the plan of Zeus to destroy man and bring a new being into existence. Prometheus obstructed the purpose of Zeus by stealing fire from the lightning of Zeus and giving it to man. Thus Prometheus was the giver of fire and all of its advantages to man. Zeus was angered by this act of Prometheus and took a terrible revenge upon him. Prometheus was chained to a rock and each day a vulture came to tear out his liver, which grew back again at night. Zeus would not allow Prometheus to die but wanted him to suffer eternally for his act. The story has a happy ending, however. Heracles, known to the Romans as Hercules, slew the vulture and released Prometheus from his chains and his agony. Zeus received him back in Olympus, and Prometheus lived on there as the wise advisor of the gods. Some writers have seen Prometheus as the symbol of all who help man in his necessity and of those who rebel against authority wrongly used. This tale influenced the English poet Shelley in his lyrical drama *Prometheus Unbound* in which there runs the theme of man's capability of casting out the evil that is in him.

Although there was a close and continuing relationship between the Greeks and their gods, the Greek notion of the gods gradually changed over the years. Human qualities became more pronounced in the gods. The more philosophic and sophisticated Greeks took the gods less seriously in a religious sense and gradually converted them into literary and philosophical symbols.

The Greeks lived close to their gods. Each city had a guardian god or goddess who was honored with festivals and ceremonies. Because they needed the help and dreaded the wrath of their gods, the Greeks frequently pleaded for divine favor and pardon with ritual and sacrifice.

1. Name the principal Greek gods and goddesses.
2. What was the attitude of the Greeks in their approach to their gods?

### The Greeks Were Independent Thinkers

The Greeks were curious, and they wanted to know about almost everything. They spent much of their time trying to obtain this knowledge. They believed that there was a rational explanation for man and his universe, and they were determined to use their brains and reasoning power to find this explanation.

The Greeks were as independent in their thinking as they were in their living. They accepted nothing as forbidden to their probing and inquiring minds; nor would they accept the conclusions of others if they did not think them right.

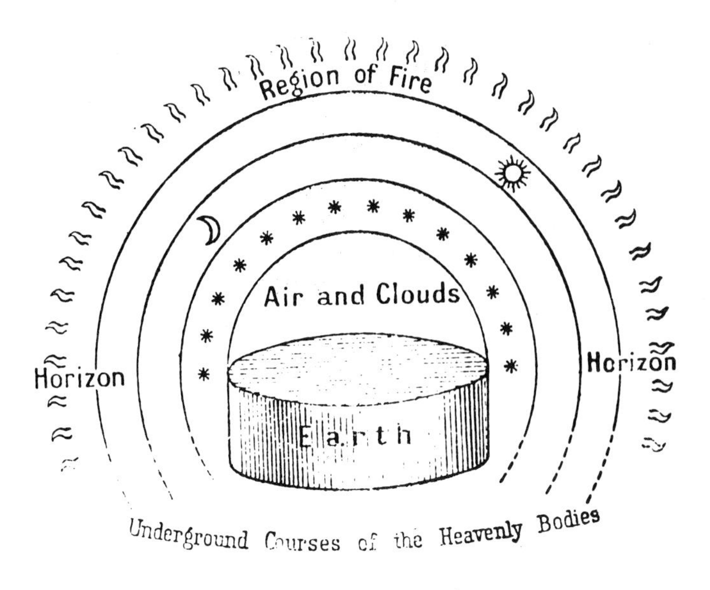


Anaximander (611-547 B.C.) was a Greek astronomer and philosopher of Miletus. His description of the universe is shown above. (Yerkes Observatory)

## The Basis of Matter

In the sixth century B.C., the Ionian Greeks, who lived along the shores of Asia Minor, began to search for that substance which was basic and essential to all the varieties of material things. After much deliberation and speculation, an Ionian named Thales decided that *water* was the one essential component of all matter. But a younger colleague, Anaximenes, disagreed and said it was *air*. Around 500 B.C., another, called Heraclitus, stated that they were both wrong; the answer was *fire*. Some years later, several Greeks, one of whom was Democritus, declared that all the previous answers were wrong and stated that all matter was composed of indivisible particles called *atoms*. Modern scientists have borrowed this Greek word to describe very tiny particles of matter. However, it is now known that atoms are made up of even smaller particles.

Some other Greeks were not satisfied with any of these answers. Pythagoras, who lived in the sixth century B.C., had a more religious and abstract bent of mind. He and his disciples came to the conclusion that harmony and proportion were the cement that held the universe together, and the essence of this cement was a nonmaterial principle called *number*. There were mathematical laws which all things, including man, must follow if there was to be harmony and good among men and in nature; for instance, there was a mathematical relationship between the length of a harp's string and its tone.

## The Sophists

By the fifth century B.C., the Greek Athenian had become more interested in man and his affairs than in the basic stuff of nature. The individual was becoming more important to himself and to others in Athens, and he wanted some knowledge about himself which would permit him to live a happier and more useful life. A group of men who were called Sophists, or "wise men," came forth to meet these needs. Today we use the word *sophistry* to describe a line of reasoning which is intended to deceive by making something not necessarily true look believable on the surface. Many of the Greek Sophists taught those seeking to get ahead in the world how to speak, debate questions, and discuss affairs in a way that would promote their advancement whether or not they spoke in the interests of truth. Some Sophists were sincere in searching for the truths which govern man and his actions, but their search always led them to the same conclusion: truth is relative. What is beautiful, true, just, and good for one man may not be regarded so by another man in another place and another time. These Sophists saw man living in a jungle, and they believed that too often might made right. They traveled much and acquainted themselves with the ways of man in other places. Today we use the word *sophisticated* to

The Parthenon, atop the Acropolis, sits high above the modern city of Athens. Built in the fifth century B.C., the Parthenon has served as a Greek temple, a Christian church, and a Moslem mosque. (Air France)

describe a person who is wise in the ways of the world.

Other men, however, challenged this reasoning as superficial for they felt that it led to a state of disorder and uncertainty rather than a constructive, orderly society. Three of these challengers were mental giants—Socrates, Plato, and Aristotle.

### Socrates

Socrates was born around 470 B.C. of a poor family of Athens. He grew into a short, bulky, ugly man, but the brilliance of his mind attracted swarms of students who listened to his conversations, tried to answer his questions, and were impressed by the closeness between his principles and his manner of living.

Socrates left no writings, but fortunately Plato, his disciple, wrote about him. Thus, something is known about the content and method of his teaching. He did not purposely teach by example, for he often admitted that he knew more than he was able to practice about right living. The aim of his teaching was, rather, to help others to gain an understanding of themselves and to arrive at philosophical truths. Perhaps his greatest teaching was summed up in the words "Know thyself."

Socrates was utterly opposed to the Sophists, for they used words to deceive—without regard for the truth—and they failed to admit to ignorance of what they did not know. There was an ultimate truth and a correct course of action for each individual, Socrates said, which was true and right wherever and whenever man lived. Further, each man has the ability within himself to discover this truth and to live by it. Even though he knows only a part of the eternal truth, man must govern his actions by the part he knows, and thus he will be moving ahead in the right direction.

To stimulate men to realize their ignorance and know the truth better, Socrates asked penerating and disturbing questions of those who came into his presence. He continued the questioning until they contradicted themselves or could find no answer. The use of the question technique to assist a person to gain insight into himself and other matters is still known as the *Socratic method.* Since that time man has found this method useful in learning and in teaching. He has also found it disturbing and shattering at times when the questions pricked some of the cherished values of his life and he found them to be empty.

Socrates' method of seeking the truth and exposing the ignorance of others gained him enemies among the Athenians. Many of them wanted him out of their sight and their hearing. He was brought to trial and accused of misguiding the youth and blaspheming the gods. He was found guilty, and when he refused to leave the city or to silence his tongue, he was condemned to death. At the age of seventy, he ended his life by drinking a cup of hemlock, and thus died a man whom death could not separate from the principles he held eternal and true.

### Plato

Plato was born in 427 B.C. He was a student and follower of Socrates. He immortalized Socrates and himself in his writings, called *dialogues*, which were discussions among various people on such subjects as government, religion, ideas, and justice. He had intended to participate in the public affairs of Athens, but the judicial murder of Socrates so shocked him that he retired from active life and founded a school, the Academy, where he taught until he died at the age of eighty.

Plato reasoned that the material world is in a constant state of change and that nothing in it ever remains the same. In nature there is always change and variety. If an object is described today, it may have changed by tomorrow so that the description is no longer true. A stringed instrument may be tuned, but its strings soon stretch or slip, and the instrument goes out of tune. Thus, Plato came to believe that knowledge could never be gained simply from what could be observed in the material world. But if man could rise above the confusing world of matter, Plato insisted, it was possible to discover a perfect, unchanging world of universal truths. These truths he called Ideas, and they represented perfection. They could not be understood by observing the real world but must be grasped only by the mind. This ideal world, he said was the only reality. Here was perfect Truth, Beauty, and Justice. In this world of ideals were the perfect man, the perfect woman, and perfect musical harmonies that were never out of pitch. These ideals did not change the way that material things change. Only in this ideal world, beyond the world of the senses, could man find universal, unchanging truth.

In Plato's world of ideals, the chief virtues were courage, wisdom, and moderation. In *The Republic,* one of his more famous dialogues, Plato described an ideal government and society which would be governed by men who had these virtues. He called these men philosopher-kings. A second class in this society was made up of soldiers, and another, the lowest, of artisans, farmers, and merchants. In Plato's ideal republic, the division of men into these various classes did not depend upon birth or wealth but upon their capacity as developed through education. In this republic, there were no slaves, and all things were held in common.

### Aristotle

The last of the three Greek philosophical giants was a man named Aristotle who was born in 384 B.C. in a more backward place than Athens called Stagira. When he was seventeen he came to Athens and became a student in Plato's Academy. Plato recognized and acknowledged his greatness of mind. Aristotle served for seven years as tutor to Alexander the Great in Macedon and afterwards returned to Athens, where he founded a school known as the Lyceum. He remained there until he died in 322 B.C.

Aristotle was more concerned with the material world than Plato had been. He did not believe, as Plato did, that the world of ideas or ideals was separate and distinct from the world of real things. He did not believe that the universal idea of a tree or a man was the only real one. To Aristotle, the world of material things and the world of these abstract ideas were equally real and true; in fact, he considered them both as part of the real world. He believed that each individual tree, man, or other material thing was *matter* and that it also expressed an idea which he called *form*. The form had been given material existence by a *first mover* or *first cause*. Thus, we speak of "man" sometimes as a class of beings with certain physical shape and certain other qualities—but the *idea* of man is given real shape in the material of which each individual man is made. Each of the individuals also is made up of the universal qualities of man, which are abstract ideas. Aristotle believed, therefore, that *form* and *matter* are part of the same thing and are inseparable.

Each kind of thing was produced by some agent, or first cause, because form always sought to be expressed in matter and this was the nature of things. Thus, animals produce other animals of their own kind; great works of art are produced by artists. But the animal or the work of art is inseparably made of both form and matter. This was Aristotle's view of the real world, and it brought together Plato's two ideas of an abstract world of ideas and a world of material things.

Another important part of Aristotle's philosophical system was the describing of great classes of things based on similarities and differences. This often (but not always) led him to observe many different examples of things (animals, people, dramas, governments, etc.) and to describe them as classes. He was one of the first great thinkers to use a systematic method of description and analysis.

Aristotle was a scientist with a craving for knowledge about almost everything. He was a great biologist, and collected huge storehouses of facts about natural life, and organized, classified, and distinguished them from each other. For instance, he divided zoology and botany into separate fields of study. He applied this same systematic method in studying a variety of subjects: what acts of man furthered his happiness; what made good and bad dramas; what was the best method of thinking; what was the best system of government. Before he wrote his book called *Politics*, he studied the constitutions of one hundred and fifty city-states.

Aristotle held that man is a political animal by nature. The state was not superimposed on man by the one or the many, but sprang from the nature of man himself. Civilized man could not exist outside a state of some kind. Aristotle believed that the best state was somewhere between an oligarchy and a democracy and that it would be controlled by a middle class—neither too rich nor too poor.

The works of Aristotle were studied for a thousand years or more after his death. During the early Middle Ages in Europe, his writings were accepted as a standard authority. St. Thomas Aquinas was impressed by him. The influence of Aristotle's methods of reasoning can be seen in the *Summa Theologica*, which St. Thomas wrote in the thirteenth century. It is still a major philosophy, especially within the Roman Catholic Church. Aristotle's influence can yet be seen in the team research and scientific method employed by scholars today to arrive at conclusions based upon massive foundations of collected and sifted data.

### Hellenistic Thought

The period from around 338 to 133 B.C. is generally referred to as the Hellenistic Age because it was a time when the thought and culture of the Greeks and of men in the Middle East were meeting and merging to produce new outlooks on man and nature, newer forms of art, and tremendous advances in science and medicine. There had been contact between men in the Middle East and the Greeks for centuries, but the conquest of the Middle East by Alexander the Great and the subsequent rule of this region by generations of Greeks made this contact more intimate and more prolonged. Each learned from the other, and from their combined learning there emerged new ideas about how man should conduct himself if he was to be happy.

**The Epicureans.** The philosophers known as Epicureans take their name from their founder, Epicurus, who lived in Athens around 300 B.C. They believed that man's purpose was to avoid mental and physical pain and to strive for peace of mind and physical pleasure. They believed that the peace of man's mind was disturbed by his fear of the supernatural, and they counseled that this fear was unnecessary because all matter, including the soul, was composed of atoms which did not survive the death of the body. There was neither reward nor punishment after death, they said, only extinction. The Epicureans urged man, therefore, to seek what pleasure he could find here and now, especially that pleasure which comes from the tranquil and serene mind. They cautioned him to seek this pleasure in moderation, for excess will also bring pain. Today we refer to an *epicure* as one who is exacting in his tastes and pleasures.

**The Stoics.** Zeno, who founded the Stoic school of thought, was also an Athenian who taught around 300 B.C. He and his followers first discussed their teachings on a porch called a *stoa*, hence the name Stoic. The Stoics also wanted peace of mind, but they found it in resignation, duty, and self-discipline rather than in material pleasures. They believed that there was a rational order in the world and that everything that happened to man for ill or for good was ultimately for the good of the universe. It was useless for man to cry out and rebel against the evils that befell him, for there was nothing he could do to avoid harm if it was necessary in the fixed scheme of things. Man was not the governor of his fate, they said. He was a part of a destined order which was inexorable in its movement toward a determined end. If he wanted peace of mind and a little happiness, he must accept whatever happened to him without bitterness or resentment and must adjust himself to bear calmly the buffets and stings of fate.

The Stoics taught that there was a brotherhood of man, and that men should live together in tolerance and equality. They spoke out against slavery and taught that men should not war against others but rather that they should aid those in need. They also urged men to take an active part in public affairs. There was much in the Stoic philosophy that was admired by the Greeks, the Romans, and later generations of men who have attempted to practice the teachings of the Stoics.

**The Cynics and the Skeptics.** The Cynics were men who believed that virtue alone should be sought by man; all else was useless. Their founder, Diogenes, who lived in the fourth century B.C., exemplified this philosophy by living a simple life. At night he slept in a barrel, and by day he sat in the sun. It is reported that Alexander the Great stood before him and asked if there was anything that he could do for him. Diogenes replied, "Yes, get out of the way of my sunshine."

The Skeptics did not believe that man could have any definite knowledge about anything. There was no use in seeking absolute truth or knowledge, for man could never obtain it. Abandon this search, suspend your judgment, they advocated, and you will have peace of mind.

1. When did the flowering of Greek thought begin?
2. What was the educational technique used by Socrates?
3. How did Aristotle combine the perfect but unrealizable world of ideas with the real world of imperfect matter?

## The Greeks Sought Excellence

The Greeks sought excellence in everything they did. They often achieved it in their buildings, sculpture, writings, and ideas about the physical laws which govern man and nature. Their minds knew no rest, for they sought perfection, and perfection is not easily found by man. The Greeks appealed in their excellence to men everywhere, for they captured in their creations much of the beauty and the tragedy that is in all men; they were magnificently human.

The Greeks had many moments of greatness throughout their history—in their seaside cities in Asia Minor, the island cities of the Aegean Sea, the colony cities of the western Mediterranean, and the peninsula cities of Greece itself. But the period between 500 and 338 B.C. was the time of their greatest sustained excellence. There are those who think that the Age of Pericles in Athens, between 461 and 429 B.C., was the golden expression of this period of bursting talent. During most of this period Athens was the cultural center of Greece, and the height of Athenian glory was reached under the rule of Pericles.

A lively picture of life and customs of the fifth century and the age of Pericles was given in the books of Herodotus, who has been called the "father of history." Although it is suspected that his inclination for the spectacular and the fantastic sometimes led him to stretch the facts, his books have been read with pleasure from that day to this. He described especially the rise of the Persian Empire and the Greek struggle against the Persian invaders.

The Persian menace was turned from Greece mostly by the courage and craft of the Athenians, but many of the Greeks living in the coastal parts of Asia Minor and in the islands of the Aegean were badly frightened. They requested the Athenians to form a league of city-states whose combined strength would hold back the Persians in the future. The Athenians accepted the request and headed a league which eventually incorporated over two hundred city-states. The Athenians began a fleet-building program assisted by the contributions of these many city-states. Soon Athens became the leading naval power in the eastern Mediterranean. As the naval power of the Athenians grew, their commerce, industry, and city also grew. At last the Athenians were beyond all doubt citizens of the greatest of all Greek cities.

The evident power of the Athenians restrained their foes, but it also disturbed their allies within the league. The other Greek city-states suspected that Athens might use this new strength to dominate them—the Greeks were as suspicious of the human failings of their own people as they were of others. It turned out as they had feared, for when they sought to withdraw from the league, the Athenians would not permit it and occasionally used force to keep them within the league. The Athenians transferred the treasury of the league from an island in the Aegean to their own city, extorted other tribute from the now subject Greeks, and regarded them as parts of their empire rather than as equal allies. The Athenians were now under the rule of all-powerful Pericles, and in their city there gathered the greatest thinkers, builders, carvers, and writers of Greece. Pericles could say with truth that Athens was the "school of Hellas." Some of the outpourings of this school of excellence have already been shown in the descriptions of Socrates, Plato, and Aristotle. And there were others who have astonished man with their excellence from that time to this.

## They Built in Proportion

The Greeks discovered that one of the essentials of excellence was to do nothing in excess. Their temples, theaters, and public buildings were ideals of moderation and balance in marble and stone. The Athenian gazed upward at the Parthenon, temple of his goddess Athena, standing serene and simply adorned with ordered Doric columns on a hill called the Acropolis, and his sense of excellence and proportion was satisfied. The Parthenon, which was built between 447 and 438 B.C., represented a majesty and dignity that was fitting for the gods and for man.

The Greeks, like the Egyptians, used columns instead of arches to support the flat roofs of their buildings. They used three types of columns: Doric, Ionic, and Corinthian. The

The classic simplicity of Greek architecture has served as a model of simplicity for centuries. Compare the Corinthian columns, above, with the Doric columns of the Parthenon, right. The Porch of the Maidens is shown below. (All photos, Air France)

Doric column was the simplest in design; the Corinthian, the most elaborate. Once, at least, they used statues of young women to support a part of a roof. On the north side of the Acropolis stood a temple called the Erechtheum. On one of the porches of this building, statues of six young women, called *caryatids*, were used in place of columns for support. The portion in which these statues were used is known today as the Porch of the Maidens.

### Heroic and Human Statues

The Greeks adorned their buildings with statues carved in heroic proportions. Many of these carvings have been lost to man, but from a few surviving fragments, from written descriptions, and from Roman copies, the genius of the Greeks is known. Among the greatest of their sculptors was Phidias, who lived during the fifth century B.C. He carved the forty-foot-high statue of Athena which stood enclosed within the Parthenon. He made her majestically beautiful with ivory, gold, bronze, and colored marble. Phidias fashioned the great statue of the seated Zeus at Olympia, the site of the Olympic games. This statue was considered one of the seven wonders of the ancient world. It is related that the onlooker was filled with peace and reverence as he looked and felt the towering kindness of Zeus which Phidias had captured in the statue's dark marble. Phidias was the artistic advisor to Pericles in that statesman's efforts to make Athens into a cultural center of beauty.

Praxiteles, who worked in the fourth century B.C., placed a winning human gentleness in the statue of the bronzed messenger-god Hermes holding the infant Dionysus. But the hands of the Greeks were not always busy creating statues of the gods; they also portrayed man himself. Myron, who also lived during the fifth century B.C., sculpted in bronze the discus thrower as he tensed to hurl the discus. There were others who portrayed with great humanity the activities of the young—a seated boy pulling a thorn from his foot, a young girl fleeing from someone or something. The Greeks were understanding sculptors of the human form as well as of gods.

### Tragic and Comic Drama

The Greeks enjoyed plays, whether tragedy or comedy. On the occasion of the festival of Dionysus, the Athenians attended three successive days of plays. During this time they

Hellenistic sculptors often captured a graceful sense of motion, as in the Winged Nike of Samothrace, above. (Sawders from Cushing) The Greek theater below is at Syracuse. (Italian State Tourist Office)

might watch as many as nine short plays each day, beginning at sunrise. They were called upon to select the best play of the day—an honor to which every playwright aspired.

The audiences watched these plays in the outdoors, sitting on seats carved from the natural rock of the hillside which curved around three sides of the orchestra section and the stage.

On the stage below, two or three male actors, dressed in elaborate costumes, walked on raised shoes to make them seem taller and spoke through masks in many voices, including those of the women. Only males performed on the Greek stage, and some were trained to play the parts of female characters. There was no scenery. At times a chorus — a group of singers and speakers in front of the stage — entered into the action of the play and described events that were happening off the stage, explained the background of the play, or told a part of the story. They and their audience reacted with pity and terror to the unfolding of some of man's greatest tragedies. They watched man struggling to free himself from the looming shadow of his own flaws of character. They reacted with pity and sadness because they saw that it was the flaws in man which moved him to commit unworthy acts and thus set in motion forces which would relentlessly return him evil for evil.

Three tragedies make up a single long story called the *Oresteia*, and they were written by Aeschylus (525-456 B.C.). The Oresteia tells the tragic tale of Agamemnon, leader of the Greek expedition against the Trojans. Agamemnon gave one of his daughters as a living sacrifice to the gods in order that the winds might not delay the journey to Troy. By this act he stained his entire family with blood. The mother of the sacrificed girl took her revenge upon Agamemnon by killing him. The son avenged his father by killing the mother, and then he went mad and was hunted down by the avengers of the gods, the Furies. Evil breeds evil from one generation to the next and brings about its own punishment.

The tragedy *Antigone* was written by Sophocles who lived from 496 to 406 B.C. Polynices, the nephew of King Creon of Thebes, revolted against his uncle and was slain. The vengeance of King Creon was yet unsatisfied and he left Polynices lying on the ground to be eaten by the beasts rather than bury him as was the sacred custom. Antigone, the sister of Polynices, defied the king's order, declaring that it was her heaven-commanded duty to bury her brother. She buried him, and Creon, in a fit of anger and pride, killed her. Afterward he realized his wrong, but it was too late; the forces of fate were in motion. Creon's son had loved Antigone, and now despairing, he killed himself. He was followed in death by his mother who also committed suicide. The actions that resulted from the pride and anger of Creon brought only sadness and sorrow to him.

*The Bacchae* was a tragedy written by Euripides (about 484-407 B.C.). The Bacchae were women followers of Dionysus, the god of wine and drunkenness. Sometimes they went to excess in their devotion to him and roamed the hills in wild abandon, destroying animals and replenishing their drink from wine-gushing rocks. One of these followers was named Agave, and she was the mother of a sober young king. Her son, grieving for his mother's actions, went to find and restrain her. The other Bacchae, in their unreasoning madness, tore his head from his body and thrust it upon a stick. The mother took the stick, held high the severed head of her son and laughed exultantly, thinking it to be the head of a slain lion. When her reason returned and she knew what she had done, the horror of her face portrayed the anguish and sickness that would be forever in her mind. By this tragedy Euripides told the onlooker that in man's mind there are hidden recesses where dark drives lurk which sometimes push him far beyond the reasonable and the sane.

The Greeks witnessed other tragedies from their hillside seats. One of the most famous of these was *Oedipus Rex*, also written by Sophocles. Aeschylus, Sophocles, and Euripides were the greatest of the Greek tragic playwrights. The Greeks did not always look at tragedies upon the stage, for balance was necessary to life. They balanced their tragedies with comedies which poked fun at the pompous, the important, and the unliked.

The most famous of comedy playwrights was Aristophanes, who lived from around 448 to 380 B.C. His comedies were very popular and are still interesting to read. One of his comedies, *The Wasps*, satirized the subject of jury duty, and another, called *The Knights*, ridiculed the tendency of Athenians to find more and more corrupt leaders.

Aristophanes also wrote a comedy called *The Frogs* in which he derided the playwright Euripides and a play called *The Clouds* which ridiculed Socrates. In this play, Socrates talked from a basket suspended in mid-air, and thus was portrayed as a man whose words were of air and impractical, without the wisdom and common sense of those whose feet were solidly planted on the earth. Aristophanes is among the earliest in a long series of writers who have criticized others for not having their feet on the ground.

## They Merged with Men of the Middle East

There was a great merging of the knowledge of the Greeks and that of men in the Middle East during the period from the fifth century to 133 B.C. During this time the Greeks continued to achieve in the arts, in science, and in medicine. Their achievements were not confined to the city of Athens, for Athens eventually declined, and with this decline the power the Athenians had held was taken by others. Men are always suspicious of those who have great power and are unsatisfied until they hold superior or at least equal power to balance that of others. The Greeks led by the Spartans were jealous and fearful of the might of the Athenians, and they formed an alliance with other city-states to destroy this power or reduce it to a balance which they could accept without fear.

The Athenian decline began in 431 B.C. when a war started between the group led by Athens and the alliance led by Sparta. By 404 B.C. the Athenians stood shorn of their glory. Their walls were down, their fleet lost, their orchards destroyed, and their numbers drastically reduced by plague and war. This war, which the Spartans won, is known in history as the Peloponnesian War. It was described in the carefully documented histories of Thucydides (c. 460-400 B.C.) who might be termed the father of thorough and scholarly history.

The victory of Sparta over Athens, however, did not bring peace to Greece. The Greeks found that they could not endure the harsh rule of the Spartans, and an alliance was formed against Sparta. The Spartans were defeated by a group headed by the city-state of Thebes in 371 B.C. Thebes in turn lost its dominance after a short time, and at last, after these many years of weakening wars, there was no city-state which had the strength to rule all Greece. There was now a balance of weakness in Greece which attracted the seeking glances of a shrewd, strong man to the north of the Greeks—Philip of Macedon.

### The Macedonians Conquer

The Macedonians were a mixture of Greeks with other, less advanced people of the north. For years the Macedonians, too, had been weak because of the quarrels of their jealous and petty aristocrats. In the fourth century B.C., however, a skillful, patient man named Philip became their king. From the time he became king in 359 B.C., Philip schemed with a ruthless passion to unify Macedon and Greece, and he was successful. He studied the wars of the Greeks and others and borrowed their best techniques for his soldiers. He armored his soldiers, gave them long spears, and positioned them in a closely massed group, called a *phalanx*, which was almost impossible for the enemy of that time to penetrate. He used cavalry and was insistent that the foot soldier and mounted soldier work together in a predetermined strategy. His strategy was good; his army was disciplined and drilled to a level near perfection; and when Philip marched to battle, he was always victorious. In the decisive battle of Chaeronea, he overthrew the combined forces of Athens and

Thebes in 338 B.C. and took from his distant cousins, the Greeks, the dominance of Greece.

With this battle, Philip of Macedon became the overlord of Greece. But he was a diplomatic man, and he permitted the city-states of Greece to retain their autonomy in local affairs, provided they preserved the peace and provided him with soldiers for his army when he was in need of them. Philip had learned to wear a velvet glove over his iron hand in his diplomatic dealings. But he did not learn how to combat the traitorous plotting of his wife; in 336 B.C. he was murdered by an assassin she had hired.

## Alexander the Great

Philip was succeeded by his son Alexander, whose remarkable military exploits earned him the name Alexander the Great. He ruled as king and conqueror from 336 to 323 B.C. Before he died at the age of thirty-three, he had created a legend which knew no age. Aristotle had tutored him for seven years in Macedon. No one knows what effect his tutoring had on this young man. Alexander was one of those men who dreamed of uniting people into one world, and he was one of those rare men who have both dreamed and acted. In his acting he conquered and united for a brief moment much of the civilized world from the forests of Macedon to the plains of India. He set forces in motion which outlived his death in Babylon in 323 B.C. and which helped to mold some of the patterns of man then and since.

Alexander took the customs and institutions of the Greeks wherever he went and attempted to blend them with the customs and institutions of the people he conquered. He stressed the ties which bind men together rather than the variety which distinguishes one man from another. He brought the Greeks and men in the Middle East together, and their ties continued after his empire was separated into three parts. Upon the death of Alexander, Macedonia continued to control many of the city-states. Egypt was ruled by the Ptolemy family. The remainder of the Middle East was governed by the Seleucid family. The rulers of these kingdoms in Egypt and the Middle East were all descendants of Alexander's generals, and they were assisted by other Greeks and Macedonians who wanted to share in their prosperity and political power. From their sharing there emerged a culture known as Hellenistic or "Greek-like."

1. How did her leadership of the Athenian league contribute to Athens' leadership in nonmilitary fields?
2. Who were the three greatest Greek playwrights?
3. What were the three parts into which the Macedonian Empire separated?

The Macedonian coin above was issued by Alexander the Great. (Chase Manhattan Bank Money Museum) The relief figures below are at a Buddhist stupa in Pakistan. They show the influence of classical art brought by the invasion of Alexander the Great. (Embassy of Pakistan)

This marble head, made in the third century B.C., represents Alexander the Great. (Courtesy of The Cleveland Museum of Art)

## Hellenistic Advances

The centers of Hellenistic advances were bustling cities such as Alexandria in Egypt and Antioch in Syria. The island cities of the Aegean and the cities of Asia Minor also became centers of this culture. In the mingled form called Hellenistic, the Greeks persisted in their pursuit of excellence. In this period, Hellenistic sculptors carved the world-renowned statutes of *Venus de Milo* and the *Nike of Samothrace*. Also of this period is a humanly real statue of an ageing, weary market woman and the horribly real statue picturing the agony of the priest Laocoön of Troy and his sons held in the coils of a large snake. In the Hellenistic period a lighthouse was built at Alexandria which reached four hundred feet into the sky, and it was called one of the wonders of the world. Tragedies and comedies continued to be written, but it was in science and medicine that Hellenistic man stormed the highest peaks of excellence. The Hellenistic period ended about 133 B.C. when the Romans completed their conquest of most of Asia Minor.

### Astronomy and Geography

With the help of the knowledge gained from the Middle East, Hellenistic man arrived at truths about the stars so startling that most men refused to believe some of them until almost two thousand years later. Aristarchus of Samos, who lived during the third century B.C., discovered and declared that the earth and the other planets revolve around the sun. He was disbelieved for many centuries. Eratosthenes, a contemporary of Aristarchus, found the earth to be spherical, not flat, and calculated its circumference to within fifty miles of its actual size. He claimed that if one sailed west from Spain he would eventually reach the coasts of India. Columbus tried it more than fifteen hundred years later. Hipparchus made his discoveries late in the second century B.C. He invented the astrolabe—an instrument for measuring distances in the sky—which Columbus used in a modified model. Hipparchus charted the heavens, and knew the approximate distance of the earth from the moon as well as the moon's diameter. Ptolemy of Alexandria summarized the works of early astronomers. This work was regarded as a classic for more than a thousand years. A Greek philosopher and scientist, Thales of Miletus (640?-546 B.C.), who preceded these men by some centuries, knew something about eclipses of the sun; he accurately predicted the date of one for the year 585 B.C.

### Mathematics and Applied Science

Euclid (c. 300 B.C.) drew upon earlier mathematical advances of the Greeks and the ideas of men in the Middle East. In his school at

Alexandria, he stated the basic principles of geometry. His name is still connected with the subject. Other Hellenistic mathematicians developed trigonometry. Archimedes, who lived from about 287 to 212 B.C., was one of Euclid's students. He was a remarkable genius who continued the mathematical work of his master and uncovered new laws of physics. Using water as a standard, he discovered the relative weight of things. His name identifies a law of specific gravity. Archimedes applied his knowledge and arrived at some interesting inventions. He demonstrated many of these inventions at the city of Syracuse in Sicily, where he lived. He knew the secrets of the pulley and the lever, and with an ingenious arrangement of them he alone once pulled a loaded ship from the sea and rested it on the beach. He was the first man of whom we have knowledge to understand and describe the laws of the lever. Archimedes devised ways of removing water from tunnels and established the basic principle of the modern conveyor belt. He knew the principle of the screw propeller and the reflecting lens. He is said to have stated: "Give me a place to stand on, and I will move the world."

Another inventor, named Hero, lived in Alexandria in the second century B.C. The list of inventions attributed to him is incredible. A few are the fire engine, a steam engine, and the use of compressed air. But man continued to work with his hands because slaves were many and cheap, and machines were scarce and expensive.

### Medicine

Hippocrates (460-377 B.C.), known as the father of medicine, founded a school of medicine. He worked on the premise that sickness is brought about by natural causes rather than by the curse and anger of the gods. Graduates of medical schools still take the Hippocratic Oath he formulated which outlines the responsibilities of a doctor. During the Hellenistic period there were many men, especially in Alexandria, who advanced the art of healing. Among the best of them was Herophilus who lived around the beginning of the third century B.C. From his careful study and examination of the human body, he made many discoveries and learned that from the heart blood is pumped through the arteries to the entire body; that the pulse is important in revealing sickness; that there is a relationship between the nerves and the brain; and that the brain is divided into many sections, each of which has its function in controlling the various parts of the body. Erasistratus, in the third century B.C., investigated the body so thoroughly that he might be called the father of physiology. He denounced the excessive use of the practice of removing blood from a person's body to effect a cure, but this practice continued under doctors in the West until modern times. These early Greek doctors undertook surgery and used drugs to deaden the pain. Hippocrates asserted what many doctors today yet claim, that rest, fresh air, and a good diet are still the best roads to a healthy life.

## A View of Greek Life

The Greeks represented a fascinating mixture of men. They were rich in the achievements of their minds and in the beauty of their art. They were not obsessed with the material comforts of life, but rather sought moderation in all things. They were especially addicted to discussing politics, and they haunted the market-places for choice gossip. They enjoyed plays, and their drama was an important part of their social and religious life. The Greeks were public-spirited, and they lavished their talent for proportion on public buildings—temples, theaters, gymnasiums, schools, and stadiums. But their daily living evidenced a simplicity and temperance that remain as ideal examples of moderation.

### The Home

The Greek lived in a plain little house, which was often built of sun-dried brick. It was brightened on the outside only by a painted door, which faced a narrow lane that sometimes smelled of the litter of discarded garbage. This home was squeezed between other simple houses like it. There were no drains, and furniture was kept to a minimum. The house was lighted with the faint flame of an olive-oil lamp. The beds were hard and had no springs.

The Greek ate and dressed simply, too. He generally ate fish, onions, and cakes of barley. His breakfast was often merely bread, and he washed his food down with wine mixed with water. He draped himself in a rectangular piece of cloth called a *tunic* which he pinned at the shoulders and belted at the waist. When he went out he merely threw another piece of cloth over his shoulders. Women dressed in a similar fashion, but their tunics were longer. Both men and women wore sandals.

### The Shop

The Greek of the city was a small-business man, a maker of pottery, a blacksmith, a weaver of cloth, a tanner of leather, a seller of food, a worker in silver, or gold, or metal—or he worked at any other occupation necessary for his life and his exports. We know of only one manufacturer who employed more than a hundred men. The typical Greek shop was tiny and stifling under the hot sun.

The Greek did not seek to expand; he sought only what was necessary to support himself and his family. His business was not his life. There were many periods of leisure when he lectured or listened to others; and he took an active role in governing the affairs of his city.

### Trade Overseas

The Greeks were forced to trade overseas, for they did not produce enough on their poor soil to feed their people. Although many of the Athenians were farmers who grew barley or wheat, much grain still had to be imported. The Greeks had grapes for wine, figs for fruit, olives for oil, goats for cheese, meat, and milk, sheep for wool, and some silver mines. But there was little else. Olive oil, wine, manufactured articles of silver, and articles made of raw materials brought from elsewhere were traded around the Mediterranean for things that the Greeks needed and could not produce themselves. The land of Greece could not produce enough to meet even the most basic requirements, so the Greek people were compelled to trade to supplement their production at home.

### The Family and Education

The family that was supported by the shop, farming, or trade consisted of a husband and wife, married sons and their wives and children, and all unmarried sons and daughters. A married daughter lived in the household of the family of her husband. The father was the head of the household and none questioned his authority. The woman in Greek society was confined mostly to the home, to weaving, spinning, cooking, and managing the domestic affairs; there was usually no place for her in public affairs. She did not go out to banquets with her husband, and even when he entertained in his own home, she was expected to remove her presence from the company of his male guests. The father arranged the marriage of his daughters, although he usually consulted with his wife. The daughter rarely saw her husband before marriage, and she was usually only fourteen or fifteen years of age when she married. The father gave each daughter a dowry which had been agreed upon with her prospective husband's family.

The rather restricted life of Greek women did not represent a scorn for them. The Greek goddess of wisdom was the female Athena, and there were several Greek poetesses whose talent was admired. Outside of the home, there were also female entertainers. But in general, within the Greek social system, woman's place was considered to be in the home rather than in public affairs.

The Greek of means was very solicitous about the future of his son. At the age of seven or eight, the boy was sent to school. Sometimes he was accompanied by a slave called a *pedagogue* who taught him manners and other useful matters. At school the boy learned reading, writing, elocution, literature, mathematics, and music. The balanced Greek required a healthy body as well as a healthy mind, and the boy also became an athlete. He hurled the discus, threw the javelin, jumped, raced, and wrestled. At about the age of fourteen a boy was apprenticed to his father if his family was poor. If his father could afford it, however, he went on to advanced studies in government, astronomy, and other fields. At the age of eighteen he went into the armed forces, for it was required of most Greeks to spend a year in the military service of their city-state. In the city-state of Athens, the Greek boy was admitted to full citizenship at the age of nineteen. Upon the death of a Greek father, the sons shared equally in the inheritance, but the daughters did not receive shares.

### Roman Rule

After the death of Alexander the Great in 323 B.C., many of the less powerful Greek cities desired to form a league which would give them the unified strength of the many while, at the same time, preserving their local independence. They formed two such leagues, each having a central government, a head, a senate, and an assembly consisting of all the citizens of each city-state in the league. Each league also had an army and a navy. The central government had little authority other than the power to establish armed services and to tax, and the great bulk of political power was retained by each city-state. The formation of these leagues was an experiment in a federal system of government. The founders of the United States of America studied with care the constitution of the more important league known as the Commonwealth of the Achaeans, for they, too, desired to write a constitution which would balance state and national power.

Unfortunately, the Greeks failed in their attempt to find strength in unity. Athens and Sparta, the two strongest city-states, refused to join in a league, and the empire-building Romans from the western part of the Mediterranean moved in upon them. By the middle of the second century B.C. the Romans were the political masters of Greece.

1. Why were the scientific and technological achievements of the Greeks not put to use?
2. Describe the social and economic life of the Greeks.
3. How did the Achaean League seek to maintain the local autonomy of its members while still presenting a unified front in foreign and military affairs?

### Conclusion

The Greeks had gods in whom they believed, but they also believed that they could reason out the why and how of nature and of man. The scope of their ideas and explanations about nature and man is almost unbelievable. They were original thinkers—trailbreakers whose paths of thought men are still following and discussing. Some men have been so astounded by the wealth of ideas searched out by their exploring minds that they have cried out in their wonder, "There is nothing that the Greeks have not touched upon." Of course, this is an exaggeration, but the statement does indicate the immense range of Greek thought. The Greeks were men of phenomenal reasoning powers.

The Greeks left for all men a fine heritage of art and science. When they glorified man in their sculptures, they taught that man is the glory of earth. When they proportioned their buildings, man learned that design without excess can be beautiful. Their tragedies and comedies did not speak merely to the Greeks but to man thereafter, and man continues to loathe and laugh as he sees himself dramatized by the Greeks on the modern stage. In their search for excellence the Greeks pierced some of the starry mysteries of the skies and solved many of the riddles of the earth. Thus they laid the foundations of many sciences upon which man has since built.

Greece declined in political power, but the respect that all men of knowledge hold for her brilliant ancient people has never dimmed. The Greeks are yet highly regarded as having fathered many fields of knowledge: medicine, geometry, areas of the natural and physical sciences, and even the field of history, with which this book deals. Then there are the magnificent Greek creations in philosophy and politics, which man has always found stimulating as well as informative and useful. Until modern times no one practiced and preached the way of democracy to the extent that the ancient Greeks did, and in much of the world today there is nothing to compare to the democratic practices of the Greeks.

The Greeks were uncommon men with an extraordinary list of accomplishments to their credit. These accomplishments can never be forgotten by man as long as he continues to read, observe, and think.

## SUMMING UP THE CHAPTER

A. Identify the following and tell why they are important.

| | |
|---|---|
| Aeschylus | Herodotus |
| Alexander the Great | Hippocrates |
| Apollo | Phidias |
| Archimedes | Philip of Macedon |
| Aristophanes | Praxiteles |
| Athena | Seluecid family |
| Diogenes | Sophocles |
| Epicurus | Thucydides |
| Euclid | Zeno |
| Euripides | Zeus |

B. Locate or explain the following and tell why they are important.

| | |
|---|---|
| Acropolis | Skeptics |
| Cynics | Sophists |
| Delphi | Stoicism |
| Parthenon | *The Republic* |
| Peloponnesian War | |

C. Indicate the significance of the following dates.
1. 336-323 B.C.
2. 338 B.C.
3. 431-404 B.C.
4. 133 B.C.

D. Chapter review questions.
1. What does the mythology concerning various Greek gods and goddesses tell you about Greek life and thought?
2. Why was Socrates put to death? If you do not know, read the account by Plato describing the trial and death of Socrates.
3. What was the political ideal of Plato?
4. What are the implications of Aristotle's view of man being by nature a political animal?
5. On what things did the Stoics and Epicureans agree? How did the Stoics' answer to the question of the meaning of life differ from that of the Epicureans?
6. What were the major concerns of the Greek thinkers in the sixth century B.C.?
7. Who were the Sophists? What were their major beliefs?
8. How do we know so much about Socrates when he never wrote anything himself?
9. Describe the political and social structure idealized by Plato.
10. What was the attitude of the Skeptics toward knowledge?
11. What were the major themes of the great Greek tragedies?
12. Describe the various military alliances of the Greeks. How did the collapse of these alliances open the way for the Macedonian conquest of Greece?
13. What was the policy of Philip of Macedon toward the conquered Greek city-states?

E. Questions for discussion.
1. What were the purposes of the Greek tragedies? How did they reflect the view of life of their time?
2. Why do you suppose the interests of Athenian philosophers changed from mathematics and physics to ethics and politics?
3. How did Aristotle's genius as a scientist, poet, and philosopher enable him to achieve the synthesis of the ideal and the real which marks his *Politics*?
4. How is Skepticism a negation of its own teachings? (Hint: What is the logical result of stating that there can be no knowledge of absolutes or first principles?)
5. Why do you suppose many of the discoveries and calculations of the Hellenistic Age were not accepted until fifteen hundred years later?
6. How would you explain the fact that it was the Athenian rather than the Spartan who finally turned back the Persian military challenge?

F. Projects for groups or individuals.
1. Read in a history of science and mathematics about the Greek contributions. Prepare a report for class describing some of the most important Greek contributions in these fields.
2. Read Plato's "Allegory of the Cave" in *The Republic,* and explain it in class.
3. Look through a volume of pictures of the art masterpieces of the Greeks. What do the subjects and their execution tell you about the concerns of the Greeks? What do they tell you about the Greek view of man? of the gods?

CHAPTER **15**

# *The Romans Claimed the World*

SOMETIME AFTER 2000 B.C. tribe after tribe of migrating Indo-Europeans discovered the passes through the Alps, which separate Italy from the remainder of western Europe. For more than a thousand years, members of these tribes straggled through the passes to settle the peninsula of Italy. Some lingered in the green, rich valley of the Po River, while others continued down the western plains which lay between the Apennine Mountains and the waters of the Tyrrhenian Sea.

Among the tribal groups which moved southward along the western levels of Italy and settled a portion of it midway down were the Indo-European people called Latins. The plain they settled was called Latium. This plain was immediately south of the Tiber River, which runs southward from the Apennines and curves westward into the sea. The Latins were the ancestors of the Romans, who, in partnership with the Greeks, fostered the civilization of the Europeans.

## Early Settlers in Italy

The Indo-European Latins who settled in Latium met with other, more civilized men who came to the peninsula of Italy later by way of the sea. Most of these were the people known today as Etruscans, Phoenicians, and Greeks.

### The Etruscans

Both the Etruscans and Greeks came to Italy by way of the sea, but the Etruscans came earlier than the Greeks, perhaps as early as 900 B.C. from somewhere in the Middle East—some historians think from Asia Minor. We say "perhaps" because the Etruscans are among history's men of mystery. Currently, puzzled scholars are searching out their origins and the meaning of their writing; but no man can yet understand their written language. The Etruscans are proving to be elusive characters. Archaeologists have found evidence, however, that the Etruscans did influence the early Latins.

The Etruscans lived in the western portion of Italy just north of the Tiber River and the plain of Latium, which was occupied by the farming Latins. They lived in cities which they enclosed with wide walls and made convenient with paved streets. They arched their gates, domed their buildings, and laid underground sewers. They used iron, worked

Much of our knowledge of the ancient Etruscans comes from remains of their tombs. The tomb shown is about 22 miles northwest of Rome. (Italian State Tourist Office)

The Etruscan urn at left is of unglazed pottery. The chair is of metal. Both are from Etruscan tombs. (Both photos, University of Pennsylvania Museum)

with other metals, dressed in cloth of quality, wore tasteful jewelry, and knew the comforts and the elegance of good furniture. They were also traders, and they imported civilized products from elsewhere. The Latins saw and admired these products. From some time before 600 B.C. until 509 B.C., the Etruscans ruled the Latins, and one of their chief cities was on the site of Rome. They introduced the Latins to their more civilized life and knowledge.

## The Greeks and Carthaginians

The Greeks came to Italy sometime after 750 B.C. and settled in colonies south of the Latins on the mainland, and on the island of Sicily, which lies in the Mediterranean like a large rock about to be kicked by the toe of Italy's boot. The Greeks gave generously to the Latins. They shared with them the alphabet which had been received from the Phoenicians and made more useful by the addition of symbols for vowels. The Greeks gave the Latins many of their gods, and they contributed other great parts of their culture to the Latins.

The Latins also knew the Phoenicians, some of whom were called Carthaginians, after their city of Carthage across the sea in North Africa. The Carthaginians traded around the peninsula of Italy. They had trading posts and colonies in western Sicily and on the islands of Sardinia and Corsica, which lay off the western coast of Italy.

## The Romans

The Latins learned from those whose civilization and power preceded them, and as they learned, they adjusted and grew into the strong and striking men called Romans. They took their name from their city of Rome which was built on the banks of the Tiber River, some fifteen or more miles inland from its mouth. This "City of Seven Hills" was the result of the combining of seven small villages perched upon seven adjacent hills. The beginning of Rome was due in great part to its profitable location as a trading center. The nearby Etruscans manufactured articles which the Latins wanted in exchange for their wheat, oats, and cattle. Trading between the Latins and Etruscans was made easier because the waters of the Tiber were shallow at this point.

The Romans had only agricultural products to barter with the Etruscans because they were mostly farming people at this stage of their development. However, they possessed the daring of the rebel and the desire to be free. Sometime around 509 B.C., they drove the Etruscans from Rome. Thus began an expansion which continued until the Roman name was feared and famed in Europe, Africa, the Middle East, and in parts of Asia.

When the Romans expelled the Etruscans, they had but a tiny piece of city and land in western Italy surrounded by many hostile and powerful tribes. Before their greatness died in the west almost a thousand years later, the Romans ruled the civilized and uncivilized world to the borders of Persia, deep into Africa, throughout western Europe, and beyond the Rhine and Danube rivers. Statesmen and schemers, military geniuses and citizen-soldiers, endowed with perseverance and blessed by luck, the Romans amassed an empire which yet captures the imagination of man.

### They Began in Italy

The Romans started on the road to an empire in Italy. They early displayed tenacity, opportunism, and statesmanship in their dealings with their Italian neighbors. They made allies of the more friendly tribes who lived around them and enlisted their help in conquering the more hostile tribes. They were often most solicitous of those whom they conquered and offered them special privileges and even citizenship in return for future allegiance and assistance in furthering Roman plans. The Romans did not offer these privileges to everyone; it depended upon their evaluation of the usefulness or potential threat of the conquered people. They first gave the privilege of citizenship to those who lived around Rome, but as their empire grew, citizenship was extended to many diverse men within their far-reaching borders. Whether friend or former foe, once the Romans had a people in alliance they never let go unless forced; and there were none stronger than the Romans at the height of their power.

During these days of their independent infancy, the Romans were fortunate to have the unwitting help of the warlike Gauls to the north who rushed upon their strong neighbors, the Etruscans. This invasion kept the fine fighters of the Etruscans occupied while the Romans further enlarged their army and territory. The Romans did not wear themselves out by fighting the Gauls. When the Gauls turned their attention toward Rome, the Romans bought them off with money, and the Gauls returned to the valley of the Po in northern Italy. Later, when the Romans were stronger, they defeated the Gauls.

The creeping hand of Roman rule in Italy moved softly, firmly, and remorselessly for several centuries; it was felt by the Etruscans, tribal brothers, and Greeks. Pyrrhus, the Greek king, tried to stop the onward march of the Romans with his military genius, his phalanxes of soldiers, and his war elephants. Although Pyrrhus lost no battle, he won no war. After one battle, he exclaimed that if he won more victories such as this, he would be a lost man. We still speak of a "Pyrrhic victory" as one gained at too high a price. By 264 B.C. the Romans held Italy from the Po River in the north to the heel and toe of its boot in the south.

### Changes Among the Romans

While the Romans were changing the political appearance of Italy, their own political appearance was also changing. When they overthrew the Etruscans and began their republic of Rome, they were divided into two classes of people: a few known as *patricians*, and a majority known as *plebeians*. The patricians were the men of property—the big landowners. The plebeians were the poor, the artisans, and the small citizen-farmers.

**The patricians.** The Roman Republic was dominated by the patricians. At the head of the government were two chief officials known as *consuls*. In the earliest days of the Republic, and for many years, the consuls were always patricians, chosen by a patrician-dominated Senate to run the government and command the army. Although the consuls were empowered to veto each other's acts, they were not inclined to diminish the political influence of the patrician class. Sometimes during a war or civil emergency, the consuls, with the consent of the Senate, would appoint a dictator to govern the country for a maximum period of six months, but he, too, was a patrician.

The Senate was an exclusive patrician club of three hundred members who were selected by the consuls. All former consuls were members of the Senate. They held a life membership and for years were dominant in the government of Rome. The patricians had the power to veto all decisions of the Assembly, where the plebeians had some representation. The Assembly elected the consuls and other officials of the Republic, but it, too, was dominated by a majority of patricians. The patricians always elected members of their own class to other official positions, such as the praetors, who were judges and who occasionally acted as consuls when the consuls were absent from Rome. Another important patrician official was the *censor* who took the census and decided who could or could not be a citizen. Two censors passed on the morals of the Roman citizens and made the lists of patrician citizens from which the senators were selected.

**The plebeians.** During the several centuries that the Romans were making gains in Italy, the plebeians were making gains in advancing their political rights as citizens. They established an assembly called the Assembly of Tribes, which they dominated. The Assembly of Tribes had the right to participate in the making of laws and in the election of officials. Each year the plebeians elected ten *tribunes* from their ranks and these tribunes had the power to veto any act of a judge. This power helped to protect the plebeians against unjust patrician treatment, and their power and social condition gradually improved. They gained the right to marry into the patrician class—which had formerly been forbidden to them. They could hold office and even become senators. Around 450 B.C. they managed to get the unwritten laws of the Romans inscribed upon twelve tables. This gave them additional protection from the patrician judges, who often interpreted the unwritten law in the interests of the patrician class.

Although the Senate continued to be an exclusive club, the divisions between patrician and plebeian gradually became less sharp. There was a greater political equality between all classes of Roman citizens. This progress toward equality among the Romans did not mean, however, that non-Romans were considered as equals. The Romans of the Republic retained an essentially aristocratic outlook. They were still unsatisfied with the extent of their power and wanted more. This led to the war with the Carthaginians.

1. Who were the most civilized people of Italy before the Romans?
2. What are some of the factors that may have contributed to the Romans' rise to power in Italy by 264 B.C.?
3. How did the patricians maintain their political control in Rome? How did the plebeians gain power?

## They Destroyed the Carthaginians

The Carthaginians had evolved from the old Phoenicians who, long centuries before, had established a trading post called Carthage on the shores of North Africa across from Sicily. Their rule over a great territory from Carthage was a tribute to the foresight of their ancestors and the endurance of their trading tradition. The power of Carthage extended over the islands of Corsica and Sardinia and the greater part of Sicily. The influence of this great city reached far back into the hinterland of Africa.

When the Romans had gained control over most of Italy, they looked suspiciously at the Carthaginians, whose influence on sea and land reached the boundaries claimed by Rome. Nor were the Carthaginians pleased with this nearness of an ambitious neighbor. They tested each other in a series of three wars over a period between 264 and 146 B.C., and the Carthaginians lost all three. The Romans

Men still wonder at Hannibal's feat in crossing the Alps with war elephants and an army. (Swiss National Tourist Office)

called these the *Punic* Wars—from the name they used to refer to the Carthaginian descendants of the Phoenicians.

**The First Punic War.** During the First Punic War, which lasted from 264 to 241 B.C., the Romans learned to fight effectively on the sea as well as on land. The Carthaginians were primarily warriors of the sea. The Romans were compelled to meet them at sea where, for much of the war, the Romans found themselves at a disadvantage. The Romans were ingenious military men, however, and they devised a way to use their legions on the sea. They built into their ships boarding bridges which swung down to make a drawbridge for their legionnaires to cross over after they had rammed an enemy ship. The addition of the marine-legionnaire to the struggle at sea turned the tide of war. A Roman army crossed to Africa and defeated the Carthaginians on land. The Romans demanded and received from the Carthaginians large sums of money and the islands of Corsica, Sardinia, and Sicily.

**The Second Punic War.** A Carthaginian general, Hannibal, played an important role in the Second Punic War, which lasted from 218 to 201 B.C. His military feats astounded and distressed the Romans at this time of their maturing might. Hannibal marched from Spain, where the Carthaginians had nourished a colony after the First Punic War. He crossed the Alps into Italy with his war elephants and his soldiers during the autumn. At first the Romans thought this feat impossible, and men still wonder how he did it. Hannibal broke army after army sent against him by the Romans, and for more than thirteen years he held out in Italy beyond the walls of the Roman cities. Hannibal did not have the equipment or supplies to conquer the cities, so the Romans confined themselves within the cities and patiently planned and waited for their moment to come. It came when a Roman general, Publius Cornelius Scipio the Elder, known as Scipio Africanus, managed to reach Africa with an army. This army threatened Carthage, and Hannibal was recalled to defend the city. He later returned to experience his first defeat and to lose the war.

Carthage was forced to destroy most of her warships and to surrender her territory in Spain and most of what she controlled in Africa as well as a great sum of money. Hannibal fled to Asia Minor, where he spent the rest of his life trying to persuade others to war against Rome. Once again the Romans had lost most of their battles, but won the war.

**The Third Punic War.** The Third Punic War lasted from 149 B.C. to 146 B.C. Some Romans, like Cato the Elder in the Senate, believed that Carthage should be completely

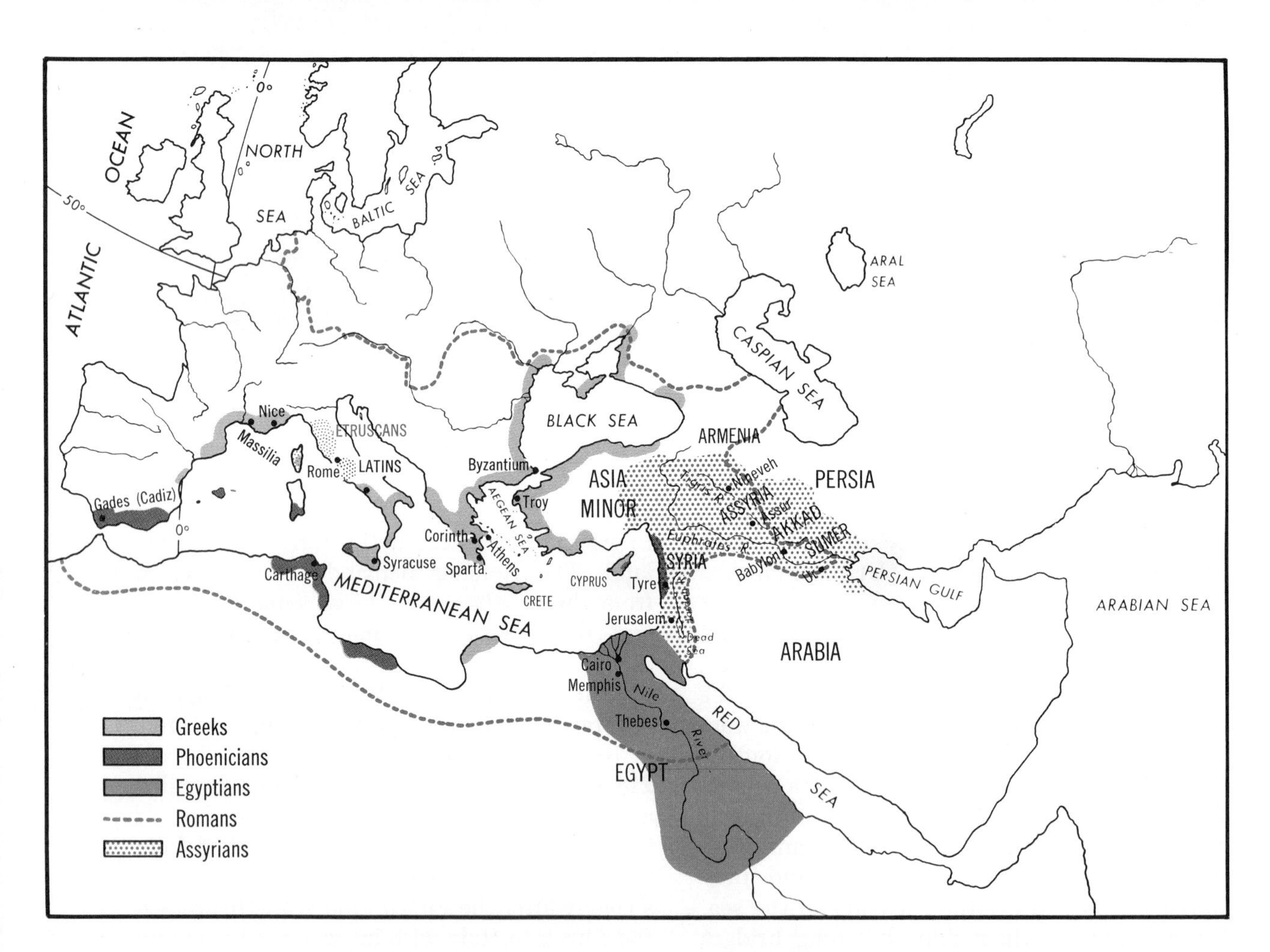


**SOME ANCIENT MEDITERRANEAN EMPIRES BEFORE ROME**

Early civilizations developed trade all around the shores of the Mediterranean Sea. In ancient times ships were a fast and easy means of transportation, while land routes were slow and difficult. The Phoenicians established colonies in all parts of the Mediterranean, and the Romans spread their empire to include all of its shores.

destroyed. Their will prevailed. The Romans began another war with Carthage and won it in the relatively short period of three years. This time Carthage was removed from the sight of man. The Romans leveled the great walls and buildings of the city and mixed them with earth by plowing up the site. To prevent any further animal or vegetable growth, they salted the earth, and blighted its future with a fearful curse.

The ship model is a second-century A.D. Roman merchant. Roman ships sailed perhaps as far as India and used a Suez canal. (Commercial Museum, Philadelphia)

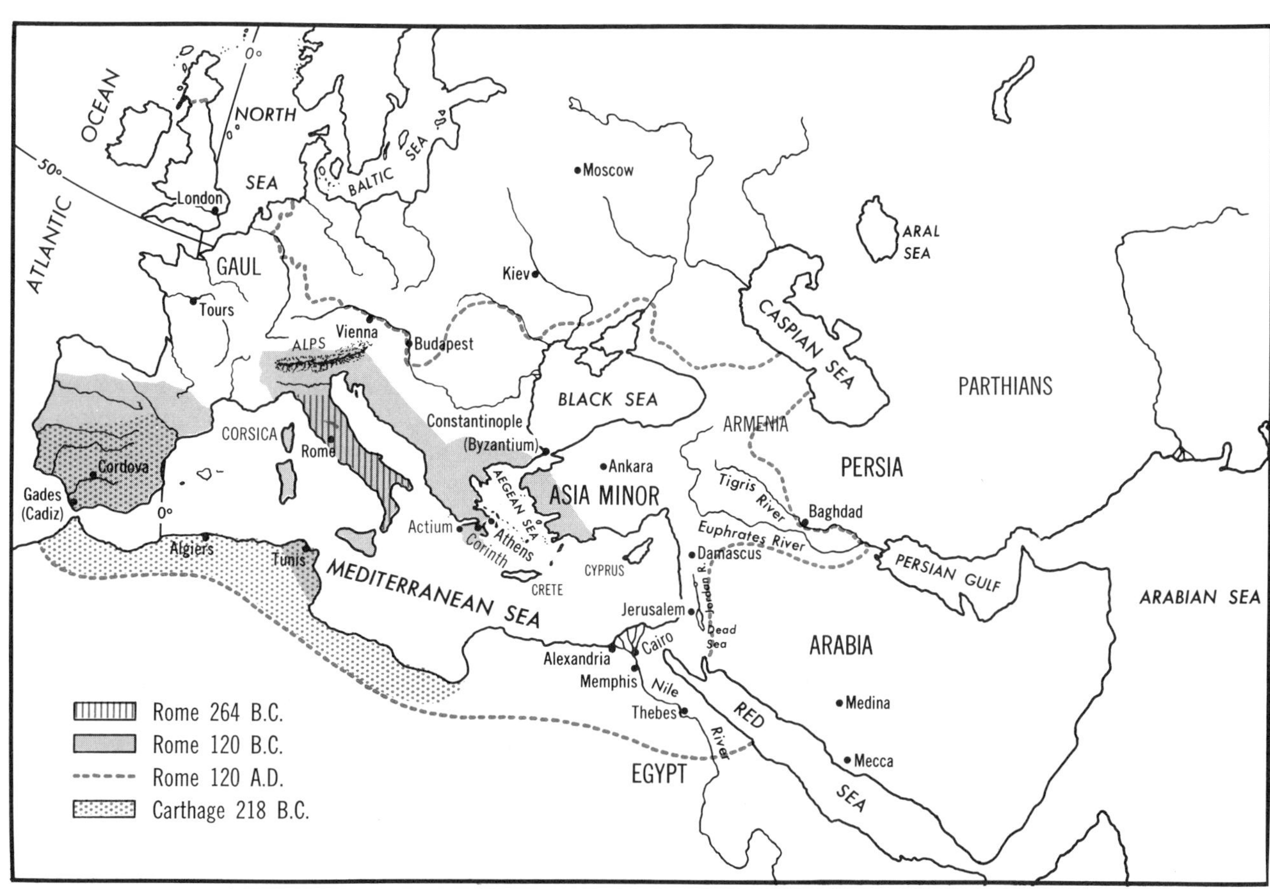


**GROWTH OF ROME FROM 264 B.C. to 120 A.D.**

Beginning on the plain of Latium, the Romans extended their dominion over much of Western Europe and the lands around the Mediterranean Sea. After the conquest of Carthage in the Punic Wars (264-146 B.C.), other lands and peoples fell in rapid succession before the Roman legions.

North Africa and Spain became Roman provinces, and the Romans stood masters of the western Mediterranean. The Romans were moving rapidly now, and kingdoms and cities tumbled before the onslaught of their arms and their demands.

Even before they destroyed Carthage, the Romans had made the eastern shores of the Adriatic Sea their domain, and around 197 B.C. Macedonia became a Roman dependency. The Romans began to meddle in the political affairs of the Middle East and infiltrated there with agents and intrigues. Egypt became subject to Roman influence and later the land of Asia Minor became a Roman province. The Romans had already taken control of the Greek city-states around 146 B.C. Thus, by the year 133 B.C., they could truly call the Mediterranean "our sea," and the people who lived on the shores of that sea were Roman subjects.

## The Republic Grows Feeble

The Romans continued to extend the size of their empire. Their control over others grew vaster despite the growing poverty of the free-citizen masses in Italy, corruption among governors, and the schemes of selfish men—all of which made Rome a city of turmoil and rotted the underpinnings of the Republic. The Romans learned, like many before and after them, that the moral fiber of man is often weakened and lost when great wealth and great power become a part of his life. So it was that from 133 to 27 B.C., the republican system of government in Rome was dying.

### The Rich

The wealthy men who governed the Romans became obsessed with obtaining more wealth and power. Bribery was normal, the buying and selling of offices routine, tax collecting a profitable profession, and governors ruled their provinces for the purpose of retiring to Rome with bags of gold and loot. Hundreds of thousands of slaves, by-products of Roman conquests, were available to work the growing expanse of the rich men's lands, to build their villas, work in their factories, clothe them, bathe them, and attend to their increasing wants. The simple, hard-working Latin ancestors who had traded the produce of their small farms with the Etruscans would probably not have recognized their blood in these descendants.

### The Poor

The rich were recognized but not liked by the small free farmers of Italy who could not compete with their masses of cheap slave labor. The small free farmers saw their holdings and homes being absorbed into Roman bigness. Former owners of little pieces of land frequently sought refuge in Rome and became part of the swarming, complaining poor who made the city seethe with their discontent. The ex-soldier sons who returned from wars that had made some men rich were upset to find their families scattered and their homes gone. They, too, swelled the misery and discord which assembled the mobs of Rome. Though the Roman masses were poor, their votes were still powerful, and they were wooed by office-seekers and demagogues with bread, money, games, and circuses. The games and circuses became institutions, and for centuries animals, men, and fortunes were sacrificed on the sands of the arenas to appease and pacify the unruly mobs of Rome.

### The Reformers

Out of the uncertainty and wretchedness of this period, some men rose to greatness, and some fell, too. Sincere reformers like the Gracchi, Gaius and Tiberius Gracchus, wanted to make the Republic more democratic by decreasing the economic and political power of the wealthy. They proposed limitations on the amount of land that could be owned by any one family and urged that farmers who had lost their lands should be resettled in colonies abroad or on state-owned lands in Italy itself. They also suggested that the poor of the city of Rome should be enabled to buy grain at cost or even more cheaply from the state. They also wanted a reduction in the power of the

Senate and an expansion of Roman citizenship to others who lived in Italy. Their proposals and actions aroused the anger of many powerful men of Rome. Tiberius Gracchus was murdered, and Gaius Gracchus was driven to suicide by those who would have suffered from reforms.

Gaius Marius and Lucius Cornelius Sulla started a tradition of rule by the military. Marius abolished the citizen-soldier army and replaced it with soldiers serving for a fixed period of time and paid by their general. The loyalty of the soldier was transferred from his state to his general. Out of this new power of the soldier there sprung one of the most famous of all Romans—Julius Caesar.

Gaius Julius Caesar (100-44 B.C.) has lived in history as general, statesman, and writer. The bust above is in the National Museum at Naples, Italy. (Charles Phelps Cushing)

### Julius Caesar

Caesar shared his rule of Rome at first with two other men, Gnaeus Pompey (called Pompey the Great) and Marcus Licinius Crassus. This rule by three men is known as a *triumvirate*. Crassus was killed in war, leaving Pompey and Caesar, each of whom wished to rule Rome alone. Pompey had expanded Rome's lands by conquering Syria and Jerusalem and had gained popularity in Rome. Caesar, too, knew that the way of the soldier was now the way to permanent power in Rome, and while he was consul in 59 B.C., he had himself appointed governor of the territory which was called Gaul. In 58 B.C., this remarkable man started a campaign which in nine years brought that part of Europe now making up Holland, Belgium, France, part of Germany, and a part of England under the government of Rome. He sent back to Rome progress reports of his victories. Caesar's *Commentaries on the Gallic Wars* still make good reading for the student learning Latin, and there are few who are not familiar with its opening words "All Gaul is divided into three parts."

Caesar's success disturbed his rival, Pompey, and others who were jealous and fearful of his rising power. In 49 B.C. he was asked to resign his office as proconsul of Gaul and return without his army to Rome. He returned, but with his army, for he was suspicious of the intentions of the Senate. He was met at the River Rubicon, separating his territory of Gaul from Italy, by a messenger from the Senate who declared him a rebel if he crossed this river leading his army. He crossed it and marched on to capture Rome. Since that time it is said of a man who has decided upon a course of action from which there is no return, "He has crossed the Rubicon."

Caesar followed Pompey to Greece and defeated his army there. He crossed over to Africa, placed Cleopatra on the throne of Egypt, and drove out an invader from Rome's Asia Minor province. He then returned to Rome and in 45 B.C. was given full power to rule Rome as a dictator for ten years. Caesar now showed his genius in statesmanship as he had previously shown his genius in war. Within a period of little more than a year he brought order out of chaos, and lifted the Romans to a new peak of organization and hope.

He carefully chose governors of provinces and officials of cities, and checked upon them with inspectors. He introduced reforms to make the system of tax collection more honest and efficient. He returned land to the landless and lifted the morale of his people. Caesar offered citizenship to those who lived outside Italy and thus knit the empire by closer ties. His reformed calendar was used by Europeans until the Gregorian corrections were made in the sixteenth century. Some nations continued to use the Julian calendar until the twentieth century. The month of July is named for Julius Caesar.

Julius Caesar was one of the those exceptional men who occasionally are born to amaze and to stimulate by their seemingly unlimited capacity to plan and to perform works of wonder. However, it is also one of man's habits to fear and to envy such as these. A group of Romans, including Caesar's friend Brutus, planned and carried out his murder on the Senate floor on the Ides (15th) of March in the year 44 B.C.

### Octavian and Marc Antony

Caesar had died, but the struggle to possess the power that was Rome passed on to others: Marc Antony, a man of impulse and huge appetites, who orated eloquently over Caesar's body and desired his undisputed authority; the young eighteen-year-old student Octavian, grandnephew and heir of Caesar, who was quietly effective, patient, and able; and Lepidus, a pygmy by the side of the other two, who soon retired from the struggle. Marc Antony ruled the East and Octavian the West after they defeated an army led by those who wished to restore power to the Senate.

Octavian (63 B.C.-14 A.D.) ruled as Augustus. (Charles Phelps Cushing)

Octavian made his headquarters in Rome. Marc Antony ruled from Egypt, where he remained with Cleopatra as his queen. For a time there was peace. But it was an uneasy peace disturbed by intrigues, jealousies, and rivalry between these two men, each of whom wanted to be the sole ruler of the Roman Empire. Then, in 32 B.C., at the urging of Octavian, Marc Antony was stripped of his authority by the Senate. War was formally declared against Egypt. It was, in reality, a war between the forces of Marc Antony and those of Octavian, and the victor would be the only ruler of the Empire.

The two opposing armies fought without a final decision, and, on Cleopatra's advice, Marc Antony decided to risk the outcome of the war on a naval battle. The engagement took place off the western coast of Greece, near Actium, which was on the Ambracian Gulf. Octavian's fleet destroyed all but about forty of the four hundred ships Antony sent against it. Marc Antony fled back to Egypt with Cleopatra, and his land forces surrendered. In the summer of the year 30 B.C., Octavian conquered Egypt. Marc Antony committed suicide, and Cleopatra also killed herself to avoid the humiliation of walking as a chained captive before the people of Rome.

Thus, Octavian became supreme in Rome. Under his rule, the spirit of the Republic died, and the age of the Roman emperors began.

1. What device enabled the Romans to defeat the Carthaginians at sea?
2. How did the Romans succeed in forcing the withdrawal and defeat of Hannibal? For what feat is Hannibal best known?

3. Who were the contenders for Caesar's power after his death?

## An Empire to Remember

When Octavian was given the title Augustus, or "exalted one," by the Senate in 27 B.C., he inaugurated a two-hundred-year period of stability and prosperity for some—a peace called *Pax Romana.* Under a series of emperors both good and bad, the citizens and subjects of Rome were unafraid of raiders from outside their borders and, in general, were satisfied with the order and the government of the Empire. The forms of the Republic were retained, but the actual power of government was the voice of a single man—the emperor. The Senate kept a name and a membership, but it always confirmed the successor chosen by the reigning emperor or by the military.

Under capable emperors like Augustus (Octavian), who ruled from 27 B.C. to 14 A.D., Nerva (96-98 A.D.), Trajan (98-117 A.D.), Hadrian (117-138 A.D.), and Marcus Aurelius (161-180 A.D.), the frontiers were protected by well-trained and well-led soldiers. Roman security was reinforced by walls running across southern Scotland and along the Rhine and Danube rivers. These excellent rulers knew the tremendous problems of administering an empire so vast that it took a man two months to cross, and they tried to find the best men to assist them in governing it. They realized that the heart of good administration is capable men.

The Roman Empire was open and bustling. Traders knew few restrictions, and buying and selling were made easier by the use of the commonly accepted Roman coins. Silks, glasses, linens, jewelry, and spices were shipped from the East to Rome over the blue-green Mediterranean, and there was little fear of pirates. Traders traveled to Rome from the provinces of Europe on broad paved roads and crossed rivers massively bridged by the genius of Roman engineering. There were changes in the countryside as forests and swamps were replaced with the stirring of seeds and stalks of grain; there was movement in the urban areas as villages grew into towns and towns into cities.

1. What was the *Pax Romana?*
2. How were the Romans able to maintain their control over all the diverse peoples and vast territories of the Empire?
3. What common cultural elements introduced throughout the Empire by the Romans tied the Empire together?

## Conclusion

The Romans were often fine administrators, and they did not intrude upon the local affairs of their subjects without good cause. The Roman Empire embraced a variety of men ranging from the cultured Egyptian to the barbarian of Europe's forest, mountain, and plain. It was an enormous empire of diverse cultures which included, among others, the sophisticated, freedom-loving Greeks, the autocrats of the Middle East, the wanderers of the African deserts, the boatmen of the Danube and Rhine rivers, the skin-clad hunters of the German forests, the horsemen of Spain, and the painted men of northern Britain. It included those who had explored in detail the art of government and those who barely knew its meaning. It gathered in those who believed in gods and goddesses, and some who believed in only one God.

The Romans wisely did not attempt to impose upon the variety of their empire a regime which would disturb the local fabric of life. The Romans adapted themselves to special customs and beliefs and to differing levels of civilization. They asked their subjects only to pay taxes, send their quotas of soldiers, acknowledge reverence for the emperor through certain ceremonies, and maintain the peace. Having done this, the Romans left their subjects alone to follow their accustomed ways of living. The system worked for centuries.

Roman tolerance and adaptability reduced the friction between the Romans and the dissimilar men they governed, but there were also other strands which tied the multitudes of the empire together. The Romans began to extend the privilege of citizenship to subjects in the provinces. By the middle of the third century A.D. a host of men called themselves citizens of Rome, though they had never viewed the city of Rome and were not of the same ancestry as the Latins. The Romans were generous in giving their name to others, who in turn were proud of their boast, "I am a Roman citizen." Roman subjects were brought closer together by a network of roads, a general acceptance of Roman law, a general use of the Latin and Greek languages, a desire of most to maintain the peace, and the binding forces of one monetary system, one capital, and one emperor. Thus the Romans fashioned and preserved an empire long remembered by man.

## SUMMING UP THE CHAPTER

A. Identify the following and tell why they are important.

| | |
|---|---|
| Augustus Caesar | Pompey |
| Cato the Elder | Pyrrhus |
| Gaius Gracchus | Tiberius Gracchus |
| Julius Caesar | |

B. Locate on a map the following places mentioned in this chapter.

| | |
|---|---|
| Actium | Gaul |
| Alps | Latium |
| Apennines | Po |
| Carthage | Tiber |
| "City of Seven Hills" | Tyrrhenian Sea |

C. Indicate the significance of the following dates.

1. 264-241 B.C.
2. 218-201 B.C.
3. 149-146 B.C.
4. 27 B.C.

D. Define or explain the following terms, relating them to this chapter.

| | |
|---|---|
| censor | praetor |
| consul | Senate |
| patrician | tribune |
| plebeian | triumvirate |

E. Chapter review questions.

1. What territories around the Mediterranean was the Roman able to call his own by 133 B.C.?
2. What brought about the decline in morality among Roman officials? Was this moral decay confined to the wealthy and official classes?
3. How did the officials and the wealthy placate the mobs of Rome?
4. How did Julius Caesar build up his popularity?
5. What elements of Roman culture and citizenship tied together the far-flung peoples of the empire?
6. Why did the Romans give citizenship to the conquered peoples of the empire?
7. What contributions were passed on to Roman civilization by the Greeks?
8. Describe the class structure of Rome.
9. Describe the course of the Punic Wars.
10. How did the existence of slavery turn the small farmer into a virtual beggar and slave? Has slavery always had this depressing effect on the poor freeman?
11. Describe the system of imperial administration initiated by Julius Caesar and the Augustan emperors.

F. Questions for discussion.

1. Why did the Roman emperors maintain the forms of the Republic? Can you think of other governments described in this book in which the outer form of a republic was kept, even though the actual government was not a republic? What does this tell you about the necessity of looking beyond mere formal institutions? Could you determine whether a republican form of government actually existed if you knew only the formal institutional arrangements? What more would you need to know?
2. How did Roman culture differ from Hellenistic culture?
3. How did the Roman generals attain political power?
4. What do the administrative and cultural devices used by the Romans to control their empire indicate about the possibilities of successful imperial systems? What relevance does the Roman Empire have to problems of the modern world?
5. How were the Romans able to weld together such a vast empire?

G. Projects for groups or individuals.

1. Describe the geography of Italy. Draw a map of Italy and surrounding areas, labeling each area, city, and geographical feature mentioned in this chapter.
2. Read Shakespeare's *Julius Caesar*. Prepare a class report on the character of Caesar and his successors.
3. Find pictures and descriptions of the Roman walls in Britain.
4. Draw a map of the Roman Empire at its height, labeling each of the major territories.

CHAPTER **16**

# *Roman Beliefs and Accomplishments*

THE ROMANS SHARED with the Greeks in laying the early foundations of Western civilization. They took the thoughts of the Greeks and others of the eastern Mediterranean—particularly the teachings of the Stoic philosophers—made them their own, and passed them along to the later European clothed in the beauty of the Roman language and adorned with the interpretations and elaboration of Roman philosophers.

The Romans evolved a system of law and justice which forms the basis of legal systems in many countries today. They were cosmopolitan in outlook and displayed a tolerance and sense of practicality in governing the many diverse peoples of their empire. At their best, the Romans showed a high sense of duty and sacrifice and a feeling for others that would merit the approval of the most virtuous among men. Their genius for organization, their feeling for the useful, and their engineering skill enabled them to build works still admired today.

The Romans preserved and polished their heritage from the Greeks and others, added their own significant contributions, and passed along traditions to Europe that still play a major role in the world today.

## Roman Spirits and Gods

The Romans spent much of their early republican life encircled by the boundaries of their families and farms. The spirits in which they believed were also closely associated with their families and farms. Dead ancestors were a part of this spirit world, but they also remained a part of the family. The male head of the family had an obligation to sacrifice to the spirits and to assume leadership in the religious ceremonies of his family.

The most important of the Roman's spirits was Vesta, the spirit of hearth and fire. As the hearth and the fire were central to the Roman household, so was Vesta the center of Roman worship. Janus, god of the door, had two faces, one for those entering and one for those leaving The *lares* protected the whole household and its fortune. The *penates* guarded the storerooms. Ceres was the goddess of the harvest. Other spirits watched over the grain from its seeding to its storing; they were as numerous as there were requirements for the production of food. The Romans honored all of them with ceremony and festival.

Under the influence of Etruscan intruders, the spirits of the Romans began to assume a human shape. The Romans tried to know better the desires of their gods and to learn the shape of the future by watching birds in flight and studying the entrails of sacrificed animals. This practice was called "taking the auspices." If the flight of the birds and the state of the entrails were favorable, the Romans knew the signs were auspicious for a contemplated undertaking, and they could proceed with confidence.

As their civilization evolved, the Romans symbolized the larger grouping of their national family by building a temple for Vesta in Rome, where this great spirit was installed as the guardian of the hearth of the total Roman family. A sacred fire always burned within this temple attended by six vestal vir-

The Pantheon, in Rome, was the center of the Roman religion. It was dedicated to all the gods. (Italian State Tourist Office) The great stones below, at Carnac, France are called dolmens. They were a center of Druidic religious ceremonies. (French Government Tourist Office) The Romans permitted a great variety of religions in their Empire.

gins, who were among the most honored and revered of the inhabitants of Rome.

The Romans were soldiers, and they favored Mars, god of war, who had brought them empire and glory. They especially honored him in the month of March, which bore his name. It was in the month of March that the Romans started their serious preparations for the coming military campaigns of the year. Long association with the Greeks led the Romans to associate the Greek gods with their own. Zeus became the Roman god Jupiter, and Hera became the Roman goddess Juno. Aphrodite, the goddess of love, was known to the Romans as Venus, and the Greek messenger of the gods, Hermes, was changed to the Roman Mercury. But the Romans did not cease accepting gods, just as they never stopped accepting useful ideas. They accepted the cult of Mithra from the Persians, the Egyptian god Isis, and Cybele, the fertility goddess of Asia Minor, among others. Before the breakup of the western portion of the Roman Empire in the fifth century A.D., the gods of many nations found a place among the temples the Romans built in their city and in their Empire.

## Philosophy, Literature, and Law

In their philosophy and literature, the Romans borrowed quite freely from others, adapted ideas to their own cosmopolitan outlook, and added their own ideas. Roman philosophers and writers were concerned with man and his relation to the universe, but they also saw man as a member of a great republic and a great empire. Civic duty and obligations to the whole of society figured strongly in their writings.

Roman law remains as one of the great achievements of ancient times, and its survival as the basis of modern codes of law is a tribute to the Roman genius for governing great numbers of diverse peoples.

### Roman Philosophers

Greek ideas about man's nature and way of life and about the nature of the universe had a great influence upon the Romans. As the Romans expanded their empire, they came into contact with a wealth of thought which had developed in Greece and the Middle East. The Romans found many ideas which were adaptable to their own needs. Greek scholars were brought to Rome, and Romans went to Greece to study.

Greek philosophical thought was studied and discussed by educated Romans. Greek ideas were clothed in the rhythm and vigor of the Latin language and flavored with the Romans' own traditions and feelings. As Roman society grew and expanded, so did Roman thought grow and develop. The Romans gave a special form and content to philosophy and evolved their own concepts of man and the universe. In doing so, they passed along some of the most important guidelines and values by which men in the Western world live today.

During the last years of the Republic, some Romans became especially interested in the teachings of the Epicureans and the Stoics.

**Lucretius.** The Roman poet Lucretius, who lived from around 98 to 55 B.C., was an Epicurean. He believed that all things, including man, are merely chance combinations of atoms. He accepted the gods but thought that they had nothing to do with man. Let us live the balanced life with purity of heart and peace of mind, he said, and be not afraid to taste the pleasures of the senses. In poetry of great beauty and strength, Lucretius urged men to cast off their fear of death and not to be like children who shudder in the darkness for fear of things which might not even exist.

The Epicurean philosophy of Lucretius, however, did not receive as much honor and acceptance among the Romans as did the teachings of the Stoics. Among the best known of the Romans who taught and practiced the teaching of the Stoics were Cicero, Seneca, Epictetus, and Marcus Aurelius.

**Cicero.** One of the most high-minded of the Romans who were attracted to the teachings of the Stoics was Cicero, who lived from 106 to 43 B.C. He studied law in Rome, and in Greece he learned about philosophy. He became one of Rome's greatest lawyers and orators and held many high offices in the government of Rome. Cicero believed in the Roman Republic and was often opposed to the imperial policies of Caesar and Octavian. He wrote much, and his speeches for many centuries have been considered to be masterpieces of style. His works *On Duties* and the *Tusculan Disputations* reflect the moral teachings of the Stoics, and his writings on government contained in *On the Republic* and *On Laws* have been read and discussed over the many centuries since they were first written. Cicero's speeches and letters mirror the mind and the heart of a man who loved Rome and who wanted all men to live more virtuously together.

Like the Stoics, Cicero believed that all men should live by the highest moral standards and that they could know the right moral way of life through the faculty of their reason. Reason made all men brothers, for it was one thing they all possessed in common. Cicero believed a virtuous life was in accord with the law of Nature, which he felt to be above and beyond man-made institutions, directing man and the universe with a purpose. Cicero came to the conclusion that there was a divinity in man which not only made him one with all men but also a part of an all-directing power which moved man and the universe. He advised men to pursue virtue, to be indifferent to pain and grief, to be guided always by reason, and to work in cooperation with others in accordance with the law of Nature.

**Seneca.** Seneca (about 3 B.C.-65 A.D.) was born in Cordoba, Spain, and studied and lived most of his life in Rome. He was a wealthy patrician, a teacher and chief advisor of the Emperor Nero, an author of scientific writings, a playwright, and a philosopher who was deeply influenced by the teachings of the Stoics. He believed that there was a divine force which was directing all things to some final and good end, and that this divinity was shared by all men, making them brothers. For this reason, he held that there were essentially no class distinctions among men, and that slaves, too, should be treated decently because they were human and part of the brotherhood of man. Seneca urged men to use their reason to practice the good life and taught that they should discipline their minds so that they might remain tranquil and untouched by whatever adversities fortune might shower upon them.

**Epictetus.** Another Stoic philosopher was Epictetus, who lived from about 60 to about 120 A.D. Epictetus was a slave who was born in Asia Minor. He was brought to Nero's court by his owner and was later freed. Like Seneca, he believed that a divine Providence was guiding the universe to a destined end. It was the duty of man, he said, to direct his will in accordance with the will of this divine plan. It was important that man should know which things were within his control and which things were not. A man might fulfill his own desires and make his own choices between alternatives—but he should not be upset by matters beyond his control. Epictetus taught that man may have serenity, peace of mind, and a true freedom only when he renounces those things that are beyond his control and is prepared to accept and endure whatever misfortunes may befall him.

Marcus Aurelius, who became Emperor of Rome, was impressed and influenced by the teachings of Epictetus.

**Marcus Aurelius.** Another man who believed in the disciplined life of the Stoics was the Emperor Marcus Aurelius, who lived between 121 and 180 A.D. In his life and in his writings, *The Meditations of Marcus Aurelius*, he taught the importance of duty and private virtue. For much of his life he fought on the frontiers of the Empire, and he knew the hardships that duty often requires. He was often tempted to shirk the routine of his duty, as he relates in his *Meditations*, but as the ant, the bee, and the spider cannot refuse the tasks which make an ordered universe, neither could he, the Emperor of Rome. He was tempted to remain under his blankets in the cold dawning at the frontier post, but when he thought of the ordered purpose for which he was ordained, he threw off his warm coverings and began the discipline of his day. He refused to be oppressed by the opinions and actions of others, and he was never tied to the money he possessed. He was conscious of the brotherhood of man and of the need to give of himself and his property. No Roman was ever more ruled by the principles he held than Marcus Aurelius.

**The Stoic appeal.** The moral teachings of the Stoics found a home in the minds and hearts of many Romans because they were in harmony with the old traditions of the Republic, which placed duty and sacrifices above comforts and the happiness of the individual. The Romans, at least during the period of their civic strength, were not much influenced by the ideas of the Epicureans, for they saw in these teachings a tendency to self-indulgence which they scorned. The Stoic insistence on the obligations of citizens to their state appealed to the Romans, for they had a tradition of duty and public-spiritedness. The Romans also thought in terms of empire, and the Stoic idea of the brotherhood of man appealed to their cosmopolitan outlook. The application of a universal law of Nature to all men was readily grasped by the Romans, who were expanding their sway over many diverse peoples. It was both democratic and practical.

1. What gods and goddesses of the Greeks were comparable to Roman gods and goddesses?
2. What were Cicero's greatest contributions to political thought?
3. Why are the *Meditations* of Marcus Aurelius important?

## Roman Literature

The Romans frequently wrote well. The excellence and eloquence of their style have been held up to generations of European writers as models. The model for the Roman writer, however, was often the Greek. Roman writers sometimes imitated Greek comedies and other forms of Greek writing, and in many cases they were influenced by the Greek philosophies of Stoicism and Epicureanism.

Virgil (70-19 B.C.) ranks among the Roman poets who, like Cicero and Marcus Aurelius, were influenced by the philosophy of the Stoics. He was also influenced by a sense of the superior destiny and greatness of the Romans. His finest creation was the epic poem, the *Aeneid*, which tells the story of Aeneas, who escaped the ruin of Troy by the Greeks and after much wandering settled in Italy, there his descendants founded the city of Rome. The *Aeneid* is the writing of a man who took deep pride in the ancestry, traditions, triumphs, and destiny of the Roman.

In the *Aeneid*, the story is told how the Greeks overcame the Trojans with a trick. They built a great wooden horse, placed a number of their warriors within its hollow body, and then pretended to halt the siege of Troy and leave. They left the horse behind. The curious Trojans pulled the large wooden horse within the city walls. That night the Greeks climbed out of their horse, opened the gate of the city, and let in the remainder of their army. Troy was taken. In referring to this trickery, one of the Trojans in Virgil's epic remarked that he feared the Greeks even when they bore gifts. Man has continued to say "Beware of Greeks bearing gifts" to express suspicion of those whose gifts might be used to conceal their real intentions.

Horace (65-8 B.C.) wrote poetry and prose and borrowed his philosophy from both the Epicureans and Stoics. He condemned neither pain nor pleasure but believed that the man of moderation was most happy. He advised man to hope when distressed and to worry a little when prosperous. This attitude and way of behaving was called the "Golden Mean." Using this formula man would be prepared for the inevitable ebb and flow of his fortunes. Another Roman poet, Ovid (43 B.C.-17 A.D.) was more concerned with man's pleasure than with his morals—a concern which is obvious in his poetry. Livy (59 B.C.-17 A.D.) wrote a history of Rome which is famous for its style, but numerous readers have questioned the truth of some of his statements. All of these writers lived around the time of Augustus, which is often referred to as the Augustan Age.

Some of the writers who wrote after this period were also quite good. Juvenal (about 60-140 A.D.) satirized the vices of Rome under the Empire. Observing the great hypocrisy and dishonesty of many men of his time, he once remarked, "Honesty is praised and starves."

Tacitus (55-117 A.D.), the best of the Roman historians, wrote a classic description of the early Germans in a work called *Germania*. By contrasting the hardiness and simplicity of the German with the softness of many Romans, he scorned the decay and the luxury of his Roman society. Tacitus had a biting pen. He reproved the Roman mother who took time for all her pleasures but spent none with her children, who knew only the silly chattering of illiterate maids. He was upset by the shallowness of Roman education and the mania of his people for the circus and chariot racing. Tacitus feared the evil times which would follow the Roman pursuit of luxury and easy living.

The Romans were, at their best, excellent writers, and their works have given to man many hours of thought and relaxation. Perhaps, however, in no way have later men benefited more than in their heritage of Roman law and justice.

1. Name some of the great engineering and architectural achievements of the Romans.
2. What is the story of the great Roman epic, the *Aeneid*?
3. What did Tacitus see as the weaknesses of his fellow Romans and their life? With whom did he contrast them?

## Roman Law

The Romans had a deep feeling and respect for law. Roman law was based upon tolerance and rationality. In its clarity and universality, it reflected the Roman genius for abstracting general principles from experience.

The first Roman code of law, called the Twelve Tables, was written about 450 B.C. It was designed for the rather simple and confined life of an early stage of the Republic. Life did not long remain simple and limited, however, and by the time of the rule of Augustus, which began in 27 B.C., the Roman Empire included a vast complex of men and customs. The Romans expanded their law as they expanded their empire, adapting it to meet newer customs and the teachings of the Stoics, and to give better justice in each particular case. Magistrates, called *praetors*, were flexible in interpreting the law in each case which came before them. Their interpretations became precedents for other praetors to follow and upon which to base further interpretations. The Roman law grew in much the same fashion that the later English common law grew—daily, gradually, and practically.

Beginning with Augustus in 27 B.C., Roman law bloomed. It became customary for the judges and others to request the opinion of respected lawyers or jurists in particular cases. The opinions of these jurists were generally accepted and upheld. These jurists were mostly swayed by the thoughts of Cicero, who believed that there was a natural law above the state, the emperor, and the senate—an eternal law which could not be repealed, forbidden, or ignored. Cicero maintained that the individual ultimately derived his just rights from this law, and that the law could be understood through man's ability to reason. Even the slave had rights which protected him from cruel treatment. Roman jurists were, in many instances, influenced in their opinions by the spirit of the law rather than its letter. The Roman jurist Ulpian declared that the jurists worshiped justice and desired always what was good and fair.

The Romans did not force their law upon the people they conquered, but in the course of time most of the people of the empire came to accept Roman law as suitable and just. Even after the death of the empire, many continued to use the law of the Romans. Many of modern man's legal ideas about such things as partnerships, private property, and contracts were first expressed by the Romans. All of the later European countries were affected by Roman law, but its impact was greatest in the Latin-speaking countries—Italy, France, Spain, and the countries of Latin America. Roman law still remains at the base of the legal system of these countries. The Romans made laws to meet their own immediate needs for justice and order, but they made so well that later nations also found Roman law suitable for their legal needs. The Romans were great organizers and knew how to use the mind's highest ability—the creation and use of abstract ideas.

But the Romans did not confine themselves to creations in the fields of philosophy, literature, and law. They also made significant contributions in art and architecture. Their paintings and works of art in bronze and marble are still admired, but they are best remembered today as builders. They built grandly and they built well, and what they built revealed magnificence of imagination and practicality.

## The Romans Were Builders

The Romans built to house their bureaucracy, to stage their circuses and games, to enclose their baths, to celebrate their military triumphs, to accommodate their emperors and nobles, to carry water to a city from mountain and river, and to display their power.

They made their buildings massive and they made them strong. Still standing in Rome

Greek originality continued under Roman rule. Hero of Alexandria, a Greek, invented this steam engine, called an aeolepile. (Smithsonian Institution)

Roman aqueducts were built in many provinces of the Empire. This aqueduct, the Pont du Gard, near Nîmes, France, was built in three tiers of arches. The lowest is still in use as a road bridge. (French Government Tourist Office)

The head of Bacchus in mosaic work is a fine example of Roman art. (University of Pennsylvania Museum)

Wherever they went, the Romans carried their culture with them. The ruins of a Roman theater below are found in Libya. (Libyan Mission to the UN)

The coin shown above is a denarius of the time of Augustus. (Chase Manhattan Bank Money Museum)

Throughout the ages, the architecture of the Greeks and Romans has been admired and copied. This structure in Nashville, Tennessee is an exact copy of the Parthenon. How does Roman architecture differ from this classic Greek example? (State of Tennessee)

are the circling walls of the giant Colosseum, where once fifty thousand or more Romans sat and screamed with excitement at the scenes of blood and death provided by the performers below. The Romans built huge baths where thousands of the poor and hundreds of the rich went to bathe and to gossip. The baths built by the Emperor Caracalla still serve a useful purpose today. During the warm summer nights, the modern Roman and his guests gather at this impressive site and listen to the thundering music of the opera.

The Romans erected great triumphal arches, some of which yet stand, to commemorate military victories. Unlike the Greeks, who used columns, the Romans were fond of the arch in their construction. They used arches in their buildings, bridges, and aqueducts. The Assyrians had built an aqueduct in the Middle East centuries before to carry water from the mountains to their capital city of Nineveh, but no man in those earlier days of history built as many or as enduring aqueducts as the Romans. They built them in the many provinces and for the city of Rome. The arches of Roman aqueducts are found in many places. There is an aqueduct still standing in southern France which is around nine hundred feet long and over a hundred and fifty feet high, an enduring proof of Roman firmness in building.

The Romans were a very sanitary people and knew the practical uses of water. They used great amounts of water. It is estimated that aqueducts brought three hundred million gallons of water daily to the people of the city of Rome. Like the Japanese, the Romans were fond of bathing, and wherever they went outside the city of Rome, they built baths—in the Middle East, North Africa, Spain, and elsewhere. They laid underground sewers and were generous in constructing latrines, which were sometimes made more attractive by marble facing. The Romans were skilled in the science of drainage and they made land more useful and life more healthful by draining swamps. In their physical hygiene the Romans were not surpassed by later Europeans until the nineteenth century.

The Romans were fine builders of bridges and roads. They made roads of stone, and sometimes lava blocks, between fifteen and twenty feet wide and several feet thick. Roman roads were built to last and were laid throughout the empire so that men might know Roman will and desires as soon as possible. Over these roads the Roman legions tramped, couriers hurried, and trading carts plodded. The Romans also compiled road maps for the convenience of the traveler. Modern men have acknowledged the Roman's skill in engineering by laying their roads over his. What the Roman found useful, modern Europeans have also found useful.

The Romans often domed their buildings. During the rule of the Emperor Hadrian (117-138 A.D.), the Pantheon was built in Rome. Its dome is one hundred and forty-two feet in diameter, rising one hundred and forty-two feet from the ground. Within domed buildings the Romans placed statues of their emperors and famous men. Sometimes their statues showed depth of character and realism, but the Roman creations could not compare with the genius of Greek sculptors.

The ruins of the Colosseum still stand in the modern city of Rome. Here gladiators fought and died to amuse the ancient Romans. Here, also, many Christians suffered martyrdom. (Moore-McCormack Lines)

## The Roman Way of Life

During the early days of their Republic, the Romans lived in a manner still untainted and unspoiled by excesses of power and wealth. They were citizen-farmers. The necessities of farming kept their bodies strong and their emotions family-centered. Within the family, the Romans learned those virtues which strengthened them and helped the state to endure and to advance. They learned to respect authority, to reverence tradition, to feel responsible for their families, and to be prepared to sacrifice their own personal interests if called upon by their greater Roman family—the city-state.

### The Soldier-Farmer

Both father and mother shared the responsibility of educating their children, but the Roman father was the head of the household. The household was very large and included married sons and their families as well as the unmarried children. The father instructed his sons in the management of the farm, in the obligations of citizenship, and in the qualities of a good soldier. The early republican Roman was required to serve in the army. He was a hardy soldier who could march for miles with a sixty-pound pack upon his shoulders. He was expected to provide his own equipment of helmet, shield, sword, and iron-tipped javelin. He fought in a legion of from three thousand to more than five thousand men, divided into *centuries*—at first made up of one hundred men, but later the number varied. Each century was headed by a leader called a *centurion.* Two consuls commanded the army, but in times of great need a dictator might command for a period of six months. The Roman general Cincinnatus was twice summoned from his farm to lead the armed forces, and afterwards returned to his plowing.

The discipline of his farming family prepared the Roman for the harsh training of the army. For falling asleep while on guard or leaving his post unguarded, the soldier was beaten and stoned by his fellow soldiers. And after this punishment, even if he escaped death, he could never return home because he had brought a terrible disgrace upon his family. The Roman soldier was also punished severely if he lost his equipment in battle, stole, lied about others, or boasted of deeds he had not performed. He was rewarded if he fought well, and the honor he received was an honor to his entire family. The expansion of Rome was due in large measure to the fighting ability of her citizen-farmer-soldiers.

### The Family and Education

The father's authority in the family was overwhelming. He had the power to punish with death if necessary. The family property was held in his name, and it passed on to his sons in equal shares after his death. The Roman woman's primary function was the bearing and rearing of children and the care of the home. But the Roman wife often had a strong influence upon her husband and upon the family. She participated in entertainment at home and frequently shared her husband's company when he went out on business and social engagements. She was commonly consulted on family decisions and played a part in the education of her sons and daughters. Even in the early days of the Republic, Roman women were respected for their vital role in the family, and later commentators recognized their help in building the Roman Empire. With the decline of republican austerity, the upper-class Roman women enjoyed greater freedom. A few of them even received a formal education.

During the later days of the Republic and the time of the Empire, there were writers who criticized the slackening of parents' attention to the moral and mental training of their children. These writers criticized the common obsession with eating, drinking, and entertainment. They condemned the Romans for their low morals, their luxurious living, and their depravity; for there was evidence that sinister forces were in movement among the flower of Roman aristocracy. The tale was often told that the mother of the Emperor Nero (54-68 A.D.) poisoned her husband, the Emperor Claudius (41-54 A.D.), in order that her son by a previous marriage might become emperor. Nero later poisoned his mother and his wife.

During this period of Rome's material peak, the wealthy Roman boy was sometimes taught at home by an educated slave or a private tutor. At times he was sent to private schools—the Romans did not provide for free public school education—and after he had graduated from these schools, he might go to the famed schools of Greece to round off his education. Octavian, who ruled as Augustus, was a student in Greece when his great-uncle, Julius Caesar, was murdered. The poor—the vast majority of the Roman citizens—did not possess the funds to give their children any academic education; they generally remained unschooled.

### Four Classes

During the later years of the Republic and the period of the Empire, the Romans were divided into four distinct classes: aristocrats, equites, plebeians, and slaves. The aristocrats were few in number, about three hundred, and they were senators, who were wealthy through well-paid official positions and extensive landed estates. The equites had originally been members of the Roman cavalry. (Latin *eques* means "horseman.") From their high military rank, they developed into a privileged social class. They had grown fat in wealth with the expansion of the Roman Empire. They were the lenders of money at high interest rates, the speculators in grain, wine, and oil, the buyers of lucrative government contracts, the corrupt tax collectors, the owners of gladiator schools, the ship owners, and the big merchants.

The wealthy Roman lived a comfortable life. He had a tasteful town house in the city and a spacious villa in the country. He built these houses with open sun-lit courtyards where he sat relaxed, shaded by awnings and fanned by slaves. There he gossiped, received his friends, and watched his children play with their boats in the courtyard pool. In the colder climates he used glass windows, had piped water, and heated his rooms with hot air circulated through pipes of tile. He had marble tables, comfortable couches and stools, wonderful statues, leaping fountains of water, and private marble baths. He acquired a taste for much food and drink, his gluttony, drunkenness, and coarse behavior at the banquet table have been described in detail by both Roman and non-Roman writers. The more sober-minded Roman saw in these excesses the beginning of the end of Rome.

The ordinary citizens were known as plebeians. Sometimes they were farmers or workers, but mostly they were the mobs of Rome. Their land had been taken by the big and the rich, and they could not compete with the cheapness of slave labor, so they became the numerous wards of the state—over three hundred thousand in number toward the end of the Republic. The city of Rome had to feed and entertain these masses if it was to be secure and at peace. The plebeians were feared in their numbers by emperors, aristocrats, and equites, who tried to keep them moderately satisfied with bread, wheat porridge, free baths, and circuses. Rome had costly temples, public buildings of marble, lovely theaters, colonnades, and parks or wide fields of green lawn called *campuses*. But it also had ugliness in its dirty alleys and in its untidy tenements of four to six stories where the plebeians lived cramped and fearful of fire.

Fires were numerous in Rome, and mostly they consumed the wood of the poorly constructed tenements. Robbery was another danger not uncommon in this city where the majority were poor. The man who walked at night by the light of his lantern was always alert to shadows which lurked and moved. The rich, of course, were guarded by armed slaves.

Cruel though the life of the plebeians was, it did not compare in its desperation to the fate of the slaves. The plebeians were free, and there was a glimpse of hope that fortune might smile on them. But the slaves, especially the slaves of the fields, mines, and circuses, saw only death's release from the bitterness of life. The slaves were the animals who worked the large lands of the rich. They were branded; they were whipped; they were chained at night with herds of others in darkened rooms or cellars. Slaves often died from overwork and exposure, or grew old and weak before they reached their prime. Some slaves worked for their masters as gladiators, and it was only the fortunate few who escaped the armed opponent or the fangs and claws of beasts.

For some of the educated slaves, life was more fortunate. They worked in the household as tutors, secretaries, managers of businesses, and in other such useful occupations. Sometimes they were lucky and had masters who treated them humanely or gave them their freedom. Some were even able to obtain and save money and thus buy their freedom, but they were a small minority. More often the Romans feared their slaves. They had reason to fear. In 104 B.C. rebellious slaves had devastated the island of Sicily, and in 73 B.C. seventy thousand of them under the leadership of a leader named Spartacus had kept Italy in turmoil for more than a year. There were around 1,500,000 slaves in Italy during the latter days of the Republic. The slaves produced most of the Romans' food, manned their industries, and made their lives more comfortable.

1. What were the most important contributions of the Romans to the Western heritage?
2. Describe the four distinct classes which divided the Romans.
3. Why was the economic position of the plebeian so precarious?

## Conclusion

The Romans left a variety of solid achievements. They fathered the French, Spanish, and Italian languages, and many Latin words have been incorporated into English, German, and other languages. They invented instruments for surgery, gave a name to the Caesarian operation—Julius Caesar is reported to have been delivered at birth by this method—and passed on to the Europeans a tradition of public hospitals and public hygiene. They acted as preservers of much that was fine in Greek art, architecture, and philosophy. The only knowledge we have of much of Greek sculpture, for example, is from Roman copies. To military men, the Romans gave some excellent examples of how to organize for war and win it; and to peaceable men the Romans gave the example of their *Pax Romana*, which lasted for several centuries.

The Romans built a structure of law which men continue to find useful in dispensing justice. Roman domes, arches, and amphitheaters are still copied, and the foundations and routes of Roman roads are still in use. Roman writings continue to be read by those who seek to improve their literary style and their knowledge. The Romans contributed much and gave their own special form to the mighty foundations of the civilization of Western man.

## SUMMING UP THE CHAPTER

A. Identify the following and tell why they are important.

| | |
|---|---|
| *Aeneid* | Lucretius |
| aqueducts | Marcus Aurelius |
| Baths of Caracalla | Mars |
| Cicero | Mercury |
| Colosseum | Ovid |
| Horace | Pantheon |
| Janus | Tacitus |
| Jupiter | Twelve Tables |
| Juvenal | Ulpian |
| Livy | Virgil |

B. Chapter review questions.
1. How was the Roman law able to adapt to the emergence of the Empire?
2. Why do you suppose the Roman was such a practical and active man whose contributions to the Western heritage were mainly practices and constructions rather than abstract ideas?
3. Describe the administration of the Roman law.
4. Describe the role of woman in the Roman family.
5. What political role did the plebeian play?
6. What was the condition and role of the educated slave?
7. What was the role of the family in Roman religion? How was the family the basic unit of society?
8. Describe the central ideas of Stoicism.

C. Questions for discussion.
1. In the mythology of the Greeks and Romans, identify the comparable gods and goddesses, and where possible, compare the legends about them. Compare them with the Chinese, Indian, and Japanese gods and goddesses and their respective mythologies. Can you draw any conclusions from this?
2. What does the importance of the various Roman gods tell you about Roman life and thought?
3. Why do you think the law was so important to the Romans?
4. Do you think Stoicism was responsible for the greatness of Cicero and Marcus Aurelius, or was their greatness something individual, something within them? Support your opinion with facts.
5. What was it about the Roman law which made it relevant to the Renaissance and caused its revival as one of the bases of modern law?

D. Projects for groups or individuals.
1. Prepare a report with illustrations of the various types of Roman architecture.
2. Compare Virgil's *Aeneid* with the *Iliad* and *Odyssey* of Homer.
3. Read selections from the *Meditations* of Marcus Aurelius in class. Point out their elements of Stoic philosophy.
4. Prepare a display of illustrations of the great architectural achievements of the Romans.
5. Use reference books to make a report on Roman law. Be sure to include and explain the terms *jus civile, jus naturale, jus gentium.*

# CHAPTER 17

# The Romans Declined—Others Rose

During the days of their greatness, Roman citizens viewed with pride and security the vastness of an empire which engulfed all of the land from the borders of Persia and the deserts of Africa to the banks of the Danube and Rhine rivers and the wall of stone running across southern Scotland. But the cycle of empire, like that of man, is one of growth, maturity, and ageing decay. The strength of the Romans gradually waned, and Roman rule passed into other hands. The Empire was divided and ruled in the West by Germanic tribes who came from beyond the Rhine and Danube and in the East by the Byzantine emperors. The center of the Christian Church in the West, however, remained in Rome.

As the Roman Empire declined, the pattern of life in Europe was shaped by the doctrines and spirit of Christianity, the political customs and social institutions of the Germans, and the remaining cultural heritage from the Greeks and Romans. The fusion of these three influences characterized that period of European historical evolution generally known as the Middle Ages or medieval period. Traditionally, the medieval period is considered to include the years between the fifth and the fifteenth centuries. The transition, however, from the Roman to the medieval way of life was not an abrupt change but a gradual process that went on over many years.

## The Decline of Rome

Shortly after 180 A.D., the strife between military factions to possess the throne of Rome caused discord and disunity within the Empire. Emperor after emperor was placed upon the throne by soldier-supporters, and then murdered and replaced by another temporarily successful candidate. From 180 to 284 A.D., twenty-six men became emperor of Rome, and twenty-five of them were assassinated. The Empire held together during this confusing scene of rapidly changing emperors, but it was weakened.

The morale and discipline of the soldiers guarding the frontiers suffered. Restless barbarian Germanic tribes breached the Danube and Rhine river barriers and sifted and sometimes streamed into the Roman-held lands. Many of these tribesmen were absorbed into the Roman legions; others found available space and settled down; but they were an advance notice to the Romans of the stirring of a hive of men who, once in swarm toward the western portion of the Empire, might not be so peacefully absorbed.

## Diocletian

The barbarian tribes were held off for a time, and the decline of Rome was delayed for some years, by the able rule of two emperors: Diocletian (284-305 A.D.) and Constantine (307-337 A.D.). Diocletian was the son of a peasant who had risen to be a general. He was a strong-willed administrator and reformer who changed the face of the Empire. He centralized the government, divided the Empire into a greater number of provinces, and grouped the provinces into thirteen administrative units called *dioceses*. The entire Empire was then divided into two parts. A Latin-speaking part included

Gaul, Spain, Britain, North Africa, and Italy; the other part was made up of Greek-speaking areas and included Greece and the Middle East. Diocletian chose a co-emperor to govern the western division, while he spent much of his time in the eastern portion of the Empire.

### Constantine

Diocletian's reforms were continued and completed under Constantine, who also legalized Christianity. Until this time, the Christians had been persecuted spasmodically, depending upon the temperament of the ruling emperor and the condition of the Empire. During the middle of the third century A.D., the juggling and the murdering of emperors left the Empire vulnerable to invaders from the outside and civil disturbances from within. At this time the Christians suffered renewed persecutions. Constantine halted this practice. The story is told that when he was battling a rival for the throne of Rome, he saw a cross blazing in the sky and under it the words: "By this sign you will conquer." He won the battle. In 313 A.D. he legalized Christianity in the Edict of Milan, and he, too, became a Christian.

Constantine built a new capital for the Roman Empire on the site of the ancient Greek city of Byzantium, and named it Constantinople. Constantine governed alone for a period, but later it became the practice to have two emperors—one in Rome, the other in Constantinople. The emperor who lived in Rome ruled the dying portion of the Empire. Many reasons for the death of western Rome have been put forward by scholars. They all agree that the demise of this part of the Empire, which they place around 476 A.D., was not a sudden, unexpected event. It was the result of a slow decay which had been weakening Rome's inner strength for several centuries.

### Reasons for Decline

The moral fiber of the Romans had disintegrated as their power and wealth expanded. Though Roman leaders paid lip service to the old virtues of responsibility and simplicity, their personal lives were often selfish and luxurious. Perhaps this decline in private morals was in part responsible for the decay of the Senate, the army, the economy, and other public institutions. The numbers of the poor continued to swell, and their lot grew more miserable. They became accustomed to depending upon handouts from the government. The government was near bankruptcy. Taxes were raised to meet the costs of government, the increased demands of the soldiers, and the rising costs of feeding the poor.

Under Diocletian and later emperors, occupations became hereditary, and the worker was bound to the fields he tilled or the industry he served. He could not move, and his sons inherited his occupation. This policy encouraged stagnation and a caste system. As plagues decimated large areas of Italy, the population decreased. There was a lack of vigor and self-reliance. The Romans had little will and desire to resist when the roving tribes from beyond the Danube and Rhine rivers moved with their families and their wagonloads of possessions into the western regions of the Empire. With the arrival of these newcomers and their occupation of the western portions of the Empire, Roman glory and control in the West withered and were lost.

## Other Men Replaced the Romans

Beyond the Danube and Rhine rivers, which generally marked the eastern boundaries of the European portion of the Empire, Teutonic, or German, tribes had been multiplying on the borders of the Baltic Sea for centuries. They spoke languages that belonged to the Indo-European language group. The resources of their land could not keep pace with their rapidly increasing numbers. Branches of these tribes occasionally broke away and moved southward into central Europe and southern Russia. From time to time they also tested the strength of Roman arms at the frontier. Over the centuries of Roman rule in Europe, some of these German people seeped through to settle lands under Roman control, and some even became valiant soldiers of the legions of

The picture shows the falls of the Rhine. For 400 years the Rhine was a boundary between the Romans and German tribes. (Swiss National Tourist Office)

Rome. The Roman historian Tacitus praised the virtues of their home life, loyalty, and courage as a contrast to the moral weakness of the Romans.

In the prime of their might, the Romans withstood the pressure fermenting from these tribes upon the threshold of their domain. But as Roman will and firmness waned, defenses were overrun in greater numbers by those who robbed, plundered, and stayed in the territory the Romans once called their own. Often these tribes had no choice but to invade the Roman land, for a savage horde of horsemen called Huns thundered upon them from Central Asia and drove them in terror along avenues which led to Rome. It will be remembered that the Indians and the Chinese also tasted the bitterness of the Huns. The seepage of Teutons into the western part of the Empire became a flood during the fourth and fifth centuries.

### The Visigoths

The first of the barbarian tribes to shatter the foundations of Roman confidence and morale were called Visigoths (West Goths). The Visigoths had moved from their Baltic homes to the shores of the Black Sea around 200 A.D. There they encountered the scourge of the Huns. They fled in haste from these terrible men, crossed the Danube, and entered the eastern portion of the Roman Empire. Suspicions and quarrels worsened relations, and in 378 A.D. the Visigoths and Romans fought a great battle at Adrianople—north of Con-

The Huns, Magyars, and Turks invaded Europe through the Danube valley. (Austrian Information Service)

stantinople. The Visigoths won this battle, and they continued to wander and to plunder in the southern Balkans. Besides being the first great victory over the Romans, the battle of Adrianople clearly showed the superiority of cavalry over the foot soldiers of Rome. After this defeat, the Romans began to use the horse more in war, and the horse continued to be important in war for the next thousand years in Europe.

At last the Visigoths roamed into Italy where, under their chief Alaric, they stormed and plundered the city of Rome about 410 A.D. The Romans shuddered and feared as they viewed these two great defeats—one in the East and one in the West—which struck down their city of Rome for the first time in almost eight hundred years.

The Visigoths moved southward toward Sicily. Alaric died on the way and he was buried in the bed of a river. The Romans granted the Visigoths a tract of land called Aquitaine in southern Gaul. They went northward across the Alps and settled down in this land. Later, they went into Spain and added much of this country to the land they ruled. In 507 A.D. the Visigoths lost their land in Gaul to a tribe called Franks, and in the eighth century, the Moslems took Spain from them. Thus the Visigoths did not survive as a nation. They were, however, an example of how the German tribes contributed to the fall of western Rome and the division of the land of Europe.

### The Huns

There were none among men who frightened Germans and Romans alike more than the Huns. Glued to their horses, hardened from childhood to the exposure of the elements, and dressed in ill-smelling tatters of animal hides or cloth, the Huns galloped in hordes from the depths of Central Asia. They stunned the Germans with the fury of their onslaught and the savagery of their deeds. Killing and enslaving the Slavs and Germans, they pushed on to grasp a great part of the Danube plain. Under the fierce leadership of Attila, who boasted that he was "the scourge of God," the Huns sought to take all Europe. The eastern emperor paid them money to stay away from Constantinople. They moved into Gaul where they were defeated in 451 by the Roman general, Aëtius. The Huns then retreated across the Rhine, and the following year marched in hordes against the city of Rome. The tale is told that they were stopped from robbing and burning Rome by Pope Leo the Great. The Huns left Italy, Attila died, and a plague decimated their numbers. They rode back to the plains of Central Asia where they had first learned their contempt for life and their capacity for endurance.

### The Teutons Flood In

Scattered and fleeing before the savagery of the Huns, the Teutonic tribes of Germany moved into many parts of Europe. The Romans could not contain them, for Roman might had grown feeble and the Romans were unable to defend even their cherished city. A German leader, Odoacer, removed the co-emperor from Rome in 476. This date has been used to mark the end of the Roman Empire in the West. The Ostrogoths (East Goths) then roved into Italy. Under their educated leader, Theodoric, they governed Italy for a time. The Ostrogoths were finally driven out, however, by the soldiers of Justinian, emperor of the eastern section of the remaining Roman Empire in the sixth century.

Earlier, a group called Vandals had rushed across Gaul and down into southern Spain, burning and looting as they swept along. In 429 they went from Spain to North Africa and possessed the land there. They built a navy, used it to capture Rome in 455, and thoroughly plundered the city of its centuries of gathered treasures. Their looting was so ruinous that the word *vandalism* has become synonymous with senseless destruction.

The Burgundians settled in the Rhone Valley of what is now France. They plunged their roots productively into this valley, and even today their descendants are famous for the goodness of their wine and the tastiness of

The Arch of Constantine, above, is in Rome. It commemorates the military victories of Constantine, who was Roman emperor from 306 to 337 A.D. (Moore-McCormack Lines) The cup at right is a fine example of Roman skill in glassmaking. (The Corning Museum of Glass)

their produce. The Lombards followed the passes of the Alps and lodged themselves firmly in the Po Valley. There is still a Lombardy in Italy. The Angles, the Saxons, and the Jutes, generally known by the shorter name of Anglo-Saxons, pirated by sea the area from the shores of the North Sea to Britain. They impressed their traditions, attitudes, and blood so solidly upon this island that we still speak of the Anglo-Saxon British, Anglo-Saxon language, and Anglo-Saxon tradition.

### The Coming of Change

The many years of invasion and rule by warlike Germanic tribes brought gradual and inevitable changes in the social, political, and economic life of Europe. The Teutonic tribesmen were warriors, farmers, and herders of animals. Their laws and customs were suited to this way of life. They knew the harshness of war and the hunt and the basic needs of the body. Their social relationships were based upon the kind of life they knew. They had not learned to build and govern cities, and they had not developed a complex economic and social structure based upon peaceful commerce. Learning was of small importance to them, and they had not been educated to the advantages of the arts and sciences. It was natural, therefore, that during the period of war and chaos in which the North European tribes replaced the Romans, there was a decline of the arts, a neglect of the skilled crafts, a stifling of commerce, and a deterioration of learning. But as time crept along and the tribesmen settled down in the territories they had wrenched from the Roman, there was a fusion of Roman and Germanic ways. The systems of feudalism and manorialism which came to characterize medieval Europe were made up of a blending of Roman and Germanic customs. The influence of both the Romans and the Germanic tribes was witnessed in the evolving Europeans.

Many Roman ideas and some of the Roman structure of government were also preserved by the Christian Church, which was emerging as a strong organized institution during this period. Moreover, the Byzantine Empire, which was governed from Constantinople, conserved and conveyed to later generations much of the best of the Greek and Roman civilizations.

1. What administrative changes did the Emperor Diocletian make to secure the Empire against the barbarians?
2. How were the Visigoths able to sack Rome in 410 A.D.?
3. Describe the various barbarian tribes who moved into the western Roman Empire.

## The Men of the Church

During the first century A.D., the Apostles and disciples of Jesus went forth upon the peaceful highways and waterways of the Roman Empire and spoke in the many tongues of man about His life and teachings. Some abandoned the highroads and sought out those beyond the Roman-guarded borders, but mostly they stayed within the boundaries of the Empire. Christian teachers and missionaries continued to spread their religion in the years that followed and Christian communities grew up in Asia Minor, Greece, Egypt, and in the city of Rome itself.

The Romans were generally tolerant of all religions, but from time to time there was persecution of the Christians. A number of Romans regarded the Christians as enemies

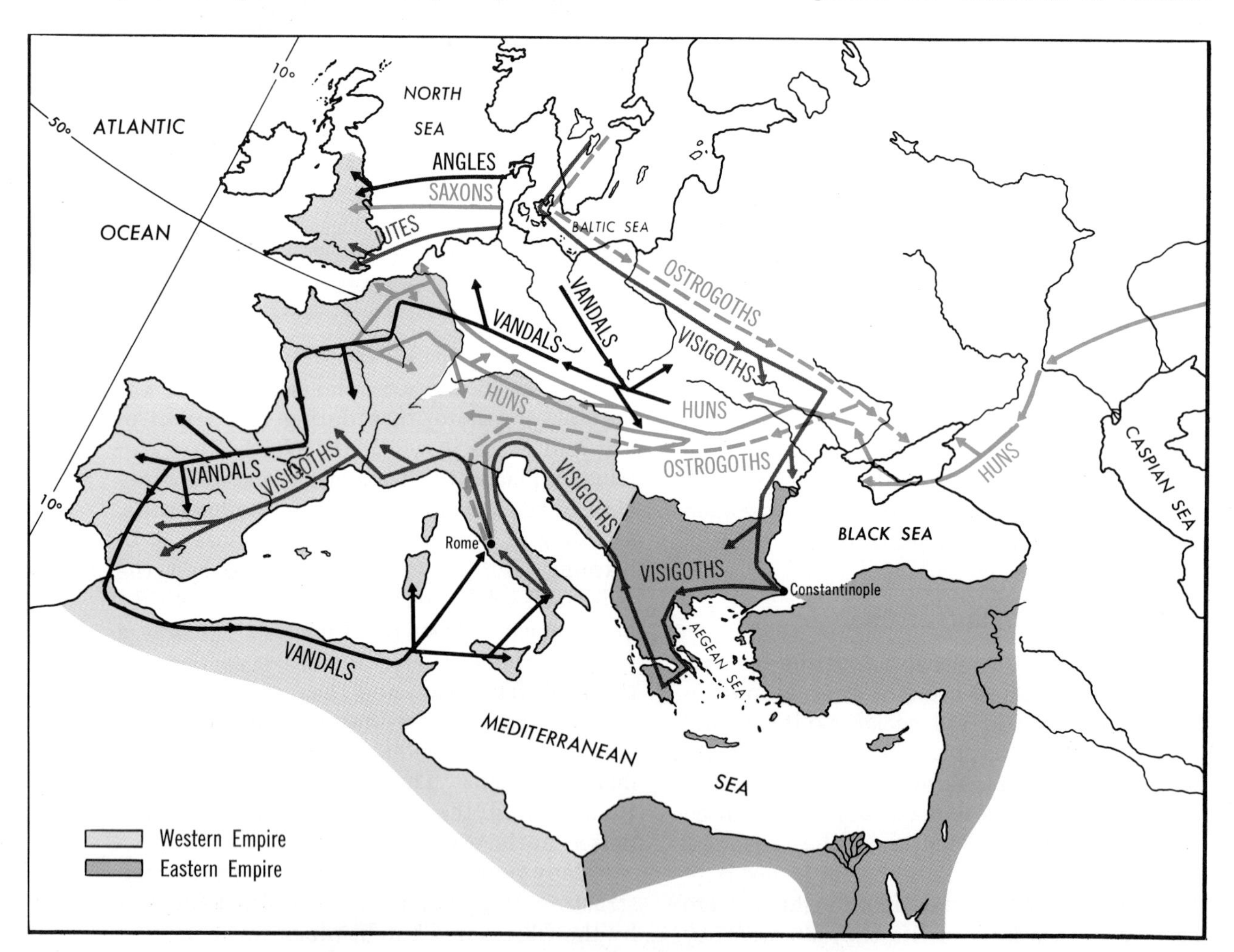


**BARBARIAN INVASIONS AND THE DIVISION OF THE ROMAN EMPIRE**

During the fourth and fifth centuries A.D. the Roman Empire crumbled before the onslaughts of invading Germanic tribes. The Empire was divided into an eastern and a western part. The Western Empire was taken by the Germanic invaders, but the Byzantine Empire, ruled from Constantinople, continued for several hundred years.

of the state because they refused to offer incense and wine before the statue of the emperor or because they refused to serve in the Roman army. But Christianity grew and spread and was legalized by the Emperor Constantine in 313 A.D. in the Edict of Milan. Under one of Constantine's successors, Theodosius (378-395 A.D.), the worship of all heathen gods was forbidden and Christianity was made mandatory. The spirits and gods of the Romans and their subjects were replaced by the Christian God, and Christianity has been the focus of European religious beliefs and attention ever since.

## Organization of a Church

As the Christians increased in numbers, they organized their Church. In their younger years —when they were few and scattered—gatherings of Christians were presided over by an overseer, known in Greek as an *episcopos*, from which the words *bishop* and *episcopal* are derived. The bishop or overseer was assisted by elders called *presbyters;* it is from this name that the words *priest* and *Presbyterian* stem. The name *Christian* comes from the Greek word *Christos*, meaning "the Anointed" or Messiah. As the Christians made more and more converts, their administrative system necessarily grew in order to better minister to the spiritual wants of Christian people everywhere.

The Christian subjects of Rome followed Roman political divisions in administering their widely spreading churches and congregations. A local group, or *parish*, of Christians was ministered to by a *pastor* who was appointed by a bishop. The bishop governed a territorial unit called a *diocese*, which incorporated many parishes. A number of dioceses were grouped within a *province*. In the capital of the province there lived a church official of higher level known in Western Europe as an *archbishop* and in the eastern part of the Roman Empire as a *patriarch* or *metropolitan*. Rome had long been the center of governmental power; it was natural for the Christians to think of the bishop of Rome as holding a central position in the organization of the Church. The position of the bishop of Rome (who was later called *pope*) was strengthened by the doctrine of "Petrine supremacy." This doctrine affirms that the pope, as the successor of Peter, to whom Christ had given the headship of the Church, is the divinely appointed head of the Church. Some early popes, such as Leo the Great (440-461 A.D.) and Gregory the Great (590-604 A.D.), strengthened this claim of papal supremacy by a vigor-

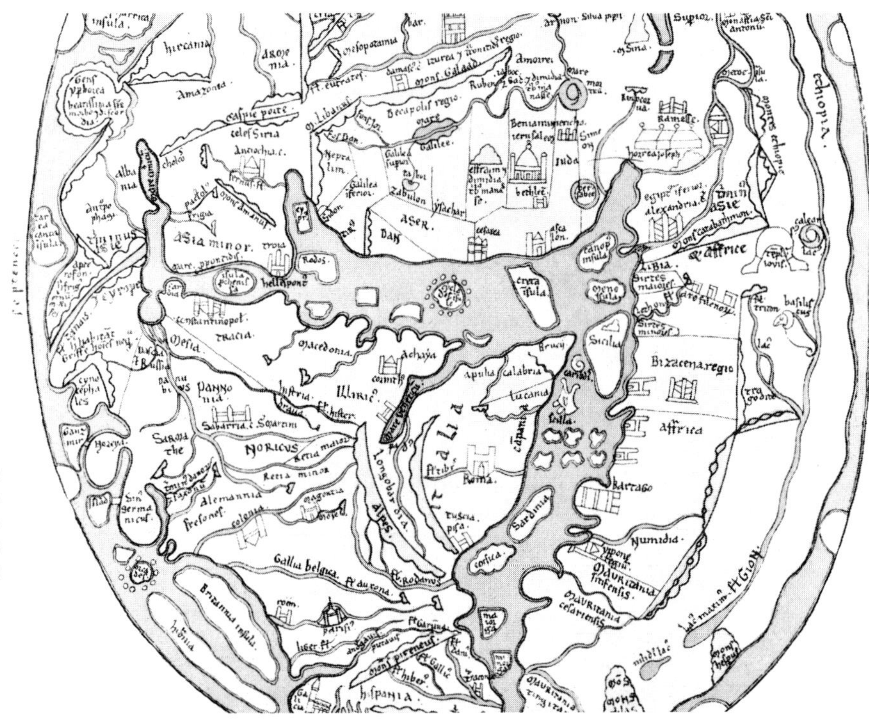


The Romans thought of the earth as being flat and drew their maps accordingly. This portion of a Roman map of the early Christian era places Rome at the center of the known world. (Library of Congress)

ous and successful assertion of their authority, at least in the western part of the former Roman Empire. The eastern Christians, however, did not accept the supreme authority of the Roman pope.

## The Eastern Christians

The Christians living in the eastern portion of the Roman Empire challenged the supremacy of the bishop of Rome. They gradually began to look to the patriarch and the emperor living in their capital of Constantinople as their leaders. The Christians of the eastern and western parts of the former Roman Empire slowly began to drift apart. As time passed, the eastern Christians began to refer to their church as the Eastern Orthodox or the Greek Orthodox Church to distinguish it from the Roman Catholic Church. Use of the Greek language in the Eastern Orthodox Church instead of Latin and differing church ceremonies are evidence of the division between the two churches over the years. This separation has lasted until the present day.

The Christians of both the East and the West survived the catastrophes which befell the Roman Empire in the fifth century. Their survival in an organized form meant not only the continuation of the Christian faith, but also the survival of much that was of value in the civilizations of Greece and Rome. In their monasteries and churches, the clergy preserved great works of the past which later flourished and further expanded the beliefs and thoughts of man about his spiritual and material world.

### Byzantine Empire

The eastern Romans and those who came after them were not merely preservers of the thoughts and works of the Greek and Roman; they also created in their own right much that was good. They often referred to themselves as Romans, spoke a special form of Greek, and were a mixture of many men and many cultures from which they evolved a culture of their own known as Byzantine. Their name was derived from the original Greek name of their capital—Byzantium.

It was on the site of Byzantium that Constantine located his capital—Constantinople. This city became the capital of the Byzantine Empire. It had a strategic location. Three sides of the city were protected by the Sea of Marmara, and the land side was protected by almost impenetrable walls. Constantinople lay next to the Bosporus, which was the waterway from the Black Sea to the Sea of Marmara, across from the coasts of Asia Minor. It marked the end of the trade routes from Asia and the beginning of the trade routes from Europe. In the hands of capable men, this geographically valuable city could be used to influence the destinies of man in Europe and the Middle East. And the Byzantines had their share of capable rulers.

### Emperors

Justinian (527-565) reunited many portions of the divided Roman Empire. His soldiers retook North Africa from the Vandals, Italy from the Ostrogoths, and the southern part of Spain from the Visigoths. He resurrected Roman law from the time of Hadrian (117-138), codified it, and thus made justice under law available to man then and in the future. Heraclius (610-641) recaptured the provinces which had been lost to the Persians in the Middle East; and he returned the supposed True Cross to its hallowed sanctuary in Jerusalem. Basil I, of Armenia, and his successors held off the vigorous Arabs who had found a unity and an ideal under the stimulus of Islam. Basil II defeated the powerful Bulgarians and protected the poor. By the time of his death in 1025 he had restored the Empire to almost the full glory of its ancient days.

### A Christian Atmosphere

The Byzantines breathed a Christian atmosphere; it was a wanted and necessary part of their lives. From the emperor down to the most ordinary man, religious matters were discussed and debated as fiercely as political

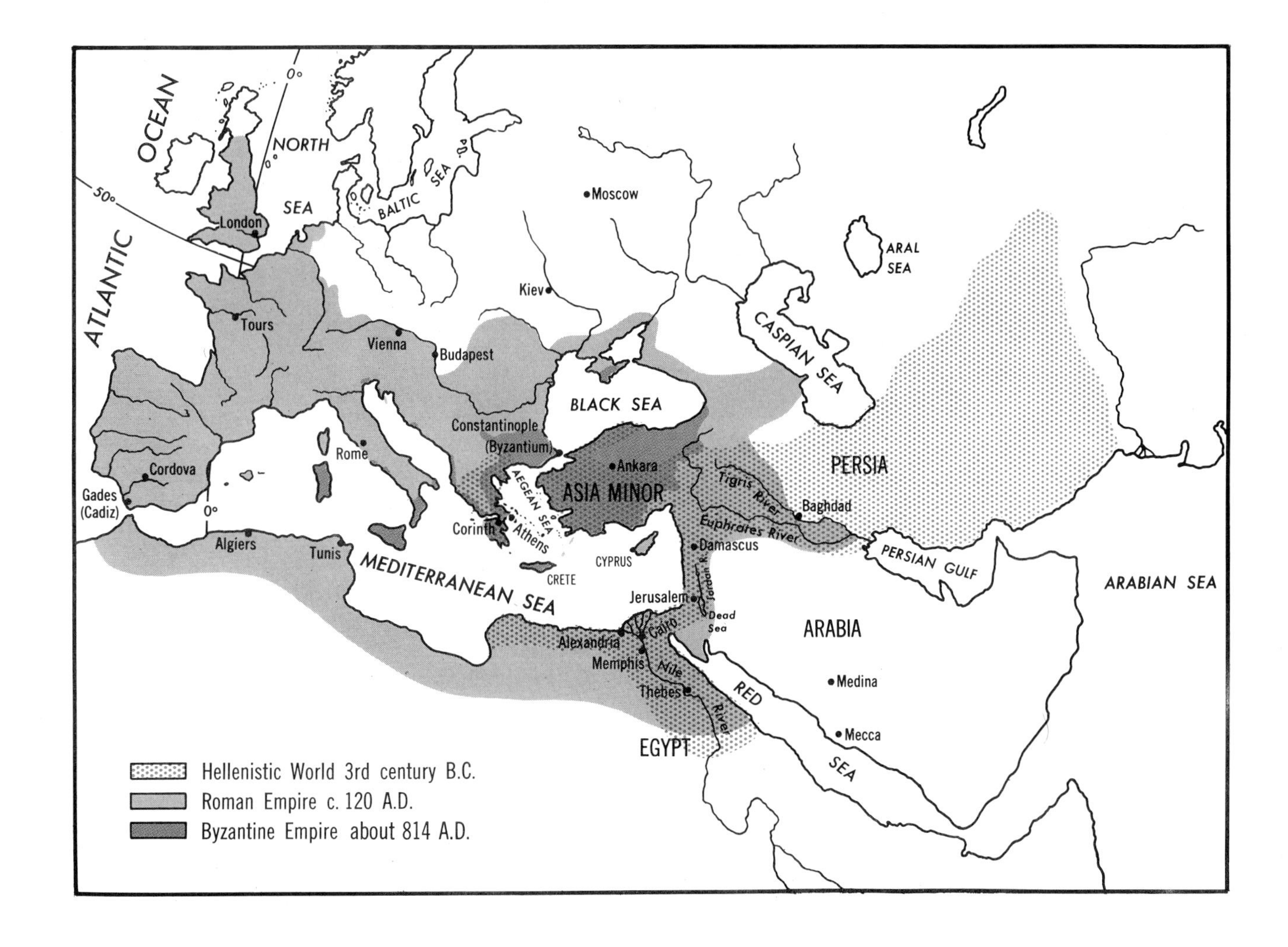


**BACKGROUND AND GROWTH OF THE BYZANTINE EMPIRE**

The lands that formed the Byzantine Empire had once belonged to the empire of Alexander the Great. For several centuries they were a part of the empire of Rome. For centuries after the fall of Rome, the Byzantine Empire continued to flourish, blending the cultures of East and West.

controversies, which indeed they often were. Religion and politics were intertwined. The emperor was not divine, but he was supported by the divine, and he was regarded by the Byzantines as God's agent. He had more to say about religious affairs than the patriarch of Constantinople, whom he selected, but there were doctrinal limits beyond which he found it wise not to venture.

The Christians debated and even bloodied each other over the question of the exact relationship between Father, Son, and Holy Ghost in the doctrine of the Trinity. They hotly disputed whether the nature of Jesus was human or divine, or both. When some emperors tried to remove icons from Byzantine worship, they encountered such fanatic resistance that they were eventually compelled to return the icons to the adoring eyes of the Byzantines. *Icons* were images of the Virgin Mary, Jesus, or the saints—painted, in bas-relief, or in mosaic—and a person who opposed their use in religious worship was called an *iconoclast* or breaker of images. We use this

The Byzantine earring of gold, pearls, and emerald, top, dates from the seventh century A.D. The pyx, or container for the Eucharist, below, is also Byzantine. It dates from the sixth century. (Both photos, Courtesy of The Cleveland Museum of Art)

word today to describe a person who attacks established beliefs as false.

## Crusaders

The Byzantines were brave, well-led, and well-equipped soldiers and sailors. They possessed the secret of Greek fire which they shot from tubes or threw in grenades; there were few who could withstand its fierce flame. They always went into battle behind a holy icon. Centuries before the Europeans thought of crusading to the Middle East, the Byzantines had been waging their own crusades. Every war was a crusade in their eyes. Their keen diplomacy was directed toward maintaining control of the Holy Land. The Byzantine missionary brothers, Cyril and Methodius, carried the Christian faith to the Slavs. They are said by some to have invented the alphabet which is still in use by the Russians, Serbs, and Bulgarians. It is called the Cyrillic alphabet in honor of Cyril. The Byzantines did not separate their religion from their politics, or daily routine of life—it was an inseparable part of their civilization.

## Christian Artists

Nowhere are the depths of Byzantine religious emotion expressed with greater feeling and beauty than in the church of St. Sophia. It was built by the Emperor Justinian in the sixth century and is a harmonious fusion of the Greek, Roman, and Middle Eastern influences. It is yet considered one of the architectural triumphs of the Byzantine Christian. The magnificent dome surmounting this church has been described as suspended from the sky by a chain rather than resting upon a solid base. The exterior was made simply, but the interior was magnificently decorated with paintings of grace and richness and with *mosaics*—small pieces of colored stone which the artists cemented together to create glowing pictures. The architecture of this church was copied by the Turks in the building of their mosques after they took Constantinople in 1453. Perhaps Justinian was correct when he boasted that he had outdone Solomon in the building of a temple.

The Byzantines fashioned exquisite icons for public and private worship. The beauty of these religious images drew from the viewer a deeper feeling for the divine. Byzantine artists and craftsmen worked with colored marble, made chairs and statues of well-carved ivory, illuminated manuscripts with vivid miniature paintings and elaborate letters, enameled book-covers, and turned out a wealth of products in gold, silver, and precious stones. Their products were welcomed and imitated in Western Europe, Russia, and the Middle East, and the influence of Byzantine creations is still obvious to the traveler in these lands.

St. Sophia, in Istanbul, is one of the finest examples of Byzantine architecture. (Turkish Tourism and Information Office) St. Peter's, in Rome, is an outstanding example of Italian Renaissance architecture. (Italian State Tourist Office)

### The Poor Suffered

The Christianity that the Byzantines professed did not always moderate the oppression and avarice of the rich and the powerful. Throughout much of the time the Empire existed, the poor were frequently made poorer and enslaved by influential landowners and merchants. As in Italy, there were those in the countryside who took advantage of the small farmer who could not pay his taxes or whose crop failed by absorbing his land into their own. It did not matter if this was done illegally; it only mattered that the land be taken. Some of the better emperors attempted to stop this practice and curb the advancing power of the big landowners. But the growth of great landholdings and the complaints of the dispossessed became a permanent part of the rural landscape of the Byzantines. The independence of many of the small farmers was lost, and this loss weakened the spirit and morale of those from whom the emperor drew his recruits for the armed services.

### A Rich Empire

The Byzantines were part of a rich empire. From everywhere the riches of trade poured into the city and the empire. Hides, furs, ivory, gold, silver, spices, jewels, slaves, wine, and foods of all varieties funneled into Constantinople daily from near and distant places. The city ranked among the most prosperous trading hubs of the world. One of the greatest sources of income in Constantinople was the export of silk.

Silk cloth was the invention of the Chinese, who tried to keep its manufacture a secret; but, like many secrets, it leaked out, first to the Indians and Persians, and later to the Byzantines. Silk is the product of the silkworm, which feeds on mulberry leaves. Large farms of mulberries were established in various parts of the empire, and the silk industry began to flourish. Because of the value of this product to the economic life of the Byzantines, silk was made a government monopoly and placed under government control. The returns were enormous.

The emperor kept a solid gold foundation under his economy by forbidding the export of gold. Byzantine coins were rarely debased, and consequently this coinage was accepted as standard throughout many parts of Europe and the East. The *bezant*, a gold coin valued at almost six dollars, circulated among the Byzantines and Europeans for more than seven hundred years without a change in value. Prosperous in their trade, dazzling in the glories of their arts, the Byzantines overawed visitors from western and eastern Europe who had not achieved such civilized splendor. The visitor from the West was impressed but he was also jealous and envious—and a certain unfriendliness between the Byzantines and the Western Europeans expressed itself on many occasions.

### Fall of the Byzantine Empire

Political differences between the popes in Rome and the Byzantine emperors existed as early as the eighth century, when the Byzantine emperor removed certain Balkan areas from the jurisdiction of the pope and gave them to the patriarch of Constantinople. Friction continued between the two in later centuries as the Normans from France invaded southern Italy. These invaders took Byzantine churches and territory, which were placed under the jurisdiction of the pope. Then a doctrinal difference between the two sets of Christians was introduced, and on this point a *schism*, or division, separated the two Christian communities in 1054. The breach has never been healed to this day.

The two Christian churches of the East and West were brought closer together, however, when the Moslem Seljuk Turks began to make inroads into the Byzantine Empire and the Holy Land. Answering the appeal of Pope Urban II in the eleventh century, crusaders from Europe went in a series of expeditions to the Middle East to fight for control of the Holy Land. In 1204, however, the Fourth Crusade, instead of sailing to the Holy Land, went to Constantinople. It stormed and plundered this Christian city as though it were the stronghold of a hated infidel. The Byzantines

The Book of Kells was made at Columba's monastery in Ireland during the 700's or 800's. It is an illuminated manuscript. (Irish Tourist Board)

The art of making tapestries has been known since ancient times, but it reached its height in Europe during the Middle Ages and Renaissance. At the left is a Gobelin tapestry from France. (French Government Tourist Office)

regained their city in 1261, but this sack of their city considerably reduced their former strength. As others increased in power around them, their relative power continued to decline. In Asia Minor, the Ottoman Turks grew stronger. In 1453, denied help from others, the Byzantine capital of Constantinople fell to the Turks and the Byzantine Empire ended. Byzantium is known today as Istanbul, and it is still under Turkish control.

1. How did the early Christians organize their Church?
2. What were some of the most important contributions of the Byzantine emperors?
3. How did the Byzantine emperors combine political and religious roles?

## The European Church in the Middle Ages

While the Byzantines were struggling to maintain unity in their empire, the Europeans were becoming less unified. Kings, knights, and daring raiders competed to divide and subdivide the territory of Europe. Everywhere there was the motion of combat. Knights in chain-mail armor rode to battle on heavy-muscled horses,

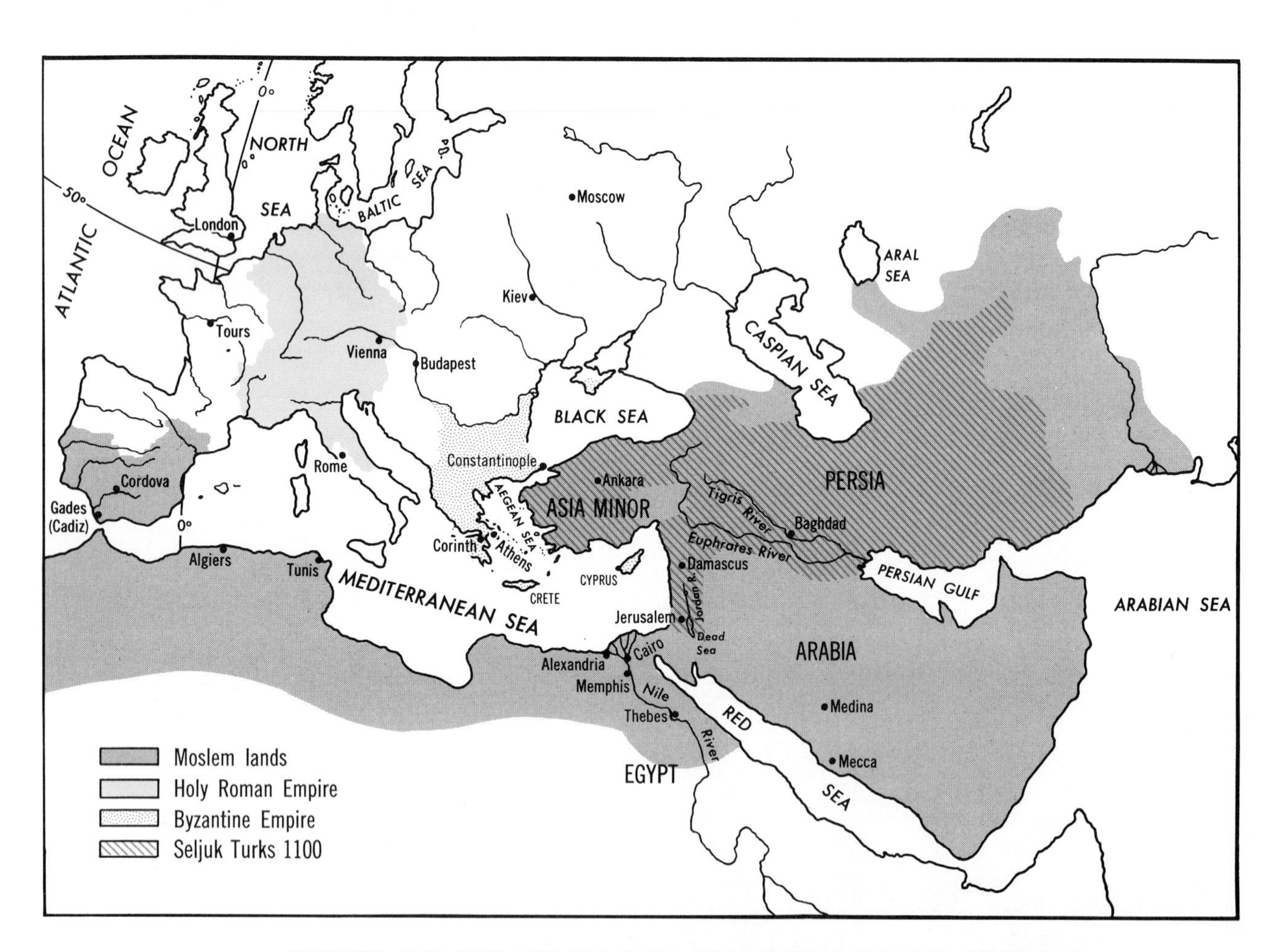


**EUROPE AND THE MIDDLE EAST AT THE TIME OF THE CRUSADES**

Between 1055 and 1057 the Seljuk Turks conquered much of the Middle East and they presented a threat to the Byzantine Empire. The map shows the extent of Moslem lands. The Holy Roman Empire was actually a collection of many tiny states, each with its own ruler, but it represented the greatest power in Europe at the time.

and bowmen and pikemen trudged behind them in deadly lines. Villages and towns huddled for protection near massive castles perched on hill and crag, and sometimes there was no protection after war engines opened the strong gates of the castles or reduced their thick walls to rubble. The sounds of Europe were the steady thump of hooves and feet marching to some war and the whispered intrigues of the powerful as they plotted for small or great pieces of land.

The Europeans who lived in the period between the fifth and the fifteenth centuries were growing, energetic men. This period of their history is known as the Middle Ages. It was not a comfortable period of time. Luxuries were few, even for the rich, and the serf was tied to a small plot of soil which he could not leave without the consent of his noble master. Pestilence and war made life uncertain for everyone. Communication between communities was made difficult by robber bands and the lack of roads.

The Europeans of this time frequently channeled their abundant energy into lusty living and were capable of the wildest enthusiasms. They were often motivated by the highest ideals, which they sometimes used to excuse the lowest of acts. Except for the churchmen, they were but little interested in books, except those that told a tale of romance or spoke of the deeds of shining knights. Even these stories were heard chiefly through the lips of wandering storytellers, for the people of Europe were generally illiterate. The Europeans of this age displayed a simplicity of action not yet made complicated by much questioning and original thought. However they possessed one thing that gave to their lives certainty and security —their Church.

### The Church, Their Security

Amidst the puzzle of scrambled political authorities and the uncertainties of existence, there stood an unshakable institution which gave the Europeans guidance in their life on earth—the Roman Catholic Church. It did not matter that life was rough, that there was much man did not know, nor that he strayed at times; the European had an inner certainty that all would end well if he remained faithful to the Church. It was the Church which gave stability to his life, hope to his future, and stored for the European and his descendants the wisdom of the past and a feeling for learning.

### The Pope, Their Father

The pope headed the Church and in the Church he held the authority of God on earth. There were some who sought to use the pope for their personal advancement and for material gain. There were also rebellious, powerful men who challenged the pope's authority to settle their quarrels. On one occasion, in 1305, the French king installed the pope in Avignon, where he and his successors lived for over seventy years, subject to the dictates of the French kings. But even away from Rome, the divine sanction of the papal office and of the pope's words were recognized. The pope was the divinely elected father of Christendom, and though some despised the man, they could not deny the authority of his office.

Strong and able popes had directed the molding of the Catholic European. Pope Gregory the Great, who reigned from 590 to 604, was the secular political ruler of the city of Rome as well as head of the Church. He expanded the membership of the Church throughout Europe. His missionaries converted the threatening Lombards in north Italy, the Anglo-Saxons in England, and the Visigoths in Spain. Before he died, he was the respected father of a greatly enlarged European family of Catholics.

Gregory VII, in the eleventh century, forced the proud Emperor of Germany, Henry IV, to journey from Germany to Italy and to stand barefoot, robed in burlap, for three wintry days outside the papal residence at Canossa in penance for his opposition to the pope's authority. Innocent III (1198-1216) regarded kings and emperors as his subordinates and described their positions in comparison to the papacy as like the dim light of the moon compared to the brilliant and powerful light of the sun.

**Weapons of consequence.** The pope had weapons of terrible consequence which he used occasionally to teach the advantages of obedience and to remind men of their duties. Chief of these weapons were *excommunication* and *interdict*. Excommunication was the cutting off of an individual from the solace and sacraments of the Church. The excommunicated Catholic was ostracized by his community of fellow Catholics.

Interdict was excommunication applied more widely to an entire country or region. If punishment, or the threat of punishment, is to be effective, it must be fitted to time and circumstance. The European during this period was a very religious man. He shuddered to think that his soul might burn in hell forever, which was a possibility if he remained under the ban of excommunication or interdict. Whether king or noble, merchant or serf, he wanted no part of a life without the comforts of the Church. Consequently, the mere threat of applying these punishments to an offender was usually sufficient to bring him back into line. The stronger popes, such as Gregory VII, did not hesitate to threaten these punishments when their will was being thwarted.

## The Clergy

Under the pope were other Church officials. The *cardinals* were the advisors of the popes, and after the eleventh century, the cardinals elected all new popes. The other ranks of officials were the *archbishops*, the bishops, and the priests. Most frequently the higher ranks of the clergy came from the nobility, while the parish priests were of peasant stock. But this statement should not hide the fact that an intelligent man of peasant blood could sometimes rise high in the ranks of the Church. There were few opportunities for the sons of the lowly born to become educated and elevate themselves to high position, but the Church offered one way, and some availed themselves of this opportunity.

Because pope, cardinal, archbishop, bishop, and priest lived and worked in the world of man, they are known as *secular* clergy. Those, however, who preferred to retire from the hustle of life and live in quiet contemplation apart from the materialism of the secular world were called *monks*, and the places in which they lived were *monasteries*. The monks were distinguished from the other clergy by the name *regular*, which stems from the Latin word *regula*, meaning "a set of rules." Strict rules governed the life of the monks, for they sought a heightened spiritual life, undistracted by material pleasures and comforts.

Women, too, went apart from the world to lead lives of prayer and contemplation or to serve in charitable works. Convents existed in the Middle East and elsewhere as early as the fourth century A.D. Often the orders established for monks formed the pattern for parallel organizations for women. The sister of St. Benedict, for instance, adapted the rules her brother had laid down for Benedictine monks to her own convent. Women have continued to organize religious orders up until the present day, and many of these orders are especially known for their work in education and in caring for the sick, the aged, the handicapped, and the needy.

The Church was the citadel of learning during the brawling period of the Middle Ages. Many of the lower clergy were poorly educated; but a number of this rank, as well as those of higher rank, were also eager teachers and scholars. The Church and the clergy were so closely identified with education in this period of uneducated laymen that all a man had to do to show that he was a member of the clergy was to read a part of the Bible.

**Contributions of the monks.** Among churchmen, it was the man of the monastery, the monk, who contributed most to the learning of the Middle Ages. Within the silence imposed by his rules and guarded by monastery walls, the monk studied, meditated, wrote, taught, and copied what he thought to be the best of the ancient classics. It must also be said, however, that due to lack of knowledge the medieval copyists often destroyed ancient manuscripts of classical works, and many of these works were lost forever.

The city of Lübeck was the head of the great Hanseatic trading league of the medieval period. Its fortified gateway, built in the 1400's is an example of northern Gothic brick architecture. (German Tourist Information Office)

The medieval marketplace was a square in the center of the town. A fine example is this square in a German town. (German Tourist Information Office)

The manuscript copyists sometimes brightened their handiwork by introducing chapters and pages with colorful and artistic large capital letters. These *illuminated* manuscripts are a part of the heritage that has been passed down from the Middle Ages. Documents and manuscripts were collected in the monasteries, and gradually libraries grew up. The monasteries also became centers of learning where schools were conducted. These libraries and schools were often the only ones to be found in most of Europe.

The monks not only studied but also worked in the fields and gardens which surrounded their monasteries. They cultivated good grapes, reclaimed land from the swamps by drainage, and set a good example of the best farming practices then known. They worked with their hands to produce clothes, tools for work, and leather goods. Some monasteries became famed for the quality of their wine and beer, and the monasteries were often used as inns by weary travelers. They were also the charitable centers of European communities, where the poor could get clothes to replace their rags, and food if they were hungry.

The Benedictine monks, whose order was founded in the sixth century by St. Benedict, were also missionaries. They went forth from their monasteries to convert the non-Christians in Europe and elsewhere. In the thirteenth century, two other orders of religious men were founded, known as Franciscans and Dominicans after the names of their founders, St. Francis of Assisi and St. Dominic. The members of these groups, generally called *friars*, went among men to minister to spiritual and physical needs. They were dedicated to a life of service.

## The Christians Stood Supreme

The Christians and their Church now stood supreme throughout most of Europe. There was a Christian Church headquartered at Constantinople and a Christian Church centered in the city of Rome. Throughout most of the European continent the non-Christian was an oddity, and the rare person who denied Christian truths was considered a heretic surely doomed to the fires of hell. All knew the truth, and the truth was Christian. The Byzantine Christians also knew much of what the Greeks, Romans, and Middle Eastern men had said about philosophy, science, and other worldly and spiritual matters. But the European Christians had little knowledge of this ancient learning, and mostly did not care. A few monks scattered here and there in Western Europe were interested in these ancient subjects, but the majority were busy with the problems of daily living or expanding their power.

Few areas of European life during the Middle Ages were not touched deeply and continuously by the Church and the clergy. The Church was interested in the care of the body as well as the soul. Body and soul are closely linked in man on earth, but during this period in Western Europe there were few aside from the clergy who were concerned about the physical wants of others. The clergy also became involved in the economic, social, and political life of man during this period, and there was a distinctive character to these aspects of man's life in Western Europe during the Middle Ages. This special character was given to life by the system of feudalism, which will be described in the next chapter.

1. What was the only unifying focus of life in the Middle Ages?
2. What weapons did the Church possess to tame rebellious secular princes?

## Conclusion

While the Christians increased in numbers and influence, the Empire of Rome declined. Restless tribes from the frontiers began a movement that led them to Rome itself and the Empire in the West was engulfed in a time of chaos. But in the Eastern capital of Constantinople, there survived an empire and a culture known as Byzantine.

The Byzantines preserved for mankind the thought and knowledge of the Greeks and Romans. They copied the ancient Greek writings on science, philosophy, and other literature, and they commented upon them. Much of this work was done by monks. The schools of Constantinople were good, and education was respected among all classes. Scholars taught in the universities, learned men worked in the government bureaucracy, and the emperors themselves were patrons of the arts and pursuers of knowledge. The Arabs profited by the stored knowledge of Byzantium before the Europeans. They passed it along to the Europeans in their own language even before the Westerners knew the works yet existed in the original Greek. Man owes a debt to the many who came before him, and he owes something special to the Byzantines, who have sometimes been shamefully bypassed in the story of man's past.

Europe from the fifth to the fifteenth century passed through a period known as the Middle Ages. Held together only by their Church, and lacking the powerful force of an empire, the Europeans of the West developed their own way of life, which was quite different from that of the Byzantine. The organization of their Church gave a form and pattern to their lives, and the men of the Church contributed greatly to social and cultural life under the system known as feudalism.

## SUMMING UP THE CHAPTER

A. Identify the following and tell why they are important.

| | |
|---|---|
| Alaric | Justinian |
| Angles | Leo the Great |
| Attila | Lombards |
| Burgundians | Odoacer |
| Constantine | Ostrogoths |
| Diocletian | Ottoman Turks |
| Gregory the Great | Seljuk Turks |
| Huns | Theodoric |

B. Define or explain the following terms, relating them to this chapter.

| | |
|---|---|
| Christos | patriarch |
| episcopos | presbyters |
| interdict | regula |

C. Indicate the significance of the following dates.

| | |
|---|---|
| 1. 313 | 5. 1054 |
| 2. 378 | 6. 1204 |
| 3. 410 | 7. 1261 |
| 4. 476 | 8. 1453 |

D. Chapter review questions.

1. Why were the Christians persecuted by the Romans?
2. Why was the capital of the Roman Empire removed to Constantinople?
3. How did the Church and the bishop of Rome fill the vacuum created by the break-up of Roman secular authority?
4. Why did the split between the Roman and Byzantine churches develop along the lines of political division of the old Roman Empire?
5. How was the Church able to preserve so much of the Roman heritage?
6. Why was silk production made a government monopoly?
7. Describe the organization of the Church. What influence did this organizational form have on the power and ideas of the Church?
8. What was the only avenue for education and advancement among the peasantry? How did this influence the Church?
9. How did Byzantine monetary policies preserve the economic stability of the Empire?
10. What caused the schism between the Byzantine and Roman churches?
11. What were the most important organizational and doctrinal differences between the Byzantine and Roman churches?

E. Questions for discussion.

1. Was there any relationship between the rise of Christianity and the barbarian conquest of the Roman Empire? Explain.
2. What were the practical effects of making occupations hereditary?
3. Why did the Church find central organization so essential?
4. What were the motives of the popes in calling for the Crusades?
5. Why do you suppose the Roman pope did not attempt to prevent the fall of Constantinople to the infidel Turks?
6. How was the secular power of the Church made effective in the Middle Ages? Would this work today? Why?

F. Projects for groups or individuals.

1. Read Tacitus' *Germania* (it is quite short). Compare his description of the Teutonic tribes with his description of the decadent Romans (in the *Annals*).
2. Prepare a chart showing the Cyrillic alphabet alongside ours. What peoples today use the Cyrillic alphabet?
3. Collect a portfolio of pictures illustrating Byzantine art and architecture.
4. Prepare a report on the religious orders which developed during the Middle Ages.

# CHAPTER 18

# *Feudalism and a New Era*

THE INVADING TRIBES that had swept over the Roman Empire in the West continued their movements into Italy and the rest of Europe for several centuries. There were no strong rulers of great parts of the continent, and the lands that had known Roman rule were disunited.

A political system called *feudalism* and an economical system called *manorialism* grew up in Europe, and under these systems, the foundations for the structure of modern Europe were gradually formed.

## Emerging Kingdoms

The Franks and the Norsemen played important roles in the development of kingdoms in Europe during the Middle Ages. In order to take up our story of these peoples, it will be necessary to go back in time to the period when the Roman Empire in the West was crumbling, and tribes from the north and east began their movements across the Roman frontiers.

### The Franks

The Franks were among the last and most important of the German tribes to enter Gaul from east of the Rhine. Under their king, Clovis, these tribesmen established themselves as the rulers of much of the area known to the Romans as Gaul. They gave their name to France. Clovis became a Christian in 496 A.D., and he encouraged the conversion of many of his people. From this time onward there was close cooperation between the Franks and the Roman Catholic Church. France has sometimes been referred to as "the eldest daughter of the Church."

The Franks ruled for several centuries, but their rulers gradually degenerated into worthless, incompetent kings who have sometimes been referred to as the "do-nothing kings." High officials in the palace took over the real functions of king. One of the greatest of these officials was Charles Martel, who lived from about 689 to 741. In 732 he defeated the invading army of the Moslem Arabs and Moors at Tours, a place about one hundred miles from Paris. He bore no title other than Mayor of the Palace, but his son Pepin did take the title of king and ruled from 751 to 768.

**Charlemagne.** The Lombards, another Germanic tribe, were threatening to take over much of Italy at this time, and the Pope called

The Vikings knew the use of metal and made implements of iron, such as this ax head. (Courtesy of the American Museum of Natural History)

upon Pepin for help. Pepin obliged, marched into North Italy, and defeated the Lombards in several battles. He compelled them to return some of the lands they had seized. These became Church states under the rule of the papacy, and they remained under papal rule for many centuries. Pepin's son, Charlemagne, continued the conquests of his father and extended the territory of the Franks until it included most of the western portion of the old Roman Empire. Pope Leo III crowned Charlemagne Emperor of Rome in 800 A.D. Once again an emperor ruled most of the West, but he was a Frank, not a Roman. His crowning was the start of a later Holy Roman Empire and gave hope to the desire of many Europeans for stability and a unified Europe.

Charlemagne held his huge empire together by the strength of his personality and ability. He placed various parts of his empire under representatives called *counts* and *dukes*, whom he supervised closely by sending royal investigators, called *messengers*, to check their administration each year. To prevent possible disloyal agreements among his representatives, the messengers were sent to a different region each year. This system worked while Charlemagne lived, and it continued to work well under his son Louis; but the empire was divided among the three sons of Louis upon his death. One son received the territory of approximately what is now Germany, another much of what is now France, and the third son received the crown of emperor and the territory comprising northern Italy, the Low Countries, Alsace, and Lorraine, which lay somewhat between the lands of the other two brothers.

This division brought constant war to Europe. The middle kingdom was absorbed into the eastern part, and the central government was weakened as local lords asserted their independence from royal authority. These divisions of Europe were made sharper by continued invasions from various directions. The Moslems had already taken Spain, Sicily, and the islands of Corsica and Sardinia. Slavs were moving in central Europe, as were the Magyars, who founded the state of Hungary. But the most terrifying raiders to the Europeans were the Vikings, often called Northmen or Norsemen. Their appearance on the western shores of Europe brought fear and subjection to many Europeans. They were raiders and traders of the sea, and their homeland was the present region of Scandinavia.

## The Vikings

The Vikings were an amazingly adventurous lot of men. They dared to venture far into the uncharted seas in their small but sturdy ships. The Norwegian branch of their family settled Iceland and, under Eric the Red, traveled the cold sea lane to Greenland. Eric's son, Leif Ericson, compelled by the same searching spirit of his father, sailed and rowed even farther westward to the American coast around 1000 A.D. But the visit of the Northmen to America made no lasting impression. It was closer to home—in England, Ireland, France, and other European lands—that they made unforgettable and lasting impressions upon the people and the land.

The Danes, another group of Vikings, visited England during the ninth and tenth centuries and conquered large portions of the country. The Anglo-Saxons resisted, and under the rule of Alfred the Great, king of the West Saxons (871-899), most of England was united. At this time the Danes held only the eastern third of the country. Alfred took a great interest in learning and translated several works from Latin himself. It was during his reign that a record of events called the *Anglo-Saxon Chronicle* was begun. This record was continued after Alfred's death and is a source of information about Anglo-Saxon history. The Chronicle was kept from the late ninth century up to the year 1154.

In the year 1016, a Dane named Canute became King of England and ruled a northern empire which included Norway, Denmark, and England. But his line did not last long, and in 1042 the Saxon Edward the Confessor took over the throne from the Danes. In 1066, another branch of the Viking family crossed over to England from France, where they had taken

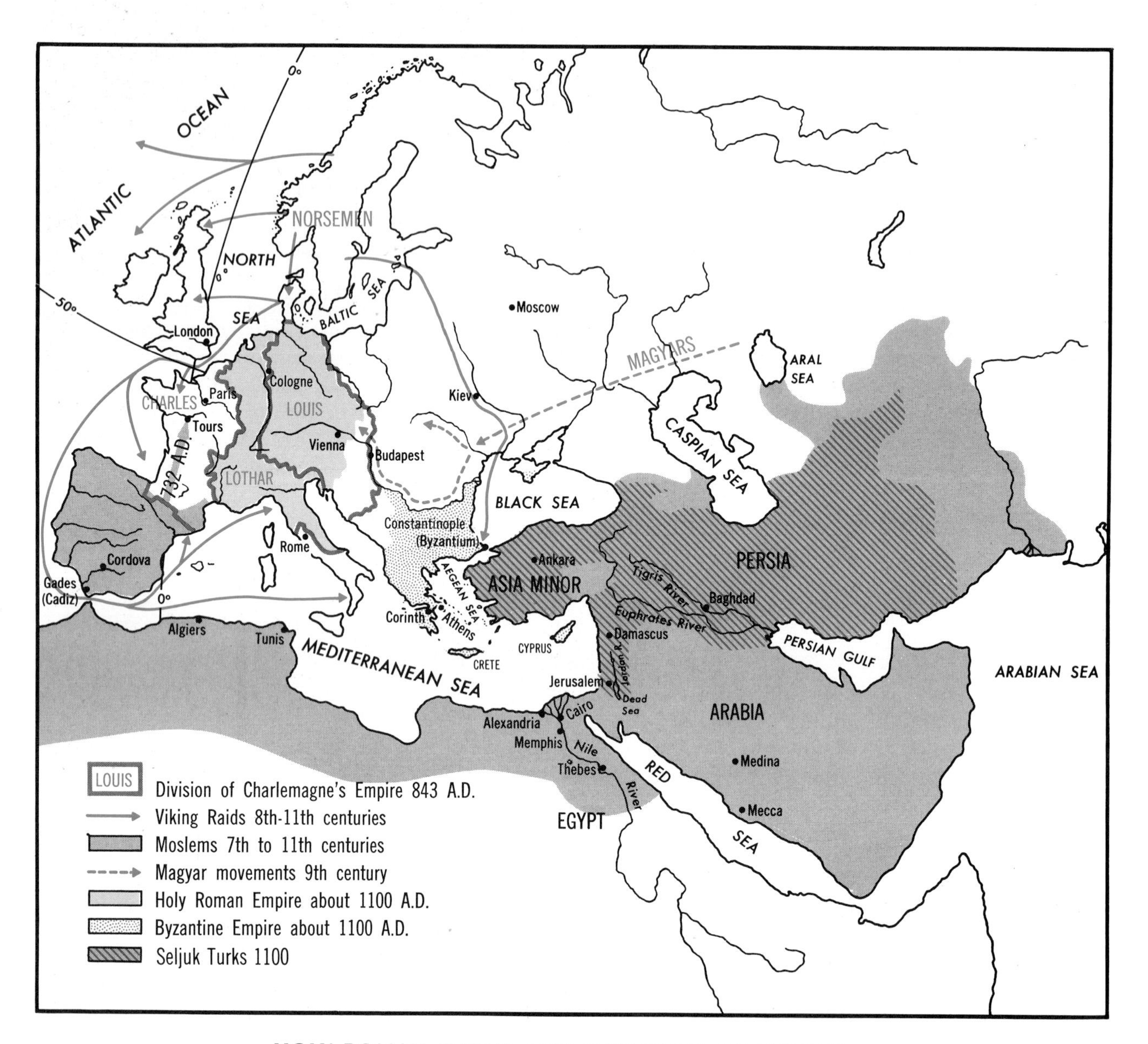


**HOLY ROMAN EMPIRE AND INVASIONS OF EUROPE, 800–1100**

Between 800 and 1100, Europe was seldom free from invaders. The Moors were driven back into Spain after their defeat at Tours, but during the next century Viking invaders attacked from the north and west, and the Moslems remained a constant threat. During the ninth century, the Magyars invaded and brought terror to southeastern Europe.

and settled that part along the lower Seine River known thereafter as Normandy—a variation of the name Northman. The Normans defeated the forces of the English king, Harold, at the battle of Hastings, and began a long rule of England. The Normans were led by William, Duke of Normandy, later called "the Conqueror." The traditions, languages, and blood of the Anglo-Saxons and the Norman-French were now intermingled.

The Normans did not cease their roving conquests with the taking of England. In the eleventh century they moved into the Mediterranean and formed a kingdom of southern Italy and the island of Sicily, which they called the Kingdom of the Two Sicilies. This kingdom endured until the middle of the nineteenth century. The Normans also played a leading role in the conquest of Constantinople and settled a few areas and islands around the Balkan peninsula.

The Vikings, or Norsemen, did not spare Ireland, which had been Christian since the revered St. Patrick converted the Irish in the fifth century. The Irish were Celts and were related to the early Britons. After their conversion to Christianity there was a period from about 700 to 1000 A.D. when the arts flowered and the poetic tastes of the Irish were fruitful under the leadership of the Church. The magnificent illuminated manuscript, the *Book of Kells*, dates back to the 700's or 800's. From the great Irish monasteries, educated monks brought Christianity and civilization to Britain and many parts of the continent of Europe. Then the restless roving giants from the north discovered this tempting civilized land. From around 800 until 1000 A.D. they warred for the prize of this green island. The Vikings were eventually defeated and absorbed by the Irish, but in the process Ireland became a disunified land. In the twelfth century the Norman-English forced their rule into parts of Ireland. From that time until the twentieth century there has often been friction between the British and many of the Irish.

1. How was the empire of Charlemagne divided among the sons of Louis?
2. What countries were conquered by the Normans?

### The Faint Outline of Later Europe

From around the year 1000, the beginnings of today's European states could be seen in faint outline. There were independent units of territory called England, Scotland, Ireland, and Wales; and the Viking kingdoms of Denmark, Norway, and Sweden. Otto had been crowned Holy Roman Emperor and ruled also over northern Italy. France had a king known as Hugh Capet; in reality he governed a very small portion of what is modern France. The Moslems controlled much of Spain, though there were some Christian kingdoms in the north of this country. A boundary line was becoming increasingly clearer between the peoples who recognized Rome as their spiritual center and those who called themselves Orthodox Christians — the Bulgarians, Serbs, Romanians, Greeks, and Russians. There was also a decentralized way of life called *feudalism* and *manorialism* which had grown amid the multiplying divisions of Western Europe.

Reliquaries are containers for objects venerated because of their association with a saint or martyr. This one dates from the thirteenth century. (Irish Tourist Board)

## Feudalism

With the gradual disintegration of the Roman Empire under the poundings of centuries of invading tribes and warring groups, local citizens were forced to rely more and more on their own resources to exist. Charlemagne brought unity to a great part of Europe for a period of time. After his death and the separations of his empire, the movement toward the independence of local areas was hastened by the visits of the Vikings. In addition, landed estates called *fiefs* were granted by kings and great nobles to other men in return for money and men to wage war.

Frequently the landed estates were too large for the lord or landholder to farm himself. In such a case, the landholder granted the use of portions of his land to others in return for certain benefits. There were also times when small landlords, frightened by the grasping hands of powerful neighbors, surrendered their land to a more powerful lord in return for his protection. The small landholder might retain the use of his land, but sometimes strong nobles seized the lands of the weaker and granted the use of them to loyal subjects. In all cases, fiefs were granted in return for special favors. Thus there came into being between the holder of the fief, called a *vassal*, and the grantor of the fief, called the *lord*, a political and social relationship generally termed *feudalism*.

This castle was the birthplace of Alfonso Henriques, first king of Portugal. How did Viking invasions hasten the growth of independent kingdoms? (Sni-Yan)

**Vassals and lords.** The feudal relationship between vassals and lords, all of whom were knights or clergy, shaped the political life of the Europeans who lived in the early Middle Ages of Europe. As a part of this feudal structure, the clergy granted or were granted fiefs, and this fact conditioned their relationship to others. Over the years, the legal use and possession of fiefs became hereditary, passing from father to son, or, in the case of clergy, with possession and use of the land remaining under the control of the clergy or the Church.

The vassal owed his lord certain duties, which were a condition of the grant of a fief. The lord also had certain obligations in this relationship. The name vassal was an honorable title, and the aristocracy that came to govern the various parts of Europe were a part of this feudal system. Theoretically, everyone was a vassal to someone, except the king, who sat at the top of the feudal pyramid. Beneath the king were the great lords, the dukes, the counts or earls, and the barons; under them were the lesser lords, and beneath them the many knights.

**Obligations for both lord and vassal.** Relationships within the feudal system often became quite confusing. For example, a lord might grant a fief to another, who was therefore his vassal; however, he might also hold a grant made by this same vassal, who therefore became his lord!

There were certain definite relationships which arose from a grant. It was a contract which placed responsibilities upon both lord and vassal. The lord promised to protect the vassal and his family and to see that they received justice in cases where his judgment was necessary. The law was a private matter which the lord administered. The vassal on his part promised to remain loyal and faithful to the lord and to render him aid when needed. This aid was frequently of a military nature and took the form of equipping and sending soldiers and of paying their expenses while they were at war.

Since military expenses were heavy, military aid was usually limited to forty days. A vassal was also required to feed and entertain the lord and his followers when they paid a visit, which the lords were accustomed to doing from time to time. The vassal was also expected to assist in the weddings of the lord's sons and daughters, in knighting ceremonies, and in other great festive occasions. Should his lord be captured in battle, the vassal had to contribute to the ransom. In those days it was more profitable to capture a noble alive than to kill him, and holding for ransom was a common occurrence.

These obligations of lords and vassals reflect the chief activities of the feudal period, for war was the sport of this time. Little wars were always being waged between the feudal lords to gain glory, to kidnap rich men who could pay ransom, or to extend the borders of their land. War was the pastime of the gentlemen called *knights*, and a test of courage for their trainees, called *squires*.

**Knighthood.** The word *chivalry* usually brings to mind a picture of a knight in armor—noble of heart, noble of posture, noble of steed—riding forth to fight evil, any evil. It recalls the image of a man who was loyal to his lord to the death, and who could not live without honor. The knight was considered to be the ideal picture of a man on horseback. Sometimes the reality did not match the ideal, but the ideal remained and has been upheld to this day by some.

It was not easy to become a knight, for a man did not inherit knighthood at birth; he earned it. Early in boyhood he was a *page*, or attendant, in the household of his lord. As a page the boy learned good manners and the courtesies of his class. When he reached his teens, he became a *squire* and learned the use of arms. He was assigned to some knight whose arms he polished and whose dress he attended. When he had proved himself in battle, he was prepared for entrance into knighthood. He was made a knight formally in a ceremony which concluded when his lord touched him upon the shoulder with the flat part of a sword and said, "I dub thee knight." In the later Middle Ages, these ceremonies became quite elaborate.

By becoming a knight a man did not become less human. There were good knights and bad knights, exceptional knights, and mediocre knights, for the touch of the sword did not change character or abilities. The knight was a man of his times—lusty times when strength of arm was more important than the cultivation of the mind, and the ability to strike a mighty blow was of greater use than the ability to read a manuscript.

When the knight rode to war, he girded himself with chain mail, carried a long, cross-hilted sword, bore a long lance, and carried a shield. During the latter part of the Middle Ages, after plate metal came into use, the armor was often so heavy that a knight had to be lifted into his saddle, and if he fell or was struck from his horse, he was unable to rise without assistance.

Knights enjoyed a *joust*, in which two horsemen fought to unseat each other with lances; and all delighted in the *tourney*, in which two groups of knights battled in a series of warlike games. The winners of these contests were awarded prizes by the lady of the tournament. The knights also delighted in hunting with dog and falcon, and they sometimes gambled with dice.

A knight's marriage was likely to be arranged for political or financial reasons, such as the inheritance or dowry his wife might bring. He expected of his wife a son who would carry on his name, inherit his land, and who might also become a knight. The knight was supposed to treat his wife with courtesy, but she sometimes knew the heaviness of his hand if she annoyed him. He was the master; she was the subordinate. Although few knights were literate, many of them enjoyed listening to love poetry and stories or poems called *romances*, which were recited by wandering troubadours. These were, however, times of roughness, and the knight was a vigorous man. It was a man's world.

## The Manor

By the tenth century, much of Europe was divided into thousands of farming units called *manors*. Agriculture was the basis of the economic life of the Europeans at this time. The relationship between those who worked on the manor and the lord of the manor is embraced under the term *manorialism*.

The lord or vassal who held a fief lived in a large house or hall which was the principal building of the manor. These fiefholders were the few, the aristocrats of Europe, the dictators of a locality, the law. Beneath and around them in scattered communities were the many—the common people—called *serfs* or *villeins*. The serf was not a slave of the lord; he was bound to the manor under a general set of customs which placed obligations upon both serf and fiefholder. There were, of course, also a few freemen at all times, and they had their own small bits of land.

A typical manor was dominated by the house or castle of the lord, around which were huddled the houses and fields of the serfs. There was a mill to grind the grain, a central oven, a blacksmith shop, pasture land, and fields. Some of the fields were worked, and others lay fallow to allow them to recover their fertility. Surrounding this manor settlement, there was often a forest which separated the manor from the outside world. These forests often harbored outlaws.

By the beginning of the eleventh century, the manor was usually a relatively self-sufficient settlement. The serfs produced the food, clothing, tools, and shelter needed by the people of the manor. Trade and commerce had dwindled to a trickle during these times of disorder, and the manor bought little from the outside world except salt, iron, and stones for the mill. Sometimes the lord of the manor might purchase a luxury, such as spice for his food or fine cloth for his wife and daughter. But these items cost money, and even the aristocrats had little money. Nobody lived in great comfort by modern standards.

**The castle.** The lord of the manor lived in the most imposing structure of the manor, which was frequently a castle. It was a menacing building of stone with high, thick walls, and it was encircled by a wide, water-filled moat. The moat was bridged only by a great gate, which was drawn up at night or when the castle was under attack. The lord needed a fortified place to defend himself and his people from marauding knights and outlaws seeking plunder.

The main room of the castle was a large, murky hall where the lord received his occasional guests and ate his food from a table of wooden planks resting on trestles. Here he delivered his judgments in the daily cases involving the people of his manor, for he was both judge and jury. The rooms of the castle were chilly and damp. During the winter the winds whistled through the small uncovered windows. Oiled paper was sometimes used to keep the elements outside, but it was poor protection. Wood burned in a great fireplace gave some warmth to the great hall, but smoke from the fire fouled the air and changed the appearance of tapestries and beams. The floor was covered with rushes, and hunting dogs fought for bones and leavings of food which the lord and his guests discarded upon the floor. Within the castle walls there were also stables for the horses and rooms for the lord's men-at-arms, servants, and guests. Beds were covered by coarse woolen blankets and were generally shared with vermin of various kinds. It was not a comfortable life even for the lord of the manor.

**The serf's home.** The castle, however, had more conveniences than the homes of the serfs, or villeins. These were small, one-room huts, which sat beside the single road which emerged from the forest and ran through the settlement. The hut had a thatched roof, and its walls were sometimes wood, sometimes stone. If there was no fireplace, a fire was built on the dirt floor, and the smoke found its slow way out through little openings in the thatched roof. A few pots, perhaps a spindle and a loom, a bag of straw for sleeping on the floor, a plank or two of wood for a table, a few rough utensils and dishes for eating—this was the home of the serf.

At night the serf shared his little hut with his animals, for if he lost them his fate would be even worse. His diet consisted of black bread, cheese, eggs occasionally, and cabbage and a few other vegetables. In the north he might drink beer; in the south, a sour wine. At times he might be entertained by wandering acrobats or storytellers, and there were holidays when he might rest from work. But, in general, his life consisted of back-breaking toil in the fields from dawn to dusk, and it was often made harder by a lack of proper and substantial food.

The workers on the manor did have a certain degree of security. The land that they farmed continued to be theirs to farm, no matter into whose hands the manor fell. The custom of the manor was often a check on the actions of the lord—he could not always do as he pleased. Also among the lords there was the idea of *noblesse oblige*—the conception that high rank and high birth carry with them an obligation to deal honorably with those of lower rank and to treat them with kindness and generosity. The lords commonly accepted their responsibility toward the people of the manor and supported them in their old age (although it should be pointed out that the life span was short), fed them in times of famine, protected them during war, and helped them when sickness struck. The serfs of the manor also had certain obligations to their lord.

**Obligations of the serfs.** Serfs cultivated strips of land which were assigned to them in the fields of arable land belonging to the manor. The number of fields belonging to the manor varied from place to place. Three- and four-field systems were common, and there were also two- and five-field systems. The number of fields depended upon the area and the nature of the crops that were grown.

The lord and each peasant had several strips of land within each field. The average size of a strip was about one acre. Each year one field was allowed to remain fallow while the others were planted with spring and autumn crops. Thus, in a three-field system one field was always left to rest every third year to regain its fertility. Wheat was grown in the warmer climates, and barley, oats, and rye in the colder areas. Since the strips of the individual peasants were scattered, and because plows and other equipment were limited, it was necessary for the serfs to work cooperatively in planting, cultivating, and harvesting the crops.

In addition to the cultivated fields, there was also common land on the manor. Meadows were used by all for grazing cattle, and wood from the forest was gathered by all to be used for fuel and for building. In all cases, the workers of the manor had an obligation to their lord to use the manor's resources carefully.

The serfs were required to cultivate the arable land assigned to the lord of the manor. This land was called the "lord's demesne." Further, at specified times during the year, the serf was obliged to pay dues in the form of his finest farming product—some grain, ducks or chickens, a pig, or some other product, depending upon the custom of the particular manor. In later centuries, a fixed sum of money was required. In addition, the lord demanded fees for the use of the village bake-oven, the mill where grain was ground into flour, and the use of the winepress and the brewery. In the blacksmith shop of the manor, horses were shod, and iron was turned into tools, weapons, and other needed utensils. The serfs also made payment in kind for these goods and services. The percentage or amount of payment received by the lord varied from manor to manor, but he always received payment in produce or in services for the goods and facilities that were supplied by the manor to the serfs.

This feudal and manorial way of life was fitted to an age when people were thrown upon their own resources to exist. It was not an easy existence; life was usually short and almost always hard, and there was little pleasure during this time of harshness. But man had his little happinesses—at weddings, knightings, and feasts—and he endured the rigors of his life with the hope that after death he might find reward and eternal happiness in heaven.

1. What was the essential relationship between the holder of a fief and the lord who granted it to him?
2. What were the mutual rights and duties of lords and vassals in the system of feudalism?
3. Who administered justice under the feudal system?
4. In what way was the manor self-sufficient? What were some of the articles that could not be produced on the manor?

## The Crusades

It was, in part, the religious beliefs and hopes of the Europeans that sent them to the Middle East to battle with the Moslems for control of the holy land of Palestine. The Arab Moslems had taken Palestine from the control of the Byzantines in the seventh century, but their religion required them to be tolerant of the Christians and the Jews, who were permitted to live in and visit the land of Palestine and to conduct business there with little interference.

Later converts to Islam—the Seljuk Turks, who came from the steppes of Central Asia—invaded the Middle East and conquered much of it, including Asia Minor. They threatened the city of Constantinople itself. The Byzantine emperor petitioned Rome for help. For a variety of reasons, Pope Urban II responded and in 1095 urged the French to embark upon a Crusade against the unbelieving Turks who were holding portions of the Middle East sacred to the Christian. The Turks were not really unbelievers, for the God of Abraham was also the God of the Moslem, the Christian, and the Jew. But it was enough for the Christian Europeans that the Turks were infidels, nonbelievers in Christianity.

The Crusader, who was identified by the cross sewn on his clothes, was motivated for many reasons to undertake this arduous journey to Palestine. He believed that his sins were forgiven if he fell in battle and that he would go directly to heaven. Those who were in debt had their debts cancelled, and the criminal who became a Crusader was pardoned. Others, more material-minded, thought of the riches they might obtain. Still others were attracted by the high adventure of the trip and the war, and became a part of the Crusade with anticipation.

The Abbey of Mont-Saint-Michel, in Normandy, was founded in 708 and was a fortified prison-fortress through much of the Middle Ages. (French Government Tourist Office)

### The First, Second, and Third Crusades

The First Crusade (1096-1099), led by the French and Normans, was successful. A kingdom of Jerusalem and some other kingdoms were established. The feudalism known in Europe was continued here, and for nearly a hundred years the Europeans governed these parts of the Middle East. They learned to live with the Moslems and the climate and, in general, became a part of the life of this region. During this period, however, the Turks began to threaten again.

The Second Crusade (1147-1149), under Louis VII of France and Conrad III of Germany, went to the Middle East, but it was a failure. In 1187 the Turks, under the famous Saladin, retook Jerusalem. Richard the Lion-Hearted of England, Philip of France, and Frederick Barbarossa of Germany headed the Third Crusade (1189-1192) to Palestine. Frederick drowned on the way, and his army turned back. Philip quarreled with Richard and returned to France, where he took advantage of Richard's absence to seize some of the English king's French lands. Richard was left alone. He had little success and did not retake Jerusalem.

### End of the Crusades

There were other Crusades later, but none so important as the infamous Fourth Crusade (1202-1204) which, starting from Venice, launched an attack against Christian Constantinople rather than against the Moslems. Constantinople was thoroughly plundered by the Crusaders.

During the twelfth century the Crusaders were driven entirely from the areas in the Holy Land which they had taken, and the Crusades ended without achieving their purpose. But the Crusades had many lasting effects upon Western Europe which the Crusaders had not foreseen when they first went to the Middle East with the cry "God wills it!"

### Results in Europe

The Crusades further stimulated the growing trade of Europe. Many European trading centers were pushed to the limit to furnish supplies for the crusading armies. The cities of Italy—Venice, Genoa, Pisa, and others—provided ships to transport many of the Crusaders to the Middle East. These ships returned laden with the enticing goods of the East, which the Europeans willingly emptied their pockets to possess. This trade, in turn, led to the growth of banking, for letters of credit and documents of exchange became useful and necessary to traders whose commerce took them far away for great periods of time and whose business affairs became increasingly complex.

The Crusades probably contributed to the emancipation of the common people and to their winning greater freedom and privileges. A number of feudal lords sold special privileges to towns and communities under their control in return for money and equipment to outfit their soldiers. The power of money became more evident. Thus, the Crusades gave impetus to the growth of a middle class and further reduced the power of the nobles. There are those who think that the Crusades speeded the movement of people to the towns and thus helped to ease the pressure of population on the land in the rural parts of Europe.

The Crusades gave the Europeans a better knowledge of geography, and introduced them to ideas and to scientific discoveries that were rather startling. Through their contacts with the educated Byzantines and Moslems the Europeans came to realize that there was much that they did not know. The Crusades were undertaken to drive the Turks from their entrenched position in the Holy Land; they eventually failed to achieve this purpose, but they did further the spread of knowledge and contribute to a ferment in Europe that was spelling the deterioration of the old order of feudalism.

### Increasing Trade and Wealth

Trade had never ceased with the decline of the Roman Empire and the economic decentralization of Europe into thousands of manors. It was curtailed, however, by the shattering of Europe into many political parts, the lack of communications, the perils of travel, and the many tolls that were imposed along roads and rivers. But there were always those who dared to face these difficulties in the hope of making a profit. Merchants and peddlers traveled lonely roads and risked the dangers of robbery to offer to the people of the manors goods they could not produce themselves—salt, oil, wine, armor, brass, tin, glass, cloth, and luxury items. There was frequently a market town which served the manors of the surrounding area, and the surplus produce of manors was marketed there. In these towns the people of the manors could buy goods they needed. There was also the yearly fair which was a holiday of buying and selling and fun.

The fair lasted sometimes for a few days, sometimes for several weeks, depending upon the time and the place, and merchants came from far and near to display their wares in booths. People from the manors and the neighborhood streamed by the booths to gape, to admire, to stop, to haggle, and to buy. The fair was an exhibition of goods from Europe and elsewhere that most of the people saw but once a year. There were wines from the south, furs from the north, linen from Flanders, silk from Italy, armor, jewelry and articles of gold and silver, soft velvet, and many other rare and luxurious goods. But the fair was not merely an opportunity to look and to buy, it was also a time of festivity. There was an atmosphere of gaiety at these fairs—acrobats and tumblers performed, plays were given, music was played, and a holiday mood prevailed. The fair was a time of laughter and joy as well as an occasion for buying and selling.

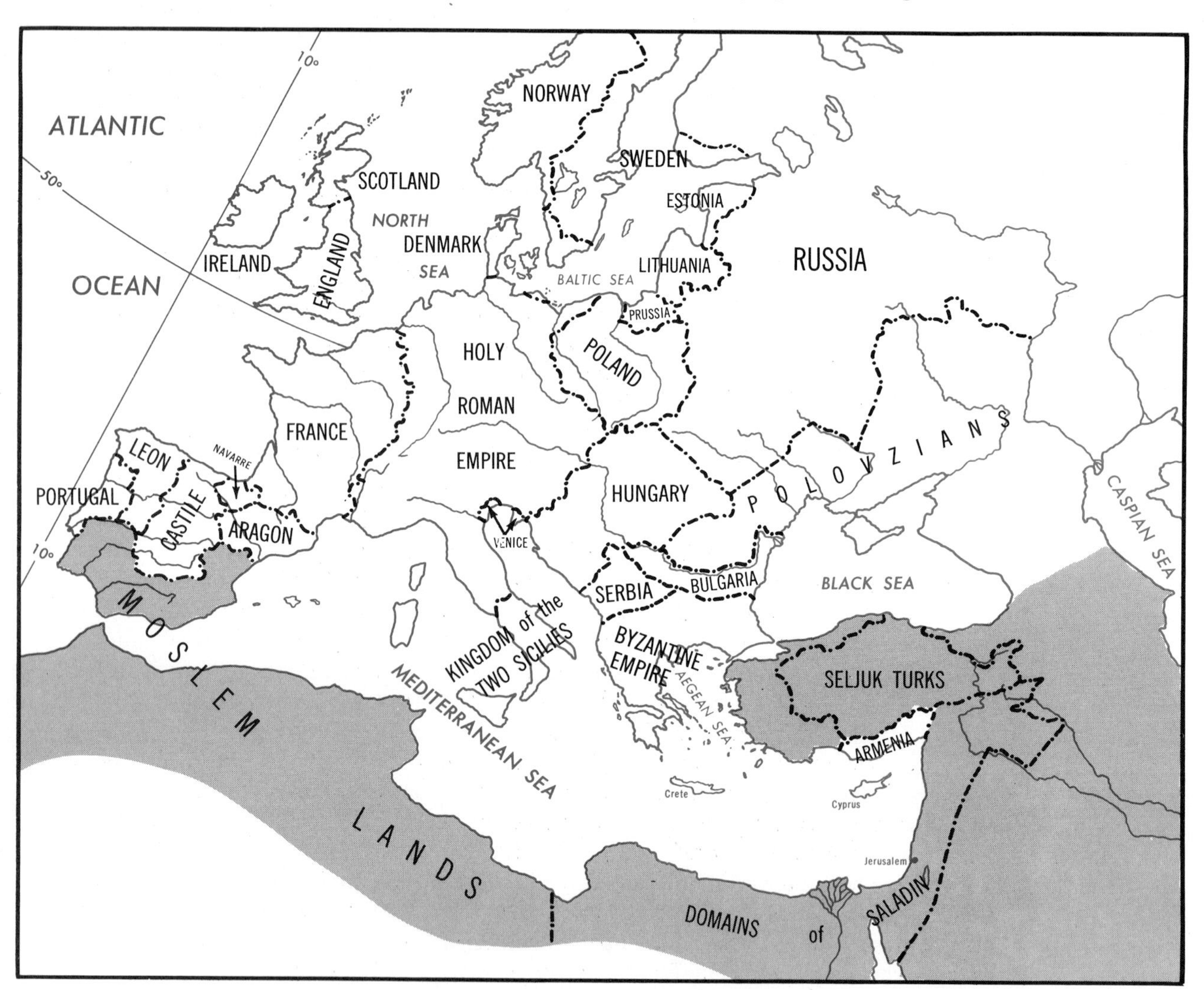


**EUROPE AT THE TIME OF THE THIRD CRUSADE (1189–1192)**

While the Crusades (1096-1270) are best remembered in history as the struggle to regain the Holy Land from the Moslem Seljuk Turks, they were part of a general struggle against Moslem expansion. By the time of the Crusades, the Moors were being driven back into southern Spain, but they were not defeated there finally until the fifteenth century. (The Polovzians were a Turkic people who occupied parts of southern Russia from the ninth to the eleventh century.)

Beginning in the twelfth century, and lasting throughout the remaining years of the medieval period, there was a steady increase in the pace of trade. The population of Europe increased, and with greater freedom and greater wealth, the people were eager to buy more goods.

Trade routes on both sea and land were expanded and grew safer, and more and more traders traveled these routes to supply the increasing demand for goods. Wool went from England to the cities of Flanders and northern France and over the Alps to Italian cities to be made into cloth and re-exported. Lumber was in demand for the growing shipbuilding industry. Convoys of ships took salt from the coast of France to the Baltic and to Scandinavia where it was used to salt fish for export; wine was carried in great quantities from southern to northern Europe; and other products were carried along the complex web of trade routes which tied all parts of Europe together.

Trade grew between the Mediterranean and the East—drugs, perfumes, spices, jewels, silk, dyes, and other products which the Europeans gradually came to prize. The Venetians built great merchant galleys and sent fleets of them to England and to Flanders carrying merchandise, and the merchants of Genoa, Pisa, and other Italian cities roamed the Mediterranean and elsewhere with their cargoes.

**Hanseatic League.** To the north, on the shores of the North Sea and Baltic Sea, the cities of Hamburg, Lübeck, Bremen, and others grew prosperous and powerful through trade. They began to recognize the advantages that a united effort would provide against the perils and the risks of the times. In the latter part of the thirteenth century, the merchants of these cities established a confederation known as the Hanseatic League. It grew into a powerful confederation of over eighty cities. The confederation provided protection for merchants, supplied maps of harbors, lighthouses, and other navigational aids, and standardized weights and measures. The cities of the League were powerful enough to wage war, and they defeated Denmark when the king of that country encroached upon their territories and their privileges. The League sent its own diplomats abroad, had its own flag, and made treaties with other powers. The Hanseatic League continued to obtain privileges for merchants in European cities, to maintain the safety of the sea lanes of the north, to make commercial law, and to improve the quality of merchandise until the sixteenth century, when it declined in power and finally vanished.

**Merchant-bankers.** From this surge of trade in the later Middle Ages, there emerged great merchant-bankers who had amassed wealth and capital from their trading ventures. These merchant-bankers increased their fortunes by lending money to kings, nobles, and high officials of the Church. These ruling groups of Europe generally had a need for extra funds to wage war, to maintain their grand state, and to finance their adventures of one kind or another. They frequently borrowed from the great merchant princes of the time. In return for their financial assistance, the merchant-bankers received considerations of various kinds—interest, special privileges, and the favor of the political rulers.

**The growth of banks.** During the period from around 1250 to 1450, groups of men began to meet the need for money-changing, for lending money, for keeping money in a safe place, and for transferring money from one region to another. They were the first European bankers. The greatest and earliest of the European bankers were the Italians. There were the Buonsignori, who established the headquarters of their banking business in Siena in the mid-thirteenth century and for many years were the bankers of the popes. Banking families emerged in Rome and other Italian cities, but perhaps the most famous of the banking cities was Florence.

Before Florence became famed for the artistic genius of its citizens, it was well known as the home of many famous banking families—the Peruzzi, the Bardi, the Cerchi, among others. The bankers of Florence transported money for kings and popes; they collected papal dues in various countries; they kept money on deposit for others; they loaned

As trade began to flourish, towns grew. Stores were sometimes built on bridges like this one in Florence, Italy. (Italian State Tourist Office)

money for commercial and political ventures; and they issued bills of exchange payable elsewhere. These Florentine bankers thus laid the foundations for the banking system which is prevalent throughout the world today. The banking business spread to other areas of Europe and, in the fifteenth century, the Fugger family of Augsburg, for example, founded a financial empire of enormous prestige and wealth.

Thus, during this period of the later Middle Ages, the growth of trade, wealth, and capital and the development of banking began to erode and to modify the manorial and feudal systems which were founded on agriculture and on chivalry and other customs. The power of wealth could make a man a member of the nobility and a political influence in the land. Obligations to the lord of the manor could be met with money as well as service, and a serf with money was not so strongly bound to the land. There was also during the later Middle Ages a growth of towns which became the strongholds of a rising middle class.

## The Growth of Towns

Trade and civilization flourish in cities. The decline of cities in the early Middle Ages was in part responsible for the decline of trade and artistic pursuits during this period. On the other hand, the growth of towns and cities during the later Middle Ages, from around 1100 to about 1450, was in great part responsible for the changes in the lives of Europeans during this time. Towns had already started a rebirth as men in Europe settled into the routine of feudalism; but the growth in population, the expansion of trade, wealth, and capital, as well as other factors, hastened the growth of towns into thriving centers of change and progress.

In response to the demands of trade and manufacturing, towns mushroomed everywhere in geographically favorable areas. Some towns, such as London and Paris, flourished beside rivers near the sea, where massive castles or monasteries gave them security; others grew around manufacturing centers, as in Flanders. As these towns grew in size, increased and more varied services were required to meet the expanding demands of the townsmen and people of the surrounding area.

**Artisans and guilds.** Shoemakers, tailors, masons, carpenters, goldsmiths, silversmiths, weavers, bakers, and other craftsmen responded to the growing needs. Gradually, they found it necessary to organize in order to safeguard the quality of their work, their wages, and other aspects of their crafts. They formed guilds, and the membership of each guild included all of those working in the same craft. These craft guilds held great power over their members. The guild fixed wages, hours, and working conditions, and even regulated the prices which could be charged for products. The guild was also a welfare agency and was always ready to assist needy members. It also disciplined members who had violated regulations. In time, the guild members developed high standards of craftsmanship and full membership in the guild was reserved for masters of their work. Those who wanted to be master workers had to undergo a long period of training.

The young boy was generally *apprenticed* to a master craftsman for some years and lived as a member of the master's family while learning his craft. The master, like a father, had full authority over his *apprentice* and provided him with the necessities of life—food, clothing, and shelter. When the apprentice was judged to be sufficiently adept at his craft, he was raised to the level of *journeyman*, which indicated that he was skillful but not yet a master. He also received a regular wage. When he felt he was ready, he could apply for full membership in the guild and the title of master workman, but he had to prove his ability before the experts of his guild.

There were also merchant guilds which regulated and protected the general trade of the town. Both the merchant guilds and the craft guilds played an important role in the commercial life of the growing cities. At their best, the guilds gave to their members protection and security, and they gave the assurance of quality to the buyer of the members' products.

**The town's appearance.** The fourteenth-century cities in which guild members and their fellow townsmen lived were usually rather small by modern standards—the population ranged from five to ten thousand people. (Cities like Paris and London had considerably more people.) But even this relatively small number of persons found themselves packed tightly within the protecting walls of the city, for the walls could not be stretched to accommodate the continually increasing number of residents.

The citizens of these cities found the same solution to their problems of space that the citizens of today's rapidly expanding cities are using—building higher. They built their houses four, five, and six stories upward. To gain more space, each additional story was extended a little farther outward so that the top floors of facing houses almost met over the narrow street below. This did give the townsmen more space, but it also made life hazardous for the passersby below. It was not uncommon for those living on the upper floors to empty their garbage and other refuse onto the street below.

Many of the towns of the fourteenth century were clean, but a great number lacked sewers and drainage facilities, and rotting garbage and refuse was a breeding ground for disease and epidemics. Frequently drinking water was polluted, and the city dwellers relied mainly on beer, ale, and wine to drink. The danger of fire was always present. In the cramped quarters of city houses, fires once started could easily spread from one dwelling to another and could not be put out quickly by the volunteer bucket brigade. There was also danger from robbers at night, and anyone out after dark had to be careful lest he be injured or robbed. The police force was inadequate and often consisted of aged men who were of little assistance in a struggle with a brawny thief.

Medieval towns were often colorful and fascinating. They were places where the hustle of trade brought novel ideas and products. Entertainers and people from strange, faraway places came to reap money and deal in the wanted products of the town. There was learning in the towns, too, and the ambitious could engage a tutor or even attend a university. Beauty was there, too, in the magnificence of the church or cathedral which spired to heaven and dominated the buildings of the town. Generally life in the town was better than the serfdom of the manor, and it certainly provided more hope.

### Cities Obtain Privileges

Gradually the people of the growing towns and cities, under the leadership of merchants and men of substance, began to obtain greater liberties and privileges from the lord or king who ruled them. Often they bought these privileges from the ruler, and at times they wrenched them from him by force. Sometimes the king granted privileges to cities because of their service to the safety of the realm. In Spain, for instance, the rulers of León and Castile granted charters embodying special privileges to the cities which protected their frontiers in the wars against the Moors. During the thirteenth and fourteenth centuries there were in Spain a number of self-governing cities—Madrid, Barcelona, and Seville among others—whose citizens enjoyed a great degree of freedom. Around this time the townspeople in France, Germany, and England were also gaining freedom from feudal control.

The townsmen gradually were released from a number of obligations, including the payment of feudal dues. They gained freedom to buy and to sell as they chose. They organized their own courts of law and thus were not at the mercy of the private law of the feudal lords. A number of towns, like those of Spain, gained the right of self-government. The type of government varied from city to city, ranging from an oligarchy of wealthy merchants to cities governed by elected officials. And often the privileges enjoyed by the people of the city extended to the countryside and villages in the neighborhood of the city.

The nobility and the clergy remained as powerful social classes, but with the evolving independence of cities in Europe a third powerful group arose whose power was centered in cities and founded upon the freedoms, the knowledge, and the wealth of their class. They came to be called the middle class or the *Third Estate* to distinguish them from the other two estates or classes, the nobility and the clergy. From the expansion of trade and wealth and the growth of towns there had now arisen a class of men the government was forced to recognize as important because of their material and other resources.

### Middle-Class Participation in Government

The kings who governed during the latter part of the thirteenth and early fourteenth centuries in Spain, France, England, Germany and elsewhere indicated their recognition of the significance of this new class. Representatives of the middle class were received at royal councils and gained a voice in assemblies, diets, and parliaments. This was a departure from established practice because formerly only the nobles and the high clergy had participated in the deliberations of these bodies. During this period the kings of Aragon and Castile in Spain began inviting the representatives of towns to meet together with the nobles and the clergy in an assembly called a *cortes*.

In 1302, Philip the Fair of France invited representatives of towns within his realm to participate in an assembly which was called to gain support for the king in a dispute with

Pope Boniface VIII. This was the first meeting of the Estates-General of France, and it is historically noteworthy as the first time others than the nobility and clergy of France took part in an assembly of national significance. In succeeding years the king called other meetings of the Estates-General to which representatives of more French towns were invited. By the middle of the fourteenth century participation by the French middle class in government had become usual. It was during this period also that representatives of the cities began to appear in the diet or Reichstag of Germany and in the Parliament of England.

No doubt the kings requested the representatives of the middle class to attend these meetings primarily because they wanted to raise money through taxation, grants, or other methods. The middle class owned property that was subject to taxation, while the clergy and the nobility were traditionally exempt from taxation. But this new group was made up of shrewd men who quickly saw the advantages of their position. They began to require additional privileges and rights from their kings in return for their agreement to requests for funds. Each of the kingdoms of Spain—León, Castile, Aragon, and others—had its own cortes at this time. Since the middle class was represented in the cortes, this class became increasingly powerful by demanding and obtaining concessions from the king. The same was true of France where the Third Estate obtained a degree of control over the money spent as well as obtaining equal taxation and other concessions. By 1357 middle class power had reached the point where the ruler of France was forced to accept proposals which gave the middle class equal power with others in government and which severely curtailed the royal power. It was practically a revolution of the middle class. But this was the peak of the political power of the middle class during this period in France. The Third Estate gradually declined in influence during the succeeding centuries as the king became dominant there and elsewhere in Europe.

In England, as elsewhere in Europe, the political power of the middle class increased during the thirteenth, fourteenth, and fifteenth centuries. The influence of the middle class was manifested in the English Parliament, which traces its origins to this period of English history.

1. Why did feudal lords and their subjects join the Crusades? What inducements were there?
2. How did the power of kings develop?
3. How was trade stimulated by the Crusades? Who succeeded in obtaining trade leadership as a result of their part in the Crusades?

### Evolution of English Institutions

The period from 1066 to around 1450 witnessed the beginning and the growth of institutions in England which were of immense significance in Europe and elsewhere for centuries thereafter. This was the period in which the foundations of English common law were laid down, in which the English system of juries and judges developed, and in which the Magna Carta was signed. During this period the English Parliament also was established. The story begins with the conquest of Anglo-Saxon England by William the Conqueror, Duke of Normandy, at the battle of Hastings in 1066.

William was a strong king, and he imposed his own feudal system upon the land of England. He took away much of the land that had belonged to the Anglo-Saxon nobles and gave it to the followers who had helped him to conquer England. In return he demanded that they give him military service for a certain period each year. He did not completely trust these nobles, however, and the manors he gave them were widely dispersed. William also required that the nobles take an oath of allegiance to himself. He retained about a sixth of the land under his own direct rule.

Under William's rule, the Anglo-Saxon courts and the office of sheriff were retained. The old council of the Anglo-Saxons, the *witenagemot*, was replaced by William's own council known as the *curia regis*. William also had a survey made of all the property of England, which was listed in the "Domesday Book." This listing of property was invaluable for purposes of taxation. The new Norman ruler attempted to centralize the government of England as far as possible. But decentralization of authority was basic to the feudal system, and the successors of William were compelled to continue their efforts to lessen the powers of stubbornly resisting nobles.

Henry I (1100-1135), began to pay his officials salaries which made them more dependent upon him. He also established a secretariat (royal chancery) and a treasury which audited the accounts of the kingdom. Henry established one system of law for all his subjects which incorporated much from both Anglo-Saxon and feudal customs and practices. After a short period of civil war he was succeeded by Henry II (1154-1189), who is regarded as one of England's most able kings.

## Writs, Judges, Juries

Henry II continued the policies of his predecessors and did much to curb the power of the feudal barons. He, too, wanted a single system of law to replace the laws of the scattered manors, and he improved the processes of the law. He made *writs*—written orders in the king's name—available to his subjects at a moderate price so that cases could be brought into the royal courts for inquiry and judgment. Many of the major crimes committed in the realm were declared offenses against the king's peace, and the offenders were tried by royal judges.

Henry II expanded the practice started by Henry I and sent judges into the countryside to try cases. Judges were assigned to regular routes in the country and went from place to place at regular intervals to hold court and judge cases. They were called *circuit* judges, and the name is still known in America. To assist the judges in uncovering the cases they should hear, the king appointed juries in each district. These juries consisted of respected persons who gave the judges the names of those men they thought had committed crimes. Today in the United States we have our grand juries who deliberate whether or not there is sufficient evidence of crime to bring a man to trial.

The king also gave authority to a jury of twelve men to function as sworn witnesses to the facts in disputes concerning land. This is the origin of the jury system which in the course of time came to be used to decide criminal cases. The jury is now a fixed institution in British and American courts. The replacement of private feudal law by the king's law assisted in the breakdown of feudalism in England and led to a betterment in government and the administration of justice.

## Magna Carta

Henry II was succeeded by his son, Richard the Lion-Hearted (1189-1199). Richard was out of the country during most of his reign fighting against the French and later against the Turks in the Middle East. Much of the royal treasury was used up in financing his wars and in ransoming him from captivity. When Richard's brother, John, followed him on the throne, he inherited a treasury made poor by these great expenses. John reigned from 1199 to 1216, and it was during his reign that the Magna Carta, the Great Charter, was signed.

King John has the reputation in history as a man given to treachery and cruelty. He schemed against his brother, Richard, and murdered a nephew in order that he might possess the throne of England. His high-handedness toward his barons and his trespassing upon their rights aroused their animosity. At last the powerful nobles organized their united might against him. On June 15, 1215, at a place called Runnymede, they forced him to sign a document which guaranteed and renewed their old feudal rights. It is known as the Magna Carta.

The Magna Carta was a document which contained the confirmation of traditional rights and privileges. It was not the affirmation of something new. King John promised in this agreement that he would not impose unusual

The Houses of Parliament stand beside the Thames River in the modern city of London, England. (Chauncey from Cushing)

taxes without the consent of his council; that the city of London would retain its old liberties; that no free man could be imprisoned, banished, or deprived of his property unless it was the judgment of a jury of his equals, or peers; and that he, the king, must give justice to all. The importance of the document lay in the establishment of the principle that there was a limitation on the power of the king; that he was not above the law; and that he could be compelled to obey the law. Although the barons thought of themselves as the main beneficiaries of the provisions of the Magna Carta, in later centuries it was interpreted in many instances to apply to all Englishmen.

## Parliament

King John was succeeded by his son Henry III (1216-1272), who became king when he was only nine years old. During Henry's youth there was peace between the king and the barons, but Henry's later actions caused the nobles to turn against him. He appointed foreigners, mostly Italian and French, to high positions in the kingdom and made great financial demands upon the nobility. The nobles rebelled. They secured control of the great council of the king and appointed a committee which issued a document known as the Provisions of Oxford. These provisions surrounded the king with a council of fifteen men and required him to accept their advice.

The institution of the *king's council* goes far back into English history. The Anglo-Saxon rulers had an assembly called *witenagemot* which was composed of high churchmen and nobles of the land who counseled the ruler on various matters, including taxes. It also sometimes acted as a court. When the Normans conquered England they replaced this assembly with their own customary council in which the great feudal lords participated. These nobles advised the king and also performed judicial functions. Originally they were merely advisors whom the king might or might not ask for advice, depending upon his whim or circumstance of the moment. But slowly the attitude grew among the nobles that the king should be required to consult the council. This attitude was formally incorporated into the Magna Carta, for instance, in the provision that there should be no unusual taxation without the consent of the king's council. Thus, when the barons assumed power over the king in 1258, they strengthened the council and declared that it should meet three times a year. They called this council by the name that has continued to be given to the English legislative body—Parliament.

When Henry failed to fulfill his agreement, civil war again broke out between the King and his barons. In 1264 the barons under the leadership of Simon de Montfort defeated the king, and a new government was established under the leadership of de Montfort. In 1265 de Montfort held an assembly which included not only the customary great lords and high clergy but also the knights and the burgesses, or representatives, of the towns. Two knights represented each county, and the more prominent towns sent two burgesses.

The knights were the rural gentry, the moderately well-to-do land owners, who were midway on the feudal social scale. They were gentlemen farmers. They might or might not be related to nobility, but they themselves never worked the land from which they derived their living. They were men of leisure in this sense, but they were busily involved in the affairs of their neighborhood. They served on juries, and they assisted the king in the collection of taxes. They were also justices of the peace and frequently served as investigators of local abuses. For years these members of the rural gentry were invaluable assistants of their kings and lords in the localities where they lived. Starting about 1254, they began to participate in assemblies dealing with national matters, especially financial matters. From that time onward it became customary to invite them to these assemblies.

The assembly of 1265 was the first one to which the burgesses or representatives of the towns were invited. The growing influence of wealth and the towns in the affairs of the nation was now recognized in England as elsewhere in Europe. From this time forward, both knights and townsmen participated with increasing frequency in the assemblies or parliaments of England. But this procedure was not regularized until 1295 when Edward I (1272-1307) was threatened by an invasion from France. Edward attempted to rally all the classes, excluding serfs, behind him by inviting to a parliamentary meeting two knights from each shire and two representatives from each borough and town. He also invited the lower as well as the higher clergy, and lesser nobles as well as the great barons. Not all attended, but enough came to make this assembly representative of the various classes of England, and to have it referred to thereafter as the "Model Parliament."

As the fourteenth and fifteenth centuries moved along, the kings were forced to call more and more upon Parliament for the money they needed to govern the realm and wage their wars. The members of Parliament learned to bargain with the kings for concessions in return. There was a growing together of the knights and the burgesses of the towns as their interests became more intimately intertwined and they learned the advantages of united action. They began to meet together in one house called the "Commons" to distinguish it from the house in which the great lords and high clergymen sat. This happened as early as 1332. Thus the Parliament of England slowly came to be divided into two houses, the House of Commons and the House of Lords. This division still holds true in England today, but the House of Commons has become, over the years, the stronger of the two bodies.

The power of Parliament continued to grow during the reigns of Edward II (1307-1327), and Edward III (1327-1377). During the reign of this latter king the Hundred Years' War began with France and the bubonic plague, or Black Death, struck England. Both of these events caused economic dislocation and led Parliament to take greater control over the finances of the kingdom. Parliament requested and obtained privileges which evolved into rights. The houses of Parliament began to criticize the king's ministers and reached a peak of power when, in 1399, the Lords and Commons removed Richard II from the throne and declared that Henry of Lancaster should rule as King Henry IV (1399-1413).

The Lancastrian line of kings, who began to rule with Henry IV in 1399, lasted until 1485. From 1455 until 1485, however, two branches of the royal house struggled to gain the throne in a series of savage conflicts known by the poetic name of "The Wars of the Roses." This name came from the fact that the house of York used a white rose as its emblem, and the red rose was associated with the house of Lancaster. The conflict was finally resolved when Henry Tudor ascended the throne in 1485 as Henry VII. Henry married the heiress of the house of York, thus uniting the two factions, and he established policies that were to keep the Tudor kings in control of powerful nobles. Under the strong Tudor rulers, the power of Parliament waned, but its position as an institution in England remained strong. In later centuries the powers and energies of Parliament were renewed and increased, and it became dominant in England. The English Parliament has served as a model for many other nations in the world who sought a truly representative government.

## France in the Later Middle Ages

While the kings of England were struggling to curb the power of their barons and the English Parliament was growing in strength, the kings of France were striving also to secure their throne and expand their rule over the country. The French kings had an especially hard task because feudalism was more thoroughly entrenched in France than in England. During much of this time the English kings controlled great portions of France, and the French kings had to fight both the English and their own nobles. In this fighting, much of the fair land of France was made ugly by bloody battles, burning, and looting. Despite these obstacles, the power of the French kings eventually increased and became stronger than that of the English monarchs.

At the end of the twelfth century, Philip Augustus of France attacked King John of England, who had antagonized his nobles, and took from him much of English-held France. Philip also won control of the large fief of Normandy. In the thirteenth century, Louis IX checked the lawlessness of his vassals and brought to France a better system of courts and law. Philip the Fair (1285-1314) increased his power at the expense of the Church. It was Philip who assembled representatives of the various classes or *estates* of the French people in 1302 to enlist their support in his quarrel with Pope Boniface VIII over taxation of the clergy. Philip was responsible for bringing Pope Clement V to live in Avignon, France, in 1305. For seventy years thereafter the papal residence was in this French city, where the popes were subject to the influence of the French kings.

The rise of the Estates-General in France more or less paralleled the beginning and growth of the English Parliament, and its powers were substantial during the latter part of the Middle Ages. The clergy, the nobility, and the commoners made up the three estates which were collectively known as the Estates-General. Like Parliament, however, the Estates-General declined in influence beginning in the latter part of the fifteenth century, as the power of the king increased.

### The Hundred Years' War

From 1337 to 1453 a long series of wars were fought on French soil between the English and the French. These wars, together, are commonly known as the Hundred Years' War.

Avignon, in France was visited by the ancient Greeks as well as by the Romans. Its old bridge still stands as a reminder of the Middle Ages. Use reference books to read the legend of this bridge. (French Government Tourist Office)

The Romans found a settlement on an island of the Seine and built a fortress there. They called it "Lutetia Parisiorum." The Roman town became the modern city of Paris. (French Government Tourist Office)

This war stemmed chiefly from English claims on the continent and claims to the throne of France. In 1337, the English king, Edward III, formally laid claim to the throne of France and sent an army to Normandy. The French refused to acknowledge his claim. The wars that followed were waged entirely on the land of France and made the countryside a scene of horror and devastation.

During the first part of the Hundred Years' War, the armies of England made great gains. At the battle of Crécy in 1346, the English footsoldiers with their powerful longbows routed the armored knights of the French. This battle presaged the end of the usefulness of the armored knight on horseback. During the course of the fighting chaos and disorder spread over the land of France, and the people of both England and France died by the thousands from bubonic plague—known to them as the Black Death—which spread from Asia and struck down millions of people in Europe. It is estimated that a third of the population of England died of the plague.

After the battle of Agincourt in 1415, Henry V of England was granted the French crown, but after his death in 1422 the war broke out again. The English had reached their greatest success under Henry V, and the remaining part of the war eventually went in favor of the French.

At first, the English seemed successful and took much of northern France in the renewed fighting. But the French were rallied by a girl called Joan of Arc, who brought them from the depths of their despair and led them to victories over the English. She had been impelled, she said, by visions and voices which told her to drive out the English. Under her leadership the French began to win battles. Even after she was captured by the English and burned at the stake as a heretic, the French found the unity and strength they needed to throw the British from their country.

After the English had gone, the French, under the shrewd King Louis XI (1461-1483), became more strongly centralized than before. After the Duke of Burgundy, a feudal lord, had been killed and his army defeated by the Swiss, Louis seized much of his land in eastern France. Louis slowly gained control of much of France from the nobles. By the time of his death, France had increased in size and the position of the king was greatly strengthened.

### Other Kingdoms

Strong kings also developed in other parts of Europe. In Spain, the Moors were slowly being pushed out by the Christian kingdoms in the north. In 1469 the marriage between Ferdinand of Aragon and Isabella of Castile brought these two kingdoms together in the war against the Moors. The last great Moorish stronghold in Granada was taken in 1492, and shortly afterward Spain was united under strong kings. Portugal also came to be governed by able kings. To the north, in Scandinavia, Sweden and Denmark became separate kingdoms. Norway, which had been a separate kingdom since the 800's, was united with Denmark during the 1300's and did not become independent again until 400 years later. In Germany and in Italy there was a central authority in name but not in fact.

#### The Holy Roman Empire

In central and eastern Europe there was the Holy Roman Empire. It was ruled by an emperor who was elected by a group of archbishops and the rulers of four of the more powerful German-speaking states that comprised the Empire. The Empire roughly embraced the central and eastern sections of Charlemagne's former empire. The Holy Roman Empire had its beginning with the crowning of Otto the Great by the pope in 962 as Holy Roman Emperor. It lasted until it was overthrown by Napoleon in 1806. But it was never a unified empire—only a league of independent German-speaking states and northern Italy. The title of Holy Roman Emperor carried great prestige but not much actual power over all the Empire. There were always quarrels and disputes between the nobles and the emperor, and between the pope and the emperor.

Some emperors were constantly meddling in north Italy and arousing the suspicions and enmity of the pope. This was the case in the reign of Frederick Barbarossa (1152-1190), known as "Red Beard," and that of Frederick II, his successor. The emperors never succeeded in uniting Italy or in really curbing the power of their nobles. Until the nineteenth century this empire remained divided into several hundred independent states, and both Italy and Germany remained politically partitioned until the latter part of that century.

1. Describe how Henry II replaced private feudal law with the king's law.
2. What was the *Magna Carta*? Who forced the king to sign it? Who benefited from it?
3. Describe the early development of Parliament.

## Conclusion

During the early Middle Ages, from around the fifth through the eleventh century, the Europeans struggled with the new problem of how to live in a divided land. The unity of their land had been destroyed when the Romans faltered in protecting it. They found their solution in feudalism and manorialism, which gave to their life a certain stability but limited their loyalty and their interest to a small piece of earth. After the eleventh century, however, events began to happen which gradually lifted their eyes from the narrow horizons of the manor to the broader vistas of the town and the state.

The Crusades, the bustle of trade, the accumulation of wealth, the multiplication of people, the growth of cities, all conspired to reduce the power of the feudal lords and increase the influence of the middle class and the flow of authority into the hands of the kings. The period from around 1100 to about 1450 is often described as the later Middle Ages. It may also be viewed as the preface to a new era.

It was during the later Middle Ages that political and economic power slipped steadily from the proud noble. This was an awakening time, and the Europeans began to see dimly

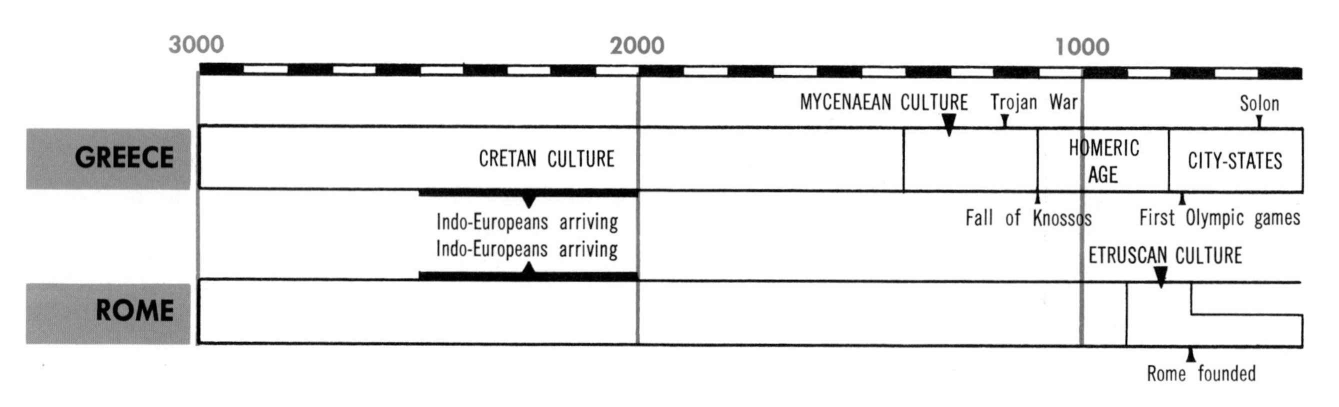


## MILESTONES

ANCIENT GREECE AND ROME

B.C.

| | |
|---|---|
| c. 3000-1200 | Cretan civilization flourishes |
| 2500-2000 | Indo-Europeans begin to migrate to Europe |
| c. 1800 | Achaeans encounter Cretans |
| c. 1400-1200 | Height of Mycenaean civilization |
| c. 1170 | Trojan Wars as related by Homer |
| c. 1200 | Fall of Knossos |
| c. 900 | Etruscans come to Italy |
| 776 | Earliest Olympic games |
| 753 | Legendary founding of Rome |
| 750-500 | Greeks colonize Mediterranean |
| 621 | Draco's code of law |
| 594 | Solon assumes power |
| c. 509 | Etruscans driven from Rome; beginning of Roman republic |
| 508 | Cleisthenes assumes power |
| 492-480 | Greco-Persian wars |
| 470-399 | Socrates |
| 461-429 | Age of Pericles |
| 450 | Twelve Tables |
| 431-404 | Peloponnesian War |
| 427-347 | Plato |

a new kind of life and a new viewpoint. An economically powerful middle class began to experiment in national assemblies and parliaments with the political and social advantages of their power; and kings employed guile and harsh measures to centralize the administration of emerging nations in themselves. There was a feeling of movement, and change, and the impulse to search. The inventions and fermentation of new ideas among the Europeans of this high Middle Age were to explode later in a great dynamic surge which would take them and their culture to the far reaches of the world.

## SUMMING UP THE CHAPTER

A. Identify the following and tell why they are important.

| | |
|---|---|
| Avignon | Estates-General |
| Battle of Hastings | Franks |
| Celts | Gaul |
| Charlemagne | Hanseatic League |
| Charles Martel | Hundred Years' War |
| Clovis | Joan of Arc |
| Louis XI | Pepin |
| Otto the Great | William the Conqueror |
| Parliament | |

B. Define or explain the following terms, relating them to this chapter.

| | |
|---|---|
| bubonic plague | page |
| estates | squire |
| fiefs | vassal |
| manor | villein |

C. Indicate the significance of the following dates.
1. 732
2. 800
3. 1066
4. 1096-1099
5. 1147-1149
6. 1189-1192
7. 1215
8. 1337-1453
9. 962-1806

D. Chapter review questions.
1. How did the papacy acquire its first secular territories?
2. Describe how Charlemagne ruled his empire.
3. What is meant when it is said that feudalism was a system of contracts?
4. Why did the manor have to be self-sufficient?

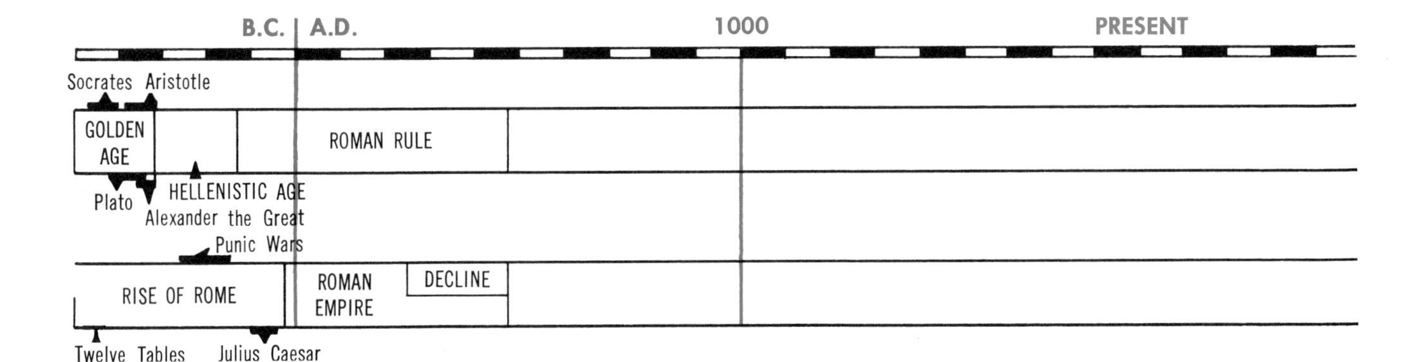


| | |
|---|---|
| 384-322 | Aristotle |
| 338 | Battle of Chaeronea |
| 338-133 | Hellenistic Age |
| 336-323 | Reign of Alexander the Great |
| 287-212 | Archimedes |
| 264-146 | Punic Wars |
| 197 | Macedonia becomes Roman dependency |
| 168 | Egypt becomes subject to Roman influence |
| 146 | Rome controls Greek city-states |
| 146-30 | Rome conquers much of Alexander's empire |
| 44 | Julius Caesar assassinated |
| 30 | Rome conquers Egypt |
| 27 | Reign of Augustus begins |

A.D.

| | |
|---|---|
| 54-68 | Reign of Nero |
| 98-117 | Reign of Trajan |
| 117-138 | Reign of Hadrian |
| 121-180 | Marcus Aurelius |
| 161-180 | Reign of Marcus Aurelius |
| 284-305 | Reign of Diocletian |
| 307-337 | Reign of Constantine |
| 313 | Edict of Milan: Christianity legalized |
| 378 | Battle of Adrianople |
| 410 | Visigoths sack Rome |
| 455 | Vandals capture Rome |
| 476 | Odoacer removes co-emperor from Rome |

5. How did the self-sufficiency of the manor make possible the entire system of feudal relationships?
6. What were the motives of the popes in calling the Crusades?
7. How were the Crusades used as a political weapon by the popes?
8. What part did trade play in the development of kingship?
9. Describe the course and results of the Hundred Years' War.
10. How did the guild system operate? How did merchant guilds differ from craft guilds?
11. How did control of the purse strings give Parliament its power? Is the power of the purse always so important?
12. How did the Crusades stimulate a revival of trade? What were the results of this?
13. How would you explain the power of the Hanseatic League? Was it a governmental body or an economic association?

E. Questions for discussion.

1. Much is heard about the man of the feudal period. What was woman's role during this time?
2. How did the medieval attitude toward marriage differ from modern attitudes?
3. Why do you suppose not even manorial lords enjoyed many comforts?
4. How did the guild come to replace the Church and the manor as the central focus of its members' allegiance? Why?
5. To what extent are modern labor and trade unions and professional associations similar to the guilds?
6. It has been said that the Holy Roman Empire was neither holy, Roman, nor an empire. Explain why this statement is true, at least in some respects. What was the origin of the name?
7. How did Italy become the leading center of trade and political power, and the intellectual heart of Europe? Was Italy a single country during the Middle Ages?
8. How did the Crusades serve as an opening wedge for the end of the Middle Ages?

F. Projects for groups or individuals.

1. Describe the relationships of feudalism, using charts, graphs, or pictorial devices.
2. Read a biography of Joan of Arc or one of the biographical novels based on her life. How was she able to rally the French against the English?
3. In a historical atlas of Europe trace the territorial changes during the Middle Ages discussed in this chapter.
4. Prepare a report detailing the explorations and settlements of the Northmen. Use maps, if you wish, to illustrate your report.
5. Describe a typical town in the Middle Ages.

# CHAPTER 19

# Concluding Thoughts About Medieval Man

MEDIEVAL MAN had inspirations, desires, and dreams which he tried to realize as best he could within the boundaries of his time and circumstance, just as all men do. His achievements were considerable.

## His Achievements

The works and thought of medieval man reflected very much the world in which he lived. Many of his works were works of the hands, and they often were inspired by the Church which gave him security in an uncertain age. There were, however, independent thinkers and men of learning and curiosity. They preserved as much of the past as they could, made their own contributions, and gradually evolved into the modern Europeans.

### A Farmer

As a serf, or villein, the man of the medieval period was bound to the earth he plowed, and life on the manor to which he belonged was burdensome and restricted. But he was not without skills, and he made a number of advances despite these limitations. He knew how to rest a portion of his land for a year so that it might regain the fertility he had taken from it. He developed labor-saving devices—such as wind and water mills—to grind his grain, cut his wood, sharpen his knives, and perform other useful tasks. Another important medieval invention was the horse collar, which made it possible to utilize work animals better and thus to improve the production of crops.

The medieval farmer was, of necessity, self-reliant, and he had a justifiable respect for the work of his hands. Physical labor was not despised, and even the educated monks worked in the gardens and vineyards of their monasteries.

### An Artisan

When trade started to increase after the eleventh century, the peasant frequently had the courage to escape from his small future on the manor to the larger future of the town. There he might learn a trade and become a skilled craftsman who made objects of quality and usefulness. He might become a woodcarver, a silversmith, a goldsmith, a maker of clocks, a mason, or a carpenter. As an artisan he joined an association called a guild, which regulated his life but in return gave him protection from the oppression of the nobles and a certain degree of economic security.

### A Builder

As a skilled artisan, the medieval man might be called upon to assist in building the great cathedral which would dominate his town. The Church was a major source of his creative inspirations, and he expended much of his artistic feelings and energy on his places of worship. At first the Europeans were influenced by Roman building designs, and their churches reflected this influence in arches and domes and in roofs supported by strong, wide walls. The windows of these churches were small, for

The towering spires and flying buttresses of the Cathedral of Chartres are characteristic of Gothic architecture. (French Government Tourist Office)

The ship model shows a "Norman cog" of the fourteenth century. This type of ship was used by the traders of the Hanseatic League. (Commercial Museum, Philadelphia)

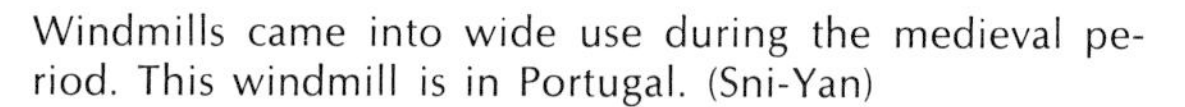

Windmills came into wide use during the medieval period. This windmill is in Portugal. (Sni-Yan)

The art of beekeeping has been known since the earliest periods of history. This etching by Pieter Brueghel the Younger shows beekeeping as it was practiced in the late medieval and Renaissance periods. (Copperplate engraving from Staatliche Museen, Berlin-Dahlem)

their builders dared not weaken the strength of the walls lest the heavy roof pressing down on the walls should cause them to collapse.

The gloomy Roman buildings did not please the builders of France and northern Europe, and they designed another type of church building which the Italians ridiculed by calling *Gothic*. The Italians meant that the design was barbarous, like the "Goth" or northern European who had conceived it. Gothic, however, is now regarded as a wonderful kind of architecture, and some of the most beautiful cathedrals and churches in Europe and the Americas have been built in this style.

The walls of Gothic churches were higher and thinner than those of Roman buildings, and the interiors were lighted by large, beautiful stained-glass windows. Gothic churches had steeply slanted roofs and spires that soared far into the sky. Their walls were braced with pointed arches of stone called *flying buttresses* so that they could withstand the outward pressure of the steep-pitched roofs without collapse. The "barbarous" Goth gave his name to an architecture that is a cherished part of Western culture.

Medieval man lavished his skill in carving statues of saints which decked the altars or complemented the outside appearance of the cathedral. Contrasted with the serene beauty of these saints were grotesquely carved devils and dragons called *gargoyles*, which were used as waterspouts to drain water from the roof. The interior of the church glowed with the soft, colored light of stained-glass windows. These windows inspired the worshiper with religious and biblical scenes made of many small bits of colored glass. These beautiful windows are among the best ever done by man. Wooden pews and altars of churches were of solid workmanship, and the walls were often adorned with paintings and mosaics.

## Schools, Teachers, and Thinkers

A few people had an opportunity to study and to learn during medieval times, and their numbers gradually increased over the years. Alfred the Great of England and Charlemagne had provided schools for the education of the sons of nobles in the early years of the medieval period. Later, however, in the eleventh century, schools became more commonplace. They were generally associated with religious institutions such as cathedrals and monasteries, but some were also connected with guilds. The early education of a student was focused on the study of the seven liberal arts: grammar, rhetoric, and logic, collectively called the *trivium*, and arithmetic, geometry, astronomy, and music, collectively called the *quadrivium*. The study of grammar was intended to give the student a solid grounding in Latin, which was the language of the Church, of most books, and the mark of an educated man during these times.

From around the twelfth century on, if he had the ambition, will, and money, the medieval student could go on to higher studies in a university. The best universities of the twelfth century were those of Bologna and Salerno in Italy, Oxford in England, and the University of Paris in France.

In the university the student might continue his studies of the seven liberal arts which led to the degree of Master of Arts. If the student obtained this degree, he was considered qualified to teach these arts to others. Or he might undertake work in the professional faculties of law, medicine, and theology. Law and theology were of great advantage to the ambitious medieval student, for they led to careers in the service of kings and the Church. The field of medicine, however, did not have the high social status that it enjoys today, and the study of medicine was not greatly advanced until the later years of the medieval period in Europe. In this age of deep religious belief, theology was the queen of sciences, and many students were inclined to study this subject.

In the latter half of the twelfth century, the works of Aristotle and the writings of the Moslems on philosophy, theology, and medicine became available to the Europeans. The rediscovery of the great Greek philosophers and the work of Moslem scholars then became a part of European learning. In medieval Europe, philosophy and theology were closely related studies in schools and universities, and the combined study of these subjects made up the philosophy called *scholasticism*. The two men who were most prominent in the founding of the philosophic system of scholasticism were the Dominican friars Albertus Magnus (1193-1280) and Thomas Aquinas (1225-1274). Thomas Aquinas, especially, attempted to reconcile and combine the philosophy of Aristotle with the doctrines of the Christian Church.

**Abelard.** If the student in medieval Europe of the twelfth century was fortunate, he might have the opportunity of studying under Peter Abelard (1079-1142), who is often referred to as the founder of the University of Paris. Abelard was a believer in the method that Socrates had used—the question method which forces the student to arrive at answers for himself rather than accept as true the authoritative statements of others.

**Thomas Aquinas.** A student in Italy during the thirteenth century might have been a classmate of St. Thomas Aquinas, who was called by his colleagues "the dumb ox" because of his slowness of speech. Aquinas may have been slow with his words, but there was nothing slow about his mind. He was much influenced by the writings and thought of Aristotle.

Aquinas was convinced that the teachings of his faith were supported by reason. Acting upon this assumption, he wrote the classic *Summa Theologica*, which systematized the Christian thought of his time. By his writing, Aquinas made Aristotle acceptable and respectable to medieval man. The teacher of Aquinas was Albertus Magnus, who also dealt with the works of Aristotle. It was generally from the teachings of Aristotle that the student of this age gathered much of his knowledge about logic and the natural sciences.

**William of Ockham.** There were other medieval philosophers, however, who did not believe that the rational approach could be used to explain religious beliefs. Chief among these were John Duns Scotus (1265?-1308) and William of Ockham (1300?-1349). Ockham sided actively with the civil rulers of Europe in their frequent attempts to deny papal authority in secular matters. He also laid important foundations of modern philosophical systems by maintaining that universal truths existed only as abstract ideas but had no reality. Ockham believed that each question should be considered in its own terms rather than as a part of a universal truth. He was, therefore, in opposition to the followers of Aristotle, who looked for great general truths. Ockham was a thinker who was far ahead of his time, and it was many centuries before later philosophers were to develop his ideas further. He is looked upon today as one of the early founders of the modern scientific method of thought and analysis.

**Roger Bacon.** Had the medieval student been a pupil of the English friar Roger Bacon, who lived between 1214 and 1294, he would have been both shocked and excited. Roger Bacon disagreed with any reasoning which first accepted something as true solely on the basis of authority or faith. He would have said: first prove by experimentation that your premise is factually correct, and then we can reason to a conclusion. This is the method scientists use today.

Roger Bacon was remarkably accurate in his predictions of the future; he foresaw the submarine, the mechanized ship, the automobile, and the airplane. They are most probably not as he saw them in his mind so many centuries ago, but he envisioned the general outline of what was to come. He wrote a book about gunpowder, and in the fourteenth century a gun to fire explosives was developed in Europe. Roger Bacon probably knew of the magnetic compass which the Arabs introduced into Europe around the twelfth century. The Europeans improved the compass and learned to find locations more accurately. This compass encouraged sailors and explorers to venture farther out on the expanses of the sea.

## Languages and Literature

Latin was a living language in Europe throughout the medieval period. It was used by Church, school, and educated men of all na-

A favorite theme of medieval literature and art was the "dance of death" which told how death leveled all social ranks. The covered bridge above is in Lucerne, Switzerland and each panel contains a different painting of the "dance of death." One of the panels is shown below. (Swiss National Tourist Office)

tions. Much of the literature of the time was composed in Latin. This medieval literature often dealt with subjects of a religious nature—religious poetry, hymns, and tales of holy men and women; but medieval writers also composed poetry and tales in Latin which were secular in content and in tone. Latin, however, was a second language of the learned, and was not known by the masses of people who spoke dialects and popular languages then evolving in Europe. It was during the medieval period that the French, Spanish, and Italian languages, which largely stemmed from Latin, came into being. In this same period, German, the Scandinavian languages, and English, which had Germanic origins among others, also developed.

Some of the earliest monuments of modern European literature were first composed during the Middle Ages. Among these were *Beowulf*, an Anglo-Saxon poem of the tenth century, the dramatic Norse sagas of the twelfth century, and the French *Song of Roland* and the Spanish *Poem of the Cid* which date from the twelfth and thirteenth centuries. Tales in prose and poetry in the popular language, called *romances*, were also enjoyed during this period. In English, some of the most popular of these stories dealt with King Arthur and his knights, and other tales, poems, and songs extolled the merits of chivalry.

Romances dealing with chivalry were pleasing entertainment for the knightly class, who saw themselves reflected in these tales of high and honorable adventures. But the members of the rising middle class, who did not share their status and their attitudes, were delighted by writings which satirized their noble rulers. The accounts of Reynard the Fox, which in part poked fun at knightly romanticism, were especially to their liking.

### He Lived for the Future

Although medieval man was not static, there were basic assumptions in his life which he believed to be eternal and unchanging. He had a spiritual outlook that conditioned his way of life and thought and made him different from the Greeks and Romans who had preceded him. The welfare of his soul was of greater importance to medieval man than the state of his body. This was constantly shown in his daily routine, his art, his learning, and his acceptance of the troubles of earth as being often unavoidable and the will of God. He was usually inclined to view life on earth as only preparatory to something finer and better in the hereafter, where he would have no problems if he but suffered in patience and remained faithful to his Church while living.

This attitude encouraged men to live for the future and to be less disposed to criticize or to question the feudal system, the short life span, poor living conditions, and secular or clerical authorities. It was an age of acceptance rather than doubt. Men were inclined to endure rather than rebel. The sojourn on earth was considered as a testing and waiting period, important only as preparation for the future.

Although the medieval period was generally one that could be described as an age of acceptance, rather than doubt, it should be remembered that this was also a lusty age. There were many men who were driven by strong ambitions—lords and kings who wanted more land and more power, and ordinary men who wanted some of the pleasures of this world before they entered the next one. Although pleasures were rude and few, medieval man also knew his moments of lightness. Students at the universities often caroused, and their drinking songs have come down to us as reminders that they sought some pleasures in this world. Moral life at courts was often lax, and even among the monks and clergy there was sometimes dissipation and worldliness.

With lessened trade and the domination of rude invaders, many of the refinements of Greek and Roman civilization had been lost, and only the Church served to preserve the cultural attainments of the past. Thus there was a great emphasis upon the spiritual life and the hereafter. This attitude, however, was mingled with a very human attitude of seeking to make the best of the present world. Medieval man had within him some remnants of his past and some promise of his future.

### The Greek Was Different

The ancient Greek, of course, would probably have disagreed with the general attitude of the medieval period, for it was quite alien to his own view of life. The Greek questioned everything, and accepted only those conclusions which he had arrived at with his reason or through experience. He was not particularly interested in luxurious living, but there was something called a balanced life, and he would have thought medieval man unbalanced.

The Greek tried to improve the beauty of form and strength of his body; he was convinced that a healthy body contributed to healthiness of mind. Further, there was a lack of independence in medieval man which would have disturbed the necessary spirit of independence in the Greek. The Greek saw beauty, dignity, and worth in man—invaluable qualities which he was concerned with emphasizing, maintaining, and furthering while he lived here and now.

### The Roman Would Not Understand

The non-Christian Roman would not have comprehended this attitude either. He was generally looking for ways and means to better his position and life on earth. He borrowed, adapted, and improved upon material conveniences and went far beyond the Greek in pampering his body. Many of the best Romans believed in the principle of moderation, in devotion to duty, and in disciplining the body, but this was in the interest of advancing the welfare of man and the state while he and it existed. Happiness hereafter did not much enter the Roman's mind until he became Christian. Both the Roman and the Greek were interested in man's life now, not his possible life afterwards.

## Medieval Man Begins to Change

Starting around the first half of the fifteenth century and continuing into the sixteenth century, the Europeans began to move closer to the Greeks and the Romans in their thoughts and actions. This period of the later Middle Ages is called the *Renaissance*, or time of rebirth. It was a period when the Europeans made a systematic effort to rediscover the thought and achievements of the Greeks and Romans which had been lost to most men in Europe since the fall of Rome in the fifth century A.D. It was a time of transition, which combined the characteristics of the medieval era and the beginning characteristics of the modern age. This modern period did not start abruptly. It had its origin during the medieval period which we have just discussed.

While medieval man held the basic view of the temporary nature and unimportance of his physical life, and looked forward to the permanency of his spiritual future, he sometimes undertook activities which had far-reaching consequences. He embarked upon the Crusades to the Holy Land, and there was a certain spiritual motivation at the basis of these expeditions. But they brought Europe into contact with the magnificent civilizations erected by the Byzantines and the Moslems.

The Europeans were impressed. The learning, science, and material advances of the Byzantines and Moslems moved the men of Europe to desire these things for themselves. The Europeans came into contact with the Moslems of Spain and marveled at their medicine, architecture, and material comforts, even though the Moslems were trying to destroy the Christians and drive them from the country. Some medieval men knew there was a more comfortable manner of life practiced by others.

After Europe had settled down into feudalism, trade began to flourish once again, and towns multiplied to handle this trade. The increased import and export of material goods brought about an expansion of wants and of wealth. There was a freer atmosphere in the towns, and discussions of ideas and novel opinions were tolerated more than in the conservative atmosphere of the rural manors. Universities began to grow, and as in all universities, there were debates, arguments, and the clash of conflicting opinions. Men wondered about their long-cherished ideas, although few dared speak about their doubts

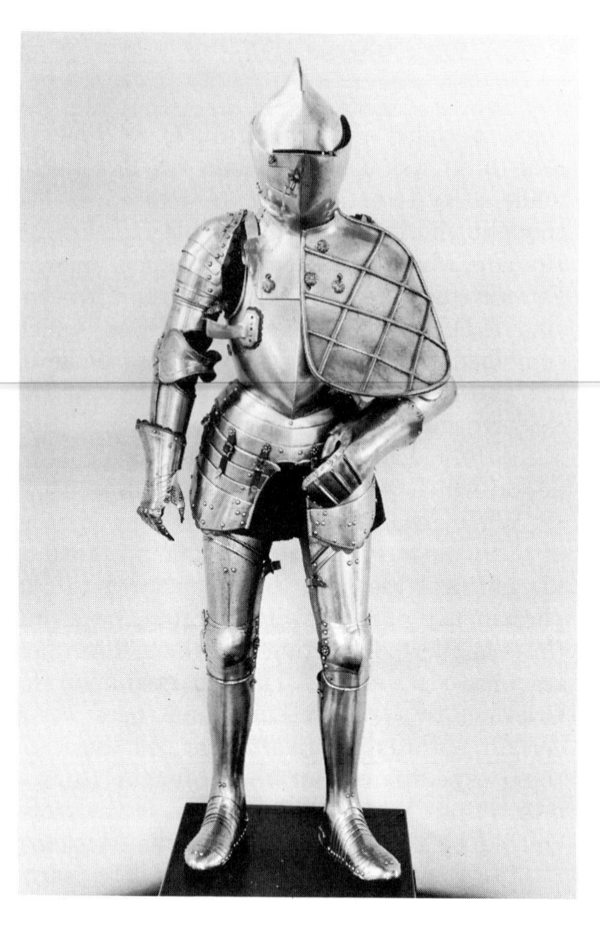

Chain mail armor, below, was most commonly used during the period of the Crusades. Plate armor, above, came into use later. (The John Woodman Higgins Armory, Worcester, Mass.)

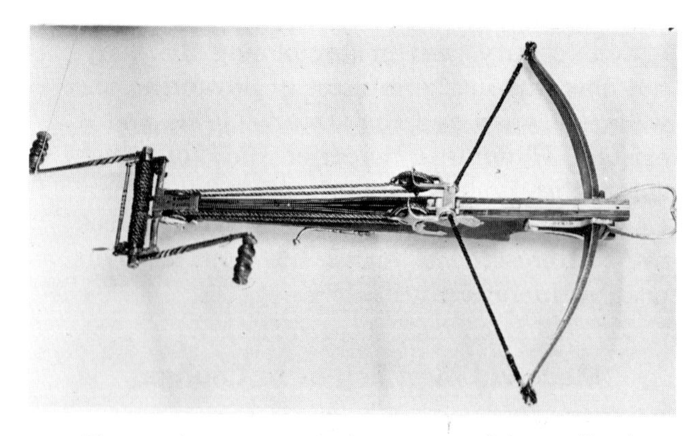

The crossbow was a popular weapon of the medieval period. A powerful crossbow could pierce plate armor. Arrows from a longbow could be shot much faster than from a crossbow, and the longbow also had a greater range. (The John Woodman Higgins Armory, Worcester, Mass.)

and questions; doubters were regarded as subversive and might be burned at the stake. In every society, towns and cities are the catalysts of civilization, and medieval towns were no exception.

Kings were jealous of the independence of their vassals, and they were ceaselessly engaged in trying to increase their own power. They eventually succeeded, but in the process they helped to introduce new ideas, new liberties, and new concepts of the rights of man. A king of England introduced the use of juries to his subjects and encouraged his people to look to the king for justice rather than to the feudal lord. In the process he strengthened his own power, but he also gave to his subjects a better way and right to justice. Kings began to look to the wealthy commoners for money to wage their wars, and the commoners took advantage of this opportunity to gain certain privileges for themselves, their middle class, and their cities.

The Church was an integral part of medieval man's life. He did not usually doubt its teachings, but he often doubted the rightness of some actions of the clergy. It was difficult to have great trust in a bishop who lived like a tyrannical and cruel feudal lord or a cardinal who was more interested in advancing his own power and wealth than in spiritual matters. There were also some popes who appeared to work exclusively for the advancement of a particular king or the possession of a particular piece of land rather than the welfare of the Christian community. All these actions caused many men to question the system of the Church, at least privately.

1. How do Gothic and Roman styles of architecture differ from each other?
2. Where were the best twelfth-century universities located? Who was Roger Bacon?
3. What was the *Summa Theologica*?

### Conclusion

The medieval period was a time in which change was slow, and the emphasis of man's thought was on a spiritual future. The attitudes of the earlier Greeks and Romans had been laid aside, but not forgotten. Their lively ideas and outlook were preserved and would come to life again. The growth of trade and towns brought a freer atmosphere. The Crusades brought new ideas and renewed contact with the Middle East. The spirit of questing and questioning found renewed life as medieval man began to look about at the world of the present, to think and ask about the here and the now.

All of these questions, ideas, and events caused a quiet ferment in the mind of medieval man. This ferment burst forth into an expression which became more intense as the years moved on to the modern age. With this expression the ideas and accomplishments of Greece, Rome, and the Middle East converged with the medieval accomplishments of Europe. From their mixing, the modern age began to take shape.

## SUMMING UP THE CHAPTER

A. Define or explain the following terms, relating them to this chapter.

| | |
|---|---|
| flying buttress | Gothic |
| gargoyle | university |

B. Chapter review questions.
   1. How did the guild benefit the artisan?
   2. What were the requirements for a Master of Arts degree in twelfth-century Europe? Have the requirements for this degree changed much in the past several hundred years?

C. Questions for discussion.
   1. Why do you suppose medieval man was willing, generally, to accept his situation in life without questioning it?
   2. Can the term *medieval* be properly applied to parts of the world other than Western Europe? What are some of the difficulties in applying the term to India, the Americas, or China?

D. Projects for groups or individuals.
   1. Read a collection of poems from the Middle Ages and write a short essay discussing the subject matter of the poems.
   2. Use several reference books and read more about William of Ockham. Find out what is meant by the term "Ockham's razor."

# SUMMING UP THE UNIT

### *Drawing together the main themes*

1. How was the Greek heritage preserved? By whom? Who transmitted this heritage back to the European? Where? When?
2. Contrast the life of the ancient Greeks and Romans with the life of the Europeans in the Middle Ages. How would you explain this vast difference?
3. Why did the man of the Middle Ages concern himself so little with the comforts of life or with bettering his condition?
4. Why do you suppose cities and towns are always the heart of a civilization and the source of ferment and change?
5. Why did the Roman law disappear in the West during the Middle Ages? What took its place?
6. Some scholars believed that one reason for the eventual decline of feudalism was the fact that the relationship between overlords and vassals was inherited. How do you think this would have contributed to the downfall of the system?
7. What economic reasons led the towns of the later Middle Ages to grant the freedom of the town to all who lived there a year and a day?
8. How was the rise of centralized authority in the person of the king related to the rise of towns? Is this relationship of centralized power and cities true today? Why or why not?
9. Explain the process whereby the Crusades led to trade, which encouraged the growth of cities, which led to the breakup of feudalism and the rise of kingship.
10. What was the source of the wealth which supported the magnificent culture of the Renaissance?
11. What stimulated the man of the later Middle Ages and the Renaissance to attempt to recover the past of Rome and Athens?
12. How did Europe, often described as only a tiny peninsula of Asia, come to be the "tail that wagged the dog"? What made this possible?
13. The breakdown of the social and political systems of the medieval period has been described as the result of their failure to give justice. Explain this in terms of 1) relations between rulers and the Church; 2) the growth of towns; 3) the rise of powerful kings; 4) the rise of the guild system; and 5) that whole complex of changes which historians call "the Renaissance."

### *Unit projects for individuals or groups*

1. Two terms were used for much the same office: *tyrant* by the Greeks, and *dictator* by the Romans. Both of these terms have been carried over into our vocabulary, but with changes in their popular meaning. Show by reference to good Latin and Greek dictionaries and to the *Oxford English Dictionary* how the meanings of these terms have changed. What other terms used in this unit have undergone similar changes in meaning? What does this tell you about the necessity of specifying which particular meaning is intended when certain words are used?
2. Collect a portfolio of illustrations of some of the great Gothic cathedrals of Europe. Does your city or town have any churches or other buildings with Gothic architecture?

## FURTHER READINGS


AUGUR, HELEN, *Book of Fairs.* Harcourt, 1939. All about fairs during the Middle Ages.

BALDWIN, MARSHALL W., *The Mediaeval Church.* Cornell U., 1953, paperback. The Church during the Middle Ages.

BOLTON, IVY M., *Son of the Land.* Messner, 1946. The adventures of a runaway serf in England.

BRAGDON, LILLIAN J., *Land of Joan of Arc.* Lippincott, 1952. Readable and interesting.

BREASTED, JAMES H., *The Conquest of Civilization,* new rev. ed. Harper, 1938. Informative chapters on early Greece.

CHUBB, THOMAS C., *The Byzantines.* World, 1959. Clear and informative.

COTTRELL, LEONARD, *The Bull of Minos.* Holt, 1958; Grossett, paperback. Cretan life is portrayed.

DAVIS, WILLIAM S., *A Day in Old Rome.* Biblio & Tannen, 1959.

———, *A Day in Old Athens.* Biblio & Tannen, 1960.

———, *Life on a Medieval Barony.* Harper, 1928. These three books describe the daily life of man in Classical Greece and Rome and on a thirteenth century manor. Interesting and readable.

DEHKES, EVELYN, *The Young Viking Warrior.* Bobbs, 1953. An interesting novel about the Scandinavian Viking.

DIEHL, C., *Byzantine Portraits,* Knopf, 1927. The Byzantines are portrayed in an informative and interesting manner.

DOYLE, ARTHUR CONAN, *The White Company.* Dodd, 1927, and various other publishers. A well-told story about English mercenaries in France and in Spain.

FOSTER, GENEVIEVE, *Augustus Caesar's World.* Scribner's, 1949. A good description of the Roman world into which Jesus was born.

FOWLER, WILLIAM W., *Social Life at Rome in the Age of Cicero.* Macmillan, 1909. How people live together is always important to an understanding of them.

GAER, JOSEPH, *How the Great Religions Began,* rev. ed. Dodd, 1956; New Am. Lib., paperback. A treatment of an important subject and important historical figures.

"Greece," *Life* (various issues, 1963). Beautiful illustrations and good commentary on ancient Greece.

HALL, JENNIE, *Buried Cities.* Macmillan, 1922. The tale of the digging up of old cities like Mycenae and Olympia of Greece, and Pompeii in Italy makes for interesting and informative reading.

HARTMAN, GERTRUDE, *Medieval Days and Ways.* Macmillan, 1937. Gives us a good look at the daily life of medieval man.

KIERAN, JOHN AND DALEY, ARTHUR, *Story of the Olympic Games,* rev. ed. Lippincott, 1961. A modern sports writer comments interestingly on old Greek sports.

LAMB, HAROLD, *Alexander of Macedon.* Doubleday, 1946.

———, *Charlemagne: The Legend and the Man.* Doubleday, 1954.

———, *Constantinople: Birth of an Empire.* Knopf, 1957.

———, *The Crusades.* Doubleday, 1945. Bantam, paperback.

The titles are explanatory. Lamb writes well, and his books show good research.

MILLS, DOROTHY, *Book of the Ancient Greeks.* Putnam, 1925.

———, *Book of the Ancient Romans.* Putnam, 1927. Books written especially for high school students.

———, *The Middle Ages.* Putnam, 1935.

POLO, MARCO, *Travels,* ed. by Manuel Komroff. Liveright, 1953. Exciting tale of the famous Venetian traveler.

POWERS, ALFRED, *Hannibal's Elephants.* McKay, 1944. Through the eyes of Hannibal's elephant keeper we see much of the great exploits and problems of the great general in fighting on Roman soil.

PYLE, HOWARD, *Men of Iron.* Harper, 1891; Globe (adapted), 1954. A story of the chivalrous Englishmen of the 1400's.

QUENNELL, MARJORIE AND CHARLES H. B., *Everyday Life in Roman Britain.* Putnam, 1952.

———, *Everyday Things in England.* 4 vols. Putnam, 1956.

These two books tell much about daily life in England during the Roman occupation, and in the period from the Norman Conquest until around 1500.

———, *Everyday Life in Anglo-Saxon, Viking, and Norman Times.* Putnam, 1955.

SCOTT, SIR WALTER, *Ivanhoe.* Dodd, and other publishers. An exciting tale focused on a time when the Normans and the Saxons were mixing in England, around 1300.

———, *Quentin Durward.* Dodd, and other publishers. Another good story at the time when Charles the Bold of Burgundy and Louis XI of France were competing for power.

SELLMAN, ROGER R., *The Crusades.* Roy, 1955. The Crusades had an impact upon the European.

TAPPAN, EVA M., *Story of the Greek People.* Houghton, 1908.

———, *When Knights Were Bold.* Houghton, 1911. Well-written stories about the Greeks and the Europeans of the Middle Ages.

THORNDIKE, LYNN, *History of Medieval Europe,* 3rd ed. Houghton, 1949. The Middle Ages are treated in a solid manner.

TREBLE, HENRY A. AND KING, K. M., *Everyday Life in Rome in the Time of Caesar and Cicero.* Oxford U., 1930.

WALLACE, LEW, *Ben Hur.* Various publishers. A Jewish boy makes an appealing and exciting hero in a tale of ancient Rome.

# UNIT IV

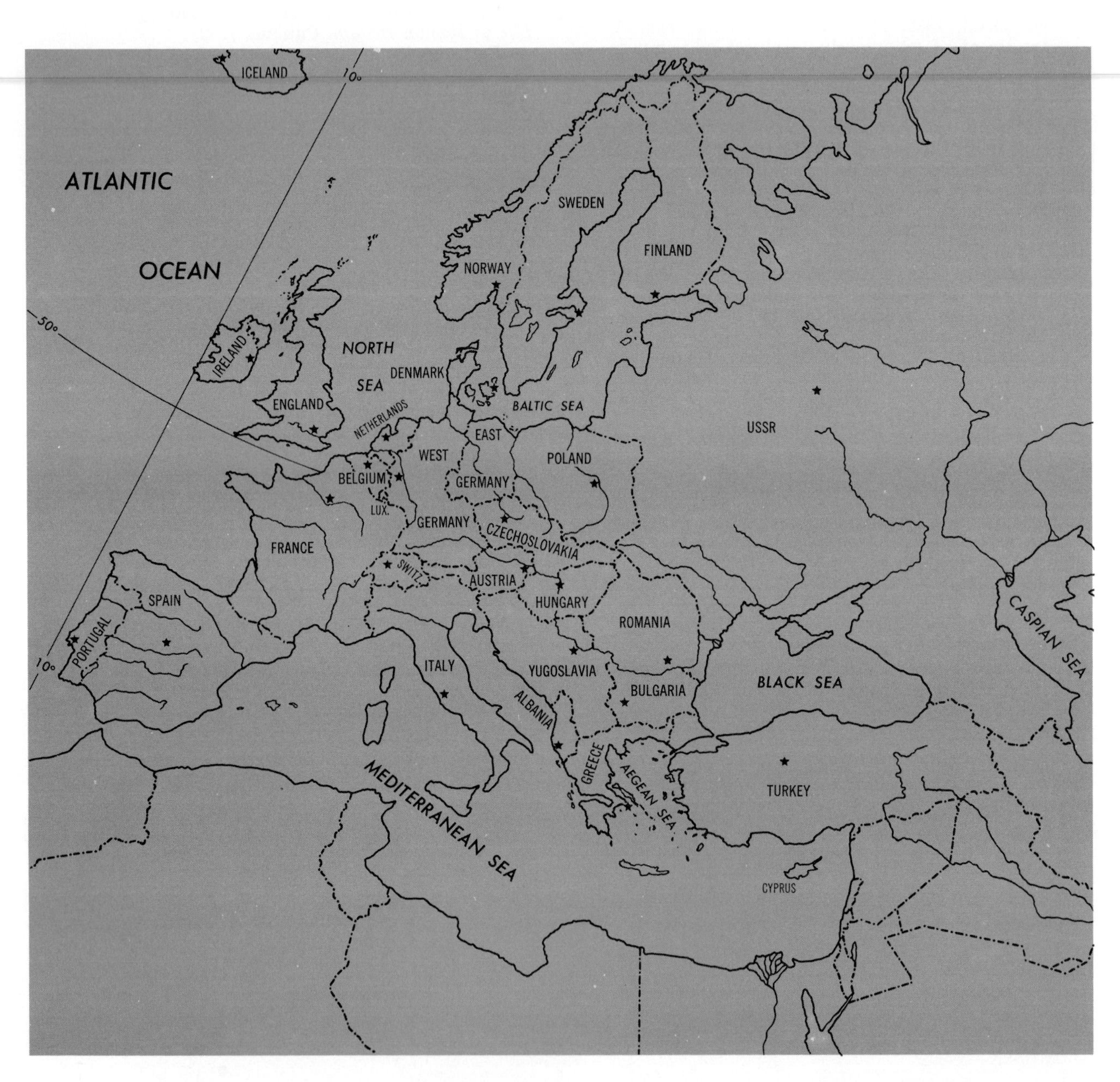


The large political map shows present-day Europe. Stars indicate capitals.

# THE EVOLUTION OF THE MODERN EUROPEAN

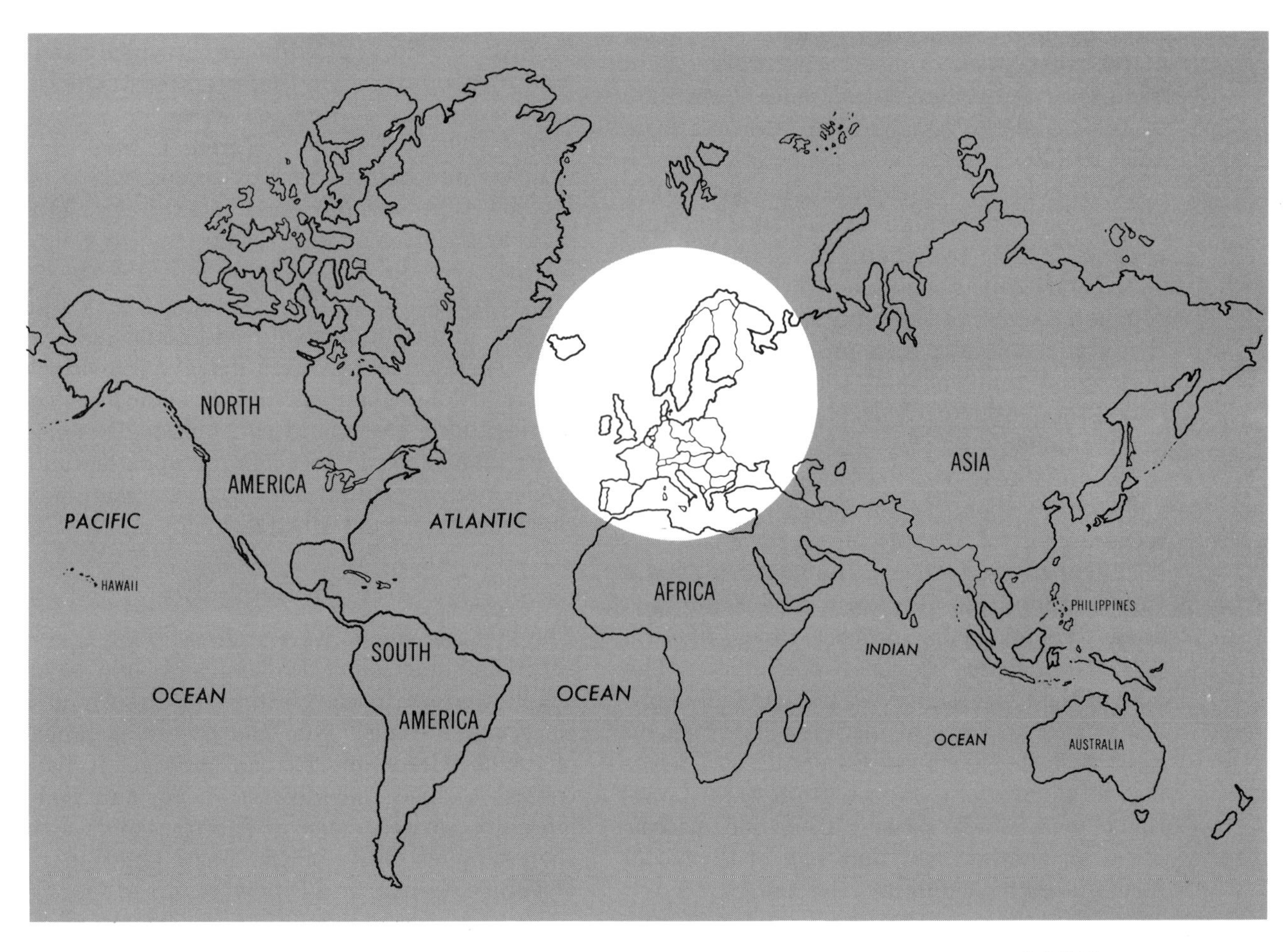

# CHAPTER 20

# An Ending and a Beginning

AROUND 1350 A PERIOD BEGAN which marked an increase in the speed of transition from medieval to modern times. During a span of around two hundred and fifty years there was an era of rapid change from older viewpoints and ways to new and somewhat different ones. This period from around 1350 to around 1600 is usually labeled with the name *Renaissance*, which literally means "rebirth." Some writers have described the Europeans of this period as being born again into the cultural brightness with which the Greeks and Romans had formerly illuminated the world. This period of rebirth has sometimes been considered in two parts: the Italian Renaissance, from 1350 to 1550, and the Northern Renaissance from 1450 to 1600.

It should be remembered, however, that names such as "Middle Ages," "Italian Renaissance," and "Northern Renaissance" are only handy labels, and they do not give the complete picture of the time. As we have seen, the later medieval period produced a number of original thinkers, and the men who produced the Gothic cathedrals cannot be called unenlightened.

There was a period of time from around 500 to 1000 when the Europeans were groping to find a way of life suitable to the chaos and disunity which followed the decline of the Roman Empire in the West. The Europeans knew dark moments in those times, but the cultural darkness was never complete. The man of the Renaissance was not suddenly born again with no trace of his immediate past in him. And the medieval European was never in a total cultural darkness. Both were transitional men, slowly passing from one manner of life to another, and they had in them elements of both the old and the new.

Man's present is always linked with his past. He is constantly rediscovering and adapting older ideas and practices for use in his present surroundings. Renaissance man found that the Greeks and Romans had placed an emphasis upon earthly life which was pleasing and gratifying. He was inspired by their example to modify his present, and in modifying it he began to build something new.

## Man of the Renaissance

The man of the Renaissance gradually emerged from the medieval atmosphere, in which there was great concern for the afterlife. Medieval man regarded his time on earth only as a period that had to be endured. It was preliminary and unimportant by comparison with the life that was promised after death. The man of the Renaissance began to think differently. He did not lose his religious spirit, but he started to believe that life on earth had its own unique importance and could also be good. He became convinced that the individual was entitled to an earthly existence which would afford immediate satisfaction. Renaissance man centered his attention upon distinctively human aspirations and interests. For this reason he is described as a *humanist*.

## The Italian Humanists

The first humanists were Italians. This is not surprising, for many Italians had long been acquainted with the cultures of the Byzantines and Moslems, who had preserved much of the old Greek and Roman heritage. Italian traders roamed the Mediterranean, and Italian ships carried many of the Crusaders and their supplies to the Middle East. The traders of Venice, Genoa, and Pisa were famed for the extent of their commerce. They specialized in trade with the Byzantines and Arabs.

During the period beginning around the middle of the fourteenth century, Italy was broken up into a number of small states ruled by men who had a genuine interest in art and letters. These rulers were interested in promoting the finer creations of man. Some members of the Medici family of Florence, especially Cosimo and Lorenzo the Magnificent—and other individuals such as Ludovico Sforza of Milan and the culturally inclined popes—vied with one another in searching out the classical Greek and Roman writings.

Increasing numbers of Italians studied ancient Greek and Roman works, and they were impressed by the emphasis the ancients had placed upon man and his life on earth. This attitude was in sharp contrast to that of the medieval writers, who focused their attention almost chiefly upon man's relationship to God. The humanists were attracted by the older outlook of the Greeks and Romans. It appealed to their human nature. Their writings began to reflect this influence.

Dante Alighieri of Florence (1265-1321) wrote in the Tuscan dialect, which was his native tongue. This was an unusual innovation because at that time Latin was the usual language of writers. Gradually Italian writers began using the Tuscan language. Thus Dante became the father of the modern Italian language. He wrote a still-famous poem, the *Divine Comedy*, which relates the story of an imaginary trip through Purgatory and Hell guided by the Roman poet Virgil. The *Divine Comedy* tells the stories of many famous historical personages encountered on this journey. Dante used his poem to criticize his society. Characteristic of the Renaissance man was his inclination to criticize the conditions of his society and to criticize the clergy.

Petrarch, who lived during the fourteenth century, had wide interests and was eager for fame. He is sometimes called the father of humanism. He was a collector of old manuscripts, a traveler, a student of archeology, and an excellent lyric poet. He was also a critic of the medieval viewpoint.

The English Renaissance reached its height in literature with the plays of William Shakespeare, above. (The Folger Shakespeare Library) Shakespeare's Globe Theatre was the showplace for his plays, below. (Model by John Cranford Adams and Irwin Smith on loan to The Folger Shakespeare Library)

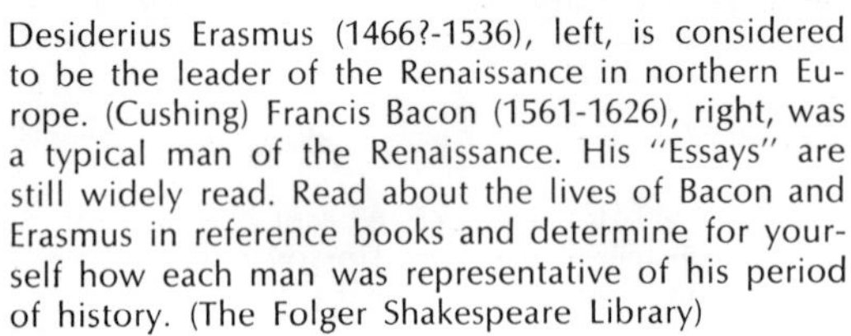

Desiderius Erasmus (1466?-1536), left, is considered to be the leader of the Renaissance in northern Europe. (Cushing) Francis Bacon (1561-1626), right, was a typical man of the Renaissance. His "Essays" are still widely read. Read about the lives of Bacon and Erasmus in reference books and determine for yourself how each man was representative of his period of history. (The Folger Shakespeare Library)

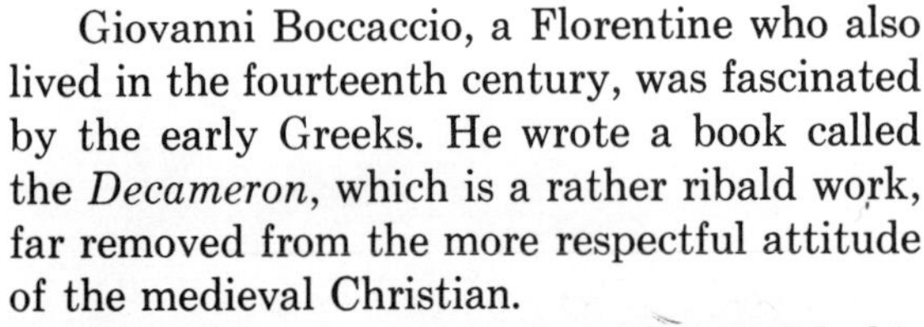

Giovanni Boccaccio, a Florentine who also lived in the fourteenth century, was fascinated by the early Greeks. He wrote a book called the *Decameron*, which is a rather ribald work, far removed from the more respectful attitude of the medieval Christian.

The political commentator Niccolò Machiavelli (1469-1527) observed the disorderly and divided state of politics in Italy and decided that a strong ruler should use any means whatever to bring peace and stability out of the chaos of his country. Machiavelli ignored morality in the choice of a means to accomplish political aims. He advised those who wanted power over other men to employ whatever methods might be required to achieve their goal, without particular concern for right or wrong. He expressed many of his political ideas in his book *The Prince*. Machiavelli looked at man and described him as he often actually is rather than in an ideal form.

Other men who followed these humanists built up libraries, wrote, spoke, and contributed to the cultural ferment which was widespread among the educated and noble classes of Italy. This knowledge did not remain confined to Italy. It moved across the Alps and seethed elsewhere in northern Europe.

## Other Humanists

Erasmus, a Dutchman who lived from around 1466 to 1536, was one of the greatest of the humanists. He held mankind in high regard and declared that man's evil came only from ignorance and the human tendency to blunder. Erasmus was ever conscious and respectful of the potential in man as evidenced by Jesus, Socrates, Cicero, and others. He traveled throughout Europe and taught at some of its best universities. Erasmus published a New Testament in Greek; it differed in some respects from the official Latin Church version, called the *Vulgate*. These differences raised doubts in the minds of some men about the official version. Erasmus was an excellent Latin scholar. He spoke with penetration about the failings of man and held that war was silly. Erasmus pricked the consciences of those who thought only the people of their own nationality were the chosen ones, and he criticized the laxity of the clergy. The title of one of his most famous works, *Praise of Folly*, indicates his sense of humor and satire.

Geoffrey Chaucer, who lived in England from around 1340 to 1400, displayed a Christian point of view in his *Canterbury Tales*. The high value of the spiritual and the chivalry of the knight shine forth in these tales; but there is also present the spirit of the Renaissance. Chaucer used the English tongue of his day, rather than Latin, to tell his stories. His tales are enlivened by descriptions of the earthiness of man.

Another Englishman, Sir Thomas More (1478-1535), criticized society by conceiving a place called Utopia, where everything was perfect. Today, when we wish to dismiss the suggestions of another as impossibly idealistic, we call them *Utopian*.

In France, François Rabelais (1494?-1553) urged man to live naturally, joyfully, and honestly. He thought that man could improve his life by study and by use of his reason. In his novels, Rabelais created two giants, one known as Gargantua and the other, his son, Pantagruel. They lived life to the fullest and on a gigantic scale. Gargantua's name is now part of the English language; sometimes a thing that is very large is described as *Gargantuan*, meaning "giantlike."

An early printing press was pictured on the title page of an edition of Horace printed at Paris in 1511, above. Use reference books to learn more about the early days of printing. (Rare Book Department, Free Library of Philadelphia)

1. Define the term *Renaissance*. How accurately does this term describe the fourteenth, fifteenth, and sixteenth centuries in European history?
2. Who were some of the great Italian humanists? Upon what classical writings was their thought based?
3. Identify the Vulgate.

## Printing

The writings of the humanists became widely known because the Europeans discovered the art of printing with movable type during the 1400's. The Chinese had been the first printers, several centuries earlier, and they had carved their writing on blocks of wood which were then inked and pressed against silk or other material. The ancient Egyptians had made a paper of the reed known as papyrus, and the Moslems living in Spain passed along to the Europeans a knowledge of how to make paper from rags. For many years the Europeans had laboriously copied manuscripts by hand. This meant that a very small number of books were produced, and that errors crept into works copied over and over again. Long hours of copying and recopying can cause a man to become bored, tired, and less attentive to his work. Then all this changed.

In the 1440's a German named Johann Gutenberg invented a method of molding individual letters from metal. As many letters as needed could be cast and arranged together in a frame, inked, and impressed upon a sheet of paper. These molded metal letters could be used over and over again. Gutenberg's invention revolutionized the making of books and made possible a great spreading of knowledge. Printing presses were much faster and more free of error than works done by hand. Although only the rich could afford books during the early days of printing, the use of printing undoubtedly helped to spread the learning of the humanists. Eventually printing made it possible to produce books for a broader reading public and contributed to the growth of literacy.

### The Artists

Incredible, magnificent, and versatile men made the art of the Renaissance a unique and permanent part of our artistic heritage. Almost everyone is familiar with at least a few of the works of such masters as Leonardo da Vinci, Michelangelo, Titian, and Dürer. Copies and photographs of their masterpieces are known throughout the world.

While medieval artists had often produced their works as offerings to God, the artists of the Renaissance were not at all disposed to work and live obscure and unknown. They were hungry for fame and material rewards here and now. Giotto, who lived from about 1276 to 1337, worked with religious themes in churches and chapels. He wanted all to know that the work was his, and he wanted good payment for his creations. He associated with the nobles and the wealthy. Giotto was a shrewd businessman who lent money at high interest and owned a debt-collection agency.

Some Renaissance artists continued to paint religious themes, but with a new approach. In their works, the humanity of man and a greater sense of his earthly nature shone forth. Even the most spiritual ideas came to be expressed in terms of physical and worldly beauty. The heavenly subjects of Renaissance religious paintings seem human in appearance and emotions. Fra Angelico (1387-1455) painted Old and New Testament subjects and scenes sacred to Christian tradition and teaching. Masaccio (1401-1428) portrayed the drama of man's emotional and spiritual life, and perhaps his greatest work is the painting of the expulsion of Adam and Eve from the Garden of Eden. The figures of Adam and Eve reflect the depths of their tragedy as the angel drives them out of Eden.

Other Renaissance artists responded to the spirit of their time and painted portraits of individuals—churchmen, kings, princes, nobles, and wealthy merchants and their families. The emphasis of the humanists upon the individual and his worldly activities brought new inspiration to the art of portrait painting. The pictures of individuals were more than just likenesses—they expressed the personalities of their subjects.

Many artists of the Renaissance found their inspiration in the lifelike beauty of Greek and Roman art. They studied anatomy and learned to depict the human body in all of its beauty. Some of them found their subject matter in the mythology of the Greeks and Romans and painted the ancient gods and goddesses. Botticelli (1445-1510) painted the *Birth of Venus* and portrayed the gods in the springtime. Scenes of important events of their own time also interested the painters of the Renaissance, and Paolo Uccelo (1396-1475) is especially remembered for his painting of a battle between the armies of Florence and Siena.

In this age of artistic greatness, none were greater than Leonardo da Vinci (1452-1519), Michelangelo (1475-1564), and Titian (1477-1576).

Leonardo da Vinci was fantastic in the scope of his talent. His paintings of *The Last Supper* and the *Mona Lisa* are widely admired. He was an observant scientist who kept notebooks in which he sketched plants, animals, fossils, and inventions ranging from two-level highways to airplanes. He was one of the world's greatest geniuses.

Michelangelo was another towering artist of this period, and his works still capture and stagger the imagination of man. He thought and worked in great dimensions. Lying on his back, he painted the ceiling of the Sistine Chapel in the Vatican to create the grandest story of the Creation ever told. Four years were required to complete the painting. He was not only a painter. He was a sculptor of gigantic figures. His statue *David* weighs ten tons. Michelangelo also chiseled the magnificent statue *Moses*, and for a chapel of the Medici family the figures *Night*, *Day*, *Dawn*, and *Twilight*. Men still gaze with awe and amazement at these works of stone which express such power and feeling. Michelangelo also designed the great dome of St. Peter's Cathedral in Rome.

The Venetian artist Titian is credited with having painted a picture a month for eighty years. He liked rich, vivid colors, and he painted all kinds of subjects: Madonnas, battle scenes, aristocrats, kings, merchants, and popes.

There were many other artists who were identified with the Renaissance in Italy. Among them were Raphael Santi (1483-1520), whose *Madonna of the Chair* and *Sistine Madonna* are regarded as masterpieces, and Benvenuto Cellini (1500-1571), whose work in silver and gold is highly treasured today. Nor was the Renaissance limited to Italy. Great artists in Germany, the Low Countries, and Spain came forth to make this whole period one of exploding talent. Albrecht Dürer (1471-1528) and Hans Holbein, his contemporary, are among the best known of the German painters. Among the seventeenth century Dutch painters were Rubens, Van Dyck, and Rembrandt. The best-remembered of the Spanish painters of this time are Velásquez (1599-1660) and El Greco (1548?-1614?). All of these artists belonged to the tradition of painting established in the Renaissance.

Renaissance artists experimented with new techniques which considerably improved the appearance of their creations. They strove to give a three-dimensional impression to the flat surface of their pictures by skillful use of colors, by the use of detail, contrast between light and shade, and the use of perspective. They sought greater accuracy in their portrayal of man and of nature, and to achieve this purpose, painters undertook the study of anatomy, botany, and physics.

Around the fifteenth century, oil paints came into wide use, and these paints made possible many new techniques. Prior to this time, paintings had been made chiefly with tempera paints (colors mixed with egg whites, milk, or some other liquid). Tempera paints were applied onto a surface which was prepared by being coated with glue. The paints were almost transparent, and very beautiful effects could be achieved with them. But it was necessary to work very quickly before the paints dried, and it was very difficult to make any changes once the paints were applied. Oil paints, on the other hand, were very slow-drying, and this made it possible for the artist to work more slowly and carefully. Because they were not transparent, it was possible to paint over mistakes with oil paints, and hence an artist could make his paintings much more nearly perfect. While the Italian artists were still working with tempera paints or painting frescoes on wet plaster, the painters of Northern Europe were developing the techniques of oil painting. Soon the use of oil paints was common throughout Europe.

Artists were very important during the flowering of the Renaissance in Europe. Their importance was witnessed by the rich and mighty who competed to obtain their services. The artist who was hired by a rich prince or noble was often richly supported and showered with official positions, money, and favors. Popes, kings, nobles, and rich tradesmen commissioned artists to adorn churches, buildings, and palaces, or to paint their portraits. The genius of the artist enhanced his own and his patron's reputation in their own time and gave them both lasting fame for centuries thereafter.

### Science and Technology

Renaissance man did not stop with the discovery of new techniques in the arts. He also questioned the world of nature and the physical laws which governed the earth, the stars, and the body of man. Leonardo da Vinci observed that plains were formed over a long period of time by soil washed down from the mountains. He questioned the dogmatic statements of the majority who proclaimed that the earth was but a few thousand years old.

Copernicus, left, and Galileo, right, advanced the study of astronomy during the Renaissance. (Yerkes Observatory, University of Chicago) Compare Galileo's drawing of the moon's surface, inset, with the photograph made by a modern telescope and camera. (Both, Yerkes Observatory, University of Chicago)

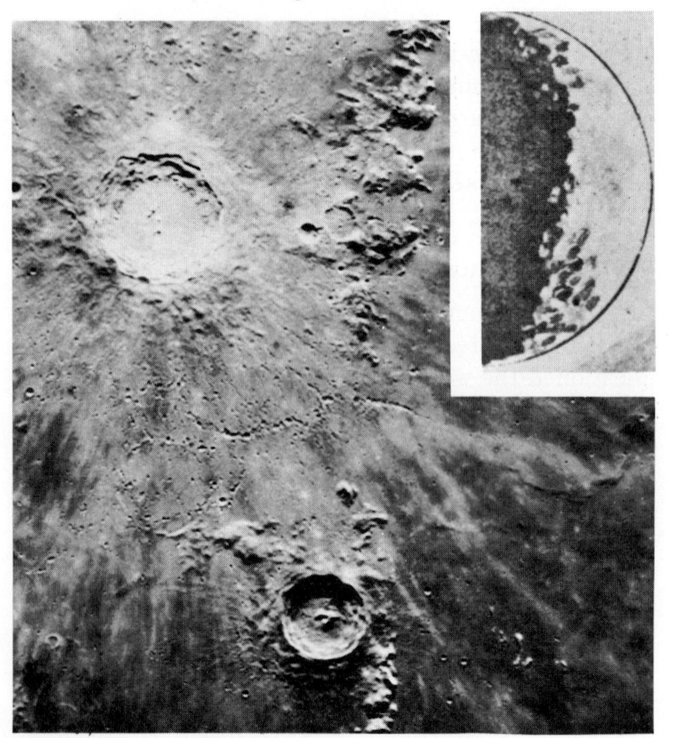

Copernicus (1473-1543) was a Polish astronomer of German ancestry who studied in Italy. He could not make his mathematics agree with the prevailing theory that the earth was stationary and the heavenly bodies revolved around it. He began to think of the earth and the other bodies of the heavens as moving around the sun. Copernicus was the forerunner of Galileo and other great experimenters and discoverers of the sixteenth and seventeenth centuries.

During this period man began to improve his technology with such advances as the printing press, a knowledge of gunpowder, deeper knowledge of geology and mining, improvements in shipbuilding, and better charts and compasses which prepared the Europeans for their great voyages of discovery. All of these served to widen man's horizons and to stimulate him to even greater efforts to know himself and his environment. Men began to look more carefully at the human body and to study the nerves, muscles, and blood circulation. They started to doubt the worth of many medieval medical practices.

Some men began to criticize and actively oppose some of the practices and teachings of the clergy. This eventually led into a period known as the Reformation, which brought conflicts between men and nations and disturbed men's consciences for centuries. The Reformation changed many medieval religious practices within the Catholic Church, and it led finally to the establishment of Protestantism as a form of Christianity practiced by millions of men.

1. Why was the invention of printing important?
2. What changes were brought about in artistic expression during the Renaissance?
3. What scientific and technological advances were made during the Renaissance?

## Man of the Reformation

The Catholic Church had been having problems with secular authorities and with certain of its own members and clergy for a long time. When the popes were able and strong and feudalism was still the accepted way of life, the Church enforced its spiritual and even political supremacy in Europe. As kings gained power and dreamed of empire and national centralized states, however, they frequently saw in the pope a threat to their political and economic strength. They often quarreled with him over the right to appoint church officials in the lands they ruled. They looked with envy upon the vast possessions of the Church which were exempt from their taxes. They were also displeased that the clergy were beyond their legal jurisdiction and could be tried only by the Church.

Growing numbers of clergy and laymen ridiculed and satirized the lax lives of churchmen, high and low. Then they began to question the doctrines which these churchmen preached but did not practice. The atmosphere of the Renaissance was one that encouraged inquiry rather than acceptance, and the Church was not spared the doubt and criticism of the Renaissance man. Further, some of the popes during this time were not conspicuous for their holiness or their interest in the welfare of the great masses of the Christian community.

Papal prestige and authority had been lowered when, from 1309 to 1377, a succession of popes lived in Avignon, France, rather than Rome. In Avignon, of course, they were subject to the influence of the French kings. The citizens of Rome and other Europeans resented this French domination over the papacy. This period is sometimes known as the "Babylonian Captivity of the popes." When the pope did return to Rome, a quarrel ensued between the French and Italian factions. The French cardinals elected another pope who moved again to Avignon. There were now two popes, one at Rome and one at Avignon. Each excommunicated the other and called him false. The European Christian was faced with the task of determining to which pope he would give his allegiance. His choice was often determined by political considerations.

The period of a divided papacy, which lasted from 1378 to 1417 is usually referred to as the Great Schism. It ended when a Church council was called and met at Constance in Germany in 1414 to settle this divided authority and to bring about a reformation within the Church. After several weary years of debate and discussion, the Council of Constance managed to have one man elected as pope, but did little about reforms except to suggest certain recommendations to the new pope.

There had been indications of a rebellious temperament among a number of clergy and laymen. John Wycliffe, a friar and teacher at Oxford, England during the fourteenth century, held that the Church should give up all its wealth. He proclaimed that the clergy were not necessary for the salvation of man. Wycliffe wrote a translation of the Bible in English. His writings were widely read and accepted. One of the men he influenced was John Huss, a Bohemian, who attacked the clergy and proclaimed these same doctrines. Huss was excommunicated and, in 1415, was burned at the stake as a heretic. But ideas and movements are difficult to burn away.

Then, on October 31, 1517, Martin Luther, a German professor of theology who was angered by the selling of indulgences, attached his Ninety-five Theses to the door of a church in Wittenberg, Saxony, and the Reformation exploded in Europe. In the Theses, Luther attacked many of the Church's teachings. The Church taught that an indulgence could remit all or part of a repentant sinner's future punishment in Purgatory. Luther took issue with the Church especially in the matter of beliefs and practices having to do with these indulgences.

After the publication of Luther's Ninety-five Theses, religious and political divisions among the Europeans multiplied wtih startling rapidity. Out of a multitude of conflicting claims, differing religious practices, and wars there emerged the third large branch of Christianity, known as Protestantism. It stands today as a major division of the Christian faith beside Roman Catholicism and Eastern Orthodoxy. Protestantism embraces a membership of over two hundred million Christians.

### Martin Luther

Martin Luther was a professor of theology and had also studied the law for a time. He was worried about the salvation of his soul and undertook to save it through rigorous fasting, pilgrimages, and other good works. But they gave him no peace of mind. At last he found a passage in the Bible telling him that faith in God would save him. Then his doubts about salvation were finally resolved. Luther was in good standing in the Church until he nailed his Ninety-five Theses to the door of All Saints' Church in Wittenberg. He was goaded into this deed by the extravagant claims of a monk named Tetzel, who was trying to raise money through the sale of indulgences.

The Church taught that every sinner who wished his sins forgiven must confess them to a priest with sorrow for having committed them, and undertake some penance which would show his sorrow. He would then receive pardon from the priest who acted as a representative of God. This is the Sacrament of Penance. But the punishment or penance the sinner performed on earth might not be sufficient, and after death the sinner might be required to undergo further punishment in Purgatory before being allowed to enter Heaven. An indulgence would remit all or part of this punishment by drawing upon all the unused good works accumulated by Jesus, His mother Mary, and the saints.

It appears that Tetzel went beyond the Church's doctrine on indulgences in his eagerness to obtain money. Martin Luther attacked the commercialism of Tetzel in rescuing sinners from Purgatory. In doing so, he also attacked some of the basic teachings of the Church which lay behind indulgences.

The officials of the Church reacted swiftly and harshly. In 1518 Luther was asked to retract some of the propositions he had made in his Theses. He refused. In 1519, in a debate with the theologian John Eck, Luther was pressed to answer whether he accepted the authority of the popes and the councils of the Church. Luther replied that their authority was not necessarily final. The controversy became bitter. The Pope condemned the teachings of Luther in 1520. Luther burned the condemnation. By this time he had arrived at the conclusion that man could achieve salvation by faith alone. He denied that a priest had the power to remit the punishment due to sin.

Luther was excommunicated and declared an outlaw. He was asked once again if he would retract his words and teachings. He replied that unless he was convicted of error on the testimony of the Scripture, he would take back nothing. It was too late for the officials of the Church and the Holy Roman Emperor Charles V to chastise Martin Luther, because Frederick III, the ruler of Saxony, protected him, and other German princes rallied to his support.

Martin Luther wrote in the German language, and his writings were widely read and accepted, especially in the northern part of Germany. He taught that the Christian could find salvation through faith alone, and that the clergy, although helpful, were not essential to salvation. He urged the Christian to seek his guidance from God in the Bible. To assist the individual in finding this guidance, he translated the Bible into German. By this teaching he actually encouraged education in Germany; it was now important for each person to read the Bible, and reading meant study and learning.

Luther's secular writings helped to stir the nationalistic spirit of the Germans and to buttress the authority of the ruling German princes. Luther deplored the fact that the Germans were required to pay taxes to Rome. He urged the princes to stop this economic drain upon German resources and to throw off the authority of the pope. A number of German princes, who resented sharing their authority with an Italian foreigner, responded to this invitation. They embraced the teachings of Martin Luther, seized the riches of Church property within their states, and declared the Lutheran Church to be the official religion of their states. It was the practice of the time that the people had no choice but to follow the religion elected by their ruler, unless they overturned his decision by force.

The teachings of Martin Luther swept beyond the borders of the German states to Norway, Denmark, and Sweden. Within the short space of slightly more than ten years, the Lutheran Church became official in Denmark and Norway, and a short time later, in Sweden.

When the Holy Roman Emperor Charles V forced his Diet—an assembly similar to a parliament—to declare the Lutheran doctrine to be heresy, a number of the Lutheran princes protested. They refused to accept this decision. It is from their protestation that the name *Protestant* stems. To this day this word describes all Christians who consider the Reformation as the formal historical date of their beginning. Wars broke out between the Protestants and the Catholics in Germany. These wars were finally ended by the Peace of Augsburg in 1555. By this time Lutheranism was entrenched in northern Germany, and Catholicism in southern Germany.

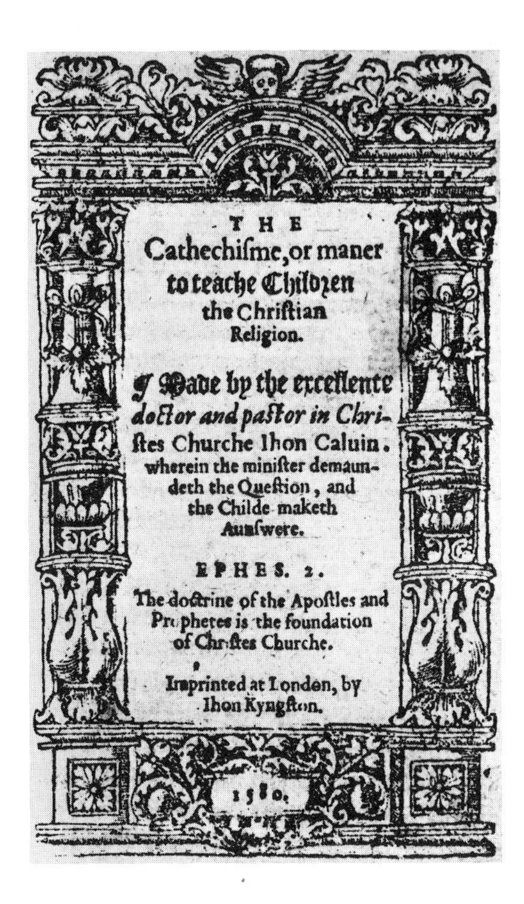

THE
Cathechiſme, or maner to teache Children the Chriſtian Religion.

¶ Made by the excellente doctor and paſtor in Chriſtes Churche Ihon Caluin. wherein the miniſter demaundeth the Queſtion, and the Childe maketh Aunſwere.

EPHES. 2.
The doctrine of the Apoſtles and Prophetes is the foundation of Chriſtes Churche.

Imprinted at London, by Ihon Kyngſton.

1580.

John Calvin (1509-1564) was a leading figure of the Reformation. The title page of his Catechism in English is shown above. (The Folger Shakespeare Library)

1. What frictions developed between the Church and the kings of Europe? Between the Church and the clergy?
2. Identify the Ninety-five Theses. Why were they written? What happened to the author?
3. Why do you think so many German princes accepted the teachings of Luther so readily? How did this strengthen their political positions?

### Ulrich Zwingli and John Calvin

Ulrich Zwingli (1484-1531), a humanist, began a quieter Protestant movement in Switzerland. He, too, saw no need of a priest nor, for that matter, of incense, candles and other ornamentation, which he conceived as superstitions. He also denied the worth of indulgences.

Under the leadership of a Frenchman named John Calvin, Protestantism made rapid progress in Switzerland and spread from there to France, Scotland, Holland, Hungary, southern Germany, and other parts of Europe.

In 1536 John Calvin published a book entitled *Institutes of the Christian Religion*, which provided the doctrinal foundation for a type of Protestantism often referred to as *Calvinism*. It is from ideas in this book that the Presbyterian Church and later Protestant groups spring. John Calvin wanted no stained-glass windows, altars, burning incense, nor other outward symbols that might distract the Christian from direct communication with God. Calvin became all-powerful in the city of Geneva. He was quite strict in prohibiting dancing, card-playing, ostentatious dress, obscenity, and frivolous and worldly vanities. He regarded religion as a very serious business that people should approach in a serious manner. Calvin taught that no one could be sure he was saved; hence it was necessary for all men to search their consciences constantly and to strive always to live a moral life.

Men came from all over Europe to Geneva to hear the doctrines of Calvin, and they returned to their own countries to spread them to others. The French who came returned to France and converted many of the middle class of the towns and cities. They were known in France as *Huguenots*. Wars were fought between the Huguenots and the French king, and finally in 1598 by the Edict of Nantes they were granted a measure of freedom of worship and were also granted political rights.

John Knox came to Geneva from Scotland and, after a period, returned there to found the Calvinist Presbyterian Church. This church replaced the Catholic Church in Scotland. Calvinist ideas flowed into England and there influenced men called Puritans, who later were among the first settlers of the British colonies in New England. These Puritans laid a deep imprint upon the thinking and the customs of the colonies which later became the United States. These teachings of John Calvin were impressive in the scope of their impact.

## England Breaks with Rome

The second Tudor king, Henry VIII, ascended the throne of England in 1509 at the age of eighteen. It was during his reign that England broke with Rome. Henry's father, the first Tudor king, Henry VII, had shown a strong determination to enhance the royal power. Through shrewd policies, he broke the power of the feudal nobles of his realm and left to his son a kingdom well along toward centralization and a full treasury. The versatile Henry VIII was an athlete, a horseman, a composer, and a musician—a man of many talents. He was beloved of the Pope in his youth, for he had written a pamphlet against the doctrines of Luther. Pope Leo X found Henry's words so valuable that he gave him the title "Defender of the Faith." Later, Pope Clement VII had cause to regret that this title had been bestowed upon the English king, for Henry was headstrong, stubborn, and ready to sweep aside anyone or anything that stood in his way. Henry quarreled with Clement VII and defied his authority because the Pope would not sanction a divorce.

One of Henry's desires was to have a male heir to his throne, but he had no son by his first wife, Catherine of Aragon, who was the widow of his brother. The Pope hesitated when Henry requested an annulment of his marriage so that he might marry Anne Boleyn. Catherine had powerful political connections, being the daughter of Ferdinand and Isabella of Spain and the aunt of the Holy Roman Emperor, Charles V. Moreover, Henry had already received a papal dispensation to marry Catherine. Henry would tolerate no hesitation. With the help of the new archbishop of Canterbury, Thomas Cranmer, a Church court declared his marriage null and void. Henry then obtained from Parliament the Act of Supremacy, in 1534, which made the king the head of the Church in England and severed ties with the pope of Rome. Pope Paul III finally excommunicated Henry in 1538.

Henry took his new wife, and others followed her. He also confiscated the properties of the monasteries and convents in England.

The elaborate costumes of the sixteenth century are shown by the dress of Mary, Queen of Scotland, shown with her second husband, Henry, Lord Darnley. Mary was executed for plotting the assassination of Elizabeth, Queen of England. (The Folger Shakespeare Library)

The plain dress of unpretentious English folk of the sixteenth century is shown at left. (The Folger Shakespeare Library)

Some properties he kept for himself, and portioned out others to his loyal followers and nobles. He tightened his control over all the affairs of the English nation. When Henry VIII died he left the throne to his ten-year-old son, Edward VI. Henry left England stronger and more centralized than when he inherited it from his father.

Edward reigned for only a few years, but in this space of time his advisors, who were influenced by Calvinism and Lutheranism from the continent, managed to carry England even farther along the Protestant way. This trend toward Protestantism was curtailed by the new queen, Mary, who succeeded Edward. She was a devout Catholic who was married to Philip II of Spain. She tried to restore England to the old faith and its former allegiance to Rome. But Mary ruled for only five years. She was succeeded by Elizabeth I, who was the daughter of Henry VIII and his second wife, Anne Boleyn.

Elizabeth I brought England to some of its greatest peaks of prestige during the forty-five years of her rule. She was called Good Queen Bess, and was a fascinating woman whose subjects gave her their hearts and their loyalty. Many a prince and king asked her hand in marriage, but Elizabeth was married to her nation, and her heart was set upon making England a sound and prosperous country. She had been raised a Protestant, and she renewed the task of making England Protestant.

During Elizabeth's reign, the Thirty-Nine Articles were published, setting forth the official doctrine of the Church of England, or the Anglican Church as it is often called. In the United States it is known as the Episcopal Church. This Church, which became the official Church of the English, was supported by state taxes. It retained a number of the ceremonies and beliefs of the Roman Catholic Church, but its head was the ruler of England, not the Roman pope. Calvinist influences were also pouring into England, but Elizabeth tried to practice a policy of toleration. She wanted to keep her realm free of the religious wars which were making chaos of much of the European continent.

1. What were the major teachings of John Calvin? From which groups were his followers primarily drawn?
2. What personal reasons led Henry VIII to sever ties with Rome? What economic and political factors buttressed this move and made it popular?
3. What was the attitude of Elizabeth I toward religious worship in England during her reign? What did she hope to accomplish by this attitude?

## The Thirty Years' War

The year 1618 marked the beginning of a war on the lands of the Germans which continued intermittently but savagely until the Treaty of Westphalia in 1648. Ill will between the Catholics and Protestants greatly contributed to the beginnings of this war. The political and economic results of these religious divisions within Germany kept the war going over a long period of time. But there were also purely political factors which brought various countries into this war. Catholic France was at this time under the guidance of Cardinal Richelieu. He secretly subsidized the Protestant Swedish armies at first, and later France entered the war publicly. Richelieu feared the power of the Hapsburg family who ruled the Holy Roman Empire.

The Hapsburg family had a long and distinguished history. Hapsburg counts had made their home originally in Switzerland about 1020, and with the passing of the centuries, their wealth and influence increased. Eventually Rudolf of Hapsburg (1273-1291) was elected Emperor of the Holy Roman Empire by the princes of Germany. From this time until the 1900's, the Hapsburgs were among the most influential rulers in Europe. Members of the Hapsburg family were emperors of the Holy Roman Empire and kings of Spain, Austria, and other European nations. Few families have rivaled them in power and prestige.

Richelieu feared the growing power of the Hapsburgs especially because they ruled both Spain and central Europe. France lay between these Hapsburg lands as if it were in the jaws of a vise. Richelieu wanted the Hapsburgs weakened to the point that they would not be a threat to France. The Danes and the Swedes sympathized with their fellow Protestants who were being massacred and slaughtered by the hired soldiers—called mercenaries—of the Catholic Hapsburgs. They were not averse to using this opportunity also for taking over some of the former Baltic possessions of the Holy Roman Empire.

The war started in Bohemia, a country which had been independent within the Holy Roman Empire, but which the Hapsburgs incorporated under the rule of the Austrian branch of their family. In their Catholic zeal, the Hapsburgs further angered the Protestant Bohemians by refusing them freedom of worship. The Bohemians rose in revolt and chose a Protestant prince as their king. The Hapsburg armies moved in, badly defeated the Protestants, and drove out their new king. Bohemia remained a province of Austria for centuries thereafter. But this seizure of Bohemia frightened the Danes, Swedes, and French. They saw that this same Hapsburg power might eventually absorb them too. Quite naturally the European Protestants were aware that if the Hapsburgs won, their religion and their continued existence would be in doubt.

The Danes, under King Christian, were the first foreign group to enter the war. They were beaten by the Catholic forces under the able leadership of two commanders, Wallenstein and Tilly. The armies of Wallenstein and Tilly were really made up of mercenaries who lived off the land where they camped and fought. Soldiers in search of plunder, and soldiers filled with religious fervor swarmed to the battlefield of Germany. The merged motivations of religion and plunder can often result in unspeakable tragedy. This was the fate of the Germans whose lives and lands were ravaged by the fanaticism and greed of these mercenaries. Farming villages and cities were sacked and burned; women were ravished; harvests were confiscated or destroyed; famine swept over the land; and disease and pestlience were rampant. Germany, within a short time, was a place of ruin and despair.

Then, under the military genius of Gustavus Adolphus, the Protestant Swedes entered the war and won victory after victory for the Protestant cause. When Gustavus Adolphus died in battle, the Protestants grew afraid. But the Catholic French, guided by the diplomatic mind of Cardinal Richelieu, went into the war against the Hapsburg-ruled Spanish and Austrians. Their entry into the struggle weakened the arms of the Hapsburgs. Eventually all the participants became weary and exhausted by this prolonged war. It ended with the Treaty of Westphalia in 1648.

### Results of the War

The Hapsburg kings were weakened by the Thirty Years' War, and their power declined in relation to that of France. The Treaty of Westphalia brought many changes to Europe. The German princes, three hundred of them, were guaranteed independence; they could make peace or war and handle their own diplomatic relations, independent of the Holy Roman Emperor. The Swedes obtained valuable and strategic lands on the Baltic coast. Holland and Switzerland were formally recognized as independent countries. France gained Alsace on the border of Germany. The state of Brandenburg-Prussia, under the Hohenzollern family, received territory which contributed to its growing might. The Protestant Calvinists were extended the same privileges as the Lutherans and the Catholics, and Protestant princes who had held Church lands in 1624 were permitted to retain them. Although religious hatreds and frictions continued, there was a general feeling that the rivalry should be restricted to more peaceful competition for the good of all.

The war left Germany a divided, desolated land and delayed its unification for several centuries. It did, however, contribute to the rising power of Prussia, whose Hohenzollern rulers were later to rule a united Germany. In 1618 the territories of Brandenburg —in which Berlin was located—and East Prussia were united. Under Frederick William, the Prussians won momentous victories in the closing days of the Thirty Years' War. Under a succession of able kings, the army was made into a fine professional force, and the economic affairs of the kingdom were well handled. By the eighteenth century Prussia was one of the most powerful of the German states and, in fact, one of the most powerful states of Europe.

### The Catholic Reformation

The religious upheaval of the Protestant Reformation did not leave the Roman Catholic Church unchanged. In addition to Martin Luther, there were many other men of the Church who called for reforms. These voices finally found an answer to their appeal in the Council of Trent, which met a number of times between 1545 and 1563. This Council firmly restated the important doctrines of Catholicism and accomplished many reforms within the Church. These reforms were intended to stem the tide of Protestantism by the correction of abuses which had led so many men to break with Catholicism. The Council strongly affirmed the supremacy of the pope in the Church. The education of priests was improved, and the religious education of laymen was also strengthened. In order to preserve and protect the faith and morals of its members, the Church began to issue an Index of Prohibited Books, listing writings the faithful should not read without special permission. Decrees were published concerning the sacraments, indulgences, Purgatory, the veneration of saints and so forth. All of these strengthened and clarified the doctrines of the Church.

Although the Protestant Reformation began originally within the Church, it soon became a political issue as well. It was accompanied by a strong movement within the Roman Catholic Church which helped to give that body much of its modern shape. The Society of Jesus (known as the Jesuit Order) was founded by St. Ignatius Loyola (1491-1556), and it was extremely helpful to the Church in carrying out reforms and in preaching against heresy. The period of great reforms continued up until the end of the Thirty Years' War, so that as Protestantism was emerging as an established movement, the Roman Catholic Church was also undergoing changes in its attitudes and policies.

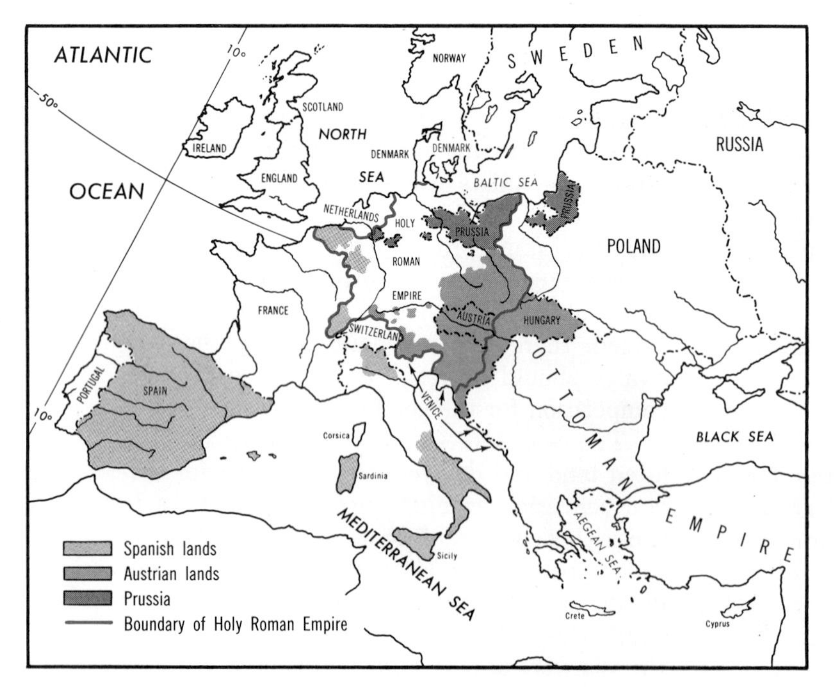


**Europe After the Thirty Years' War, 1648**

In 1648 the Thirty Years' War was ended by the Treaty of Westphalia. From this time until its end in 1806, the Holy Roman Empire existed in name only. Each of the several hundred German states conducted its own affairs independently. The period of the Thirty Years' War marked the beginning of the slow growth of Prussia that led eventually to the unification of Germany.

1. Where did the Thirty Years' War begin? What were the primary causes of this war? Why did it last so long?
2. What part did Gustavus Adolphus play in the Thirty Years' War?
3. What are some of the most important consequences of the Catholic Reformation?
4. How did the Thirty Years' War contribute to the rise of Prussia?
5. What was the Council of Trent?

## Conclusion

For centuries man had quietly accepted the hardships of his life as bordering on the inevitable. His religious faith told him that there awaited a paradise which would have no end. Temporary evils must be suffered with the right attitude if the timeless delights of eternity were to be attained. Then, during the

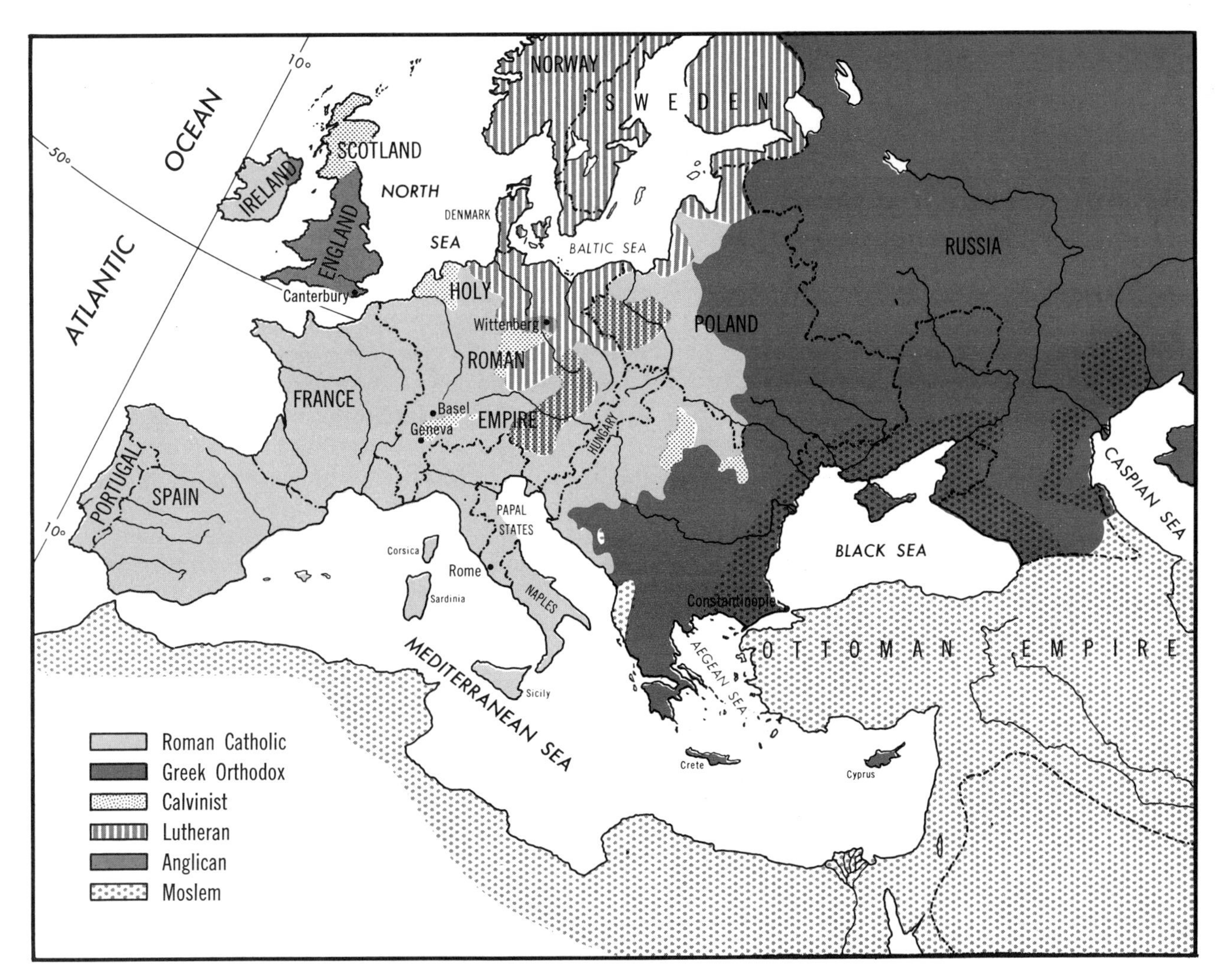


**THE RELIGIOUS DIVISIONS OF EUROPE ABOUT 1550**

The Protestant Reformation brought about religious divisions in Europe that led to a long series of religious wars. In some cases a state church made one religion dominant (as in England), while in other states, several forms of Protestantism existed side by side with Catholicism. What effect did the Protestant Reformation have upon the Holy Roman Empire?

The reforming Protestants sought simplicity and disapproved of images and decorations in churches. The stone carvings on the Cathedral of Berne, Switzerland, escaped destruction during the upheaval of the Reformation. (Swiss National Tourist Office)

fourteenth century, the European began to question this attitude. He wondered if man might not enjoy some satisfaction and happiness while yet alive. He looked back to the ancient Greeks and Romans and was attracted by their emphasis on the physical world of man. They had believed that man might find some happiness on earth, and they had found beauty in mankind. The European, too, began to discover this potential for happiness and this beauty. As the centuries unfolded, this attitude of questioning and seeking increased in depth and intensity. A new acceptance of man's earthly nature replaced the old attitudes, and this spirit grew as the modern European evolved.

Although he became engrossed with the material side of life, the European did not lose his concern for the spiritual nature that was a part of him. He was a questioning man now, and he began to re-examine customary beliefs and practices. During the 1500's the branch of Christianity known as Protestantism began. A primary purpose for all Protestants of this period, and thereafter, was to remove accumulations of practice and doctrine which often seemed to obscure the original teachings of Jesus. The Protestants maintained that they were restoring its former purity and simplicity to Christianity. In searching out this past purity, they emphasized the spirit rather than the letter of the law. They also stressed the responsibility of the individual to look to the Bible for the truths and the guidance of God. This emphasis led to the translation and publication of the Bible in many languages. Because many people were illiterate, it was necessary to teach them to read. This necessity encouraged the expansion of schools and education.

The Protestants were convinced that the Roman Catholic Church had gradually introduced certain ceremonies and teachings which were alien to the beliefs and practices of the first Christians. They differed among themselves, however, in determining which were alien and which were not. Many Protestants—for instance, the Calvinists and the Puritans—felt that statues of saints, the burning of incense, the use of stained-glass windows in churches, and praying with beads were all practices that were foreign to Christianity. The Anglicans of England, however, found these objects and practices quite acceptable and in the Christian tradition. Many did not believe that bread and wine were actually changed by the priest at Mass into the substance of the real body and blood of Christ. Martin Luther, for instance, thought that a mysterious change took place, though not in the same way as the Church taught. Most Protestants denied that it was necessary to obtain forgiveness of sin and remission of punishment from a priest, but a number of Anglicans still believe it is essential.

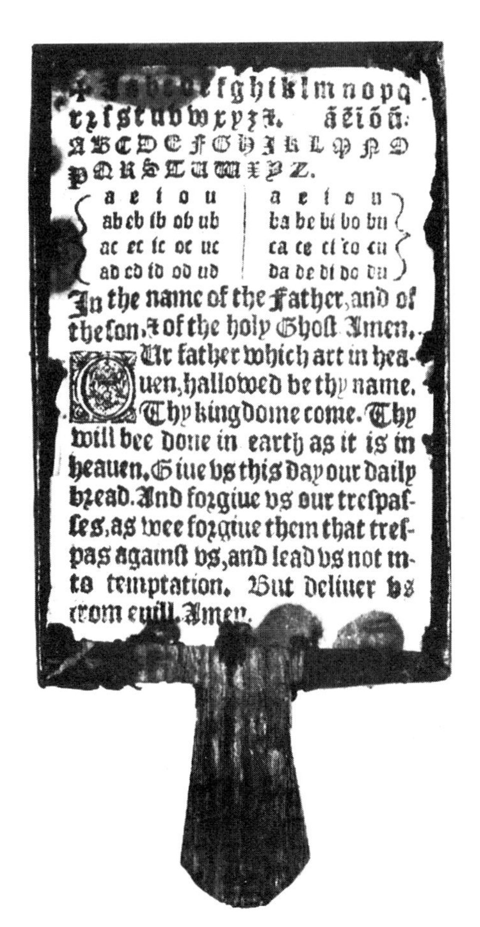

a e i o u | a e i o u
ab eb ib ob ub | ba be bi bo bu
ac ec ic oc uc | ca ce ci co cu
ad ed id od ud | da de di do du

In the name of the Father, and of the Son, & of the holy Ghost Amen.
Our father which art in heauen, hallowed be thy name. Thy kingdome come. Thy will bee done in earth as it is in heauen. Giue vs this day our daily bread. And forgiue vs our trespasses, as wee forgiue them that trespas against vs, and lead vs not into temptation. But deliuer vs from euill. Amen.

The Protestant reformers encouraged their followers to read the Bible for themselves, and education grew during the 1500's. The hornbook at right is typical of those used to teach reading in Elizabethan schools. It is made of a sheet of parchment mounted on wood and covered by a thin sheet of transparent horn. (The Folger Shakespeare Library)

These differences of opinion and belief led to divisions within Protestantism which led to the formation of many different *denominations*. These divisions are a source of regret and sorrow to many Protestants. There are now continuing efforts to find a unity which will bring these denominations all closer together.

The religious upheaval known as the Reformation left some permanent secular marks on the history of man. It contributed to the disappearance of the medieval way of life, and to the formation of a middle class which in turn formed the bases of modern democracies. It continued the process started in the Renaissance of questioning the most fundamental aspects of life. Max Weber, the German historian, reasoned that because of its stress upon saving, thrift, and hard work, the Reformation contributed to the growth of capitalism. He cited the Dutch, Germans, English, and the New England Yankees to support his argument.

It is most probable that the Reformation helped to strengthen the growing feeling of nationalism in Europe. The religion of a people became rather closely identified with politics in the state. Rulers were often suspicious of those people within their realm who professed a different religion from their own or from that of the majority. French kings generally suspected the French Protestants, known as Huguenots. The princes of north Germany and the Scandinavians were suspicious of the Catholics within their midst, as were the English rulers. The English became convinced of the subversive nature of the Catholics when Spain—a strongly Catholic country—sent the ships of its Armada against England in 1588. People began to refer to their nations as being either Catholic or Protestant, a fact which demonstrated the mixing of politics and religion.

The birth and growth of Protestantism played a major role in the religious, economic, social, and political evolution of man in the West. Protestantism continues today to influence and mold the lives of millions of men throughout the world.

## SUMMING UP THE CHAPTER

A. Define or explain the following terms, relating them to this chapter.

| | |
|---|---|
| denomination | indulgences |
| Gargantuan | mercenaries |
| Huguenot | Utopian |
| humanist | |

B. Identify the following and tell why they are important.

| | |
|---|---|
| Act of Supremacy | Johann Gutenberg |
| Calvinism | Martin Luther |
| Dante Alighieri | Petrarch |
| Erasmus | *The Prince* |
| Geoffrey Chaucer | Tetzel |
| Good Queen Bess | Thirty Years' War |
| Hapsburgs | Thirty-Nine Articles |
| Henry VIII | Treaty of Westphalia |

C. Identify the following dates and indicate their importance.
   1. October 31, 1517
   2. 1378-1417
   3. 1555
   4. 1588
   5. 1618-1648

D. Chapter review questions.
   1. What is the humanist view of man? Explain the views of important humanists in your answer.
   2. Name four of the great artists of the Renaissance. What are their most famous works?
   3. What are the most significant dates in the history of the Christian Church between 1309 and 1555? Why are these dates important?
   4. Explain what Calvin may have meant in opposing "outward symbols that might distract the Christian from direct communication with God."
   5. Trace the history of Protestantism in England.
   6. What were some of the political, economic, and social results of the Protestant Reformation?
   7. In what ways was the Renaissance both a beginning and an end? In what ways was it a transition to something new?

E. Questions for discussion.
   1. What were the major sources of the revival of classical thought which characterized the Renaissance? How did the Middle Easterners and North Africans play a role in bringing the heritage of Rome and Greece to Europe?
   2. The Florentine diplomat and historian Machiavelli has become a symbol of political and diplomatic cunning and dishonesty. Do you believe this reputation was deserved, or was Machiavelli merely a realist? Support your answer with a discussion of his views on the political art.
   3. How would you explain the concern of the Renaissance humanist with personal fame? Explain in terms of the philosophical bases of humanism and the classical origins of the Renaissance.
   4. One of the most important features of the Italian Renaissance was the patronage, or support, of art and artists (and even of scientists) by those with wealth. To what extent do you believe this accounted for the great advances of the Renaissance and for the magnificence and quantity of artistic achievement? Compare Renaissance patronage of the arts in Europe with other times and places in the world, including the present.
   5. Explain how the political, economic, and social history of Italian city-states contributed to the intense feeling of the Italian for his city.
   6. How do you account for the many denominations within Protestantism, while most other major religions have relatively few? What has been the effect of these divisions?

F. Projects for individuals or groups.
   1. Read several of Chaucer's *Canterbury Tales.*
   2. Prepare a report on the artistic masterpieces of Leonardo da Vinci. Prepare a report on his scientific and technological achievements.
   3. Draw maps of Europe before and after the Thirty Years' War. Note the areas which passed from the control of one country to another and those whose independence was recognized.
   4. Read a historical novel dealing with the Italian Renaissance. Report in class on some of the important features of Renaissance life and thought which are brought out in the book.

# CHAPTER 21

# *Discoverers and Claimers*

Beginning in the fifteenth century the Europeans launched upon voyages of discovery which, during the next two and a half centuries, took them into all the world. These explorations and discoveries brought changes to the Europeans as well as to the people whose lands they visited, claimed, and settled. The European discoverers risked the dangers of uncharted waters in their zeal to spread the word of God, in their craving for trade and wealth, and in their desire to find new lands. Many Europeans believed that the world was flat, and that frightening beasts lived in the wastes of unknown waters; they had no desire to gamble away their lives and resources upon perilous ventures of the sea. Other men, however, thought of the seas as pathways to the conversion of souls and to the wealth of spices produced in the faraway Indies. For whatever their reasons might be, there were always at least a few to equip and man the ships of this great age of discovery.

## Early Explorers

Five of the nations of Europe are remembered today for their early lead in exploration. Their ships went out in all directions, and their explorers charted new seas and also laid claim to great parts of the newly discovered lands. Often these claims led to conflicts and disagreements. The nations that led in the age of exploration were Portugal, Spain, the Netherlands, France, and England.

### The Portuguese

Prince Henry of Portugal (1394-1460) was a religious man who sought to spread his Catholic faith, but he was also envious of the Venetians, who were harvesting great wealth from their monopoly of the spice trade of Europe. Spices were essential for seasoning meat, which was usually rancid and often tainted in those days of no refrigeration. Spices were extremely expensive, for they had to come a long way from the East by ship and camel. Along the way they passed through the hands of many traders who grasped a percentage of their value. The Venetians had a monopoly of the spice trade in Europe, and by the time they obtained spices from the Arabs in the eastern Mediterranean, the spices were already worth more than twenty times their original value. Henry assembled the best seamen and ships and began a thorough preparation for finding a direct seaway from Portugal to the Indies. Because of his great interest in exploration, Henry is remembered in history by the title "the Navigator."

In the early 1400's Henry's captains began to sail in short jumps down the west coast of Africa, establishing trading posts as they went along. While making discoveries southward along the coast of Africa, they also discovered sources of cheap labor. They became slave traders. Trading in human flesh was not compatible with the teachings of Christianity, but man has often shown that he can reconcile the conflict between principle and profit. Henry died before his captains reached the sources of the spices, but movement south along the coast of Africa continued.

The kings of Portugal who came after Henry the Navigator continued to follow his policy of encouraging exploration. In 1486 the Portuguese navigator Bartholomew Diaz was blown out to sea in a storm. When he next sighted land it was to the west rather than to the east—he had rounded the tip of southern

Africa. His king, John II, was elated when he heard the news. He promptly named this tip the Cape of Good Hope, for the Portuguese were now in good hope that the spice trade would soon be their monopoly. Their hope was fulfilled. A few years later, a daring man named Vasco da Gama rounded this cape of hope, reached the east coast of Africa, and crossed the Indian Ocean to the shores of southern India. There he filled two ships with precious spices. When he returned to Lisbon two years later, in 1499, his spices were worth sixty times the cost of the voyage. Prince Henry's gamble paid off with handsome dividends, and for many years Portugal reaped the benefits of the foresight, courage, and skill of her rulers and her sailors who laid the foundations of a widespread empire.

The Portuguese continued exploring, trading, and setting up their trading stations in strategic areas, for they had found the sea a road to riches. By chance or by intention, a captain named Pedro Cabral discovered Brazil in 1500 and immediately claimed it for the king of Portugal. It was the accepted custom in those days for the European to claim as his own the people as well as the lands he discovered across the sea. Regardless of the height of their culture, they were considered his unless they had the might to withstand his firearms, his strength, or his leadership in war and politics. The European rulers feared only fellow Europeans, who had warred with each other for centuries over lands and resources each coveted.

New disputes arose as lands were discovered and claimed in other parts of the world. The Portuguese and the Spanish requested the Pope to settle disputes over their areas of discovery. In this settlement the Portuguese received all lands within a line three hundred miles east of the Cape Verde Islands; the Spanish received everything west of this line. A year later, in 1494, a treaty between the two countries shifted the line farther west. The Dutch, French, and English refused to accept this division and proceeded to take everything they could, whether it was east or west of this line.

The main effort of the Portuguese was in Asia. They established a base in Goa on the western shore of India, which they kept until recent years. From here they fanned out to Ceylon, Malaya, Indonesia, Macao in China, and even to Japan, where they initiated trade. They had little influence upon the mass of the people with whom they traded, but for a number of years they were the only Europeans the people of Asia knew. The Portuguese were also interested in the souls of the Asians they had discovered, and some of the first European missionaries to these far lands were brought there by the Portuguese. The Portuguese trading posts were gradually gobbled up by the Dutch, the English, and others who followed the sea paths they had first explored. Today only a few remnants of their old trading posts still remain—Macao on the coast of China, Timor in Indonesia, Mozambique in East Africa, Angola in West Africa, and a few other pieces of land and islands elsewhere. Though their country was small, and at times their deeds were motivated by greed, the Portuguese captains and sailors had iron in their adventurous spirits.

### The Spanish

The Spanish were neighbors of the Portuguese, and they shared with them the wish to bring their Catholic beliefs to the "heathen." They also shared a desire for the wealth to which the sea lanes led. But their ambitions had to wait until the Moslem Moors were driven from the land of Spain. After this aim had been achieved, the Spanish, too, set forth upon voyages of discovery, colonization, and wealth. In their very first venture, one of their captains, Christopher Columbus, a Genoese, discovered America in 1492.

Columbus (1451-1506) was convinced that the earth was round. This belief had also been held by a number of Greeks centuries before. But Columbus had difficulty finding wealthy people who were willing to subsidize his theory. Finally, Queen Isabella of Spain was convinced that Columbus could reach the riches of the East by sailing west. She gave him three ships to test their mutual theory. The sailors who went with Columbus did not share this theory. They began to want to turn back and were on the verge of mutiny. On the very night that these sailors had decided was to be the last of their fruitless western voyage, a light from land was sighted. On October 12, 1492, they found the land from which this light originated—one of the islands of the Bahamas.

Columbus thought he was offshore of the Indies, but he had actually discovered an immense new uncharted land—the Americas. He went on to find Cuba and Santo Domingo, and then returned to Spain. He had not found the spices of the Indies, but he carried some Indians back to Spain as well as some strange plants and animals. The Spanish were somewhat disappointed that Columbus did not bring back the spices which spelled riches, but they were excited with what he had found. They sent him back three times with settlers who started a colonization which left the Spanish imprint deep in Latin America. Columbus died, however, thinking that he had reached the Indies.

The Spanish were now on fire with the possibilities of exploration. The lands and peoples of the Americas came quickly under their domination. Ponce de León discovered Florida in 1513. Balboa crossed the narrow strip of Panama in 1513, and when he gazed at the broad Pacific, he knew that this was a new land and not the Indies.

In 1519 a heroic captain who was not destined to return set out from Spain with his small fleet—Ferdinand Magellan, a Portuguese in the service of Spain. He maneuvered through a dangerous passage at the southern tip of South America — later named for him, the Strait of Magellan—and entered into an ocean so calm he called it Pacific. He had not yet seen this ocean in its more rebellious moods. He crossed its wide expanse and came upon the Philippine Islands. There Magellan met his death while fighting some of the inhabitants, but one of his men took command. The voyage was continued across the Indian Ocean and around the Cape of Good Hope. At last, in 1522, one ship arrived back in Spain manned by eighteen men—all that were left of the original five ships and two hundred and forty-three men that had started out about three years before. It had been a journey of unimaginable hardships, during which the crew ate sawdust and ox-hides softened in sea water to stay the pangs of hunger. To supplement their food supply, they bought rats at half-a-crown each and drank foul, yellow water. But they had proved that the earth was round. Theirs was the first ship to circumnavigate the globe.

Christopher Columbus (1451-1506) claimed the lands that he discovered for Spain. North America had been visited by the Vikings long before the arrival of Columbus, but they made no permanent settlements. (Courtesy of Pan American Union)

The Spanish claimed and settled large reaches of land in North and South America as well as the islands of the Philippines in Asia. From these new lands, gold and silver poured into the treasury of Spain. These riches from the New World were used to further Spain's interests in Europe, but without much success.

### The Dutch

The Dutch lived in a part of Europe known as the Low Countries. These Low Countries now make up the lands of Holland and Belgium. The inhabitants of the Low Countries were industrious, thrifty people who wasted no land and lost no opportunity to make themselves prosperous. By the sixteenth century their cities and ports were centers of industry, banking, and trade. Their ships were familiar in all the major and minor ports of Europe. They not only sailed the surface of the sea, but claimed part of its floor by their system of dikes which gradually pushed the waters farther from their shores. The Dutch were also independent and stubborn in their religious and political opinions.

In the 1500's the Holy Roman Emperor, Charles V, added the Netherlands, of which the Dutch were residents, to his large empire. Later it became a part of the empire of his son, Philip II, who also ruled Spain. The Dutch who lived in the northern part of the Netherlands became, for the most part, Calvinists. This conversion infuriated the Catholic Philip. He sent armies against them and curtailed their religious and secular privileges. The Dutch were determined to resist, and they warred on under their leader, William the Silent, Prince of Orange. Although William was assassinated before freedom was gained, he remained a symbol of persistence to his people and is considered the founder of the Dutch Republic.

The Dutch of the seven northern provinces of the Netherlands formed the Union of Utrecht in 1579 to continue the struggle against Spain. In 1581 these provinces declared their independence from Spain as the Republic of the United Netherlands. They never again permitted the Spanish to rule them. However, it was not until the Treaty of Westphalia in 1648 that the independence of Holland was formally recognized.

From the time of their declaration of independence, the Dutch made the seas swarm with their privateers and their large merchant ships, which were the best of that time. They preyed on Spanish and Portuguese shipping and trading posts. Their greatest triumph at sea was the seizure of Portugese trade in Asia, especially the spice trade of the Indies. They formed the Dutch East India Company and channeled their trade activities through it. The Dutch managed to seize most of the islands of the East Indies, permitting the Portuguese to hold only Timor. Moving inland from their coastal settlements, the Dutch gradually extended their dominance over all the lands and peoples of these islands. So strong was their hold that the East Indies remained Dutch possessions from the seventeenth to the twentieth century. The Dutch made this realm a rich island empire by introducing coffee plantations and developing production of rubber, palm oil, sugar, and other commodities. Only after World War II did the area that the Dutch ruled become the independent Republic of Indonesia.

By around 1600 the Dutch had ten thousand ships operating on the seas, and they were producing them at the rate of one a day. They did not confine themselves to Asia. They whaled in the Arctic. They hired Henry Hudson to find a northwest passage to the Indies. On this mission he sailed up the river that now bears his name and went as far as present-day Albany, New York. The Dutch settled the present site of New York and called it New Amsterdam. They found their way into the Caribbean, and they struggled with the Portuguese for a part of Brazil. They planted a colony on the Cape of Good Hope, and their descendants still make up the majority of the white population in South Africa.

The Dutch were a great power during the seventeenth century, and they are today a prosperous nation, although their empire overseas has now been reduced to rather small pieces of land scattered around the globe.

1. Name three great Portuguese sailors. For what is each famous? Whose discovery do you consider to be the most important? Why?
2. What were the limits of Spanish explorations and conquests in the Americas? What type of administration did the Spanish establish in their conquered territories?
3. What were the important Dutch explorations and colonies in Asia and the Americas? How successful were they?

## The English

The English were late getting started on their voyages of exploration, but once under way, they persisted until they had fashioned an empire upon which the sun did not set. This empire was not built overnight but was the culmination of several centuries of steady growth. The English today still govern areas in faraway parts of the world, but for the most part their former large overseas possessions have now become independent nations. At the height of its empire, England ruled more people than any nation in history. This empire beyond the island shores of Great Britain began when the Italian explorers John and Sebastian Cabot were sent to North America in 1497. The Cabots sailed in search of a northwest passage to the Indies. They explored the North American coast from Hatteras to Labrador and laid the foundation for England's future claim to this coastline. The

When Francis Drake landed at the La Plata River in 1578, the playful Indians found his hat amusing and stole it. (From Theodor de Bry, "America," 1595, courtesy of The Folger Shakespeare Library)

Henry VIII, above, and Elizabeth I, below, were the two great Tudor rulers of England during the Renaissance. (Both, National Portrait Gallery, London)

English did not immediately follow up these discoveries, but waited until the latter part of the sixteenth century to begin their serious colonization and trade.

There were daring men of the sea among the English, and some of the finest adventure stories of any age have been written around the exploits of men like John Hawkins and Francis Drake. On a voyage between 1577 and 1580, Francis Drake was the first Englishman to circumnavigate the earth. On his way, he stopped at the California coast. The English were primarily interested in the trade of Asia, and they focused their attention mainly upon India. For many years they operated through a private chartered company of investors called the East India Company. This company raised the money and provided the ships and supplies for voyages in the hope that returns would be profitable. Queen Elizabeth chartered the first company in 1600 and gave it a monopoly of all eastern trade.

At first the English were rather slow in expanding their trade within India. At this time the Mogul emperors were still strong and able to limit the activities of the English and others. But the English secured various strong coastal positions for trading posts. By late in the seventeenth century they were entrenched in Madras, Bombay, and Calcutta. During this period Mogul power waned, and the English took advantage of this opportunity to pit one ruler against the other. Slowly the English expanded their political and economic power until they controlled a substantial part of India. All this was done by the East India Company, which put armies in the field and governed India much like a regular government. The excesses of the East India Company led the English government to take over political power, but it was this private company which had built an empire in India.

The English went on to explore other parts of Asia, and as the centuries moved along, they took over Ceylon, Malaya, Burma, North Borneo, Hong Kong, and other islands of Asia. Their first and main base, however, was India. The profits they reaped from this trade were enormous and helped to stimulate the industry of England and the growth of one of the world's largest merchant marine and war fleets. The English, like other European powers of this period, insisted that English goods travel in English ships and that the colonies buy English-manufactured goods in return for their raw materials and other products.

In 1584 the gentleman-adventurer Sir Walter Raleigh tried to start an English colony in Virginia, which was named for Queen Elizabeth. He failed. In 1607, however, under the leadership of the resourceful Captain John Smith, the first permanent English settlement in the United States was started at Jamestown, Virginia. In 1620 a shipload of Puritans, whom we know today as the "Pilgrim Fathers," crossed the Atlantic in the *Mayflower* and landed at Plymouth in New England. Gradually a line of English colonies grew along the eastern coast of present-day United States reaching from Georgia to Maine. By the eighteenth century, these colonies had built up an economy founded on agriculture and supported by a growing trade with England and the West Indies. This growth of colonial economy, however, never really satisfied the English, who had hoped to make a fine profit from the colonists they had placed upon the shores of North America.

The English also explored and claimed land in South America, and a number of islands in the Caribbean. In America and in India, however, they found the French to be energetic and ambitious rivals.

### The French

The French also proved to be good explorers. They claimed vast stretches of land and water in various parts of the world. For a time they held the land of Canada and much of what is present-day United States west of the Mississippi. Our state of Louisiana takes its name from the territory that was named for the French king Louis XIV. During the reign of this king, and under the guidance of the finance minister, Jean Baptiste Colbert, the French also formed an East India Company to compete in India with the British. The French established a trading post at Pondicherry on the southern coast of India near Madras and spread to other parts of India, where they set up trading stations.

In both North America and India, the competing interests of the French and the British led them into war with one another. France and England became two of the greatest of the world's landowners as the Spanish and the Portuguese declined under the sea and land blows from the English, French, and Dutch. France under Louis XIV was also land-hungry in Europe, and the succession of wars between France and other countries of Europe had their reactions in the territories abroad.

1. What part did the East India Company play in British explorations?
2. What lands did the British claim in the Americas?
3. In which part of the Americas did the French colonize? What was the extent of their interest in India?

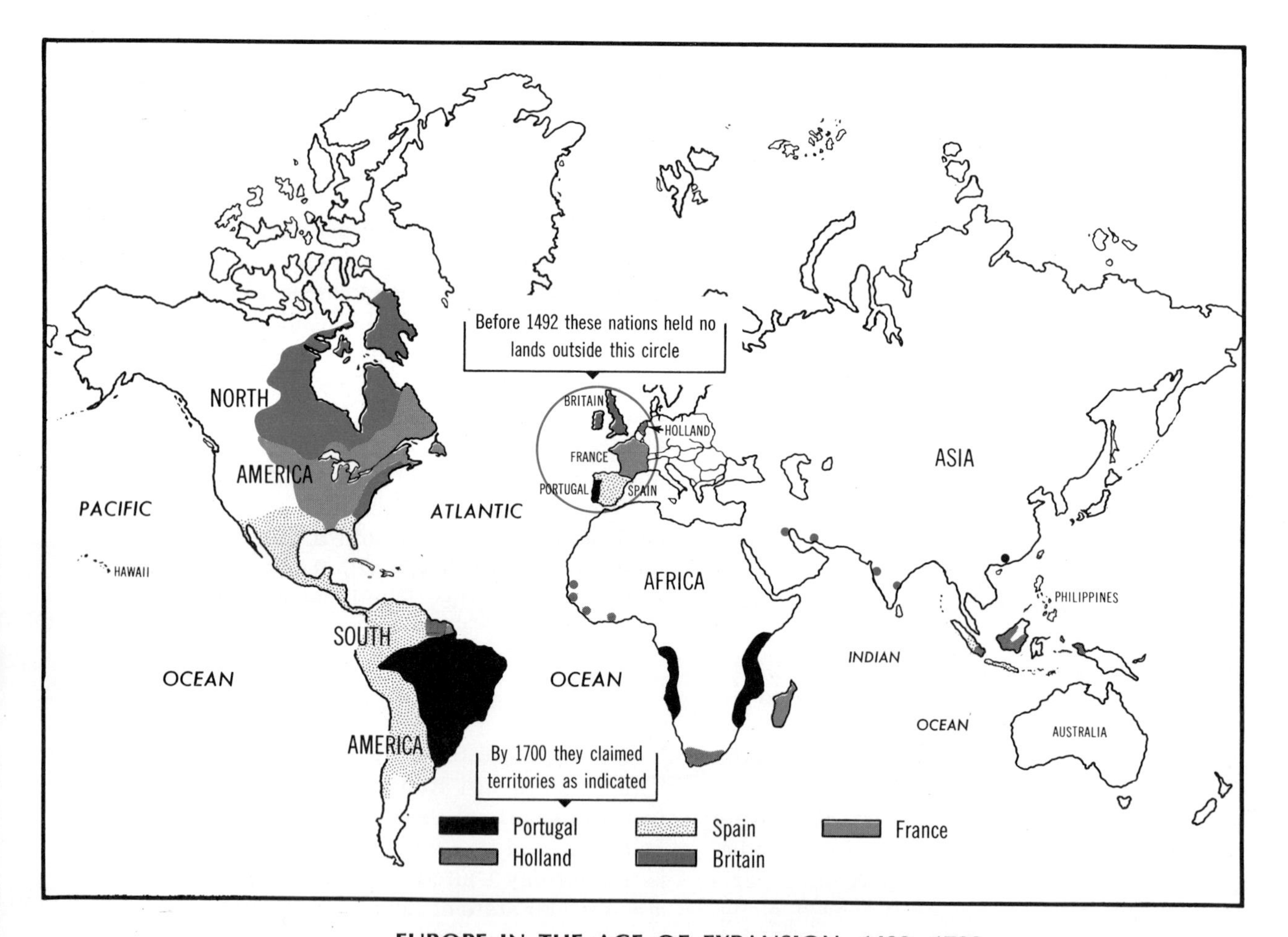


**EUROPE IN THE AGE OF EXPANSION, 1492–1700**

After the voyages of the great discoverers had opened up ways to Asia and the New World, the major nations of Europe vied in claiming and settling new lands. How do you account for the fact that there was less penetration into Africa than in the Americas?

### Kings Compete in Europe

During the centuries that the Europeans were mapping, grabbing, and ruling possessions overseas in the name of their kings, the kings were scheming how to take or defend territories in Europe that they regarded as vital to their existence and power. From the sixteenth century onward, it was rare for a war to remain isolated in Europe. There were a few isolated wars, but the European countries were so close together that wars usually became general. The interests of European countries were so interlocked that a drastic move by one of the kings, especially if he was powerful, sooner or later involved most of the others. European rulers were very suspicious of one another, and the more powerful one became, the greater the fear and suspicion of the others. If a ruler became too powerful, the others continued the age-old practice of ganging up on him, lest he should attack first and overwhelm them. The kings of Europe also had problems with the Turks who were threatening Vienna in Austria. In addition there was continual trouble with the nobles who had not yet been completely subdued, and with religious quarrels which continued to plague the politics of Europe. All of these factors kept the Europeans in turmoil from the sixteenth century into the eighteenth century. Kings with ambitions and a sense of duty to their kingdoms did not live easy lives.

Charles V (1500-1558) was Holy Roman Emperor from 1519 to 1556. He ruled Spain as Charles I. His was the greatest empire in Europe. When he abdicated, his possessions were divided between his son Philip and his brother Ferdinand. The Hapsburgs were a major ruling family of Europe from the 1200's until the twentieth century. (Cushing)

#### Charles V: Holy Roman Emperor

One of the greatest of the European rulers was Charles V, who became Holy Roman Emperor in 1519 at the age of nineteen. He was a member of the Hapsburg family. Through his Spanish mother, he inherited the vast possessions of Spain; from his father he inherited Burgundy and the Low Countries; and from his grandfather, he inherited the Austrian empire of the Hapsburgs. He was the ruler of Spain and all Spanish possessions in the New World, half of Italy, Burgundy and the Low Countries of Holland and Belgium, Germany, Austria, and part of Hungary. The wealth of the Americas poured into his treasury in a continuous stream of gold and silver. He commanded large armies of soldiers and officials.

No other ruler in all Europe ranked as high as Charles V. But he had little time for leisure to enjoy the music, the literature, or the quiet pursuits of the scholar for which he longed. The people he governed allowed him no peace of mind, and there were many who wanted no part of his rule. The Turks plunged deep into Hungary and menaced the city of Vienna in Austria. As soon as Charles had stopped this threat, he was forced to ride swiftly to Italy where rebellious nobles threat-

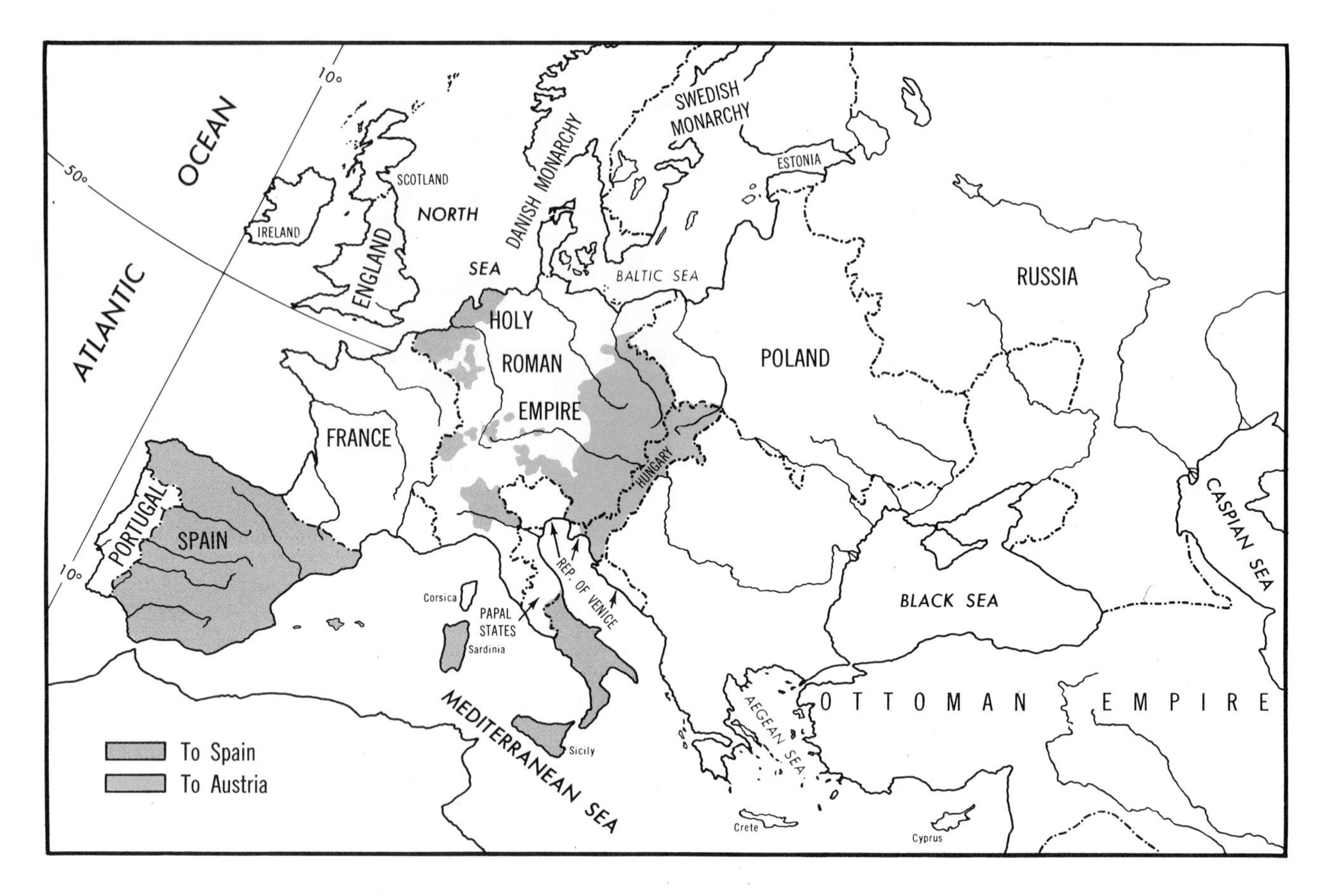


**DIVISION OF THE EMPIRE OF CHARLES V BETWEEN SPAIN AND AUSTRIA**

As Holy Roman Emperor and King of Spain, Charles V ruled one of the largest empires the world has ever known. In addition to the lands shown on the map, Charles ruled all of the lands claimed by Spain in the New World. In 1557 he retired to a monastery in western Spain. His empire was divided between his son, Philip II of Spain, and his brother Ferdinand.

ened to become independent. The French wanted his power curtailed, and they threatened his western borders with their troops. The revolt of the Lutherans and the Lutheran-minded princes promised to tear apart the Germans. On the high seas, the English, the Dutch, and growing bands of pirates plundered his treasure ships and harassed his settlements.

Charles V managed to retain the borders of his empire until 1555. Then, exhausted by his efforts and the cares of empire, he divided his vast possessions between his son Philip II and his brother Ferdinand. He retired to a monastery, where he at last enjoyed a measure of peace and happiness during the remaining two years of his life.

### Philip II: King of Spain

Philip II ruled a country great in wealth and ships, and famed for the disciplined and fighting quality of its soldiers. His share of his father's inheritance included parts of Italy, France, the Spanish Americas, the Philippines, and the Netherlands or Low Countries. His uncle, Ferdinand, inherited the remainder of the empire, including Austria and Germany. They generally acted together because of their family relationship and common Roman Catholic religion.

Philip II was firmly determined to make Spain first in importance and to stamp out Protestantism, which was a threat to both his political and religious purposes, He, too, found that his aims brought him only continuous wars and problems. In using the terrors and tortures of the Inquisition in Spain and in the Netherlands, he aroused anger, revenge, and revolt. The *Inquisition* was a Church tribunal set up to discover, punish, and prevent heresy. The Spanish Inquisition conducted its inquiries with extreme severity.

During the reign of Philip, the Dutch declared their independence, held his soldiers at bay, and destroyed many of his ships. The revolt of the Moors in Spain also drained his treasury and his resources. In 1580, Philip seized the vacant Portuguese throne and thus brought upon himself the anger and the problems of the Portuguese people. He was forced to spread thin his sea power in order to defend the overseas empire of Portugal. Portuguese possessions and ships were simply additional prey for the Dutch, the French, and the English.

Philip was married to Mary, Queen of England, and together they attempted to restore Catholicism in England. This action aroused the enmity of the English, who were now determined to be independent of the Roman pope. When Elizabeth became ruler of England, she supported the Church of England. She also supported raiding rovers of the sea, like Drake and Hawkins, who kept her enemies off balance and spread the might of England to far shores and peoples. Her famous sea captains stepped up their attacks upon Spanish shipping, and Elizabeth secretly welcomed their harassment of the Spanish. Her treasury was enriched by the cargoes of Spanish treasure they placed at her feet.

In 1588 Philip sent an armada of ships, which he considered invincible, to remove the English pirates and heretics from the sight of man. But Elizabeth's magnificent captains, by superior seamanship and gunnery, and aided by a providential storm, destroyed most of Philip's invincible fleet. From that time, his enemies became more daring and confident, and Spanish sea power began to decline. As the Spaniards declined, the French increased in power. Other countries then combined their efforts to restrict the French advance at home and abroad.

### Henry IV: The French King

Henry IV of France had formerly been the leader of the Huguenots—the French Protestants—under the title Henry of Navarre. But when the throne of France became vacant, he embraced Catholicism and, in 1589, became Henry IV of France. He was a tolerant and wise king. With the assistance of an able Huguenot, the Duke of Sully, Henry started France on the road to greatness in Europe.

In 1598 he issued the Edict of Nantes, which gave to the Huguenots freedom to worship as they pleased and permitted them to retain their armed fortifications and self-government. Until this time the Protestant Huguenots had experienced harsh persecutions at the hands of Catholic rulers. At one time, many thousands of them were murdered—over three thousand men, women, and children had been massacred in Paris alone—but Henry's tolerant policy removed this religious division from France for the time being.

Henry IV was interested in the welfare of the people. Under Sully's wise guidance, taxes were systematized and industries encouraged. Commerce advanced, and the extension of overseas colonies was stimulated. Quebec was founded during this period. Henry was assassinated in 1610, but he left France prosperous and more centralized.

### Louis XIII and Cardinal Richelieu

Louis XIII was a child of about nine when his father, Henry IV, died. His reign of thirty-three years lasted from 1610 to 1643. While he was still a child, his mother, Marie de Médicis, was regent, and France faltered, but when Cardinal Richelieu became his advisor and mentor, the country took a long stride toward greatness. Richelieu worked for the glory of France and his king. Not even the advancement of the Church, of which he was a high official, was permitted to interfere with increasing the greatness of France.

Under Richelieu's guidance, Louis XIII embarked upon an ambitious policy of diplomacy. To stem the power of the Catholic Hapsburgs, France aided the Protestant Germans. This

The Spanish Riding Academy in Vienna is a reminder of the days of Hapsburg power in Austria. It was founded by Prince Eugene of Savoy (1663-1736) who fought against the Turks at Vienna in 1683 and was active in the coalition against Louis XIV of France. (Austrian Information Service)

alliance of power was of immense importance in contributing to the decline of Hapsburg power and the decline of the Holy Roman Empire. The Huguenots within France were permitted to worship in peace, but they were completely subject to the authority of the king, and their fortified towns and cities were destroyed.

Richelieu and Louis XIII were ruthless in their treatment of those who thought themselves independent of the king. Under Richelieu's direction, the power of the nobles was curbed, and they were watched and supervised by members of the middle class, who were sympathetic to the king. Supervisors called *intendants* were appointed to oversee local administration, and this reform further reduced the power of the nobles.

Richelieu also contributed to the cultural growth of France by establishing the French Academy in 1635. The Academy served to encourage French literature, and it has continued to function up to the present. When Louis XIV succeeded Louis XIII to the throne of France, he inherited a country that had been made strong by Richelieu, and he also inherited a trained advisor, Cardinal Mazarin (1602-1661).

### Louis XIV

At the age of five, in 1643, Louis XIV inherited the throne of a prosperous and mighty France. During his reign France reached to even greater heights of power and prestige in Europe. The rule of Louis XIV was given a sound foundation by Cardinal Mazarin, who continued the policies of Richelieu until his death in 1661. At that time Louis XIV assumed control of the destiny of France, and he ruled with ambition and with strength. He had excellent advisors. One of them, Jean Baptiste

Colbert, his finance minister, filled the treasury, improved the economy of the country, and encouraged the establishment of French colonies overseas. Louis also had some excellent military commanders, and he used his military forces often.

Much of the reign of Louis XIV was filled with war. Between 1667 and 1713 Louis engaged in four wars which, at various times, caused most of Europe to combine in alliances against France. The other nations of Europe feared France, for it was stronger than any individual country, but not stronger than combinations of countries. Louis wanted, by his wars, to expand the territory of France and to increase his power in Europe.

The first of these wars was in 1667-1668, and it was fought with Spain to bring the land that is modern Belgium under French control. The second war, 1672-1678, was fought against the Dutch. In this war, France was allied with Sweden, some German states, and, for a time, England. The Dutch were supported by Spain, the Holy Roman Empire, and Brandenburg-Prussia. Louis gained territory from this war and through skillful diplomacy. At this time France reached the zenith of its power.

Louis was not content, and in 1688 he launched his third war, this time against the Germans. The rulers of Europe were alarmed, and some of the most powerful of them united against France in the League of Augsburg—comprised of Spain, the Holy Roman Empire, Sweden, Holland, and England. On sea Louis lost power to the English, and on land the conflict was a draw. This war ended in 1697. The fourth and final war started over Louis' attempt to place his grandson, Philip of Anjou, on the throne of Spain. It lasted from 1701 to 1713 and was fought in America and elsewhere as well as in Europe. This war arrayed Holland, England, Austria, Portugal, Savoy, and some German states against France. When the war was settled by the Treaty of Utrecht in 1713, Louis made some gains, but he also was forced to make concessions.

The Treaty of Utrecht provided that a Bourbon (a member of the family of Louis) might rule in Spain, but not both Spain and France. England obtained from France the Hudson Bay, Newfoundland, and Nova Scotia in America, and from Spain the colony of Gibraltar at the meeting point of the Atlantic Ocean and the Mediterranean Sea. The Austrians obtained the area now called Belgium and parts of Italy. Louis, through his wars and diplomacy, had not obtained all he desired, but he had increased the territory of France, though the financial burden upon his people was severe.

Under Louis XIV, France became the cultural center of Europe. Not far from Paris Louis built the palace of Versailles, which housed the most brilliant court in Europe. To Versailles came European kings, princes, and nobles, great and small, to look, admire, and try to imitate in their own courts at home. Visitors to France saw performances of the plays of Molière, Racine, and Corneille, and they were stimulated and influenced. The French language became the second language of the educated non-French, and gradually French became the common language of diplomacy. The content and style of French culture became a part of the culture of other Europeans, and its influence is still prominent today in Europe and in other parts of the world.

Louis XIV is famed not only because he made French culture kingly in Europe but also as a towering example of those kings of his time who believed that their power was absolute and supported by Divinity. It is generally believed today that Louis never said "I am the State," but this phrase certainly expresses the spirit of his attitude. He and other kings of Europe in his time thought that they ruled by divine right, that God had planned their birth and position, and that their decrees were buttressed by divine authority. This was not the first time in history that men had founded their rule upon divine authority. It will be recalled that ancient rulers in the Middle East had based their authority upon this belief and, sometimes, went further and called themselves divine. Several of the Roman emperors had also considered themselves to be gods.

Louis and other kings of his time did not

regard themselves as gods, but they did consider themselves as God's agents on earth. They believed that they were chosen, anointed, and appointed to their high earthly positions by a power beyond man and that it was the duty of their subjects to obey commands without questioning. According to their belief, rebellion and opposition directed against royal power were, in a real sense, rebellion and opposition against God.

Although belief in the divine right of kings was shared, in theory at least, by a number of the kings' subjects, there were also many who did not think that the king's will was always the will of God. The nobility, the clergy, and the rising middle class held tenaciously to privileges more ancient than the rights of the ruling king, and when a king trespassed upon these privileges, he frequently met opposition. Though the absolute kings of this time and later never reached the degree of regimentation and control of their subjects which authoritarian modern rulers have achieved, they did hasten the centralizing process then underway in Europe in government, economy, administration, and other aspects of national life.

1. What evidence exists to show that Charles V was a conscientious ruler?
2. Trace the relations of Philip II with England.
3. In what ways did France become the cultural center of Europe? Under whose reign?

The great palace of Versailles housed the court of Louis XIV. It was a center of European culture during the reign of Louis, who gathered about him many of the greatest writers, musicians, and artists of the day. (French Government Tourist Office)

## Forerunners of Global War

European explorers staked claims to the many lands and islands they discovered on their voyages. They settled them with their colonists, exploited their resources, and founded on them a European way of life. They also made these new possessions the battlegrounds of their wars. The great wars fought in Europe during the seventeenth and eighteenth centuries were duplicated in the colonies, although often under other names. The wars fought by England, France, and Spain in North America are excellent examples of this extension of European wars.

### War in the Americas

Under the name "King William's War," the English and the French fought the War of the League of Augsburg (1688-1697) on North American soil. Calling it Queen Anne's War, the English fought the French and the Spanish in America during the drawn-out War of the Spanish Succession in Europe (1701-1713). The War of the Austrian Succession (1740-1748) began in Europe and was waged in America under the name King George's War.

When Charles VI, Holy Roman Emperor, died in 1740, his daughter Maria Theresa inherited the Austrian throne. Frederick II of Prussia and some German princes thought this a fine opportunity to take some of the Hapsburg territory that they had long desired. But Maria Theresa, the Empress, was not a weak woman. To the surprise of Frederick and his German allies, she battled valiantly and successfully. The war moved from small beginnings to a full-scale conflict which pulled in most of the great powers of Europe. Inevitably it spread to the Americas. There it pitted the French and the Spanish, who had joined with Prussia, against the English and the Dutch, who supported Maria Theresa. When the war was finally concluded in 1748, Frederick II retained Silesia, which had been under the rule of Maria Theresa. This led to further conflict, which also spread to the Americas.

Maria Theresa wanted revenge upon the Prussians who had taken her land of Silesia and had plunged Austria into a war of hardship. With diplomatic cunning, she gathered Spain, France, Sweden, Russia, and Saxony into an alliance with her against Prussia. Supported by this formidable combination, she

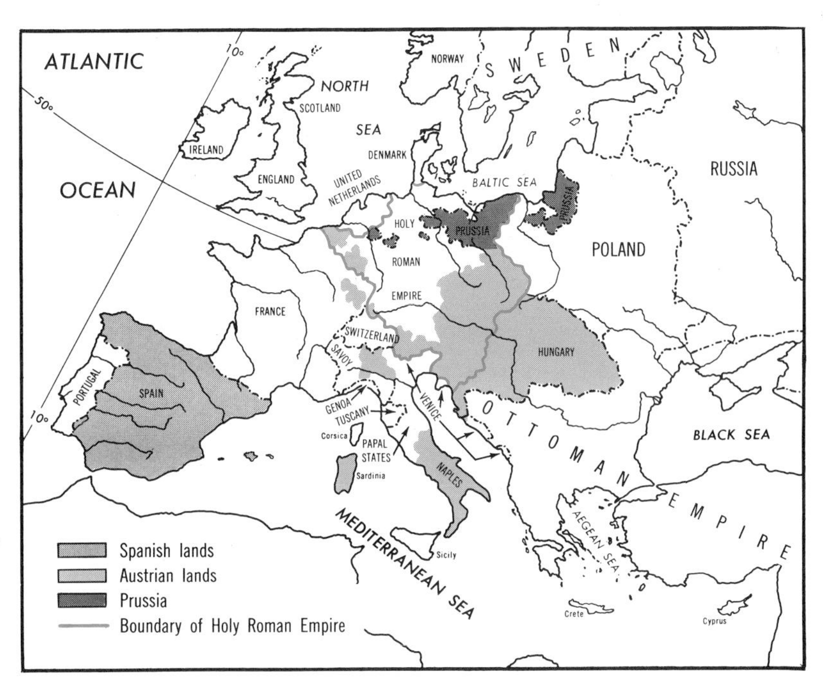


**Europe After the War of the Spanish Succession, 1714**

The War of the Spanish Succession was known in America as Queen Anne's War. After this war, by skillful diplomacy, Louis XIV had his grandson made king of Spain, with the provision that Spain and France were never to be united. The map shows the division of Spanish and Austrian lands after the war.

started in 1756 what was known to Europeans as the Seven Years' War. England supported Prussia, which once again pitted the French against the English in North America in a war known as the French and Indian War. The war continued until it was settled by the Peace of Paris in 1763.

No European lands changed hands, but in America the English made great gains by the French and Indian War. By the treaty terms, the French ceded to the English their land in Canada and all the land they had claimed east of the Mississippi. Spain was forced to give England the territory of Florida. Now England was dominant in North America from the eastern coasts to the Mississippi River.

## War in India

The English were ever conscious of the importance of their sea lanes, which were lifelines to colonies and trading posts, especially the extremely lucrative stations in India. The French were trying to wrest the trade of India from the English, particularly in southern India, where the French had brought many of the native rulers to their side. At the time when the Mogul Empire was breaking up both the French and the English took advantage of India's weakness to further divide, weaken, and rule the Indians.

Under the leadership of Robert Clive, the English made large gains in India during the mid-1700's. Clive had gone to India as a clerk for the East India Company and was transferred to the military division of his company. By his ability to manipulate and scheme and through his daring in war, Clive weakened the French hold in India. He laid the founda-

The Castle of Schönbrunn in Vienna was rebuilt in its present form during the reign of Maria Theresa, who, from 1740 to 1780 was the wise and able ruler of Austria. The Castle, below, is surrounded by a park and gardens. A number of its rooms, like the one above, are decorated with Gobelin tapestries from France. Maria Theresa's daughter, Marie Antoinette, became Queen of France and was beheaded during the Revolution. (Both pictures, courtesy of Austrian Information Service)

tions for the complete control of India by the British. At the end of the Seven Years' War, the French could still trade in India, but they had no fortifications or armed camps there.

The feats of arms and diplomacy which won India for the English were first performed by the employees of the private firm of the East India Company. But the company was not equipped to govern a country so complex and so vast as India. In 1784, India was placed under the British Crown. The later influence of the British in India has already been discussed in the Asian unit of this book.

The English also took areas from the Spanish and the French elsewhere in the world. At the end of the Seven Years' War, they were supreme among those who claimed territory in the lands discovered since the fifteenth century. Much of the credit for the vigor of the English in waging wars with other European nations must go to William Pitt, the statesman who headed the government of England several times during the 1750's and 1760's. Pitt brought a new morale and a new positive direction to the men who were fighting for empire overseas.

1. In what sense were the European wars also fought in the Americas?
2. How successful was the Empress Maria Theresa as a political and governmental leader?
3. What new products did the Europeans obtain from Asia? From the Americas?

## Conclusion

The Europeans emerging from the Middle Ages were possessed by a restlessness which led them to explore the unknown parts of the earth. They cast their lot upon the seas and reaped wealth, fame, and power as well as war, loss, and death. To the lands and the peoples they conquered, they brought their religion, their more advanced technology, and certain benefits of their civilization as well as greed, battle, and subjugation. In their voyaging and colonizing, the Europeans were driven not by a single motive but by many. Their record of piracy and brutality, of treachery, deceit, and greed beyond bounds is not one that can be read with pride. The deeds of the European conquerors, however, were partly redeemed by some who expressed spiritual concern and human compassion for the subjugated peoples. Some of these humane men and idealists, in their words and deeds, laid the foundations of hope, freedom, and tolerance in the new worlds that were discovered.

The Europeans' discoveries led them to enjoy and to use products they had never known before. From the Indians of the Americas, they learned the uses of tobacco, potatoes, maize, and chocolate. They used their new lands in the Americas to produce sugar, molasses, cotton, and indigo. From these lands they received lumber, furs, and other raw materials. Spices, teas, silks, rugs, carvings, and many other products of the skilled hands of the Asians began to make the lives and homes of the Europeans more comfortable and more beautiful. This increase of trade stimulated the growth of their industries, and enlarged their capacity for shipbuilding. The size of European cities grew to match the growing trade between Europe and the worlds that had been found.

The Europeans' intellectual horizons were broadened by their explorations. Along with the new lands, the Europeans also discovered new and different ways of looking at life. They did not accept these new ways at first, but gradually some new ideas and practices proved to be so practical that they were studied and sometimes adopted. The Europeans began to think in terms of improved ways to govern, and they developed new ideas about man and his relationships. Some believe that all this explosion of discovery was the force that brought about the industrial revolution, the Western-structured global unity which came later, and the surge of capitalism.

Certainly the age of exploration and discovery contributed to a far-reaching development of ideas and achievements in politics, economics, science, and industry. New and revolutionary ideas about the freedoms of man also followed upon and accompanied these voyages of discovery.

## SUMMING UP THE CHAPTER

A. Identify the following and tell why they are important.

| | |
|---|---|
| Bartholomew Diaz | John Cabot |
| Cardinal Mazarin | Louis XIV |
| Cardinal Richelieu | Pedro Cabral |
| Christopher Columbus | Prince Henry |
| Edict of Nantes | Vasco da Gama |
| Ferdinand Magellan | Walter Raleigh |
| Francis Drake | William Pitt |
| Jean Baptiste Colbert | William the Silent |

B. Identify the following dates and indicate their importance.

1. October 12, 1492
2. 1519
3. 1555
4. 1584
5. 1588
6. 1607
7. 1713

C. Chapter review questions.

1. What inspired the Portuguese to make their early voyages?
2. Evaluate Spanish rule in the Americas. Do you feel the Spanish took more than they gave?
3. Who were some of the great explorers in the service of the Spanish crown? What territories did they discover?
4. Explain the following statement: "The English fashioned an empire upon which the sun did not set."
5. What discoveries did the English make in the Americas? Relate these chronologically to the discoveries of other European powers.
6. Compare the policies of France, Spain, and England in exploring and settling the Americas.
7. What were Philip II's goals for Spain? What difficulties did he meet? How successful was he?
8. What important advances were made during the reign of Henry IV? Who was Henry's chief minister?
9. What were the consequences of Louis XIV's plan to expand the borders of France? Explain the reactions of the other countries of Europe.
10. When did the Seven Years' War take place? Who were the opponents? What was the outcome?
11. What factors motivated the Portuguese, Spanish, Dutch, English, and French to explore Asia and the Americas? Did the differences among the Europeans account for differing approaches toward lands acquired abroad?
12. List the lands in Asia and the Americas originally claimed by the Portuguese, the Spanish, the Dutch, the English, and the French. By 1800 what territories were still held by these countries?
13. Which of the European countries do you feel were the best administrators of foreign territories? Why?
14. Compare Philip II and Louis XIV as rulers.
15. What were the major highlights of the history of France between 1589 and 1763?

D. Questions for discussion.

1. Why were the British so late in beginning their explorations in comparison with the other European countries?
2. What justifications do you think the Portuguese offered for the slave trade they carried on?
3. What use do you suppose was made of the vast quantities of gold obtained from the Americas? How did the gold affect the power struggles among the European countries?
4. Why did the French stress a policy of trade, while the English pinned their hopes on colonization? Why was the latter more successful?
5. How did the numerous European wars of the seventeenth and eighteenth centuries permit the British to gain ascendency in North America?

E. Projects for groups or individuals.

1. Sketch a map showing the territories Charles V divided between his son and his brother in 1555.
2. Make a chronological chart listing the various rulers of several major countries of Europe during the 1500's and 1600's and the significant events in their reigns.
3. Read a biography of any of the great political leaders of Europe during this period, and report to the class.
4. Chart the voyages of several of the great explorers.
5. Prepare a report on the British East India Company.

# CHAPTER 22

# *Exploding Ideas — Revolutionary Changes*

DURING THE seventeenth, eighteenth, and nineteenth centuries, the everyday life of the Europeans changed drastically. There were also revolutionary changes in European attitudes toward government. The questioners of the Renaissance, the religious reformers, and the adventurers of the seas had set the Europeans in motion, and the pace of discovery and change gradually accelerated with the passing years.

Changes in the politics, economy, and social order of Europe did not move at the same rate of speed in each country. Sometimes the spirit of change exploded in violent revolutions which quickly demolished the established order; in other cases, there was a more or less peaceful evolution into something different. Reaction and progress were often found side by side within one country, and the rate of progress can be painfully slow as it moves against strong opposing currents.

The revolutionary political and philosophical ideas that began in Europe in the eighteenth century spread quickly to the New World and are continuing to spread their ferment throughout the world today. These political revolutions were matched by revolutionary developments in industry, science, and technology, which are still going on and which greatly affect all men everywhere. Just as the Europeans had reached out for colonies and conquest in earlier centuries, European ideas born in the modern period have reached out to seize the minds and change the lives of men throughout the world. This process is still going on.

## Continued Evolution of Rights in England

The English did not win greater personal liberties and a share in their government overnight. Their rights were cemented into custom and law over centuries of time. The slow progress of the growth of freedom can be traced from the later Middle Ages when the institution of Parliament started its long evolution. In this same period the laws were made uniform in England, and justice came to be better administered; the idea of juries began to take form, and many ancient privileges were restated and confirmed during this time.

The Tudor rulers of the sixteenth century, from Henry VIII to Elizabeth I, the last of her line, were powerful and not inclined to increase the privileges of the English nobles and commoners. But the Tudors were generally shrewd enough to realize that they could not reduce the Englishman's rights without causing internal trouble.

The Stuart kings of the first half of the seventeenth century, James I (1603-1625) and Charles I (1625-1649), who succeeded the Tudors, were not as sensitive to the feelings of the English people about their privileges. Under the Stuart rulers, there was a constant pull and tug between the will of the king and the will of Parliament and religious groups—mostly Puritans. The will of Parliament and the Puritans prevailed, and their rights increased.

James I, who was also King of Scotland, followed Elizabeth on the throne of England. James believed that he ruled by divine right and that his authority was absolute. This belief antagonized the members of Parliament, for they, too, believed that they had a certain authority, including control of the purse and a voice in foreign policy. James also discriminated against the nonconformist Puritans—a name which at that time embraced Low Church Anglicans, Presbyterians, Congregationalists, and others who were influenced by the religious simplicity and stern spirituality of John Calvin. The Puritans were an influential group both inside and outside Parliament, and their opposition contributed to the difficulties James encountered in ruling. His discrimination against the Puritans caused some of them to migrate to the freer environment of Holland and the Americas, while others stayed in England and voiced their opposition both secretly and openly.

Charles I, below, was beheaded for treason. (National Portrait Gallery, London)

James was usually in need of money because of his own extravagance and because of the inflation of prices during this period. But Parliament was not disposed to grant him the money he requested. The members of the House of Commons were his most influential opponents, and they disliked his friendliness with Spain, his religious intolerance of the Puritans, and his conception of kingly power. They remained negative and cold toward the King's financial needs. Perhaps they would have granted him money in return for more voice in his government, but this was contrary to James' view of kingship. He impatiently dissolved Parliament and ruled for some years without its presence.

By his policies and attitudes, James aroused resentment and suspicion among the members of Parliament and the Puritans which burst into violence upon his successor, Charles I. But James will long be remembered and praised by millions of Christians for his authorization and support of a committee of scholars who translated the Old and New Testaments of the Bible into sounding and majestic English prose. Their creation was finished in 1611, and it is yet known as the King James Version of the Bible.

## Charles I

The rash and determined policies of Charles I brought civil war to the English, expanded their liberties, and cost Charles his head. Charles I was even more fixed than his father, James I, in the belief that he ruled by divine right. He looked upon the autocratic rule of the French kings as his model. But Charles, also, found it necessary to call Parliament into session to raise money. Before the members would give it to him, they forced him, in 1628, to consent to a statement called the Petition of Right. The Petition of Right became another great foundation stone supporting the rights of the Englishmen. In this petition, the following limitations on the king were approved: no taxes could be collected without the consent of Parliament; martial law could not be applied in time of peace; Englishmen could not be forced to quarter soldiers in their homes; and no person could be imprisoned without a trial. Charles agreed to the conditions, but he was furious, and he dismissed Parliament. He refused to call it back into session for about eleven years.

Charles, like his father, hated the Puritans and he persecuted them so severely that many emigrated to the Americas. He had those who opposed him brought before the Star Chamber, a court which tried people without jury. He also imposed hated taxes on towns and levied outrageous fines to obtain the money he often squandered. Charles especially antagonized the Scots. They invaded England, and Charles was forced to call Parliament together once again to find the needed funds for his armies. The Parliament which convened in 1640 was in a resentful and rebellious mood, for the House of Commons was controlled by Puritan leaders. They passed legislation stating that Parliament could not be dismissed without their consent, and that the special courts that Charles had set up to collect fines were unlawful. Charles had to agree, but he led troops to the House of Commons to arrest some of its leaders. They escaped, and in 1642 Charles fled London. Open war broke out between Parliament and the king.

## Oliver Cromwell

Charles was defeated by the Roundheads—so called because they cut their hair short in scorn of the long flowing locks of the Cavaliers who supported Charles I. The Roundheads were under the leadership of the stern and disciplined Puritan, Oliver Cromwell. They had Charles beheaded for treason in 1649. That a king could be executed for treason was an entirely new concept to the English. Until this time only a man who conspired against the king had been considered a traitor; but no one had acted upon the idea that a king might be a traitor to his own people.

Oliver Cromwell (1599-1658) made England over into a Commonwealth ruled by a Council, but later he became the sole dictator under the title of Lord Protector. He had been helped in his overthrow of the king by the more moderate Protestants—the Presbyterians and the Low Church Anglicans—who wanted a constitutional monarchy rather than the complete overthrow of the monarchy. But Cromwell controlled the army, and his will prevailed. He ruled now through a tightly organized minority and could have been king, but he refused the title.

Cromwell was a man who would brook no attempt to lessen the power of England, and he sought to maintain and increase English power on land and on sea. He ordered that goods imported to England or her colonies be carried only in English ships. This law struck heavily at the Dutch, whose ships were handling many of England's imports. Cromwell also warred against Spain and seized from her Jamaica in

Oliver Cromwell ruled England with an iron hand as Lord Protector (1653-1658). He was succeeded by his son Richard. (National Portrait Gallery, London)

the Caribbean. He beat the army of the Scots and repressed a Catholic rebellion in Ireland with such severity that his name is still hated in much of Ireland. When Cromwell died in 1658, he was succeeded by his son Richard, who lacked his father's strength. The English had had enough of Puritan rule and troubles. Parliament, supported by the army, recalled Charles II from exile in 1660.

### The Restoration

The period between 1660 and 1688 is known as the *Restoration*—the re-establishment of the monarchy in England. Two Stuarts, Charles II, followed by his brother James II, ruled during this period. They were the sons of Charles I. Charles II did not dispute with Parliament because he wanted no more of travels in exile. Life in England became gayer as the theaters, dancing, card playing, and other frivolities forbidden by the Puritans were once again permitted. But the English were suspicious of Charles' friendship toward France and of his Catholic tendencies.

James II ascended the throne upon the death of Charles and ruled from 1685 until 1688. James was publicly a Catholic and in 1687, by a "declaration of indulgence," granted freedom of worship to Catholics and dissenters in England. This and other actions made the majority suspicious. They thought that James was scheming to return Catholicism to England and to restore the former authority of the king. A faction in Parliament known as the Whigs decided to change kings, and they started what is known as the Glorious Revolution.

### The Glorious Revolution

The Whigs, a coalition of great lords and London merchants, negotiated with William of Orange in Holland, who was married to Mary, the Protestant daughter of James II. William accepted their proposition to come to England with Mary and occupy the English throne. He landed in 1688 on England's coast with fourteen thousand soldiers who were largely unnecessary, for James had no support and fled to France. Before formally accepting the reign of William and Mary, Parliament had them agree in 1689 to a document known as the Bill of Rights.

This Bill of Rights is regarded by the English as one of the greatest monuments in the evolution of their freedoms. It also had a profound effect upon the Constitution of the United States, and a number of the rights enumerated in this bill were incorporated into the first ten amendments to the United States Constitution. The Bill of Rights stated, among other provisions, that laws could not be suspended without the consent of Parliament; that taxes for the use of the crown could not be levied without Parliament's consent; that Parliament's agreement was needed for maintaining a standing army in England during peacetime; that freedom of speech should not be questioned and books should not be censored; that Parliament should meet frequently; and that the imposition of excessive bail, fines, and the use of cruel and unusual punishment should be outlawed.

By the Bill of Rights, the English Parliament gained supremacy, and individual freedoms of speech, writing, and justice were broadened. But the Englishman was not yet completely free nor did he share fully in the affairs of his government. In 1689 Parliament also passed the Act of Toleration, which allowed freedom of worship to all Protestants who were not Anglican. This act, however, did not include Roman Catholics.

The supremacy of Parliament over the king was confirmed by the Act of Settlement which spelled out who would inherit the throne of England if William and Mary, or Mary's sister Anne, should die without heirs. The throne would then go to the son of Sophia, granddaughter of James I and wife of the Elector of the House of Hanover in Germany. This happened. After the death of Mary and William, Anne was named queen. During Queen Anne's reign, England and Scotland were united under the name of Great Britain in 1707. When Anne died childless, George of Hanover, the son of Sophia, started the new line of English kings.

Parliamentary government continued to evolve in England. The names *Whig* and *Tory* became identified with parties in Parliament. The king chose his ministers from the majority party. Thus the leaders of the majority party gradually came to control the executive as well as the legislative branches of English government. Parliament gained other powers, such as those of declaring war and removing bad judges from the bench. The custom solidified into an unwritten law that no act of Parliament could be vetoed by the reigning sovereign. By the middle of the eighteenth century, the English had built the foundations and the framework of their structure of freedom which persist to the present day.

What the English accomplished had its effect in other parts of Europe and in the Americas, where English colonists were bunched along the eastern coasts of North America.

1. Why was James I such an unpopular ruler? For what accomplishment is he remembered?
2. What was the Petition of Right? Under what circumstances and by whom was it recognized?
3. What important events took place under the leadership of Oliver Cromwell? What groups supported Cromwell?
4. What important advances were made during the Glorious Revolution?

## The Americans Revolted

The English colonists who settled the eastern seaboard of the land that is now the United States were proud of their freedoms. Liberal writers and philosophers led some of them to think more deeply about their rights and freedoms. One of the writers who influenced the thinking of the new Americans was the Englishman John Locke.

### John Locke

The Americans read and agreed with the political statements in the *Two Treatises of Government*, which Locke wrote in 1690 to defend the Glorious Revolution. In this work he developed a basic political philosophy. Man lives in a state of nature, said Locke, which is ordered and regulated by the natural law of reason. This law of reason "teaches all mankind who will but consult it, that being all equal and independent, no one ought to harm another in his life, health, liberty, or possessions . . . ." But men are often biased and irrational where their own interests are concerned, and there is a need for an impartial judge to decide between them and a power to support his decrees. Locke suggested, therefore, that men form a voluntary association—he called it a *compact*—which would guarantee the property, the safety, and the peace of all. It was a theory of government based upon the consent of the governed. If the governors and the judges who were selected should act arbitrarily, they could be resisted. Men were "free, equal, and independent."

These concepts found swift approval in the minds and hearts of many in the American colonies, and they were formally incorporated into one of the Americans' most cherished documents—the Declaration of Independence. In this document Thomas Jefferson substituted the phrase "pursuit of happiness" for Locke's concept of "property."

### Voltaire and Montesquieu

Among the French writers whose words and ideas appealed to the American reader were Voltaire and Montesquieu. Voltaire (1694-1778) was a sharp critic of the authoritarian ways of his society. The rasp of his ideas caused sensitive nerves in Europe to shudder and delighted the many who suffered injustices. Voltaire's tolerance and idea of freedom were expressed in his *Essay on Tolerance* when he said "Think for yourselves and let others enjoy the privilege to do so too." Voltaire suffered imprisonment and exile because of his views, but he was never afraid to be outspoken. His whole life was evidence that he believed in freedom of expression for all men, including those with whom he disagreed.

Montesquieu (1689-1755) wrote a work called *The Spirit of the Laws* from which the framers of the United States Constitution borrowed the idea of dividing the government

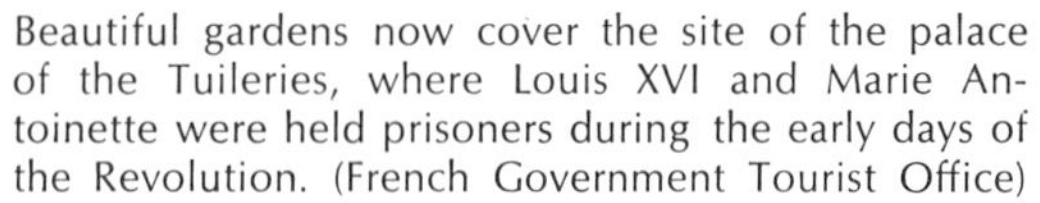

Beautiful gardens now cover the site of the palace of the Tuileries, where Louis XVI and Marie Antoinette were held prisoners during the early days of the Revolution. (French Government Tourist Office)

We remember the latter part of the eighteenth century best as the time of the American and French revolutions. It was also a period of great artistic achievement. Beethoven (1770-1827) and Mozart (1756-1791) are two of the great musicians who lived in this troubled period. The statue of Mozart, above, stands in Vienna. (Austrian Information Service)

The Place de la Concord in Paris commemorates the peace achieved after the French Revolution. (French Government Tourist Office)

into three branches: executive, legislative, and judicial. To avoid a possible dictatorship and to maintain a balance in government, the framers of the United States Constitution agreed with Montesquieu that it was necessary to separate the powers of the government so that each might act as a check upon the other.

The words of these and other writers found a response in the hearts of the French as well as the Americans, and the fact that the Americans successfully accomplished their revolution helped to stimulate the French to rebel against their own rulers.

## The French Revolution

By the latter part of the eighteenth century, there was an agitation of ideas among the French intellectuals and middle classes. There was also a stir of discontent among the farming peasants and the city poor. Louis XIV and Louis XV had squandered the treasury of France upon wars and displays of magnificence. The burdens of a heavy taxation fell heavily upon the middle class and the impoverished as the reigning monarch, Louis XVI, sought to maintain the requirements and the appearance of his office and to repay the debts he had incurred for war. Unemployment, an empty treasury, and a growing harshness of life plagued the people, who looked bitterly at the extravagance of the king and nobles who paid no taxes.

Many of the literate French had agreed with Voltaire when he aimed his cutting satire at the autocracy of an unenlightened monarch and the privileged position of nobles and clergy. They knew about Montesquieu's idea of the separation of powers. Many of them believed, with Rousseau, that man was basically good but had been corrupted by the society in which he lived. Rousseau (1712-1778) believed that education and political reforms could restore men to their natural state of goodness. In his book *The Social Contract* Rousseau discussed the ideal state. He insisted that monarchs ruled, not by divine right, but because this right was given by the people. Rousseau thus attacked the idea of the divine right of kings and upheld the idea that the people should choose their own rulers.

The French looked at the United States government, founded on the basic equality of man, and they responded with passion to the inflaming content of the Declaration of Independence. They were mentally prepared for daring changes when, in desperation, Louis XVI called a meeting of the old Estates-General in 1789 to raise urgently needed funds. The Estates-General was the French national assembly, in which clergy, nobility, and commoners were represented. Although it was comparable in some ways to the Diet of the Holy Roman Empire or the English Parliament, it had much less power. The chief function of the Estates-General was simply to approve royal legislation.

Louis XVI had his first indication of the growing radical attitude when the Third Estate, made up mostly of the middle classes and the intellectuals who represented the commoners of France, refused to sit separately from the First Estate, which represented the clergy, and the Second Estate, which represented the nobles. It will be recalled that the Third Estate began to participate in the Estates-General in the fourteenth century. Sitting separately, as was the old custom, the conservatively inclined members of the First and Second Estates could outvote the representatives of the commoners. But together, and voting as individuals, the Third Estate could match the votes of the other two groups. Louis refused their request for a joint meeting, but the Third Estate was not to be denied. The members of the Third Estate took an oath —called the "Tennis Court Oath" because it was taken on a tennis court when all halls were closed to them—never to disband until they had written a new constitution for France. Louis conceded, and all representatives of the three estates met together under the name of the National Assembly.

By this time the submerged inferno of resentment and hate among those long-oppressed by the privileged few was churning near the surface of expression. When the people of

Paris learned that the king was secretly bringing in troops to intimidate the National Assembly, they formed into a fearsome mob. This mob stormed and captured the Bastille, a prison which was also a fortress and a dark symbol of all the wrongs done the commoners by the ruling class. This happened on July 14, 1789, and that date is now celebrated as Bastille Day. The French consider this date as the beginning of their independence.

The Revolutionary flag, the *tricolor* of blue, white, and red, soon flew over the city of Paris. Throughout France the passions of revolution spread as hated masters were driven from castles and chateaus, old officials were killed, and the records of old obligations were burned. The spark of revolution was now a leaping flame in France. It would not be confined until the French had altered their government, laid the foundations for a newer way of life, varied the face of Europe, and changed the political and social attitudes of other Europeans.

Meeting in an atmosphere charged with change and violence, the National Assembly swept away the ancient feudalistic structure of government. Serfdom and special obligations to king, noble, and church were abolished, and the special privileges of the old governing class were removed. It was decreed that henceforth anyone could hold public office and that all should be taxed fairly. These sweeping changes were capped with a stirring statement known as the Declaration of the Rights of Man, which proclaimed the principles of the Revolution. This statement follows in the tradition of the English Bill of Rights and the American Declaration of Independence. It made all men equal before the law and asserted that every man had a right to participate in the formation of this law either personally or through representatives. No man could be arrested or imprisoned except in cases prescribed by law. The Assembly affirmed in strong language the right of man to express his ideas and opinions without restraint.

In 1791 the National Assembly wrote a constitution for France which turned the absolute monarchy into a limited one. A government of three separate branches—executive, legislative, and judicial—was established, following the principles of Montesquieu. Thinking they had finished their job, the members of the National Assembly disbanded in 1791, and later a Legislative Assembly was elected in accordance with the provisions of the new constitution.

The moderate middle class was opposed in this Legislative Assembly by more radical groups led by Jean Paul Marat, Georges Jacques Danton, and Maximilien Robespierre. The radical leaders wanted a republic rather than a limited monarchy. Their opposition was aided by the military successes of the Prussians and the Austrians who had organized an army to restore the monarchy in France. Emotions flamed in Paris. A mob attacked the residence of the king, who fled to the protection of the Legislative Assembly. The Austro-Prussian army continued to move toward Paris, and extremist elements killed several thousand royalists and clergy imprisoned in Paris. Their actions have since been known as the September Massacres (1792). In this charged atmosphere, the Assembly called for a new National Convention to draw up another constitution.

The National Convention governed France for the next three years, 1792-1795. Three major groups sat in the National Convention: The Girondins, the Jacobins, and those called the Plain of the Marsh. The Girondins were the more conservative republicans representing the higher middle class; the Jacobins represented a part of the middle class and the more radical reforming interests of the peasants and workers; and the members of the Plain of the Marsh swayed between the opposing forces of these two groups.

The Girondists controlled the Convention until about the middle of 1793. Under their leadership, the monarchy was abolished in September 1792, and Louis XVI was tried, convicted, and executed for treason in January 1793. Under Girondist leadership, however, France suffered military reverses in the field, and one of the chief Girondist generals, Dumouriez, defected to the enemy. These events, coupled with a lack of capable and determined leadership, provided the Jacobins with the opportunity of capturing the leadership of the Convention from the Girondists.

Under the leadership of such men as Maximilien Robespierre, Lazare Carnot, and Louis Antoine Saint-Just, the Jacobins established a revolutionary government. This revolutionary government was headed by two chief committees—the Committee of Public Safety and the Committee of General Security. These committees administered the government, waged war abroad, and secured the internal safety of the country against counter-revolutionaries.

Because of the harshness of its measures against internal and external enemies, the revolutionary government of the Jacobins has frequently been called the Terror. Many people suspected or accused of treason were killed by the guns of firing squads or decapitated by the guillotine—an instrument favored then for beheading those believed to be enemies of the government. Those who lost their heads under the razor edge of the guillotine included Marie Antoinette, the Queen of France, as well as leaders of the Girondist faction, Danton and his followers, and an assortment of royalists and others believed to be enemies of the government. The revolutionary government finally came to an end in July of 1794 when a group called the "Thermidorians," who were fearful of Robespierre and more moderately inclined in their politics, sent Robespierre and his chief followers to the guillotine.

Modern scholars who have studied this period of French history do not generally find the justice of the Revolutionary Tribunal faulty for its time, and some feel that Robespierre has been unjustly distorted in historical accounts. These scholars call attention to his popular sympathies, patriotism, moderation, honesty, humanitarianism, and his ability to lead and to organize.

In 1795 the National Convention put into effect a new republican constitution which established a legislature of two houses and placed the executive power of government in the hands of five men, known as *Directors*. Their government was thereafter known as the *Directory*. The Directory controlled France from 1795 until 1799. It was not a particularly honest or efficient ruling group. In 1799, Napoleon Bonaparte, a man of military genius, dismissed the Directors with the help of his army and some other leaders. In the same year he became the First Consul of France, and in 1804 he became Emperor of France.

1. What factors fostered an atmosphere of independence in America?
2. Describe the ideas of Locke, Voltaire, and Montesquieu. In what ways are they similar?
3. What was the immediate impact of the American Revolution on the world? What has been its impact through the years?
4. Recount the events which led to the storming of the Bastille.
5. Describe France during the three years the National Convention ruled. What type of government was this? Who was in control?

### Napoleon Bonaparte

Napoleon Bonaparte (1769-1821) was born on the island of Corsica, which then belonged to France. He studied at military schools in Brienne and Paris. When the Revolution exploded in France, he proved to be so able that in 1796 he was given command of the French forces struggling against the Austrians in Italy. His marriage to Josephine de Beauharnais, who had influence with the Directory, also helped to obtain this appointment for him. During a swift campaign he won a reputation for military genius and skillful diplomacy in bringing an end to a war which gave France command of much of northern Italy. This left France with but one fighting opponent—England. Napoleon persuaded the Directors to approve his scheme of striking at England by hurting English trade in the East through an expedition to the Middle East.

Napoleon was not merely a soldier. He was also a man with a feeling for culture and a desire to uncover the mysteries of antiquity. On his conquest of Egypt and Syria he took

Napoleon Bonaparte (1769-1821) led France to peaks of power and depths of defeat. Under Napoleon, the central government of France was strengthened. He is still a favorite national hero. (Cushing)

with him archaeologists and other experts. By this act he advanced man's knowledge about ancient Egypt. Near the town of Rosetta, on the mouth of the Nile, one of Napoleon's officers found a stone containing inscriptions in Greek, hieroglyphics, and demotic, which was the later alphabetical form of Egyptian writing. After several years of study the scholar Jean François Champollion was able to announce in 1821 that he had deciphered the Egyptian writings. His accomplishment made it possible for other scholars to read ancient Egyptian hieroglyphics and thus added greatly to man's knowledge of the past.

The Middle Eastern campaign, however, was not a complete success. Admiral Nelson, the great British naval hero, destroyed Napoleon's fleet while it was at anchor in Abukir Bay in 1798, thus cutting off his communications and supplies from France.

A year later Napoleon returned home, leaving his army in Syria and Egypt. Upon his return he was even more popular, for he gave glorious reports of the great victories he had won for France in the Middle East. During the period from 1799 to 1804, known as the *Consulate*, the authentic genius of Napoleon flowered in peace as well as in war.

Napoleon defeated his enemies by brilliant diplomacy and war strategy. By 1801 the Austrians gave up and sued for peace. In 1802 even that stubborn enemy, England, made peace with him. Napoleon had little success in establishing or administering French colonies overseas. At one time, his ambitions extended to the new world of the Americas, where he dreamed of a vast colonial empire built around Haiti, in the Caribbean, and the Louisiana Territory, which he had forced Spain to cede to him in 1801. However, the continued resistance of the Haitians and an outbreak of yellow fever decimated his troops there. In 1803, he sold the Louisiana Territory to the United States for $11,000,000—one of the best bargains the Americans have negotiated in their history. Napoleon reluctantly discarded his grandiose scheme for an empire overseas.

Napoleon reorganized and centralized the government of France during the period when he was Consul. The economic reforms of this period brought greater prosperity to France and inspired in the French people an emotional attachment to their land and to Napoleon. Secure in the affection and support of his people, Napoleon asked and received their approval to become Emperor. In 1804 the Pope came to Paris to crown Napoleon in the cathedral of Notre Dame. When he was about to place the crown on Napoleon's head, this shrewdly unpredictable man took it from the Pope's hands and crowned himself. The power expressed by this simple gesture was not lost on the Europeans who saw it or later heard the incident related by others.

From 1804 to 1815 Emperor Napoleon I was the dominant man of Europe. He was engrossed mainly with war and conquest during these years, and his most tenacious enemy was England. War broke out between England and France again in 1805, and Napoleon prepared to cross the channel and destroy this annoying disturber of his sea lanes. England, however, controlled the seas with men of greater experience and ships of better quality than those of the French. At the battle of Trafalgar, off the coast of Spain, Admiral Nelson destroyed many of the French and Spanish ships with not one loss of his own vessels. In achieving this great sea victory, Nelson lost his life. He is still honored by the British as one of the greatest of their numerous heroes of the sea. By Nelson's victory, England became the undisputed mistress of the waters, and Napoleon found the English Channel impossible to cross.

Checked by England's control of the seas, Napoleon turned his attention to the interior of Europe where his empire was threatened by the armies of Austria, Russia, and later Prussia. From 1805 to 1807 he defeated in succession the Austrians, Russians, and Prussians, and occupied the city of Berlin. He reached the summit of his glory when, in 1807, he met the Tsar of Russia, Alexander I, at Tilsit in East Prussia and divided up Europe between the two of them. By this settlement Napoleon became either directly or indirectly the ruler of Europe to the borders of Russia, the Ottoman Empire, and Sweden. Napoleon now reigned supreme in Europe. But there were forces at work undermining his rule, and he gave greater strength to these forces by continuing his military adventures, thereby draining the strength and resources of France.

England had established a blockade of Napoleon's empire. However great quantities of English goods continued to pour into the continent, carried by smugglers. Meanwhile the industries and economy of France and other European nations suffered from Napoleon's policies of economic control and his draining of the wealth of other countries to support the French at war. By his continual nibbling at various parts of Europe, Napoleon further aroused the enmity of the Spanish, Austrians, Prussians, Russians, and others.

In 1808 Spanish civilian fighters began to ambush French troops, using hit-and-run tactics to fight Napoleon's forces. This kind of war came to be known as guerrilla warfare, deriving its name from the Spanish word for war, *guerra*. The British sent an expeditionary force to Spain under the command of the Duke of Wellington. The Peninsular War, which then began, drew from Napoleon 300,000 troops. But even the presence of this large number of soldiers was insufficient to forge a real victory there. Then Napoleon made one of his biggest mistakes. In 1812 he tried to conquer Russia. He assembled an army of 500,000 soldiers, and marched across the wide plains of Russia to Moscow. The strategy of the Russians, however, consisted of one long retreat, so that they lost very few men while Napoleon was advancing. The French losses, however, were very heavy, for they could not keep their armies supplied over such a great distance, and the Russians left behind as little as possible in the way of food and supplies. By the time Napoleon reached Moscow his troops had been reduced by a third. The Russians had withdrawn from the city, and fires broke out in the wooden buildings of Moscow. The French were thus deprived of shelter and forced to withdraw from Moscow. With supplies running out and the Tsar refusing to meet his terms, Napoleon began a retreat which became a horrible nightmare. Lack of discipline among discouraged troops, exhausting distances, the onslaught of winter, and the harassing blows of a tracking enemy felled more than three-fourths of Napoleon's army.

Encouraged by Napoleon's failures in Spain and Russia, all of Europe entered into a coalition against him. In October 1813 he was defeated at the battle of Leipzig in Saxony. The following April the coalition forces occupied Paris, and the Emperor Napoleon abdicated. He was exiled and was given the small island of Elba off the coast of Italy to rule as his own.

With Napoleon in exile, a political conference was held. Representatives of the leading monarchs of Europe were sent to the Congress of Vienna in 1814. Although a meeting of all

**The Empire of Napoleon**

At the height of his power, Napoleon held much of Western Europe.

the representatives never took place, much work was done in committees. England, Austria, Prussia, and Russia were the chief powers at these meetings. Through skillful diplomacy, Talleyrand, who had been a leading diplomat under Napoleon, won a major voice for his country. Talleyrand obtained very easy terms of peace for France. The dominant figure at the Congress, however, was Clemens Metternich, prime minister of Austria.

Among the chief aims of the Congress was the restoration of the monarchs who had been overthrown by Napoleon. Another major objective was the establishment of a "balance of power" in Europe to insure that no nation could become powerful enough to threaten the others.

As a result of the conferences at the Congress of Vienna, the map of Europe was redrawn. Territories were swapped without regard for their inhabitants by the rulers and politicians who wanted compensation for losses they had suffered at the hands of Napoleon.

But Napoleon was not yet finished. In March, 1815 he returned to France, and the people rallied to his cause. Once again the coalition was formed against him, and on June 18, 1815 at the battle of Waterloo, he was again defeated. He was exiled to the small island of St. Helena where he died in 1821.

Napoleon ranks high among those who have been successful in conquering others. There are those, especially among the non-French, who speak of him as a despot, a man possessed of an insatiable ego, a tyrant who brought bloodshed, pain, and misery to untold numbers of people. They say the world would have been better had he not been born. But among the French he is yet regarded as one of the greatest of their heroes. They point to the institution of the Napoleonic Code which became the one law of France. Though based on the old Roman law, the Napoleonic Code also

The statue of a lion atop a great mound marks the site of Napoleon's defeat at Waterloo. (Belgian Tourist Bureau)

contained principles born of the French Revolution. The French refer with pride to Napoleon's introduction of a system of public education in their country. They praise his centralization of the French government. As early as the Revolution, France had been divided into administrative units called departments. Napoleon further improved this system and strengthened the central administration of government. Each department was governed by a prefect, and within the departments each town or city had a single head of government. The French still speak with wonder of the rapid improvement Napoleon made in the French system of communications, which assisted greatly in bringing a new unity to the country.

Napoleon continued the process of changing the attitude of the French provincial into one of the French national, which the Revolution had started. When the revolutionary government conscripted men for the armies, they appealed to their love of France and of the new principles which made everyone an equal part of the nation. These appeals developed in the Frenchman a spirit of patriotism. Napoleon also appealed to this love of country in his leadership of the French people. Thus the citizens of France became conscious of the oneness of their culture and their land. The Frenchman was constantly reminded that it was for the glory and honor of his own country that he was asked to fight and to sacrifice. The French have never lost this love of country.

1. What important advances did Napoleon bring about in France during the period from 1799 to 1804? How did the French people reward him?
2. Trace the relations between the British and the French during the reign of Napoleon.

## Industrial Revolution

Man has been inventing and tinkering with machines since far back in his history. The Chinese, Indians, Egyptians, Hellenistic Greeks, and others made machines for use and to satisfy their curiosity. Some of the Greeks displayed extraordinary imagination in putting together a broad variety of machines ranging from the fire engine to the sewing machine, but they regarded such machines simply as interesting toys for amusement. They did not make much use of their machines, and most of their mechanical inventions died with them. Later, during the Renaissance, a few men also showed great inventiveness. Leonardo da Vinci had a fertile mind for inventions. He filled his scrapbook with sketches for airplanes and other machines and ideas which seem modern beyond belief. But, like the Greeks, da Vinci was ahead of his time.

There is an element of mystery in the way that man follows certain directions in his evolution. Certainly the conditions of his environment must be favorable if he is to advance far along any particular evolutionary or revolutionary path. Conditions were favorable for the English, who began to rapidly change the whole fabric of their lives in the 1700's with new machines and new ideas. Conditions were also favorable for the Europeans on the continent and the North Americans who followed the trail the English were blazing.

## The English Invented New Machines

The Englishmen of the mid-eighteenth century lived on an island tightly secured by the finest fleet in the world. They were well supplied by the cargoes brought to fine harbors by a great fleet of merchant ships. Communications within England were excellent, for the island kingdom was not extensive, and roads and canals criss-crossed it. The atmosphere in which the English conducted their business was becoming increasingly free, and their wealth was piling into a large surplus. They were interested in schemes and investments which could utilize this surplus profitably, thus continuing the accumulation of wealth. The demands of markets at home and overseas were growing and the English had to find speedier methods of production to meet the requirements of expansion. They found the solution in new machines.

Until this time most of England's production had come from the hands of numerous small shopkeepers, and from the homes of people who combined farming or some other occupation with work at home in their spare hours. They worked under contract to a manufacturer who furnished the raw materials and paid them for their labor. But hand labor was too slow to keep pace with the demands of trade, especially in the making of cotton cloth. In 1733 a man named John Kay patented an instrument for weaving called the "flying shuttle." With this shuttle it was possible to weave cloth faster than the thread could be spun. This was the beginning of a rapid process which has yet to end—the process of one invention leading to another, and another, and another. This was the process that led to our great technology of today and may produce an even greater one in the future.

The first great series of inventions of the Industrial Revolution had to do with the textile industry. A laborer, James Hargreaves, invented a machine which increased the spinning of thread eight times over the old spinning wheel. A man named Richard Arkwright brought the use of water power to spinning. Another man, Samuel Crompton, improved on Arkwright's invention, and the weavers now found that they could not keep pace with the spinners. But a clergyman, Edmund Cartwright, found a method of using water power for weaving, and the production of cotton textiles soared again.

The use of these rapid methods of manufacturing brought about a shortage of raw fiber from which the cotton thread came, for the seeds of the cotton had to be removed by hand, and this was a slow process. Then, in 1793, Eli Whitney, an American, invented a machine called a cotton gin to remove the seeds. This invention increased production by around fifty times. Later the gin was improved to the extent that it became a thousand times more productive than the output of one man. The cotton gin made more raw cotton available to the spinning and weaving machines, and production took another great leap forward. Naturally cotton became more valuable, and it became the main export crop of the United States.

The machines were showing their produc-

James Watt's steam engine was familiarly known as "Old Bess," left. Eli Whitney's cotton gin helped to revolutionize an industry. Both models are in the Smithsonian Institution, Washington, D. C. (Smithsonian Institution)

tive worth, and new sources of power were sought and found to run them even more rapidly and efficiently. First, man had used his hands alone to do his work. Then he found a way to run his machines by water power, provided by rivers and streams. In 1769 a Scot named James Watt invented a steam engine which could provide power for machines. The steam engine gave man greater freedom in selecting sites for the home of his machines—the factory. Men began to go to factories and work full time tending the machines. What had formerly been a sideline done at night and in spare hours now became a full-time occupation. The steam engine needed fuel, and on their island the English had the fuel—coal. Coal now became the black gold of the earth, and the English learned to mine it with care and efficiency.

But the machines had barely begun to make their demands upon the mental and physical energies of man. A strong, durable metal was needed to construct machines, and that metal was iron. The machines were hard-working and needed parts which would have the strength to withstand the continuous strain put upon them. Steel had been known since ancient times, even before the Christian era, but it was very expensive and could be made only in small quantities. The earliest kind of steel was probably made in a *crucible*, or large container in which it could be heated to a very high temperature. This process had been lost, however. It was rediscovered in 1740 by Benjamin Huntsman, an Englishman. But steel was still very expensive to make. In the 1850's Henry Bessemer, an Englishman, and William Kelly, an American both experimented with blowing air through molten iron to remove impurities and make steel. At about the same time, Robert Mushet, of England, discovered that the addition of manganese would strengthen steel.

The discoveries of these men made it possible to produce steel cheaply in large quantities. Coal, iron, and steel became the basic ingredients of the Industrial Revolution. As the number of machines increased, other machines were needed to make machine parts, and thus began the machine-tool industry.

Machines came to be used for all kinds of manufacturing, and machines were also invented to improve transportation on sea and on land. An American, Robert Fulton, made a steam-propelled ship in 1807 which paddled up the Hudson River. Soon steam was propelling ships on rivers and seas in all parts of the

Samuel P. Langley was a pioneer inventor of heavier-than-air machines. His airplane is shown above. Popular music celebrated the laying of the first telegraph cable across the Atlantic, left. (Both, Library of Congress)

world. Around 1825 an Englishman, George Stephenson, ran a steam-driven locomotive on iron rails in England. This was the beginning of the railway, which has played a vital role in improving the communications and transportation of man.

## Inventions Elsewhere

After the English had started the Industrial Revolution, it did not stay in England but spread to Western Europe and the United States. In these countries other men continued to invent and create on the foundations laid in England. In 1800 Alessandro Volta, an

Italian, invented a battery which produced an electric current. A Frenchman, André Ampère, gave man an understanding of the magnetic aspects of this current. In 1832 an American, Samuel Morse, used the discoveries of Volta and Ampère to build an electrical telegraph.

Other Americans were also inventive. Many of their inventions were improvements upon European inventions or represented practical applications that improved production in industries. Certainly they needed to be practical and productive to cope with the challenge of their resource-laden land. They built roads and canals, and by 1869 had conquered the expanses of plains, deserts, and mountains with a railroad which linked their eastern and western coasts. Inventions tumbled in incredible quantities from their gifted minds and hands. Thomas Edison perfected the electric light bulb and gave to man the phonograph and the motion picture, among other inventions. Charles Goodyear vulcanized rubber, and George Westinghouse made the railroads safe with his air-brake. George Eastman further improved the processes of photography which had been invented by the Frenchmen Niepce and Daguerre. The internal combustion engine, which Europeans had first developed, was improved by American inventors, making possible the production of great numbers of automobiles and the development of airplanes.

The Americans have often been wasteful of their rich resources, but no one can doubt their technological skill and their mastery of efficient production.

## Revolution in Agriculture

Supporting and accompanying the Industrial Revolution was the revolution in producing food and raw materials for the manufacture of cotton cloth, woolens, linens, and other materials. The population in Europe and the Americas was mounting with increasing rapidity, and the mouths of men and machines were devouring with voracious appetites the fruits of the earth. In 1798 Thomas Malthus had published *An Essay on the Principle of Population* in which he stated that human beings multiplied faster than their production of food increased. In the resulting competition for this insufficient supply of food, he said, a number of people died. According to Malthus' theory, there was possibly a threat to man's survival if the population outgrew the food supply. Man had to find ways to induce the earth to bear more if he was to thrive and see his industry grow and mature. He found them.

During the 1700's and 1800's there were many inventions and discoveries that contributed to the revolution in agriculture. Jethro Tull, an Englishman, invented a horse-drawn cultivator for loosening the soil and a drill for planting seeds. Crop rotation, which had been practiced by the ancient Romans and also during the Middle Ages, was greatly improved by the methods of another Englishman, Charles Townshend. Townshend found that wheat, turnips, clover, and barley in rotation improved and retained the fertility of the soil.

More scientific approaches to the breeding of animals came into use during this time also. Among the pioneers in scientific animal breeding was Robert Bakewell, who in the late 1700's developed new breeds of sheep and cattle. Bakewell learned that inbreeding (breeding back into the same blood lines) could be used to improve the characteristics of animals. Through his experiments with breeding animals in a systematic way, Bakewell contributed to man's understanding of the laws of genetics and heredity.

While the iron plow had been in use even before the Christian era, not many new machines were introduced in agriculture until the period of the agricultural revolution. Following upon the English inventors, Americans began to make their contributions to the rapid changes in agriculture. In the 1830's Cyrus McCormick patented a reaper, and steam powered threshing machines came to be used in harvesting grain. In 1837 John Deere introduced a steel plow. Besides being stronger than iron plows, the steel plow presented a self-cleaning surface which made it possible to make clean, even furrows in the thick, rich soil of the prairies.

Eventually machines were designed which

did many things at once, and today in much of the world huge combines harvest great seas of ripened wheat, while other machines gather and process many other kinds of fruits and vegetables.

Up until the end of the nineteenth century, the majority of Americans were engaged in agriculture. Today the agricultural population is a small minority. This same proportion also prevails in much of Western Europe. It is the few, rather than the many, who, aided by machines, produce food and raw materials on great farms in much of the Western world today.

In much of the Western world, the theory that Thomas Malthus expressed in 1798 has proved not to hold completely true. Throughout Europe and the Americas, improvements in agricultural methods have made it possible for food production to keep pace with a rapidly increasing population. Between 1850 and 1964, the world population increased three times over, from 1,000,000,000 to over 3,000,000,000. In parts of the non-Western world, food production has lagged and much of the population is not adequately fed. But it is possible that the revolution in agriculture will still come to these areas, at least in some degree.

1. What were the conditions which led up to what we call the Industrial Revolution? What discoveries made the Industrial Revolution possible?
2. What was the significance of John Kay's discovery of the flying shuttle?
3. What factors gave impetus to the revolution in agriculture? Which factors do you feel were most important?

## Revolution in Science

In a very real sense, the eager, seeking spirit of the scientist preceded and sustained the technical advances associated with the industrial and agricultural revolutions of the eighteenth and nineteenth centuries. This same searching spirit of inquiry continues to stimulate and to nourish the technology of the twentieth century. From around the middle of the sixteenth century until now, the patient labors, the careful experiments, and the bold, inspired hypotheses of scientists have produced mighty advances in technology, a deeper understanding of the earth and universe, and a clearer picture of the complexities of man himself.

The methods and procedures of science have always been a combination of imagination, hard work, and the use of man's ability to reason. Ancient philosophers sought to find explanations of the natural world, and their systems of thought remained models throughout the medieval period. In these early periods, there was a great effort to find out *why*. *Why* does an animal produce other animals of its own kind? *Why* do the planets revolve around the sun? *Why* does water run downhill? Often it proved impossible to answer the question of *why*.

Modern science, however, does not often concern itself with the question of *why*, but rather with the question of *how*. It is often possible to observe and describe what actually does happen, and to tell the way in which it happens, without ever knowing *why* it happens. Modern scientists, unlike the ancient philosophers, do not often look for the ultimate causes of things—but they are very interested indeed in finding logical ways to describe the *way* in which things occur. They live in an exciting world where every new discovery raises many new questions and opens up new paths for the mind to explore. Science is more than mere experimentation and observation. It is a way of looking at the world and of seeking to find truth.

**Copernicus and Galileo.** The beginning of the revolution in science is often associated with the publication *On the Revolutions of the Heavenly Orbs* by Nicolaus Copernicus in 1543. In this work, Copernicus stated that the earth went about the sun and that the earth spun on its own axis. This was a radical departure from the idea stated by the Greek astronomer Ptolemy, in the second century A.D., that the sun and the planets revolved around the earth. Ptolemy's theory had been accepted for more than a thousand years, and Copernicus delayed publication of his book for many years because its ideas were so revolutionary. Later,

Galileo Galilei (1564-1642), an Italian, constructed his own telescope and saw moons revolving around the planet Jupiter. His observations backed up the theory of Copernicus. For publishing these radical findings he was brought before the Inquisition. Threatened by punishment, he promised to keep quiet about his observations. Galileo also experimented with falling bodies and uncovered an important law. He measured the acceleration of gravity by rolling small metal spheres down parchment-lined grooves on an inclined plane, timing them with a water-clock.

**Newton and others.** Sir Isaac Newton (1642-1727), an Englishman, was a magnificent scientist. He proclaimed his theories of motion and gravitation which provided an explanation of the way that objects fall and the way that planets revolve around the sun instead of wandering off into some other part of space. His physical laws of movement were stated in terms of the masses of bodies and the distances between them, and these laws became a basis used by later scientists to reach new conclusions about nature and the universe. Newton, like all great scientists, was not an overly dogmatic man. He stated that he had merely explained a process, for he neither knew the cause nor the nature of gravity.

Scientific advances began to multiply as more and more discoveries and inventions were made. A Dutch naturalist, Anton van Leeuwenhoek (1632-1723), made simple microscopes and described tiny cells of living matter. His discoveries started man on a field of investigation which has not ceased. Antoine Lavoisier (1743-1794), a Frenchman who lost his head to the revolutionists' guillotine, uncovered the basic principles of burning and gave man an explanation of fire. John Dalton (1766-1844), the English chemist and physicist, stated that all matter is composed of tiny particles, which we call atoms.

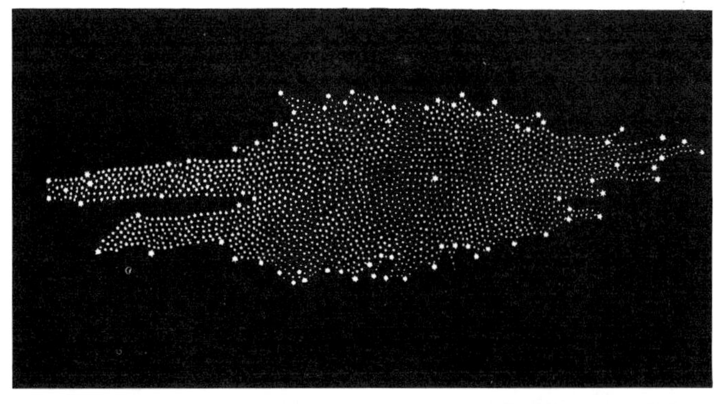

William Herschel (1738-1822) was a pioneer in modern astronomy, especially in the study of nebulae. His "galactic system" is shown at top. Below, a spiral nebula photographed through a modern telescope. (Yerkes Observatory; Mount Wilson and Palomar Observatories)

**Mathematics.** The science of mathematics was further developed and provided better ways to express logical ideas and relationships. René Descartes (1596-1650), a French mathematician, created analytical geometry. Newton and Leibnitz continued Descartes' achievements by developing calculus. Later, about 1830, Bolyai of Hungary and Lobachevsky of Russia invented new systems of geometry which were very different from the geometry of Euclid. The relationships that could be expressed through the non-Euclidean geometry formed an important basis for the theory of relativity which was stated by Albert Einstein in the twentieth century. George Boole (1815-1864) invented a kind of algebra which has been useful in stating and solving problems in logic and probability.

**The Enlightenment.** During the sixteenth, seventeenth, and eighteenth centuries, the scientific triumphs of reason and the discovery of "natural laws" ordering the universe also influenced the thinking of the social philosophers and ushered in a period known as "The Enlightenment" in the eighteenth century.

The thinkers and observers of man's society in this period assumed that there were "natural laws" governing the social life of man, and that they could be discovered by the use of reason and the scientific method. Once these laws were discovered, man could progress to a better society by bringing his life into accord with the natural order. This concept influenced such thinkers as Voltaire, Locke, Montesquieu, Rousseau, and Adam Smith (1723-1790), who wrote the *Wealth of Nations*—a basic economic work which is still studied today. The attitudes of these, and many other intellectuals, resulted in political, economic, social, and even religious changes in both Europe and the Americas.

**Geology and biology.** One of the greatest advances of the scientific revolution was an increased understanding of geology and biology. Carolus Linnaeus (1707-1778) had founded the modern study of biology and provided a system of classifying plants and animals according to family, genus, species, etc. in the eighteenth century. Then, in 1833, Sir Charles Lyell published *Principles of Geology*, which showed that it had taken millions of years for the wind, the ice, and other forces of nature to shape the present features of the earth. Encouraged by Lyell, in 1859 Charles Darwin published his *The Origin of Species*. In this book he observed that all living things had evolved from ancient beginnings. He also expressed the theory that those kinds of plants

Jean Jacques Rousseau (1712-1778) was born in Geneva, Switzerland. This island in Lake Geneva is named in his honor. (Swiss National Tourist Office)

and animals that were best suited to survive had lived and reproduced while others died out. This process, in which the best-equipped forms of life survived, Darwin call "natural selection."

Since the publication of Darwin's observations man has continued to probe the mysteries of evolution and heredity. Darwin believed, like Jean Lamarck (1744-1829), that acquired characteristics were inherited, but later findings such as those of August Weismann (1834-1914), have indicated that only those characteristics already in the germ plasm of the parents are inherited by their children. The Austrian monk Gregor Mendel (1822-1884) and Hugo De Vries (1848-1935) of Holland were led by the results of their research to the opinion that evolution occurs quickly because of mutations within a single generation, making the offspring different from the parents in a distinctive way. There are those today who think that the increasing radioactivity in the atmosphere will speed up changes by mutation in earth's life. Perhaps future generations will observe a more rapid change in man, animal, and plant.

Modern technology has given man a great degree of control over his environment. Above, an airplane sprays insecticides to control mosquitoes. Below, vaccination helps to control disease. (Both, USDA)

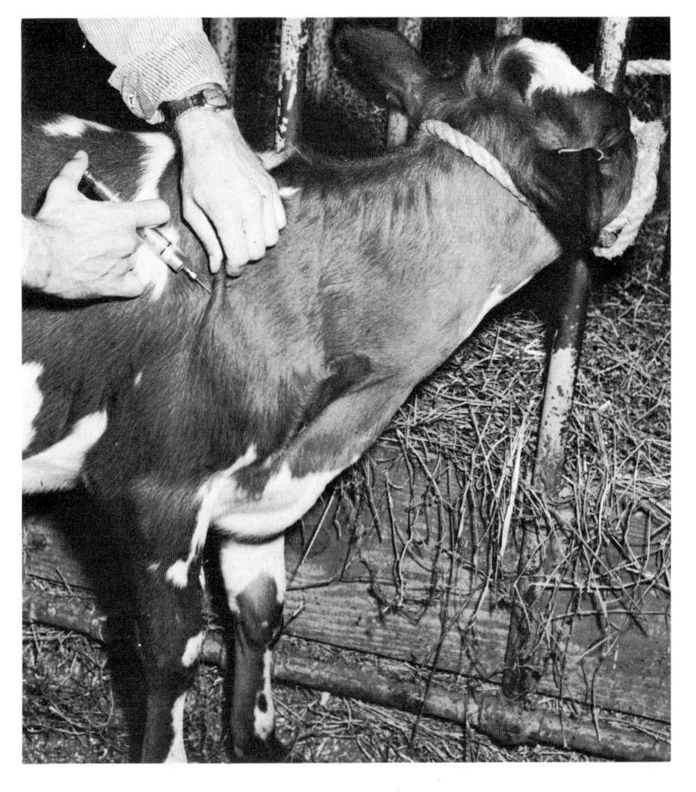

**Medicine.** During the seventeenth century, an English doctor, William Harvey, had described the circulation of the blood in the body, and in the eighteenth century Edward Jenner, another English doctor, discovered a vaccine for smallpox, one of the greatest killers of the time. The great advances that followed these pioneers came more and more rapidly and continue even up to the present. The Frenchman Louis Pasteur discovered the world of germs and learned that the deadliness of many bacteria could be killed by heat. Pasteur and the German Robert Koch (1843-1910) worked independently, but arrived at the same conclusions—germs were the cause of many diseases. Pasteur gave man the process of pasteurization and the use of innoculations against hydrophobia and anthrax. Koch searched out the germs of tuberculosis and cholera among others.

The search for the causes of disease went on. The malaria parasite, which has destroyed armies and weakened empires (the Romans are an example), was discovered by Alphonse Laveran in 1880. In 1897 Sir Ronald Ross showed that it was a mosquito which spread the parasite. The natives of eastern Peru had known for a long time that the bark of the cinchona tree was effective against malaria. Quinine was extracted from this bark and became widespread in the treatment of this malaria. Later, atabrine and other drugs were developed to combat this scourge. But malaria was not wiped out in many parts of the world until it was found that DDT, first made in Germany in 1874, destroyed the larvae of the mosquito. During the Second World War and afterwards it has been used extensively in great parts of the world with remarkable results.

In the scientific revolution, men became curious about the fundamental functions of life and the basic structures of living matter. Theodor Schwann (1810-1882) and others found that cells were basic to all living things whether complex or simple. Karl Ernst von Baer (1792-1876) began the science of embryology, and those who followed him have continued this study of man and other animals in the earliest stages of their development.

The names of patient, brilliant, and often brave men and women who have contributed to the advancement of the life and health of man during the nineteenth and twentieth centuries could fill volumes. Lister in 1830 improved the microscope and thus contributed to the success of Pasteur and Koch in their studies of the small world of germs. His son, Joseph Lister (1827-1912), substantially reduced the danger of operations by cleansing instruments and wounds with a solution of carbolic acid and sewing up wounds with catgut also treated with carbolic acid. The use of antiseptics grew out of Lister's practices and has saved thousands of lives.

In 1842, Dr. Crawford Long, of Georgia, used ether to ease the pain and the shock of a patient undergoing surgery, and in 1846 Charles Jackson, a chemist, and William Morton, a dentist, also experimented with the use of anesthesia. Since that time the advances in this field of medicine have been remarkable. Dr. Walter Reed (1851-1902), an American Army surgeon, proved that yellow fever was spread by a mosquito, and ways were developed to reduce its spread. Conrad Roentgen (1845-1923), a German physicist, discovered the X-ray and broadened the knowledge of other fields as well as medicine. Florence Nightingale (1820-1910), lifted the nurse from a state of little respect to the honorable title of "Angel of Mercy." More recently, Dr. Jonas Salk and Dr. Albert Sabin have given their names to vaccines which have drastically curbed the blight of polio.

These are but a few of the many whose research and discoveries have revolutionized the field of medicine and rescued man from disease and from death. And today thousands of men and women continue to work in laboratories, in hospitals, in small offices and busy clinics, in universities, and in lonely outposts that man may live longer, relieved of the scourge of pain and disease.

**The mind of man.** Throughout his history man has alternately applauded and deplored the products of his mind. Within its yet unfathomable depths, the mind of man has conceived an abundance of good which has glorified him and an ocean of evil which has shamed him. Its wisdom has uplifted him; its folly has stunned him; and he has frequently thought of it as a battleground where the forces of light and darkness warred for a supremacy over his actions. But until recent years no one really thought of the mind as a part of the total physical being which could be studied and analyzed in much the same way that the digestive and circulatory systems and other noticeable features of the body have been studied.

It was a German, Wilhelm Wundt (1832-1920), who fathered psychology as a science and stressed the physical foundations of thought. Influenced by his teaching, Ivan Pavlov (1849-1936), a Russian, experimented with the reactions of animals. Among his experiments was one with dogs. He fed them after ringing a bell, and after a period of time he found that their mouths would water on merely hearing the sound of the bell. He called this response a "conditioned reflex" and suggested that it was a key aspect of all human behavior. There are those today who hold that if man is exposed long enough to a certain environment and conditions, he will eventually respond to these influences in an almost automatic manner. Pavlovian psychology is especially honored in Communist Russia where the leaders are attempting to make a new man—the Communist man.

There were those, however, who did not think of man's behavior as merely the response to outside influences. They conceived of man as an individual with certain basic inner drives — power, self-preservation, and sex. The founder of this school of thought was Sigmund Freud (1856-1939). He saw man as an individual who, prevented by society from expressing these drives, buried his desires in the unconscious or subconscious part of his mind. But they were not dead and frequently revealed themselves in abnormal behavior and in nervous and mental disorders. Freud recommended that each mental case be treated on an individual basis. He thought that when the individual recognized the long-buried reasons for his behavior, he would be helped. There are many today who believe that his analysis and solution are essentially correct, and his suggested treatment is widely used at present in aiding those who suffer from mental disorders.

The mentally ill are a growing legion in modern times, and the twisting depths of the mind are but little known. Within the mind there are unknown possibilities for evil—and an immeasurable capacity for good.

**Atomic science.** There were also those who looked into the basic core of matter and found that it could be considered as energy. Men like Hermann von Helmholtz (1821-1894), William Thomson (1824-1907), and Max Planck (1858-1947) told man how energy was conserved, dissipated, and released. Marie Curie (1867-1934) discovered radium and opened up a new field for research. Physicists studied light waves, the X-ray, electricity, and other forms of radiant energy and saw that they were related.

From the time of the Greeks there had been some who thought that all matter was composed of atoms, but they thought of these atoms as indivisible and indestructible. Now it was discovered that the atom itself could be split and that it could give off tremendous amounts of energy. Albert Einstein (1879-1955), one of the great geniuses of the modern age, made the shocking announcement that there was a relationship between the mass of matter and energy. He gave to the world a formula, $E = mc^2$, which stated the relationship of mass and energy. His formula was proved correct when the atom bomb was born at the University of Chicago during the Second World War. Men like Enrico Fermi (1901-1954), Niels Bohr (1885-1962), and Harold Urey (1893- ) have continued to probe the unknown expanses of the physical universe and to startle man with their findings and theories.

## The Reaction

How did men react to the new views of reality uncovered by science? Some men, like Herbert Spencer (1820-1903) and the American sociologist W. G. Sumner (1840-1910), saw Darwin's idea of the survival of the fittest displayed in the social system of our times. They saw the thrifty, the intelligent, and the strong as rich and propertied leaders. The unfit and the less able were the poor. The English biologist Thomas Huxley (1825-1895) was led to the idea of *agnosticism*, which is the belief that neither God nor the ultimate nature of the universe is knowable. Friedrich Nietzsche (1844-1900), the German philosopher and poet, came to advocate the destruction of such virtues as humility, pacificism, and charity toward the unfortunate. He stressed, instead, courage, strength, loyalty, and the elimination of all those qualities which would prevent man from becoming a "superman."

On the other hand, this great sea of doubt caused the leaders of the Roman Catholic Church and Protestants like Reinhold Niebuhr, to reinforce the philosophical bases of their faith, and to proclaim that God still remained the center and the ultimate end of

The theories of Albert Einstein (1879-1955) helped to revolutionize the modern study of physics. (Yerkes Observatory, University of Chicago)

Robert Hutchings Goddard (1882-1945) was the father of modern rocketry and space flight. Below are two of his rocket models. (Smithsonian Institution)

man's existence. It led Alfred North Whitehead (1861-1947) and Bertrand Russell (1872- ) to the conclusion that science could advance the development of man. They expressed the idea that the discoveries of science should not be used for selfish or destructive ends, but for the benefit of all mankind. Science was not to be worshiped, but neither was it to be condemned. It was not the whole truth, but it was the only illuminating truth about reality that we had at this moment. And there were practical reactions from Americans such as Charles Peirce (1839-1914), William James (1842-1910), and John Dewey (1859-1952) who thought that truth should meet the test of practicality. The quest for knowledge, they said, had one main end—to better the lot of man on earth.

The terrible potential destructiveness of their discoveries gave many scientists a sense of guilt and pushed them into a mighty conflict with their consciences. Was it right for them to place the means of the destruction of all mankind into the hands of men who were yet far from angels and who were sometimes maddened with a lust for power? Could they in good conscience go on creating without thought of the impact of their creations upon the spirit and the body of man? Or did they have a real responsibility to help fashion a moral and social climate among men which would favor a sane and constructive use of science? Scientists of our century have found these problems of social and moral responsibility to be very perplexing.

The nonscientist, man in general, also began to become aware of the real changes science had made in his life. Could he, without danger to himself and his family, continue to live by old guidelines in this world so greatly altered by science? Must he not throw off his complacent and passive acceptance of the products of the scientist and the technician? Was it not necessary to question the effect of scientific advancement upon his way of life? Man's scientific genius had changed his world, but had it changed his viewpoint and attitude of mind? These are questions that have preoccupied man especially in this century.

## The Machine Brought Social Changes

In industry, agriculture, science, and medicine, man began revolutions which drastically changed his daily life and his society. The machines he invented and used were placed together in buildings called factories. Workers left the homes, where they had worked with smaller and less efficient machines, and congregated for most of their daylight hours in the factories. People built their homes within walking or riding distance of the factories. Tailors, shoemakers, food merchants, and a variety of other tradesmen were required to service the needs of growing communities. These communities required law and order and a government. Gradually the communities became cities. Cities grew up around the machines.

The factory workers came first from among the poor, the landless, and the children. But gradually workers began to pour into the factory from the countryside and the farm. They all crowded together in undistinguished rows of small soot-smeared houses. Wages were low. Working conditions were bad for adults and worse for children. Child labor was permitted and encouraged because there was no need to pay the children much. The machine received more attention than the human—its value was regarded as higher. Around the machines there grew poverty, slums, diseases, and death.

In the country, on the farm, and in the small shop with a limited but steady market, the world rarely intruded. It did not matter that the price of raw materials was high, that trade abroad had dwindled, or that war had taken away trading posts or the sources of supply. The farmer and the shopkeeper managed to get enough to eat and to wear. But when the farmer or owner of a small shop moved to the city and the factory, he became subject to all the political and economic forces which turned or stopped the machines. Many events affected the machine: overproduction and not enough buyers to keep the machine going; a revolution or war which cut off a substantial portion of the raw materials needed; tangled finances within a country, which made it difficult to get credit. Because of these many complex factors, the machines were often stopped, factories were closed, and the workers were laid off. Around the machines there grew a dependence and an interdependence among men.

The workers became increasingly upset and frustrated at the insecurity of their lives and the worsening conditions under which they lived and worked. Under the strain of their troubled lives, they became conscious of the need for unity and collective action if they were to survive the new machine age. They banded together and formed labor unions which negotiated for all of them with the owners of the machines. These unions helped to improve working conditions and wages and won reductions in the number of hours of work demanded, for they spoke collectively, not individually. Collectively the workers became politically powerful, and their votes began to speak and to be heard in government. Around the machines, there grew unions of the laboring classes.

Money was needed to buy, improve, replace, and house machines. Few men had the large amounts of money to do this. They borrowed from banks. They borrowed from governments. But still more and more money was needed to keep pace with expanding needs, growing competition, increasing costs of labor, raw materials, and transportation. The owners of factories found the money they needed by selling stock in their enterprises to the general public. The profits they made were shared in the form of dividends, distributed among those who had bought their stock. Around the machines, there grew corporations and a system of capitalism.

The middle class — merchants, bankers, manufacturers—started to exert greater political power in England during the nineteenth century. Political reforms were pushed through Parliament giving to this class greater voting privileges and representation in the House of Commons. Public education expanded. Under the influence of the statesmen William Gladstone and Benjamin Disraeli reforms were extended to the working classes. By the beginning of the twentieth century, most men in England had the right to vote. There were other advances providing for injured workmen,

Clara Barton (1821-1912) was the founder of the American Red Cross. (American Red Cross)

aged workmen, and the ill and unemployed. These welfare provisions have continued to be part of the evolving society of the European as well as the Englishman and the American.

There were many individuals who reacted positively and wonderfully to the social needs of humanity created by this new era of the scientist, the technician, and the machine. There was William Booth (1829-1912), who saw the plight of those who dwelled in the slums of London and founded the Salvation Army to assist them. There was Jane Addams (1860-1935), who searched out the reasons for crime and poverty. Hull House in Chicago is a memorial to her work. There was Henri Dunant (1828-1910) of Switzerland, whose desire for better treatment of prisoners of war led to the organization of The International Red Cross. In 1881, Clara Barton founded a Red Cross Committee in the United States.

Recognizing the key role of education in this fast-expanding era of knowledge, governments made it free and compulsory—at least up to certain levels—in much of the world. Some men established foundations — Ford, Carnegie, Rockefeller, among many others—to promote the surge of science, to investigate more thoroughly man and his nature, and to search for ways that would permit man to live more realistically and with greater peace of mind amidst the complexities of his age. Others organized labor unions to negotiate higher salaries and better conditions of work, and in the United States the forty-hour week, pensions, health benefits, and good salaries, are concrete examples of their success. The AFL-CIO is the huge symbol of the unity of labor. Concerned with the insecurity and frustration that accompanied advancing age, forward-looking men and women advocated and made into law social security programs, old-age pension plans, and other measures designed to make the life of senior citizens more gracious and more bearable. Around the machine there grew political, economic, and social reforms.

1. How does the approach of modern scientists differ from the approach of the ancient philosophers?
2. What was "The Enlightenment"? What events led up to it?

## Socialism Is Introduced

The European and the American are still engrossed with their technology, and it continues to influence their entire way of life. One of the political developments of the machine age which began in Europe in the nineteenth century and lives on today is the doctrine of *socialism.* Essentially, socialism is the idea that all should own the means of production —the land, the factory, the mine—and also the means of distribution of the goods produced—the railroads, the trucking lines, the boats, or any other transportation system. Since the government represents all the people, in practice socialism meant government ownership and management of the means of production and distribution. This theory and practice is in opposition to *capitalism,* which advocates the private ownership of the means of production and distribution.

There are several kinds of socialists. The more democratic and moderate socialists seek to attain their political and economic ends through democratic means. They work through political parties and advocate laws passed by a representative legislative body with the approval of the majority of voters. They do not attempt to gain their purposes through force, such as the violent overthrow of a government; nor do they encourage revolutions of the minority against the majority. The moderate socialists work within the democratic systems of their countries. The revolutionary socialists, such as the Communists, believe that only by violence can they succeed in imposing their system upon the people. They are followers of Karl Marx and are often called Marxists. Marx was a German who obtained most of his ideas while observing the growing machine age in England. His theories are now practiced in Eastern Europe, Russia, China, and a few other places in the world.

The European worker is frequently a member of the moderate socialist or labor party, although there are also Communist parties in most European countries. Communists are a minority in most European countries, but in France and in Italy, the party has millions of members. Communism is a disturbing problem to the more moderate socialists and other political parties. Around the machine there grew ideologies and political parties—socialism and Communism.

1. What social changes were brought about by the machine?
2. Define socialism. Describe the aims of the moderate and the revolutionary socialists.

## Conclusion

Ideas about freedom—the rights of the individual and the manner in which men should be governed—began a rapid growth during the seventeenth century and this growth continued through the eighteenth and nineteenth centuries. At the same time there was also a rapid development of new ideas and techniques in science, industry, and agriculture. In England men had started early to question the right of their kings to wield unlimited power and began a gradual process of limiting this power. A representative system of government was set up by which selected men congregated at certain intervals in an assembly called a Parliament. This Parliament represented the interests of the people in dealing with the ruling monarch.

At first Parliament had represented only a small number of the people and imposed few limitations on the power of the king. But as more and more men realized the inviting possibilities of freedom, they broadened their representation in Parliament and further restricted the authority of their king. Man legalized his right to speak freely, to refuse his home to the king's soldiers in time of peace, to practice the religion of his choice, and to demand a trial by jury.

But freedom did not always evolve gradually elsewhere. It was often seized by violence and paid for with blood. The English colonists of North America became angered by their lack of representation at home and in England. They resented the curtailment of their liberties and they revolted. The Americans won representation and freedoms by the use of force, and they stirred the world by the audacity of their deeds and the ringing words of their Declaration of Independence. The impact of their words and their success had a striking effect among the French who had been long oppressed. French anger and longing to be free burst forth in a furious revolution shortly after the American revolt. The French Revolution spurred the European on the continent to demand rights and freedoms for himself and thus changed his political life. At the same time nationalism grew. The people of each nation thought of themselves as a group with a common culture and a common background whose integrity must be defended with fervor and whose interests were all-important. The European took his nationalism abroad and taught all men its importance.

The European today is still passionate about the need for freedom. He remains a nationalist, but his ideas about national government are changing as they develop. Many Europeans feel that the government should provide welfare services which will make life economically more secure. They agree to certain government restrictions upon the activities of those engaged in industry and commerce. Nationalism is yet a powerful force, but there are many who desire a greater unity among European nations and some who even advocate a United States of Europe.

During these dynamic, moving centuries, the European's questions were not limited to his personal liberties; he also became interested in easing his work and improving the production of goods and food. His interest led him to develop machines which have been his servants, although at times demanding ones. By means of the machine, life was made more comfortable and it became possible to feed much of the multiplying population. But the machine also changed the economic, social, political, and cultural environment. This change was so radical that it is referred to as the Industrial Revolution. There were also agricultural and scientific revolutions. Man became more interested in the mysteries of nature, in astronomy, chemistry, biology, and the natural and physical sciences. He became seriously engaged in the never-ending task of finding the keys to nature's almost unlimited secrets. His discoveries made life more convenient and rewarding; but they brought fear to man too. Into his hands were placed discoveries awesome in their power to destroy, and man feared lest his imperfections cause him to use this power unwisely, thus destroying himself. This fear is yet a part of man's life, but it is tempered by the hope of a better life which these new-found powers might also bring.

## SUMMING UP THE CHAPTER

A. Define or explain the following, relating them to the chapter.

| | |
|---|---|
| Act of Settlement | Petition of Right |
| Act of Toleration | Restoration |
| Bastille Day | Roundheads |
| Battle of Trafalgar | Scientific Revolution |
| Bill of Rights | Tennis Court Oath |
| Cavaliers | Third Estate |
| natural selection | |

B. Identify the following dates and tell why they are important.

1. 1599-1658
2. 1603-1625
3. 1628
4. 1649
5. 1660-1688
6. 1689
7. 1707
8. 1789
9. 1799

Identify the following and tell why they are important.

Eli Whitney
James Hargreaves
James Watt
John Locke
Albert Einstein
Friedrich Nietzsche
Alfred North Whitehead
Reinhold Niebuhr
William Harvey
Ivan Pavlov

C. Chapter review questions.

1. Why was the English revolution of 1688 called the "Glorious Revolution"?
2. What part did Robespierre play in French history?
3. What was the background of William and Mary before they reigned in England?
4. Compare the Tudor and Stuart monarchs.
5. Explain what the French meant by their slogan, "Liberty, Equality, Fraternity."
6. How did French nationalism develop? When?
7. Discuss the most important events in the political and legal decline of the English monarchy and the rise of Parliament.
8. Explain why Great Britain is known as a constitutional or limited monarchy.
9. Discuss how one invention rapidly led to others at an ever-increasing pace in the Industrial Revolution.
10. Why did the English lead the Industrial Revolution? What part do you think the economic system and form of government played in English leadership?
11. Why were so many of the great advances in agricultural technology American rather than European? What part did the relative population and size of the labor force play in these advances?
12. How did the Industrial Revolution affect the development of cities?
13. What is a nation? What distinguishes a nation from a country, or from a city, or a state? (Use your dictionary to compare meanings.)
14. What were John Locke's major political ideas? How did his concept of "natural rights" differ from the traditional Christian idea of natural law?
15. How was the assent of William and Mary to the Bill of Rights obtained? What were the major provisions of this charter of liberty?

D. Questions for discussion.

1. How were the provisions of the English Bill of Rights incorporated in the American Declaration of Independence? How does this show that the Americans were fighting not so much for new liberties as for the traditional "rights of Englishmen"?
2. Although the Americans were inspired in their struggle for liberty by the philosophies of Locke and Rousseau, their major argument was a legal one, within the framework of the English law. Contrast

this argument with the French Revolutionists' denial of all legal authority.

3. Discuss Rousseau's concept of the "social contract." How does the Reign of Terror of the French Revolution show that Rousseau was naive in believing that self-rule was a guarantee of freedom? What does this tell you about the nature of man as a political animal? Compare the views of Rousseau with those of Machiavelli.
4. What does the evolution of Cromwell from political and military leader to dictatorial "Protector" tell you about the dangers of concentrating power in the hands of one man?
5. Compare the Glorious Revolution, the American Revolution, and the French Revolution in terms of basic ideas and social and political consequences. Which has served as the model for revolution in the twentieth century?
6. Why do you suppose science and invention progressed at a relatively slow rate for centuries, then suddenly blossomed forth in the Renaissance and Industrial Revolution? What part do you think economic and political systems played in this?

E. Projects for groups or individuals.

1. Read some of the writings of the British statesman Edmund Burke on the American and French revolutions. Compare Burke's views with those of Thomas Paine.
2. Read a biography of Napoleon and prepare a report for the class.
3. Prepare a report on the Palace of Versailles. Discuss its size and describe its grounds and galleries. What are some of the great historical events which have taken place there?
4. Select one of the inventions mentioned in this chapter and discuss some of its consequences; for example, did the invention stimulate other new inventions? Cause new industries to rise? Reduce the costs of products? Make products more widely available?

# CHAPTER 23

# The Scandinavians

In northern Europe there live men who have often been moved to explore and to adventure the unknown. Their past is one of roving deeds, their marriage with the sea has been both productive and disturbing, and their present is one of civilized advances. They are the Scandinavians.

Scandinavia includes the lands called Norway, Sweden, Denmark, Iceland, Greenland, and Finland. The ancient roots of the peoples of these lands, however, reach into times far removed from these modern names. Agriculture was practiced in Sweden, Norway, and Denmark as early as 3000 B.C. and copper and bronze were used there about 1500 B.C. Later, the technique of making iron was learned from neighbors to the south. Near the end of the first century A.D., Tacitus, the Roman historian, spoke of the *Suiones*, who later gave their name to Sweden, and of the *Fenni*, who were the ancestors of the Finns. But northern Europe developed separately and remained largely unknown to other Europeans until, around 700 A.D. Then, with an audacity rarely matched by man, the Scandinavians dared the oceans, the rivers, and the coasts beyond their borders to explore, to plunder, to trade, and to settle. They then became known from the eastern shores of the Mediterranean to the islands of the North Atlantic as Vikings and Norsemen.

Following the lakes and rivers of western Russia, the Vikings of Sweden wandered southward to the Black Sea and sailed its waters to the city of Constantinople, then the capital of the Byzantine Empire. By this feat they opened the Baltic to the trade and knowledge of the East and contributed to the beginnings of the Russian nation. This achievement is described in more detail in the story of early Russia, pages 458-460. Although joined on occasion by the Vikings of southern Sweden, it was the Vikings of Norway and Denmark who spearheaded the voyages to the islands of the North Atlantic, the mainland of Western Europe, and the continent of North America. Unafraid of the stormy might of the sea, these daring men sailed their packs of long, narrow ships to England, Scotland, Ireland, France, Iceland, Greenland, and other lands. Wherever they went, there were few who could withstand their strength and skill in battle. They conquered, settled, ruled, and merged their blood and their customs with those of the peoples they had defeated.

There are those who formally mark the end of the Viking Age around 1050 A.D., but there is not yet an ending to that Viking urge to seek far horizons nor of that courage to venture into the unexplored. Modern Scandinavians who have dared the unknown include Roald Amundsen, who discovered the South Pole in 1911, Fridtjof Nansen (1861-1930), the humanitarian-scientist, who gave to man a knowledge of the Arctic, and Thor Heyerdahl, who, in 1947 challenged the ocean on the raft *Kon-Tiki* to show that the Indians of South America might have also voyaged to the islands of the Pacific in the same way. There was also Adolf Nordenskjöld who found the Northwest Passage from Europe to Asia, and Sven Hedin, who charted the wastes of the Gobi Desert. But these later men of adventurous spirit are known as Norwegians, Swedes, Danes, or Finns. Even before the end of the Viking Age, the Vikings had begun to become separated into various political units and separate nations.

Left, modern Scandinavians demonstrate horns from the Viking bronze age, 500-400 B.C. Center, this statue of Leif Ericson commemorates the great Icelandic discoverer. Right, longships like this one, found at Oseberg, were used by Vikings over a thousand years ago to navigate the seas. (Danish Information Office; Embassy of Iceland; Mittet Foto, Oslo)

Vikings in Sweden set these stones in the shape of ships about 500 A.D. (American Swedish News Exchange)

Runes were the alphabetic characters used by Teutonic peoples before the Roman alphabet was introduced. Many examples of them are still found carved on stones. (American Swedish News Exchange)

## Norway

Norway traces its beginning as a separate country to about 900 A.D., when King Harald Haarfager united a number of small kingdoms into a larger whole. In succeeding centuries, Norwegian kings expanded the territory under their sway by adding Greenland, Iceland, and other North Atlantic islands to their kingdom. Then, in the fourteenth century, Norway was joined with Denmark, and for around 400 years its affairs were dominated by that country, which had become one of the strongest powers in northern Europe. This domination came to an end in 1814 when the Danes were forced to cede Norway to Sweden after the defeat of Napoleon, with whom they had been allied.

This new rule was resented by the Norwegians, and a compromise was reached which permitted them to retain their parliament and self-government in domestic affairs. They recognized the Swedish king as their sovereign, and their foreign affairs were controlled by Sweden. But the Norwegian people preferred complete independence and remained unhappy with this arrangement. In 1905, they separated from Sweden and chose as their king a prince from Denmark. From that time to this, with the exception of a few years of German occupation during the Second World War, the Norwegians have retained control of their land and their destiny.

The Norwegians have fashioned a democratic state. Their king is a constitutional monarch who governs together with a Council of State headed by a Prime Minister. There is a parliament, called *Storting*, which is elected every four years and in which is vested all legislative power. Every Norwegian over the age of twenty-three is permitted to vote, and the Norwegians are proud of the fact that in 1913 theirs became the first independent country to give women the right to vote.

Norway occupies the western part of the Scandinavian Peninsula, and its area is slightly larger than that of Italy. It is a land made rugged and beautiful by tall mountains and green valleys, and by deep sea-inlets of grandeur called fjords which gash much of Norway's 1,100 miles of coast. Norway shares with Sweden and Finland the title "Land of the Midnight Sun," for almost half of Norway is within the Arctic Circle. In the northern reaches of the land the sun does not set from about the middle of May until the end of July. Norway is a land of glaciers, wintry snowdrifts, and spreading forests, and it is sparsely settled because most of the land is inhospitable to cultivation.

The rugged coasts of Norway are deeply cut by sea-inlets called fjords. (Norwegian Information Service from Embassy of Sweden)

Many of the 3,600,000 Norwegians live in cities like Oslo, the capital, and Bergen, Trondheim, and Stavanger, which are centers of commerce, industry, and administration. Others live in towns and hamlets near the sea where fishing sustains their life, and there are the decreasing few who stubbornly cling to their small farms scattered around the country. In the twentieth century Norway has been changing from an agricultural to an industrialized country. The key industries are wood-processing and the production of electro-metallurgical products based on abundant resources of cheap water power. But the Norwegian has never lost his interest in the resources of the sea. He lives today, as in the past, on the surface of the sea, and gathers from its depths a wealth of fish and whales. Norwegian ships also transport the cargoes of other lands. The Norwegians have been wedded to the sea for a long, long time.

## Sweden

During the centuries following the end of the Viking Age around 1050 A.D., the Swedes continued to evolve their political, economic, social, and religious way of life. Roman Catholicism was introduced into the land by missionaries from England and northern Germany, and churches still stand which were built in the twelfth and thirteenth centuries. Around the middle of the fourteenth century a national code was written which spelled out the powers of king, council, and citizen. Late in that century, the Swedes negotiated the Kalmar Union which placed their country under Queen Margaret of Denmark. With this Union all of Scandinavia was united under one ruler, for Norway was joined with Denmark at this time. After Margaret's death, however, the actions of her successors disturbed the Swedes, and they dissolved the Union in the fifteenth century.

The struggle between the Danes and the Swedes continued until, under the leadership of the nobleman Gustav Eriksson Vasa (1496-1560), the Danish king was defeated. Gustav Vasa was elected king of Sweden in 1523. With his election as king Sweden began its modern history as an independent national state. Gustav impressed the stamp of his personality upon Sweden and made it strong. It was during his reign that the Lutheran Church became accepted in Sweden, and today it is still the State Church.

But the history of Sweden continued stormy, and there was often fighting against foes in Russia, Poland, Denmark, and elsewhere. The Swedes built a great military machine which was sometimes led by men of genius. Such a one was Gustavus Adolphus (1594-1632), the grandson of Gustav Vasa. He led his army to brilliant victories during the Thirty Years' War, and when he died in battle, Sweden was acknowledged one of the great military powers of Europe.

Another great leader was Charles XII (1682-1718). Threatened by the combined power of Russia, Poland-Saxony, and Denmark, he defeated each of them in battle. He lost his fine army, however, when he made the same mistake Napoleon later made in trying to invade the heartland of Russia. After the death of Charles XII, Sweden lost most of her possessions south and southeast of the Baltic, and in 1809 Russia seized her Finnish possessions.

After a revolution following the loss of Finland, Marshal Bernadotte of France was elected successor to the throne and later assumed it as Charles XIV (1818-1844). Sweden, having fought against Napoleon, was awarded Norway in recompense for her loss of Finland to Russia, but the union between Sweden and Norway was dissolved in 1905. Since this period, the Swedes have evolved their cultural and economic way of life in comparative peace. Sweden remained neutral during the First and the Second World Wars.

Over these long years of war and peace, the Swedes gradually evolved democratic institutions. The Swedish king today, like the English king, is a constitutional monarch. A Council of State headed by a Prime Minister really governs the country. The Swedish parliament, called *Riksdag,* consists of two chambers, and they have equal power. The members of the First Chamber are elected for a term of eight years by provincial and local councils. The members of the Second Chamber are elected for a term of four years by direct popular vote. All Swedish citizens over the age of 21 may vote. There are a number of political parties in Sweden, and the citizen has a wide choice of political views to select from when he casts his vote.

The land area of Sweden is the largest in Scandinavia—173,000 square miles. Its population of approximately 7,500,000 is also greater than that of any other Scandinavian country. Sweden has several cities which are important to its political and economic life. There is Stockholm, the capital, and Göteborg and Malmö, great seaports which are essential to important sea-borne trade. Upsala, a cultural and educational center, traces its beginnings back to about 500 A.D. Other cities include Örebro, where shoes are made, Norrköping, known for its textiles, Västerås, where electrical equipment is manufactured, and Visby on the island of Gotland, which was a Hanseatic trading town during the Middle Ages. There are farms, too, mostly in south and south-central Sweden where the climate is like that of New England in the United States. The farm population, however, is decreasing as farms become more mechanized and industry attracts greater numbers of people from the countryside to the city. Some

The glaciers and snow-covered mountains of northern Sweden attract skiers, above. Below, Sweden has excellent schools and illiteracy is almost unknown there. (Swedish Information Service from Embassy of Sweden)

Swedes live and work in the forests which cover much of the land and provide the leading export—pulp and paper. Others labor and live near the mines from which comes some of the world's best iron ore as well as copper, manganese, and lead.

Sweden has a long expanse of land stretching over 900 miles from the gentle fields and lovely chateaus of Skåne in the south to the far north where the borders of Sweden and Finland meet. In this land the Swedes have created an environment which is a tribute to their constructive use of resources, their sense of balance, and their advanced social consciousness.

## Denmark

The Dane, like the other Scandinavians, has known the exulting moments of triumph and the bitterness of defeat. It is believed that Gudfred became the first Danish king around the year 810 A.D., but that it was Gorm the Old (883?-940) who really made Denmark into one kingdom. The Danes learned the taste of defeat when they were conquered by Henry I of Germany in 934 A.D., but they also knew victory and empire when Canute the Great (994?-1035) conquered England between 1016 and 1018 and formed an Anglo-Scandinavian kingdom. After some years, the Danes lost their power in England, but Denmark continued to be an important power in northern Europe.

In the late fourteenth century, the Danes were ruled by a great and good queen named Margaret, who became the queen of Sweden as well as Norway and Denmark. But the successors of Queen Margaret were not as successful as she in ruling, and as the years passed Denmark lost much of the territory it had formerly governed. The Danish provinces in present-day Sweden were lost, and in 1814 Denmark was forced to cede Norway to Sweden as the penalty for siding with Napoleon.

The Danes have tried during the modern period to remain at peace, and Denmark was neutral during the First World War. The Danes also tried to remain outside the Second World War, but Hitler made this impossible by sending troops that occupied Denmark in 1940. It was during this war that Iceland declared itself independent of Denmark. Greenland, however, the largest island in the world, and the Faeroe Islands remain a part of Denmark. Today, Denmark, like Norway and Iceland, belongs to the North Atlantic Treaty Organization (NATO), which groups most of the Western European countries and the United States in a defensive alliance. The Danes have now forsaken the policy of neutrality which proved of so little value during the Second World War.

The Danes, too, have developed a democratic way of life. Their king is a constitutional monarch and shares legislative power with parliament. The Danish parliament,

Copenhagen, the capital of Denmark is one of the most beautiful cities of Scandinavia. It was the seat of a university as early as 1478 and has long been a leading cultural center of Scandinavian literature and art. (Danish Information Office)

Left, the round church on the island of Bornholm, Denmark, dates from the eleventh century. The loopholes high up on the walls, just under the roof, show that this building was used as a fortress as well as a church. Kronborg Castle was the setting for Shakespeare's "Hamlet." A performance of the play is presented here every summer. (Danish Information Office)

The coasts of Denmark offer ample opportunities for fishing. Cod, herring, and mackerel are the chief fish caught by commercial fishermen. A Danish fishing harbor and auction shed are shown below. (Danish Information Office)

called *Folketing*, consists of one legislative house of 179 members who are chosen by popular election every four years. There is a prime minister appointed by the king, and a cabinet. Both men and women have the right to vote.

The Danes have made their land area of 16,619 square miles—exclusive of the Faeroe Islands and Greenland—a richly productive bit of earth. Denmark is famed for the milk, butter, eggs, bacon, cattle, and poultry which are sources of much of the Danish agricultural income. It is estimated that as much as thirty per cent of the Danish population is engaged in agriculture. Danish farmers also cultivate barley, oats, rye, turnips, sugar beets, and a variety of other vegetables and fruits. The Danes have never lost their interest in the sea, and they continue to harvest its fish and roam its surface in their merchant ships.

A good number of Danes also live in cities, and the capital, Copenhagen, is the great political, economic, and cultural center of Denmark. Of the total population of 4,581,000, over 900,000 Danes live in this city.

The Dane is a craftsman and a designer of taste and imagination, and his artistry is revealed in the bold shapes of his silver, in the clean lines of his furniture, and in the high quality of his porcelains and ceramics.

1. To what countries does the term *Scandinavia* refer?
2. What was the Kalmar Union? Why was it dissolved?
3. What period in Swedish history is marked by the election of Gustav Vasa as king?
4. Describe the governments of Sweden, Norway, and Denmark. How are the parliaments of these countries similar? How do they differ?

Finland's great folk epic, the "Kalevala," has been translated into many languages. Longfellow used the meter of this epic for his "Hiawatha." The scene below from the "Kalevala" was painted by Aksel Gallen-Kallela. (Finnish National Travel Office)

## Finland

The Finns came to their present homeland of trees and lakes during the early centuries of the Christian era. Some came by way of the Karelian Isthmus in the southeast; others crossed over the Gulf of Finland from the lands grouped around the Baltic Sea. Some scholars assert that far back in time there were strains of the Mongolian family of man in the ancestry of the Finns. Today the people of Finland are best described as a mixture of Scandinavian-Baltic peoples. The name for Finland is *Suomi* in Finnish, which is related to only two other European languages—Estonian and Hungarian. These languages, along with a few minor languages, make up what has been called the Finno-Ugric language family. This family of languages may possibly have some distant relation with Turkish and a few other languages.

Swedes—between eight and nine per cent of the population—also live in Finland. They are the descendants of Swedish settlers who came to the coastal areas in prehistoric times and of Swedes who came later, when Finland was an integral part of Sweden. For six centuries or more Swedish was the official language of the country. Today it remains the second official language of the state and is taught in all high schools.

Olavinlinna Castle in eastern Finland's lake region was built in the fifteenth century. (Finnish Tourist Association)

The *Kalevala*, the great folk epic of the Finns, which was collected and published in the first half of the nineteenth century, tells much about the early life and characteristics of the Finns. They were hunters and fishermen, clearers of the forest, and planters of crops. They were hardy men who matched their strength against the toughness of their environment and won. They were men who lived intimately with nature and were sensitive to its moods and its beauty. The Finns loved song and music, and their bards composed lyrics about their life and their heroes. All of these characteristics can still be seen in the Finns of today. Even when joined with Sweden under a common king in the twelfth century, they remained a people of independent spirit who preserved their liberties and freedoms.

From around the middle of the twelfth century until 1809 Finland was a part of the Swedish kingdom. Swedish became the language of administration and of culture, and Swedish law was paramount in the land. But Finland also became a battleground in the many conflicts between Russia and Sweden during these centuries. Sweden gradually declined in power relative to Russia, and in 1809 Finland became a Grand Duchy under the rule of the tsar of Russia. Until 1917 the Finns were subjects of the tsar of Russia. On December 6, 1917 the Finns declared their independence of Russia, but they had to fight a bitter civil war before their independence was truly secure. In this conflict, the Finns were divided into two factions—the "Reds," supported by the Russian Communists, and the "Whites," supported by Germany. The "Reds" were defeated in 1918 and in 1919 a constitution was adopted. Since this date the Finns have lived under the rule of their own elected government. But they have continued to have problems with the Russians to the south and east.

In 1939, when the Finns would not agree

to certain territorial demands of the Russians, Soviet armies invaded Finland. The Finns defended themselves gallantly against the massive attacks of the Russians but finally had to sue for peace in 1940. They were required to cede some of their land to the Russians, and this loss left the Finns with a bitter feeling toward the USSR. Consequently, when Germany invaded Russia in 1941, the Finns seized upon the opportunity to take back the land that had been taken from them by the USSR. And they held it until 1944, when the Russians again seized this land and more. In the peace terms that followed, the Finns lost about 12 per cent of their pre-war territory and were required to pay an indemnity in Finnish products which amounted to about 570 million dollars. Since this time relations between the Russians and the Finns have been regulated by treaties, but there is no doubt that the Finns must pay careful attention to the policies and desires of their huge neighbor, the Soviet Union.

Finland is a democracy with a constitution which, among other provisions, contains guarantees of personal liberties, and assures freedom of speech, religion, association, and freedom of the press. All Finnish citizens are equal before the law. There is a president who is elected for a term of six years, and a single-chamber diet, called *Eduskunta*, whose members are elected for a term of four years. There is universal suffrage in the country.

Finland is a country of thousands of lakes. It is estimated that lakes and rivers make up one-tenth of the 130,165 square miles of the total area of the country. But the great green wealth of Finland is its trees, which cover almost two-thirds of the land. Industries based upon wood, paper, pulp, furniture, and box factories produce about one-third of the country's total industrial output. Water power is used to produce electricity, for Finland has neither coal nor oil. Finnish farms are generally rather small, and wheat and rye are the main crops. Finland is rapidly becoming industrialized, and about a third of the population of 4,500,000 live in towns and cities. Helsinki is the capital and largest city.

The Finns are an industrious people who use with care the resources of their land. The Finnish nation has been famed for honesty and has paid to the last cent its debts. The Americans, the Russians, and others know from experience that this is true. Though the Finns have been saddled in the past with large debts and war reparations, they have, while repaying them, managed to lift their own standard of living. Through thrift, hard work, careful planning, and ability, the Finns have made a better material life for themselves and their children.

## Iceland

Prior to 900 A.D., the Norwegian Vikings discovered and settled an island in the North Atlantic that has been long known as Iceland. These early explorers and settlers had a strong sense of independence and a deep feeling for democracy. In 930 A.D. they drew up a constitution which created a general assembly known as the *Althing*. There is still a parliament known as the Althing in Iceland, and it is held to be the oldest legislative body in the world, having existed for more than a thousand years. Thus was created the independent republic of Iceland. But many among the Icelanders continued to challenge the sea and seek new lands. From here Eric the Red went out to Greenland in 982 A.D., and from here, too, Leif Ericson sailed and rowed to discover the shores of North America around 1000 A.D.

The Icelanders continued to rule their country until about 1262, when they came under the domination of Norway. In the fourteenth century, both Norway and Iceland fell under the rule of Denmark. Iceland remained a part of the kingdom of Denmark until 1941, when the Althing voted to drop all ties with Denmark. In 1944 the modern Republic of Iceland was proclaimed. Iceland has no king, but it has, rather, a president, who is elected by popular vote every four years. There are also a prime minister and a cabinet. Legislative power is vested in the Althing, which consists of an upper and a lower house. All citizens over the age of 21 may vote.

A church now stands on the site where Iceland's parliament was born in the valley of Thingvellir. Iceland's parliament, the Althing, originated in the tenth century and claims the distinction of being the oldest legislative body of its kind. Right, a statue of Ingolfur Arnarson, the first settler of Iceland, who came from Norway in 874 A.D. (Embassy of Sweden)

Iceland is a large island, slightly smaller than the state of Virginia in the United States. It lies near the Arctic Circle, and on much of its surface there are fields of snow and glaciers. There are also volcanoes, geysers, and hot springs which provide heat to warm homes and hothouses. Iceland is a land which resists cultivation, and most of the 185,000 persons cluster near the coasts where the earth is fertile and where food from the sea is available. The fishermen of Iceland gather in fish—cod, halibut, and herring—which are the basis for the country's chief export industry. The farmers of Iceland grow hay, potatoes, and turnips. They also herd sheep. The chief city

and capital is Reykjavik, where over 72,000 of the population live.

### The Scandinavians Have Given Much

The Scandinavians have preserved much of the old Norse literature and thus contributed beyond measure to our understanding of their cultural development. There is, among the most important pieces of this literature, the *Edda*, which is a collection of poems about the early Norse heroes and Norse gods such as Odin, god of war and wisdom, and Loki, god of mischief and discord. In addition to the *Edda*, there is the poetry of the *scalds*, poets who sang of mighty deeds and pictured the horses, swords, and ships of the Norsemen in vivid language. There are also the *sagas*, monumental epics of great heroes and narratives which often embrace the life of an entire family. In these magnificent sagas there are excellent descriptions of the lusty life and the fantastic heroism of the old Scandinavians. Theirs is an impressive literature.

The later Scandinavians have continued to write works of merit. The fairy tales of the Dane Hans Christian Andersen have delighted generations of the world's children, and the philosophy of the Danish writer A. S. Kierkegaard is still a subject of controversy and discussion. There are the fine writings of the Norwegians Henrik Isben, Jonas Lie, B. Bjørnson, Sigrid Undset, and Knut Hamsun; of the Swedish authors August Strindberg and Selma Lagerlöf; and of the Finnish giants, J. L. Runeberg, the national poet of Finland, and Väinö Linna who, in three great works, pictured man's fate in Finland from about 1900 to 1945.

The Scandinavians have created great music for man. Millions of listeners have been entranced by the tone poems and symphonies of the Finn Jean Sibelius, the compositions of the Norwegian Edvard Grieg, and the Dane Carl Nielsen.

Among the most impressive Scandinavian works of art are the magnificent figures of Gustav Vigeland in Sculpture Park at Oslo, Norway. And all who behold Eriksen's statue of the *Little Mermaid* rising from the waters of the harbor at Copenhagen are touched by its quiet tenderness. There are also the achievements of the Icelandic sculptor, Einar Jónsson, and the Swedish sculptor, Carl Milles, whose fountains are known in the United States as well as Sweden. And there are also the fine paintings of Ernst Josephson and Carl Fredrik Hill of Sweden, of Edvard Munch of Norway and Jon Stefansson and Johannes Kjarval of Iceland. Scandinavia has also produced designers of merit, whose talent is revealed in the loveliness of their architecture and in the woodwork, metalwork, glassware, and other materials shaped by their hands. Scandinavian craftsmanship is also evident in drama, theatrical productions, and films.

The Scandinavians have contributed much to the advance of science. There was Carl von Linné, commonly called Linnaeus, who might be called the founder of modern biology, and later there were the Swedish chemists Jons Jakob Berzelius and Svante Arrhenius. There was the Danish scientist Niels Bohr, who pioneered in nuclear physics, the Norwegian mathematician Niels Henrik Abel, and Gerhard Armauer Hansen, also a Norwegian, who uncovered the bacillus of leprosy. These are but a few of the Scandinavian scientists who have advanced the knowledge of man about himself and his universe.

The Scandinavians continue to encourage the artist, the scientist, and the peacemaker, through the bestowal of Nobel prizes which are among the highest honors man can achieve in the world. Alfred Nobel (1833-1896), a Swedish humanitarian, inventor, and manufacturer, willed that the income from most of his great fortune should be divided into five shares and awarded annually to those men and women who had contributed the greatest benefit to mankind in physics, chemistry, physiology and medicine, literature, and in work for peace.

1. What are the two official languages of Finland? What is the *Kalevala*?

The house where Hans Christian Andersen spent much of his youth is a national shrine in Denmark. Andersen's stories have been read in all parts of the world for over 100 years. (Danish Information Office)

Below, the eleventh-century bowl is a fine example of the vigorous ornamental style of the Vikings. Right, "Galloping Horse" was painted by Edvard Munch in 1912. (Both, Embassy of Sweden)

2. To what U. S. state does Iceland compare in size? Describe the geography of Iceland.
3. Who are some well-known Scandinavian composers? Authors? What are some of the Scandinavian contributions to the advance of science?
4. What is the purpose of the Nordic Council?

## Conclusion

Throughout his history the Scandinavian has played a manly role in helping to shape the past, the present, and the future of others; but nowhere outside his borders has he played a more important part in the unfolding of a people's history than in the United States of America. Since the year 1638, when a mixed group of Swedes and Finns settled in Delaware, Scandinavians have been emigrating to America. During the nineteenth and twentieth centuries thousands upon thousands of them came to this hemisphere. Some settled in the East; many found an environment similar to their homeland in Michigan, Illinois, Wisconsin, Minnesota, and the Dakotas and made these states their new homes; and others spread their numbers in the West. They cleared the forests, farmed the fields, multiplied, and made their blood and their culture a part of the American heritage. Their names have graced the Declaration of Independence. They have died on battlefields to preserve American freedoms. Their hands have built schools, railroads, canals, and highways. Their brains have helped to develop industry, education, government, and culture in this country. The Scandinavians have contributed sinew, intellect, and heart, to the making of the United States of America.

The Scandinavians have also given to man an example of peaceful, constructive cooperation. Scandinavian nations have quarreled among themselves in the past, but in recent times there has been a close and growing cooperation among them. Workers may cross borders freely in search of work, and there are no passport requirements for Scandinavians. These nations have coordinated much of their social legislation, and have standardized certain of their laws concerning property, as well as standardizing educational systems and school textbooks. In 1953, a Nordic Council was established which provides a forum for consultation on matters of common interest to the governments and the parliaments of the Scandinavian countries. The recommendations and actions of this Council are bringing about a greater degree of political, economic, cultural, and social unity, among the Scandinavian people.

The Scandinavian has been long interested in international organizations whose purpose is to advance the peaceful progress of man. He supported the old League of Nations and, more recently, has worked energetically to make the United Nations a worthy and useful organization. Trygve Lie, a Norwegian, was the first Secretary-General of the UN, and, in 1953, was followed by the Swede, Dag Hammarskjöld, who died in a plane crash in 1961 while on a mission of peace in the Congo.

The Scandinavian continues his civilized advance. The order, the prosperity, and the social consciousness evidenced in his lands are a tribute to his progressive, constructive character.

## SUMMING UP THE CHAPTER

A. Define or explain the following terms, relating them to this chapter.

| | |
|---|---|
| Althing | Riksdag |
| Folketing | Storting |
| Fenni | Suiones |
| fjord | Suomi |
| Kon-Tiki | |

B. Identify the following and tell why they are important.

| | |
|---|---|
| Alfred Nobel | Linnaeus |
| Canute the Great | Marshal Bernadotte |
| Charles XII | Queen Margaret |
| Fridtjof Nansen | Roald Amundsen |
| Gustav Vasa | Thor Heyerdahl |
| Gustavus Adolphus | |

C. Chapter review questions.

1. Trace the history of Norway from 900 A.D. to the present time.

2. Why was Denmark forced to cede Norway to Sweden in 1814?
3. How successful were the Danes in their effort to remain neutral during World War II? Do the Danes still maintain a policy of neutrality?
4. What is the "green wealth" of Finland? What portion of the country's total production comes from this source?

D. Questions for discussion.

1. Trace the history of Iceland. Why do you suppose the *Althing*, oldest such legislative body in the world, has lasted for more than a thousand years?
2. Iceland is sometimes described as "the Land of Frost and Fire." Why is it so called? What per cent of the country is actually covered by ice? Compare the climate and geography of Iceland and Greenland. Do you think the countries are appropriately named?
3. Contrast the geography of Denmark with that of Norway and Sweden. How does the amount of coastline of Denmark compare with that of the United States?
4. How would you explain the fact that Denmark has one of the highest standards of living in the world?
5. What significant reasons can you give for Norway's change from an agricultural to an industrialized country during the twentieth century?
6. Why do you suppose Sweden has chosen to maintain a policy of neutrality?
7. What prompted Alfred Nobel to bequeath his fortune to "those who most benefited mankind"? What were the terms of his will?

E. Projects for groups or individuals.

1. Prepare a map showing the locations of the Scandinavian countries. Indicate the major cities (population over 100,000) in each country.
2. Read an account of the life of Alfred Nobel. Report to the class on the Nobel Prizes for the current year. Include in your report the stipulation made by Nobel regarding eligibility. What country has had the greatest number of winners? What in your opinion is the most significant award made since the prizes were first given in 1901?

# CHAPTER 24

# *Europe Warred and the World Followed*

LIKE MANY MEN throughout history the Europeans have often squandered their energies and resources in war. There have been relatively few moments in their development when they were not engaged in battle somewhere at home or abroad. As they extended their technical knowledge and their dominance overseas, they enlarged the size of their battlefields and multiplied the numbers of those slain and maimed in war. During the late nineteenth century the Europeans completed their appropriation of much of the world. After this, when they decided to fight in their homelands, their decision affected those whom they dominated and influenced elsewhere. Thus the world was drawn into the Europeans' struggles.

There have been two world wars in the twentieth century: World War I, which began in 1914, and World War II, which began in 1939. Each one started among the Europeans. Both brought horrible agonies to mankind. But the second war was more ruinous than the first because scientific and industrial advances made possible the creation of weapons of vast destruction. It is ironic that man has probably directed more of his mental energies and resources toward destruction than toward constructive goals.

## Causes of World War I

The causes which pushed the Europeans to fight had their sources in the past as well as the present. They stemmed from nationalism, imperialism, the arms race, and alliances between nations.

### Nationalism

The word *nationalism* includes within its meaning a sense of the unity, the common interests, and the independence of a nation. Inherent in nationalism is a sense of exclusiveness which is often defined by geographic borders and sharpened by a common language, culture, and tradition which separate those within from those outside these borders. Basic to its meaning is the preservation of self-government and the cultural institutions of each nation-state. Nationalism has been a vital force in preserving the identity and the diverse cultural riches of nations. It has also been a powerful force in causing one nation to subjugate others and destroy their cultures and their identities.

At its best, nationalism has been synonymous with peaceful patriotism—an attachment to the ideals, culture, and history of a country. And man's love for his country has frequently motivated him to high nobility in word and in deed. But nationalism has also been used by the ambitious and the misguided as an excuse for violence, hatred, and the extension of the ideology and the power of a nation. For centuries nationalism has had a key role in the shaping of man's life, and it continues today to be a major factor in the evolving life and destiny of nations.

When the Europeans lived in many separate small groups under the system of feudalism, their loyalties were directed toward feudal rulers rather than toward all of the large group of people who lived within a broad geographic area and who shared a common language and culture. But in the later Middle Ages larger territorial groupings were formed and a sense of national consciousness began to grow. As strong kings centralized their rule and unified their territories, the character of modern nationalism began to be visible in the development of national economies, literature written in national languages, and the shared feeling for a common culture and tradition held by the people of each nation.

In the late eighteenth century nationalism played a major role in the making of modern nations and the shaping of the affairs of man. The French Revolution and the years of rule by Napoleon intensified the national consciousness of the French. The military excursions of Napoleon throughout Europe made other Europeans more conscious of their separateness as nationalities and of their need for unity. There came to be a definite meaning and firmness in the voices that now said, "I am French," "I am English," "I am Dutch," "I am a Swede, Dane, or Norwegian." In the nineteenth century, the Germans and the Italians, still divided, also moved toward a national unity and consciousness.

**Prussia unites the Germans.** Beginning during the Thirty Years' War, Prussia began to rise to power under the leadership of its ruling family, the Hohenzollerns. Under Frederick II, called Frederick the Great (1712-1786), Prussia seized the province of Silesia from Austria and later took part of Poland. Then, after the invasion of the German states by Napoleon's armies, the spirit of German nationalism began to grow. Prussia played an important part in the defeat of Napoleon at Waterloo, and as a result of the Congress of Vienna in 1814-1815 took part of Saxony and other lands along the Rhine. The movement for German unity continued during the 1800's until finally most of the Germans united under the Prussian king in 1871.

The man who led the Germans to unification was Otto von Bismarck, sometimes known as "the Iron Chancellor" because he remarked that the larger political problems were settled ultimately by the iron of weapons and the blood of man. He used a devious diplomacy, however, to attain his purposes. Bismarck was a cautious man who made concessions to others when he saw he could not gain his ends directly or immediately. When Bismarck became chief minister of Prussia in 1862, Germany was a confederation of thirty-eight states under the domination of Austria. Bismarck set about the task of freeing these states and uniting them under Prussian leadership into a German empire.

With the assistance of some capable generals, Bismarck made his army into one of the best in Europe. Quietly he made an agreement with France and Italy to remain neutral in case he warred with Austria. Then, when his army was ready, in 1866, he provoked Austria into declaring war on Prussia. In seven weeks of fighting, Bismarck's army vanquished the Austrian forces. With the conclusion of this war, Prussia was dominant in Germany, and all the German states except Bavaria, Baden, and several others were united with Prussia in a North German confederation.

Bismarck united most of the Germans against France in the Franco-Prussian War (1870-1871). After winning this war, the German Empire was declared on January 18, 1871, and William of Prussia was declared emperor. Ironically, this empire was proclaimed in the palace of the French kings at Versailles. The German states that had remained outside the confederation joined with the others in the new German Empire.

Bismarck was not lenient with France in his peace terms, for he regarded the French as his main enemy. He forced them to cede the provinces of Alsace and Lorraine to Germany and to pay an indemnity of around one billion dollars. The French never forgot this humiliating loss, and they revenged themselves on the Germans after Germany lost the First World War (1914-1918).

Bismarck had worked well with the Prussian king William I, but shortly after William's death his grandson, William II, became the Kaiser, or Emperor, of Germany. Bismarck was eased out of power, and William II ruled as he chose. He was not as far-seeing or as skilled a diplomat as Bismarck. Under his rule

Camillo Benso di Cavour (1810-1861), left, and Giuseppe Mazzini (1805-1872), right, differed in their methods, but both worked for a unified and independent Italy. (Both, Cushing)

Germany was eventually led into World War I, and at the end of that war William II was forced to abdicate in 1918.

**The Italians unite.** Italian unification was forged by the tireless efforts of three men: Giuseppe Mazzini, idealist, scholar, and poet; Giuseppe Garibaldi, sailor, farmer, and man of action; and Camillo di Cavour, aristocrat, diplomat, and government leader. Differing in their methods and the type of government they wanted—Mazzini and Garibaldi desired a republic of Italy; Cavour wanted a limited monarchy—the three were one in their aim for a unified nation. They were nationalists.

Mazzini (1805-1872) knew only exile and prison cells during much of his life. While in exile in Switzerland he organized a secret socety known as Young Italy. In 1848 his followers seized Rome and Venice and founded republics. However, the Austrians recovered Venice and the French restored Rome to its former state. Mazzini continued to live in exile, but the currents of nationalism continued to swirl around him and gain strength from his dedication and idealism.

Garibaldi (1807-1882) was a member of Young Italy. When discovered by the police, he escaped death and fled to South America, where he worked and fought beside those who wanted change there. He returned to Italy to help found a republic in Rome in 1848. He went into exile again and retired to his farm when the republic fell, but he returned several times to take an active part in Italian political life. Garibaldi was a patriot loved by the Italians in his own time, and he remains a favorite hero today. He was not interested in title, glory, or wealth. He wanted an Italy where the Italians could live free, independent, and unified, and where he could have a share in the government that ruled. He asked nothing more than this.

Cavour (1810-1861) was more sophisticated than Mazzini or Garibaldi. He schemed and planned for Italian unity in the rarefied atmosphere of the ruling cliques of Europe. In 1852 he became Prime Minister of the Kingdom of Sardinia, which included the northeast portion of Italy called Piedmont and the island of Sardinia. Cavour aimed to make his kingdom powerful enough to drive Austria from Italy, and he wanted his king, Victor Emmanuel II, to become a constitutional king of Italy. Cavour made an agreement with Emperor Louis Napoleon of France, a nephew of Napoleon Bonaparte, that if Austria declared war on Piedmont, France would come to the assistance of Italy. As a reward, he promised to cede the lands of Nice and Savoy to France. Cavour then induced Austria to declare war on Piedmont. The combined French and Italian forces drove the Austrians from Lombardy in north Italy. They would have taken Venezia, but uprisings of revolutionists in north Italy frightened Louis Napoleon, so he made a separate peace with Austria. By the terms of this peace, Venezia was left to Austria, and the other northern Italian states, except Lombardy, remained under their former rulers.

But the fires of nationalism were still burning brightly in Italy. They were reflected in the "redshirts," the followers of Garibaldi, as he emerged from his tiny farm and led a thousand of them in an invasion of the island of Sicily. The people of the Kingdom of the Two Sicilies, into which the southern Italians were grouped, rallied around Garibaldi, and shortly he controlled all of southern Italy. In the meantime, Cavour, fearful that Garibaldi might take Rome and other papal states, marched south and met him in Naples. The humility of Garibaldi was magnificent, and his desire for a united Italy was overwhelming. He surrendered to Cavour the territories of the south which he had conquered. The surrender of these states made it possible for all of Italy to be one nation. Garibaldi returned to his small farm, and Victor Emmanuel II became king of all Italy except the city of Rome. In 1871 the Italian forces occupied Rome and it became the capital of a united Italy.

With the unification of Germany and Italy, nationalism was triumphant in most of Europe. But out of its triumph was to come jealousy as well as pride, separateness as well as unity, hate as well as love, and distrust as well as trust. One of its outcomes was a looking outward as well as inward, and this led to a new imperialism.

1. What part did nationalism play in unifying Germany?
2. How did Bismarck loosen the German states from Austria? How many of these states were there?
3. Who were the three leaders in the movement for Italian unification? What did each contribute to the movement?

## Imperialism

There began in the mid-1800's another great expansion of European control abroad which lasted into the twentieth century. The leaders of Germany, France, Italy, Belgium, and England looked beyond their continent and saw lands that were tempting in their weakness and promising in their potential wealth. The nations of Europe embarked upon a policy of acquiring these lands for themselves. In the struggle for territorial possessions, there were meetings that led to quarrels and sometimes to violence. The competition for empires intensified the distrust with which the nations of Europe regarded one another.

The desire of nations to increase their dominion over others is as old as all of history. Since the earliest recorded times there has been no age without some rulers who wished to extend their sway over larger portions of the earth and greater numbers of people. The nationalism of the nineteenth century gave a new content, a new frame of reference, and a new impetus to the empire-building urge of the nations of Europe of that time. It also shaped the attitudes of nations since that time. Today we speak of imperialism not only in terms of territorial expansion but also as the attempt of any nation to extend its economic, political, and cultural aims and to impose them upon others. Most of the nations of Europe have relinquished the widespread empires that they held at the beginning of this century, but the accusations "imperialist" and "colonialist" are still in use among the nations of the world.

With the rise of nation-states in Europe there also arose a struggle for power among these states. In this struggle, it was inevitable that the political and national interests of nations should lead them into conflict with one another. The most powerful nations were at an advantage in these conflicts, and it was natural, therefore, that each nation should strive to increase its power in every possible way. The European nations of the nineteenth century generally tried to acquire territories in various parts of the world that had strategic value as military bases.

Economic forces also contributed to the outward drive of the nations of Europe. The growing industries of Europe needed greater amounts of raw materials and larger markets for their products. Overseas possessions provided many opportunities for safe and profitable investment of surplus capital, and manufacturers and merchants could sell their goods in these areas, too, without the bother of tariffs. The nations of Europe had raised high walls of *tariffs*—duties on imports—in Europe, and they refused access to their colonies to others. The English, however, were an exception in that they followed a policy of free trade.

And still another reason was proclaimed by the nations of Europe for their expansion—the mission of bringing European civilization to the backward countries and peoples of the world. This viewpoint was held sincerely by some, and was perhaps proclaimed with tongue in cheek by others—but it was loudly and often expressed in Europe as well as among the people of newly acquired areas throughout the world. And with this pretext and this justification the English dominated India and Egypt, the French ruled in Algiers, the Russians in Turkestan, the Germans in Southwest Africa, and other civilized nations of Europe took over territories in Africa, the Middle East, and Asia. There is no doubt that some altruistic and humane Europeans did bring a number of the best aspects of their civilization to the people of these areas. There is no doubt also that the empire-builders brought a grinding subjugation and many features of European life that were unwanted.

For these and other reasons the Europeans of this time went beyond their own borders and assumed domination over others. They were so successful that by the beginning of the twentieth century they dominated most of the world. But for their empires they paid a heavy price in anxiety, suspicions, and antagonisms. In no area was the price higher than in their mounting military budgets.

## The Arms Race

In the latter part of the nineteenth century, the Europeans started an arms race which has not yet ceased. Under Prussian leadership, the Germans demonstrated the advantage of a general military staff to plan and organize for war. They also proved the value of conscription of all able-bodied men to provide adequate manpower to carry out the policies of the leaders and the plans of the general staff. All nations have copied these two innovations, and they are now customary everywhere.

The German army was the best on land, but the British navy was the best at sea. The Germans thought it necessary to rival the British navy, and the British, French, and Americans were forced to keep pace with their building to maintain naval superiority. Industries were geared to produce better and greater quantities of arms. National budgets were increased to meet increased defense needs. The arms race, far from bringing a sense of security to nations, only added to the tenseness of the atmosphere of Europe. Arms were not enough. The Europeans needed even more power for their security, and they found it in alliances.

## Alliances

In order to increase their total power, the nations of Europe began to form alliances. Germany proposed a defensive alliance with Austria-Hungary, promising that one would come to the aid of the other if either was attacked by another nation. Austria-Hungary agreed. This agreement was known as the Dual Alliance. Germany turned to Italy and proposed the same conditions. Italy agreed, and the Dual Alliance became the Triple Alliance. France was now alone in Europe and frantically sought for allies to counterbalance those of Germany. Bismarck had managed to keep France without allies as long as he controlled the diplomacy of Germany, but the policies of William II assisted in bringing Russia and France together. England, fearful of Germany's growing strength, also thought it advantageous to unite with France.

In 1907 there were two great power blocs facing each other: the Triple Alliance of Germany, Austria-Hungary, and Italy; and the Triple Entente of France, England, and Russia. Tensions now stemmed from the relationship of groups of nations rather than single ones.

Perhaps none of the nations of Europe wanted war. Certainly they did not want the war they got. But all wanted things they could not have *without* war, and all had formed alliances and engaged in an arms race to be prepared for war. When the war came in 1914, it spattered their lands with blood and changed the maps of the world.

Trench warfare was characteristic of World War I. (U. S. Signal Corps)

## World War I

World War I began in Europe, but it eventually involved countries in all parts of the world. More than 65,000,000 men and women were mobilized during the course of this war, and new and terrible weapons were used for the first time. Although at the time it was called "the war to end wars," later events proved that it was only a prelude to an even greater conflict. Many of the same problems led to both world wars, and it is necessary to understand these wars in order to understand the world we live in today.

### The Beginning of the War

The First World War mushroomed from the assassination of Archduke Franz Ferdinand, heir to the Austro-Hungarian throne. He was killed on June 28, 1914 by a Bosnian who was a member of the Black Hand Society, a group of nationalists which also included many high-ranking Serbians. Bosnia was a province fronting the Adriatic Sea which Austria had annexed and which the Serbians thought should belong to them. Bosnia and Serbia, along with Romania, Bulgaria, Albania, Greece, and Turkey, were a part of that section of southeast Europe known as the Balkans.

The Balkans were considered a powderkeg because nationalistic feelings were often violently expressed there. These expressions of nationalism attracted the attention of larger powers that had an interest in what happened to these lands and their people. Germany was interested because she wanted to run a railroad through the Balkans to Constantinople and on to Baghdad and the head of the Persian Gulf. This railroad was intended to give Germany overland access to the trade of the

The airplane was used in combat by both Allies and Central Powers in World War I. The plane shown is a French S.P.A.D. (U. S. Army Air Forces)

Middle East and Asia. England was interested because such an undertaking would threaten the Suez Canal, which the British considered their lifeline. For this reason also, England did not want either Germany or Russia meddling with Turkey or the Middle East. Russia was interested because the Turks controlled the only channel between the Black and Mediterranean seas. Many of the people of the Balkans were Slavs, and the Russians regarded them with a protective, paternal eye. Austria-Hungary was interested because these lands bordered her southern boundaries, and their nationalism sometimes threatened her, just as she threatened them.

This was the situation when Archduke Franz Ferdinand was killed in 1914. Austria-Hungary immediately made excessive demands of Serbia, some of which the Serbians refused to meet. Austria-Hungary then declared war on Serbia. The Russians mobilized, and Germany declared war on Russia. When the French refused to state that they would remain neutral, Germany declared war on France. The Belgians remained neutral, but the easiest land passage to France was through Belgium. Germany invaded Belgium, and as a result Eng-

Tanks were first developed by the British during World War I. They were referred to as "water tanks" to keep their purpose secret. (U. S. Signal Corps)

land declared war on Germany and Austria-Hungary. World War I had begun, and it spread in Europe and abroad. There were few parts of the world untouched by its consequences.

Italy had been secretly promised some spoils from the war if she joined with France, England, and Russia. She accepted and deserted her former alliance. These nations came to be known as the Allies. Japan saw an opportunity to profit, and she joined the Allies. Romania and Greece also joined the Allies. Turkey and Bulgaria joined with Germany. Germany and the nations associated with it were known as the Central Powers. The war leaped overseas to the British dominions and drew in Canada, Australia, New Zealand, and others. Eventually, in 1917, the United States entered the conflict, and thus the globe was encircled with the flame of war.

## A Look at the War

World War I lasted from 1914 to 1918. It was, for much of the time, a struggle for a few yards or miles of muddy, gun-beaten land on the eastern front of France. Soldiers lay in trenches protected by barbed wire in front of them and listened for the enemy. Patrols ventured cautiously beyond the barbed wire, probing the enemy's position and intention. The Germans developed great guns, some of which had a range of seventy miles. With these guns they knocked out steel and concrete fortifications and even shelled Paris itself. The British were the first to build and use tanks, which proved to be powerful weapons of attack in a conflict that had bogged down in trench warfare. Both sides built airplanes, and in this war nations started to learn the military possibilities of air power. They also fought at sea. German submarines sent millions of tons of shipping to the depths of the sea and took a toll of thousands of lives. But the British ruled the surface of the sea, and they bottled up the German navy. Overseas, the Allies were victorious everywhere. Germany lost her island possessions and her colonies and spheres of influence in Africa and Asia.

The tide of war changed in Europe when the United States, under President Woodrow Wilson, threw her might behind the Allies. Gradually the nations aligned with Germany began to break away and sue for peace. The German people rebelled against the slaughter of war. They forced the Kaiser to abdicate and on November 11, 1918, the chancellor of the new socialist government of Germany, signed an armistice, or truce. This day is yet celebrated in the United States and elsewhere as Armistice or Veterans' Day.

## After the War

World War I—like all wars—left its aftermath of misery and disaster. But improved weapons had made this war more destructive than previous wars. Nearly 8,500,000 were killed, and over 20,000,000 were wounded. Hospitals were filled with the disfigured and those yet unhealed, and there were many whose minds had been shocked, never to return to sanity. The fields where battles were fought, especially in France, had been torn and pitted, and forests had been stripped by exploding shells; those which failed to explode made the land dangerous to till for years afterward. Economies were shattered, politics were in upheaval, and society was in disorder.

Men heard the words of President Woodrow Wilson, the idealist among the victors, describing this war as "a war to end wars" and pleading for the need to make "a world safe for democracy." Men of good will gave Wilson their hearts and their assent, and the defeated were heartened by his words "peace with justice." Wilson's Fourteen Points called, among others things, for freedom of the seas, freedom to trade, freedom and a voice for those subjected by European colonial powers, and reduction of armaments. Many thundered their approval. But among the victors there were those, both leaders and common men, who did not agree with all of Wilson's Fourteen Points. Woodrow Wilson obtained his League of Nations, which the United States later refused to join, but the other victors also obtained their demands in the treaty of peace. The

The American officials at the Peace Conference after World War I were headed by President Woodrow Wilson, center. (Cushing)

leaders of the victorious Allies were Georges Clemenceau of France, David Lloyd George of England, and Vittorio Orlando of Italy.

**Treaty terms.** The treaty of peace was signed reluctantly by the Germans at Versailles in France on June 28, 1919. Germany was required to pay five billion dollars in two years, and in 1921 the total bill was set at thirty-three billion dollars. Germany returned Alsace and Lorraine to France and agreed to leave the Rhineland unfortified. She also agreed to have the Saar valley—rich in coal deposits—administered by the League of Nations. Some German territory was given to Belgium, another slice to Denmark, and Poland received a corridor of land which cut west and east Prussia in two. All German colonies were divided among the victors under a mandate of the League of Nations. Germany's army was limited, the general staff was disbanded, and the manufacture of arms was restricted. At this moment Germany really tasted the bitter fruits of defeat, and this bitterness was to be an element in her return later to the way of war.

The Treaty of Versailles changed the face of Europe by adding new states and decreasing the territories of the defeated nations. Austria and Hungary were split. Austria became a small republic. Hungary became a kingdom without a king. The new nations of Czechoslovakia and Yugoslavia were created to satisfy Slavic nationalism. Four new states—Finland, Estonia, Latvia, and Lithuania — split from Russia, and the victors recognized them as independent. Though the treaty makers tried to follow nationality lines in drawing national borders, it was impossible, and a number of minorities were left in the various countries. German minorities in other countries were later to furnish an excuse for Hitler's invasions.

Postwar conditions worsened in Europe, especially in Germany and Italy. These worsening conditions, plus the problems created by the treaty provisions, and other continuing

The International Court of Justice meets at The Hague. It was an organ of the League of Nations and is now a part of the United Nations. (United Nations)

problems of long standing eventually led the Europeans to World War II.

1. Describe conditions in Europe generally, and in Central Europe in particular, just before the assassination of Archduke Franz Ferdinand. What were the major causes of this tension?
2. What were the terms of the peace treaty after World War I? What was the name of the treaty?
3. What countries were on the side of the Allies in World War I? Who were the Central Powers?

### The Conditions That Led to War Again

The death, destruction, and disorder of the war brought Communism to the Russians, Fascism to the Italians, and Nazism to the Germans, and out of their coming dictators emerged in Russia, Italy, and Germany. The freedoms that Woodrow Wilson had hoped would spring from the war failed to live in the atmosphere of poverty and despair which followed the world conflict. Instead there was the spawning of dictatorial leaders and authoritarian philosophies which generally followed the slogan of Mussolini's Fascists: "Believe! Obey! Work!"

#### Mussolini and Fascism

The Italians were discontented and frustrated after the war. Although they had been among the victors, they did not receive all the spoils of war they had been promised in a secret treaty; for instance, they did not receive the city of Fiume and other territories along the east coast of the Adriatic and elsewhere in the world which they had expected. Italy suffered from inflation, widespread labor disputes, unemployment, and a grinding poverty which angered the people. The Italians looked to their government for help, but the government changed hands rapidly as one group after the other tried to cope with the nation's problems and failed. Then into the lives of the insecure Italians came a stocky man of determined features. His name was Benito Mussolini, and he told the Italians loudly that he had the answers to their problems. Follow him, he told them, and he would make them proud, secure members of a great nation. Many of the people believed him. Mussolini became Prime Minister of Italy in 1922 at the invitation of King Victor Emmanuel III. He started another kind of life for the Italians under his personal direction and with the assistance of the Fascist party which he had founded.

Mussolini was *Il Duce*—the leader—and his word was the law and will of Italy until he was executed by a band of partisans in the latter days of World War II. Mussolini, the son of a blacksmith, had educated himself. He joined the Socialist party but broke with it when the party refused to sanction the First World War. He fought in the Italian army and returned to organize his Fascists amidst the postwar chaos of Italy. Army veterans and frustrated nationalists were the backbone of his party. The Fascists took their name from the rods and ax, called *fasces,* which were the symbol of authority in ancient Rome. The Fascists, sometimes known as the Blackshirts, were anti-Communist and anti-Socialist, and they brawled with both of these groups, breaking up their meetings and silencing their speakers.

Under Fascist rule, political opponents were constantly in danger of arrest, and political prisoners were often tortured or killed. Great quantities of castor oil were forced down the throats of political opponents, many were beaten with rubber hoses, and a number were murdered. Strikes by the workers' parties were broken by Fascist troops, and the Fascist actions against the threat of the workers' parties attracted a number of followers from the middle class and among the large industrialists. The Fascists soon became economically and politically powerful.

Within a year or so after coming into power, Fascist party members ruled everywhere in Italy. Only the Fascist party was legal. Although the Chamber of Deputies and the Senate were left as the outward trappings of parliamentary government, it was *Il Duce* who ruled through his Grand Council of the Fascist party. In this Fascist state, men of various occupations—farming, industry, transportation, and others—were grouped into thirteen syndicates or corporations. Each of these syndicates was represented in the government. This differed from countries like the United States where men were represented geographically and on the basis of numbers rather than by their occupations. The Italian syndicates were all controlled at the top by Mussolini, who was Minister of Corporations. Even the employers and the employees were organized into a syndicate or corporation. This system is sometimes referred to as a *corporate state.* Private property existed, but it was always subject to seizure and use by the state if necessary.

Mussolini did not win and hold power by free elections. The Fascist government of Italy was a *totalitarian* government—one that permits the existence of only one political party. This government curtailed freedom with its secret police, its authority from above, its abolishment of opposition, and its strict supervision of the political life of the Italian people. The Fascists did, however, restore order, discipline, and a feeling of security to many Italians—man has been often known to trade his freedoms for security. Marshes were drained and converted into farms, and many new roads were built. But there was also flagrant corruption among the Fascists.

Mussolini envisioned founding a new Rome, and he searched for an empire. The army, navy, and air force were strengthened and prepared for war. In 1935 Italy invaded and occupied Ethiopia. Mussolini also joined Hitler in meddling in the Spanish Civil War in the 1930's. He dreamed of a great empire that would be his if Hitler and he won the Second World War. Mussolini's ambitions, however, brought him only an ignominious death and defeat to his country when the Allies won the war.

## General Franco Came to Power

Another authoritarian government came to Europe when General Francisco Franco defeated the republican forces in Spain and occupied Madrid in 1939. When this event happened Spain had long since lost her status as a great power in Europe. The decline of Spain had begun when the great Armada that Philip II sent against England was destroyed in 1588. With the slow progression of the following centuries, the Spanish overseas empire—once the greatest in the world—had shrunk in size. Uprisings, independence movements, and defeat in wars with other nations led to the loss of most of Spain's huge holdings abroad. As the flow of gold, silver, and other wealth from her colonies practically ceased, Spain became a weak, second-rate power. Napoleon conquered the country, and internal conflicts and economic problems continued to harass the Spanish people during the 1800's and 1900's.

Spain was neutral during the First World War. War contracts and trade brought a measure of industry to the country and prosperity to some, but the great mass of the working class were desperately needy. Antagonisms and conflicts grew between the vast numbers of the poor and the favored few who really controlled the country—the large landowners, the military, and the clergy. Thousands of Spaniards began to think as anarchists, as socialists, as syndicalists, as Communists of various kinds, and as republicans. All of these movements together made up the political "left" in Spain. Conditions worsened, and, although Alfonso XIII reigned as a constitutional monarch, General Primo de Rivera became the dictator of the country in 1923. He imposed martial law upon the state. But the people continued to seethe at the harshness of their lives, and in 1931 a republican-socialist government came to power and proclaimed Spain a republic.

The new republican leaders separated Church and State, made the schools secular institutions, planned the break-up of large landed estates, and attempted in other ways to change the traditional political, economic, and cultural structure of Spain. But divisions continued to widen between the "leftists" and the "rightists," and there were dissensions among the "leftists" themselves. In 1936 the "leftists," including the Communists, united in a Popular Front and won the election. The "rightists," fearing the abolishment of the system and ideology they believed in, attempted under the leadership of General Francisco Franco to overturn the government in 1936. Their attempt led to a bloody civil war which lasted from 1936 to 1939.

General Franco was supported by the same groups which had supported the monarchy—the landowners, the military, and the clergy. There was also a strong rightist party called the *Falange* (phalanx), founded in 1932, which modeled itself much along the lines of the Fascist party in Italy. The members of this party brought additional support to Franco. Further, Mussolini and Hitler saw in Franco a welcome ally in their drive for power in Europe and the world. They sent him substantial help in the form of weapons, tanks, airplanes, and men. The Soviet Union entered the struggle and sent aid to the republican armies, and liberals and leftists from many parts of the world volunteered their services and fought in international brigades against Franco's forces. Thus, for three years an international ideological war was waged which made of Spain a land of terror and death. The Spanish Civil War was a prelude to the carnage of World War II.

In 1939 General Franco occupied Madrid and began a rule which has lasted to the present day. He is the *Caudillo*, the leader. He is the Chief of State, the Prime Minister, and the head of the Falange party. There is a *Cortés*, or parliament, but its power is subordinate to that of General Franco. And though Franco has indicated in a succession law that Spain is a monarchy, no king has yet been selected to succeed him. Spain is not yet a great power in the world, but the country is beginning to participate more in the various international bodies of the world and to speak with its vote and voice in their assemblies. It is a country of more than 30,000,000 people, and there is in these people the potential to make of Spain once again a growing force among the nations of the world.

### Hitler and Nazism

Adolf Hitler will be long remembered as one who loosed upon humanity torrents of blood and the tortures of hate. He bequeathed to mankind a legacy of political conditions so dangerously tangled that we are yet laboriously attempting to unravel their twisted strands. Hitler, like Mussolini in Italy, rose to supreme power in Germany from the sickness of spirit and the despair which gripped the German people in the years following World War I. The Germans, like the Italians, were ready for a leader to follow, one who offered them hope again. In Hitler's spellbinding oratory the Germans heard the words they wanted to hear. Many Germans believed and blindly followed where he led. They had *Der Führer*, "the leader," and he would make them proud and secure once again.

Immediately after World War I, the Germans established a federal republic named after the town of Weimar where the constitution was written. The Weimar Republic had an elected president and a parliament of two houses: a lower house known as the *Reichstag* and an upper house known as the *Bundesrat*. In the lower house, parties were represented in proportion to the number of votes they had received. The upper house represented the seventeen states which made up Germany. The premier or prime minister was called a chancellor in Germany. He came from the majority party in the lower house, as did his cabinet, which ruled the executive branch of government. The Weimar Republic had a stormy history. It was beset by multiplying parties which represented all shades of opinion ranging from the extreme right to the extreme left. It was also harassed by economic conditions that made life in Germany a nightmare.

In the troubled years that followed World War I, the Communists were repressed in their attempt to take the government by force. The monarchists also tried and were foiled. Liberal leaders were murdered. Strikes became commonplace, and unemployment soared. Money became cheaper than the paper it was printed on. No people, not even the Chinese after World War II, experienced an inflation as disastrous as that of Germany. It is estimated that twenty-five cents of American money in 1923 was worth one trillion marks—German money is calculated in marks—and that the smallest bill printed in Germany at this time was for five million marks. Germans went to the banks with baskets and collected their salaries in large bags. For those who had their savings in bonds, banks, and pensions, there was bitter disappointment and despair: their money which had formerly been worth hundreds and thousands of dollars was now worth a few cents.

This inflation was curbed in 1924. Conditions improved somewhat until 1929, when a world-wide depression struck the Germans heavily, just as it did the Americans and others in the world. The Germans started to give their favor in growing numbers to the extremists of the right and the left. The party of Adolf Hitler, the National Socialists, made great gains.

Hitler was born in Austria in 1889. He fought in the First World War, won an Iron Cross for bravery, and attained the rank of corporal. He rebelled at the terms of the peace treaty and joined with those who wanted to overthrow the republic. He was put in jail for a period of time during which he wrote a book called *Mein Kampf*, "My Battle," which later became the Nazis' bible. During this time he founded the National Socialist German Workers' party, the name of which was shortened to Nazi party. His followers were often called "brownshirts," after the color of their uniforms. He promised the German people an improvement in their welfare, security, and economy. He preached repeal of the Versailles treaty and the return of lost territories and colonies. He told the German people that they were a "master race," the great and pure Aryans, and that all who were not Aryans were inferior. (The Aryans, it will be recalled, were an ancient Indo-European language group, and if they ever were a race, that race was mingled with others thousands of years ago.) Many of the Germans believed Hitler's teachings and promises, and they made his party the largest in the lower house of the legislature. In 1933 President von Hindenburg appointed Hitler Chancellor of Germany, and the Nazis quickly seized full power.

Hitler soon made Germany over into a centralized, totalitarian state ruled by him and his Nazi party. The Nazis controlled every facet of German life. Concentration camps—places for the confinement of prisoners of war, persons with feared political beliefs, and refugees — were built and packed with people Hitler and his Nazis did not like. These included Communists, socialists, the liberal-minded, and the Jews. Under some of the more fanatic Nazis, these camps were turned into scenes of horror where gas ovens extinguished the lives of millions of Jews. The Jews were singled out for the special hatred of the Nazi.

Hitler started a vast public works program, but his greatest emphasis was put upon the manufacture of military equipment — guns, planes, tanks, warships, submarines, and the other instruments of war. His foreign policy risked war, and he considered his need for guns more important than the German people's need for food.

Hitler's goal was world empire, but first it was necessary to retrieve the territories which the Germans had lost in the last war. In 1936 Hitler tested the will of the British and the French to fight by marching into the Rhineland, a part of Germany which was to remain unfortified by the terms of the Versailles treaty. Nothing was done to stop him. He began to build his Nazi party in Austria, Czechoslovakia, and wherever there were German minorities. Nazi party groups in these countries prepared the way for his coming. He entered Austria in March of 1938 and proclaimed it part of the German Reich. He began a war of nerves, crying that the three million Germans in Czechoslovakia must belong to Germany.

Neville Chamberlain, who was then Prime Minister of Great Britain, went to Germany in 1938 and met with Hitler at Munich. Chamberlain yielded to Hitler's demands in the

War crimes trials after World War II revealed Nazi atrocities. (Warsaw Ghetto, German photographer unknown, exhibit at Nuremberg Trial)

hope of forestalling a war. To this day, the word *Munich* is used to refer to an instance of appeasement or unresisting surrender. Czechoslovakia melted away as Germany, Poland, and Hungary claimed parts of it as their own. In 1939 Hitler made a pact with Stalin, the Communist dictator of Russia, in which they pledged nonaggression in war and divided eastern Europe between them. Then on September 1, 1939 Hitler invaded Poland. Two days later England and France declared war on Germany. World War II had begun.

### World War II

France and England were not as well prepared for war as the Germans under Hitler. During the years after World War I, the French declined in power relative to that of the Germans. The only ally France could depend upon in terms of power support was Great Britain. But the British had their own problems during this period. The economy of France was weak, and inflation became a curse. The French population remained stationary and even declined. The French trusted in a great fortification complex of steel, stone, and guns called the Maginot Line to guard their borders against the Germans. In their blind trust the French neglected to consider the possibility of a new kind of war. When it came, France was unprepared and surprised.

Great Britain, too, had experienced political and economic difficulties during the postwar years. The British were losing markets to the Americans and the Japanese. Most of the British investments abroad had been spent to fight World War I, and taxes after the war fell heavily upon the great fortunes and the great estates. In British factories, machines were getting old and needed to be replaced by more efficient ones. The colonies and overseas territories were becoming increasingly demanding of more freedom to run their own affairs. All of these internal matters demanded attention and financing. Little attention was paid to preserving the high efficiency of the British military services. Great Britain also was not prepared to fight the battle which Hitler had begun.

While the French and the English moved into and around the Maginot Line, Hitler moved quickly elsewhere. In April 1940 Hitler conquered Norway and Denmark. This victory so startled the British that they requested Neville Chamberlain's resignation. Winston Churchill became their wartime leader. Then with screaming dive bombers and roaring tanks, Hitler took Holland, Belgium, and Luxembourg in quick succession. The Germans rolled the English expeditionary force back to the beaches of Dunkirk on the English Channel. The British managed to return most of their forces to England, but most of their equipment was left on the beach. Then the Germans turned on the French army and flanked the Maginot Line. On June 22, 1940 the French signed an armistice with Germany. In the meantime, Italy had entered the war on the side of Germany, and in September 1940 the Japanese joined with Hitler and Mussolini.

England was now fighting the war alone. After besieging the British with a week of bombing, Hitler offered them peace with their empire intact provided that Britain would recognize the dominance of Germany and Italy. Churchill refused the offer, and the British fought on with stubborn determination. On December 7, 1941 the Japanese bombed Pearl Harbor in Hawaii and thus brought war to the United States. The Japanese quickly seized the Philippines and a number of other Pacific islands as well as Burma. The Germans had invaded Russia on June 22, 1941. These two events gave the British two powerful allies. This combination of forces was to bring about the eventual defeat of Hitler.

In the fall of 1942 the British stopped the Germans in North Africa, and the Americans landed to join forces with them. By February of 1943, the German army attacking Stalingrad was compelled to surrender. The Germans were defeated in Africa in May 1943. Two months later, the Allied armies landed in Sicily, and with its conquest Mussolini was forced to resign his post of Prime Minister.

The bombing of Pearl Harbor on December 7, 1941 was the immediate cause for the United States' entry into World War II. (Official U. S. Navy Photo)

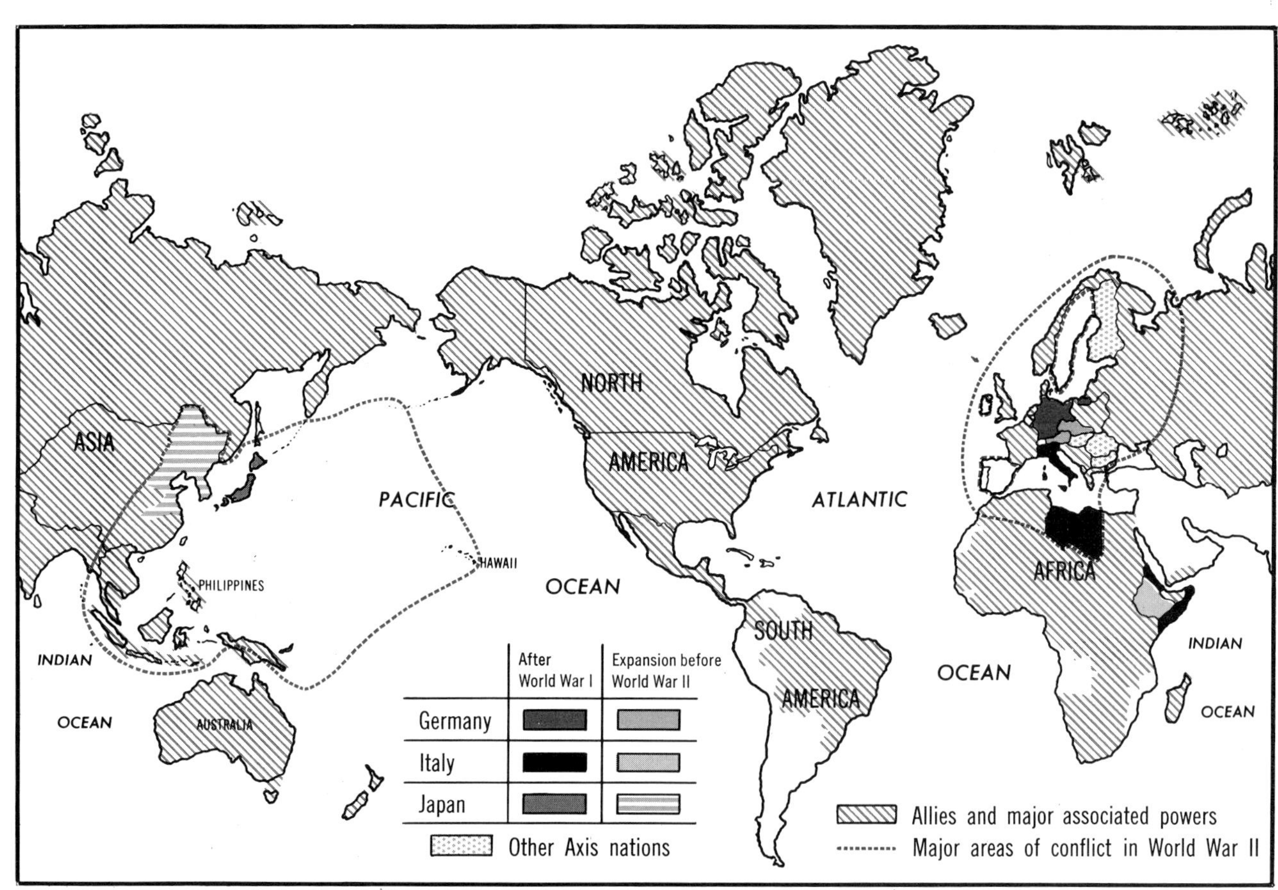


**ALLIED AND AXIS POWERS IN WORLD WAR II, 1939–1945**

In the years preceding World War II, the Axis powers began policies of expansion that finally led to hostilities. Compare the territory they held before this war with the territory they hold today. List and discuss some of the major results of this war in terms of information shown on the map.

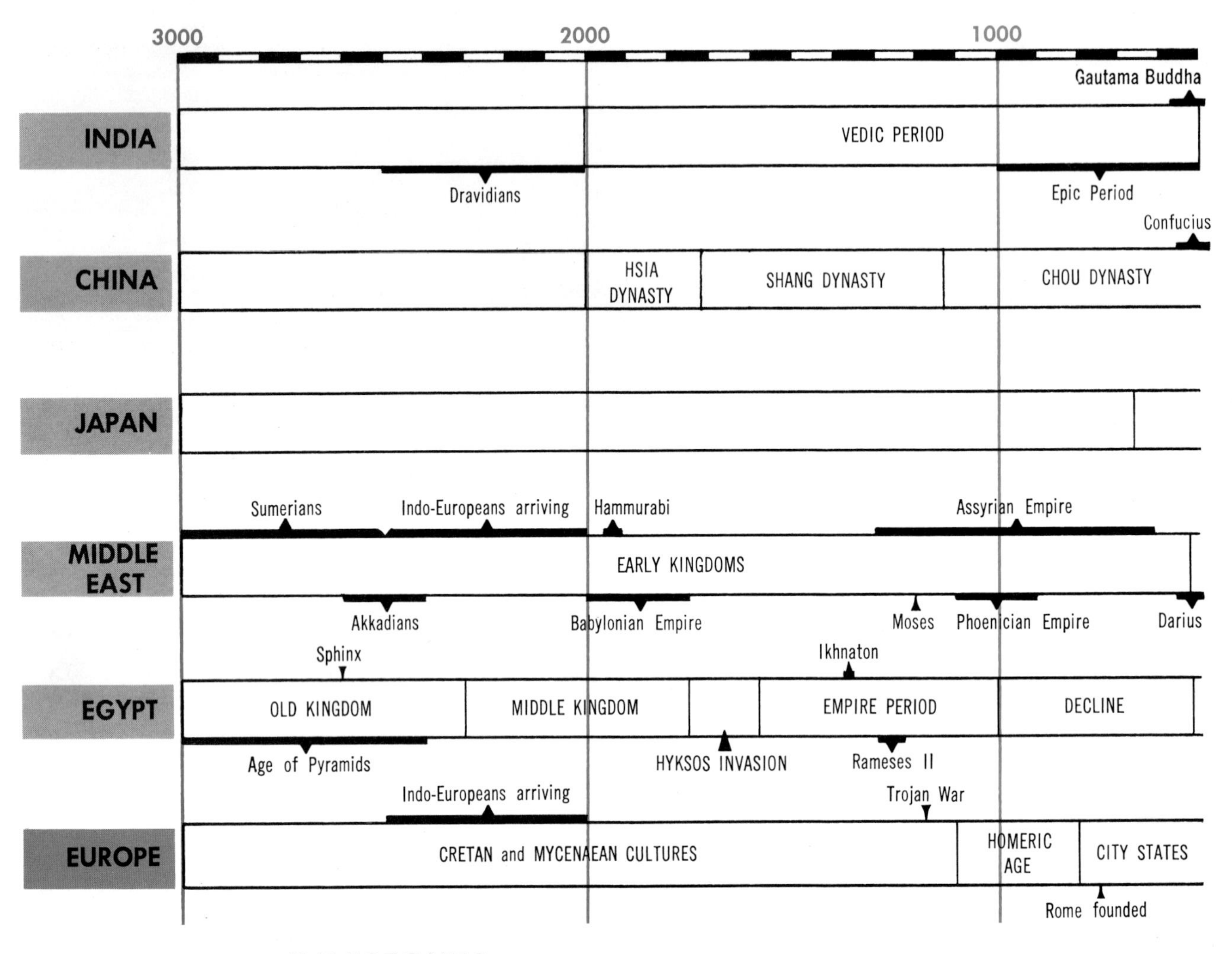


## MILESTONES

MEDIEVAL AND MODERN EUROPE

A.D.

| | |
|---|---|
| 711 | Moslems take Spain from Visigoths |
| 732 | Martel defeats Moslem Arabs at Tours |
| 800 | Charlemagne crowned Emperor of Rome |
| 930 | Iceland's constitution creates Althing |
| 962 | Beginning of Holy Roman Empire |
| c. 1000 | Lief Ericson sails westward to American coast |
| 1016-1035 | Reign of Canute the Great |
| 1054 | Split between Eastern and Western Christians |
| 1096-1270 | The Crusades |
| 1215 | Magna Carta |
| 1295 | Marco Polo returns from Far East |
| c. 1350-1600 | Renaissance |
| 1337-1453 | Hundred Years' War (England and France) |
| 1394-1460 | Prince Henry the Navigator |
| 1440s | Gutenberg: printing with movable type |
| 1453 | Turks take Constantinople; end of Byzantine Empire |
| 1492 | Fall of Granada, last Moorish stronghold |
| 1492 | Columbus discovers America |
| 1498 | Vasco da Gama reaches India |
| 1517 | Martin Luther: Ninety-five Theses |
| 1534 | Act of Supremacy (England breaks with Rome) |
| 1536 | Calvin publishes Institutes |
| 1545-1563 | Council of Trent: Catholic Reformation |
| 1555 | Peace of Augsburg ends German religious wars |
| 1588 | Spanish Armada defeated by England |
| 1598 | Edict of Nantes (religious toleration in France) |
| 1618-1648 | Thirty Years' War (renewal of German religious wars) |
| 1628 | Petition of Right (England) |
| 1642-1660 | Commonwealth followed by Protectorate (England) |
| 1643-1715 | Reign of Louis XIV (France) |
| 1648 | Treaty of Westphalia ends Thirty Years' War |
| 1649 | Charles I beheaded (England) |
| 1660 | Restoration (England) |
| 1689 | English Bill of Rights |
| 1713 | Treaty of Utrecht ends War of the Spanish Succession |

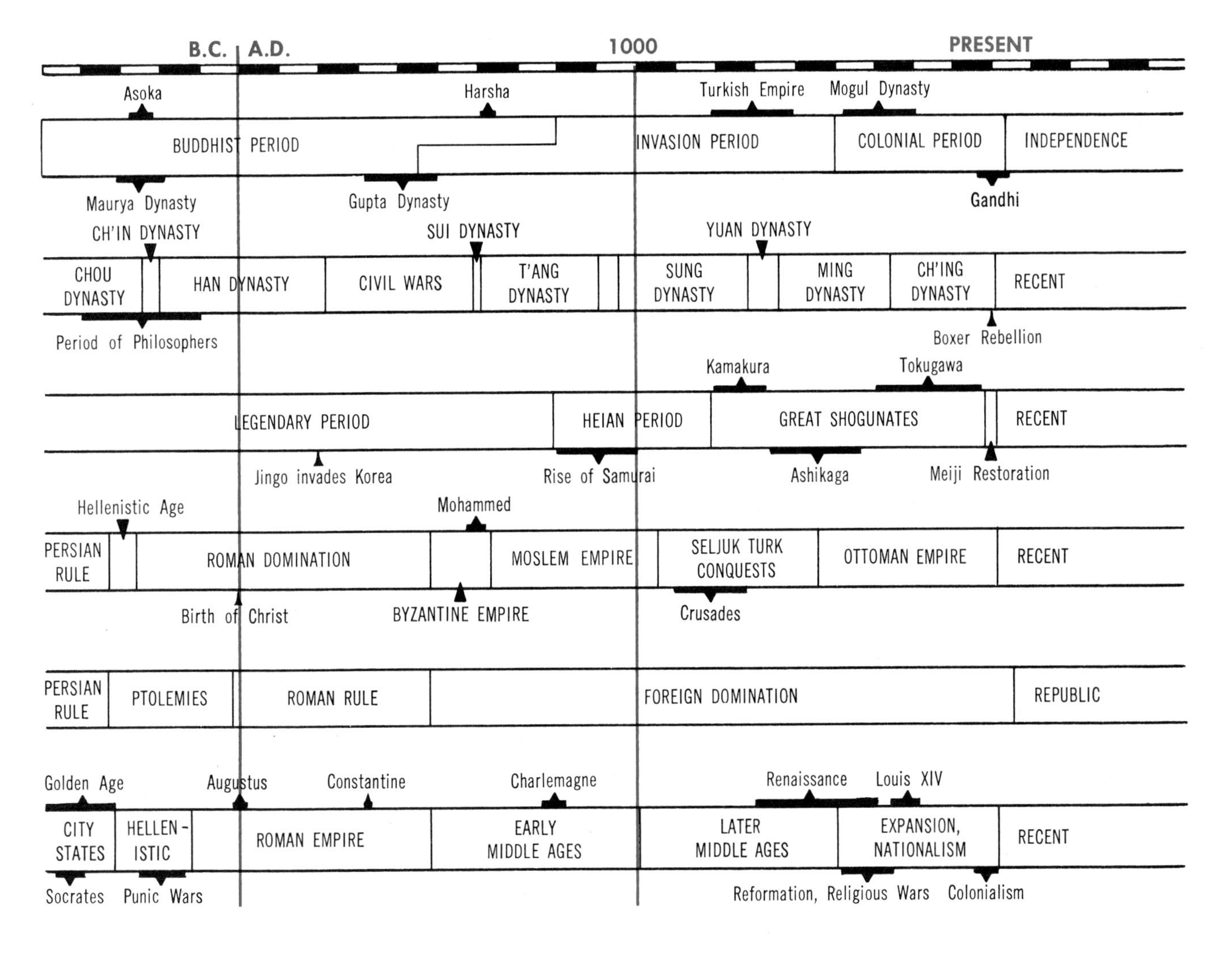


| | |
|---|---|
| 1763 | Peace of Paris ends Seven Years' War |
| 1769 | Watt's steam engine |
| 1789 | Beginning of French Revolution |
| 1804 | Napoleon crowned Emperor of France |
| 1809-1882 | Charles Darwin |
| 1815 | Battle of Waterloo |
| 1822-1884 | Gregor Mendel |
| 1848 | Garibaldi helps found republic at Rome |
| 1870-1871 | Franco-Prussian War |
| 1871 | Rome becomes capital of a united Italy |
| 1871 | German Empire declared |
| 1882 | Triple Alliance formed |
| 1907 | Triple Entente formed |
| 1914-1918 | World War I |
| 1919 | Treaty of Versailles |
| 1929 | World-wide depression begins |
| 1933 | Hitler becomes Chancellor of Germany |
| 1936-1939 | Spanish Civil War |
| 1936 | Hitler marches into Rhineland |
| 1938 | Munich Conference |
| 1939 | World War II begins |
| 1945 | United Nations established |
| 1945 | Germany and Japan surrender unconditionally |
| 1947 | Truman Doctrine |
| 1948 | Marshall Plan |
| 1949 | NATO formed |
| 1956 | Hungarian revolt |
| 1957 | Six nations form European Common Market |
| 1961 | Berlin Wall built |

On August 6, 1945 the first atomic bomb to be used in warfare was dropped on the Japanese city of Hiroshima. Over four square miles of the city were destroyed by this one bomb. A second bomb was dropped on Nagasaki three days later, and the following day the Japanese government asked for peace. (U. S. Strategic Bombing Survey)

After World War II the West German Federal Republic was established with a new constitution. West German economic recovery was phenomenal. Below, Kongresshalle in Berlin, used for international conventions. (German Tourist Information Office)

Soon Italy declared war on Germany, but the Germans made it difficult for the Allies to take Italy.

By the beginning of 1944 the German armies to the east were forced back to Poland. On June 6, 1944 the Allies landed in Normandy in France, and by August they were in Paris. The Russians launched an attack from the east, and by April 1945 the Russian and American armies met. On May 7, 1945 the Germans surrendered unconditionally.

Then the Allies, especially the Americans, turned their attention to defeating the Japanese. The Japanese had it all their own way until spring of 1942 when they were turned back by the naval battles of the Coral Sea and Midway Island. Under the overall command of General Douglas MacArthur, the Allies began gradually to leap from island to island toward the Philippines and Japan. In October of 1944 the Americans landed in the Philippines and in six months recaptured them from the Japanese. It was on August 6, 1945, however, that the single most important event of the war occurred. An atomic bomb was dropped on the Japanese city of Hiroshima. Three days later another bomb hit the city of Nagasaki. The next day the Japanese asked for peace, and on September 2, 1945, they signed an unconditional surrender aboard the *U.S.S. Missouri* in Tokyo Bay. With their signature, the hostilities of World War II officially came to an end.

1. What were the main sources of Mussolini's support in his rise to power?
2. What economic, social, and political conditions stemming from Germany's defeat in World War I made it easy for Hitler to rise to power?
3. What was the title of the "bible" of the National Socialists?

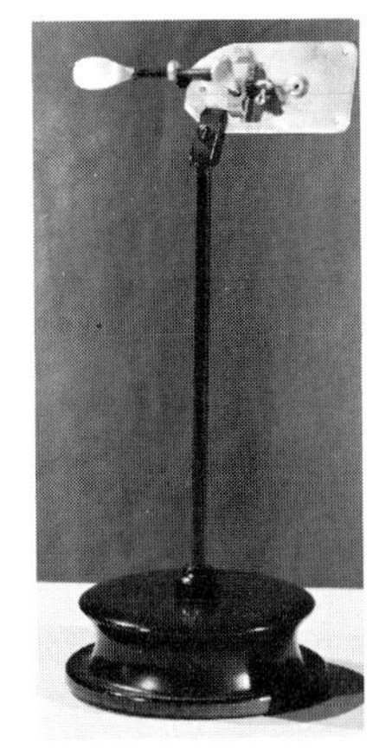

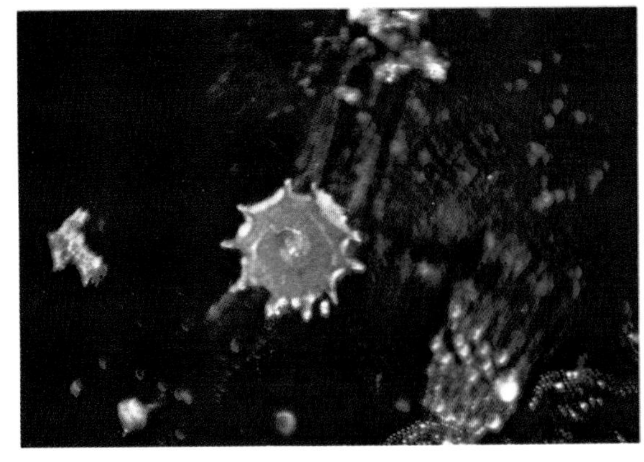

Technological advances have made war a threat to the survival of mankind, but they have also brought much good. Leeuwenhoek's simple microscope, left, opened up the study of a world of tiny organisms. Modern microscopes are used to study organisms multiplied hundreds of times, right, and aid in the control of disease. (Bausch & Lomb Inc. Rochester, N. Y.; Shell Oil Co.)

## The Legacy of World War II

World War II left an even more devastated world than the previous war. Weapons were much more powerful, bombs were larger, and airplanes carried bombs to cities where civilians lived and worked. No one within the range of a plane escaped the deadly touch of war. This war was more widespread, involved more people, and touched off more changes than any previous war in history. After the war there were rapid changes among the dependent peoples who suddenly emerged from colonial subjection to independence. India, Burma, Vietnam, Malaya, Indonesia, the Philippines, and a number of countries of the Middle East and Africa have all obtained their independence since the end of World War II. There are few colonies remaining in the world today, and most of these are in the process of becoming independent.

There have also been some changes in attitudes toward war. War now involves atomic and hydrogen bombs, and there is real doubt that mankind could survive a nuclear war. Under the circumstances, there is a stalemate of terror at this time, for no man dares to begin a war which would amount to suicide. Another change is in the attitude of the free people of the West and the Communists. During the war they were in alliance. After the war, under the direction of Stalin, the Communists seized every opportunity to stir up trouble in various parts of the world, to break promises, and to occupy territory not their own. In general they created many real problems for the democratic people who desired to see freedom, security, and peace reign once again in the world.

Since World War II, rockets have been used for peaceful purposes and have helped to advance man's knowledge. Left, an astronaut is recovered after an orbital flight. Right, high-altitude photographs help in weather study. (NASA)

With the conclusion of World War II, there was an economic collapse in Europe. The Communists became powerful in France, Italy, and other European countries. They tried to assume control of the governments of the Europeans. There was armed conflict in Greece, for instance, which further worsened the political and economic instability of the Europeans. The United States feared that the Europeans might fall even more completely under the Communist sway—all of eastern Europe was Communist.

Then, in 1947, President Harry S. Truman proclaimed his policy of support for the free nations resisting domination by armed minorities and outsiders. It was called the Truman Doctrine. Truman's administration then began the Marshall Plan, named for General George C. Marshall, Secretary of State. This plan was designed to help European nations in their economic recovery from the war. Its aim was to free the nations of Europe from the main internal causes of Communism. Under this plan the United States sent more than eleven billion dollars worth of food, machinery, and other products to aid European nations in lifting hunger, poverty, and desperation from their people. In 1949 the North Atlantic Treaty Organization (NATO) was formed. It included most of the nations of Western Europe and the United States. NATO was designed to deter Russia from attacking any of the powers that were members. These measures all helped, and gradually the Europeans worked themselves into the prosperity and bustling industrial atmosphere that they enjoy today. In this process Western Germany became one of the most prosperous states of Europe.

After the war, armies of occupation stayed in Germany, and the Nazi leaders were prosecuted as war criminals. A democratic form of government was established in Western Germany. Gradually this government became more and more independent of allied supervision as it proved its sincerity and desire for freedom. East Germany, however, was occupied by the Russians and a Communist regime was established there. Berlin remains a divided city. The western part of the city is under a three-power occupation of the democracies, while East Berlin is under the Communists.

Six nations—Belgium, France, Italy, Luxembourg, The Netherlands, and West Germany—joined together to create a common market in coal and steel. Under a plan offered by Robert Schuman of France, they formed the European Coal and Steel Community. Production and trade are regulated in the member nations by a nine-member council which levies taxes on coal and steel and can fine firms or individuals who violate its regulations. In 1957 these same six nations formed the European Common Market, which has as its object the removal of barriers to free circulation of goods and capital among the member nations. Under the European Common Market, workers will be permitted to move freely from one country to another, and a uniform economy will be established for all. England and the remaining non-Communist countries of Europe wanted to join this common market of Europe, but President de Gaulle of France opposed British entry into the community. It is interesting to note that Germany, the foe of yesterday, is welcomed by France today in the Common Market, while England, its ally of yesterday, is rejected.

One of the significant changes during the years since the war has been the increase in international organizations, especially the United Nations and its many specialized branches. In April 1945, representatives of fifty nations met in San Francisco to draw up a charter for the United Nations which became effective on October 24, 1945. Among the purposes of this charter are: to maintain international peace and security; to settle international disputes by peaceful means; to develop friendly relations among nations based upon respect for the equal rights and self-determination of peoples; to seek international cooperation in solving the economic, social, cultural, and humanitarian problems of man; and to strive for the fundamental freedoms of all without distinction as to race, sex, language, or religion.

The principle organizations of the United Nations are the General Assembly, the Security Council, the Secretariat, the Economic and Social Council, the Trusteeship Council, and the International Court of Justice. Each member nation is represented in the General Assembly and has one vote. The Security Council, most powerful of the UN organizations, is composed of eleven nations, five of whom are permanent members—Russia, Britain, France, China, and the United States; the other six are elected by the General Assembly. The job of the Security Council is to handle international disputes and try to settle them peacefully. The five permanent members also possess a veto power; that is, if any one of them vetoes an action, the Council cannot act. The Secretariat carries out the daily routine of administrative tasks of the UN. The Economic and Social Council has the overall task of working for the improvement of economic and social conditions of man everywhere. The Trusteeship Council watches over people and territories not yet independent and sees to it that territories held under mandate are developing education, individual rights, and freedom of speech and worship. The International Court of Justice decides on disputes brought before it by member nations and renders advisory opinions on matters of international law.

Perhaps the most effective work of the United Nations has been done in the specialized agencies which carry out particular functions. Among the most important are: the Food and Agriculture Organization (FAO); the UN Educational, Scientific, and Cultural Organization (UNESCO); World Health Organization (WHO): International Labor Organization (ILO); UN International Children's Fund (UNICEF); International Civil Aviation Organization (ICAO); International Bank for Reconstruction and Development (IBRD); International Monetary Fund (IMF); International Telecommunications Union (ITU); and the World Meteorological Organization (WMO). The headquarters of these various agencies are scattered throughout the world. Much of their work has been useful because these agencies have not been directly concerned with the political and security affairs of nations, but rather with more concrete functions in physical and scientific fields.

1. What was the Marshall Plan? When was it begun?
2. What do the letters NATO stand for? What countries are members? What are the goals of NATO?
3. Name the major organs of the United Nations. Describe the structure and function of each.
4. Name some of the specialized agencies of the United Nations. How has their relative isolation from the more political organs of the UN permitted them to operate effectively?

## Conclusion

The Europeans have rarely known a time without the destruction and bloodshed of war. Because of their advanced technology, military experience, and intimate connections with the rest of mankind, their wars have been extremely ruinous and widespread. The individual European has no desire for war, especially since atomic bombs have become a part of man's weapons for war. Many European nations joined in a feeble attempt to contain and restrict war through the international organization known as the League of Nations, which was established after World War I. The League of Nations never had a real chance to enforce peace—the United States was not a member, and the Germans, Italians, and Japanese paid no attention to its counsels. The League had no way to control nations except through the voluntary efforts of its members, and no nation was prepared to go to war unless compelled. The League was not successful in stopping the invasions of other nations by Japan, Italy, and Germany.

After World War II, the nations of Europe helped to establish the United Nations and have participated in its activities to this day. Many Europeans hope that the United Nations may be of assistance in preventing future wars. But the European nations do not think that the United Nations is the answer to all international problems. They have sometimes

In a shrinking world made smaller by faster communications and transportation, the contrast between highly developed nations and underdeveloped nations appears to be greater. The advanced science of the United States, Western Europe, and the Soviet Union deals with revolutionary new devices such as the laser, above. These devices produce intense light rays which promise to have applications in industry, communications, and medicine. In other parts of the world, technology has lagged far behind, and life is based on subsistence agriculture. Left, small farmers of Iraq depend upon primitive spades to till their soil. (Western Electric, above; FAO, left)

boycotted it when it infringed upon matters that were regarded as domestic questions. The Europeans place more trust in other institutions.

Many Europeans believe that a regional organization in Europe, and perhaps an alliance with the United States, is a greater deterrent to war than the United Nations. They also continue to place their trust in the loyalty of the people, and in national armies, navies, and air fleets. Nationalism is not dead; it continues to play an important role in the relations among nations. But most Europeans today agree that a world war must be avoided, for once started it is apparently impossible to isolate and keep a war confined to a single region. Eventually a war would draw in all men and involve most of the world.

## SUMMING UP THE CHAPTER

A. Define or explain the following terms, relating them to this chapter.

| | |
|---|---|
| corporate state | Maginot Line |
| fascism | nationalism |
| imperialism | tariffs |
| inflation | totalitarian |
| Kaiser | |

B. Identify the following and tell why they are important.

| | |
|---|---|
| Balkans | Mazzini |
| Cavour | *Mein Kampf* |
| der Führer | Shuman Plan |
| Dual Alliance | Treaty of Versailles |
| Garibaldi | Triple Alliance |
| Il Duce | Triple Entente |
| "Iron Chancellor" | Truman Doctrine |
| League of Nations | Weimar Republic |

C. Identify the following dates and indicate their importance.

1. 1871
2. June 28, 1914
3. November 11, 1918
4. May 7, 1945
5. August 6, 1945
6. September 2, 1945
7. October 24, 1945

D. Chapter review questions.

1. When did the nation-state develop? What part did the Napoleonic wars play in developing nationalism?
2. How did Bismarck unite the Germans? Evaluate Bismarck as a political leader.
3. Who were the great unifiers of Italy? Describe their connections with each other.
4. How did technological advances in World War I change the entire nature of war?
5. Discuss the idealism of Woodrow Wilson. Why do you suppose Wilson's ideas failed to win acceptance?
6. What were the terms of peace forced upon the Germans at Versailles? How did these terms lead to the economic collapse of Germany?
7. What new nations were created in Europe following World War I? Which of these nations are still in existence?
8. Describe the government structure of the Weimar Republic.
9. How did the policy of appeasement by the rest of the world encourage Hitler to push his conquests forward?
10. In what ways was the Second World War more devastating than the First World War? How did the technology of these wars cause greater destruction of civilian populations and production facilities than previous wars had done?
11. What were the purposes of the Marshall Plan? Did this aid have a political purpose?
12. By what countries was Germany occupied after the Second World War? What parts of Germany are still occupied?
13. What is the European Common Market? What are its goals, both immediate and long-range?
14. Who are the permanent members of the United Nations Security Council? What is the purpose of the Security Council? What happens if a member uses its veto power?

E. Questions for discussion.

1. Compare the unification of Italy and Germany, paying particular attention to the rise of national consciousness, the leadership, and the methods of the nation-builders. Do you believe there was any connection between these factors and the rise to power of Hitler and Mussolini?
2. Discuss the policies of Bismarck in terms of the philosophy of Machiavelli.
3. How did the development of formal alliances tend to make wars among the European nations less likely and at the same time insure that any war which did occur would be wider in scope? Do you believe that World War I was a world-wide war because of alliances, or would it have become world-wide anyway?
4. What does the rise of Hitler and Mussolini tell you about the attraction of radical promises to disillusioned and despairing peoples?
5. How did Mussolini envision the corporate state? How does such a centrally organized and controlled state almost inevitably become totalitarian?

F. Projects for groups or individuals.

1. Sketch a map showing the territories which changed hands as a result of World War I.
2. Show on a map the occupation zones of Germany. Show the four-power occupation of Berlin on a separate map of the city.
3. Prepare a file of newspaper clippings on the development of the European Common Market.
4. Prepare a report on one of the specialized agencies of the United Nations.

## SUMMING UP THE UNIT

### Drawing together the main themes

1. How successful has the United Nations been? Why has it not been more successful? Do you think it will ever be able to settle all disputes among nations peacefully?
2. Is imperialism an extension of nationalism? How did the imperialism of the nineteenth and twentieth centuries differ from earlier European colonialism? Would you say this tendency is a natural part of all political and economic systems? Explain your answers.
3. Why have the founders of modern Italy succeeded where others for centuries have failed? Would you say that Machiavelli was extremely foresighted in perceiving that the freedom of the Italian cities and states could only be achieved in a unified nation? Was it necessary to resort to Machiavellian tactics in order to succeed?
4. Describe the history of Franco-German relations from the Reformation to the present. Be sure to note the religious conflicts, great wars, peace settlements, and competition.
5. The French Revolution has often been seen as the great turning point in Western political history, and it has been claimed that one can identify the modern liberal and conservative on the basis of their differing views of the French Revolution. How do you think this is possible? In what ways is it impossible?
6. How would you explain the fact that wars based on religious differences tended to be so intense? In your answer, discuss not only the conflicts growing out of the Reformation and Catholic Reformation, but also the Crusades and non-European religious wars.
7. How did the Renaissance mark a change in the European's attitude toward man? What is this attitude called?
8. How has nationalism changed since World War II? What are the causes of this change? What do you see evolving?
9. Around what functions did the city evolve from the late Middle Ages to the time of the Industrial Revolution? How did the large modern city develop?
10. How did the movement from the farm or small craft shop to the city and the factory change man's life? How did it change his living conditions? Was man more independent, or less, as a result? What effect has this had on government?
11. How did the economics of large enterprises lead to the development of the joint stock company?
12. What was the significance of the new middle class that was created by the modern economic system? What have been the political consequences of the rise of the middle class?
13. Did man in Europe—also in the United States or in the Communist world—see in regional organization the real hope of the future?

### Unit projects for groups or individuals

1. Read Machiavelli's *The Prince*. (It is quite short.) What does the author tell a ruler he must do to be successful?
2. Read a modern novel about European history and prepare a class report on it.
3. Draw a series of maps illustrating the historical development of European nations and changes in territory during the period from the Renaissance to the present.
4. Read a historical novel dealing with the Italian Renaissance. Report in class on some of the major features of Renaissance life and thought which are brought out in the novel.

### FURTHER READINGS

BARNOUW, ADRIAAN J., *The Land and People of Holland*. Lippincott, 1961.

BENN, F. LEE, *Europe Since 1914: In Its World Setting*, 8th ed. Appleton, 1954. Good reference work.

BERRY, ERICK, *The Land and People of Finland*. Lippincott, 1959.

———, *The Land and People of Iceland*. Lippincott, 1959.

BRAGDON, LILLIAN, *The Land and People of France*. Lippincott, 1960.

———, *The Land and People of Switzerland*. Lippincott, 1961.

BUCHANAN, FREDA M., *The Land and People of Scotland*, rev. Lippincott, 1962.

BULLOCK, ALAN, *Hitler: A Study in Tyranny*, rev. ed. Harper, 1960; Bantam, paperback. One of the best biographies of Hitler.

CARR, ALBERT Z., *Men of Power*. Viking, 1940, rev. 1956. Sketches of powerful men such as Frederick the Great and Napoleon.

CARRINGTON, C. E., *The British Overseas: Exploits of a Nation of Shopkeepers*. Cambridge U., 1950. Detailed account of the building of the English empire.

CHANDLER, ANNA CURTIS, *Story-Lives of Master Artists*, rev. ed. Lippincott, 1953. Contains portraits of Renaissance artists.

CHRISTENSEN, ERWIN O., *A History of Western Art*. New Am. Lib., 1959. Good coverage.

COMMAGER, HENRY S., *Pocket History of the Second World War.* Pocket Books, paperback. Brief and good.

DAVENPORT, MARCIA, *Garibaldi: Father of Modern Italy.* Random, 1957. The story of the brave and colorful Garibaldi, during Italy's fight for unification.

DAVIS, WILLIAM STEARNS, *Life in Elizabethan Days.* Harper, 1930. A vivid portion of English history.

DE KRUIF, PAUL, *Microbe Hunters.* Harcourt, 1932; Pocket Books, paperback, 1959. A popular account that places the development of modern medical science in its historical perspective.

DICKENS, CHARLES, *A Tale of Two Cities.* Various editions. Classic tale of individuals caught up in the excesses of the French Revolution.

DUMAS, ALEXANDRE, *Three Musketeers.* Various editions. A tale of adventure during the times of Richelieu and Louis XIV.

EISENHOWER, DWIGHT, *Crusade in Europe.* Doubleday, 1948; Dolphin, paperback. The Commander-in-Chief of the Allied forces in Europe tells the story of World War II. Amply illustrated with maps, diagrams, and photographs.

FISHER, HERBERT ALBERT, *Napoleon.* Oxford U., 1945. A brief but good biography of Napoleon.

FORBES, R. J., *Man, the Maker: A History of Engineering and Technology,* rev. ed. Abelard, 1958. The title is explanatory.

FORESTER, C. S., The various Hornblower books covering the period when England was fighting to contain Napoleon.

GIANAKOULIS, THEODORE, *The Land and People of Greece,* rev. ed. Lippincott, 1964.

GRANT, MADELEINE P., *Louis Pasteur: Fighting Hero of Science.* McGraw, 1959. Good biography of a great scientist.

GUNTHER, JOHN, *Inside Europe.* Harper, 1940.

———, *Inside Europe Today,* rev. ed. Harper, 1962; Pocket Books, paperback. A view of the conditions and personalities of Europe by a keen observer and excellent writer.

HALL, ELVAJEAN, *The Land and People of Norway.* Lippincott, 1963.

HARTMAN, GERTRUDE, *Machines and the Men Who Made the World of Industry.* Macmillan, 1939. Stories of inventors and their machines.

HEWES, AGNES DANFORTH, *Spice Ho!* Knopf, 1947. A good novel about the struggle for Asia's wealth of spices.

HOGBEN, LANCELOT, *From Cave Painting to Comic Strip.* Chanticleer, 1949. Man has been communicating with pictures for a long time.

HUME, RUTH F., *Great Men of Medicine.* Random, 1961. Stories of founders of modern medicine.

ICENHOWER, JOSEPH B., *Man Against the Unknown: The Story of Exploration.* Winston, 1957. This story places emphasis upon the personal feats of the explorers rather than upon the events themselves.

KOHN, HANS, *Nationalism: Its Meaning and History.* Anvil Book, Van Nostrand, 1955. Excellent summary of a vital topic.

KOSTICH, DRAGOS D., *The Land and People of the Balkans.* Lippincott, 1962.

LAMPREY, LOUISE, *Building an Empire.* Stokes, 1941. Well-told account of the building of the British Empire.

Editors of LIFE, *Life's Picture History of World War II.* Time, Inc., 1951. Pictured well and written well.

LODER, DOROTHY, *The Land and People of Belgium,* rev. Lippincott, 1963.

———, *The Land and People of Spain,* rev. Lippincott, 1963.

LOWELL, EDWARD J., *Eve of the French Revolution.* Houghton. France from 1589 to 1789.

LUCAS, MARY SEYMOUR, *Vast Horizons.* Viking, 1943. From the Crusades to the nineteenth century the Europeans went forth to other lands. Excellent maps and other aids for the reader.

MATTINGLY, GARRETT, *The Armada.* Houghton, 1959; also paperback. How England defeated the mighty fleet of Spain and went on to become supreme upon the seas.

MAY, ARTHUR J., *Europe and Two World Wars.* Scribner's, 1947. Period from 1914 to 1946.

MEGARO, GAUDENS, *Mussolini in the Making.* Houghton, 1938. His early career.

MONTGOMERY, ELIZABETH R., *The Story Behind Great Inventions.* Dodd, 1953. Stories of the development of many types of inventions. Biographical sketches of the inventors are included.

MOON, PARKER T., *Imperialism and World Politics.* Macmillan, 1926. Good solid work on this subject.

NANO, FREDERIC C., *The Land and People of Sweden,* rev. Lippincott, 1964.

O'BRIEN, ELINOR, *The Land and People of Ireland.* Lippincott, 1953.

RAYNAL, MAURICE, *The Nineteenth Century: From Goya to Gauguin.* Skira, 1951. Excellent treatment of nineteenth-century painting.

SABATINI, RAFAEL, *Scaramouche.* Various editions. An adventure story during the French Revolution.

SLOSSON, PRESTON, *Europe Since 1815.* Scribner's, 1954. General history of modern Europe.

STREET, ALICIA, *The Land of the English People,* rev. Lippincott, 1963.

TAYLOR, ALAN J. P., *Struggle for Mastery in Europe, 1848-1918.* Oxford U., 1954. Excellent reference work for this period.

TUNIS, EDWIN, *Oars, Sails, Steam.* World, 1952. The development and history of ships throughout the ages. Pen and ink drawings accompany this.

WHITE, THEODORE H., *Fire in the Ashes: Europe in Mid-Century.* Sloane, 1953. An excellent book on postwar Europe and the "Cold War." It requires a wide background of political and economic history.

WINWAR, FRANCES, *The Land of the Italian People,* rev. ed. Lippincott, 1961.

WOHLRABE, RAYMOND A. AND KRUSCH, WERNER, *The Land and People of Austria.* Lippincott, 1956.

———, *The Land and People of Denmark.* Lippincott, 1961.

———, *The Land and People of Germany.* Lippincott, 1957.

———, *The Land and People of Portugal,* rev. Lippincott, 1963.

The creations of European artists are an important part of our cultural heritage. Above, Pieter Brueghel's "Peasant Dance" reflects Flemish customs and costumes of the sixteenth century. (Kunsthistorisches Museum of Vienna)

Gentile Bellini (1429?-1507) painted with tempera as well as with oil colors. His "Procession in St. Mark's Square" shows the cathedral in Venice. (Scala)

El Greco was the foremost Spanish painter of the sixteenth century. His "Assumption of the Virgin" illustrates the popularity of religious themes. (Art Institute of Chicago)

Most famed of the Dutch school of painting was Rembrandt van Rijn, who painted this portrait of himself with his wife Saskia. (Deutsche Fotothek Dresden)

Claude Monet (1840-1926) was one of the greatest painters of the school of French impressionists. At right, Monet's painting of the old St. Lazare railroad station in Paris. (Art Institute of Chicago)

# UNIT V

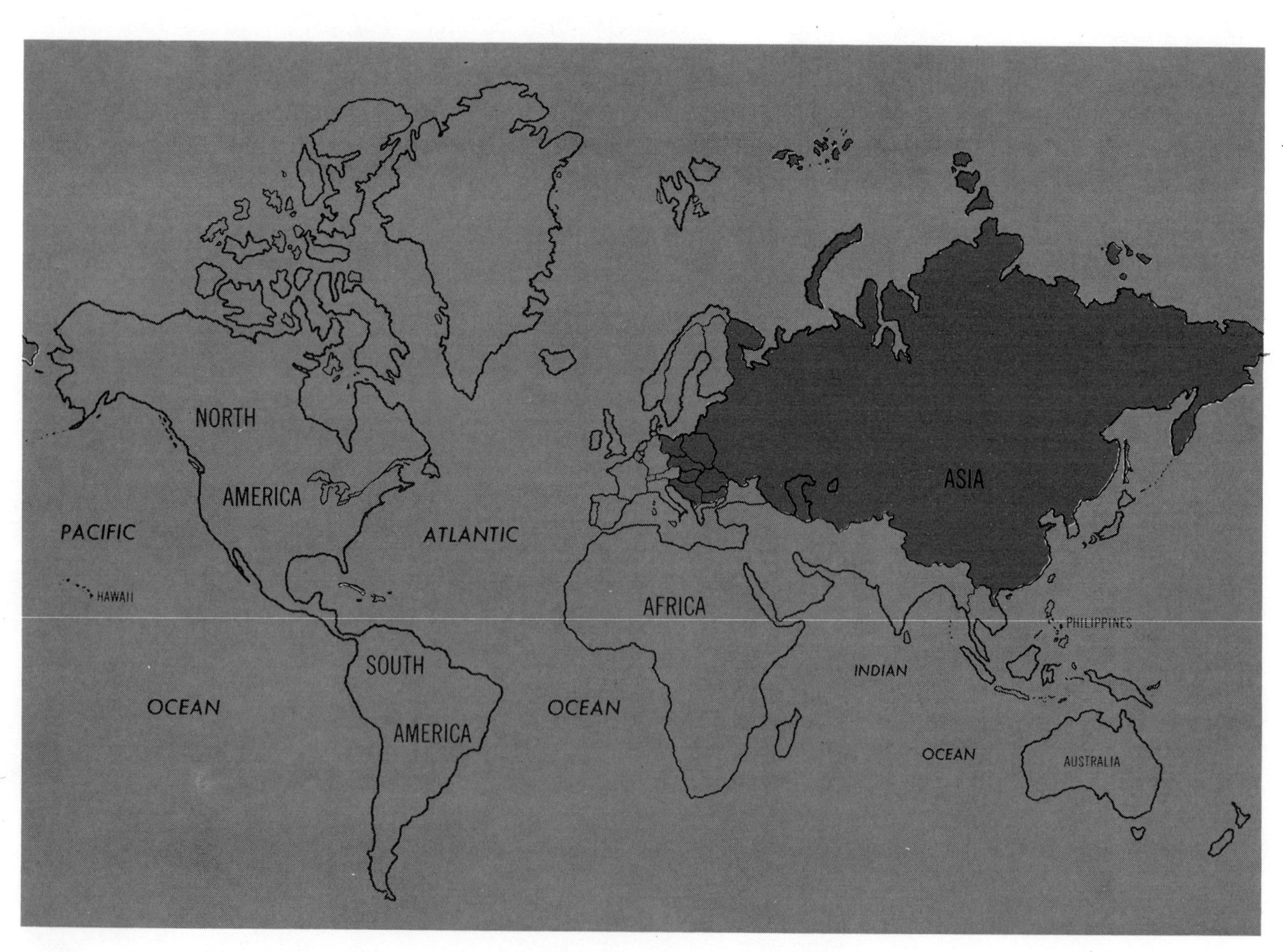

NORTH
AMERICA
PACIFIC
HAWAII
ATLANTIC
AFRICA
ASIA
PHILIPPINES
SOUTH
AMERICA
OCEAN
OCEAN
INDIAN
OCEAN
AUSTRALIA

# THE COMMUNIST WORLD

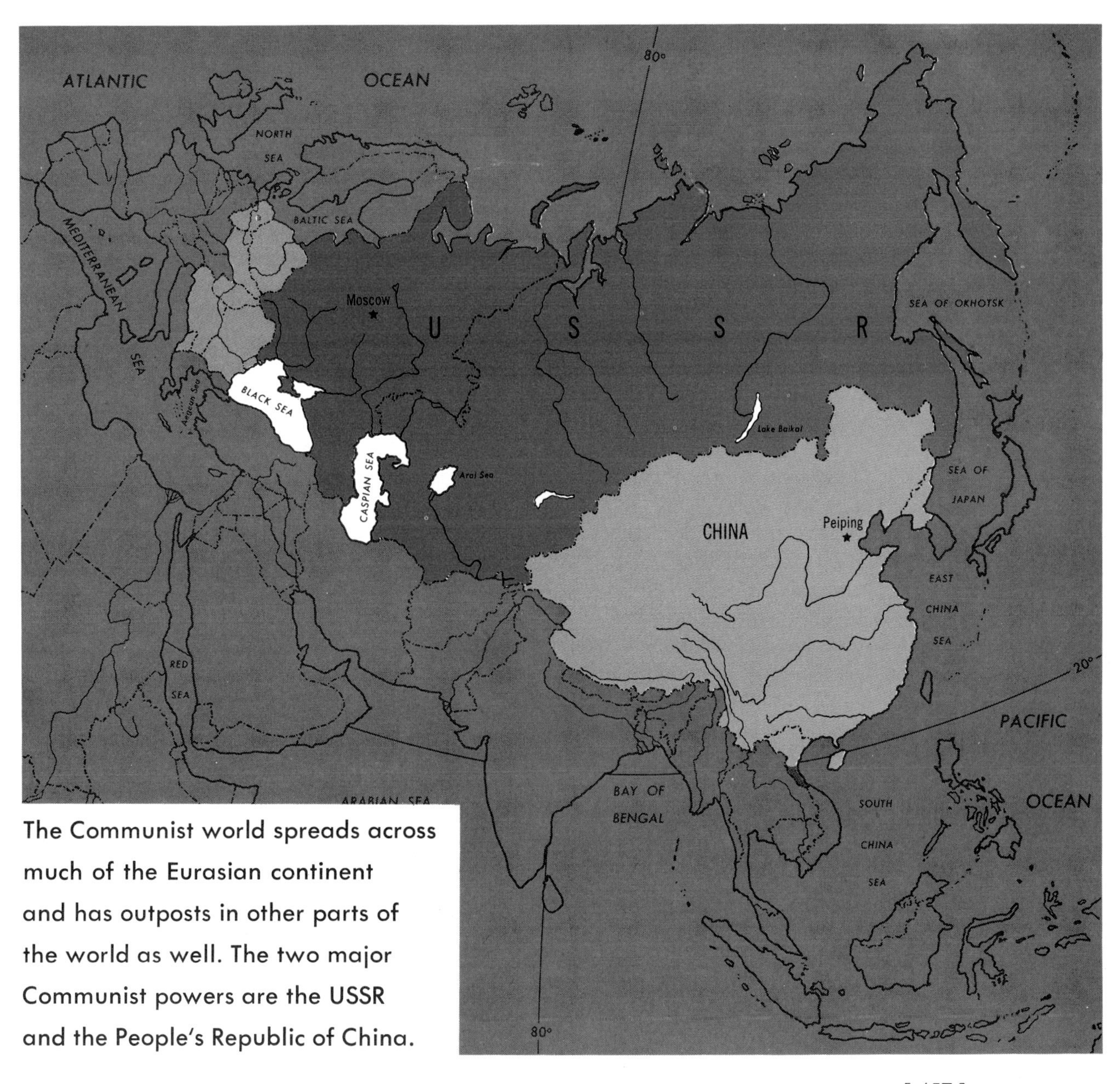


The Communist world spreads across much of the Eurasian continent and has outposts in other parts of the world as well. The two major Communist powers are the USSR and the People's Republic of China.

# CHAPTER 25

# *The Making of the Soviet People*

THE PEOPLE OF THE USSR (Union of Soviet Socialist Republics) belong to many families of man. They are Russian Slavs, Ukrainian Slavs, Byelorussian Slavs, Armenians, Tatars or Mongols, Georgians, Uzbeks, Moldavians, and many others. One has a round face, his eyes wide apart, his cheekbones high; another's face is lean, his eyes dark, his upper lip mustached; some are fair, some dark, and some the softened color of ivory. The Soviet people are a part of the many-colored book of the families of man. In their veins is the blood of the Vikings of Scandinavia, the Turks of Central Asia, the Mongols of the Far East, and possibly the Scythians. But the greatest numbers are descendants of the Slavs.

Some authorities estimate that there are 169 separate nationalities in the USSR, each distinguished from the others by ancient ancestry, language, or customs and traditions. Generally, they live distinct from one another, tied together largely by a common Communist rule. The Communist rulers are mostly Russians, and most Russians are descendants of the Slavs. The Russian people are a mixture of their non-Communist past and their Communist present. Our understanding of them will deepen with a brief probing of their setting in history.

## The Slav

The early Slav was a hunter and farmer of the forests, a fisherman of river and lake, and a trader in furs, wax, and honey. Our earliest knowledge of the Slavic people is from the time when they lived in and around a land known as the Pripet Marshes. These marshes were located near the western borders of Russia in the area now known as Byelorussia. No one knows when the Slavs came here, but there is evidence that they were trading with the Romans as early as the second century A.D. Perhaps around this time, or somewhat later, they began to build towns and to protect them with walls of earth and wood. There were so many of these towns that the Vikings named this the "land of cities." The tribes of Slavs were ruled by local leaders. There was disunity in the land, for these tribes warred among themselves; and greedy-minded neighbors sought the goods of the tribes to increase their own wealth and took the people to be their slaves.

The Slavs were not alone. To the north and northeast of them, farther along in the depths of the forests, were Finnish tribes who were ancestors of the present-day Finns. To the north and northwest were the Vikings of Scandinavia—members of that same family of man who went out from Denmark, Norway, and Sweden and helped to change the map of Western Europe. The Vikings wandered southward to the land of the Slavs, from the Baltic Sea to rule and to trade. To the west were the Poles, another branch of the Slavic family, and also the Lithuanians and the Germans. These people, too, became interested in trade and sometimes in taking territory.

The Russian Slavs felt safest living in the forest. Although they shared these forests with

Modern Russian artists have often painted the activities of working people in the Soviet Union. Above, Arkadi Plastov's painting "Haying" is an example of modern Soviet art. (Sovfoto)

the bear, the lynx, and the wolf, these animals were less dangerous than the man-packs that roamed the plains to the south. The forests of the Slavs were extensive, and they continue to stand today in massed ranks from Norway to the Pacific, roofing the vast land of the USSR. Some authorities estimate that they make up one-fifth of the world's total forests.

To the south of the forests were the flat grasslands, the steppes of the Ukraine. A Russian author has described the unplowed expanses of these grasslands as "measureless waves of wild grass" with a surface "like a gold and green sea." Much of this grassland is plowed today, and from the fertility of its deep-layered black earth the people of the USSR harvest wheat for the bread that is essential to their diet. Once this grassland was the green home of the nomad and his animals, who had wandered here from the poorer lands farther south and from the dryer steppes of the east, which stretched in almost unrelieved flatness to the great wall of China itself. The Soviet Union is a land of flatness broken only by the Urals, which many regard as the eastern border of Europe and the western border of Asia. The Slav looked out from his forests to the southeast and toward the Caspian lowlands with fear. From this direction there were always men, careless of life and eager for spoils, erupting from the vastness of the inhospitable steppes. For centuries the Slav felt the lash of their rule and paid the tribute they exacted. He knew them by the names of Hun, Turk, and Tatar.

### Kiev: First Russian State

Legend has it that the people of Novgorod, near the Gulf of Finland, requested the Vikings to come and rule them. According to this legend, the Vikings established a unified government under a chief named Rurik. This was around the year 862. The Slavs moved eastward and southward to the area where Kiev, the capital of the Republic of the Ukraine, is now located on the Dnieper River. The Vikings followed and about 882 established the first unified Russian state. For seven hundred years thereafter all Russian rulers held themselves to be descendants of Rurik.

The Vikings gradually extended their control southward, eastward, and northward. At the same time their blood mingled with that of the Slavs, who outnumbered them. The Vikings who came to Russia were eventually absorbed into the Slavic family. In the meantime, they traveled with merchandise and slaves down the Dnieper River to the Black Sea, and from there boated to the capital of the Byzantine Empire—Constantinople. Thus the Scandinavian Vikings opened a trading route from the Baltic Sea and the Gulf of Finland to Constantinople via the rivers and lakes of Russia. Through this trade route all of that area was opened to the culture, the crafts, and the knowledge of Asia, the Middle East, and the Mediterranean.

It was, however, the culture and the religion of the Byzantine Empire which most influenced the Slavs, and they became a part of the Eastern Orthodox Church. Their architecture was modeled after the Byzantine, and the Byzantines also gave them the old Roman law and, some believe, the Russian alphabet.

The rulers of the Kiev state became powerful and prosperous, and through marriage they became interconnected with the leading kings and princes of Europe. The daughter of Yaroslav the Wise was married to an English king; and the daughter of King Harold of England was the wife of Vladimir Monomakh, who ruled Kiev from 1113 to 1125. The mother of Vladimir Monomakh was the daughter of a Byzantine emperor. Vladimir's sister was the wife of Henry IV, the Holy Roman Emperor.

Kiev was a city of splendor and of many churches in the twelfth century, and few cities of Western Europe could compare to it. After the death of Yaroslav in 1054 the realm was weakened by disunity among his sons. His grandson, Vladimir Monomakh, consolidated the principality, but after his death war began to drain the Kiev state of its strength. In the 1200's when the Tatars, under the leadership first of Genghis, then of Batu Khan, swept into Russia, there were none strong enough to withstand their onslaught.

### The Tatar or Mongol

Deep in the fastness of the eastern steppes, in 1162, there was born among the wandering Mongols or Tatars the greatest of their leaders—Genghis Khan. He was a man of his own time and environment in ruthlessness, cruelty, and endurance. But he was a man of all times in his genius for war, in his sense of organization, and in his ability to choose the right man for the work he wanted done. With daring, with dash, and with discipline, Genghis gradually brought the teeming, warring tribes of the steppes from China to Russia under unified rule. This was a heroic accomplishment, for the people of the steppes were fiercely independent and loath to acknowledge any leader who did not prove himself their master. They did not take easily to discipline and unity, but under the iron command of Genghis Khan the roving men of the steppes became followers always ready to carry out the will of their master.

Peace came to the lawless steppes. Caravans traveled in increasing numbers across its unfolding distances—it is about 5400 miles from the western to the eastern borders of the steppes within Russia today. Daily the messengers of the Khan traveled from far and near bringing information and taking orders to his officials. The Khan spared cities when they submitted and accepted his rule without revolt; but if the cities rebelled, he spared no one, man, woman, or child, unless perhaps they were useful or beautiful. His successive victories, his terrible revenges, and his awesome might spread fear far and wide.

Genghis Khan penetrated even into the territories of the Western Europeans, and he encouraged the thought there that he was the scourge of God. The mention of the name Tatar or Mongol was enough to make women and children hysterical and to paralyze the arm of the warrior. This was the psychological weapon of Mongol success in battle.

Another reason for the Khan's success was the careful preparation he made in scouting out the weaknesses and the strength of his opponent. Before striking at the West, Genghis Khan commissioned his eldest son, Juji, to scout western Russia and its neighborhood in detail. Around 1221-1222, while Juji's force was encamped in the southern part of the Ukraine, the Russians went forth to battle the Tatars. The Tatars did not seek this fight, for they were primarily concerned with obtaining information about Europe, and they were outnumbered. But when their envoys were killed, and their advance guard was attacked, they fought back. The Russian force was practically annihilated, and the Tatars ate their victory banquet on heaped stacks of Russian bodies.

After this battle the Tatars left Russia, and it was not until 1237 that they returned under the leadership of Batu the son of Juji. The army he led came to be called "the Golden Horde," so named because of the splendor of the tent in which Batu lived. Starting in 1237 and continuing for about six years, the Tatars under Batu conquered Russia, Poland, Hungary, Serbia, and Bulgaria. The Tatar conquerors made the land desolate—a wilderness of burned cities, a litter of skulls and bones, a cemetery for the homeless and the orphan. Batu found the land relatively prosperous and populous. He left it bleak and lonely.

The Tatars soon discovered, however, that the dead and those chained by poverty pay little tribute. They began to encourage trade, discourage lawlessness, and promote the growth of cities. Their capital of Sarai was located on the lower reaches of the Volga River. In this city the Tatars received tribute,

Ulan Bator, capital of Outer Mongolia, has a number of modern buildings but few autos. The descendants of the Tatars live mainly in this republic of the USSR. (Wide World photo)

issued orders, and ruled with a firmness demanded by the diversity and the vastness of the land they controlled. But they were also tolerant. The religion of the Russians was protected, and the Russian way of life was left undisturbed so long as the Tatars received tribute and obedience.

This was the time of the Renaissance farther west in Europe, but the currents of change were kept from Russia by the walls of Tatar arms. The development of a modern state and modern society in Russia had to wait until some centuries later.

The Tatars governed Russia until 1480, when Ivan III, the Grand Duke of Moscow (who is remembered as Ivan the Great) refused to pay tribute any longer. The rulers of Moscow, with patience and cunning, had gradually grown strong enough to overthrow their Tatar rulers, and they became the governors of a great piece of western Russia.

The Tatars did not disappear abruptly, however, from the Russian scene, and remnants of their rule lingered at Kazan on the middle Volga, at the mouth of the Volga, and in the Crimean peninsula on the Black Sea. The Tatars were also forced out of China and areas of the Middle East which they had conquered. They began once again their undisciplined wandering of the steppes. Some of them became Buddhists, and the loving commands of this religion transformed many into men to whom violence was unthinkable and murder undreamed.

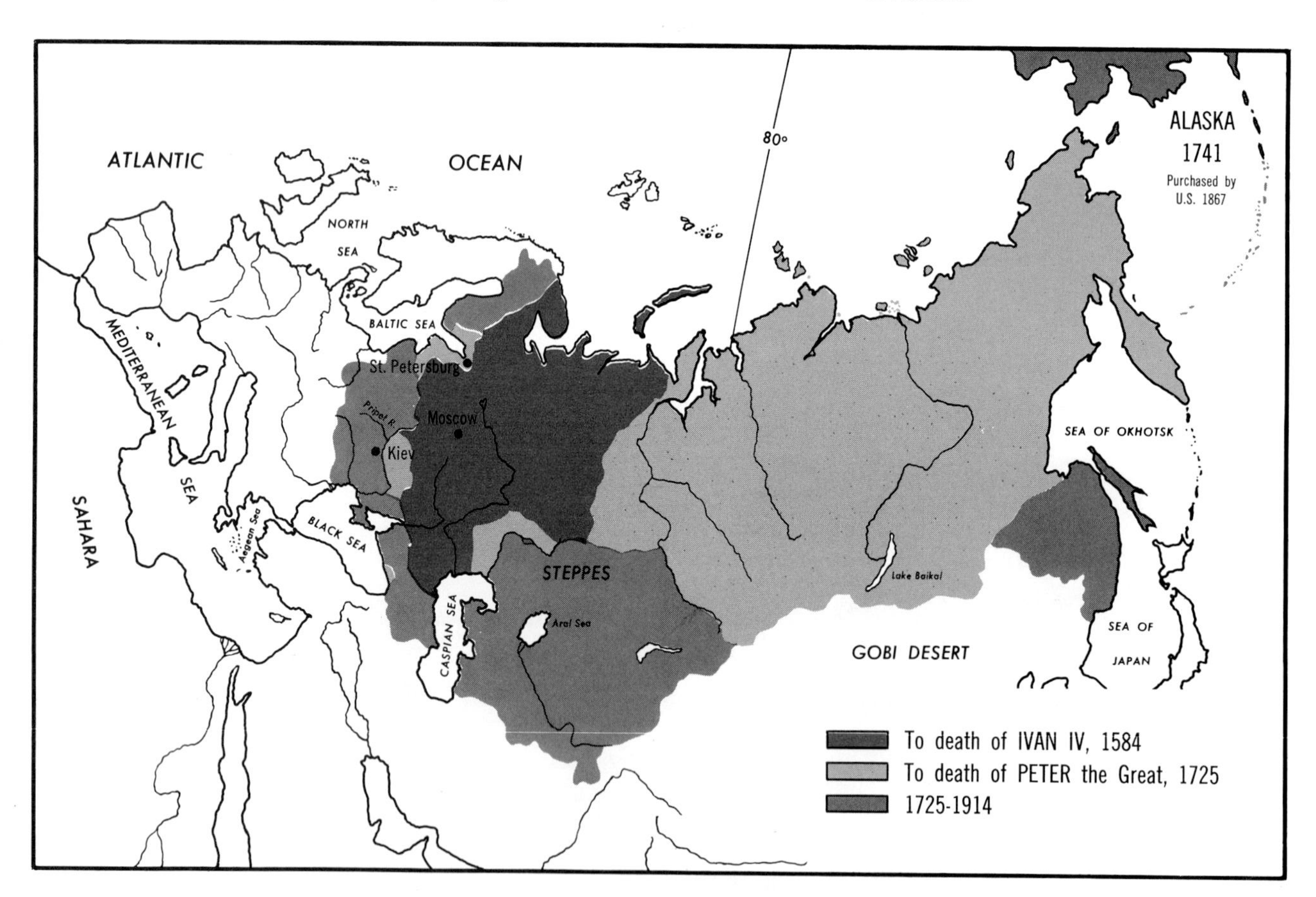


**THE EXPANSION OF RUSSIA FROM 1584 TO 1914**

In which direction was Russian expansion greatest? Why was expansion toward the West difficult? How did Peter the Great obtain his "window on the West"?

The Tatars live today mainly in a republic of the Soviet Union commonly called Outer Mongolia. Some of them live farther south in an area known as Inner Mongolia, which is dominated by China, while still others live in the Crimea and on the lower Volga.

1. What was the earliest Russian state?
2. Describe the physical geography and climate of the USSR.
3. Why was Genghis Khan successful in his conquests?
4. How long did the Tatars govern Russia? What led to their eventual overthrow?

### Moscow: The Age of the Tsar

Moscow, the present capital of the Soviet Union, was an unimportant place deep in the forest during the early days of Russian history. While the Tatar ruled, shrewd, scheming princes made it into an important center of Russian political life. Through marriage, mortgage, inheritance, and other means the princes of Moscow enlarged their landholdings and their power. They strengthened this power by obtaining the exclusive right to collect tribute due the Tatar from the other independent and semi-independent Russian principalities. Thus the eyes of the Russians were turned upon Moscow as the center of native power. The Moscow princes kept their land intact by not dividing it among all sons, as was the customary practice. Instead, they bequeathed it to the senior son of the family. Finally, under the leadership of Ivan the Great, the Tatars were overthrown. This was in 1480, and this date begins the age of the tsar in Russia.

Ivan the Great (1440-1505) married Zoë, the niece of the last Byzantine emperor. He thus laid claim for the Russian tsars to the rights and the personal power of the Byzantine emperor. Ivan surrounded himself with Byzantine ceremony. Etiquette, protocol, and precedence or rank became extremely important in obtaining office and in conducting oneself in Russian society. This formal correctness is still a part of the Russian's behavior and attitude, and ritual is yet an essential aspect of the Russian Church.

The church of St. Basil the Beatified was built in Moscow about 1560. It is an example of later Byzantine architecture. (Dr. T. D. Jones from Charles Phelps Cushing)

Ivan imitated the Byzantine emperor by building a palace apart from his subjects. He took the Byzantine double eagle as his seal and assumed the Byzantine title of *autocrat*, symbolizing the supremacy of his power. He was also called *tsar*, the Russian word for *caesar* or "emperor." He also asserted the divinity of God behind his rule. The present leaders of Russia also assert the rightness and the supremacy of their rule but they do not claim to rule by divine right. Ivan centralized the government of Russia, and this centralization has continued from his day to this.

The tsars were supported by the Church, which was a great and growing force in Russia. Formerly, the Russian Church had looked

The walled fortress of the Kremlin is over 450 years old. The palaces of the Kremlin once housed the tsars of Russia and now contain offices of the Soviet government. (Wide World photo)

to Constantinople for guidance and leadership, much as the Roman Catholics of Europe looked to Rome. But Constantinople had fallen to the Turk, and the leaders of the Russian Church found it necessary to establish their own center in Moscow. A close alliance knitted the tsar and the Church together, and this closeness continued until about the time of Peter the Great in the eighteenth century.

Ivan IV (1533-1584) known in English as "the Terrible," continued the concentration of power in the hands of the tsar. He broke the power of the old nobles, who threatened his purpose, and a new class of military-service landholders arose. These landholders owed their estates to the tsar in return for their service to him in time of need. Gradually, under Ivan the Terrible and other tsars, all hereditary estates became service estates, closely controlled by the tsar.

Ivan expanded the Russian borders. He drove the Tatars from Kazan on the middle Volga and brought the territory along the Volga to the Caspian Sea under Russian rule. He thus opened for the Russians the way to Siberia and the steppes all the way to the Pacific Ocean. He tried to open a door on the Baltic Sea for Russia but was prevented by the stiff opposition of the Poles and the Swedes.

From boyhood, Ivan had found himself surrounded with intrigue and attempts at assassination. Gradually, he became convinced that there was no one he could trust. He began to strike out at those around him and to punish offenders with severity and without restraint. The slightest suspicion that someone was disloyal often resulted in the extermination of the person's entire family. Ivan's black-clothed policemen roamed the countryside with power to punish those who were suspected of treason. They used their power with such cruelty that whole villages were emptied when townsmen and peasants fled to escape the persecution of Ivan's police. There was misery in the land. Ivan capped some of the extremes of his rule by striking his eldest son in anger, a blow which resulted in his son's death. Despite these faults, there are many historians today who regard Ivan's long-term good for Russia as being greater than his evil. They question whether he was any more terrible than William the Conqueror of England or others faced with the plottings and disloyalty of powerfully entrenched nobles.

Ivan was succeeded by his second son, Theodore I. Under the influence of his brother-in-law, Boris Godunov, Theodore made it more difficult for the peasant to leave the land he tilled. Before the time of Theodore, peasants contracted with landlords to work on the land and to pay so much in produce after each harvest. But the peasant always had the right of departure from the land if he so desired. From the time of Theodore onward, however, it became more and more difficult for peasants to leave the land they farmed. Eventually, in 1649, they were bound to the soil as serfs.

The peasants did not escape from this

bondage until 1861 when serfdom was abolished. In this respect Russia was several centuries behind the countries of Western Europe, which had freed themselves from serfdom some centuries earlier. It is interesting to note, however that in the United States the institution of slavery had not yet ended at this time.

Theodore had no heir, and from about 1604 until 1613 civil war and an invasion by the Poles, who occupied Moscow for a time, kept Russia in turmoil. This period is referred to as the "Time of Troubles." Then, in 1613, a man named Michael Romanov was chosen tsar. This Romanov dynasty continued to rule Russia until the last tsar abdicated in 1917. He was killed by the Communists in 1918. Under the Romanovs, Russian society and government took a rigid form, and few dared to act on their own initiative without an order from the superior above them in the hierarchy. This attitude also characterizes many Communist officials, who carefully keep to the paths charted by their superiors without the slightest change from the plotted course. Most Western Europeans and Americans are often inclined to act on their own, when they feel it is advantageous, and to seek permission afterwards.

## The Cossacks

During the sixteenth and seventeenth centuries the Russians swelled their land space. The Ukraine was a frontier land after the fall of Kiev, and it was occupied by Tatar, Turk, and Pole at various times. Each sought to milk the Ukraine of its resources. Under these trying circumstances, the Ukrainians became independent-minded and self-reliant. Their life was in contrast to the servitude which bound the life of the peasant elsewhere in settled Russia. They were called Cossacks, "free adventurers," and their numbers were constantly reinforced by the discontented, the rebellious, and offenders who fled the law from elsewhere in Russia. The Cossacks were, in spirit and in action, very close to the scouts, the trappers, and the frontiersmen who opened and defended the western lands of the United States.

In 1648 they drove the Poles from most of the Ukraine, and a few years later they offered to unite with Moscow. Gradually the leading Ukrainian Cossacks became a part of the noble class, while the poorer ones became the trusted agents of the tsar in quelling revolts within the country. There were different Cossack groups along the Don River, the Ural River, and the Terek River and in other places where the land was open and the environment a challenge. They, too, were daring and fearless warriors, and their deeds shine in the pages of Russian history. It was a Cossack leader, Yermak, who led a small band of Cossacks across the Ural mountains in 1581 and fought and schemed his way over the broad expanse of Siberia.

## Siberia

Siberia is a land of long, cold winters and short summers, as is much of the Soviet Union. Most of the USSR lies in a northerly latitude, and the roar of icy winds and the silence of falling snow are familiar, chilly companions of the people. The season for growing food is short, and farmers work furiously during this brief period to plant and harvest their crops before they are forced to retire from the cold to their small homes and the warmth of their wood-burning stoves. For many people of the USSR, the fur coat and hat and felt boots are necessary for survival during the rigors of winter. It was primarily the riches of fur in Siberia which first drew the Russian to this vast land.

Siberia is a land of diversity. In the far north there is an Arctic wasteland where the Eskimo lives. Farther south, fur-bearing animals roam its great spread of forest. South of the forest are the steppes and grasslands which have been trampled for centuries by wandering herds of animals and men. Still farther south lies earth which can be tilled to produce grain and vegetables. Rivers—the Ob, the Yenisei, the Lena—cross its vastness and run for thousands of miles northward to the

Arctic, while the Amur meanders thousands of miles eastward to the Pacific. There are lakes, and one, Lake Baikal, is believed to be the deepest fresh-water lake in the world. There are tremendous known mineral resources in this land, and much yet to be discovered. Into this rich and varied land the Russian went, and the USSR continues to pour its wealth of manpower into Siberia today.

Once the Russians had possession of Siberia, they used it for various purposes. It was a fine source of lumber, and wood is still the common material for building there today. Wood is even used to surface roads. Siberia was a place of refuge for peasants who sought to escape the severity of their lives under brutal landlords, and it was also a secure prison for criminals and political enemies of the tsars. Under the Communist leader Stalin it became a slave-labor camp for millions. The present regime is making an intensive effort to explore and exploit its resources. Animals and men still roam the unfenced plains of Siberia, but farms, towns, and cities are multiplying on its flat earth. Siberia is now feeling the bustle of men and machines as industrialization grows there.

1. How did the princes of Moscow keep their land intact?
2. How did the tsars acquire the authority of Byzantium?
3. Describe the character of Ivan the Terrible.
4. Who were the Cossacks?

## Peter the Great

During the period when Russia was ruled by tsars, there was none more colorful, more gargantuan in his appetites, more overflowing in his energy, more strange and fascinating in character than Peter the Great. He ruled Russia from 1689 to 1725. Like some of the other tsars, he had periods of danger and difficulty during his childhood and teens, for there were those who sought his throne.

Peter grew up in the countryside just outside Moscow, and he grew into a giant of a man, six feet six inches in height. He had a passion for the practical and the useful, and he had the knack of giving his full attention to whatever he was learning or doing at the moment. He loved to tinker and work with his hands, and this fondness for manual work never left him, even after he became tsar. While still a young man, he came to know the foreign quarter of Moscow, where he developed an interest in Western technology which never deserted him. He was not possessed by a need to keep himself apart from foreigners, and he did not have the suspicion of them which marked many Russian rulers before and after him.

Under the tsars who preceded Peter, foreigners were often kept isolated from the Russians. If an unauthorized Russian was seen conversing or visiting with a foreigner, he was suspect. Marriage between Russians and foreigners was discouraged. One Danish ambassador managed to meet a Russian woman, and eventually they were married, but the wife was not allowed to leave the country. The Russians were anxious to know the foreigner and his works, but they also bore a certain distrust of him and kept him segregated as though he carried a dangerous contagion. The foreigner met only the trusted few in the Russian hierarchy. Even the food and the supplies he needed to sustain himself in Russia were supplied only by authorized Russian officials. Many foreigners who have lived in Communist Russia have also experienced this official suspicion and distrust, and their meetings with Russian citizens have been restricted. This attitude is not recent in Russian history; it is a part of an old heritage.

Peter the Great was different. He did not fear the foreigner; he was attracted. He was so pulled toward the modern developments in Western Europe that he made a grand tour there in 1697 and 1698. He did not travel with ceremony, in the grand manner of kings, but as a worker and a learner. He worked as a laborer in the shipyards of Holland and England and studied with enthusiasm the technical advances of the European. He did not seek to penetrate the reasons behind the technology, nor the bases of the developing social, economic, and political ways of Western Europe. He did not dream of curtailing his personal power nor of giving political power to the Russian people, but he did want the new knowledge that might advance Russia in power and in greatness. He was an autocratic patriot.

Peter was impulsive, and when he returned from Europe, he seemed determined to modernize Russia within his own lifetime. He dramatized his will for rapid change by shortening the traditional long Russian coat to the more modern knee-length one. Anyone found wearing the long coat was forced to kneel where he was and have it cut off at the knee. Beards were sacred to the Russian, but Peter insisted that they be cut off. Anyone caught by him or his guards wearing a beard had it immediately removed with scissors or razor. Selected men were sent to the West to learn about ships and navigation.

Peter wanted a coast and a port, but to get them he was forced to fight the Swedes. His army was beaten badly in its first encounter with the Swedish army under the command of Charles XII. He later managed, however, to secure a part of the Baltic seacoast to the north at the mouth of the Neva. In this barren land of swamp, marsh, and fog, he built his new capital, St. Petersburg. Thousands died that a city might rise in this damp, disease-ridden land, but Peter was determined to have his "window on the West," and his will prevailed. St. Petersburg became a European-Russian city, where Western customs, thought, and achievements merged with those of Russia. The old city of St. Petersburg is now called Leningrad, and Moscow is today the capital of the Soviet Union. Leningrad, however, is still an important symbol and historical landmark for the modern Russian.

Peter made changes in many phases of Russian life. He modernized the army and built the first Russian navy. He opened up the Baltic Sea to Russia, advanced trade and industry, surveyed the country's natural resources, and tried to better agricultural production. He made it possible for the humble to rise in his bureaucracy through merit, opened

Peter the Great (1672-1725) was one of the greatest of the tsars of Russia. He introduced Western civilization to his country and made Russia a major power in Europe. (Charles Phelps Cushing)

schools for the children of the nobility, and generally encouraged learning. Peter insisted that every landowner must be registered and must pay his required service to the state.

Under Peter's rule, able outsiders were brought into the ranks of the nobility, and all were made dependent upon the tsar. Western European forms of administration were copied, and ministries were placed under committees called "colleges." When the Patriarch of the Russian Church died, Peter imposed the same committee system on the Church. He did not want the people to think that any one person, even the spiritual leader of the Russians, ranked near or next to the tsar in power. He bound the serf more tightly to the soil by his policies, took a census of his people, and imposed a poll or "head" tax on every "soul" in Russia.

There is little about this giant of a man that can be called common. Giant passions and urges drove him in many directions and often warred within him. He might labor at the lathe in the early hours of the morning, attend to affairs of administration and reform all day, and convene fantastic drinking bouts at night. He was a skilled shipbuilder, blacksmith, printer, carpenter, and shoemaker. (A pair of boots he made for himself is still preserved.) Conqueror, patriot, great lover and great hater—Peter the Great was all of these. Suspicious of treason, he killed his eldest son and heir by torture, and lived on to weep bitterly for his deed. Outsiders have called him mad. The Russians say he cannot be judged by the minds of ordinary men. He was not ordinary.

After Peter the Great, Western influences, knowledge, and customs—especially French customs—flowed in upon the Russian, slowly changed his thought, and pushed him into closer contact with the Western European. Russia became important to Western Europe and loomed large in the political affairs and schemes of European statesmen. At times the Russian ruler was a person of foreign extraction. The most noted one was a German princess called Catherine.

### Catherine the Great

One of Russia's most successful rulers was Catherine II (the Great) who ruled from 1762 to 1796. She was the daughter of a German prince and became the ruler of Russia on the death of her husband, Peter III. Although a German, she tried hard to make herself over into a Russian. She was an astute politician and led Russia in conquests that increased both its land and power.

Catherine warred with the Turks, and took from them the northern coasts of the Black Sea which they had long controlled. She schemed with Maria Theresa of Austria and Frederick the Great of Prussia to erase Poland from the map. On several occasions Russia, Austria, and Prussia robbed Poland of its land and divided the spoils among themselves. Under Catherine's leadership, Russia fought to gain land and retain power in Finland. Her grandson, Alexander I, took all of Finland from Sweden in 1808-1809.

Catherine was aware of the currents of reform then moving in Western Europe, and she welcomed foreigners and their ideas to Russia. She brought French culture to Russia, improved education of the nobles, and introduced vaccination against smallpox. But, like her predecessors, she was an autocrat who did not wish her political power challenged. After a frightening revolt of Cossacks and serfs in 1773, she reorganized local government but continued to subject her people to strong central control. The small reforms that Catherine attempted did not reach down to the majority of her subjects, the serfs. The nobles, the landlords, and the intellectuals advanced, but the peasants remained in their slavery.

### Other Rulers

As the nineteenth century crawled toward the twentieth, ideas that were strange, but often attractive, continued to pour into Russia from Western Europe. There began a long conflict between the traditional and the new. Nicholas I, who began his reign in 1825, carried on the dictatorial tradition of the tsar and tried to keep the radicalism of Western Europe from Russia with censorship and police. Other tsars followed his example. Although Alexander II (1855-1881) freed the serfs in 1861, most of his reforming ideas stayed in the dreaming stage. The last tsar, Nicholas II, who ruled from 1894 to 1917, tried also to stem these dangerous and alien ideas. But, like all the others, he failed, for there were those ready to go into exile, to prison, and to death so that their ideas might live. The tsars during the nineteenth and twentieth centuries could not crush the fires of discontent which were burning both secretly and openly in Russia. These fires burst into a devouring flame in 1917; the tsar and his family were killed the next year. The Communists took over the leadership of the Russians.

1. What were the most important accomplishments of Peter the Great?
2. Why was it so important for the Russians to have a Baltic port?
3. How successful were the reforms brought about by the great Russian tsars?

## Conclusion

The Russian of today is a part of his past, just as all men are. Into his making have gone his forests, his rivers, his sweep of steppes, the harsh governor, and the harsh invader. He has long known an uncertainty of life from inside and outside his borders. The ruler was never sure how long he would rule; the peasant never knew how long he could endure. There was within all Russians a great appetite for life which only the few could satisfy. The stretching land gave to some a release from the slavery of a small patch of earth. Those who explored its vastness bequeathed to modern Russia one-sixth of the world's land surface.

The Russian did not progress into the modern world at the same rate of speed as his fellow Europeans in the West, for the tsars generally distrusted challenges to tradition. But there were those who were willing to sacrifice much that reforms might come to Russia, and in 1917 their will to change proved stronger than the tsar's will to conserve. It was then that the Communists assumed control of the destiny of the Russian and the other nationalities that make up the Soviet Union.

## SUMMING UP THE CHAPTER

A. Locate the following places on a map and tell why they are important.

| | |
|---|---|
| Baltic Sea | Moscow |
| Byelorussia | Novgorod |
| Dnieper River | Siberia |
| Kiev | St. Petersburg |
| Lake Baikal | Ukraine |

B. Identify the following and tell why they are important.

| | |
|---|---|
| Batu Khan | Nicholas I |
| Boris Godunov | Peter the Great |
| Catherine the Great | Theodore I |
| Ivan III | Vladimir Monomakh |
| Ivan IV | Yaroslav the Wise |
| Juji Khan | Zoë |
| Michael Romanov | |

C. Define or explain the following terms, relating them to this chapter.

| | |
|---|---|
| autocrat | Slav |
| colleges | Time of Troubles |
| Cossacks | tsar |
| Golden Horde | window on the West |
| Russ | |

D. Identify these dates and indicate their importance.

| | |
|---|---|
| 882 | 1689-1725 |
| 1162 | 1762-1796 |
| 1480 | 1825 |
| 1604-1613 | 1894-1917 |
| 1613-1917 | |

E. Chapter review questions.

1. Describe the major groups of peoples of the USSR today.
2. How does the variety of cultural groups in the USSR compare with that of the United States?
3. Who were the earliest known peoples of Russia?
4. Where is Kiev located? Why do you suppose it was the first site of a Russian state?
5. What was the medium of first contact between Russia and the rest of the world?
6. Who conquered the steppes of Asia? When did this occur?
7. When was European Russia brought under Tatar control? By whom? How?
8. How long did the Tatar rule last?
9. Describe the climate, land features, and natural resources of Siberia. How has Siberia been developed, and what has been its role in recent years?
10. What were the reasons for Peter the Great's interest in Western technology?
11. Why did not the reforms of the great Russian tsars reach below the nobility and aid the peasants?

F. Questions for discussion.

1. What was the primary cultural influence on Kiev, and through Kiev on all Russia? What were some of the most important results of that influence?
2. What is meant when it is said that under the tsars Moscow became the "Third Rome"? Is this idea still present in Russian thought? In what form?
3. What would you say is the proper historical judgment of Ivan the Terrible?

G. Projects for groups or individuals.

1. Trace the derivation of the term *autocrat.*
2. Read a biography of either Peter the Great or Catherine the Great, and report on it in class.

CHAPTER **26**

# *Conflicting Ideologies*

THE RUSSIAN PEOPLE have for long been Christians. Christianity was brought to Russia during the late 980's when Vladimir I ruled at Kiev. (He was the great-grandfather of Vladimir Monomakh, who was mentioned in Chapter 25.) Vladimir wanted his people to follow some religion, but he was unable to choose between the Moslem, Jewish, and Christian faiths. At last, he gathered a group of his wise men and sent them on a journey to find the best religion for the Russian people. They examined the Roman Catholic, the Jewish, and Moslem faiths and were not impressed. Then they looked into the Eastern Orthodox religion, which was centered in Constantinople, and they were overwhelmed by the ritual, the sincerity of worship, and the magnificence of the church of the Byzantine. Returning to Vladimir they spoke of their experience in the glorious church of Saint Sophia, describing the beauty and spiritual elevation they had sensed there.

Their description was enough for Vladimir. He and his nobles were baptized, and at his command thousands upon thousands of his subjects walked into the Dnieper River and were baptized by its waters. The Dnieper might be called "The River of Baptisms." From that time on, the Russian people gave their devotion and their loyalty to the Eastern Orthodox faith.

## The Russians and the Orthodox Church

The life of the Russians was vastly changed by the Orthodox Church. Morals, family and national attitudes, laws, language, literature, and art were all shaped and colored by the conversion of the Russians to the Orthodox Church. The Byzantine influence is yet evident today in the richness of the interiors and in the onion-shaped domes which crown Russian churches. The icon, the religious image originated by the Byzantine, was made into glorious forms which were Byzantine and Russian at the same time.

Many modern Russians argue that the conversion to the Orthodox Church held back the development of Russian intellectual questing. Some critics, both foreign and Russian, declare that by becoming a part of the Orthodox Church the Russians were cut off from the political, economic, scientific, and industrial revolutions of Western Europe. They argue that this separation delayed by centuries the evolution of the Russians into a modern people. Others deny this sweeping assertion. They state that the conversion brought hope, love, and civilization, and that it was a strong and vital force in molding the Russian character. There is no question that, from the time of Vladimir, the Church became closely intertwined with Russian society.

The clergy grew into a new and powerful class in Russia, and their influence was felt from the top to the bottom of Russian society. Slowly monasteries grew up throughout the land and became centers of culture and education. This network of monasteries brought religion to all of Russia. The monks became owners of much land, and as their wealth increased they became more closely tied to the tsar and the nobles. This had a corrupting influence on the Church, which became a partner of the tsar. Finally Peter the Great abolished the position of the single patriarch and established a synod, or group, to govern the Church. Thus the clergy became even more closely bound to the tsar and his rule.

The photograph above shows buildings destroyed during the Russian Revolution. (Wide World photo)

The painting at right depicts soldiers of the tsarist government firing on the peaceful workers who marched before the Winter Palace in St. Petersburg, January 22, 1905. (Wide World photo)

From 1721 to 1917, the clergy were often regarded as agents of the state. Their wealth and their close ties to the tsar and his system of rule condemned them in the eyes of the revolutionists who took over Russia in 1917. The Church is still regarded with suspicion by the present rulers of the Soviet Union.

The parish priest, however, was generally very close to the peasant. He was himself a peasant, often uneducated, and he worked in the fields like a peasant. The Russian priest was distinguished by his ordination and his training, but in all else he was of the people. Unlike the priests of the Roman Catholic Church, the Orthodox priests were allowed to marry. The Orthodox priests lived closely among their people. It was not uncommon to see a priest amongst the rebellious people when they arose to combat the unbearable rule of the landlord and the noble. There were saintly ones also among the monks and the priests, and the Russian Church has its list of saints and holy men and women.

The Russian Orthodox Church did not grow and develop, however, without rifts and open conflict. When Nikon became Patriarch of Moscow in 1652, he instituted some changes in the liturgy and service of the Church. There were those among the clergy and their followers who resisted change in their ritual and tradition with an unbelievable firmness. These dissenters were persecuted horribly by both Church and secular authorities. Thousands of them were tortured and killed. The dissenters came to be called "Old Believers." They considered it their mission to preserve the old and traditional form of the Russian Church. They split into various small groups, some of which live on in Russia and in other parts of the world.

There were a few Roman Catholics in Russia, and after its birth Protestantism came to Russia and influenced the minds of some. Most of these Protestants today are Baptists —estimated at around three million—but they still have some of the subtle characteristics of the Orthodox. When the Communists became the rulers of Russia, the clergy and the openly religious had a difficult time.

**Communism and the Church.** The Communists, by reason of their philosophy, believe the basic assumption of religion to be false. They disliked the Russian clergy and hated the Church because it had been tied with the reactionary regime which they had helped to overthrow. The Communists nationalized Church property, seized Church valuables, forbade priests to teach and conduct schools, sent many into exile, and imprisoned many, including the Patriarch Tikhon. Churches were made over into museums or taxed so heavily that many closed.

To the Communists, the clergy were enemies of the state, dangerous men who might attempt to overthrow Communism in Russia. Under Stalin, the Communist leader from the late 1920's until 1953, the persecution continued. Many of the clergy were killed and others exiled. For a time the children of priests could not obtain a higher education, nor could any child under eighteen be taught religion except in the privacy of the home and in groups of not more than three. Only the man who cared little for his career and his life dared to practice his religion openly during these times.

When the Second World War broke out, relations with the Church improved because all the forces in Russia had to be mobilized to defeat the strong German enemy. Since that time the persecution of the clergy and the religious man has eased considerably. But there is still a profound difference between the teachings of the Church and the dogmas of the Communists. The man in Russia to whom religion is a faith works under a handicap. It is the rare religious man who succeeds in climbing to the top of his profession. The official philosophy of the USSR does not admit a God, and the Communists unceasingly attempt through propaganda and force to erase from the minds and hearts of the people a belief in what they call the "mythical Christ."

It is never an easy task, however, to remove religion and God from the minds of men who have long believed. There are many millions of Russians who still believe and practice their cherished religion. Even the children of party members are baptized and taught the old beliefs in their homes. Many who profess to be Communists still want a cross on their graves after death, and some Communists still remember the feast days and sometimes attend church. Bibles are read, prayers are said, icons are kissed, and God is yet worshiped in Russia. Thorough as they are, the Communists have not succeeded in tearing religion from the people they rule.

1. When did Russia first become Christianized?
2. What happened to the Russian churches and clergy when the Communists took over?
3. How successful have the Communists been in destroying the religious faith of the Russian people?

## Communism and the Soviet People

A number of citizens of the USSR believe in the doctrine called Communism, and they have organized themselves into a party through which they rule. Adult members of the Communist party comprise only about four per cent of the population, but if the Communist youth and other organizations sympathetic to their cause are added to their number, the percentage is significantly increased. The Communist party is an elite group, however, and is strongly entrenched at the top of political, economic, social, and cultural life. There is no phase of society which is not directed and influenced by the beliefs and purposes of Communism. To understand the Soviet people today, it is necessary to understand something about the deep conviction which moves the Communist to act in his own special way.

### The Coming of Communism

Despite the censorship and secret police of the tsar during the nineteenth and early twentieth centuries, modern ideas from Western Europe circulated among the Russians and found followers there. These ideas spoke of the rights of man, the right to a better earthly life, the right to share in government, and the right to be released from fear and oppression. The Russians were receptive to these ideas, for they had been long repressed and oppressed.

There were volcanoes of discontent throughout the countryside. In their anger and despair, the peasants burned and pillaged the possessions of their noble lords and fled, carrying their tools for tilling the soil. There were volcanoes of discontent in the cities. During the late nineteenth century, some industrial development had started in Russia: mines were dug, railroads built, factories multiplied, and cities grew as Russians from the rural parts swarmed to the cities to man the machines. But the workers met misery in the cities, for wages were low, housing was only slums, and conditions of work were nearly unbearable. Among the industrial workers, too, there flamed the dangerous fires of dissatisfaction. Moving among them, fanning the fires of their discontent and organizing them, were the more literate revolutionaries who were dedicated to reform and determined to change the Russian system by violence if necessary.

**Nicholas II.** The last tsar, Nicholas II, was not a particularly bright despot. He relied upon the traditional means of the gun, the prison, exile, and police to stem the rush for change. When, in 1905, the industrial workers of St. Petersburg marched in a peaceful procession to his Winter Palace to request some relief from their pitiful conditions, his guards responded with bullets. The workers knew then that it would take something stronger than petition to obtain the changes they wanted. They organized themselves into councils called *soviets*, and during that year there were strikes and mutinies among the armed forces and restlessness among the Poles, the Finns, the Jews, and other minorities.

Nicholas was frightened, and he promised reforms, including an elective assembly called a *duma*, which would play a role in making the laws of the country. But he was not sincere in his intentions, and nothing was done to quell the passions of discontent.

It was World War I which brought mat-

Nicholas II (1868-1918), the last tsar of Russia, is shown above with his family. Nicholas abdicated in 1917 and was executed with his whole family after the Bolsheviks seized power. (Charles Phelps Cushing)

ters to a head. The Russians were not prepared for this war, and many of their soldiers marched into battle unarmed and badly equipped. This was mainly because much of the money appropriated by the tsarist regime went into the pockets of grafters who furnished inferior equipment or none at all. Droves of Russians were killed, wounded, or captured by the efficient German armies. The war drained the people of their scarce resources. Starvation and disease made life a nightmare.

The people looked to the tsar for hope, and saw an indecisive man and a royal court where a mysterious monk, Gregory Rasputin, held sway over the mind of the empress. From the throne there could be no positive solution to the people's problems. It was too much for the Russians, and in February 1917, the workers, the soldiers, and the leaders of the duma rebelled. They established a provisional government which promised a constitution and reforms. Nicholas abdicated, and this was the end of the rule of tsars in Russia.

**Bolshevik rebellion.** The provisional government lasted only until October 1917, when the Communists, or Bolsheviks as they were then called, seized power in the capital and other major cities of Russia. They had worked energetically under the leadership of Vladimir Ilich Lenin. Lenin had been brought to Russia from exile in Switzerland by the Germans in the hope that he would remove Russia from the war. The Bolsheviks took control of the soviets, or councils, and enlisted the help of the soldiers in overthrowing the government. They were, as history shows, successful.

The Communists made peace with Germany and began a fight of several years to preserve the power they had seized. Civil war and the intervention of foreign forces kept them almost continuously in battle. Finally, the White Russians—generally supporters of the tsar—were defeated and foreign troops were withdrawn. By the latter part of 1920, the Communists ruled all of Russia. They then began seriously to transform the life of the Russians on the basis of Communist ideas and assumptions.

**Spread of Communism.** After the Communists mastered Russia, they used the resources and opportunity there to spread the Communist philosophy, often by force, to other parts of the world. After World War II, the Poles, the Czechs, the East Germans, the Romanians, the Bulgarians, the Yugoslavs, the Albanians, the mainland Chinese, the North Koreans, the North Vietnamese, and the Cubans all came to be governed by the Communist minorities among them. Further, in practically every country of the world there are Communist parties, sometimes large and important, sometimes small and unimportant. But they are always active and convinced that the world of tomorrow belongs to them. The men who have embraced the dogmas of Communism ring the world, and they declare that they will not rest until they have brought all the rest of the world under Communist domination. The free nations of the world, of course, are determined that this ambition will not be fulfilled.

People stand in long lines to visit the tomb of Lenin in Moscow's Red Square. (Charles Phelps Cushing)

### Communist Ideas

The ideas of two Germans, Karl Marx and Friedrich Engels, were expanded, interpreted, and organized by Lenin to make up the philosophical foundations of Russian Communism and the Communist movement in other parts of the world thereafter. The primary sources of these ideas are contained in the *Communist Manifesto*, written by Marx and Engels and published in 1848, and in *Das Kapital*, written by Marx alone in 1867. Lenin wrote a great deal, and one of his best-known books, written in 1917, was called *Imperialism, The Final Stage of Capitalism.*

A Western European, Karl Marx, first conceived Communism; but it was first adopted and put into practice by Eastern Europeans in Russia. Communism was intended for those who lived in the age of the machine; yet it became dominant among those who were mostly workers of the soil. Before Communism could exist, there was supposed to be a propertied middle class, which was called the *bourgeoisie.* But Communism made its strongest gains in countries like Russia and China where the middle class was almost nonexistent; and it is weakest where the middle class is strongest. The development of Communism is a good example of the differences between a doctrine and its results in practice. But man has often been known to make theory fit the opportunity and the current scene. The opportunity and the scene were right for the Russian Communists when they seized power in 1917.

The Communists believe that changing systems of production have shaped the life of man throughout history. They point to the development of economic systems based on slavery, then serfdom, and finally capitalism. In each period they point to an exploiting class—slave owner, feudal lord, or capitalist. In each period there was also an exploited class which struggled to attain a greater equality of wealth. Thus, the Communists see history as primarily a moving drama of conflicts between those who have and those who have not, between class and class. Communists believe that the latest phase of this struggle is between monopoly capitalism and the people. They believe that the heads of great monopolies control not only the major financial resources but also governments, which are forced to invest in the monopolies to keep them operating.

Capitalism is, for the Communists, a bad word. They regard this system which permits man to make a profit on the goods he manufactures and sells as highly injurious to the proletariat and to the society as a whole. Profits are wrong, say the Communists, because the value of goods depends upon how much labor was expended in making them, and upon nothing else. Profit, said Lenin, is the difference between the wages paid the laborer and the amount the product is sold for. Therefore, the capitalist, in order to make more profit, does not pay the laborer the full value of the product but the lowest amount he possibly can.

Prior to the advent of the atomic bomb, the Communists taught that there was only one way in which capitalism could be overturned—and that was by violence. Currently, the leaders of the USSR, at least, hold that Communism will triumph without the necessity of a major war. They declare that there are definite stages man must pass through before attaining the perfect society. First, the workers overthrow the capitalists, and then they become the rulers. After the capitalist bourgeoisie are destroyed, their system should be replaced by socialism. This stage is called the "dictatorship of the proletariat." It requires taking over the means of production: the factories, the machines, and the transportation system. Once this has been done, there should be no necessity for a state, and theoretically speaking, the state will wither away and no longer exist. Everyone would then produce according to his abilities and be rewarded according to his needs. This, the Communists say, is the ultimate and the best system in man's evolving life; there can be no better; this is the perfection man has been working toward since his beginning. This is the Communist credo in essence.

The Communists have called religion the "opium of the people," and they see no God in the long evolution of man—merely man's economic life and his class struggle which have brought him to where he is today. This claim has met with strong objections from those who point to the directing hand of God, the urges of man's soul, and the variety of other passions, both good and bad, which move man to action. Men of every religious faith have demonstrated the error of Communism in denying the spiritual to man. Nor can all conflicts be attributed only to economic causes. Objectors point to the desires to hold political power and domination over others, which is as frequent, and even more evident, in man's history as greed and the desire for wealth. They also point to the fact that wherever the socialist stage of Communism is practiced, the state has not withered away but rather grown stronger. The social state strait-jackets the proletariat more than the so-called capitalist nations do. Objectors point to the continuing development under capitalism of wide ownership of the means of production, and they cite as examples the millions who own part of the American Telephone and Telegraph Company, General Motors, General Electric, and other large corporations. Many of these owners also work in the factories and plants of which they hold shares. The managers as well as the laborers depend upon their wages for existence. Marx and Lenin did not foresee this economic evolution of man.

Many people fear and object to the explicit command in Communism to use violence in seizing power. Their fear seems particularly justified in this dangerous age of the atomic bomb. The widespread fear and suspicion of Communism are due to the methods of subversion and force which its followers advocate and frequently practice. It is almost entirely because of this suspicion of intent that the great and small nations of the world remain armed to the fullest extent possible. Because of this suspicion, tension and anxiety disturb the mind of modern man. Tension was eased somewhat in recent years with the proclamation by Premier Nikita Khrushchev that he believed in coexistence and would carry on the struggle with the capitalist nations in the less dangerous fields of economics and politics. The Chinese Communists disagreed with him and clung to the old doctrine that only violence would bring about the complete success of Communism. This attitude caused a deep rift between the Russian and the Chinese Communists, and the Communist world was forced to choose between them. Most of the Communist nations of Europe followed the lead of Russia.

Despite the flaws in its theory, however, Communism did come to Russia, China, and other countries of the world, and in these places its followers are attempting to make it work.

1. How large a proportion of the Russian people are active Communists?
2. How did Tsar Nicholas II react to the 1905 Winter Palace revolt?
3. What are the *soviets*?

## The Communist Party

The Communists have gained control over the vast spread of the USSR through their party, which is the only political party permitted. There are approximately 8,000,000 members in the Communist party, and around 30,000,000 in its youth organizations who are preparing to be full members. In the Komsomol, the Communist organization for youth, teenagers learn to be good party members and spend most of their leisure time in disciplining themselves and working for party aims. They live a stern life, and deviation from the morality of Communism will ruin their future chances for a career in the USSR. But if the young Communist shows talent for administration, for carrying out orders, and in acting as an example for others, he has a good chance of rising high, perhaps even to the Central Committee of the Communist Party. He may often start upon his adult career as a secretary of the party at a local level.

In October, 1964, Alexei Kosygin, left, became Premier of the USSR, and Leonid Brezhnev, right, became First Secretary of the Communist party. Both posts were formerly held by Nikita Khrushchev. (Wide World photo)

Secretaries are extremely important within the party. At the head of the party is the First Secretary, and the primary source of his strength stems from this fact. This was the position held by Joseph Stalin who rose to supreme power in the USSR in 1926 and stayed there until 1953, mainly on the basis of control of the Communist party through the Secretariat. This was also the position of Nikita Khrushchev, who became First Secretary in 1953 and Premier of the Soviet Union in 1958, retaining control until he was ousted in 1964.

The secretary is that person who administers and supervises an organization in accordance with the policies laid down by a higher committee or assembly and carries out the expressed will of its members. Stalin managed to become First Secretary of the Communist party while Lenin ruled between 1917 and 1924. He used this position to place his men in strategic positions throughout the party organization. And the most strategic position was that of secretary at the various levels of the Communist party hierarchy. A brief look at the organization of the party will help in understanding the secretary's power.

The foundations of the party are the 360,000 cells of Communist party members. Every Communist must belong to a cell, and these cells honeycomb the whole Soviet society. At the lowest level, cells elect *bureaus*, which carry on the work of the cell between meetings. Each bureau in turn appoints a *secretary* to actually do the administrative work of the cell. The lowest cells elect representatives to *city* or *district conferences*. These send representatives to *provincial conferences*, and they to *republic congresses*. Highest of all is the All Union Congress which meets at least once every four years and is made up of representatives from republic congresses. At every level, working upward, there are smaller committees, like the bureau of the cell, and each of them selects a secretary. At the top of the committees is the Central Committee of the Communist Party, and it, too, has a secretary. This was the position held by Stalin and by Khrushchev. In the Communist party organization, the secretary at each level controls the small bureaus and committees which select him. He, in turn, is subordinate to the secretary above him on up to the First Secretary, who controls all. Thus the First Secretary through his subordinate secretaries controls the entire party, and through the party, the government.

### The Party and the Government

Formally speaking, the Communist party and the government of the Soviet Union are two distinct organizations. In reality, however, the important men of the Communist party also occupy the important positions in the government. This placement of Communists in the key governmental offices insures that the policies of the party also become the policies of the government. The party makes the policies; the government serves as an instrument to carry them out. All questions about Soviet life—commerce, agriculture, transportation, conditions of work, housing, social and cultural life—are first discussed and decided in the higher levels of the party. These decisions are then passed along to the government to be administered. Since the top men who made the decisions are also the top men of the government, there is little chance for disagreement.

There are two houses of representatives in the Soviet government—the Soviet of the Union and the Soviet of Nationalities. The members of these two houses are elected by the people. They have equal power, and when they meet together for two weeks each year they are known as the Supreme Soviet of the Union of Soviet Socialist Republics. Theoretically the Supreme Soviet holds ultimate power in the USSR. The Supreme Soviet elects the thirty-two members of the Presidium of the Supreme Soviet, which acts for it when it is not in session. It also appoints a group called the Council of Ministers, which is the administrative part of government. The functions of the Council of Ministers are similar in nature to those of the cabinet of the American, British, and other governments.

The Communist party places its members in key government positions by controlling the selection of candidates offered for election to the Supreme Soviet and by controlling the elections. Candidates to be placed upon the ballots are screened, and one official name is ultimately offered for each position. Generally the candidates are Communists. Some non-Communists are also given a place on the ballot, but they are a small minority. The voter is given a ballot with one candidate for each office, and he is required to vote. Almost 100 per cent of eligible Soviet citizens vote in elections.

On election day the voter may either put his official ballot in an open voting place or go to a secret ballot place. If he votes secretly, the supposition is that he is crossing out the name of the official candidate and writing in another name. Thus, the use of the secret ballot makes a citizen the object of official suspicion. Use of the secret ballot is not playing the election game according to the party's rules. Few voters are this daring, and the official candidates are elected by an overwhelming majority. Thus, the great majority of the Supreme Soviet are Communists who have been chosen by the party, which is controlled by secretaries. Naturally, they will inevitably elect and appoint to the key government posts the ruling members of their party.

It must be remembered that the highest organization, in reality, of both the party and the government has the same name—Presidium. In the party, the Presidium of the Central Committee acts for the Committee when that group is not in session. It has fourteen members and several alternates, and the very highest members of the party compose its membership. It is the center of power in the Soviet Union. At the top of the government is the Presidium of the Supreme Soviet. The Presidium of the Supreme Soviet is also composed of the top Communist leaders, who have been elected to it by the Supreme Soviet. Thus, the party and the government of the USSR are intertwined, and it is the Communist party which controls. The secretaries control the party and the First Secretary controls the secretaries. This was the method by which Stalin and Nikita Khrushchev controlled the Soviet Union. It must be noted, however, that although the party apparatus is supervised by the Secretariat, major decisions regarding the party are made by the Presidium and the Central Committee.

## Chinese Communism

The People's Republic of China, which is the formal name of Communist China, has essentially the same party and governmental structure as the USSR. Soviet Communism is the model for all Communists. The Chinese Communist uses different names to describe the various organs of his government, but, as in the USSR, the leaders of the Communist party also control the government.

Theoretically, the highest authority in the People's Republic of China is the National People's Congress, which corresponds to the Supreme Soviet of the USSR. This Congress is supposed to meet once a year to represent the interests of the people. But, as in the case of the Supreme Soviet of the USSR, the members of the People's Congress are carefully screened by the Communist party before nomination and election.

Three Communist leaders who helped to seize control from the Nationalists in 1949 are shown above. From left to right, Chou En-lai, Mao Tse-tung, and General Chu Teh. (Cushing)

The People's Congress elects a Standing Committee consisting of a chairman, sixteen vice-chairmen, and sixty-two members. This committee acts for the Congress between meetings. The Congress also appoints a Chairman of the People's Republic, who is the formal head of the country. But Chinese state organs are subject to party commands, and the actual power is vested in the Standing Committee of the Politbureau of the party, which consists of seven men, the most important of whom is Mao Tse-tung.

The daily administration of government is carried out by the members of a State Council headed by the premier of China, who is appointed by the Chairman of the Republic. This council is similar to the Council of Ministers in the USSR. The leading members of the Standing Committee, the Chairman of the Republic, the Premier, and the leading members of the State Council are all dominant members of the Chinese Communist party, which therefore controls the government.

The overriding power of the Communist party in China is witnessed by the fact that the single most powerful man in China is Mao Tse-tung. Mao holds no official government position, but he controls the Republic through his position as Chairman of the Central Committee of the Communist party.

In order to give a more democratic appearance to the political life of China, several small political parties other than the Communist party are permitted to exist. Some of their numbers are picked for the lesser important government posts, but they, too, are carefully screened before appointment. All parties are collectively grouped into what is called a United Front dominated by the Communist party.

1. How large is the Communist party in the USSR? How large is the party youth corps?
2. Describe the organization of the Soviet Communist party. How does authority flow from top to bottom through the party hierarchy?
3. Describe the formal institutional structure of the Soviet government. Describe its interaction with the Communist party.

## Conclusion

The Russians were a religious people centuries before a minority among them became Communists. Religion brought to the Russians, as it has brought to many men throughout history, a promise of eventual relief from the burdens of life, a richness of ritual and ceremony, a beauty of art and architecture, the beginnings of a written language and education, and monasteries which for hundreds of years were centers of culture and civilization.

The Eastern Orthodox Church gradually became centered in Moscow instead of Constantinople, and it became the State Church. It was one of the main pillars supporting the tsar, who headed the institution of monarchy in Russia. This had unfortunate results at times for religion and for the clergy of Russia. It was not uncommon for the tsar to assert his authority over the patriarch who headed the Russian Orthodox Church. On one occasion Peter the Great abolished the position of patriarch and headed the Church with a "college" or committee of men who were of his own choice.

The Church became so closely identified with the state that when the Communists came to power in 1917, they thought of the Church and the tsar as inseparable. Those who followed the teachings and rituals of the Church were regarded as enemies of the state. From that time to this, the Church has had a continuing history of persecution and harassment in the USSR, especially during the period prior to the Second World War. Since the end of that war, the Church has been tolerated, and a certain accommodation has been worked out between the Church and the government. But the Church is still suspect by the Communists, for they do not believe in God. It is frustrating for the Communists to see that so many Russians, either openly or secretly, still persist in believing in the God which Communist philosophy denies.

The Communists who rule the Soviet Union do not look forward to a paradise in the hereafter but concentrate rather on trying to create a Communist paradise on earth. They look at the history of man and see in it only the economics of man. They see all of history as a never-ending struggle between the classes who have and the classes who have not. They believe that this struggle will cease when there is a classless society in a Communist nation. They trust no one but the members of the Communist party to rule, and they justify this party dictatorship as necessary for the making of the Communist man. The Communists rule through the few, not the many. Although a large number of men make up the Supreme Soviet, they are all carefully selected by the few who control the Communist party. Their decisions are also manipulated by this small group. The citizens of the USSR live under a strict authority which bases its decisions upon the dogmas of Communism.

## SUMMING UP THE CHAPTER

A. Identify the following and tell why they are important.

| | |
|---|---|
| Bolsheviks | Mao Tse-tung |
| *Communist Manifesto* | Karl Marx |
| *Das Kapital* | Nikon |
| Friedrich Engels | Old Believers |
| *Imperialism, The Final Stage of Capitalism* | Rasputin |
| | Joseph Stalin |
| Lenin | Vladimir I |

B. Define the following terms, relating them to this chapter.

| | |
|---|---|
| bourgeoisie | opium of the people |
| bureau | proletariat |
| cell | united front |
| class struggle | soviets |

C. Identify the following institutions and tell their organization, functions, and importance.

| | |
|---|---|
| Central Committee | Presidium |
| Council of Ministers | Soviet of Nationalities |
| | Soviet of the Union |
| duma | Supreme Soviet of the USSR |
| Komsomol | |

D. Identify these dates and indicate their importance.

| | |
|---|---|
| 1652 | February 1917 |
| 1848 | October 1917 |
| 1867 | 1917-1924 |
| 1905 | 1926-1953 |

E. Chapter review questions.

1. Compare the ties of the Russian Orthodox Church under the tsars with the ties of the Roman Catholic Church to the rulers of Europe. What, if any, differences were there? When did these ties end in Western Europe? in Russia?
2. Why did the Communists seek to destroy the clergy? Why did they seek to destroy religion itself?
3. How did World War I bring about conditions in Russia which made a revolution virtually inevitable?
4. Who forced the abdication of the Romanov tsar? What sort of a government did they set up? How long did it last? Who then gained control?
5. What are the basic Communist beliefs about economics? Why is this called "economic determinism"?
6. What is the Communist definition of "profit"? Relate this to the "labor theory of value."
7. What is the "dictatorship of the proletariat"? What is its historic function, according to the Communists? What groups of people are called "the proletariat"?
8. Why do Communists believe violence is necessary to eliminate the capitalist system? Has this view changed among the Communist leaders of the USSR?
9. What is the stage which the Communists call *socialism*? When does it become possible?
10. What is the Communists' definition of the state? How does the state "wither away," according to Communist theory?
11. What does the Communist mean when he says that Communism is the "final stage" in the economic evolution of man? What enables him to be so certain of this?
12. Why are the world's churches so opposed to Communism?
13. How does Mao Tse-tung control China when he has no official position in the government?

F. Questions for discussion.

1. To what extent have Marx's predictions about the course of capitalism been proved wrong by actual history?
2. Have the Russian Communists changed their views about the necessity of violence to overthrow capitalism? What is their policy called? How do the Chinese Communists view this?
3. Do you believe that man is primarily an economic being? Why?
4. What is the relationship between the Communist party and the government of the USSR?
5. Through what steps in the electoral process does the Communist party gain its control of the government?
6. What is the sole avenue of advancement in the Soviet Union?
7. Why is it important to study not only formal institutional arrangements, but also actual power relationships in a governmental system if one wants to really understand the system? Give specific examples.

# CHAPTER 27

# *Soviet Economy, Society, Arts, and Education*

THE REVOLUTION that swept over Russia in 1917 brought more than a change of rulers. Every aspect of Russian life was violently changed by the new Communist rulers. They wished not only to reshape the outer forms of the government and social system but also to shape a new kind of society and a new kind of man to fit their system—the ideal Soviet man.

## The Communist Economy

The Communists are necessarily very concerned with the economic framework within which man works. In the Soviet Union today the state owns and controls the resources of the nation. The coal and other minerals, the mines, factories, transportation system, and power plants, as well as most of the retail trade, the marketing system, the commerce both domestic and foreign, and most of the land—all are owned or controlled by the state. There is still private property in the USSR. A man may own his automobile; he may own his home and its furnishings, but not the land on which his house is built; and a few people still have small shops and small farms. But these are a small fraction compared to the property of the state. Soviet Russia has a state-controlled and state-owned economy.

### The Collective Farmer

The Soviet Union has had many difficulties in producing enough food to feed its expanding population. In line with Communist ideology, the USSR has attempted to solve food problems by the establishment of collective farms. A collective farm is called a *kolkhoz.* There are, on the average, about 250 families on a collective farm. They work together cooperatively in handling the chores of the farm and are divided into groups who are given special tasks to do. For instance, there are groups who milk cows, others who run tractors, others to feed the hogs and take care of other animals, and still others who seed and cultivate. The produce that results from these collective efforts is sold to the state at a price fixed by the state, although some may be sold on the open market. The money received from this united effort is shared among the farmers, minus deductions such as insurance, building funds, and the cost of machinery and certain other items. But the Soviet leaders have also found that it is necessary to give the peasant-farmers other incentives if they are to produce in the quantity and quality wanted.

The members of collective farms are permitted to have private gardens, the produce of which they may use as they see fit and sell if they wish. These private gardens are usually fenced-in plots of ground varying in size, depending upon the region. The garden is located behind the house or hut in which the peasant lives. Here he grows his vegetables or whatever else he needs to eat or feels he can sell for the money he so desperately needs. The peasant is also permitted to own a cow, several sheep, a pig, and all the poultry he can raise.

It is common knowledge that the peasant lavishes more care and work on the private garden that is all his than upon the collective farm of which he has only a small share. It is estimated that privately owned hens produce almost 80 per cent of the eggs consumed in the USSR, and half the meat and milk come from privately owned animals. Perhaps as much as 40 per cent of the vegetables consumed in the Soviet Union are supplied from these backyard gardens which belong wholly to the individual farmers. The products of backyard gardens are sold on the open market rather than in state stores.

The Russian peasants did not willingly herd themselves into collective farms; they were forced into them by Stalin. Premier Khrushchev said that Stalin never saw the countryside and the village after 1928, except on films which had been carefully doctored for his benefit. Stalin was determined, however, that the farmers of the USSR must work in a collective manner. The wealthier peasants, called *kulaks*, who employed others to work for them, along with others who resisted Stalin's will, were sent into exile, imprisoned, and finally liquidated as a class. This had an unfortunate effect upon agriculture because the kulaks were the backbone of the farming class. In their anger and despair when collectivization was begun, they broke their tools, killed their animals, burned their homes, and left a shortage of livestock in Russia from which the country has not yet recovered.

Stalin was ruthless with the farmer-peasants, and he killed and exiled millions of them. In 1932-33 he seized the little grain and food they had, and millions upon millions starved to death. He fashioned a famine which rivaled the devastation of some of history's greatest destroyers.

Nikita Khrushchev, who was premier from 1958 to 1964, was closer to the peasant and the farm. He instituted reforms designed to improve the conditions and morale of the farmers. He gave them more money for the produce raised on collective farms and increased the size and reduced the number of collectives. The local authorities were given the choice of planting what they thought best and

Above, achievements of a collective farm are posted on a signboard outside the chairman's home. Outstanding workers are pictured. Below, the silo was built as part of the Russian drive to raise corn as cattle feed. (Stockwell from Cushing)

were allowed to handle the manner of production instead of being dictated to from the central planning committee in Moscow, as was formerly the practice. Khrushchev abolished the tractor stations which Stalin had established to be his centers of power and control in the countryside. The stations were given to the collectives to use and to control. All of these reforms helped, but the agricultural problem plaguing the Soviet Union has still not been solved.

The problem is one of geography as well as of rapid change. Where the land is good in the USSR, the rainfall is uncertain. Much of the farmland lies above 50° north latitude. (Compare this with Chicago.) The winters are long and cold, and the summers short and hot. Crops must be grown quickly in these short summer periods. Soviet scientists are working desperately to develop quick-growing crops and improve the use of the land and the little water that is available. But the process is slow and frustrating. At the present time, it takes about 34,000,000 farmers to feed the Soviet people. This estimate is in sharp contrast to the United States, where about eight per cent of the population feed the rest and have a large surplus as well. Of course, the United States is better favored geographically than the USSR, but its farmers are also using better seeds and fertilizer, and the land is used more efficiently. Khrushchev was intensely interested in the agriculture of this country when he visited here some years ago.

Most farms in the USSR are cooperatively run, but there are also state farms called *sovkhoz*. On these farms the members of the collective are paid like factory workers, but generally in produce rather than in money. Everyone is not paid equally. Each is paid according to the kind and amount of work he does. This is true of all aspects of Soviet economic life. The skilled worker may receive a base pay of $300.00 per month, while the cleaning woman or street sweeper will make about $30.00 per month. The manager of a factory will make more than the workers, and his superiors, in turn, will receive more than he does.

1. How were the Soviet collective farms organized? How successful were these farms in increasing agricultural production?
2. How did the liquidation of the *kulaks* by Stalin cause a complete breakdown of Soviet agriculture? How were the majority of the *kulaks* liquidated? Has Soviet agriculture recovered fully from this breakdown yet?
3. What reforms on the farms did Khrushchev initiate to solve the agricultural problem? Were these reforms successful?

## The Planner and Industry

From the early beginning of their rule until now, the Communists of the USSR have tried to plan everything, and they have planned for industry as well as agriculture. In addition to planning for collective farms and setting quotas for each, the Communists have also given much of their attention to the planning of industry. They set long-range plans in terms of several years. For instance, the first five-year plan ran from 1928 to 1932 and emphasized the expansion of industry: steel, machines, and machines for making machines. The latest plan is for seven years, and the goal is to catch up with and surpass the United States in every economic area.

The top planning commission located in Moscow is known as *Gosplan*. Under Gosplan are regional councils which coordinate the plans of all industries in the region. And then there are the local factories themselves. Plans go up from the low levels and plans come down from the high levels, and it is those plans which come down from Gosplan which are the ultimate authority for the factory. Yearly quotas and production plans are set for each factory.

The Communist leaders of the USSR can plan and expect their directions to be followed because the state owns all the factories. This is extremely different from those countries where free enterprise is the system and millions of different owners control the various industries. It would be impossible, except perhaps in times of war emergency, to plan the economy of the United States and tell the owners what and how much they can produce.

This would be in opposition to the free-enterprise system.

There is another difference between the Communist economies and the free-enterprise system. Up to now the Communists have concentrated on building up industries to service other industries rather than the people. They have not been concerned with making goods for the consumer—sewing machines, refrigerators, pleasure cars, clothes, television and radio sets, and other items of this nature. They have, rather, concentrated on making power plants and dams, trucks, steel, and machine tools. The present population must suffer so that the future may be insured. Suffering has its limitations, however, and there are indications that the people of the USSR would like to enjoy some pleasures today.

Because of the concentration upon building for the future, the ordinary citizen of the USSR has a rather low standard of living compared to the citizen of Europe or America. It must also be noted, however, that his standard of living has improved over that of his father and grandfather under the tsars. But, like humans everywhere, once the Soviet people know these better standards of living, their demands increase rather than decrease, and this human factor is operating in the USSR today.

Soviet industry has improved under the planned strict austerity and determined drive of the Communists, but Soviet wages are low, and the workers are not permitted to strike to raise them. The Communist will explain that a strike is impossible because the worker would be striking against himself, since ultimately he owns the factory in which he works. There are unions in the USSR, and they have the freedom to complain about conditions of work, the poorness of food in the cafeteria, and other matters of this kind. But the workers are not free to impose their will through the weapon of nonwork.

The prices of food and consumer goods are sometimes high. Eggs cost around $1.45 per dozen, sugar over 70 cents per pound, chicken $1.21 per pound, a cheap suit over $110.00, a cotton dress over $30.00, and an automobile almost $5,000.00. The average worker pays heavily for the things that make his life more comfortable. Yet the average income of about 40 per cent of Soviet families has been estimated to be no more than $200.00 per month, and 50 per cent of the Soviet families have even less.

Right, Moscow's subway is decorated with ornate columns and lights. (Stockwell from Cushing). Below, Moscow's Open Market is one of the few examples of free enterprise in the USSR. (Cushing)

## Soviet Society

The Communist declares that history has been an unfolding drama of conflict between different classes in man's society. He further declares that the triumph of Communism will mean the abolishment of classes and therefore the disappearance of conflict within the Communist society, Man, however, does not always evolve according to the pat requirements of a formula, and new classes have emerged under the rule of Communism. There may not be private ownership of the means of production, but there are those who control production, and they are the dominant class wherever Communism is practiced. Among the people of the USSR today there are layers of classes, and this fact is obvious both to them and to outside observers.

### Economic and Social Groupings

At the top of Soviet society are the members of the Presidium of the Communist party and the Presidium of the Supreme Soviet, the members of the Council of Ministers, and ranking Communist leaders and officials. At this level also are the ranking generals, and the most outstanding artists, writers, and scientists. They are few. They are not even one per cent of the population. They live in fine houses, are driven in chauffeured cars, and have villas in the country and at the seaside. They eat well and are served well. The state supplies their needs lavishly, for they are in a real sense the state.

The next highest group consists of the second-level governing Communists, the managers of industry, the planners of the future, the high administrative officials, the best engineers, the university professors, the good artists and scientists. They are paid well, and at times their salaries may be more than $20,000 a year. They, too, have country houses, called *dachas,* know the pleasures of vacations in mild climates, attend the operas and the ballets, patronize culture, and generally enjoy the good life. They are slightly less than ten per cent of the total population of the country.

Lower down the scale are the technicians, the foremen of the factories, the better-paid clerks, and others of like rank. Often they live with their families in a single room in the city or in a small village house in the country. In the city apartments they frequently share a common kitchen and a common toilet with many other families. Both the husband and the wife work in order to make ends meet, and there is rarely anything left out of their combined monthly salary for entertainment. Much entertainment, however, is very cheap or even free, such as movies and the theater. The Soviet people, especially the Russians, also spend much of their time in reading, and there are many books available to them. This class makes up between 30 and 40 per cent of the population. The combined salaries of husband and wife might range around $200.00 per month.

At the bottom are the poorer ones, who comprise the vast remainder of the Soviet people. For this great mass of people the food is poor and housing is poor. There is much sickness among them, although medical service is free. They do not starve, but their life is hard, and they must be frugal and budget their scarce funds very carefully if they are to carry on even in a minimum way. The daily routine of making a living occupies most of their thinking. However, a great number of them feel that life is improving somewhat, and they hope for the future of their children. The Russian people have a great love for their children and will sacrifice beyond measure so that they may be better clothed, better fed, and better educated.

There is a growing gap between the levels of Soviet society. Members of a group tend to associate only within that group and to follow similar ways of life. There is a way to climb to a higher level, and that is by means of the ladder of merit in the Communist party. The young, ambitious, loyal, intelligent Communist has a good chance of lifting himself and his family to the upper reaches of Soviet society. But there is little chance for individual advancement otherwise.

## Nationalities

There are many varying ethnic groups within the Soviet Union. Some estimates indicate that there are as many as 169 groups distinguishable by language, cultural, and racial differences. All of these are grouped within fifteen republics, each of which represents a major nationality grouping. The greatest of these is the Russian Soviet Federated Socialist Republic, which contains about 100,000,000 "Great Russians." Other republics in which the Slavs are the majority are the Ukrainian Soviet Socialist Republic, which contains around 40,000,000 "Little Russians," and the Byelorussian Republic, embracing around 8,000,000 "White Russians."

Other republics located in the Baltic region, in the Caucasian mountain area, and in Central Asia were fashioned to provide a sense of autonomy to those who were non-Slav—the Latvians, the Estonians, the Georgians, the Moldavians, the Kazakhs, the Uzbeks, and others.

The history of a number of these peoples goes back farther than the history of the Slavs, and they cherish their own languages, cultures, and distinct ways of life. As the Russian or the Slav came to dominate them over the slow passage of the years, they were resentful and bitter, and they dreamed of independence and release from the Slav's rule. Under the tsars they were frequently persecuted, and their will to be free became even more fixed and determined. There were frequent revolts and bloodshed. When the Russians turned against the tsar in 1917, many of these other groups joined in the struggle. They saw in the downfall of the tsar an opportunity to be free and independent once again. But the Russian Communists soon imposed their rule in Russia, and they were determined that none of these groups should have independence. The Communists did, however, try to meet some of their requirements by establishing republics for the major nationalities where a degree of cultural autonomy was given them.

These groups were permitted to retain their languages in schools and in their newspapers, and to keep their individual styles of dress, their arts, and their cultural ways of life. But the content of their teaching, their written word, and their economic way of life were Communist. In form they could be themselves; in content they were socialist. Many remained resentful because they wanted more than the Communists permitted them. When the Germans invaded the Soviet Union in the early period of World War II, a number of these groups joined forces with the Germans. When the German armies fell back, however, the Soviet rulers took their revenge. The rebellious groups were uprooted from their traditional lands and scattered far and wide throughout the immense expanse of the USSR. Many still hide a smoldering hatred for the Slavs who control them. But there is little they can do about it, for they have neither the numbers of men nor the military might to challenge the power of the majority. And with the movement of the years, they are being tied even more closely to the national state of the Soviet Union.

Since the 1930's all non-Russian speaking nationalities have been required to teach Russian in the schools. There is little chance for a non-Russian to rise high in his profession or in the government if he does not speak Russian. Industrialization is carrying the population into the cities and bringing a certain sameness of life to Russian and non-Russian alike.

Groups yet remain distinct from one another within the Soviet Union, but the movement of the Slav throughout the USSR, the similarity of indoctrination everywhere, the same content of teaching in schools, and propaganda in newspapers are all tending to reduce the differences between the peoples of the various nationalities. Eventually they may become alike in culture, just as they are already alike in government. In the meantime, however, it is chiefly the descendants of the Slavs who rule and enjoy the better life, and there is still jealousy, envy, and resentment on the part of the non-Slavic nationalities who want a greater degree of independence and freedom for themselves.

Soviet women take part in almost every kind of work. Above, a woman agronomist shows off tomatoes being raised in a greenhouse. (Stockwell from Cushing) Below, a woman operates a soft-drink stand on a sidewalk of Kiev. (Cushing)

## The Soviet Woman

The woman of the USSR is an extraordinary person. There are few fields of labor, skilled or unskilled, professional or nonprofessional, where she is not found working constructively, energetically, and faithfully. She sweeps the streets, she shovels snow, she digs ditches and builds buildings, and swinging high on platforms of wood she paints the buildings she has helped to build. She drives buses, trucks, and tractors. She works in the fields, in the factories, in the office buildings, and everywhere that there is work to be done. She works as the equal of man in labor long thought to be the exclusive domain of the male, and she receives equal pay for equal work.

Soviet women have flocked into professional fields of work, and the vast majority of the doctors of the USSR are women. Women are also a sizable minority in the engineering field, in the technology of agriculture, and in the field of economics. The woman of the Soviet Union is not the same woman who lived under the tsars when the male thought of her as lacking a brain. She is a part of the Communist party, and she has risen high in its ranks, but only one woman has risen as yet to the Presidium of the party. That is still an almost exclusively male club.

There are few women who do not work in the Soviet Union. Women make up about 45 per cent of the total labor force, and someday they may outnumber the men at work. The woman of the USSR is still devoted to her family, however, and like many other modern working mothers and wives, she has problems in bringing up her family and working at the same time. This is not easy to do, but the government has tried to ease the burden.

There is a great network of nurseries and kindergartens where a mother may take her little children in the morning on her way to work. She picks them up in the evening on the way home. This not only makes it possible for mothers to work but also makes it possible for the State to begin implanting Communist ideas in the minds of children at an early age. The government encourages large families and gives financial assistance and prestige to mothers. The Soviet woman is valuable to the continued progress of the country.

1. What do the Communists mean when they talk about the "class struggle"?
2. Describe class structure in the Soviet Union. How does this contradict Marxist theory?
3. Describe the life of the Soviet woman.

## The Arts

In the past, the Russians produced great music and literature, and their tradition has continued in the Soviet Union. Among the world-famous Russian musicians are Tchaikovsky, Rimski-Korsakov, Moussorgsky, and Borodin, whose compositions are an enduring part of man's musical heritage. In these modern days there have been the composers Dimitri Shostakovich, Aram Khachaturian, and Sergei Prokofiev. Russia has long turned out fine musicians, and music has continued to be treasured by the Soviet government.

The ballet is an art in which Russia has reigned supreme for many years. Many Soviet cities have their own special ballet groups, but the finest of all performs in the Bolshoi Theater in Moscow. Competition to become a member of this group is keen among Soviet dancers, who study and practice for long, long years in the hope that they may become members of this select group. When the ballet performs, the theater is always crowded, and the performance is as close to perfection as man can achieve in this form of art.

The Russians are prodigious readers of books. They read at every opportunity—in the subway, at home, in the parks, and on trains and buses. Whenever he has an opportunity, the Russian opens his book. Russians read whatever they can find of interest, but mostly they enjoy the classics. They read their own great writers of the past, Dostoevski, Tolstoy, Pushkin, Turgenev, and others, and they read and especially like Shakespeare, Mark Twain, Jack London, and Victor Hugo. During Stalin's rule, the Communists insisted that all writing be tied to the interests of the state and the party, and this made rather boring reading for even the Communist. When boy met girl and the main subject of their conversation in the book was how they could produce more boots, cars, or machines, Russians as well as foreigners generally found the dialogue unexciting.

Writers who showed too much originality or expressed criticism of the regime under Stalin were chancing exile and possibly death. While Stalin lived, the modern Soviet writer stayed close to the party line and the triumphs of socialism, or he did not write for long. When Stalin died, there was some relaxation of the rules, and Soviet writers began to grow more daring in their novels and books. But there was still a censorship of manuscripts, and Boris Pasternak's book *Doctor Zhivago* was refused publication in the USSR. It was only because a copy of the manuscript fell into the hands of an Italian publisher that the world knew of this book. Pasternak was forced to refuse the Nobel prize for literature and was attacked savagely for the writing of this work.

The Soviet writer at present is not exposed to as much danger as he was when Stalin lived, but he is still required to stay within rather narrow bounds. Writers are under the control of the Writers Union, and the leaders of this union are servants of the party. It is their job to keep the writers in line with party policy.

But there are signs of rebellion against the restraints placed upon writers, and these signs may burst into print again. The government and policies of the Communists are evolving, and the people of the USSR today are not the same as the Russians of yesterday. They may yet successfully win for themselves greater freedom to write and to speak.

## Education in the USSR

Under the tsars, most Russians were illiterate. The Communists have made over the masses of people into a reading and writing public. Eight years of schooling are compulsory for all, but the student who stops his

The Russians are proud of their achievements and show great curiosity in examining a model of a Sputnik. (Stockwell from Cushing)

One of the tallest buildings in the Soviet Union is the 32-story central building of the Moscow Lomonsov State University at Lenin Hills. (Hoffman from Cushing)

schooling at this point can never hope to rise high in the country. Even the secondary or high school graduate cannot look forward to a promising career. It is the university graduates and the graduates of specialized technical schools for whom the future holds great promise. The competition to obtain advanced education is as keen in the Soviet Union as it is in other parts of the world.

The Communist leaders knew early that if they were to have an industrialized country, and one that would rank among the powers of the world, it was necessary to have a body of citizens who could read and write. There was great need for those who could delve into the mysteries of nature and the universe and for those who could teach at lower and higher levels. To achieve this purpose, they knew that education must be provided.

At the higher levels, the Communists were chiefly interested in producing engineers and scientists; they still are. Subjects in the humanities are neglected, and there are few who study these fields. Students who are lucky enough to enter the university and study engineering or science are given special allowances and find good positions when they graduate. Others are not so favored.

The vast majority of Soviet students, however, do not enter a university. Most have only a primary education, a lesser number a secondary education, and only a small percentage receive a university education. The primary school students, or those between the ages of nine and fourteen, receive their indoctrination in Communism in an organization known as the Pioneers. It is somewhat similar to the youth organizations of the West in its emphasis on camping and related activities. But the young Pioneers are also grounded in some basic Communist ideas. At the secondary level, young people in the USSR receive intensive courses in civics and other studies. At the university level they take courses in Marxism-Leninism every year.

There are those high up in the Kremlin who feel that too many students are going to the universities. The Communists are thinking in terms of polytechnical education, meaning that all students must spend time in doing manual work, either in a factory or in agriculture. The Soviet Union has a labor shortage, and the students are one group which the planners could tap to cover their shortage of manpower. Premier Khrushchev believed that it would be good for students to get their hands dirty at manual labor, and there is a plan calling for many of the students to work for several years before entering the university. It is possible for working students to study correspondence courses at night after work and thus earn university credits.

Education is important to the advance of the USSR. The Soviet leaders feel that ideological indoctrination plus a type of social and political training will be likely to produce the "New Soviet Man." It is for this important reason that the Communists have placed so much emphasis upon education. Another reason, of course, is that trained minds are needed if the USSR is to grow and develop as planned. Engineering and scientific fields have been especially emphasized. This emphasis has paid high dividends in a tremendous industrial expansion and in scientific achievements which at times have amazed the world. No one will question the remarkable exploits of the Soviet Union in space.

Education is the road to a career, and the young Soviet citizen wants the economic promise of this career. Engineering and science are the two primary roads to the future he wants. But there is a growing number of students who are also interested in the arts, in music, in the social sciences, and in the other fields that deal with man as man. These students are demanding more opportunities for study in the fields of their interests. The youth of the USSR, like youth in other parts of the world, tend to be a bit rebellious and questioning about the dogmas that they are taught. They are inclined to resent the planning of their lives. As a consequence, the Communist leaders are finding the youth a growing problem.

1. Name several of the best-known Russian composers.
2. What are the two Soviet youth organizations? What are their roles in Soviet society?
3. What effect has the Soviet labor shortage had on education?

## Conclusion

In economics, in society, in the arts, and in education, the Communists are trying to fashion the "New Soviet Man." This Soviet man is one who will live as the teachings of Communism say he should live. He will be free of the biases of capitalism and obedient to those who dictate in the name of the proletariat. However, the Communists are having difficulties in shaping this ideal man. Theoretically he should have been an inevitable development under Communist rule; but in practice the man of the Soviet Union remains a human who is often obstinate in his attitudes and in his tastes.

The Soviet man, like all men, is proving difficult to mold permanently into one rigid pattern of thought and action. Throughout his history man has often refused to accept the inevitable and, instead, has continued to evolve his economics, his society, his arts, and his education. Man does not stand still. He moves on to something else. The man of the USSR today is not standing still; he is progressing to another future. Perhaps it is not the future that the orthodox Communists have planned for him.

## SUMMING UP THE CHAPTER

A. Define or explain the following terms, relating them to this chapter.

| | |
|---|---|
| dacha | kulaks |
| five-year plan | Pioneers |
| Gosplan | sovkhoz |
| kolkhoz | |

B. Identify the following and tell why they are important.

| | |
|---|---|
| Borodin | Pushkin |
| Dostoevski | Rimski-Korsakov |
| Khachaturian | Shostakovich |
| Moussorgsky | Tchaikovsky |
| Pasternak | Tolstoy |
| Prokofiev | Turgenev |

C. Chapter review questions.

1. What is the underlying reason for state planning? Why do such attempts at economic planning so often fail?
2. How successful has forced industrialization been in the USSR?
3. How is Communism supposed to arrive at a "classless society"? Has Soviet society actually become classless?
4. What concessions did the Communists make to the various Russian nationalities? How successful were they in satisfying these minorities?
5. Who takes care of Soviet children while their parents work?
6. Why do you suppose education is much more competitive in the USSR than in the United States? Do you consider this a weakness, or a strength, in the Russian educational system? Compare the Soviet and American systems.
7. What effect has Russia's emphasis on scientific and technical education had on humanistic attitudes in the USSR?
8. What steps have the Russians taken to prevent artistry and creativity from drying up? What measures do we have of the success of such efforts?
9. Why have Russian university students been required to work in the factories and fields? What does this tell you about the Russian labor shortage?
10. What has been the emphasis in Communist economic planning? How has this affected the average Russian?
11. What are the major nationalities within the Soviet Union? How are they organized under the Communist system? Why has this been necessary?

D. Questions for discussion.

1. Do people tend to work harder for themselves than for others? To what extent are man's main motivations economic? How would you compare the Communist theories about human nature with the theories of the free-enterprise system?
2. What class structure has developed in Communist Russia? What are the differences, if any, between these classes and those in capitalist countries? What conclusions would you draw from this?
3. How are industrialization and the city tending to eliminate many of the former sources of individualism and opposition to the Soviet Communist regime? What effect do you anticipate this will have on the Soviet system?
4. Why do you suppose Soviet women engage in all the occupations men do? What fields are dominated by women? Do you think this would be the free choice of Russian women? Why?
5. Why do you suppose Russia has for a century produced so many of the world's greatest writers, composers, artists, and performers? Is this great creative activity something inherent in the Russian people, the product of the now-passed tsarist tradition, or the product of Communist society? In other words, what are the sources of artistic genius in any culture?
6. What has been the effect of Communist censorship and "socialist realism" on creative genius in the USSR?

E. Projects for groups or individuals.

1. Compare the percentages of the Russian population engaged in agriculture, service fields, and industrial factory work with the percentages in the same categories in the United States and one or two other countries. What does this tell you about the nature and efficiency of the economy of each?
2. What great musicians from the USSR have played extensive tours in the West in recent years? What Soviet ballet troupes and musical ensembles have appeared recently in the United States?
3. Compare the extremes of wealth and position, the gap between the classes, and the percentages of the population in the various classes in the USSR with the same for the United States. What do you find? What does this tell you about the Soviet claim of economic and social equality?

CHAPTER **28**

# *Communism Beyond the Soviet Union*

THE COMMUNIST is a member of a world-wide movement, and his ideology is shared by many men throughout the world. The creators of Communism—Marx, Engels, Lenin, Leon Trotsky, Stalin, and others—thought of it as a way of life for all men. They and their successors mobilized strong resources to make this way of life a reality everywhere.

As early as 1919, a Communist International, commonly called the *Comintern,* was established to promote Communism and revolution among all men. In rousing fighting language, the Comintern called upon workers of the world to unite against the capitalist and the imperialist. All men were urged to bind themselves together in a World Federation of Soviet Republics. Organizers and propagandists were sent forth into the world to convince men of the rightness of Communist claims and the need to shake off capitalistic chains. They found those who listened, believed, and acted, and Communism took root and grew in many parts of the world. Today there is no non-Communist ruler who says with certainty, "There is no Communist in my country."

Communists have become dominant in a number of countries outside of the Soviet Union, and Communist parties have been established in most countries of the world. Communism and its followers girdle the globe. When Communists gather for an international meeting in one of the countries they dominate, they exhibit the many faces and speak the many tongues of man.

Whether at home or abroad, Communists are closest to those who think as they do. Regardless of difference in race and nationality, there is a remarkable similarity in the words, opinions, and actions of Communists throughout the world. The Communist is a part of a world-wide body, and he is strongly bound to it by faith, by discipline, and by purpose. Communism is truly an international movement.

With the chief exceptions of Cuba and North Vietnam, the Communist-dominated countries are grouped around the borders of the Soviet Union. They are commonly referred to in a group as *satellites,* meaning that they are minor or secondary bodies linked in an orbit to the main body of the USSR. The most faithful of the non-Russian Communist leaders are those who live near the borders of the USSR in Europe. Due to its importance and power, Communist China cannot be regarded as a satellite of the USSR.

The Communist minorities who govern eastern European satellites came to power during and after the Second World War with the help of Soviet arms and organizers. As the massive Soviet armies pushed the Germans back and occupied the lands of eastern Europe, Communist rule was imposed upon the people in each of these countries. The power of the democratic majority parties was weakened through force and deception, and the influence of the Communists increased until, eventually, all of eastern Europe, except Greece, became Communist-ruled.

## Poland

The citizens of Poland are ruled by a Communist government. Communists seized control of Poland in 1945 and they have ruled the country ever since that time.

The Pole is originally of the same tribal family as the Russian—he is a Slav. But over the years since the tenth century—the century from which he generally dates his history—differences of belief and opinion have separated the Pole from the Russian. Over 95 per cent of the Poles are Roman Catholic and recognize the pope as the supreme father of their religion. This common religion has been a unifying force in Poland, and it marks a boundary between the Poles and the Eastern Orthodox Russians. In the course of their history, both Poles and Russians have overstepped the limits of this religious boundary. As a consequence, war and suspicion have characterized their relations with each other.

Because of geographic location, Poland has also been long harassed by Germany. A band of Germans known as the Teutonic Knights seized a part of north Poland in the Middle Ages and made it a part of the Prussian state they were establishing along the Baltic Sea. The Prussians were driven out in the 1400's by the Polish king, Ladislas II, and then the Poles went on to the heights of their power in the late 1600's. They defeated the Russians in battle, and in 1683, under the able leadership of their king, John Sobieski, saved Europe from the onrushing Turks who had neared the Austrian city of Vienna.

Polish peasants still ride to market in old style wagons, some with auto tires. A Soviet army is maintained in Poland, but Poland has a degree of autonomy. (Wide World photo)

Beginning in the 1700's, however, the Poles were subjected to the greedy schemes of those who surrounded them—the Prussians, the Austrians, and the Russians. In 1772 these nations began to divide the lands of Poland among themselves, and by 1795-96 there was no longer a nation called Poland. But it remained a reality in the hearts of Polish patriots, and after the First World War, in 1918, the Poles got back their land and their independence. Ignace Paderewski, a world-famous pianist, became the first premier.

Still Poland rarely knew peace. Polish and Russian Communist troops clashed in 1920 and it was only after the Russians were defeated that they temporarily stopped their violence against Poland. Then, in 1939, the German Nazis and the Russian Communists plotted the partition of Poland again. By force of arms they overran the country and divided it between them. For a time Poland was completely under German control when Hitler attacked the USSR a few years later. Then the Soviet troops turned back the Germans, and they saw to it that Poland became a state ruled by Communist Poles who were bound to the Soviet Union by ideology, politics, and economics. And once again the land of Poland was cut up according to the needs of Soviet politics.

In eastern Poland, the USSR took almost 70,000 miles of former Polish territory which was populated by almost 11,000,000 people. In return, Poland was given about 39,000 square miles of former German territory in the west. Throughout its history, Poland has been partitioned on various occasions by Russia, Germany, and other nations. The Poles have known invasions from north, east, south, and west. They have became suspicious of the intentions of their neighbors, and they are not an easy people to govern. A Soviet army is maintained on Polish soil, but it also leaves the Poles to practice a Communism which is less strict than the Communism practiced in the USSR.

The Communist leader of Poland is Wladyslaw Gomulka, and he has permitted religion in the schools and religious liberty, provided the Church stays out of politics. Even the Polish Communists generally have their children baptized, and many marry in the Church. Poland is a Communist state, and its 1952 constitution is modeled after that of the Soviet Union, but there is a certain freedom of expression. Polish Communism is marked by emphasis upon the national economy and culture and a determination to allow the people of Poland to remain separate and distinct from those of the USSR.

Poland has a population of around 30,000,000. The formal name of the country is the People's Republic of Poland, and the capital is Warsaw. Poland possesses good resources of iron ore, coal, zinc, copper, lead, and other minerals, and the country is advancing in industrialization.

The Pole has always remained a Pole, no matter who governed his country. The Pole has for centuries shown an independence of spirit and a pride in his country and his culture. He has testified to these feelings with his blood on numerous occasions. He may presently be tied to Russia by politics and economics, but he wants those ties to be as flexible as possible.

Ancient castles, bridges, towers, and statues make Prague, Czechoslovakia one of the most attractive capital cities behind the Iron Curtain. (Wide World photo)

### Czechoslovakia

The Czechoslovakians are also mostly of the Slavic family of man. The two largest groups in the country are the Czechs, who number about 8,000,000, and the Slovaks, who number around 3,500,000. There are also large minorities of Hungarians, Germans, Poles, and Ukrainians in the country. The capital of Czechoslovakia is Prague. The total population of the country is around 13,750,000.

Czechoslovakia became formally an independent country in 1918 as part of the peace settlement after the First World War. Its history, however, goes back to the 900's when the people of three countries, Bohemia, Moravia, and Slovakia, were separate divisions of an old Moravian empire. At a later date, Bohemia and Moravia became members of the Holy Roman Empire, and most of the country was governed by Austria until Austria was defeated in the First World War.

Tomáš G. Masaryk and Eduard Beneš were the founders of the new republic, and Masaryk became its first president. As an independent democratic country Czechoslovakia had a short history of about twenty years. Hitler dissolved the state in 1939, and parts of it were divided between Germany, Hungary, and Poland. In 1945 the army of the USSR occupied Czechoslovakia, and after a few years the country became a Communist-dominated state with a constitution modeled after that of the Soviet Union. It is now known formally as the Czechoslovak Socialist Republic.

Czechoslovakia was an industrialized country when the Communists took it over, and it has continued to turn out industrial products in increasing quantities. It is well known for its munitions, steel, glass, shoes, textiles, and other products. Although the country has oil, uranium, coal, iron ore, and other resources, it still must depend upon the Soviet Union for raw materials to keep the economy expanding. It is one of the countries that the USSR depends upon to help in its foreign assistance to other nations.

About 75 per cent of the people are Roman Catholic, and the remainder are Protestant and Eastern Orthodox. But the ruling group is Communist.

1. Name the "satellite" countries of East Europe, and the order in which they became Communist-dominated.
2. Describe the history of Polish partition and rule by the Germans and Russians.
3. When was Czechoslovakia created as an independent nation? How long did its independence last?

East Berliners met in a mass demonstration to hear a Cuban Communist party leader speak against the United States' blockade of Cuba in 1962. East Germany seems drab and poor in comparison to the thriving republic of West Germany. (United Press International)

## East Germany and Berlin: Contrast Between Two Systems

After the Second World War, Germany was divided into two parts: the eastern part occupied by Soviets, and the western part occupied by the allied powers of England, France, and the United States. Berlin, the former capital of Germany, lay in the Russian-occupied zone, and it was divided up into sectors governed by the USSR, the United States, France, and England. The part now governed by France, England, and the United States is known as West Berlin, and the section governed by the USSR is now called East Berlin.

In 1955, France, England, and the United States recognized the area of Germany they had occupied as an independent republic. It became the Federal Republic of Germany, commonly referred to as West Germany. Its capital is Bonn. The East German Democratic Republic was proclaimed in 1949 in the Russian-occupied part of Germany. Its capital was located in East Berlin, the sector of the city the Russians controlled. East Germany is recognized by the Communist bloc of nations, but it is not legally recognized by most of the Free World nations. East Germany has a territory of about 41,000 square miles and a population of approximately 17,000,000. It is smaller than West Germany, which has about 96,000 square miles and a population of about 56,900,000.

East Germany is extremely important to the power of the USSR in Western Europe. It is estimated that there are around half a million Soviet soldiers in East Germany and huge supplies of war equipment. Because of this, East Germany is supervised rather closely. Though it is recognized as an independent country, there is a Soviet High Commissioner, who is the ultimate authority in the country. From the very beginning, the USSR has had many difficulties in governing and supporting East Germany.

Grave economic problems have curtailed the economic growth of East Germany and contributed to restlessness among the people. This has embarrassed the governments of East

Germany and the USSR because next-door is the prosperous, booming state of West Germany. Under a scorned capitalist system, West Germany has renewed itself from the ruins of war and become one of the world's great industrial nations. In East Germany, under the Communists, there is stagnation, poverty, and austerity. The contrasting results of two systems in action have depressed the Communists and exalted the West. Nowhere is this more evident than in Berlin itself, where the two systems meet in open display.

On the one side, in West Berlin there are new glittering buildings rising daily from the debris of war; while in East Berlin the rubble of war still covers much of the ground in ugly heaps. In West Berlin there is a rush of workers to busy factories, offices, and shops, and everywhere the pulse of life beats firmly. The man of West Berlin has a spring to his stride, an assurance in his voice, and a certain manner that bears the message of hope. In East Berlin there is a grayness in man and in the environment, a listlessness of face and act which tells of no ambition and little hope. Housing in East Berlin is scarce and poor, the shops carry little to buy, and what there is costs much. Life is regimented, and the people live in fear of the police. The East Berliner frequently has only one hope, one purpose—to escape.

Since the establishment of East Germany, there has been a continuous migration from there to West Berlin and West Germany. In all, it is estimated that almost four million persons have gone from East to West Germany. At least 50 per cent of these escapees were under 25 years of age. A large percentage of them were professional men—engineers, doctors, professors, and skilled technicians.

This outward flood of skilled men and women from East Germany has aggravated its economic problems and brought shame on the system which drove them out. The Communists took various measures to prevent the exodus of their manpower. Finally, in 1961, they sealed off East Berlin and East Germany from the West by walls of stone and barriers of barbed wire. Fewer get through now, but there are those who still try. Some are lucky, and some are shot.

Because the presence of Western powers in Berlin was agreed upon at the conclusion of the defeat of Germany, the Russians and East Germans can do little to remove this prosperous showcase of another system from inside their boundaries. The Communist rulers of East Germany have tried all kinds of harassments—stopping the surface supply routes from West Germany, trying to limit the air routes, putting the unrecognized East Germans in charge of administrative matters, and threatening to make a separate peace treaty. But the Western powers have stubbornly maintained their legal right to be in Berlin. There is no doubt that Berlin is a source of friction between the USSR and the West, and there is always the danger that this friction may spark a conflict which might lead to a general war. Both sides would prefer to have the question settled in some way, but up to now no workable formula has been found to resolve this question.

West Berlin is an island of capitalist prosperity within a land made drab and poor by the Communist system. It is a temptation and a reality which the Communists want very much to remove from the sight of those they govern.

1. Describe the division of Germany following World War II.
2. When did the West German Federal Republic become independent?
3. What is the relation between East Germany and the USSR?

## Bulgaria

Bulgaria takes its name from an Asian tribe, akin to the Huns, known as Bulgars. The Bulgars invaded the country during the seventh century and mixed with Slavic people who were already there. Historically, the Bulgarians never had the same suspicion or animosity toward Russia which characterized the Poles.

The Bulgarians often looked to Russia for aid when threatened by others, and they generally practiced the same Eastern Orthodox religion as the Russians. The Bulgarians have been Christian since the 800's, but there are also about 75,000 Moslems in the country. The Moslem Turks conquered and governed the country beginning in 1393. During the late 1800's, the Russians aided the Bulgarians in overthrowing their Turkish rulers. Finally, in 1908, Bulgaria became an independent country. It was ruled by its own tsar until 1946, when the monarchy was abolished.

Bulgaria was allied to Germany during most of the Second World War. At the conclusion of the war, it was occupied by Soviet troops. The same pattern was followed as elsewhere. A Communist government was established there in 1946, and Georgi Dimitrov became the first Communist premier.

Bulgaria is primarily an agricultural country. Its main exports are grains, tobacco, potatoes, and fruit. The Bulgarians are attempting to build up an industrial base in the country, and they are succeeding. Bulgarian foreign policy is patterned after that of the USSR, and is not, for the most part, a problem to the Soviet Union. The capital of Bulgaria is Sofia, and the nation's population is around 7,900,000.

### Romania

Romania has a long history. The land was occupied by the Romans from about 101 A.D. to 274 A.D., and the Romanian language has a Latin base. Romania has been invaded often, and for many years it was under the domination of the Turks. The Romanian people have been influenced by the Romans, the Slavs, the Greeks, and the Turks, and these influences may be observed in the Romanian language. Romania became independent of the Turks in 1877, but was occupied by Soviet troops during the Second World War. In 1947 Romania became a Communist-led state and has remained under Communist rule since that time.

The people of Romania are mostly Eastern Orthodox in religion. Agriculture is the most important industry, but Romania has some excellent natural resources, including oil, and is rapidly on the way to developing manufacturing industries. Its capital is Bucharest. The country has a population of about 18,500,000.

### Hungary

The Hungarians have known the heavy hand of invaders, as have the other peoples of Eastern Europe who have been exposed to the raids of man from both the east and the west. It was the Slavs and the Germans who settled the land of Hungary first, but they were overcome by the terrible thrusts of the Huns and the Magyars who descended upon them from the steppes of the East. In 1001 Hungary became a kingdom, under Stephen I, and around the same time it became a Christian nation. The vast majority of the Hungarian people are Roman Catholic, but there is a small Protestant minority. In the 1500's the country was conquered by the Turks, who were driven out later by the combined efforts of the Hungarians and the Austrians. Hungary became a part of the dual monarchy of Austria-Hungary in 1867. Except for a short Communist rule under the Bolshevik leader Béla Kun after the First World War, Hungary remained a monarchy until World War II. After the war, in 1947, a Communist government was established.

The Soviet Union received a bad shock when, in 1956, the Hungarian people expressed dissatisfaction with their Communist governors by a violent rebellion. Revolution spread quickly throughout the country. The Communists, however, do not approve of revolution when it is against themselves. Soviet armed forces, tanks, and troops sped quickly to put down the revolt with harshness and finality. Thousands upon thousands were killed and wounded in conflict with the Soviet troops, and other thousands were executed and imprisoned. Almost 200,000 people fled the country for refuge elsewhere. The rebels were brave, daring, and almost successful, but they were poorly armed and could not withstand the hundreds of thousands of Soviet troops nor the waves of their armored tanks.

The Russians were infuriated because the Hungarian rebellion made it necessary for them to reveal the steel hand with which they controlled. They would have preferred not to show this hand that really ruled. The Hungarians are quiet now, and living conditions have greatly improved. Next to Poland, Hungary is one of the most liberally governed of the satellites.

Hungary is primarily an agricultural land and is well known for its good wines. In recent years industry has been expanded, and industrial exports are becoming increasingly important to the economy of the nation. The capital of Hungary is Budapest, and the population of the nation is around 10,000,000 people.

### Yugoslavia

The Yugoslav is a mixture of various strains of man—the Serb, the Croat, and the Slovene, among others. Yugoslavia was formed of these three main groups after the First World War, and the country was ruled by Peter I of Serbia. In 1941 the Germans invaded the country, and from that time until near the end of the Second World War, Yugoslavia was a place of conflict. A national liberation movement was established under the leadership of Josip Broz, later known as Marshal Tito, and he waged a fierce guerrilla war against the Germans all during the war. Tito was a Communist, and in 1945 he proclaimed the country a republic. Since that time Yugoslavia has been a Communist country. Marshal Tito is the present ruler of Yugoslavia's 18,800,000 people.

In Yugoslavia, too, the Soviet Union received a severe shock from which it has not yet wholly recovered. Tito refused to bow always to the will of Stalin in foreign policy or to have his national policies dictated by the USSR. He started to practice policies different from those of Stalin. Tito was denounced by the USSR in 1948, and there was an organized international Communist effort to unseat him and raise more obedient men to the seats of power in the country. Tito survived these attacks and launched upon a neutralist policy in the Cold War between the West and the Communist World. He accepted aid from the United States and other non-Communist countries and followed an independent line.

When Premier Khrushchev came to power in the USSR in the years following the death of Stalin in 1953, he embarked upon a policy of wooing Marshal Tito back into the Communist fold. Khrushchev apologized to Tito for the former policies of Stalin and offered to work more cooperatively with Yugoslavia. Tito did not return completely to the Russian Communist camp, but there was a distinct improvement of relations between the two countries. There was no easing of relations between Yugoslavia and the Chinese Communists, however. The Chinese continued to regard Tito as a traitor to the Communist cause and spoke of his errors as a conservative religious person might speak of heresy.

Yugoslavia was traditionally an agricultural country, but Tito has striven to turn it into more of an industrial country. He has been succeeding, and gradually the economy of the country is becoming more balanced. Tito continues to need economic assistance from the outside and has accepted aid from the United States and other free nations. But the growing rapport between Premier Khrushchev and Marshal Tito made a number of American government officials suspicious of Tito's future intentions.

Marshal Tito is one of the prominent neutralists of the world. He has attempted to steer a middle course between the opposing blocs in the Cold War. He is friendly with Nasser of Egypt and others who espouse neutralism in foreign policy. In the Yugoslavian capital of Belgrade, the neutralists have met on several occasions to define and publicize their common purposes.

### Albania

The smallest of the Communist countries is Albania. It has a population of only around 1,600,000 persons living in an area of about 10,630 square miles. Its capital city is Tiranë.

Albania has been fought over for many centuries. In modern days the Turks, Italians, and others have controlled and coveted its territory. In 1946 it became a Communist country under the control of General Enver Hoxha. Here too, the USSR has had a problem. The Albanians broke off relations with the Soviet Union in 1961 in protest against the policy of peaceful coexistence with the West and other questions of doctrine. The Albanians insisted that war with the capitalist countries was inevitable, and they condemned many of the policies of Khrushchev and his supporters. After the break with the USSR, Albania and Communist China maintained close relations and joined in alliance with each other. They constantly joined together in denouncing the more peaceful policies of Premier Khrushchev with regard to the West.

Albania has a majority of Moslems, but there are also members of the Eastern Orthodox and Roman Catholic faiths in the country. Albania is not a strong country, and it is having problems with its larger neighbor, Yugoslavia. Although it is small, Albania can be annoying, and larger countries dare not move against it lest an international explosion burst forth.

1. Describe the historic ties between Bulgaria and Russia.
2. What is Communist Yugoslavia's relationship with the USSR?
3. What is Albania's position in the struggle between Russia and China for leadership of world Communism?

## Communism in Asia

In the chapters on Asia, the Communist countries of Asia have been noted and described. They are Communist China, North Korea, and North Vietnam. A good part of Laos is under Communist control, as are parts of South Vietnam. These countries appear to be more influenced by their close Communist neighbor, China, than by the USSR. The Communists control a great many people in Asia, and there is evidence that their numbers are growing there. Poverty, worsening conditions of living, and the constant subversive activities of Communists in the Asian countries are all contributing to the slide of millions into the hands of Communist leaders. Most of the Asian Communists are oriented toward China rather than toward the USSR.

## Communist Goals Elsewhere

In countries not ruled by Communists, there are Communist parties. In some countries, such as France, Italy, and Indonesia, these parties have millions of members. Even in countries where Communism has been outlawed, there are many thousands of Communists who work in secret ways to achieve their purposes. They have made their greatest gains in countries whose people have long lived without hope of attaining the good life. In these countries, many people have grasped at the shining promises of Communism with the eagerness of the dying who would be saved.

Once enveloped in the dogma and the discipline of the party, there are few who leave. Those who do leave it live in fear and in uncertainty, for the party has been known to take cruel revenge. Once a member of the party, a man is expected, indeed commanded, to sacrifice everything for its aims. And the chief aim is ultimate domination of the world by the Communist party. The Communists believe that any means justifies this end. There is a time for softness and a time for violence, a time for cooperation with others and a time to remain separate—only the ultimate goal shines steady and unchanging: the coming of Communism.

The successes of the Communists have alarmed a large part of the non-Communist world. After the Second World War the nations of the Free World began to take collective action to offset Communist expansion. The United States led this movement. Afraid that all of Europe might fall to the Communists, President Truman proclaimed a doctrine supporting free people everywhere who were resisting subjection by armed minorities and outside groups. The Marshall Plan was begun to solve some of the internal problems of hunger, poverty, and lack of hope, which had made Communism seem so appealing in many countries. Economic aid was given to underdeveloped countries through the Marshall Plan. Recently an Alliance for Progress program was initiated for Latin America, where Communists have been multiplying. Money, goods, and technical skills have poured

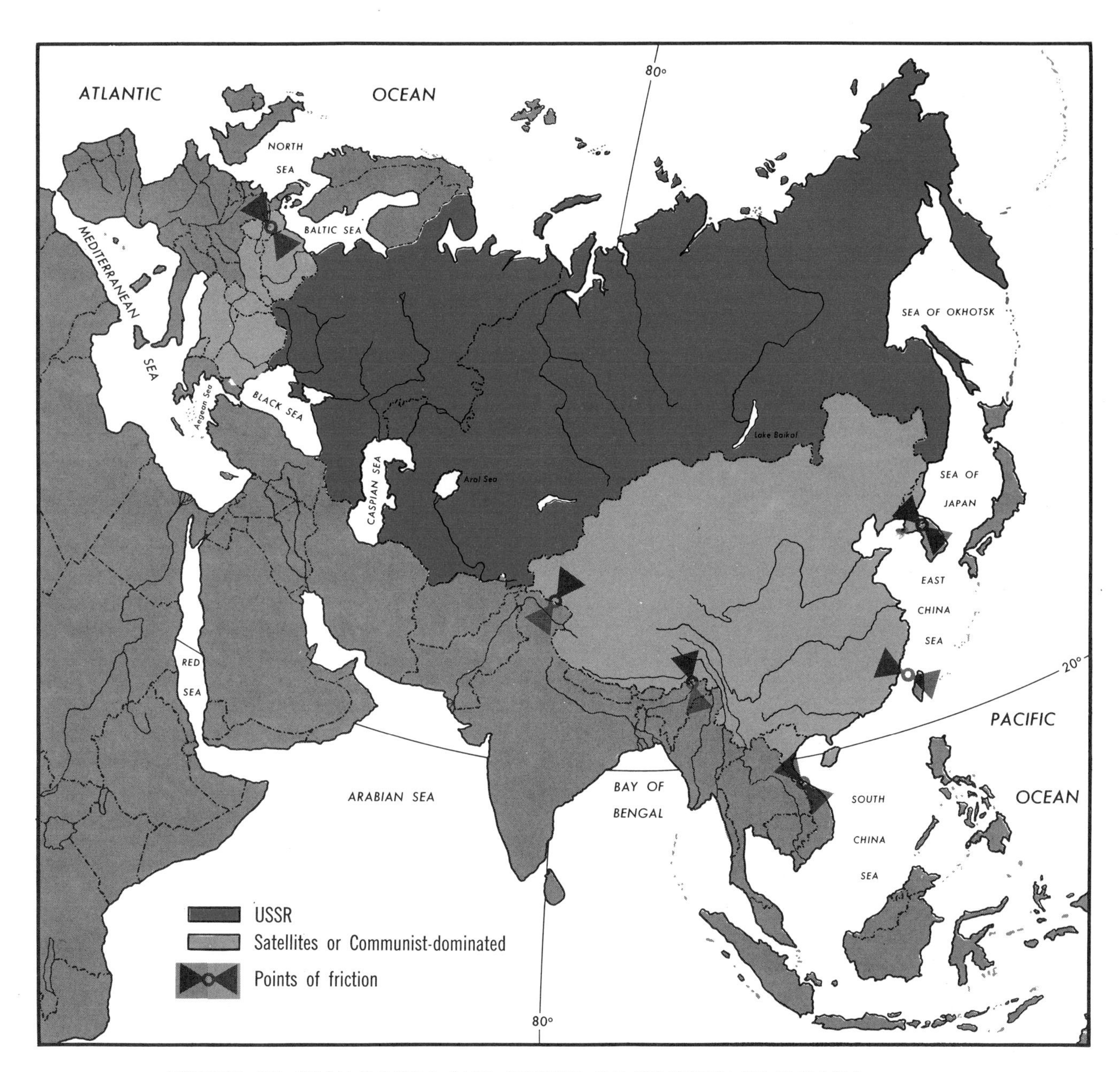


**EXTENT OF COMMUNISM AND POINTS OF FRICTION IN EURASIA**

Compare this map with the map on page 462. Are there any similarities between the spread of Communism since 1918 and the growth of Russia before 1914? In what ways does the spread of Communism differ from previous Russian national expansion? The points of friction represent military clashes.

from the United States in unimaginable quantities in the hope of stopping this Communist growth. The program of aid worked quite well in Western Europe, but in other parts of the world the issue is yet in doubt.

The external threat of the USSR was met by the North Atlantic Treaty Organization (NATO), which has its headquarters in Europe. Two other regional security pacts are also directed against the spread of Communism: the Central Treaty Organization (CENTO) for the Middle East and the Southeast Asia Treaty Organization (SEATO). From shortly after the Second World War until the present, the powerful nations of the world have been divided into two opposing camps—the Communist World and the Free World.

The Communists have persisted in their efforts to make all men Communist. The Free World citizens have persisted in their efforts to keep men free. Tension and anxiety have grown among men, for all fear the possibility of atomic war. Many kinds of war have become man's unwanted companions and disturbed his complacency and peace of mind. There is the war of nerves, the war of words, and the war of violence. Above all, men have feared that war might erupt in radioactive dust which would include all of the world in its poison. All these wars and threats of war have been given a chilly collective name—the Cold War.

There are those within the Communist World who do not agree on how far this war should go. The Russian has built his industry and economy to the point where he could have much to lose if bombs fell upon him. Under Nikita Khrushchev, the USSR began to advocate a lessening of tensions between the Communist nations and the Free World. The Russian Communists preached a doctrine of coexistence, which meant no atomic war, but they continued competition in all other ways.

The Chinese Communists disagreed with Khrushchev in method, although not in their ultimate goal. They maintained that the old doctrine of Communism was still valid: that capitalism will never be overthrown except by violence. The Chinese Communists can rely upon their numbers—700,000,000—to survive in some portion the destroying power of the atomic bomb. The USSR dominates only slightly over 200,000,000 people, and the Russians do not share either the confidence or the poverty of the Chinese. Soviet leaders have been reluctant to risk a war they probably will not survive. Over this question, an ever-widening gulf has developed between the Communists of the USSR and the Communist Chinese. To what future it will lead, no one knows.

In the Communist World only the officials and the appointed are permitted to voice solutions to the questions of the Cold War. But in the world where the voice is free, a multitude of men have offered their answers to solving the tense relations between the Free World and the Communist World. Often the answers that they propose are contradictory, and conflicting. This, too, has led to confusion, uncertainty, and irritation. Deep in his consciousness the man of the Free World recognizes the stalemate of terror which the atomic bomb represents. He knows that he must prevent atomic war while yet maintaining his freedoms and his defenses against Communist domination. He knows that he must continue to seek knowledge, to ponder, to be strong, and most of all to be patient, for these are mighty problems which only patience and time can solve.

## Conclusion

The Russian Communists were led to ring their country with satellites for a number of reasons. For a long time, since the process first began in Moscow, the Russians have been expanding their borders. The USSR now controls directly one-sixth of the world's land surface, and its movement into eastern Europe and elsewhere is but the continuation of this swelling tendency. For some time, even prior to the coming of Communism to Russia, Russian leaders wanted loyal buffer states between themselves and the larger powers of Western Europe. Such states served as protection because they could absorb the first heavy blows of an invader. The Communist leaders of Russia inherited the desire for satellites from their non-Communist ancestors. Then, too, there is the aim of making the whole world Communistic. Few opportunities are neglected in trying to achieve this aim. The Communists believe that they hold the ultimate truth of man's life. Like all who believe they are destined to impose the truth upon others, they are extremely active in spreading their beliefs to all corners of the globe.

Toward the conclusion of the Second World War the USSR succeeded in sending troops into the countries of eastern Europe and into Manchuria and North Korea in eastern Asia. The Soviet rulers inevitably used their might and their opportunity to establish Communist governments in occupied lands. They have used their might and their influence to tie these areas closer to their political and economic purposes ever since. Some nations, like China and Yugoslavia, have proved more nationalistic and stubborn than loyal to domination by the USSR, and there are rifts growing within the former union among them.

As time moves along, the Soviet Union is finding it difficult to retain control over the satellites that make up the Communist frontiers. It has often been necessary to woo these satellites with compromise, with concessions, and with relaxed control; but the USSR has no intention of freeing them from ultimate control unless they win independence by force of arms. The Soviet leaders have realistically recognized the power of force, and it is a part of their doctrine. Only the power of armed force or the threat of destruction to themselves will tear from the Russian Communists the Communist-ruled lands they have placed between themselves and those they consider to be enemies.

## SUMMING UP THE CHAPTER

A. Locate the following cities on a map and tell what countries they are in.

| | |
|---|---|
| Belgrade | Prague |
| Bonn | Sofia |
| Bucharest | Tiranë |
| Budapest | Warsaw |

B. Identify the following and tell why they are important.

| | |
|---|---|
| Béla Kun | John Sobieski |
| Eduard Beneš | Josip Broz Tito |
| General Enver Hoxha | Ladislas II |
| Georgi Dimitrov | Stephen I |
| Ignace Paderewski | Tomáš Masaryk |

C. Identify these dates and indicate their importance.

| | |
|---|---|
| 101-274 | 1908 |
| 1001 | 1918 |
| 1683 | 1956 |
| 1867 | 1961 |
| 1877 | |

D. Chapter review questions.

1. How were the Communist governments of eastern Europe installed? To what extent were they the product of Russian occupation of countries after World War II?
2. What has been the economic effect on East Germany of the mass escapes to West Germany and West Berlin? What have the East German and the Soviet governments done to stop this flow of people to the West?
3. Why do you suppose the leaders of the USSR have not reacted more vigorously to Albania's defiance of Russian leadership?
4. Why was the Hungarian revolt of 1956 such an embarrassment to the USSR?
5. What is meant when the satellite nations of eastern Europe are referred to as "buffer states"?
6. What satellites have attempted to become independent of Soviet domination? How successful have they been?
7. What other Communist countries have sought to take leadership of world Communism away from the USSR? How successful have they been?

E. Questions for discussion.

1. Why is the existence of West Berlin such a threat to the Communists? What has been the reaction of the East German and Soviet governments to this threat?
2. How did eastern Europe come under Soviet domination and control at the end of World War II? What boundaries are marked by the Elbe River? By the Oder-Neisse Line?
3. What role has traditional Russian imperialism played in the drive of the USSR to control eastern Europe? Which would you say was the more important in this drive—Communism or Russian imperialism?

F. Projects for groups or individuals.

1. Read a biography of the great Polish pianist-statesman, Ignace Paderewski and report on it in class.

2. On a map of Europe trace the boundary line between East and West Germany. What natural boundary does it follow? Why?

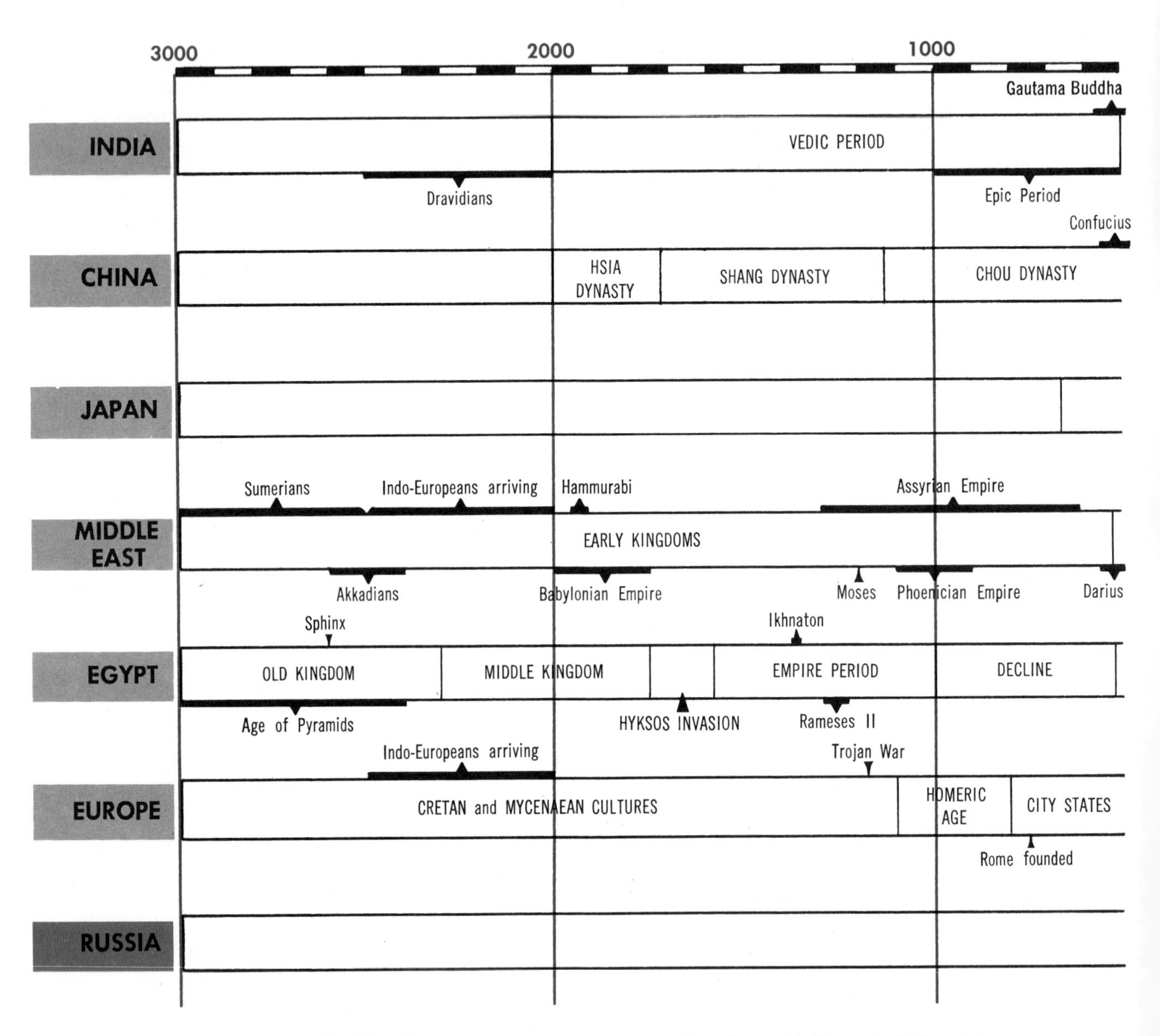


## MILESTONES

RUSSIA

A.D.

| | |
|---|---|
| c. 862 | Rurik establishes government at Novgorod |
| c. 882 | Vikings control Kiev |
| late 980s | Vladimir I brings Christianity to Russia |
| 1015-1054 | Reign of Yaroslav the Wise |
| 1162-1227 | Genghis Khan: united tribes of steppes |
| c. 1237-1243 | Golden Horde conquers Russia |
| 1480 | Ivan III overthrows Tatars |
| 1533-1584 | Reign of Ivan the Terrible |
| 1604-1613 | Time of Troubles |
| 1613-1917 | Romanov dynasty |
| 1689-1725 | Reign of Peter the Great |
| 1762-1796 | Reign of Catherine the Great |
| 1812 | Napoleon invades Russia |

3. Prepare a map showing the divided city of Berlin, with its British, French, and American occupation zones. Also show the rail, highway, and air "corridors" or access routes to West Berlin from West Germany. Why are these so important?
4. Prepare a report on the 1956 Hungarian revolt. Why was it unsuccessful?

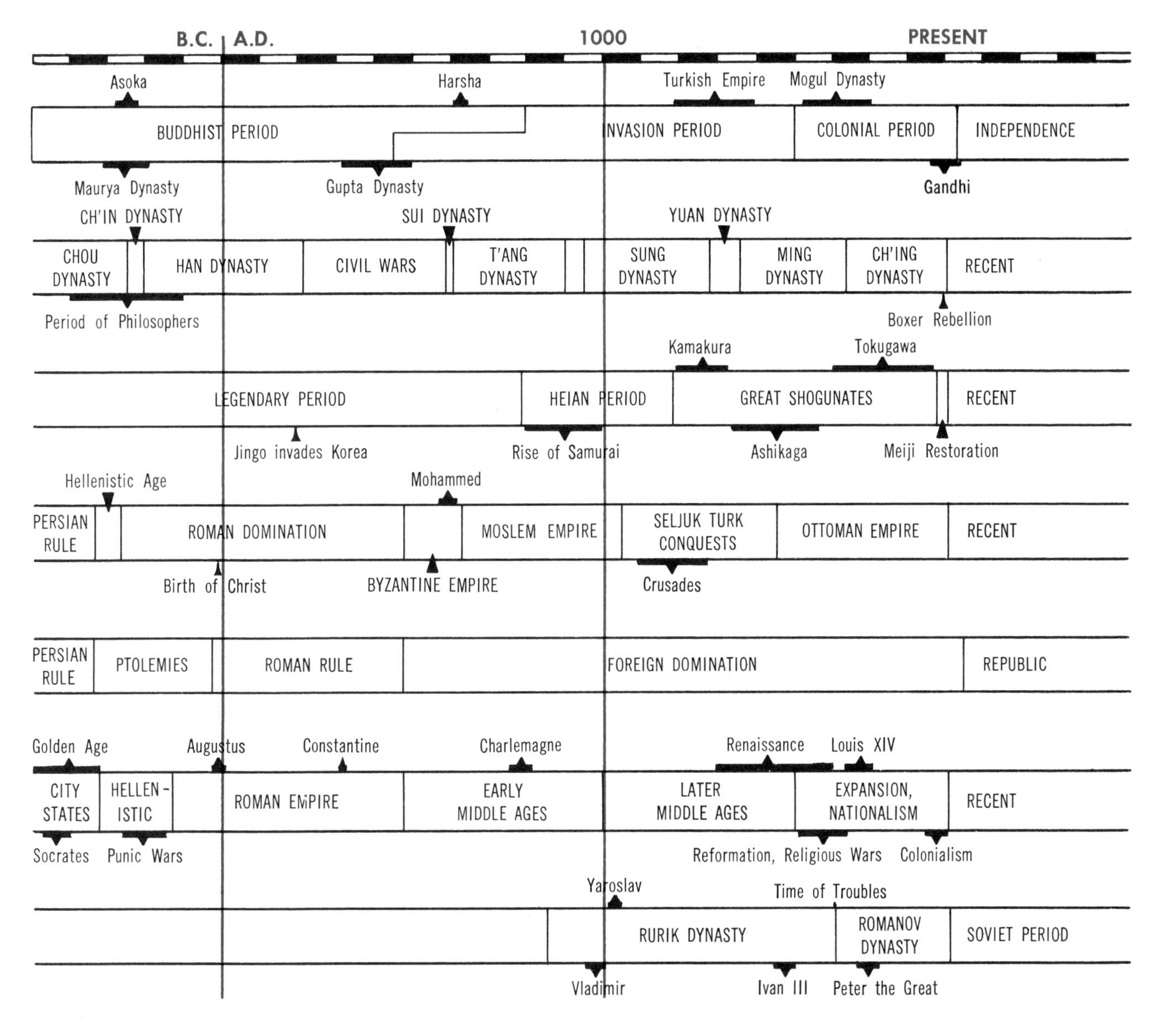


| | |
|---|---|
| 1848 | Communist Manifesto |
| 1861 | Serfs freed |
| 1904-1905 | Russo-Japanese War |
| 1917 | Revolutions end Tsarist rule |
| 1917-1924 | Lenin rules |
| 1926-1953 | Stalin holds supreme power |
| 1928 | First five-year plan begins |
| 1941 | Germany invades Russia |
| 1948 | Berlin blockade |
| 1953 | Khrushchev becomes First Secretary |
| 1957 | Russians place first satellite in space |
| 1958 | Khrushchev becomes Premier of Soviet Union |
| 1964 | Khrushchev falls from power |

## SUMMING UP THE UNIT

### *Drawing together the main themes*

1. What was the Comintern? Why was it dissolved? What succeeded it?
2. What was the purpose of the Marshall Plan? How successful was it? How was it extended?
3. What are the three major regional alliances of the Free World?
4. What is the Alliance for Progress?
5. What strategic considerations make it possible for the Chinese Communists to advocate a "hard" policy toward the non-Communist world, even including nuclear war?
6. What is meant when it is said that Communism in practice is a totalitarian system?
7. In what countries are there large Communist parties?
8. What appeal does Communism have in the underdeveloped countries? What steps has the Free World taken to minimize this appeal?
9. What has been the position of the United Nations in the struggle between the Communist world and the Free World? How is the effectiveness of the UN limited in this area? What is meant when it is said that the UN is a "sounding board," "talking place," or a "forum" for all sides? What valuable results have been obtained from even this limited role?
10. Compare the rigidity of Romanov rule with that of China under the Manchus, and Japan under the Tokugawas. What similarities do you find in style of rule, reaction to the West, technology, and the final opening up of the country to foreign influences?
11. Compare the Russian Revolution with the French and American revolutions. Why is the Russian Revolution more similar to the French than to the American Revolution?
12. What has been the effect of industrialization and the growth of cities on the individualism of the Soviet people? Has the effect of industrialization and the growth of cities been the same elsewhere in the world? What about the Far East? Africa? The United States?
13. What does the Russian Communists' failure to mold the ideal socialist man tell you about human nature? About the theory of Marxism?
14. If Communism is inevitable, as Marxist theory proclaims, why do the Communists work so hard to assist in bringing about this "inevitable" future?

### *Unit projects for groups or individuals*

1. On an outline map of the USSR locate all of the land features discussed in this unit, and locate and label all of the cities.
2. Make a list of some outstanding Russian composers of the tsarist period and of some of the best-known modern Soviet composers. Listen to records of the music of several of these composers; read something about their lives in reference books.
3. Read several accounts of the Berlin Airlift of 1948-49 and prepare a report detailing the reasons behind the airlift. Be sure to include a description of the physical details of the airlift itself—length of flights, amount of freight carried, number of planes involved, etc.
4. Read and report on one of the books listed in the bibliography for this unit.

### FURTHER READINGS


ALEXANDER, ROBERT J., *Communism in Latin America.* Rutgers U., 1957. Good discussion of a real problem and danger in the American hemisphere.

BAKER, NINA BROWN, *Peter the Great.* Vanguard, 1943. Biography of a fascinating Russian tsar.

BARGHOORN, F. C., *The Soviet Image of the United States.* Harcourt, 1950. The USSR looks at the United States.

BLUNDEN, GODFREY, *The Room on the Route.* Lippincott, 1947. A novel which shows how Communist terror shatters the individual.

CALDWELL, JOHN C., *Communism In Our World.* Day, 1956. A primer on Communism for young people.

CRANKSHAW, EDWARD, *Khrushchev's Russia.* Peter Smith, 1960; Penguin, paperback.

CROSSMAN, R. H., ed. *The God That Failed.* Harper, 1950; Bantam, paperback. Various well-known persons tell how Communism failed them. Helps students to understand the attraction and then rejection of Communism by intellectuals.

EINAUDI, M., and others, *Communism in Western Europe.* Reynal and Hitchcock, 1948. Communism has had members and supporters in Western Europe for some time.

FISCHER, JOHN, *Why They Behave Like Russians.* Harper, 1947. History also influences the behavior of the Russians.

HARCAVE, SIDNEY S., *Russia, a History,* 4th ed. Lippincott, 1959. Especially good account since 1917.

KELLY, ERIC, *The Land of the Polish People,* rev. ed. Lippincott, 1964.

KENNAN, GEORGE F., *Russia and the West under Lenin and Stalin.* Little, 1961. A keen analysis of the course of Soviet-Western relations. A difficult but challenging book.

KRAVCHENKO, VICTOR A., *I Chose Freedom.* Scribner's, 1946. A Russian official tells why he escaped to the West.

LENGYEL, EMIL, *Siberia.* Random, 1943. Russia expanded into a tremendous stretch of land.

LESSNER, ERWIN C., *Cradle of Conquerors: Siberia.* Doubleday, 1955. The steppes that Russia controls today were alive with people in very early times.

LIBRARY OF CONGRESS, *Communism in Action.* U. S. Govt. Printing Office, 1946. A good description.

MAZOUR, ANATOLE G., *Russia: Past and Present.* Van Nostrand, 1951. Contains much on the religion, the arts, and culture of Russia.

NAZAROFF, ALEXANDER, *The Land of the Russian People*, rev. ed. Lippincott, 1960.

ROBERTS, HENRY L., *Russia and America.* Harper, 1956; New Am. Lib., paperback. The two countries have a tense and continuing relationship.

ROSTOW, W. W., and others, *The Dynamics of Soviet Society.* New Am. Lib., paperback, 1954. Several scholars probe the Russian's behavior.

SALISBURY, HARRISON E., *American in Russia.* Harper, 1955. A clarification of the character of the Soviet system.

SEEGAR, ELIZABETH, *Pageant of Russian History.* McKay, 1950. A carefully presented account of Russian history from its beginnings up until 1945.

SIENKIEWICZ, HENRY, *With Fire and Sword.* Various editions. The Poles have been fighting the Russians for a long time. This is a novel about them in the seventeenth century.

SLONIM, MARC, *Outline of Russian Literature.* Oxford U., 1958; New Am. Lib., paperback. The Russian has written, and sometimes well.

THOMSON, GLADYS SCOTT, *Catherine the Great and the Expansion of Russia.* Macmillan, 1950. Good biography for the general reader of an interesting woman ruler and the social background of eighteenth century Russia.

TOLSTOY, L., *Anna Karenina.* Mod. Lib. and various other editions. A famous author writes a classic tale which pictures both country and city people of Russia in the nineteenth century.

———, *War and Peace.* Various editions. Another classic work which revolves around the invasion of Russia by Napoleon.

ULAM, ADAM B., *Titoism and the Cominform.* Harvard U., 1952. There are some Communists who do not wish to be dictated to by the Russian leaders.

WILMOT, CHESTER, *Struggle for Europe.* Harper, 1952. Perhaps Eastern Europe need not have been lost to Communism.

WREN, MELVIN C., *The Course of Russian History.* Macmillan, 1958. A popular history textbook.

# UNIT VI

The countries of North and South America
had their beginnings as parts of
Indian empires and as colonies
of European nations.
European cultures transplanted to
the New World grew and changed
in their new environment.
The cultures and peoples of the
Americas today present
a study in diversity.

# THE TWO AMERICAS

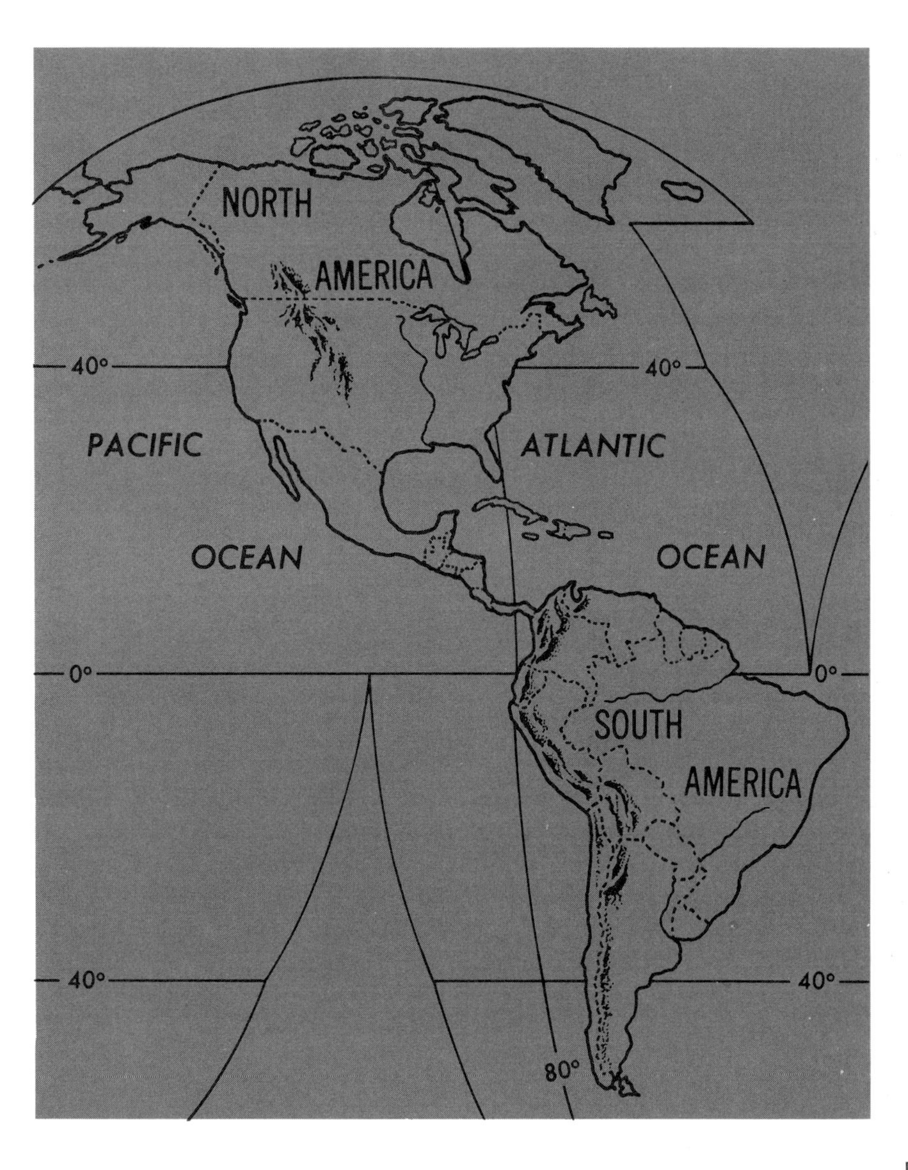

# CHAPTER 29

# Man in the Americas

IT WAS THE Indians who first settled and spread over the sweeping lands of the Americas. They were named *Indians* because the European explorers who came to America thought that they had reached the land of India. Most scholars believe that Indians came to the Americas by way of the Bering Strait, far to the north. It is believed that the Eskimos, who live on the Arctic coasts of North America, also came by this route. Others believe it possible that there may have been boat trips across the Pacific by peoples of South Asia and the islands. All agree that Indians have lived in the Americas for thousands of years. Over this sweep of time, the Indians gradually peopled the varieties of America's environments with the varieties of their tribes.

## The Indian Peopled North America

The Indian settled in the Northwest where the trees are tall and bunched and the rivers rich in fish. Here he built houses of logs and hollowed out the trunks of trees for his boats. He roamed from place to place in the area west of the Rocky Mountains in search of deer and fish for his food. Or he gathered seeds and nuts which he pounded into flour to make bread, weaving baskets to contain the food he gathered. He wandered into the Southwest—into the lands that are Utah, Nevada, New Mexico, Arizona, Colorado, and northern Mexico—and here he ceased to wander and became a farmer of corn. There were few trees in these lands, and the Indian made his house of earth. He found the high passes through the Rocky Mountains and followed them to rove the stretching plains that lie between the Rockies and the Mississippi River. He moved with the millions of buffalo that grazed these vast plains of grass, for they were the source of his food, and their hides made coverings for his tents and leather for his other needs. After the Spaniards came and left some of their horses, the Indians found them and began to ride them. The use of horses made life more convenient and hunting more profitable.

The Indian crossed the wide Mississippi and made his home on the banks of lakes and rivers and in the thick woodlands of eastern Canada. He moved into northeast and southeast United States. In the north, where it was cold, the Indian woman was skillful in making soft, warm clothes from the hide of the deer and the skin of the beaver. Where there was maple, the Indian tasted the sweetness of its sap, and he also knew which fruits and berries were good to eat and which nuts could be used for food. He fished the rivers, the lakes, and the ocean, and when he stalked wild game his step was as quiet as the falling leaf. He killed his game with bow and arrow, with a spear, or sometimes with a club, and he used knives, hatchets, arrow heads and spear heads made of flint. He cultivated corn, called *maize*, and pounded it into meal with a large pestle of hard wood. The bark of the plentiful trees supplied material to make dwellings and canoes, and the birch canoe is yet well known in eastern North America.

The Indian lived as a member of a tribe, and the family was basic to his society. He believed in spirits, and some of these spirits were believed to possess the animals of the forest and the plain, while others dwelled in the quiet depths of the river and the lake. They could be heard in the myriad sounds of the woods and in the roar of the storm, and

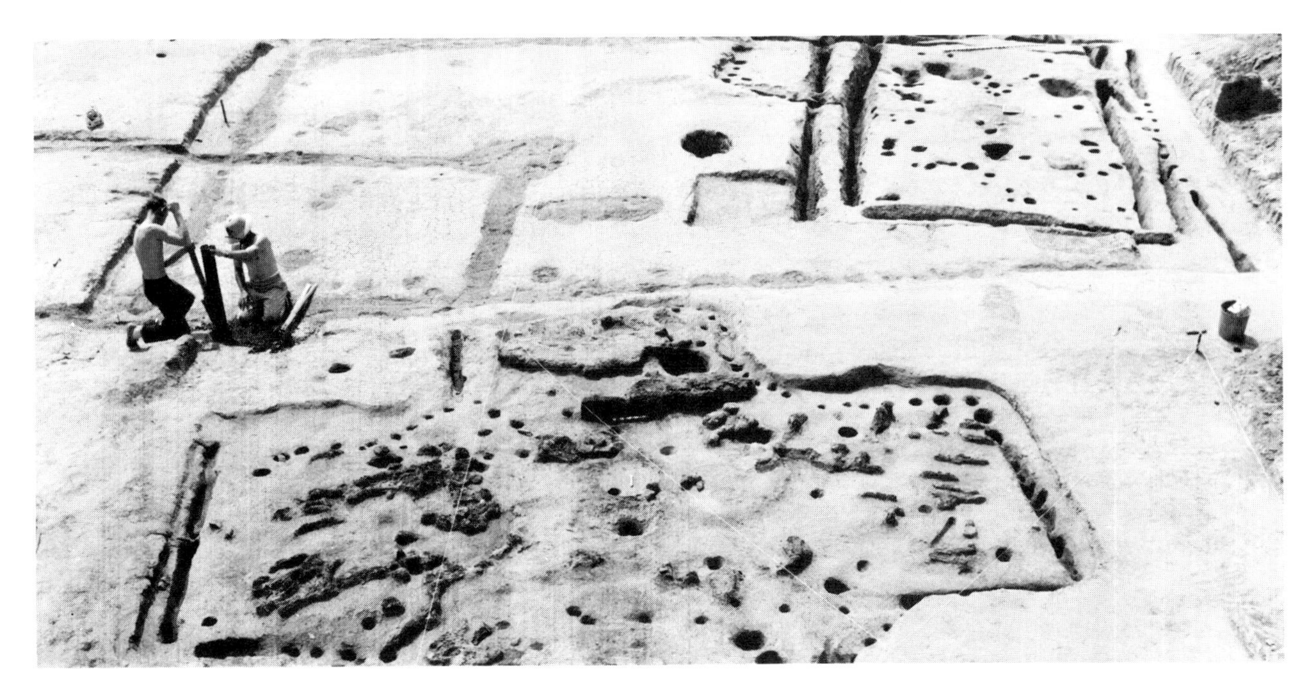

their power could be seen in the majesty of the sky and in the fertility of the earth. The Indian called upon the spirits to protect him from harm, to cure his sickness, and to make his hunt rewarding. He also had his moments of relaxation and his feasts, and he watched the young, energetic ones dance around the fire to the beat of the drum and the piping of flutelike instruments. He did not write, but passed his tales along from generation to generation by word of mouth. And he felt his customs to be right because they were sanctioned by antiquity. He had a fondness for decoration, and the clothes the Indian woman made were often brightened with the dyed quills of porcupines and the gaudy feathers of birds.

The Indian who lived in the land that is now Canada and the United States did not, however, reach the heights of civilization attained by some of his brothers in Mexico, Guatemala, and Peru.

North American Indians built villages and buried their dead in mounds as long ago as 1000 B.C. Above, the site of an ancient Indian village in Illinois. (Illinois State Museum) Below, Indian rock carvings in the Petrified Forest and wampum, which was used as money. (National Park Service; Chase Manhattan Bank Money Museum)

### Indian Civilizations of Latin America

There were three groups of Indians who achieved a high degree of civilization in Latin America — the Mayas, the Aztecs, and the Incas.

The Mayas spread their civilization from the area now called Guatemala to the Yucatan peninsula in Mexico. They reached the peaks of their glory from around 300 or 500 A.D. to about the year 1000. In general, they lived peacefully in cities which were independent of each other. In these cities, the priest-scholars ruled, and they knew the mysteries of mathematics, including the use of the zero. The Indians of India and the Indians of the Americas arrived at the use of the zero independently of each other. The Mayas built observatories and became fine astronomers. They created a calendar which was more accurate than the European calendar of the same time, and they developed a kind of hieroglyphic writing. Mayan temples were built atop great terraced pyramids, and the sculptured work in stone which embellished temples and cities is yet regarded with wonder. Merchants of these Mayan cities traveled on roads paved with stone and boated by sea to their trading destinations. Mayan artisans wove cloth, fashioned lovely jewelry, and made vases of beauty and usefulness. The majority of the Mayas were farmers, and their principal crop was corn. When the Spaniards first visited Yucatan in the 1500's, the Maya had already been conquered by the Aztec.

The Aztec learned much from the Maya, but his civilization, in terms of quality of achievement, was not as great as that of the

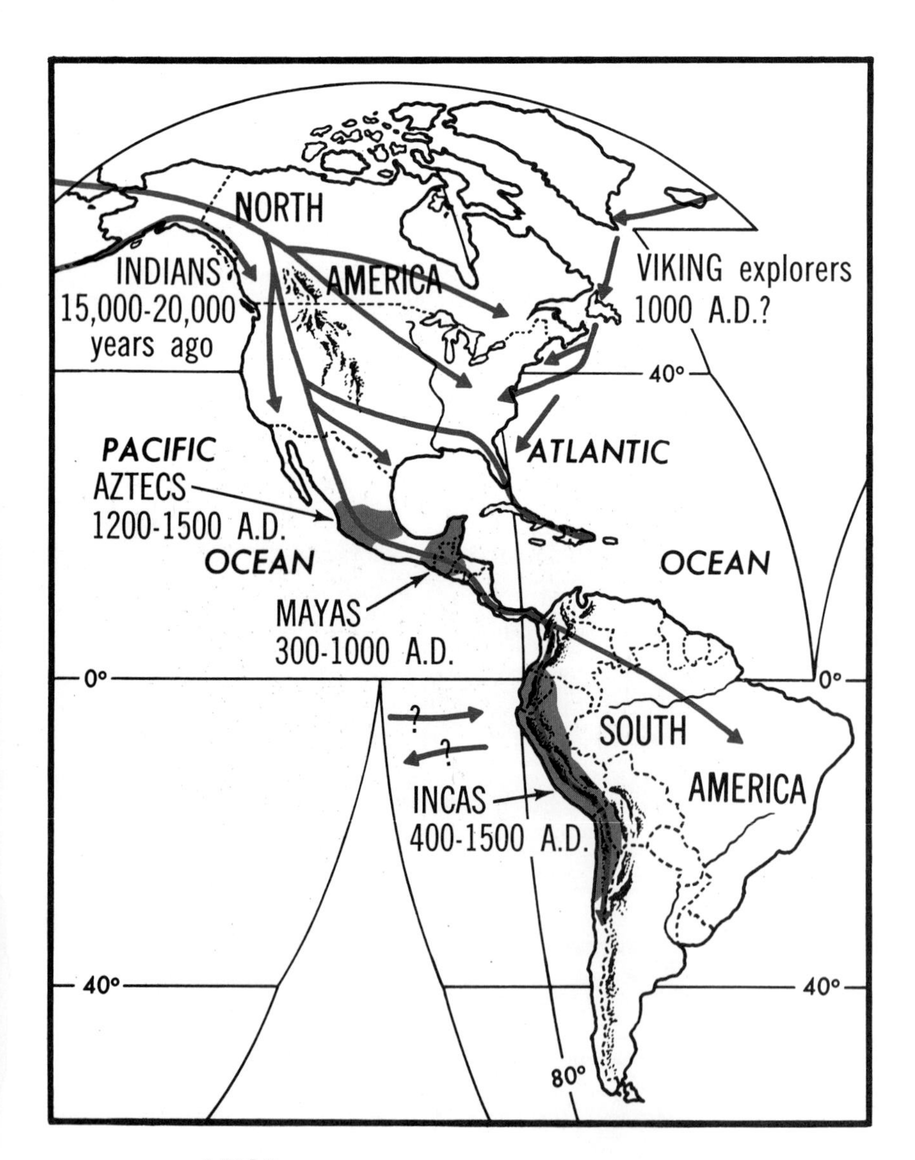


**Early Indian Empires and Viking Explorers in the Americas**

Before the voyages of Columbus, great Indian empires flourished in the Americas. Vikings had explored the eastern coast of North America by 1000 A.D., but their attempts to establish colonies failed. Much of the rich cultural heritage of the Indians was destroyed by conquering Europeans.

Maya. He, too, wrote with pictures, sculptured, painted, wove cloth, and possessed a calendar, though it was inferior to that of the Maya. The Aztec government was a well-organized system, ruling an empire that stretched from the Gulf of Mexico to the Pacific Ocean. There were courts which were empowered to judge the lowly and the high alike. The Aztecs, too, were ruled by a king who was also a priest, and the war god they worshiped demanded human sacrifices by the thousands. The main Aztec city was called Tenochtitlán, located on the high elevation where Mexico City stands today. The Aztecs were skilled engineers, and their buildings, dykes, bridges, and irrigation works were well built. Labor for these works came from many thousands of slaves and servants who dug canals, tilled the fields, and dragged the stones for temples.

The third great civilized Indian group of the Americas made up the Inca empire. The Inca capital was the city of Cuzco in Peru. Inca civilization flourished from around 400 A.D. to the 1500's when it was crushed by the Spaniards. At the height of their glory the Incas controlled the western parts of South America from Ecuador to Chile and northwestern Argentina. Inca messengers ran swiftly along roads which pierced the mountains and across bridges suspended over deep ravines. Along the way were rest houses for the convenience of the traveler. The Incas had a centralized government headed by an emperor who was considered to be descended from the sun god. Under the emperor there were governors who ruled parts of the empire. The Incas practiced a system in which property was held by the community.

The Incas had an advanced technology and knew surgery and the manufacture of bronze. In building, they joined huge blocks of stone so closely together that to this day a knife edge cannot be pushed between many of them. They domesticated the mountain animals called llamas, which bore their loads and gave wool from which cloth was made. The Incas terraced the mountainsides for growing their crops, of which the potato is the best

Corn was a basic agricultural product of the American Indians, and it is still a favorite food in both the Americas. Hundreds of products are made in modern factories from corn. Above, well filled-out ears of corn. Below, an ear of corn found in a prehistoric Indian grave in South America. (USDA, both)

The Pueblo, Maya, Inca, Aztec, and some Caribbean Indians knew the art of weaving and made beautiful textiles. Use reference books to learn when weaving was first known in various parts of the world. Above, an Inca doll illustrates the use of the A-frame loom. Right, Mayan stone carvings show a high degree of skill. (University Museum, Philadelphia; Standard Oil Co., N. J.)

The Aztecs built their temples atop huge pyramids of earth and stone. Many of these pyramids remain near Mexico City. (American Airlines)

known today. They knew the value of fertilizer and irrigation. Although the Incas never developed a written language, their achievements were great enough to still arouse our wonder.

There were also Indians elsewhere in Latin America. They lived in the rainy, tangled jungles of the Amazon, on the plains of Argentina and the coasts of Brazil, and on the lush islands of the Caribbean. But none rivaled in population or in civilization the Mayas, the Aztecs, and the Incas.

After the Europeans came to their land, the Indian civilizations died. Their rule was shattered, their wealth was confiscated, and their numbers diminished. The European came to North, Central, and South America, and with his coming the Indian lost his domination in the land. The Americas became the home of the transplanted European who gradually assumed the name American.

1. How did the Indian get his name? Who gave this name to him?
2. Describe the social organization of the Mayas, the Aztecs, and the Incas.
3. Describe the effects that the coming of the Europeans had upon the various Indian cultures in the Americas.

## The Spaniard Came

Toward the end of the 1400's, three Spanish ships under the command of Christopher Columbus reached the islands of the Caribbean. Following this discovery, the Spaniards began to come to this promising land in great numbers. The Spaniards, however, were not the first Europeans to come to the Americas. The dramatic discoveries of the Norwegian, Helge Ingstad, in 1963 show that the Norwegian Vikings visited Canada as early as 1000 A.D., and perhaps even earlier. Other Europeans may have also reached this land before Columbus, but their discoveries were not followed by colonization.

By the mid-1500's Spain controlled much of the territory in South, Central, and North America and was destined to govern and to seed these lands with Spanish culture. The Spaniard came as an explorer, determined to expand the boundaries of Spain. He came as a soldier to enforce the rule of Spain. He came as an adventurer in search of wealth and power, and gold and silver were his primary concern. He came as a colonist to make a new home away from Spain. He came as a farmer, taking over much of the best agricultural land and introducing new crops and domesticated animals. He also came as a missionary to convert the souls of the heathen Indians and to replace the temples and the ceremonies of the pagan with the churches and the ritual of the Catholic.

Spanish explorers found the islands of the Caribbean, trudged across the narrows of Panama to the Pacific, touched upon the outskirts of Central America, and cautiously scouted the lands now named Colombia, Venezuela, and Ecuador. They threaded their way southward through Peru and Chile on land squeezed narrow between the high ramparts of the Andes mountains and the thundering surges of the Pacific Ocean. They explored the thousands of twisting miles of the Amazon River and gasped for breath in the thin air of Bolivia. Spanish farmers settled in Paraguay, and Spaniards founded the city of Buenos Aires near the mouth of the Río de la Plata in Argentina. The Spaniards landed in Mexico, reached into California, viewed the majesty of the Sierra Nevada and Rocky mountains, rode their horses over the grassy plains west of the Mississippi, and were gripped with awe when they gazed at that immense chasm in the earth known as the Grand Canyon. Spaniards landed on the warm sands of Florida, and they sailed their ships into the yawning mouth of the Mississippi. They claimed for Spain all this immense expanse of land.

Spanish soldiers and adventurers followed the trails of the explorers and sometimes they, too, were explorers who broke new trails. They were incredible in their daring and sometimes brutal in their treatment of the Indian. Hernando Cortez took six hundred men in 1519 to conquer Mexico, where the armies of the warlike Aztecs outnumbered his force by as much

A church in Taxco, Mexico, left, and the ruins of a Spanish mission in New Mexico, above, are reminders of the Spanish colonial period of Latin America and our own Southwest. (American Airlines; National Park Service)

as ten or even twenty to one. Cortez burned the boats that brought him so that there might be no retreat for his soldiers. Cortez and his men were received with gifts and courtesy by the Aztecs, but Cortez seized the Aztec king Montezuma and massacred the Aztec people in battle. He was aided in this conquest by thousands of the Indians who were enemies of the Aztecs. Cortez had won these Indians over to his cause by his diplomatic skill. Within the space of a few years he ruled all the land and people the Aztecs had once governed. Francisco Pizarro seized the chance of a civil war among the Incas and subdued them between the years 1531 and 1533 with his treachery and the savagery of his fighting men. Everywhere the Indian was reduced to the status of a subject, a servant, and a slave.

Colonists from Spain settled on grants of land given to them by their king, and they made these lands into great plantations and ranches where the Indians were forced to work without wages. Their labor was the tax the Spaniards demanded of the Indians. The Spaniards especially wanted the gold and silver they had uncovered in the Americas, and they forced the Indians to labor long hours in the mines. On the islands of the Caribbean, the Spaniards established sugar plantations which changed the Indian agriculture based on maize, potatoes, manioc, beans, squash, and agave. The Spaniards also grew cotton, and they also required the Indian to labor on the cotton plantations. The Indian suffered, sickened, and died from the severity of his work and from the alien germs that the Spaniard had brought from his homeland. Faced with a labor shortage, and forbidden by the Spanish crown to enslave the Indians, the Spaniards imported slaves from Africa to work their fields and mines. Thus the Negro became an integral part of the humanity of America.

The Spaniards brought cattle, horses, sheep, pigs, citrus fruits, wheat, barley, and other plants and animals to the Americas. They, and the other nations of Europe, received from the Americas maize, the potato, and the tomato, to name only a few. This giving and receiving between the Spaniards and the early Americans is but one of many examples of the exchanges between men of different parts of the world which have resulted in a blending of cultures.

Spanish missionaries accompanied the explorers, the soldiers, the adventurers, and the settlers. The Spaniard and his Church were inseparable, and they were always together abroad as at home. Wherever the Spaniard ruled, the people must be Christian. As Spanish control was expanded over the Indians, Catholic missions, sometimes utilized as forts, were built. These missions became the religious centers of the Indians' new way of life. They also served as cultural centers for Spain and were valued by the Spanish administrators because they helped to keep the Indians more peaceably inclined. Indians cultivated the mission gardens and fields and made them relatively self-supporting. There were many among the mission priests who became attached to their new flocks and tried with some success to protect the Indians from the greed and the ill-treatment of the lay Spaniard. In the process of making this new land his, the Spaniard also seeded it with his religion.

### Others Came

Around 1500, a Portuguese captain, Pedro Álvares Cabral, landed on the shores of northeast Brazil. Cabral claimed he was blown off his course while on the way to India—a story historians accept with some suspicion, for some believe that Cabral deliberately sailed westward. He claimed the land for Portugal, and other expeditions came after him to claim more, until Portugal possessed about half of South America.

Brazil is a territory almost as large as the United States and is slightly over three million square miles in area. This land, first claimed by the Portuguese, is named for a wood found there which produced a dye for cloth. This wood was known in Europe as *brazilwood.*

Here, too, the Indians were exploited, and they died by the thousands from overwork and the diseases brought by the Europeans. The Portuguese solved their labor problems by enslaving some Indians and bringing in thousands of Negro slaves to work plantations, mine the earth, transport loads of merchandise, and to be servants for their households. Together with the Indian, the Portuguese, and the mixtures of Indian and Portuguese, the Negro became a large and familiar part of the Brazilian landscape. The Portuguese, like the Spaniards, brought Catholic missionaries to the lands they conquered, and Catholicism has been the dominant religion in Brazil since the colonial period.

The British, the French, and the Dutch visited the shores and islands of Central and South America, and they disputed with the Spaniards and the Portuguese for control of these lands. Piracy and war disturbed the normal routine of life as each tried to capture or to retain the earth and the wealth of this tempting new world. On the shores of northeastern South America three territories are still known as British, French, and Dutch Guiana. The British and French also claimed and kept some of the islands of the Caribbean. It was in North America, however, that the British and the French seized the greatest areas of American territory.

Spanish milled dollars, below, were called "pieces of eight" and were the chief circulating medium in most of the world during the last half of the eighteenth century. (Chase Manhattan Bank Money Museum)

The site of Jamestown, Virginia is now a national park, above. Among the earliest settlements of present-day United States were Jamestown, in 1607, Plymouth, Massachusetts, in 1620, and Saint Augustine, Florida, in 1565. (National Park Service) The Canadian city of Quebec, below, was first settled in 1608. (Canadian Pacific Railway)

## The British and the French Came

The British and the French started to make voyages of discovery shortly after the Portuguese and the Spanish. Although much of the Atlantic coastline of the United States had been claimed by the British at the end of the fifteenth century, it was not until 1607 that they established a permanent settlement in Jamestown, Virginia. From that time onward, however, they came in numbers and settled a narrow strip of land facing the Atlantic Ocean from the rugged shores of New England on the north to the gentler lands and climate of the southland. They settled Bermuda in 1609 and founded tobacco plantations on Barbados and other islands in the 1620's. The Cabots led English exploration in the north, looking for a Northwest Passage to the Orient. The passage was not found, but soon there was an English fishing industry in the waters off Newfoundland.

In 1524, an Italian named Verrazano sailed up and down the North American coasts looking for a shorter passage to Asia. He reported back to the king of France that he had failed to find one. Many explorers of that time searched for a sea passage through the Americas that would shorten the way to India. Some ten years later, a Frenchman named Jacques Cartier found the St. Lawrence River, and claimed the lands around it for France. Shortly after 1600 Samuel de Champlain also explored the lands bordering the St. Lawrence, and in 1608 he established a colony at Quebec. From this time onward, until the British took control of Canada in 1763, the French attempted to make this land another France. The French colonies in the Caribbean, however, were of equal if not greater importance during the seventeenth and eighteenth centuries.

During the seventeenth and early eighteenth centuries, far-roving French adventurers, traders, trappers, and missionaries moved into the wild inland of America and uncovered its virgin richness. They roamed the shores of the Great Lakes, and, under La Salle, paddled down the wide Mississippi to the Gulf of

The American West was claimed at various times by Spain, France, and England. Above, the stagecoach in Virginia City, Nevada, about 1866. (Library of Congress)

Mexico. All this land, from the Appalachian Mountains in the east to the Rockies in the west, was claimed for France. But only the city of New Orleans and the province of Quebec became and remained French until the latter part of the eighteenth century.

Under the determined will of Louis XIV in the seventeenth century, soldiers and settlers were sent to Quebec in increasing numbers, and it became a new France in custom, in language, and in religion. Boatloads of brides from France were sent to the colonies to help establish French families in the New World. French settlers lined the St. Lawrence with their farms, and towns and villages grew, each dominated by its sturdy stone church. The experience of the farmer became as important as the lore of the hunter of furs to the economy of the land. The hop and skip of the playing child and the clump of the booted farmer on the cobblestones of new towns and cities sounded loudly in a land which for centuries had known only the quiet pad of the moccasined Indian and the silent passage of animals. By the time that the English took over control of the country in 1763, the French Canadian was rooted so deeply in the soil of Quebec that the English were forced to govern him by his own law and to respect his French customs. The separateness of the French community in Canada has lasted from that time to this.

English colonists, however, settled most of New Brunswick and Nova Scotia, and these other parts of that vast country became English in language, in law, and in customs.

1. When did the Spaniards come to the Americas? In what parts of the Americas did they primarily settle?
2. When did the Portuguese first come to the Americas, and where did they settle?
3. Where did the French settle in the Americas? What became of their settlements in Canada?

## They Supplanted the Indian

The North American colonists replaced the Indian as ruler, just as the Spaniards and the Portuguese had done in Latin America.

The Indians of the Great Plains hunted bison and depended upon these animals for their living. As European settlers moved westward, the Indians were deprived of their hunting grounds. (National Park Service)

As the numbers of the colonists increased and pressed upon the frontiers to the west, the Indians were pushed into other territory. The Indians were a proud and courageous people, and they fought back. Many knew the sound of their war cries, the flaming of their arrows, and the surprise of their attack. But the transplanted Europeans were too many, too well armed and organized. Slowly they reduced the Indian population and territory. The advance westward by the new Americans was inexorable, and the Indians fell back and were ground under. The movement did not cease until it reached the far western limits of North America.

The greatness of the Indians declined, and they knew of their former freedom to roam the far reaches of this land only through the tales of their elders. They were herded into restricted areas called *reservations*, and even here they were not entirely safe from the land-hungry and the prejudiced.

Thus, the Indian, who had once been the only family of man to tread the spaciousness of the Americas, gave way to the newcomer from Europe. An evolving new variation of man became prominent in the Western Hemisphere—the American of European descent.

## The American Landscape

The land discovered and settled by the new Americans was varied and vast. It ranged in climate from the extremely cold to the extremely hot. It was a challenging land which demanded much of man, but the rewards were great for those who accepted its challenge, endured its rigors, and overcame its obstacles. And the obstacles were often formidable.

## The Latin American's Landscape

The Latin American lives and works on a spread of mixed landscape which extends for around seven thousand miles from the southern borders of Texas to Cape Horn at the southern tip of South America. This land stretches so far south that its southern portions are farther from the eastern United States than are the majority of the European countries. The Latin American occupies lands more than twice the size of the United States, over seven million square miles. His lands are marked by a variety of forms—mountain, plateau, jungle, desert, plain, and river. One of the most striking features of his land is its mountains and highlands.

**Mountain and highland.** A number of the people of Latin America live high above sea level in foothills and mountain valleys, on mountain slopes, and on flattened mountain plateaus. The mountains of South America are especially impressive, some new and arrogantly high, and glaring here and there with the torches of their volcanoes. Others are old and rounded, subdued by the ceaseless winds and erosion of the centuries. No other mountain chain except the Himalayas of Asia surpasses in mightiness the Andes Mountains of western South America. Towering to dizzy heights, the snow-capped peaks of the Andes stretch for four thousand miles from Chile in the south to Venezuela and Colombia in the north. Along these thousands of miles, the ridges are sometimes split into two's and three's, and the Andes range bulges to a width of around 600 miles. One of its peaks, Aconcagua, rises to a height of around 23,000 feet, making it the tallest point of land in the Americas. Man cannot live permanently on the highest parts of the Andes, but he does live on some of the high plateaus and in valleys. He has learned to terrace the mountain slopes for his food and mine deep into the mountains for minerals.

In eastern South America—in Brazil and in the Guianas—there are also humps of highland where the Latin American has found it profitable and comfortable to live. In Central America and in Mexico he has also settled in high altitudes where the air is cooling and stimulating. Mexico City, the capital of Mexico, is located on a high plateau slung between two mountain ranges, one on the east and one on the west. This is not the only Latin American capital perched high above sea level, for a number of other countries have placed their political centers in the high altitudes.

**Jungle and desert.** The Latin American prefers to live in the more temperate climate

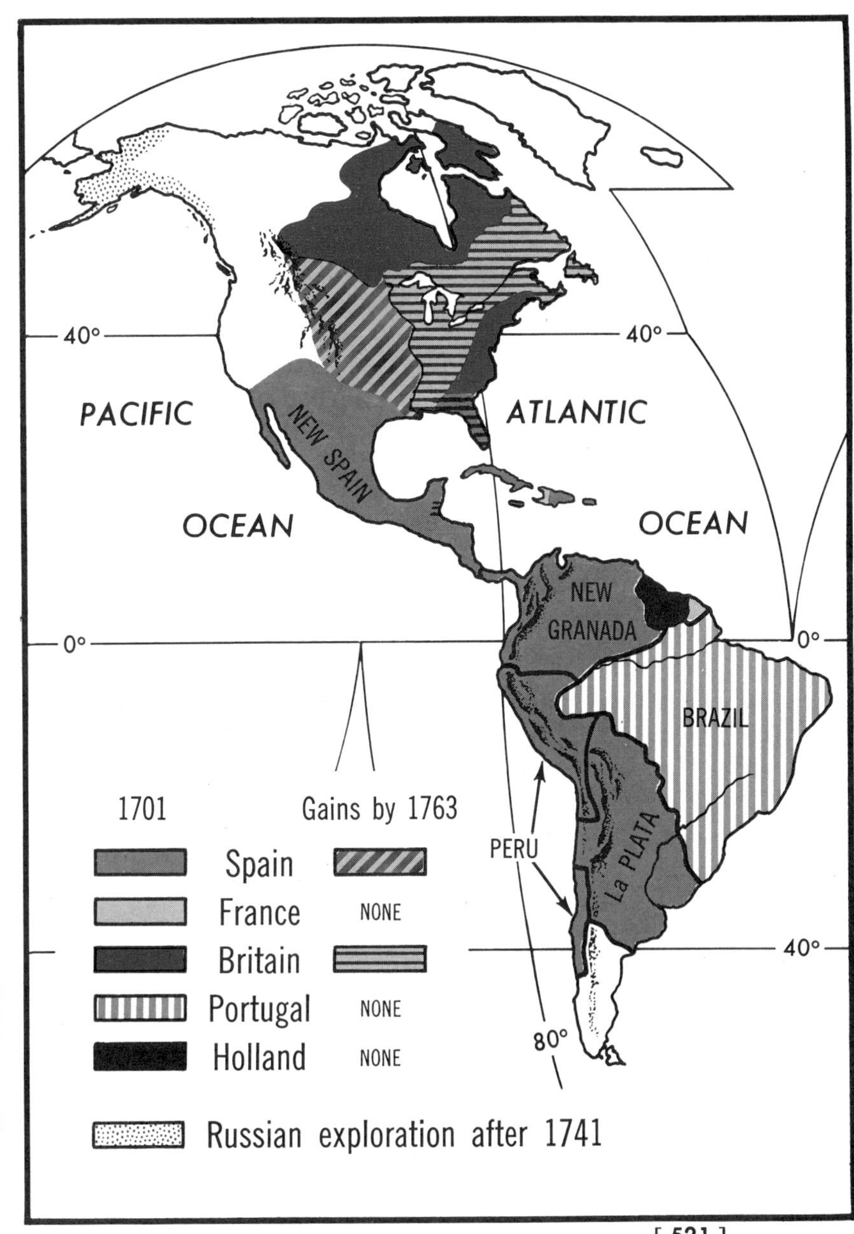


**Colonial America (1701-1763)**

During the eighteenth century there was a series of wars between the great colonial powers of Europe. Under different names these wars were also fought in the New World. The map shows how territory changed hands between 1701 and 1763. By the time of the American Revolution France had lost her great empire in the Americas.

of the highland because most of his land lies within the tropical lowlands where life can be precarious and short. In Mexico, in Central America, in Brazil, and in other parts of Latin America, there are repelling areas of damp and darkened jungle and rain forest. Here there is the endless drip of rain and almost perpetual twilight, for the sun rarely shines through the massed green ceiling of the close-growing trees. The tropical rain forest is a place of rapid birth, rapid growth, and rapid decay, and there is a dramatic closeness between life and death. There is savagery here, and there is danger everywhere—in the coils of the boa constrictor and the anaconda, in the vampire bat that must have blood, in the poisonous bite of the spider, in the bite of the disease-bearing mosquito, and in the prowling jaguar and puma. In the waters are voracious piranha, fish that can strip the flesh from man and animal within seconds. There are also eels that shock with electricity, fish that bear poison in their bodies, and the toothed menace of alligator and crocodile. There is disease in these tropical jungles, and little food, and soil that cannot be tilled for long. Men do live in a few of these jungle regions, in coastal Mexico and Yucatan, for instance, but generally life is safer and healthier in the higher places.

There are also deserts in Latin America, and places where the rain rarely falls. Mexico, Brazil, Argentina, Chile, and Peru all have arid regions, but the greatest of these dry areas is the desert which runs for around 1,800 miles along much of the coast of Peru and northern Chile. Men live in the river valleys of the Peruvian desert, where the soil is productive, and there are mining camps in the desert of Chile. Here and elsewhere, modern Americans are making portions of the desert bloom. There are also dry regions in the highlands, and food cannot be grown there. But not all of Latin America's land is inhospitable for growing food and herding cattle.

**Temperate plain and plateau.** The geographic heartland of Argentina is an area of fertile, grassy plains called the *Pampa,* which makes up about one-third of the country. Here wheat and other crops grow in the richness of watered soil, and cattle graze in great herds tended by the picturesque cowboys called *gauchos.* Elsewhere—in Brazil, in Uruguay, and in Paraguay—there are also green plains where cattle feed and multiply, and golden grain glints in the sunshine. In Venezuela, in Colombia, and in other countries, there are plains and coastlands suitable for the raising of animals and the planting of crops. On the low-lying Caribbean islands, there is also a concentration of population.

In the countries carrying the running ramparts of the Andes Mountains, many farmers plant their crops on high plateaus and terraced mountainsides. On a great plateau in Mexico, which slopes from eight thousand feet into the western highlands of the United States, farmers grow cotton, wheat, corn and beans, and there are large cattle ranches. In Central America and in Mexico and Peru as well as in the islands of the West Indies, there are fertile soils where sugar, rice, and other tropical products grow in lush abundance.

**Rivers.** Rivers are also important in the Latin American landscape. Among the greatest of the world's rivers is the Amazon, of Brazil. It has been estimated that this river drains around 40 per cent or more of the land of South America. Five hundred or more rivers, some of them streaming for over a thousand miles, feed their waters into the Amazon. These feeding waters come from Peru, Bolivia, Venezuela, Colombia, the Guianas, and Ecuador, as well as from Brazil. As it nears the ocean, the width of the Amazon extends at times to forty miles. Into the Atlantic Ocean, through a mouth fifty miles wide, it pours one-fifth of the total river waters of the world. Its length extends for four thousand miles, and only the Nile of Africa is a few hundred miles longer. But the Amazon holds many times more water than either the Nile or the Mississippi. The basin to which it gave its name is mostly a land of swamp, jungle, and heat, and the numbers of people who live around its shores are few and scattered. There are, however, many products of value in this basin—rubber, oils, medicinal herbs, minerals, and other items of value to man.

The Amazon has placed great obstacles in the path of those who would pluck the wealth of its basin. The river is navigable by ocean steamer as far as Manaos, a distance of about 1,000 miles, and by riverboats as far as Iquitos, Peru. However, the natural difficulties of jungle, swamp, and heat in the Amazon Basin pose problems which have yet to be overcome.

The next largest river system is the one which drains over a million square miles of land in Argentina, Paraguay, south Brazil, and Uruguay, into the estuary or funnel-shaped bay of the Río de la Plata. The Paraná, the Uruguay, and the Paraguay rivers all drain into the Río de la Plata. The Plata flows across an area temperate in climate and abundant in rainfall, and from this area the pampas roll westward to the Andes.

Farther north is the Orinoco River, which drains the great plains of southern and central Venezuela and has tributaries in Colombia. The Orinoco and the rivers and streams that feed its waters drain an area of around 600,000 square miles. Finally, there is the Magdalena River system, which drains a large area of Colombia and runs northward into the Caribbean.

Plans are made and dreams are dreamed to make all of these river systems more useful to man by dredging, dams, and flood control. Some work has been done to improve their use, but there is much more that remains to be done. These rivers have been useful to the Latin American, giving him a cheap means of transportation and communication, water for his fields, and fish for food. Hydroelectric power has been developed along a few of the rivers, and they may be even more useful in the future.

**There are resources.** There is an abundance of mineral resources in Latin America. If properly exploited, these resources could contribute to the betterment of all the people in this region. Some of the most valuable of these resources, oil and iron ore, are being exploited in Venezuela. Dotting the waters of Lake Maracaibo in Venezuela are thousands of derricks marking wells which tap the immense oil reserves beneath the waters of the lake. The various companies which produce oil return 50 to 60 per cent in royalties to Venezuela. Most of the companies are owned in the United States, but 75 per cent of their employees are citizens of Venezuela. In 1941 Bethlehem Steel uncovered over a billion tons of iron ore in the jungles of the Orinoco valley, and U. S. Steel has discovered a mountain of iron ore at Cerro Bolívar. Southern Venezuela is also rich in manganese, bauxite, coal, and other minerals.

In Mexico there is oil which is exploited as a government monopoly. Bolivia is known for its resources of tin, Chile for copper and nitrate fertilizer. Both Peru and Mexico have gold and silver mines. Brazil, one of the largest of the American nations, has vast resources, much yet untapped. These include diamonds, manganese, gold, copper, iron, oil, nickel, bauxite, and coal. Its valuable forest products include fibers, rubber, and wax. Brazil has reserves of almost every mineral known to man. The problem of Brazil is that its interior is sparsely populated and communications are limited. The vast expanse of interior Brazil must be populated before its resources can be tapped.

The main occupation of many of the people of Latin America is still agriculture. Land is important from a social point of view, and the large landowner is a man of great prestige. It is traditional in Latin America to invest in land, and most Latin Americans with money still prefer to invest their surplus capital in land. Other enterprises are left to the foreign capitalist, the new immigrant, or the government. Having both temperate and tropical climates, Latin America produces a wide selection of products. In the temperate zones and altitudes found in parts of Uruguay, southern Brazil, and Mexico to a degree, the Latin American herds cattle and grows wheat, corn, flax, barley, oats, and other grains. In the tropical countries, he produces bananas, sugar cane, coffee, tobacco, pineapples, citrus fruits, coca, rice, cacao, and manioc, the tapioca plant. Some of these areas, for instance Central America and the islands of the Caribbean, emphasize one crop for export, such as sugar or bananas. This specialization and dependence upon one-crop agriculture often leads to economic difficulties when the prices of these products decline in the world market or the crop is not good in a particular year.

**Industry.** Before World War II, there was relatively little industry in Latin America. Since that time, however, industrialization has been extensive in many countries. One example is the state of São Paulo in southern Brazil, which has become one of Latin America's fastest growing and largest industrial centers. Around 50 years ago, the city of São Paulo had a population in the thousands, but today its population ranges around 4,000,000. It is now the ninth largest city in the world. With the city as its heart, this state is estimated to produce over 50 per cent of the paper, textiles, and chemicals of the country. But elsewhere in much of Brazil, the only occupations are agriculture and mining. In these areas, settlements are sparse, and the people live in poverty. Outside of countries like Argentina, Brazil, Mexico, Chile, and Uruguay, which have some industry, there is little industry. The resources are there, and there is a need, but widespread industry is a thing of the future for most of Latin America.

1. How large is the land area of Latin America? Describe the chief land features of South America.
2. Identify the Pampa and describe life in this region.
3. What is the greatest river of Latin America? Describe it briefly in a few sentences, noting especially its length. What are some of the other great rivers of Latin America?

## Landscape of the North American

North of the lands occupied by the Latin American are two huge pieces of American territory on which live the Canadian and the American of the United States. The territory on which the U. S. American lives lies between that of the Latin American and that of the Canadian. This geographic fact is one of the reasons why contacts between the Latin American and the Canadian have been relatively few and their knowledge of each other relatively limited. When the Latin American speaks of the "North American" he is usually referring to the U. S. American or the Canadian, but not the Mexican. Latin Americans have had a long and close relationship with the Americans of the United States. Both in Latin America and in the rest of the world, people have come to associate the name American with the U. S. American and to think of his land as dominant in North America. Even the Canadian and the Latin American have contributed to this association by such statements as "I am a Canadian" or "I am Brazilian" to distinguish themselves from the "American" of the United States. Because of the prominence of the U. S. American in North America, the Canadian and his land have often been cast into the shadow. As a result, many people lack a knowledge of the land and people of Canada. Canada is important and its spread of land is overwhelming.

**The Canadian landscape.** The Canadian rules a land that runs for around 4,000 miles east and west along the northern borders of the United States and bulks northward to the far distances of the Arctic. Canada covers a vastness of earth and water of almost four million square miles. It is the second largest country in the world in land area.

The observer gazes at a map of the land of Canada and receives a striking impression of hugeness. Great stands of trees, over a million square miles of them, cover much of the land with an immense canopy of greenery. These trees also provide the Canadian with an important source of revenue in lumber and in paper and pulp products. Every year Canadian forests produce around ten million tons of pulp and paper, and much of this goes into the daily newspapers the North American reads. Sparkling, deep, inviting lakes dot the land, many of them from fifty to over one hundred miles long. These lakes are frequently visited by the fisherman, the vacationer, and the artist in search of beauty and pleasure. Canada also has great and vital rivers, the most important of which is the St. Lawrence. This river, with its great Seaway, permits ocean-going vessels to go over 2,000 miles inland from the Atlantic. The St. Lawrence is, in a sense, the moving heart of eastern Canada as well as of industrial and urban centers on the Great Lakes in the United States. There are also numerous lesser streams teeming with fish. Many of the rivers and streams of Canada tumble over waterfalls as they flow down to the Atlantic and Pacific oceans. On its eastern and western coasts the land of Canada reaches to both of the world's largest oceans.

Water is another profitable asset to the Canadian, for about six per cent of Canada's total area is fresh water. From this fresh water there comes a rich harvest of fish—trout, pickerel, perch, and whitefish. Rivers are also a source of power and are of use in irrigating crops. From the surrounding oceans, there is an additional harvest of fish—cod, salmon, herring, and haddock—as well as lobsters, clams, and oysters.

Agriculture is important to the economy of Canada, and almost 300,000 square miles of Canadian land are used to produce food. On the interior plains in the provinces of Manitoba, Saskatchewan, and Alberta millions of tons of wheat are grown, and Canada ranks fourth among the wheat producers of the world. Cattle, hogs, and tons of sugar beets are also sources of a remarkable income. In the provinces of Ontario and Quebec, the dairy industry is important, and agriculture is the important basis of livelihood. In the east coast provinces of Prince Edward Island and New Brunswick, potatoes are the important crop. And fruit is produced all over the country, apples being the most profitable fruit crop. Canada also produces oats, barley, and corn, and the poultry industry is also important. Canada has a fortunate combination of skillful farmers and fertile soil, and there is usually a large surplus of food which is exported in quantity to other nations. Canadian trade with the United States and Great Britain far exceeds trade with other countries.

Canada is a huge storehouse of minerals. Buried in its earth is a fantastic hoard of valuable minerals—gold, silver, lead, copper, iron, zinc, cobalt, tungsten, and molybdenum. No other nation surpasses Canada in the production of nickel, asbestos, and gold, and it is believed that the Canadian northwest possesses the greatest reserve of the world's uranium. These mineral products are exported to other countries in great quantities, especially to the United States.

The space controlled by Canada is immense, but the population is small, around 18,500,000. Most of this population is concentrated along the southern borders near the United States. Here, too, are the chief large cities of Canada, including Montreal, the largest city, and Ottawa, the capital. If the number and distribution of Canadian population were represented as dots on a map, the greatest concentration would appear in the southeastern portions of the country—in the provinces of Nova Scotia, Prince Edward Island, New Brunswick, Quebec, and Ontario. Dots would appear only as scattered clusters in the south-

The lakes and rivers of Canada are an important natural resource. Rivers provide a means of transportation as well as hydroelectric power. Canada's many lakes are used for fishing and boating. (Canadian Government Travel Bureau)

ern reaches of the middle provinces of Manitoba and Saskatchewan and in the western provinces of Alberta and British Columbia. The vast majority of Canadians live within 200 or 300 miles of the U. S. borders. Only a small percentage of the population is found in the Yukon and in the great expanse of Northwest Territories and the lowlands around Hudson Bay.

The Canadians are a mixture of men, but mostly they came originally from the British Isles and France. The descendants of the original French settlers are concentrated in the province of Quebec, and French is still spoken there. The descendants of British settlers are found throughout the provinces of Canada. In order to increase the population, Canada has encouraged immigration. Over the years large numbers of immigrants have come from Germany, the Ukraine, Scandinavia, Poland, the Netherlands, Italy, Russia, and other lands. There also remains in Canada a small number of the descendants of the Indians, and there are some Eskimos in the north.

Most Canadians live in the southern regions because these regions have the best soil, and the climate there provides a longer and better growing season for crops. Canada, like Russia, lies largely in the northern latitudes, and the climate is not as favorable as that of the United States, which is in the middle latitudes. But Canadians are well aware of their reserves of natural riches, and of the need of a greater population to fully develop their potential. They have seen in their neighbor, the United States, what a large and skillful population can produce in a large and resource-rich land.

**The U. S. American and his land.** No man has been more fortunate in the capacity and the beauty of his land than the man who lives in the United States. Fertile and productive land begins stretching westward from the Atlantic coastal plain and ascends gradually

There is a great variety in the land features of the United States. The Grand Canyon, carved by the Colorado River is a favorite spot for sightseers. (American Airlines)

Canada and the United States have a great variety of people. Above, an Eskimo boy attends school in Canada's Northwest Territory. (National Film Board photo by G. Lunney)

over the gentle mountains and hills of the Appalachians and the Piedmont Plateau. From the Appalachians to the Rockies, north to Canada and south to the Gulf of Mexico, lies one of the finest and greatest of the world's agricultural regions. The West is a region of mountains—the Rockies, the Sierra Nevadas, and the Cascades—but near the Pacific Ocean good rainfall and a moderate climate permit the production of an abundance of food for man. But this is not all the land of the United States. Far to the north is the great and often cold state of Alaska; and across thousands of miles of Pacific Ocean lies the warm lushness of the state of Hawaii. This great expanse of around 3,600,000 square miles places the United States fourth in land area among the nations of the world.

Great river systems such as the Mississippi-Missouri in the Midwest, the Hudson in the East, and the Colorado in the West have been of tremendous importance to the U. S. American. They have provided water for hydroelectric power and for use in irrigating crops, and they have provided an easy means of transportation. The United States and Canada also share the Great Lakes, the largest body of fresh water in the world. On the waters of these lakes, a commerce of raw material and industrial products moves from port to port along spacious coasts. Ships from the ocean also move into their fresh waters through the St. Lawrence Seaway. In the high mountains there are also deep blue lakes and swift streams rich in game fish. And there are roaring waterfalls, the greatest of which is Niagara

The people of North America are blessed with rich natural resources. Left, a trawler hauls in fish on the Great Bank of Newfoundland. (National Film Board) Potatoes were cultivated by Indians of the Americas and introduced into Europe by the discoverers of the New World. Today modern machines are used to harvest this important food crop, below. (USDA)

Falls, which is harnessed to provide electricity.

The United States has huge resources of minerals, forests, and rich earth for farming. Iron ore, lead, copper, zinc, sulfur, and gold and silver have poured from its earth in the past, and there are still great stores of coal, though much has been mined. There are also great reserves of oil and natural gas, and these have been exploited in enormous quantities. The U. S. American has not been content merely to view and admire these riches in his possession but has torn them from the earth and used them extravagantly.

The United States is the greatest steel producer in the world. It uses 40 per cent of the world's electricity, produces between 40 and 50 per cent of the world's aluminum, and with skill and imagination, its farmers have coaxed the earth into producing fantastic quantities of food. The United States' output of products for the consumer is almost beyond count in number and beyond conception in variety. The technical ingenuity and inventive mind of the U. S. American are known and admired all over the world, and he has long been man's leader in the area of technology.

And the man who has done all of this represents every region and practically every country of the world. The United States has been rightly called a "melting pot" of the nations. Its population has grown from a few million of mostly English descent at the time of the Revolutionary War to more than 190,000,000 at present. These millions of men have been restless on this land, moving from the east to the west, from the north to the south, from the west to the east, and from the south to the north. They have been always doing, and making, and revising, and from their restless minds have come the great use and modification of the land on which they live.

1. Describe the Canadian landscape. In your answer, include facts concerning boundaries, land area, natural resources, and major crops.
2. Briefly describe the various land features of the United States. In what area would you prefer to live? Why?
3. Identify the two major streams of culture and tradition in the Americas.

## Conclusion

For thousands of years the Indian was the only family of man known in the Americas. His numbers were spread thinly over the sweeping surface of North America and clustered more thickly in certain parts of Latin America. In Mexico, in Central America, and in Peru the Indian produced civilizations greater than those of his brothers to the north. Some of his civilized advances were remarkable, and we gaze with admiration at some of the products of his skill which still remain. But civilized or not, the Indian fell back and was subdued by the European who discovered his coasts.

The Spaniard came and stamped much of Latin America with his personality and his culture. The Portuguese came, and the Brazilian is of his heritage. The English, the French, the Dutch, and others came and settled mostly in North America. Gradually, the English settlers came to dominate much of this northern region, and it came to partake of many English ideas. The lands that these groups of Europeans explored, seized, and settled upon were extensive in size, wide-ranging in their diversity, challenging in their character, rich in their resources, and frequently magnificent in their beauty.

There began to flourish early in the Americas two different streams of culture and tradition: one had its sources in the Latin, as represented by the Spaniard and the Portuguese; the other sprang from the differing evolution of the British. These differing cultures and traditions have long been a subject of contrast, of controversy, and of misunderstanding between the American of the North and the American called Latin. For many years, and even today, the Latin American frequently feels culturally closer to the European of Latin descent than he does to the citizens of the United States and Canada, who inhabit the same hemisphere and are called by the same name—American.

## SUMMING UP THE CHAPTER

A. Define or explain the following terms, relating them to this chapter.

| | |
|---|---|
| gauchos | Pampa |
| Indians | reservations |

B. Identify or locate the following and tell why they are important.

| | |
|---|---|
| Aconcaqua | Jamestown |
| Andes | Mayas |
| Aztecs | Orinoco |
| Bering Strait | Río de la Plata |
| Cuzco | St. Lawrence |
| Great Lakes | Tenochtitlán |
| Incas | Yucatan |

C. Identify the following and tell why they are important.

| | |
|---|---|
| Francisco Pizarro | Montezuma |
| Hernando Cortez | Pedro Cabral |
| Jacques Cartier | Samuel de Champlain |

D. Chapter review questions.

1. Compare the civilizations of the Incas, Aztecs, and Mayas. During what periods of history did they flourish, and in what parts of Latin America can their remains be found?
2. How did the various peoples who came to the Americas treat the Indians? What was the eventual result for the Indian civilization? How do you account for the different ways the Europeans treated the Indians?
3. Contrast life in the various types of landscape in Latin America. In your answer, consider the hardships the people have to endure.
4. What are the most important river systems of the Americas?
5. Who are the Americans?
6. What are Canada's major assets? How do the Canadians provide for their livelihood and where does the majority of the population live?

E. Questions for discussion.

1. What theory do you think best explains how the Indians first came to the Americas?
2. Why do you suppose the civilization of the Indians of North America did not reach the heights of the Indian civilizations in Latin America?
3. What were the most important contributions (if any) of the Indians to the culture of the United States?

F. Projects for individuals or groups.

1. Trace on a map of the Americas the areas settled by the various peoples of Europe and the dates of the first known settlements.
2. On an outline map of Canada indicate distribution and density of population by using dots.
3. Prepare a report for classroom presentation on the life of the Indians in North America or Latin America before the coming of the Europeans.
4. Make a collection of illustrations of North American Indians. If possible, include reproductions of paintings of Frederic Remington and Samuel Chamberlain.
5. Read a book on one of the early Indian civilizations of Latin America and report on it in class.

CHAPTER 30

# New Nations in the Americas

ALTHOUGH OF VARYING cultures and traditions, the Latin Americans and the Americans of English background eventually became determined to free themselves of control by European rulers and their representatives. They wanted relief from what they regarded as oppressive government. They wanted independence and greater freedom in their private and public activities. The first among the new Americans to rebel against the European overlord and gain independence were the Americans of the United States.

## The American Revolution

Strong beliefs and traditions concerning freedom were brought by English colonists to North America. The English colonists had, in many instances, come to America to escape the restrictions in England upon their worship, their speech, and their actions. In the new land that they settled, their disposition to be free was reinforced and enlarged.

The colonists were on their own, with little help from England. They had to measure their wits against the wiles of the wilderness, which did not distinguish between the titled or the untitled, the rich or the poor, but yielded only to the cunning of mind and hand. An atmosphere of equality developed in this land. The hewer of wood, the tiller of the field, and the hunter of game were as important—and frequently as much needed—as the cultivators of the mind. But there were always those among them who studied the evolution of democracy and freedom in the homeland and adapted the principles expressed by political philosophers to their own special conditions.

In the works of Locke, Montesquieu, Voltaire, and others, these thoughtful Americans read about how man should look at his political self and his government. These philosophical ideas gave a deeper meaning and impetus to the developing American convictions and to the need for freedom.

The people of the Thirteen Colonies lived in an environment vibrant with freedom and they were schooled in self-reliance. These inheritors of long-evolving rights were convinced of the worth of the individual in theory and in practice. They rebelled against the threats to their freedoms from an authoritarian parliament and king. They felt that the American colonist was taxed unjustly by the British government; that his person was being endangered by trials without jury; and that he was being treated as a subject who had no voice in determining the laws which governed him, nor the right to appeal their recall if he thought them unjust. The colonists also wanted the right to carry on trade freely, to develop their lands in the West, to handle their own relations with the Indians, and to establish banks and issue money.

Continuous quarrels and violence began to color relations with the government and representatives of England. Finally, convinced that the governors in England would not change their attitude or practice, the Thirteen Colonies formally declared their independence of England with the Declaration of Independence on July 4, 1776. These colonies represented about one half of the English colonies in the New World, and the other colonies remained loyal to England.

The English resisted with the might of their navy and their armies. The Americans have been described as a "rabble in arms," but in their favor they had the will to win, the

Political cartoons helped to express the revolutionary sentiments of the American colonists. The cartoon above was published in London in 1774. (Library of Congress)

help of the French, and the leadership of George Washington and other devoted and able men. Spain also came into the war as an ally of France and captured Florida and invaded the Mississippi Valley. The colonies won the war and confirmed their declaration of independence with the surrender of General Cornwallis to the Americans at Yorktown, Virginia, in 1781. Peace negotiations between the British and the Americans dragged on for two more years and were finally settled by a peace treaty signed in Paris in 1783. The United States was born.

The rights for which the American of the United States fought and died were revolutionary for that time, and are yet revolutionary for many today. They were the inalienable rights of man's nature, and therefore could not be taken from man. They held each man to be of equal worth and of equal dignity, deserving of equal treatment and opportunity. They proclaimed that all men were equal before the law. There was no legal distinction between one man or another regardless of rank, wealth, or social status. The colonists demanded for themselves the right of national self-determination. The government born of these beliefs was a government of the people, by the people, and for the people, and the rulers were the people's representatives. These rulers were servants who were elected, and they existed to serve the people. The individual, under this government, was important, and his importance has not diminished from that time to the present.

From the moment of his independence until now, the rights and ideas which the American made a reality have served as ideals for men elsewhere. Uncounted millions have looked at the freedoms of the American of the United States and have been moved to gain freedom for themselves.

1. Where did the colonists of the thirteen colonies that formed the United States learn about freedom? How did life in the colonies enforce their ideas about freedom?
2. What were the grievances of the Americans against the British king and Parliament that led to the War of Independence?
3. What were the "inalienable rights" for which the American colonists fought?

## The Latin American Gained Independence

For several centuries after their first discoveries and conquests, the Spaniards and Portuguese continued to plant their culture and their control deep in American soil. While the French, Dutch, and English competed in the parts of North America that are now Canada and the United States, they were not successful in colonizing much of the region we call Latin America today. It was, however, the French possession of Haiti that led the way toward independence in Latin America. Haiti became free in 1804, and was soon followed by the Spanish and Portuguese possessions in the New World as the century progressed. By the end of the 1800's the greatest part of Latin America was free and independent. Today only the French, Dutch, and British possessions in the Guianas and a few islands of the Caribbean still remain under foreign control.

Assisted by the officials of his court, the king of Spain governed the people of the Spanish colonies in an authoritarian manner. There was no higher appeal from his decisions. He governed in Latin America through representatives called viceroys and slightly less powerful officials called captains-general. Around the time the Latin American nations began their struggle for independence, the Spanish colonies were divided into four areas called viceroyalties. These were governed by viceroys in the name of the king. The four viceroyalties were the United Provinces of the Río de la Plata (Argentina, Paraguay, and parts of Uruguay and Bolivia); New Granada (Colombia, Venezuela, Panama, and Ecuador); New Spain (Mexico); and Peru. There were also areas governed by captains-general: Chile, Cuba, Guatemala (Guatemala, El Salvador, Honduras, Nicaragua, and Costa Rica), and Santo Domingo (Haiti and Dominican Republic), which was lost to France toward the end of the eighteenth century.

The representatives of the king of Spain governed in an authoritarian way, and there was no appeal from their decisions except to the king in Madrid. The important posts in the colonies were held by officials born in Spain. Spanish colonists born in America, called *Creoles* (Spanish, *criollos*), sometimes held official positions, but never those of great influence. Persons of mixed Spanish and Indian blood, called *mestizos*, the Indians, and the Negro slaves were the ruled ones who had nothing to say about the manner in which they were governed. All power was held by a small elite group of Spaniards and Creoles who frequently used their position to enrich themselves and Spain. These rulers had little interest in furthering the advancement of the great mass of the people who produced their wealth. Only a few Creoles had any part in the colonial government, and of course the Indians and mestizos had none at all. But in the 1700's there were those among the ruled, especially the educated Creoles, who began to think about changing their political situation.

Fresh, electrifying ideas and movements in the United States, in France, and elsewhere in the late eighteenth century began to make the people of Latin America restless and daring. They were excited by the explosion of revolutions among the English settlers in North America and the French in Europe. The cry of respect for the dignity of man, which generated these revolutions, appealed to them. They were stirred to seek the proper respect for their own dignity, and they began to rebel violently against their overlords. The Spanish Americans were eventually successful, and during the 1800's they won their freedom from Spain. The Portuguese colony of Brazil also became independent during this period, as did the French colony of Haiti. From that time until this, the Latin Americans have lived in independent countries, some small and some large, but all fiercely proud of the dignity and freedoms their liberators gained for them.

### The Liberators

Latin Americans are often vivid, dramatic personalities, and none were more flaming in their vividness or more exciting in the dramas of their lives than the leaders of the Spanish American revolutions. They were of all the families of man in Latin America: Creole, mestizo, Indian, Negro, mulatto. These leaders were often well educated and born of families with wealth. They heard how the ordinary people—the farmers, the merchants, and the scouts—of North America had transformed themselves into soldiers fighting for the right to govern themselves. The Latin Americans were gripped with amazement and admiration. They saw these untrained civilians, badly equipped and sometimes badly led, fall and fail in battles; and they watched them rise and persevere and finally defeat the power and the professional fighting men of England. The Americans of Spanish America were spurred by the glowing success of those who would not admit any limitations to the human spirit. They witnessed the sudden breaking of the revolution in France, and a fever of purpose seized them as they read the declaration of the French on the rights of man. They looked about them and were shamed and angered at the daily, degrading insults to their dignity as men suffered at the hands of their rulers. At last they were fired to strike back and to restore the dignity and rights of their fellowmen. Revolution began in Latin America.

**Francisco Miranda.** Francisco Miranda, one of the earliest great leaders of rebellion, was born in Caracas, capital of the present nation of Venezuela. His father was an immigrant from the Canary Islands who had prospered as a merchant in this new land, and he gave his son a good education. Miranda became a revolutionist as a very young man, and he used his education and military ability in the cause of freedom in France and in Venezuela.

He came with a Spanish expedition to the United States during the American Revolution and became acquainted with a number of the leaders of the new American republic. In 1792-93 he rose high in the military councils of the French revolutionists. But Miranda deserted the French revolution when he witnessed the excesses of their revenge and their insatiable need for the blood of victims. He traveled to England, to the United States, and elsewhere seeking aid to realize his dream of a Latin America free of the burden of Spain.

Miranda organized secret societies, wrote, and plotted continually to make Latin America independent. With soldiers recruited in North America, he sailed from New York and landed on the coast of Venezuela in 1806 to begin the revolution. But this attempt failed. Miranda escaped to London and continued to sound the bugle of revolt. There were those who heard, and they revolted. In 1810 Miranda returned, and Venezuela was declared independent of Spain in 1811. Miranda and the Venezuelan revolutionists began to draft a constitution modeled after that of the United States and influenced by the French declaration of the rights of man. But the Spanish governors had not given up and they defeated Miranda in 1812. His former followers were disgusted. They deserted Miranda, and the Spaniards captured him. He died in a prison in Spain in 1816. The flame of his life was gone, but the fire of his purpose flamed on in the hearts of others.

**Simón Bolívar.** The man known as "the Liberator" in Latin America was also a wealthy Creole, who traveled widely in Cuba, in Europe, and in the United States. Simón Bolívar was born in Caracas, Venezuela, in 1783 and inherited a fortune from his parents. As a young man, while living in Spain, he married the daughter of a Spanish nobleman and in 1802 took her back to the Americas. She died there in less than a year, and his grief was great, for he had loved her greatly. Bolívar went to Europe, where he tried to flee the pain of his lost love in the wildness of his pleasures, but there was no escape and he sometimes thought of suicide. During this period of his life, he met his old teacher, Simón Rodríguez, who had been exiled from Latin America because of the dangerous liberal ideas he held and taught. Rodríguez gave Bolívar a new purpose to live for, the freedom of the Latin American. Standing with his teacher on one of the hills of Rome, Bolívar swore an oath to deliver his people from the rule of the Spaniard. From that moment forward he knew no physical or spiritual rest until he had wrested from the Spaniards the lands they ruled in Latin America. He dreamed of a free, united Latin America, and he lived to see the land free, but not united.

Bolívar returned to Venezuela and helped to bring about its first declaration of independence on July 5, 1811. He joined with Miranda in fighting the royalist forces who crushed the bud of this first independence. Bolívar escaped and returned in 1813 to retake the capital of Caracas but was forced to flee again the next year. He continued the struggle in the land now known as Colombia, but the rebels would not unite in the face of their common enemy. In their disunity they were defeated. Bolívar was again forced to flee and went to Jamaica and then Haiti in exile. For two years he continued to work on behalf of his purpose. In 1817 he landed again in Venezuela and began anew his liberation of northern South America. Along the lands of the lower Orinoco River, he trained recruits, some of whom came from Europe and America. From among his own people, Bolívar recruited most of his troops, and among these were many *llaneros* (cowboys) from the Orinoco Plain, as well as a number of Negro troops. Bolívar had freed his own Negro slaves, and he lost most of his fortune in the struggle for liberty. In 1819, with about 3,000 men, he began a march to Bogotá, the capital of the viceroyalty of New Granada. Bolívar's march on Bogotá ranks with the epic marches of history.

Bolívar's army marched for hundreds of miles, mauled by the forces of nature which took their sacrifice of men and animals. Some died in the flooding rivers and in the dankness of the swamp, and others fell stunned by the burning rays of the sun. Torrents of rain drenched them, their clothes became tatters of rags, and their shoes rotted on their feet. But always there was Simón Bolívar urging and leading them on. They reached the towering Andes mountains, weakened already by the torments of their march. But they began to climb the miles of rugged mountain heights. Battered scarecrows of men and animals, led by an oath-bound man, they pitted the endurance of their courage and their will against this mighty barrier of nature, and they won. But the cost was high. The trail of their passage was marked by the graves of over a thousand of their comrades and the bones of many horses. Those who reached the final heights of the mountain staggered in the final stages of exhaustion, and they had not yet met the main enemy in battle.

From somewhere, perhaps in the voice and the spirit of Simón Bolívar, the army found strength to march on. Sixty miles from Bogotá, at a place called Boyacá, they fought the larger army of the royalists and were victorious. A few days later, on August 7, 1819, at the head of men whose endurance of body and spirit no man can know and ever forget, Simón Bolívar rode into the capital city of Bogotá and declared it free. Bolívar became the president of the new republic of Colombia.

But Bolívar's oath was not yet completely fulfilled, for there were still royalist armies in northern South America, in Peru, and elsewhere, and his oath included all. He continued the work of liberation and the expansion of freedoms in South America. In 1821 he advanced into Venezuela and drove most of the royalists from the region. His trusted lieutenant, José Antonio de Sucre, a Venezuelan, marched into the mountains to defeat another Spanish force and occupy Quito, Ecuador, in 1822. On July 26-27, in 1822, Simón Bolívar went to Guayaquil, Ecuador, and held a conference with José de San Martín, a patriot of Argentina who had led the struggle for liberation in Chile and Peru. Their conference did not bring agreement, and San Martín withdrew from the revolutionary movement and returned to Argentina.

Bolívar persisted in his harrying of the royalists and drove them from the mountains of Peru. With the able assistance of the young military genius Sucre, Bolivia was liberated. The republic of Bolivia is named after Bolívar. By 1825, the Spanish royalists were defeated in South America, and Bolívar had indeed met the full requirements of his oath. Military genius, far-seeing planner and organizer, writer and speaker, inflexible in purpose, dedicated fighter for freedom—Simón Bolívar has a shrine in the hearts of all Latin Americans and men everywhere who know what he accomplished for the dignity of man.

**José de San Martín.** Just as Bolívar was the liberator of northern South America, San Martín was the liberator of the south. He was born in Argentina in 1778, the son of a Spanish soldier. José de San Martín was educated in Madrid for a military career, and he showed a great talent as a soldier. He served in the Spanish army in Europe and in North Africa. When he came back to his homeland in Argentina in 1812, he was already a successful commander. He offered his services to the government of Buenos Aires, which had already proclaimed its independence from Spain. San Martín was given command of an army. At a place called Mendoza, he organized an expedition against the Spaniards who controlled Chile and Peru.

Recruits rallied to the banner of revolt—Chilean exiles, eager revolutionists from the area governed by Buenos Aires, and some fighting men from Europe. They all discovered in San Martín a capable leader, organizer, and planner. Among those who joined his expedition was Bernardo O'Higgins, the son of a Chilean mother and an Irish soldier of fortune who had risen to become Viceroy of Peru. O'Higgins had tried rebellion in Chile earlier but had failed. Linked with San Martín, he was destined to succeed.

San Martín was a hero of integrity and honesty, and he had no ambition to become an official of the countries of Latin America. He only wanted them to be free; he asked nothing for himself. This sincerity of intention and simplicity of purpose attracted all to give him their devotion and their help. His headquarters at Mendoza was a beehive of preparation. Here cannon balls were made from church bells, and the rawness was drilled out of recruits. Women gave their jewelry to be exchanged for the necessities of war, and plans were laid for the crossing of the high Andes mountains of the south. It was San Martín who gave to Bolívar the proof that the Andes could be crossed by an army. He scaled the mountains in 1817 to attack the Spanish armies in Chile, two years before Bolívar made his successful attempt.

San Martín feared the frightening heights of the Andes more than he did the soldiers of the ruling Spaniard. But the mountain peaks separated him from Chile, and he had to conquer them before he could conquer the Spaniard. His was a historic passage over the bleak, snow-covered Andes. Though San Martín lost many animals, he lost few men in this rugged crossing, for he had made careful preparations. In February of 1817 he met and defeated the main Spanish army not far from Santiago, the present capital of Chile. He entered the capital city in triumph on February 12. Humble and unambitious, he refused the leadership of Chile, stepping aside for the Irish-Chilean, Bernardo O'Higgins. Gradually the royalists were cleared from northern Chile, and the formal independence of Chile was declared on February 12, 1818. He then turned his attention to the conquest of southern Chile, which was accomplished by a decisive defeat of the Spaniards in April of 1818.

After freeing Chile, San Martín moved on to liberate Peru. With ships, he blockaded the ports of the royalists. Powerful propaganda from the printing press rallied public opinion behind the justice of his cause. The Spanish viceroy left his center in Lima and took his armies into the mountains. San Martín entered Lima in July of 1821 and received from its citizens the title of "Protector." On July 28, 1821 Peru was declared a free and independent country.

For one reason or another, San Martín did not continue as a military leader at this time. Perhaps he felt he had not sufficient forces to fight the Spanish royalists in the highlands—much of his army and navy had returned to Chile—perhaps because of ill health, or even because of politics, he withdrew from military activity. He did, however, continue to prepare and send out propaganda against the royalists. He thought it better, under the circumstances, to join forces with Bolívar, and it was then they had their historic meeting at Guayaquil in Ecuador. San Martín, the man of few words and great humility, saw no possibility of harmony with two leaders on the scene. He quietly withdrew, leaving Bolívar in command of the area. He returned to Mendoza, paid the last respects to his wife who had died, took his infant daughter, and went to Europe. He spent the remaining years of his life in voluntary exile from the lands he had helped to free and died in France in 1850.

There was magnificence in this man of quiet words and thunderous deeds. He stands high among the heroes who led the Latin American to freedom. San Martín exiled himself from the lands of the Americas, but not from the memory of the Americans.

1. Name the Spanish viceroyalties and the areas ruled by captains-general. How were these areas governed?
2. Trace Francisco Miranda's efforts to win independence for Venezuela. Was he successful?
3. What countries did Simón Bolívar help to liberate? List the date that each attained independence.
4. What part did José de San Martín play in liberating South America? What connection did he have with Bolívar?

## The Mexican Liberators

In the viceroyalty of New Spain, of which Mexico was the major part, there were also men of spirit and of courage who fought for freedom. Among the first of them was a priest, Miguel Hidalgo. His sympathies lay with the oppressed: the Indian, the mestizo, the poor Creole. He wanted to raise their standards of living, and he wanted to give them greater hope. In the early 1800's he led forth a revolutionary army that almost toppled the viceroy of New Spain. Hidalgo was neither military man nor organizer, but he became the focus of all those who sought justice and hope. His followers at one time reached an estimated 80,000. He was successful for a time, and came within a few miles of Mexico City, but the undisciplined mob that had gathered around him was not destined to capture it. In 1811 Hidalgo's unruly followers were defeated by the disciplined troops of the royalists. Hidalgo was shot as a rebel, and his head was displayed in a cage as an example of the penalty for rebellion.

But Hidalgo had started something, and there were others who were also willing to risk their heads for the cause of freedom from oppression. The revolt was continued by another Mexican, José María Morelos, a mestizo priest who wanted only Mexicans to govern. For a time he, too, was successful, and in 1813 Mexico was declared an independent country. But in 1815 Morelos was captured and killed. Although guerrilla warfare continued after his death, the independence of Mexico had to wait for some years longer.

In February of 1821, Agustín de Iturbide, a Creole commander who had deserted the royalist cause, signed an agreement with Vicente Guerrero, chief of the guerrilla troops south of Mexico City. Their joint forces compelled the surrender of the royalist forces in Mexico, and Mexico's independence was acknowledged. Iturbide became the Emperor of Mexico on July 21, 1822, and promised to reign under a constitution. But the monarchy did not last for long. In 1824 Iturbide was forced to abdicate, and Mexico was proclaimed a republic. Until around the 1850's the country was torn by revolts and long dominated by a man known as Antonio López de Santa Anna. It was in the 1850's that Benito Juárez—a man held by the Mexicans to be their finest liberal reformer—became the president of Mexico.

Juárez was born of a poor Indian family, and he knew only the barren hillsides of Mexico while he was a boy. But there was in him that will, a quality of some men of all races, to educate himself so that he might someday be an influence for good in his country. He became a lawyer and later was the leading figure in Mexico's highest court of justice. In 1858, a year after the adoption of a new Mexican constitution, Juárez was elected to the position of president of Mexico. But his position was not a restful one. Powerful forces were opposed to the liberal constitution under which Juárez ruled, and they resisted him with intrigue and violence. He won against internal opposition, but Mexico was almost bankrupt. Then the French tried to make Mexico theirs, and in 1864 sent Maximilian, a young Austrian prince, to be Emperor of Mexico. French troops were sent to support him. The United States objected that this invasion violated the Monroe Doctrine. A Mexican army finally defeated Maximilian's forces, and after its own Civil War, the United States was influential in bringing about the withdrawal of the French from Mexico. Juárez became once again the real president of the country. The Mexicans today hail Benito Juárez as one of the greatest, if not the greatest, of their liberal reformers. Benito Juárez

Above, Francisco Miranda (1750?-1816) was one of the earliest great leaders of the rebellion of Latin America against Spain. Right, Simón Bolívar (1783-1830) is known throughout Latin America as "the Liberator." (Pan American Union)

Left, José de San Martín (1778-1850) helped to pave the way for Bolívar's success. Below, Benito Juárez (1806-1872) served five terms as President of Mexico and made many liberal reforms. (Pan American Union)

was Mexico's selection to stand in the Hall of Heroes of the Pan American Union with other founding fathers of the Americas.

While other Latin Americans were gaining their independence, the Central Americans also revolted. With the assistance of Mexican armies, they, too, threw off the hold of Spain and became a part of the new Mexican empire. However, they soon broke with Mexico and in 1823 established a Central American Federation, which lasted until 1838. Then this federation also dissolved, and the separate states of Guatemala, Nicaragua, Honduras, El Salvador, and Costa Rica were formed. Panama, another Central American country remained a part of Colombia until 1903, when, with the assistance of the United States it declared itself independent.

## Brazilian Evolution

During the period of revolution in the Spanish-governed parts of Latin America, the Brazilians protested the rule of Portugal from time to time. But in Brazil there were never any large-scale outbursts which affected the entire country. Brazilian independence evolved in a different way. The conquests of Napoleon in Spain and his threat to Portugal not only ignited revolutions in the Spanish-ruled parts of Latin America but also played a key role in conditioning the political development of Brazil.

During the time of Napoleon's rise to power, the Braganza family reigned in Portugal. The ruling queen was insane, and her son, Dom João, ruled as regent. He was an indecisive man. When Napoleon invaded Portugal in 1807, Dom João fled from Portugal to Brazil. There have been few transfers from one kingdom to another to match this one. João gathered together around fifteen thousand of his followers and court officials, and on a fleet of 37 vessels he took with him the treasury of Portugal as well as art, jewels, and a library estimated at around 60,000 books. He landed in Brazil the same year and was welcomed.

Since Brazil was now his kingdom of residence, Dom João removed the commercial restrictions which had hampered it previously. He founded a printing press and a bank, encouraged the expansion of industry, opened a public library, and opened the ports to friendly nations—they had previously been closed. Brazil was declared to be an equal part of the empire, and in general the Brazilian felt that he was now a member of an independent

Rio de Janeiro, right, was the capital of Brazil when that country gained its independence from Portugal in 1822. (Brazilian Government Trade Bureau)

power instead of a colony. Although the court officials were snobbish, looked down upon the colonials, and were not well liked, they did bring a certain sophistication, culture, and appreciation of the arts and sciences.

After the fall of Napoleon, liberal forces began to emerge in Portugal. By 1820 they were demanding that Dom João should return to Portugal if he wanted to keep his throne. At the same time, the Brazilians learned of the liberal movement in Portugal and demanded more rights for themselves and a limitation on the powers of the king. There were uprisings, and a mob assembled in Rio de Janeiro, the capital. Dom Pedro, the son of Dom João, spoke to the crowd. Dom Pedro assured them that the constitution to be established in Portugal would have the consent of the Brazilians. But conditions worsened in Rio, and in 1821 the king at last left for Portugal. He took back with him much of the treasury of Brazil, the jewels, and his courtiers. His eldest son, Dom Pedro, stayed in Brazil with his family.

After Dom João returned home, the Portuguese Cortes, or parliament, began to limit the freedoms of the Brazilians rather than expand them. Under the leadership of José Bonifacio, the Brazilians persuaded Dom Pedro to stay in Brazil and rule as their constitutional king. On September 7, 1822, Pedro declared Brazil independent of Portugal and shortly afterwards was proclaimed Emperor of Brazil. The country remained a monarchy until the republic was proclaimed on November 15, 1889.

### Independence in the Caribbean

The Caribbean islands of Cuba and Puerto Rico continued under Spanish rule until the conclusion of the Spanish-American War. At the conclusion of this war in 1898, Puerto Rico was ceded to the United States, and Cuba became independent. Independence came sooner to the island of Hispaniola, which was discovered by Columbus in 1492. The western third of the island came under French control in 1697, and is known today as Haiti. The eastern part of the island continued for some years under Spanish rule and is now known as the Dominican Republic.

The great majority of the people of Hispaniola were Negroes and mulattoes. The Negroes had been brought there in large numbers from Africa to work as slaves on the great plantations. In the French section of the island there were over 400,000 black and mulatto slaves, around 35,000 Frenchmen who governed them, and about 35,000 freedmen of color. In the Spanish part there were about 40,000 Spaniards out of a total population of 125,000. When the revolution broke out in France in the 1790's, the slaves and freedmen of color, under the leadership of Toussaint L'Ouverture, turned against the whites. For about a decade, civil war and bloodshed turned this island into an inferno of hate and chaos. Finally, in 1804, under the leadership of Jean Jacques Dessalines, Haiti became an independent country.

The independence of the Dominican Republic was first declared in 1821. The country was almost immediately overrun by Haiti and did not become free again until 1844. Later the Spaniards ruled it again for a few years. It has been independent, however, without interruption since 1865.

Thus independence from Spain, from Portugal, and from France was achieved in Latin America. With the chief exception of Brazil, independence had to be gained through violence. Neither England in the U. S. part of North America nor Spain and France in Latin America were inclined to relinquish control of the colonies peacefully. The American revolutionaries had to gain their independence by force. But the English, being a practical people, learned their lesson well. When the Canadians began to become discontented with their lack of freedom, the English gave it to them without a violent struggle.

1. Who was Juárez? What was his family background? What were his ambitions, and was he able to fulfill them?
2. How did Brazil gain independence? What role did Dom Pedro play?
3. Briefly trace the history of the island of Hispaniola from 1492 to 1865.

### Canada Won Self-Rule

Canada evolved rather peacefully into a self-governing country. Canada was originally settled by the French, but in 1763 came under the control of Great Britain. The Catholic French were alarmed lest the Protestant English curb their religion and disrupt their customary mode of living. The English quieted this alarm by passing the Quebec Act which, among other provisions, permitted the French to have freedom of worship and to retain their legal code and their customs.

Then, when the American Revolution erupted, many American colonists—some estimate a third of the population—were in sympathy with Britain. When the revolutionists were successful, many of these British sympathizers fled to Canada and settled in the Maritime Provinces of Nova Scotia and New Brunswick, and in great numbers along the upper St. Lawrence, in the province now known as Ontario. Many settlers also came from England to settle in this "upper" region, and Quebec began to be known as Lower Canada, and Ontario as Upper Canada. This new group of settlers in Upper Canada began to cry for self-rule and more participation in the government. Others in the provinces of Nova Scotia, New Brunswick, Prince Edward Island, and Quebec also raised the cry for more actual control of their governments.

It was the practice of the English to govern each of the provinces separately through a royal governor sent out from England. From the few prosperous and leading members of the community, the governor selected a council to assist him in administering the territory he ruled. Elected assemblies represented the people, but the governor and the council could veto the acts passed by these representatives. The people resented the power of the governor and his council. They began to stir with some violence and to demand that they be represented on this executive level. Threats of an uprising in both Upper and Lower Canada in 1837 led the English to fear another revolution. The Earl of Durham was sent to Canada to investigate and make recommendations.

Durham's recommendations were realistic and liberal. He recommended that the Canadians be given greater political freedoms and responsibilities in governing themselves. He indicated that if this were done, the Canadians would probably continue to grow and develop within the British Empire. In 1840 the English united Upper and Lower Canada into one large province. This province was permitted to have an elected legislature of two houses, but it remained under a governor who selected his council. The Canadians were close to responsible and truly representative government. Ten years later, in 1850, the British quietly told the royal governors they sent out to assent to the majority will of the legislature. The governors were also instructed to choose their council or cabinet from the majority of the legislature. Thus the British practice of naming a ruling cabinet from the majority party evolved in Canada.

Then there began to emerge the feeling that there should be a greater unity among all those who lived in the large territory north of the United States. Canada consisted then of the united provinces of Upper and Lower

The St. Lawrence Seaway serves both Canada and the United States. It is symbolic of the good relations between the two countries. (National Film Board)

Canada (Ontario and Quebec). But there were other independent provinces—Newfoundland, Nova Scotia, New Brunswick, Prince Edward Island—and scattered settlements growing in the stretching plains of middle Canada and in the Pacific-washed territory of the far west. And to the north and northwest were the immense wilderness lands controlled by the Hudson's Bay Company. The Canadians felt that political unity in this vast land would give them greater strength and further their economic development.

The separate colonies sent representatives to a conference in Quebec, where they drew up a constitution for a United Canada. The British approved this constitution in an act called the British North America Act, and it became law on July 1, 1867. Canada became known as the Dominion of Canada and celebrates its birth as a nation on July 1, which is known as Dominion Day. (The word *Dominion* was finally dropped from the name of the country in 1949.) It is interesting to note also that the birth of Canadian independence marks in a real sense the birth of the British Commonwealth of Nations which continues to tie Britain and many of her former colonies with very loose bonds.

But not all who lived in Canada were incorporated into provinces. A period of time had to pass before the population was sufficient in much of the land of Canada to form new provinces. And there was one old settlement, Newfoundland, which preferred to remain separate from the rest until 1949, when it finally united with Canada. There are now, in all, ten provinces and two large territories in Canada.

Thus, the Canadians evolved a system of representative government and unity as a nation. Canada has a central government which is quite similar to that of Great Britain. It has a legislature of two houses, the Senate and the elected House of Commons. Members of the Senate are appointed for life by the cabinet. The prime minister and the cabinet are selected from the majority part of the House of Commons. The important house is the House of Commons. Canada also has a federal system of government, like the United States: each province has its own government, with power to administer and legislate for the people of the province. There is often tension also between the French and British Canadians. While all the provinces are united under the federal government in Canada, the provinces also maintain a good deal of autonomy and separateness. This sometimes places harsh strains upon the unity of the federal government.

1. What groups of people came to Canada, and in what areas did each settle?
2. Briefly describe the development of the British system of government in Canada during the 1800's. What were the attitudes of the Canadians toward the British rule?
3. Name and describe briefly the provinces of Canada.

## Conclusion

The Europeans who discovered, claimed, and settled the Americas did not realize that their actions would lead to the birth of independent American nations. The English settlers along the Atlantic coastline of the United States brought with them a sense of the importance of their individual rights and freedoms. These ideas had long been evolving in their original homeland. The power of the king of England was limited by certain individual rights of his subjects, and these rights could not be disturbed without the risk of civil war. It was the stubborn attempts of the rulers in England to control the colonists too strictly that aroused their anger and caused them to revolt. The revolt of the Thirteen Colonies, the revolution in France, the spread of new ideas about freedom, and the oppression of European rulers spurred the Latin Americans to rebellion.

Under leaders who were magnetic in their appeal, daring in battle, and sacrificing in character, the Latin Americans gained independence from their former masters. New nations were established in Latin America. Some of the revolutionary leaders dreamed of a unified Latin America as well as independence. But forces beyond the control of any leader pushed the people into many separate states rather than one. In the areas governed by the Spanish and the French the people used force to gain their freedom, but the Brazilians managed to obtain independence without significant violence.

In Canada self-government evolved in a most peaceful and constitutional way. The Canadians would probably have used violence if necessary, but Britain gave way gracefully, and in this giving retained friendship and political ties with Canada. Thus nations were born in the Americas, and these nations grew to have importance throughout the world.

## SUMMING UP THE CHAPTER

A. Identify the following and tell why they are important.

Antonio López de Santa Anna
Augustín de Iturbide
Benito Juárez
Bernardo O'Higgins
Francisco Miranda
José de San Martín
José María Morelos
Lord Durham
Maximilian
Miguel Hidalgo y Costilla
Simón Bolívar
Toussaint L'Ouverture

B. Identify these dates and indicate their importance.

1. 1781
2. July 5, 1811
3. February 12, 1818
4. July 28, 1821
5. July 1, 1867
6. November 15, 1889
7. 1898

C. Chapter review questions.

1. Describe the Spanish system of colonial rule prior to liberation. How were the various groups such as the Indians, Creoles, and mestizos treated? Did these groups participate to any degree in the government?
2. What part did the American Revolution play in the movement for independence in Latin America?
3. Describe Bolívar's march on Bogotá. What drove Bolívar to make this march? Compare this with San Martín's long march. Which was more successful?
4. What do you consider to be the greatest qualities of San Martín?
5. Trace the course of the independence movement in Mexico from 1800 to the withdrawal of the Emperor Maximilian. Who were the most important figures in Mexico's history during this period? Which would you say was the greatest leader? Why?
6. What modern nations were formed upon the dissolution of the Central American Federation? When did this federation exist? Why was it important?
7. What was the significance of Dom João's move from Portugal to Brazil in 1807? Why did he return to Portugal in 1821?
8. How did the islands of the Caribbean gain their independence?
9. What is a federal system of government?
10. Trace the evolution of political rule in Canada from the passage of the Quebec Act to July 1, 1867.
11. What were the major causes of revolution in the Americas?

D. Questions for discussion.

1. In what sense was the wilderness of North America a great equalizer, an environment susceptible only to ability and hard work?
2. Why do you suppose it was the educated and wealthy Creoles who often led the revolutions of Latin America? Who led the American Revolution? The French Revolution?
3. How would you explain the fact that the revolutions of the Americas were won by untrained citizen-soldiers who defeated armies of professional soldiers?
4. Discuss the Durham Report and its provisions. How did this set the tone for Canadian government from that day to this? Why is the policy set forth in the Durham Report and the British North America Act so important for the other former colonies of Great Britain around the world?
5. How would you explain the willingness of the British to grant independence and self-government to Canada without a fight when only three generations before they had fought to prevent the United States from becoming independent?
6. What factors led to the failure of the Latin Americans to obtain a unified continental government? Was this dream of Bolívar realistic?
7. How do you account for the fact that Brazil gained her independence without violence?

# CHAPTER 31

# The American Increased and Evolved

THE EARLY COLONISTS had come to the Americas for many reasons. Some came for adventure, others to spread their faith, and others in search of land, economic improvement, or personal freedom. The vast lands of the New World attracted men from all parts of Europe with their promise. The revolutions in which the colonies gained their independence did not put an end to this immigration, but rather led to an increase. And men still come from all parts of the world to mingle their hopes and their futures with those of the people who are called North and South Americans.

## In Canada and the United States

During the nineteenth and twentieth centuries, millions upon millions of immigrants from Europe congested and shaped the great cities of the eastern seaboard of the United States and Canada. From the east they spread out into the vastness of the interiors of these two countries. The United States received the greatest numbers of these immigrants. They came from Italy, Germany, Denmark, Sweden, Norway, Ireland, Scotland, England, Greece, and Eastern Europc. Smaller groups came from the Middle East, and from Asia came the Japanese and the Chinese, who at first settled mostly in California and then scattered themselves eastward over the land. Thousands of Africans were brought to the United States forcibly as slaves before the overseas slave trade ended in 1808, and most of them worked the plantations of the South. After they were freed in the 1860's, many of them moved north and west.

There was a merging in the United States, and to a certain degree in Canada, of the strains of many different nationalities of man, and in their mixture they made, and were made into, the American. In the ancestry of the average citizen of the United States there is likely to be the blood of the English, Irish, German, Italian, Greek, Scandinavian, or eastern European, or any combination of these and other nationalities. In addition, there are the Indian and Negro strains which distinguish two important minority groups. The cultures and the traditions which they brought with them also mixed, harmonized, and became, in many instances, a part of the evolving culture and way of life of the American in the United States and Canada.

The U. S. American, to a large degree, and the Canadian, to a lesser degree, are today mixtures of the immense diversity that is man. This process of mixing has produced types of men who are different and distinct in many ways from other men—the Canadians and the Americans of the United States.

## In Latin America

People continued to pour into Latin America from abroad after the former colonies had gained their independence. It is estimated that more than 10,000,000 immigrants entered the various nations of Latin America from around 1885 to the mid-twentieth century. Some calculate that from Italy alone over 4,000,000 immigrants have streamed into Latin America since the early part of the nineteenth century. Other millions departed from Spain, Portugal, Germany, France, and the Slavic lands and went mostly into the countries of Argentina, Brazil, Chile, Uruguay, and Mexico. But all of the Latin American countries received them in their thousands and in their hundreds.

They came from the countries washed by the eastern waters of the Mediterranean Sea, from parts of the Middle East and, as in North America, from China and Japan. Some estimate that there are about one-half million Japanese in Brazil, most of them in the state of São Paulo. There they cultivate vegetables and fruit, have their own restaurants, their grocery stores, and their bookshops. In their customs and culture they contribute to the flowering diversity of Brazilian life.

Mostly, however, the newcomers were Latin in culture and in temperament, and the Spanish and Portuguese culture that they found was not alien to them. There were differences, but there was also a basic similarity, and the Latin Europeans melted easily into the Latin American way of life and became a part of it. From both Latin and non-Latin immigrants there flowered important contributions to the economic and cultural life of the Latin American. The newcomers were willing to experiment and to try something new. They developed new breeds of animals, planted new varieties of grain and vegetables, and manufactured useful articles for trade abroad and consumption at home. Some made wine, built dairy industries, or founded banks, and others worked as laborers, as mechanics, as peddlers of the street, or became professional men. There were artists among them, writers of merit, and creators of other forms of beauty. And from the energy and the imagination of these new Americans there streamed a new vitality into the life of the Latin Americans.

Thus, those who arrived later from Europe and other regions of the world joined the Indians, the Spaniards, the Portuguese, and the Negroes. All of these diverse peoples are today encompassed by the name Latin American.

## The Society of the Latin American

From the beginning of their occupation of Latin America, the Spaniards continued the system of class they had known in Spain. The conquering Spaniards brought to this land their system of feudalism, and they became the lords of large tracts of land worked by Indian serfs. In many respects, the Spaniards simply replaced the ruling class that the Indians had already known in their own society. An aristocracy based on land ownership evolved.

After the revolutions, serfdom with its system of reciprocal obligations and responsibilities was abolished, but in practice the system continued. The workers were now called *peones* and the masters *patrones*. The legal basis of binding the peon to the land was the tribute that had been owed to landowners in colonial days. Then, during the nineteenth century, many peons found themselves bound to the land by debt. They were forced to buy all of their necessities from the landowner, and they remained constantly in his debt. The peons were forced to work for many long years, even their lifetimes, to repay their debts. Even today there are evidences of this system in parts of Latin America. Thus, in the beginning of Latin American history, there were two well-defined classes in Latin America: the Indian and Negro laborers and the landowning whites from Spain and Portugal. The Spaniards and Portuguese were also linked to the ruling officials and large merchants of the cities.

Between the ruling, landowning European group and the lowly Indian, there gradually emerged another group of men called *mestizos*. The mestizo was the offspring of the white European and the Indian. They were not regarded as being as lowly as the Indian, for they had European blood; however, they were not regarded as being as high as the European, for they had Indian blood. The term mestizo is often today used to refer to a full-blooded Indian who has adopted European ways. In the colonial period, the mestizos found their occupations as artisans, small merchants, mechanics, and similar trades. They generally had little opportunity to obtain an education, and this was another distinctive difference between the Spanish and Portuguese elite, who were educated, and the uneducated Indians and mestizos.

Then among the white Europeans themselves there arose class divisions. The children born in the New World of European parents were given the name *Creole*, and this label indicated that they were born in the Americas rather than Europe. This geographic fact of birth made them socially inferior to the European-born colonists, who controlled the positions of influence in the colonies. It was extremely difficult for the Creoles to rise to the highest offices of the land, although they could and did occupy minor government positions. They generally received some education and a number of them were extremely well educated. If their families possessed wealth, they frequently went to Europe to study and to complete their education. Naturally, the Creoles resented this inferior status and the obstacles in the path of their careers. From their class came many of the prominent revolutionists who rebelled against the ruling Spaniards in Spanish America.

The revolutions which abolished the rule of the Spanish-born did not lift the Indian, the Negro, and the mestizo from the bottom of the Latin American social system. Although the leaders in movements for independence promised that all would be Americans and equal, this did not prove to be the case. In many parts of Latin America the Indians, Negroes, and mestizos still have the lowest social position. The Indian still works in the fields and on the plantations. His wages are low, his poverty is grinding, and his future often seems bleak. For the most part he has continued to live according to the traditions of his ancestors, and he has been loath to change. The Indian has an abiding love for his village and community, and he rarely goes far beyond its bounds. He often lives in a hut bare of modern conveniences and transports his goods on his back or in a cart pulled by an ox or donkey. The mestizos are only slightly better off than the Indians in many parts of Latin America. Their numbers have also been increased by poor Portuguese and Spanish immigrants who settled among them and mingled with them. Negroes are farm laborers, sharecroppers, or city workers. Because of their low economic position many Indians, Negroes, and mestizos remain illiterate. Cultural differences and the failure of governments to encourage or provide schools have also contributed to the lack of education. Negroes, Indians, and mestizos have continued to find their social and economic status galling and bitter.

Not all the poor live in the rural areas. The people of the countryside are beginning to discover the enticements of urban life and have started to trek to the city. Behind the surface appearance of prosperity—the skyscraper, the luxury shop, the rush of traffic, and the growth of apartment buildings—the newcomers are building their slums. With scraps of wood, iron, and discarded rubbish, they patch together frail houses in unplanned huddles on hillside and lowland around the city. They search the heaps of garbage for food, and they do not know the convenience of running water, sewers, and electricity. Disease is everywhere among them. Some find the work they seek, some do not, and all live deep in poverty's depths. Only the hardiest and the luckiest of their babies survive.

The city dwellers are exposed to the trends and modern currents of the outside world. A few watch television, and almost everyone hears the news of the world over radio or reads it in newspapers. Progress is reflected in the changing physical shape of the cities. They are becoming modern, industrialized, and traffic-jammed—a scene of hurrying crowds of office workers, shoppers, and construction workers, accompanied by the sounds of great activity. There is a housing storage, and large numbers of people live in cramped apartments. They dream of a future home somewhere in the city or its outskirts. These city-dwellers respond to the currents of change in their attitudes and opinions. Despite the steady influx of those from the countryside, those who live in the city still remain a minority in most countries, however, and their way of life and thought is far distant from that of the country people.

But the process of change and advance goes on in Latin America, and those who have been lowly are starting to grope for that which will make their life easier and more rewarding. Technology and the machine are coming to their villages and their homes, and their children are beginning to go to school in greater numbers. Many Indian villagers in Mexico, Peru, and elsewhere have shown great ingenuity in setting up their own schools, given the opportunity. As they learn, they will demand more. The climb, however, to education and to a better life may require a long period of time, for the Indians, Negroes, and mestizos are many, and the resources of Latin America have not yet been fully realized.

Still at the top of the social structure, separated by a wide gulf from the poor Indian, the Negro and the mestizo, are the descendants of the Spanish and the Portuguese. The descendants of the later European immigrants also rank high in the Latin American social structure. A relatively small group owns most of the land, and its members are the managers of great enterprises, controllers of the banking system, arbiters of society, and rulers of the Latin American countries. It is this elite group which sets the tone of fashion, literature, art, economics, and politics. It is they who travel abroad and who know and are known by the world.

## The Family

Families still remain close in Latin America. The traditional strong ties are yet binding among many upper and middle-class Latin American families. Ideally, the family embraces all the close relatives, and, as in the past, they still live within a single household when the circumstances and the economy permit it. Important questions are discussed at length among the family members, and businesses are often family enterprises. When problems arise which might reflect upon family pride, the members of a family present a united front to the public.

The father is the head of the family and, from a legal and public point of view, the most important member of it. It is he who makes the final decision in all important questions, and even minor ones, whether they be social, political, or economic. The male is of high value throughout Latin America, and the son of the family is frequently pampered and spoiled, while the female of the family is disciplined, secluded, and watched lest she affront the accepted customs of a society which places limitations on her actions.

## The Woman of Latin America

Old Spanish custom kept the female from the eyes of the public. The old-style Latin American houses were built to keep her hidden from the eye and the touch of the male stranger and friend. Her bedroom was in the inner parts of the house, and her windows were barred. Her visits on the outside were chaperoned by a trusted woman of respectable age, and she was not left to grow too old before her marriage was arranged for her. The ideal wife cared for her husband, ordered the affairs of his household, was docile, obedient, and understanding of the sometimes wayward ways of the male. She did not intrude herself upon her husband's public affairs, though she might influence his decisions in private. She was given very little education while young, and even today Latin Americans sometimes consider the education of girls to be less important than that of boys.

These traditions and customs concerning the place of the woman in private and public life are yet prevalent in Latin America. But there are changes. The surge of the woman toward full equality with the male in North America and in other parts of the world has also had its impact in Latin America. Many Latin American women now demand an education, plan for a public career, insist upon their rights as human beings, and fight fiercely any implication that they are secondary to the male. Industrialization, changes in economy, and the movement to the cities are all tending to increase the importance and the status of women within and outside the family. Women are becoming increasingly influential in family decisions, and they are seen now in growing numbers embarking upon careers in government, in business, and in the professions. The modern Latin American woman now has the right to vote, and, though still bound by long-cherished traditions and habits of thought, is starting to become prominent in political and economic life.

### North American Contrast

The society of the United States and Canada is quite different in tradition and in practice from that of Latin America. The original English colonists did not bring feudalism to the North American shores, nor did they use Indian serfs as the human foundation of their agricultural production. There grew up among these early settlers a feeling of equality rather than a consciousness of class distinctions. The ragged, unwashed scout, trapper, and farmer might be unrefined and illiterate, but they were extremely well educated in finding the dim trails of the forest, in following the elusive game, and in clearing fields and producing food and commercial products. In fact, there developed in the United States a greater admiration for the man who worked with his hands—the doer—than for the intellectual and the man of books. In the eyes of the Latin American, the latter stood higher.

There developed from this early tradition and base, particularly in the United States, a society of men who thought of themselves as the equal of any man, and to whom class distinction was alien and unwanted. There developed also a passion for making things, for inventing and tinkering, and for exploiting the immense resources of the land. The wealth of the lands of the United States and Canada found its way eventually into the hands of the many, and there evolved in these countries a great majority of the middle class and minorities of the very poor and the very rich. This middle class came to dominate the society of the countries and to make impossible the cultural, social, and economic cleavages which divide the society of Latin America.

Nor was there the same patriarchal family system in the United States and Canada that characterized Latin American society. The man was important, but so was the female. Pioneer families went out into the wilderness to make new homes for themselves in Canada and the United States. It was necessary for the woman to be as strong and as responsible as the male in coping with the unimaginable difficulties which beset them. Families were usually on their own, and when the children married they usually went off to found families and homes of their own, separate from the old homestead. As the Canadian and the U. S. American developed their countries, the bulk of the population began to move into the cities, and there was little place for the

American women of the United States began earlier than women of most countries to make their way in what had previously been the "man's world" of business. American inventiveness produced a practical typewriter in the last quarter of the nineteenth century. By the early 1900's many young women were using these machines in offices. (Library of Congress)

large family in the narrow confines of the city.

Women continued to gradually evolve their equality with men. Despite the traditional prejudice of the male and the conservatism of many women, some began to embark upon careers and to enter professions previously the preserve of the male. Increasing numbers of women followed their example as the years passed, and today many American women are members of the government, hold high professional rank, and are engaged in a multitude of activities that take them far beyond the exclusive care of the family and the home which is the primary concern of most Latin American women.

Thus, in the Americas there evolved two distinct societies which reflect the contrasting traditions of the people who settled this hemisphere. As time goes on, however, the society of Latin America tends to move closer to the society of North America. How far this trend will go, and how quickly, is a question that only the future can answer.

## Contrasting Mental Pictures

There are many sharp and obvious differences between the Latin American and the North American. These differences are often multiplied and intensified by mental images of each other that are often misleading and sometimes quite incorrect.

### The Latin American Pictures

The Latin American has frequently pictured in his mind an image of the American of the United States, and his image is of a man somewhat different from himself. He has thought of this American man as rather unrefined and more interested in technology, science, and the machine than in art, literature, philosophy, and intellectual matters that concern the humanity of man. He conceives of this American as a cog of the machine, a prisoner of the clock, an impersonal unit of an organization, and a man addicted to the exclusive pursuit of wealth. He views the U. S. American as a rather cold, inhibited individual who does not show forth the warmth of his humanity openly and with frankness. He may think of the Canadian as possessing some or all of these qualities also, for he does not know the Canadian well, and in creating his image tends to link together the Americans who live north of him.

Examples of this image of the North American can certainly be found among many North Americans of both Canada and the United States. Both Canadians and U. S. Americans have themselves written about, commented on, and sometimes criticized some of these traits in their own character. But the North American is also creative. No one can question the advances and skill of North American architects who pioneered the skyscraper, blended ancient and modern forms, and attracted students from all parts of the world. North American painters have done magnificent work, and their creations have been recognized by the Europeans as fresh and provocative. North American authors and poets have written works of stature and endurance which have made a place for them among the masters of literature. And American musicians have won acclaim throughout the world. There is creativity among the North Americans, and any image of them should include these features which are becoming increasingly important in their lives.

### The North American Pictures

There is a real lack of knowledge on the part of most North Americans about the Latin American. What pictures they have are rather sketchy and also misleading. Nor do all picture the Latin American in the same way. But a composite image might include the following features. He is romantic; a man of dark and magnetic eyes, whose exquisite courtesy is both touching and sophisticated. He dances to exciting rhythms. He woos with the soft serenade of the guitar, frequently becomes violent, and makes revolution a way of political life. He is impractical and prefers to talk rather than to do. He works little but sleeps and plays much. Time for him is unimportant. These are some of the pictures which flash into the minds of many North Americans who know the Latin American only from movies, travel folders, some popular novels, and an occasional meeting. The U. S. Americans who live in southern California and the Southwest often meet the Mexican migrant worker, and they may have other images which are not always complimentary and are limited to the very poor of Mexico. Tourists who visit the Caribbean islands may picture the Negro who sings calypso songs and dances to strangely complicated rhythms.

These pictures are partly true, but not complete. The personality of the Latin American is frequently warming and stimulating. He is often a warm-hearted, spontaneous individual with a zest for living and a high sense of his dignity as a man. He is an individualist. He is warm-hearted and outgoing. When he meets a friend, he embraces him, and he is not ashamed to show the intensity of his feelings and emotions in public. The core of his human philosophy is that emotions are of man and should not be hidden. Nor will he publicly hurt others if it can possibly be avoided, for he prizes dignity. In ceremony and in etiquette he extends to others that dignity that he demands for himself. He is often helpful and generous, and he is sensitive to what might give hurt to others. His friendship can be soothing and calming, and his social relationships are often harmonious and graceful.

There is that flame in him that draws some, but which repels the cold and impersonal man. He has little affection for the machine and sees in it an inhumanity that is alien to him. He insists that the machine exists for him, not he for the machine. He also refuses to have life dictated by a clock. Punctuality is not for him a virtue but a fault, because he thinks man should be the master of time and not its prisoner. The Latin American is an exciting personality. Indeed, in his insistence upon the dignity and freedom of man, he has helped to preserve the importance of man in this new world of the machine. It was man who made the Americas of the past and present, and it is man who is shaping the Americas of the future.

## Reasons for the Contrast

The economic evils that have brought despair to so many Latin Americans have not been duplicated on a large scale in the United States or Canada. The great size of a middle class has made for stability of government in these two countries, for there are not the extremes of wealth and poverty that exist in the nations of Latin America.

Nor are the rigid class distinctions, which are an integral part of Latin American society, evident to such a great degree in these two countries. The laws of both Canada and the United States have placed no restrictions upon any citizen because of birth, wealth, or education, and both countries have a long tradition of permitting the individual to move freely in society. While there are, of course, some groups who consider themselves above or apart from others, the snob is, more often than not, an object of contempt or laughter. The North Americans generally have little feeling for the aristocracy of blood, but they have a great respect for the aristocracy of work and accomplishment.

The Canadian and the American of the United States have not been beset by the dictator, the elite, and military men who desire to rule their countries. Safeguards have been incorporated into their constitutions and political attitudes which make extremely difficult, if not impossible, the rise and rule of a dictator. Naturally, there are those among them who would desire this post of power, but they have small chance of success. Nor have the military been permitted to usurp the rule of the country. It is the tradition of the people of these North American countries to keep the military subordinate to the civil authority, and presidents and prime ministers have slapped military hands which strayed beyond their domain. Among the military men themselves, this tradition of civilian control is upheld and observed. The military generally have no inclination to go beyond the powers assigned by their government.

There are other contrasts between the North American and the Latin American. To own land is not as great a mark of prestige in North America as it is in Latin America. Agriculture has become a science in both Canada and in the United States, and the machine is characteristic of agricultural work, rather than the man as in Latin America. This agriculture is diversified, not specialized as in some Latin American countries. The concentration on industry in the United States and, to a degree, in Canada, also differentiates these Americans from their mainly agricultural neighbors to the south. This difference becomes less, however, as industrialization increases in Latin America.

## Religion of the Latin American

Most of the people of Latin America are Roman Catholics. One of the primary reasons for the voyages of the Spanish explorers to non-Christian portions of the world was to spread the Catholic faith. Wherever explorers and settlers went, they were generally accompanied by missionaries, and the dominant building in the towns, villages, and cities they constructed were the churches. Government and Church officials worked closely together, for the Catholic Church was virtually a State Church, and the only one permitted in Spanish-held territory.

The Indians were converted, and mission churches became a familiar part of their landscape. Catholic ritual became an inseparable part of their spiritual life. The Indian Catholic is generally a loyal, devoted member of his Church. Although he may not know the fine theological distinctions familiar to the educated Latin American, he also does not question the teachings of his religion. The Indian Catholic, however, sometimes holds beliefs and attitudes derived from preconquest religions. Also, among some descendants of Negro slaves, anthropologists have discovered the use of symbols and the continuation of beliefs of an African religious heritage.

Most of the Europeans who immigrated to Latin America came from the Latin areas of Europe, and these, too, were members of the Catholic faith. Thus, the later influx of Catholic immigrants also contributed to the preservation and domination of the Catholic faith in Latin America. There are few places in Latin America where the Mass, the burning of candles, the vivid statues of saints, and the bent figures of praying women are not daily scenes in the life of the Latin American.

But there were those, including Catholics, who resented the closeness of Church and State in Latin America. They opposed the conservative character of Church officials, which they believed to be an obstacle in the path of progress and social advance. During the nineteenth and early twentieth centuries, the liberal political parties fought for a separation of Church and State. Because they were anticlerical, they were often accused of being opposed to the Church. This charge still hangs over these political parties today.

Some Latin Americans have accepted Protestant Christianity, and there are vigorous and influential Freemasons among them. There are also Jewish religious communities in Latin America.

The clamor for reform and the antagonism of competing doctrines are now disturbing the religious life of Latin America. In the second half of the twentieth century, however, a vigorous, socially conscious lay movement is underway based upon the papal encyclical *Rerum novarum.* This movement is especially concerned with labor, agrarian reform, and the strength of political democracy through the Christian Democratic Party.

## Religion of the North American

In some ways, the English, who dominated the settling of North America, were similar to the Spaniards and Portuguese who dominated the colonization of American lands farther south, and in other ways they were different. Among the English there were some who came in search of wealth—gold, silver, and land; and some were moved by the same urge for adventure and escape that motivated many of the Spaniards and Portuguese. But many Englishmen were spurred to ship themselves to North America for other reasons.

Many of the English settlers came to America to find the freedom to worship God as they chose. In general, there was no common effort on the part of colonists or government to impose a certain religion upon others. The settlers had come here to escape the interference of government in their religious beliefs, and most of them brought to America's shores a strong conviction that government should not meddle in the religion of the individual. These ideals eventually became a fundamental part of the constitutional foundations and personal convictions of the U. S. American and the Canadian. For this reason, no one religion became the religion of the State, as was the case in much of Latin America.

The French Catholics who had originally settled in Canada became very concerned about their religious freedom when the English took over control from France. But the English soon guaranteed freedom of religion and relieved this anxiety.

Although there are no State churches in Canada and the United States, there have been religious problems which have irritated and perplexed the peoples of these two countries. One of the most vexing questions involving religion in both countries revolves around the subject of education, and whether or not government aid should be given church-run schools, and if so, to what extent. Because of the separation of Church and State, this problem raises large constitutional issues and debates. State support of church schools is also an issue in Latin American politics.

1. From what countries did most of the immigrants to the United States come? What countries supplied most of the immigrants to Latin America?
2. To what extent has economic class in Latin America been influenced by race? In what other parts of the world is there also economic grouping based to some degree on race?
3. Describe the family structure of Latin America. What changes are taking place which affect the position of women in Latin American society?

## Arts of the Americas

While Latin America and North America differ greatly in colonial background and later political development, they also share much in common. Both shared in the struggle of colonies against European mother countries; both have also shared, generally, in the desire to avoid European interference in the Western Hemisphere. Both have also had similar problems and similar advantages in their complex racial and cultural mixtures. The majority of both Latin Americans and North Americans are regarded as citizens of Christian countries, although the Protestants predominate in North America and the Catholics in Latin America.

It is in their cultures, with their great variations and differences, that North Americans and Latin Americans have also found much in common. The Indian and the Negro contributed to both; a great mixture of immigrants from all parts of the world brought their own contributions; and the people of both the Americas have shared much through their common love of music, painting, design, and literature. The same urges that have moved all men of all times to express their joys, sorrows, longings, and convictions through creativity have also found expression in the Americas and have been a basis for a kind of brotherhood among the people of the Western Hemisphere.

### Latin American Arts and Artists

The educated Latin American is often a very enlightened man. He is able to converse intelligently about classical and modern literature. He demands of his operas the same perfection of performance required by the most sophisticated audiences of Europe. He enjoys and appreciates good paintings, and, when he has money buys them. He is fond of the good life, and if he has sufficient money, his home is frequently furnished with elegance and taste. Latin American architecture is among the world's best, and the startling beauty Latin Americans have created with concrete and steel has drawn the awe and the admiration of men everywhere. Perhaps nowhere have these architectural exploits been more dramatically displayed than in the creation of Brasilia, the new capital of Brazil.

**Brasilia: City of lovely forms.** On an isolated, barren plain in the interior of Brazil, the city of Brasilia was officially made the new capital of the country in April 1960. Rio de Janeiro, the former capital near the sea, was believed to be too removed from the enormous heartland of Brazil. Brazilian leaders were convinced that an inland capital would be a unifying political and cultural center and a stimulus for the economic development of a largely undeveloped hinterland. Accordingly, in 1956, President Juscelino Kubitschek announced the plan to build a new capital. He gave to Oscar Niemeyer, Brazil's most famous architect, the contract to design the government buildings and final authority over the designs of all structures to be built there. Under Niemeyer's direction, Brazilian architects created forms in concrete, glass, steel, and bronze which make Brasilia seem as much a part of an alien future as the wilderness around it is of an alien past.

The city is shaped like an airplane or a bird in flight, and this concept of motion is carried out in the tapering pillars, the curving ramps, the sweep of vistas of glass, and the skyward-slanting concrete beams of its buildings. Two of the most imaginative buildings are the bowl-like structures which house Brazil's two chambers of deputies. These structures sit like one inverted and one open dish on the flat roof-table of a low building. Especially magnificent are the statues that adorn the city. Here a woman of bronze washes her hair in the falling waters of a fountain; there an impressive woman of stone stands blindfolded and beyond passion, reminding man

The architecture of Latin America has attracted the admiration of men everywhere. Left, the murals of the Library of the University of Mexico reflect the influence of Indian art. (American Airlines) Below, Brasilia was planned to open up the interior of Brazil. (Brazilian Government Trade Bureau)

that his justice must be more than animal. And sentinels of skyscrapers defy an unbroken land and the stormy challenges of nature, telling man that there is a future for the creative and the courageous.

There are few who doubt the beauty of the city's form, but there are some who doubt its practicality. They complain that it was not built for man to work and live in, and they speak of the cramped space of their offices, the limitations of their living quarters, and the lack of those conveniences which modern man requires. Others dislike its distance from the civilization and gaiety of Rio. Government officials feel isolated from the main pulse of life which beats in the more populous communities nearer the sea. But Brasilia is now the capital of Brazil, and although it may not be suitable for some who must live there, it is a breathtaking vision for visitors.

**Other creations.** Creativity in Latin America is not confined to Brazil. Throughout Venezuela, Mexico, Argentina, Chile, and other nations, Latin American architects have built structures which rank among the world's greatest in imagination and in design. And in the past the Spanish and the Indians also contributed to the man-made landscape of Latin America.

The Spanish built their houses looking inward to patio and courtyard, and they reinforced the privacy of their homes with barred windows and surrounding walls. The seclusion of the home is yet valued in Latin America, and many of the houses there reflect this aspect of Spanish design. The Spanish also covered the countryside and the cities with their churches and cathedrals, and these were generally the most prominent buildings in the locality. Many of them still stand, mellowed and graced with age, giving the beholder a feeling of the sanctity and the importance which the devout Spaniard sought to impart to his house of worship. There are yet mission churches built of adobe and stone in the former Spanish possessions in the western and southwestern parts of the United States, and many of them are still used as houses of worship.

From the Indian, the modern Latin American has inherited a sense of color and design. In many parts of Latin America the Indian woman weaves cloth for shawl and dress on her crude loom. The patterns of this handmade cloth are attractive and warm with blended colors. Both male and female make baskets, mats, and interesting hats and decorate gourds of interesting shapes. The Indians have long practiced the art of making pottery. Before the coming of the Spanish, the Mayas, Aztecs, and Incas erected monuments in stone and sculptured forms which still merit the praise of man. During the colonial period, many Indian artisans worked in the building of great colonial churches and cathedrals. The designs and religious images that they carved in stone reflect the quality and character of their native art.

The heritage of the Indian, the Spaniard, and the mixtures of man in Latin America have combined to produce a distinct art in this region of the world.

**Music and festivals.** There are few people in the world who do not tap their feet or clap their hands in response to the exciting strains of Latin American music. It was the folk music of the Latin American which first went forth to delight and excite man elsewhere in the world. Songs such as "La Cucaracha," "Ay, Ay, Ay!", and "La Paloma" are still sung with gusto in many parts of the world. The smooth flow of the tango, the catching beat of the samba and the rhumba, and other rhythms which have emerged from Latin America have become part of the musical and dancing patterns of the world. Into the creation of this heady music have gone the folk songs of the Indian, the drum rhythms of the Negro, and the melodic strains and intensity of the Spaniard. But folk songs and popular music were not the only contributions of the Latin American. He also reached to more formal musical expressions, and in his reaching he became an artist in the finest sense of the word.

The Mexican composer, Carlos Chávez, has composed music which is a tribute to his Indian descent and heritage as well as his

The festivals and entertainments of Latin America are among the most colorful in the world. The bullfights in Mexico City, left, attract thousands of spectators. (American Airlines) Carnival in Rio, above, is a three-day celebration. (Brazilian Government Trade Bureau)

genius. Manuel Ponce of Mexico is familiar to many through his composition "Estrellita," and the Cuban composer, Ernesto Lecuona, is known to many outside his country. Perhaps one of the most famous of the Latin American composers and conductors is Heitor Villa-Lobos, a Brazilian who has written and composed an enormous amount of fine music. Out of Latin America there have also come musicians of exceptional talent, such as Claudio Arrau of Chile, Teresa Carreño of Venezuela, and Jésus María Sanromá of Puerto Rico.

Music is a part of the Latin American's life, and though he may not play an instrument or compose, he appreciates its importance to the good life of man. Latin American symphony orchestras and opera companies are often housed in palace-like structures. Strolling musicians are also found in many parts of Latin America. In Venezuela it is a custom to gather a group of musicians from the street, crowd them into car or taxicab, and tour the city, accompanied everywhere with music. Occasionally a stop is made to serenade outside the homes of friends and family. Sometimes the touring orchestra may not be appreciated, especially if the hour is late, but most people seem to enjoy this musical custom, even the neighbors. There is music and gaiety in the life of the Latin American, and he also exhibits this quality of his life in his celebrations and in his festivals.

No Latin American festival is more famous or more fevered than the three-day celebration prior to Ash Wednesday in Rio de Janeiro. It is called *Carnival.* Business stops, government practically comes to a standstill, and there is no time for anything but fun, laughter, dancing, and music. For these three days the streets of Rio are the possession of marching, whirling, singing, clapping figures in gay costumes. There are balls and dancing everywhere, and practical jokes are the rule of the day. Confetti, masked dancers, the scent of perfume, and the flirtatious eye are all part of a parade of color which defies description.

Mosaic sidewalks lead to the Opera House in Rio de Janeiro. (Brazilian Government Trade Bureau)

For this brief period the city of Rio is one big carnival. Festivals such as this are also held in other Latin American villages and cities. In the heart of the Latin American there is the wish to be joyful, and this desire is frequently expressed in his daily life.

**Painting.** The painters of Latin America have expressed their feelings about heaven, earth, and man in creations of striking lines and colors. Some have painted the tortured body of Christ and the agony of the cross, while others have made smiling heavenly figures who were far removed from the pains of man. Some have revealed the nobility of their heroes, while others have portrayed on a grand scale the figures of the tyrants who temporarily ruled them. Some have painted as though apart from the struggles and the strivings of man, while others have sensed that the hands of all men were wielding their brushes. Some were seized with the greatness of their heritage and their traditions, and they sought to teach and to reform through their paintings. Two of the greatest and the best known of these teaching, reforming painters were the Mexican artists Diego Rivera (1886-1957), and José Clemente Orozco (1883-1949).

Rivera is best known for his huge murals which told the story of the Mexican's legends, traditions, history, and heritage. He wanted the peon and peasant, who were largely illiterate, to know and to appreciate their past. Upon this foundation of knowledge he hoped to build their loyalty to the nation-state of Mexico then evolving. Rivera wanted all other Mexicans to feel the fire of nationalism which was aflame in him. He painted the torment of their lives, their poverty, and their hopelessness. Through these vivid pictures he sought to shake the people from their apathy and to make them stern, enduring supporters of the Mexican Revolution. One of the best of his murals, *Liberation of the Peon*, shows the directness and the intensity of his attack upon the old social and economic system in Mexico. Soldiers are portrayed cutting the rope from the bound wrists of a peon whose naked body shows the scars of the lash and the faintness of exhaustion. In the background, burning brightly, is the *hacienda* or large house of the peon's master. It is obvious that the revolutionists are righting the wrongs done by the landlord. In Rivera's paintings, the Mexicans saw the history of their lives.

Orozco was even stronger in the violence of his paintings than Rivera. He hated the brutality which man too often inflicted upon man, and the sufferings of the Indian in Mexico moved him to portray the evil of man in horrible forms. Man the monster, man the starving, and man in skeleton forms make man the observer shudder and draw back from the horror that man can be. Orozco intended for his paintings to shock. They were nightmares of dark truths which he saw in man. They were drawn from his observation of man in Mexico, but they were universal in their application.

**Writers.** The educated Latin American has an unusual gift for words. He uses them generously to express his ideas both in speech and in writing. The best of his speakers and his writers have reached high peaks of beauty, passion, and eloquence in their words. There was Rubén Darío, thought by many to be the finest of the Latin American poets. He was born in the small Central American country of Nicaragua and in him flowed the blood of the Spaniard, Indian, and Negro. He spent much of his life in travel and lived in various parts of Latin America, especially Argentina, where he is revered and regarded as a native son.

It was Darío, and other writers of his time in the late nineteenth and early twentieth centuries, who helped to bring to the Latin Americans a consciousness of the ties that knitted them together as a regional family. Writers like José Martí of Cuba, José Asunción Silva of Colombia, José Enrique Rodó of Uruguay, Amado Nervo of Mexico, to mention a few, were masters of literary style who wrote about subjects that appealed to all Latin Americans. They emphasized the cultural bonds that held the Latin Americans together as a unit and distinguished them from the rest of the world. They stressed the unity that was beyond physical and political differences. One aspect of their regional thinking was a common conception that the Yankee to the north was a threat to the cultural and political life of Latin America.

An example of this common thinking is found in the interpretations of the work of the Uruguayan writer Rodó, who published an essay entitled *Ariel* in 1900. In this essay "Ariel" represented the Christian-Hellenic tradition and "Caliban" stood for crude materialism. It is true that Rodó mentioned the example of materialism in the United States, but his chief purpose in writing this essay was to call upon Latin American youth to maintain a high cultural level. He pointed out that the North American feeling for liberty and technical genius might be studied by Latin Americans, but not necessarily North American cultural values.

Many readers, however, believed that Rodó intended to contrast a "materialistic" United States and a "culturally superior" Latin America in his essay. This interpretation led many Latin Americans to think of the United States as culturally inferior to Latin America. This attitude still persists among Latin Americans today.

There were other writers who expressed a bitter fear of the United States. José Martí, the Cuban revolutionary, was fearful lest the United States lay greedy hands upon Latin American countries. Francisco García Calderón of Peru wrote of Anglo-Saxon invaders, and Ismael Enrique Artigas of Colombia lashed out at Yankee offenses against Latin Americans.

Until recently, most of the great Latin American writers wrote as though they were divorced from the real environment in which they lived. Unlike the painters Rivera and Orozco, they did not conceive it to be their purpose to consider the hard realities of the masses. They thought of their writing as being on a higher plane which was not touched with the commonness of life. They had little social consciousness. Some were even subsidized by dictators, for there was little danger that subversive thoughts or activities would result from their writings. In recent years, however, Latin American writers have turned more of their attention to the real environment in which they live. Some writers are describing actual conditions and prescribing reforms. They are attempting to do through their writings what the recent Mexican artists have done through their paintings.

Among the greatest of the Latin American writers, one whose importance has not diminished with the passage of time, is Joaquim Maria Machado de Assis. Born in poverty of a Negro laborer and a Portuguese

In 1945 Chilean poetess Gabriela Mistral was presented the Nobel Prize for literature by King Gustaf of Sweden. (Wide World photo)

woman, his genius took him to the height of success in Brazil. He founded the Brazilian Academy of Letters and wrote numerous poems and books of merit. Some of his works have been translated into English. Another great Brazilian work, called *Os Sertões,* published in English under the title of *Rebellion in the Backlands,* was written by Euclides da Cunha. It is a story of the hardships of the backwoods environment which shaped the character of the cowboy of northeastern Brazil. Another modern Latin American who has won admiration throughout the world is the Chilean poetess Gabriela Mistral, who was awarded the Nobel prize for literature in 1945.

1. What have been some of the major themes of Latin American writers?
2. What were the reasons advanced by President Kubitschek and his supporters for moving the capital of Brazil to Brasilia?
3. What are the main sources of the music of Latin America?

## Creativity of the U. S. American

The U. S. American has sometimes been termed "uncultured" by his fellow man in other nations. Especially during the colonial period and when the country was young, its people must frequently have seemed rough, unrefined, and lacking in those values and attitudes which are the foundations required for building a great culture. And even today, there are those in Asia, Africa, Europe, and Latin America who see only the inventive genius, the tearing energy, the drive for money, and that scorn for the impractical which are an important part of the U. S. American temperament. But these are only a part of the whole American, and he also has other qualities that his critics have failed to see. These critics have not known the trapper who paused, like a statue of buckskin, to pay a tribute of silence to the bursting glory of a sunrise; nor have they seen the pioneer wife who sought solace and beauty in the worn pages of her Bible. These critics did not hear the unforgettable words of Thomas Jefferson in the Declaration of Independence, or the silencing simplicity of Abraham Lincoln's Gettysburg Address. They have not felt the powerful pulse of the city in the poetry of Carl Sandburg, or the deep life of nature in the words of Henry Thoreau. They have not watched the millions who throng to the museums, art galleries, and concert halls of the United States. The creative arts are an essential part of American life.

**Distinguished painters.** The U. S. American has been painting since the early days of his history. There were John Copley (1738-1815), Charles Willson Peale (1741-1827), and Gilbert Stuart (1755-1828) who are remembered for their portraits. Stuart is especially remembered for his portraits of George and Martha Washington. Not all confined themselves to portrait painting, however. There was the famous Benjamin West (1738-1820), who portrayed historical scenes in a graphic manner. Many are acquainted with his paintings *The Death of General Wolfe* and *Penn's Treaty with the Indians.*

There were also painters who revealed the magnificence of the American landscape with precise detail. Some of these belonged to a group called the "Hudson River School," but they did not confine themselves to the scenery around the Hudson River. They painted the crags of Yosemite, the grandeur of the Rocky Mountains, and the falling torrents of Niagara, as well as the beauty of the Catskills in New York. Some of the more prominent members of this school were Thomas Cole (1801-1848), George Inness (1825-1894), and Albert Bierstadt (1830-1902).

A number of American painters have become internationally famous, and one of the most successful of them was James Whistler (1834-1903). Perhaps his best-known work is the painting of his mother which he called simply *An Arrangement in Grey and Black.* John Sargent (1856-1925), during his lifetime, was a much-admired artist. Thomas Eakins (1844-1916) did not enjoy the wide fame of Sargent in his lifetime, but today he is thought to have been one of the greatest American painters. He knew the human body as only a doctor can and gave it immortality as only a true artist can. And there was Winslow Homer (1836-1910), who painted *Prisoners from the Front* during the Civil War, *The Life Line* bearing men just beyond the grasping waves of the ocean, and the peace of the country in the seascapes from his Gloucester, Massachusetts farm.

Then in the first part of the twentieth century a group led by Robert Henri (1865-1929) rebelled against the usually accepted subjects for painting. They sought a broader expression and chose as their subjects the more common and sometimes more sordid aspects of American life. Slums, saloons, poolrooms, and the people of the street or passengers of a ferry often provided subjects for their paintings. Someone called them the "Ashcan School," and the name stuck, but sometimes these painters achieved very fine art. *The Wake of the Ferry* by John Sloan (1871-1951) is regarded as an extremely good painting.

The American painter was heir to a European heritage of art, and his paintings were often influenced by the trends that originated in Europe. The French, especially, have for many years been leaders in this field. American painters absorbed the techniques and ideas of Impressionism, Expressionism, Cubism and other schools born in Europe and applied them to the American scene. Marsden Hartley (1877-1943), Arthur G. Dove (1880-1946), and John Marin (1870-1953) were three pioneers of these art forms in the United States. Marin portrayed the exciting movement and the mighty restlessness of the city using the techniques of these new French schools of painting. The watercolors *Lower Manhattan* and *The Singer Building* are stimulating products of his art.

In the 1930's some painters began to rediscover the special qualities and customs of the people and their landscape outside the city. There was John Curry (1897-1946), whose *Baptism in Kansas* and *The Tornado* are well known. Thomas Benton, born in 1889, painted graphically the people and the landscape of the South, the Middle West, and Southwest. There are few who do not delight in the *Ride of Paul Revere* and *American Gothic* painted by Grant Wood (1892-1942). All of these men came from the heartland of America. Benton was a native of Missouri, Wood was a son of Iowa, and Curry belonged to Kansas.

American painters have viewed the American scene with a variety of attitudes. Some have pictured the brute faces of the poor and the meanness of their lives, while others pictured beaches as hills of bodies and the landscape as heaps of junked cars. Some have striven to describe the irrationality of man and to probe the subconscious motives that move him. This type of painting is called Surrealism, and Salvador Dali, a native of Spain, is its leader in the United States. There are those who express themselves in the most abstract manner, such as Jackson Pollock (1912-1956), and there are those called primitive who have talent but little training, such as Anna Mary Robertson ("Grandma" Moses). The U. S. American continues to express his emotions, his attitudes, and his values through painting, and he is beginning to lead as well as follow in this field of the creative arts.

**Famous sculptors.** The U. S. American has also sculptured. John Rogers (1829-1904) molded forms in red plaster, and many people have admired *Checkers Up at the Farm.* Augustus Saint-Gaudens (1848-1907) is noted for the lifelike quality of his statues. Among his most admired works are *The Standing Lincoln,* in Chicago, and the figure of a weeping seated woman, *The Adams Monument,* in Washington, D. C. Lorado Taft (1860-1936) sculptured groups of symbolic figures, and some of his better-known works are the *Fountain of Time* in Chicago, and the *Thatcher Memorial Fountain* in Denver.

Modern American sculptors, like modern American painters, have also made abstract works of art. In addition to stone, marble, and wood, they are doing fine work with steel, aluminum, lead, wire, and other materials. It was Alexander Calder who invented the *mobile,* which is made up of suspended objects that move into changing relationships with each other, when stirred by the air currents. Some of the better known recent American sculptors are David Hare, Herbert Ferber, Richard Lippold, Theodore Roszak, and José De Rivera.

**Original architects.** Even in his colonial days the U. S. American built warm, livable, and often lovely houses. Each year thousands of Americans and non-Americans visit the restored city of Williamsburg, Virginia and are charmed by the serenity and grace that mark the buildings of this colonial town. A bright-

Eero Saarinen's design for the Trans World Airlines terminal at John F. Kennedy International Airport, New York. is a striking example of modern American architecture. (The Port of New York Authority)

ness of interior, the mellowed colors of aged brick walls, and a graciousness of structure draw man to look and to admire. The American has continued to build inviting, comfortable, and frequently beautiful homes which are envied by millions who live in other parts of the world. In fact, many Asians consider that an American house would be a part of their paradise on earth.

The U.S. American architect has very often been a leader rather than a follower. American buildings were among the first in modern times to scrape the skies in story after story that reached to incredible heights. The American architect Louis Sullivan (1856-1924) is associated with the beginnings of the skyscraper in the United States. His phrase "form follows function" became the guideline for most American architects and helped to establish the idea that what is useful may also be beautiful. Better kinds of structural concrete and steel, and new kinds of materials, such as structural aluminum, also contributed to the flowering of American architecture. These new materials gave greater freedom and flexibility to the architect in designing his buildings. As the population increased, land within cities became scarcer. It became necessary to build upward in space. Skeletons of steel with skins of glass, which revealed rather than hid their structures, leaped into the skylines of Chicago, New York, and other cities. Tall towers of light—delicate yet strong—they were both useful and beautiful. The Seagram Building in New York, which was designed by Miës Van Der Rohe is a shining example of the modern skyscraper.

Probably the most famous and the most controversial of modern American architects was Frank Lloyd Wright (1869-1959). There was nothing small about this man. Gifted with imagination, skilled in engineering, strong of character, and stubborn in his convictions, he was magnificent in success and great in failure. Ever mindful of the earthliness of man, he grafted buildings onto the earth which have stimulated other men to wonder, to criticize, to admire, and to imitate. Wright designed industrial plants and offices in which men work, and the buildings of the Johnson's Wax Company of Racine, Wisconsin are examples of his genius. He designed halls to house the art treasures of man, and the Guggenheim Museum in New York is itself a work of art. He built homes for man to dwell in, and they became a part of the hill, the stream, the waterfall, the desert, and the plain. In material and in design, Wright's buildings belonged to that special earth upon which they were built.

**Authors of renown.** The U. S. American has written much, and has often written well. He has written in many styles and for many purposes, from the colonial period to the present day. Cotton Mather (1663-1728) and Jonathan Edwards (1703-1758) expressed the religious concerns of the New England Puritans. Benjamin Franklin (1706-1790) was a humanitarian, man of science, statesman, businessman, and thinker whose writings still give pleasure and sound advice. Franklin was a moral man, who was yet tolerant and liberal toward others, and the range of his thought covered everything from the essay "On the Causes and Cure of Smoky Chimneys" to ethics and common sense in *Poor Richard's Almanac*. Our most intimate and appealing view of Franklin today is through his *Autobiography*. Michel Guillaume Jean de Crevecoeur (1735-1813), an immigrant from France, wrote a sensitive series of essays *(Letters from an American Farmer)* describing the people and life of his times. The spirit of freedom that guided the American Revolution was expressed through the speeches of Patrick Henry and Thomas Paine's *Common Sense*, *The Rights of Man*, and *The Crisis*. This love of freedom is immortalized in the *Declaration of Independence*, drafted by Thomas Jefferson. Contributions by Alexander Hamilton, James Madison, and John Jay to *The Federalist* laid further foundations for the American government through their ordered and reasoned discussions.

During the first half of the 1800's American writers became interested in telling good, imaginative stories in which the individual, his emotions, and his environment were impor-

Edgar Allan Poe (1809-1849) left a legacy of beauty and imagination in his poetry. (Brady-Handy Collection, Library of Congress)

Nathaniel Hawthorne (1804-1864) was a neighbor of Thoreau and Emerson. (Brady-Handy Collection, Library of Congress)

tant. This was a part of the movement known as romanticism which also prevailed in Europe during those years. This was the period when the American began to create real literature. With pleasing humor and extraordinary style, Washington Irving (1783-1859) wrote tales that have captured the imagination of generations of readers. Who can forget Rip Van Winkle's long sleep or the ghostly "Legend of Sleepy Hollow"? The richness of Irving's images in *The Alhambra* set a standard still admired today for descriptive writing. With a feeling for the sea and the frontier, James Fenimore Cooper (1789-1851) created exciting stories. Natty Bumppo in *The Deerslayer* and Hawkeye in *The Prairie* are heroes who still live. *The Last of the Mohicans* and *The Pioneers* pay tribute to the nobility of character of the Indian. During this period, Edgar Allan Poe (1809-1849) lived his brief and tragic life, but left behind a legacy of great beauty and imagination. Two of his best-loved poems are "The Raven" and "The Bells" and they influenced other American writers as well as poets of Europe. Poe also wrote fine short stories and became one of the early creators of the detective story with "The Murders in the Rue Morgue."

Two giants of thought and word lived in and around Boston during the 1800's. They were Ralph Waldo Emerson (1803-1882) and Henry David Thoreau (1817-1862). These men sought beauty and truth, and they felt themselves surrounded by eternal unseen principles which they tried to grasp through intuition and communion with nature. Generations of men have been inspired and uplifted by Emerson's challenging *Essays* and have looked with Thoreau in *Walden* at the deep, rich life of nature.

Other poets and novelists also adorned America during this century. Nathaniel Hawthorne (1804-1864) and Herman Melville (1819-1891) are outstanding novelists whose works are still of great importance. Hawthorne is most often remembered by *The Scarlet Letter* and *The House of the Seven Gables*. Melville's masterpiece was *Moby Dick*. Henry Wadsworth Longfellow (1807-1882) is best known for his long poems "Evangeline," "Hiawatha," and "The Courtship of Miles Standish"; and John Greenleaf Whittier (1807-1892) is especially remembered for such poems as "Snow-Bound," "Maud Muller," and "The Barefoot Boy." The great poet of democracy, Walt Whitman (1819-1892) has grown in stature with the passing of time. Some of his best poems are grouped under the title *Leaves of Grass*. Exquisite in images and singing in word, Whitman holds a special place among the poets of America.

And as the 1800's moved toward the 1900's, other Americans continued to strike the minds of men with their words. Harriet Beecher Stowe (1811-1896) directed much sympathetic attention to the plight of Negro slaves in *Uncle Tom's Cabin* and created portraits of them that would live for many years. Louisa May Alcott (1832-1888) told a tale in *Little Women* which still enchants young and old. Emily Dickinson (1830-1886) created loveliness of word and thought in striking images and original rhythms that still have a great influence on modern poets. Mark Twain, who was born Samuel Langhorne Clemens (1835-1910), made the American boy eternal in *The Adventures of Tom Sawyer* and *The Adventures of Huckleberry Finn*, and won worldwide acclaim for his other novels, short stories, and essays. And O. Henry, who was William Sydney Porter (1862-1910), penned short stories that became American classics.

As the American burst into the twentieth century, he was often driven by a ruthless greed and hunger to seize wealth and power. Sometimes he seemed to ignore the sufferings of those who were less fortunate. And as the American art of writing matured, novelists began to portray the American scene with a sharp eye and to search the American soul with skilled strokes of the pen. Theodore Dreiser (1871-1945) saw the American individual hurt, shattered, and lost in his drive for success, and Dreiser told of this plight in *An American Tragedy*. Sinclair Lewis (1885-1951) found the American imprisoned and unhappy in a web of petty social convention, and he described him harshly as a *Babbitt*.

William Faulkner was awarded the 1949 Nobel Prize for literature. Other Americans who have won this prize are Eugene O'Neill, Sinclair Lewis, Pearl Buck, Ernest Hemingway, and John Steinbeck. (Wide World photo)

And there were those who grieved with the poor in a land where wealth sometimes seemed to be king: Erskine Caldwell in *Tobacco Road*, and John Steinbeck in *The Grapes of Wrath*.

After World War I, there was a group of writers who have been called "the lost generation." Many old social values seemed no longer to be true after that war, and these writers were seeking new directions and new values. They wrote with great vigor, held strongly to a sense of justice, and detested sham. Among these were John Dos Passos *(U. S. A.)*, Ernest Hemingway *(The Sun Also Rises)*, and F. Scott Fitzgerald *(The Great Gatsby)*. And there was William Faulkner whose characters lived, agonized, and died on a small piece of the Southland. There was also Thomas Wolfe, whose intensely personal novels expressed in language of highly poetic tone the longings and ambitions of youth.

Thomas Edison, shown above with his tinfoil phonograph in 1878, thought of this invention at first as only a business machine. George Eastman's Kodak camera, below, made photography a popular hobby. Today great music is available everywhere in recordings, and photography is an admired art form. (National Park Service; Eastman Kodak Company)

Perhaps one of the strongest characteristics of American literature was a broad humor mixed with compassion. Humorous writing had begun to flower with such writers as Mark Twain and Booth Tarkington, and in later days it flourished with humorists such as Clarence Day, Robert Benchley, and James Thurber, who laughed and mourned at the same time.

The American was ripening with age, and his writing talent continued to grow. Eugene O'Neill, Maxwell Anderson, Thornton Wilder, and Robert Sherwood wrote plays that shocked and won praise for their tragedy and tenderness. The singing of poets touched all the land with melodies of thought and word. Edwin Arlington Robinson, Amy Lowell, Edna St. Vincent Millay, Vachel Lindsay, T. S. Eliot, Carl Sandburg, Robert Frost, Stephen Vincent Benet, Archibald MacLeish, and a host of others sent forth in musical waves of words their feelings about man, society, and nature.

The American continues to write what is in his mind and heart, and often there is thunder in his line and beauty in his goal. He writes as a novelist, a poet, a critic, a journalist, a philosopher, and a statesman, and his words are of concern to the world as well as America, for he is concerned with all the world of man.

**Art and invention.** A fascinating characteristic of American cultural life has been the combination of creativeness with a keen business sense in a marriage that is often discordant but always exciting. The inventiveness and love of business that many critics have seen as materialistic have also played an important role in the U. S. American's contributions to creative arts and the appreciation of beauty. No inventions of modern times have had greater impact on the arts than the phonograph, radio, and the moving picture camera—and all of these were developed chiefly in the United States.

Thomas Edison, who invented a phonograph in 1878, thought of it first as a business machine, but its first great success was in entertainment. Within a few years the popular music of the day was available on phonograph cylinders and discs, and soon the greatest performers of the finest music were available everywhere through recordings. In the first few years of the century millions of records of the greatest opera stars, pianists, violinists, and other musicians were sold. This wide distribution of the works of fine musicians helped to bring an appreciation of music to parts of a land that had only recently emerged from the pioneer stage—and the phonograph formed the basis of one of our richest money-making industries!

Edison also invented a successful motion picture camera, and he was a pioneer in the early making of movies for entertainment. The nickelodeons did not display great art, but they accustomed the public to seeing dramatic performances with the eye of the camera. Within a few years, many skilled actors of the day were performing before the movie cameras in adaptations of literary classics and new stories especially written for the screen. Today the dramatic art of the cinema is an essential part of our culture and has proved capable of admirable achievements.

The radio utilized many inventions of the American inventor Lee De Forest. Radio and its later offspring, televisiòn, contributed widely to creativity and culture in the United States and in all the world. Radio and television, like the movies, have flourished chiefly as profit-making business enterprises, and many critics have found them to be of little value. Yet, at their best, they have offered entertainment that combined the finest of writing, performing, and musical arts: great plays, operas, and music performed by the best actors, singers, and orchestras. We have only begun to appreciate their possibilities, and we may still expect real contributions from these products of invention that have helped to further the arts.

**A very special music.** There is music in the U. S. American. From the beginning of his history he has sounded in music the joys, the sorrows, the yearnings, the needs, the love, and the worship of his heart. The Indian, with flute, drum, and rattle made music and sang to celebrate victory in war and luck in the hunt. Colonists brought with them from Europe their hymns of praise and thanks to God, and their work-songs that made labors easier. In stately homes the wealthy colonists danced to the measures of the minuet, and in the secluded mountain cabins of Virginia, Kentucky, and Tennessee, voices lilted the songs first heard in their English homeland. The early American listened to French and

As the first transcontinental railway was laid across the United States, a camera car followed the workmen to record their progress. John Henry and Casey Jones are famous railroad folklore characters celebrated in songs. (Library of Congress)

Work songs associated with the building of canals and railroads in the 1800's have became a part of our heritage of American folk music. Left, a part of the Chesapeake and Ohio canal, built in 1850. (National Park Service)

Spanish songs in old New Orleans, stirred to the strains of the Spanish guitar in Texas and New Mexico, and bellowed the French-Canadian song of "Alouette" around the waters of the Great Lakes. He labored as a slave and poured forth in "spirituals" his African melodies and rhythms and his special feeling for God.

Wherever the Americans went to settle and live, and whatever they did, their music went with them and often expressed their attitudes. They fiddled and danced to the "Arkansas Traveler," built waterways and sang "The Erie Canal," laid railroads to the rhythms of "John Henry," and mourned the brave engineer "Casey Jones." They traveled West to the tune of "Oh! Susanna" and dug gold in California while humming "Clementine." They eased the hardship of their cattle drives with "The Old Chisholm Trail," showed their affection for horses in "Old Paint," and expressed their love for the spacious West in "Home on the Range."

The melodies of Stephen Foster (1826-1864) touched the hearts of many and won an enduring fame. "My Old Kentucky Home," "Old Folks at Home," and "Jeanie with the Light Brown Hair" have continued to be loved for their simple tenderness. Americans marched away to the tragic War Between the States singing "Dixie" or "The Battle Hymn of the Republic." Later they waltzed to "Sweet Rosie O'Grady," voiced their sentiment in "Silver Threads Among the Gold," caught a

Benjamin West (1738-1820) was born in Pennsylvania and was a self-taught artist. He gained fame in London, where he was a charter member and president of the Royal Academy. "Penn's Treaty with the Indians," left, is one of his many famous historical paintings. (The Pennsylvania Academy of the Fine Arts)

Thomas Eakins (1844-1916) is widely admired for the realism and accuracy of his paintings, which expressed the vitality of American life. At right, Eakins' "Between Rounds." (Courtesy of The Philadelphia Museum of Art) The paintings of George Caleb Bingham (1811-1879) showed scenes of everyday American life, especially of the Middle West. Below, Bingham's "Stump Speaking" portrays a political orator of the last century. (Courtesy of The Boatmen's National Bank, St. Louis)

The Metropolitan Opera of New York is a showplace for world-famed performers. Above, a performance of "Carmen." (Metropolitan Opera Archives)

spirit of the city in "The Sidewalks of New York," and dreamed of the quiet countryside in "On the Banks of the Wabash."

As the twentieth century moved along, the pace of life and music began to quicken. The music of the Southern Negro began to move northward, up the Mississippi to Chicago and along the Eastern seaboard to New York's "Tin Pan Alley." As early as the 1890's a type of dance music known as ragtime had been popular, and in 1911 Irving Berlin published the well-known "Alexander's Ragtime Band." Then in 1914, the American Negro composer William C. Handy published his famous "St. Louis Blues." Among his other famous blues were "Memphis Blues" and "Yellow Dog Blues." Negro musicians began to move north, especially from New Orleans, and out of the ragtime music, the "blues," and perhaps the spiritual, there was born that special type of music called jazz. By the 1920's it was widely known and was especially associated with the United States.

As jazz became a popular form of music, the dance orchestra became dominant upon the popular music scene, and great band leaders and performers leaped to fame. Paul Whiteman, Fletcher Henderson, "Duke" Ellington, and other orchestra leaders became widely known. Crowds were drawn to the clarinet of Benny Goodman, the trombone of Jack Teagarden, the piano of "Count" Basie, and the trumpet of Louis Armstrong. They were not merely technical masters of instruments, but composers too, who improvised with creative abandon as they played. Jazz is no longer confined within the borders of the United States. It is now a part of the music of all men.

The musical theater had developed in Europe, but it took a special form and a special American character in the United States. Victor Herbert, who came to America from Ireland, was among the first of a long list of great American composers who wrote music for the stage. His musical comedies *Naughty Marietta* and *Babes in Toyland*, and his songs such as "Ah, Sweet Mystery of Life" and "The Italian Street Song," are yet prized in America and elsewhere. There were other composers who followed him, and their music was tuneful and lasting. There was Rudolf Friml and his *Vagabond King*, Sigmund Romberg's *The*

*Student Prince*, Jerome Kern's *Show Boat*, George Gershwin's *Of Thee I Sing*, Cole Porter's *Kiss Me Kate*, Richard Rodgers' *South Pacific*, Frederick Loewe's *My Fair Lady*, and Leonard Bernstein's *West Side Story*. These are but a few of the composers whose musical shows have pleased man with their music. The American musical comedy, which was originally inspired by European operettas, became an artistic form in its own right.

American composers have also written enduring music of a more formal kind. "To a Wild Rose" by Edward MacDowell is known to every listener and player of the piano, and in his *Indian Suite* there is the ancient music of the Indian. Charles W. Cadman (1881-1946) studied deeply and was touched by the music of the Indian, and his opera *Shanewis* is based upon an old Indian tale. John Carpenter (1876-1951) composed the ballad "Skyscrapers." Deems Taylor wrote, among others, the opera *Peter Ibbetson*, Howard Hanson the opera *Merry Mount*, and Gian-Carlo Menotti the opera *Amahl and the Night Visitors*. William Schuman, Randall Thompson, and Samuel Barber are known for their symphonies, and Aaron Copland is famous for his musical interpretations and descriptions of the American scene. And these are but a few of those Americans who have composed magnificent music. Today almost every major American city supports a symphony orchestra or some other musical organization. Music is an essential part of the rich and varied life of the U. S. American.

The music of America is a mixture and blending of the American heritage from men of all ages and all parts of the world. It is the melodies of the Indian, the harmonies of Bach, and the rhythms of Africa and Latin America. It is of Italy, France, England, Greece, Germany, Spain, and many other countries. It is the music of a multitude of churches. It is the music of the miner tunneling for coal and gold, of the farmer plowing the earth, of the cowboy riding the wide range, and of the city man walking and living in the narrow confinement of his crowded world.

It is of all the great sweep of America: North, East, South, and West. It is the music of a growing, maturing American.

1. Why is Louis Sullivan often called the father of modern architecture?
2. What have been the major subjects of American painters? Of American writers?
3. What musical forms are uniquely American?

## Conclusion

The Latin American has been frequently seized with the frenzy of creation. He has expressed his creativity in stone, steel, and concrete, as well as with pen and brush. He has painted with sympathy the sorrows and frustrations of the poor. He has been unforgettably dramatic in his prose and in his poetry. He has made melodies and rhythms which hasten the pulse and move the feet. He is an artist in many forms. All of the young and the old who dance with gladness in the traditional fiestas, and all who know and respect their culture and ancient heritage, are expressing the art of Latin America. But the Latin American is also a culturally evolving man, and the present and the future are as much a part of his artistry as the influence of the past.

Until recently the voice of the U. S. American in the humanities and in the arts was only a whisper in the world. His accomplishments in the creative arts were drowned out by the roar of his machines and his own loud boasts about them. They were frequently obscured by the spectacular bigness of his land and his construction. And often, the U. S. American spent his energies in making this country a material paradise, a symbol and refuge for those who would be free. But there were always those who strove for more, who used hand and brain to make the beautiful as well as the useful, and to catch fragments of eternity as well as moments of immediate comfort. Quietly they created, inevitably they grew, and almost suddenly the eyes of man saw in the American the creativity of the artist as well as the holder of wealth, and the builder of beauty as well as freedom.

## SUMMING UP THE CHAPTER

A. Define or explain the following terms, relating them to this chapter.

| | |
|---|---|
| Ashcan School | mobile |
| Carnival | patrón |
| Creole | peón |
| hacienda | primitive |
| mestizo | |

B. Chapter review questions.

1. Describe the class system of Latin America. To what extent was it derived from the Spanish class system? What changes have there been in the class system, and how significant have they been?
2. What effect did independence from Spain have on the Indian and the mestizo of Latin America?
3. Describe the traditional role of the woman in Latin America. To what degree does this represent the role of the modern woman of the upper classes? Of the modern woman of the lower classes?
4. Compare the role of the family in the United States with that of the family in Latin America. How would you explain the differences? Which family structure do you think is better? Why?
5. What explanations can you find for the American woman having extended her life so far beyond the home? Do you think this is good or bad? Why?
6. What are the historical reasons for the dominant role of the Roman Catholic Church in Latin America?
7. Why did not the Roman Catholic Church dominate in North America as it did in Latin America?
8. What efforts have been made by the English-speaking Protestant majority in Canada to guarantee to the French Catholics the preservation of their cultural and religious heritage?
9. What were the apparent reasons for the creation of the monumental capital city of Brasilia? What criticisms have been made of it?
10. How does the culture of the United States reflect the variety of origins of its people?
11. What influence did the phonograph have in shaping the musical appreciation of the American people? How has it raised the performance standards demanded of musical artists? What problems has it created for the performing artist? How has it, at the same time, lowered the standards of performance?

C. Questions for discussion.

1. What are some of the major problems of Latin America today? Which do you feel are most important? Most basic?
2. Look up the word *culture* in an unabridged dictionary. When we speak of the "culture" of a country, what do we mean? Who generally is the possessor and preserver of this culture? Compare the culture of the United States with that of Latin America. How would you account for the differences?
3. Describe the class structure of the United States. What historical factors might explain this structure?
4. Why do you think anti-intellectualism has often played a prominent part in American life? What problems and dangers has this created for the United States?
5. What is meant when it is said that the people of the United States belong to a "middle class" society? What has this meant in terms of the distribution of economic wealth? Who are the people that set the dominant social, intellectual, and artistic standards of the United States?
6. Can you find any similarities between the creation of the Brazilian capital, Brasilia, and the creation of the U.S. federal city of Washington, D.C.? Who was responsible for laying out the plan of each?

D. Projects for groups or individuals.

1. Prepare a report on current problems in relations between Church and State in the United States.
2. Make a collection of pictures of the city of Brasilia. Locate the city on a map.
3. Listen to the *Bachianas Brasilieras No. 5* of Heitor Villa-Lobos. Can you identify any specifically Indian, African, or Spanish influences in this composition?
4. Collect pictures of some of Diego Rivera's murals and mosaics. Compare his style and subjects with those in the murals of the American artist, William Benton.
5. Look through a folio album of the art of Colonial and early Federal America. What were the subjects and techniques of the artists of these periods?
6. Prepare a report on the subjects and styles of any of the significant "schools" of American painters.
7. If your school library does not have many books on art, compile a collection of representative American art from magazines and other sources.
8. Prepare a report on the colossal sculptures on Mount Rushmore in the Black Hills by Gutzon Borglum.

The Mayan vase at right was made between 600 and 900 A.D. It was found in Guatemala and is considered to be one of the finest known examples of Mayan painting. (University Museum, Philadelphia) Machu Picchu is a ruined Inca city high in the Andes Mountains of Peru. It was discovered in 1911. The remaining stone walls show an advanced architecture. (Pan American Airways)

CHAPTER **32**

# *Disunity-Dictators-Revolutionists*

SIMÓN BOLÍVAR dreamed of a unity among all Latin Americans. This dream was shared by others among the original revolutionists, and it was to encourage unity that San Martín removed himself from the politics of Latin America. The dream of a unified Latin America has continued to live among Latin Americans from the time of their revolutions to the present. But it is yet an unrealized dream, and the same barriers to unity that existed in the past still exist today.

## Reasons for Disunity

There was a political unity in the colonial period among the Latin Americans who were ruled by Spain, Portugal, and France. It is ironic that when colonial authority in the American hemisphere was destroyed, this political unity was also destroyed. There were several reasons why this happened. The lands that gained their independence from Spain and Portugal were a vast expanse of enormous distances humped with steep-sided mountains. Great areas of these lands were covered with dense jungles and strewn here and there with impassable swamps. All of these land features made travel very difficult. Communication between the various parts of Latin America was limited, and mostly the people grew up and lived in isolation from one another. The people of each country knew their locality, their rulers, and their neighbors, and that was all. They had an interest and a certain loyalty to the particular stretch of earth on which they lived, but they knew little of other peoples and places.

Differences in the composition of population also separated the people of the various Latin American countries. In Chile, Argentina, Uruguay, and Costa Rica, the European family of man was predominant, while in countries such as Mexico and Peru, the Indians were the majority. The Portuguese were rulers in Brazil, as were the French and Dutch in their colonies, although they did not make up the greatest part of the population. In some countries a considerable number of the people were of mixed European and Indian descent. The Negro was dominant in Haiti and also made up a large percentage of the population in Cuba and Brazil.

Then, too, there were ambitious and power-hungry men who sought to govern in the areas they were freeing from Spain and other colonial powers. Jealousy and envy, quarrels, and a scramble for position among leaders all tended to drive the new nations apart rather than together. Greater Colombia, which Bolívar had put together for a time, fell apart into the three countries of Venezuela, Colombia, and Ecuador. Panama later became independent. Paraguay maintained its separateness, as did Chile, Bolivia, and Peru. Uruguay arose out of the rivalry between Brazil and Argentina. The Central American confederation eventually became the present states of Costa Rica, Guatemala, El Salvador, Nicaragua, and Honduras. In the Caribbean there were the countries of the Dominican Republic and Haiti. Later, Cuba become another independent country. Thus Latin America became a land of twenty-two nations, including English-speaking Jamaica and Trinidad. These nations

The importance of Latin America to United States interests is sometimes symbolized by the Panama Canal. The picture at right shows the first tugboat to pass through Gatun Locks, September 26, 1913. (Pan American Union)

have gone their separate ways since their birth. The relations between these nations have not always been friendly, and this factor, too, has tended to make them somewhat suspicious of each other on occasion.

Argentina and Brazil quarreled over the land that is now Uruguay; Paraguay and Bolivia fought a war over the area known as the Gran Chaco; and the area of Ecuador has been decreased by her neighbors. The history of the countries of Central America is one of constant bickering, invasion, and suspicion, increased by fear of the "colossus to the north," which for some of them is not the United States but Mexico. Latin American history has also been marked by plots and attempts to overthrow governments. Thus, for many reasons the countries of Latin America have continued in their separate paths of political and economic development. In Latin America, as in many other parts of the world, geographic closeness has frequently led to hate, suspicion, and even war between neighbors rather than to understanding and friendship. The unfortified border between the United States and Canada has long been cited as an example of the ideal relationship between nations, but there have been incidents and suspicions of intentions even in the relationship between these countries. Some Canadians and some U. S. Americans have also expressed distaste for neighbors along their common border. The Latin American, in his geographic setting, has behaved no differently from other men in the past and present.

### Military Power and the Dictator

The nations of Latin America had to fight for independence and to defend their sovereignty

Handicraft industry plays an important role in the economy of much of Latin America. Almost every village and city of Mexico has its open-air market, where locally made goods are sold. (Mexican National Tourist Council)

Latin America has a wealth of natural resources. Above, oil prospectors take a sample from the ground in the jungle of Colombia. (Socony Mobil Oil Company, Inc.)

The drying of coffee, a chief product of Latin America, requires much manual labor. Heavy manufacturing industries have not yet been developed in much of Latin America. (Pan American Coffee Bureau)

after independence. As a consequence, military men became and remained important as leaders. The general, the colonel, and the major were drawn into politics from almost the very birth of their countries, and it is mostly they who have ruled the independent nations of Latin America. Men sit in power in many countries of Latin America today because they hold control over the military. In recent years military groups, or *juntas*, seized control of Argentina and Peru, and these military leaders have had a powerful voice in the decisions of those who have been elected to office. All Latin Americans know that a displeased military group might depose elected officials at any time. This has become a habit of the military in Latin America.

Out of this conflict for independence, this drive for power in the various localities, and this military habit, there was born a multitude of dictators, who, at one time or another, have ruled every country of Latin America. Mexico had Porfirio Diaz, who ruled from 1877-1911 with only one short interruption. Venezuela finally threw out Perez Jiménez in 1958, and Generalissimo Rafael Trujillo of the Dominican Republic was assassinated in 1961. Haiti now has François Duvalier, who came to power in 1957, and Paraguay is firmly governed by General Alfredo Stroessner. The dictators of Latin America have appeared in all kinds of physical shapes: short, tall, fat, plump, or lean, and they have been of various strains of man, mixed and so-called "unmixed."

Their personalities have varied from the sophisticated and the educated to the primitive and the illiterate. Their rule has been sometimes acclaimed and sometimes despised. Some have been benevolent; many have been cruel. Some have tried to better conditions in their countries; but many have been interested only in bettering their personal fortunes and glorifying themselves in statues and in paintings. In appearance, in tastes, in education, and even in their personalities, it would be difficult to say that all had something in common. But all were the same in that they governed in an authoritarian manner, either alone or in the company of a small group, and their basic support was the bayonets of their soldiers. They were all dictators.

1. Why were communication and travel in Latin America difficult during the period of Spanish rule?
2. What differences in the composition of population separated the people of the various Latin American countries?
3. How did the military originally become involved in politics in Latin America? What do military rulers generally have in common?

### The Reasons

After hearing the long roll call of dictators in Latin America many have exclaimed, "Why? How could it have happened?" There are a number of answers. When the Latin Americans broke free from Spanish control, the leaders of their revolt were the wealthy and educated Creoles, the owners of business interests in the colonies, and the military leaders; in other words, the small elite of the former colonies assumed the control that the colonial masters had been forced to relinquish. The rulers in the new countries were mostly of European parentage, and they continued the practice of governing from above. Constitutions were written, often in beautiful language, eloquently proclaiming the same fundamental freedoms and rights of man that had been proclaimed shortly before by the revolutionists of the United States and France. But too often they remained written statements of an ideal which did not become a reality for most of the people.

These rights did not become a reality for the masses because the poorer ones of the great mass—the peons, who were mostly Negroes, mestizos, and Indians—had little if any conception of rights and freedoms. The Indians had been ruled in an authoritarian manner by their own chiefs and kings. They and the mestizos were governed in the same way by the Spaniards who conquered the land. They were told what to do, how to act, and how to speak; they were not asked their opinion. They were not consulted on the law or the government of their locality; it was handed down to them from above. Although they might dislike some of the actions of their leaders, they did not usually question the rightness of those above them. On the few occasions when they protested openly, their uprisings were suppressed.

They lacked the experience and the tradition of their fellow men to the north in the United States and Canada, where the people demanded that assemblies of their representatives ask popular approval in making and carrying out the law. The Americans of the north were quick to anger and rebel when their liberties were threatened. There were some unsuccessful rebellions in Latin America, but they did not lead to the establishment of representative government. For the most part, the masses of Latin America continued to be ruled by the one or the few, just as they had been under their ancient Indian chiefs.

The Spanish had fought desperately against Moslem Moors and Protestant reformers to preserve their lives and continue the Catholicism of their land. They were not disposed to expose the Indians and others in the New World to heresy and to doubt. They had a mission to convert the heathen to the Catholic faith, and once he was converted, they wanted no straying from the fold. The Latin American was kept isolated and insulated from all those thoughts which might cause him to question his secular and religious authorities, but not entirely, for there was in him at times a stirring of dangerous ideas. Generally, his religion also reinforced the authoritarian tradition he had always known.

Then, too, there was a cry for law and order after the expenditure of blood and sacrifice in the wars of independence. Villages had been burned, cities looted, fields trampled, ports blockaded, food stolen, and businesses closed. Disorder plagued the land. There were the homeless to be housed, the hungry to be fed, the sick and the wounded to be tended, the roads and sea lanes to be opened. The spawn of disorder, the lawless and the opportunist, also had to be repressed. Soldiers of disbanded armies often turned brigands, and the new governments did not have sufficient funds to pay new armies to keep the peace. They had already borrowed heavily from foreign governments. When they could not repay their debts, they were unable to borrow more. Somehow the ugly wounds of war had to be healed. This need seemed more pressing than those human rights which few among the people knew about anyway. It seemed natural to the Latin Americans that they should give their loyalty to that one or those few who promised them release from suffering and an orderly government in the land. That the government ruled without votes or advice seemed unimportant. The healing of their economic sicknesses was all-important.

From that time to this, the pledge of stability, order, and security has been the excuse of every man or group of men who have placed themselves in high Latin American positions of power. The military who recently took over in Peru and Ecuador reasoned publicly that it was a preventive measure to curb the lawlessness of the leftists. The military dictators declare that none but they can give stability to their people. In some cases, the army has been the only force that could maintain law and order. This promise of stability has been the justification of practically every man who has set himself up as the destined leader of his people without asking their consent. Often such a man believes in his own promises. He cannot understand when others do not share his belief. And law, order, and stability do have an appeal to a people who have been mangled by violence and who seek a time of peace to recover from the horrors of their experience.

For these and other reasons, in some Latin American countries the dictator and his band of followers have become an almost permanent aspect of political life. Most of these dictators have not been motivated to impose any particular political philosophy upon their people, but rather have been concerned with preserving things as they were. The rich continued to be rich and the poor continued to be poor. The few continued to be educated; the many continued to be illiterate. The wide social separation between the ruling elite and the ruled majority continued to be a chasm which was rarely if ever bridged. The dictator was occupied most of the time in shoring up his office and his power, for he never really felt secure.

In fairness, it should be noted that there were dictators who represented movements of change. There were liberal party dictators such as Justo Rufino Barrios of Guatemala, in the nineteenth century, and conservatives such as Vargas, Perón, and others in the twentieth century who wanted changes in the social and common life of the people.

In some countries there were quarreling factions among the elite who governed, and there were always groups of elite who were out of power and wanted to supplant the dictator and his followers. They sometimes succeeded, and the Latin Americans have witnessed the many comings and goings of dictators and military groups. Governments have frequently been of short duration, and revolutions and instability have been characteristic of the political scene. The history of some of the Central American countries reflects this scene. Arturo Araujo was elected president of El Salvador in 1931, and in less than a year he was replaced by General Maximiliano Hernández Martínez who lasted until 1944. Then another military group ruled for five months, succeeded by a regime which endured for about three years. Since that time some elected representatives have ruled the country, but these governments were interspersed with military juntas. As a general rule changes of rulers did not change the economic and social setting of the land. They were usually only the replacement of one man and one group by another man and another group—something more of the same thing.

1. Why did the Indian lack any conception of political rights and political freedom as the Europeans understood them? How did this affect his attitude toward government?
2. How did religious institutions reinforce the authoritarian tradition in Latin America?
3. How does military rule almost inevitably lead to political instability in Latin America?

### More Far-reaching Revolutions

Others among the Latin Americans have engaged themselves in revolutions which were designed to change the economic, social, and political institutions of their countries. During the past thirty or forty years, the Chilean has striven and finally obtained government-supported schools for his children. Education is compulsory for all between the ages of 7 and 15. The Chilean government also offers welfare services of various kinds. The Uruguayan has evolved a stable democratic system of government which operates with little or no violence, supports an extensive educational system, and is concerned with the welfare of the people. Costa Rica has made primary education compulsory, and higher education free, and higher education is also free in Uruguay and Argentina. Voting is obligatory in Costa Rica, and the country has been governed in a democratic manner for years under an elected president and chamber of deputies. Voting is also compulsory in a number of other Latin American countries.

The Mexican started in 1911 to change radically the old edifice of his society and has continued the evolving of his political, economic, and social life to the present day. Starting with the reforms under Francisco Madero, who became president in 1911, and the later, more radical reforms of others, the Mexican government broke up the large estates and divided them among the peasants and the poor. The Mexican government has recognized the value of the old achievements of the Indian and has acted to restore and preserve the monuments of Indian history. This has helped to restore the Indian's pride in himself and his ancestors. The Mexican people are guaranteed fixed maximum hours of work, and workers have the right to strike and to organize unions. The Mexican people, both men and women, are also guaranteed the right to vote in elections. The president is elected for six years. Mexico has several political parties, of which the most powerful at this time is the Party of Revolutionary Institutions (PRI).

During recent years there has been an in-

Young Communists in Caracas seek recruits with a sign reading "Youth for a bigger sports awakening—Join the Communist Youth." (Wide World photo)

creasing ferment of real revolutionary changes throughout the length and breadth of the land the Latin American calls his own. Many Latin Americans are thinking thoughts and doing deeds dangerous to the established elite who have governed in their own rather than the people's interests. The masses of the people have become exposed now to the possibilities of enlarging their human rights and bettering their standards of living. They are stirring and restless, and they are expressing their restlessness in ways that are disturbing to those who seek a gradual change. Many Latin Americans want immediate changes, and no one is making a greater effort to steer the restless people into a sudden and violent change than the Communists of Latin America.

## The Communist

Sensing that the time is now ripe for him to take charge of the destiny of the Latin American, the Communist is beginning to speak and to act in Latin America with audacity, with strength, and with confidence. During the Betancourt administration in Venezuela, Communists raided the homes and properties of American businessmen and sat immune from prosecution in the national congress. The Communist leaders in Lima have had great control over thousands of students and intellectuals, and they are patiently and coldly trying to inch Peru along the way Cuba has taken. Brazilian students are urged by Communist leaders to fight "U. S. imperialism." The Communist is a university student in Peru, a guerrilla in the isolated valleys of Colombia, a smuggler of arms from Bolivia, a leading architect in Brazil, a professor of eminence in Chile, a member of an estimated 40,000-strong party in Argentina, an organizer of the peasants in Central America, and a man of considerable influence in Mexico. He is everywhere, promising, pleading, building his party and working with other leftists who are not Communists. He infiltrates secretly, speaks openly, and receives funds from both the Communist giants, China and the USSR.

The actual number of party members is relatively small, but the Communists have increased their actual strength by working in collaboration with other leftist parties. Such a combination is often called a "front party." For instance, in a municipal election in Chile in 1963, the Communists participated in a coalition with others called Popular Action Front. The Front candidate polled about 28 per cent of the votes in this election. The Communists also work with that strong and growing group of men and women in Latin America who are anti-U. S., believe in socialism, and find no real flaws in the USSR. New Fidelista groups, named after Fidel Castro, head of the revolutionary Cuban government, have sprung up all over Latin America. They are especially useful when under Communist control. The revolution in Cuba, which is

Marxist and anti-American in tone, gave a lift and a surge to all those who seek radical changes in the society of Latin America.

## Cuba and Fidel Castro

By successfully establishing a revolutionary-leftist government ninety miles off the shores of the United States, and by sustaining that government while at the same time baiting the Yankee, Fidel Castro made himself a hero and an example to thousands upon thousands of Latin Americans. He gave to the Communists of other countries the vision of success, and this possibility enticed them to redoubled efforts to do as he had done. If Fidel Castro could establish an unfriendly regime on an island that the United States had always declared was in her vital sphere of interest, would not their chances be good in an area much farther removed from the United States?

It is true that the United States has always had a close and continuing interest in what happened to Cuba. As far back as 1808, the United States declared that the interests of Cuba and the United States were intimately connected. The U. S. government did not want the island to come under the domination of any strong European power other than Spain either commercially or politically. For geographic reasons, many U. S. American statesmen wanted to join Cuba to the United States. It is located in a strategic position at the mouth of the Gulf of Mexico and lies athwart the line of communications between the United States and its Caribbean neighbors. In the hands of a strong enemy, the island of Cuba could become a serious threat to the United States. During his term of office, President Polk entered into negotiations to buy the island from Spain, as did President Pierce during his term. Revolutions plagued the island colony, but Spain managed to hold on to it. Finally the United States intervened in the Cuban war of rebellion against Spain. At the conclusion of the Spanish-American War in 1898, when the United States defeated Spain, Cuba received her independence.

The United States was still fearful that another strong power might take over control of Cuba. The United States succeeded in having the Platt Amendment incorporated into the Cuban constitution in 1901. A reading of the principal provisions of the Platt Amendment is sufficient for an understanding of the significance of Cuba to the United States. The amendment provided that Cuba was not to permit a foreign power to secure partial or complete control of the island; that she was not to incur too large an indebtedness; that the United States was at liberty to intervene for the purpose of preserving order and maintaining Cuban independence; and that Cuba would sell or lease to the United States sites for naval and coaling stations.

Fidel Castro of Cuba has attempted to export Communist revolution to other countries of Latin America, where his followers are known as "Fidelistas." (Wide World photo)

The new Cuban republic became subject to misrule at times over the years, and revolt, controversies over elections, and other disturbances created an atmosphere harmful to the interests of the Cuban people and to the interests of the United States. At times the United States sent troops to intervene in Cuba at the request of the Cuban government. However, no troops were sent after the abolition of the Platt Amendment in the 1930's. After World War II Cuba fell into the hands of a dictator, Fulgencio Batista. During the 1950's, opposition to Batista intensified under the leadership of Fidel Castro. Batista fled the country in January 1959, and Fidel Castro became premier and real ruler of Cuba. Soon it became evident that Cuba under Castro was swinging to the extreme left. He instituted land reforms, nationalized tobacco and cattle lands, brought all private enterprises under the control of a Central Planning Board, and nationalized all banks, industries, and foreign-owned companies, of which the greatest number were U. S.-owned.

Fidel Castro announced publicly his belief in Marxism, appointed many known Communists to positions of power, and welcomed the immediate deluge of personnel and goods from countries of the Communist bloc. He permitted the erecting of missile sites pointed at the United States on Cuban land, executed a number of those opposed to his regime, and continued to hurl invective and charges at the United States. Castro openly espoused the cause of the USSR and the Communist bloc against the United States. He went further and exported his revolution to the rest of Latin America.

There are few if any countries of Latin America where there are not Fidelistas who seek to carry out in their countries the revolution that Castro brought to Cuba. They have brought new life and new blood to the work of the Communists. However, many became disillusioned with Castro when he went all the way over to the Communist bloc, and some of his followers came to differ with him over economic and defense policies. A great number of his followers, however, were dedicated and fanatical. These followers of Castro are an influential force within the Communist apparatus in Latin America. In Colombia the Fidelista party is the United Front for Revolutionary Action, and its numbers exceed those of the old-line Communists. In Venezuela the Fidelistas make up the Movement of the Revolutionary Left. In Brazil the movement is centered in the peasant leagues of Brazil's barren and poverty-burdened northeast. In other countries it is found among the students, the intellectuals, the peasants, and all classes of society.

Fidel Castro does not stop with exporting his ideas. He advances funds to support the activities of his followers in Latin America and brings many of them to Cuba, where they are trained in revolutionary tactics. The revolutionaries are taught the use of arms and the making of bombs, and they are instructed in the infiltration of positions of power within their countries. Cuba under Fidel Castro has become a center of revolutionary activity, with tentacles reaching out to every country of the hemisphere. It is also a mecca for those of Latin America who see in Castro the founder of a new revolutionary explosion in the hemisphere. Cuba is a shining example to all who want to begin revolutions in their own lands.

The Fidelistas and the Communists are fraternal allies, and together they are bringing the pressure of new and more radical revolutions to Latin America.

### Their Opponents

There are those who believe the rule of the new liberators would be worse than the present system, though the more democratic and concerned among them admit that the present system may need overhauling. The military who now hold great power in Latin America, and their supporters, argue that it is necessary for them to retain power. They argue that the present government is the only bulwark against a take-over by the Communists or the Fidelistas. They say that there is no middle class with influence nor any other group capable of curbing the power drive of the revolutionists. The military leaders insist that if they retire from the struggle, a vacuum will result which will be filled by the Communists.

There are many among the officials of the Roman Catholic Church who might agree, for they have seen what the Communists have done to the Church in the areas they control. The attitude of Fidel Castro has also been very harsh toward the priests and bishops of Cuba. There are others, however, among the officials who feel that the new radicals can be curbed ultimately only by democratic and social reforms, and they plead for a more liberal policy in the Church. In some countries, rigorous Christian Democratic parties (non-Communist) have pursued vigorous reform programs. In others these parties are more conservative. Whether conservative or liberal, the Roman Catholic Church is a powerful influence in Latin America, and its opposition to the Communists and the Fidelistas carries weight.

There is a growing number of democratic Latin Americans who believe strongly that rule by one or a few should be abolished. They feel that rule by Communists or Fidelistas should be prevented, and they advocate the type of democracy that is practiced in Canada and the United States. These are democrats who desire social, political, and economic reforms for the people. They are striving to achieve these aims through democratic processes.

The statesmen of the United States generally support this type of thinking. These statesmen lend their support to the efforts of Latin American leaders who follow a path of democratic and social change. Unfortunately, there are too few of these leaders, and there is often little choice between the extremists of right and left. This is one of the reasons why the United States has embarked upon a massive aid program called Alliance for Progress. The United States has allied itself with the Latin American nations in a program to improve the standards of living of the Latin Americans and thus give greater stability and hope to these people. Given stability and an improved standard of living, it is hoped that the true democratic processes will have a chance to evolve and to work among all the Latin Americans.

But the issue at this moment is in doubt. There are many groups working among the Latin Americans, and each considers its own interests as primary and its own opinions as the only valid ones. Latin America is today the scene of evolving, conflicting movements among people. What will emerge from the contest among these competing forces is a question that only the future can answer.

1. What techniques do the Communists employ in Latin America? Who are their supporters?
2. What interest does the United States have in Cuba? When did the U.S. first show an interest in Cuba?
3. Why are Castro in Cuba and his followers in other nations of so much importance in the entire American hemisphere?

## Relations Between the U. S. and Latin America

Over the long history of relations between the Latin American and the U. S. American, there have been friendship and animosity, understanding and misunderstanding, progress and retreat, calmness and anger. There have been periods of name-calling and periods of embrace, for a common name and hemisphere tie the two together, while differences of tradition and personality tear them apart. The things they hold in common and the things that distinguish them from one another have been amply manifested over the years they have lived together in the hemisphere of the Americas.

The revolution of the U. S. Americans was a stimulus and an inspiration to the Latin Americans who sought release from the hold of Spain, Portugal, and France. They read with hope the words which justified this revolution and the constitution which guaranteed freedoms and gave the foundation for a future political system. When the Latin Americans began their revolution against their European rulers, the United States sympathized and encouraged them. In 1823, President Monroe, by proclaiming the Monroe Doctrine, sought to keep from the hemisphere those Europeans who might stifle American aspirations to be free. Monroe warned the Europeans off, stating that the American continents "are henceforth not to be considered as subjects for future colonization by any European powers. . . ." This statement was appreciated by the Latin American revolutionists, and they thought of the U. S. American as a brother revolutionist. However, when U. S. statesmen intervened in Latin American problems on the basis of the Monroe Doctrine, many Latin Americans resented their actions. They feared that the doctrine might be only a cloak for United States expansion.

As Europe became more industrialized in the nineteenth century, its merchants and manufacturers became interested in foreign areas where they could obtain raw materials, loan out surplus money for interest, or make investments which would pay lucrative dividends. The Europeans discovered good sources of raw materials as well as fine loan and investment possibilities in Latin America. Naturally, they expected regular returns on the money they invested, but in a number of cases the dictators who had borrowed money refused to pay. Frequent and rapid changes in government brought others to power, and they failed to pay the debts contracted by the former rulers.

Whenever this occurred, the Europeans were furious, and they threatened these delinquent nations with warships and soldiers. The statesmen of the United States were alarmed. They saw the scene of revolutions, wars, and political factionalism in Latin America as an invitation to foreign powers to exploit these conditions for their own purposes. The United States feared that this chaos would be utilized by non-American countries to gain territorial control or for the purpose of weakening the ties of Latin American countries with the United States. Either of these courses of action would weaken the position of the United States in the hemisphere. Reacting to the pressure from abroad, and confident that they were acting in harmony with the historic policy of the United States, American statesmen began to act with vigor in cautioning the Europeans to take no territory in this hemisphere. The United States began to actively police those areas where political and economic unrest were tempting the Europeans to military action.

**Theodore Roosevelt.** No American statesman acted with more vigor and determination than Theodore Roosevelt. He was concerned primarily with this hemisphere, and his feeling of responsibility to its people and lands took precedence over all other thoughts in his policies. He understood the Monroe Doctrine to embody the concept of American responsibility to this hemisphere. He did not think it a doctrine of the past. He felt it must be modified and kept alive to meet the changing needs of national life.

The repudiation of debts by Latin American countries and the possibility that Europeans might take territory in this hemisphere placed Roosevelt in a dilemma. He did not feel he could prevent the collection of an honest debt, but he was also bound that there should be no territorial expansion by a European power under cover of collecting a debt. The Europeans claimed the right under international law to intervene in the collection of debts. Roosevelt found a solution by enunciating the Roosevelt Corollary to the Monroe Doctrine. The essence of it was that when a country in this hemisphere refuses to pay her just debts, the United States must assume the economic supervision of that country and enforce the payment of honest obligations. The United States would police the countries of the Western Hemisphere in economic matters. Under this justification, Roosevelt sent soldiers and marines into various countries, especially of the Caribbean and Central America, where he felt chaos and disorder were threatening the peace and relations with outside powers.

President Roosevelt declared his extended interpretation of the Monroe Doctrine in 1904, and on several occasions from then until 1934 the United States intervened in some Latin American countries. The Latin Americans did not like these actions, and many began to resent what they called the "bullying" tactics of the giant Yankee to the north. They called attention to the war between the United States and Mexico (1846-1848) in which the United States won territory in California and the Southwest. They cited the intervention in Cuba after the Spanish-American War, declared that the Panama Canal

Delegates to the first Pan American meeting were photographed in front of the United States State Department. (Pan American Union)

was really taken by force, and became convinced that the United States had embarked upon a policy of political and economic imperialism. Few, if any, responsible leaders in Latin America have often seriously suspected the intentions of the United States. However, the record has left a popular heritage of suspicion which Latin American demagogues have exploited to serve their own purposes.

**The Good Neighbor Policy.** Starting in the 1920's, the United States tried to reassure the Latin Americans that they had no imperialistic ideas about the lands to the south. President Franklin Roosevelt, after his election in 1933, developed what came to be called the "Good Neighbor" policy. The United States agreed in a treaty with the other American nations that no nation had the right to intervene in the affairs of another nation, and when troubles flared in various countries to the south, the United States stayed out of direct interference in their problems. Then, with the nations of Latin America, the United States encouraged and supported the Pan American movement.

As early as 1890, a Pan American Union had been established with headquarters in Washington, D. C. This Union was developed further during the 1930's, during the Second World War, and during the later crises of the Cold War. Most of the nations of the Americas joined together in a collective organization known as the Organization of American States (OAS). One of the primary purposes of this organization was to protect each nation from aggression on the part of others. The nations of the Americas have now joined in a closer cooperation for the purpose of meeting together problems originating inside and outside the hemisphere.

There are still those, especially the Communists and the Fidelistas, who suspect the intentions of the United States in Latin America. But as time goes on, and the moderating forces of peace and cooperation soften the angriness of the past and the economic evils of the present, a greater degree of understanding and appreciation of each other's problems will grace the relations between these Americans.

## The Canadian and the Latin American

The relations between the Canadian and the Latin American, on the whole, have been cordial. The Canadian has been oriented in the past more toward the United States, Great Britain, and the Commonwealth of Nations founded by the British. He has had little

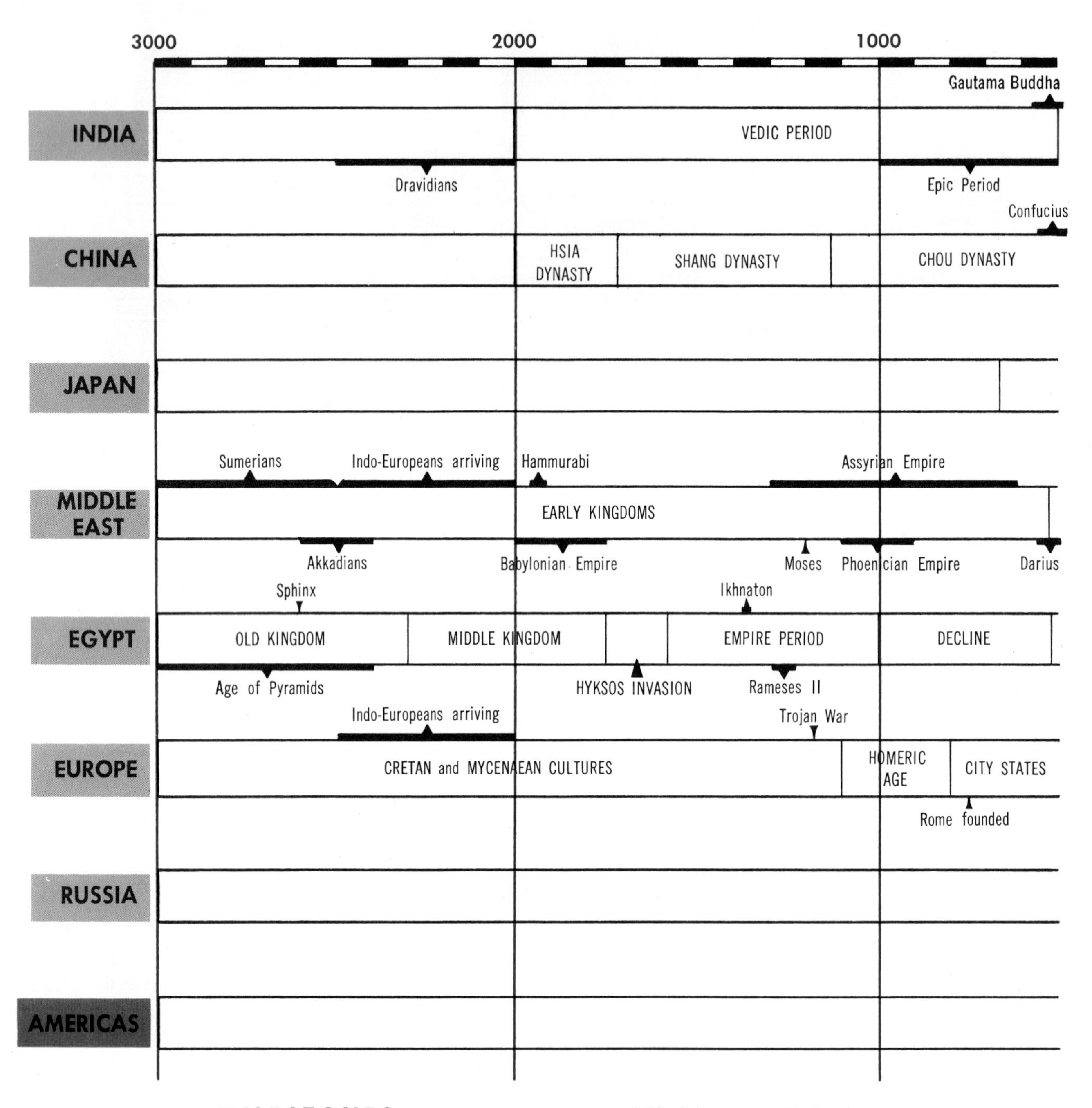


## MILESTONES

### THE AMERICAS

A.D.

| | |
|---|---|
| c. 300-1000 | Height of Mayan civilization |
| c. 400-1500 | Height of Inca civilization |
| c. 1100-1500 | Aztec civilization flourishing |
| 1492 | Columbus discovers Hispaniola |
| c. 1500 | Cabral discovers coast of Brazil |
| 1519 | Cortez conquers Mexico |
| 1531-1533 | Pizarro conquers Incas |
| c. 1534 | Cartier claims St. Lawrence area for France |
| 1607 | Jamestown colony settled |
| 1608 | Champlain founds colony at Quebec |
| 1620 | Pilgrims land at Plymouth |
| 1763 | British take control of Canada |
| 1775-1783 | American Revolution |
| 1776 | U. S. Declaration of Independence |
| 1803 | Louisiana Purchase |

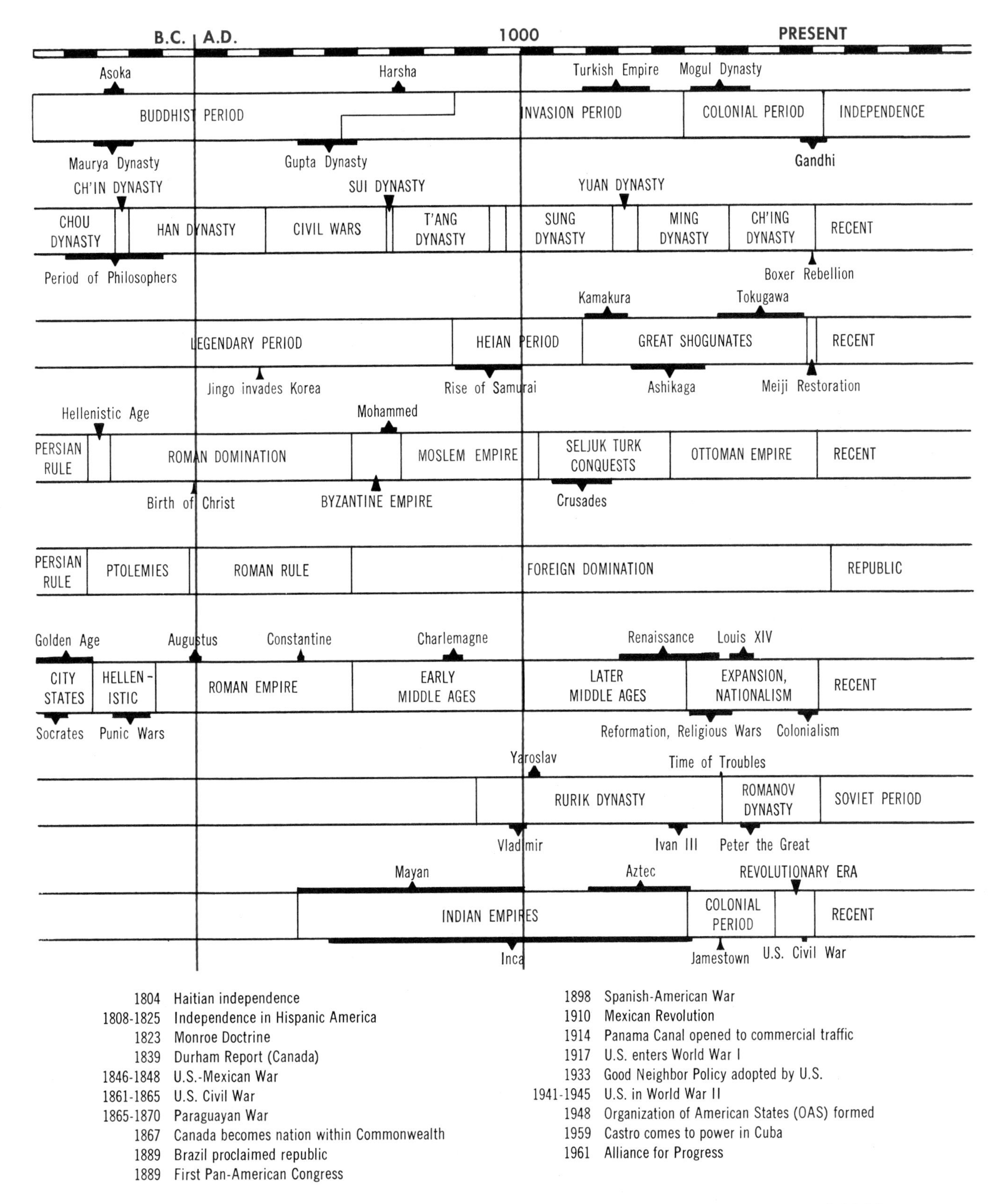


| | |
|---|---|
| 1804 | Haitian independence |
| 1808-1825 | Independence in Hispanic America |
| 1823 | Monroe Doctrine |
| 1839 | Durham Report (Canada) |
| 1846-1848 | U.S.-Mexican War |
| 1861-1865 | U.S. Civil War |
| 1865-1870 | Paraguayan War |
| 1867 | Canada becomes nation within Commonwealth |
| 1889 | Brazil proclaimed republic |
| 1889 | First Pan-American Congress |
| 1898 | Spanish-American War |
| 1910 | Mexican Revolution |
| 1914 | Panama Canal opened to commercial traffic |
| 1917 | U.S. enters World War I |
| 1933 | Good Neighbor Policy adopted by U.S. |
| 1941-1945 | U.S. in World War II |
| 1948 | Organization of American States (OAS) formed |
| 1959 | Castro comes to power in Cuba |
| 1961 | Alliance for Progress |

interest in Latin America politically, economically, or socially and has had relatively few intimate contacts with the Latin American. As a consequence, there have been few opportunities for discord to color relations between Canada and the nations of Latin America. Canada has no geographic boundaries with the countries of Latin America. Canada, unlike the United States, has not felt called upon to guarantee the territorial integrity of Latin America from outside intruders. It has not joined in the Organization of American States, though it is an American nation. But Canada does have defense agreements with the United States and participates in other international organizations which also include the Latin Americans.

However, a change of attitude is stirring among the Canadians. The Catholic French Canadians have shown a special interest in establishing closer relations with Latin America. The Canadians are beginning to realize the importance of fellow Americans to the south, and they are starting a program of more intimate relations with them. There are indications that Canada will join the Organization of American States, and it has sent a number of delegations of various kinds to visit and to speak with the Latin Americans about their common problems. With this change in the Canadian attitude, it is likely that relations between Canada and the Latin American will ripen and increase.

1. What is the Monroe Doctrine? What led to its proclamation? What is its present status?
2. What is one of the primary purposes of the Organization of American States?
3. Describe the tone of Latin American-Canadian relations. How would you account for this attitude?

## Conclusion

The Latin Americans originally sought independence from Spain and other colonial rulers and a unity of all Latin Americans. They gained their independence, but lost political unity. Divisive geographic conditions, social forces, the hunger for power, continued unfriendly relations among neighboring countries, and other causes led to disunity rather than unity. The Latin Americans were accustomed to an authoritarian tradition and, for the most part, had little or no experience with the political rights associated with self-government. While educated Latin Americans knew the ideas of freedom and liberal thought that swept over Europe and North America, the great masses of the illiterate had no way of learning these ideas. Out of the great need for law, order, and stability there emerged a strong military and the rule by the few and the dictator.

This rule by an elite and by dictator continued a system which rewarded the few and oppressed the many. The Latin American witnessed a continuous turnover of rulers but saw little change in his political, economic, and social system. However, in some countries, there gradually evolved real revolutionary changes which brought advances in political and economic life. In recent years there has been a ferment for radical changes among the people in all the countries of Latin America. Radical and revolutionary groups have arisen to influence the direction these restless people will take. Many of these groups are not Communist. The Communists and Fidelistas, however, have been very active in all revolutionary movements.

The Communists and the Fidelistas have frequently united as fraternal allies to bring revolutionary changes to the countries of Latin America. They have been aroused and stimulated by the success of Fidel Castro in carrying out his Cuban revolution. Leftist groups in Latin America have been encouraged by Castro's actions in defiantly challenging the near and great might of the United States, in lining up his little island with the Communist bloc of nations, and in continuing to support Communist activities in Latin America. Leftists in other nations have moved rapidly to take advantage of the material and psychological opportunities offered by Castro's success. One of the psychological weapons of their arsenal is anti-Americanism; that is, opposition to the United States.

The relations between the Latin American and the American of the United States have not always been calm and cordial. The Latin American has often suspected and accused the U. S. American of having designs upon his territory and his resources. The U. S. American has often been called an imperialist by Latin Americans. The anti-U. S. Latin American repeats without pause the history of wars between Latin American countries and the United States. He points to the seizure of Latin American territory, and the policing of Latin American land. He calls attention to the present U. S. investments in Latin America and cites them as a modern example of imperialism. Recognizing the deterioration of relations between the United States and Latin America, United States statesmen began a "Good Neighbor" policy. That policy has continued to the present day. Much has been done to improve relations, but much yet remains to be done. Friendship among peoples of differing countries and cultures requires continuous nurturing and attention.

There is a growing closeness between the peoples of Latin America and North America despite the efforts of those who would deny this friendship. Time, patience, knowledge, understanding, tolerance, and assistance are the qualities needed to found, to preserve, and to make permanent warm relations among all Americans.

## SUMMING UP THE CHAPTER

A. Identify the following and tell why they are important.

| | |
|---|---|
| Alliance for Progress | Greater Colombia |
| Fidelistas | Monroe Doctrine |
| Francisco Madero | OAS |
| Fulgencio Batista | Pan American Union |
| Gran Chaco | Popular Action Front |

B. Identify these dates and indicate their importance.

| | |
|---|---|
| 1. 1823 | 3. 1898 |
| 2. 1846-1848 | 4. 1904 |

C. Chapter review questions.

1. Why was the political unity of Latin America destroyed by the end of Spanish rule?
2. How has geographic closeness sometimes led to friction among the nations of the Americas?
3. What factors account for the tradition of military leaders in Latin America? Do you feel there will be a break with this tradition in the foreseeable future?
4. Describe some of the economic, social, and political changes brought about in Latin America by revolution. In your answer pay particular attention to Mexico.
5. What was the Platt Amendment? Why was it important?
6. Trace in broad terms the political history of Cuba.
7. What influence is Fidel Castro having in the countries of Latin America?
8. Why did the United States feel it necessary to police the activities of many Latin American countries?
9. Explain the significance of Theodore Roosevelt's corollary to the Monroe Doctrine.
10. When and under what circumstances was the Organization of American States established? What other inter-American organizations are there?

D. Questions for discussion.

1. What were the major factors which prevented Latin America from becoming a group of large nations instead of a score of separate nations?
2. How has regional organization in recent years done much to overcome some of the most serious problems of Latin America?
3. What future do you see for military rule in Latin America? What factors might lead to a lessening of the importance of rule by military dictators?
4. What role has Communist China played in Latin America? What is the relationship between Cuba and Communist China?
5. Describe the relations of the United States with Latin America during the Theodore Roosevelt administration.
6. Why was the American Revolution successful in bringing about democratic government in the United States, while similar revolutions in Latin America often paved the way for dictatorships?

E. Projects for groups or individuals.

1. Draw an outline map of Latin America and illustrate how the nations of Latin America were carved out of the colonial empires.
2. Read a biography or other account of any of the dictators of Latin America and report on it to the class.
3. Prepare a report for classroom presentation on the Good Neighbor Policy.
4. Make a chart illustrating the rapidity of changes of government in Latin America, noting the length of each rule.

## SUMMING UP THE UNIT

### *Drawing together the main themes*

1. Why and by whom were the Negroes brought to the Americas?
2. What peoples came to the Americas and where did they found their settlements?
3. Compare the landscape of North America with that of Latin America.
4. In what sense is the United States a "melting pot" of peoples?
5. What improvements did Dom João make in Brazil between 1807 and 1821? Did Brazil retain all the privileges it had gained when João returned to Portugal? Why?
6. Compare the American and Canadian experience in gaining independence from Great Britain. How do you account for these differences?
7. Who were the great revolutionary leaders of the Americas? Identify them briefly and tell of their importance. In your opinion, do any of these leaders stand out above the rest? Why?
8. What factors account for the fact that the countries of Latin America have followed separate paths of political and economic development? Which of these factors do you feel are most important?
9. What factors in Latin American life and history have reinforced the authoritarian tradition and aided military rule?
10. Why has change been so slow in coming to Latin America?
11. What has delayed the development of the mineral resources of Latin America? What minerals have been discovered in quantity in each of the countries of Latin America?
12. How do governments which oppress the people play into the hands of the Communists and Fidelistas, and make it easier for them to secure support?
13. Trace the history of United States involvement in Latin American affairs. What significant changes in policy can you pinpoint?
14. Which American nations do you believe have best preserved the contributions of Indian cultures?
15. Compare the attitudes of North Americans and Latin Americans toward the arts, education, intellectual pursuits, economic and social reform.
16. What is the Latin American's view of the role of the military? How does the North American's attitude toward the military differ?
17. How do you account for the contrast between the American of the United States and the Latin American?
18. Why do Latin Americans fear the economic power of the United States? Do the Canadians also fear it?
19. Why do you suppose the United States did not prevent Castro's rise to power in Cuba or attempt to unseat him after he came to power and began attacking the United States verbally? What would have been the effect on the other countries of Latin America if the United States had actively intervened? What has the OAS done in cooperation with the United States to keep Castroism under control?
20. How has the greatly increased leisure time of the North American contributed to an appreciation of the arts? How else has this leisure been used?

### *Projects for individuals or groups*

1. Make a collection of travel folders, maps, and pictures of cities of historical interest in the Americas.
2. Use other history books and reference books to do research and prepare a series of maps showing important campaigns and the locations of famous battles in the struggle for independence in the Americas.
3. Read a biography of one North American statesman and one Latin American statesman of the same period. Make a book report in which the lives of the two men are compared. Show how each is a product of his own environment.
4. Prepare a report on the uses of leisure time. Give evidence to show whether or not machines have increased leisure for most people. Interview your classmates to determine how they use their leisure time. How do their uses compare with those revealed by your research? At the end of your report, draw some conclusions about possible future uses of leisure.
5. Use current news sources and write a short description of international relations between American nations.

### FURTHER READINGS

*LATIN AMERICA*

BAILEY, BERNADINE, *Famous Latin-American Liberators.* Dodd, 1960. Vivid stories of courageous founders of Latin-American independence.

BAILEY, HELEN M. AND NASATER, ABRAHAM P., *Latin America: The Development of Its Civilization.* Prentice-Hall, 1960. Especially good on Latin-American culture, arts, and way of life.

BAITY, ELIZABETH C., *Americans Before Columbus,* rev. ed. Viking, 1961. Covers Indians from period before Columbus until their conquest; well illustrated and contains a glossary.

BOWEN, J. DAVID, *The Land and People of Peru.* Lippincott, 1963.

BROWN, ROSE, *The Land and People of Brazil,* rev. ed. Lippincott, 1960.

COLLIER, JOHN, *Indians of the Americas.* Norton, 1947; New Am. Lib., paperback. A valuable book which shows that the Indian had much to contribute to the white man's thought; it also gives an account of what has been done to develop the Indian's culture and creative gifts.

HALL, ELVAJEAN, *The Land and People of Argentina,* rev. ed. Lippincott, 1962.

INMAN, SAMUEL G., *Latin America: Its Place in World Life,* rev. ed. Harcourt, 1942. Good to date (1942).

LARRALDE, ELSA, *The Land and People of Mexico,* rev. ed. Lippincott, 1964.

MASUR, GERHARD, *Simón Bolívar.* U. of New Mexico, 1948.

MORISON, SAMUEL E., *Christopher Columbus, Mariner.* Little, 1955.

PECK, ANNE M., *Pageant of Middle American History.* McKay, 1947.

———, *Pageant of South American History,* rev. ed. McKay, 1958, 1962. Both books are good general histories.

PERKINS, DEXTER, *The United States and the Caribbean.* Harvard U., 1947. Good description of national problems (to date), culture, and way of life in Caribbean. Excellent background of U.S. role in connection with the people of these lands.

———, *History of the Monroe Doctrine,* rev. ed. Little, 1955. The Monroe Doctrine has been long the foundation of U.S. policy with regard to Latin America. It is yet a living policy.

RIPPY, J. FRED, *Historical Evolution of Hispanic America.* Crofts, 1945. The author is especially well informed.

VAILLANT, GEORGE C., *Aztecs of Mexico,* rev. by Suzannah B. Vaillant. Doubleday, 1941; Penguin, paperback. An expert gives an account of the life of the Aztecs in a style suitable for the general reader. A vivid, well-documented survey.

VON HAGEN, VICTOR W., *Realm of the Incas.* New Am. Lib., paperback. Good description of some fantastic achievements by the Incas.

WOHLRABE, RAYMOND A. AND KRUSCH, WERNER, *The Land and People of Venezuela,* rev. ed. Lippincott, 1963.

*CANADA*

BURT, ALFRED L., *A Short History of Canada for Americans.* U. of Minnesota, 1944. Readable and good.

CREIGHTON, DONALD G., *History of Canada: Dominion of the North.* Houghton, 1958. Excellent general history.

PECK, ANNE M., *Pageant of Canadian History.* McKay, 1943. The various provinces and their industries are described simply.

ROBERTS, KENNETH, *Oliver Wiswell.* Doubleday, 1940. An historical novel dealing with the American Revolution and told from the point of view of a colonel loyal to the Crown. A bold and swiftly moving narrative.

ROSS, FRANCES A., *The Land and People of Canada,* rev. ed. Lippincott, 1964.

WADE, MASON, *French-Canadian Outlook.* Viking, 1946. The viewpoint and ideas of the French-Canadians are important in understanding Canada.

*UNITED STATES*

ALLEN, FREDERICK L., *Since Yesterday.* Bantam, 1961, paperback. One of the best descriptions of American social, cultural, and economic life.

———, *The Big Change.* Harper, 1952; Bantam, paperback. Some of the greatest changes in American life took place in the first half of the twentieth century.

BAILEY, THOMAS A., *Diplomatic History of the American People,* 6th ed. Appleton, 1958. Important to an understanding of the U.S. American.

BELOFF, MAX, *Thomas Jefferson and American Democracy.* Macmillan, 1949; Collier, paperback. Jefferson applied his freedom of thought and attitude to the making of a democracy.

CHRONICLES OF AMERICA SERIES, 4 Vols. Yale U.

BROGAN, DENIS, *The Era of Franklin D. Roosevelt.* 1951.

FAULKNER, HAROLD U., *From Versailles to the New Deal.* 1950.

NEVINS, ALLAN, *The New Deal and World Affairs.* 1950.

———, *The United States in a Chaotic World.* 1950. Cover modern American history since World War I.

LEWIS, SINCLAIR, *Babbitt.* Harcourt, 1949; New Am. Lib., paperback.

MORGAN, EDMUND S., *Birth of the Republic, 1763-1789.* U. of Chicago, 1956. Early days in the history of the United States.

NEVINS, ALLAN, *Fremont: Pathmarker of the West.* 2 Vols. Ungar, 1955. Fremont blazed a trail which millions followed.

PRATT, FLETCHER, *Ordeal by Fire.* Sloane, 1948. Published as *Short History of the Civil War.* Pocket Books, paperback.

RADIN, PAUL, *Story of the American Indian,* rev. ed. Liveright, 1944. The Indian was the earliest American.

ROBERTS, KENNETH, *Arundel.* Doubleday, 1933.

———, *Rabble in Arms.* Doubleday, 1947. Two interesting stories about the fight for independence.

SANDBURG, CARL, *Abraham Lincoln: The Prairie Years and The War Years.* Harcourt, 1954.

SMITH, BRADFORD, *The Islands of Hawaii,* rev. Lippincott, 1960. Crossroads of the Pacific for many nations and races, Hawaii has a rich and fascinating culture.

TWAIN, MARK, *The Adventures of Huckleberry Finn.* Various editions.

———, *The Adventures of Tom Sawyer.* Various editions. Two of the all-time favorites by the great American novelist, essayist, and humanist.

# UNIT VII

The African continent is divided among many new nations. Most of the new nations of Africa have gained their independence in the period since World War II.

# ATTENTION TURNS TO AFRICA

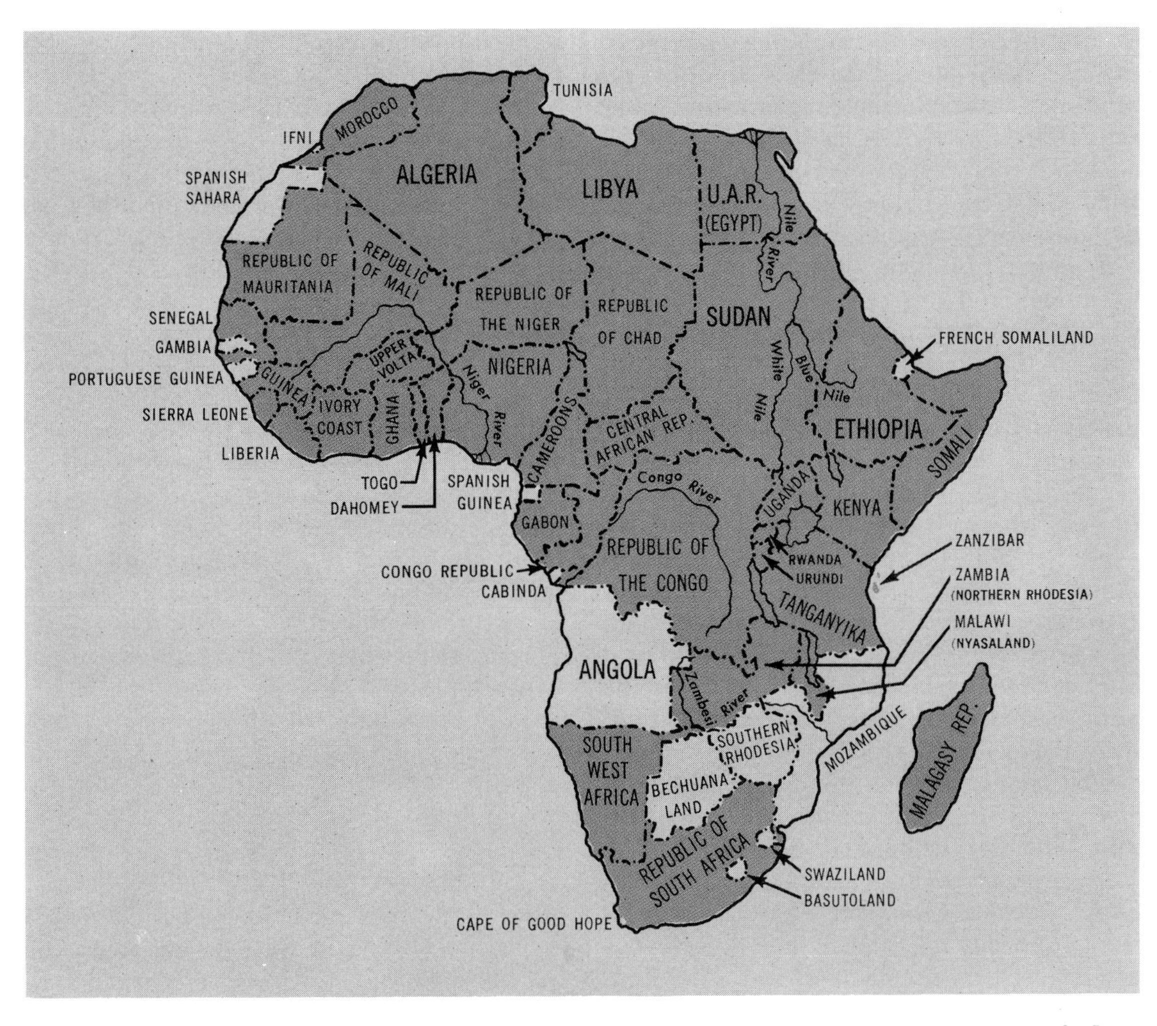

# CHAPTER 33

# *Man in Africa*

MAN IN ALL of his varieties lives on the continent called Africa. Those who live north of the Sahara, along the borders of the Mediterranean Sea, have been shaped and influenced since ancient times by the Egyptians, Phoenicians, and the Arabs of the Middle East, as well as by the Greeks, the Romans, and others of Europe. To the south, separated from these North Africans by the wide wastes of the Sahara, is the heart of Africa.

The families of man in Africa have diverse features and shades of skin, and their members are distinguished from each other by varieties of dress, custom, language, and other cultural features. There are the six-foot tall Masai warriors with hair ocher-reddened, who stride like kings, holding lordly spears, over the grasslands of East Africa where their cattle graze. In contrast are the Pygmies, between four and five feet tall, who live and hunt in the depths of the jungle and rain forest of the Congo. There are the descendants of the mating between the Arab and the African who live on the east coast of Africa, for example the people of Zanzibar. Islam is the religion of these people. There is the Nigerian who makes his home in the country or in the capital, Lagos, and his religion is Christian. There is the colorful ricksha puller of Durban, South Africa, who is a delight to the eye with his large, vivid headdress and many-colored beads. And in all parts of the world there are the officials and diplomats of newly independent African countries.

The families of man in Africa speak hundreds of different languages and belong to many different tribal and national groups. They are called by many names—Bantu, Ghanaian, Nigerian, Ethiopian, Sudanese, Congolese, Luo, Kikuyu, Bushman, and others—but each is known by the name African.

The name African does not mean a sameness of form, language, culture, climate, or environment, but it gathers together under one name all those who live within the approximately 11,500,000 square miles of the African continent. At its widest point, Africa runs for 4,600 miles east and west (nearly half again the distance from New York to San Francisco) and 5,000 miles north and south (six times the distance from Dallas to Minneapolis). This continent contains over 260,000,000 people who, like all people, would like to be understood and recognized. Africa was long called "the dark continent" and the African was long ignored, long exploited, and long insulated from the revolutionary advances and outbursts of man in other parts of the world. He has suddenly burst from the cocoon of isolation and cried out, "I, too, am a man. I, too, want the freedoms that other men have achieved."

The diverse, hidden people of Africa have shouted loudly, and their actions have drawn the attention of other people. The rest of the world listens, looks, and sees that the Africans have the same needs that all other men have. Some had thought they knew the African well; others had been uncaring, thinking him of little moment; while still others knew him only through the veil of the half-truth. But all began to see him for the first time clearly when he cried "Freedom." And in seeing him clearly there came the first glimmer of understanding and recognition of the African as a man.

## Background and Separation

The earth of Africa has supported men for centuries beyond knowledge, but it was only in the middle of the twentieth century that most of mankind first began to know and to recognize the African. Man lived in Africa unimaginable ages ago, and this fact is witnessed by the pieces of skeletons picked up and pieced together with patience and skill by modern searchers into the past called archaeologists. In a place called Olduvai Gorge, located in Tanganyika, East Africa, the British archaeologist L. S. B. Leakey has found the remains of tool-making men. Some scientists have estimated the oldest of these to be around 1,750,000 years of age. Leakey has also found tools of a kind called Chellean, and a skull of the kind of man, who made these tools. These men are believed to have also lived in Asia and in Europe almost 500,000 years ago. Little is known of the evolution of these ancient men, but stone tools and weapons found in their dwelling place and near the skeletons of slain animals tell a story of a hunting and fishing people. There is yet much mystery in the early history of man in Africa, for evidence of ancient life there was rarely found until recently.

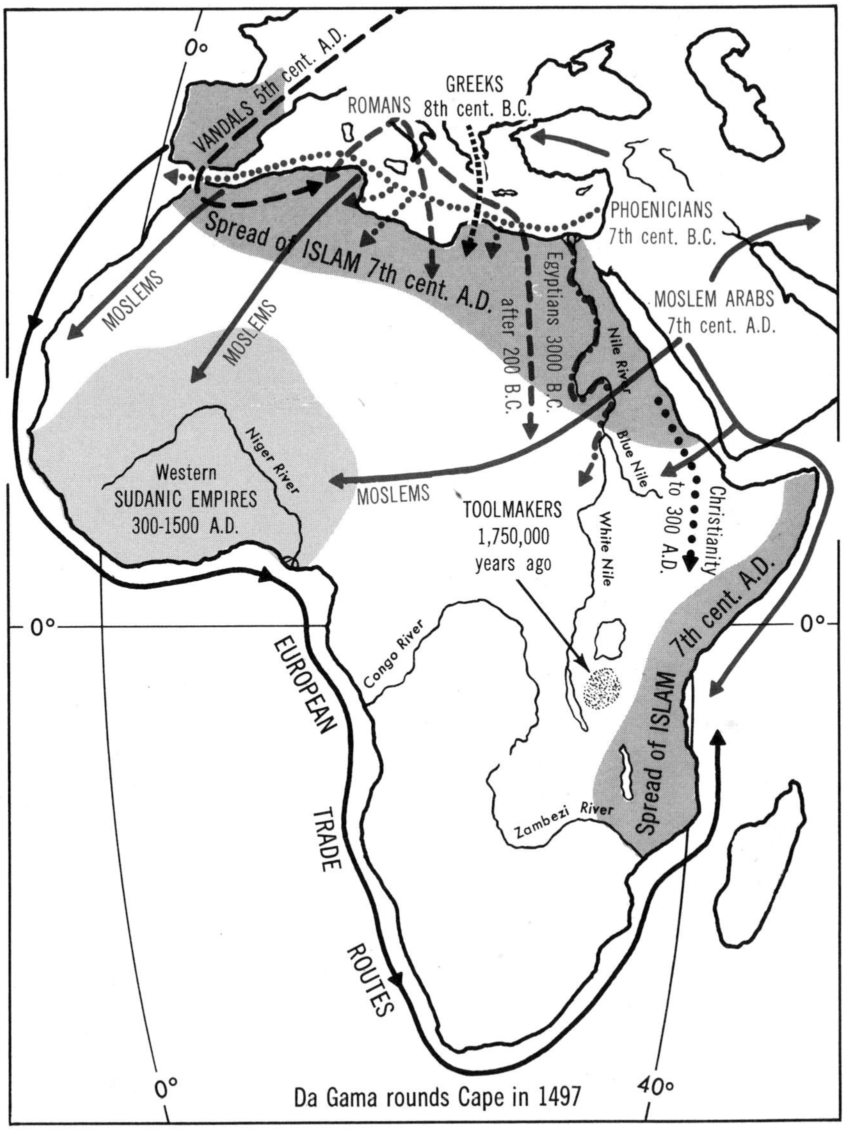

**Ancient Civilizations and Movements of Peoples in Africa**

Northern Africa was well known to the ancient peoples around the Mediterranean Sea, and Islam was carried to parts of Africa south of the Sahara. However, there was little penetration into the continent below the Sahara until the coming of modern European colonial powers.

Left, ricksha men of Durban, South Africa wear colorful costumes. (Moore-McCormack Lines) Below, the vast potential power of Africa's rivers is only beginning to be tapped by dams and hydroelectric plants. (East Africa Tourist Travel Association)

Bronze castings, such as the one at right, were made in the Benin kingdom of western Africa during the 1500's. The bronzes of Benin exhibit a high degree of technical skill. (Chicago Natural History Museum)

Some surmise that the Negro family of man did not even originate in Africa but migrated there from somewhere in Asia, perhaps 30,000 years ago. The Egyptian had some contact with the men of Africa south of the Sahara, and even had some Negro slaves around four or five thousand years ago. In general, however, most of the Negroes of Africa were free and had never heard of Egypt. Some think that the African Negro started farming around 4000 B.C. As man evolved in Africa, he started to plant crops, to herd cattle, and to produce a diversity of people who speak different languages and differ greatly in appearance. These people of Africa, like all men everywhere, developed a special harmony between themselves and the landscape on which they lived.

The landscape has often been a barrier between the families of man in Africa. There are extensive, threatening deserts, and their barren expanses effectively cut off communication between great populated regions. Largest of these deserts is the Sahara in North Africa, which bulks its waterless stretches of sand, stone, and shale between the Negro families of man to the south and those who live along the fringes of the Mediterranean. The Sahara is not, however, entirely barren. There are oases, islands among the sands, where water bubbles from underground sources and men can live. Voyaging men of the Sahara stop at these oases to rest and to water their long caravans of camels which bear on their backs the trade of the desert. Herders of sheep and of goats also live there. The Sahara has known the sound of battle and the sand-muffled raids of those seeking plunder. But mostly the Sahara has been a barrier between the man living south of it and the man living north of it.

The North Africans—the Moroccans, the Algerians, the Tunisians, and the Libyans—have little in common with the Africans to the south, but they have much in common with man in the Middle East in ancestry and in religion. They are mostly Moslems, and their culture has been greatly influenced by that of the Middle East. These North Africans have, for centuries, looked toward the trade of the Mediterranean, and toward the peoples and lands across from them in southern Europe, which also borders a common sea. On the lands of North Africa are ancient remains of visitation and occupation by the Phoenicians, Greeks, Romans, Vandals, and Arabs, as well as the later French, Italians, and Spanish. The North Africans have not been isolated from the world of man but have been very much a part of it from almost the beginning of man's known history. For these and other reasons, it has become customary to think of Africa proper as that part south of the Sahara, sometimes called Sub-Saharan Africa. This portion of our story of man will deal mainly with the man who lives south of the Sahara.

## South of the Sahara

Man south of the Sahara lives mostly on a great plateau which slants from around six thousand feet above sea level in the east to about three thousand feet in the west. It is the altitude of this plateau which makes living more bearable and more comfortable for the African, for much of Africa lies along or near the equator.

### Savannah, Animal, and Man

About half of the land south of the Sahara is grassy, almost treeless land because there is not enough rain to permit the growth of a forest. Such land is called *savannah.* But there are large areas of Africa, especially in the east and in the south, where the rainfall is adequate for the growth of some trees. In these areas there is a parklike landscape of trees standing in clumps or scattered separately upon a surface of tall-growing grass. It is in this type of savannah that the wild game, the lion, zebra, giraffe, elephant, rhino, waterbuck, and many other varieties of animals have lived. Today, in these areas, there are many very large national parks which are forbidden to the hunter.

For long centuries the wild animals of Africa grazed or preyed upon other animals for food over a wide expanse of savannah, but in this modern era their numbers began to decrease. A number of wild animals had commercial value. The ivory of the elephant's tusk, the horn of the rhino, the hair of the giraffe's tail, and unique features of other animals became good trading items. Men killed them by the thousands to make money. In some areas the European governments killed large numbers of animals because they were diseased and their diseases were transmitted to cattle. Multiplying people and their multiplying cattle gradually took over more and more of the grazing land of the wild animals. As food became insufficient, the wild animals died. For these and other reasons, large game preserves were established in East, Central, and South Africa where the animals could be protected from the advances of civilization and from the gun and the greed of man. In these great parks, the wild animals are most important. When the sightseer enters their home he is told by signs that no hunting is permitted, that he proceeds at his own risk, and that "elephants have the right of way." Whether man can prevent all of the species of Africa's animals from becoming extinct is still a question. Poachers, moved by a desire to make money, still trap and kill them, and civilization continues to advance. But some men are trying to save the animals by setting aside protected lands for their exclusive use on the savannah.

### Rain Forests

The African has frequently been pictured in books, movies, and in lectures as a dweller of the jungle, where trees grow to heights of a hundred feet or more and bar the sun with their interlaced tops. Below is a place of gloom where shadowy shapes furtively creep and slithering snakes coil and uncoil, while monkeys and birds make the treetops raucous with

Much of Africa's wildlife is now protected in large national parks. (South African Tourist Corporation)

the sounds of their chatter and their calls.

Some Africans do live in areas like this, called *rain forests*, but these rain forests make up only about fifteen per cent of the land of Africa. Much of this fifteen per cent lies around the Congo River, along the coasts of Guinea and Ghana in West Africa, and in parts of Nigeria. There are also rain forests in the eastern section of the island of Madagascar, off the southeast coast of Africa, and in a few other places. In these forests, the rain falls heavily and frequently. The air is close, the humidity high, and dampness is everywhere. Most of such an area is properly called rain forest rather than jungle. A jungle is any area of thick and tangled vegetation which grows close to the ground, as for instance along river banks. The floor of the rain forest has relatively little dense vegetation because the massive green ceiling of intertwined branches and leaves keeps the sun out.

## Lakes, Rivers, and Mountains

In Africa there are great lakes which rival in size the lakes in other parts of the world. Most of these lakes are in East Africa. Lake Victoria is second in size to Lake Superior in the United States, which is the largest body of fresh water in the world. Besides this lake there are others called Albert, Tanganyika, Edward, and Nyasa. These lakes are places of beauty and are also useful. They are especially important as the birthplaces of great rivers which serve the African as a means of communication and provide water for irrigation of food crops.

Starting from Lake Victoria, the Nile, the longest river in the world, runs for more than four thousand miles to the sea. The Nile is essential to the Sudanese and the Egyptians, and they think of it as their center of life. Its waters are increased along the way by the

Left, Murchison Falls, on the Nile, cascades downward for 130 feet. The beautiful waterfalls of African rivers are obstacles to river traffic. (East Africa Tourist Travel Association) Below, a village in Basutoland, high in the Drakensberg Mountains. (South African Tourist Corporation)

Blue Nile, which begins in the high reaches of Ethiopia and feeds into the main stream of the Nile. In the northwest of Africa is the Niger; cutting through the center of Africa is the mighty Congo; and to the southeast is the Zambezi.

Running from the highlands to the narrow coastal plains rimming Africa, these rivers thunder down steep falls, raising a lacy spray shot with droplets of water turned to the colors of the rainbow. Watching the magnificence of the Victoria Falls leaping downward for 354 feet, the famous English explorer, David Livingstone, exclaimed that it was a scene for the "angels in their flight" to pause and admire. Another waterfall of grandeur and beauty is Murchison Falls on the Nile flowing out of Lake Victoria. These falls fashion a permanent rainbow of mist as they cascade downward for 130 feet. But few Africans have seen these beautiful sights, and the waterfalls are unfortunately obstacles to traffic on the rivers. It is difficult or impossible to navigate most of the length of African rivers because of the rapids and the waterfalls, and this is a deterrent to river commerce.

There are some mountains in Africa, and among the most famous are the "Mountains of the Moon," which lie between western Uganda and the Republic of the Congo. The natives call these mountains "Ruwenzori," the "Rainmaker." Only thirty miles north of the equator, their highest peaks rise to more than 16,000 feet and are covered with snow. Explorers who have climbed these heights describe them as eerie places which resemble the imagined landscape of an alien planet rather than earth.

1. The peoples of Africa are many; describe a few of them and give illustrative examples of their diversity.
2. Give a short description of the various ways of life in the Sahara region of Africa.
3. What uses were found by the European and the native African for animal life in the savannah?

## The Africans Developed

Over many centuries of time, the Africans spread their various ways of life over a broad sweep of land. Early African history is extremely vague, due to a lack of historical records. It is thought that thousands of years before the beginning of the Christian era, the ancestors of the Negro families of man moved northward and westward from an area around Kenya and settled in an area between the rain forest and the desert. In those early days the Sahara was not as extensive a desert as it is today, and the earth there was hospitable in many places to settlement by men. Here continued the development of the physical and cultural characteristics of the people of Africa.

**Farming.** Around 4000 B.C. Africans began to cultivate the land. They grew rice, millet, and sorghum and developed cotton and palms for oil. They grew peanuts, watermelons, and other food products. From the people of the Middle East, the Africans learned to grow wheat, barley, flax, olives, onions, and other vegetables. As the centuries moved along, they learned from others, perhaps the Asians, about bananas, ginger, sugar cane, yams, and other products. In the more modern period, the Europeans introduced maize, tomatoes, tobacco, and other cereals, fruits, and vegetables. Like the developing men in other regions of the world, the Africans were both originators and borrowers.

Farming is still the primary occupation of the African people. The African farmer is very mobile. When the fertility of his savannah soil declines, he moves with his entire village to another area which has regained its fertility or where the earth is virgin. There he begins a new farm and a new home. This practice is generally known as "shifting agriculture." The African farmer of the savannah shifts his land cultivation from place to place.

The African also farms in rain forests. Here too, he is continually on the move, for rain forest soil cannot support him long. The rain is so heavy that it washes the minerals from the earth, especially when the land is cleared for agriculture. The African farmer of the rain

Left, a woman works a field in the savannah using a primitive hoe. (FAO) Below, more than 80% of Nigeria's population is employed in agriculture, which not only produces the country's food but accounts for 90% of its export trade. Increased production is needed to raise the standard of living and to keep pace with the growing population. The government sponsors a farm-settlement scheme and teaches young farmers the use of modern equipment. (FAO)

forest plants his crops in one field for only a year or two. Then the land cannot produce sufficient food. The farmer moves on to another part of the forest, cuts down the trees, burns the underbrush, and thus fashions a clearing where he begins another temporary village and farm. As on the savannah, fields must be shifted often in the rain forest. There are other parts of Africa which are semiarid, and here the rains are infrequent and uncertain. Most of these areas lie between the Sahara and the parklike savannah, and others are in southern and southwestern Africa. Here, too, the farmer is constantly moving, a nomad who roams from place to place looking for better soil to till and better grass and water for his cattle.

**Herding cattle.** In the eastern and southern parts of the savannah the African found it good to domesticate and herd cattle. He often killed and ate these cattle in the performance of rituals of a religious, political, and legal nature. The cattle also became symbols of wealth and social status—the more a man had, the higher his standing in the community. Cattle were kept for prestige and to barter for other things their owners wanted. The tall Masai, who herd cattle by the many thousands, frequently use them as a source of food without killing them. The cattle are milked, and their blood is also drunk. Blood is drawn by pricking a large vein, draining off a cup or so of blood, and then stopping the flow with a smear of mud. Thus the herder has a continuous source of living food.

**Iron working.** Around the fifth century B.C., the secrets of making iron spread from Egypt up the Nile into the hinterland of Africa. The Egyptians and other Middle Eastern people had learned these secrets from

The photograph shows all the implements used in preparing and cooking corn meal, known as "mealie meal." (FAO)

the Hittites, who introduced the manufacture of iron into the Middle Eastern world. At a place called Meroe, not too far removed from Khartoum, the modern capital of the now independent nation of Sudan, the manufacture of iron became a vital industry. Perhaps the West Africans learned the techniques of making iron from the Carthaginians, who were transplanted Phoenicians from the Middle East. At any event, the Africans of the savannah were making iron tools for work and iron weapons for war around 300 B.C.

**Migrations.** Around the beginning of the Christian era, the Bantu-speaking people who lived near the Cameroons Highlands began a great migration into Central, East, and South Africa. This movement continued for over 1,500 years. The Bantu-speaking people were better organized for war and peace than the Pygmies, the Bushmen, and others whose lands they overran. Over the many centuries, they gradually imposed their rule, their language, and much of their culture and characteristics upon a vast area of Africa. They pushed into the Congo basin, occupied the great lake country, settled parts of Tanganyika and Kenya, and moved into the Rhodesias.

During the 1600's and 1700's the Bantus met with the Dutch Boers who were moving northward from their former Cape Colony on the tip of South Africa. This fantastic and long-continued movement of people rivals any migration of man anywhere. The fact that most of the Africans now living south of the equator speak a Bantu language is evidence of the deep and lasting imprint the Bantus made on much of Africa south of the Sahara.

**Traders and builders of empires.** The Africans south of the Sahara have long been engaged in trade. They traded with their fellows and traded with those who lived north of the Sahara—the Egyptians, the Carthaginians, and the Berbers. They sent north their gold, wild animals, ivory, and slaves, and in return they received metals, cloth, salt, and other products they lacked and wanted. As this trade grew, it also helped to stimulate the growth of cities and states.

One of the most conspicuous examples of trade and growth of empire was in the western Sudan. There, the Africans who lived around the Niger River exchanged their gold and slaves for the salt mined by the Berbers in northern Sahara. This trade started sometime between the second and fifth centuries A.D. and continued up to modern colonial times and the present. Cities and busy trading centers sprang up to handle this expanding trade, and, around 500 A.D., there began an impressive succession of Sudanic states which centered largely around the city of Timbuktu. At their peak the rulers of these states controlled or influenced areas extending from Senegal to Nigeria and from the forest zone to Algeria. Perhaps initially stimulated by North Africans, these states were chiefly made up of African Negro peoples.

The earliest, and one of the greatest of these empires, was known as the Empire of Ghana. With the slow turning of the centuries Ghana extended its political control to include the Niger Valley and much of western Sahara. Although weakened by the conquests of the African Moslems in the eleventh century, it continued to exist in name until the thirteenth century. The independent state of Ghana now continues the name of this old and important empire. There were later African empires in this region. There was the Empire of Mali, which from the twelfth to the fifteenth centuries ruled from the Atlantic Ocean to the borders of modern Nigeria. There were the Songhai who conquered Timbuktu in the fifteenth century. The Africans, like other men of the past and present, were empire builders.

The African plowed and planted his earth, drove his cattle over its surface, and settled it in mighty surges of migrations. He produced utensils for living and weapons for death. He boated along rivers to visit and to war, and he mined the earth for minerals to trade. He dotted the land with his villages and his cities and added to its diversities the varieties of his customs and his languages. He impressed upon this landscape his own special development and made it African.

But there were also non-Africans who helped to shape the culture and the attitudes of modern Africa.

## Other Men Came

Africa south of the Sahara was visited on a number of occasions by men from elsewhere, but not until the late 1800's was there any great penetration beyond the coastal lands by outsiders. In ancient times the Greeks and the Phoenicians traded with Africans of the south, and the Romans knew these people as slaves. Africa was a continent from which there was always something new and strange emerging to cause amazement among the Romans. The Persians, during the period of their expansion, knew the African of the east coast, and traded with him. The Chinese too, probably visited the east coast of Africa during one of their rare long sea voyages. It was the Arabs, however, who, in the seventh century A.D., under the impetus of their expansion, came to know Africa better and more extensively than any outsiders up to that time.

**Arabs.** During the seventh century the Moslem Arabs began an expansion that carried them across the broad expanse of North Africa, into other regions, and down the eastern coast of Africa. Under Arab domination and stimulus, trade increased from the borders of the Mediterranean Sea southward across the Sahara to the west Sudan. And thus began increasing contact between the African to the south and the Arab-ruled north. Together with trade went the religion of Islam, and many Africans embraced it. An instance of its penetration is the hinterland, or back country, of Nigeria, where the majority of the people are Moslem.

The Arabs did not go too far inland from their coastal strongholds, however, except on raiding expeditions for slaves. Generally, they were content to transmit ivory, spices, slaves, and other goods from their trading centers back to the Middle East. From there goods were funneled to other parts of the world. The Arab brought with him the religion of Islam and other features of his culture, and he frequently mated with the African. An example of the merging of all these features in the life of the East African is the island city of Zanzibar off the east coast of Africa.

**Europeans.** The Arabs dominated most of the Africans' trade and contacts with the outside world until the coming of the European in the 1400's. It was the Portuguese who led this new penetration of Africa. They slowly made their way down the west coast of Africa, establishing trading posts as they went along. Eventually they rounded the southern tip of Africa, discovered the east coast, and from there found the way to India. The Portuguese were rewarded by gaining a monopoly of the spice trade which had formerly been the exclusive possession of the Arabs. The English, the Dutch, the French, and other Europeans slowly began to discover the routes of the Portuguese and to settle themselves and their trading centers on Africa's coasts.

1. Compare the life of the farmer with that of the cattleman living in the savannah. Which life would you prefer to live? Which life do you think most Africans would prefer to live if they had a choice?
2. What contacts did the African south of the Sahara have with visitors from Europe, the Middle East, and Asia before the 1800's?
3. When and for what purposes did the Arabs come to Africa? What did they contribute to the evolution of civilization in Africa?

## The Slave Trade

The Europeans, as had many others in ancient times before them, discovered that great sums of money could be made in the African slave trade. The Europeans had also discovered the New World of the Americas, and they wanted the profits that could be made growing sugar, cotton, rice, and other products on colonial plantations. But they lacked labor, for the American Indian was not numerous in some places, and moreover the hard labor and the

Beginning in the 1500's and lasting until the 1800's, the slave trade brought Africans to all parts of the New World. Above, a sale of slaves in New Orleans, from an engraving made in 1842. (Library of Congress) Below, diamonds from the mines at Kimberley are part of the natural wealth of Africa. (South African Tourist Corporation)

diseases brought by the Europeans resulted in many deaths and weakening sicknesses. Accordingly, in the 1500's and 1600's European and American slave ships went from Africa to the Americas. They brought slaves to the West Indies, to Brazil and to the plantations of the southern United States. The story of the slave trade is not a pretty tale, and it reflects the depths to which man will sink at times to gain wealth.

African chiefs and traders cooperated in obtaining slaves. Guns, ammunition, food, gold, metal tools, and cheap cloth, beads, or trinkets of jewelry were all objects that might be exchanged for slaves. African raiders sold able-bodied men and women who had been captured or tricked into the chains of slavery, and the African traders as well as the Europeans often grew rich from this profitable trade. As more and more slaves were required to work the fields and handle the many other occupations which were found for them, the trade boomed. The trade in slaves from Africa continued for about 400 years, and there are those who think that as many as 20,000,000 slaves were taken from West Africa to other parts of the world while the trade lasted. Many of them came to the Americas. It is said that for every slave working in the Americas, another had died on the way to this land. But these are all blind guesses, for the slaver did not always talk about those many who had died in the cramped, stifling holds of his ship where they were chained together in close-packed numbers. The slaver crammed as many as he could into his slow-moving ship, for he knew the voyage was long to the Americas and there would be some who would not survive.

There have been vivid descriptions of the tortures and the sufferings of the men and women who were enslaved. Some were thrown into the sea to drown when the ship captain feared the illegal nature of his cargo might be discovered; and those who reached their destination were often harshly or cruelly treated.

There were a number of Englishmen, at home and in the American colonies, who were opposed to the slave trade. In the late 1700's the British colony of Sierra Leone was made a haven for freed slaves, and its capital was named Freetown. After the Revolutionary War, several of the new states of the United States passed laws prohibiting the slave trade, and in a number of states the institution of slavery was abolished before 1800.

Early in the nineteenth century both England and the United States passed laws making the slave trade illegal for their citizens. In 1822 freed slaves from the United States landed in the territory of Liberia which had been reserved for them, and thus began the oldest independent republic in Africa. But because the profits of the trade were high and enforcement of the law difficult, many continued to trade in African slaves around the world. It was not until later in the 1800's that the practice lessened and eventually ceased.

## European Domination

All during the 1800's, Europeans continued to penetrate the interior of Africa and to learn more about this previously "dark" continent. There were those interested in finding African products of value which might replace the trade in slaves; some were naturally curious about the interior of Africa; others were moved by the spirit of adventure. Europeans, singly and in groups, began to move cautiously into the interior from the coasts. They followed rivers to their sources, found and named lakes after their sovereigns, and uncovered resources which led to profit and to fame. The names of these explorers and adventurers are many and they came from various European countries. Perhaps the name of David Livingstone, an Englishman, is best known to English-speaking peoples. In the 1850's he crossed the continent from east to west, followed the Zambezi, and named the Victoria Falls. A journalist, Henry Stanley, was sent by a New York paper to find Livingstone when he had not been heard from for two years. Stanley found him deep in the heart of Africa in 1871, and their meeting has become famous for Stanley's greeting, "Dr. Livingstone, I presume?" Stanley himself went on to become a famous explorer, and he also aided the Belgians in accomplishing their colonial aims in the Congo.

Gradually the possibilities of Africa began to interest the Europeans more and more. In the latter part of the 1800's, governments started to parcel out the land among themselves and to grab as much of it as they thought desirable. Inevitably, their holdings increased, and by the beginning of the twentieth century nearly all of the land of Africa was under the political and economic domination of European nations.

1. Why did the European traders deal in slaves? To what parts of the world did they take their slaves?
2. Explain how slavery exemplified man's inhumanity toward man in Africa as well as in other lands.
3. Name two great African explorers described in this section of your book. How did their motives differ from those of most of the Europeans who went to Africa?

## Conclusion

With the coming of the European, the African found the interior of his continent taken over and ruled by outsiders for the first time in his long history. Europe and Africa were brought into close contact, and this contact had a great impact on the peoples of both continents. But the long-range effects were probably greater for the African than for the European. Many scholars regard the coming of the European to Africa as so important that they divide the history of Africa into two main divisions: prior to the coming of the European, or up to about 1500; and after his coming, or from 1500 to the present.

In the latest period of African history, the many political, economic, and social ideas that had changed the life of man in Europe and elsewhere have been brought to the masses of people in Africa. Before this time the African had lived in seclusion, apart from the rest of the world. It was inevitable that the African should respond to these new, exciting, promising ideas and seek to make them a reality in his own life. The European brought political and economic domination to the African, but he also brought change, ambition, and the desire to imitate. His coming brought the beginning of a new kind of life.

## SUMMING UP THE CHAPTER

A. Define or explain the following terms, relating them to this chapter.

| | |
|---|---|
| "angels in their flight" | oasis |
| archaeologist | rain forest |
| dark continent | savannah |

B. Identify or locate the following and tell why they are important.

| | |
|---|---|
| Lake Victoria | Pygmies |
| L. S. B. Leakey | Sahara Desert |
| Masai | Zambesi |
| Nigerian | Zanzibar |

C. Chapter review questions.

1. What do you consider to be the greatest development in Africa since 1900?
2. Where and by whom were the earliest traces of man found in Africa?
3. How has the landscape of Africa helped to shape the character of the African peoples and provide them with diverse modes of living? In your answer you may want to compare life within the various regions — savannah, rain forest, semiarid lands, desert.
4. What human qualities motivated man to set up the game preserves in Africa? In what parts of Africa are these preserves located?
5. Why did some of the Africans cooperate with the Europeans in securing men and women to be sold as slaves in other parts of the world?

D. Questions for discussion.

1. Why do you suppose this book has very little to say about the evolution of early African civilization?
2. Why do you suppose the people of some nations have been interested in colonization while those of other nations have not? Compare the roles of European Christians and Middle Eastern Moslems in the colonization of Africa.
3. What theories might an anthropologist offer to account for the variety of African tribes?

E. Projects for groups or individuals.

1. Read *I Married Adventure* by Osa Johnson, and make a report on this book to the class.
2. Draw a map of Africa and label the major climatic regions. Show the major rivers, lakes, and mountains in each region.
3. Prepare a report on the early Arab voyages along the coasts of Africa.
4. See if you can capture in a short essay the African's feeling toward his great rivers and lakes which provide him with material and spiritual satisfaction.
5. Collect pictures of life in Africa. Plan a display for your class that will show the peoples and landscape of the African continent in all their variety.

CHAPTER **34**

# *The African Began to Know the New*

WHEN THE European began seriously to investigate and develop the resources of Africa, he brought changes to the African's economy, culture, and social life. The pace of these changes was rather swift. European powers spent only a little longer than fifty years colonizing and exploring before the African began to regain his rule over most of the continent in the middle years of the present century. Yet, in those few years, the seeds of change were planted and began to grow. Some of the most obvious changes were in the African's way of making a living and in his general economy.

## Changes in Economy

The African has mostly been a farmer. When Europeans began to probe the interior lands, they saw the African living in villages and tilling land cleared from the forests or the grassy savannah. These villages and farms were often impermanent because the soil played out quickly and forced the African to move along to richer earth. The African had learned not to demand too much of his rather poor earth. He took from the land only what he needed to support his family. He rarely had or wanted a surplus. Nor did he grow

Rice production has been stepped up in Liberia by the use of improved methods and mechanical equipment. How does this differ from traditional African agriculture? (Liberian Information Service)

commercial crops that other men in the world desired, for he was insulated from the remainder of mankind. He did not know the customs and desires of other men, except, of course, the desire of some to trade or to make him a slave. Over the long course of time, the African had learned to live within the limitations of his land. By trial and error he had found an adequate working relationship with his environment.

A new factor entered into this environment and began to disturb and change the African's relationship with his land. European colonial governments reserved much of the African land they ruled for the exclusive use of European settlers, who were beginning to discover the good possibilities of this continent. This was true of the rulers of South Africa, Southern Rhodesia, Northern Rhodesia, Kenya, and other areas. The introduction of this alien practice modified the African's relationship with the land by limiting the amount of land available for farming. There were other European legal and business ideas and customs which also affected the African's relationship to the land.

The African knew nothing of the customary European practices and ideas concerning ownership of property. When he started to do business with this newly met acquaintance, he often found himself with a loss instead of a profit. In line with their usual custom, the Europeans offered to buy good land from the African chiefs, and the chiefs often accepted their offers. Unfortunately for the African, there was a serious misunderstanding in these transactions. The Europeans naturally thought of this contract and sale as a permanent change in the ownership of the land. The Africans, on the other hand, had never thought of their earth as being the personal property of any one person. They considered the land rather as community property to be used by the various members

Liberian villagers celebrate a festival with dancing and music. (Liberian Information Service)

Europeans were attracted by the rich mineral resources of Africa. Above, Johannesburg, with gold mine dumps in the foreground. (South African Tourist Corporation)

of the tribe or the village just as long as they farmed it. The result was that in East Africa, in Kenya, and in the Rhodesias for instance, more of the land was withdrawn from the use of the African people.

It is true that the land which the European took for himself and farmed was frequently managed in a profitable and efficient manner. He terraced and contoured the land in a modern way and raised a surplus of commercial crops and cattle for export. But it is also true that many Africans were compelled to become squatters on pieces of this land. In return for this privilege the Africans had to give a certain amount of labor to the European owners. The vast majority of European settlers had their farms and ranches in East Africa, in Kenya, in North and South Rhodesia, in Tanganyika, and in South Africa. The malaria-bearing mosquito, the inhospitable nature of the rain forest and the jungle, and the many tropical diseases discouraged the Europeans from farming in parts of West Africa such as Nigeria and Guinea. There are American-owned rubber plantations in Liberia, but cocoa in Ghana and peanuts in Gambia are grown mostly on small African-owned farms.

The Europeans also began to mine the mineral wealth of the continent, as for example in the Congo and some parts of Northern Rhodesia. And for all these enterprises able-bodied labor was needed. This change of the African from an independent farmer to a worker for wages also changed his relationship with the land, for the practice of leaving his village and his tribe to work for someone else was not in his tradition. For all these and other reasons, the harmony which the African had built up over the years with his land be-

The introduction of manufacturing industries has greatly changed the Africans' way of life. Left, an African employee in a nail factory. (East Africa Tourist Travel Association)

gan to be disturbed. His relationship to the land changed, and this led to changes in his way of living.

## A New Economic Environment

As the European deepened his investigations of the African earth, he uncovered vast and rich resources which were quickly exploited. There were diamonds and gold in South Africa, copper in the Rhodesias, copper, uranium ores and other minerals in the Congo, iron ore in Liberia, and minerals in other parts of Africa. Settlements of Europeans and Africans grew up around the mine shafts as European administrators and engineers and hundreds of thousands of African laborers congregated to take from the earth its riches of resources. Commerce grew as merchants came to provide the services and the goods required by these new congregations of man. Cities and great ports grew to handle the increasing exports and imports of Africa. In East and South Africa these new merchants frequently came from India, and gradually they came to control much of the retail and wholesale trade in these areas, especially in East Africa. The Indians came to have a middle status between the rulers, the English in this case, and the Africans. Because of their literacy and education, they often filled minor posts in the English bureaucracy. Dams were built on the rivers to obtain the hydroelectric power needed to run machines and light cities. Modern civilization of the West, with its differences of appearance, custom, and attitude, began to intrude with increasing force on the African way of life.

As more Africans began to work for wages, money became important to their way of life. Wages for the African were much lower than for the European or the Indian, but even this small amount was used to buy products of the West from the European and Indian merchants. European dress became customary in the cities, and a few Africans began to live in houses with electricity and some modern conveniences. This was a real change, for most

Africans still live in mud huts with thatched roofs. The floors of these huts are of earth, and the furnishings are few. Most of them do not have electricity nor the material conveniences which make the homes of the more materially advanced non-African comfortable and inviting. But the African, like all men, wants these things when they are available. Especially in West Africa, Africans have begun to engage in commercial undertakings to gain money for themselves and to provide the goods now being demanded in increasing quantities. But those who live in the city and those who can buy the consumer goods of the West are still a minority. It is, however, in the direction of this minority that many of the Africans now desire to move.

1. Describe the Africans' ways of making a living prior to the arrival of the Europeans. What new and different practices did the Europeans introduce which affected the Africans' relationship with the land?
2. What did the European colonizers expect from their African possessions? What were the results of their policies?
3. Why did the Africans leave their villages and farms? What changes did this bring about in their lives?

## Changes in Culture

The coming of the European also brought about changes in the culture of the African. There have been many modifications of African religious, artistic, and social ways since the beginning of the twentieth century. The process of adaptation and orientation to the newer currents of thought flowing in from the outside goes on at increasing speed.

### Religion

The African was and is a religious man. He, like most other men, gave considerable thought and attention to that which was of the spirit in his life. He wondered about the birth of the universe and of man, and many

Planned villages with modern conveniences are springing up in many parts of Africa. (Liberian Information Service)

of his fellowmen gave varying answers to these mysterious questions. The African was told of an unseen world of spirits around him, and though these spirits might differ from tribe to tribe and from village to village, they were all deemed powerful. They had a strong influence upon the African and upon all aspects of his life. It was often necessary to placate them lest they bring harm to him and his family. Sometimes there were those possessed of a dangerous spirit, and it was necessary for a man skilled in such matters, the medicine man or priest of the native religion, to drive these dangerous spirits from their bodies. The medicine man was a most influential figure in the life of the African, sometimes even more powerful than the chief. When he put on his mask and his ornaments, there were few who did not fear him and give him a wide berth. He was often the only one in the village or tribe who was skilled in rude medicine, for the African frequently saw a close connection between the spirit world and the diseases that affected him. The medicine man and the world of spirits originally known by the African declined in power among those Africans who were converted to the religion of Islam.

Islam, which had its origin among the Arabs of the Middle East, swept like a religious flame to Asia, to Egypt, and across the sweeping deserts of North Africa. In the seventh century, it went with Islamic converts southward across the Sahara to West Africa. There many Africans saw in it a spirituality they were seeking, and they were converted. Islam continues to meet the spiritual desires of many there today. It is the fastest spreading religion in West Africa according to some commentators. Islam went up the Nile from Egypt, and much of the country of the Sudan is Moslem today. It was carried by Arab traders to the shores of Africa farther south and east, and there are numerous Moslems among the East Africans. One of the reasons given for the spread of Islam in Africa is its emphasis upon the brotherhood of men and the basic equality of men. It is said that Mohammed, the founder of Islam, married an African woman to teach his followers that all races are as one within the family of Islam. The insistence of Islam that all Moslems should be able to read the Koran gave rise to religious schools where children were taught to read this holy book in Arabic. This practice gave at least a minimum of education to the African at a time when he had little and helped to fortify his faith. Islam has been a great and growing force in Africa for centuries, and it continues to exert a powerful appeal to the spiritual nature of the African.

When the non-Moslem European came to the continent of Africa, he brought with him his Christian religion. This was not the first time that Christianity had been known in parts of Africa. There is a tradition that some of the early Christian converts also carried this religion up the Nile from Egypt to other African lands. Many of the Ethiopians are Coptic Christians, who practice a form of Christianity introduced into Ethiopia from Egypt around the fourth century A. D.

But it was the European missionary who brought his religion, both in the Catholic and in the Protestant forms, to much of Africa. Many of the first great explorers were Christian missionaries. David Livingstone, the English medical missionary, crossed Africa from east to west and fought against the slave trade wherever he found it. In the colonies governed by the French, the Portuguese, the Italians, and the Spanish, the missionaries were mostly Catholic. In the colonies of the English and in South Africa, both Protestant and Catholic missionaries strove to make the African Christian, and with some success. Starting in the 1800's both groups also built schools, hospitals, orphanages, and other welfare institutions, and under the colonial governments it was largely the Christian missions that provided most of the welfare services for the African. Perhaps the single most famous example today of the spiritual power which moved these men and women to explain their religion through example is Albert Schweitzer. Schweitzer is a world-famous theologian, musician, and physician who has dedicated his life to operating a hospital at Lambaréné in the jungles of Gabon.

Those Africans who were converted to Christianity were also changed in various other aspects of their culture. They were required to give up their original worship and the relations with their old spirits. Thus they lost many cultural aspects of their lives which revolved around the spirit world. They were required to give up polygamy, or the practice of having more than one wife. Not that most Africans had more than one wife—they were too poor. But to have more than one wife was a sign of prestige and influence in the locality. In most instances, the Africans were required to wear more clothing, the women especially, since it had long been the practice of most Africans to wear as few clothes as possible where the weather permitted. In no area, however, were the missionaries more influential in changing the attitudes and customs of the African than through education.

1. In what sense was the medicine man both a religious and a medical figure? Explain the type of religion he practiced.
2. How was Islam brought to Africa? What accounted for its ready acceptance?
3. Where were the earliest traces of Christianity found in Africa? When did most of the Christians come to Africa and what significant contributions did they make? What aspects of African culture did this change?

### Education

Many of the schools in Africa are private schools. The vast majority of these private schools were founded by missionaries and are run by missionaries. When the Europeans arrived in Africa south of the Sahara, they found the Africans generally illiterate, except for a few who knew Arabic. A large number of Africans remain illiterate today, but the number has diminished due to the opening of schools by the missionaries. In some parts of Africa as many as 80 per cent of the schools are private. It must be also remembered that many of these schools were supported by colonial governments.

There were drawbacks in the educational systems that arose under colonial governments. In the Belgian Congo, the Africans were rarely given any opportunity for education beyond the elementary level. As a consequence, when independence came on June 30, 1960, there were very few educated Congolese leaders available to replace the former Belgian rulers. In the French and English colonies, only an elite few were trained beyond the secondary level. Although the colonial governments did begin to subsidize the mission and other private schools, there were relatively few schools operating in proportion to the population. However, the minority who were fortunate enough to learn to read and write, and to absorb some elementary knowledge about the world they lived in, were changed to some extent by this knowledge.

The educated Africans came to have some knowledge of European history and practices. In fact, it has been said that because the Africans were taught with French and English textbooks, they knew much more about Europe than about their own vast continent. The Africans who went to school became European in many ways and in some respects lost contact with the culture of their own locality. They learned to prize European culture and ideas more than those of Africa. Many of them began to copy the ways of the particular European who governed or taught them. This, too, led to a separation of the educated from their own families and villages. The French in their educational system tried to make the African a Frenchman, but the English did not try to assimilate or Anglicize him, though it was inevitable that the Africans they taught should speak with an English accent and learn a number of English attitudes. Some observers have noted that there is greater understanding between the French-taught African and the Frenchman, and between the English-taught and the English, than there is between these educated groups and other Africans. Africans speaking French and Africans speaking English have the same problems of communication and philosophy that plague the relations between the European English and

The African learns music, the rhythm of drums, and dancing from earliest childhood. Above, a spirited tribal dance. (South African Tourist Corporation) Colorful designs are painted on the clay walls of many villages in southern Africa, left. (South African Tourist Corporation)

French. But education did bring a greater unity among the educated minorities within the various colonial areas.

Africans have spoken many different languages for centuries, and communication between regions has been impossible for this reason. The French and the English governed vast and diverse territories within Africa. Within these areas, those who learned English or French could converse with other Africans in these tongues although their native languages were different. Then, too, the common system of colonial administration and customs helped to bring about greater understanding and communication between tribes and language groups.

Many of the present republics of Africa gained their independence during the 1950's and 1960's, and the new governments have placed great emphasis on education. African leaders know that only through education can their people advance toward the civilization they want. The governments of new African countries are pouring huge sums of money into building educational facilities, and they are receiving help from other countries and international organizations. But their problems are vast, their resources scarce, and much time must elapse before they can hope for a satisfactory educational system.

## Music and the Arts

The African learns music, the rhythm of drums, and dancing from earliest childhood. For centuries he has communicated with others over the distances of tangled jungle and rolling savannah with the rhythmic musical beat of drum and hollowed log, and they have replied with the same musical rhythm. The African's sense of rhythm is also revealed in the weaving of his body and the beat of his feet as they create the intricate patterns of his dance. There are few men who are not held spellbound by the colorful drama of graceful men and women dancing wildly or calmly to the beat of the drum and the clapping of hands. The tribal dance is an outburst of emotion which releases the creativeness of the African and stimulates the imagination of the observer.

Rhythm is a basic part of all music. Underlying and giving meaning to the sound of brass, the murmur of woodwinds, or the beat of the drum, there is always rhythm. And complex rhythm is the trademark of African music. The African was brought forcibly to the Americas, but he took the Indian and Spanish music of Latin America and gave it his own individuality. The blending of them all is Latin American music. The African came to the southland of North America, and he took the music he found there and gave jazz to the world. And jazz has now become a part of the world repertory of music. The rhythm of the African has become an admired part of his culture throughout the world.

In recent years the non-African has learned to appreciate and to admire the creative art of the African, formerly called "primitive" but now regarded as sophisticated. Slender, elongated figures created by the African are often blended harmoniously in the decoration of the most modern apartments and buildings. African art stands proudly in the museums of the world, and many see in it an expressiveness and beauty of which the creator should be justly proud. Before the birth of Christ, the Africans of northern Nigeria were making jewelry of fine quality and beautiful sculptured figurines. And during the fifteenth century, Nigerian artisans made figures of gods and men that are prized today for their workmanship. In this modern age some African artists of great talent are exhibiting in the world's showplaces of art, while others, untaught but creative, wander the countryside painting masterpieces which only the fortunate few have an opportunity to see.

1. Compare the British, French, and Belgian systems of education in Africa. Which system do you think assisted the African to the greatest degree?
2. In what way did the teachings of the Europeans influence the development of unity in Africa?
3. How has the African expressed himself artistically?

## Changes in Society

The African today is a man of many societies. In Africa there are societies centered around hunting and fishing; other societies revolve around the herding of cattle, and these cattle are a symbol of wealth and status as well as a source of food; and there are roving societies which move freely, seeking desirable locations, ignoring the national boundaries of states, which are unimportant to nature. The structure of African societies is complex. It is the outcome of the centuries, and it embraces many groups. Each of these groups is made up of those who speak the same language, follow the same customs, and know the approximate limits of their territory. Each such group is known collectively as a tribe. The societies of Africa are made up of many, many tribes, and the people of each tribe have constructed customs and practices around the land they farm and the village they inhabit. In the yet remote parts of the African continent, some tribes continue to believe and to act much as their ancestors did for years beyond man's knowledge. In the cities and among the educated elite, many Africans are shrugging off the accumulated traditions of the centuries and living a social life similar to that of the European. The complexity and variety of his social life reveal the African as not the one, but the many.

The physical features of Africa have tended to keep its people separated from each other, and contact between tribes has frequently been of a warlike rather than of a peaceful nature. This, too, furthered the separateness among Africans. Thus, the African evolved in special ways conditioned by the uniqueness of his environment, his occupation, and the countless factors which condition the evolving of all men. But, like all men of diverse color, nationality, occupation, and environment, the Africans also had something in common.

Members of tribes were very social in their attitudes, and the community was of greater importance than the individual. The individual had his role to play so that the group might survive and remain harmonious. Tribe members were educated to this responsibility from an early age. Children were taught their responsibilities to the family, the village, and the tribe. They knew their duties and the acceptable relationships to their elders, their relatives, their fellow tribesmen, and outsiders. They knew the changing patterns of these relationships as they reached each stage of youth, maturity, and old age. These relationships were fixed and certain within the tribe and the locality, and this certainty gave stability and a degree of security to life. While societies might vary, the members of any particular group shared a common standard of behavior in differing situations; they knew what was expected and demanded of them.

One of the most basic responsibilities was, of course, to the family. In Africa, as in most early agricultural societies, the family included the married sons and their families—and sometimes daughters—and often numerous other close relatives. Kinship was important, and it was the responsibility of each to see that this family group was maintained in as secure a manner as possible. Even those Africans who have left the village and the family for work elsewhere in the cities, mines, and industrial plants, feel responsible for the maintenance of the family from whom they are temporarily separated. Many of them return permanently to the warmth of the family after several years of working separated from it.

The African has traditionally felt a deep-seated sense of responsibility to preserve the wholeness of the customs of his locality and his tribe. Customs grew from the need to further the purposes of the group in the most effective and harmonious way possible. Each member, as a valuable part of the group, understood that they were designed as much for him as for anyone else. Many representatives of the European powers in Africa considered the native African only as a possible source of labor and called him "barbarous," "ignorant," and "primitive." These Europeans were, themselves, too poorly informed to realize that the African had a well-developed sense of social responsibility and obligation to the society of which he was a member.

Because the African was unfamiliar with European culture and civilization, it was not necessarily true that he was inferior or incapable of understanding and learning. The Europeans, on the other hand, were equally ignorant of African culture and society. Throughout his history man has shown a genius for working out a variety of ways to live in harmony with his fellows and his landscape, and what man has the objectivity to say which is better for a particular time and place?

## The African Woman

The woman of Africa, like the male of Africa, has her own special responsibilities within the closely knit local society. She has the care of the home, the cooking, the cleaning, and the care of children, but she does more. She carries the water, works in the fields, cuts trees, gathers firewood, and is often seen in the marketplace selling food or articles made by her family during the times when work is slack. She is a familiar figure walking the roads and trails with a burden balanced on her head and a baby slung on her side or bundled tightly to her back. She is not a luxury in the household but a worker performing duties as essential as those of the male, and sometimes more so.

The African woman is frequently an individual of strong character who knows her role in society and asserts it with firmness and with dignity. In those tribes which practice polygamy, there may be several wives in one household. Because this is the accepted custom, these wives do not generally object to it, and are often proud of their position, for a man who can afford several wives has high social status. There are, of course, bickerings, jealousies, and rivalries in a household of many wives and family members, and a wife may complain of her husband's poor choice in selecting a new wife, but she does not generally complain of the system.

The African woman may live veiled from the eyes of man; she may walk unconcerned, clad only in a loincloth; or she may spend most of her life within the boundaries of some lonely forest village or travel to the ends of the earth with her diplomat husband. In certain instances, women wield great political influence and may become local chiefs. But whatever her lot, the African woman has an independence of spirit and of action within the role her society has given her.

## Transition, Clash, Uncertainty

With the introduction of the European into the environment, there came inevitable changes in the old and numerous societies of the African. Under the impulse of trade and administration, cities grew at strategic points along the seashores and on the rivers. The African went to these cities to live and to work. And he discovered that living in a city is far different from living in the countryside. In cities, the African encountered certain working hours, certain expected ways to dress, certain polite requirements demanded by the ruling European, and certain laws which had to be obeyed.

These urban ways of living were different from what the African had known before. Here in the city, surrounded by the many who did not know him, there was a freedom from tribal restraint which had bound the African to certain ways in his rural home. He found himself

The African has discovered that living in a city is far different from living in the countryside. Below, modern buildings on the city square of Nairobi. (East Africa Tourist Travel Association)

The impact of European culture upon traditional African ways has been great, and many Africans have found it difficult to adjust to life as wage-earners in cities and modern industries. Left, the production of rubber is important to the economy of Liberia. A worker is hanging sheets of rubber to dry. (Liberian Information Service) Above, African commerce extends to all parts of the world through busy ports on rivers and coasts. (United Nations)

associating with men whose tribes were different from his own, and this too was a new and often broadening and strange experience. The African was discovering that there were other ways of living, and that his old way was not the only way.

In the cities, European systems of law and courts were established. An act that might have been permissible or even desirable in tribal society could be condemned and punished by the laws of the Europeans. Under the old tribal traditions, the African might revenge himself on another member of his society who had wronged him; but in the city he could not take the law into his own hands. Members of a tribe might wander about freely within their own area, but in the city entrance to many places was prohibited. There were pressing crowds of people here, and living quarters were cramped. The African saw many things he had never known before—cars, large buildings, and shops with glass windows—but he also found different customs and strange new laws. There were policemen everywhere, and many things were prohibited which had been permitted in the less crowded and simpler life of the countryside. The African had to learn how to live in the city and to adapt to a new way of life. In order to do this, he had to compromise.

In his search to find social solutions which were satisfying in his new special situation, the African in the city frequently offended those of his tribe and his family at home. In the city, he might, for instance, marry someone of another tribe, and in a manner not sanctioned by his tribe. He was married in the city, but he was not legally married in the eyes of his family and his tribe. There were other things he did which did not have the approval of his tribe and family, and thus he was confronted with a social dilemma. Tribal life had continued in the same old ways without changing; but city life had brought new and different ways of living. Many Africans still have not found a good solution to the dilemmas presented by the demands of the modern city and the demands of the society and the family back home.

Change from a secure and accepted way of life to a new and untried way is always agonizing and frustrating. The uncertainty that comes with change often creates a conflict within man which is very real and very difficult to resolve. Most Africans are trying to resolve this uncertainty today.

1. Discuss the relationship of the African to his family, his tribe, and his locality. What basic factors and attitudes have helped to produce such a close relationship?
2. What strange customs did the African find when he moved to the city? Was he able to adjust to these new customs?
3. Do you feel that the African's loyalty to family, tribe, and locality has impeded his transition to modern ways?

## Conclusion

Before the penetration of the European into the interior of Africa, the African had worked out a rather harmonious relationship with his landscape and his fellowmen. He knew his earth, and he knew the reasonableness of the customs of his societies. He had his customary ways of working within the limitations of his environment, of dealing with his world of spirits, and of living in groups. All of these ways were known, certain, and secure.

In the mid and late 1800's, the new, strong, strange outsider, the European, intruded upon the African scene. Suddenly the scene began to change, and the African was required to modify his traditional ways of life. He became confused, puzzled, and sometimes angered, as he tried to change what he had thought was unchangeable. The African today is engaged in meeting this problem of change, and it is a hard problem for the many who still live in the old ways. But the few who lead know that the present and the future command a change. In time, the African will find his solution, and certainty will descend once again upon his society and his landscape. In the meantime he lives between the old and the new, and his way of life consists of experiment, adaptation, and compromise.

## SUMMING UP THE CHAPTER

A. Chapter review questions.

1. How and in what areas did the Europeans obtain land in Africa? What did they do with this land, and how did the Africans react?
2. What natural resources, including minerals, did the Europeans exploit? In what parts of Africa were these resources found?
3. When and why did Indians migrate to Africa? Did they receive greater economic gains than the Africans? In what sense were they a "middle layer" of society in Africa?
4. What important changes did the Europeans initiate in the economic life of the African? What were the consequences of these changes?
5. In what sense did a European education draw the African both closer to his own country and yet at the same time draw him away from it?
6. Describe as many different types of society within Africa as you can. In each case evaluate the changes brought about by the Europeans.
7. Try to capture the spirit of the African woman in a few short descriptive paragraphs. Mention and describe her social position and function within the family and the tribe. Where possible, place your explanation in a historical context.
8. Prior to the coming of European missionaries, what were the religions of Africa? What function other than religious did the European missionaries perform?
9. What type of music is typically African? How has African music been adapted as a part of the music of other lands?
10. Define polygamy and explain its significance for the African. Where is polygamy still practiced?

B. Questions for discussion.

1. What was the role of the Indian in the economic development of Africa? Compare his role with that of the Chinese in much of Southeast Asia.
2. How would you explain the fact that the African lacked the concept of property as a personal possession before the coming of the Europeans? Has this situation changed today?
3. How did education bind the African to Europe? How did colonial education and rule both unify and divide the Africans? Is this influence still present today?
4. How did the social and legal customs of cities create conflicting pressures on the Africans who came there to work? What has been the result of this conflict between old and new ways?
5. How do you suppose so much of the trade of Africa came to be carried on by women? Is this true in any other societies that you know of?

C. Projects for groups or individuals.

1. Listen to some jazz records and to some records of typical African music. See if you can detect rhythms that they have in common. What relation does Latin American music have to African music?
2. Prepare a report on Islam in Africa.
3. Collect pictures of African art objects and write short descriptions explaining their significance and comparing them with Asian, American, and European art forms.
4. Sketch a map of Africa and label each major region to show principal products.

# CHAPTER 35

# *The Political African*

PRIOR TO the coming of the European, a variety of political systems and attitudes had evolved in Africa. African rulers were tribal chiefs, and some of these chiefs held their positions because they were mighty in war and able in their leadership. Often the chief was chosen because of his ability rather than because of his ancestry. The selection of such a chief might be based upon strength, skill with weapons, and keenness of mind. There were also chiefs who inherited their ruling position without earning it, and their right to rule was founded upon royal birth or seniority in the family. They might be good and just; or they might be fat and pompous, never venturing outdoors except borne high on platforms carried by their subjects and shaded by large umbrellas. Some might be very ordinary of mind and body, but they ruled by right of birth. Other chiefs were elected by councils of elders or by all the able-bodied warriors of a tribe. There were also those who seized power without consultation and ruled brutally in their own interest. And there were other leaders who were kind, responsible, and sincere in their efforts to make their people happy and contented.

In many instances the African had traditional checks upon the power of those who ruled him. In other instances it depended upon the personality of the ruler whether he was restrained or unrestrained in his use of power. In a number of localities no important decision was taken without being first discussed in council or among the people; in other places the decision was made by one or a few, and the people were required to support it. In some parts of the continent the authority was quick to punish an offender, and the causes or circumstances of his crime were of minor importance. Among other Africans the judge was important, and all aspects of the case were taken into consideration before a judgment was rendered; and the people did not always consider an accused guilty before an investigation.

The Africans shared a common continent, but their political systems were many. When the Europeans came, their political systems began to assume dominance over the traditional African customs and ways of thinking.

## European Political Dominance

Prior to the 1800's the European had been content to nibble the outer edges of the African continent, but in the 1800's he began cautiously to devour larger chunks. Liking the taste, between 1880 and 1900 he swallowed practically all of it, leaving only Liberia and Ethiopia untouched. At the beginning of the twentieth century, almost everywhere one looked in Africa the flag of some European country was flying. In most places it was the flag of England or France, but here and there, scattered over various parts of the continent, the flags of Italy, Spain, Portugal, Belgium, and Germany were also seen.

In taking territory, the European did not follow old tribal boundaries but rather seized land as time and circumstance permitted. At times European leaders met and agreed peacefully to a certain division of African territories. At other times there was strife, as in the case of the Sudan south of Egypt, when the English were forced to fight the inhabitants and menace the French before they made it their own. Sometimes settlers and traders went independently into East, West, and North Africa and cried to their governments for help when they encountered unfriendly Africans. Their governments generally responded quickly with sailors and soldiers and, once in, very often stayed to make the occupation permanent. Sometimes European powers assumed a protectorate over African territory to prevent other Europeans from grabbing it. It was not generally a planned affair; it just happened. But the desire was there, and when the opportunity for an additional acquisition arose and the politics were favorable, the European grabbed. An interesting tale of how European colonies and control began and expanded is the early history of the Republic of South Africa.

### South Africa: An Instance

The Portuguese were the first to round the southern tip of Africa in the 1400's. It was the Dutch, however, who first saw the potential use of this tip as a stopover and provisioning place for their ships engaged in trade with India. In 1652 the Dutch East India Company sent colonists there with instructions to grow vegetables and other foodstuffs for the ships traveling between Europe and the Indies. The colonists flourished and multiplied, and their settlement became known as the Cape Colony. English sailors, whose dogged courage and splendid seamanship made England mistress of the seas, had keen eyes for strategic spots along their sea lanes and were attracted by the colony. While warring with Napoleon during the early 1800's, England seized the Cape Colony. Many of the descendants of the original Dutch settlers resented this English occupation of their colony and showed their resentment by leaving. Loading all their belongings and their families into wagons, they journeyed into the lands north of the Cape to found new homes. It was at this time that they encountered the migrating Bantu-speaking people.

The Dutch settlers were known as Boers, which in the Dutch language means farmers, but they were not mere farmers. They were tough, rugged, and fearless men and women, and they were crack marksmen. The Boers were stubborn, and this stubbornness kept them going until they had conquered the wilderness and founded two states of their own, still known as the Transvaal and Orange states. They might have lived undisturbed, ruling and living as they wished, but gold was discovered in the Transvaal. This was a magnet that drew unwanted outsiders, especially the disliked English. To prevent a flood of foreigners from outnumbering them, the Boers closed their land to all outsiders. This action infuriated some Englishmen, especially those who thought in terms of empire. They wanted the English flag to fly from the Cape on the south to Egypt on the north. Such a one was Dr. Leander Jameson, who organized a band of raiders and attacked Boer territory. He was captured, but his action made the Boers even more suspicious that the English were planning to seize their territory.

Relations between the Boers and the English worsened and finally broke into open warfare. The war lasted from 1899 to 1902, and the Boers fought savagely and well. But the might of England was too great, and the Boers were conquered. Their states came under English rule, and the entire area became the Union of South Africa.

But the Boers soon won independence to govern themselves when England granted the Union self-rule in 1910. Because of their great numbers, the Boers had the majority of votes, which assured them control of the government. The English minority were grouped mostly in the areas known as Cape Province and Natal. Unfortunately, the Afrikaners, as the descendants of early Dutch and other European settlers were called, were stubborn in their determination to keep the Africans from participating in the government. They wanted to retain the rule of the white minority over the black majority. This policy has been carried to extremes in recent years by a segregation policy called *apartheid*. This policy has brought upon the Afrikaners the anger of all Africans and the condemnation of much of the world. The unbending will of the Afrikaners, which conquered a wilderness and aroused the admiration of the British, is still unbending in opposing equality for the Africans in their midst. A quality of man that may be a virtue

The Boer War was fought from 1899 to 1902 between Dutch farmers and British troops in South Africa. Right, troops outside Kimberley during the siege of that city. (Wide World photo)

in one time and circumstance may also be a fault in another era and situation.

1. What political systems and political attitudes had evolved prior to the coming of the Europeans?
2. Under what circumstances and by what methods did Europeans acquire land in Africa?
3. What conflicts developed between the Dutch and the British and the Dutch and the Africans in the Union of South Africa? What were the causes of these conflicts?

### Differing Colonial Attitudes

The colonial governments of the various European powers differed in their political approach and rule in Africa. In the English-ruled areas of East Africa, Southern and Northern Rhodesia, Nyasaland, and Kenya, and in other areas where the English settlers had come to farm, mine, and make their homes, there was a definite separation of the whites from the blacks. Hotels, clubs, restaurants, and residential areas patronized by the whites were prohibited to the Africans. The Africans were a ruled majority who had no share in government and who were not consulted about the management of local affairs. The society of these areas was made up of three layers: at the top was the small group of whites who ruled and owned the best resources of the land; in the middle were the Indian merchants and minor bureaucrats; and at the bottom were the native Africans.

In English-ruled areas of West Africa, where there were few English settlers and few Indians, there were only two classes: the few white administrators and the great African majority. But there was still inequality, for the best positions were always held by whites, and here, too, white establishments were often barred to the African.

The English, however, did not attempt to involve themselves too directly in the affairs of the African. For the most part they tried to rule indirectly through the traditional tribal African chiefs. The English did not seek officially or deliberately to change the customary patterns of African political society. They tried, rather, to keep these institutions intact so that there might be continued stability and fewer political problems to cope with. But it was inevitable that the traditional political systems of the African should be changed, for there was a new white ruler, and he was higher than the chief. This new ruler prohibited many actions and brought alien political institutions to which the African was compelled to adapt himself. All of these factors introduced changes into the African's way of thinking and into his social system.

The French practiced a policy which has generally been described as "assimilation." They wanted to absorb the African they ruled into their traditional culture and society. They wanted to make him French. For this reason they governed more directly than the English. It was the aim of the French to change the culture and the attitude of the African, not to perpetuate them. The French in general were not consciously race-prejudiced, so in official dealings and, on the whole, in social relation-

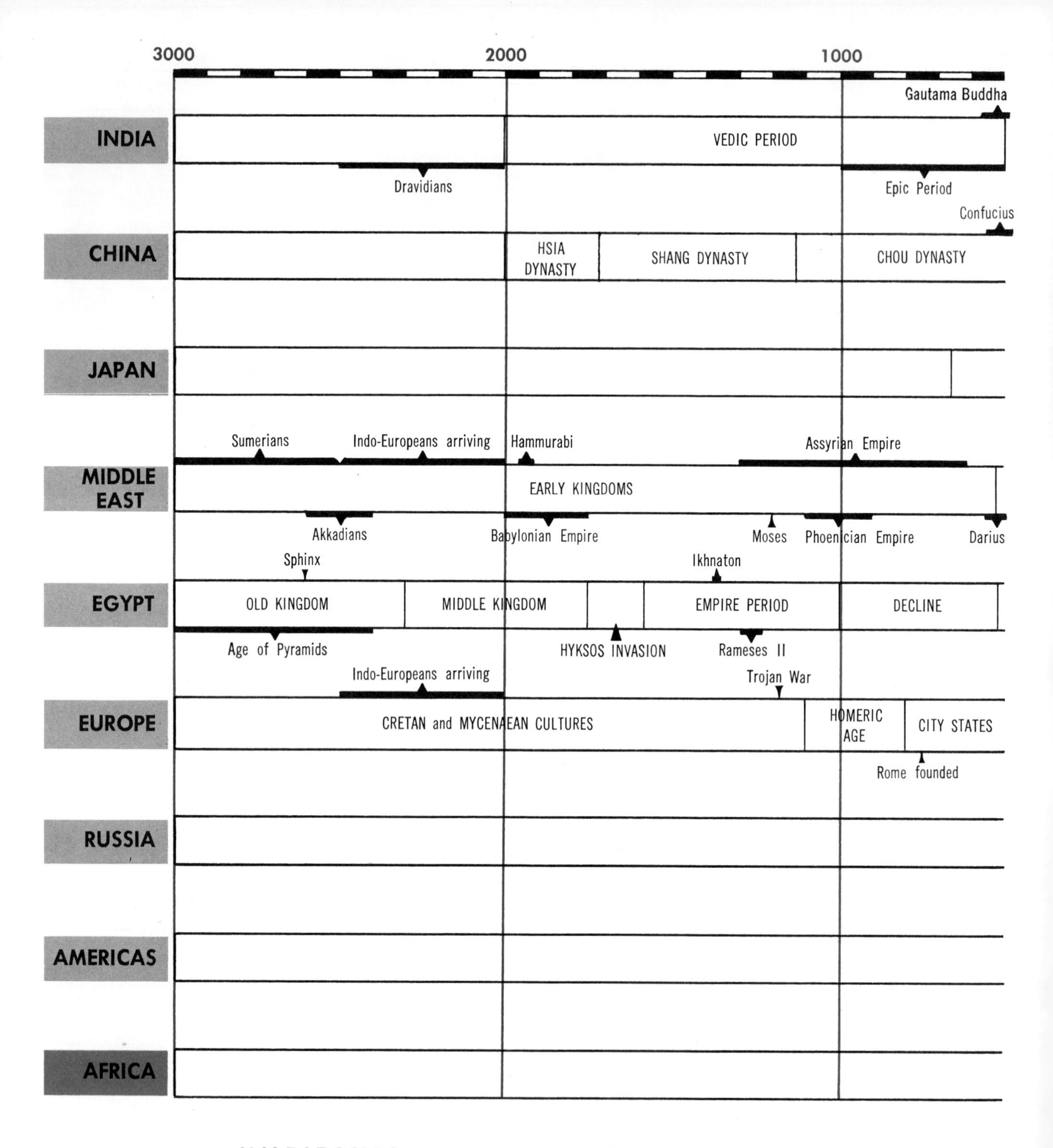


## MILESTONES

### AFRICA

B.C.

| | |
|---|---|
| 4000 | Africans begin cultivating land |
| 3000-2000 | Egyptians have contact with African Negroes |
| c. 1000-700 | Phoenicians visit and settle in North Africa |

A.D.

| | |
|---|---|
| c. 300s | Christianity introduced to Ethiopia |
| c. 300-1200 | Ghana empire flourishing |
| 600s | Arabs spread Islam to Africa |
| c. 1100-1400 | Empire of Mali flourishing |
| 1400s | Portuguese establish trading posts |
| 1486 | Diaz rounds tip of Africa |
| 1497 | Vasco da Gama sails along east coast on way to India |

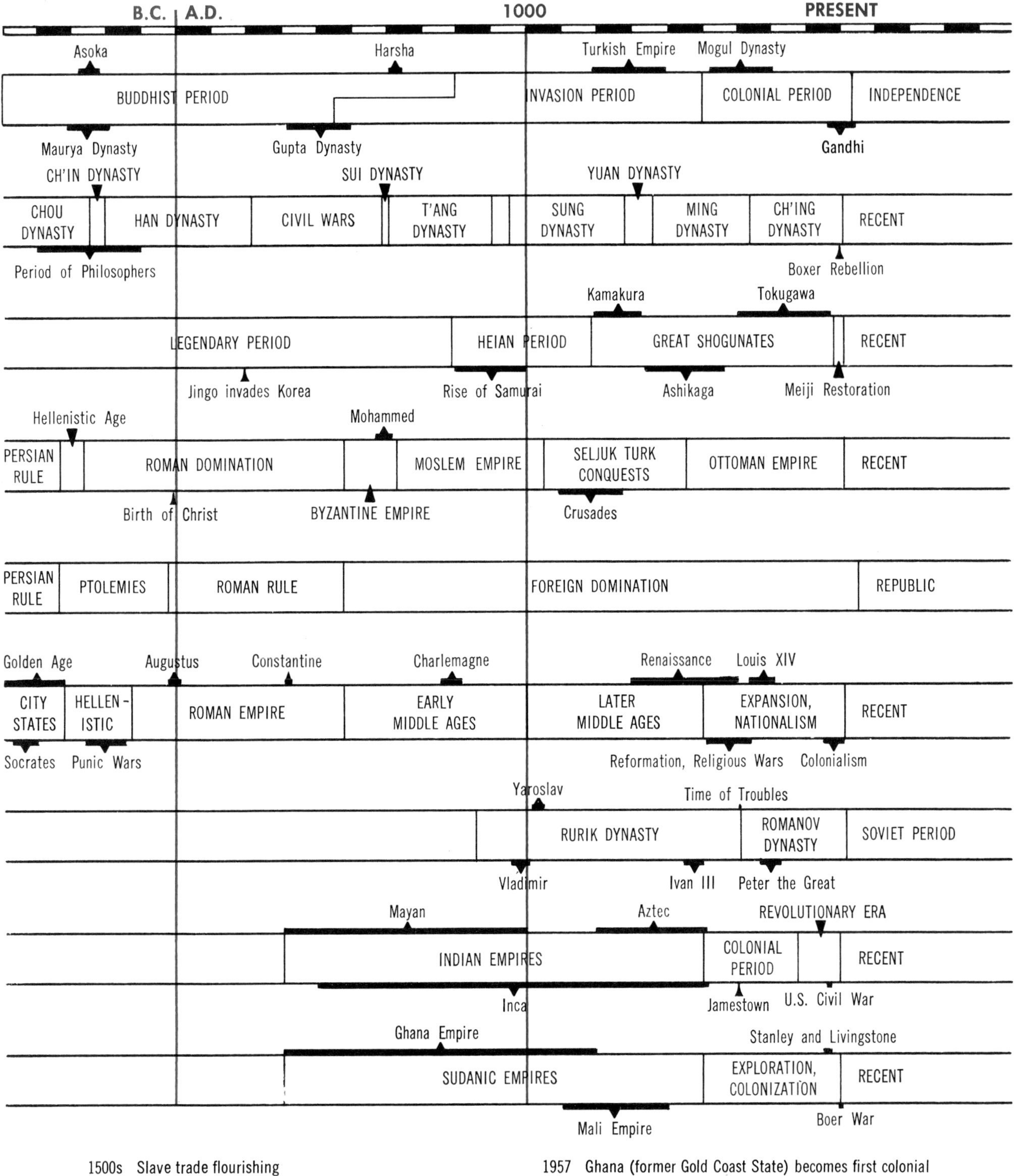


| | |
|---|---|
| 1500s | Slave trade flourishing |
| late 1700s | Sierra Leone: haven for freed slaves |
| 1847 | Liberia declared republic |
| 1850s | Livingstone crosses continent |
| 1870s | Stanley explores Africa |
| 1899-1902 | Boer War |
| 1910 | Union of South Africa granted self-rule |
| 1935 | Mussolini invades Ethiopia |
| 1957 | Ghana (former Gold Coast State) becomes first colonial area to win independence |
| 1958 | Guinea proclaimed independent republic |
| 1960 | Many African countries attain independence |
| 1963 | Formation of Organization of African Unity |

ships the color of the African's skin was not a mark against him. In French-ruled territories there was some success in training and assimilating an educated elite. The present African leaders of a number of the former French-ruled areas are very French in philosophy, language, and in general orientation. But the French did not assimilate the masses of Africans they governed—perhaps because the task was too great, perhaps because they feared to be outnumbered.

The French ruled a large expanse of West and Equatorial Africa, divided into two parts: French West Africa with its capital at Dakar, now the capital of the newly independent country of Senegal; and French Equatorial Africa with its capital at Brazzaville, now the capital of the independent country of the Republic of Congo. In addition, the French ruled under international mandate the two trust territories of Cameroun and Togoland, which are also located in West Africa and are now independent. Off the southeast coast of Africa was the French-ruled island of Madagascar, which is larger in size than France itself. It is now independent and is known as the Malagasy Republic.

The Belgians, who governed the vast, rich land called the Congo, were interested originally and primarily in taking what they could of the resources of the area and in making a profit. Gradually, however, they evolved a more paternalistic system and attitude which promised the Congolese a better economic future and a rising standard of living. In return, the Belgians demanded obedience and order. They wanted the Africans to have some education, but not beyond the elementary level. They thought of them as children to be cared for when good and to be punished when bad. It was the expectation of the Belgian rulers that their African subjects would remain in this condition of childhood. There was no official color bar in the Belgian Congo, but in practice there was segregation.

The Portuguese and the Spanish had little race prejudice, but neither did they have any inclination to advance the economic and educational levels of the Africans whom they governed. They exploited, but they returned little. Their colonial administration was rather slow-moving, stagnant, and lifeless. Neither great progress nor great violence marked Spanish and Portuguese rule. The Germans lost their few African colonies when they lost the First World War, and the few areas controlled by Italy were taken at the conclusion of the Second World War.

The Second World War witnessed a change in the attitude of the main colonial powers in Africa. The British and the French began to think more in terms of what they could do to assist the African in his economic, social, and political advancement. They began to give economic assistance to their colonies and to spur industrialization there. Chosen native leaders were taken into the colonial administration, and the Africans were given a greater representation in government. There was the thought that a developing African middle class might take some part in government at a vague time in the future. The British and French increased their budgets for education in the colonies and trained more Africans in technical skills. The better educated among the native Africans were sent abroad for advanced studies in universities and in colleges. An increased number of European professional men began going to the colonies to train the Africans in medicine, law, engineering, administration, agriculture, and education. Much of this change in thinking and in action was caused by the Africans themselves.

### The African Became Demanding

The ruling presence of the European in Africa drastically affected the political attitudes and aspirations of the African. Under European rule, the power of the chiefs and the old authorities was weakened. There began to arise a generation of Africans armed with new knowledge, new vigor, and new purpose. Even in the English colonies, where the policy was to rule indirectly, the powers of chiefs were ultimately limited. When a chief broke the rules of the European, he was deposed and another put in his place who was more pliable and less inclined to cause trouble. This action was not lost on the African people, and some, especially those being educated in the new knowledge of the European, held the chief's authority in contempt. The educated Africans started to plan for the day when they, with their new knowledge and new direction, would lead their people to a better material life and equality with all men.

These Africans had been trained and educated in European-run schools. They had learned of the poverty of the European during the Middle Ages, of the cultural advancement of his Renaissance, and of his industrial, agricultural, and scientific revolutions. They saw how the European, with his knowledge and machines, turned the raw materials of Africa and other parts of the world into usable wealth. The Africans learned, and they yearned. Some of them went to Europe and saw there the differences in standards of living between their own and that of the Europeans. They fingered cloth of quality, window-shopped the abundance of goods that could be bought, and gazed at enormous factories turning out a tremendous range of products quickly and abundantly. They saw houses and apartments which were luxurious by comparison with the homes of Africa but were ordinary in Europe. They walked the streets and saw that all were well-clothed by African standards. They entered restaurants where the food that was discarded would have fed many of their people. They rode in cars, buses, and trains that linked all parts of Europe together. The Africans freely entered any establishment, and there was no bar because of their color. They wondered. They thought. And they returned to Africa and tried to make their dreams a reality.

But there were few Africans who understood what these returned travelers were talking about. Those who had remained at home preferred to discuss the incidents of their ordinary routine of life. They could not share the dream of a new life. This smothering of their dreams caused the new Africans great depression and frustration. They sometimes wondered whether it might have been better to have known less and dreamed less. Many of them buried their dreams deep in the unconscious and tried to resign themselves to cooperating with the European administrators and accepting the limitations of their lives. Others, however, retained their determination to make of Africa a better land for all and patiently bided their time. They lived for the day when more Africans would begin to know what they knew, to yearn as they had yearned, and to will the purpose that they had willed. And it happened.

In the years after the First World War, more and more Africans attended schools, left the villages to work in the mines, and visited and lived in growing modern cities. The Second World War broke out, and Africa became more important as a producer of raw materials and a focus for commerce. It was a strategic staging area for troops, a home for airfields, and a recruitment station for troops. Africans worked the mines in greater numbers, increased the population of ports, became merchant seamen, and found themselves as soldier-tourists in various parts of the world. They saw what others before them had seen and began to desire as others before them had desired. From among them arose vigorous and demanding leaders who could speak so that many would understand. They were leaders who could dream aloud and find their dreams echoed in the minds of increasing numbers of other Africans. Time and opportunity had increased the number of Africans who dreamed and demanded more from the European for themselves. Their pressure was insistent and continuous, and the European rulers responded to their will. Since the Second World War great progress has been made in helping the Africans materialize their dreams of equality, an improved standard of living, and independence from colonial rule.

### Independence Came First to West Africa

Independence came to the African with a rush. It came first to the African of West Africa who was not forced to compete with white settlers and consequently was able to advance his political aspirations at a more rapid pace. Political parties were founded, and their leaders organized the people of the villages and the cities. The great numbers of these parties and their insistent cry for independence persuaded the colonial rulers to grant independence and retire from their rule as peacefully as possible. The territory governed by the British and known as the Gold Coast was the first of the colonial areas to win independence. In 1957 it became the independent country of Ghana and a member of the British-founded Commonwealth of Nations.

England had started earlier to prepare the people of Ghana for independence. Led by Kwame Nkrumah, a party had been established there called the Convention People's Party (CPP). This party propagandized actively for freedom from colonial rule. In 1951 the English gave Ghana home rule, and Nkrumah later became its first prime minister. Gradually, greater and greater powers were transferred to the new government until, in 1957, it became fully sovereign and independent.

The following year, in 1958, a French West African possession became the independent

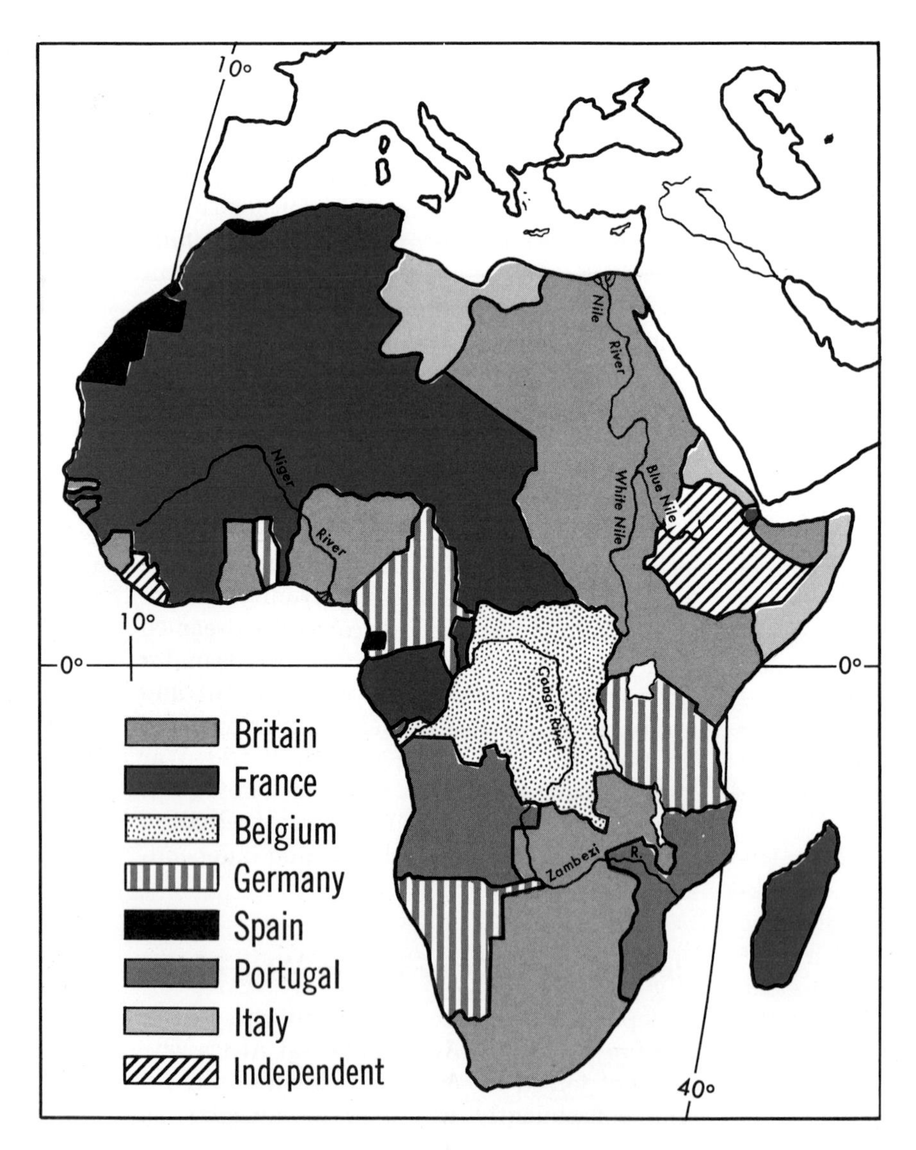


**Colonial Africa Before World War I**

Which European countries held the greatest territories in colonial Africa?

Republic of Guinea. In 1958 General de Gaulle was the premier of France, and it was his wish that all the French territories in Africa join together with France in what he called the French Community. They would have autonomy in their domestic affairs, but France would take the lead in foreign affairs and in defense.

A constitution was drawn up stating these provisions and submitted to a vote of the people of the French African territories. If any territory voted "Yes" it would continue to receive French economic aid. If any territory voted "No" it received independence immediately, but there would be no future help from France. The people of Guinea, under the leadership of Sékou Touré, were the only group to vote "No," and de Gaulle kept his promise. He gave them immediate independence, stripped the country of all French property there—even the desks of the administrators—and cut Guinea off from all French economic assistance. This action plunged the new country into a chaotic economic condition from which it has not yet fully recovered. Recently, relations between France and Guinea have improved, and the French have given aid to this former colony.

The remaining twelve territories, for example Malagasy Republic, Gabon, Senegal, Chad, Central African Republic, Congo, and others, although voting "Yes" to de Gaulle's proposals, continued to ask for more and more freedoms. Finally, by 1960 France had recognized the complete independence of all of them. But they also continued to be members of the French Community, and France has kept large economic aid flowing to them. The majority of these nations could not exist in a reasonable manner without this sustaining help from France.

In the meantime, England had also agreed to the independence of Nigeria, which has the largest population of the African countries, estimated at over 35,000,000 people. Among the influential Nigerian leaders who had formed parties were Sir Abubakar Tafawa Balewa, Dr. Nnamdi Azikiwe, and Obafemi Awolowo. These men and their followers cooperated with the British in building gradually an African constitutional form of government in the territory. Nigeria became a fully independent nation in 1960. The British UN trust territory of the Cameroons voted in the northern section to join with Nigeria, and in the southern part to join with the new country of Cameroun. This division was approved by the UN in 1961. Then the British territory of Sierra Leone became independent and a member of the Commonwealth of Nations in 1961. With the independence of Sierra Leone, the British had left in West Africa only Gambia. Then, in October 1963, Gambia became a self-governing country.

### Congo and Chaos

Independence began to come quickly, first in national affairs, and then completely in both national and international matters. Although it came peacefully in many areas, there was violence in others. Resentment long contained,

Below, Kwame Nkrumah, first president of Ghana. (Wide World photo)

King Baudouin of Belgium flew to Léopoldville for the formal ceremonies marking the Congo's attainment of independence in 1960. Above, King Baudouin is seen with Joseph Kasavubu, first president of the Republic of the Congo. (Wide World photo)

and a lack of preparation, made the Republic of the Congo an area of danger for the whites. Belgium had not adequately prepared the Congolese for the responsibilities of independence and self-government. Many of them had received a good primary school education, and thousands were trained to do skilled labor; under Belgian rule the Congolese had been presented with housing, pensions, and other economic benefits; but they had not been given the advantages of advanced education.

Only sixteen persons out of millions of Congolese in 1959 had a university education. Few had been permitted to leave the country, and fewer still to participate in running the country. The Belgian rulers had theorized that a minimum of education and a certain economic stability would preserve and continue their rule. They reasoned that it would be possible to prevent dangerous thoughts of independence and equality. But the Belgian theory did not work.

Pressures from within the country and pressures from the outside forced the Belgian government to grant independence to the Congo in a hurried fashion in 1960. The poorly organized administration of the new country broke down very quickly. Africans who had thought that independence meant an immediate economic heaven found themselves worse off than before. They rioted, stole, and killed, and the Congo became a jungle of man's unrestrained passions. The army, called the *Force Publique*, which the Belgian government had trained to help in policing the territory, was officered by Belgians. The native Congolese soldiers, trained to be tough, bullying, and fearless, began to revolt and demanded the ouster of their Belgian officers. The government agreed. All over the country the soldiers deposed their white officers and elected leaders from their own ranks. Discipline evaporated, and there were instances of atrocities. Law and order could no longer be maintained.

Belgian paratroopers returned to fight against the *Force Publique*, and Belgian planes bombed and strafed African villages. This led to Congolese reprisals on scattered white communities, and the crisis in the Congo widened and deepened. Divisions appeared between the central government and the provinces. Katanga Province, center of much of the exploited wealth of the Congo, declared itself virtually independent of the central government's authority.

Thus chaos came to this vast land which rivals India in size, and the United Nations moved in to try to maintain the peace and operate welfare services for the people. Belgians had fled by the thousands, and there were few left to man the public services and the machinery of the bureaucracy. The Congo Republic is still heaving from the shock and the chaos of those first days of independence. But the Congo, with its 14,000,000 people, is gradually becoming the scene of law and order.

1. Describe the British system of colonial government and the British attitude toward the native African. How did the system vary in different areas? Give specific examples.

2. What did the French mean by "assimilation"? Were they successful in this policy? If not, why?
3. How did European control undermine the African authorities? Did one European colonial system affect African authority less than the others? If so, which one?

## The Continuing Struggle for Independence and Equality

The fires of independence and equality were not confined to West Africa and the Congo but also swept to East Africa. Sudan declared its independence of joint Egyptian and British rule in 1955 and this independence was approved by Egypt and Britain in January, 1956. Former British Somaliland became independent in 1960 and then united with a former Italian colony to form the nation of Somalia. Tanganyika, a former trusteeship territory governed by England under a mandate of the United Nations, became independent in December of 1961. Uganda became independent in 1962, and the exotic island of Zanzibar became independent in 1963.

But independence has not come easily in parts of East Africa. There are areas where the European settled rather heavily and where inequality between the races has aroused hatred and bloodshed. The Europeans were and are determined to protect their property and what they regard as their homes. The African is just as determined to have independence and equality. Both groups are prepared to fight if necessary to accomplish their diverging goals. One of the bloodiest African protests against the white settler was the uprising of the Mau Maus against the whites of Kenya.

It was in 1953 that a secret society was formed among several of the African tribes in Kenya. The tribal group known as the Kikuyu were the majority. It was the intent of this society to terrorize the whites and to obtain more land and more freedom for its member tribes. No one knows the exact numbers of the Mau Mau, but at one time the British had jailed 60,000 of those suspected of belonging to the society. The leaders of this secret society exacted a terrible oath from all who joined the society, and many were forced to join whether they liked it or not. Those who refused were killed in a horrible manner.

Until the Mau Maus were finally crushed and many killed, the white settlers and their families lived in constant fear. Settlers were often butchered in their sleep, at their work, or while eating. The Europeans could not trust their African servants, who might be Mau Maus or under the terror of that group. Men and women worked their farms with guns strapped to their waists. Even when visiting the city of Nairobi, the capital of Kenya, they carried guns to the shops and while walking the streets. It was like a scene from the wild West of America in the second half of the 1800's. It was also a lesson that few forgot, and its legacy of fear still gnaws deep in the vitals of the white settlers of East Africa.

But independence came to Kenya despite the protests of the white settlers, for England was determined that the African would eventually rule in the former English colonies. African ministers were taken into the government, and in 1961 the Kenya National Union Party won a majority of the membership in the legislature. Kenya became independent on December 12, 1963.

The white settlers of Northern and Southern Rhodesia were and are as bitterly opposed to independence under the rule of an African majority as their fellow whites in Kenya. There is great mineral wealth in the Rhodesias. Northern Rhodesia has copper, manganese, gold, zinc, and other resources. Southern Rhodesia exports to the United States around 50 per cent of the chrome ore used by this country. In addition there are gold, asbestos, coal, and other resources. The center of resistance to African rule is in Southern Rhodesia, where there are about 175,000 European settlers who have developed an extensive farming, dairying, and cattle industry. They fear that the fruits of their labor will be taken from them if the African comes to power.

Beginning in 1953 the territories of Northern and Southern Rhodesia and Nyasaland were joined in a federation, but the Africans resented it and regarded it as a device to obstruct their march to independence. African pressures were felt more strongly in Northern Rhodesia and Nyasaland, for they were protectorates of England, and there was more freedom of political action in these two territories than in Southern Rhodesia which is self-governing. In 1963 a series of conferences in Great Britain led to the dissolving of the Federation on January 1, 1964, and the new beginning of three separate states. Nyasaland has taken the new name of Malawi (Dawn). Northern Rhodesia has adopted the new name of Zambia. Southern Rhodesia has retained its former name. Malawi and Zambia are under the control of the African majority, but Southern Rhodesia continues under the rule of the minority whites.

Farther south, surrounded by the territory of the Republic of South Africa, are three small English-controlled territories: the colony of Basutoland and the protectorates of Bechuanaland and Swaziland. There is a gradual transition to a form of self-rule in these small territories also. The English have embarked upon a policy of eventually granting independence to all of their former African possessions. They have been trying to carry out this policy with a minimum of friction between whites and blacks in East Africa. But emotional questions often burst forth with an intensity of passion, and the English are trying to solve them peacefully with that practical genius for which they are famed.

The most aggravating and troublesome problem in Africa, and a potential scene of exploding violence, is the Republic of South Africa. Here live around 3,000,000 whites, 500,000 Asians, almost 11,000,000 Africans called Bantus, and about 1,500,000 persons of mixed African and European ancestry called Coloureds. Of the whites, the descendants of the Boers are in the majority, and they control the government. These whites of Dutch ancestry are generally known today as Afrikaners. They have instituted a rigid system of segregation, or *apartheid*, which keeps whites, Asians, Coloureds, and Bantus separated from each other. The groups are separated especially in housing, education, and job opportunity and advancement. Whites do employ the others in various capacities and need their labor, but the majority of the population, the non- or mixed-white, are not represented in the government and do not in any sense enjoy equality. This has brought upon the government of South Africa criticism from both inside and outside the country and has particularly infuriated the African elsewhere in Africa.

The ruling group, however, has not yielded in its intention. In an effort to bring pressure on the South African government, many Asians and Africans have instituted boycotts of South African goods throughout the world. South African trade with many of these people is small, however, and the boycotts are only partial and ineffective. As yet this action has not resulted in any official change of purpose and action on the part of the Afrikaners.

South Africa is a country rich in minerals and has a good industry and a good communications network. Its agricultural production is excellent. It is one of the richest countries in the world in the output of gold and diamonds and also has uranium, coal, copper, tin, iron, lead, and other minerals. South Africa alone has over forty per cent of the total production of minerals in all Africa. The white South Africans have much at stake here, and they fear that they will lose much of their wealth if the Bantus should obtain a majority rule in South Africa.

But there is the moral question of the rights of man involved here as well as an economic question. An ideal solution requires that political and economic as well as human rights be secured. This is, of course, easy to state but difficult to apply to the specific situation. But there is no man-made problem that cannot be man-solved. Some have predicted a volcano of destruction in South Africa unless the ruling cliques soften the rigidity of their purpose and permit the flowering of freedom in this republic.

1. Identify the Mau Mau movement. When and where did it operate? Who were its followers?

What were the factors which led to its development?

2. Identify the areas in Africa where serious conflicts are likely to break out. What factors are the causes of current tensions?

## Unity and Disunity

For those Africans who have them, independence and equality have not yet brought the fullness of economic rewards nor the complete unity they desire within their borders and their continent. The boundaries of African nations are generally the same artificial boundaries that were imposed by the European powers when they controlled the greatest part of the continent. These boundaries cut across the old tribal groups and often include rival tribes. These divisions are still plaguing the independent African leaders of today. Ethiopia and Somalia have disputed their borders; Morocco has asserted that the independent country of Mauritania is really her territory; and Ghana has border problems with Togo. Groupings of African nations also reveal their various differences.

Groups of African nations have formed alliances which differed in their approach to the economic, social, and political problems of their continent and of the world. At Casablanca, in 1961, Morocco, Mali, Algeria, Guinea, Ghana, and Egypt formally joined in an association. They are often referred to as the "Casablanca Powers." They desired the political unification of all Africa, indicated their suspicion of the continuing colonial ambitions of the former Western overlords of Africa, declared their intention to foil these ambitions everywhere in Africa, and sought greater independence from these former colonial governments. Their revolutionary tendencies and their neutral approach to the problems of the Cold War brought them applause and favor from the Communist Bloc.

At Tananarive, in September of 1961, thirteen former French states joined in a union called the Afro-Malagasy Union (U.A.M.). They were more conservative than the Casablanca Powers in attempting to solve their many problems. They sought to maintain their close ties, especially in the economic field, with France and other countries of Europe; and they were not really concerned with the formation of an African "superstate." The countries of this Union are frequently referred to as the "Brazzaville group."

Another larger grouping of African countries, consisting of the Brazzaville group, Nigeria, Liberia, Ethiopia, Sierra Leone, and others, met in Monrovia in May 1961. They advocated a more evolutionary and gradual "unity of aspirations and actions" among African nations. They desired to develop along practical, peaceful ways toward the economic and political well-being they all sought. At Lagos, in 1962, the members of this "Monrovia group" approved the charter of an Inter-African and Malagasy States Organization (I.A.M.O.). The approving countries represented over 100,000,000 independent Africans, and their aim was an organization that would represent their region of Africa much as the Organization of American States (O.A.S.) represented the interests of American nations. This aim was achieved in organization and in spirit when the heads of the Casablanca Powers, the Brazzaville group, the Monrovia group, and of other African nations met in Addis Ababa in May 1963 and began the Organization of African Unity (O.A.U.), which brought them all together in one regional organization.

In opening this meeting, the Emperor of Ethiopia reminded his listeners that there were still great differences among them and that the formal union they sought must come gradually. To speed up this transition period between the disunity of the present and the formal union of the future, he advocated that they "seize on those areas of agreement and exploit them to the fullest. . . ." Although there was some disagreement from those who wanted union immediately, an agreement was reached which followed to a large degree the spirit and content of the Lagos Charter. The O.A.U. Charter was formally registered at the United Nations in October 1963, and the O.A.U. is now recognized as one of the great regional organizations of the world. The Administrative Secretariat of the O.A.U. is located at Addis Ababa in Ethiopia.

The O.A.U. has gained the adherence of all independent African states, and it is the wish of many that the charters of all former groupings of African states be abolished. The members of the U.A.M., however, have indicated that they prefer to retain the advantages of their union until they see how the new organization will work out. In response to criticism, however, they have replaced the old name of U.A.M. with the new organizational name of Afro-Malagasy Union for Economic Cooperation (UAMCE).

Some Africans as well as non-Africans feel that eventually there will be about four or five regional groupings of autonomous states within Africa. In April 1964, the new island country of Zanzibar united with Tanganyika. Perhaps such groups will evolve a cooperation among themselves in customs, in trade, in economic development, and in other areas. No one, however, foresees that this will come about quickly.

Many Africans believe that there is a common African personality, and that this personality is deeper and more basic than the differences which separate independent nations. They claim that only in the unification of all Africa can this African personality flower and bring prosperity, health, and happiness to all who are African. It is these Africans who speak and yearn for Pan-African cooperation which will tie them together in a secure, mighty, unified force.

1. Identify the two rival alliances which seek to organize Africa's relations with the rest of the world. Name the countries in each group, and discuss their general orientation.
2. What major political evolution has taken place in Africa in recent years? Has this evolution been completed?

## Conclusion

The African has evolved politically from an exclusive loyalty toward chief and tribe to the larger loyalty of nation, which includes a diversity of tribes and cultures. He is no longer merely a tribesman; he is also a nationalist. The pattern of government in most of the new African republics has followed the examples of the former European rulers, especially the British and the French. The new national patriotism, however, has not entirely cut off the ties of the African to the tribe, the family, and the culture which bred him, nursed him, and supported him in his making of new nations. Any real independence must be an African independence based upon clinging native traditions as well as the political contributions of the European. The form may be European, but the spirit that gives it life and attitude still emerges from the old earth of Africa. The past is yet living within the political structure of the African who is working now to harmonize his past and his present.

In the countries where the African is now independent there is no longer a problem of equality. He is the ruler in these countries now, and he is equal with everybody who lives there. In the areas that are not independent, there is still a problem of inequality between the white and the black. The African is fighting to erase the barriers that make him unequal. The problem of inequality is most acute at this time in the Republic of South Africa.

In countries where he is independent and in areas where he is yet subject, the African is also fighting to lift his standard of living. He has seen the good things of life and he wants them for himself. He is as demanding of his own leaders as he is of foreign masters in seeking to better his livelihood. One of the greatest, if not the greatest, of the problems facing the newly independent countries of Africa is this question of raising the standard of living. This burning problem has political overtones of great significance.

Socialism has great appeal to many of the Africans, for they see in it the possibility that everyone might reap the benefits of their earth, and not merely the chosen or lucky few. It is for this reason that Communism is not as scorned in Africa as it is in many countries of the world. In fact, many of the African countries would take aid from the USSR, China, and other Communist countries if it were offered. Guinea was given much help from the USSR, and a number of Communist Chinese technicians have worked there since the country gained independence. Both Russia and China, as well as other Communist-bloc nations, have taken many Africans to their countries for training, education, and indoctrination. In the French-governed areas of Africa a number of French Communists worked long before independence to make the African a Communist in ideology and in action. Communism is a force in Africa, although its economic appeal has been stunted somewhat by the large economic aid given by France and Britain to their former territories, by international assistance, and by aid from the United States.

The African is beset by all the political currents that now sweep the earth, whether of neutrality, of Communism, or of the democracy of the West. With independence and equality the African has also taken the responsibility of governing and directing his country in the manner he thinks best for all the people. At present, he is generally following the pattern of Western democracy as taught him by his former European governors, but he is also prepared to change should he not find it suitable for the maturing of his human needs.

## SUMMING UP THE CHAPTER

A. Identify or locate the following and tell why they are important.

| | |
|---|---|
| Afrikaners | Kwame Nkrumah |
| Boers | Monrovia States |
| Brazzaville Group | Nairobi |
| Casablanca Powers | Pan-Africanism |
| Charles de Gaulle | Sékou Touré |
| CPP | The Orange |
| French Community | Transvaal |

B. Define or explain the following terms, relating them to this chapter.

| | |
|---|---|
| apartheid | protectorate |
| assimilation | self-rule |
| federation | trust territory |

C. Chapter review questions.

1. How did the methods by which Europeans gained and controlled territory in South Africa compare with methods used elsewhere in Africa?
2. Compare the various systems of European colonial administration in Africa. Which system do you feel best prepared the African peoples for independence?
3. What changes did World War II bring to Africa?
4. What new aspirations did the African acquire from his European education and travels? How did he react when he found that these were out of his reach without independence?
5. Compare the French and British policies toward the independence of their colonies. How did the African colonies react to their respective policies?
6. Identify the "three layers" of much of African society. What function does each perform? Is this pattern typical for all of Africa?

D. Questions for discussion.

1. What motives impelled the Europeans to colonize Africa? To what extent was colonization the result of competition among the European powers? Of power politics?
2. Through whom did the English rule their African colonies? Compare this colonial administration with the Roman rule of Europe and the Mediterranean.
3. How did French policy differ from English policy in regard to race and native cultures? Which policy do you think was more realistic and successful?
4. What do you believe might have been the reasons that led the colonial powers to change their policies so radically following World War II?
5. The policies of European colonial powers broke down the old political authorities of the tribe and the family. How did this bring about the rise of new leaders and centers of power? How did it lead to eventual collapse of authority of the European powers themselves?

E. Projects for groups or individuals.

1. On an outline map of Africa, shade in different colors the territories ruled by the various European powers from the late 1800's up to 1960. It may be necessary to draw a series of maps, as some of the colonies changed hands.
2. Point out historical events behind current news stories about Africa.
3. Prepare a report on Spain's colonies in Africa. How and when were these colonies acquired, and what is their status today?

# SUMMING UP THE UNIT

### *Drawing together the main themes*

1. How have events in Africa shown the crucial importance of education to self-government?
2. Compare the changes which have taken place in Africa in the past fifty years with those which took place in Japan during the last half of the nineteenth century. In what ways is this a useful comparison?
3. What explanations can you give for the primitive culture of Africa at the time the Europeans first came there? What conditions which led to the advancement of civilization in other cultures had not been present in Africa?
4. Why did the African not resist the European colonists and slavers?
5. How would you explain the close ties that exist between some former colonial powers and their former colonies? What African nations maintained close ties with their former masters after independence? To what extent are such ties primarily economic? To what extent are they cultural?
6. Describe the process by which Europe came to dominate Africa. How similar was this to the European role in the Middle East? In Asia? In the Americas? What general patterns of colonialism emerge? What would explain the differences?
7. It is often said that the American Revolution has served as a model for other colonial revolutions. What influence do you believe the American Revolution had on the nations of Africa?
8. Those territories in which the number of white Europeans was large in proportion to the number of Negro Africans were the last to gain their independence. What does this fact tell you about the nature of racial conflict? Can you demonstrate with statistics and facts that relative proportions of different races are a factor in racial conflicts elsewhere?
9. Do you believe the violence of the African's struggle for freedom from European domination has been justified? What other ways might have been used to awaken the Europeans to the situation in Africa? What are the long-term effects of such violence?
10. What has been the place of the African nations in the struggle between the free world and the Communist nations? Why is neutralism so attractive to the African? What is meant when the nations of Africa are referred to as "uncommitted"?
11. Who were the leaders in putting an end to the African slave trade?
12. Describe the chief natural resources of Africa and relate them to the geography, economy, and society of the continent.
13. What are some of the various ethnic and cultural groups whose members might be called *Africans?* What does this tell you about the danger of confusing a race with a nationality?
14. Trace the course of the Nile from its headwaters to the Mediterranean. What major sources flow into this river, and where do they originate?
15. In what ways did African slaves enrich the cultures of the Americas?
16. In the past, how has the Sahara acted as a cultural, racial, and economic dividing line between the northern part of Africa and sub-Saharan Africa? Is the importance of the Sahara as a barrier any less today?
17. Given that only limited areas of African land are suitable for intensive agriculture, what do you see as the economic position and role of Africa in the future? Aside from human resources, what natural resources compensate for the lack of agricultural land in Africa?

### *Projects for individuals or groups*

1. Read a biography of David Livingstone or Henry Stanley.
2. Prepare a report for classroom presentation on one or more of the African tribes. In your report, be sure to cover such topics as geographical habitat, language spoken, customs, livelihood, political systems, and art. If possible, bring pictures to show the class.
3. Look through several travel books on Africa. Compare a number of passages in the books to see if any of them describe a picture of Africa that may not be accurate.
4. Read an account of the slave trade and report on it to the class.
5. Read Alan Paton's novel *Cry, The Beloved Country* and report to the class on this white South African's view of the treatment of the Bantu by the Afrikaner authorities.
6. Conduct a panel discussion on the subject of justice as it applies to the problems of independence and equality in Africa.

## FURTHER READINGS

AWOLOWO, OBAFEMI, *AWO: The Autobiography of Chief Obafemi Awolowo.* Cambridge U., 1960, also paperback. Reveals the thinking and emotions of an African leader today.

BOWLES, CHESTER, *Africa's Challenge to America.* U. of Calif., 1957. A prominent American's view of the relationship between Africa and America.

CARTER, GWENDOLEN, *Independence for Africa.* Praeger, 1960, paperback. Africa's drive for independence, its acceptance by the outside world, and the conflicts arising from these are explained.

COHEN, SIR ANDREW, *British Policy in Changing Africa.* Northwestern U., 1959. The British still play an important role in Africa.

DAVIDSON, BASIL, *Lost Cities of Africa.* Little, 1959. Africa before the coming of the European.

———, *Black Mother, The Years of the African Slave Trade.* Little, 1961. An unhappy but important event in the history of Africa.

EATON, JEANETTE, *David Livingstone, Foe of Darkness.* Morrow, 1947. The adventurous story of a man who was an explorer, missionary, and enemy of slavery.

FLEMING, EDITH, *Africa and Its Peoples.* Chicago Natural History Museum, 1958. A booklet about some of the African's cultures.

FORMAN, BRENDA-LU AND HARRISON, *The Land and People of Nigeria.* Lippincott, 1964.

GATTI, ATTILIO AND ELLEN, *The New Africa.* Scribner's, 1960. Good general work.

GOLLOMB, JOSEPH, *Albert Schweitzer: Genius of the Jungle.* Vanguard, 1949. Schweitzer is an example of the heights of goodness to which man can climb.

GUNTHER, JOHN, *Inside Africa.* Harper, 1955. A vivid picture of all of Africa in the 1950's.

HAILEY, LORD, *African Survey,* rev. ed. Oxford U., 1957. Probably the best of the general reference works on Africa.

JUDD, PETER, ed., *African Independence.* Dell, 1962, paperback. Excellent collection of material by various authors.

KAULA, EDNA MASON, *The Land and People of Tanganyika.* Lippincott, 1963.

MERRIAM, ALAN P., *Congo: Background of Conflict.* Northwestern U., 1961. The problems of a populous and potentially great African nation.

MODUPE, PRINCE, *I Was a Savage.* Harcourt, 1958. Autobiography of an African, pointing out the conflicts which result in an exposure to Western ways and education.

OTTENBERG, SIMON AND PHOEBE, *Cultures and Societies of Africa.* Random, 1960. African cultures are many and varied.

PATON, ALAN, *Cry, The Beloved Country.* Scribner's, 1948, also paperback.

———, *The Land and People of South Africa,* rev. ed. Lippincott, 1964. These two books give in well-chosen words a feeling and knowledge of the people, land, and problems of South Africa.

RUTHERFORD, PEGGY, ed., *African Voices: An Anthology of Native African Writing.* Vanguard, 1959; Grosset, paperback. It is necessary to listen to the Africans speak if there is to be an understanding of the African.

SALE, J. KIRK, *The Land and People of Ghana.* Lippincott, 1963.

SELIGMAN, C. G., *Races of Africa,* 3rd ed., Oxford U., 1957. A valuable book about the people of Africa.

WINGERT, PAUL, *Sculpture of Negro Africa.* Columbia U., 1950. The African is an artist and this books tells of his artistry.

# EPILOGUE

FROM SHADOWY DEEPS of time man has slowly crawled and walked into the here and now. His journey was a long and painful one. Death was often his escort and survival a daily question. During the murky, distant ages of his slow maturing, man competed with animals better equipped with fang and claw and strength than he to defend themselves against hungry predators. The destroying forces of nature—the storming winds, the blaze of the sun, the sudden flood, the creeping coldness—all took their toll of his numbers. Many of his kind died, struck down by hunting animals or the rages of nature. But there were always some who survived to pass along their experience and to mix their varieties in new breeds.

Man learned to shelter himself against the fearful elements of nature and to protect himself with sharpened stone, with club and spear, or bow and arrow against the charge of animals seeking food. With these weapons he became one of the dangerous hunters of the plain and forest, and his food became more plentiful. And the shelter, the weapons, and the greater supply of food permitted more of his species to survive and to multiply.

But man's existence was still precarious, for he was yet a wanderer of the earth who must pursue the wandering animals he hunted or search for the places nature favored with her berries, nuts, and fruit. Then he discovered that if he seeded the earth with grain and watered it, there would emerge fields of food sufficient to feed himself, his family, and more. And when he could do this, he stopped wandering, and his numbers grew to fill villages, towns, and cities. Man's primary problem was then changed into the question of how he could live in some kind of harmony with groups of his own fast-breeding kind. He had learned to survive the forces of nature; now he was forced to adjust himself to the forces of society. He has found this adjustment a most difficult task ever since.

Learning to live in a close and continuous relationship with other men required the individual to place certain restrictions upon his actions, his movement, and even his words. Only in this way was it possible to have a measure of freedom from disorder and from conflicts. The social life of man could create a dangerous jungle even as nature and the wild animal had. Living in a complex society often proved to be a challenge to survival.

Through trial and error, men evolved ways of living together with the least possible friction, and thus began a social system. In order to obtain a measure of security and stability, groups of men gave their approval to an authority who commanded their obedience, and thus began a political system. A legal system grew because laws were necessary if groups of people were to live together. In the early days, and even in much of the earth today, farming was the chief means of livelihood. As agriculture developed, it became possible for fewer men to support the populations of towns by working in the fields. Thus, as some men were freed from the work of cultivating the land or hunting animals for food, they began to make their livelihood by providing services and products that others needed. A division of labor grew up, and a new kind of economic system.

Man learned about this time to express his thoughts in a written language as well as the spoken one he already had, and he became a recorder of passing events. He also used his new-found writing ability to express the depths of his thoughts, the wonder of nature, and the endless varieties of human behavior. He sought to express himself in sculpture, in painting, in building, and in other forms of art, and he started a flow of creativity which has never ceased. Man had long believed in a spiritual world which he did not fully comprehend, and he began to deepen his spiritual understanding. Religions became important to his total life. And all of these ideas, actions, and attitudes evolved to shape the complex pattern of man today.

## The Continuing Quest

In all the successive periods of his historical life, man produced civilizations which are monuments to his need to change himself and his surroundings. Often his attempts were successful, and these are listed among man's greatest triumphs—great masterpieces of art, the achievements of technology, the highest accomplishments of the human mind. But man's attempts to improve or change himself and his surroundings were also sometimes failures—and the ravaged bodies and war-scarred landscape of our planet have too often testified to these failures. On every continent of the earth there is evidence of one kind or another of man's continuing drive to know and of his passion to create upon the foundations of knowledge. Experiments with nature, scrutiny of the heavens, creation of works of art, and speculations about his own nature and that of the world have all played a part in making the man of today.

The pace of man's restless searching has grown faster and faster. In the past fifty years, greater scientific advances have been made than in all the previous thousands of years of man's recorded history. This increasing pace of man's advance can be seen in examples based upon the lives of a few of the characters in our story of man. Napoleon had no better roads than those used by Julius Caesar, and the early nineteenth-century French general could travel no faster than ancient Romans in their horse-drawn chariots. Yet within one long lifetime, shortly afterwards, Queen Victoria of England saw the development of rapid travel by railways and the beginning of man's attainment of flight in airplanes. A few years later, when Sun Yat-sen began his creation of modern China, the airplane was just a toy; yet he lived to see it becoming a threatening instrument of war and a promising means of rapid transportation. And within only a few short years the atomic bomb was developed, with its threat of world-wide destruction and its faint promise of atomic power that could bring hope of a better life to much of the world's population.

The rapid advance of the physical sciences that began in the last century has continued at a dizzying pace. The study of tiny particles of matter has shown that the atom, once thought to be the smallest indivisible unit, is a complex structure made up of even smaller particles. As the nature of these particles comes to be better understood, man may gain an entirely new concept of matter and the universe. And as the secrets of the reproduction of cells are studied, man comes to have a better understanding of genetics. With such an understanding, it might be possible to control or alter the nature of species of animals or plants at will.

Man's understanding sometimes approaches very near to the processes that make life in its simplest forms possible. New drugs and antibiotics are giving man a control of many diseases that formerly took a great toll of his numbers, and the span of human life has been lengthened by many years in much of the world. Some nations are already faced with the numerous problems of an ageing population. And the quest is not limited to the tiny planet of Earth. Rockets have probed the moon and the nearest planets. Very soon, rockets may be embarking upon the first manned flights to our nearest neighbors in space.

Nor is man's quest limited simply to seeking further understandings in the physical sciences and technology. Along with this rapid progress in the sciences, new philosophical and social problems have arisen. It has become more apparent than ever that our understanding of man's spiritual and social nature is necessary if we are to survive as a species. Thus, there has come to be a new and greater need for humanists—men who will make science and learning the tools of man and use them to fulfill man's purposes. Man has needs beyond those that can be measured in physical terms. These needs must be understood and met before man can reach his fullest and noblest possible attainments.

Today men of various faiths are seeking to lessen the doctrinal antagonisms which have kept them in a tense relationship for centuries. There are those who dare prison and violence to bring respect to the different races of man. Through newspapers, magazines, books, TV, and radio, people are made aware from hour to hour, and day by day, of the immediate events in most of the world which are of interest and significance. Thus, every advance in transportation, communications, and understanding of man's innermost nature has brought a greater realization of the links that bind all men together.

### The Challenge

We have seen that man today is engaged in making a new world for himself and his children. He is changing his physical, social, and cultural surroundings at breakneck pace, and, unthinking, he is frequently leaving a great wreckage in his wake. And this is his challenge. How can he advance without destroying? How can he change without losing that which is precious to his being? How can he create, as he must, without bringing pain and unhappiness to others?

Every advance that man makes brings with it new challenges and often overwhelming responsibilities. Man prepares to go to the moon —and possibly to pit it with new craters of war. He looks through telescopes at worlds so far away that they have perished before their light reached earth—but with the naked eye man often cannot see his brothers on earth dying near him in rat-plagued slums. On his planet, which is less than the point of a pin in the universe, man often acts with the pride of a god. The Asian, African, European, and American are within seconds of each other by radio and telephone—yet they remain separated by centuries of misunderstanding and ignorance. One part of the world erects monuments of swollen garbage cans to its magnificent agricultural production; in another part of the world, thousands die of starvation. While some of the most primitive men are still struggling to emerge from the stone ages, other men consult psychiatrists to try to solve some of the problems that have risen in a complex civilization. And even today most men still persist in separating the ills of the mind from the ills of the body and the society of which the mind is a part. "Civilized" men made reckless by anger and heedless by greed have often turned their machines into instruments of destruction and misery. And in some cases, the sleek, efficient machines that mine coal, make steel and manufacture other goods, and perform computations have not only replaced men but have also condemned those they replaced to a shabby and unrewarding existence.

The remarkable development of automation is an example of one way in which man's cultural development has lagged behind technological advances—resulting in disquiet, insecurity, and sorrow for many.

Machines can, indeed, do many jobs more quickly, more efficiently, and more cheaply than man, and most people will admit that our fantastic machines represent another great leap in the technological progress of man. They are building cars, mining coal, making steel, analyzing statistics, computing the flow of shipping, calculating the grading of highways, picking the spots for television commercials, predicting economic and political trends, selecting personnel, ferreting out income tax evaders, caring for much of the banker's business, and doing thousands of other jobs formerly done by man. Some computers repair themselves; and they are doing in seconds and in minutes tasks which would require many men days, months, or years to complete. And all acknowledge that the era of automation is just beginning.

But what about the frustrations, the fears, the insecurities, the hopelessness of the men who have been cast out by the machine from the only work they know? Thousands of former coal miners in West Virginia, Kentucky, Illinois, and Pennsylvania do not look with friendliness upon the machines that have reduced their lives to useless puttering and the weekly dole. And workers in other industries have also found themselves replaced by machines or struggling in unequal competition with them. The machines that man's inventiveness first created to make life easier have brought problems to challenge him.

The machines that do work have not been alone in bringing problems. Other inventions that man has created have also contributed to his difficulties. First printing, then radio, and later TV opened up seemingly endless possibilities for communication and education. But the same presses that could be used to print worthwhile books could also be used to produce materials not fit to print. Television has given to millions of people a look at far-off lands, at history in the making, and has also brought them the pleasure of fine entertainment. But the same television that can be so useful and entertaining has also exposed the eyes and minds of the susceptible to vulgarity, dishonesty, and scenes of crime, violence, and the worst that is in man. Have our media of mass communication—printing and television—tainted the minds of the young or encouraged crimes and abnormal behavior? There are those who insist that they have. Our communications media have a great potential for educating man and bringing him constructive entertainment. Man himself will decide whether they help him to advance or to decline. This is one of his great challenges.

An almost unbelievable control of the mind and the physical environment has also been made possible through the advances of science and technology. Propaganda has been developed into an artful skill which can be used to sway and control the minds of masses of people. Modern chemists have also produced drugs which have strange and powerful effects upon the nervous system and the mind. Captured soldiers and political prisoners have been "brainwashed" so that their freedom of will was weakened. The more that is understood of the human mind, the more we realize its weaknesses as well as its strengths.

Attempts to control physical environment, like those to control the mind, have also brought challenges. In many cases the attempts to alter natural processes or control them have not only been destructive but have presented a threat to the future of our species. The same X-rays that destroy diseased cells may also destroy healthy ones or cause undesirable mutations in future generations. The same pesticide which destroys disease-bearing mosquitoes and insects that ruin crops may also destroy beneficial forms of life and pollute man's sources of food and water. Atomic power can be produced to provide useful energy—or to make bombs that threaten all of the life on earth. The disposal of wastes from atomic energy plants already poses a great problem, for these wastes remain dangerously radioactive for many years. There is a complex interdependence among the many forms of life on earth. The destruction of one relationship within the chain might upset the great overall balance.

While some nations have made great strides and advances in science and technology, others have lagged far behind. The resulting differences are reflected in an imbalance of social, political, and economic development among the peoples of the world. Unevenness of attainment and widely different standards of living are causing frustration, envy, jealousy, and antagonisms. The world is yet tense, and among its peoples and nations there is yet friction which leads to disorder and possibly to conflict. Technical advances have given man control over the awesome power of the atom, and this same power might completely destroy his species. The tools and toys of science and technology have, in many cases, brought people and nations closer together. Often, however, they have only served to emphasize the wide gulfs that divide men and nations.

Man's adjustment to the world he has created will require the greatest exercise of skill and ingenuity. Many men have more leisure today than formerly, but do they use it to stagnate or to grow? Others are pushed to the point where hearts collapse and the decay of age comes early. The young are eager to seize the wealth of opportunity this new age provides, but an increasing number are finding their "kicks" in actions that are too often harmful. Cities reach their boundaries and their conveniences far into the countryside—

and shadow their earth with a smog which is sometimes deadly. Factories produce an unending stream of products desired by man, and pollute with their waste products the water he uses for drinking and swimming. The accumulated knowledge of man has been made available to all who care to read in this flood-tide of books, but many prefer to read man's accumulation of trash, which has also been made available. The challenges are many and urgent.

Must the achievements and glories of the past be lost in this alteration of the physical and cultural fabric of man? In much of the world the freedoms of man have waned under the suffocating pressure of rigid doctrines and regimentation. In other places there is the tendency to control the life of man more strictly in the interests of efficiency and uniformity. Sculptured masterpieces are hidden by the rising waters of a new dam, and lovely dwellings which house the memory of wonderful deeds crumble under the swinging hammer of a wrecking crew. And forgotten in the modern rush are many of the values which have passed the test of time—thoughts made of imperishable stuff, and ideals of intrinsic worth. There is the need to preserve all that is good of man, and the challenge to make it a part of his living present.

There is a commonality of man, but there is not a commonality of ideals and ways of achieving them. The dying may bequeath their eyes to the living blind, but the newly seeing will not view life as their benefactors saw it. A man may give of his blood that another may live, but the intermingling of their blood does not result in a merging of ideas. A man and a woman may marry, but they remain two distinct personalities. Together, they produce a child, but the child is not the same person as either of the parents. What seems right and proper to one individual or group seems strange and perhaps wrong to others. Interpretations of the meaning and ends of life vary widely. And as in the past, so in the present, this diversity of attitudes and individuals distinguishes one species on earth—man.

Today man's clashing, mingling viewpoints are reflecting his past, making his present, and shaping his future. Living man is a witness to his past, and a prophecy of his future. He is the latest creation of all men who have preceded him, and the seed of all men who will follow him. This dot of time he now occupies is his to use as he chooses. His choice will affect the future, for it is always linked to the present and the past. It is within man's power to create a more glorious future. And this is his finest challenge.

## MAJOR PUBLISHERS OF BOOKS LISTED IN BIBLIOGRAPHIES

ABELARD-SCHUMAN LTD., 6 W. 57th St., New York 19, N. Y.
AFFILIATED PUBLISHERS (see Pocket Books)
APPLETON-CENTURY-CROFTS (see Meredith)
ASIA SOCIETY, 112 E. 64th St., New York 21, N. Y.
ASSOCIATION FOR ASIAN STUDIES, Ann Arbor, Mich.
BANTAM BOOKS, INC., 271 Madison Ave., New York 16, N. Y.
BIBLIO & TANNEN BOOKSELLERS & PUBLISHERS, INC., 63 4th Ave., New York 3, N. Y.
THE BOBBS-MERRILL CO., INC. (see Howard W. Sams)
CAMBRIDGE UNIVERSITY PRESS, 32 E. 57th St., New York 22, N. Y.
CHANTICLEER PRESS, INC., 424 Madison Ave., New York 17, N. Y.
CHICAGO NATURAL HISTORY MUSEUM, Roosevelt Rd., Lake Shore Dr., Chicago 5, Ill.
CITADEL PRESS, 222 Park Ave. S., New York 3, N. Y.
COLLIER BOOKS (see Crowell-Collier)
COLUMBIA UNIVERSITY PRESS, 2960 Broadway, New York 27, N. Y.
CORNELL UNIVERSITY PRESS, 124 Roberts Pl., Ithaca, N. Y.
THOMAS Y. CROWELL CO., 201 Park Ave. S., New York 3, N. Y.
THE CROWELL-COLLIER PUBLISHING CO., 640 5th Ave., New York 19, N. Y.
CROWN PUBLISHERS, INC., 419 Park Ave. S., New York 16, N. Y.
THE JOHN DAY CO., INC., 62 W. 45th St., New York 36, N. Y.
DELL PUBLISHING CO., INC., 750 3rd Ave., New York 17, N. Y.
DODD, MEAD & CO., 432 Park Ave. S., New York 16, N. Y.
DOLPHIN BOOKS (see Doubleday)
DOUBLEDAY & CO., INC., 501 Franklin Ave., Garden City, N. Y.
DUFOUR EDITIONS, Chester Springs, Pa.
FREE PRESS OF GLENCOE, INC. (see Crowell-Collier)
GINN & CO., Statler Bldg., Back Bay P. O. 191, Boston 17, Mass.
GLOBE BOOK CO., INC., 175 5th Ave., New York 10, N. Y.
GROSSET & DUNLAP, INC., 1107 Broadway, New York 10, N. Y.
GROVE PRESS, 64 University Pl., New York 3, N. Y.
HARCOURT, BRACE & WORLD, INC., 757 3rd Ave., New York 17, N. Y.
HARPER & ROW, PUBLISHERS, 49 E. 33rd St., New York 16, N. Y.
HARVARD UNIVERSITY PRESS, 79 Garden St., Cambridge 38, Mass.
HAWTHORN BOOKS, INC. (see Prentice-Hall)
HOLT, RINEHART & WINSTON, INC., 383 Madison Ave., New York 17, N. Y.
HOUGHTON MIFFLIN CO., 2 Park St., Boston 7, Mass.
HUMANITIES PRESS, 303 Park Ave. S., New York 10, N. Y.
INDIANA UNIVERSITY PRESS, 10th and Morton Sts., Bloomingdale, Ind.
ALFRED A. KNOPF, INC., 501 Madison Ave., New York 22, N. Y.
J. B. LIPPINCOTT CO., E. Washington Sq., Philadelphia 5, Pa.
LITTLE, BROWN & CO., 34 Beacon St., Boston 6, Mass.
LIVERIGHT PUBLISHING CORP., 386 Park Ave. S., New York 16, N. Y.
LONGMANS, GREEN & CO. (see David McKay)
MCGRAW-HILL BOOK CO., INC., 330 W. 42nd St., New York 36, N. Y.
DAVID MCKAY CO., INC., 119 W. 40th St., New York 18, N. Y.
THE MACMILLAN CO. (see Crowell-Collier)
MENTOR BOOKS (see New American Library)
THE MEREDITH PUBLISHING CO., 1716 Locust St., Des Moines 3, Iowa
JULIAN MESSNER, INC., 8 W. 40th St., New York 18, N. Y.
MODERN LIBRARY, INC. (see Random House)
WILLIAM MORROW & CO., INC., 425 Park Ave., New York 16, N. Y.
JOHN MURRAY PUBLISHERS LTD., 50 Albemarle St., London W 1, England
NEW AMERICAN LIBRARY OF WORLD LITERATURE, INC., 501 Madison Ave., New York 22, N. Y.
NORTHWESTERN UNIVERSITY PRESS, 1840 Sheridan Rd., Evanston, Ill.
W. W. NORTON & CO., INC., 55 5th Ave., New York 3, N. Y.
OXFORD UNIVERSITY PRESS, INC., 417 5th Ave., New York 16, N. Y.
PANTHEON BOOKS, INC. (see Random House)
PENGUIN BOOKS, INC., 3300 Clipper Mill Rd., Baltimore 11, Md.
POCKET BOOKS, INC., 630 5th Ave., New York 20, N. Y.
FREDERICK A. PRAEGER, INC., 64 University Pl., New York 3, N. Y.
PRENTICE-HALL, INC., Englewood Cliffs, N. J.
PRINCETON UNIVERSITY PRESS, Princeton, N. J.
G. P. PUTNAM'S SONS, 200 Madison Ave., New York 16, N. Y.
QUADRANGLE BOOKS, INC., 180 N. Wacker Dr., Chicago 6, Ill.
RAND MCNALLY & CO., 8255 Central Park Ave., Skokie, Ill.
RANDOM HOUSE, INC., 457 Madison Ave., New York 22, N. Y.
HENRY REGNERY CO., 14 E. Jackson Blvd., Chicago 4, Ill.
THE RONALD PRESS CO., 15 E. 26th St., New York 10, N. Y.
ROUTLEDGE & KEGAN PAUL LTD., 68-74 Carter Lane, London E. C. 4, England
ROY PUBLISHERS, INC., 30 E. 74th St., New York 21, N. Y.
RUTGERS UNIVERSITY PRESS, 30 College Ave., New Brunswick, N. J.
ST. MARTIN'S PRESS, INC., 175 5th Ave., New York 10, N. Y.
HOWARD W. SAMS & CO., INC., PUBLISHERS, 4300 W. 62nd St., Indianapolis 6, Ind.
CHARLES SCRIBNER'S SONS, 597 5th Ave., New York 17, N. Y.
SKIRA ART BOOKS (see World Publishing Co.)

WILLIAM SLOANE ASSOCIATES (see William Morrow)
PETER SMITH, 20 Railroad Ave., Gloucester, Mass.
THE STACKPOLE CO., Telegraph Press Bldg., Cameron and Kelker Sts., Harrisburg, Pa.
STECHERT-HAFNER SERVICE AGENCY, INC., 31 E. 10th St., New York, N. Y.
TAPLINGER PUBLISHING CO., INC., 119 W. 57th St., New York 19, N. Y.
THEATRE ARTS BOOKS, 333 Ave. of the Americas, New York, N. Y.
CHARLES E. TUTTLE CO., INC., 28 S. Main St., Rutland, Vt.
TWAYNE PUBLISHERS, INC., 31 Union Sq. W., New York 3, N. Y.
FREDERICK UNGAR PUBLISHING CO., INC., 131 E. 23rd St., New York 10, N. Y.
UNIVERSITY OF CALIFORNIA PRESS, Berkeley 4, Calif.
UNIVERSITY OF CHICAGO PRESS, 5750 Ellis Ave., Chicago 37, Ill.
UNIVERSITY OF LONDON PRESS LTD., Ashby Rd., London S. E. 4, England
UNIVERSITY OF MINNESOTA PRESS, 2037 University Ave., S. E., Minneapolis 14, Minn.
UNIVERSITY OF NEW MEXICO PRESS, Albuquerque, New Mexico
VANGUARD PRESS, INC., 424 Madison Ave., New York 17, N. Y.
D. VAN NOSTRAND CO., INC., 120 Alexander St., Princeton, N. J.
THE VIKING PRESS, 625 Madison Ave., New York 22, N. Y.
VINTAGE BOOKS (see Random House)
THE WORLD PUBLISHING CO., 2231 W. 110th St., Cleveland 2, Ohio
YALE UNIVERSITY PRESS, 149 York St., New Haven, Conn.

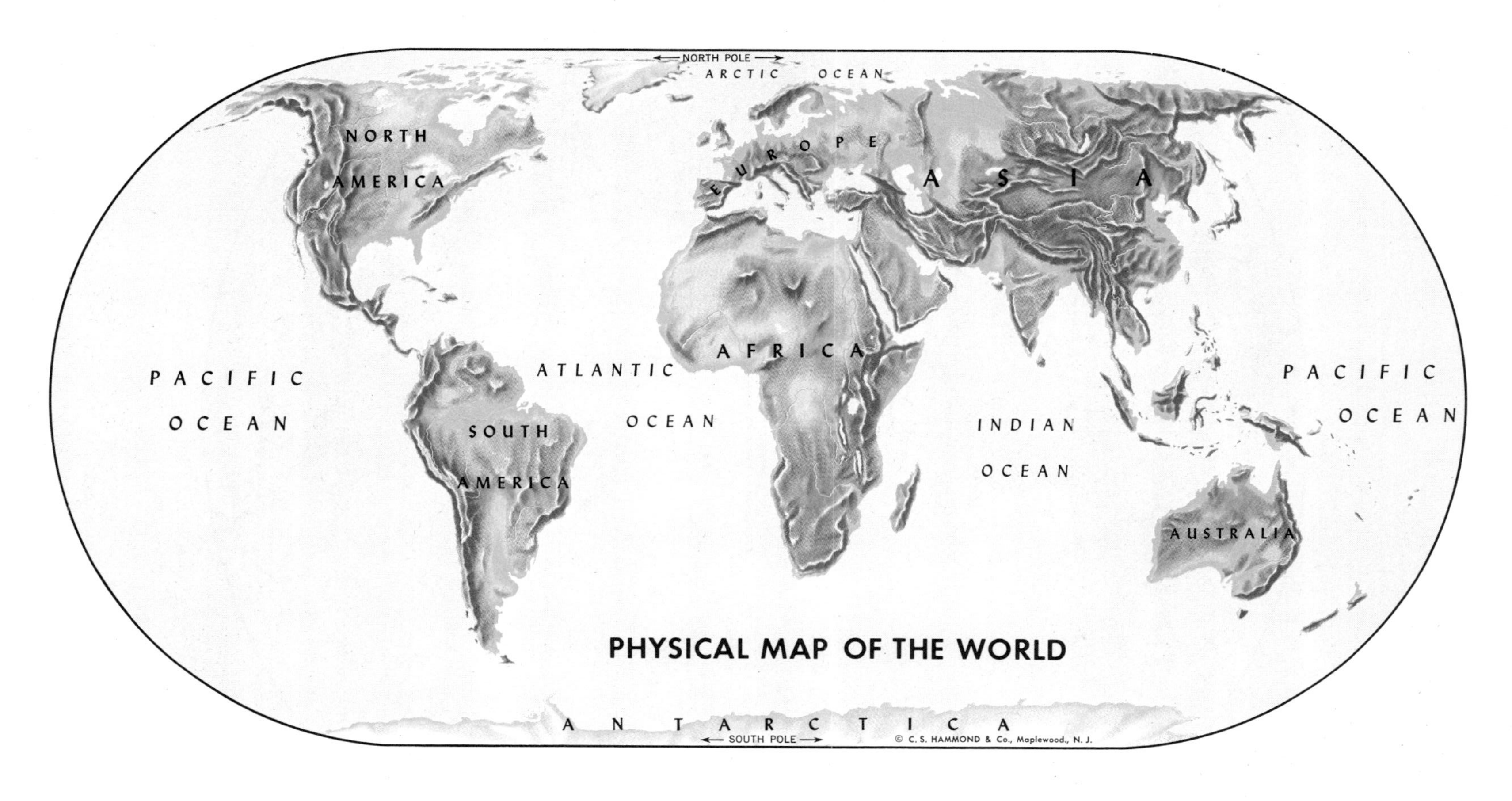
NORTH POLE
ARCTIC OCEAN
NORTH AMERICA
EUROPE
ASIA
PACIFIC OCEAN
ATLANTIC OCEAN
AFRICA
SOUTH AMERICA
INDIAN OCEAN
PACIFIC OCEAN
AUSTRALIA
PHYSICAL MAP OF THE WORLD
ANTARCTICA
SOUTH POLE
© C. S. HAMMOND & Co., Maplewood, N. J.

# THE WORLD

## Western Hemisphere

SCALE OF MILES

0 500 1000 1500 2000

SCALE OF KILOMETRES

0 500 1000 1500 2000

Capitals of Countries ◉

International Boundaries — · — · —

# THE WORLD

## Eastern Hemisphere

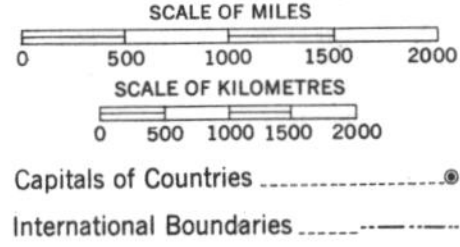

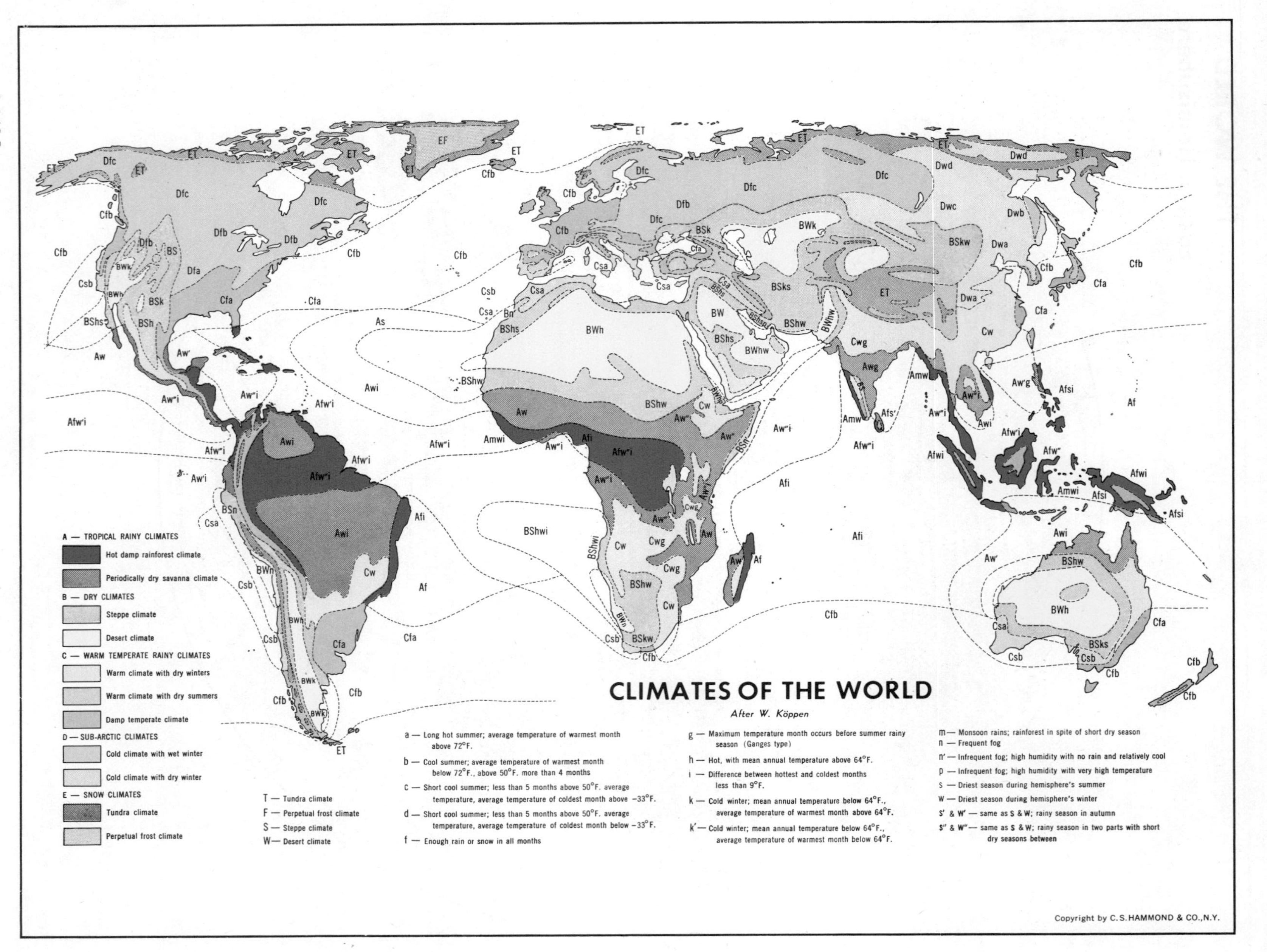

CLIMATES OF THE WORLD
After W. Köppen
A — TROPICAL RAINY CLIMATES
Hot damp rainforest climate
Periodically dry savanna climate
B — DRY CLIMATES
Steppe climate
Desert climate
C — WARM TEMPERATE RAINY CLIMATES
Warm climate with dry winters
Warm climate with dry summers
Damp temperate climate
D — SUB-ARCTIC CLIMATES
Cold climate with wet winter
Cold climate with dry winter
E — SNOW CLIMATES
Tundra climate
Perpetual frost climate
T — Tundra climate
F — Perpetual frost climate
S — Steppe climate
W — Desert climate
a — Long hot summer; average temperature of warmest month above 72°F.
b — Cool summer; average temperature of warmest month below 72°F., above 50°F. more than 4 months
c — Short cool summer; less than 5 months above 50°F. average temperature, average temperature of coldest month above −33°F.
d — Short cool summer; less than 5 months above 50°F. average temperature, average temperature of coldest month below −33°F.
f — Enough rain or snow in all months
g — Maximum temperature month occurs before summer rainy season (Ganges type)
h — Hot, with mean annual temperature above 64°F.
i — Difference between hottest and coldest months less than 9°F.
k — Cold winter; mean annual temperature below 64°F., average temperature of warmest month above 64°F.
k′ — Cold winter; mean annual temperature below 64°F., average temperature of warmest month below 64°F.
m — Monsoon rains; rainforest in spite of short dry season
n — Frequent fog
n′ — Infrequent fog; high humidity with no rain and relatively cool
p — Infrequent fog; high humidity with very high temperature
s — Driest season during hemisphere's summer
w — Driest season during hemisphere's winter
s′ & w′ — same as s & w; rainy season in autumn
s″ & w″ — same as s & w; rainy season in two parts with short dry seasons between
Copyright by C. S. HAMMOND & CO., N.Y.

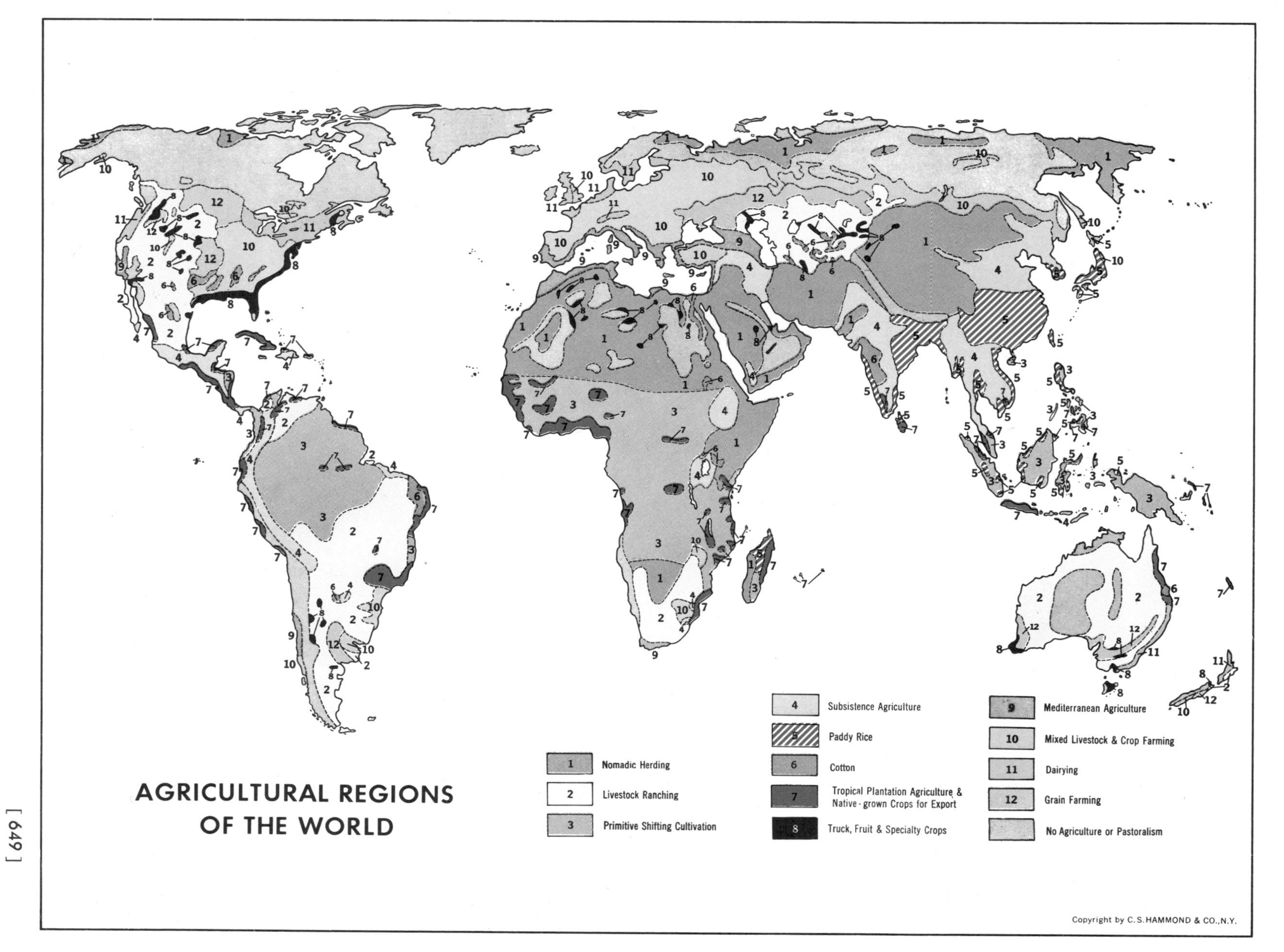
AGRICULTURAL REGIONS
OF THE WORLD
1 Nomadic Herding
2 Livestock Ranching
3 Primitive Shifting Cultivation
4 Subsistence Agriculture
5 Paddy Rice
6 Cotton
7 Tropical Plantation Agriculture & Native-grown Crops for Export
8 Truck, Fruit & Specialty Crops
9 Mediterranean Agriculture
10 Mixed Livestock & Crop Farming
11 Dairying
12 Grain Farming
No Agriculture or Pastoralism
Copyright by C. S. HAMMOND & CO., N.Y.

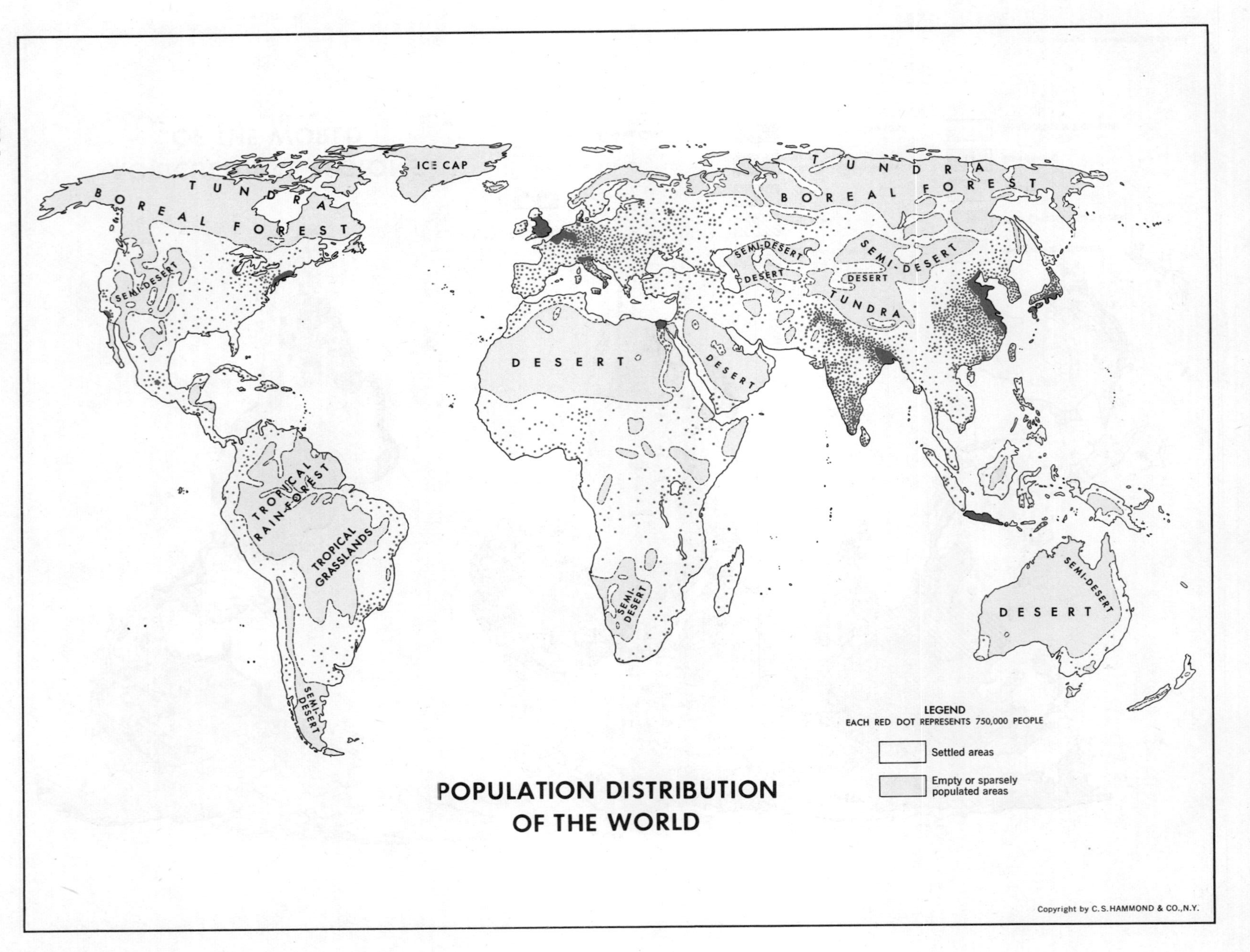


# POPULATION DISTRIBUTION OF THE WORLD

Copyright by C.S. HAMMOND & CO., N.Y.

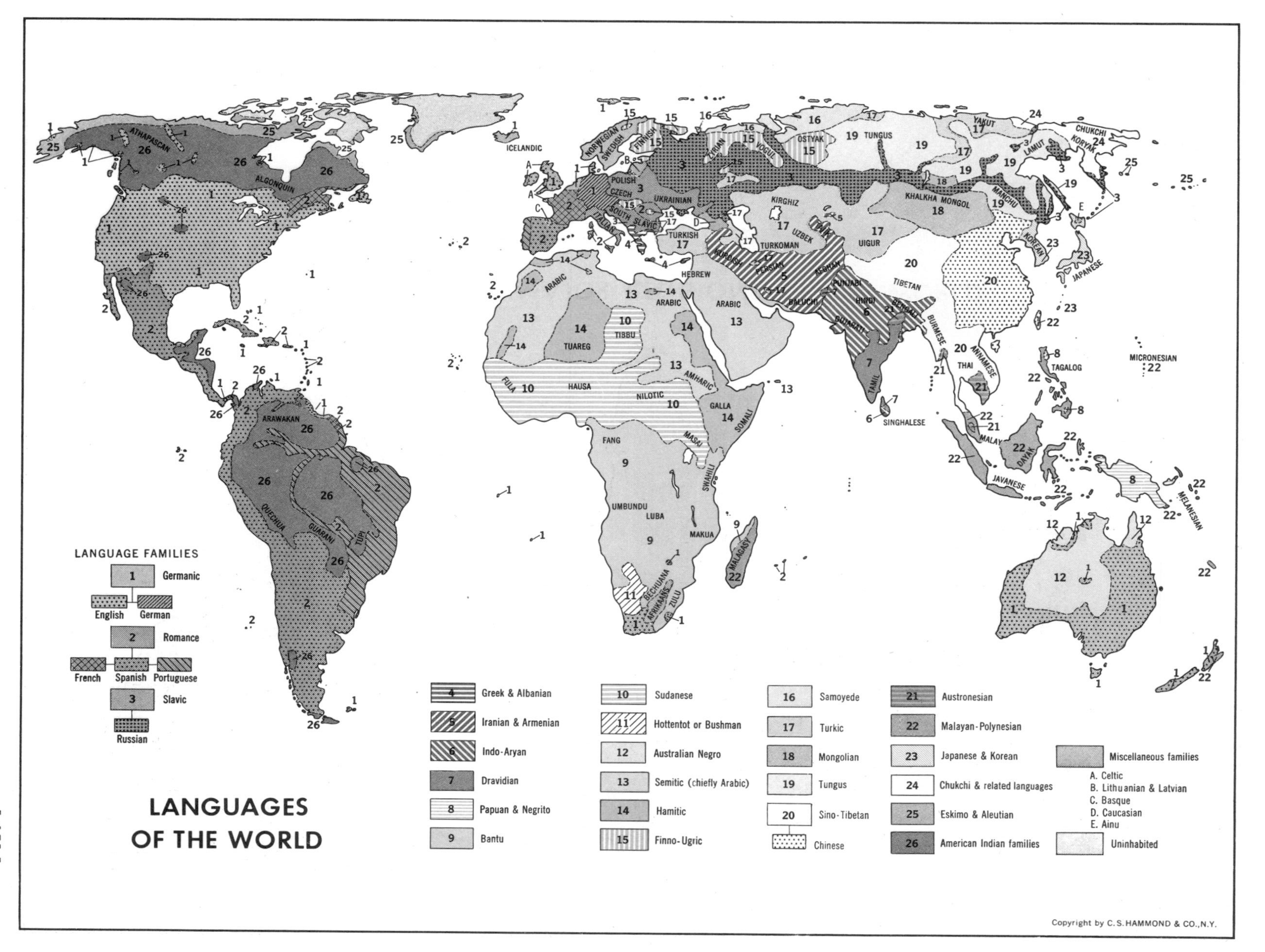
LANGUAGE FAMILIES
1 Germanic
English
German
2 Romance
French
Spanish
Portuguese
3 Slavic
Russian
LANGUAGES OF THE WORLD
4 Greek & Albanian
5 Iranian & Armenian
6 Indo-Aryan
7 Dravidian
8 Papuan & Negrito
9 Bantu
10 Sudanese
11 Hottentot or Bushman
12 Australian Negro
13 Semitic (chiefly Arabic)
14 Hamitic
15 Finno-Ugric
16 Samoyede
17 Turkic
18 Mongolian
19 Tungus
20 Sino-Tibetan
Chinese
21 Austronesian
22 Malayan-Polynesian
23 Japanese & Korean
24 Chukchi & related languages
25 Eskimo & Aleutian
26 American Indian families
Miscellaneous families
A. Celtic
B. Lithuanian & Latvian
C. Basque
D. Caucasian
E. Ainu
Uninhabited
ATHAPASCAN
ALGONQUIN
ICELANDIC
NORWEGIAN
SWEDISH
FINNISH
POLISH
CZECH
UKRAINIAN
SOUTH SLAVIC
ITALIAN
TURKISH
HEBREW
KURDISH
PERSIAN
TURKOMAN
UZBEK
KIRGHIZ
TAJIK
AFGHAN
BALUCHI
PUNJABI
HINDI
BENGALI
GUJARATI
TAMIL
SINGHALESE
ZYRIAN
VOGUL
OSTYAK
TUNGUS
YAKUT
LAMUT
CHUKCHI
KORYAK
MANCHU
KHALKHA MONGOL
UIGUR
TIBETAN
BURMESE
THAI
ANNAMESE
KOREAN
JAPANESE
TAGALOG
MICRONESIAN
MALAY
DAYAK
JAVANESE
MELANESIAN
ARABIC
TUAREG
TIBBU
FULA
HAUSA
NILOTIC
AMHARIC
GALLA
SOMALI
MASAI
SWAHILI
FANG
UMBUNDU
LUBA
MAKUA
BECHUANA
AFRIKAANS
ZULU
MALAGASY
ARAWAKAN
QUECHUA
GUARANI
TUPI
Copyright by C. S. HAMMOND & CO., N.Y.

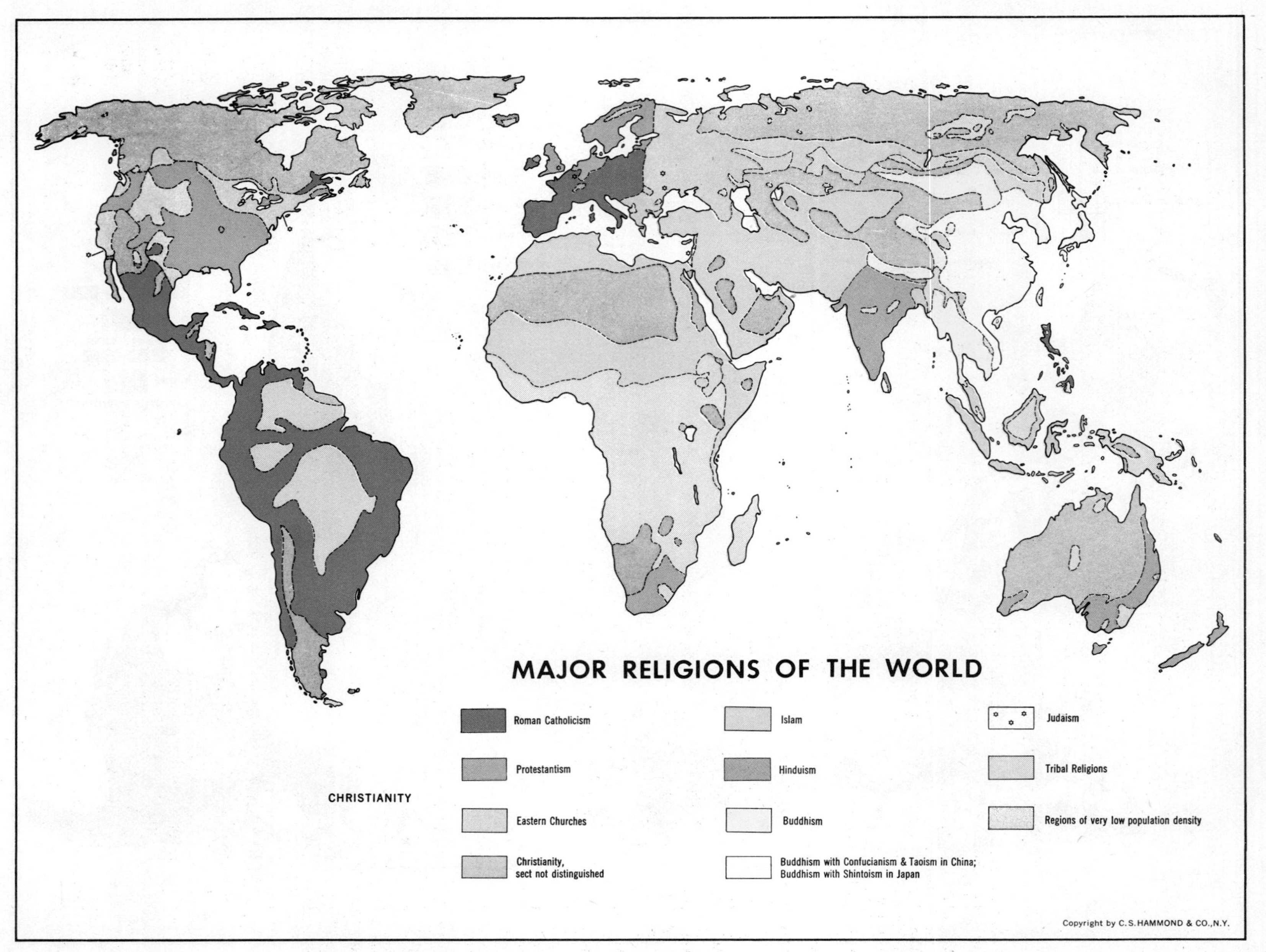
MAJOR RELIGIONS OF THE WORLD
CHRISTIANITY
Roman Catholicism
Protestantism
Eastern Churches
Christianity, sect not distinguished
Islam
Hinduism
Buddhism
Buddhism with Confucianism & Taoism in China; Buddhism with Shintoism in Japan
Judaism
Tribal Religions
Regions of very low population density
Copyright by C.S.HAMMOND & CO.,N.Y.

# INDEX

Key to pronunciation

ə *abut*; ᵊ kitten; ər *further*; a back; ā bake; ä cot, cart; aů *out*; ch *chin*; e less; ē *easy*; g *gift*; i trip; ī life; j *joke*; ŋ *sing*; ō *flow*; ȯ *flaw*; ȯi *coin*; th *thin*; *th this*; ü loot; ů foot; y *yet*; yü *few*; yů *furious*; zh *vision*; *k* German *ich*; œ French *boeuf*; œ̄ French *feu*; ue German *füllen*; ue̅ French *rue*; $^{n}$ indicates that a preceding vowel or diphthong is pronounced with nasal passages open as in French *un bon vin blanc*; ʸ indicates the final sound of French *digne*.

The system of indicating pronunciation is used by permission. From Webster's Seventh New Collegiate Dictionary, copyright 1963 by G. & C. Merriam Co., Publishers of the Merriam-Webster Dictionaries.

Page references to illustrations are in italic type